LIVY

XIV

SUMMARIES, FRAGMENTS, AND OBSEQUENS

GENERAL INDEX

404

LIVY

WITH AN ENGLISH TRANSLATION

IN FOURTEEN VOLUMES

XIV

SUMMARIES, FRAGMENTS,
AND OBSEQUENS

TRANSLATED BY

ALFRED C. SCHLESINGER, Ph.D.
ASSOCIATE PROFESSOR OF CLASSICS IN OBERLIN COLLEGE

WITH A GENERAL INDEX TO LIVY BY

RUSSEL M. GEER
PROFESSOR OF CLASSICAL LANGUAGES IN TULANE UNIVERSITY

CAMBRIDGE, MASSACHUSETTS
HARVARD UNIVERSITY PRESS
LONDON
WILLIAM HEINEMANN LTD
MCMLXXXVII

American ISBN 0–674–99445–0
British ISBN 0 434 99404 9

Printed 1959
Revised and reprinted 1967
Reprinted 1987

Printed in Great Britain by
Richard Clay Ltd, Bungay, Suffolk

CONTENTS

	PAGE
TRANSLATOR'S PREFACE	vii
SUMMARIES OF BOOKS XXXVII–XL	2
SUMMARIES OF BOOKS XLVI–CXLII	10
FRAGMENTS	171
TABLE OF CHANGES IN NUMBERING OF FRAGMENTS	236
JULIUS OBSEQUENS	237
FOREWORD TO INDEX	321
LIST OF ABREVIATIONS	323
INDEX	327
TABLE OF PARALLELS	558

MAPS—

1. SPAIN — *At end*
2. CITY OF ROME

TRANSLATOR'S PREFACE

The Periochae, or Summaries, and Obsequens are based for their text on Rossbach (Leipzig, Teubner, 1910). The Oxyrhynchus Summaries have been inserted after the more familiar Summaries of the same Books; the comparison of the two Summaries for such Books as appear in both collections will be found to be of interest. However, a few very scanty fragments from the end of the Oxyrhynchus papyrus will be found by themselves, following the Summary of Book CXLII.

The attempt has been made to give a fairly full report on the text of the traditional Summaries. For the Oxyrhynchus Summaries, the critical notes cover only those additions or corrections to the MS. which seem either to Rossbach or to the present editor to be problematical; the numerous additions made by scholars to the broken text are indicated, but for the names of the scholars to whom these emendations should be credited, the reader is referred to Rossbach.

References in the footnotes to the Summaries are intended to set these scraps of Livy's history in some amount of context, comprising both the extant primary sources and the historical narratives (including Plutarch's biographies) which are better preserved than Livy. An attempt has been made to provide cross references, not only between Summaries, but between Summaries, Fragments, and Obsequens; but the reader is warned not to trust the editor too far, if complete collection of information on a specific point is desired. In some of the cross references, the Oxyrhynchus Summaries are referred to as "O", with the number of the Book following, *e.g.*, O–LII.

The fragments are based on the collections of Weissenborn (Leipzig, Teubner, 1851, reprinted in 1911), Martin Hertz (Leipzig, Tauchnitz, 1863), and H. J. Mueller (Berlin, Weidmann, 1881). At the cost of some clumsiness, the numbering of the Weissenborn series has been maintained, in the hope that, with the appended table of changes in numbering in Hertz' edition, references elsewhere to the fragments of Livy could be found conveniently in this volume. It will be obvious that very few critical notes have been included for the text of the fragments, in the belief that reference to the sources cited will suffice the reader who wishes to scrutinize the text closely.

The present editor considers that a fragment of Livy should consist of a quotation from a lost, not an extant, book, and should probably, if not certainly, refer to Livy's own language, not simply make use of Livy's facts. If the reader prefers a somewhat broader definition, the notes on what the preceding editors have included as fragments may be useful.

TRANSLATOR'S PREFACE

For the grammarians' fragments, reference is given to the *Grammatici Latini* of Keil (Leipzig, Teubner, 1857–80; cited as K). Charisius will be found in the first volume, Priscian in the second and third, the anonymous writer in the fifth, and Agroecius and Beda in the seventh.

The present editor has not seen Hertz' discussion *De fragmentis T. Livi commentarium* (Bratislava, 1864).

In the critical notes on Obsequens, the reader's indulgence is asked for an idiosyncrasy—namely, that the symbol "MS." is used, although the only source of our text is the Aldine *editio princeps*. The intention was to avoid creating a new symbol; and since Rossbach thinks that the text was not much studied or emended before printing, there may be some propriety in the symbol used.

The notes on Obsequens may give a lead to those whose curiosity, like the editor's, is piqued by these oddities. Book II of Pliny's *Natural History* gathers together much of this lore.

It has seemed desirable to include maps of Spain, and of the city of Rome, since previous volumes of the L.C.L. Livy have had no occasion to show very much in these areas. The map of Spain will be particularly useful with fragment 18, the most important fragment; and the map of the city may serve to illustrate Obsequens; further light on the communities of Roman citizens mentioned in the latter will be thrown by the maps of Italy in previous volumes of this Livy. The map of Spain is based on Kiepert's *Atlas Antiquus*; the outline of the map of Rome is based on Richter, *Topographie von Rom*, Iwan Müller's Handbuch III, Nordlingen, Beck, 1883, by kind permission of the publishers.

SIGLA MSS. PERIOCHARUM

N = (Nazarianus) Palatinus-Heidelbergensis 894, saec. ix.
B = Bernensis A 92, saec. ix.
P = Parisinus 7701, saec. xii.
Π = codex a P. Pithoeo collatus.
R = editio princeps, ca. A.D. 1469.
G = Leidensis Gronovianus 107, saec. xv.
Gu = Guelferbytanus 175, saec. xv.

Alfred Cary Schlesinger

July 1, 1952
Oberlin College

LIVY

FROM THE FOUNDING OF THE CITY

SUMMARIES

T. LIVI

AB URBE CONDITA

PERIOCHAE LIBRORUM XXXVII–XL

OXYRHYNCHEAE

col. I [Liber XXXVII]

in Hispa]nia Romani caesi.

A.U.C. 565 M. Fulvio] Cn. Manlio coss.

Aetoli]s pax iterum nec data nec negata est.[1] P. Licinius pontif]ex maximus Q. Fabium praetorem, quod flamen Quirin]alis erat, proficisci in Sardiniam inhib]uit.[2] Antiocho regi pax data. Lusitani vastati.] Bononia colonia de s.c.[3] deducta. Acilius Glabrio] censuram petens minantibus accusa]tionem competitoribus proposito [4] destiti]t.

Liber XXXVIII

Ambra]cia capta.

Gallog]raecis in Pamphylia proelio vastatis Phrygi]a liberata. Origiacontis captiva nobilis [5]

[1] nec data nec negata est *sugg. Rossbach*: data est MS.

[2] inhibuit *sugg. Rossbach*: . . . ant MS.

[3] Bononia colonia de s.c. *Rossbach*: rhodonia desoli MS.

[4] competitoribus proposito *edd.*: compellitoribus conposito MS.

[5] captiva nobilis *Grenfell-Hunt*: captiannobilis MS.

LIVY

FROM THE FOUNDING OF THE CITY

SUMMARIES OF BOOKS XXXVII–XL

FROM OXYRHYNCHUS

Book XXXVII

In Spain the Romans were slaughtered.[1] In the consulship of Marcus Fulvius and Gnaeus Manlius, the B.C. 189 Aetolians were for the second time neither granted nor refused peace. Publius Licinius the chief pontiff prevented Praetor Quintus Fabius from setting out for Sardinia, because he was *flamen* of Quirinus. Peace was granted to King Antiochus. The Lusitanians were ravaged. The colony of Bononia was founded in accordance with a decree of the senate. Acilius Glabrio on seeking the censorship was threatened with prosecution by his rivals and abandoned his undertaking.

Book XXXVIII

Ambracia was occupied. The Galatians in Pamphylia were crushed in battle and Phrygia was set free. Origiaco's wife,[2] a prisoner of high rank, killed a centurion

[1] The summary begins with xlvi. 7–8. The peace with Antiochus and the founding of Bononia are the only items duplicated in the other Summary.

[2] The translation follows the complete text (where the Galatian king's name is written Orgiago, genitive, Orgiagontis), rather than the unsatisfactory wording of this Summary; see critical note.

centuri]onem, cuius vim passa erat, aurum ad ⟨se⟩ mittendam] poscentem occidit caputque eius ad virum reportavit.] Campanis conubium datum e[s]t.
Inter Achae]os et Lacedaemonios cruenta [pr]oelia.
A.U.C. 566 M. Messala C. L]ivio Salinatore coss.
pretiosa p]raeda ex Gallograecia per Thra[eciam
avecta. L. M]inucius Myrtilus et L. Manliu[s
dediti legat]is Carthaginiensium, qui
pulsati eran]t.
A.U.C. 567 M. Lepido C. Fl]aminio coss.
P. Scipio] Africanus a Quintis Petillis die
dicta in Li]terninum [1] abit. Qui ne revocaretur,
Gracchus t]rib. pl. intercessit. L. Cornelius
col. II Scipio dam[natus furti crim]ine.[2]

Liber XXXIX

Per C. Flami[nium M. Aemiliu]m coss. Ligures
perdomiti. V[iae Flaminia e]t Aemilia munitae sunt.
Latinorum [xii milia hom]inum coacta
ab Roma re[dire. Manlius cu]m de Gallo-
graecis in[temperate triumf]ar[et, pe]cunia
quae trans[lata erat, priva]tis p[e]r[s]oluta.
A.U.C. 568 Sp. Postum⟨i⟩o [Q. Marcio co]ss.
Hispala Fa[ecenia meretric]e et pupillo
Aebutio, qu[em T. Sempronius] Rutilus
tutor et ma[ter Duronia ci]rcumscribserant,
indicium re[ferentibus Ba]ccha[n-
alia subla[ta in Italia. His]pani
subacti. At[hletarum cert]amina
primum a Fu[lvio Nobilior]e edita.
Gallis in Ital[iam profectis Ma]rcellus
p]ersuasit [ut domum redire]nt. L. Cornelius

[1] Literninum *edd.*: . . . tratum MS.
[2] furti crimine *Rossbach*: . . . ine *vel* . . . eni MS.

who had assaulted her, when he demanded gold for her release; and she carried his head back to her husband. The Campanians were given the right to intermarry with Romans. Bloody battles took place between the Achaeans and the Spartans.

In the consulship of Marcus Messala and Gaius Livius Salinator, the valuable booty from Galatia was brought off by way of Thrace. Lucius Minucius Myrtilus and Lucius Manlius were surrendered to the Carthaginian envoys whom they had struck. B.C. 188

In the consulship of Marcus Lepidus and Gaius Flaminius, Publius Scipio Africanus went into exile at Liternum after a day for his trial had been set by the Quinti Petillii. Gracchus, a tribune of the people, vetoed his being summoned back. Lucius Cornelius Scipio was condemned on a charge of embezzlement. B.C. 187

Book XXXIX

The Ligurians were brought to subjection by Consuls Gaius Flaminius and Marcus Aemilius. The Flaminian and Aemilian roads were built.[1] Twelve thousand Latin persons were compelled to return home from Rome. When Manlius celebrated an extravagant triumph over the Galatians, the money which was carried in the procession was entirely paid out to individuals.

In the consulship of Spurius Postumius and Quintus Marcius, on evidence given by Hispala Faecenia, a courtesan, and Aebutius, a ward, against whom his guardian Titus Sempronius Rutilus and his mother Duronia had plotted, the rites of Bacchus were abolished in Italy. The Spaniards were repressed. Contests of athletes were presented for the first time by Fulvius Nobilior. Marcellus persuaded certain Gauls, who had migrated into Italy, to return home. Lucius Cornelius B.C. 186

[1] The Aemilian Way was a continuation of the Flaminian Way properly so-called; the road built by this Flaminius was a shorter alternative to the Flaminian Way built by his father; see above, XXXIX. ii. 6.

Scipio pos[t bellum Antiochi] ludos votivos conl[ata pecunia feci]t.

A.U.C. 569 Appio Claud[io M. Semproni]o coss. Ligures fu[gati, vi oppida ab i]llis accepta.

A.U.C. 570 P. Claudio Pulchr[o L. Porcio Li]cino coss. hominum ad ∞[∞ a Q. Naevio ven]efici damnati. L. Quintius Fla[mininus cos. in] Gallia, quod Philipp[o Poeno, scorto] suo, desiderante gladia[torium specta]culum col. III sua manu Boiu[m nobilem occiderat, a M. Catone [1] cen[sore senatu motus est. Basilica [2] Porcia [facta.

A.U.C. 571 M. Claudio Marcello [Q. Fabio Labeone coss. P. Licini Crassi po[ntificis maximi ludis funebribus [epulum datum. Tabernaculis po[sitis in foro id quod vate[s c]ecin[e]rat [evenit tabernacula in foro futura. I[n Hispania prospere dim[icatu]m.[3] Han[nibal apud Prusiam rege[m per] le[gatos Romanos expetitus veneno pe]rit.

L[IBER XL

A.U.C. 572 L. A[emilio C]n. Baebio [coss. in Liguras] bellum r[enovatum et Hispanos.[4] Bella v]el lites in [Graecia et Asia composita. Thessala] Theoxen[a cum viro filiisque in mare [f]ugien[s se iecit. Demetrius fictis criminibus [5] [accusatus a fratre per patrem coactu[s venenum haurire.

[1] a M. Catone *Grenfell-Hunt*: alanatòne MS.

[2] Basilica *Grenfell-Hunt*: uastaita MS.

[3] In Hispania prospere dimicatum *Luterbacher*: in senatu de rebus exteris diiudicatum *Rossbach*.

Scipio gave games, with contributed money, in celebration of the war with Antiochus.

In the consulship of Appius Claudius and Marcus Sempronius, the Ligurians were routed and six towns were taken over from them by storm. B.C. 185

In the consulship of Publius Claudius Pulcher and Lucius Porcius Licinus, about two thousand persons were convicted by Quintus Naevius of poisoning. Lucius Quinctius Flamininus was removed from the senate by Marcus Cato, because he had, while consul in Gaul, killed with his own hand a prominent Boian, when Flamininus' minion, the Carthaginian Philip, regretted missing a gladiatorial show. The Porcian basilica was built. B.C. 184

In the consulship of Marcus Claudius Marcellus and Quintus Fabius Labeo, a banquet was given at the funeral celebration of Publius Licinius Crassus, the chief pontiff. Booths for this were placed in the forum, thus fulfilling the prophecy of a soothsayer that there would be booths in the forum. There was a successful campaign in Spain. The surrender of Hannibal was demanded at the court of Prusias by Roman envoys, and Hannibal died by poison. B.C. 183

Book XL

In the consulship of Lucius Aemilius and Gnaeus Baebius, campaigns against the Ligurians and Spaniards were again undertaken. Wars and disputes were settled in Greece and Asia. The Thessalian Theoxena, fleeing with her husband and children, cast herself into the sea. Demetrius was accused by his brother on false charges and was compelled by his father to drink poison. B.C. 182

---

[4] In Liguras bellum renovatum et Hispanos *Rossbach*: Hispani bellum paraverunt *Kornemann*: spectare bellum Philippus *Luterbacher*, *qui* et Romanorum satellites interficere coepit *proxima linea suppl.*

[5] fictis criminibus *Grenfell-Hunt*, *Kornemann*: ficti egrimonibus MS.

A.U.C. 573 P. Lentulo M. Baebio [coss.
in agro L. Nerylli sc[ribae libri Numae inventi.
A.U.C. 574 A. Postumio C. [Calpurnio coss.
cum Liguribus His[panisque prospere pugnatum.
L. Livius trib. pl. quot [annos nati quemque
magistratum pete[rent, rogavit. Annalis dictus est.
A.U.C. 575 Q. Fulvio L. Manlio c[oss.
M. Lepidi et Fulvii No[bilioris censorum composita inimicitia.[1]

[1] *Desunt* 9 *vel* 10 *columnae.*

SUMMARIES

In the consulship of Publius Lentulus and Marcus Baebius, the books of Numa were found on the property of Lucius Neryllus,[1] a clerk. B.C. 181

In the consulship of Aulus Postumius and Gaius Calpurnius, successful campaigns were conducted against the Ligurians and Spaniards. Lucius Livius,[2] tribune of the people, passed a law defining the age at which a man might stand for each office. He received the nickname Annalis. B.C. 180

In the consulship of Quintus Fulvius and Lucius Manlius, the enmity of Marcus Lepidus and Fulvius Nobilior was brought to an end at the beginning of their censorship. B.C. 179

[1] The name is given as Petilius in Book XL itself.
[2] Correctly called Villius in XL. xliv. 1.

PERIOCHAE

LIBRORUM XLVI–CXLII

A.U.C. 587–594 XLVI. Eumenes rex Romam venit, qui Macedonico bello medium egerat. Ne aut hostis iudicatus videretur, si exclusus esset, aut liberatus crimine, si admitteretur, in commune lex [1] lata est, ne cui regi Romam venire liceret. Claudius Marcellus consul Alpinos Gallos, C. Sulpicius Gallus consul Liguras subegit. Legati Prusiae regis questi sunt de Eumene, quod fines suos popularetur, dixeruntque eum conspirasse cum Antiocho adversus populum Romanum. Societas cum Rhodiis deprecantibus iuncta est. Lustrum a censoribus conditum: censa sunt civium capita $\overline{\text{CCCXXXVII}}$ [2] XXII. Princeps senatus M. Aemilius Lepidus. Ptolemaeus Aegypti rex, pulsus regno a minore fratre missis ad eum legatis restitutus est. Ariarathe, Cappadociae rege, mortuo filius eius Ariarathes regnum accepit et amicitiam cum populo Romano per legatos renovavit. Res praeterea adversus Liguras et Corsos et Lusitanos vario eventu gestas et motus Syriae mortuo Antiocho, qui filium Antiochum puerum admodum

[1] commune lex *edd.*: communem res N, P.
[2] $\overline{\text{CCCXXXVII}}$ N: $\overline{\text{CCCXXVII}}$ P, R.

---

[1] The summaries of these Books from Oxyrhynchus, as far as they are preserved, will be found after the summaries of the same Books belonging to the complete series.

[2] 167 B.C. Cf. Polybius XXX. 19 (20, 17).

[3] 166 B.C. Cf. the Fasti, *C.I.L.*[2] I. 1, pp. 146 and 175.

[4] 164 B.C. Cf. Polybius XXX. 30 (31. 6), who says that "envoys from Asiatic cities" accused Eumenes of making arrangements with Antiochus. The senate took no action.

[5] 164 B.C. Cf. Polybius XXX. 31 (31. 7).

[6] 164 B.C. The censors were Quintus Marcius Philippus

SUMMARIES

OF BOOKS XLVI–CXLII[1]

XLVI. King Eumenes came to Rome, after straddling in the Macedonian War. To prevent its seeming that he was adjudged an enemy, if he was shut out, or that he had been acquitted, if allowed to enter, a general regulation was passed that no king should be permitted to come to Rome.[2] Consul Claudius Marcellus defeated the Gauls of the Alps; Consul Gaius Sulpicius Gallus, the Ligurians.[3] Envoys from King Prusias complained that Eumenes was devastating Prusias' territory, and said that he had conspired with Antiochus against the Roman People.[4] An alliance with the Rhodians was entered into at their request.[5] The half-decade was formally ended by the censors. The count of citizens was three hundred and thirty-seven thousand and twenty-two. The chief of the senate was Marcus Aemilius Lepidus.[6] B.C. 167–160

Ptolemy, king of Egypt, was expelled from his kingdom by his younger brother, but was restored when an embassy was sent to the latter.[7] On the death of Ariarathes, the king of Cappadocia, his son Ariarathes succeeded to the throne and through an embassy renewed the treaty of friendship with the Roman People.[8] The book also includes campaigns conducted against the Ligurians, Corsicans, and Lusitanians with varying success, as well as an upheaval in Syria on the death of Antiochus, who

and Lucius Aemilius Paulus. For Lepidus see above, XLIII. xv. 6, and the note; also below, XLVII.

[7] 164–3 B.C. See below, XLVII; the kingdom was divided, the younger Ptolemy receiving Cyrenaica. Cf. Polybius XXXI. 17–20 (26–8, 25–7).

[8] 163 B.C. Cf. Polybius XXXI. 3 (14), and XXXII. 1.

A.U.C. 587–594 reliquerat, continet. Hunc Antiochum puerum cum Lysia tutore Demetrius Seleuci filius, qui Romae obses fuerat, clam, quia non dimittebatur, a Roma avectus[1] interemit et ipse in regnum receptus. L. Aemilius Paulus, qui Persen vicerat, mortuus.[2] Cuius tanta abstinentia fuit, ut, cum ex Hispania et ex Macedonia immensas opes rettulisset, vix ex auctione eius redactum sit, unde uxori eius dos solveretur. Pomptinae paludes a Cornelio Cethego consule, cui ea provincia evenerat, siccatae, agerque ex his factus.

A.U.C. 594–601 XLVII. Cn. Tremellio pr. multa dicta est, quod cum M. Aemilio Lepido pontifice maximo iniuriose contenderat; sacrorumque quam magistratuum ius potentius fuit. Lex de ambitu lata. Lustrum a censoribus conditum est: censa sunt civium capita $\overline{\text{CCCXXVIII}}$ CCCXVI.[3] Princeps senatus sextum[4] Aemilius Lepidus. Inter Ptolemaeos fratres, qui dissidebant, foedus ictum, ut alter Aegypto, alter Cyrenis regnaret. Ariarathes, Cappadociae rex, consilio Demetrii Syriae regis et viribus pulsus regno, a

[1] avectus *add. Rossbach*: *om.* MSS.
[2] Aemilius Paulus . . . mortuus *Frobenius*: aemilio paulo . . . mortuo N, P, Π, R.
[3] CCCXVI N, P, G: CCCXIIII B; CCCXXII Gu.
[4] princeps senatus sextum *Jahn*: princeps sex MSS.

---

[1] The elder Antiochus died in 163 B.C. Polybius XXXI. 2 (12), 11–15 (19–23), tells a dramatic story of Demetrius' escape from Rome; he held that his place as hostage should have been taken by the son of the new king, his brother, after the death of their father.
[2] 160 B.C. Cf. Polybius XXXI. 22 (XXXII. 8); Diodorus XXXI. 25.
[3] 160 B.C
[4] 159 B.C. For Tremellius, cf. XLV. xv. 9, which records another clash with the "regulars" of the senate.

left a son Antiochus, a very young boy. This boy Antiochus and his guardian Lysias were killed by Demetrius, the son of Seleucus, who had been a hostage at Rome and had sailed away secretly, because he was not released. Demetrius was received as king.[1] Lucius Aemilius Paulus, who had conquered Perseus, died. His scrupulousness was so great that, although he had brought back vast wealth from Spain and Macedonia, the sum raised at the auction of his effects was hardly large enough to repay his wife's dowry.[2] The Pomptine Marshes were drained and made arable by Consul Cornelius Cethegus, to whom this task had been officially assigned.[3] B.C. 167–160

XLVII. A fine was imposed on Praetor Gnaeus Tremellius, because he had unlawfully opposed Marcus Aemilius Lepidus, the chief pontiff, and the claim of religion won the day over that of civil administration.[4] A law on bribery was passed.[5] The half-decade was formally ended by the censors. The number of citizens was three hundred and twenty-eight thousand, three hundred and sixteen. Aemilius Lepidus was chief of the senate for the sixth time.[6] B.C. 160–153

An agreement was made by the brothers Ptolemy, who were at odds, that one should rule Egypt, the other Cyrene.[7] Ariarathes, king of Cappadocia, was expelled from his kingdom on the initiative and by the power of Demetrius, king of Syria, and was restored by the senate.[8]

[5] 159 B.C. A previous law in 181 B.C. is mentioned in XL. xix. 11. When Polybius says (VI. lvi) that bribery is a capital crime at Rome, he is perhaps referring to a feature of the law of 159.

[6] 159 B.C. It seems likely that the census figures have been confused in transmission. Lepidus' first designation as *princeps senatus* was in 179 B.C., XL. li. 1, so that this should be his fifth term. Cf. *Summary* XLVI, note 6.

[7] Cf. above, XLVI, note 7.

[8] 158 B.C. Cf. Polybius XXXII. 10–12 (L.C.L.).

A.U.C. 594–601 senatu restitutus est. Missi a senatu, qui inter Masinissam et Carthaginienses de agro iudicarent. C. Marcius consul adversus Dalmatas primum parum prospere, postea feliciter pugnavit. Cum quibus bello confligendi causa fuit, quod Illyrios, socios populi Romani, vastaverant; eandemque gentem Cornelius Nasica consul domuit. Q. Opimius consul Transalpinos Liguras, qui Massiliensium oppida[1] Antipolim et Nicaeam vastabant, subegit. Praeterea res in Hispania a compluribus parum prospere gestas continet. Consules anno quingentesimo nonagesimo octavo ab urbe condita magistratum kal. Ian.[2] inire coeperunt. Mutandi comitia causa fuit, quod Hispani rebellabant. Legati ad disceptandum inter Carthaginienses et Masinissam missi nuntiaverunt vim navalis materiae se Carthagine deprehendisse. Aliquot praetores a provinciis avaritiae nomine accusati damnati sunt.

A.U.C. 600–604 XLVIII. Lustrum a censoribus conditum est: censa sunt civium capita $\overline{\text{CCCXXIIII}}$. Semina tertii Punici belli referuntur. Cum in finibus Carthaginiensium ingens Numidarum exercitus duce Arcobarzane Syphacis nepote

[1] oppida *Frobenius*: oppidum N, P, Π, R.
[2] kal. Ian. *add. Drakenborch*: *om.* MSS.

---

[1] Cf. Appian, *African Wars* 69.
[2] Marcius (Figulus), 156 B.C. Cf. Appian, *Illyrian Wars* 11 Nasica, 155 B.C.; for his triumph, see *C.I.L.*[2] 1, 1, p. 176.
[3] 154 B.C. Cf. Polybius XXXIII. 9–10 (L.C.L.).
[4] The Lusitanians went on the warpath in 154 B.C.; the Celtiberians were stirred to revolt in 153 B.C. by Roman restrictions and the revival of treaty demands, cf. Appian, *Iberian Wars* 47.
[5] 153 B.C.; the date of Rome's founding by this reckoning is 750 B.C., as it is by that of Polybius. The adjustment of the civil year may have been necessary because the calendar had now been set in order, cf. XLIII, Appendix. While

A commission was sent by the senate to settle the ownership of territory as between Masinissa and the Carthaginians.[1] B.C. 160–153

Consul Gaius Marcius campaigned against the Dalmatians, at first without success, but later victoriously. The cause of the war with this people was that they had plundered the Illyrians, who were allies of the Roman People. Consul Cornelius Nasica subdued the Dalmatians.[2] Consul Quintus Opimius subdued the Ligurians west of the Alps, who had been ravaging Antipolis and Nicaea, towns of the Massilians.[3] The book also contains an account of the unsuccessful campaigns in Spain waged by several commanders.[4] In the five hundred and ninety-eighth year after the founding of the city, the consuls began to enter upon their office on January first. The reason for changing the elections was the uprising of the Spaniards.[5] The envoys sent to settle the dispute between the Carthaginians and Masinissa reported that they had discovered a large supply of ship timber at Carthage.[6] Several praetors were prosecuted on a charge of peculation by the provinces, and were convicted.

XLVIII. The half-decade was formally ended by the censors; there were counted three hundred and twenty-four thousand citizens.[7] An account is given of the preliminaries of the Third Punic War. When it was reported that a large army of Numidians under Arcobarzanes, the B.C. 154–150

the calendar was fast, the year had actually begun near mid-winter, though the calendar gave March as the month.

[6] The summarizing process makes it seem that these envoys were those mentioned above; cf. note 1; but the dates should be 157 and 153 respectively, and there probably were two embassies according to Livy. Appian mentions only one, and may be following Polybius, while Livy also used Roman sources; cf. his stories of the relations of Rome with Perseus, XLII. xxxvi and xlviii, and with Rhodes, XLIV. xiv. 13 and the note.

[7] 154 B.C. The censors were Marcus Valerius Messalla and Gaius Cassius Longinus.

A.U.C. 600–604 diceretur esse, M. Porcius Cato suasit, ut Carthaginiensibus, qui exercitum specie contra Masinissam, re[1] contra Romanos accitum in finibus haberent, bellum indiceretur. Contra dicente P. Cornelio Nasica placuit legatos mitti Carthaginem, qui[2] specularentur quid ageretur. Castigato senatu Carthaginiensium, quod contra foedus et exercitum et navales materias haberent, pacem inter eos et Masinissam facere voluerunt, Masinissa agro, de quo lis erat, cedente. Sed Gisgo Hamilcaris filius, homo seditiosus, qui tum in magistratu erat, cum senatus pariturum se iudicio legatis dixisset, ita populum concitavit bellum adversus[3] Romanos suadendo, ut legatos quo minus violarentur fuga explicuerit. Id nuntiantes infestum iam senatum Carthaginiensibus infestiorem fecerunt. M. Porcius Cato filii in praetura mortui funus tenuissimo, ut potuit — nam pauper erat —, sumptu fecit. Andriscus, qui se Persei filium, regis quondam Macedoniae, ingenti adseveratione mentiretur, Romam missus. M. Aemilius Lepidus, qui princeps senatus sextis iam censoribus lectus erat, antequam expiraret praecepit filiis, lecto se strato linteis[4] sine purpura efferrent; in reliquum funus ne plus quam aeris decies[5] consumerent; imaginum specie, non sumptibus nobilitari magnorum virorum funera solere. De veneficiis quaesitum. Publilia et Licinia, nobiles feminae, quae viros suos consulares

[1] re *Hertz*: regem N, P, R.
[2] qui *Rossbach post Pithoei* qui ibi: quibus N, P, Π.
[3] ita populum concitavit bellum adversus *Jahn*: ita bellum concitavit adversus MSS.
[4] strato linteis *Perizonius*: strato sine linteis MSS.
[5] decies B: decus MSS: denos R: D *Orelli*.

---

[1] If the summary preserves Livy's order, these events were in 153 B.C. On Cato's attitude here and below, cf. Plutarch, *Marcus Cato* xxvi and xxvii.

[2] This matter is alluded to by Cicero, *De Senectute* 68, 84. It perhaps occurred in 152 B.C., and the younger Cato may have been praetor-elect.

grandson of Syphax, was in Carthaginian territory, Marcus Porcius Cato advocated that war should be declared on the Carthaginians, because they had an army in their territory which they had brought in ostensibly against Masinissa, but actually against the Romans. After a speech in opposition by Publius Cornelius Nasica, it was voted to send an embassy to Carthage to investigate what was taking place. After rebuking the Carthaginian senate for having an army and ship timber contrary to treaty, the embassy wished to make peace between Carthage and Masinissa, since Masinissa was retiring from the disputed territory. But when the senate said that it would comply with the decision of the ambassadors, Gisgo son of Hamilcar, a riotous fellow who then held a magistracy, so stirred up the people by advocating war against Rome that flight alone saved the envoys from mishandling. Their report of this made a hostile senate still more hostile to Carthage.[1] B.C. 154–150

When Marcus Porcius Cato's son died during his praetorship, his father conducted his funeral at very small expense, according to his means, for he was a poor man.[2] Andriscus, who insisted vehemently on the lie that he was the son of Perseus, the former king of Macedonia, was sent to Rome.[3] Marcus Aemilius Lepidus, who had been chosen chief of the senate by six pairs of censors, instructed his sons on his death-bed to bear him to the grave on a bier spread with linens without purple; for the rest of the funeral, said Lepidus, they were not to spend more than a million *asses*, for the dignity of the funerals of great men was properly enhanced not by expenditure, but by the parade of ancestral portraits.[4] An investigation of poisonings was held. Publilia and Licinia, women of social position, were alleged to have murdered their

[3] Andriscus appealed to Demetrius of Syria as his relative, who disposed of him by sending him to Rome. He later escaped; see below, XLIX.

[4] Cf. above XLVII, note 6. His sixth designation as *princeps* was in 154 B.C.; it is not mentioned in the Summaries. His death occurred in 153–2 B.C.

A.U.C. 600–604 necasse insimulabantur, cognita causa, cum praetori praedes vades dedissent, cognatorum decreto necatae sunt. Gulussa Masinissae filius nuntiavit Carthagine dilectus agi, classem comparari et haud dubie bellum strui. Cum Cato suaderet, ut his bellum indiceretur, P. Cornelio Nasica dicente nihil temere faciundum, placuit decem legatos mitti exploratum. L. Licinius Lucullus A. Postumius Albinus consules cum dilectum severe agerent nec quemquam gratia dimitterent, ab tribunis plebis, qui pro amicis suis vacationem impetrare non poterant, in carcerem coniecti sunt. Cum Hispaniense bellum parum prospere aliquotiens gestum ita confudisset civitatem Romanam, ut ne hi quidem invenirentur, qui aut tribunatum exciperent aut legati ire vellent, P. Cornelius Aemilianus processit et excepturum se militiae genus, quodcumque imperatum esset, professus est; quo exemplo omnes ad studium militandi concitavit. Lucullus consul, cum Claudius Marcellus, cui [1] successerat, pacasse omnes Celtiberiae populos videretur, Vaccaeos et Cantabros et alias incognitas adhuc in Hispania gentes subegit. Ibi P. Cornelius Scipio [2] Aemilianus, L. Pauli [3] filius, Africani nepos, sed [4] adoptivus, provocatorem barbarum tribunus militum occidit et in expugnatione Intercatiae [5] urbis maius etiamnum periculum adit; nam

[1] cum C.M. cui *Sigonius*: cui C.M. MSS.
[2] P. Cornelius Scipio *Gronovius*: P. Cornelius Africanus Scipio MSS.
[3] L. Pauli *Aldus*: L. Corneli Pauli MSS.
[4] sed *Frobenius*: et MSS.
[5] Intercatiae *Sigonius*: inter captae MSS.

---

[1] According to Valerius Maximus VI. iii. 8, Publilia's husband was Postumius Albinus, presumably the consul of 151 B.C. Valerius gives the name as "Publicia," and speaks of Postumius as "Consul." Licinia's husband was Claudius Asellus.

husbands, who were ex-consuls. After a hearing on the case the women assigned real estate to the praetor as bail, and were put to death by decree of their own kinsmen.[1] B.C. 154–150

Gulussa the son of Masinissa reported that recruiting was under way at Carthage, a fleet was being prepared, and obviously war was in the making. Cato advocated declaring war on Carthage; Publius Cornelius Nasica declared that no hasty move should be made; and it was voted that ten envoys should be sent to investigate.[2]

When Consuls Lucius Licinius Lucullus and Aulus Postumius Albinus were conducting the levy strictly and exempting no one as a favour, they were thrown into prison by tribunes of the people, who were unable to obtain exemption for their friends. When numerous failures in the war in Spain had caused such confusion in the Roman state that no one could be found even to undertake service as military tribune, or to accept a post as staff-officer, Publius Cornelius Aemilianus came forward and announced that he would accept any form of military service to which he should be assigned; by this public-spirited action he aroused everyone to eagerness for military service.[3] Though Claudius Marcellus was thought to have reduced all the Celtiberian tribes, Consul Lucullus, his successor, subdued the Vaccaei, Cantabri, and other previously unknown Spanish tribes. In the same region, Publius Cornelius Scipio Aemilianus, son of Lucius Paulus, and adopted grandson of Africanus, while serving as military tribune, killed a native challenger, and in the storming of the city of Intercatia exposed himself to an even greater danger, for he was the first to surmount

[2] The account of these repeated embassies is confusing; Gsell, *Histoire Ancienne de l'Afrique du Nord*, (1918), III. 333–5: Appian represents the events of 150 B.C. as the first occasion for Roman action against Carthage; G. suggests that Livy has followed, not Polybius, but a Roman annalist who built up Rome's case against her rival.

[3] 151 B.C. Cf. Polybius XXXV. 4. 1–14 for the horror stories from Spain which circulated at Rome; cf. also Appian, *Spanish Wars* 49, Orosius IV. xxi. 1.

A.U.C. 600–604 murum primus transcendit. Ser. Sulpicius Galba praetor male adversus Lusitanos pugnavit. Cum legati ex Africa cum oratoribus Carthaginiensium et Gulussa Masinissae filio redissent dicerentque et exercitum se et classem Carthagine deprehendisse, perrogari sententias placuit. Catone et aliis principibus senatus suadentibus, ut in Africam confestim transportaretur exercitus, quoniam Cornelius Nasica dicebat nondum sibi iustam causam belli videri, placuit, ut bello abstinerent, si Carthaginienses classem exussissent et exercitum dimisissent; si minus, proximi consules de bello Punico referrent. Cum locatum a censoribus theatrum exstrueretur, P. Cornelio Nasica auctore tamquam inutile et nociturum publicis moribus ex senatus consulto destructum est, populusque aliquamdiu stans ludos spectavit. Carthaginienses cum adversus foedus bellum Masinissae intulissent, victi ab eo annos habente XCII et sine pulpamine mandere et siccum gustare panem [1] tantum solito, insuper Romanum bellum meruerunt. Motus praeterea Syriae et bella inter reges gesta referuntur. Inter quos motus Demetrius Syriae rex occisus est.

(Liber XLVIII)

col. IV adversus Ca[rth]aginienses. Lusitani va[stati.
C. Corneliu[s Ceth]egus, quod P. Decim Su

[1] mandere et siccum gustare panem *Madvig*: manderet sigustaret pane NP.

---

[1] 151 B.C. A fuller account is given by Appian, *Spanish Wars* 49–55. Marcellus made peace with his opponents to forestall Lucullus; the latter made war without authorization or scruple, acquired some booty and many hard knocks.

the wall.[1] Praetor Servius Sulpicius Galba fought unsuccessfully against the Lusitanians.[2] B.C. 154–150

When the envoys returned from Africa with representatives of the Carthaginians and with Gulussa the son of Masinissa, they reported that they had discovered both an army and a fleet at Carthage. The senate decided to poll the opinions of all the senators. Although Cato and other leading senators urged that an army should be taken to Africa at once, Cornelius Nasica said that he did not believe that there was as yet proper cause for war. Therefore it was voted to refrain from war if the Carthaginians burned their fleet and disbanded their army; if this was not done, the next consuls were to put the question of war with Carthage. When a theatre, contracted for by the censors, was being built, on motion of Publius Cornelius Nasica it was torn down by order of the senate, on the ground that it was inexpedient and would be injurious to the public character; and for some time thereafter the people stood to see theatrical performances.[3] When the Carthaginians attacked Masinissa contrary to the treaty, they were beaten. Masinissa was at that time ninety-two years old; his habit was to eat and enjoy plain dry bread without a relish.[4] The Carthaginians furthermore incurred war with Rome. The book also describes revolts in Syria and wars waged by the kings. In these disturbances Demetrius king of Syria was killed.[5]

(Book XLVIII)

. . . against the Carthaginians. The Lusitanians were ravaged. Gaius Cornelius Cethegus was condemned to a

[2] This apparently refers to Galba's campaign of 152 B.C., cf. Appian, *Spanish Wars* 58.

[3] 151 B.C. There are frequent references to this, including Valerius Maximus II. 4. 2, Velleius I. 15. 3, Augustine, *City of God* II. 5, and Appian, *Civil Wars* I. 28.

[4] Cf. Polybius XXXVI. 16 (L.C.L.).

[5] 150 B.C. Demetrius' fate is recorded by Polybius III. 5, Justinus XXXV. 1, Josephus, *Antiquities* XIII. 58 ff.

a[dd]ictam [1] ingenu[a]m stupraverat DCl damnatus. *add.* PSI. 12. 1291? *Macdonald.*

A.U.C. 605 XLIX. Tertii Punici belli initium altero et sescentesimo ab urbe condita anno, intra quintum annum quam erat coeptum, consummati. Inter M. Porcium Catonem et Scipionem Nasicam, quorum alter sapientissimus vir in civitate habebatur, alter optimus vir etiam iudicatus a senatu erat, diversis certatum sententiis est, Catone suadente bellum et ut tolleretur delereturque Carthago, Nasica dissuadente. Placuit tamen, quod contra foedus naves haberent, quod exercitum extra fines duxissent, quod socio populi Romani et amico, Masinissae, arma intulissent, quod filium eius Gulussam, qui cum legatis Romanis erat, in oppidum non recepissent, bellum his indici. Priusquam ullae copiae in naves imponerentur, Uticenses legati Romam venerunt se suaque omnia dedentes. Ea legatio velut omen grata patribus, acerba Carthaginiensibus fuit. Ludi Diti patri ad Tarentum ex praecepto librorum facti, qui ante [2] annum centesimum primo Punico bello, quingentesimo et altero anno ab urbe condita facti erant. Legati triginta Romam venerunt, per quos se Carthaginienses dedebant. Catonis sententia

[1] *de nomine non liquet.* P. Decimam Sulpicio *Kornemann*: P. Decio Subuloni *Luterbacher.* addictam *Kornemann.*
[2] ante *add. Gronovius*: *om.* MSS.

---

[1] Münzer (*Klio* 5 (1905) 136f.) thinks that P. Decius Subulo was the object of the assault, cf. Valerius Maximus 6.1.10; Cicero, *de Oratore* 2.253.277; *a. ictam* in the MS is then left unexplained, and ingenu[u]m is to be read. If a woman is involved, Cethegus was fined, perhaps, for treating her as a slave, cf. Quintilian III. vi. 25.
[2] 149 B.C., reckoning from 750 B.C. as the year of Rome's founding; see above, XLVII note 5, p. 15.
[3] Polybius XXXVI. 2 (1b) says that the Romans were

fine of six hundred sesterces for debauching a free bondwoman bound to Publius Decius Subulo.[1]

XLIX. The beginning of the Third Punic War fell in the six hundred and second year after the founding of the city—a war which was concluded within five years from its beginning.[2] A contest of opposing opinions took place between Marcus Porcius Cato and Scipio Nasica, one of whom was considered a man of the greatest wisdom in the state, while the other had even been adjudged by the senate to be a man of greatest excellence. Cato urged war and the removal and destruction of Carthage, while Nasica opposed him.[3] It was voted, however, that whereas the Carthaginians had a navy contrary to the treaty, whereas they had led their army beyond their own territory, whereas they had attacked Masinissa, a friend and ally of the Roman people, and whereas they had not received Masinissa's son Gulussa, who had accompanied the Roman envoys, within their walls, war should be declared on Carthage. Before any troops had been put aboard ship, envoys of Utica came to Rome to put themselves and all they had in the hands of the Romans. This embassy was pleasing as an omen to the senate, and bitter to the Carthaginians.[4] B.C. 149

Games in honour of Father Dis were celebrated at the Tarentum, as prescribed by the Sibylline Books; similar games had been celebrated one hundred years before in the First Punic War, in the five hundred and second year after the founding of the city.[5]

Thirty envoys came to Rome to convey the surrender of Carthage. The opinion of Cato prevailed that the senate

considering the effect of their actions on international opinion at this time.

[4] Utica's action is recorded by Polybius XXXVI. 3 (1) and Appian, *African Wars* VIII. xi. 75.

[5] The Tarentum was a spot on the Campus Martius, with a subterranean altar to Father Dis and Proserpina. See also below, p. 31 note 2.

A.U.C. 605 evicit,[1] ut in decreto perstaretur, et ut consules quam primum ad bellum proficiscerentur. Qui ubi in Africam transierunt, acceptis quos imperaverant trecentis obsidibus et armis omnibus instrumentisque belli, si qua Carthagine erant, cum [2] ex auctoritate patrum iuberent, ut in alio loco, dum a mari decem milia passuum ne minus remoto, oppidum facerent, indignitate rei ad bellandum Carthaginienses compulerunt. Obsideri oppugnarique coepta est Carthago a L. Marcio M'. Manilio [3] consulibus. In qua oppugnatione cum neglectos ab una parte muros duo tribuni temere cum cohortibus suis irrupissent et ab oppidanis graviter caederentur, a Scipione Africano [4] expliciti sunt; per quem et castellum Romanorum, quod nocte expugnabant, paucis equitibus iuvantibus liberatum est, castrorumque, quae Carthaginienses omnibus copiis ab urbe pariter egressi oppugnabant, liberatorum is ipse praecipuam gloriam tulit. Praeterea cum ab inrita oppugnatione Carthaginis consul — alter enim Romam [5] ad comitia ierat [6] — exercitum duceret adversus Hasdrubalem, qui [7] cum ampla manu saltum iniquum insederat, suasit primo consuli, ne tam iniquo loco confligeret. Victus deinde complurum, qui et prudentiae et virtuti eius invidebant, sententiis et ipse saltum ingressus est. Cum, sicut praedixerat, fusus fugatusque esset Romanus exercitus et duae cohortes ab hoste obsiderentur, cum paucis equitum turmis in saltum reversus liberavit eas et incolumes reduxit. Quam virtutem eius et Cato, vir promptioris ad vituperandum linguae, in senatu sic prosecutus est, ut diceret reliquos, qui in Africa militarent, umbras volitare,[8] Scipionem vigere, et populus Romanus

[1] evicit *Halm*: pervicit R, devicit MSS.
[2] cum *Jahn*: tum N, tunc P, tunc cum R.
[3] M'. Manilio *Sigonius*: M. Manlio NPR.
[4] Africano PR: Orfitiano NΠ.
[5] Romam R: Roma NΠ; Romae P.
[6] ierat R, erat NPΠ.
[7] qui *add.* R: *om.* MSS, *Rossbach*.
[8] volitare *Sigonius*: militare MSS.

should stand by its decision and that the consuls should set out to war as soon as possible. When the consuls had crossed into Africa, they received the three hundred hostages they had ordered, and all the weapons and engines of war which were at Carthage. They then ordered, on the authority of the senate, that the Carthaginians should build a town elsewhere, but not less than ten miles from the sea. By these insulting terms they drove the Carthaginians to fight. The siege and assault of Carthage was begun by Consuls Lucius Marcius and Manius Manilius.[1] During this siege, when two tribunes with their units rashly broke through the walls where they were carelessly held, and were suffering heavy losses from the townspeople they were extricated by Scipio Africanus. He also relieved with the aid of a few cavalrymen a Roman fort which the Carthaginians were storming at night; and when the latter sallied from the city in full force and made a general attack on the Roman camp, Scipio received the chief credit for saving the day. Furthermore, when the consul—for the other consul had gone to Rome for the elections—led his army from its fruitless blockade of Carthage against Hasdrubal, who lay in wait at a difficult pass with abundant forces, Scipio at first advised the consul not to fight on such unfavourable terrain. The opinions of the majority who were jealous both of his wisdom and of his valour prevailed over him, and he entered the pass with the others. When the Roman army was routed and put to flight as he had predicted and two units were trapped by the enemy, he re-entered the pass with a few troops of cavalry, freed the Romans, and brought them back unharmed. This valour of Scipio's even Cato, a man whose tongue was readier for invective, praised in the senate so highly as to say that the others who were serving in the army in Africa were flitting shadows, while Scipio alone was alive; moreover, the Roman people hailed him with such approval B.C. 149

[1] Appian, *African Wars* xi. 76–xiv. 96 gives the speeches of the consul and of the final envoys from Carthage.

A.U.C. 605 eo favore complexus, ut comitiis plurimae eum tribus consulem scriberent, cum hoc per aetatem non liceret. Cum L. Scribonius tribunus plebis rogationem promulgasset, ut Lusitani, qui in fidem populo R. dediti ab Ser. Galba in Gallia venissent, in libertatem restituerentur, M. Cato acerrime suasit. Extat oratio in[1] annalibus ipsius inclusa. Q. Fulvius Nobilior ei,[2] saepe ab eo in senatu laceratus, respondit pro Galba. Ipse quoque Galba, cum se damnari videret, complexus duos filios praetextatos et Sulpicii Galli[2a] filium, cuius tutor erat, ita miserabiliter pro se locutus est, ut rogatio antiquaretur. Extant tres orationes eius, duae adversus Libonem tribunum plebis rogationemque eius habitae de Lusitanis, una contra L. Cornelium Cethegum, in qua Lusitanos prope se castra habentis caesos fatetur, quod compertum habuerit equo atque homine suo ritu immolatis per speciem pacis adoriri exercitum suum in animo habuisse.

Andriscus quidam, ultimae sortis homo, Persei regis filium se[3] ferens et mutato nomine Philippus vocatus, cum ab urbe Romana, quo illum Demetrius Syriae rex ob hoc ipsum mendacium miserat, clam profugisset, multis ad falsam eius fabulam velut ad veram coeuntibus, contracto exercitu totam Macedoniam aut voluntate incolentium aut armis occupavit. Fabulam autem talem finxerat: ex paelice[4] se et[5] Perseo rege ortum, traditum edu-

[1] in R: et in NPII: et est in *Rossbach*.
[2] ei *Jahn*: et MSS.
[2a] Gali *Mommsen*; Sulpi Cali MSS.
[3] se *add.* R, *edd. variis locis*: *om.* MSS.
[4] paelice MSS.: Laodice *Wilcken*.
[5] et *add. edd.*: *om.* MSS.

---

[1] Cato was quoting the *Odyssey*, X. 495, in his praise of Scipio. The election of Scipio as consul is again mentioned below in L, in the proper chronological sequence (147 B.C.). Appian, *African Wars* xiv. 98, 99 also describes the feats of Scipio.

that the majority of tribes at the elections voted him into the consulship, although this was illegal because of his age.[1] B.C. 149

When Lucius Scribonius, tribune of the commons, proposed a resolution that freedom should be restored to Lusitanians who had been sold in Gaul by Servius Galba after having surrendered at discretion to the Roman People, Cato most vigorously supported the resolution. His speech survives, as part of his *History*. Quintus Fulvius Nobilior, who had often been assailed by Cato in the senate, answered him on behalf of Galba. Moreover, Galba himself, seeing that he was being condemned, spoke in his own defence so pitiably, clasping his two young sons and the son of Sulpicius Gallus, whose guardian he was, that the resolution was defeated. Three speeches by Galba survive: two were delivered against Libo the tribune of the commons and his resolution about the Lusitanians; the third was against Lucius Cornelius Cethegus, in which Galba admits that he massacred the Lusitanians who were encamped near him, because, he says, he had discovered that they had sacrificed a horse and a man according to their custom and planned to attack his army under cover of the truce.[2]

A certain Andriscus, a man of the lowest class, styling himself the son of King Perseus, and changing his name to Philip, fled secretly from the city of Rome, to which Demetrius, King of Syria, had sent him precisely because of this false claim of his. Many followers rallied about his lying account as if it were true, and with the army he had collected he seized all of Macedonia either with the consent of the inhabitants or by force. This was the tale he had invented: he was the son of King Perseus and a concu-

[2] 149 B.C. All the orations mentioned were delivered on the same occasion. Galba's speeches are mentioned by Cicero, *De Oratore* I. 227 and *Brutus* 89, by Valerius Maximus, VIII. i. 2, by Appian, *Spanish Wars* 60, and in the *Oxyrhynchus Summary* XLIX below. The establishment of the permanent *quaestio repetundarum* (court of malfeasance) in this year was a consequence of this agitation.

A.U.C. 605 candum Cretensi cuidam esse, ut in[1] belli casus, quod ille cum Romanis gereret, aliquod velut semen regiae stirpis extaret. Hydramyti[2] se educatum usque ad duodecimum aetatis annum, patrem eum esse credentem, a quo educaretur, ignarum generis fuisse sui. Adfecto deinde eo, cum prope ad ultimum finem vitae esset, detectam tandem sibi originem suam falsaeque matri libellum datum signo Persei regis signatum, quem sibi traderet, cum ad puberem aetatem venisset, obtestationesque ultimas adiectas, ut res in occultato[3] ad id tempus servaretur. Pubescenti libellum traditum, in quo relicti sibi duo thensauri a patre dicerentur. Tum scienti mulierem[4] se subditum esse, veram stirpem ignoranti edidisse genus atque obtestatam, ut prius quam manaret ad Eumenen res, Perseo inimicum, excederet his locis, ne interficeretur. Eo se exterritum, simul sperantem aliquod a Demetrio auxilium in Syriam se contulisse atque ibi primum, quis esset, palam expromere ausum.

Liber XXXXV[I]III

L. Marcio Censorino M. Manilio coss.
bellum Punicum tertium exortum. Utic[enses
b]enigne locavere auxilia.[5] Carthagin[i]e[nses

[1] in *add. edd.*, *om.* MSS.
[2] *sic* NΠ.
[3] occultato *Rossbach*: occupato NPΠ: occulto GR.
[4] scienti mulierem *edd.*: scienti mulieri NP: scientem mulierem R.
[5] locavere auxilia *Rossbach*: locavelauxiliate MS: locant auxilia *Kornemann*.

---

[1] Wilcken would read here "Laodice," the name of Perseus' queen, cf. XLII. xii. 3. At this time, Laodice was at the court of her brother Demetrius, cf. below, L; one wonders if Andriscus would have ventured to claim kinship with her practically to her face.

bine,[1] and had been given to a certain Cretan to rear, so that in spite of the accidents of the war which Perseus was then waging against Rome, some scion, as it were, of the royal stock might survive. He had been brought up at Hydramitis [2] until he was twelve, believing that his father was the man who was rearing him, and without knowledge of his own family. Then when his foster father fell ill and was almost on his death-bed, he finally revealed to Andriscus his parentage and gave his foster mother a writing sealed with the seal of King Perseus, which she was to give to the boy when he reached maturity. His foster father added his dying entreaties that the matter should be kept secret until that time. On reaching maturity, Andriscus was given the writing in which it was said that two hoards of treasure had been left him by his father. At that time he knew that he was a foster son, but did not know his true parentage; his foster mother revealed to him his lineage and begged him, in order to avoid assassination, to depart from that region before the news leaked out to Eumenes, the enemy of Perseus. Frightened by this entreaty, Andriscus said, and also hoping for some aid from Demetrius, he had made his way to Syria and there had first dared to declare who he was.[3] B.C. 149

Book XLIX

In the consulship of Lucius Marcius Censorinus and Marcus Manilius, the Third Punic War began. The people of Utica hospitably provided quarters for the troops sent to their aid.[4] The Carthaginians offered their surrender.

[2] It is possible that Hydramia in Crete is meant; but Adramyttion in Asia Minor is often taken to be the city referred to (so Lucian, *Against an Ignoramus* 20 and Ammianus Marcellinus XIV. xi. 31).

[3] The further story of Andriscus is told below in L and LII. For the portion related above, cf. Diodorus XXXII. 15.

[4] As will be seen from the critical note, this version is conjectural.

A.U.C. 605 i]n [d]edicionem venerunt. Iussi omn[i]a [sua in alium locum tr[ansferr]e mo[ti ira ad arma redierunt. Roman[os obses]s[i Carthaginienses [1] pepulerunt. Scipio [trib. mil. fugientes defendit. Aemiliani fidem P[oeni suspexerunt.[2] Aemiliani virtute exer[citus, qui obsessus in saltu a Poenis erat, liber[atus.

per Charidemum poe [. . . Ser. Galba de Lusitanis reus product[us. Liberaverunt eum fili, quos flens com[mendabat. Ab Andrisco, q]ui se Philippi filiu[m ferebat, Macedonia per arma occupata.

Manilio et Marcio c[oss. quarti ludi saeculare[s], factos quos opo[rtuit Diti ex Sibyllae carminibus, [Tar]en[ti facti sunt.[3]

A.U.C. 601–606 L. Thessalia, cum et illam invadere armis atque occupare Pseudophilippus vellet, per legatos Romanorum auxiliis Achaeorum defensa est. Prusias rex Bithyniae, ⟨homo⟩[3a] omnium humillimorumque vitiorum, a Nicomede filio, adiuvante Attalo rege Pergami, occisus, habebat alterum filium, qui pro superiore ordine dentium enatum habuisse unum os continens dicitur. cum III [4] legati [5] ad pacem inter Nicomeden et Prusiam faciendam ab Romanis [6] missi essent,

[1] *suppl. Rossbach*: Romanorum consules Poeni obsessi *Kornemann*: Romani urbem obsedere. Poeni eos *Luterbacher*.

[2] suspexerunt *Rossbach*: admirati sunt *Kornemann*.

[3] *suppl. Wissowa*: dicunt, ludos saec. fact., quos oportuit fieri ex Sib. carm. Cn. Lentulo L. Mummio coss. *Kornemann*: plerique prodiderunt Man. et M. coss. ludos saec. fact. quos oportebat ex Sib. carm. dis centesimo quoque anno fieri *Luterbacher*. [3a] *suppl. Heraeus*.

[4] cum tres *Lovelianus*: cum in NP.

[5] legati *Gronovius*: legatos MSS.

[6] ab Romanis *Gronovius*: ad Romanos MSS.

When ordered to convey all their possessions to another site, they were roused to anger and resorted to arms again. The Carthaginians, being blockaded, repelled the Romans. Scipio as tribune of the soldiers protected the routed men. The Carthaginians admired the good faith of Aemilianus. By the valour of Aemilianus the army which had been trapped in a defile by the Carthaginians was released . . . through Charidemus[1] . . . Servius Galba was put on trial for his conduct towards the Lusitanians. His acquittal was secured by his sons, whom he presented with tears to his judges. Macedonia was seized by force of arms by Andriscus, who claimed that he was the son of Philip. In the consulship of Manilius and Marcius, the fourth[2] centennial festival which was required, according to the prophecies of the Sibyl, as an offering to Dis, was held at the Tarentum. B.C. 149

L. When the false Philip attempted to invade and seize Thessaly, this district was defended by Roman deputies at the head of Achaean troops.[3] Prusias King of Bithynia, a man of unlimited and basest defects of character, was killed by his son Nicomedes, aided by Attalus King of Pergamum. Prusias had a second son, who is said to have had a single continuous bone growing in place of his upper row of teeth.[4] Three envoys were sent by the Romans to arrange peace between Nicomedes and Prusias; B.C. 150–148

[1] Charidemus is unknown; he may have been a poet, but the letters *poe* might also indicate something Carthaginian (*Poenus*, etc.).

[2] Cf. Censorinus 17. 10; apparently in the time of Augustus a schedule of supposed *ludi saeculares* was drawn up, to justify his celebration of 17 B.C. as the fifth of the series; the first two were placed in 509 and 408 B.C. respectively; the third was the celebration of 249 B.C. mentioned in the first *Summary* XLIX above.

[3] 150 B.C. The Roman commander was Scipio Nasica, according to Zonaras IX. 28.

[4] Cf. Pyrrhus, Plutarch, *Pyrrhus* iii. 4; also Pliny, *N.H.* VII. xvi. 69; Herodotus IX. 83. 5.

A.U.C. 604–606 cum unus ex his multis cicatricibus sartum[1] caput haberet, alter pedibus aeger esset, tertius ingenio socors haberetur, M. Cato dixit eam in legationem, nec caput nec pedes nec cor habere. In Syria, quae eo tempore stirpe generis parem Macedonum regis, inertia socordiaque similem Prusiae regem habebat, iacente eo in ganea et lustris Hammonius regnabat, per quem et amici omnes regis et Laodice regina et Antigonus Demetri filius occisi sunt.[2] Masinissa Numidiae rex maior nonaginta annis decessit, vir insignis. Inter cetera iuvenalia opera, quae ad ultimum edidit, adeo etiam veneris usu[3] in senecta viguit, ut post sextum et octogesimum annum filium genuerit. Inter tres liberos eius (maximus natu Micipsa, Gulussa, Mastanabal, qui etiam Graecis litteris eruditus erat) P. Scipio Aemilianus, cum commune his regnum pater reliquisset et dividere eos arbitro Scipione iussisset, partes administrandi regni divisit. Item Phameae[4] Himilconi, praefecto equitum Carthaginiensium, viro forti et cuius praecipua opera Poeni utebantur, persuasit ut ad Romanos cum equitatu suo transiret. Ex tribus legatis, qui ad Masinissam missi erant, M. Claudius Marcellus coorta tempestate fluctibus obrutus est. Carthaginienses Hasdrubalem, Masinissae nepotem, quem praetorem habebant, hominem proditionis suspectum in curia occiderunt; quae suspicio inde manavit, quod propinquus

[1] sartum *Jahn*: sarsum MSS.: sparsum R.
[2] occisi sunt *edd.*: occisum NPR.
[3] veneris usu *Seyffert*: versus MSS.: nervis *Britzlmayr, Rossbach.*
[4] Phameae *edd.*: phamae NP².

---

[1] Cf. Polybius XXXVI. 14 (L.C.L.).
[2] The king was Alexander Balas. On Hammonius, see also Josephus XIII. 106 ff. For Laodice, cf. above p. 28, note 7. She was sister to Demetrius, and may have married him.
[3] 149–8 B.C. On Masinissa, cf. Polybius XXXVI. 16 (L.C.L.). Mastanabal was not alone among his brothers as to his education, cf. Diodorus XXXIV. 35. Scipio's division of the

one of these had a head strewn with many scars, another was gouty, and the third was considered stupid in nature. Marcus Cato's comment on that embassy was that it had neither head nor feet nor wits.[1] In Syria, which at that time had a king who was in ancestry the equal of the kings of Macedonia but in idleness and sluggishness resembled Prusias, the kingship was exercised by Hammonius, while the titular king took his ease in cook-shops and brothels. Hammonius put to death not only all the friends of the king, but Queen Laodice and Antigonus the son of Demetrius.[2] B.C. 150–148

Masinissa King of Numidia died aged more than ninety, a distinguished man. Among other youthful exploits which he performed during his last years, he was so vigorous even sexually in his old age as to beget a son after he was eighty-six. He left his kingdom undivided to three sons, Micipsa, the eldest, Gulussa, and Mastanabal, who had also been educated in Greek culture, and ordered them to divide it according to the judgment of Publius Scipio Aemilianus. Scipio accordingly assigned the shares of the kingdom which each should rule.[3] Scipio also induced Phameas Himilco, commander of the Carthaginian cavalry, a brave man who was of extraordinary service to the Carthaginians, to desert with his force to the Romans.[4] Of three envoys who had been sent to Masinissa, Marcus Claudius Marcellus was drowned at sea in a storm.[5] The Carthaginians suspected Hasdrubal, the grandson of Masinissa, who was serving then as their general, of treachery, and killed him in their senate-house.[6] This suspicion grew from his relationship to

kingdom is described in Appian, *African Wars* 106 (based on Polybius) and in Zonaras IX. 27.

[4] 148 B.C. Himilco's successes against the Romans and Scipio's feat of winning him over are related by Appian, *African Wars* 97, 99, 100, 104, 107–9.

[5] 148 B.C. Many items in Marcellus' career are mentioned by Livy from XLI. xiii. 4 (177 B.C.) to XLVIII.

[6] This Hasdrubal is mentioned by Appian, *African Wars*, 93 and 111.

A.U.C. 604–606 esset Gulussae Romanorum auxilia iuvantis. P. Scipio Aemilianus cum aedilitatem peteret, consul a populo dictus. Quoniam per annos consuli fieri non licebat, cum magno certamine suffragantis plebis [1] et repugnantibus ei [2] aliquamdiu patribus, legibus solutus et consul creatus. M'. Manilius [3] aliquot urbes circumpositas Carthagini expugnavit. Pseudophilippus in Macedonia, caeso cum exercitu P.[4] Iuventio praetore, ab Q. Caecilio victus captusque est, et revicta [5] Macedonia.

L[IBER L

Per socios popu[li R. Andriscus ex Thessalia pulsus
in ultim[a]m T[hraciam.[6] De tribunis pl.
lat[a est] l[ex] At[inia. Prusia occiso Nicomedes re-
col. V gno Bithy]niae potitus [7] est. Ad Attalum regem
Pergami] et Prusiam ⟨am⟩endati [8] sunt legati Marc[us Licinius
poda]gricus, A. Hostilius Mancinus capite
icto test]a quondam, L. Manlius Volso stolidus.
Cunctari] legationem dixerunt, M. Cato respondit

[1] plebis *Perizonius*: legis NPΠR.
[2] ei *Jahn*: et MSS.
[3] M'. Manilius *Sigonius*: M. aemilius NPΠR.
[4] P. *Gruter*: m. NPR.
[5] revicta *Rossbach*: relicta NPR: recepta *Leidensis*.
[6] Thraciam *Rossbach*: c . . . MS.
[7] potitus *Kornemann*: positus MS.
[8] Pergami et Prusiam amendati *Rossbach*: in pugnamentas MS: in Pergamenos missi *Grenfell-Hunt*: deductum in pugnam *Gundermann*: a Romanis in Pergamum *Kornemann*: et Prusian Pergamum *Reid*.

Gulussa, who was assisting the Roman auxiliaries. When Publius Scipio Aemilianus stood for the aedileship, he was elected consul by the people. Since he was under age to be made consul lawfully, there was a great struggle between the commons, who campaigned for him, and the senators, who for some time resisted him, before he was exempted from the statutes and declared consul.[1] Manius Manilius stormed several cities surrounding Carthage.[2] After the false Philip had crushed Praetor Publius Iuventius and his army in Macedonia, he was conquered and captured by Quintus Caecilius, and Macedonia was reconquered.[3]

B.C. 150–148

Book L

Andriscus was driven out of Thessaly into outer Thrace by the allies of the Roman People. The Atinian law concerning the tribunes of the people was passed.[4] When Prusias was assassinated, Nicomedes laid hold on the crown of Bithynia. There were sent abroad as envoys to King Attalus at Pergamum and to Prusias, Marcus Licinius, who was gouty, Aulus Hostilius Mancinus, who had once been hit on the head by a jar, and Lucius Manlius Volso, a blockhead. People said that the embassy was delaying, and Marcus Cato answered that it had neither

[1] Cf. Appian 112; Velleius I. 12. 3; Cicero, *Philippic* XI. 17.

[2] Cf. the *Oxyrhynchus Summary* L, below. Appian 108–9 does not mention successes won by Manilius, so that these " cities " must have been quite unimportant.

[3] Cf. Obsequens 19 below; Velleius I. 11. 2; Diodorus XXXII. 9b.

[4] If the restoration is correct, this is the law which admitted tribunes of the people to the senate, cf. Gellius XIV. 8. 2. Members of the Atinian family had been praetors, but had held no higher magistracy; there may have been a family interest in making senatorial rank more accessible, cf. below, LIX.

eam nec caput] nec pedes nec cor habere.[1] M. Sca[n]tiu
repuls]am tulit in stupro deprehensus.[2]
A.U.C. 606 Sp. Albino L. Piso]ne coss.
Masinissa ult]imae senectutis liberos IIII
et XL virile]s reliquit decedens. Cuius regnum legit]imis filis per Aemilianum distributum.
Marcellus leg[atus ad Masinissam missus
perit in mari. Ha]sdrubal, quod adfinis Masinissae erat,
a suis in cur]ia subsellis occisus [3] est. Scipio Aemilianus
consul creat]us.
A M'. Manilio] in Africa pr[os]pere dimicatum [es]t.
Iuventi pr. in] Thessalia exercitus caesus.
Andriscus a] Metello captus. Sacrarium
Opis et laur]us foci maximo incendio
inviolata.]

A.U.C. 607–608 LI. Carthago, in circuitum $\overline{\text{XXIII}}$ [4] patens, magno labore obsessa et per partes capta est, primum a Mancino legato, deinde a Scipione consule, cui extra sortem Africa provincia data erat. Carthaginienses portu novo, quia vetus obstructus a Scipione erat, facto et contracta clam exiguo tempore ampla classe infeliciter navali proelio pugnaverunt. Hasdrubalis quoque, ducis eorum, castra

[1] habere *Kornemann, Rossbach*: haberent MS.

[2] repulsam tulit . . . deprehensus *Grenfell-Hunt*: . . . am tulit . . . deprehensi MS: de in stupro deprehensis *Warde Fowler*.

[3] subsellis occisus *Kornemann*: subselli socius MS.

[4] $\overline{\text{XXIII}}$ *H. J. Mueller*: XXIII passus MSS. (passuum *Leidensis*): XXIII milia quidem passuum R.

---

[1] It is not clear that this restoration is correct; Scantius may have proposed a law concerning those caught in sex-offences (*de in stupro deprehensis*).

[2] Polybius XXXVI. 16. 5 (L.C.L.) says ten sons; Appian, *African Wars* 106, seems to follow him, but mentions that many of Masinissa's sons died during his lifetime, so that the

head nor feet nor wit. Marcus Scantius was rejected for office because he had been caught in a sexual offence.[1]

In the consulship of Spurius Albinus and Lucius Piso, Masinissa, dying in extreme old age, left forty-four sons.[2] His kingdom was divided among his legitimate sons by Aemilianus. Marcellus, sent as envoy to Masinissa, was lost at sea. Hasdrubal, because he was related to Masinissa, was beaten to death with benches in the senate-house by his own people. Scipio Aemilianus was elected consul. A successful campaign was conducted in Africa by Manius Manilius. The army of Praetor Iuventius was crushed in Thessaly. Andriscus was taken prisoner by Metellus. The shrine of Ops and a laurel belonging to the hearth were unharmed by a huge conflagration.[3] B.C. 148

LI. Carthage, extending in a circumference of twenty-three miles, was besieged with great toil, and portions of it were captured, first by the staff-officer Mancinus, and then by Consul Scipio, to whom Africa had been assigned without the lot as his field of operations.[4] The Carthaginians built a new harbour because the old one had been blocked by Scipio; in a brief space of time they secretly formed a substantial fleet, but failed to win the naval battle.[5] Also the camp of Hasdrubal, their general, placed in B.C. 147–146

restoration may be as Livy stated the matter. Another possibility is that the figure of four refers to legitimate sons (including the famous four-year-old, cf. the first *Summary* L), and another figure referred to other sons.

[3] Cf. below, Obsequens 19. The shrine was part of the *regia*, the religious successor to the king's palace.

[4] 147 B.C. Appian, *African Wars* 113, follows Polybius in minimizing the success of Mancinus, to the greater glory of Scipio; but Mancinus was elected consul in 145, presumably on the reputation gained before Carthage. Cf. also Zonaras IX. 29. Scipio was given Africa by the senate, according to Valerius Maximus VIII. 15. 4, by decree of the people, according to Appian 112.

[5] Appian 121 f.

A.U.C. 607–608 ad Nepherim oppidum loco difficili sita cum exercitu deleta sunt a Scipione, qui tandem expugnavit septingentesimo anno quam erat condita. Spoliorum maior pars Siculis, quibus ablata erant, reddita. Ultimo urbis excidio, cum se Hasdrubal Scipioni dedisset, uxor eius, quae paucis ante diebus de marito impetrare non potuerat, ut ad victorem transfugerent, in medium se flagrantis urbis incendium cum duobus liberis ex arce praecipitavit. Scipio exemplo patris sui Aemilii Pauli, qui Macedoniam vicerat, ludos fecit transfugasque ac fugitivos bestiis obiecit. Belli Achaici[1] semina referuntur haec, quod legati Romani ab Achaeis pulsati sint Corinthi, missi ut eas civitates quae sub dicione Philippi fuerant ab Achaico concilio secernerent.

[Liber LI]

A.U.C. 607 P. Cornelio C. Livio] coss.
Clausa Cartha]gine in captivos[2] crudelissime
Poeni saevie]re. Obsidentes Romani no-[3]
cent Carthag]inem crebris proeli⟨s⟩.

[1] Achaici *Gronovius*: achaicis MSS.
[2] captivos *Gundermann*: appius MS.
[3] Obsidentes Romani no- *Grenfell-Hunt, Rossbach*: obsidentiis romanos non MS.

---

[1] Nepheris was taken in the winter of 147–6; Hasdruba was by then in Carthage as commander, cf. Appian 126; Polybius XXXVIII. 7 f.; Zonaras IX. 30. The last days of Carthage are described by Appian, 128–31, and Polybius, XXXVIII. 19–22 (L.C.L.).

[2] Cf. Appian 133; Diodorus XXXII. 25; Cicero *Verres* II. i. 11, ii. 85 ff., iv. 73 ff.; Plutarch, *Sayings of Scipio* 6 (L.C.L. *Moralia* III, p. 187). The implication that the wealth of Carthage consisted largely of loot from Sicily is presumably an unfortunate result of the process of summarization.

[3] Polybius XXXVIII. 20. 7–10 (L.C.L.); Appian 131.

[4] Appian 135; Valerius Maximus II. vii. 13.

difficult terrain near the city of Nepheris, was destroyed along with its garrison by Scipio, who finally took Carthage in the seven-hundredth year after its founding.[1] The greater part of the spoils were given back to the Sicilians from whom they had been taken.[2] At the final storming of the city, when Hasdrubal surrendered to Scipio, Hasdrubal's wife, who a few days before had been unable to persuade her husband to desert to the conqueror, hurled herself and her two children from the citadel into the midst of the flames of the burning city.[3] Scipio, taking his cue from his father Aemilius Paulus, the conqueror of Macedonia, celebrated games and exposed the deserters and fugitive slaves to the wild beasts.[4] The preliminaries of the Achaean War are recorded as follows: Roman envoys were struck by the Achaeans at Corinth—envoys sent to separate from the Achaean League those states which had been under the control of Philip.[5] B.C. 147–146

Book LI

In the consulship of Publius Cornelius and Gaius Livius, while Carthage was blockaded the Carthaginians inflicted the most savage cruelties on prisoners.[6] The besieging Romans damaged Carthage by frequent attacks. B.C. 147

[5] 148–7 B.C. Personal politics in the Achaean League led to attacks on Sparta by the League, which had gained confidence in dealing with Rome because its troops had put down Andriscus in Macedonia. Rome took the occasion to demand that Sparta, Argos, Corinth, Orchomenus, and Heracleia by Mount Oeta should be dropped from the Achaean League. The mistreatment of the Roman envoys was due to rabble-rousing by Achaean leaders; the lower classes had long been discontented and in difficulties; it is possible that the usual Roman preference for the well-to-do had become apparent. The embassy here referred to was probably that of the spring of 146 B.C., the third Roman embassy which had been disregarded and discourteously treated.

[6] Cf. below, Obsequens 20 and Appian, *African Wars* 118.

A.U.C. 607 Per Critola]um pr. Corinthi legati Romanorum violati. Lu]sitani subacti.
Cn. Corne[lio L. Mummio coss.
col. VI A.U.C. 608 p]er Scipion[em Carthago expugnata et d]irepta. Qu[i cum etiam arcem inflammavisset, ux[or Hasdrubalis se ipsa cum duobus fil[iis in medium iecit incendium, ne in potestate[m victoris veniret. Scipio exemplo Aemili, a q[uo Perseus victus erat, ludos fecit.

A.U.C. 606–610 LII. Cum Achaeis, qui in auxilio Boeotos et Chalcidenses habebant, Q. Caecilius Metellus ad Thermopylas bello conflixit; quibus victis dux eorum Critolaus mortem sibi veneno conscivit. In cuius locum Diaeus, Achaici motus primus auctor, ab Achaeis dux creatus ad Isthmon a L. Mummio consule victus est. Qui omni Achaia in deditionem accepta Corinthon ex senatus consulto diruit, quia ibi legati Romani violati erant. Thebae quoque et Chalcis, quae auxilio fuerant, dirutae. Ipse L. Mummius abstinentissimum virum egit, nec quicquam ex his operibus ornamentisque, quae praedives Corinthos habuit, in domum eius pervenit. Q. Caecilius Metellus de Andrisco

---

[1] Apparently the first stirrings of the rise of Lusitania under Viriathus.

[2] The battle was actually fought at Scarpheia in Locris, as the Achaean commander did not have the courage to attempt the defence of Thermopylae. Critolaüs disappeared during the battle, according to Pausanias VII. xv. 4. Metellus also cut to pieces an Arcadian contingent and one from Patras; Pausanias VII. xv. 5–6; Polybius XXXVIII. 16. 4 (L.C.L.).

[3] Polybius XXXIX. 8. 6 (L.C.L.); Pausanius VII. xvi. 1–4. Aurelius Victor 60 calls the site of the battle Leucopetra; but this locality in the Isthmus of Corinth is not mentioned elsewhere.

[4] Cf. Pausanias VII. xvi. 7 f. The standard modern interpretation is that Roman commercial interests wanted to eliminate their chief Greek competitor.

Roman envoys were molested by General Critolaus at Corinth. The Lusitanians were defeated.[1] B.C. 147

In the consulship of Gnaeus Cornelius and Lucius Mummius, Carthage was stormed and plundered by Scipio. When he also set fire to the citadel, the wife of Hasdrubal cast herself with her two sons into the midst of the flames, in order not to put herself in the power of the conqueror. Scipio followed the precedent set by Aemilius, the conqueror of Perseus, in giving games. col. VI B.C. 146

LII. Quintus Caecilius Metellus fought a battle at Thermopylae against the Achaeans, who had the support of Boeotia and Chalcis. After the defeat of the Achaeans, their leader Critolaus committed suicide by poison.[2] In his place Diaeus, the original sponsor of the Achaean uprising, was made commander and was defeated at the Isthmus by Consul Lucius Mummius.[3] The latter secured the surrender of all Achaea and in accordance with a decree of the senate destroyed Corinth, because the Roman envoys had been mistreated there.[4] Thebes and Chalcis, which had supported the Achaeans, were also destroyed.[5] Lucius Mummius himself played a part of extreme self-denial, and none of the works of art and adornments, in which Corinth was very rich, were introduced into his house.[6] Quintus Caecilius Metellus celebrated a triumph B.C. 148–144

[5] This is an exaggeration. The walls of these cities were torn down, some citizens executed, and fines imposed on Thebes for the benefit of Heraclea and Euboea, see Polybius XXXIX. 4–6 (L.C.L.); Pausanias VII. xvi. 9 f.

[6] On the excellent conduct of Mummius, cf. Polybius XXXIX. 6; his refusal to keep booty is mentioned by Cicero, *de Officiis* II. 76, Strabo VIII. 381, and others. The stories of Mummius' lack of culture seem to be rhetorical (perhaps originally political) inventions or exaggerations. He gave Corinthian works of art to many communities, even in Spain (*C.I.L.* I². 626–32), cf. *Oxyrhynchus Summary* LIII below; this presumably occurred when Mummius was censor in 142 B.C.

A.U.C. 606–610 triumphavit, P. Cornelius Scipio[1] Aemilianus de Carthagine et Hasdrubale. Viriathus in Hispania primum ex pastore venator, ex venatore latro, mox iusti quoque exercitus dux factus, totam Lusitaniam occupavit, M. Vetilium praetorem fuso eius exercitu cepit; post quem C. Plautius praetor nihilo felicius rem gessit; tantumque terroris is hostis intulit,[2] ut adversus eum consulari opus esset et duce et exercitu. Praeterea motus Syriae et bella inter reges gesta referuntur. Alexander, homo ignotus et incertae stirpis, occiso, sicut ante dictum est, Demetrio rege in Syria regnabat. Hunc Demetrius Demetri filius, qui a patre quondam ob incertos belli casus ablegatus Cnidon fuerat, contempta socordia inertiaque eius, adiuvante Ptolemaeo Aegypti rege, cuius filiam Cleopatram in matrimonium acceperat, bello interemit. Ptolemaeus graviter in caput vulneratus inter curationem, dum ossa medici terebrare conantur, expiravit, atque in locum eius frater minor Ptolemaeus, qui Cyrenis regnabat, successit. Demetrius ob crudelitatem, quam in suos per tormenta

[1] Cornelius Scipio *Jahn*: C. Africanus Scipio MSS.
[2] is . . . intulit *edd.*: his . . . impulit NPΠ.

---

[1] Both triumphs are mentioned by Appian, *African Wars* 135; for Metellus', see also Valerius Maximus VII. i. 1; for Scipio's, Valerius Maximus IV. iii. 13, *C.I.L.* I². 1, p. 176, and Cicero, *de Republica* VI. 11.

[2] The campaigns of 147 and 146 are summarized here, see Appian, *Spanish Wars* 60–67. The consul was Q. Fabius Aemilianus, cf. below, LIII.

[3] This contradicts L above, where Livy apparently took seriously Alexander's claim to be the son of Antiochus Epiphanes (so also Josephus XIII. 35, *I Maccabees* 10); Diodorus XXXI. 32a and Justinus XXXV. i. 6–9 speak of Alexander's low birth.

over Andriscus, and Publius Cornelius Scipio Aemilianus, another over the Carthaginians and Hasdrubal.[1] B.C. 148–144

In Spain, Viriathus, first turning from shepherd to hunter, then from hunter to brigand, presently became commander, too, of a regular army, seized all of Lusitania, and captured Praetor Marcus Vetilius after the rout of his army. Next, Praetor Gaius Plautius had no better success, and this enemy raised up such a threat that a consul and a consular army were required against him.[2]

In addition the book contains an account of the disturbances in Syria and the wars waged between the kings. Alexander, a man of no reputation and of doubtful parentage,[3] was ruling in Syria after killing King Demetrius, as has been previously mentioned. This Alexander was slain in war by Demetrius, son of Demetrius, who had at one time been sent away to Cnidus by his father because of the doubtful fortunes of war; he had scorned Alexander's sluggishness and indolence, and had received assistance from Ptolemy, King of Egypt, whose daughter Cleopatra he had taken in marriage.[4] Ptolemy was severely wounded in the head, and when, in an attempt at healing the wound, the doctors tried to trepan the skull, the king died. His younger brother Ptolemy, the ruler of Cyrene, succeeded to the throne.[5] Because of the cruelty which Demetrius employed in torturing his subjects, he was defeated in battle by a

148–7 B.C. When Ptolemy saw Alexander's misrule, and Hammonius, Alexander's henchman, tried to assassinate him, he abandoned Alexander, took Cleopatra away from him, and gave her to Demetrius. Diodorus XXXII. 9c, Josephus XIII. 103–109, *I Maccabees* 10–14, Justinus XXXV. i. 6–11, and Appian, *Syrian Wars* 67 tell of Demetrius' victory and Alexander's death. The battle was fought at Antioch on the Oenoparas, Strabo XVI. 751.

[5] Ptolemy's death is related by *I Maccabees* 11, 14 ff., and Josephus XIII. 119. On the younger Ptolemy's arrangements with his brother, cf. above, Summaries XLVI and XLVII.

A.U.C. 606–610 exercebat, ab Diodoto quodam, uno ex subiectis, qu Alexandri filio bimulo admodum regnum adserebat, bello superatus Seleuceam confugit. L. Mummius de Achaeis triumphavit, signa aerea marmoreaque et tabulas pictas in triumpho tulit.

LIBER LII

L. Mummius [1] C[orinthum diruit. Diaeus
uxore o[ccisa se necavit. A Lusitanis Romanorum
per<i>uria u[ltis gravis clades
accepta.
A.U.C. 609 Q. Fabio Max[imo L. Hostilio coss.
M. Petron[ius et L. Apuleius legati in Asiam,
adversu[s Viriathum Fabius cos. missus est.
A.U.C. 610 Ser. Galba L. [Cotta coss.
Q.[2] Metell[us, qui pr. Andriscum vicerat, consulatum [post duas repulsas aegre obtinuit.
Qui invis[us plebi ob nimiam severitatem
petituru[s . . .[3]
Syria va[stata bellis regum populus R.
c[on]tent[us fuit legatis ad eos missis.[4]

[1] Mummius *Grenfell-Hunt*: mumanus MS.
[2] Q. *Rossbach*: L. MS.
[3] petiturus Hispaniam conviciis laceratus est *sugg. Rossbach*: petitur vehementissime consulatus *Kornemann*: sed tertium petiturus mitior factus est *Luterbacher*.
[4] Syria vastata *Grenfell-Hunt, cetera Rossbach*: quod inter reges contentum est *Kornemann*: est inter reges contentione orta *Luterbacher*.

---

[1] Demetrius had dismissed his Syrian troops, keeping his Cretan mercenaries. A revolt, largely of the unemployed troops, at Antioch brought on the persecutions.

certain Diodotus, one of those subjects, who pressed the claim to the throne of Alexander's son, an infant of only two years. Demetrius took refuge in Seleucia.[1] Lucius Mummius celebrated his triumph over the Achaeans, and carried in the triumphal parade paintings, and statues of bronze and marble.[2] B.C. 148–144

Book LII

Lucius Mummius destroyed Corinth. Diaeus killed his wife and then himself.[3] A severe loss was inflicted by the Lusitanians, who avenged the false oaths of the Romans.

In the consulship of Quintus Fabius Maximus and Lucius Hostilius, Marcus Petronius and Lucius Apuleius were sent as ambassadors to Asia,[4] and Consul Fabius was sent to oppose Viriathus. B.C. 145

In the consulship of Servius Galba and Lucius Cotta, Quintus Metellus, who when praetor had conquered Andriscus, barely won election as consul after being twice rejected. On asking for Spain, he was the target for abuse because he was hated by the commons for his undue strictness.[5] When Syria was ravaged by wars between the kings, the Roman People did no more than send envoys to them.[6] B.C. 144

[2] Vergil, *Aeneid* VI. 836–7 speaks of a triumph over Achaeans and Corinthians, cf. Cicero, *Murena* 31. *C.I.L.* I^2. 626 says only " he returned in triumph to Rome."

[3] Cf. Pausanias VII. xvi. 6.

[4] Polybius XXXII. 16 (28) mentions an embassy by Gaius Petronius and Lucius Apuleius; the difference in one name and the discrepancy, as it seems, of ten years in date make this restoration uncertain.

[5] The reading is conjectural (see critical note), but is based on *de Viris Illustribus* 61. 3 and Valerius Maximus VII. v. 4.

[6] If the restoration is correct, the implication that the Romans might have been expected to intervene directly in Syria at this time would seem to be a notion of the epitomator rather than of Livy.

A.U.C. 611-613 LIII. Appius Claudius consul Salassos, gentem Alpinam, domuit. Alter Pseudophilippus in Macedonia a L. Tremellio quaestore cum exercitu caesus est. Q. Caecilius Metellus pro cos. Celtiberos cecidit, et a Q. Fabio pro cos. pars magna Lusitaniae expugnatis aliquot urbibus recepta est. Acilius[1] senator Graece res Romanas scribit.

[Liber LIII

A.U.C. 611 Q. Metello [Appio Claudio coss.
Rethog[enis transfugae Centobrigenses
liberos to[rmentorum ictibus obiecerunt.
Proposito a[bstitit Metellus.[2]
col. VII occidit. A Tyresio, quem devici[t, gla]dium
dono accepit saguloque rem[isso am]ici-
ti]ae dextram dedit.
M]etellus cos. a Lusitanis vex[atus est.
S]igna statu⟨a⟩s tabulas Corinth[ias L. M]ummius
distribuit circa oppida et Rom[am ornavit.

[1] Acilius *Hertz*: c. iulius NPR.
[2] *Periit una columna.*

---

[1] 143 B.C. Appius Claudius Pulcher took advantage of the strife between the Salassi and the Libicans for the gold-mines of Eporedia, cf. Strabo IV. 205, Dio frg. 74. 1 f. The Salassi were not really "subdued" till Imperial times. Claudius wanted a military victory and got it after some losses; he was refused a triumph by the senate, celebrated it at his own expense, and was protected by his daughter, a Vestal, from a tribune who would have halted him, cf. Valerius Maximus V. iv. 6.

[2] 142 B.C. Cf. Varro, *de Re Rustica* II. iv. 1; Eutropius IV. 15.

[3] 142 B.C. For Metellus, cf. Velleius II. v. 2, Appian, *Spanish Wars* 76. The activity of Quintus Fabius Servilianus fell in 141 B.C., cf. below, LIV, and Appian, *Spanish Wars* 67.

[4] Reference to Gaius Acilius and his history is found in Cicero, *de Officiis* III. 115, Plutarch, *Romulus* xxi. 7, Dionysius III. 67.

SUMMARIES

LIII. Consul Appius Claudius subdued the Salassi, an Alpine tribe.[1] A second false Philip in Macedonia was slain in the rout of his army by Quaestor Lucius Tremellius.[2] Quintus Caecilius Metellus as proconsul slaughtered the Celtiberians, and a large part of Lusitania was recovered by Quintus Fabius the proconsul, when he had stormed several cities.[3] Acilius, a senator, wrote a history of Rome in Greek.[4] B.C. 143–141

Book LIII

In the consulship of Quintus Metellus and Appius Claudius, the people of Centobriga exposed the children of Rethogenes, a deserter, to the shots of the siege-artillery. Metellus gave up his undertaking.[5] . . . killed. He received a sword as a present from Tyresius, whom he conquered, gave in return a cloak, and clasped his hand in friendship.[6] Consul Metellus was harassed by the Lusitanians.[7] Lucius Mummius distributed statues, monuments, and paintings from Corinth among the towns and adorned Rome with them.[8] B.C. 143

[5] Cf. Valerius Maximus V. i. 5. Rethogenes seems again to have left the Roman side, cf. Valerius Maximus III. ii, ext. 7, perhaps because he had a personal relationship to Metellus which did not include the latter's political opponent Scipio. Following this item a column of text has been lost.

[6] The Roman concerned is Quintus Occius, a staff-officer, cf. below, *Ox.* LIV, and Valerius Maximus III. ii. 21. His exploits bear a resemblance to those of young Manlius (VIII. vii. 1–22) and Lucius Sicinius Dentatus (Aulus Gellius II. xi. 1), which suggests that the story of Occius may have been built up as a publicity measure to compensate for the poor Roman record in these years.

[7] Metellus campaigned against the Celtiberians (above, first LIII) and it is not clear what he had to do with the Lusitanians. This epitomator mentions the latter with notable frequency.

[8] Cf. above, first LII, end.

A.U.C. 613 Cn.] Caepione Q. Pompeio coss.
Q. Fabius Maximus Lusitanis ca[esis
Viriathum fugavit.

A.U.C. 613–615 LIV. Q. Pompeius consul in Hispania Termestinos subegit. Cum isdem et Numantinis pacem a p. R. infirmatam [1] fecit. Lustrum a censoribus conditum est: censa sunt civium capita $\overline{\text{CCCXXVIII}}$ CCCCXLII. Cum Macedonum legati questum de D. Iunio Silano praetore venissent, quod acceptis pecuniis provinciam spoliasset, et senatus de querellis eorum vellet cognoscere, T. Manlius Torquatus, pater Silani, petit impetravitque, ut sibi cognitio mandaretur; et domi causa cognita filium condemnavit abdicavitque. Ac ne funeri quidem eius, cum suspendio vitam finisset, interfuit, sedensque domi potestatem consultantibus ex instituto fecit. Q. Fabius pro cos. rebus in Hispania prospere gestis labem imposuit pace cum Viriatho aequis condicionibus facta. Viriathus a proditoribus consilio Servilii Caepionis interfectus est et ab exercitu suo multum comploratus ac nobiliter sepultus, vir

[1] infirmatam *Gronovius*: ab infirmitate NPII.

---

[1] 141 B.C. Pompeius' success was very temporary. He made the treaty with the Numantines to save face after an unsuccessful siege, and then proceeded to repudiate it, denying before his successor and at Rome that he had ever made it. Cf. Appian, *Spanish Wars* 76–79.

[2] The censors were Scipio Africanus and Lucius Mummius, cf. XL. li. 4, Cicero, *Brutus* 85.

[3] 140 B.C., see the *Oxyrhynchus Summary* below. Junius was born a patrician and adopted into a plebeian family—the

SUMMARIES

In the consulship of Gnaeus Caepio and Quintus Pompeius, Quintus Fabius Maximus crushed the Lusitanians and routed Viriathus. B.C. 141

LIV. Consul Quintus Pompeius subdued the Termestini in Spain, and made with them and the Numantines a peace-treaty which was repudiated by the Roman People.[1] The half-decade was formally closed by the censors.[2] The count of citizens was three hundred and twenty-eight thousand, four hundred, and forty-two. Envoys of the Macedonians came to complain of Praetor Decimus Junius Silanus that he had taken bribes and robbed the province. The senate was prepared to investigate their complaints, when Titus Manlius Torquatus, the father of Silanus, successfully requested that the investigation be delegated to him. Having tried the case at his home, he condemned his son and banished him from his sight. When Silanus ended his life by hanging, his father did not even attend the funeral, but sat at home and was at the service of those who wished his advice, as his custom was.[3] Proconsul Quintus Fabius won successes in Spain, but marred his record by making a peace with Viriathus which recognized his independence.[4] Viriathus was assassinated by traitors instigated by Servilius Caepio; he was deeply mourned by his army and given a magnificent burial. He was a great man and a great B.C. 141–139

earliest known instance of this. The Junii Silani took great pride in the relationship thus acquired, and claimed the Manlii as ancestors, cf. Tacitus, *Annals* III. 76. The condemnation of this Silanus is mentioned also by Cicero, *de Finibus* I. 24 and Valerius Maximus V. viii. 3. Manlius was an expert in jurisprudence, as is intimated in the last sentence.

[4] 140 B.C. Fabius' good fortune apparently ran out, and he was compelled to make peace as indicated, or leave the field to his successor, Servilius; the peace was repudiated through the influence of the latter, cf. Appian 69–75. Florus I. xxxiii. 17, and *de Viris Illustribus* 71. 2 give Popilius, consul in 139 B.C., as the leader against the treaty.

A.U.C. 613–615 duxque magnus et per quattuordecim annos, quibus cum Romanis bellum gessit, frequentius superior.

Lib[er] LIV

Pompeius cos. a Numantinis d[evictu]s. In Scordiscis cladis accepta.
A.U.C. 614 Q. Cae]pione [C.] Laelio Sapiente [1] c[oss. Appius Claudius evicit, ne duos [delectus] annus haberet. T. Manlius Torquatus D. S[ila]num filium suu[m d]e Macedonia damn[avit, f]uneri non interfuit eademque die [i]n do[mo] sua consultantibus respondit.
C]aepio cos. intellegens Ti. Claudium Assellum [2] tr⟨i⟩b. pl. interpellantem profectionem s]uam l[i]ctore⟨m⟩ stri⟨n⟩gens ensem deterruit.[3]
Q.] Fabius Maximus a Vir⟨i⟩atho devictus de-f]ormem cum hostibus pacem fecit. Q. Occius oppress]us [i]nsidiis Lusitanorum fortissime [cecidit. M. Porc]inae devota [4] est aqua Anio. Aqua Marcia in Capi]tolium contra Sibyllae carmina perducta.]

[1] Sapiente *Grenfell-Hunt*: Salasso MS.
[2] intellegens Ti. Claudium Assellum *Grenfell-Hunt, Rossbach*: indelegem ti. claudi amassilium MS.
[3] suam lictorem stringens ensem deterruit *Rossbach*: strigemreddeterbuit MS: lictores derigendo *Luterbacher*: "Lictor, stragem redde" *Gundermann*.
[4] *suppl., divisit M. Stuart.*

---

[1] The assassins were three friends of Viriathus, who had been sent by him to negotiate with Servilius. The latter promised them great rewards, but refused to pay them for the crime. The "fourteen years" go back to the beginning of the Celtiberian War; Viriathus' own resistance lasted eight years, according to Appian 75. Cf. Diodorus XXXIII. 21.
[2] Apparently a punitive expedition from Illyricum failed; no further reference to this matter is known.

leader, and in the fourteen years in which he waged war against the Romans, he had the advantage more often than not.[1] B.C. 141–139

Book LIV

Consul Pompeius was thoroughly beaten by the Numantines. A disaster befell the Romans among the Scordisci.[2]

In the consulship of Quintus Caepio and Gaius Laelius the Wise, Appius Claudius successfully recommended that one year should not see two levies.[3] Titus Manlius Torquatus condemned his son Decimus Silanus for his conduct in Macedonia, did not attend his funeral, and on that very day gave answers to those who consulted him in his home. Consul Caepio, perceiving that Tiberius Claudius Asellus, tribune of the commons, was trying to prevent his departure, drew his sword and frightened off the lictor.[4] Quintus Fabius Maximus, after his defeat by Viriathus, made a disgraceful peace with the enemy. Quintus Occius fell most valiantly when trapped by an ambush of the Lusitanians.[5] The Anio aqueduct was sacrificed to M. Porcina. The Marcian aqueduct was continued to the Capitol contrary to the Sibylline prophecies.[6] B.C. 140

[3] This Claudius is presumably the consul of 143 B.C. and father-in-law of Tiberius Gracchus. His resolution against double levies may have been a first move to relieve the commons.

[4] This tribune seems to have been antisenatorial; Scipio, as censor in 142, had tried to demote him from his tribe, but Mummius, the other censor, restored him; Claudius in turn during his tribunate brought Scipio to trial, cf. Gellius III. iv. 1 and IV. xvii. 1, Cicero, *de Oratore* II. 258, 268.

[5] Cf. above, *Ox.* LIII, page 47 note 6.

[6] According to Frontinus, *Aqueducts* I. 7, repairs to the Old Anio and the building of the Marcia were begun in 145 B.C.; debate on the propriety of bringing water to the Capitol continued till 140 B.C., when, says Frontinus, the influence of Marcius Rex, original officer in charge, carried the day. M. Aemilius Lepidus Porcina opposed extending the Anio.

col. VIII A.U.C. 615

Cn. Pisone C. Po⟨pi⟩lli[o coss.
Chaldaei urbe ⟨e⟩t It[alia abire iussi sunt.
A. Gabinius, verna[e nepos, legem tulit ut
suffragium per ta[bellam ferretur.
Servilius Caepio a[b equitibus quos Viriatho
obiecerat claus[us [1] praetorio et paene ustus.
Audax Minurus ⟨D⟩ita[lco a Caepione corrupti
Viriathum iugula[verunt.

A.U.C. 512–618

LV. P. Cornelio Nasica, cui cognomen Serapion fuit ab inridente Curiatio tribuno plebis impositum, et Dec. Iunio Bruto consulibus dilectum habentibus in conspectu tironum res saluberrimi exempli facta est. Nam C. Matienius accusatus est apud tribunos plebis, quod exercitum ex Hispania deseruisset, damnatusque sub furca diu virgis caesus est et sestertio nummo veniit. Tribuni plebis quia non impetrarent ut sibi denos, quos vellent, milites eximere liceret, consules in carcerem duci iusserunt. Iunius Brutus consul in Hispania iis, qui sub Viriatho militaverant, agros et oppidum dedit, quod vocatum est Valentia. M. Popilius a Numantinis, cum quibus pacem factam irritam fieri senatus censuerat, cum exercitu

[1] clausus *Rossbach*: clauo MS.

---

[1] Their soothsaying was the difficulty, cf. Valerius Maximus I. iii. 3.

[2] Gabinius had served under Metellus in Macedonia and was at this time a tribune, cf. Cicero, *de Legibus* III. 35, Polybius XXXVIII. 12. 1 f. (L.C.L.).

[3] Cf. Dio XXII. frg. 78.

[4] 138 B.C. On the nickname, which came to be generally used, cf. Valerius Maximus IX. xiv. 3; Pliny, *Natural History* VII. 54 and XXI. 10.

[5] Frontinus IV. i. 20 describes this as happening to "deserters" at this time, cf. *Ox. Summary* below.

[6] Cicero, *de Legibus* III. 20 gives this as the action of the above-mentioned (Gaius) Curiatius, who first clashed with the consuls over a distribution of grain, Valerius Maximus III. vii. 3. The *Oxyrhynchus Summary*, below also mentions

In the consulship of Gnaeus Piso and Gaius Popillius, the Chaldaeans were ordered to leave Rome and Italy.[1] Aulus Gabinius, grandson of a home-born slave woman, carried a law that electoral votes should be cast by ballot.[2] Servilius Caepio was shut up in his headquarters and almost burned by the cavalry whom he had exposed to Viriathus.[3] Audax, Minurus, and Ditalco were bribed by Caepio to cut Viriathus' throat. B.C. 139

LV. While Consuls Publius Cornelius Nasica[4] (whose nickname was Serapio—a name given him in mockery by Curiatius, a tribune of the commons) and Decimus Junius Brutus were holding the levy, an occurrence took place which gave very salutary instruction to the recruits who were looking on. For Gaius Matienius was accused before the tribunes of the commons of having deserted from the army in Spain, and on being condemned was put in the yoke and given a prolonged beating with rods, and was sold into slavery for one sestertius.[5] Because tribunes of the commons did not succeed in obtaining the right to choose ten men apiece for exemption from the levy, they ordered the consuls taken to the gaol.[6] Consul Junius Brutus in Spain gave to those who had served under Viriathus land and a town, which is called Valentia.[7] Marcus Popilius and his army were routed and put to flight by the Numantines, after a peace treaty made with them had been declared void by the senate.[8] When B.C. 142–136

Servius Licinius as a tribune concerned. Nasica was a consistent antidemocrat, cf. his role in suppressing Tiberius Gracchus, Plutarch, *Tiberius Gracchus* xiii. 3.

[7] This may not have been Brutus' first act in Spain, cf. the account below of his campaigns, and also LVI; but if Valentia was the present Valencia, the removal of Viriathus' men to the east coast would have been a good early move.

[8] Popilius was consul in 139, and was in Spain as proconsul, cf. Appian, *Spanish Wars* 79, and Frontinus III. xvii. The repudiated treaty was the treaty of Pompeius, cf. above LIV, and note 4, p. 49.

A.U.C. 612–618 fusus fugatusque est. C. Hostilio Mancino consule sacrificante pulli ex cavea evolaverunt; conscendenti deinde navem, ut in Hispaniam proficisceretur, accidit vox "mane, Mancine": quae auspicia tristia fuisse eventu probatum [1] est. Et victus enim a Numantinis et castris exutus, cum spes nulla servandi exercitus esset, pacem cum his fecit ignominiosam, quam ratam esse senatus [2] vetuit. $\overline{XXXX}$[3] Romanorum ab quattuor milibus Numantinorum victa erant. Decimus Iunius Lusitaniam expugnationibus urbium usque ad Oceanum perdomuit; et cum flumen Oblivionem transire nollent, raptum signifero signum ipse transtulit et sic, ut transgrederentur, persuasit. Alexandri filius, rex Syriae, decem annos admodum habens, a Diodoto, qui Tryphon cognominabatur, tutore suo, per fraudem occisus est corruptis medicis, qui illum calculi dolore consumi ad populum mentiti, dum secant, occiderunt.

Lib[er LV

A.U.C. 616 P. Sc[i]pione D. Iunio [coss.
interfectores Viri[athi urbe pulsi sunt, praemium
negatum. C[um ex cu]ria [P. Scipionem et
Decim. Bru[tum coss.] S. Licini[us et C. Curiatius
trib. pl. in carc[er]em [c]oll[ocavissent,
precibus populi mul[t]a re[missa . . ., qui
trib. pl. pro commodis pop[uli agebat et

[1] probatum G: promptum *MSS. vetera.*
[2] senatus *add.* GR: *om. vetera.*
[3] $\overline{XXXX}$ *Jahn:* $\overline{XXX}$ NPΠR.

[1] Mancinus attempted to withdraw from Numantia by night, because the discipline of his army was bad, and there were rumours of uprisings in his rear. The Numantines happened to catch him leaving. The numbers involved are probably exaggerated, but the emended reading is based on Florus I. xxxiv. 2. The repudiation of the treaty by which Mancinus' force was released from the trap was not in accord

Consul Gaius Hostilius Mancinus was offering sacrifice, the chickens flew out of the coop; when thereafter he was going aboard ship to leave for Spain, the cry was heard "Stay, Mancinus!" That these were omens of evil was demonstrated by the outcome. For Mancinus was both defeated by the Numantines and stripped of his camp; when no hope remained of saving his army, he made with them a disgraceful peace, confirmation of which was refused by the senate. Forty thousand Romans were beaten by four thousand Numantines.[1] Decimus Junius thoroughly subdued Lusitania by storming its cities all the way to the Ocean. When his men refused to cross the River Oblivion, he seized the standard from its bearer, carried it across, and thus induced the soldiers to pass over.[2] The King of Syria, son of Alexander, who was only ten years old, was killed by treachery on the part of his guardian Diodotus, whose nickname was "The Luxurious"; Diodotus bribed the doctors, who represented to the people that the boy was wasting away from suffering with a stone, and killed him on the operating table.[3] B.C. 142–136

Book LV

In the consulship of Publius Scipio and Decimus Junius, the murderers of Viriathus were driven from Rome and refused a reward.[4] When Sextus Licinius and Gaius Curiatius, tribunes of the commons, took Consuls Publius Scipio and Decimus Brutus from the senate-house to the gaol, at the entreaty of the people the fine was remitted . . ., who as tribune of the commons had been working for the good of the people, and who died to B.C. 138

with Roman pride in Roman good faith. Cf. Plutarch, *Tiberius Gracchus* v; Appian, *Spanish Wars* 79–80; and for the sequel, below, LVI.

[2] 137–136 B.C. Brutus had to reconquer some peoples who revolted after Mancinus' defeat had damaged Roman prestige.

[3] 142 B.C. Cf. Appian, *Syrian Wars* 68.

[4] Cf. Orosius V. 4. 14; Eutropius IV. 16.

A.U.C. 616 omnibus luct⟨u⟩i expiravit, co[e]un[te plebe elatus. De-
sertores in comitio virgis cae[si sunt et sestertiis
singulis venierunt.
P. Africanus cum L. Cottam [accu]sar[et, iudices ob
magnitudinem nom[inis eum] cad[ere noluerunt.
Lusitani vastati. A N[uman]tin[is clades accepta.
Diodotus Tryphon An[tioc]hum [regem occi-
dit Suriaque potitus e[st.
A.U.C. 617 M. Aemilio C. Hostilio M[an]cino [coss.
Decimus Brutus in Hispania re b[ene gesta
Oblivionis flumen planus trans[iit.

A.U.C. 618–620 LVI. Decimus Iunius Brutus in Hispania ulteriore feliciter adversus Gallaecos pugnavit. Dissimili eventu M. Aemilius Lepidus pro cos. adversus Vaccaeos rem gessit clademque similem Numantinae passus est. Ad exsolvendum foederis Numantini religione populum Mancinus, cum huius rei auctor fuisset, deditus Numan-

---

[1] It is impossible to restore the name of this tribune.

[2] *I.e.*, Cotta was acquitted. This interpretation of the over-abbreviated text is based on references to this affair in Cicero, *pro Murena* xxviii. 58; *Divinatio in Caecilium* xxi. 69; Valerius Maximus VIII. i. *acquittal* 11 (Valerius speaks of a trial "before the people," and it should be noted that the words in our text indicating a court are restored). The view of the acquittal here given is the pro-senatorial view; Appian, *Civil Wars* I. iii. 22 cites the case as typical of the bribery and corruption of senatorial courts. Probably both the prosecution and the acquittal were politically motivated. The date of the trial has been usually given as 132–129 B.C., because Cicero refers to Scipio as twice consul, and conqueror of Numantia; from our text, it is clear that this date must be abandoned, and that Cicero, who wanted to emphasize the great reputation and prestige of Scipio, did not bother to

everyone's grief, his funeral was escorted by a gathering of the commons.[1] Deserters were beaten with rods in the assembly place and sold into slavery for a sestertius apiece. When Publius Africanus accused Lucius Cotta, the judges were unwilling to let the defendant lose because of the greatness of the prosecutor's reputation.[2] The Lusitanians were ravaged. A disaster was inflicted by the Numantines.[3] Diodotus the Luxurious killed King Antiochus and took possession of Syria. B.C. 138

In the consulship of Marcus Aemilius and Gaius Hostilius Mancinus, Decimus Brutus after a successful campaign in Spain made no bones about crossing the River Oblivion.[4] B.C. 137

LVI. Decimus Junius Brutus conducted a successful campaign against the Gallaeci in Farther Spain.[5] The outcome was otherwise when Pro-consul Marcus Aemilius Lepidus marched against the Vaccaei: he suffered a reverse comparable to that before Numantia.[6] In order to release the Roman People from the binding force of the treaty with Numantia, Mancinus was surrendered to the Numantines as the man responsible for this arrangement, B.C. 136–134

note that he had not yet performed his second great feat of arms.

[3] Details about the mopping-up in Lusitania and the customary lack of success before Numantia are not known.

[4] It is not clear what meaning is to be given to *planus*, referring to Brutus; some editors prefer to change the Latin; I have given a somewhat far-fetched interpretation, which seems to make better sense than the more usual meaning "flat, on the level, not elevated," which is commonly applied to things, and which Rossbach seems to favour, and the possible meaning "bare-footed."

[5] The final success of Brutus was in 134 B.C., cf. Appian, *Spanish Wars* 73–75, 99, where the name Sextus is incorrect; Strabo III. 152 f.; Velleius II. v. 1.

[6] 136 B.C. Lepidus undertook the campaign on his own initiative; he was recalled and fined by the senate, cf. Appian 80–83.

A.U.C. 618–620 tinis non est receptus. Lustrum a censoribus conditum est; censa sunt civium capita $\overline{CCCXVII}$ DCCCCXXXIII. Fulvius Flaccus consul Vardaeos in Illyrico subegit. M. Cosconius [1] praetor in Thracia cum Scordiscis prospere pugnavit. Cum bellum Numantinum vitio ducum non sine pudore publico duraret, delatus est ultro Scipioni Africano a senatu populoque Romano consulatus; quem cum illi capere ob legem, quae vetabat quemquam iterum consulem fieri, non liceret, sicut priori consulatu legibus solutus est. Bellum servile in Sicilia ortum cum opprimi a praetoribus non potuisset, C. Fulvio consuli mandatum est. Huius belli initium fuit Eunus servus, natione Syrus; qui contracta agrestium servorum manu et solutis ergastulis iusti exercitus numerum implevit. Cleon quoque alter servus ad septuaginta milia servorum contraxit; et iunctis copiis adversus exercitum Romanum bellum saepe gesserunt.

[1] Cosconius *Sigonius*: cossonius NPΠ: Cesonius BR.

---

[1] The " binding force of the treaty " was, as indicated by the Latin word, the religious taboo involved in a broken oath. Breach of the arrangement by which Mancinus' force was released from a trap was not in accord with Roman pride in Roman good faith; a sufficient commentary is furnished by the words credited by Livy to the Samnites after the similar occasion at the Caudine Forks (IX. xi). Mancinus was restored to full status at Rome by action of the Roman assembly. Cf. Plutarch, *Tiberius Gracchus* v; Appian 80, 83; Velleius II. i. 4 f.

[2] 134 B.C. The censors were Appius Claudius Pulcher and Quintus Fulvius Nobilior.

[3] Cf. Appian, *Illyrian Wars* ii. 10.

[4] 135 B.C. Cosconius seems to have continued as governor of Macedonia for several years, since his name appears on inscriptions referring to the disturbances in 133 B.C. after the

but was not received by them.[1] The half-decade was formally closed by the censors; the number of citizens enumerated was three hundred and seventeen thousand, nine hundred and thirty-three.[2] Consul Fulvius Flaccus overcame the Vardaei in Illyricum.[3] Praetor Marcus Cosconius fought successfully against the Scordisci in Thrace.[4] Since the Numantine War was dragging along through the fault of the commanders and to the shame of the State, the consulship was offered to Scipio Africanus on the initiative of the senate and the Roman People. He was forbidden to accept this office by a law which ruled that no one should be consul a second time, but as in his first consulship, Scipio was exempted from legal restrictions.[5] A slave revolt arose in Sicily, and when the praetors could not suppress it, command was assigned to Consul Gaius Fulvius.[6] The instigator of this revolt was Eunus, a slave of Syrian nationality; he assembled a force of rural slaves, opened the workhouses, and raised his numbers to those of a regular army. Another slave, Cleon, also assembled as many as seventy thousand slaves, and when the forces had joined, they frequently took the field against the Roman army.[7] B.C. 136–134

Pergamene kingdom was given to Rome. The Scordisci were raiding from the north-west.

[5] The law against a second consulship seems to have been passed in 151 B.C. Since Scipio was granted neither troops nor funds for his campaign, his appointment must have been less universally supported than the above statement would indicate.

[6] Cf. Orosius V. ix. 6. Gaius Fulvius (Flaccus) was consul in 134 B.C. with Scipio.

[7] The beginning of the revolt was perhaps in 136 B.C. Eunus won his leadership by charlatanry, but was supported by some of the poorest freemen, as well as slaves. Diodorus XXXIV. 2 gives the greatest number involved as 200,000; the figure of 70,000 is given as the total by Orosius V. vi. 4, and was perhaps misunderstood by the epitomator. Cleon was Cilician in nationality. The final sentence seems curiously flat; Rossbach suggests reading " fought savagely " (*saeve* for *saepe*).

A.U.C. 620 LVII. Scipio Africanus Numantiam obsedit et corruptum licentia luxuriaque exercitum ad severissimam militiae disciplinam revocavit. Omnia deliciarum instrumenta recidit; duo milia scortorum a castris eiecit; militem cotidie in opere habuit et triginta dierum frumentum ad septenos vallos ferre cogebat. Aegre propter onus incedenti dicebat: "cum gladio te vallare scieris, vallum ferre desinito". Alii scutum parum habiliter ferenti, amplius eum scutum iusto ferre, neque id se reprehendere, quando melius scuto quam gladio uteretur. Quem militem extra ordinem deprehendit, si Romanus esset, vitibus, si extraneus, virgis cecidit. Iumenta omnia, ne exonerarent militem, vendidit. Saepe adversus eruptiones hostium feliciter pugnavit. Vaccaei obsessi liberis coniugibusque trucidatis ipsi se interemerunt. Scipio amplissima munera missa sibi ab Antiocho rege Syriae, cum celare aliis imperatoribus regum munera mos esset, pro tribunali accepturum [1] se esse dixit omniaque ea quaestorem referre in publicas tabulas iussit: ex his se viris fortibus dona esse daturum.[2] Cum undique Numantiam obsidione clusisset et obsessos fame videret urgeri, hostes, qui pabulatum exierant, vetuit occidi, quod diceret velocius eos absumpturos frumenti quod haberent, si plures fuissent.

A.U.C. 621 LVIII. Tib. Sempronius Gracchus tribunus plebis cum legem agrariam ferret adversus voluntatem senatus et equestris ordinis, ne quis ex publico agro plus quam mille

[1] accepturum *Freudenberg*: ea accepturum MSS.

[2] se viris f.d. esse daturum *Halm*: se veris f.d. se daturum N: severis, *etc.* P.

---

[1] 134–133 B.C. Cf. Appian 84–98, presumably based on Polybius. The existence of Polybius' eye-witness account may explain the detail of Livy's story.

[2] This side-issue of Scipio's campaign may derive its high colour from a Roman annalist. According to Appian, *Spanish Wars* xiv. 87, Scipio ravaged the crops of the

LVII. Scipio Africanus besieged Numantia and recalled his army to the most stringent military discipline, after it had been corrupted by being allowed to indulge itself.[1] Scipio cut off all apparatus of pleasure; he cast out of camp two thousand prostitutes; he kept the soldiery at work daily and compelled them to carry thirty days' grain and seven stakes apiece. When someone had difficulty in marching because of his load, Scipio would tell him, "When you know how to entrench yourself behind your sword, you may stop carrying your rampart with you." To another who was having difficulty in carrying his shield, Scipio said, "You are carrying a shield larger than the regulation; I don't blame you; you're better at managing a shield than a sword." If a soldier was caught out of ranks, Scipio had him beaten with vines, if a Roman, and with rods, if a foreigner. He sold all the baggage animals, so that they might not relieve the soldiers of their loads. He won frequent successes against enemy sallies. The Vaccaei when besieged slaughtered their wives and children and committed suicide.[2] When magnificent gifts were sent to Scipio by Antiochus the King of Syria, although it was the custom of other commanders to conceal gifts from kings, Scipio declared that he would receive the gifts with public formality, and he ordered the quaestor to enter all the gifts in the official accounts; from these, said Scipio, he proposed to give presents to brave men. When he had completed the circumvallation of Numantia and saw that the besieged were hard pressed by hunger, he gave orders that the enemy who came out to forage should not be killed, because he said that they would the sooner exhaust what grain they had if there were more of them. B.C. 134

LVIII. Tiberius Sempronius Gracchus, a tribune of the commons, carried a land law against the desires of the senate and the order of knights, to the effect that no one B.C. 133

Vaccaei, to prevent their helping Numantia, but made no attempt on their cities.

A.U.C. 621 iugera possideret, in eum furorem exarsit, ut M. Octavio collegae causam diversae partis defendenti potestatem lege lata abrogaret seque et C.[1] Gracchum fratrem et Appium Claudium socerum triumviros ad dividendum agrum crearet. Promulgavit et aliam legem agrariam, qua sibi latius agrum patefaceret, ut idem triumviri iudicarent, qua publicus ager, qua privatus esset. Deinde cum minus agri esset quam quod dividi posset sine offensa etiam plebis, quoniam eos ad cupiditatem amplum modum sperandi incitaverat, legem se promulgaturum ostendit, ut his, qui Sempronia lege agrum accipere deberent, pecunia, quae regis Attali fuisset, divideretur. Heredem autem populum Romanum reliquerat Attalus, rex Pergami, Eumenis filius. Tot indignitatibus commotus graviter senatus, ante omnis T. Annius consularis,[2] qui cum[3] in senatu in Gracchum perorasset, raptus ab eo ad populum delatusque plebi, rursus in eum pro rostris contionatus est. Cum iterum tribunus plebis creari vellet Gracchus, auctore P. Cornelio Nasica in Capitolio ab optimatibus occisus est, ictus primum fragmentis subsellii, et inter alios, qui in eadem seditione occisi erant, insepultus in flumen proiectus. Res praeterea in Sicilia vario eventu adversus fugitivos gestas continet.

[1] C. *add. Sigonius*: *om.* NPIIR.
[2] consularis *Drakenborch*: cos. NPR.
[3] cum *add.* R: *om.* MSS.

---

[1] The limit is usually stated as 500 *iugera*; the figure above is perhaps the total allowed to a family or household group, cf. *C.A.H.* IX, p. 23.

[2] 133 B.C. Cf. Plutarch, *Tiberius Gracchus*. Tiberius' action against Octavius was based on a justified sense that a tribune, traditionally a defender of the commons, should not act for the "haves" against the "have-nots"; but balancing one magistrate against another was a key-principle of the Roman constitution. Roman political tact—the instinct for adjusting to the grievances and rights of others—begins to break down at this point; the partisan spirit led to civil war within fifty years. Losses in Spain may have made acute the problems Tiberius was striving to solve.

should occupy more than a thousand acres of public land [1]; Gracchus then went so insane as to remove from office by special enactment his colleague Marcus Octavius, who was supporting the other side of the controversy [2]; Gracchus also had himself, his brother Gaius Gracchus, and Appius Claudius his father-in-law elected as the board of three in charge of distributing the land. He also proposed a second land law, in order to put more land at his disposal, that the same commissioners should judge which land was public and which private. Then when there was less land than could be divided up without incurring the hostility of the commons too, because Gracchus had stirred them up to be greedy enough to hope for a large amount, he declared that he would propose a law that the fortune which had belonged to King Attalus should be divided among those who ought to receive land under the Sempronian Law. For Attalus, son of Eumenes, King of Pergamum had made the Roman People his heir.[3] B.C. 133

The senate was deeply stirred by so many actions ignoring its prestige; the ex-consul Titus Annius was especially moved.[4] After he had delivered a speech in the senate against Gracchus, he was summoned before the people by the latter, and accused before the commons; Annius again made a public address against Gracchus from the Rostra. When Gracchus wished to be elected tribune of the commons for the second time, he was killed on the Capitol by men of the "upper class" led by Publius Cornelius Nasica. Gracchus was first struck down with pieces of a bench, and then with others who were killed in the same riot was thrown unburied into the river. The book also contains an account of the campaigns conducted in Sicily against the fugitive slaves with varying success.

[3] Attalus died of disease (Strabo XIII. 624) or sunstroke (Justinus XXXVI. iv. 5). His bequest to Rome is attested by Pergamene inscription 249.

[4] Titus Annius (Luscus) had been consul in 153 B.C. Cf. Plutarch, *Tiberius* xiv. Annius' speech against Tiberius is quoted by Festus 316 (= 416 Lindsay).

A.U.C. 621–625 LIX. Numantini fame coacti ipsi se per vicem traicientes[1] trucidaverunt, captam urbem Scipio Africanus delevit et de ea triumphavit, quarto decimo anno post[2] Carthaginem deletam. P. Rupilius[3] consul in Sicilia cum fugitivis debellavit. Aristonicus Eumenis regis filius Asiam occupavit, cum testamento Attali regis legata populo Romano libera esse deberet. Adversus eum P. Licinius Crassus consul, cum idem pontifex maximus esset,[4] quod numquam antea factum erat, extra Italiam profectus proelio victus et occisus est. M. Perperna consul victum Aristonicum in deditionem accepit. Q. Pompeius Q. Metellus, tunc primum uterque ex plebe facti censores, lustrum condiderunt: censa sunt civium capita $\overline{\text{CCCXVIII}}$ DCCCXXIII, praeter pupillos[5] pupillas et viduas. Q. Metellus censor censuit, ut cogerentur omnes ducere uxores liberorum creandorum causa. Extat oratio eius, quam Augustus Caesar, cum[6] de maritandis ordinibus ageret, velut in haec tempora scriptam in senatu recitavit.

[1] traicientes *Rossbach*: tradentes MSS.
[2] quarto decimo anno post R: post XIIII annos MSS.
[3] Rupilius *Sigonius*: autilius NPΠ: Rutilius G: C. Attilius R.
[4] esset *add. edd.*: *om.* MSS.
[5] pupillos *add. Mommsen*: pupillos et R: *om.* MSS.
[6] cum *add.* GR: *om. vetera.*

---

[1] 133 B.C. Cf. Appian, *Spanish Wars* 96–98.
[2] 132 B.C. Cf. Diodorus XXXIV. ii. 20–23; Valerius Maximus II. vii. 3; VI. ix. 8; IX. xii. ext. 1.
[3] Aristonicus, a natural son of Eumenes, laid claim to the kingdom on the death of Attalus in 133 B.C. After being checked by the Ephesians, he adopted the cause of the oppressed slaves and proletariat, and promised an equalitarian state. He won great successes, including the defeat of Crassus

LIX. The Numantines, being hard pressed by hunger, thrust one another through and slew themselves; Scipio Africanus captured and destroyed the town and celebrated his triumph over it, in the fourteenth year after the destruction of Carthage.[1] Consul Publius Rupilius brought an end to the war in Sicily against the fugitive slaves.[2] Aristonicus, a son of King Eumenes, seized Asia, although it was to be autonomous after it had been bequeathed to the Roman People by the will of King Attalus. Consul Publius Licinius Crassus, who was also chief pontiff—a situation which had never arisen before—left Italy to oppose Aristonicus, was beaten in battle, and was killed. Consul Marcus Perperna overcame Aristonicus and received his surrender.[3] Quintus Pompeius and Quintus Metellus, censors both of plebeian origin—the first time this had happened—formally closed the half-decade; there were enumerated three hundred and eighteen thousand, eight hundred and twenty-three citizens, not counting wards of both sexes, and widows.[4] Censor Quintus Metellus proposed that everyone should be compelled to marry in order to produce children. His speech is preserved, and was read by Augustus Caesar before the senate as though written for the present day, when the emperor was discussing the problem of marriage B.C. 133–129

(Dives Mucianus). The latter was consul in 131 B.C.; he was a partisan of the Gracchi; as consul he used his power as chief pontiff to bar his colleague, who was also a priest, from the command in Asia, but disregarded the restriction on himself, as hinted in the text. His defeat occurred in 130 B.C., as he was about to retire from the province. Perperna, consul in 130 B.C., was a plebeian and a "new man." He died shortly after the defeat of Aristonicus, who was later executed at Rome.

[4] 129 B.C. His plebeian status did not prevent Metellus (Macedonicus) from being a determined opponent of the Gracchi. In fact, the election of two plebeians to the most dignified of offices would indicate that the distinction between patrician and plebeian had lost all importance, even as a technicality.

A.U.C. 621–625 C. Atinius [1] Labeo tribunus plebis Q. Metellum censorem, a quo in [2] senatu legendo praeteritus erat, de saxo deici [3] iussit; quod ne fieret, ceteri tribuni plebis auxilio fuerunt. Cum Carbo tribunus plebis rogationem tulisset, ut eundem tribunum pleb., quotiens vellet, creare liceret, rogationem eius P. Africanus gravissima oratione dissuasit; in qua dixit Ti. Gracchum iure caesum videri. C.[4] Gracchus contra suasit rogationem, sed Scipio tenuit.[5] Bella inter Antiochum Syriae et Phraaten Parthorum regem gesta nec magis quietae res Aegypti referuntur. Ptolemaeus Euergetes cognominatus, ob nimiam crudelitatem suis invisus, incensa a populo regia clam Cypron profugit; et cum sorori eius Cleopatrae, quam filia eius virgine per vim compressa atque in matrimonium ducta repudiaverat, regnum a populo datum esset, infensus filium, quem ex illa habebat, in [6] Cypro occidit caputque eius et manus et pedes matri misit. Seditiones a triumviris Fulvio Flacco et C. Graccho et C. Papirio Carbone agro dividendo creatis excitatae. Cum P. Scipio Africanus adversaretur fortisque ac validus pridie domum se recepisset, mortuus in cubiculo

[1] Atinius *Frobenius*: atilius NPΠ.
[2] in *add. Rossbach*: *om.* MSS.
[3] saxo deici *edd.*: saxa fieri NPΠ: saxo ferri B.
[4] C. *add. Gronovius*: *om.* MSS.
[5] tenuit *Frobenius*: censuit MSS.
[6] in *add.* Norvicenis, R, *om. vetera.*

---

[1] On Metellus' speech, cf. Suetonius, *Augustus* 89; Gellius I. vi., where the speech is wrongly ascribed to Metellus Numidicus.

[2] 131 B.C. Cf. Cicero, *de Domo Sua* 123; Pliny, *Natural History* VII. xliv (142–6). Atinius also tried to confiscate Metellus' property by dedicating it to a god, but failed.

[3] On Carbo's oratory at this time, cf. Cicero, *de Oratore* II. 170, and *de Amicitia* 96. Carbo belonged to the party of the Gracchi, but changed over after the death of Gaius. The exact saying of Scipio about Tiberius is quoted by Velleius II. iv. 4: "If he planned a *coup d'état*, he was justly killed."

among the upper classes.[1] Gaius Atinius Labeo, tribune of the commons, ordered Censor Quintus Metellus, who had passed him by in revising the roll of the senate, to be thrown from the Tarpeian Rock; the other tribunes of the commons came to the aid of Metellus to prevent this from taking place.[2] When Carbo, a tribune of the commons, proposed a law that it should be permissible to re-elect a man tribune of the commons as often as he chose, Publius Africanus argued against the law in a very weighty speech, in the course of which he said that he thought that Tiberius Gracchus had been killed justly. Gaius Gracchus on the other hand argued for the law, but Scipio carried the day.[3] B.C. 133–129

An account is given of the wars between King Antiochus of Syria and King Phraates of Parthia,[4] and of the no less disturbed situation in Egypt. Ptolemy, surnamed the Benefactor, being hated by his people because of his excessive cruelty, fled secretly to Cyprus after his palace had been set on fire by the populace. When the crown was given by the people to his sister Cleopatra, whom he had divorced after violating and marrying her virgin daughter, Ptolemy in his anger killed in Cyprus the son he had had by Cleopatra and sent the head, hands, and feet to the child's mother.[5]

Civil disturbances were incited by the board of three—Fulvius Flaccus, Gaius Gracchus, and Gaius Papirius Carbo—elected to divide the land. After Publius Scipio Africanus had appeared in opposition, and had returned home that day in vigorous good health, he was found

[4] Antiochus VII Euergetes Sidetes campaigned against Phraates II in 130 B.C. with great success, but was defeated and killed in the following year.

[5] The involved matrimonial arrangements, of which Livy shows the worst aspect, did not prevent Ptolemy and the two Cleopatras, mother and daughter, from ruling Egypt jointly from 143–2 B.C. to 132–1. Cf. Valerius Maximus IX. i. ext. 5. The story of Ptolemy's revenge is told also by Diodorus XXXIV. 14 and Justinus XXXVIII. viii. 13–14.

A.U.C. 621–625 inventus est. Suspecta fuit, tamquam ei venenum dedisset, Sempronia uxor hinc maxime, quod soror esset Gracchorum, cum quibus simultas Africano fuerat. De morte tamen eius nulla quaestio acta. Defuncto eo acrius seditiones triumvirales exarserunt. C. Sempronius consul adversus Iapydas[1] primo male rem gessit; mox victoria cladem acceptam emendavit virtute Decimi Iunii Bruti, eius qui Lusitaniam subegerat.

A.U.C. 629–633 LX. L. Aurelius consul bellantes Sardos subegit. M. Fulvius Flaccus primus Transalpinos Liguras domuit bello, missus in auxilium Massiliensium adversus Salluvios Gallos, qui fines Massiliensium populabantur. L. Opimius praetor Fregellanos, qui defecerant, in deditionem accepit, Fregellas diruit. Pestilentia in Africa ab ingenti lucustarum multitudine et deinde necatarum strage fuisse traditur. Lustrum a censoribus conditum est: censa sunt civium capita $\overline{\text{CCCXCIIII}}$ DCCXXXVI. C.[2]

[1] Iapydas *Sigonius, Gruter*: Iapygas NPΠR.
[2] C. *add. Frobenius*: *om.* MSS.

---

[1] 129 B.C. Suspicion of foul play was widespread and eagerly adopted as a partisan weapon; but it was directed against Carbo as much as against the Gracchan ladies, and seems to have had no genuine foundation in fact, cf., *e.g.*, Cicero, *de Amicitia* v. 10–12. 14 and the *scholia Bobiensia* on *pro Milone* p. 283.

[2] Besides annoying the large landholders, the commissioners were infringing on the autonomy of the " allies " in Italy by questioning the land-tenure of non-Romans.

[3] 129 B.C., cf. *C.I.L.* I²., p. 48 (Sempronius Tuditanus triumphs over the " Iapudes "), and Appian, *Illyrian Wars* 10.

[4] 126–3 B.C., cf. Plutarch, *Gaius Gracchus* i. Aurelius celebrated his triumph in 122 B.C., *C.I.L.* I²., pp. 49, 53.

[5] 125 B.C. Fulvius was a strong supporter of the Gracchi and had come out in favour of extending Roman citizenship to the Latin allies, cf. Plutarch, *Gaius Gracchus* xv. 1 and *C.I.L.* I²., p. 49. The Salluvii are sometimes called Ligurians, some-

next day dead in his bedchamber. His wife Sempronia was suspected of having poisoned him, chiefly on the ground that she was the sister of the Gracchi with whom Scipio had been quarrelling. However, no judicial investigation of his death was held.[1] After his death, the disturbances centring around the Board of Three blazed up more fiercely.[2] Consul Gaius Sempronius at first met with no success against the Iapydae; presently the loss incurred was cancelled by a victory won through the ability of Decimus Junius Brutus, the man who had conquered Lusitania.[3] B.C. 133–129

LX. Consul Lucius Aurelius subdued the Sardi who went to war.[4] Marcus Fulvius Flaccus was the first to overcome the transalpine Ligurians in war; he had been sent to help the people of Marseilles against the Salluvian Gauls who were ravaging the territory of Marseilles.[5] Praetor Lucius Opimius received the surrender of the Fregellans, who had revolted, and destroyed Fregellae.[6] It is recorded that a plague arose in Africa from the great number of locusts and the masses of them that were killed.[7] The half-decade was formally closed by the censors; there were enumerated three hundred and ninety-four thousand, seven hundred and thirty-six citizens.[8] B.C. 126–121

times distinguished from them, *e.g.*, Strabo IV. vi. 3; culturally at least they were close to the Gauls. Cf. below, LXI.

[6] 125 B.C. The revolt arose over the question of granting citizenship, or at least the right of appeal to the Roman People, to the Latin allies.

[7] 125 B.C. Additional details are given below, Obsequens 30. Other plagues of locusts are mentioned above, XXX. ii. 10, XLII. ii. 5 and x. 7, see also Orosius V. xi. 2 ff.

[8] The censors were Lucius Cassius Longinus Ravilla, famed for his enunciation of the judicial principle "Cui bono?" and Gnaeus Servilius Caepio (Frontinus, *Aqueducts* I. 8; Cicero, *Verres* II. I. 143; *pro Roscio Amerino* 84).

A.U.C. 629–633 Gracchus, Tiberii frater, tribunus plebis, eloquentior quam frater, perniciosas aliquot leges tulit, inter quas frumentariam, ut senis et[1] triente frumentum plebi daretur; alteram legem agrariam, quam et frater eius tulerat[2]; tertiam, qua equestrem ordinem, tunc cum senatu consentientem, corrumperet, ut sescenti ex equite[3] in curiam sublegerentur et, quia illis temporibus trecenti tantum senatores erant, sescenti equites trecentis senatoribus admiscerentur, id est ut equester ordo bis tantum virium in senatu haberet. Et continuato in alterum annum tribunatu legibus agrariis latis effecit, ut complures coloniae in Italia deducerentur, et una in solo dirutae Carthaginis; quo ipse triumvir creatus coloniam deduxit. Praeterea res a Q. Metello consule adversus Baleares gestas continet, quos Graeci Gymnesios[4] appellant, quia aestatem nudi exigunt. Baleares a teli missu appellati, aut a Balio[5] Herculis comite ibi relicto, cum Hercules ad Geryonen navigaret. Motus quoque Syriae referuntur, in quibus Cleopatra Demetrium virum suum et Seleucum filium, indignata, quod occiso patre eius a se iniussu suo diadema sumpsisset, interemit.

[1] senis et *Weissenborn*: sexis et NPΠ: sesis cn Vossianus: semis et Norvicensis R.
[2] tulerat G: fuerat *vetera*.
[3] equite Gudianus: equitem *vetera*.
[4] quos . . . Gymnesios *Jahn*: quas . . . Gymnesias MSS.
[5] Balio *edd.*: blato NPΠ, Balteo Norvicensis R.

---

[1] 123–2 B.C. Plutarch, *Gaius Gracchus* v. says that Gaius planned to add an equal number (three hundred) to the senate. The price of grain, 6 *asses* per peck (*modius*), was intended to be a reasonable cost price, cf. Polybius II. 15. 1, and *Cambridge Ancient History* IX, pp. 58 f. The African colony was to be founded near, not at, ancient Carthage, on a site appropriate for agriculture.

[2] 122–1 B.C., cf. *C.I.L.* I²., pp. 49 and 176. This seems to have been a formal taking over of the islands by Rome, on the

Gaius Gracchus, the brother of Tiberius and a better speaker than his brother, carried as tribune of the commons several ruinous laws, among which were: a law on the grain supply, that grain should be sold for six and one-third *asses* to the commons; a second law concerning land, such as his brother also had carried; and a third law, as a means of seducing the order of knights, which was at that time in harmony with the senate, to the effect that six hundred of the knights should be joined to the body of the senate and, since at that time there were only three hundred senators, that these three hundred senators should be amalgamated with six hundred knights, which meant that the order of knights would have a two-to-one majority in the senate. When Gracchus was continued as tribune for a second year, he passed land laws and brought about the foundation of several colonies in Italy and one on the site of destroyed Carthage; for the last, he himself was appointed to the Board of Three and founded the colony.[1] B.C. 126–121

In addition, the book contains an account of the campaign of Consul Quintus Metellus against the Baleares, whom the Greeks call Gymnesians, because they spend the summer unclothed. They are called Baleares because of hurling missiles, or else after Balius, a companion left behind there by Hercules when he sailed after Geryon.[2] An account is also given of the disturbances in Syria, during which Cleopatra put to death her husband Demetrius, and then her son Seleucus, because she resented his assuming the crown without her permission, after she had killed his father.[3]

ground that some inhabitants were practising piracy. The first derivation of the name "Baleares" is from the Greek *ballein,* to hurl a missile, cf. Diodorus V. xvii, where a second story is told of Hercules.

[3] 125 B.C. According to Appian, *Syrian Wars* 69, Cleopatra feared that Seleucus might avenge his father; Justinus XXXIX. i. 9 agrees with Livy; but the reasons are not mutually exclusive.

A.U.C. 631–634 LXI. C. Sextius pro cos. victa Salluviorum gente coloniam Aquas Sextias condidit, ob aquarum copiam e caldis frigidisque fontibus atque a nomine suo ita appellatas. Cn. Domitius pro cos. adversus Allobrogas ad oppidum Vindalium feliciter pugnavit. Quibus bellum inferendi causa fuit, quod Toutomotulum Salluviorum regem fugientem recepissent et omni ope iuvissent, quodque Aeduorum agros, sociorum[1] populi Romani, vastassent. C. Gracchus seditioso tribunatu acto cum Aventinum quoque armata multitudine occupasset, a L. Opimio consule ex senatus consulto vocato ad arma populo pulsus et occisus est, et cum eo Fulvius Flaccus consularis,[2] socius eiusdem furoris. Q. Fabius Maximus consul, Pauli nepos, adversus Allobrogas et Bituitum Arvernorum regem feliciter pugnavit. Ex Bituiti exercitu occisa milia CXX; ipse cum ad satisfaciendum senatui Romam profectus esset, Albam custodiendus datus est, quia contra pacem videbatur ut in Galliam remitteretur. Decretum quoque est, ut Congonnetiacus filius eius comprehensus Romam mitteretur. Allobroges in deditionem accepti. L. Opimius accusatus apud populum a Q. Decio tribuno plebis, quod indemnatos cives in carcerem coniecisset, absolutus est.

[1] sociorum *add.* R: *om.* MSS.
[2] consularis *Sigonius*: cos. MSS.

---

[1] 123–2 B.C. Sextius (Calvinus) was consul in 124. Cf. Strabo IV. 180; Velleius I. xv. 4; *C.I.L.* I²., p. 53. Aix en Provence was a colony in Livy's day, but was not founded as such by Sextius.

[2] The battle took place in 121 B.C., but Domitius (Ahenobarbus) had been active in the campaign as consul of the preceding year. Cf. Appian, *Gallic Wars* 12, Florus I. xxxvii. 4.

[3] Livy's view of these events was evidently thoroughly senatorial; cf. Plutarch, *Gaius Gracchus* xiii–xviii.

[4] 121 B.C. Fabius joined Domitius as the Arverni, rivals of the Aedui for the hegemony of Gaul, came to the aid of the

LXI. Proconsul Gaius Sextius conquered the Salluvian tribe and founded the colony of Aquae Sextiae, which was named after the abundance of waters from hot and cold springs, and after the name of the proconsul.[1] Proconsul Gnaeus Domitius fought successfully against the Allobroges before the town of Vindalium. The reason for waging war on them was that they received Toutomotulus the king of the Salluvii, when he had fled, and assisted him with all their power; also that they had devastated the land of the Aedui, allies of the Roman People.[2] Gaius Gracchus, after passing a riotous tribuneship, proceeded also to seize the Aventine with an armed mob, and was routed and killed by Lucius Opimius the consul, in accordance with a decree of the senate, after the people had been summoned to arms. Along with Gracchus was killed Fulvius Flaccus, an ex-consul, and his comrade in like madness.[3] Consul Quintus Fabius Maximus, grandson of Paulus, fought successfully against the Allobroges and Bituitus the king of the Arverni.[4] One hundred and twenty thousand of Bituitus' army were killed; after the king himself had set out for Rome to make his peace with the senate, he was placed in custody at Alba, because his return to Gaul seemed not to be in the interest of peace. It was also decreed that his son Congonnetiacus should be arrested and sent to Rome.[5] The surrender of the Allobroges was accepted. Lucius Opimius was accused before the people by Quintus Decius, tribune of the commons, on the ground that he had cast citizens into prison without a trial, but he was acquitted.[6]

B.C. 123–120

Allobroges. Cf. *C.I.L.* I². 1, p. 53, where the king's name is given as Betultus. The battle fought by Domitius (above) may have followed this battle, cf. Strabo IV. 191.

[5] According to Valerius Maximus IX. vi. 3, Bituitus was captured by treachery. Congonnetiacus appears to have been released and put on the throne as an ally of Rome, if the Contoniatus of Diodorus XXXIV. 36 is the same man.

[6] 120 B.C. Decius' first name is given as Publius in Cicero, *de Oratore* II. 132, 134–5.

A.U.C. 636–639 LXII. Q. Marcius consul Stynos, gentem Alpinam, expugnavit. Micipsa Numidiae rex mortuus regnum tribus filiis reliquit, Adherbali Hiempsali Iugurthae, fratris filio, quem adoptaverat. L. Caecilius Metellus Dalmatas subegit. Iugurtha Hiempsalem fratrem petit bello, qui victus occiditur.[1] Adherbalem regno expulit. Is a senatu restitutus est. L. Caecilius Metellus Cn. Domitius Ahenobarbus censores duos et triginta senatu moverunt. Praeterea motus Syriae regumque continet.

A.U.C. 640–643 LXIII. C. Porcius consul in Thracia male adversus Scordiscos pugnavit. Lustrum a censoribus conditum est: censa sunt civium capita $\overline{\text{CCCXCIIII}}$ CCCXXXVI. Aemilia, Licinia, Marcia, virgines Vestales, incesti damnatae sunt, idque incestum quem ad modum et commissum et deprehensum et vindicatum sit, refertur. Cimbri, gens vaga, populabundi in Illyricum venerunt: ab his Papirius Carbo consul cum exercitu fusus est. Livius Drusus

[1] occiditur *Jahn*: occidit MSS.

---

[1] Marcius was consul in 118 B.C., and celebrated a triumph over this tribe, "the Ligurian Stoeni," *C.I.L.* I^2. 1, p. 53.

[2] 118 B.C. Jugurtha was adopted in 120 B.C.

[3] Metellus was consul in 119 B.C., and celebrated his triumph in 117 B.C., cf. *C.I.L.* I^2. 1, p. 53; he received the surname Delmaticus.

[4] Cf. Sallust, *Jugurtha* xi.–xiii.

[5] 115 B.C. The censors were Metellus Delmaticus and the Domitius of LXI, cf. Cicero, *in Verrem* II. I. 143. Cf. below LXIII.

[6] This probably refers to the attack by Antiochus IX Cyzicenus on his elder half-brother Antiochus VIII Grypus, who was on the throne of Syria, cf. Justinus XXXIX. ii. 7–10; Appian, *Syrian Wars* 69.

SUMMARIES

LXII. Consul Quintus Marcius routed the Styni, an Alpine tribe.[1] Micipsa king of Numidia at his death left his kingdom to three sons, Adherbal, Hiempsal, and Jugurtha, his brother's son, whom he had adopted.[2] Lucius Caecilius Metellus subdued the Dalmatians.[3] Jugurtha assailed his brother Hiempsal in war; the latter was conquered and killed. Jugurtha drove Adherbal out of his kingdom. This prince was restored by the senate.[4] Lucius Caecilius Metellus and Gnaeus Domitius Ahenobarbus as censors removed thirty-two from the senate.[5] In addition, the book contains the disturbances in Syria and among the kings.[6]

B.C. 118–115

LXIII. Consul Gaius Porcius lost a battle against the Scordisci in Thrace.[7] The half-decade was formally closed by the censors; the number of citizens counted was three hundred and ninety-four thousand, three hundred and thirty-six.[8] Aemilia, Licinia, and Marcia, Vestal Virgins, were condemned for unchastity; an account is given of the manner in which this offence was committed, detected, and punished.[9] The Cimbri, a nomad tribe, came plundering into Illyricum; they routed Consul Papirius Carbo and his army.[10] Consul Livius Drusus

B.C. 114–111

[7] 114 B.C. From Eutropius IV. xxiv. one would conclude that the battle was fought in Macedonia. The Scordisci pushed on to Delphi (Appian, *Illyrian Wars* 5) and to the Adriatic (Florus I. xxxix. 3 f.).

[8] For this censorship cf. above LXII.

[9] 114 B.C. Cf. Dio XXVI, fr. 87; Plutarch, *Roman Questions* 83 (284); Valerius Maximus III. vii. 9, VI. viii. 1; Orosius V. xv. 20–22; and below, Obsequens 37. The pontifices condemned Aemilia only in 115 B.C.; a special court was set up in the following year to secure the condemnation of the others.

[10] 113 B.C. The defeat of Carbo was near Noreia, cf. Strabo V. 214; Appian, *Gallic Wars* I. 13 speaks of Teutoni, but seems to refer to this occasion. Cf. also Plutarch, *Marius* xvi; Velleius II. xii; Tacitus, *Germania* 37.

consul adversus Scordiscos, gentem a Gallis oriundam, in Thracia feliciter pugnavit.

A.U.C. 642–645 LXIV. Adherbal bello petitus ab Iugurtha et in oppido Cirta obsessus contra denuntiationem senatus ab eo occisus est, et ob hoc bellum Iugurthae indictum, idque Calpurnius Bestia consul gerere iussus pacem cum Iugurtha iniussu populi et senatus fecit. Iugurtha fide publica evocatus ad indicandos auctores consiliorum suorum, quod multos pecunia in senatu corrupisse dicebatur, Romam venit; et propter caedem admissam in regulum quendam nomine Massivam, qui regnum eius populo Romano invisi adfectabat, cum[1] periclitaretur causam capitis dicere, clam profugit et cedens urbe fertur dixisse "o urbem venalem et cito perituram, si emptorem invenerit!" A. Postumius legatus infeliciter proelio adversus Iugurtham gesto pacem quoque adiecit ignominiosam, quam non esse servandam senatus censuit.

A.U.C. 645–647 LXV. Q. Caecilius Metellus consul duobus proeliis Iugurtham fudit totamque Numidiam vastavit. M. Iunius Silanus consul adversus Cimbros infeliciter pugnavit. Legatis Cimbrorum sedem et agros, in quibus consisterent, postulantibus senatus negavit. M. Minucius pro cos. adversus Thracas prospere pugnavit. L. Cassius

[1] adfectabat cum *Jahn*: adfectabat Romae interfectum cum MSS.

---

[1] Drusus was consul in 112 B.C. In 112–1, he held back the Scordisci, as Gaius Caecilius Metellus had in the year 113; but it remained for Minucius Rufus in 110–108 B.C. to beat the Scordisci back decisively, see below LXV, and their final defeat occurred in 88 B.C.

[2] 112 B.C. Cf. Sallust, *Jugurtha* xx.–xxviii.

[3] 111 B.C. Sallust, *Jugurtha* xxviii. 4–xxix. 7.

[4] Sallust, *Jugurtha* xxx.–xxxv.; for Jugurtha's comment, xxxv. 10; Appian, *Numidian Wars* 1.

[5] 109 B.C. Sallust, *Jugurtha* xxxvi.–xxxix. 3.

fought successfully in Thrace against the Scordisci, a people of Gallic descent.[1]

LXIV. Adherbal was assailed in war by Jugurtha, besieged in the town of Cirta, and put to death, contrary to the proclamation of the senate. On this account, war was declared against Jugurtha,[2] and Consul Calpurnius Bestia was ordered to conduct it. He concluded with Jugurtha a treaty unauthorized by the people and the senate.[3] Jugurtha was summoned and came to Rome under safe-conduct to reveal the sponsors of his plots, because it was being said that he had corrupted by bribes a large number of senators. He proceeded to murder a certain prince, Massiva by name, who was laying claim to Jugurtha's kingdom because the latter was in bad odour with the Romans. On this account Jugurtha was in danger of standing trial for his life, and fled secretly. As he left the city he is said to have remarked, "O venal city! How soon it will perish if it find a purchaser!"[4] Aulus Postumius, a staff officer, lost a battle to Jugurtha and further perpetrated a disgraceful peace treaty, which the senate voted not to ratify.[5]

B.C. 112–109

LXV. Consul Quintus Caecilius Metellus routed Jugurtha in two battles and devastated all Numidia.[6] Consul Marcus Junius Silanus lost a battle to the Cimbri.[7] The senate refused the demand of envoys of the Cimbri for an abode and land on which to settle.[8] Proconsul Marcus Minucius fought successfully against the Thracians.[9] Consul Lucius Cassius and his army were slaughtered in

B.C. 109–107

[6] 108 B.C. Cf. Sallust xl.–lxix; Plutarch, *Marius* viii; Appian, *Numidian Wars* 3.

[7] 109 B.C. Cf. Velleius II. xii, Vegetius III. 10.

[8] Cf. Florus I. xxxviii (III. 3), who seems to place the request before the battle.

[9] 109–8 B.C. Minucius was consul in the preceding year; the Scordisci were still the chief disturbers, cf. above LXIII, note 1.

A.U.C. 645–647 consul a Tigurinis Gallis, pago Helvetiorum, qui a civitate secesserant, in finibus Nitiobrogum [1] cum exercitu caesus est. Milites qui ex ea caede superaverant, obsidibus datis et dimidia rerum omnium parte, ut incolumes dimitterentur, cum hostibus pacti sunt.

A.U.C. 648–649 LXVI. Iugurtha pulsus a C. Mario Numidia, cum auxilio Bocchi Maurorum regis adiutus esset, caesis proelio Bocchi quoque copiis, nolente Boccho bellum infeliciter susceptum diutius sustinere vinctus [2] ab eo et Mario traditus est; in qua re praecipua opera L. Cornelii Syllae, quaestoris C. Marii, fuit.

A.U.C. 649–652 LXVII. M. Aurelius Scaurus, legatus consulis, a Cimbris fuso exercitu captus est; et cum in consilium ab his advocatus deterreret eos, ne Alpes transirent Italiam petituri, eo quod diceret Romanos vinci non posse, a Boiorige [3] feroci iuvene occisus est. Ab iisdem hostibus Cn. Manlius consul et Q. Servilius Caepio pro cos. victi proelio castris quoque binis exuti sunt, militum milia octoginta occisa, calonum et lixarum quadraginta secundum Antiatem apud Arausionem.[4] Caepionis, cuius temeritate clades accepta erat, damnati bona publicata sunt,

[1] Nitiobrogum *Mommsen*: Allobrogum MSS.
[2] sustinere vinctus GR: sustinere noluit vinctus *vetera*: sustinere voluit *Jahn*.
[3] a Boiorige *Freinsheim*: abolorege NP: a Bolo rege R.
[4] Antiatem apud Arausionem *Gronovius, Zangemeister*: aprausionem NPΠ.

---

[1] 107 B.C. Cf. Caesar, *Gallic War* I. vii. 12; Appian, *Gallic Wars* I. 3; Orosius V. xv. 23 ff. The division of the defeated party's goods recalls Hector's thought in *Iliad* XXII.

the territory of the Nitiobroges by the Tigurine Gauls, a canton of the Helvetians, who had withdrawn from that state. The soldiers who survived this slaughter arranged with the enemy to be released unharmed after giving up hostages and half of all their possessions.[1] B.C. 109–107

LXVI. Jugurtha was driven from Numidia by Gaius Marius. When Jugurtha received the assistance of Bocchus king of the Moors, Bocchus' forces were also slaughtered in battle, and Bocchus was unwilling longer to endure the war that he had so unfortunately undertaken. He therefore threw Jugurtha in chains and handed him over to Marius; in this operation the services of Lucius Cornelius Sulla, Marius' quaestor, were outstanding.[2] B.C. 106–105

LXVII. Marcus Aurelius Scaurus, a staff officer of the consul, was taken prisoner by the Cimbri when his army was routed; he was summoned before their council, and when he tried to discourage them from crossing the Alps to enter Italy, on the ground that the Romans could not be conquered, he was killed by Boiorix, a savage youth.[3] At Arausio these same enemies conquered in battle Gnaeus Manlius the consul and Quintus Servilius Caepio the proconsul, stripped them both of their camps, and killed eighty thousand soldiers and forty thousand servants and camp followers, according to Valerius Antias.[4] Caepio, through whose rashness the disaster had been incurred, was condemned and his property confiscated, for the first B.C. 105–102

[2] Cf. Sallust lxxx, lxxxvii–cxiii; Plutarch, *Marius* ix f.; Appian, *Numidian Wars* 4 f.

[3] 105 B.C. Boiorix may have been the chieftain of the Cimbri, cf. Plutarch, *Marius* xxv. Cf. Granius Licinianus, p. 11 Flemisch; Velleius II. xii. 2; Tacitus, *Germania* 37; Orosius V. xvi. 2 f.

[4] Cf. references in note 3; also Plutarch, *Marius* xix, *Lucullus* xxvii; Cicero, *pro Balbo* 28; Valerius Maximus IV. vii. 3; Dio XXVII fr. 91. 1–4.

A.U.C. 649–652 primi post regem Tarquinium, imperiumque ei abrogatum. In triumpho C. Marii ductus ante currum eius Iugurtha cum duobus filiis et in carcere necatus est. Marius triumphali veste in senatum venit, quod nemo ante eum fecerat; eique propter metum Cimbrici belli continuatus per complures annos est consulatus. Secundo et tertio absens consul creatus quartum consulatum dissimulanter captans consecutus est. Cn. Domitius pontifex maximus populi suffragio creatus est. Cimbri vastatis omnibus, quae inter Rhodanum et Pyrenaeum sunt, per saltum in Hispaniam transgressi ibique multa loca populati a Celtiberis fugati sunt, reversique in Galliam in Vellocassis se Teutonis [1] coniunxerunt.

A.U.C. 652–653 LXVIII. M. Antonius praetor in Ciliciam maritimos praedones [2] persecutus est. C. Marius consul summa vi oppugnata a Teutonis et Ambronibus castra defendit. Duobus deinde proeliis circa Aquas Sextias eosdem hostes delevit, in quibus caesa traduntur hostium ducenta milia, capta nonaginta. Marius absens quinto consul creatus est. Triumphum oblatum, donec et Cimbros vinceret, distulit.

[1] in Veliocassis se Teutonis *Mommsen*: inbellicosis et teutonis NP.

[2] praedones GR: praedones, id est piratas *vetera*.

---

[1] 104–3 B.C. Cf. Cicero, *de Oratore* II. 124, 198–9; Orosius V. xvi. 1–7. The confiscation was one of several measures that were aimed at Caepio, though stated in general terms, because of his exaggerated aristocratic bias; this also caused the "rashness," or lack of co-operation, which produced the disaster.

[2] 104 B.C. Cf. Sallust, *Jugurtha* cxiv, Plutarch, *Marius* xii. One son of Jugurtha, Oxyntas, was used in 90 B.C. by a Samnite to impress the Numidians on the Roman side of the Social War, cf. Appian, *Civil Wars* I. 42.

time since King Tarquin, and he was cashiered.[1] In the triumph of Gaius Marius, Jugurtha with his two sons was led before the triumphal chariot and was killed in the gaol.[2] Marius entered the senate in his triumphal dress, which no one previously had done. Because of dread of the war against the Cimbri, Marius' consulship was renewed for several years. The second and third times he was away when elected, and he achieved a fourth consulship by a pretence of making no campaign for it.[3] Gnaeus Domitius was elected chief pontiff by vote of the people.[4] The Cimbri devastated all the land between the Rhone and the Pyrenees, crossed through a pass into Spain, and there after devastating many districts were routed by the Celtiberians. They returned to Gaul and in the land of the Vellocasses joined the Teutoni.[5] B.C. 105–102

LXVIII. Praetor Marcus Antonius pursued the sea brigands into Cilicia.[6] Consul Gaius Marius defended his camp against furious assaults by the Teutoni and Ambrones. Thereafter in two battles near Aquae Sextiae he destroyed these same enemies; in these battles it is recorded that two hundred thousand enemies were killed and ninety thousand captured. Marius was elected in his absence consul for the fifth time.[7] He postponed the triumph offered him until he should conquer the Cimbri B.C. 102–101

[3] Marius' entry into the senate is mentioned in Plutarch, *Marius* xii. 5. On Marius' elections as consul, cf. Plutarch xiv.

[4] Apparently in 103 B.C. Domitius had introduced a law that the people should elect priests of the principal colleges from candidates nominated by these colleges. Cf. Valerius Maximus VI. v. 5; Cicero, *pro Deiotaro* 31.

[5] 103–2 B.C. See Obsequens 43; Plutarch, *Marius* xiv.

[6] 102 B.C., cf. Cicero, *de Oratore* I. 82; Plutarch, *Pompey* xxiv; below, Obsequens 44. Dynastic disturbances in Syria gave occasion both for the piratical activity, and for Roman interference so near the centre of Seleucid power; see below, end of this Summary.

[7] Cf. Plutarch, *Marius* xvi–xxii.

A.U.C. 652–653 Cimbri cum repulso ab Alpibus fugatoque Q. Catulo procos., qui fauces Alpium obsidebat et ad flumen Atesim castellum editum insederat cohorte reliqueratque,[1] quae tamen virtute sua explicata fugientem procos. exercitumque consecuta est, in Italiam traiecissent, iunctisque eiusdem Catuli et C. Marii exercitibus proelio victi sunt, in quo caesa traduntur hostium centum quadraginta milia, capta sexaginta. Marius totius civitatis consensu exceptus pro duobus triumphis, qui offerebantur, uno contentus fuit. Primores civitatis, qui ei[2] aliquamdiu ut novo homini ad tantos honores evecto inviderant, conservatam ab eo rem publicam fatebantur. Publicius Malleolus matre occisa primus in culleo insutus in mare praecipitatus est. Ancilia cum strepitu mota esse, antequam Cimbricum bellum consummaretur, refertur. Bella praeterea inter Syriae reges gesta continet.

A.U.C. 654 LXIX. L.[3] Apuleius Saturninus, adiuvante C. Mario et per milites occiso A. Nunnio competitore, tribunus plebis

[1] et ad flumen . . . cohorte reliqueratque *Rossbach*: flumen . . . relinqueret *ceteris omissis* MSS.
[2] ei *Jahn*: et MSS.
[3] L. *Sigonius*: Cn. NPII.

---

[1] Cf. Plutarch, *Marius* xxiv.
[2] The text is uncertain, probably due to omissions, see critical note; the present version is based on Plutarch, *Marius* xxiii.
[3] Cf. Plutarch, *Marius* xxv–xxvii.
[4] Cf. Plutarch, *Marius* xxvii. 6, xliv. 5; *C.I.L.* I^2. 1, pp. 177, 195.
[5] Cf. Cicero, *pro Rabirio Perduell.* 27; Juvenal viii. 250.
[6] That Malleolus was the first to incur this punishment seems to be a special assertion of Livy's, meaning presumably that this was the first clearly historical occasion. In Dionysius IV. 62 and Valerius Maximus I. i. 13, this punishment is said to have been used by Tarquin the Proud on the occasion of a serious crime against religion; it is more usually associated

also.[1] The latter drove back from the Alps and put to flight Proconsul Quintus Catulus, who was trying to block the Alpine passes, and who had left a lofty fort at the Atesis River which he had garrisoned with one cohort. This cohort, however, extricated itself by its own unaided gallantry and overtook the fleeing proconsul and his army.[2] The Cimbri had by this time crossed into Italy, and were beaten in battle by the combined forces of the above-mentioned Catulus and Gaius Marius. In this battle it is recorded that one hundred and forty thousand of the enemy were killed and sixty thousand were captured.[3] Marius was hailed with the unanimous applause of the whole state, but was satisfied with a single triumph instead of the two which were offered him at that time.[4] The leading men of the state, who had for some time held a grudge against him as a man without family background who had been elevated to posts of such importance, now admitted that the state had been preserved by him.[5] B.C. 102–101

Publicius Malleolus, who had killed his mother, was the first to be sewn into a sack and hurled into the sea.[6] The report is given that the sacred shields were shaken and rattled before the conclusion of the Cimbric War.[7] The book also includes the wars waged in the royal family of Syria.[8]

LXIX. Lucius Apuleius Saturninus, who had the support of Gaius Marius, and whose rival Aulus Nunnius was B.C. 100

with parricide, *e.g.*, Cicero, *pro Roscio Amerino* 70. In either case the intention was to cleanse the country of a portentous defilement. Cf. Orosius V. xvi. 23; Auctor ad Herennium I. 13.

[7] Cf. below, Obsequens 44a (101 B.C.).

[8] The dynastic struggle in Syria, cf. above LXII, page 75, note 6, continued, and was complicated by rivalry for the throne of Egypt, cf. Justinus XXXIX. iv. 4. Cf. also the first item of this Summary.

(For a brief fragment of the *Oxyrhynchus Summary*, see below, p. 172.)

A.U.C. 654 per vim creatus, non minus violenter tribunatum, quam petierat, gessit; et cum legem agrariam per vim tulisset, Metello Numidico, quod in eam non iuraverat, diem dixit. Qui cum a bonis civibus defenderetur, ne causa certaminum esset, in exilium voluntarium Rhodum profectus est, ibique audiendo et legendo magnos viros avocabatur. Profecto C. Marius, seditionis auctor, qui sextum consulatum pecunia per tribus sparsa emerat, aqua et igni interdixit. Idem Apuleius Saturninus tribunus plebis C. Memmium candidatum consulatus, quoniam adversarium eum [1] actionibus suis timebat, occidit. Quibus rebus concitato senatu, in cuius causam et C. Marius, homo varii et mutabilis ingenii consiliique semper secundum fortunam, transierat, oppressus armis cum Glaucia praetore et aliis eiusdem furoris sociis [2] bello quodam interfectus est. Q. Caecilius Metellus ab exilio ingenti totius civitatis favore reductus est. M'. Aquilius pro cos. in Sicilia bellum servile excitatum confecit.

[1] eum Jahn: eius NPΠ.
[2] sociis *add.* R: *om.* MSS.

---

[1] Cf. Appian, *Civil Wars* I. 28, who mentions that Saturninus had been tribune before (in 103 B.C., cf. Cicero, *pro Sestio* 37); Plutarch, *Marius* xxix.

[2] The land law was for the benefit of Marius' veterans, cf. Plutarch xxix, Appian, *Civil Wars* I. 29–31; Saturninus also planned to make the veterans citizens in colonies, cf. Cicero, *pro Balbo* 48. The city populace rioted in opposition to this extension of their privileges, and Saturninus conducted counter-riots. A special clause requiring the senate to uphold the law was perhaps aimed at Metellus, whom both Marius and Saturninus hated. On Metellus' behaviour, cf. also Cicero, *ad Familiares* I. ix. 16; Seneca, *Epistles* xxiv. 4. (L.C.L.).

[3] On Marius' election, cf. Plutarch xxviii; Velleius II. xii. 6.

slain by the soldiers, was elected tribune of the commons by violence.[1] He conducted his tribunate as lawlessly as his campaign; after passing a land law by violence, he indicted Metellus Numidicus because he had not sworn to uphold it. The better class of citizens rallied to Metellus' defence, but to avoid being a cause of strife, he went into voluntary exile at Rhodes, and there found distraction in hearing and reading distinguished philosophers.[2] After Metellus left, Gaius Marius, the man responsible for the civil strife, who had bought his sixth consulship by strewing money among the tribes, banned Metellus from fire and water.[3] The same Apuleius Saturninus, tribune of the commons, killed Gaius Memmius, a candidate for the consulship, because he feared him as an opponent of his proceedings.[4] The senate was aroused at these crimes; and Gaius Marius too, being a man of shifting and changeable nature, and one to shift his policy as chance directed, had come over to their side. Saturninus, along with Praetor Glaucia and other comrades in the same madness, was put down by military force and killed in a sort of war.[5] Quintus Caecilius Metellus was brought back from exile to the loud applause of the whole state.[6] Proconsul Manius Aquilius put an end to a slave war which had arisen in Sicily.[7] B.C. 100

[4] Memmius was anti-senatorial; Glaucia, named below as an associate of Saturninus, was a candidate for the consulship.

[5] Considering that Marius did not wish to be dominated by Saturninus and Glaucia, and that he may even have disapproved at this time of continued murdering of opponents as a political measure, the charge of shiftiness seems overdone; but Marius was not a shrewd or long-sighted political calculator. Cf. Plutarch, *Marius* xxx; Appian, *Civil Wars* I. 32 f.; Cicero, *pro Rabirio Perduell.* 28; Velleius II. xii. 6.

[6] Cf. Plutarch, *Marius* xxxi; Valerius Maximus IV. i. 13, V. ii. 7; Appian, *Civil Wars* I. 33.

[7] Aquilius had served under Marius and was consul with him in 101 B.C. The campaign against the slaves took some time; Aquilius killed their leader in a duel, but was severely wounded. Cf. Diodorus XXXVI. 10; Florus II. vii.

A.U.C. 655–663

LXX. Cum M'.[1] Aquilius de pecuniis repetundis causam diceret, ipse iudices rogare noluit; M. Antonius, qui pro eo perorabat, tunicam a pectore eius discidit, ut honestas cicatrices ostenderet. Indubitate absolutus est. Cicero eius rei solus auctor. T. Didius pro cos. adversus Celtiberos feliciter pugnavit. Ptolemaeus Cyrenarum rex, cui cognomen Apionis fuit, mortuus heredem populum Romanum reliquit, et eius regni civitates senatus liberas esse iussit. Ariobarzanes in regnum Cappadociae a L. Cornelio Sylla reductus est. Parthorum legati, a rege Arsace missi, venerunt ad Syllam, ut amicitiam populi Romani peterent. P. Rutilius, vir summae innocentiae, quoniam legatus C. Mucii pro cos. a publicanorum iniuriis Asiam defenderat, invisus equestri ordini, penes quem iudicia erant, repetundarum damnatus in exilium missus est. C. Sentius praetor adversus Thracas infeliciter pugnavit. Senatus cum impotentiam equestris ordinis in iudiciis exercendis ferre nollet, omni vi eniti coepit, ut ad se iudicia transferret, sustinente causam eius M. Livio Druso tribuno plebis, qui ut vires sibi adquireret, perniciosa spe largitionum[2] plebem concitavit. Praeterea motus Syriae regumque continet.

[1] M'. *Sigonius*: M. MSS.
[2] largitionum *Gruter*: largitionem MSS: largitionis R.

---

[1] Aquilius was guilty, cf. Cicero, *pro Flacco* 98; on his acquittal, cf. *de Oratore* II. 124, 188, 194–6.

[2] 97 B.C. Didius was consul in 98 B.C. Cf. Obsequens 47 f.; Appian, *Spanish Wars* 99.

[3] Probably 96 B.C. Cf. Justinus XXXIX. 5; Tacitus, *Annals* XIV. 18.

[4] 92 B.C. Cf. Justinus XXXVIII. 3. 3; Plutarch, *Sulla* v; Appian, *Mithridatic Wars* x. 57. Ariobarzanes was pro-Roman, and was opposed by Tigranes of Armenia and Mithridates of Pontus.

LXX. When Manius Aquilius was standing trial for extortion, he was unwilling to make an appeal to the jury, but Marcus Antonius, who was concluding his speech in defence of Aquilius, tore the shirt from his chest in order to display his honourable scars. Aquilius was acquitted with no hesitation. Cicero is the only writer who tells of this incident.[1] Proconsul Titus Didius fought successfully against the Celtiberians.[2] Ptolemy king of Cyrene, whose personal name was Apion, died and left the Roman People as his heir; accordingly the senate decreed that the cities of that kingdom should be independent.[3] Ariobarzanes was restored to the throne of Cappadocia by Lucius Cornelius Sulla.[4] Envoys of the Parthians, sent by king Arsaces, came to Sulla to seek the friendship of the Roman People.[5] Publius Rutilius, a man of unblemished conduct, was hated by the order of knights, because as deputy of Proconsul Gaius Mucius he had protected Asia against the injustice of the tax gatherers. Since the knights had control of the courts, Rutilius was condemned for extortion and sent into exile.[6] Praetor Gaius Sentius lost a battle to the Thracians.[7] The senate refused to endure the licence of the order of knights in managing the courts, and began to bend every effort to transfer control to the senate itself. The cause of the senate was supported by Marcus Livius Drusus, tribune of the commons, who stirred up the commons with the ruinous hope of gratuities in order to strengthen his position.[8] The book also includes disturbances in Syria and among the kings.[9] B.C. 99–91

[5] Sulla was at the border of Armenia, south of which were the Parthians. Cf. Velleius II. xxiv; Plutarch, *Sulla* v.

[6] 92 B.C. Cf. Velleius II. xiii. 2; Dio XXVIII. fr. 97; Orosius V. xvii. 12–3. Rutilius had served in Asia in 97 B.C. under Quintus (not Gaius) Mucius Scaevola.

[7] 92 B.C. Cf. Orosius V. xviii. 30; Sentius continued as governor of Macedonia, and his later victory is mentioned in Cicero: *in Pisonem* 84; *in Verrem* II. III. 217.

[8] 91 B.C. Cf. below, LXXI; Velleius II. xiii; Appian, *Civil Wars* I. 35. Drusus was a nephew of Rutilius.

[9] Cf. above, LXVIII.

A.U.C. 663 LXXI. M. Livius Drusus tribunus plebis, quo[1] maioribus viribus senatus causam susceptam tueretur, socios et Italicos populos spe civitatis Romanae sollicitavit; iisque adiuvantibus per vim legibus agrariis frumentariisque latis iudiciariam quoque pertulit, ut aequa parte iudicia penes senatum et equestrem ordinem essent. Cum deinde promissa sociis civitas praestari non posset, irati Italici defectionem agitare coeperunt. Eorum coetus[2] coniurationesque et orationes in consiliis principum referuntur. Propter quae Livius Drusus invisus etiam senatui factus velut socialis belli auctor, incertum a quo domi occisus est.

LXXII. Italici populi defecerunt Picentes, Vestini, Marsi, Paeligni, Marrucini, Samnites, Lucani. Initio belli a Picentibus moto Q. Servilius pro cos. in oppido Asculo[3] cum omnibus civibus Romanis, qui in eo oppido erant, occisus est. Saga populus sumpsit. Ser. Galba a Lucanis comprehensus, unius feminae opera, ad quam devertebatur, e[4] captivitate receptus est. Aesernia et Alba coloniae ab Italicis obsessae sunt. Auxilia deinde Latini nominis et[5] exterarum gentium missa populo Romano et expeditiones invicem expugnationesque urbium referuntur.

[1] quo *Jahn* : qui NPΠ.
[2] coetus *Duker* : coitus MSS.
[3] Asculo *add.* GR : *om. vet.*
[4] e *add. Jahn* : *om.* MSS.
[5] et *add. Rossbach* : *om.* MSS.

---

[1] 91 B.C. Cf. Diodorus XXXVII. x. 1–3, xi, xiii. 1 f.; Cicero, *de Oratore* III. i, ii. 1–5; Velleius II. xiii f.; *de viris illustribus* lxvi. 1 f.; Appian, *Civil Wars* I. v. 35 f., whose account is somewhat distorted to fit Appian's conception of the Social War as part of the civil wars.

LXXI. Marcus Livius Drusus, tribune of the commons had undertaken to support the cause of the senate; in order to bring greater resources to the maintenance of this task, he stirred up the allies and the peoples of Italy to hope for Roman citizenship. With the assistance of the Italians he carried by force laws on the distribution of land and grain, and also pushed through a law on the courts, to the effect that control of the courts should be equally shared by the senate and the order of knights. When after these events the promised grant of citizenship for the allies could not be effected, the Italians were enraged and began to promote a revolt. Their gatherings and conspiracies, and the speeches in conference of their leading men are reported in the book. These events made Livius Drusus detested even by the senate as being a promoter of rebellion among the allies; he was cut down in his own home by an unknown assassin.[1] B.C. 91

LXXII. The following Italian peoples rebelled: the Picentes, Vestini, Marsi, Paeligni, Marrucini, Samnites, and Lucanians.[2] The opening move of the war was made by the Picentes; in the town of Asculum, Proconsul Quintus Servilius and all the Roman citizens who were in the town were killed.[3] The Roman people donned military cloaks. Servius Galba was arrested by the Lucanians and was released from captivity by the action of a lone woman with whom he had been lodging. The colonies of Aesernia and Alba were besieged by the Italians. An account is given of the troops sent by the Latin Name and foreign nations to the relief of the Roman People; also recorded are campaigns and the storming of cities by both sides.

[2] 91 B.C. A coin gives a list mentioning also the Frentani and Hirpini and omitting the Lucanians, cf. *C.A.H.* IX, p. 185.

[3] Cf. Velleius II. xv, Diodorus XXXVII. xiii. 2, Appian, *Civil Wars* I. v. 38 f. Servilius, a praetor or propraetor acting *pro consule*, attempted to browbeat the Asculans, and so touched off the massacre.

A.U.C. 664 LXXIII. L. Iulius Caesar consul male adversus Samnites pugnavit. Nola colonia in potestatem Samnitium venit cum L. Postumio praetore, qui ab his interfectus est. Complures populi ad hostes defecerunt. Cum P. Rutilius consul parum prospere adversus Marsos pugnasset et in eo proelio cecidisset, C. Marius legatus eius meliore eventu cum hostibus acie conflixit. Ser. Sulpicius[1] Paelignos proelio fudit. Q. Caepio legatus Rutilii cum obsessus prospere in hostes inrupisset et ob eum successum aequatum ei cum C. Mario esset imperium, temerarius factus et circumventus insidiis fuso exercitu cecidit. L. Iulius Caesar consul feliciter adversus Samnites pugnavit. Ob eam victoriam Romae saga posita sunt. Et ut varia belli fortuna esset, Aesernia colonia cum M. Marcello in potestatem Samnitium venit. Sed et C. Marius proelio Marsos fudit, Hierio[2] Asinio praetore Marrucinorum occiso. C. Caecilius in Gallia Transalpina Salluvios rebellantes vicit.

A.U.C. 665 LXXIV. Cn. Pompeius Picentes proelio fudit et[3] obsedit; propter quam victoriam Romae praetextae et alia magistratuum insignia sumpta sunt. C. Marius cum

[1] Servius Sulpicius Moguntina: sex. sul NPR.
[2] Hierio *Rossbach*: hirno MSS: Herio *Gronovius*.
[3] fudit et obsedit GR: fudit obsedit *vet.*, *Rossbach*: fudit . . obsedit *Jahn*.

---

[1] 90 B.C. Caesar was attempting to relieve Aesernia, cf. above, LXXII.

[2] Cf. Appian, *Civil Wars* I. v. 42. Nola was not a colony. The Samnites held it till 80 B.C., cf. Velleius II. xvii. 1, Plutarch, *Sulla* viii.

[3] The battle was fought east of Rome, cf. Ovid, *Fasti* VI. 563–6, which gives the date of June 11, and may have been part of an attempt to relieve Alba Fucens (above, LXXII). Marius was in the neighbourhood and retrieved the situation by prompt action, cf. Appian, *Civil Wars* I. v. 43, Orosius V. xviii. 13.

LXXIII. Consul Lucius Julius Caesar lost a battle to the Samnites.[1] The colony of Nola came into the hands of the Samnites, along with Praetor Lucius Postumius, who was put to death by them.[2] Numerous peoples deserted to the enemy. After Consul Publius Rutilius had fought unsuccessfully against the Marsi and had fallen in that battle, his deputy Gaius Marius was more successful in a battle against the enemy.[3] Servius Sulpicius routed the Paeligni in battle.[4] Quintus Caepio, a deputy of Rutilius, was besieged and made a successful sally against the enemy; because of this success his authority was made equal to that of Gaius Marius. Caepio thereupon grew reckless, was lured into an ambush, and fell in the rout of his army.[5] Consul Lucius Julius Caesar fought successfully against the Samnites.[6] Because of this victory, military cloaks were laid aside at Rome. That the fortunes of war might be fickle, the colony of Aesernia, along with Marcus Marcellus, fell into the hands of the Samnites.[7] For the Romans again, Gaius Marius routed the Marsi in a battle, after Hierius Asinius the general of the Marrucini had been slain.[8] Gaius Caecilius subdued a rebellion of the Salluvii in Transalpine Gaul.[9] B.C. 90

LXXIV. Gnaeus Pompeius routed the Picentes in battle and besieged them. Because of this victory, purple-bordered togas and the other distinctions of the magistrates were donned at Rome.[10] Gaius Marius fought B.C. 89

[4] Perhaps the Servius Galba of LXXII.

[5] Cf. Appian, *Civil Wars* I. v. 44; *C.I.L.* I². 708. Caepio and Marius were recognized as in command, jointly, of the northern theatre of operations after the death of Rutilius.

[6] Cf. Appian, *Civil Wars* I. v. 42.

[7] Cf. Appian, *Civil Wars* I. v. 41.

[8] The name of the Italian commander is often given as Herius, cf. Appian, *Civil Wars* I. v. 40, Velleius II. xvi. 1.

[9] The praetor's name may have been Caelius, cf. *RE.* III. 1188 and 1255; Broughton, *Magistrates* II. 25.

[10] 89 B.C. Pompeius, as consul, commanded on the northern front, near which he seems to have owned property.

A.U.C. 665 Marsis dubio eventu pugnavit. Libertini tunc primum militare coeperunt. A.[1] Plotius legatus Umbros, L. Porcius praetor Etruscos,[2] cum uterque populus defecisset, proelio vicerunt. Nicomedes in Bithyniae, Ariobarzanes in Cappadociae regnum reducti sunt. Cn. Pompeius consul Marsos acie vicit. Cum aere alieno oppressa esset civitas, A. Sempronius Asellio praetor, quoniam secundum debitores ius dicebat, ab his, qui faenerabant, in foro occisus est. Praeterea incursiones Thracum in Macedoniam populationesque continet.

LXXV. A. Postumius Albinus legatus cum classi praeesset, infamis crimine perduellionis[3] ab exercitu suo interfectus est. L. Cornelius Sylla legatus Samnites proelio vicit et bina castra eorum expugnavit. Cn. Pompeius Vestinos in deditionem accepit. L. Porcius consul rebus prospere gestis fusisque aliquotiens Marsis, dum castra eorum expugnat, cecidit. Ea res hostibus victoriam eius proelii dedit. Cosconius et Lucanus Samnites acie vicerunt, Marium Egnatium, nobilissimum hostium ducem, occiderunt compluraque eorum oppida in deditionem acceperunt. L. Sylla Hirpinos domuit, Samnites pluribus proeliis fudit, aliquot populos recepit,

[1] A. *edd.*: Aurelius NPΠR.
[2] Etruscos *Duker*: umbros *vet.*: marsos GR.
[3] perduellionis *Rossbach*: perditiones N, per deditionis P.

---

[1] Cf. Appian, *Civil Wars* I. vi. 49; the freedmen garrisoned the coast of Latium.
[2] Cf. Orosius V. xviii. 17.
[3] Cf. Appian, *Mithridatic Wars* ii. 11.
[4] Cf. Appian, *Civil Wars* I. vi. 52.
[5] Cf. Valerius Maximus IX. vii. 4; Appian, *Civil Wars* I. vi. 54.
[6] Cf. below, LXXVI and LXXXI.
[7] 89 B.C. Cf. Plutarch, *Sulla* vi. 9. Postumius' real offence was cruelty to his own men, who were spared punishment by Sulla.

indecisively with the Marsi. At this time, freedmen first began to serve in the army.[1] Aulus Plotius, a deputy, defeated the Umbrians in battle, and Praetor Lucius Porcius overcame the Etruscans, since both peoples had revolted.[2] Nicomedes was brought back to the throne of Bithynia, and Ariobarzanes to that of Cappadocia.[3] Consul Gnaeus Pompeius won a battle against the Marsi.[4] B.C. 89

The state was labouring under the burden of debts; Praetor Aulus Sempronius Asellio was slain in the forum by usurers because he was deciding cases in favour of debtors.[5] The book also includes raids and ravaging in Macedonia by the Thracians.[6]

LXXV. Aulus Postumius Albinus commanded the fleet as deputy; being discredited by charges of treason, he was put to death by his own troops.[7] Lucius Cornelius Sulla as deputy conquered the Samnites in battle and stormed two camps of theirs. Gnaeus Pompeius received the surrender of the Vestini.[8] After successful campaigning, and having on several occasions routed the Marsi, Consul Lucius Porcius fell while storming a Marsian camp. This misfortune gave the enemy the victory in that battle.[9] Cosconius and Lucanus conquered the Samnites in battle, killed Marius Egnatius, the most conspicuous leader of the enemy, and received the surrender of a large number of Samnite cities.[10] Lucius Sulla overcame the Hirpini and routed the Samnites in several battles; he received the

[8] See below, LXXVI.

[9] This occurred early in the year.

[10] Appian, *Civil Wars* I. vi. 52 gives an account of Cosconius' successes in Apulia which cannot quite be adjusted to Livy's. The name of the other commander is sometimes conjectured to be Lucanius (a member of Pompeius Strabo's staff in this year had that name), or Lucceius (so R and Gronovius). For Marius Egnatius' successes in the previous year, cf. Appian, *Civil Wars* I. v. 41 and vi. 45.

A.U.C. 665 quantisque raro quisquam alius ante consulatum rebus gestis ad petitionem consulatus Romam est profectus.

LXXVI. A. Gabinius legatus rebus adversus Lucanos prospere gestis et plurimis oppidis expugnatis in obsidione hostium castrorum cecidit. Sulpicius legatus Marrucinos cecidit, totamque eam regionem recepit. Cn. Pompeius pro cos. Vestinos et Paelignos in deditionem accepit. Marsi quoque a L. Cinna [1] et Caecilio Pio [2] legatis aliquot proeliis fracti petere pacem coeperunt. Asculum a Cn. Pompeio captum est. Caesis et a Mamerco Aemilio legato Italicis Silo Poppaedius dux Marsorum, auctor eius rei, in proelio cecidit. Ariobarzanes Cappadociae, Nicomedes Bithyniae regno a Mithridate Ponti rege pulsi sunt. Praeterea incursiones Thracum in Macedoniam populationesque continet.

A.U.C. 666 LXXVII. Cum P. Sulpicius tribunus plebis auctore C. Mario perniciosas leges promulgasset, ut exules revocarentur et novi cives libertinique in tribus [3] distribuerentur et ut C. Marius adversus Mithridatem Ponti regem

[1] Cinna *Jahn* : pinna *vet.* : murena GR.
[2] Pio *Sigonius* : pinna NPΠR.
[3] in tribus *add.* R, *edd.* : *om.* MSS : in XXXV tribus *Halm.*

---

[1] Sulla began his campaign on the coast below Naples, moved north-east against the Hirpini, a faction of whom provided a legion among his forces, and then north-west into Samnium, cf. Appian, *Civil Wars* I. vi. 50 f.

[2] 89 B.C. Cf. LXXV; Sulpicius was either Servius Sulpicius Galba, cf. LXXIII or Publius Sulpicius Rufus, cf. LXXVII; Orosius V. xviii. 25 also gives the *nomen* only.

[3] The exact course of events described here, and above, is not made clear, but cf. Appian, *Civil Wars* I. vi. 48. No

surrender of several peoples; and after achieving successes of a magnitude seldom equalled by anyone else before becoming consul, set out for Rome to seek the consulship.[1] B.C. 89

LXXVI. The deputy Aulus Gabinius achieved successes against the Lucanians and stormed a very large number of cities; he fell while besieging a camp of the enemy. The deputy Sulpicius crushed the Marrucini, and recovered that whole region. Gnaeus Pompeius as proconsul received the surrender of the Vestini and Paeligni.[2] The Marsi also were broken by the deputies Lucius Cinna and Caecilius Pius in several battles and began to ask for peace. Asculum was taken by Gnaeus Pompeius.[3] When the Italians suffered a further defeat at the hands of the deputy Aemilius Mamercus, Poppaedius Silo, the commander of the Marsi and ringleader of the revolt, fell in the battle.[4] Ariobarzanes of Cappadocia and Nicomedes of Bithynia were driven from their kingdoms by Mithridates king of Pontus.[5] The book also includes raids and plundering by the Thracians in Macedonia.[6]

LXXVII. Publius Sulpicius, tribune of the commons, instigated by Gaius Marius, proposed ruinous laws—that the exiles should be recalled, that new citizens and freedmen should be distributed among the tribes, and that Gaius Marius should be appointed commander to oppose B.C. 88

notice is taken, at least in the Summary, of the offer of Roman citizenship which conceded much to the rebels, until it appears as the first item of Summary LXXX, long after it took effect.

[4] Silo retired to Samnium after his Marsians were knocked out of the war, and scored some success before this close of his career.

[5] Nicomedes was replaced by his younger brother, Socrates; Mithridates' son took the throne of Cappadocia. Cf. Appian, *Mithridatic Wars* ii. 10.

[6] Cf. below, LXXXI.

A.U.C. 666 dux crearetur, et adversantibus consulibus Q. Pompeio et L. Syllae vim intulisset, occiso Q. Pompeio [1] Q. Pompei consulis filio, genero Syllae, L. Sylla consul cum exercitu in urbem venit et adversus factionem Sulpicii et Marii in ipsa urbe pugnavit, eamque expulit. Ex qua duodecim a senatu hostes, inter quos C. Marius pater et filius, iudicati sunt. P. Sulpicius cum in quadam villa lateret, indicio servi sui retractus et occisus est. Servus, ut praemium promissum indici [2] haberet, manumissus et ob scelus proditi domini de saxo deiectus est. C. Marius filius in Africam traiecit. C. Marius pater cum in paludibus Minturnensium lateret, extractus est ab oppidanis; et cum missus ad occidendum eum servus natione Gallus maiestate tanti viri perterritus recessisset, impositus publice navi delatus est in Africam. L. Sylla civitatis statum ordinavit, exinde colonias deduxit. Q. Pompeius consul, ad accipiendum a Cn. Pompeio procos. exercitum profectus, consilio eius occisus est. Mithridates, Ponti rex, Bithynia et Cappadocia occupatis et pulso Aquilio legato Phrygiam, provinciam populi Romani, cum ingenti exercitu intravit.

[1] Q. Pompeio *add. Sigonius, Hertz*: occisoque pompei NPR, occisoque pompeio Gu.

[2] promissum indici *Gronovius*: promissi indicii NPΠR.

---

[1] 88 B.C. The first measure was obvious; the second was Sulpicius' real and much-needed contribution to the settlement of the Social War; the third was presumably the political price for support of the second by an anti-senatorial group of considerable influence.

[2] The greater violence was on the side of the consuls; but Livy, like our other authorities, *e.g.*, Plutarch, *Sulla* viii, and Appian, *Civil Wars* I. vii. 55 f., quotes the senatorial tradition. Cf. frs. 15 and 16.

[3] Cf. Valerius Maximus III. viii. 5; Velleius II. xix. 1.

Mithridates King of Pontus.[1] When the consuls Quintus Pompeius and Lucius Sulla opposed him, Sulpicius met them with violence, and Quintus Pompeius, son of Consul Quintus Pompeius and son-in-law of Sulla, was killed, whereupon Consul Lucius Sulla entered the city with an army and, battling the party of Sulpicius and Marius in the city itself, drove them out.[2] Of this party twelve, including Gaius Marius senior and junior, were adjudged public enemies by the senate.[3] While Publius Sulpicius was hiding in a certain country-house, he was dragged out and killed on information given by his own slave. The slave was given his freedom, in order to pay him the reward promised to an informer, and was thrown from the Tarpeian Rock because of his crime in betraying his master.[4] Gaius Marius junior crossed over to Africa. The elder Marius hid in the swamps belonging to Minturnae, but was dragged out by citizens of that town. A slave of Gallic nationality was sent to kill him, but withdrew appalled by the dignity of so great a man. Marius was put aboard a ship by the town and carried to Africa.[5] B.C. 88

Lucius Sulla established order in the state, and thereafter sent out colonies.[6] Consul Quintus Pompeius set out to take over the army of Proconsul Gnaeus Pompeius, and was murdered at the instigation of the latter.[7] Mithridates King of Pontus seized Bithynia and Cappadocia and routed the deputy Aquilius; he then entered Phrygia, a province of the Roman people, with a large army.[8]

[4] Cf. Velleius II. xix. 1; Valerius Maximus VI. v. 7; Plutarch, *Sulla* x. 2, Appian, *Civil Wars* I. vii. 57–60.

[5] Cf. Plutarch, *Marius* xxxv. 5–xl; Velleius II. xix. 2–4; Appian, *Civil Wars* I. vii. 60–62; Valerius Maximus II. x. 6; Juvenal x. 276–82. The common people showed their devotion to Marius, and were presumably responsible for the change of official attitude.

[6] Cf. Appian, *Civil Wars* I. vii. 59.

[7] Cf. Appian, *Civil Wars* I. vii. 63.

[8] Cf. Appian, *Mithridatic Wars* iii. 17–20.

A.U.C. 666 LXXVIII. Mithridates Asiam occupavit; Q. Oppium procos., item Aquilium legatum in vincula coniecit, iussuque eius, quidquid civium Romanorum in Asia fuit, uno die trucidatum est. Urbem Rhodum, quae sola in fide populi R.[1] manserat, oppugnavit et aliquot proeliis navalibus victus recessit. Archelaus praefectus regis in Graeciam cum exercitu venit, Athenas occupavit. Praeterea trepidationem urbium insularumque, aliis ad Mithridatem aliis ad populum Romanum civitates suas trahentibus, continet.

A.U.C. 667 LXXIX. L. Cornelius Cinna consul cum perniciosas leges per vim atque arma ferret, pulsus urbe a Cn. Octavio collega cum sex tribunis plebis imperioque ei abrogato corruptum Appii Claudii exercitum in potestatem suam redegit et bellum urbi intulit, arcessito C. Mario ex Africa cum aliis exulibus. In quo bello duo fratres, alter ex Pompei exercitu alter ex Cinnae, ignorantes concurrerunt, et cum victor spoliaret occisum, agnito fratre ingenti lamentatione edita, rogo ei extructo, ipse se supra rogum transfodit et eodem igne consumptus est. Et cum opprimi inter initia potuisset, Cn. Pompeii fraude, qui utramque partem fovendo vires Cinnae dedit nec nisi profligatis optimatium rebus auxilium tulit, et consulis segnitia confirmati Cinna et Marius quattuor exercitibus,

[1] fide populi Romani *edd.*: fidem pr. NΠ.

---

[1] 88 B.C. Cf. Appian, *Mithridatic Wars* iv. f. 22–9; Plutarch, *Sulla* xi; Dio, XXX–XXXV, fr. 101.

[2] 87 B.C. Cf. Appian, *Civil Wars* I. viii. 64 f. The issue was the admission of the new (Italian) citizens to all tribes. The counterviolence of Octavius' followers was extreme, cf. Cicero, *in Catilinam* III. x. 24, *pro Sestio* xxxv. 77.

LXXVIII. Mithridates seized Asia; he cast into chains Quintus Oppius the proconsul, and also Aquilius the deputy; by Mithridates' order, every Roman citizen in Asia was slaughtered on a single day. He assailed the city of Rhodes, which alone remained loyal to the Roman People, but retired after being beaten in several naval battles. Archelaus the King's officer came into Greece with an army and seized Athens. The book also includes the turmoil in the cities and islands, as some tried to draw their states to the side of Mithridates, others to that of Rome.[1] B.C. 88

LXXIX. When Consul Lucius Cornelius Cinna was passing ruinous laws by violence and force of arms, he along with six tribunes of the commons, was driven from the city by his colleague Gnaeus Octavius.[2] After Cinna was deprived of his authority, he brought the army of Appius Claudius under his control by bribery and made war on the city of Rome, after summoning Gaius Marius, along with the other exiles, from Africa.[3] In this campaign two brothers, one of Pompeius' army, the other from that of Cinna, came unwittingly to blows; when the winner was stripping his slain rival, he recognized his brother, broke into loud laments, and when he had built his brother's pyre, he stabbed himself on it and was consumed in the flames with his victim. B.C. 87

Although the struggle could have been crushed at its outset, Cinna and Marius were strengthened not only by the treachery of Gnaeus Pompeius, who lent strength to Cinna by cultivating both sides, and did not come to the aid of the better sort till their situation was desperate,[4] but also by the inertia of the consul. The rebels besieged Rome with four armies, two of which were entrusted to

[3] Claudius' status as commander (propraetor) was in some doubt, cf. Cicero, *de Domo Sua* xxxi. 83, and the position of Cinna as consul carried some weight.

[4] Pompeius was not a man of principle, and had been snubbed by the aristocracy; cf. above, LXXVII.

A.U.C. 667 ex quibus duo Q. Sertorio et Carboni dati sunt, urbem circumsederunt. Ostiam coloniam Marius [1] expugnavit et crudeliter diripuit.

LXXX. Italicis populis a senatu civitas data est. Samnites, qui soli arma recipiebant, Cinnae et Mario se coniunxerunt. Ab his Plautius legatus cum exercitu caesus est. Cinna et Marius cum Carbone et Sertorio Ianiculum oppugnaverunt et fugati ab Octavio consule recesserunt. Marius Antium et Ariciam et Lanuvium colonias expugnavit. Cum spes nulla esset optimatibus resistendi propter segnitiam et perfidiam et ducum et militum, qui corrupti aut pugnare nolebant aut in diversas partes transiebant, Cinna et Marius in urbem recepti sunt; qui velut captam eam caedibus ac rapinis vastaverunt, Cn. Octavio consule occiso et omnibus adversae partis nobilibus trucidatis, inter quos M. Antonio eloquentissimo viro, C. Lque [2] Caesare, quorum capita in rostris posita sunt. Crassus filius ab equitibus Fimbriae occisus. Pater Crassus, ne quid indignum virtute sua pateretur, gladio se transfixit. Et citra ulla comitia consules in sequentem annum se ipsos renuntiaverunt; eodemque die, quo magistratum inierant, Marius S. Licinium senatorem

[1] Marius *add. edd.* : *om.* MSS.
[2] Lque *Hertz* : L MSS. : Caesaribus *Gronovius*.

---

[1] Cf. Appian, *Civil Wars* I. viii. 66 f.; Plutarch, *Marius* xli f.

[2] 87 B.C. A belated mention of this important step, first taken in 89 B.C.

[3] Metellus Pius, responsible for containing the Samnite rebels, had been recalled with part of his force, to defend Rome against Cinna, cf. Plutarch, *Marius* xlii. 3; Appian, *Civil Wars* I. viii. 68.

[4] The death of Pompeius, the most experienced soldier, is not mentioned (cf. Appian, *Civil Wars* I. viii. 68; Velleius II. xxi. 4); the other commanders were better as civilians than as leaders of a forlorn hope; and the soldiers may have

Quintus Sertorius and Carbo. Marius stormed the colony of Ostia and cruelly sacked it.[1] B.C. 87

LXXX. The citizenship was granted by the senate to the peoples of Italy.[2] The Samnites, who alone took up arms again, joined Cinna and Marius. The deputy Plautius and his army were beaten by these Samnites.[3] Cinna and Marius, along with Carbo and Sertorius, attacked the Janiculum, were routed by the consul Octavius, and retired. Marius stormed the colonies of Antium, Aricia, and Lanuvium. When no hope of holding out remained to the better sort, because of the inertia and treachery both of the commanders and of the soldiers,[4] who because of bribery either refused to fight or deserted to the opposite side, Cinna and Marius were received in the city, and proceeded to ravage it with slaughter and plundering as if they had captured it. Consul Gnaeus Octavius was killed, and all the outstanding men of the opposing party were slaughtered, among them Marcus Antonius, a most eloquent man, and Gaius and Lucius Caesar; their heads were placed on the Rostra. The younger Crassus was killed by the cavalry of Fimbria. The elder Crassus stabbed himself with his sword, to avoid suffering a fate unworthy of his valour.[5]

Without the slightest formality of election, Cinna and Marius announced themselves as consuls for the following year. On the very day on which they entered on their magistracy, Marius ordered Sextus Licinius, a senator,[6]

been understandably unenthusiastic about dying in a last-ditch stand for the privileges of their betters.

[5] The elder Crassus had been active in the preceding fighting; for his death, cf. Cicero, *pro Sestio* xxi. 48, *de Oratore* III. iii. 10, *Tusculan Disputations* V. xix. 55; and possibly *pro Scauro* iii. 1. 2.

[6] Velleius II. xxiv. 2 calls him "Lucilius, who had been tribune of the commons the preceding year," and makes Laenas, a tribune, responsible for his death, cf. also Plutarch, *Marius* xlv. 1 ("Sextus Lucinus").

A.U.C. 667 de saxo deici iussit editisque plurimis sceleribus idibus Ianuariis decessit, vir, cuius si examinentur cum virtutibus vitia, haud facile sit dictu, utrum bello melior an pace perniciosior fuerit. Adeo quam rem publicam armatus servavit, eam primo togatus omni genere fraudis, postremo armis hostiliter evertit.

LXXXI. L. Sylla Athenas, quas Archelaus praefectus Mithridatis occupaverat, circumsedente et cum magno labore expugnante[1] urbi libertatem et quae habuerat reddidit. Magnesia, quae sola in Asia civitas in fide manserat, summa virtute adversus Mithridaten defensa est. Praeterea excursiones Thracum in Macedoniam continet.

A.U.C 668 LXXXII. Sylla copias regis, quae Macedonia occupata in Thessaliam venerant, proelio vicit, caesis hostium centum milibus et castris quoque expugnatis. Renovato deinde bello iterum exercitum regis fudit ac delevit. Archelaus cum classe regia Syllae se tradidit. L. Valerius Flaccus consul, collega Cinnae, missus, ut Syllae succederet, propter avaritiam invisus exercitui suo a C. Fimbria legato ipsius, ultimae audaciae homine, occisus est, et imperium ad Fimbriam translatum. Praeterea expugnatae in Asia urbes a Mithridate et crudeliter direpta provincia, incursiones Thracum in Macedoniam referuntur.

[1] expugnante Gu.: expugnare *vet.*: expugnavit GR: expugnaret *Jahn.*

---

[1] Livy's fairness mixes here with the senatorial bias of his sources.

[2] 87–6 B.C. The Summary does not mention the pillage and slaughter immediately following the Roman entrance, cf. Plutarch, *Sulla* xiv., Appian, *Mithridatic Wars* vi. 38 f.

[3] 87 B.C. Cf. Appian, *Mithridatic Wars* ix. 61.

[4] These raids were presumably directed by Mithridates, through his son Ariarathes, who was trying to establish himself in Thrace; the earlier raids mentioned in LXXIV and LXXVI may have been instigated by Mithridates.

to be cast from the Tarpeian Rock; and after committing innumerable crimes, Marius died on the thirteenth of January, a man about whom it would be hard to say, if his vices and virtues are scrutinized together, whether the excellence of his services in war outweighed the damage he did in peace, or the reverse. So true is it that as a soldier he saved the state, and as a civilian first confounded that same state with all manner of trickery, and in the end made devastating war on it.[1] B.C. 87

LXXXI. Lucius Sulla besieged Athens, which had been seized by Archelaus, Mithridates' officer; when after severe exertions Sulla captured the town, he left it its autonomy and its property.[2] Magnesia, the only city in Asia which had remained loyal, was defended against Mithridates with the utmost valour.[3] The book also contains raids by the Thracians into Macedonia.[4]

LXXXII. Sulla defeated in battle the King's troops which had seized Macedonia and entered Thessaly; one hundred thousand of the enemy were killed and their camp was stormed also. When the war flared up again after that, Sulla again routed and destroyed the King's army. Archelaus surrendered himself and the King's fleet to Sulla.[5] Consul Lucius Valerius Flaccus, the colleague of Cinna, was sent to replace Sulla; being hated by his army because of his greed, Flaccus was killed by his own staff officer Gaius Fimbria, a man of utmost recklessness, and the command transferred to Fimbria.[6] The story is also told of the storming of cities in Asia by Mithridates, the cruel plundering of that province,[7] and raids of the Thracians into Macedonia. B.C. 86

[5] 86 B.C. Cf. Plutarch, *Sulla* xv–xxiii; Appian, *Mithridatic Wars* 41–45, 49 f.

[6] Cf. Appian, *Mithridatic Wars* viii. 51 f.; Dio XXX–XXXV, fr. 104.

[7] Cf. Appian, *Mithridatic Wars* xii. 46–48.

A.U.C. 669–670 LXXXIII. Flavius Fimbria in Asia fusis proelio aliquot praefectis Mithridatis urbem Pergamum cepit, obsessumque regem non multum afuit, quin caperet. Urbem Ilium, quae se potestati Syllae reservabat, expugnavit ac delevit et magnam partem Asiae recepit. Sylla compluribus proeliis Thracas cecidit. Cum L. Cinna et Cn. Papirius Carbo a se ipsis consules per biennium creati bellum contra Syllam praepararent, effectum est per L. Valerium Flaccum principem senatus, qui orationem in senatu habuit, et per eos qui concordiae studebant, ut legati ad Syllam de pace mitterentur. Cinna ab exercitu suo, quem invitum cogebat naves conscendere et adversus Syllam proficisci, interfectus est. Consulatum Carbo solus gessit. Sylla cum in Asiam traiecisset, pacem cum Mithridate fecit ita, ut his cederet provinciis: Asia, Bithynia, Cappadocia. Fimbria desertus ab exercitu, qui ad Syllam transierat, ipse se percussit impetravitque de servo suo, praebens cervicem, ut se occideret.

A.U.C. 670 LXXXIV. Sylla legatis, qui a senatu missi erant, futurum se in potestate senatus respondit, si cives, qui pulsi a Cinna ad se confugerant, restituerentur. Quae condicio cum iusta senatui videretur, per Carbonem factionemque eius, cui bellum videbatur utilius, ne conveniret effectum est. Idem Carbo cum ab omnibus Italiae oppidis coloniisque obsides exigere vellet, ut fidem eorum contra Syllam obligaret, consensu senatus prohibitus est. Novis civibus senatus consulto suffragium datum

---

[1] 85 B.C. Cf. Appian, *Mithridatic Wars* viii. 53; below, fr. 17, Obsequens 56b.

[2] 84 B.C. Cf. Appian, *Civil Wars* I. ix. 76–8.

[3] Cf. Plutarch, *Sulla* xxiv; Appian, *Mithridatic Wars* viii. 54–8.

LXXXIII. Flavius Fimbria routed in battle several officers of Mithridates in Asia, captured the city of Pergamum, and narrowly failed to capture the King in the course of the siege. Fimbria stormed and destroyed the city of Ilium, which was waiting to hand itself over to Sulla, and recovered a large part of Asia.[1] Sulla cut the Thracians to pieces in numerous battles. When Lucius Cinna and Gnaeus Papirius Carbo, self-appointed as consuls for two years, were preparing a campaign against Sulla, Lucius Valerius Flaccus, the chief of the senate, made a speech in the senate and with the help of those who were pressing for harmony brought it about that envoys were sent to Sulla to discuss peace. Cinna was put to death by his army, which he was trying to force against its will to embark and set out against Sulla. Carbo held the consulship without colleague.[2] When Sulla crossed over to Asia, he made peace with Mithridates on condition that the latter evacuate the following provinces; Asia, Bithynia, and Cappadocia.[3] Fimbria was abandoned by his army, which deserted to Sulla; he stabbed himself, offered his neck to his slave, and persuaded the latter to kill him.[4] B.C. 85–84

LXXXIV. Sulla replied to the envoys who had been sent by the senate that he would submit to the authority of the senate, if the citizens who had taken refuge with him after being driven out by Cinna were reinstated. Although this stipulation seemed fair to the senate, agreement was prevented by Carbo and his party, who thought that war was more to their interest. The same Carbo wished to demand hostages from all the towns and colonies of Italy, in order to secure their loyalty against Sulla, but he was prevented by the united sentiment of the senate.[5] The right to vote was given by decree of the senate to the new B.C. 84

[4] Cf. Plutarch, *Sulla* xxv; Appian, *Mithridatic Wars* ix. 59 f.; Velleius II. xxiv. 1.

[5] 84 B.C. Cf. Appian, *Civil Wars* I. ix. 77.

A.U.C. 670 est. Q. Metellus Pius, qui partes optimatium secutus erat, cum in Africa bellum moliretur, a C. Fabio praetore pulsus est, senatusque consultum per factionem Carbonis et Marianarum partium factum est, ut omnes ubique exercitus dimitterentur. Libertini in quinque et triginta tribus distributi sunt. Praeterea belli apparatum, quod contra Syllam excitabatur, continet.

A.U.C. 671 LXXXV. Sylla in Italiam cum exercitu traiecit missisque legatis, qui de pace agerent, et ab consule C.[1] Norbano violatis eundem Norbanum proelio vicit. Et cum L. Scipionis, alterius consulis, cum quo per omnia id egerat, ut pacem iungeret,[2] nec potuerat, castra oppugnaturus esset, universus exercitus consulis sollicitatus per emissos a Sylla milites signa ad Syllam transtulit. Scipio cum occidi posset, dimissus est. Cn. Pompeius, Cn. Pompei eius, qui Asculum ceperat, filius,[3] conscripto voluntariorum exercitu cum tribus legionibus ad Syllam venerat, ad quem se nobilitas omnis conferebat, ita ut deserta urbe ad castra veniretur. Praeterea expeditiones per totam Italiam utriusque partis ducum referuntur.

A.U.C. 671–672 LXXXVI. Cum C. Marius C. Marii filius consu ante annos XX per vim creatus esset, C. Fabius in Africa propter crudelitatem et avaritiam suam in praetorio suo

[1] C. *Sigonius*: cn. MSS.
[2] ut pacem iungeret *edd.*: pacem iungere MSS.
[3] filius *Rossbach*: scriptus NPΠ: privatus *Gronovius*.

---

[1] A formal ratification of preceding promises, unless Livy meant some extension of the franchise, or an increase in its practical importance through opening more tribes to the new citizens.

[2] Cf. Plutarch, *Crassus* vi. 2.

[3] 83 B.C. Cf. Velleius II. xxv. 2, 4; Appian, *Civil Wars* I. x. 84 misstates the location.

citizens.[1] Quintus Metellus Pius, who had taken the side of the better sort, began to stir up war in Africa, but was defeated by Praetor Gaius Fabius; [2] a decree of the senate that all armies everywhere should be disbanded was passed by the party of Carbo and the followers of Marius. Freedmen were distributed among the thirty-five tribes. The book also contains the preparations for the campaign which was being drummed up against Sulla. B.C. 84

LXXXV. Sulla crossed to Italy with his army; he sent envoys to discuss peace, and when they were mistreated by Consul Gaius Norbanus, Sulla conquered this same Norbanus in battle.[3] When Sulla was about to attack the camp of the other consul, Lucius Scipio, with whom he had made every effort to come to terms without success, the entire army of the consul, on being invited by soldiers sent by Sulla, carried their standards over to Sulla. Although Scipio might have been executed, he was released.[4] Gnaeus Pompeius, son of the Gnaeus Pompeius who had taken Asculum, enrolled a volunteer army and came to Sulla with three legions.[5] All the leading men made their way to Sulla, so that the pilgrimage to his camp left Rome deserted. In addition, an account is given of the marching and counter-marching of the commanders of both factions all over Italy. B.C. 83

LXXXVI. Gaius Marius, son of Gaius Marius, was made consul by violence before he was twenty.[6] In Africa Gaius Fabius was burned alive in his headquarters because B.C. 83–82

[4] Cf. Appian, *Civil Wars* I. x. 85; Velleius II. xxv. 2; Plutarch, *Sulla* xxviii. 1–3.

[5] Cf. Appian, *Civil Wars* I. ix. 80; Plutarch, *Pompey* v.–viii.; Velleius II. xxix.

[6] 82 B.C. Marius' age is given as twenty-seven by Appian, *Civil Wars* I. x. 87, and as twenty-six by Velleius II. xxvi. 1. The "violence" seems to be actually unconstitutionality, because he had not held the praetorship.

A.U.C. 671–672 vivus exustus est. L. Philippus legatus Syllae Sardiniam Q. Antonio praetore pulso et occiso occupavit. Sylla cum Italicis populis, ne timeretur ab his velut erepturus civitatem[1] et suffragii ius nuper datum, foedus percussit. Itemque ex fiducia iam certae victoriae litigatores, a quibus adibatur, vadimonia Romam deferre iussit, cum a parte diversa urbs adhuc teneretur. L. Damasippus[2] praetor ex voluntate C. Marii consulis cum senatum contraxisset, omnem, quae in urbe erat, nobilitatem trucidavit. Ex cuius numero Q. Mucius Scaevola pontifex maximus fugiens in vestibulo aedis Vestae occisus est. Praeterea bellum a L. Murena adversus Mithridaten in Asia renovatum continet.

A.U.C. 672 LXXXVII. Sylla C. Marium, exercitu eius fuso deletoque ad Sacriportum, in oppido Praeneste obsedit, urbem Romam ex inimicorum manibus recepit. Marium erumpere temptantem reppulit. Praeterea res a legatis eius eadem ubique fortuna partium gestas[3] continet.

LXXXVIII. Sylla Carbonem, eius[4] exercitu ad Clusium ad Faventiam Fidentiamque caeso, Italia expulit; cum Samnitibus, qui soli ex Italicis populis nondum arma posuerant, iuxta urbem Romanam ante portam Collinam debellavit, reciperataque re publica pulcherrimam victoriam crudelitate, quanta in nullo hominum fuit, in-

[1] civitatem *edd.*: civitates NPΠ.

[2] Damasippus *Frobenius*: damasicius *vet.*: damascius NR.

[3] fortuna partium gestas *edd.*: fortunam partium gesta MSS.

[4] eius Lovelianus 2: eum Π, cum NP.

---

[1] 83 B.C. Cf. Cicero, *in Verrem* II. I. xxvii. 70; Valerius Maximus IX. x. 2. His *cognomen* was Hadrianus.

[2] 82 B.C. Philippus had been censor in 86 B.C., during the Marian regime.

[3] Cf. Appian, *Civil Wars* I. x. 88; Velleius II. xxvi. 2 f.

of his cruelty and greed.[1] Lucius Philippus, a staff officer of Sulla, seized Sardinia after the defeat and death of Praetor Quintus Antonius.[2] Sulla came to terms with the peoples of Italy, to preclude his being regarded as a threat to their recently gained status as citizens with the right to vote. Again, out of confidence in the victory which was now assured, he ordered men who brought suits before him to deposit their bonds at Rome, although the city was still in the possession of the other party. Praetor Lucius Damasippus assembled the senate by decision of Consul Gaius Marius, and butchered all of the leading men who were in Rome. Among these, Quintus Mucius Scaevola, the chief pontiff, was cut down as he fled in the entry to the temple of Vesta.[3] The book also includes the renewal by Lucius Murena of war in Asia against Mithridates.[4] B.C. 83–82

LXXXVII. Sulla routed and destroyed the army of Gaius Marius at Sacriportus, besieged Marius in the town of Praeneste, and recovered the city of Rome from the hands of his enemies. When Marius attempted to break out, Sulla drove him back.[5] The book also includes the operations of Sulla's deputies, conducted everywhere with the same outcome to the respective sides. B.C. 82

LXXXVIII. Sulla routed Carbo's army near Clusium, near Faventia and near Fidentia and drove Carbo out of Italy;[6] he fought to a finish under the walls of Rome before the Colline Gate with the Samnites, who alone of the Italian peoples had not yet laid down their arms.[7] After Sulla had restored the state, he befouled a most glorious victory by cruelty greater than any other man had

[4] 83–2 B.C. Cf. Appian, *Mithridatic Wars* ix. 64.

[5] 82 B.C. Cf. Appian, *Civil Wars* I. x. 89 f.

[6] Cf. Appian, *Civil Wars* I. x. 89 and 92; Velleius II. xxviii. 1.

[7] Cf. Appian, *Civil Wars* I. x. 93; Velleius II. xxvii. 1–3; Plutarch, *Sulla* xxix.

A.U.C. 672 quinavit. Octo milia dediticiorum in villa publica trucidavit; tabulam proscriptionis posuit, urbem ac totam Italiam caedibus replevit, inter quas omnes Praenestinos inermes concidi iussit, Marium, senatorii ordinis virum, cruribus bracchiisque fractis, auribus praesectis et oculis effossis necavit. C. Marius Praeneste obsessus a Lucretio Ofella,[1] Syllanarum partium viro, cum per cuniculum captaret evadere saeptum exercitu, mortem conscivit. Id est, in ipso cuniculo, cum sentiret se evadere non posse, cum Telesino, fugae comite, stricto utrimque gladio concurrit; quem cum occidisset, ipse saucius impetravit a servo, ut se occideret.

A.U.C. 672–674 LXXXIX. M. Brutus a Cn. Papirio Carbone, Cossyra quam adpulerant,[2] missus nave piscatoria Lilybaeum, ut exploraret, an ibi iam Pompeius esset, et circumventus navibus, quas Pompeius miserat, in se mucrone verso ad transtrum navis obnixus corporis pondere incubuit. Cn. Pompeius in Siciliam cum imperio a senatu missus Cn. Carbonem, qui flens muliebriter mortem tulit, captum occidit. Sylla dictator factus, quod nemo umquam fecerat, cum fascibus viginti quattuor processit. Legibus[3] novis rei publicae statum confirmavit, tribunorum plebis potestatem minuit et omne ius legum ferendarum ademit. Pontificum augurumque collegium ampliavit, ut essent quindecim; senatum ex equestri ordine supplevit; pro-

[1] Ofella *Sigonius*: afella NPΠR.
[2] Cossyra quam adpulerant *Rossbach*: quem corcyram adpulerant *vet.*: qui Corcyram adpulerat GR.
[3] Legibus *Gronovius*: rebus MSS.

---

[1] On Sulla's cruelty, cf. Plutarch, *Sulla* xxx–xxxii; Appian, *Civil Wars* I. x. 95; Velleius II. xxviii. The Marius of this section was Marcus Marius Gratidianus.

[2] Cf. Plutarch, *Sulla* xxxii.; Appian, *Civil Wars* I. x. 94; Velleius II. xxvii. 4–6.

[3] For Brutus' previous career as a Marian, cf. Appian, *Civil Wars* I. vii. 60; Plutarch, *Sulla* ix. 2.

ever displayed. He butchered eight thousand men, who had surrendered, in the Civic Villa; he set up a proscription list; and filled the city and all Italy with slaughter. Among other enormities he ordered all the Praenestines, who were disarmed, to be cut down, and put Marius, a man of senatorial rank, to death after breaking his legs and arms, cutting off his ears, and gouging out his eyes.[1] When Gaius Marius was besieged in Praeneste by Lucretius Ofella, a man of Sulla's party, he tried to escape by a tunnel which was blocked by the hostile army, and determined on death. That is, in the very tunnel, when he realized that he could not escape, he and Telesinus, his companion in flight, both drew their swords and dashed at each other; Marius killed Telesinus and, being himself wounded, persuaded his slave to kill him.[2] B.C. 82

(For a fragment of the *Oxyrhynchus Summary*, see below, p. 172.)

LXXXIX. Marcus Brutus was sent by Gnaeus Papirius Carbo in a fishing-vessel from Cossyra, to which they had put in, to Lilybaeum to see whether Pompey was already there. When cut off by the ships which Pompey had sent, Brutus turned his point against himself and, bracing his sword on a thwart of the vessel, fell with all his weight upon it.[3] Gnaeus Pompeius was sent to Sicily as a military commander by the senate; he captured and put to death Gnaeus Carbo, who met his death weeping like a woman.[4] Sulla was made dictator, and appeared in public with twenty-four *fasces*—an unprecedented action. He strengthened the constitution by new legislation, diminished the power of the tribunes of the commons, and took from them entirely the power of introducing legislation. He added to the colleges of pontiffs and augurs, to make them fifteen in number; he recruited the senate from the order of knights; he deprived the sons of the B.C. 82–80

[4] Cf. Appian, *Civil Wars* I. xi. 96; Plutarch, *Pompey* x. 3 f.

A.U.C. 672–674 scriptorum liberis ius petendorum honorum eripuit et bona eorum vendidit, ex quibus plurima priva[1] rapuit. Redactum est sestertium ter milies quingenties. Q. Lucretium Ofellam[2] adversus voluntatem suam consulatum petere ausum iussit occidi in foro; et cum hoc indigne ferret populus Romanus, contione advocata se iussisse dixit. Cn. Pompeius in Africa Cn. Domitium proscriptum et Hiertam, regem Numidiae, bellum molientes victos occidit et quattuor et viginti annos natus, adhuc eques Romanus, quod nulli contigerat, ex Africa triumphavit. C. Norbanus consularis proscriptus in urbe Rhodo cum comprehenderetur, ipse se occidit. Mutilus, unus ex proscriptis, clam capite adoperto ad posticias aedes Bastiae uxoris cum accessisset, admissus non est, quia illum proscriptum diceret; itaque ipse se transfodit et sanguine suo fores uxoris respersit. Sylla Aeserniam in Samnio recepit. XLVII legiones in agros captos deduxit et eos his divisit. Volaterras, quod oppidum adhuc in armis erat, obsessum in deditionem accepit. Mitylenae quoque in Asia, quae sola urbs post victum Mithridaten arma retinebat, expugnatae dirutaeque sunt.

A.U.C. 675–677 XC. Sylla decessit, honosque ei a senatu habitus est, ut in campo Martio sepeliretur. M. Lepidus cum acta Syllae temptaret rescindere, bellum excitavit. A Q.

[1] priva *Rossbach* : prima MSS.
[2] Q. Lucretium Ofellam *Sigonius* : quingentisque lucretium afellam NPΠ.

---

[1] 81–80 B.C. Cf. Appian, *Civil Wars* I. xi. 98–100; Plutarch, *Sulla* xxxiii.
[2] 82 B.C. Cf. Appian, *Civil Wars* I. xi. 101.
[3] 80 B.C. Cf. Plutarch, *Pompey* xi–xiv, who calls the Numidian King Iarbas.
[4] Cf. Appian, *Civil Wars* I. x. 91.

proscribed of the right to stand for office, and auctioned off their property, a very large amount of which he pocketed for his own use. The proceeds were three hundred and fifty million sesterces.[1] Quintus Lucretius Ofella dared to seek the consulship against Sulla's wishes; Sulla ordered him to be cut down in the Forum; and when the Roman People took this amiss, Sulla called a public meeting and announced that he had ordered the deed.[2] Gnaeus Pompeius conquered and killed in Africa Gnaeus Domitius, one of the proscribed, and Hierta, King of Numidia, who were stirring up a war. At the age of twenty-four, while still a Roman Knight, Pompey celebrated a triumph for his African campaign—an unprecedented honour.[3] When the ex-consul Gaius Norbanus, a proscribed man, was arrested in the city of Rhodes, he killed himself.[4] Mutilus, one of the proscribed, came secretly with muffled head to the rear door of the house belonging to his wife, Bastia; he was not admitted, his wife saying that he was proscribed; and so he stabbed himself and besprinkled his wife's doorway with his blood.[5] Sulla recovered Aesernia in Samnium. He took forty-seven legions to captured territory, and divided it among them. He besieged Volaterrae, a town which was still up in arms, and received its surrender.[6] Also, in Asia Mytilene, the only city which remained in arms after the defeat of Mithridates, was stormed and destroyed.[7] B.C. 82–80

XC. Sulla died, and the honour of being buried in the Campus Martius was decreed to him by the senate.[8] When Marcus Lepidus tried to repeal the measures of Sulla, he awakened a war. He was driven from Italy by his col- B.C. 79–77

[5] Cf. Granius Licinianus, p. 32 F; Papius Mutilus was a Samnite leader, commander at Nola until it fell at this time, 80 B.C.

[6] Cf. Granius Licinianus, p. 32 Flemisch.

[7] 80 B.C. Cf. Suetonius, *Julius* ii.

[8] Cf. Appian, *Civil Wars* I. xii. 105 f.; Plutarch, *Sulla* xxxvii f.

A.U.C. 675–677 Catulo collega Italia pulsus et in Sardinia frustra bellum molitus perit. M. Brutus, qui Cisalpinam Galliam obtinebat, a Cn.Pompeio occisus est. Q. Sertorius proscriptus in ulteriore Hispania ingens bellum excitavit. L. Manlius proconsul et M. Domitius legatus ab Hirtuleio quaestore proelio victi sunt. Praeterea res a P. Servilio procos. adversus Cilicas gestas continet.

A.U.C. 677–679 XCI. Cn. Pompeius cum adhuc eques Romanus[1] esset, cum imperio consulari adversus Sertorium missus est. Sertorius aliquot urbes expugnavit plurimasque civitates in potestatem suam redegit. Appius Claudius procos. Thracas pluribus proeliis vicit. Q. Metellus pro cos. L. Hirtuleium quaestorem Sertorii cum exercitu cecidit.

A.U.C. 679 XCII. Cn. Pompeius dubio eventu cum Sertorio pugnavit, ita ut singula ex utraque parte cornua vicerint. Q. Metellus Sertorium et Perpernam cum duobus exercitibus proelio fudit; cuius victoriae partem cupiens ferre Pompeius parum prospere pugnavit. Obsessus deinde Cluniae Sertorius adsiduis eruptionibus non leviora damna obsidentibus intulit. Praeterea res ab Curione[2] procos. in Thracia gestas adversus Dardanos et Q. Sertorii

[1] eques Romanus *Sigonius*: aequester *vet.*: eques Gu: Questor Leidensis, R.

[2] ab Curione *Gronovius*: ap. cursone NP: ab curisone Π: a P. Cursore Leidensis, R.

---

[1] 78–7 B.C. Cf. Appian, *Civil Wars* I. xiii. 107; Plutarch, *Pompey* xvi.

[2] Cf. Plutarch, *Pompey* xvi; Appian, *Civil Wars* II. xvi. 111.

[3] 79–8 B.C. Cf. Plutarch, *Sertorius* xii. 3 f. Eutropius VI. 1, Orosius V. xxiii. 3 f. Domitius was governor of Nearer Spain in 79; Manlius was governor of Transalpine Gaul in 78, and had entered Spain to help against Sertorius.

[4] Servilius had been consul in 79. Cf. Sallust, *History* II, fr. 87.

league Quintus Catulus and met his end in Sardinia while vainly engineering a campaign.[1] Marcus Brutus, who was in possession of Cisalpine Gaul, was slain by Gnaeus Pompeius.[2] Quintus Sertorius, a proscribed man, raised a great war in Farther Spain. Lucius Manlius, a proconsul, and Marcus Domitius, a deputy, were defeated in battle by Quaestor Hirtuleius.[3] The book also includes the successes achieved by Proconsul Publius Servilius against the Cilicians.[4] B.C. 79–77

XCI. Although Gnaeus Pompeius was as yet a Roman knight, he was sent against Sertorius with consular authority. Sertorius stormed several cities and brought a very large number of communities under his control.[5] Proconsul Appius Claudius conquered the Thracians in a number of battles.[6] Proconsul Quintus Metellus routed Lucius Hirtuleius, Sertorius' quaestor, and his army.[7] B.C. 77–75

XCII. Gnaeus Pompeius fought indecisively with Sertorius; the fact was that one wing of each side was victorious. Quintus Metellus routed in battle Sertorius and Perperna and their two armies; Pompey wanted to share in this victory, but fought with slight success. Later, Sertorius was blockaded in Clunia but by repeated sallies inflicted on the besiegers as much damage as he received.[8] The book also includes the achievements of Proconsul Curio in Thrace against the Dardanians,[9] and the many acts of cruelty committed by Quintus B.C. 75

[5] 77–6 B.C. Cf. fr. 18, Appian, *Civil Wars* I. xiii. 108; Plutarch, *Pompey* xvii.

[6] 77–6 B.C. Cf. Florus I. xxxix. 6; Eutropius VI. ii. 2; Orosius V. xxiii. 19.

[7] 75 B.C. Cf. Orosius V. xxiii. 10 and 12; Frontinus II. vii. 5.

[8] 75 B.C. Cf. Plutarch, *Sertorius* xix; *Pompey* xix; Appian, *Civil Wars* I. xiii. 110.

[9] Cf. Sallust, *History* II. 80; Eutropius VI. ii. 2; Orosius V. xxiii. 20; below, XCV.

A.U.C. 679 multa crudelia in suos facta continet; qui plurimos ex amicis et secum proscriptis crimine proditionis insimulatos ccoidit.

A.U.C. 679–680 XCIII. P. Servilius procos. in Cilicia Isauros domuit et aliquot urbes piratarum expugnavit. Nicomedes Bithyniae rex populum Romanum fecit heredem, regnumque eius in provinciae formam redactum est. Mithridates foedere cum Sertorio icto bellum populo Romano intulit. Apparatus dein regiarum copiarum pedestrium navaliumque; et occupata Bithynia M. Aurelius Cotta consul ad Calchedona proelio a rege victus; resque a Pompeio et Metello adversus Sertorium . . . omnibus belli militiaeque artibus par fuit, . . . et ab obsidione Calagurris oppidi depulsos coegerit diversas regiones petere, Metellum ulteriorem Hispaniam, Pompeium Galliam.

A.U.C. 680–681 XCIV. L. Licinius Lucullus consul adversus Mithridaten equestribus proeliis feliciter pugnavit et aliquot expeditiones prosperas fecit poscentesque pugnam milites a seditione inhibuit. Deiotarus Gallograeciae tetrarches praefectos Mithridatis bellum in Phrygia moventes cecidit. Praeterea res a Cn. Pompeio in Hispania contra Sertorium prospere gestas continet.

A.U.C. 681 XCV. C. Curio procos. Dardanos in Thracia domuit. Quattuor et septuaginta gladiatores Capuae ex ludo Lentuli profugerunt et congregata servitiorum ergastu-

---

[1] Cf. Appian, *Civil Wars* I. xiii. 109, 112; *contra*, Plutarch, *Sertorius* xviii. 6.

[2] Cf. above, XC; Eutropius VI. iii; Orosius V. xxiii. 21; Cicero, *in Verrem* II. III. xc. 210 f.

[3] 75 or 74 B.C. Cf. Appian, *Mithridatic Wars* x. 71; *Civil Wars* I. xiii. 111.

[4] 74 B.C. Cf. Appian, *Mithridatic Wars* x. 71; Plutarch, *Sertorius* xxiii f. The alliance with Sertorius may have been an earlier preliminary, cf. *C.A.H.* IX, p. 322.

Sertorius upon his men; for he killed very many of his friends and fellow victims of the proscription on trumped-up charges of treachery.[1] B.C. 75

XCIII. Proconsul Publius Servilius overcame the Isaurians in Cilicia and stormed several cities of the pirates.[2] Nicomedes King of Bithynia made the Roman People his heir, and his kingdom was converted into a province.[3] Mithridates made a treaty with Sertorius and attacked the Roman People. The muster of the King's forces, infantry and naval; the seizure of Bithynia, and the defeat in battle near Chalcedon of Consul Marcus Aurelius Cotta by the King;[4] the achievements of Pompey and Metellus against Sertorius . . . he was a match for them in all the arts of war and campaigning . . . he drove them away from the siege of the city of Calagurris and compelled them to make off in different directions, Metellus to Farther Spain, Pompey to Gaul.[5] B.C. 75–74

XCIV. Consul Lucius Licinius Lucullus fought successful cavalry battles against Mithridates, made several victorious marches, and, when his soldiers demanded battle, restrained them from mutiny.[6] Deiotarus, Tetrarch of Galatia, crushed the officers of Mithridates when they stirred up war in Phrygia.[7] The book also includes the successful campaign of Gnaeus Pompeius in Spain against Sertorius.[8] B.C. 74–73

XCV. Proconsul Gaius Curio overcame the Dardanians in Thrace.[9] Seventy-four gladiators of the troupe of Lentulus escaped from Capua, collected a mob of slaves and prisoners from the workhouses, and began a war B.C. 73

[5] 74 B.C. Cf. Appian, *Civil Wars* I. xiii. 112; Plutarch, *Sertorius* xxi, *Pompey* xix f.

[6] Cf. Plutarch, *Lucullus* vii.

[7] 74 B.C. Cf. Appian, *Mithridatic Wars* xi. 75.

[8] 73 B.C. Cf. Appian, *Civil Wars* I. xiii. 113.

[9] Cf. above, XCII.

A.U.C. 681 lorumque multitudine, Crixo et Spartaco ducibus bello excitato, Claudium Pulchrum legatum et P. Varenum praetorem proelio vicerunt. L. Lucullus pro cos. ad Cyzicum urbem exercitum Mithridatis fame ferroque delevit; pulsumque Bithynia regem, variis belli ac naufragiorum casibus fractum, coegit in Pontum profugere.

A.U.C. 682 XCVI. Q. Arrius praetor Crixum fugitivorum ducem cum viginti milibus hominum cecidit. Cn. Lentulus consul male adversus Spartacum pugnavit. Ab eodem L. Gellius consul et Q. Arrius praetor acie victi sunt. Sertorius a M. Perperna et M'. Antonio et aliis coniuratis in convivio interfectus est, octavo ducatus sui anno, magnus dux et adversus duos imperatores, Pompeium et Metellum, vel frequentius victor, ad ultimum et saevus et prodigus. Imperium partium ad Marcum translatum, quem Cn. Pompeius victum captumque interfecit, ac recepit Hispanias decimo fere anno quam coeptum erat bellum. C. Cassius pro cos. et Cn. Manlius praetor male adversus Spartacum pugnaverunt, idque bellum M. Crasso praetori mandatum est.

A.U.C. 682–683 XCVII. M. Crassus praetor primum cum parte fugitivorum, quae ex Gallis Germanisque constabat, feliciter pugnavit, caesis hostium triginta quinque milibus et ducibus eorum Casto [1] et Gannico. Cum Spartaco dein

[1] Casto *Jahn*: caesis MSS: *om.* R.

---

[1] 73 B.C. Cf. Appian, *Civil Wars* I. xiii. 116; Plutarch, *Crassus* viii f.; Orosius V. xxiv. 1; Gaius Claudius Glaber was a praetor: Florus II. viii. 3–5.

[2] Cf. Appian, *Mithridatic Wars* xi. 73–6; Plutarch, *Lucullus* ix–xi.

under the leadership of Crixus and Spartacus. They defeated in battle the deputy Claudius Pulcher and Praetor Publius Varenus.[1] Proconsul Lucius Lucullus destroyed the army of Mithridates near the city of Cyzicus by starvation and sword; after driving from Bithynia the King, who was broken by various disasters of war and shipwreck, Lucullus compelled him to seek refuge in Pontus.[2] B.C. 73

XCVI. Praetor Quintus Arrius crushed Crixus, the leader of the runaways, together with twenty thousand men. Consul Gnaeus Lentulus lost a battle to Spartacus. The same leader defeated Consul Lucius Gellius and Praetor Quintus Arrius in battle.[3] Sertorius was killed at a banquet by Marcus Perperna, Manius Antonius, and other conspirators, in the eighth year of his leadership—a great leader, more often than not the victor over two generals, Pompey and Metellus, but towards the end savage and prodigal. The command over his faction was transferred to Marcus, whom Gnaeus Pompeius conquered, took prisoner, and put to death; Pompey recovered Spain in about the tenth year after the war was begun.[4] Proconsul Gaius Cassius and Praetor Gnaeus Manlius lost a battle to Spartacus, and this campaign was entrusted to Praetor Marcus Crassus.[5] B.C. 72

XCVII. Praetor Marcus Crassus first fought a winning battle with a portion of the runaway slaves, which was made up of Gauls and Germans, and killed thirty-five thousand of the enemy, as well as their leaders Castus and Gannicus. Then Crassus fought to a finish with Spartacus, B.C. 72–71

[3] 72 B.C. Cf. Plutarch, *Crassus* ix; Appian, *Civil Wars* I. xiv. 117. Strictly speaking, Arrius was propraetor, having been praetor the previous year.

[4] Cf. Plutarch, *Sertorius* xxv–xxvii, *Pompey* xx; Appian, *Civil Wars* I. xiii. 113–5.

[5] Cassius was proconsul of Cisalpine Gaul and was trying to block Spartacus' escape northward; cf. references in note 3.

A.U.C. 682–683 debellavit, caesis cum ipso sexaginta milibus. M. Antonius praetor bellum adversus Cretenses parum prospere susceptum morte sua finiit. M. Lucullus pro cos. Thracas subegit. L. Lucullus in Ponto adversus Mithridaten feliciter pugnavit, caesis hostium amplius quam sexaginta milibus. M. Crassus et Cn. Pompeius consules facti (s. c.[1] Pompeius, antequam quaesturam gereret, ex equite Romano) tribuniciam potestatem restituerunt. Iudicia quoque per M. Aurelium Cottam praetorem ad equites Romanos translata sunt. Mithridates desperatione rerum suarum coactus ad Tigranen Armeniae regem confugit.

A.U.C. 684–686 XCVIII. Machares filius Mithridatis, Bospori rex, a L. Lucullo in amicitiam receptus est. Cn. Lentulus et L. Gellius censores asperam censuram egerunt, quattuor et sexaginta senatu motis. A quibus lustro condito censa sunt civium capita $\overline{\text{DCCCC}}$. L. Metellus praetor in Sicilia adversus piratas prospere rem gessit. Templum Iovis in Capitolio, quod incendio consumptum ac refectum

[1] s.c. *Rossbach* : sicut MSS.

---

[1] 71 B.C. Cf. fr. 21; Plutarch, *Crassus* x f.; Appian, *Civil Wars* I. xiv. 118–20.

[2] Antonius held a special commission against the pirates, cf. Cicero, *in Verrem* II. III. xci–xciii, 213–6; Velleius II. xxxi. 3; Plutarch, *Antony* i.

[3] 72 B.C. Lucullus (Marcus Terentius Varro Lucullus) extended Roman rule as far as the lower Danube, cf. Eutropius VI. viii, x; Orosius VI. iii. 4; Ammianus Marcellinus XXVII. iv. 11.

[4] 72 B.C. Cf. Appian, *Mithridatic Wars* xii. 79–81; Plutarch, *Lucullus* xvii; *C.A.H.* IX, pp. 363 f.

[5] 71 B.C., for the year 70. Cf. Plutarch, *Pompey* xxii f., *Crassus* xii; Cicero, *in Verrem* I. xv. 44 f.

[6] Cf. Velleius II. xxxii. 3; his first name was actually Lucius, cf. Asconius, p. 15 Kiessling-Scholl = p. 17 Clark. The courts were composed, under Cotta's arrangement, of one-third senators, one-third knights, and one-third *tribuni*

who was killed along with sixty thousand men.[1] Praetor Marcus Antonius undertook a campaign against the Cretans with little success and closed it with his death.[2] Proconsul Marcus Lucullus subdued the Thracians.[3] Lucius Lucullus fought successfully against Mithridates in Pontus, and killed over sixty thousand of the enemy.[4] Marcus Crassus and Gnaeus Pompeius were elected consuls, Pompey in accordance with a decree of the senate while a Roman knight, before he had held the quaestorship. These consuls restored the power of the tribunes.[5] The juries were also transferred to the Roman knights by Praetor Marcus Aurelius Cotta.[6] Mithridates was compelled by his hopeless situation to take refuge with Tigranes King of Armenia.[7] B.C. 72–71

XCVIII. Machares, son of Mithridates and King of Bosporus, was given the status of friend by Lucius Lucullus.[8] Gnaeus Lentulus and Lucius Gellius the censors conducted a severe censorship, removing sixty-four from the senate. When they closed the half-decade, there were enumerated nine hundred thousand citizens.[9] Praetor Lucius Metellus conducted a successful campaign against pirates in Sicily.[10] The temple of Jupiter on the Capitol, which had been destroyed by fire and restored, B.C. 70–68

aerarii apparently equivalent to knights in position; all three groups were subject to review by the censors, or others, cf. *C.A.H.* IX, pp. 339 f.

[7] 72 B.C. Cf. Appian, *Mithridatic Wars* xii. 82; Plutarch, *Lucullus* xix.

[8] 70 B.C. Cf. Appian, *Mithridatic Wars* xii. 83; Plutarch, *Lucullus* xxiv. 1.

[9] The censorship was restored as part of the alteration of Sulla's constitution. Cf. Cicero, *pro Cluentio* xlii. 120; Plutarch, *Pompey* xxii. 5.

[10] Cf. Orosius VI. iii. 5. Metellus is frequently mentioned by Cicero in the Verrine Orations as the governor of Sicily who succeeded Verres and tried to restore good government, although he also worked to protect Verres from prosecution.

A.U.C. 684–686 erat, a Q. Catulo dedicatum est. L. Lucullus in Armenia Mithridaten et Tigranen et ingentes utriusque regis copias pluribus proeliis fudit. Q. Metellus procos. bello adversus Cretenses mandato Cydoniam urbem obsedit. C. Triarius legatus Luculli adversus Mithridaten parum prospere pugnavit. Lucullum, ne persequeretur Mithridaten ac Tigranen summamque victoriae imponeret, seditio militum tenuit, quia sequi nolebant. Id est duae[1] legiones Valerianae, quae impleta a se stipendia dicentes Lucullum reliquerunt.

A.U.C. 687 XCIX. Q. Metellus procos. Cnoson et Lyctum et Cydoniam et alias plurimas urbes expugnavit. L. Roscius tribunus plebis legem tulit, ut equitibus Romanis in theatro quattuordecim gradus proximi adsignarentur. Cn. Pompeius lege ad populum lata persequi piratas iussus, qui commercium annonae intercluserant, intra quadragesimum diem toto mari eos expulit; belloque cum his in Cilicia confecto, acceptis in deditionem piratis agros et urbes dedit. Praeterea res gestas a Q. Metello adversus Cretenses continet et epistulas Metelli et Cn. Pompeii invicem missas. Queritur Q. Metellus gloriam sibi rerum a se gestarum a Pompeio praeverti,[2] qui in Cretam miserit legatum suum ad accipiendas urbium deditiones. Pompeius rationem reddit hoc se facere debuisse.

[1] duae *Rossbach* : quae MSS.
[2] praeverti *Rossbach* : praeterii N : preteriri PΠR.

---

[1] The temple of Jupiter Capitolinus was burned in 83 B.C. Restoration was begun by Sulla, but Catulus as pontifex completed it, cf. Cicero, *in Verrem* II. IV. xxxi. 69; Valerius Maximus VI. ix. 5.

[2] 69 B.C. Cf. frs. 22, 23; Plutarch *Lucullus* xxiv f.; Appian, *Mithridatic Wars* xii. 84 f.

[3] Cf. Appian, *Sicily*, fr. vi. 2; Velleius II. xxxiv. 1.

[4] 68 B.C. Cf. Appian, *Mithridatic Wars* xiii. 88 f.; Plutarch, *Lucullus* xxx, xxxii–xxxv. Appian passes over the

was dedicated by Quintus Catulus.[1] Lucius Lucullus routed Mithridates and Tigranes and huge forces of both kings in several battles in Armenia.[2] Proconsul Quintus Metellus was given charge of the war against the Cretans and besieged the city of Cydonia.[3] Gaius Triarius, a staff officer of Lucullus, fought with slight success against Mithridates. A mutiny of the soldiers, who were unwilling to advance, kept Lucullus from pursuing Mithridates and Tigranes and putting the finishing touches to his victory. That is, two of Valerius' legions deserted Lucullus, saying that their term of service had expired.[4] B.C. 70–68

XCIX. Proconsul Quintus Metellus stormed Cnossus, Lyctus, Cydonia, and a large number of other cities.[5] B.C. 67 Lucius Roscius, tribune of the commons, passed a law reserving the first fourteen rows in the theatre for Roman knights.[6] Gnaeus Pompeius was ordered by a law passed by the popular assembly to pursue the pirates, who had cut off the traffic in grain. Within forty days he had cleared them from all the seas. He brought the war against them to an end in Cilicia, received the surrender of the pirates and gave them land and cities.[7] The book also includes the achievements of Quintus Metellus against the Cretans, and an exchange of letters between Metellus and Gnaeus Pompeius. Quintus Metellus complains that the glory of his achievements has been stolen by Pompey, who sent his officer to Crete to receive the surrender of cities. Pompey makes a statement to show that his action was justified.[8]

mutinies, cf. his section 90. For the troops of Valerius Flaccus, violently taken over by Fimbria, cf. above, LXXXII f.

[5] 68–7 B.C. Cf. above, XCVIII, note 3; fr. 24.

[6] 67 B.C. Cf. Velleius II. xxxii. 3; Dio XXXVI. xlii. 1; Cicero, *pro Murena* xix. 40.

[7] Cf. Appian, *Mithridatic Wars* xiv. 94–6; Plutarch, *Pompey* xxiv–xxviii; Velleius II. xxxii. 4.

[8] 67 B.C. Cf. Appian, *Sicily* vi; Florus I. xlii. 4–6; Valerius Maximus VII. vi, ext. 1; Plutarch, *Pompey* xxix; Dio XXXVI. xviia, xviii f., xlv. 1.

A.U.C. 688 C. C. Manilius tribunus plebis magna indignatione nobilitatis legem tulit, ut Pompeio Mithridaticum bellum mandaretur. Contio eius bona. Q. Metellus perdomitis Cretensibus liberae in id tempus insulae leges dedit. Cn. Pompeius ad gerendum bellum adversus Mithridaten profectus cum rege Parthorum Prahate amicitiam renovavit, equestri proelio Mithridaten vicit. Praeterea bellum inter Phraaten Parthorum regem et Tigranen Armeniorum, ac deinde inter filium Tigranen patremque gestum continet.

CI. Cn. Pompeius Mithridaten nocturno proelio victum coegit Bosporum profugere. Tigranen in deditionem accepit eique ademptis Syria Phoenice Cilicia regnum Armeniae restituit. Coniuratio eorum, qui in petitione consulatus ambitus damnati erant, facta de interficiendis consulibus oppressa est. Cn. Pompeius cum Mithridaten persequeretur, in ultimas ignotasque gentes penetravit; Hiberos Albanosque, qui transitum non dabant, proelio vicit. Praeterea fugam Mithridatis per Colchos Heniochosque et res ab eo in Bosporo gestas continet.

A.U.C. 689–691 CII. Cn. Pompeius in provinciae formam Pontum redegit. Pharnaces filius Mithridatis bellum patri intulit. Ab eo Mithridates obsessus in regia cum veneno sumpto

---

[1] 66 B.C. Cf. Plutarch, *Pompey* xxx, and especially Cicero, *pro Lege Manilia*, a reference to which editors are tempted to find in the second sentence of this Summary.

[2] Cf. Justinus XXXIX. v. 3, and references above, XCIX, page 123, note 8.

[3] Cf. Appian, *Mithridatic Wars* xv. 98.

[4] Cf. Dio XXXVI. xlv. 3, l–li.

[5] 66 B.C. Cf. Dio, XXXVI. xlix; Plutarch, *Pompey* xxxii. 5–9; Appian, *Mithridatic Wars* xv. 99–101 gives a slightly different account.

[6] Cf. Dio XXXVI. li–liii; Appian, *Mithridatic Wars* 104 f., Plutarch, *Pompey* xxxiii.

C. Gaius Manilius, tribune of the commons, to the great indignation of the leading men passed a law to entrust the Mithridatic War to Pompey. His address was excellent.[1] Quintus Metellus completely subdued the Cretans and established regulations for an island which up to that time had been free.[2] Gnaeus Pompeius set out to wage war against Mithridates, renewed the friendship with Phraates King of the Parthians, and defeated Mithridates in a cavalry battle.[3] The book also includes the war fought between Phraates King of the Parthians and Tigranes King of the Armenians, and thereafter the war between the younger Tigranes and his father.[4] B.C. 66

CI. Gnaeus Pompeius defeated Mithridates in a night engagement and compelled him to flee to Bosporus.[5] Pompey received the surrender of Tigranes and restored the rule of Armenia to him after depriving him of Syria, Phoenicia, and Cilicia.[6] A conspiracy, formed by those who had been condemned for bribery in their campaign for the consulship, and aimed at the assassination of the consuls, was suppressed.[7] While Gnaeus Pompeius was in pursuit of Mithridates, he penetrated to most remote and unknown tribes; he conquered in battle the Hiberi and Albani, who tried to deny him passage. The book also includes the flight of Mithridates through the Colchians and Heniochi, and his actions in Bosporus.[8]

CII. Gnaeus Pompeius organized Pontus as a province.[9] B.C. 65–63
Pharnaces son of Mithridates made war on his father. He besieged Mithridates in his palace; Mithridates took poison, but had little success in bringing about his own

[7] Cf. Sallust, *Catiline* xviii; this was late in 66 B.C. Autronius and Sulla were the condemned consuls-elect.

[8] Cf. Dio XXXVI. liv; XXXVII. i–v; Appian, *Mithridatic Wars* xv. 102 f.; Plutarch, *Pompey* xxxiv f.

[9] Cf. Strabo XII. iii. 1–2, 6, pp. 541, 543; Velleius II. xxxviii. 6.

A.U.C. 689–691 parum profecisset ad mortem, a milite Gallo nomine Bitoco, a quo ut adiuvaret se petierat, interfectus est. Cn. Pompeius Iudaeos subegit; fanum eorum Hierosolyma, inviolatum ante id tempus, cepit. L. Catilina bis repulsam in petitione consulatus passus cum Lentulo praetore et Cethego et compluribus [1] aliis coniuravit de caede consulum et senatus, incendiis urbis et opprimenda re publica, exercitu quoque in Etruria comparato. Ea coniuratio industria M. Tullii Ciceronis eruta est. Catilina urbe pulso de reliquis coniuratis supplicium sumptum est.

A.U.C. 692–696 CIII. Catilina a C. Antonio procos. cum exercitu caesus est. P. Clodius accusatus, quod in habitu mulieris in sacrarium, quo [2] virum intrare nefas est, clam intrasset et uxorem Metelli pontificis stuprasset, absolutus est. C. Pontinus praetor Allobrogas, qui rebellaverant, ad Solonem domuit. P. Clodius ad plebem transit. C. Caesar Lusitanos subegit; eoque consulatus candidato et captante rem publicam invadere conspiratio inter tres civitatis principes facta est, Cn. Pompeium, M. Crassum, C. Caesarem. Leges agrariae a Caesare consule cum magna contentione, invito senatu et altero consule M. Bibulo, latae sunt. C. Antonius pro cos. in Thracia parum

[1] compluribus *Jahn*: cum pluribus NPΠ.
[2] quo *Gruter*: in quo MSS.

---

[1] 63 B.C. Cf. Appian, *Mithridatic Wars* xvi. 110 f., where the name of the "Gaul" is given as Bituitus; Dio XXXVII. x–xiv; fr. 25.

[2] Cf. Dio XXXVII. xv f.; Josephus, *Antiquities* XIV. ii. 3 (29)–v (79) = fr. 26; *War* I. vi. 2 (127)–vii (158). The capture of Jerusalem by Antiochus Epiphanes is overlooked.

[3] Cf. Cicero, *In Catilinam* I–IV, Sallust, *Catiline*.

[4] 62 B.C. Cf. Sallust, *Catiline* lix–lxi; Dio XXXVII. xxxix f.

[5] 62 B.C. Cf. Cicero, *ad Atticum* I. xii. 3, xiii f., xvi, xviii; Plutarch, *Caesar* x, *Cicero* xxviii f.; Dio XXXVII. xlv. The reference to Metellus appears to be a misunderstanding

death, so begging a Galatian soldier named Bitocus to help him, he received his death-blow from him.[1] Gnaeus Pompeius subdued the Jews; he captured their holy city Jerusalem, which had previously remained inviolate.[2] After Lucius Catilina had twice suffered defeat in the consular elections, he conspired with Praetor Lentulus, Cethegus, and many others to slaughter the consuls and the senate, set fire to the city, and destroy the commonwealth; an army was also made ready in Etruria. This conspiracy was extirpated by the energy of Marcus Tullius Cicero. Catiline was driven from the city, and the other conspirators were executed.[3] B.C. 65–63

CIII. Catiline and his army were slaughtered by Proconsul Gaius Antonius.[4] Publius Clodius was accused of having secretly entered in women's garb a shrine which no man might lawfully enter, and there debauching the wife of Metellus the pontiff; but Clodius was acquitted.[5] Praetor Gaius Pontinus subdued the Allobroges, who had risen in arms, near Solo.[6] Publius Clodius transferred to the commons.[7] Gaius Caesar subdued the Lusitanians; when he was standing for the consulship and plotting to attack the constitution, a clandestine agreement was made by three leading public men, Gnaeus Pompeius, Marcus Crassus, and Gaius Caesar. Agrarian laws were passed by Gaius Caesar as consul after much strife against the opposition of the senate and the other consul Marcus Bibulus.[8] Gaius Antonius as proconsul met with little B.C. 62–58

of the charge of incest with his sister Clodia which was made at Clodius' trial, cf. Plutarch. Metellus Celer was an augur, not a pontiff.

[6] 61 B.C. Cf. Cicero, *de Provinciis Consularibus* 32; Dio XXVII. xlvii f., XXXIX. lxv. 1, who gives the name of the city as Solonium.

[7] 59 B.C. Cf. Cicero *de Domo Sua* xxix. 77, *pro Sestio* 16, *ad Atticum* II. xii. 1, VIII. iii. 3; Suetonius, *Julius* xx, *Tiberius* ii; Plutarch, *Cato* xxxiii.

[8] Cf. Dio XXXVII. lii–liv; Plutarch, *Caesar* xi–xiv, *Pompey* xlvii f., *Crassus* xiv; Suetonius, *Julius* xviii–xx.

A.U.C. 692–696 prospere rem gessit. M. Cicero lege a P. Clodio tribuno plebis lata, quod indemnatos cives necavisset, in exilium missus est. Caesar[1] in provinciam Galliam profectus Helvetios, vagam gentem, domuit, quae sedem quaerens per provinciam Caesaris Narbonensem[2] iter facere volebat. Praeterea situm Galliarum continet. Pompeius de liberis Mithridatis et Tigrane Tigranis filio triumphavit Magnusque a tota contione consalutatus est.

A.U.C. 696–698 CIV. Prima pars libri situm Germaniae moresque continet. C. Caesar cum adversus Germanos, qui Ariovisto duce in Galliam transcenderant, exercitum duceret rogatus ab Aeduis et Sequanis, quorum ager possidebatur, trepidationem militum propter metum novorum hostium ortam adlocutione exercitus inhibuit et victos proelio Germanos Gallia expulit. M. Cicero Pompeio inter alios se exerente[3] et T. Annio Milone tribuno plebis ingenti gaudio senatus ac totius Italiae ab exilio reductus est. Cn. Pompeio per quinquennium annonae cura mandata est. Caesar Ambianos, Suessionas, Viromanduos, Atrebates, Belgarum populos, quorum ingens multitudo erat, proelio victos in deditionem accepit; ac deinde contra Nervios unius ex his civis[4] cum magno discrimine pugnavit eamque gentem delevit, quae bellum gessit, donec ex $\overline{\text{LX}}$

[1] est. Caesar *add.* R : *om.* MSS.
[2] Narbonensem *Gronovius* : narbonem MSS.
[3] se *add. Walter* : *om.* MSS.
[4] civis *Rossbach* : civitatis MSS.

---

[1] 61–0 B.C. Cf. Obsequens 61a, Dio XXXVIII. x.

[2] 58 B.C. Cf. Dio XXXVIII. xii–xvii; Plutarch, *Cicero* xxx–xxxii; Cicero, *ad Atticum* II. xviii–xxv, and his two orations *On His Return*.

[3] 58 B.C. Cf. Caesar, *Gallic War* I. i–xxix.

[4] Cf. Plutarch, *Pompey* xlv. It is not clear why Pompey's triumph is entered at this point, nor why Mithridates himself was not mentioned as the opponent. Certainly Pompey had adopted the name *Magnus* long since.

success in a campaign in Thrace.[1] Marcus Cicero was sent into exile by a law passed by Publius Clodius as tribune of the commons, on the charge of having put citizens to death without a trial.[2] Caesar set out for his province of Gaul and conquered the Helvetians, a nomad people, which was seeking an abode and wished to travel through Caesar's province of Narbonese Gaul. The book also includes a description of the regions of Gaul.[3] Pompey celebrated a triumph over the sons of Mithridates and Tigranes son of Tigranes, and was unanimously hailed as The Great by an assembly.[4] B.C. 62–58

CIV. The first part of the book contains a description of the geography and customs of Germany. Gaius Caesar led his army against the Germans who had crossed over into Gaul under the leadership of Ariovistus. Caesar's help was invited by the Aedui and Sequani, whose territory was being occupied. A panic among his soldiers, caused by their fear of the unfamiliar enemy, was checked by Caesar in a speech to his army; he defeated the Germans in battle and drove them from Gaul.[5] At the instance of Pompey, among others, and of the tribune of the commons Titus Annius Milo, Marcus Cicero was brought back from exile, amid great rejoicing on the part of the senate and of all Italy.[6] Supervision of the grain supply for a period of five years was assigned to Gnaeus Pompeius.[7] Caesar conquered in battle and received the surrender of the Ambiani, Suessiones, Viromandui, Atrebates, and the Belgian tribes, whose numbers were huge. Thereafter he fought at great risk against the Nervii, one of the latter peoples, and so wiped out this tribe which had made war, that of sixty thousand fighting men, five hundred remained, B.C. 58–56

[5] 58 B.C. Cf. Caesar, *Gallic War* I. xxxi–liv, and for a description of Germany, VI. xxi–xxviii.

[6] 57 B.C. Cf. Cicero's two orations *post Reditum*; Appian, *Civil Wars* II. iii. 16; Plutarch, *Cicero* xxiii.

[7] Cf. Plutarch, *Pompey* xlix. f.

A.U.C. 696–698 armatorum D [1] superessent, ex DC senatoribus tres tantum evaderent. Lege lata de redigenda in [2] provinciae formam Cypro et publicanda pecunia regia M. Catoni administratio eius rei mandata est. Ptolemaeus Aegypti rex ob iniurias, quas patiebatur a suis, relicto [3] regno Romam venit. C. Caesar Venetos, gentem Oceano iunctam, navali proelio vicit. Praeterea res a legatis eius eadem fortuna gestas continet.

A.U.C. 698–699 CV. Cum C. Catonis tribuni plebis intercessionibus comitia tollerentur, senatus vestem mutavit. M. Cato in petitione praeturae praelato Vatinio repulsam tulit. Idem cum legem impediret, qua provinciae consulibus in quinquennium, Pompeio Hispaniae, Crasso Syria et Parthicum bellum dabantur, a C. Trebonio tribuno plebis, legis auctore, in vincula ductus est. A. Gabinius procos. Ptolemaeum reduxit in regnum Aegypti, eiecto Archelao, quem sibi regem adsciverant. Victis Germanis in Gallia Caesar [4] Rhenum transcendit et proximam partem Germaniae domuit; ac deinde Oceano in Britanniam primo parum prospere tempestatibus adversis traiecit, iterum [5] felicius; magnaque multitudine hostium caesa aliquam partem insulae in potestatem redegit.

[1] D *Zangemeister* : a MSS.
[2] in *add. edd.* : *om.* MSS.
[3] relicto *add. Halm, Rossbach* : *om.* MSS.
[4] Caesar *Jahn* : caesis MSS.
[5] iterum felicius *Gronovius* : iterum parum felicius MSS.

---

[1] Cf. *Gallic War* II. xii–xxxiii.
[2] Cf. Plutarch, *Cato* xxxiv–xxxviii.
[3] 56 B.C. Cf. Plutarch, *Cato* xxxv; Dio XXXIX. xii–xvi; Cicero, *ad Familiares* I. i–vii, *ad Quintum Fratrem* II. ii f.
[4] Cf. *Gallic War* III; Crassus and Labienus were the subordinates chiefly active at this time.

and of six hundred senators only three escaped.[1] When a law was passed concerning the establishment of Cyprus as a province and the confiscation of the royal funds, Marcus Cato was assigned to administer the matter.[2] Ptolemy King of Egypt left his kingdom and came to Rome because of the wrongs he had suffered at the hands of his people.[3] Gaius Caesar conquered in a naval battle the Veneti, a tribe adjoining the Ocean. The book also includes the successes achieved by his staff officers with good fortune to match their commander's.[4] B.C. 58–56

CV. When the elections were blocked by the vetoes of Gaius Cato, tribune of the commons, the senate put on mourning.[5] Marcus Cato suffered a defeat in his campaign for the praetorship when Vatinius received the preference.[6] When the same Marcus Cato was blocking the law by which the consuls were assigned provinces for a five-year period, the Spains being given to Pompey, Syria and the war with Parthia to Crassus, Cato was taken into custody by Gaius Trebonius, tribune of the commons and the sponsor of the law.[7] Proconsul Aulus Gabinius restored Ptolemy to the throne of Egypt, after expelling Archelaus, whom the Egyptians had chosen as King.[8] After conquering the Germans in Gaul, Caesar crossed the Rhine and subdued the nearest portion of Germany. After that, he crossed the Ocean to Britain, at first with little success because of unfavourable weather, but on a second occasion with better fortune; he slaughtered a large number of the enemy and acquired control over a certain portion of the island.[9] B.C. 56–55

[5] 56 B.C. Cato acted in the interest o Pompey and Crassus, cf. Dio XXXIX. xxvii. 3.

[6] Cf. Plutarch, *Pompey* lii. 2, *Cato* xlii.

[7] 55 B.C. Cf. Dio XXXIX. xxxiv f.; Plutarch, *Pompey* lii. 3; *Cato* xliii.

[8] Cf. Cicero, *in Pisonem* xxi. 48–50; Dio XXXIX. lv–lix; Josephus, *Antiquities* XIV. vi. 2 (98 f.), *War* I. viii. 7 (175).

[9] Cf. *Gallic War* IV–V. xxiii; frs. 29, 30.

A.U.C. 700–701 CVI. Iulia Caesaris filia, Pompeii uxor, decessit, honosque ei a populo habitus est, ut in campo Martio sepeliretur. Gallorum aliquot populi Ambiorige duce, rege [1] Eburonum, defecerunt; a quibus Cotta et Titurius legati Caesaris circumventi insidiis cum exercitu, cui praeerant, caesi sunt. Et cum aliarum quoque legionum castra oppugnata magno labore defensa essent, inter quae [2] eius, cui in [3] Treveris praeerat Q. Cicero, ab ipso Caesare hostes proelio fusi sunt. M. Crassus bellum Parthis inlaturus Euphraten flumen transit, victusque proelio, in quo et filius eius cecidit, cum reliquias exercitus in collem recepisset, evocatus in conloquium ab hostibus velut de pace acturis, quorum dux erat Surenas, comprehensusque et ne quid vivus pateretur repugnans, interfectus est.

A.U.C. 701–702 CVII. C. Caesar Treveris in Gallia victis iterum in Germaniam transit, nulloque ibi hoste invento reversus in Galliam Eburonas et alias civitates, quae conspiraverant, vicit et Ambiorigem in fuga persecutus est.[4] P. Clodii a T. Annio Milone, candidato consulatus, Appia via ad Bovillas occisi corpus plebs in curia cremavit. Cum seditiones inter candidatos consulatus Hypsaeum Scipionem Milonem essent, qui armis ac vi contendebant, ad comprimendas eas Cn. Pompeio legato . . .[5] et a senatu consul tertio factus est absens et solus, quod nulli alii umquam. . . .[6] Quaestione decreta de morte P. Clodii Milo iudicio damnatus in exilium actus est. Lex lata est,

[1] rege *add. Gronovius, Rossbach* : om. MSS.
[2] inter quae *Drakenborch* : interque NPR.
[3] cui in *Madvig* : quin N : qui in P.
[4] est *add. edd.* : *om.* NPR.
[5] lacunam indicavit *Rossbach.*
[6] lacunam indicavit *Sigonius.*

---

[1] 54 B.C. Cf. Plutarch, *Pompey* liii. 1–4, *Caesar* xxiii. 4; Dio XXXIX. lxiv.
[2] Cf. *Gallic War* V. xxvi–lii.

CVI. Julia, Caesar's daughter and Pompey's wife, died, and the people voted her the distinction of being buried in the Campus Martius.[1] Several peoples of Gaul, under the leadership of Ambiorix King of the Eburones, revolted. They trapped Cotta and Titurius, Caesar's staff-officers, in ambush and killed them along with the army which they commanded. The camps of other legions also were besieged, and were defended with great difficulty, among them the camp among the Treveri commanded by Quintus Cicero; but Caesar himself routed the enemy in battle.[2] Marcus Crassus crossed the Euphrates with the intention of invading Parthia, and was beaten in a battle in which his son also fell. When Crassus had withdrawn the remnants of his army to a hill, he was summoned to a parley by the enemy, whose leader was Surenas, as if they meant to discuss a truce; Crassus was then seized, and when he resisted, to avoid suffering indignity while alive, he was killed.[3] B.C. 54–53

CVII. After overcoming the Treveri in Gaul, Caesar crossed into Germany again, found no enemy there, and on returning to Gaul, overcame the Eburones and other states which had banded together, and pursued Ambiorix in his flight.[4] When Publius Clodius was slain on the Appian Way near Bovillae by Titus Annius Milo, who was standing for the consulship, the commons burned Clodius' body in the senate house. There were riots caused by the candidates for the consulship, Hypsaeus, Scipio, and Milo, who were contending with armed force; Gnaeus Pompeius was deputized to check these riots . . . and he was made consul for the third time by the senate in his absence and without colleague, which had never been done for anyone else. An investigation of the death of Publius Clodius was voted; Milo was condemned by the court and sent B.C. 53–52

[3] 54–3 B.C. Cf. Plutarch, *Crassus* xvi–xxxiii; Dio XL. xii–xxvii.

[4] 53 B.C. Cf. *Gallic War* VI. vii–x, xxix–xliv.

A.U.C. 701–702 ut ratio absentis Caesaris in petitione consulatus haberetur, invito et contra dicente M. Catone. Praeterea res gestas a C. Caesare adversus Gallos, qui prope universi Vercingetorige Arverno duce defecerunt, et laboriosas obsidiones urbium continet, inter quas Avarici Biturigum et Gergoviae Arvernorum.

A.U.C. 702–703 CVIII. C. Caesar Gallos ad Alesiam vicit omnesque Galliae civitates, quae in armis fuerant, in deditionem accepit. C. Cassius,[1] quaestor M. Crassi, Parthos, qui in Syriam transcenderant, cecidit. In petitione consulatus M. Cato repulsam tulit, creatis consulibus Ser. Sulpicio M. Marcello. C. Caesar Bellovacos cum aliis Gallorum populis domuit. Praeterea contentiones[2] inter consules de successore C. Caesari mittendo, agente in senatu M. Marcello consule, ut Caesar ad petitionem consulatus veniret, cum is lege lata in tempus[3] consulatus provincias obtinere deberet, resque a M. Bibulo in Syria gestas continet.

A.U.C. 703–705 CIX qui est civilis belli primus.
Causae civilium armorum et initia referuntur contentionesque de successore C. Caesari mittendo, cum se dimissurum exercitus negaret, nisi a Pompeio dimit-

[1] Cassius *Frobenius*: caesius NPΠR.
[2] contentiones *Aldina*: continet MSS.
[3] in tempus *Gronovius*: in id tempus MSS.

---

[1] 52 B.C. Cf. Dio XL. xlviii–lv; Plutarch, *Pompey* liv f., *Cicero* xxxv; Appian, *Civil Wars* II. iii. 21–4; Asconius, pp. 28 f., 31 Riessling-Scholl = pp. 32 f., 35–6 Clark; Cicero, *pro Milone*.
[2] Cf. Plutarch, *Caesar* xxix; Appian, *Civil Wars* II. iv. 25; Dio XL. li. 2.
[3] Cf. *Gallic War* VII. i–liii.
[4] 52 B.C. Cf. *Gallic War* VII. lxviii–xc.
[5] Cf. Cicero, *Philippics* XI. xiv. 35; Josephus, *Antiquities* XIV. vii. 3 (119–122).

into exile.[1] A law was passed that Caesar should be allowed to stand for the consulship while away from Rome, despite the objection and eloquence of Marcus Cato.[2] The book also includes the achievements of Caesar against the Gauls, who seceded almost without exception under the leadership of Vercingetorix, an Arvernian; the toilsome sieges of certain cities are described, including Avaricum of the Bituriges and Gergovia of the Arverni.[3] B.C. 53–52

CVIII. Gaius Caesar conquered the Gauls at Alesia and received the surrender of all the states of Gaul that had taken up arms.[4] Gaius Cassius, the quaestor of Marcus Crassus, inflicted great loss on the Parthians, who had crossed into Syria.[5] In standing for the consulship, Marcus Cato received a setback when Servius Sulpicius and Marcus Marcellus were elected consuls.[6] Gaius Caesar subdued the Bellovaci and other Gallic peoples.[7] The book also includes the strife between the consuls over sending out a successor to Gaius Caesar; Consul Marcus Marcellus proposed in the senate that Caesar should return to stand for the consulship, although according to the law which had been passed he was obliged to command his provinces till the time when he became consul.[8] The book also includes the achievements of Marcus Bibulus in Syria.[9] B.C. 52–51

CIX. Which is the First on the Civil War. B.C. 51–49

The causes and first steps of the civil war are described, and the strife over sending out a successor to Gaius Caesar, since he refused to discharge his armies, unless Pompey

[6] For 51 B.C. Cf. Plutarch, *Cato* xlix f.; Dio XL. lviii.

[7] 51 B.C. Cf. *Gallic War* VIII, especially vii–xxii.

[8] Cf. Plutarch, *Caesar* xxix; Appian, *Civil Wars* II. iv. 25 f.; Dio XL. lix; Cicero, *ad Familiares* VIII. i. 2, ii. 2; viii. 4–9.

[9] Cf. Dio XL. xxx. 1; Cicero, *ad Atticum* VI. i. 14, v. 3, viii. 5; VII. ii. 8.

A.U.C. 703–705 terentur. Et C. Curionis tribuni plebis primum adversus Caesarem, dein pro[1] Caesare actiones continet. Cum senatus consultum factum esset, ut successor Caesari mitteretur, M. Antonio et Q. Cassio tribunis plebis, quoniam intercessionibus id senatus consultum impediebant, urbe pulsis . . .[2] mandatumque a senatu consulibus et Cn. Pompeio, ut viderent, ne quid res publica detrimenti caperet. C. Caesar bello inimicos persecuturus cum exercitu in Italiam venit, Corfinium cum L. Domitio et P.[3] Lentulo cepit eosque dimisit, Cn. Pompeium ceterosque partium eius Italia expulit.

A.U.C. 705 CX qui est civilis belli secundus.

C. Caesar Massiliam, quae portas cluserat, obsedit et relictis in obsidione urbis eius legatis C. Trebonio et D. Bruto, profectus in Hispaniam L. Afranium et M.[4] Petreium legatos Cn. Pompeii cum septem legionibus ad Ilerdam in deditionem accepit omnesque incolumes dimisit, Varrone quoque legato Pompeii cum exercitu in potestatem suam redacto. Gaditanis civitatem dedit. Massilienses duobus navalibus proeliis victi[5] post longam obsidionem potestati Caesaris se permiserunt. C. Antonius legatus Caesaris male adversus Pompeianos in Illyrico rebus gestis captus est; in quo bello Opitergini

[1] dein pro *Sigonius* : depr. N : de p. R. P.
[2] *lacunam indicavit Rossbach, perisse putavit* Caesar sine exercitu Romam venire iussus.
[3] P. *Perizonius* : L. MSS.
[4] M. *Sigonius* : C. MSS.
[5] victi *ed. Mediolanensis* : vicit NPΠR.

---

[1] 51 B.C. Cf. Appian, *Civil Wars* II. iv. 27; Dio XL. xii 3 f.; Plutarch, *Caesar* xxx; Cicero, *ad Familiares* VIII. xi. 3, *ad Atticum* VI. ii. 6, iii. 4; Caesar, *Gallic War* VIII. lii. 4.

discharged his.[1] The book also includes the moves of Gaius Curio, a tribune of the commons, first against Caesar, and then in his favour.[2] When a decree of the senate was passed that a successor to Caesar should be sent out, Marcus Antonius and Quintus Cassius, tribunes of the commons, were driven from the city because they tried to block this decree of the senate with their vetoes, and the consuls and Gnaeus Pompeius were charged by the senate to see to it that no harm befell the commonwealth.[3] When Gaius Caesar entered Italy with an army to make war on his personal enemies, he captured Corfinium, together with Lucius Domitius and Publius Lentulus, set these men free, and drove out of Italy Gnaeus Pompeius and the others of his faction.[4] B.C. 51–49

CX. Which is the Second on the Civil War.

Gaius Caesar besieged Marseilles, which had closed its gates to him; he left his staff officers Gaius Trebonius and Decimus Brutus in charge of the siege, set out for Spain and received at Ilerda the surrender of Lucius Afranius and Marcus Petreius, deputies of Gnaeus Pompeius, together with their seven legions. He let them all go unharmed; Varro, also a deputy of Pompey, along with his army, was brought under Caesar's control. He granted citizenship to the people of Gades. The people of Marseilles, after losing two naval battles, put themselves after a long siege into Caesar's hands.[5] Gaius Antonius, Caesar's deputy, met with ill success against the followers of Pompey in Illyricum, and was taken prisoner; in this campaign some Opitergini from across the Po, who were B.C. 49

[2] 51–50 B.C. Cf. Appian, *Civil Wars* II. iv. 26–29; Dio XL. lxi f.; Velleius II. xlviii. 3 f.; Valerius Maximus IX. i. 6.

[3] 49 B.C. Cf. Caesar, *Civil War* I. i f.; Dio XLI. i–iii; Appian, *Civil War* II. iv. 32 f.; Plutarch, *Caesar* xxix–xxxv; Suetonius, *Julius* xxix–xxxiv; Velleius II. xlix.

[4] Cf. Caesar, *Civil War* I. vii–xxviii, and the secondary sources cited in note 3; fr. 32.

[5] 49 B.C. Cf. Caesar, *Civil War* I. xxxiv–lviii. Cf. below, p. 139, note 6.

A.U.C. 705 Transpadani, Caesaris auxiliares, rate sua ab hostium navibus clusa, potius quam in potestatem hostium venirent, inter se concurrentes occubuerunt. C. Curio, legatus Caesaris in Africa, cum prospere adversus Varum Pompeianarum partium ducem pugnasset, a Iuba rege Mauretaniae cum exercitu caesus est. C. Caesar in Graeciam traiecit.

A.U.C. 706 CXI qui est civilis belli tertius.

M. Caelius [1] Rufus praetor, cum seditiones in urbe concitaret novarum tabularum spe plebe sollicitata, abrogato magistratu pulsus urbe Miloni exuli, qui fugitivorum exercitum contraxerat, se coniunxit. Uterque, cum bellum molirentur, interfecti sunt. Cleopatra regina Aegypti ab Ptolemaeo fratre regno pulsa est. Propter Q. Cassii [2] praetoris avaritiam crudelitatemque Cordubenses in Hispania cum duabus Varronianis [3] legionibus a partibus Caesaris desciverunt. Cn. Pompeius ad Dyrrachium obsessus a Caesare et, praesidiis eius cum magna clade diversae partis expugnatis, obsidione liberatus translato in Thessaliam bello, apud Pharsaliam acie victus est. Cicero in castris remansit, vir nihil minus quam ad bella natus. Omnibusque adversarum partium, qui se potestati victoris permiserant, Caesar ignovit.

[1] Caelius *Sigonius*: caecilius NPΠR.
[2] Cassii *Xylander*: cati NPΠ: Catuli R.
[3] Varronianis *Gronovius*: varianis MSS.

---

[1] Cf. Appian, *Civil Wars* II. vii. 47; Dio XLI. xl. 2; for the Opitergini, cf. Lucan IV. 462–581 and the scholia; Florus II. xiii. 33.

[2] Cf. Caesar, *Civil War* II. xxiii–xliv; Appian, *Civil Wars* II. vii. 44–6.

[3] Cf. Caesar, *Civil War* III. ii–vii.

auxiliaries of Caesar's, attacked each other and perished rather than fall into the hands of the enemy when their raft was surrounded by enemy ships.[1] Gaius Curio, Caesar's deputy in Africa, scored a success against Varus, the leader of Pompey's party, but was slain in the defeat of his army by Juba King of Mauretania.[2] Gaius Caesar crossed over to Greece.[3] B.C. 49

CXI. Which is the Third on the Civil War. B.C. 48

Praetor Marcus Caelius Rufus stirred up riots in the city by inciting the commons with the hope of a cancellation of debts; he was deprived of office and driven from the city, and joined Milo the exile who had assembled a force of runaway slaves. Both men were put to death while trying to stir up war.[4] Cleopatra, Queen of Egypt, was driven from the throne by her brother Ptolemy.[5] Because of the cruelty and greed of Praetor Quintus Cassius, the people of Cordova in Spain and two of Varro's legions deserted Caesar's cause.[6] Gnaeus Pompeius was besieged by Caesar at Dyrrachium and after storming the latter's fortifications with great loss to the defending side, released himself from the siege, moved the theatre of operations to Thessaly, and was beaten in battle at Pharsalia.[7] Cicero, a man destined by nature for anything rather than war, remained in Pompey's camp.[8] All those on the opposing side who put themselves into the victor's hands were pardoned by Caesar.[9]

[4] 48 B.C. Cf. Caesar, *Civil War* III. xx–xxii and Dio XLII. xxii–xxv, who differ as to details; Cicero, *ad Familiares* VIII. xvii. Milo and Caelius tried to operate in Campania and southern Italy.

[5] Cf. Caesar, *Civil War* III. ciii. 2; Plutarch, *Caesar* xlviii. 5.

[6] Cf. Caesar, *Civil War* II. xix–xxi. This Varro was the noted scholar, some of whose work is preserved. Cassius was propraetor. Cf. *Bellum Alexandrinum* 48–54; fr. 37.

[7] Cf. Caesar, *Civil War* III. xxx–xcix; frs. 33–34.

[8] Cf. Plutarch, *Cicero* xxxviii f.; fr. 34a.

[9] Cf. Plutarch, *Caesar* xlvi; Velleius II. lii. 4–6; Suetonius, *Julius* lxxv. 2.

A.U.C. 706–707 CXII qui est civilis belli quartus.

Trepidatio victarum partium in diversas orbis terrarum partes et fuga referuntur. Cn. Pompeius cum Aegyptum petisset, iussu Ptolemaei regis, pupilli sui, auctore Theodoto praeceptore, cuius magna apud regem auctoritas erat, et Pothino occisus est ab Achilla,[1] cui id facinus erat delegatum, in navicula, antequam in terram exiret. Cornelia uxor et Sex. Pompeius filius Cypron refugerunt. Caesar post tertium diem insecutus, cum ei Theodotus caput Pompeii et anulum obtulisset, infensus est et inlacrimavit; sine periculo Alexandriam tumultuantem intravit. Caesar dictator creatus Cleopatram in regnum Aegypti reduxit et inferentem bellum Ptolemaeum isdem auctoribus, quibus Pompeium interfecerat, cum magno suo discrimine evicit. Ptolemaeus dum fugit, in Nilo navicula subsedit. Praeterea laboriosum M. Catonis in Africa per deserta cum legionibus iter et bellum a Cn. Domitio adversus Pharnacen[2] parum prospere gestum continet.

A.U.C. 707 CXIII qui est civilis belli quintus.

Confirmatis in Africa Pompeianis partibus, imperium earum P. Scipioni delatum est, Catone, cui ex aequo deferebatur imperium, cedente. Et cum de diruenda urbe Utica propter favorem civitatis eius in Caesarem deliberaretur, idque ne fieret M. Cato tenuisset, Iuba suadente ut dirueretur, tutela eius et custodia mandata est Catoni. Cn. Pompeius[3] Magni filius in Hispania contractis viribus,

[1] Achilla *edd.*: archelao MSS.
[2] Pharnacen *Sigonius*: prahaten MSS.
[3] Cn. Pompeius *Sigonius*: in pompei MSS.

---

[1] 48 B.C. Cf. Plutarch, *Pompey* lxxvii–lxxx; *Caesar* xlviii; Caesar, *Civil War* III. ciii–cvi; Dio XLII. i–viii, xiii; fr. 39a.

[2] 48–7 B.C. Cf. Caesar, *Civil War* III. cvi–cxi, *Alexandrine War* i–xxxiii. On Caesar's (second) dictatorship, cf. Dio XLII. xx. 3 and xxi.

[3] Cf. Plutarch, *Cato* lvi.

CXII. Which is the Fourth on the Civil War. B.C. 48–47

An account is given of the panic and flight of the defeated side to various parts of the world. When Gnaeus Pompeius made for Egypt, he was killed by Achillas, to whom the crime had been assigned, in a small boat before he set foot on land, by order of King Ptolemy, Pompey's own ward, instigated by Pothinus and Theodotus the king's tutor, whose influence with the king was great. Cornelia, Pompey's wife, and Sextus Pompeius, his son, took refuge in Cyprus. The third day thereafter Caesar arrived in pursuit, and when Theodotus brought him Pompey's head and ring, he was indignant and burst into tears.[1] In spite of rioting, Caesar entered Alexandria safely. Caesar was made dictator, restored Cleopatra to the throne of Egypt, and when Ptolemy attacked him at the instigation of the same men at whose advice he had killed Pompey, Caesar won through after incurring great personal risk. While Ptolemy was fleeing, his boat sank in the Nile.[2] The book also includes the toilsome march of Marcus Cato with his legions through the deserts of Africa,[3] and a campaign conducted with little success by Gnaeus Domitius against Pharnaces.[4]

CXIII. Which is the Fifth on the Civil War. B.C. 47

When Pompey's partisans had entrenched themselves strongly in Africa, supreme command was conferred on Publius Scipio, after Cato had declined an offer of joint command. A discussion took place as to rasing the city of Utica because this commonwealth favoured Caesar; Marcus Cato maintained that this should not be done, while Juba argued that it should be destroyed; Cato was appointed protector and warden of the city.[5] Gnaeus Pompeius, the son of Pompey the Great, assembled forces

[4] Cf. Dio XLII. xlv f.; Strabo XII. iii. 14. 547; [Caesar], *Alexandrine War* xxxiv–xl.

[5] Cf. Plutarch, *Cato* lvii f.; Velleius II. liv. 2–4; Appian, *Civil Wars* II. xii. 87; [Caesar], *African War* iv. 4; Dio XLII. lvi f.

A.U.C. 707 quarum ducatum nec Afranius nec Petreius excipere volebant, bellum adversus Caesarem renovavit. Pharnaces Mithridatis filius, rex Ponti,[1] sine ulla belli mora victus est. Cum seditiones Romae a P. Dolabella tribuno plebis, legem ferente de novis tabulis, excitatae essent et ex ea causa plebs tumultuaretur, inductis a M. Antonio magistro equitum in urbem militibus octingenti ex plebe [2] caesi sunt. Caesar veteranis cum seditione missionem postulantibus dedit, et cum in Africam traiecisset, adversus copias Iubae regis cum discrimine magno pugnavit.

A.U.C. 707–708 CXIV qui est civilis belli sextus.

Bellum in Syria Caecilius Bassus, eques Romanus Pompeianarum partium, excitavit, relicto a legione Sexto Caesare, quae ad Bassum transierat, occisoque eo. Caesar Scipionem praetorem Iubamque vicit ad Thapsum castris eorum expugnatis. Cato audita re cum se percussisset Uticae et interveniente filio curaretur, inter ipsam curationem rescisso vulnere expiravit, anno aetatis quadragesimo octavo. Petreius Iubam seque interfecit. P. Scipio in nave circumventus honestae morti vocem quoque adiecit: quaerentibus enim imperatorem hostibus dixit, "imperator se bene habet." Faustus et Afranius occisi. Catonis filio venia data. Brutus legatus Caesaris in Gallia Bellovacos rebellantes proelio vicit.

[1] rex Ponti *ed. Moguntina*: ex ponto NPΠR.
[2] octingenti e plebe *Frobenius*: octingentis aplebe MSS.

---

[1] Cf. Dio XLIII. xxix f.; Appian, *Civil Wars* II. xii. 87.
[2] [Caesar], *Alexandrine War* lxv–lxxviii; Dio XLII. xlv–xlix; Appian, *Civil Wars* II. 91; *Mithridatic Wars* xvii. 120 f.
[3] 47 B.C. Cf. Dio XLII. xxix–xxxiii; Plutarch, *Antony* ix. 1 f.; [Caesar], *Alexandrine War* lxv. 1.
[4] Cf. [Caesar], *African War* i–vii; Dio XLII. lvi–lviii.

in Spain; neither Afranius nor Petreius would accept the command, and so Pompeius himself renewed the war against Caesar.[1] Pharnaces, son of Mithridates and King of Pontus was conquered without the slightest delay in the campaign.[2] When disturbances were stirred up in Rome by Publius Dolabella, tribune of the commons, who proposed a law to cancel debts, and as a result the commons were rioting, Marcus Antonius, the Master of the Horse, brought troops into the city and slew eight hundred of the commons.[3] When veterans mutinously demanded their discharge, Caesar granted it, and after crossing to Africa fought at great risk against the troops of King Juba.[4] B.C. 47

CXIV. Which is the Sixth on the Civil War. B.C. 47–46

Caecilius Bassus, a Roman knight of Pompey's party, stirred up war in Syria, after Sextus Caesar had been deserted by his legion, which went over to Bassus, and had been killed.[5] Caesar defeated Praetor Scipio and Juba at Thapsus and stormed their camp. When Cato at Utica heard of this defeat, he stabbed himself; his son intervened and tried to care for him, but he tore open the wound again while the nursing was going on and breathed his last, in the forty-eighth year of his age. Petreius killed Juba and himself. Publius Scipio was surrounded on his ship, and added to his honourable death a saying to match: for when his enemies called for "the general," he said, "The general is doing nicely." Faustus and Afranius were killed. Cato's son was granted a pardon.[6] Brutus,[7] Caesar's deputy in Gaul, won a battle over the rebellious Bellovaci.

[5] 47 B.C. Cf. Appian, *Civil Wars* III. xi. 77, IV. viii. 58; Dio XLVII. xxvi. 3–7; Cicero, *ad Familiares* XII. xviii. 1.

[6] 46 B.C. Cf. *African War*, lxxix–lxxxvi, lxxxix, xciii–xcvi; Dio XLIII. i–xiii; Appian, *Civil Wars* II. xiv. 96–100; Plutarch, *Caesar* liii f.; *Cato* lviii. 7–lxxiii; fr. 45.

[7] This was Decimus Brutus, cf. Appian, *Civil Wars* III. xiv. 98.

A.U.C. 708–709 CXV qui est civilis belli septimus.

Caesar quattuor triumphos duxit, ex Gallia, ex Aegypto, ex Ponto, ex Africa, epulum et omnis generis spectacula dedit. M. Marcello consulari senatu rogante reditum concessit; quo [1] beneficio eius Marcellus frui non potuit, a Cn. Magio cliente suo Athenis occisus. Recensum egit, quo censa sunt civium capita $\overline{\mathrm{C}}$L. Profectus in Hispaniam adversus Cn. Pompeium, multis utrimque expeditionibus factis et aliquot urbibus expugnatis summam victoriam cum magno discrimine ad Mundam urbem consecutus est. Necatus est Cn.[2] Pompeius, Sex. effugit.

A.U.C. 709–710 CXVI qui est civilis belli octavus.

Caesar ex Hispania quintum triumphum egit. Et cum plurimi maximique honores ei a senatu decreti essent, inter quos ut parens patriae appellaretur et sacrosanctus ac dictator in perpetuum esset, invidiae adversus eum causam praestiterunt, quod senatui deferenti hos honores, cum ante aedem Veneris Genetricis sederet, non adsurrexit, et quod a [3] M. Antonio consule, collega suo, inter Lupercos currente diadema capiti suo impositum in sella reposuit, et quod Epidio Marullo et Caesetio Flavo tribunis plebis invidiam ei [4] tamquam regnum adfectanti facientibus [5]

[1] quo *Gronovius*: qui MSS.
[2] Necatus est Cn. *add. Rossbach*: *om.* MSS.
[3] a *add. Gryphius*: *om.* MSS.
[4] ei *edd.*: et NPIIR.
[5] facientibus *add.* MacDonald: *om.* MSS.

---

[1] 46 B.C. Cf. Dio XLIII. xix–xxii; Appian, *Civil Wars* II. xv. 101 f.; Plutarch, *Caesar* lv; Suetonius, *Julius* xxxvii–xxxix.

[2] Cf. Cicero, *pro Marcello*; Cicero, *ad Familiares* IV. xii. 2, where the assassin's name is given as Publius Magius Cilo, and described as an intimate friend, *ad Atticum* XIII. x. 3; Valerius Maximus IX. xi. 4.

[3] This was a review of the list of those receiving the grain dole, and reduced their number by over half, cf. Suetonius,

CXV. Which is the Seventh on the Civil War. B.C. 46–45

Caesar conducted four triumphs, for the campaigns in Gaul, in Egypt, in Pontus, and in Africa; he gave a banquet and all sorts of shows.[1] He permitted the return of the ex-consul Marcus Marcellus, at the request of the senate; Marcellus was unable to profit by this kindness of Caesar's, since he was killed at Athens by his client Gnaeus Magius.[2] Caesar conducted an enumeration in which one hundred and fifty thousand citizens were counted.[3] Caesar set out for Spain to attack Gnaeus Pompeius, and after much marching and countermarching by both sides and the storming of several cities, won a complete victory at great risk near the city of Munda. Gnaeus Pompeius was killed, Sextus escaped.[4]

CXVI. Which is the Eighth on the Civil War. B.C. 45–44

Caesar celebrated his fifth triumph for the campaign in Spain.[5] When a great abundance of the highest distinctions were voted him by the senate, among which were the title of Father of the Fatherland, inviolability, and dictatorship for life,[6] occasions for a grudge against him were created because he did not rise from his seat before the temple of Mother Venus when the senate came to present him with these distinctions, because he laid in his chair a crown placed on his head by Consul Marcus Antonius, his colleague, who was running with the Luperci, and because when Epidius Marullus and Caesetius Flavus, tribunes of the commons, tried to excite a grudge against him, on the ground that he was aiming at monarchy, they

Julius xli. 3; Plutarch, *Caesar* lv. 3; Dio XLIII. xxi. 4, xxv. 2; Appian, *Civil Wars* II. xv. 102.

[4] 46–45 B.C. Cf. [Caesar], *Spanish War*; Dio XLIII. xxix–xl; Appian, *Civil Wars* II. xv. 103–105.

[5] October, 45 B.C. Cf. Dio XLIII. xlii; Suetonius, *Julius* xxxvii; Velleius II. lvi. 2.

[6] 44 B.C. Cf. Dio XLIII. xliii–xlv, XLIV. iv–vii; Suetonius lxxvi; Appian, *Civil Wars* II. xvi. 106; Plutarch, *Caesar* lvii.

A.U.C. 709–710 potestas abrogata est. Ex his causis conspiratione in eum facta, cuius capita fuerunt M. Brutus et C. Cassius et ex Caesaris partibus Dec. Brutus et C. Trebonius, in Pompeii curia occisus est viginti tribus vulneribus, occupatumque ab interfectoribus eius Capitolium. Oblivione deinde caedis eius a senatu decreta, obsidibus Antonii et Lepidi de liberis acceptis coniurati a Capitolio descenderunt. Testamento Caesaris heres ex parte dimidia institutus est C. Octavius, sororis nepos, et in nomen adoptatus.[1] Caesaris corpus cum in campum Martium ferretur, a plebe ante rostra crematum est. Dictaturae honos in perpetuum sublatus est. Chamates, humillimae sortis homo, qui se C. Marii filium ferebat, cum apud credulam plebem seditiones moveret, necatus est.

A.U.C. 710 CXVII. C. Octavius Romam ex Epiro venit (eo enim illum Caesar praemiserat bellum in Macedonia gesturus) ominibusque[2] prosperis exceptus et nomen Caesaris sumpsit. In confusione rerum ac tumultu M. Lepidus pontificatum maximum intercepit.[3] Et M. Antonius consul cum impotenter dominaretur legemque de per-

[1] adoptatus *Rossbach* : adoptatus est MSS.
[2] ominibusque *Frobenius* : omnibusque MSS.
[3] tumultu M. Lepidus pontificatum maximum intercepit *Sigonius* : tumultum lepidum pontificem tum maximum interfecit NPΠ.

---

[1] Cf. Dio XLIV. viii–xi; Suetonius lxxviii f.; Plutarch, *Caesar* lx f.

[2] Cf. Dio XLIV. xiii–xix; Suetonius lxxx–lxxxii; Appian, *Civil Wars* II. xvi. 111–117; Plutarch, *Caesar* lxiii–lxvi; frs. 46–48.

[3] Cf. Appian, *Civil Wars* II. xvii. 119, xix. 142; Dio XLIV. xx–xxxiv.

[4] Cf. Appian, *Civil Wars* III. i. 10 f., xiii. 94; Suetonius, *Julius* lxxxiii. 2; Nicolaus of Damascus, *Life of Caesar* xiii, xvii; Pliny, *Natural History* XXXV. vii. 21. These sources give Octavian's share as three-fourths.

were expelled from office.[1] For these reasons a conspiracy was formed against him, the ringleaders of which were Marcus Brutus, Gaius Cassius, and of the followers of Caesar, Decimus Brutus and Gaius Trebonius. Caesar was done to death in Pompey's senate-house with twenty-three wounds, and the Capitol was seized by his assassins.[2] Thereafter when amnesty for this murder had been voted by the senate, and hostages had been delivered to them from among the sons of Antony and Lepidus, the conspirators came down from the Capitol.[3] By Caesar's will, Gaius Octavius, his sister's grandson, was named his heir with half the estate, and was adopted as his son.[4] While Caesar's body was being carried to the Campus Martius, it was burned by the commons before the Rostra.[5] The office of dictator was banned forever.[6] Chamates, a fellow of the lowest station, who claimed to be the son of Gaius Marius, began to cause disturbances among the credulous commons and was executed.[7] B.C. 45–44

CXVII. Gaius Octavius came to Rome from Epirus (for Caesar had sent him ahead there because he was planning on a campaign in Macedonia) and being received with favourable omens also took the name of Caesar.[8] Amid political confusion and rioting Marcus Lepidus pre-empted the office of chief pontiff.[9] Consul Marcus Antonius also exercised a reckless tyranny, carried by violence a law concerning changes in the assignment of B.C. 44

[5] Cf. Cicero, *ad Atticum* XIV. x. 1; *Philippics* II. xxxvi. 90–1.

[6] Cf. Cicero, *Philippics* I. i. 3, II. xlv. 115.

[7] April, 44 B.C. Cf. Appian, *Civil Wars* III. i. 2, who calls the adventurer Amatius.

[8] Cf. Appian, *Civil Wars* III. ii. 12–14; Velleius II. lix. 6; Obsequens 68; Suetonius, *Augustus* viii, xcv; Dio XLV. iv. 4.

[9] Cf. *Res Gestae Divi Augusti* 10; Appian, *Civil Wars* II. xviii. 132; V. xiii. 131; Dio XLIV. liii. 6–7, who says that Antony tried in this way to side-track Lepidus.

A.U.C. 710 mutatione provinciarum per vim tulisset et Caesarem quoque petentem, ut sibi adversus percussores avunculi adesset, magnis iniuriis adfecisset, Caesar et sibi et rei publicae vires adversus eum paraturus deductos in colonias veteranos excitavit. Legiones quoque quarta et Martia signa ab Antonio ad Caesarem tulerunt. Deinde et complures saevitia M. Antonii, passim in castris suis trucidantis qui [1] ei [2] suspecti erant, ad Caesarem desciverunt. Dec. Brutus, ut petenti Cisalpinam Galliam Antonio obsisteret, Mutinam cum exercitu occupavit. Praeterea discursum utriusque partis virorum ad accipiendas provincias apparatusque belli continet.

A.U.C. 711 CXVIII. M. Brutus in Graecia sub praetexto rei publicae et suscepti contra M. Antonium belli exercitum, cui P. Vatinius praeerat, cum provincia in potestatem suam redegit. C. Caesari, qui privatus [3] rei publicae arma sumpserat, pro praetore [4] imperium a senatu datum est cum consularibus ornamentis adiectumque, ut senator esset. M. Antonius Dec. Brutum Mutinae obsedit; missique ad eum a senatu legati de pace parum ad componendam eam valuerunt. Populus Romanus saga sumpsit. M. Brutus in Epiro C. Antonium praetorem cum exercitu potestati suae subegit.

[1] trucidantis qui *Gronovius*: trucidati quia MSS.
[2] ei *Jahn*: et MSS.
[3] privatus *Gronovius*: primus NPΠR.
[4] pro praetore *Rossbach*: pro pr N: pro P.R. P: pro Po. Ro. R: propraetoris *Sigonius*.

---

[1] Cf. Suetonius, *Augustus* x; Appian, *Civil Wars* III. iii. 22–3; Cicero, *Philippics*, *e.g.* II. xlii. 109; Dio XLV. v–ix.

provinces, and inflicted great wrongs on Caesar, too, when he sought Antony's support against the assassins of his great-uncle.[1] Caesar therefore began to acquire resources against Antony, both for his own benefit and for that of the state, by calling out the veterans who had been settled in colonies. The Fourth and Martian legions also transferred their allegiance from Antony to Caesar. Thereafter many more persons deserted to Caesar because of the savagery of Marcus Antonius, who butchered right and left those in his camp whom he suspected.[2] Decimus Brutus occupied Mutina with his army, in order to head off Antony, who was making for Cisalpine Gaul.[3] The book also includes the scattering of men on both sides to take over provinces, and the preparations for war. B.C. 44

CXVIII. In Greece Marcus Brutus gained control over the army commanded by Publius Vatinius, and the province as well, on the pretext of the public welfare and of the campaign against Marcus Antonius which had been undertaken.[4] Gaius Caesar, who had as a private citizen taken up arms for the state, was given authority as propraetor with the insignia of a consul by the senate, with the further provision that he be a senator.[5] Marcus Antonius besieged Decimus Brutus in Mutina; and envoys sent him by the senate to treat for peace had little success in arranging it. The Roman people donned military cloaks.[6] Marcus Brutus in Epirus reduced Praetor Gaius Antonius and his army to submission.[7] B.C. 43

[2] Cf. Cicero, *ad Atticum* XVI. viii; *Philippics* III. ii–iii. 3–7; iv. 10; XIII. viii. 18.

[3] Cf. Cicero, *ad Familiares* XI. vi; *Philippics* III. iv. 8; Appian, *Civil Wars* III. viii. 49.

[4] 43 B.C. Cf. Dio XLVII. xxi. 4–7; Plutarch, *Brutus* xxv f.

[5] Cf. *Res Gestae* 1; *Philippics* V. xvii. 46.

[6] Cf. *Philippics* V. xiii. 36 f.; VI. ii–iii. 3–9; Dio XLVI. xxxi. 2.

[7] Cf. Appian, *Civil Wars* III. xi. 79, and the references in note 4, above.

A.U.C. 711 CXIX. C. Trebonius in Asia fraude P. Dolabellae occisus est. Ob id facinus Dolabella hostis a senatu iudicatus est. Cum Pansa consul male adversus Antonium pugnasset, A. Hirtius consul cum exercitu superveniens fusis M. Antonii copiis fortunam utriusque partis aequavit. Victus deinde ab Hirtio et Caesare Antonius in Galliam confugit et M. Lepidum cum legionibus, quae sub eo erant, sibi iunxit; hostisque a senatu cum omnibus, qui intra praesidia eius essent, iudicatus est. A. Hirtius, qui post victoriam in ipsis hostium castris ceciderat, et C.[1] Pansa ex vulnere, quod in adverso proelio exceperat, defunctus, in campo Martio sepulti sunt. Adversus C. Caesarem, qui solus ex tribus ducibus supererat, parum gratus senatus fuit, qui Dec. Bruto obsidione Mutinensi a Caesare liberato triumphi honore decreto Caesaris militumque eius mentionem non satis gratam habuit. Ob quae C. Caesar reconciliata per M. Lepidum cum M. Antonio gratia Romam cum exercitu venit et perculsis adventu eius his, qui in eum iniqui erant, cum XVIIII annos haberet, consul creatus est.

CXX. C. Caesar consul legem tulit de quaestione habenda in eos, quorum opera pater occisus esset; postulatique ea lege M. Brutus C. Cassius Dec. Brutus absentes damnati sunt. Cum M. Antoni[2] vires Asinius quoque Pollio et Munatius Plancus cum exercitibus suis adiuncti ampliassent, et Dec. Brutus, cui senatus ut persequeretur Antonium mandaverat, relictus a legionibus suis, profu-

[1] C. *Sigonius*: l. MSS.
[2] Antoni *Hahn*: antonius NPΠ.

---

[1] 43 B.C. Cf. Appian, *Civil Wars* III. iii. 26; Cicero, *Philippics* XI. i–iv. 1–10; vii. 16; xii. 29–31, who seems to be quoting horror-rumours; Dio XLVII. xxix. 1–4.

[2] Cf. Appian, *Civil Wars* III. ix. 66, x. 76; Dio XLVI. xxxv–xxxix. 1.

CXIX. Gaius Trebonius was killed in Asia by the treachery of Publius Dolabella. For this crime Dolabella was adjudged an enemy by the senate.[1] When Consul Pansa suffered a reverse against Antony, Consul Aulus Hirtius came up with his army and by routing the troops of Marcus Antonius, brought into balance the fortunes of the two sides. Antony, being defeated thereafter by Hirtius and Caesar, fled into Gaul and acquired the support of Marcus Lepidus and the legions which he commanded; Antony was declared an enemy by the senate together with everyone who was within his lines. Aulus Hirtius, who after his victory had fallen in the very camp of the enemy, and Gaius Pansa, who died of the wound received in the battle he lost, were buried in the Campus Martius.[2] The senate showed too little gratitude towards Gaius Caesar, the only survivor of the three commanders; for it voted the distinction of a triumph to Decimus Brutus who had been freed from siege at Mutina by Caesar, but made an insufficiently grateful reference to Caesar and his men. For this reason Gaius Caesar came to terms with Marcus Antonius through the mediation of Marcus Lepidus, came to Rome with his army, and stunning those who were ill-disposed towards him by the arrival of this force, was elected consul at the age of nineteen.[3] B.C. 43

CXX. Consul Gaius Caesar passed a law to bring to justice those concerned in the murder of his father; Marcus Brutus, Gaius Cassius, and Decimus Brutus were cited under that law and condemned by default.[4] Asinius Pollio and Munatius Plancus also joined Marcus Antonius with their armies and enlarged his strength. Moreover, Decimus Brutus, whom the senate had commissioned to pursue Antony, fled when deserted by his legions and was put to

[3] Cf. Velleius II. lxii–lxv; Dio XLVI. xxxix–xlix. On D. Brutus' triumph, cf. *Philippics* VI. iii. 8.

[4] 43 B.C. Cf. *Res Gestae* 2; Appian, *Civil Wars* III. xiv. 95; Dio XLVI. xlviii–xlix; Velleius II. lxix. 5.

A.U.C. 711 gisset caesus iussu Antonii, in cuius potestatem venerat, a Capeno Sequano interfectus est. C. Caesar pacem cum Antonio et Lepido fecit ita, ut tresviri rei publicae constituendae per quinquennium essent ipse et Lepidus et Antonius, et ut suos quisque inimicos proscriberent. In qua proscriptione plurimi equites Romani, CXXX senatorum nomina fuerunt, et inter eos L. Pauli, fratris M. Lepidi, et L. Caesaris, Antonii avunculi, et M. Ciceronis. Huius occisi a Popillio legionario milite, cum haberet annos LXIII, caput quoque cum dextra manu in rostris positum est. Praeterea res a M. Bruto in Graecia gestas continet.

CXXI qui editus post excessum Augusti dicitur.

C. Cassius, cui mandatum a senatu erat, ut Dolabellam hostem iudicatum bello persequeretur, auctoritate rei publicae adiutus Syriam cum tribus exercitibus, qui in eadem provincia erant, in potestatem suam redegit, Dolabellam in urbe Laodicia obsessum mori coegit. M. quoque Bruti iussu C. Antonius captus occisus est.

CXXII. M. Brutus adversus Thracas parumper [1] prospere rem gessit, omnibusque transmarinis provinciis exercitibusque in potestatem eius et C. Cassii redactis coierunt Smyrnae uterque ad ordinanda belli futuri consilia. M. Messalae Publicolam fratrem vinctum communi consilio condonaverunt.

[1] parumper *P. la Roche* : parum MSS : *del. Xylander.*

---

[1] Cf. Appian, *Civil Wars* III. xiv. 97–98, where the executioner of Decimus is named as Camilus, a chieftain; Dio XLVI. liii.

[2] Cf. below, fr. 50; Dio XLVI. lv–lvi, XLVII. i–xix; Appian, *Civil Wars* IV. i–vi, 1–51; Plutarch, *Antony* xix–xx; *Res Gestae* 7; Obsequens 69.

[3] Cf. Dio XLVII. xx–xxxvi; Plutarch, *Brutus* xxiv–xxviii.

[4] 43 B.C. Cf. Dio XLVII. xxviii–xxx; Appian, *Civil Wars* IV. viii. 58–62.

death by order of Antony, into whose power he had come, being struck down by Capenus, a Sequanian.[1] Gaius Caesar made terms with Antony and Lepidus, providing that he, Lepidus, and Antony, should be a board of three for regulating the commonwealth for a term of five years, and that each should proscribe his personal enemies. In this proscription, there were included a very large number of Roman knights, and the names of one hundred and thirty senators, among them Lucius Paulus, the brother of Lepidus, Lucius Caesar, the uncle of Antony, and Marcus Cicero. The last was slain at the age of sixty-three by Popillius, a legionary soldier, and his head and right hand were also placed on the Rostra.[2] The book also includes the achievements of Marcus Brutus in Greece.[3] B.C. 43

CXXI. Which is Said to have been Published After the Death of Augustus.

Gaius Cassius had been commissioned by the senate to conduct a campaign against Dolabella when the latter was declared an enemy; armed with the authority of the state, he gained control of Syria with three legions which were in that province, blockaded Dolabella in the city of Laodicea and compelled him to die.[4] Also, by order of Marcus Brutus, Gaius Antonius was taken prisoner and executed.[5]

CXXII. Marcus Brutus for a time conducted a successful campaign against the Thracians, and when all the overseas provinces and armies had been brought under his control and that of Gaius Cassius, the two men met at Smyrna to determine plans for the coming war.[6] By common agreement they pardoned their prisoner Publicola at the plea of his brother Marcus Messala.[7]

[5] Cf. Plutarch *Brutus* xxviii; Dio XLVII. xxi, xxiii f. tells a somewhat different story; also Appian, *Civil Wars* III. xi. 79; Cicero, *ad Brutum* I. ii. 3.

[6] Cf. Dio XLVII. xxv, xxxii–xxxv; Plutarch, *Brutus* xxviii–xxxv.

[7] Cf. Dio XLVII. xxiv. 3–6.

A.U.C. 711–712 CXXIII. Sex. Pompeius Magni filius collectis ex Epiro proscriptis ac fugitivis cum exercitu diu sine ulla loci cuiusquam possessione praedatus in mari Messanam oppidum in Sicilia primum, dein totam provinciam occupavit occisoque Pompeio Bithynico praetore Q. Salvidenum legatum Caesaris navali proelio vicit. Caesar et Antonius cum exercitibus in Graeciam traiecerunt, bellum adversus Brutum et Cassium gesturi. Q. Cornificius in Africa T. Sextium, Cassianarum partium ducem, proelio vicit.

A.U.C. 712 CXXIV. C. Caesar et Antonius apud Philippos vario eventu adversus Brutum et Cassium pugnaverunt, ita ut dextra utriusque cornua vincerent et castra quoque utrimque ab his, qui vicerant, expugnarentur. Sed inaequalem fortunam partium mors Cassii fecit, qui cum in eo cornu fuisset, quod pulsum erat, totum exercitum fusum ratus mortem conscivit. Altera dein die[1] victus M. Brutus et ipse vitam finiit, exorato Stratone fugae comite, ut sibi gladium adigeret.[2] Annorum erat circiter XL, . . .[3] inter quos Q. Hortensius occisus est.

A.U.C. 713 CXXV. Caesar relicto trans mare Antonio (provinciae ea[4] parte imperii positae ei cesserant[5]) reversus in Italiam veteranis agros divisit. Seditiones exercitus sui, quas

[1] dein die *Jahn*: deinde MSS.
[2] adigeret *Gruter*: adiceret MSS.
[3] idemque fecerunt principum Romanorum circiter XL *add. Sigonius*.
[4] ea *Jahn*: ex NPΠR.
[5] ei cesserant *Jahn*: recesserat NPΠ.

---

[1] 43–2 B.C. Cf. Appian, *Civil Wars* IV. xi. 83–5; Dio XLVIII. xvi–xviii.
[2] Cf. Dio XLVII. xxxvii. 1–2; Appian, *Civil Wars* IV. xi. 86.
[3] 42 B.C. Cf. Dio XLVIII. xxi. 1–4, who calls Sextius a follower of Antony; Appian, *Civil Wars* IV. vii. 53, where Sextius acts for Octavian. Sextius was appointed by Julius

CXXIII. Sextus Pompeius, son of Pompey the Great, gathered proscribed men and runaway slaves from Epirus and for a long time engaged in piracy in the Mediterranean with his force without possessing any base; he first seized the city of Messana in Sicily, then the whole island, and after slaying Praetor Pompeius Bithynicus, defeated Quintus Salvidenus, the deputy of Caesar, in a naval battle.[1] Caesar and Antony with their armies crossed over to Greece to conduct the war against Brutus and Cassius.[2] Quintus Cornificius won a battle in Africa against Titus Sextius, the leader of the party of Cassius.[3] B.C. 43–42

CXXIV. Gaius Caesar and Antony fought a battle at Philippi against Brutus and Cassius with an outcome incongruous in that each right wing won and the victorious part of both sides proceeded to storm the opposing camp. The balance of fortune was destroyed by the death of Cassius, who was on the wing which was routed and committed suicide, thinking that the whole army was routed. On the second day of battle, Marcus Brutus was also beaten and put an end to his life, begging Strato who was accompanying him in flight to drive a sword through him. His age was about forty . . . among whom Quintus Hortensius was killed.[4] B.C. 42

CXXV. Caesar left Antony overseas (the provinces situated in that part of the empire had yielded to him), returned to Italy and assigned lands to his veterans.[5] He checked at great risk disturbances in his army which B.C. 41

Caesar, so that the reference to Cassius is a copyist's error; Sextius probably sided with Antony, served Octavian when the latter was not at odds with Antony, and had no opportunity to strike for Antony against Octavian.

[4] 42 B.C. Cf. Dio XLVII. xxxvii–xlix; Appian, *Civil Wars* IV. xi. 87, xvii. 138; Plutarch, *Brutus* xxxviii–liii; *Antony* xxii; Velleius II. lxx f.

[5] 41 B.C. Cf. Appian, *Civil Wars* V. i. 1–11 (Antony); ii. 12–13; Dio XLVIII. iii, vi.

A.U.C. 713 corrupti[1] a Fulvia M. Antonii uxore milites adversus imperatorem suum concitaverant, cum gravi periculo inhibuit. L. Antonius consul, M. Antonii frater, eadem Fulvia consiliante bellum Caesari intulit. Receptis in partes suas populis, quorum agri veteranis adsignati erant, et M. Lepido, qui custodiae urbis cum exercitu praeerat, fuso hostiliter in urbem irrupit.

A.U.C. 713–714 CXXVI. Caesar cum esset annorum viginti trium, obsessum in oppido Perusia L. Antonium conatumque aliquotiens erumpere et repulsum fame coegit in deditionem venire ipsique et omnibus militibus eius ignovit, Perusiam diruit. Redactisque in potestatem suam omnibus diversae partis exercitibus bellum citra ullum sanguinem confecit.

A.U.C. 714–716 CXXVII. Parthi Labieno, qui Pompeianarum partium fuerat, duce in Syriam inruperunt victoque Decidio Saxa M. Antonii legato totam eam provinciam occupaverunt. M. Antonius cum ad bellum adversus Caesarem gerendum . . .[2] uxore Fulvia, ne concordiae ducum obstaret, pace facta cum Caesare sororem eius Octaviam in matrimonium duxit. Q. Salvidenum consilia nefaria adversus Caesarem molitum indicio suo protraxit, isque damnatus mortem conscivit. P. Ventidius Antonii legatus Parthos proelio victos Syria expulit Labieno eorum duce occiso.

[1] corrupti *Ascenius*: correpti MSS.

[2] gerendum . . . uxore *H. J. Müller*: gerendum uxore MSS: gerendum incitaretur ab uxore R, *Gronovius*: gerendum profectus esset, mortua *E. Schwartz*.

---

[1] Cf. Dio XLVIII. iv–xiii; Appian, *Civil Wars* V. ii. 14, iii. 24, 27–31. Appian says that Octavian's troubles with the army antedated the break with Antony; cf. Suetonius, *Augustus* xiv.

soldiers bribed by Fulvia, the wife of Marcus Antonius, had stirred up against their general. Consul Lucius Antonius, brother of Marcus Antonius, on the advice of the same Fulvia, attacked Caesar in war. Having joined to his faction the peoples whose land had been assigned to the veterans, he routed Marcus Lepidus, who was in charge of the defence of Rome with his army, and made an armed incursion into the city.[1] B.C. 41

CXXVI. When Caesar was twenty-three years old, he besieged Lucius Antonius in the city of Perusia and beat back several attempts to break out; when hunger compelled Antonius to surrender, Caesar pardoned him and all his soldiers but destroyed Perusia. He brought under his control all the armies of the opposing side, and concluded the war without bloodshed.[2] B.C. 41–40

CXXVII. The Parthians invaded Syria under the command of Labienus, who belonged to Pompey's party; they defeated Decidius Saxa the deputy of Marcus Antonius and overran that whole province.[3] When Marcus Antonius . . . to make war against Caesar . . . his wife Fulvia, so that there should be no obstacle to agreement between the leaders, he came to terms with Caesar and married Octavia, Caesar's sister.[4] Antony exposed the fact that Quintus Salvidenus, on his own evidence, had undertaken dastardly schemes against Caesar; Salvidenus was condemned and committed suicide.[5] Publius Ventidius, Antony's deputy, defeated the Parthians in battle and drove them out of Syria, after Labienus their leader B.C. 40–38

[2] 41–40 B.C. Cf. Dio XLVIII. xiv–xvi. 1; Appian, *Civil Wars* V. iv. 32, vi. 50; Velleius II. lxxiv.

[3] 40 B.C. Cf. Dio XLVIII. xxiv. 4, xxvi; Justinus XLII. iv. 7; Strabo XII. viii. 9 (574); XIV. ii. 24 (660).

[4] Cf. Plutarch, *Antony* xxx f.; Dio XLVIII. xxviii f.; Appian, *Civil Wars* V. vi. 56, vii. 65; frs. 51–53.

[5] Cf. Dio XLVIII. xxxiii. 2 f.; Appian, *Civil Wars* V. vii. 66; Velleius II. lxxvi. 4; Suetonius, *Augustus* lxvi. 2.

A.U.C. 714–716 Cum vicinus Italiae hostis Sex. Pompeius Siciliam teneret et commercium annonae impediret, postulatam cum eo pacem Caesar et Antonius fecerunt ita, ut Siciliam provinciam haberet. Praeterea motus Africae et bella ibi gesta [1] continet.

A.U.C. 716–717 CXXVIII. Cum Sex. Pompeius rursus latrociniis mare infestum redderet nec pacem, quam acceperat, praestaret, Caesar necessario adversus eum bello suscepto duobus navalibus proeliis cum dubio eventu pugnavit. P.[2] Ventidius legatus M. Antonii Parthos in Syria proelio vicit regemque eorum occidit. Iudaei quoque a legatis Antonii subacti sunt. Praeterea belli Siculi apparatum continet.

A.U.C. 718 CXXIX. Adversus Sex. Pompeium vario eventu navalibus proeliis pugnatum est, ita ut ex duabus Caesaris classibus altera, cui Agrippa praeerat, vinceret, altera, quam Caesar duxerat, deleta expositi in terram milites in magno periculo essent. Victus deinde Pompeius in Siciliam profugit. M. Lepidus, qui ex Africa velut ad societatem belli contra Sex. Pompeium a Caesare gerendi traiecerat, cum bellum Caesari quoque inferret, relictus ab [3]

[1] ibi gesta *Sigonius* : ingesta NPΠ.
[2] P. *Sigonius* : lNPΠR.
[3] relictus ab *Frobenius* : relicto NPR.

---

[1] 39 B.C. Cf. Dio XLVIII. xxxix f.; Frontinus II. v. 36; Plutarch, *Antony* xxxiii. 4.
[2] 40–39 B.C. Cf. Plutarch, *Antony* xxxii; Dio XLVIII. xxx. 4, xxxi, xxxvi–xxxviii; Appian, *Civil Wars* V. viii. 67–73; Suetonius, *Augustus* xvi. 1.
[3] 40–38 B.C. Cf. Dio XLVIII. xlv. 1–3; Appian, *Civil Wars* V. iii. 26.

lost his life.[1] Since Sextus Pompeius, an enemy at the borders of Italy, held Sicily and interfered with the traffic in grain, Caesar and Antony made peace with him at his demand, the terms being that he should hold Sicily as a province.[2] The book also includes the uprising in Africa and the campaigns conducted there.[3] B.C. 40–38

CXXVIII. When Sextus Pompey again made the sea dangerous through acts of piracy, and did not maintain the peace to which he had agreed, Caesar undertook the inevitable war against him and fought two drawn naval battles.[4] Publius Ventidius, the deputy of Marcus Antonius, won a battle with the Parthians in Syria, and killed their king.[5] The Jews were also subdued by Antony's deputies.[6] The book also contains the preparations for war in Sicily.[7] B.C. 38–37

CXXIX. Naval battles with divergent outcomes were fought against Sextus Pompeius: of two fleets of Caesar's, the one, commanded by Agrippa, was victorious, the other, led by Caesar himself, was destroyed, and the soldiers who had been set ashore from it were in grave danger. Later, Pompeius was beaten and fled into Sicily.[8] Marcus Lepidus crossed over from Africa as if to join forces with Caesar in waging the war against Sextus Pompeius, but when he also attacked Caesar, he was deserted by his army, and lost his B.C. 36

[4] 38 B.C. Cf. Dio XLVIII. xlv. 4, xlix. 1; Appian, *Civil Wars* V. ix. 77–87; the account given by these writers tells of defeats suffered by Octavian.

[5] Cf. Dio XLIX. xix–xxi; Velleius II. lxxviii. 1; Justinus XLII. iv. 7–10; the "king" was Pacorus, actually the crown prince.

[6] Cf. Dio XLIX. xxii. 3–6; Josephus, *Antiquities* XIV. xvi. (468–491). Cf. *Summary* CII. and fr. 26.

[7] 37 B.C. Cf. Dio XLVIII. xlix. 2–5; Appian, *Civil Wars* V. ix. 92.

[8] 36 B.C. Cf. Dio XLIX. i–xi. 1; Appian, *Civil Wars* V. x. 96, xii. 122.

A.U.C. 718 exercitu, abrogato triumviratus honore vitam impetravit. M. Agrippa navali corona a Caesare donatus est, qui honos nulli ante eum habitus erat.

CXXX. M. Antonius dum cum Cleopatra luxuriatur, tarde Mediam ingressus bellum cum legionibus XVIII et XVI equitum Parthis intulit, et cum duabus legionibus amissis, nulla re prospere cedente retro rediret, insecutis subinde Parthis et ingenti trepidatione et magno totius exercitus periculo in Armeniam reversus est XXI diebus CCC milia fuga emensus. Circa VIII hominum tempestatibus amisit. Tempestates quoque infestas super tam infeliciter susceptum Parthicum bellum culpa sua passus est, quia hiemare in Armenia nolebat, dum ad Cleopatram festinat.

A.U.C. 718–720 CXXXI. Sex. Pompeius cum in fidem M. Antonii veniret, bellum adversus eum in Asia moliens, oppressus a legatis eius occisus est. Caesar seditionem veteranorum cum magna pernicie motam inhibuit, Iapydas [1] et Dalmatas et Pannonios subegit. Antonius Artavasden [2] Armeniae regem fide data perductum in vincula conici iussit, regnumque Armeniae filio suo ex Cleopatra nato dedit, quam uxoris loco iam pridem captus amore eius habere coeperat.

[1] Iapydas *Sigonius* : iapygas NPΠ.
[2] Artavasden *Frobenius* : artunden NPΠ.

---

[1] Cf. Dio XLIX. xi. 2, xii; Appian, *Civil Wars* V. xi. 98 104; xiii. 122–128; Velleius II. lxxx.
[2] Cf. Dio XLIX. xiv. 3; Velleius II. lxxxi. 3.

position on the Board of Three, but successfully begged for his life.[1] Marcus Agrippa was presented by Caesar with a naval crown, a distinction never previously conferred on anyone.[2] B.C. 36

CXXX. While Marcus Antonius was revelling with Cleopatra, he at long last invaded Media and attacked the Parthians with eighteen legions and sixteen thousand cavalry. He lost two legions and retired after meeting with no success in any of his enterprises; the Parthians thereupon followed at his heels, but after great consternation and grave risk to his whole army, he returned to Armenia, covering in his flight three hundred miles in twenty-one days. He lost about eight thousand men in storms. He encountered this unfavourable weather, in addition to the Parthian campaign which he had so unluckily undertaken, by his own fault, since he was unwilling to winter in Armenia, in his hurry to join Cleopatra.[3]

CXXXI. Although Sextus Pompeius put himself under the protection of Marcus Antonius, he took steps to make war on him in Asia, and being surprised by Antony's deputies, was killed.[4] Caesar checked an uprising among the veterans which caused great damage, and subdued the Iapydae, Dalmatians, and Pannonians.[5] Antony enticed Artavasdes king of Armenia by giving him his word, and then ordered him to be thrown into chains; Antony gave the throne of Armenia to his son born of Cleopatra, with whom he had long been madly in love, and whom he now began to treat as his wife.[6] B.C. 36–34

[3] 36 B.C. Cf. Plutarch, *Antony* xxxvi–li; Dio XLIX. xxii–xxxiii.

[4] 36–35 B.C. Cf. Dio XLIX. xviii; Appian, *Civil Wars* V. xiv. 133–144.

[5] 35 B.C. Cf. Dio XLIX. xxxiv–xxxvii; Appian, *Illyrian Wars* iv. 18; Suetonius, *Augustus* xx.

[6] 34 B.C. Cf. Dio XLIX. xxxix–xli; Plutarch, *Antony*, liv. 4; Velleius II. lxxxii. 3 f.

A.U.C. 720–723 CXXXII. Caesar in Illyrico Dalmatas domuit. Cum M. Antonius ob amorem Cleopatrae, ex qua duos filios habebat, Philadelphum et Alexandrum, neque in urbem venire vellet neque finito IIIviratus [1] tempore imperium deponere bellumque moliretur, quod urbi et Italiae inferret, ingentibus tam navalibus quam terrestribus copiis ob hoc contractis remissoque Octaviae sorori Caesaris repudio, Caesar in Epirum cum exercitu traiecit. Pugnae deinde navales et proelia equestria secunda Caesaris referuntur.

A.U.C. 723–725 CXXXIII. M. Antonius ad Actium classe victus Alexandriam profugit; obsessusque a Caesare in ultima desperatione rerum, praecipue occisae Cleopatrae falso rumore impulsus se ipse interfecit. Caesar Alexandria in potestatem redacta, Cleopatra, ne in arbitrium victoris veniret, voluntaria morte defuncta, in urbem reversus tres triumphos egit, unum ex Illyrico, alterum ex Actiaca victoria, tertium de Cleopatra, imposito fine civilibus bellis altero et vicesimo anno. M. Lepidus Lepidi, qui triumvir fuerat, filius, coniuratione adversus Caesarem facta bellum moliens oppressus et occisus est.

A.U.C. 725–727 CXXXIV. C. Caesar rebus compositis et omnibus provinciis in certam formam redactis Augustus quoque cognominatus est; et mensis Sextilis in honorem eius

[1] IIIviratus *Gruter* : eius ratus MSS.

---

[1] 34–33 B.C. Cf. Dio XLIX. xxxviii. 2–3; Appian, *Illyrian Wars* v. 25–8.

[2] 33–31 B.C. Cf. Dio L. i–xiv. 2; Plutarch, *Antony* liii–lxii.

[3] 31 B.C. Cf. Dio L. xiv. 3, xxxv; Plutarch, *Antony* lxiii–lxxvii; Velleius II. lxxxiv–lxxxvii. 1.

[4] 30 B.C. Cf. below, fr. 54; Plutarch, *Antony* lxxviii–lxxxvi; Horace, *Epodes* 9 and *Odes* I. 37; Velleius II. lxxxvii. 1.

CXXXII. Caesar overcame the Dalmatians in Illyricum.[1] Marcus Antonius because of his passion for Cleopatra, by whom he had two sons, Philadelphus and Alexander, was unwilling to return to Rome or to lay down his command when his term on the Board of Three ended; he organized a campaign of invasion against Rome and Italy, and gathered huge forces on sea as well as on land for this purpose, and sent a notice of divorce to Octavia, Caesar's sister. Caesar crossed with an army to Epirus. A description is given of the ensuing naval battles and cavalry engagements, in which Caesar was victorious.[2] B.C. 34–31

CXXXIII. Marcus Antonius was defeated at sea off Actium and fled to Alexandria; when besieged by Caesar and reduced to complete hopelessness, he was driven to suicide above all by the false report that Cleopatra had been killed.[3] When Caesar had reduced Alexandria, and Cleopatra had died a voluntary death to avoid falling into the hands of the victor,[4] Caesar returned to Rome to celebrate three triumphs, one for the campaign in Illyricum, a second for his victory at Actium, and the third over Cleopatra.[5] He made an end of the civil wars in their twenty-second year.[6] Marcus Lepidus, son of the Lepidus who had been on the Board of Three, formed a conspiracy against Caesar and while taking steps towards war was caught and killed.[7] B.C. 31–29

CXXXIV. When Gaius Caesar had brought about a peaceful settlement and had arranged a definite organization for all the provinces, he was also given the title of Augustus and the month called Sixth was renamed in his B.C. 29–27

[5] 29 B.C. Cf. *Res Gestae* 4; Suetonius, *Augustus* xxii; *C.I.L.* I²., pp. 76, 180, 248; Dio LI. xxi. 5–9.

[6] This inclusive reckoning seems to set 50 B.C., when the Senate took steps against Caesar, as the beginning year of the civil wars.

[7] 31–30 B.C. Cf. Dio LIV. xv. 4; Appian, *Civil Wars* IV. vi. 50; Suetonius, *Augustus* xix; Velleius II. lxxxviii.

A.U.C. 725–727 appellatus est. Cum ille conventum Narbone egit, census a tribus Galliis, quas Caesar pater vicerat, actus. Bellum adversus Basternas et Moesos et alias gentes a M. Crasso . . .[1] referuntur.

A.U.C. 726–729 CXXXV. Bellum a M. Crasso adversus Thracas et a Caesare adversus Hispanos gestum refertur, et Salassi, gens Alpina, perdomiti.

Librorum CXXXVI et CXXXVII periochae desunt.

A.U.C. 739–741 CXXXVIII. Raeti a Tib. Nerone et Druso, Caesaris privignis,[2] domiti. Agrippa, Caesaris gener, mortuus. A Druso census actus est.

A.U.C. 742 CXXXIX. Civitates Germaniae cis Rhenum et trans Rhenum positae oppugnantur a Druso, et tumultus, qu ob censum exortus in Gallia erat, componitur; ara dei[3] Caesaris ad confluentem Araris[4] et Rhodani dedicata, sacerdote creato C. Iulio Vercondaridubno Aeduo.

[1] *lacunam indicavit Hertz, Jahn.*
[2] privignis *Gronovius*: privigno MSS.
[3] ara dei *Rossbach*: ardi NPΠ.
[4] Araris *Ascensius*: maris NPΠR.

---

[1] January, 27 B.C. was the time when Augustus offered to retire and received these honours; Livy appended the account of the settlement directly to the account of the civil wars. Cf. *Res Gestae* 34; *C.I.L.* I²., p. 231; Ovid, *Fasti* I. 589 f.; Dio LIII. iii–xvi; Macrobius, *Saturnalia* I. xii. 35.

[2] April 27 B.C. Cf. Dio LIII. xxii. 5.

[3] 29 BC.. Crassus, the son of the triumvir, had been consul in the first half of 30, cf. Dio LI. iv. 3, and for the campaign, Dio LI. xxiii–xxvii; Florus II. xxvi.

[4] 28 B.C. Cf. references for CXXXIV, note 3.

[5] 27–5 B.C. Cf. Dio LIII. xxv f.; Suetonius, *Augustus* xx, xxvi. 3, lxxxi.

honour.[1] When he held assizes at Narbo, a census was conducted of the three Gauls, which his father Caesar had conquered.[2] The book also describes the war waged against the Bastarnae and Moesians and other tribes by Marcus Crassus. . . .[3] B.C. 29–27

CXXXV. An account is given of the war waged by Marcus Crassus against the Thracians,[4] of that waged by Caesar against the Spaniards,[5] and of the final conquest of the Salassi, an Alpine tribe.[6] B.C. 28–25

The Summaries of Books CXXXVI and CXXXVII are missing.

CXXXVIII. The Raeti were overcome by Tiberius Nero and Drusus, the stepsons of Caesar.[7] Agrippa, Caesar's son-in-law, died.[8] Drusus conducted the census.[9] B.C. 15–13

CXXXIX. The states of Germany situated on the near and farther sides of the Rhine were attacked by Drusus, and the uprising that arose in Gaul over the census was settled.[10] An altar of the divine Caesar was dedicated at the confluence of the Arar and the Rhone, Gaius Julius Vercondaridubnus, an Aeduan, being appointed the priest. B.C. 12

[6] 25 B.C. Cf. Strabo IV. vi. 7 (205); Dio LIII. xxv. and fr. 79.

[7] 15 B.C. Cf. Horace, *Odes* IV. 4 and 14; Strabo VII. i. 5 (292); *Res Gestae* 26; Dio LIV. xxii; Velleius II. xcv; *C.I.L.* I²., pp. 244, 248, 323.

[8] March, 12 B.C. Cf. Dio LIV. xxviii; Velleius II. xcvi. 1; Pliny, *Natural History* VII. viii. 45 f.

[9] 13 B.C. This was a census of the three provinces of Gaul, of which Drusus was now the governor.

[10] 12 B.C. Cf. Dio LIV. xxxii. and *C.I.L.* XIII. 1668. ii. 35–38. The trouble over the census may have been occasioned by a Roman demand for financial ratings. The dedication of the altar of Caesar on August 1 (cf. Suetonius, *Claudius* ii, where the year is wrongly given), furnished an occasion for calling the Gauls together at Lyons and quieting them.

A.U.C. 741–743 CXL. Thraces domiti a L. Pisone,[1] item Cherusci Tencteri[2] Chauci aliaeque Germanorum trans Rhenum gentes subactae a Druso referuntur. Octavia soror Augusti defuncta, ante amisso filio Marcello; cuius monimenta sunt theatrum et porticus nomine eius dicata.

A.U.C. 743–744 CXLI. Bellum adversus transrhenanas gentes a Druso gestum refertur, in quo inter primores pugnaverunt Chumstinctus et Avectius tribuni ex civitate Nerviorum. Dalmatas et Pannonios Nero frater Drusi subegit. Pax cum Parthis facta est signis a rege eorum, quae sub Crasso et postea sub Antonio capta erant, redditis.

A.U.C. 745 CXLII. Bellum adversus Germanorum trans Rhenum civitates gestum a Druso refertur. Ipse ex fractura, equo super crus eius conlapso, XXX die, quam id acciderat, mortuus. Corpus a Nerone fratre, qui nuntio valetudinis evocatus raptim adcucurrerat, Romam pervectum et in

[1] L. Pisone *Sigonius*: caepione NPΠ.
[2] Cherusci Tencteri *Gronovius*: ce rusti cenchrei NP.

---

[1] 13–11 B.C. Cf. Dio LIV. xxxiv. 5–7; Velleius II. xcviii.
[2] 12 B.C. Cf. Dio LIV. xxxii. 2 f.; Suetonius, *Claudius* i. 2; Strabo VII. i. 3–4 (290 f.); Tacitus, *Germania* xxxiv; *Annals* II. viii.

CXL. The Thracians were subdued by Lucius Piso[1]; an account is also given of the subjugation by Drusus of the Cherusci, Tencteri, Chauci, and other German tribes across the Rhine.[2] Octavia the sister of Augustus died,[3] having previously lost her son Marcellus; he has memorials in the theatre and colonnade dedicated in his name.[4] B.C. 13–11

CXLI. An account is given of the war conducted by Drusus against the tribes across the Rhine, in which two of the most conspicuous fighters were Chumstinctus and Avectius, tribunes from the state of the Nervii.[5] Nero, Drusus' brother, subdued the Dalmatians and Pannonians.[6] Peace was made with the Parthians, on the restoration by their king of the standards captured from Crassus and later from Antony.[7] B.C. 11–10

CXLII. An account is given of the war waged by Drusus against the German states across the Rhine. Drusus himself died of a broken leg, sustained when his horse fell on it, on the thirtieth day after the accident. His body was conveyed to Rome by his brother Nero, who had arrived posthaste on news of his illness; burial B.C. 9

[3] 11 B.C. Cf. Suetonius, *Augustus* lxi, who sets the date a year or more later; Dio LIV. xxxv. 4. Marcellus' death occurred in 23 B.C. Cf. Vergil, *Aeneid* VI. 868–886; Propertius III. xviii; Dio LIII. xxx. 4–6.

[4] For the buildings, cf. *Res Gestae Divi Augusti* 21; Dio LIV. xxvi. 1; Pliny, *Natural History* VIII. xxv (65).

[5] 11–10 B.C. Cf. Dio LIV. xxxiii, xxxvi; Florus II. xxx. 23–25; Orosius VI. xxi. 15–17; and above, CXL, note 2.

[6] 11–10 B.C. Cf. *Res Gestae* 30; Dio LIV. xxxiv. 3, xxxvi. 3; LV. ii. 4.

[7] Since this occurred in 20 B.C., it is not clear why Livy mentioned it only at this point. Cf. *Res Gestae* 29; Dio LIV. viii. 1–3; Suetonius, *Tiberius* ix. 1; *Augustus* xxi. 3; Velleius II. xci. 1; Ovid, *Fasti* V. 579–94, *Tristia* II. 227 f.; Strabo XVI. i. 28 (748); Justinus XLII. v. 10 f.

A.U.C. 745 tumulo C. Iulii reconditum. Laudatus est a Caesare Augusto vitrico, et supremis eius plures honores dati. Clades Quinctilii Vari.[1]

Clades Quinctilii Vari II *solus.*

---

[1] 9 B.C. Cf. Dio LV. i–ii (penetration of Drusus to the Elbe); Strabo VII. i. 3 (291) and *C.I.L.* I²., p. 248, for his death; Valerius Maximus V. v. 3; Pliny, *Natural History* VII. xx (84); Suetonius, *Tiberius* vii. 3; Tacitus, *Annals* III.

was in the tomb of Gaius Julius. The eulogy was pronounced by Caesar Augustus, his stepfather, and many distinctions were conferred on him at his funeral.[1] Disaster to Quintilius Varus.[2] B.C. 9

v, for Tiberius and the funera procession; above references and Ovid, *Fasti* I. 597, *Tristia* IV. ii. 39, for burial and honours, which included an altar in Germany (Tacitus, *Annals* II. vii), a triumphal arch near Rome, statues, and a cenotaph in Mainz (Dio; Suetonius, *Claudius* i. 3).

[2] Cf. Obsequens 72 and the note; Velleius II. cxvii–cxx; the date was A.D. 9.

FRAGMENTS

FRAGMENTA OXYRHYNCHI REPERTA

1. f]amili

. . . .

. . . .

rom

A.U.C. 653 C. Marius] v c[os.

isme

cu]stodia

2. sullanis

m eum

enonre

LIBER LXXX]VIII [1]

A.U.C. 672 C. Mario Cn. Papirio co]ss.

Sulla cum] Samin[itibus ante portam Collinam debell]avit p[ulcherrimam

3. uir

4. st

[1] *Sic Rossbach ex imagine photographica: at Kenyon litteras in papyro dispicere negat.*

MINOR FRAGMENTS FROM OXYRHYNCHUS

1.

In the fifth consulship of Gaius Marius B.C .101

2. pertaining to Sulla

Book LXXXVIII [1]

In the consulship of Gaius Marius and Gaius Papirius, Sulla ended the war against the Samnites at the Colline Gate, (and stained a) most glorious (victory with utmost cruelty [2]). B.C. 82

3.

4.

[1] The existence of this numeral is not certain, see critica note.

[2] The words in parenthesis are Rossbach's conjecture for completing the sentence. Nothing can be made of the other lines of letters.

LIBRORUM DEPERDITORUM FRAGMENTA

Liber XII?

1. Servius ad Vergil. *Aen.* I. 456: Livius "ni Pyrrhus unicus pugnandi artifex, magisque in proelio quam bello bonus."

Liber XIII?

2. Servius ad Vergil. *Aen.* I. 476: Curribus falcatis usos esse maiores, et Livius et Sallustius docent.

3. Priscian XV, p. 69K: Livius in XIII, "Privato nos tenuissemus."

[Liber XIV]

4. *Cf. infra, fr.* 81.

FRAGMENTS

From Book XII?

1. Servius, note on *Aeneid* I. 456: Livy: " if Pyrrhus had not been a consummate master of tactics, but excellent in a battle rather than in a campaign."

References to the campaigns of Pyrrhus in Italy are found in *Summaries* XII and XIII. The Roman opinion that Pyrrhus was weak on strategy may have arisen from their natural inability to perceive that war with Rome was to Pyrrhus a side issue, an excuse for establishing suzerainty over " Great Greece "—south Italy and Sicily.

From Book XIII?

2. Servius, note on *Aeneid* I. 476: Both Livy and Sallust inform us that our ancestors used scythed chariots.

Archæological evidence for chariot fighting in Italy seems to be lacking, unless the use of a chariot as the general's vehicle in a triumph is such evidence. The war with Pyrrhus would provide a good loophole for the insertion of such a picturesque detail by some annalist, especially a Greek who knew his Xenophon.

3. Priscian XV, p. 69K: Livy in Book XIII: " We should have kept out of public life."

[From Book XIV]

4. See below, fr. 81.

Liber XVI ?

5. Servius ad Vergil. *Aen.* I. 343 : Sichaeus Sicharbas dictus est ; Belus, Didonis pater, Methres ; Carthago a Cartha, ut lectum est ; quod invenitur in historia Poenorum et in Livio.

6. Servius ad Vergil. *Aen.* I. 366 : Carthago est lingua Poenorum nova civitas, ut docet Livius.

7. Servius ad Vergil. *Aen.* I. 738 : Bitias classis Punicae fuit praefectus, ut docet Livius.

Liber XVII

8. Priscian XIV, p. 44K : " Pridie Nonas, Pridie Idus," Livius ab urbe condita XVII.

Liber XVIII

9. Charisius, p. 95K : Imberbi autem dicuntur, non imberbes. Sic enim et Varro de actionibus scenicis V, " imberbi iuvenes " ; sed et Cicero " imberbum perduxit," non imberbem, et Kalendis Ianuariis de

From Book XVI?

5. Servius, note on *Aeneid* I. 343: Sichaeus is called Sicharbal; Belus, the father of Dido, Methres; Carthage was named from Cartha, as the name is given. This information is found in the history of the Carthaginians, and in Livy.

For the name which Vergil changed, presumably for metrical reasons, to Sichaeus, cf. Justinus XVIII. 4. 5, who draws on Timaeus, cf. *F.H.G.* I. 197, fr. 23. The city after which Carthage is supposed to have been named (but see below, fr. 6) is called Cartha in Servius, *Aeneid* IV. 670, Carthada in Solinus xxvii. 10. *Summary* XVI mentions the founding of Carthage.

6. Servius, note on *Aeneid* I. 366: " Carthage " means " Newtown " in the Carthaginian language, as Livy informs us.

This is one ancient etymology confirmed by modern scholars.

7. Servius, note on *Aeneid* I. 738: Bitias was the admiral of the Carthaginian fleet, as Livy informs us.

From Book XVII

8. Priscian XIV, p. 44K: " The day before the Nones; the day before the Ides "—Livy, *From the Founding of the City*, Book XVII.

From Book XVIII

9. Charisius, p. 95K: Moreover, one speaks of " imberbi," not " imberbes." For so says not only Varro in the fifth book of his *On Theatrical Performances*: " imberbi iuvenes " (beardless youths); but Cicero as well says " imberbum perduxit " (he induced the beardless boy), not " imberbem," and in his speech of January first *On the Agrarian Law*, uses " imberba

lege agraria, "imberba iuventute." Titus Livius autem XVIII imberbes vulgariter.[1] Beda, *de orthographia*, p. 276K: Titus Livius autem "imberbis" singulariter. Anon. ap. Barth, *Adversaria* XXXVII. 14: Varro "imberbi iuvenes"; ita et Cicero; sed contra Titus Livius.

10. Valerius Maximus I. 8, ext. 19: Serpentis quoque a T. Livio curiose pariter ac facunde relatae fiat mentio. Is enim ait in Africa apud Bagradam flumen tantae magnitudinis anguem fuisse ut Atilii Reguli exercitum usu amnis prohiberet; multisque militibus ingenti ore correptis, compluribus caudae voluminibus elisis, cum telorum iactu perforari nequiret, ad ultimum ballistarum tormentis undique petitam silicum crebris et ponderosis verberibus procubuisse, omnibusque et cohortibus et legionibus ipsa Carthagine visam terribiliorem. Atque etiam cruore suo gurgitibus imbutis, corporisque iacentis pestifero afflatu vicina regione polluta, Romana inde summovisse castra. Dicit etiam beluae corium centum viginti pedum in urbem missum.

[1] *ita* N: licet libius inberbis vulgariter dixerit p: Historiarum XVIII *ed. prin.*: imberbis singulariter *Keil*: imberbes singulariter, imberbi vulgariter *Putsch.*

iuventute' (beardless young men). But Titus Livius in his eighteenth Book uses "imberbes" commonly. Beda, *On Orthography,* p. 276K: Titus Livius, however, uses "imberbis" in the singular. Unknown author, quoted by C. von Barth, *Adversaria,* XXXVII. 14: Varro uses "imberbi iuvenes," so does Cicero; but Titus Livius does the opposite.

The text of Charisius is somewhat uncertain, see the critical note, but the general, and somewhat minor, point that Livy treats *imberbis* as a third-declension word seems clear. No context is extant for Cicero's words from *de Lege Agraria* I. fr. 1.

10. Valerius Maximus, I. viii. ext. 19: Let me mention also the serpent described by Titus Livius no less exactly than eloquently. For Livy says that in Africa at the Bagradas River, there was a snake of such size that it kept the army of Atilius Regulus from using the river. It caught many of the soldiers in its huge jaws, and crushed large numbers of them in the coils of its tail. Hurled missiles could not penetrate its skin, but at last when it was attacked on all sides with missiles from the catapults, it succumbed to the continuous heavy blows of the stones. Both legions and auxiliary troops without exception regarded it as more to be feared than Carthage itself. Even after death the pools were stained with its blood, and the area round about was defiled with the poisonous stench of the exposed body, till it drove the Roman camp away from there. Livy also says that the monster's skin, measuring one hundred and twenty feet, was sent to Rome.

Liber XIX

11. Censorinus, *de Die Natali*, xvii. 10: Tertii ludi (saeculares) fuerunt, Antiate Livioque auctoribus, P. Claudio Pulchro C. Iunio Pullo consulibus.

12. Servius ad Vergil. *Aen.* VI. 198: Est in Livio quod, cum quidam cupidus belli gerendi a tribuno plebis arceretur ne iret, pullos iussit adferri. Qui cum missas non ederent fruges, irridens consul augurium ait, "Vel bibant"; et eos in Tiberim praecipitavit. Inde navibus victor revertens ad Africam in mari cum omnibus quos ducebat exstinctus est.

Liber XX

12a. Scholium in codicem Parisiensem Latinum 3858 = Krueger-Mommsen, *Hermes* IV. (1870) 371–6 = Mueller, fr. 12: Livius libro vicesimo: P. Cloelius [1] patricius primus adversus veterem morem intra septimum cognationis gradum duxit uxorem. Ob hoc M. Rutilius plebeius sponsam sibi praeripi novo exemplo nuptiarum dicens seditionem populi concitavit, adeo ut patres territi in Capitolium perfugerent.

[1] Cloelius *Krueger*: Celius MS.

FRAGMENTS

From Book XIX

11. Censorinus, *On the Birthday*, xvii. 10: The third Festival of the Age occurred, as (Valerius) Antias and Livy tell us, in the consulship of Publius Claudius Pulcher and Gaius Junius Pullus.

12. Servius, note on *Aeneid* VI. 198: The story is told in Livy that when a certain consul who was anxious to conduct a campaign was prevented from departing by a tribune of the commons, the consul ordered the chickens to be brought. When these failed to eat the grain scattered before them, the consul, mocking the omen, said, "Let them drink, then", and flung them into the Tiber. After that as he was triumphantly returning in his fleet to Africa he lost his life at sea, along with all his men.

The year was 249 B.C. *Summary* XIX identifies the omen-defying consul as the Claudius of this year, but makes his fate less directly a vindication of the omen. Cf. also XXII. xlii. 9; *Summary* XLIX, p. 31 and note 2; and especially Polybius I. xlix. 3–li. 12.

From Book XX

12a. Note in margin of Paris Latin MS. 3858: Livy in Book XX: Publius Cloelius, a patrician, was the first to go against the ancient custom by marrying a wife within the seventh degree of relationship. On this account, Marcus Rutilius, a plebeian, complained that his betrothed was taken from him by an unprecedented sort of marriage; he stirred up a riot of the people so severe that the senators in terror took refuge on the Capitol.

The rule of marriage here recorded forbade marriage between second cousins, or those more closely related. Nothing further is known about this incident.

12b. Servius ad Vergil. *Aeneid.* VI. 860 = Mueller, fr. 13: varie de hoc loco tractant commentatores, Numae legis immemores, cuius facit mentionem et Livius.

Liber XLIX

13. Censorinus, *de Die Natali*, xvii. 11: De quartorum ludorum (saecularium) anno triplex opinio est. Antias enim et Varro et Livius relatos esse prodiderunt L. Marcio Censorino M'. Manlio consulibus, post Romam conditam anno sexcentesimo quinto.

Liber LVI

14. Priscian XVIII, p. 344K: Livius LVI ab urbe condita: Q.[1] Pompeium morbum excusasse ferunt, ne cum interesset deditioni animos Numantinorum irritaret.

[1] Q. *Hertz*: Qui MS.

12b. Servius on Vergil, *Aeneid* VI. 860: Commentators advance various views on this line, forgetting the law of Numa, of which Livy also makes mention.

Servius quotes this law as decreeing that the first *spolia opima* (spoils taken by a Roman commander from an enemy commander) were to be dedicated to Jupiter Feretrius (as done by Romulus, cf. Livy I. x. 4–7), the second to Mars (as done by Cossus, cf. IV. xx. 5–11), and the third to Quirinus (as done by Marcellus). Since this law is not mentioned in the earlier passages, it must have appeared in the account of Marcellus' feat, cf. *Summary* XX.

From Book XLIX

13. Censorinus, *On the Birthday*, xvii. 11: As to the fourth Festival of the Age, three opinions are held. For (Valerius) Antias, Varro, and Livy have stated that the festival was revived in the consulship of Lucius Marcius Censorinus and Manius Manlius, in the six hundred and fifth year after the founding of Rome.

Cf. *Summaries* XLIX, pp. 23 and 31, and the note, p. 31, note 2, on variations in the reckoning as to the founding of Rome. The year was 149 B.C.

From Book LVI

14. Priscian XVIII, p. 344K: Livy, *From the Founding of the City*, Book LVI: "They relate that Quintus Pompeius made illness his excuse, so that he might not inflame the spirits of the Numantines by being present at the surrender."

This evidently was the Pompeius who had made a treaty with the Numantines that was repudiated by Rome, cf. *Summary* LIV. He returned to Spain as *legatus* in 136 B.C.; cf. Valerius Maximus III. vii. 5.

Liber LXXVII

15. Plutarch, *Sulla* vi: Καὶ παρελθὼν εἰς τὴν πόλιν ὕπατος μὲν ἀποδείκνυται μετὰ Κοΐντου Πομπηΐου, πεντήκοντα ἔτη γεγονώς, γαμεῖ δὲ γάμον ἐνδοξότατον Καικιλίαν τὴν Μετέλλου θυγατέρα τοῦ ἀρχιερέως· Ἐφ' ᾧ πολλὰ μὲν εἰς αὐτὸν ᾖδον οἱ δημοτικοί, πολλοὶ δὲ τῶν πρώτων ἐνεμέσων, οὐκ ἄξιον ἡγούμενοι τῆς γυναικὸς ὃν ἄξιον ὑπατείας ἔκριναν, ὥς φησιν ὁ Τίτος.

15a. Suidas, *s.v.* Σύλλας: ὅτι ἐπὶ Σύλλα τοῦ ὑπάτου ὁ ἐμφύλιος Ῥωμαίων ἀνήφθη πόλεμος. ἐπισημῆναι δὲ τὴν τῶν μελλόντων κακῶν φορὰν Λίβιός φησι καὶ Διόδωρος. ἐξ ἀνεφέλου τοῦ ἀέρος καὶ αἰθρίας πολλῆς ἦχον ἀκουσθῆναι σάλπιγγος ὀξὺν ἀποτεινούσης καὶ θρηνώδη φθόγγον. καὶ τοὺς μὲν ἀκούσαντας ἅπαντας ἔκφρονας ὑπὸ δέους γενέσθαι, τοὺς δὲ Τυρρηνῶν μάντεις μεταβολὴν τοῦ γένους καὶ μετακόσμησιν ἀποφήνασθαι σημαίνειν τὸ τέρας. εἶναι μὲν γὰρ ἀνθρώπων η' γένη, διαφέροντα τοῖς βίοις καὶ τοῖς ἤθεσιν ἀλλήλων· ἑκάστῳ δὲ ἀφωρίσθαι χρόνον ὑπὸ τοῦ θεοῦ, συμπεραινόμενον ἐνιαυτοῦ μεγάλου περιόδῳ. τῆς γοῦν προτέρας περιόδου τελευτώσης καὶ ἑτέρας ἐνισταμένης κινεῖσθαί τι σημεῖον ἐκ γῆς ἢ οὐρανοῦ θαυμάσιον,' ᾧ δῆλον εὐθὺς τοῖς τὰ τοιαῦτα σοφοῖς γίνεσθαι ὅτι καὶ

FRAGMENTS

From Book LXXVII

15. Plutarch, *Sulla* vi: When he (Sulla) entered the city, he was declared consul together with Quintus Pompeius, Sulla being at the age of fifty, and he made a very distinguished marriage with Caecilia, the daughter of Metellus, the chief pontiff. On account of this, the popular party composed many lampoons against him, and many of the leading citizens were indignant, considering that the man whom they had judged worthy of the consulship was not worthy of the lady, as Titus puts it.

88 B.C.; this was Sulla's fourth marriage, and he divorced Cloelia to make it possible, which may have had something to do with the objections felt by some senators; Caecilia Metella now married for the second time.

15a. Suidas, article "Sulla": In Sulla's consulship, the Roman civil war broke out. Livy and Diodorus say that there were portents of the harvest of evils to come. From cloudless air and a wide expanse of clear sky, the blast of a trumpet was heard, uttering a shrill and lamentable sound. Those who heard it were one and all beside themselves with fear. But the Etruscan soothsayers pronounced that the portent indicated a change of the race and a new era. For, they said, there are eight races of men, differing in their modes of life and their characters from each other. An epoch has been assigned to each race by God, ending with the completion of a cycle of the Great Year. At any rate, as the former cycle ends and another sets in, some miraculous sign from earth or heaven is sent forth, from which it becomes clear to those expert in these matters that men have been τρόποις ἄλλοις καὶ βίοις ἄνθρωποι χρώμενοι γεγόνασι, καὶ θεοῖς ἧττον τῶν προτέρων μέλονται.

16. Augustine, *de Civitate Dei* II. xxiv: Sulla cum primum ad urbem contra Marium castra movisset, adeo laeta exta immolanti fuisse scribit Livius, ut custodiri se Postumius haruspex voluerit, capitis supplicium subiturus nisi ea quae in animo Sulla haberet diis iuvantibus implevisset.

Liber LXXXIII

17. Augustine, *de Civitate Dei* III. vii: Eversis quippe et incensis omnibus cum oppido simulacris solum Minervae simulacrum sub tanta ruina templi illius, ut scribit Livius, integrum stetisse perhibetur.

Liber XCI

18. *Fragmentum ex codice Vaticano*: Nocte[1] tamen insequenti ipso pervigilante in eodem loco alia excitata turris prima luce miraculo hostibus fuit.

[1] Nocte *add.* *Iuvenatius*: *om.* MS.

born whose ways and manner of life are different, and for whom the gods care less than for the former race.

The whole passage is given as a quotation from the authors cited. It occurs almost word for word in Plutarch's *Sulla* vii. 3–4, but Plutarch allows for a change to a more godly race, as well as the Hesiodic deterioration which stands alone in Suidas. In accordance with Boissevain, Cassius Dio, I, p. cxxi, I do not regard this passage as a fragment of Dio, as Hertz places it.

16. Augustine, *City of God* II. xxiv: When Sulla had first advanced toward Rome against Marius, the entrails as he sacrificed portended such good fortune, so Livy writes, that Postumius the soothsayer offered himself as a prisoner doomed to suffer death if Sulla, with the aid of the gods, did not wholly accomplish what he purposed.

Cf. Plutarch, *Sulla* ix. 3. *Summary* LXXVII includes Sulla's march, but not this incident.

From Book LXXXIII

17. Augustine *City of God,* III. vii: For, if you please, when all the idols were overthrown and burned along with the city, the image of Minerva alone is said to have stood intact amid the utter destruction of her temple, so Livy writes.

The reference is to the sack of Troy by Fimbria, cf. *Summary* LXXXIII; Obsequens 56b.

From Book XCI

18. *A fragment from a Vatican MS*: However, during the following night, while Sertorius himself kept watch, another tower was erected on the same spot, and at dawn struck the enemy with wonder.

Simul et oppidi turris quae maximum propugnaculum fuerat, subrutis fundamentis, dehiscere ingentibus rimis et tum conflagrare immisso facium [1] igni coepit; incendiique simul et ruinae metu territi Contrebienses de muro trepidi refugerunt; et ut legati mitterentur ad dedendam urbem ab universa multitudine conclamatum est. Eadem virtus quae irritantes oppugnaverat victorem placabiliorem fecit. Obsidibus acceptis pecuniae modicam exegit summam armaque omnia ademit. Transfugas liberos vivos ad se adduci iussit; fugitivos, quorum maior multitudo erat, ipsis imperavit ut interficerent. Iugulatos de muro deiecerunt.

Cum magna iactura militum quattuor et quadraginta diebus Contrebia expugnata, relictoque ibi L. Insteio cum valido praesidio,[2] ipse ad Hiberum flumen copias adduxit. Ibi hibernaculis secundum oppidum quod Castra Aelia vocatur aedificatis ipse in castris manebat; interdiu conventum sociarum civitatium in oppido agebat. Arma ut fierent pro copiis cuiusque populi per totam provinciam edixerat; quibus inspectis referre cetera arma milites iussit, quae aut itineribus crebris aut oppugnationibus et proeliis inutilia [3] facta erant, novaque viris per centuriones divisit. Equitatum quoque novis instruxit armis, vestimentaque praeparata ante divisa, et

[1] tum conflagrare immisso facium *post alios Weissenborn* tu . . . o . . . um MS: tugurium conflagrare correptum *Niebuhr*.

[2] cum valido (*sive* modico) praesidio *add. Kreyssig* : *om.* MS.

[3] et proeliis inutilia *add. Niebuhr* : *om.* MS.

At the same time, the tower which was the city's chief bulwark began to gape with great cracks as its foundations were undermined, and then was set on fire as blazing torches were thrown in. Terror-stricken by the threat of fire and collapse together, the people of Contrebia in panic fled back from the wall, and the whole crowd set up a shout that envoys should be sent to surrender the city. That same valour which had caused them to attack those who challenged them made the conqueror the readier to give terms. When he had received hostages, he exacted a moderate sum of money, and deprived them of all their weapons. He ordered the free deserters to be brought to him alive; the runaway slaves, whose number was far greater, he ordered the townspeople themselves to kill. The slaves' throats were cut, and they were thrown from the wall.

Contrebia was reduced after forty-four days with a large loss of soldiers. Sertorius left Lucius Insteius in the town with a strong garrison, and led his own force to the Ebro River. There he constructed winter quarters by the town called Camp Aelia, and remained there with his forces; by day he held a conference in the town of the cities allied with him. He issued an order that throughout the province arms should be manufactured according to the capacities of the several peoples. After he had inspected the new weapons, he ordered his soldiers to turn in the arms they had which had become unserviceable either because of the frequent marches or because of sieges and battles. He distributed the new weapons to his men through their centurions, equipped his cavalry also with new arms, distributed clothing which had been previously prepared, and issued pay.

stipendium datum. Fabros cura conquisitos undique exciverat quibus officina publica instituta uteretur,[1] ratione inita quid in singulos dies effici possit. Itaque omnia simul instrumenta belli parabantur; neque materia artificibus praeparatis ante omnibus enixo civitatium studio,[2] nec suo quisque operi artifex deerat.

Convocatis deinde omnium populorum legationibus et civitatium, gratias egit quod quae imperata essent in pedestres copias praestitissent[3]; quas ipse res in defendendis sociis,[4] quasque in oppugnandis urbibus hostium gessisset exposuit et ad reliqua belli cohortatus est paucis edoctos quantum Hispaniae provinciae interesset suos partes superiores esse. Dimisso deinde conventu, iussisque omnibus bono animo esse atque in civitates redire[5] suas, principio veris M. Perpernam cum viginti milibus peditum, equitibus mille quingentis, in Ilercaonum gentem misit ad tuendam regionis eius maritimam oram, datis praeceptis quibus itineribus duceret ad defendendas socias urbes, quas Pompeius oppugnaret, quibusque ipsum agmen Pompei ex insidiis adgrederetur.

Eodem tempore et ad Herennuleium, qui in isdem locis erat, litteras misit et in alteram provinciam ad L. Hirtuleium, praecipiens quem ad modum bellum

[1] instituta uteretur *add. edd.*: *om.* MS.
[2] enixo civitatium studio *Niebuhr*: nixo . . . undio MS.
[3] in pedestres copias praestitissent *Niebuhr*: . ede . . res . . . sti . . . MS.
[4] in defendendis sociis *add. Niebuhr*: *om.* MS.
[5] bono animo esse atque . . redire *add. Niebuhr*: *om.* MS.

He diligently searched out smiths from all about, and brought them in for the service of the military workshop which he had set up, after drawing up a schedule of what could be produced day by day. And so all the sinews of war were being made ready at the same time; there was no lack of materials for the artisans who were supplied first of all by the strenuous zeal of the cities, nor was any sort of artisan lacking for his peculiar task.

He then called together embassies from all the tribes and cities, and presented his thanks because they had furnished the supplies for the infantry forces which had been demanded. He laid before them his achievements in defending his allies and in storming cities of his enemies, and encouraged them to continue in the war after a brief explanation of the advantages to the province of Spain if his side had the upper hand. He thereupon dismissed the gathering, bidding them all be of good cheer and return to their states.

As spring opened he sent Marcus Perperna with twenty thousand infantry and fifteen hundred cavalry to the tribe of Ilercaones to defend the seacoast of that region; he gave Perperna instructions as to the routes he was to use in coming to the rescue of allied cities which Pompey would attack, as well as those routes from which he was to attack Pompey's own column from ambush.

At the same time he also sent dispatches to Herennuleius,[1] who was in the same region, as well as to Lucius Hirtuleius in the other province, instructing

[1] The name is usually given as Herennius, cf. Plutarch, *Pompey* xviii. 3 and Sallust, *History* II. xcviii. 6, and has presumably been corrupted here by " Hirtuleius " below.

administrari vellet; ante omnia ut ita socias civitates tueretur, ne acie cum Metello dimicaret, cui nec auctoritate nec viribus par esset. Ne ipsi quidem consilium esse ducere adversus[1] Pompeium; neque in aciem descensurum eum credebat. Si traheretur bellum, hosti cum mare ab tergo, provinciasque omnes in potestate haberet, navibus undique commeatus venturos; ipsi autem, consumptis priore aestate quae praeparata fuissent, omnium rerum inopiam fore. Perpernam in maritimam regionem superpositum ut ea quae integra adhuc ab hoste sint, tueri posset et si qua occasio detur, incautos per tempus adgressurum.

Ipse cum suo exercitu in Berones et Autricones progredi statuit, a quibus saepe per hiemem, cum ab se oppugnarentur Celtiberae urbes, imploratam esse opem Pompei compererat missosque qui itinera exercitui Romano monstrarent; et ipsorum equitibus vexatos saepe milites suos, quocumque a castris per oppugnationem Contrebiae pabulandi aut frumentandi causa progrederentur.[2] Ausi tum quoque erant Arevacos in partes sollicitare.[3] Edito igitur exemplo[4] belli consilium se initurum utrum prius hostem, utram provinciam petat,[5] maritimamne oram ut Pompeium ab Ilercaonia et Contestania arceat,

[1] adversus *Niebuhr* : . . versus MS.
[2] progrederentur *add. Niebuhr* : *om.* MS.
[3] sollicitare *add. Niebuhr* : *om.* MS.
[4] igitur exemplo *add. Niebuhr* : *om.* MS.
[5] petat *add. Niebuhr* : *om.* MS.

them how he wanted the war to be managed, especially that Hirtuleius was to protect the allied cities in such a way as not to meet Metellus in battle, since he was no match for Metellus either in personal prestige or in military power. Sertorius said that he had no intention of meeting Pompey head on, nor did he believe that Pompey would offer battle. If the war were prolonged, the enemy would receive provisions by ship from all directions, since he had the sea at his back and all the provinces under his control. Sertorius, on the other hand, having used up during the previous summer the accumulation of supplies, would lack everything. Perperna, said Sertorius, had been given command in the seaward region so that he might be able to protect whatever was so far undamaged by the enemy, and might attack them when they were momentarily off their guard, if some opportunity presented itself.

Sertorius himself with his own forces decided to march against the Berones and Autricones, who had, as he had learned, frequently begged aid from Pompey during the winter, while Sertorius was assailing the Celtiberian cities. Moreover, these peoples had sent men to show the Roman army the roads, and with their cavalry had often harassed Sertorius' soldiers whenever during the siege of Contrebia they had gone out from camp to gather fodder or grain. At that time also these tribes had had the audacity to invite the Arevaci to change sides. He thought therefore that he would furnish a sample of his campaigning before deciding which enemy and which province to make for, and whether to turn to the sea coast, in order to keep Pompey away from Ilercaonia and Contestania, both of which tribes were Sertorius' utraque socia gente, an ad Metellum et Lusitaniam se convertat.

Haec secum agitans Sertorius praeter Hiberum amnem per pacatos agros quietum exercitum sine ullius noxa duxit. Profectus inde in Bursaonum et Cascantinorum[1] et Graccuritanorum fines, evastatis omnibus proculcatisque segetibus, ad Calagurim Nasicam, sociorum urbem, venit; transgressusque amnem propinquum urbi ponte facto castra posuit. Postero die M. Marium quaestorem in Arevacos et Cerindones misit ad conscribendos ex iis gentibus milites, frumentumque inde Contrebiam, quae[2] Leucada appellatur, comportandum, praeter quam urbem opportunissimus ex Beronibus transitus erat, in quamcumque regionem ducere exercitum statuisset; et C. Insteium, praefectum equitum, Segoviam et in Vaccaeorum gentem ad equitum conquisitionem misit, iussum cum equitibus Contrebiae sese opperiri. Dimissis iis ipse profectus, per Vasconum agrum ducto exercitu, in confinio Beronum posuit castra. Postero die cum equitibus praegressus ad itinera exploranda, iusso pedite quadrato agmine sequi, ad Vareiam, validissimam regionis eius urbem, venit. Haud inopinantibus iis noctu advenerat. Undique equitibus et suae gentis et Autriconum.[3] . . .

[1] Cascantinorum *Iuvenatius* : Casuantinorum MS.
[2] quae *add. Niebuhr* : *om.* MS.
[3] Autriconum *edd.*: Autric . . . MS.

allies, or whether to turn against Metellus and Lusitania.

With these thoughts in mind, Sertorius led his army up the Ebro River through friendly territory in a peaceful and harmless fashion. He then advanced into the territory of the Bursaones, Cascantium, and Graccuris, ravaging everything and trampling the crops, and arrived at Calaguris Nasica, a town of his allies. He crossed the river near the city on a bridge which he had built and pitched camp. Next day he sent his quaestor Marcus Marius to the Arevaci and Cerindones to enroll soldiers from among those tribes, and to transport grain from there to the Contrebia which is called Leucada, past which city there was the most convenient passage out from the Berones, no matter to which region he might decide to lead his forces. He also sent Gaius Insteius, his cavalry commander, to Segovia and among the tribe of the Vaccaei to recruit cavalry, giving him orders to await him with the cavalry in Contrebia. After these officers had been sent off, Sertorius himself set out, led his army through the territory of the Vascones, and pitched camp on the border of the Berones. The next day he went in advance with cavalry to reconnoitre the roads, and ordered the infantry to follow in squared column; he reached Vareia, the strongest city of that region. His arrival by night was by no means unexpected by the Berones. From all about, cavalry both of their own tribe and of the Autricones . . .

The events described in this fragment took place in 77 and 76 B.C. Calaguris Nasica, the more westerly of the two towns named Calaguris, is mentioned in XXXIX. xxi. 8 and *Summary* XCIII. Sertorius' spring campaign was planned to eliminate

19. Frontinus, *Strategemata* II. v. 31: Hoc primum proelium inter Sertorium et Pompeium fuit. Decem milia hominum de Pompeii exercitu amissa et omnia impedimenta, Livius auctor est.

19a. Asconius in Cicero. *pro Cornelio* lix f. Clark = fr. 23 Mueller: Neque apud Sallustium neque apud Livium neque apud Fenestellam ullius alterius latae ab eo (C. Cotta) legis est mentio, praeter eam quam in consulatu tulit invita nobilitate, magno populi studio, ut iis qui tribuni plebis fuissent, alios quoque magistratus capere liceret.

Liber XCIV

20. Servius ad Vergil. *Aen.* IX. 715: Livius in libro nonagesimo quarto Inarimen in Maeoniae partibus esse dicit, ubi per quinquaginta millia terrae igni exustae sunt. Hoc etiam Homerum significasse vult.

the threat from disaffected tribes sandwiched in among his allies, and so to establish a solid base area in north central Spain. He moved westerly, near the north boundary of this area at the Pyrenees, and sent his officers to the south-west. Cf. *Summary* XCI.

19. Frontinus, *Stratagems* II. v. 31: This was the first battle between Sertorius and Pompey. Ten thousand persons and all the baggage were lost by Pompey's army, as Livy informs us.

19a. Asconius, note on Cicero, *pro Cornelio*: There is no reference, either in Sallust or in Livy or in Fenestella, to any law passed by him (Gaius Cotta) other than the one which he passed in his consulship over the opposition of the office-holding class, but with the eager support of the people, to the effect that those who had been tribunes of the commons should be allowed to hold other magistracies too.

This occurred in 75 B.C., and was Cotta's measure of conciliation to prevent further rioting over a scarcity of grain.

From Book XCIV

20. Servius, note on *Aeneid* IX. 715: In his ninety-fourth book, Livy says that Inarime is in a portion of Maeonia, where for fifty miles the countryside is scorched with fire. Livy's opinion is that Homer also meant this region.

Maeonia, synonymous with Lydia to the poets, meant north-east Lydia to the geographers, cf. Ptolemy V. ii. 16. In this area, along the Hermus River, Strabo (XIII. iv. 5 (626)) speaks of a region called Catacecaumene ("destroyed by fire") which is no doubt the volcanic area Livy had in mind. The reference had some connection with the campaigns of Lucullus against Mithridates.

The ancient error by which Homer's *ein Arimois, Iliad* II. 783, (among the Arimi) became "Inarime" is well known. Vergil's Inarime was in the volcanic area near Naples.

Liber XCVII

21. Frontinus, *Strategemata* II. v. 34 : Triginta quinque milia armatorum (fugitivorum a Crasso devictorum) eo proelio interfecta cum ipsis ducibus (Casto et Gannico) Livius tradit, receptas quinque Romanorum aquilas, signa sex et viginti, multa spolia inter quae fasces cum securibus.

Liber XCVIII

22. Plutarch, *Lucullus* xxviii. 7 : Λιούϊος δ' εἴρηκεν, ὡς οὐδέποτε Ῥωμαῖοι πολεμίοις ἀποδέοντες τοσούτῳ πλήθει παρετάξαντο· σχεδὸν γὰρ οὐδ' εἰκοστὸν ἀλλ' ἔλαττον ἐγένοντο μέρος οἱ νικῶντες τῶν ἡσσημένων.

23. Plutarch, *Lucullus* xxxi. 8 : Φησὶ δὲ ὁ Λιούϊος ἐν μὲν τῇ προτέρα μάχῃ πλείονας, ἐν δὲ ταύτῃ γνωριμωτέρους πεσεῖν καὶ ληφθῆναι τῶν πολεμίων.

Liber XCIX

24. Servius, *ad Vergil. Aen.* III. 106 : Creta primo quidem centum habuit civitates, unde Hecatompolis

From Book XCVII

21. Frontinus, *Stratagems* II. v. 34: Livy relates that thirty-five thousand armed men (of the escaped slaves conquered by Crassus) were killed in that battle along with their commanders (Castus and Gannicus). Five Roman eagles were recovered and twenty-six military standards, and much booty, among which were *fasces* with axes.

This victory of Crassus is mentioned in *Summary* XCVII.

From Book XCVIII

22. Plutarch, *Lucullus* xxviii. 7: Livy, moreover, has said that the Romans never entered a battle against foes so overwhelmingly superior in numbers; for, at a rough estimate, the victors were not even the twentieth part of the conquered, but rather less.

This refers to the battle for the relief of Tigranocerta, October 6, 69 B.C. The calculation of numbers may involve crediting the enemy with the total combined forces of Tigranes and Mithridates, though the latter was not present.

23. Plutarch, *Lucullus* xxxi. 8: Livy says that in the former battle greater numbers of the enemy fell and were captured, but in this battle, higher-ranking persons.

The second battle was in 68 B.C., on the Arsanias River, as Lucullus was making for Artaxata. Cf. Dio XXXVI. v. f.

From Book XCIX

24. Servius, note on *Aeneid* III. 106: In early times, indeed, Crete had a hundred city-states; on this account it was called Hecatompolis (a hundred cities).

dicta est; post viginti quattuor; inde, ut dicitur, duas, Gnosson et Hierapytnam, quamvis Livius plures a Metello expugnatas dicat.

Liber CII

25. Agroecius, *Ars de Orthographia*, p. 115K: Livius de morte Mithridatis: "quod cum diluisset."

26. Josephus, *Antiquities of the Jews* XIV. iv. 3: Καὶ γὰρ ἁλούσης τῆς πόλεως περὶ τρίτον μῆνα, τῇ τῆς νηστείας ἡμέρᾳ, κατὰ τὴν ἐννάτην καὶ ἑβδομηκοστὴν καὶ ἑκατοστὴν ὀλυμπιάδα ὑπατευόντων Γαΐου Ἀντωνίου καὶ Μάρκου Τουλλίου Κικέρωνος οἱ πολέμιοι μὲν εἰσπεσόντες ἔσφαττον τοὺς ἐν τῷ ἱερῷ, οἱ δὲ πρὸς ταῖς θυσίαις οὐδὲν ἧττον ἱερουργοῦντες διετέλουν, οὔτε ὑπὸ τοῦ φόβου τοῦ περὶ τῆς ψυχῆς, οὔτε ὑπὸ τοῦ πλήθους τῶν ἤδη φονευομένων ἀναγκασθέντες ἀποδρᾶναι, πᾶν δ' ὅτι δέοι παθεῖν τοῦτο παρ' αὐτοῖς ὑπομεῖναι τοῖς βωμοῖς κρεῖττον εἶναι νομίζοντες ἢ παρελθεῖν τι τῶν νομίμων, ὅτι δὲ οὐ λόγος ταῦτα μόνον ἐστὶν ἐγκώμιον ψευδοῦς εὐσεβείας ἐμφανίζων ἀλλ' ἀλήθεια, μαρτυροῦσι πάντες οἱ τὰς κατὰ Πομπήϊον πράξεις ἀναγράψαντες· ἐν οἷς καὶ Στράβων καὶ Νικόλαος καὶ πρὸς τούτοις Τίτος Λίβιος, ὁ τῆς Ῥωμαικῆς ἱστορίας συγγραφεύς.

Later, it had twenty-four, and later still, only two, Cnossus and Hierapytna, so we are told, although Livy says that Metellus stormed a larger number.

Some Roman lack of information, or a hyperbole, must be behind the alleged reduction of Cretan cities to two; references to a larger number are reasonably continuous.

From Book CII

25. Agroecius, *Skill in Spelling*, p. 115K: Livy on the death of Mithridates, "When he had washed this out."

26. Josephus, *Antiquities of the Jews* XIV. iv. 3: For when the city was taken during the third month, on the day of the fast, in the 179th Olympiad and the consulship of Gaius Antonius and Marcus Tullius Cicero, the enemy on breaking in went to cutting the throats of those in the temple. But those in charge of the sacrifices none the less continued their sacred service, and were not compelled to run away either by fear for their lives or by the multitude of those who were already being slaughtered. They deemed it better to await whatever suffering they must endure by the very altars, rather than to transgress any point of the law. That this is no mere story, parading praise of a fictitious piety, but rather the truth, is supported by the testimony of all who have recorded the achievements of Pompey. Among these are Strabo and Nicolaüs, and in addition Titus Livius, the author of the history of Rome.

The capture of Jerusalem is mentioned in *Summary* CII, together with the Catilinarian conspiracy. There is a brief allusion in Strabo XVI. ii. 40 (762). The "fast" was probably the sabbath, as interpreted by some Gentile, cf. Marcus *ad loc.* VII. 480 and 700–1. (L.C.L.).

26a. Scholium Bernense in Lucan. *Pharsalia* II. 593: Livius de Iudaeis: "Hierosolymis fanum cuius deorum sit non nominant, neque ullum ibi simulacrum est, neque enim esse dei figuram putant."

Liber CIII

27. Q. Serenus, *de Medicina* xxxix. 725–32:

Horrendus magis est, perimit qui corpora, carbo.
Urit hic inclusus, vitalia rumpit apertus;
Hunc veteres quondam variis pepulere medelis.
Tertia namque Titi simul et centesima Livi
Charta docet, ferro talem candente dolorem
Exsectum, aut poto raporum semine pulsum,
Infecti dicens vix septem posse diebus
Vitam produci, tanta est violentia morbi.

[Liber CIV]

28. *Cf. infra, fr.* 82.

Liber CV

29. Tacitus, *Agricola* x: Formam totius Britanniae Livius veterum, Fabius Rusticus recentium, eloquentissimi auctores, oblongae scutulae vel bipenni assimulavere.

30. Iordanes, *de Rebus Geticis* ii: Britanniae licet

26a. Note on Lucan, *Pharsalia* II. 593 (Usener, 85): Livy on the Jews: "As to the temple at Jerusalem, they do not say to which of the gods it belongs, nor is there any image there; for they believe that there is no such thing as a bodily form of a god."

From Book CIII

27. Quintus Serenus, *On Medicine* xxxix. 725–32: More to be dreaded is that which destroys bodies—the malignant tumour. This burns when enclosed, and when open, snaps the thread of life. This the ancients aforetime repulsed with various remedies. For the one hundred and third book of Titus Livy shows that this great misery has been cut out with the hot knife, or repelled by a draught of turnip seed; the book says that it is hardly possible to prolong life for seven days, once the victim is attacked, such is the violence of the disease.

The Serenus of this treatise is often identified with the younger Serenus Sammonicus, who lived about 200 A.D., was noted as a poet, and was interested in medicine, but the identification is not certain. Cf. also fr. 88.

[From Book CIV]

28. See below, fr. 82.

From Book CV

29. Tacitus, *Agricola* x: The shape of Britain as a whole has been compared to an oblong shield or a double-axe by Livy in earlier times, and by Fabius Rusticus more recently—both most eloquent authors.

30. Iordanes, *History of the Goths* ii: Although no one

magnitudinem olim nemo, ut refert Livius, circumvectus est, multis tamen data est varia opinio de ea loquendi.

Liber CIX

31. Orosius VII. 2: Septingentesimo condicionis suae anno quattuordecim vicos eius (Romae) incertum unde consurgens flamma consumpsit, nec umquam, ut ait Livius, maiore incendio vastata est, adeo ut post aliquot annos Caesar Augustus ad reparationem eorum quae tunc exusta erant magnam vim pecuniae ex aerario publico largitus sit.

32. Orosius VI. 15: Caesar Rubicone flumine transmeato mox ut Ariminum venit, quinque cohortes, quas tunc solas habebat, cum quibus, ut ait Livius, orbem terrarum adortus est, quid facto opus esset edocuit.

32a. Scholium Bernense in Lucan. *Pharsalia* III. 182: Livius in primo libro belli civilis ait: "nam Athenienses de tanta maritima gloria vix duas naves effecere."

32b. Scholium Bernense in Lucan. *Pharsalia* III. 59: Ut ait Livius, Marcum Catonem expulit provincia.

in early times, as Livy says, sailed around the whole extent of Britain, that did not prevent many people from delivering different opinions on the subject.

The author's name also appears as Iornandes in the MSS. *Summary* CV ends with mention of Caesar's campaign in Britain.

From Book CIX

31. Orosius VII. 2: In the seven-hundredth year of its existence, Rome had fourteen of its streets devastated by a fire of unknown origin, nor was it ever ravaged by a greater blaze, so Livy says. As a result, Caesar Augustus several years later donated a large sum of money from the public treasury to the rebuilding of the structures consumed at that time.

32. Orosius VI. 15: When Caesar had crossed the Rubicon, he presently came to Ariminum, and there explained his plan of action to the five cohorts which were all that he had at that time—with which, as Livy puts it, he assailed the whole world.

Cf. Caesar, *Civil War* I. vii f.; Caesar's force is usually referred to as one legion; whether the "five cohorts" is an estimate of actual strength present, or a piece of rhetoric without military foundation does not appear, but cf. *Civil War* I. xi. 4. William of Malmesbury, *Historia Novella* II § 478 Stubbs, follows Orosius.

32a. Note on Lucan, *Pharsalia* III. 182 (Usener, 100): In the first book on the civil war, Livy says: "for the Athenians barely mustered two ships as relics of their great reputation for sea-power."

32b. Note on Lucan, *Pharsalia* III. 59 (Usener, 92): As Livy says, he drove Marcus Cato from the province.

The reference is to Curio, cf. Caesar, *Civil War* I. xxx. 5; Plutarch, *Cato* liii; Appian, *Civil Wars* II. vi. 40 f.

Liber CX?

32c. Scholium Bernense in Lucan. *Pharsalia* IV. 354: Livius: "et duces sumus in bello inutiles,[1] per quos tibi licuit sine sanguine vincere. Quod Caesari pulcrum est, petimus: quibus armatis pepercisti, deditis consulas."

32d. Scholium Bernense in Lucan. *Pharsalia* V. 494: Livius de hoc: "veniant si modo mei sunt."

Liber CXI

33. Scholium ad Lucan. *Pharsalia* VII. 471: Ut ait Titus Livius, "Primus hostem percussit nuper pilo sumpto primo C. Crastinus."

33a. Scholium Bernense ad Lucan. *Pharsalia* VII. 470 (ed. Usener, p. 270):

De quo Titus Livius dixit tunc fuisse evocatum, proximo anno deduxisse primum pilum Gaium Crastinum qui a parte Caesaris primus lanceam misit.

34. Plutarch, *Caesar* xlvii: Ἐν δὲ Παταβίῳ Γάϊος Κορνήλιος, ἀνὴρ εὐδόκιμος ἐπὶ μαντικῇ, Λιβίου τοῦ συγγραφέως πολίτης καὶ γνώριμος, ἐτύγχανεν ἐπ' οἰωνοῖς καθήμενος ἐκείνην τὴν ἡμέραν. Καὶ πρῶτον μέν, ὡς Λίβιός φησι, τὸν καιρὸν ἔγνω τῆς μάχης,

[1] inutiles *H. J. Mueller*: milites MS: et duces ulli usui in bello milites *Usener*: ei denique fuimus in bello milites *Novák*.

---

[1] Apparently from a message of Caesar in Epirus to Antony in Italy, cf. Caesar, *Civil War* III. 25. 3.

From Book CX?

32c. Note on Lucan, *Pharsalia* IV. 354 (Usener, 132): Livy's words are: "and we are incompetent as commanders in war, since it is on our account that you were able to win without bloodshed. Our request redounds to Caesar's credit, for we ask that you make provision, after their surrender, for those whom you spared while they were still embattled."

This is presumably from a speech by Afranius at the final surrender in Spain, cf. Caesar, *Civil War* I. 72 and 84 f.

32d. Note on Lucan, *Pharsalia* V. 494 (Usener, 174): Livy's words on this subject are: "Let them come, if only they are my men."[1]

From Book CXI

33. Note on Lucan, *Pharsalia,* VII. 471: As Titus Livius says, "The first to strike the enemy was a man who had recently become a First Centurion, Gaius Crastinus."

33a. Note from a Berne MS. on Lucan, *Pharsalia* VII. 470: About him Titus Livius said that Gaius Crastinus, who was the first on Caesar's side to hurl a lance, was at that time a veteran recalled to service, and in the previous year had been First Centurion.

Cf. Caesar, *Civil War* III. xci, xcix. The second quotation clarifies the use of "recently" in the first.

34. Plutarch, *Caesar* xlvii: In Padua Gaius Cornelius, a man of high reputation for soothsaying, a fellow citizen and acquaintance of Livy the historian, happened to be watching the omens on that day. In the first place, as Livy tells, he recognized the

καὶ πρὸς τοὺς παρόντας εἶπεν, ὅτι καὶ δὴ περαίνεται τὸ χρῆμα, καὶ συνίασιν εἰς ἔργον οἱ ἄνδρες. Αὖθις δὲ πρὸς τῇ θέᾳ γενόμενος, καὶ τὰ σημεῖα κατιδὼν ἀνήλατο μετ' ἐνθουσιασμοῦ βοῶν, "Νικᾷς, ὦ Καῖσαρ." Ἐκπλαγέντων δὲ τῶν παρατυχόντων περιελὼν τὸν στέφανον ἀπὸ τῆς κεφαλῆς ἐνωμότως ἔφη, μὴ πρὶν ἐπιθήσεσθαι πάλιν ἢ τῇ τέχνῃ μαρτυρῆσαι τὸ ἔργον. Ταῦτα μὲν οὖν ὁ Λίβιος οὕτω γενέσθαι καταβεβαιοῦται.

34a. Scholium Bernense in Lucan. *Pharsalia* VII. 62: Titus Livius eum (Ciceronem) in Sicilia aegrum fuisse tradit eo tempore quo Pharsaliae pugnatum est et ibi eum accepisse litteras a victore Caesare, ut bono animo esset.

Liber CXII

35. Scholium in Cicero. *pro Ligario*, ed. Orelli-Baiter, p. 415: Interea, sicut dixit Livius, oppressus est Tubero et Pansa; fugerunt ad Pompeium cum quaererentur. Inter has moras supervenit Curio ad Africam.

36. *Cf. infra, fr.* 43a.

37. Priscian VI. 22, p. 213K: Inveni tamen apud Livium in CXII ab urbe condita in *d* desinens bar-

moment when the battle began, and said to the bystanders, " Now the affair is going forward, and the gentlemen are going into action." And later, turning to his observations and beholding the signs, he leaped up inspired, crying out, " Yours is the victory, Caesar." When the bystanders were dumbfounded, he removed the wreath from his head and said with an oath that he would not replace it until the fact bore witness to his art. These things Livy definitely affirms to have taken place in this manner.

This striking story also appears in Dio XLI. lxi. 5; Obsequens 65a; Gellius XV. xviii. 1–3.

34a. Note on Lucan, *Pharsalia* VII. 62 (Usener, 223): Titus Livius says that he (Cicero) was in Sicily, because of ill-health, at the time when the battle at Pharsalus took place, and that he received there a letter from the victorious Caesar, bidding him be of good cheer.

The reference to Sicily is a mistake, mechanical or otherwise, of the commentary on Lucan, cf. *Summary* CXI ("Cicero stayed in the camp"—also inexact); Cicero, *On Divination* I. 68.

From Book CXII

35. Note on Cicero, *For Ligarius,* ed. Orelli-Baiter, p. 415: Meantime, as Livy tells us, Tubero and Pansa were suppressed; they fled to Pompey while search was being made for them. During these delays Curio appeared on the scene in Africa.

Cf. xxi in the oration itself; also Caesar, *Civil War* I. xxxi.

36. See below, 43a.

37. Priscian VI. 22, p. 213K: However, I have found in Livy in Book CXII of *From the Founding of the City* a foreign name ending in *d*, the name of the king of

barum nomen regis Maurorum Bogud, cuius genetivum secundum tertiam declinationem Bogudis protulit, ut: Castra quoque diversis partibus Cassius et Bogud adorti haud multum abfuere quin opera perrumperent.

38. *ibid.*: Quo tempore firmandi regni Bogudis causa exercitum in Africam velociter traicere conatus sit.

39. *ibid.*: Cassius gessisset cum Trebonio bellum, si Bogudem trahere in societatem furoris potuisset.

39a. Scholium Bernense in Lucan. *Pharsalia* VIII. 91: Hunc locum poeta de Livio tulit, qui Corneliam dicit dixisse Pompeio: "vicit, Magne, felicitatem tuam mea fortuna. Quid enim ex funesta Crassorum domo recipiebas nisi ut minueretur magnitudo tua?"

40. Scholium ad Lucan. *Pharsalia* X. 471: Legati, quos rex miserat, duo fuerunt, quorum unus erat Dioscorides et alter Serapio. Ex his unus occisus est, ut Titus Livius meminit libro quarto (belli civilis).

the Moors, Bogud, of which Livy gives a genitive of the third declension, Bogudis, as follows: Cassius and Bogud also attacked the camp from different directions and were not far from breaking through the entrenchments.

In 47 B.C., Cassius Longinus, a Caesarian propraetor in Spain, quarrelled with his quaestor, Marcellus, who seceded with part of the troops. Cassius summoned Bogud to help him overcome Marcellus, who had succeeded in shutting Cassius up in the town of Ulia. The strife was finally settled by the armed intervention of the governor of Nearer Spain, Lepidus. Cf. [Caesar], *Alexandrine War* lxii–lxiv.; below, fr. 43*a*. For previous events, cf. *Summary* CXI.

38. *ibid.* At the time when he attempted to transport an army rapidly to Africa for the purpose of strengthening Bogud on his throne.

39. *ibid.* Cassius would have waged war against Trebonius, if he had been able to induce Bogud to be his partner in madness.

Trebonius was sent to Spain in 46 B.C. by Caesar to supersede Cassius and quiet the disaffection he had caused, cf. *Alexandrine War* lxiv. 2; Dio XLIII. xxix. 1.

39a. Note on Lucan, *Pharsalia* VIII. 91 (Usener, 259): The poet took this passage from Livy, who relates that Cornelia said to Pompey, "My luck, Magnus, has overthrown your good-fortune. For what did you receive from the ill-starred house of Crassus except the diminution of your greatness?"

40. Note on Lucan, *Pharsalia* X. 471: The envoys whom the king had sent were two, one of them being Dioscorides and the other Serapion. One of these was killed, as Titus Livius mentions in the fourth book (of the civil war).

Cf. Caesar, *Civil War* III. cix.

41. *ibid.* X. 521: Arsinoe soror Ptolemaei fuit; hanc Ganymedes quidam spado puellae acceptissimus in castra Achillae perduxit, cuius iussu Achilles occisus est et exercitui praepositus Ganymedes. Hunc postea Caesar victis Aegyptiis in triumpho duxit, ut meminit Livius in libro quarto belli civilis.

42. Seneca, *de Tranquillitate Animi* ix: Quadringenta millia librorum Alexandriae arserunt, pulcherrimum regiae opulentiae monumentum. Alius laudaverit, sicut Livius, qui elegantiae regum curaeque egregium id opus ait fuisse.

Liber CXIII

43. Priscian VI. 22, p. 214K: Idem in CXIII oppidi nomen in *d* desinens per accusativum casum neutro genere protulit (Livius): et ipse circa Pulpud oram tuebatur.

Liber CXIV

43a. Priscian V. 10, p. 146K: et Bogud, nomen barbarum, quod Livius in centesimo quarto decimo declinavit Bogudis.

41. Note to Lucan, *Pharsalia* X. 521: Arsinoe was the sister of Ptolemy; she was brought over to the camp of Achillas by a certain eunuch, Ganymede, who was much favoured by the girl. On her order Achillas was killed and Ganymede put in charge of the army. Later on, he was led in Caesar's triumph after the conquest of Egypt, as Livy mentions in the fourth book of the civil war.

Cf. Caesar, *Civil War* III. cxii; *Alexandrine War* iv, xxiii; Dio XLII. xxxix f.; xlii; XLIII. xix.

42. Seneca, *On Tranquillity of Mind* ix: Four hundred thousand volumes were burned at Alexandria, a most handsome memorial to royal wealth. Let someone else praise such a collection, as Livy does, who says that this was a distinguished achievement of the good taste and solicitude of kings.

This appears to be an early example of the false equation of the burning of some books during Caesar's campaign—with the total destruction of the great Library.

From Book CXIII

43. Priscian VI. 22, p. 214K: Likewise in Book CXIII (Livy) exhibited the name of a town ending in *d* in the accusative case and neuter gender: "And he himself was guarding the shore in the vicinity of Pulpud."

In Keil, Supplement p. 123, the name appears as Pudpud. Weissenborn gives Palpud. It is not mentioned elsewhere.

From Book CXIV

43a. Priscian V. 10, p. 146K: Also Bogud, a foreign name, which Livy in Book CXIV declined *Bogudis*.

44. *Cf. infra, fr.* 83.

45. Jerome, *in Hoseam,* Migne 25 (= Jerome 6). 861: Optarem mihi contingere quod T. Livius scribit de Catone, cuius gloriae neque profuit quisquam laudando nec vituperando quisquam nocuit, cum utrumque summis praediti fecerint ingeniis. Significat autem M. Ciceronem et C. Caesarem, quorum alter laudes, alter vituperationes supra dicti scripsit viri.

Liber CXVI

46. Plutarch, *Caesar* lxiii: Ἦν γάρ τι τῇ Καίσαρος οἰκίᾳ προσκείμενον, οἷον ἐπὶ κόσμῳ καὶ σεμνότητι τῆς βουλῆς ψηφισαμένης ἀκρωτήριον, ὡς Λίβιος ἱστορεῖ. Τοῦτο ὄναρ ἡ Καλπουρνία θεασαμένη καταρρηγνύμενον ἔδοξε ποτνιᾶσθαι καὶ δακρύειν· ἡμέρας δ' οὖν γενομένης ἐδεῖτο τοῦ Καίσαρος, εἰ μὲν οἷόν τε, μὴ προελθεῖν, ἀλλ' ἀναβαλέσθαι τὴν σύγκλητον.

47. Servius ad Vergil. *Georg.* I. 472: Malum omen est quotiens Aetna, mons Siciliae, non fumum sed flammarum egerit globos; et, ut dicit Livius, tanta flamma ante mortem Caesaris ex Aetna monte defluxit ut non tantum vicinae urbes, sed etiam Regina civitas, quae multo spatio ab ea distat, adflaretur.

Bogud was a chieftain of Mauretania, recognized as king by Caesar, together with Bocchus, perhaps his brother, cf. frs. 37–9 above. Keil, Supplement p. 123, has a reference to the name as a type of ending.

44. See below, fr. 83.

45. Jerome, *Commentary on Hosea* II, preface: I should choose to have it true of me, as Titus Livius writes of Cato, that his fame was neither helped by anyone's praise, nor hurt by anyone's censure, although the authors of both were men endowed with the highest abilities. He means, of course, Marcus Cicero and Gaius Caesar, the former of whom wrote a eulogy, the latter an excoriation, of the aforesaid gentleman.

From Book CXVI

46. Plutarch, *Caesar* lxiii: For there was a gable ornament attached to Caesar's house by vote of the senate as a decoration and mark of dignity, as Livy relates. Calpurnia in a dream saw this shattered, and thought that she called on the gods and wept; so when day broke, she begged Caesar, if it was possible, not to go out, but to postpone the session of the senate.

Cf. Obsequens 67.

47. Servius, note on *Georgics* I. 472: It has been an evil omen whenever Etna, the Sicilian mountain, has ejected balls of fire instead of smoke. As Livy tells us, before the death of Caesar such flame flowed from Mount Etna that not only the neighbouring cities, but even the town of Regium, which is a long distance from the mountain, felt the blast.

For an eruption of Etna as a bad omen, cf. Obsequens 26, 29, and 32.

48. Seneca, *Naturales Quaestiones* V. 18: Quod de Caesare maiore vulgo dictitatum est et a T. Livio positum, in incerto esse utrum illum magis nasci reipublicae profuerit an non nasci, dici etiam de ventis potest.

Liber CXVIII

49. Priscian IX. 40. p. 477K: Livius in CXVIII: Adversus interfectores C. Caesaris ultoribus manum comparans concibat.

Liber CXX

50. M. Seneca, *Suasoriae* VI. 17 (VII): Titi Livi: M. Cicero sub adventum triumvirorum cesserat urbe, pro certo habens id quod erat, non magis Antonio eripi se quam Caesari Cassium et Brutum posse. Primo in Tusculanum fugit, inde transversis itineribus in Formianum, ut ab Caieta navim conscensurus, proficiscitur. Unde aliquotiens in altum provectum cum modo venti adversi retulissent, modo ipse iactationem navis caeco volvente fluctu pati non posset, taedium tandem eum et fugae et vitae cepit; regressusque ad superiorem villam quae paulo plus mille

48. Seneca, *Investigations into Nature* V. xviii. 4: What has been commonly said about the elder Caesar, and is recorded by Titus Livius—that it cannot be decided whether it was better for the commonwealth for him to be born, or never to be born—this can also be said about the winds.

Cf. *Summary* CXVI for the death of Caesar.

From Book CXVIII

49. Priscian IX. 40, p. 477K: Livy in Book CXVIII: "He was causing a stir by raising a force for the avengers against the assassins of Gaius Caesar."

Cf. *Summary* CXVIII and *Res Gestae Divi Augusti* 1.

From Book CXX

50. Seneca the Rhetorician, *Suasoriae* VI. 17 (VII): From Titus Livius: Marcus Cicero had taken his departure from the city shortly before the arrival of the Board of Three; he was convinced of what was actually the case, that he could no more be saved from the clutches of Antony than Cassius and Brutus could be from those of Caesar. First he fled to his Tusculan estate, thence he set out by cross-country routes for his place at Formiae, for he planned to take ship at Caieta. From that port he put out to sea several times, but sometimes contrary winds drove him back, and again he was unable to bear the tossing of the ship, as a ground swell heaved it. Finally a weariness both of flight and of life came upon him; he went back to his upper country house, which is a little more than a mile from the sea, and said,

passibus a mari abest, "Moriar," inquit, "in patria saepe servata." Satis constat servos fortiter fideliterque paratos fuisse ad dimicandum; ipsum deponi lecticam et quietos pati quod sors iniqua cogeret iussisse. Prominenti ex lectica praebentique immotam cervicem caput praecisum est. Nec satis stolidae crudelitati militum fuit. Manus quoque, scripsisse in Antonium aliquid exprobrantes, praeciderunt. Ita relatum caput ad Antonium iussuque eius inter duas manus in Rostris positum; ubi ille consul, ubi saepe consularis, ubi eo ipso anno adversus Antonium, quanta numquam humana vox cum admiratione eloquentiae auditus fuerat. Vix attollentes prae lacrimis oculos homines intueri trucidata membra eius poterant. Vixit tres et sexaginta annos, ut si vis abfuisset ne immatura quidem mors videri possit; ingenium et operibus et praemiis operum felix; ipse fortunae diu prosperae et in longo tenore felicitatis magnis interim ictus vulneribus, exsilio, ruina partium pro quibus steterat, filiae morte, exitu tam tristi atque acerbo, omnium adversorum nihil ut viro dignum erat tulit praeter mortem; quae vere aestimanti minus indigna videri potuit quod a victore inimico nil crudelius passus erat quam quod eiusdem fortunae compos ipse fecisset. Si quis tamen virtutibus vitia pensarit, vir magnus acer

Let me die in the fatherland I have so often saved." It is definitely known that his slaves were ready to fight bravely and loyally, but he bade them set down the litter and endure without rebellion what a hostile fortune forced upon them. As he thrust his head out of the litter and held his neck steady, he was decapitated. Nor was this enough for the brutish cruelty of the soldiers. They also cut off his hands, reproaching them for having written something against Antony. Thus the head was brought back to Antony and by his order placed between the two hands on the Rostra. There Cicero in his consulship, and again often as ex-consul, and again that very year in opposing Antony, had been heard with admiration for his eloquence such as had never been accorded to another human voice. People could hardly raise their eyes for their tears, in order to look at his butchered parts.

He lived sixty-three years, so that if he had suffered no violence, his death would not have seemed to be even untimely. His nature was fortunate both in its achievements and in its rewards for achievement; he enjoyed a long-continued good fortune and a prolonged state of prosperity, yet was from time to time smitten with severe blows, his exile, the downfall of the party he represented, the death of his daughter, and his own sad and bitter end. None of his adversities did he bear in a manner worthy of a gentleman except his death; and this, if one weighs the matter accurately, might seem the less undeserved, because he suffered from a victorious personal enemy nothing crueler than he would himself have done, had he attained to the same success. However, if one balances his faults against his virtues, he was a memorabilis fuit, et in cuius laudes persequendas Cicerone laudatore opus fuerit.

Liber CXXVII

51. Acro ad Horat. *Sat.* I. v. 29: Quoniam inter Augustum et Antonium reliquiae adhuc erant dissensionis, Cocceius Nerva, proavus Nervae qui postea imperavit Romae, mandavit Augusto ut mitteret qui de summa rerum tractarent. Ergo missus est Maecenas cum Agrippa, qui utrumque exercitum in una castra coegerunt, ut ait Livius[1] lib. CXXVII. Intelligendum autem quod Fonteio misso ab Antonio Augustus Maecenaten et ceteros ad eundem locum emiserit.

52. Porphyrio, *ibid.*: Dissensione orta inter Caesarem Augustum Antoniumque Cocceius Nerva, avus eius qui postea Romae imperavit, petiit a Caesare ut aliquem qui de summa rerum tractaret mitteret Tarracinam. Et primum Maecenas, mox et Agrippa congressi sunt, hique pepigerunt fidem confirmatissimam et in una castra conferri signa utriusque exercitus iusserunt. Hoc et T. Livius lib. CXXVII refert, excepta Capitonis mentione.

53. Commentator Cruquii, *ibid.*: Ab Antonio missus fuerat Fonteius Capito legatus, ab Augusto Maecenas intercedente Cocceio Nerva, proavo Nervae imperatoris, qui et Augusto et Antonio gratus erat,

[1] Licinius *Hauthal, Berlin, 1866.*

man of greatness, energy, and distinction—a man, the complete exposition of whose merits would demand a Cicero as eulogist.

From Book CXXVII

51. Acron, note on Horace, *Satires* I. v. 29: Since there still remained certain left-overs of dispute between Augustus and Antony, Cocceius Nerva, the great-grandfather of the Nerva who was later Emperor of Rome, enjoined on Augustus that he should send envoys to discuss the whole situation. Accordingly, Maecenas was sent with Agrippa, and they gathered both armies into one camp, as Livy says in Book CXXVII. We are to understand, however, that after Fonteius had been sent by Antony, Augustus sent out Maecenas and the others to the same place.

52. Porphyrion, on the same: When a disagreement arose between Caesar Augustus and Antony, Cocceius Nerva, the grandfather of the man who was later Emperor of Rome, asked Caesar to send to Tarracina someone to discuss the whole situation. And first Maecenas, then presently Agrippa joined them, and these pledged faith with all solemnity and ordered the standards of both armies to be brought together in one camp. This is also related by Titus Livius in Book CXXVII, except for the mention of Capito.

53. Commentator Cruquii, on the same: Fonteius Capito had been sent as envoy by Antony, Maecenas and Agrippa by Augustus after the intervention of Cocceius Nerva, the great-grandfather of the Emperor Nerva, who was in the good graces of both Augustus and Antony. The terms on which

cum Agrippa. Ea autem condicione convenerant legati ut de summa rerum tractarent, exortamque dissensionem inter duos hos imperatores componerent; quod et fecerunt et utrumque exercitum iuxta Brundisium in una castra cum magna laetitia coegerunt, ut infert Livius lib. CXXVII.

Liber CXXXIII

54. Commentator Cruquii ad Horat. *Od.* I. xxxvii. 30: Livius refert Cleopatram, cum ab Augusto capta indulgentius de industria tractaretur, dicere solitam "Non triumphabor."

Liber CXXXV

55. Apponius, *in Canticum Canticorum* xii p. 237 (Rome, 1843): Caesar Augustus in spectaculis populo[1] nuntiat, regressus a Britannia insula, totum orbem terrarum tam bello quam amicitiis Romano imperio subditum.[2]

Liber CXXXVI

56. Censorinus, *de Die Natali* xvii: Eodem anno ludos saeculares Caesar ingenti apparatu fecit, quos

[1] spectaculis populo *edd.*: spectaculis Romano populo MS.
[2] imperio subditum *edd.*: imperio pacis abundantia subditum MS.

the envoys came together were that they should discuss the whole situation, and settle the disagreement which had arisen between the above-mentioned commanders. They proceeded to do so, and moreover gathered both armies near Brundisium into one camp, amid great rejoicing, as Livy notes in Book CXXVII.

The "omission" of Fonteius Capito by Livy seems to be due to a confusion on the part of the commentators between the negotiations of 40 B.C., described by Livy in Book CXXVII, cf. *Summary*, and those of 37 B.C., in which Fonteius was probably Antony's agent. For Nerva, cf. Appian, *Civil Wars* V. vii. 60–4.

From Book CXXXIII

54. Commentator Cruquii, on Horace, *Odes* I. xxxvii. 30: Livy tells us that Cleopatra, while she was a prisoner of Augustus and was intentionally being treated with considerable liberality, used to say, "I will not be shown in a triumph."

The notes of Acron and Porphyrion (cf. preceding frs.) contain the same information, and add the Greek of Cleopatra's remark, Οὐ θριαμβεύσομαι. *Summary* CXXXIII contains a very brief mention of Cleopatra's attitude and death.

From Book CXXXV

55. Apponius *on Song of Songs* xii: Caesar Augustus announced to the people at the shows given on his return from the island of Britain, that the whole world was subjected to Roman rule, whether by war or by diplomacy.

From Book CXXXVI

56. Censorinus *On the Birthday*, xvii. 10: This same year Caesar gave the Festival of the Age with great

centesimo quoque anno—is enim terminus saeculi—fieri mos.

Ex Incertis Libris

57. Seneca, *de Ira* I. xx. 6: Quod apud disertissimum virum T. Livium dicitur, "Vir ingenii magni magis quam boni."

58. Plinius, *N.H.* I, praef.: Profiteor mirari me T. Livium, auctorem celeberrimum, in Historiarum suarum quas repetit ab origine urbis quodam volumine sic exorsum: satis iam sibi gloriae quaesitum, et potuisse se desinere, ni animus inquies pasceretur opere.

59. Plinius, *N.H.* III. i. 4: T. Livius ac Nepos Cornelius latitudinis (freti Gaditani) tradiderunt ubi minus, septem millia passuum, ubi vero plurimum, decem millia.

60. = 68.

61. Servius ad Vergil. *Aen.* II. 148: Verba sunt, ut habemus in Livio, imperatoris transfugam recipientis in fidem, "Quisquis es, noster eris."

62. Guilielmus Malmesburiensis, *Rerum Anglicarum* V. § 412, p. 488 ed. Stubbs: "Imperatorem me mater mea, non bellatorem peperit."

magnificence; it is the custom to give these every hundred years, for that is the end of an age.

The year was 17 B.C. The interval was never regularly observed, in spite of Censorinus' quotations (above, frs. 11 and 13) from Livy and others; Augustus seems to have conceived the proper interval as being 110 years.

From Books not Identifiable

57. Seneca, *On Wrath* I. xx. 6: As is said in the works of Titus Livius, a very talented gentleman, "A man of great, rather than good, character."

58. Pliny, *Natural History* I, preface: I must say I am surprised that Titus Livius, that most famous author, in a certain book of his Histories, in which he went back to the beginnings of Rome, began as follows, "I have now earned fame enough, and might make an end, except that my restless mind feeds on the work."

59. Pliny, *Natural History* III. i. 4: Titus Livius and Cornelius Nepos give as the width of the strait of Gibraltar seven miles, where it is narrowest, and ten miles where it is widest.

Modern measurement gives a minimum width of 14 kilometers, or about nine and a half Roman miles.

60. = 68.

61. Servius, note on *Aeneid* II. 148: These are the words, as we find in Livy, of a commander taking a deserter under his protection, "Whoever you are, you shall be ours."

62. William of Malmesbury, *History of England* V. § 412, p. 488 ed. Stubbs:

"My mother bore me to be a general, not a warrior."

This is given by William as a saying of Scipio, and might be from Livy.

63. Gelasius Papa, *Epist. adv. Andromachum* (Baronii *Annal. Eccles.* 35 [anno 496]) : Dic mihi, cum saepe numero in Romanis historiis legatur, Livio auctore,[1] saepissime in hac urbe exorta pestilentia infinita hominum millia deperiisse, atque eo frequenter ventum ut vix esset unde illis bellicosis temporibus exercitus potuisset ascribi, illo tempore deo tuo Februario minime litabatur? An etiam cultus hic omnino nihil proderat? Illo tempore Lupercalia non celebrabantur? Nec enim dicturus es haec sacra adhuc illo tempore non coepisse, quae ante Romulum ab Euandro in Italiam perhibentur illata. Lupercalia autem propter quid instituta sint (quantum ad ipsius superstitionis commenta respectant) Livius secunda decade loquitur; nec propter morbos inhibendos instituta commemorat, sed propter sterilitatem, ut ei videtur, mulierum, quae tunc acciderat, exigendam.

64. Servius ad Vergil. *Aen.* IV. 242 : Secundum Livium legati pacis caduceatores dicuntur.

65. Servius ad Vergil. *Aen.* VI. 861 : Livius argentum grave dicit, id est massas.

66. Servius ad Vergil. *Aen.* VII. 10 : In hoc summo (promontorio Circeo) oppidum fuit, quod et Circeium dictum et Circei. Nam utrumque Livius dixit.

67. *Cf. infra, fr.* 84.

68. Servius ad Vergil. *Georg.* III, initium : Scimus concessum esse scribentibus ut iteratione prooemii legentium reficiant interdum laborem, nam et Livius

[1] auctore *Carafa* orare V (= Vat. lat. 3787 saec. XI) oratore *Günther*.

63. Pope Gelasius, *Letter refuting Andromachus*, Corpus Scriptorum Ecclesiasticorum Latinorum 35. 1, pp. 456 f.:

Tell me, since we read often in the history of Rome, on the authority of Livy, that at very frequent intervals an epidemic arose in this city and slew numberless thousands of persons, and many times matters came to such a pass that there was hardly a source from which in those war-filled times an army could be enrolled, was there at that time no ceremony at all in honour of your god Februarius? Or was even this worship of no value at all? At that time were the Lupercalia not performed? For surely you will not say that these rites had not yet begun in that period, since they are said to have been introduced into Italy by Evander before the time of Romulus. Moreover, as to the reason why the Lupercalia were established (in so far as they are connected with the falsehoods of superstition itself), Livy gives information in his second group of ten books; and he records that they were established, not to check diseases, but to eliminate, so he supposes, the sterility of women that had at that time befallen them.

64. Servius, note on *Aeneid* IV. 242: According to Livy, ambassadors for peace are called "bearers of Mercury's rod."

65. Servius, note on *Aeneid* VI. 861: Livy speaks of "massive silver," that is, bullion.

66. Servius, note on *Aeneid* VII. 10: On this height (Cape Circeium) there was a town, which was called both Circeium and Circei. For Livy used both.

67. See below, fr. 84.

68. Servius, prefatory note to *Georgics* III: We know that writers have the privilege of occasionally relieving the labour of their readers by inserting a fresh

frequenter innovat principia, ut incensa a Gallis urbe, et completis consulibus.

69. *Cf. infra, fr.* 85.

70. *Cf. infra, fr.* 86.

71. Incertus auctor, *de Dubiis Nominibus*, Keil V. p. 592: Vepres generis feminini, ut Titus Livius: has vepres.

72. *Cf. infra, fr.* 87

73. Seneca, *Controversiae* IX. i. 14 (xxiv): T. Livius tam iniquus Sallustio fuit ut hanc ipsam sententiam "Res secundae mire sunt vitiis obtentui" tamquam translatam et tamquam corruptam dum transfertur obiceret Sallustio. Nec hoc amore Thucydidis facit ut illum praeferat. Laudat quem non timet et facilius putat posse a se Sallustium vinci si ante a Thucydide vincatur.

74. Seneca, *Controversiae* IX. ii. 26 (xxv): T. Livius de oratoribus qui verba antiqua et sordida consectantur et orationis obscuritatem severitatem putant

preface, for Livy frequently makes a fresh start, as after the burning of the city by the Gauls, and at the end of a consular year.

For Livy's fresh starts, cf. the opening of Book VI (as mentioned by Servius), Book XXI, and above, fr. 58. The annalistic practice of marking the start of each consular year hardly seems worthy of Servius' attention in this connection, but I do not know how to interpret his final phrase in a different sense. Weissenborn prints *completis consulibus* as a separate fr. 60.

69. See below, fr. 85

70. See below, fr. 86.

71. Unknown author, *On Nouns of Uncertain Gender*, Keil V, p. 592: *Vepres* (briar) is of feminine gender, e.g. in Titus Livius, " these (*fem.*) briars."

72. See below, fr. 87.

73. Seneca the Rhetorician, *Argumentation* IX. i. 14 (xxiv): Titus Livius was so hostile to Sallust that he reproached Sallust for this very epigram, " Success is a wonderful cloak for faults," on the ground that it was a translation and spoiled in the translating. Nor does he do this out of affection for Thucydides, in order to give him the better of it. He praises the man he is not afraid of, and thinks that Sallust can be more easily beaten by himself if he is first beaten by Thucydides.

Sallust's epigram is found in the Oration of Lepidus (*Histories* I. 55 Maurenbrecher) sec. 24; the Greek quoted by Seneca, but not included above, does not appear in our Thucydides; the sentiment, in slightly different words, is found in [Demosthenes] *On the Letter of Philip* 13.

74. Seneca the Rhetorician, *Argumentation* IX. ii. 26 (xxv): Concerning orators who pursue obsolete and vulgar words and mistake obscurity for austerity, Titus

aiebat, Militiadem rhetorem eleganter dixisse, "ἐπὶ τὸ λεξικὸν[1] μαίνονται."

75. Quintilian, *Institutio Oratoris* VIII. ii. 18: In hoc malum a quibusdam etiam laboratur, neque id novum vitium est, cum iam apud T. Livium inveniam fuisse praeceptorem aliquem qui discipulos *obscurare* quae dicerent iuberet, Graeco verbo utens, σκότισον. Unde illa scilicet egregia laudatio, "Tanto melior; ne ego quidem intellexi."

76. Quintilian, *Institutio Oratoris* X, i. 39: Fuit igitur brevitas illa tutissima quae apud Livium in epistola ad filium scripta, "legendos Demosthenem atque Ciceronem; tum ita ut quisque esset Demostheni et Ciceroni simillimus.

77. Quintilian, *Institutio Oratoris* VIII. iii. 53: Vitanda μακρολογία, id est longior quam oportet sermo, ut apud Livium: "Legati non impetrata pace retro, unde venerant, domum reversi sunt."

78. Incertus auctor, *de Generibus Nominum*, p. 591K: Scalper, generis masculini, sicut culter, ut Titus Livius, quamvis quidam scalprum dicant.

[1] λεξικὸν *Bursian*; λεξιον MS: δεξιὸν *Madvig*: τῷ πλησιον *Weissenborn*.

Livius used to say that Miltiades the professor had put it neatly: "They have a passion for the dictionary."

An alternative emendation gives: "They are raving against their neighbour."

75. Quintilian, *Oratorical Studies* VIII. ii. 18: Certain persons even undergo toil to attain this evil, nor is this vice an innovation, since I find even in Titus Livius that there was a certain instructor who bade his students "darken" what they had to say, using the Greek word *skotison.* From the same source comes, if you please, that glorious praise, "So much the better; I didn't understand it myself."

76. Quintilian, *Oratorical Studies* X. i. 39: The safest thing, then, was the epigram written by Livy in a letter to his son, "Read Demosthenes and Cicero; after that, the more each author is like Demosthenes and Cicero, the better."

Cf. also Quintilian II. v. 20 for an abbreviated version of this reference.

77. Quintilian, *Oratorical Studies* VIII. iii. 53: Long-windedness is to be avoided, that is, any expression longer than is proper, as in Livy: "The envoys, having failed to obtain peace, returned back home, whence they had come."

Substantially the same statement is found in Charisius, III p. 271K (and cf. p. 449K). Hertz points out that, while the exact words are not found in the extant books of Livy, similar expressions occur in IX. ii. 10; XXIV. xx. 3; XXIV. xl. 9; and XXXVIII. xvi. 6.

78. Anon. *On Nouns of Doubtful Gender*, p. 591K: *Scalper* (chisel) is of masculine gender, like *culter* (knife), as in Titus Livius, although some say *scalprum.*

79. Plinius, *Naturalis Historia* III. xix. 132: (Alpis patere tradit) in latitudinem autem Cornelius Nepos $\overline{\mathrm{C}}$, Titus Livius $\overline{\mathrm{III}}$ stadiorum, uterque diversis in locis.

80. Iona, *vita S. Columbani*, Migne 87. 1015C: ut Livius ait, nihil tam sanctum religione tamque custodia clausum quo penetrare libido nequeat.

---

[1] The attribution of this fragment to Livy is questioned by Mueller. He also includes as his fr. 67 the reference in Tacitus, *Annals* IV. 34, to the freedom enjoyed by Livy to praise Brutus, Cassius, and especially Pompey. Other passages cited by Hertz and Mueller as fragments, but referable also to extant text, are the following: Quintilian I. vii. 24 = fr. 78M, use of the spelling *sibe* and *quase*; Priscian XVIII. 231, = fr. 68H, 79M, phrase *in milites*, cf. *in pedites*, XXXIV. lii. 11; Priscian XVIII. 292 = fr. 69H, 80M, *assertio*, cf. *adsertor*, III. xlvi. 7; fr. 70H, 81M, fourth declension neuters. Cf. also Hertz frs. 65–7 on *clipeum*, *callis* (fem.), and Livy's "teen" numerals; fr. 71, text and attribution doubtful.

The last clause is not included by Keil, but appears in the citation by Haupt, *Ovid's Halieutica, etc.*, p. 101. The neuter *scalprum* appears, e.g., in XXVII. xlix. 1.

79. Pliny, *Natural History* III. xix. 132: Moreover, the width of the Alps is said to extend over one hundred miles by Cornelius Nepos, and three thousand stades by Titus Livius, each of whom refers to a different region.

As pointed out by Rackham, L.C.L., Pliny, vol. II, p. 98, the figure given for Livy's measurement, 360 Roman or 333 English miles, assuming an Olympic stade of 178·6 metres, is too large; something like DL or DC would be preferable, as corresponding to the figure of seventy miles given by Pliny as a minimum, after he has mentioned one hundred miles as a somewhat under-estimated maximum. It seems likely that Livy took his Greek measurement from Polybius.

80. Jonah, *Life of Saint Columban*, Migne 87, 1015C As Livy says, nothing is made so holy by awe, or kept so remote by watchfulness, that lust cannot reach it.[1]

FRAGMENTS SOMETIMES ATTRIBUTED TO LIVY

81. Anon. *On the Seven Wonders of the World,* in Haupt, *Ovidii Halieutica, etc.*, pp. xxviii and 70 f. = fr. 4W. This contains a list of the principal mountains of Sicily, and is assigned to Livy; but elsewhere the quotation appears as from Julius Titianus, see Hertz I. xii.

82. Note on Lucan, *Pharsalia* I. 319 = fr. 28W. This is a comment on Pompey's superintendence of the grain supply. The letters *lv* in the MS. represent the name of the author quoted, but the quotation is not from Livy, but Boethius, *Consolation* III, prose iv.

83. Appian, *Civil War* III. xi. 77 = fr. 44 Weissenborn. Perizonius proposed reading " Livy " in place of " Libo " in this passage, but the emendation is generally rejected.

84. Priscian VIII, p. 382K. = fr. 67W. Weissenborn reads " Livius " for " Aelius " as the source for this quotation, but the rather technical legal language does not sound like Livy.

85. Nonius Marcellus, p. 308 L. Mueller, Leipzig, Teubner, 1888 = fr. 69W. A garbled quotation is assigned by the MSS. to Titus Livius, but Mueller assigns this to Livius Andronicus, since one MS. cites " Ajax Bearing a Whip " as the work cited, i.e., a tragedy after Sophocles (=Warmington, *Remains of Old Latin*, fr. 16–17).

86. Nonius Marcellus, p. 599 Mueller = fr. 70W. Again the MSS. name Titus Livius, but the quotation sounds poetic, and is assigned by Mueller to Andronicus.

87. Sallust, *Histories* II. 43 ed. Maurenbrecher = fr. 72W. This badly broken fragment shows the names of Publius Lentulus Marcellinus, King Apion, and Quintus Metellus Creticus, and was formerly assigned to Livy, cf. Weissenborn *ad loc.*, but is now given to Sallust, cf. Hertz I. p. xii.

88. Anon. *de Dubiis Nominibus* p. 575K: Cancer, the swelling, is of neuter gender, as in Livy, " the evil is wont to hide—the incurable cancer." It is tempting to put this

alongside fr. 27; but there is a suggestion of metre in the Latin *immedicabile cancer*, and the text is uncertain.

89. Beda, *de Orthographia* p. 292K: "Torque" is a noun of common gender, for in the story of Marius, Livy makes "torque" of masculine gender, and Cicero makes it feminine.

If we read "Manlius" for "Marius," this would refer to VII. x. 11, but there was a Gaul connected with Marius, cf. Summary LXXVII.

90. Anon. *de Dubiis Nominibus* p. 572K: The phrase "laxisque bracis" (slack trousers), quoted as from Livy, is found in Ovid, *Tristia* V. vii. 49, which may indicate that textual emendation is in order.

TABLE OF CHANGES IN NUMBERING OF FRAGMENTS

(The numbers of the Weissenborn edition are kept, except as indicated.)

Weissenborn	Hertz	Loeb	Weissenborn	Hertz	Loeb
1–3			61	58	
4	om.	81	62	om.	
5–12	4–11		63	12	
13–15			64–66	59–61	
om.	16	15a	67	om.	84
16–27	17–28		om.	62	77
28	74	82	om.	63	80
29–30	29		68	64	
31–35	30–34			65–71*	
36	42	43a	69–70	om.	85–6
37–43	35–41		om.	72	78
44	om.	83	71	73	
45–50	43–49		72	om.	87
51–53	50		73–75	76–78	
54–59	51–56		76	75 †	
60=68					
om.	57	79			

* These fragments in Hertz are grammarians' quotations from Livy; since the words quoted can be found in extant Books, they are here omitted from the fragments. Cf. note 1, p. 232.

† Chronological notes from Cassiodorus are included by Hertz, but without numbering; since these do not reproduce Livy's words, they are not included here.

JULIUS OBSEQUENS

IULII OBSEQUENTIS

AB ANNO URBIS CONDITAE DV PRODIGIORUM LIBER

A.U.C. 564

L. Scipione C. Laelio coss.

1. Iunonis Lucinae templum fulmine ictum ita ut fastigium valvaeque deformarentur. In finitimis pleraque de caelo icta. Nursiae sereno nimbi orti et homines duo exanimati. Tusculi terra pluit. Mula Reate peperit. Supplicatio per decem pueros patrimos matrimos totidem virgines habita.

A.U.C. 566

M. Messala C. Livio coss.

2. Luce inter horam tertiam et quartam tenebrae ortae. In Aventino lapidum pluviae novendiali expiatae. In Hispania prospere militatum.

A.U.C. 568

Sp. Postumio Albino Q. Marcio Philippo coss.[1]

3. Sacrum novendiale factum quod in Piceno lapidibus pluit ignesque caelestes multifariam orti

[1] Sp. Postumio Albino Q. Marcio Philippo coss. *add. Oudendorp*: *om.* MS.

---

[1] References are to the passages of Livy on which Obsequens drew, unless otherwise indicated.

JULIUS OBSEQUENS

A BOOK OF PRODIGIES AFTER THE 505TH YEAR OF ROME

CONSULSHIP OF LUCIUS SCIPIO AND GAIUS LAELIUS B.C. 190

1. The temple of Juno Lucina was struck by lightning, in such a way that the gable and the doors were damaged. In neighbouring towns many things were struck by lightning. At Nursia storm-clouds gathered from a clear sky, and two persons were killed. At Tusculum there was a shower of earth. A mule at Reate produced a colt. A day of prayer was observed by ten boys with living fathers and mothers, and as many girls. (XXXVII. iii. 2–6.[1])

CONSULSHIP OF MARCUS MESSALA AND GAIUS LIVIUS B.C. 188

2. Between the third and fourth hour of the day, darkness set in. On the Aventine, showers of stones were atoned for by a nine-day observance. There was a successful campaign in Spain. (XXXVIII. xxxvi. 4.)

CONSULSHIP OF SPURIUS POSTUMIUS ALBINUS AND QUINTUS MARCIUS PHILIPPUS B.C. 186

3. A nine-day observance was held because there had been a shower of stones in Picenum, and because lightning bolts, appearing in many places, had

A.U.C. 568 levi afflatu complurium vestimenta adusserunt. Aedes Iovis in Capitolio fulmine icta. In Umbria semimas duodecim ferme annorum inventus[1] aruspicumque iussu necatus. Galli qui Alpis transierunt in Italiam sine proelio eiecti.

A.U.C. 571

M. Claudio Q. Fabio Labeone coss.

4. In area Vulcani per biduum, in area Concordiae totidem diebus sanguinem pluit. In Sicilia insula nova maritima.[2] Hannibal in Bithynia veneno periit. Celtiberi subacti.

A.U.C. 572

L. Aemilio Paulo Cn. Baebio Tamphilo coss.

5. Procellosa tempestas strage[3] in urbe facta signa aenea in Capitolio deiecit, signa in circo maximo cum columnis evertit, fastigia templorum aliquot a culmine abrupta dissipavit. Mulus tripes Reate natus. Aedes Apollinis Caietae fulmine icta.[4]

A.U.C. 573

P. Cornelio Cethego M. Baebio Tamphilo coss.[5]

6. In area Vulcani et Concordiae sanguinem pluit. Hastae Martis motae. Lanuvii simulacrum Iunonis Sospitae lacrimavit. Pestilentiae Libitina non suf-

[1] inventus *C. Barth*: natus MS.
[2] maritima MS: mari nata *Scaliger*.
[3] tempestas strage *Oudendorp*: tempestate strages MS.
[4] icta *Sigonius*: ictae MS.
[5] P. Cornelio Cethego M. Baebio Tamphilo coss. *add. Hearn*: *om.* MS.

---

[1] Livy says the temple of Ops.
[2] That is, all the dead could not be buried.

scorched the clothes of many persons by a slight blast of heat. The temple of Jupiter[1] on the Capitol was struck by lightning. In Umbria, a hermaphrodite about twelve years old was discovered, and by order of the soothsayers was put to death. Gauls who had crossed the Alps into Italy were expelled without a battle. (XXXIX. xxii. 3–5.) B.C. 186

Consulship of Marcus Claudius and Quintus Fabius Labeo

B.C. 183

4. There was a rain of blood for two days in the precinct of Vulcan, and for the same length of time in the precinct of Concord. Off Sicily, a new island in the sea arose. Hannibal died of poison in Bithynia. The Celtiberians were overcome. (XXXIX. xlvi. 5; li; lvi. 6; Orosius IV. xx. 30.)

Consulship of Lucius Aemilius Paulus and Gnaeus Baebius Tamphilus

B.C. 182

5. A windstorm wrecked buildings in the city, overthrew bronze statues on the Capitol, overturned statues with their columns in the Circus Maximus, tore the roofs off the top of several temples, and scattered them. A mule with three feet was born at Reate. The temple of Apollo at Caieta was struck by lightning. (XL. ii. 1–4.)

Consulship of Publius Cornelius Cethegus and Marcus Baebius Tamphilus

B.C. 181

6. There was a rain of blood in the precinct of Vulcan and that of Concord. The spears of Mars moved. At Lanuvium the image of Juno the Deliverer shed tears. The plague overwhelmed Libitina.[2] On

A.U.C. 573 fecit.[1] Ex Sibyllinis supplicatum cum sex mensibus non pluisset. Ligures proelio victi deletique.

A.U.C. 575

Q. Fulvio L. Manlio [2] coss.

7. Nimbis continuis in Capitolio signa aliquot deiecta. Fulmine Romae et circa plurima decussa. In lectisternio Iovis terrae motu deorum capita se converterunt; lanx [3] cum integumentis quae Iovi erant apposita decidit. De mensa oleas mures praeroserunt.

A.U.C. 576

M. Iunio A.[4] Manlio coss.

8. Incendio circa forum cum plurima essent deusta, aedes Veneris sine ullo vestigio cremata. Vestae penetralis ignis extinctus. Virgo iussu M. Aemilii pontificis maximi flagro caesa negavit ulterius interiturum.[5] Supplicationibus habitis in Hispania et Histria bella prospere administrata.

A.U.C. 577

C. Claudio Ti. Sempronio Gracco coss.[6]

[1] suffecit *ed. Iuntina* : sufficit MS.
[2] L. Manlio *Hearn* : C. Manlius MS.
[3] lanx *Cuper* : lana MS. : laena *Scheffer*.
[4] A. *Hearn* : Gn. MS.
[5] interiturum *Scheffer* : interitorum MS.
[6] Ti. Sempronio Gracco *add. Lycosthenes* : *om.* MS.

advice of the Sibylline Books, there was a day of prayer after rain had failed for six months. The Ligurians were conquered in battle and crushed. (XL. xix. 1–5; xxix. 2; xxviii. 1–7.) B.C. 181

Consulship of Quintus Fulvius and Lucius Manlius B.C. 179

7. A succession of storms threw down several statues on the Capitol. A great amount of damage was done by lightning in Rome and round about. At the banquet spread for Jupiter, the heads of the gods turned about during an earthquake; the platter with its lids which was placed before Jupiter fell down. Mice nibbled the olives on the table. (XL. xlv. 3 [Obsequens omits some items]; lix. 7–8.)

Consulship of Marcus Junius and Aulus Manlius B.C. 178

8. When a large area around the forum was devastated by fire, the temple of Venus was burned without leaving a trace. The home fire of Vesta went out. The Vestal was whipped by order of the chief pontiff, Marcus Aemilius, and declared that the fire would never go out again. After days of prayer had been observed, successful campaigns were carried out in Spain and Histria. (*Summary* XLI; Histrians, XLI. ii–xi; Vestal, cf. XXVIII. xi. 6; Plutarch, *Numa*, x. 4; M. Aemilius (Lepidus), chief pontiff, XL. xlii. 12.)

Consulship of Gaius Claudius and Tiberius Sempronius Gracchus B.C. 177

(Items lost from the Obsequens MS. at this point are found in XLI. xiii. 1–3.)

A.U.C. 578

Cn. Cornelio Q. Petillio coss.[1]

9. Cum immolassent victimas consules, iecur extabuit. Cornelius ex monte Albano rediens membris captus ad aquas Cumanas mortuus, Petillius contra Ligures dimicans occisus est.

A.U.C. 579

M. Lepido Q. Mucio coss.

10. Gravi pestilentia hominum boumque cadavera non sufficiente Libitina cum iacerent, vulturius[2] non apparuit. Celtiberi deleti.

A.U.C. 587

Q. Aelio Paeto M. Iunio coss.[3]

11. Romae aliquot loca sacra profanaque de caelo tacta. Anagniae terra pluit. Lanuvi[4] fax ardens in caelo visa. Calatiae in agro publico per triduum et duas noctes sanguis manavit. Rex Illyrici Gentius et Macedoniae Perses devicti.

A.U.C. 588

M. Marcello C.[5] Sulpicio coss.

12. In Campania multis locis terra pluit. In Praenestino cruenti ceciderunt imbres. Veienti

[1] Cn. Cornelio *add. Oudendorp*: *om.* MS.; Q. Petillio *Scheffer*: Lucio Petellio MS.
[2] vulturius *Scheffer*: ulterius MS.
[3] Aelio, Iunio *Hearn*: Aemylio, Iulio MS.
[4] Lanuvi *Perizonius*: Lavini MS.
[5] C. *Oudendorp*: P. MS.

---

[1] Items omitted by the Obsequens MS. between the years 175 and 167 include those mentioned in XLI. xxviii. 2; XLII. ii. 4–6; XLIII. xiii. 3–8; XLIV. xviii. 6. P. Mucius was consul this year, Quintus in 174.

Consulship of Gnaeus Cornelius and Quintus Petillius

B.C. 176

9. After the consuls had offered sacrifice, the liver melted away. Cornelius suffered a stroke on his way back from the Alban Mount and died at the spa of Cumae, while Petillius was killed in battle against the Ligurians. (XLI. xiv. 7; xv. 1–4; xvi. 3–4 [other prodigies, xvi. 6]; xviii. 8–11, 14.)

Consulship of Marcus Lepidus and Quintus Mucius

B.C. 175

10. During a serious plague of men and cattle, corpses lay exposed because Libitina was overwhelmed, but no vulture appeared. The Celtiberians were crushed. (XLI. xxi. 5–7; xxvi.[1])

Consulship of Quintus Aelius Paetus and Marcus Junius

B.C. 167

11. At Rome several places, both consecrated and common, were struck by lightning. At Anagnia there was a shower of earth. At Lanuvium a blazing meteor was seen in the sky. At Calatia on land owned by the state blood trickled for three days and two nights. King Gentius of Illyricum and King Perseus of Macedonia were conquered. (XLV. xvi. 5–7.)

Consulship of Marcus Marcellus and Gaius Sulpicius

B.C 166

12. In Campania there was a shower of earth at many points. In the territory of Praeneste bloody rain fell. In the territory of Veii wool grew from

A.U.C. 588 lana ex arboribus nata. Terracinae in aede Minervae mulieres tres, quae operatae sedebant, exanimatae. Ad lucum [1] Libitinae in statua equestri aenea ex ore et pede aqua manavit diu. Galli Ligures deleti.

Comitia cum ambitiosissime fierent et ob hoc senatus in Capitolio haberetur, milvus volans mustelam raptam de cella Iovis in medio consessu patrum misit. Sub idem tempus aedes Salutis de caelo tacta. In colle Quirinali sanguis terra manavit. Lanuvii fax in caelo nocte conspecta. Fulmine pleraque discussa Cassini et sol per aliquot horas noctis visus. Teani Sidicini puer cum quattuor manibus et totidem pedibus natus. Urbe lustrata [2] pax domi forisque fuit.

A.U.C. 589

Cn. Octavio T. Manlio coss.

13. Pestilentia fameque ita laboratum ut ex Sibyllinis populus circa compita sacellaque operaturus sederit. In aede Penatium valvae nocte sua sponte adapertae, et lupi Esquiliis et in colle Quirinali meridie apparuerunt exagitatique fuerunt. Urbe lustrata nihil triste accidit.

[1] lucum *Scheffer*: locum MS.
[2] lustrata *Stephanus*: strata MS.

trees. At Terracina in the temple of Minerva three women, who were seated after performing rites, lost their lives. At the grove of Libitina, water dripped for a long time from the mouth and foot of a bronze equestrian statue. The Ligurian Gauls were crushed. B.C. 166

When elections occurred marked by great corruption, and for this reason a session of the senate was being held on the Capitol, a kite came flying and dropped into the midst of the assembled Fathers a weasel that it had caught inside the temple of Jupiter. About this same time the temple of Safety was struck by lightning. On the Quirinal hill, blood oozed from the ground. At Lanuvium a meteor was seen in the sky by night. Several things were knocked to pieces by lightning at Cassinum, and the sun was seen for several hours at night. At Teanum Sidicinum a boy was born with four hands and as many feet. After the city had been purified there was peace at home and abroad. (Ligurians, *Summary* XLVI; bribery, cf. *Summary* XLVII, 159 B.C.)

Consulship of Gnaeus Octavius and Titus Manlius B.C. 165

13. There was such suffering from disease and hunger that on instructions from the Sibylline Books the people took seats at the cross-roads and shrines for the performance of rites. In the temple of the Penates the doors opened of their own accord at night, and wolves appeared at noon on the Esquiline and on the Quirinal Hill, and were driven out. After the city had been purified, no disaster occurred.

A.U.C. 591

Ti. Gracchо M'.[1] Iuventio coss.

14. Capuae nocte sol visus. In agro Stellati fulgure vervecum de grege pars exanimata. Terracinae pueri trigemini nati. Formiis duo soles interdiu visi. Caelum arsit. Antii[2] homo ex speculo acie orta combustus. Gabiis lacte pluit. Fulmine pleraque decussa in Palatio. In templum Victoriae cygnus inlapsus per manus capientium effugit. Priverni puella sine manu nata. In Cephallenia tuba[3] in caelo cantare visa. Terra pluit. Procellosa tempestate tecta diruta stragesque agrorum facta. Crebro fulminavit. Nocte species solis Pisauri adfulsit. Caere porcus humanis manibus et pedibus natus, et pueri quadrupedes et quadrumanes nati. Ad forum Aesi[4] bovem flamma ex ipsius ore nata non laesit.

A.U.C. 592

P. Scipione Nasica C.[5] Marcio coss.

15. Anagniae caelum nocte arsit. Fulmine pleraque decussa. Frusinone bos locutus. Reate mulus tripes natus. Cn. Octavius, legatus in Syria, per Lysiam, tutorem Antiochi pueri, in gymnasio occisus.

[1] Ti. *Jahn* : T. MS.; M'. *Hearn* : M. MS.
[2] Antii *Heinsius* : Concii MS. : Compsae *Kapp.*
[3] tuba *Perizonius* : turba MS.
[4] Aesi *Scheffer* : Esii MS. : fluvium Aesin *Oudendorp.*
[5] Nasica C. *Oudendorp* : Nasi. Gn. MS.

Consulship of Tiberius Gracchus and Manius Iuventius B.C. 163

14. At Capua the sun was seen by night. On the Stellate Plain part of a flock of wethers was struck dead by a thunderbolt. At Tarracina, male triplets were born. At Formiae two suns were seen by day. The sky was afire. At Antium a man was burned up by a ray of light from a mirror. At Gabii there was a rain of milk. Several things were overthrown by lightning on the Palatine. A swan glided into the temple of Victory and eluded the grasp of those who tried to capture it. At Privernum a girl was born without any hands. In Cephallenia a trumpet seemed to sound from the sky. There was a rain of earth. A windstorm demolished houses and laid crops flat in the fields. There was frequent lightning. By night an apparent sun shone at Pisaurum. At Caere a pig was born with human hands and feet, and children were born with four feet and four hands. At Forum Aesi an ox was uninjured by flame which sprang from its own mouth.

Consulship of Publius Scipio Nasica and Gaius Marcius B.C. 162

15. At Anagnia the sky was afire at night. Several things were overthrown by lightning. At Frusino an ox spoke. At Reate a three-footed mule was born. Gnaeus Octavius, an envoy to Syria, was assassinated in a gymnasium at the instigation of Lysias, the guardian of the boy Antiochus. (Octavius, Appian, *Syrian Wars* viii. 46. The assassin was Leptines, and Appian does not involve Lysias.)

A.U.C. 598

L. Lentulo C. Marcio coss.

16. Procellosa tempestate in Capitolio aedes Iovis et circa omnia[1] quassata. Pontificis[2] maximi tectum cum columnis in Tiberim deiectum. In circo Flaminio porticus inter aedem Iunonis Reginae et Fortunae tacta, et circa aedificia pleraque dissipata. Taurus ad immolationem cum duceretur ob haec ipsa corruit. Dalmatae Scordisci[3] superati.

A.U.C. 600

Q. Opimio L.[4] Postumio coss.

17. In provinciam proficiscens Postumius consul cum immolaret, in plurimis victimis caput in iocinere non invenit; profectusque post diem septimum aeger Romam relatus expiravit. Compsae[5] arma in caelo volare visa. Fulmine pleraque decussa. A Gallis et a Lusitanis Romani per arma graviter vexati.

A.U.C. 602

M. Claudio Marcello L. Valerio Flacco coss.

18. Turbinis vi in campo columna ante aedem Iovis decussa cum signo aurato; cumque aruspices

[1] omnia *add. Rossbach* : *om.* MS.
[2] pontificis *Mommsen* : pontis MS.
[3] Scordisci *Scheffer* : Scordis MS.
[4] Q., L. *Jahn*; L., Q. MS.
[5] Compsae *Cuper* : Consae MS.

Consulship of Lucius Lentulus and Gaius Marcius

B.C. 156

16. A violent storm racked the temple of Jupiter on the Capitol and everything near it. The roof of the chief pontiff's house with its columns was thrown down into the Tiber. In the Flaminian Circus a colonnade between the temple of Queen Juno and that of Fortune was struck, and several buildings near it were shattered. When a bull was being led to sacrifice because of these very portents, the animal collapsed. The Dalmatian Scordisci were defeated. (Presumably the Scordisci entered Illyricum on a raid, cf. *Ox. Summary* LIV, 141 B.C., and LVI, 135 B.C.)

Consulship of Quintus Opimius and Lucius Postumius

B.C. 154

17. As Consul Postumius was offering sacrifice on his departure for his field of operations, he found no head on the liver in a very large number of victims; he set out, but seven days later he was brought back to Rome ill, and breathed his last. At Compsa weapons appeared to fly through the sky. Several things were overthrown by lightning. The Romans received severe military setbacks from the Gauls and Lusitanians. (Gaul and Spain, *Summary* XLVII; Polybius XXXIII. viii–x.)

Consulship of Marcus Claudius Marcellus and Lucius Valerius Flaccus

B.C. 152

18. On the Campus Martius a column with a gilded statue in front of the temple of Jupiter was overthrown by a violent whirlwind; when the soothsayers

A.U.C. 602 respondissent magistratuum et sacerdotum interitum fore, omnes magistratus se protinus abdicaverunt. Quod Ariciae lapidibus pluerat, supplicatio habita, item[1] quod Romae multis locis species togatorum[2] visae adpropinquantium oculos eludebant. In Lusitania varie, in Gallia prospere pugnatum.

A.U.C. 606

SPURIO POSTUMIO L. PISONE COSS.

19. Vasto incendio Romae cum regia quoque ureretur, sacrarium et ex duabus altera laurus ex mediis ignibus inviolatae steterunt.[3] Pseudophilippus devictus.

A.U.C. 607

P. AFRICANO C. LIVIO[4] COSS.

20. Amiterni puer tribus pedibus, una manu natus. Romae et circa fulmine pleraque icta. Caere sanguinis rivi terra fluxerunt et nocte caelum ac terra ardere visum. Frusinone aurum sacrum mures adroserunt. Lanuvii inter horam tertiam et quintam duo discolores circuli solem cinxerunt rubente alter, alter candida linea. Stella arsit per dies triginta duos. Et cum Carthago obsideretur, in captivos Romanorum per Hasdrubalem barbaro more saevitum, mox Carthago per Aemilianum diruta.

[1] supplicatio habita, item *Scheffer*: ita supplicatio habita MS.

[2] togatorum *Freinshem*: togarum MS.

[3] inviolatae steterunt *Oudendorp*: inviolata est et erunt MS.

[4] C. Livio *Oudendorp, Pighius*: et Laelio MS.

made answer that there would be deaths among magistrates and priests, all the magistrates resigned forthwith. Because there had been a rain of stones at Aricia, a day of prayer was observed, and another because at many places in Rome apparitions of men in togas were seen that vanished from the sight of persons approaching them. Fighting went on in Spain with varying outcome, and in Gaul, with good success. (Claudius in Spain, *Summary* XLVIII; Polybius XXXV. ii. f.) B.C. 152

Consulship of Spurius Postumius and Lucius Piso B.C. 148

19. In a huge fire at Rome, the Regia also was burned, but the sanctuary and one of a pair of laurel trees came out of the midst of the fire unscathed. The false Philip was overthrown. (*Summaries* L and *Ox.* L.)

Consulship of Publius Africanus and Gaius Livius B.C. 147

20. At Amiternum a boy was born with three feet and one hand. At Rome and near by several things were hit by lightning. At Caere streams of blood flowed from the earth and at night heaven and earth seemed to be on fire. At Frusino mice gnawed the sacred gold. At Lanuvium between the third and the fifth hour two halos of different colours encircled the sun; one made a red line, the other a white. A comet blazed for thirty-two days. While Carthage was being besieged, barbaric outrages were inflicted by Hasdrubal on Roman prisoners, and presently Carthage was rased by Aemilianus. (*Summary Ox.* LI.)

A.U.C. 611

Appio Claudio Q.[1] Metello coss.

21. Amiterni puer tribus pedibus natus. Caurae sanguinis rivi e terra fluxerunt. Cum a Salassis illata clades esset Romanis, decemviri pronuntiaverunt se invenisse in Sibyllinis, quotiens bellum Gallis illaturi essent, sacrificari in eorum finibus oportere.

A.U.C. 612

L. Metello Q. Fabio Maximo coss.

22. Fames et pestilentia cum essent, per decemviros supplicatum. Lunae androgynus natus praecepto aruspicum in mare deportatus. Tanta fuit Lunensibus pestilentia ut iacentibus in publicum passim cadaveribus, qui funerarent defuerint. In Macedonia exercitus Romanus proelio vexatus: adversus Viriathum dubie dimicavit.

A.U.C. 614

Q.[2] Caepione C. Laelio coss.

23. Praeneste et in Cephallenia signa de caelo cecidisse visa. Mons Aetna ignibus abundavit. Prodigium maioribus hostiis quadraginta expiatum. Annus pacatus fuit Viriatho victo.

[1] Q. *Hearn*: P. MS.
[2] Q. *Oudendorp*: Gn. MS.

CONSULSHIP OF APPIUS CLAUDIUS AND QUINTUS METELLUS B.C. 143

21. At Amiternum a boy was born with three feet. At Caura streams of blood flowed from the ground. When the Salassi inflicted a disaster on the Romans, the Board of Ten announced that they had found a provision in the Sibylline Books that, whenever the Romans were about to launch a campaign against Gauls, they were required to offer sacrifice in enemy territory. (*Summary* LIII; Dio XXII. fr. 74. 1; Orosius V. iv. 7 [293].)

CONSULSHIP OF LUCIUS METELLUS AND QUINTUS FABIUS MAXIMUS B.C. 142

22. Since there was famine and an epidemic, an observance of prayer was offered by the Board of Ten. At Luna a hermaphrodite was born, and on the instructions of the soothsayers was cast into the sea. There was such a plague among the people of Luna that though the corpses were lying about everywhere in civic areas, men to perform burial were lacking. In Macedonia a Roman army suffered losses in battle; against Viriathus another fought without success. (*Summaries* LIII and *Ox.* LIII; Orosius V. iv. 8–14 [293], but Orosius places the epidemic at Rome.)

CONSULSHIP OF QUINTUS CAEPIO AND GAIUS LAELIUS B.C. 140

23. At Praeneste and in Cephallenia it seemed that images had fallen from the sky. Mount Aetna showed much fire. This portent was expiated with forty full-grown victims. The year was peaceful after the defeat of Viriathus. (*Summary* LIV.)

A.U.C. 617

M. Aemilio C. Hostilio Mancino coss.

24. Cum Lavinii[1] auspicaretur, pulli e cavea in silvam Laurentinam evolarunt neque inventi sunt. Praeneste fax ardens in caelo visa, sereno intonuit. Terracinae M. Claudius praetor in nave fulmine conflagravit. Lacus Fucinus per milia passuum quinque quoquo[2] versum inundavit. In Graecostasi et comitio sanguine fluxit. Esquiliis equuleus cum quinque pedibus natus. Fulmine pleraque decussa. Hostilius Mancinus consul in portu Herculis cum conscenderet navem petens Numantiam, vox improviso audita, " Mane, Mancine." Cumque egressus postea navem Genuae conscendisset, anguis in navi inventus e manibus effugit. Ipse consul devictus, mox Numantinis deditus.

A.U.C. 618

L. Furio S.[3] Atilio Serrano coss.

25. Regium paene totum incendio consumptum sine ullo humano fraudis aut neglegentiae vestigio. Puer ex ancilla quattuor pedibus manibus oculis auribus et duplici obsceno natus. Puteolis in aquis calidis rivi manarunt sanguine. Fulmine pleraque deiecta. Puer aruspicum iussu crematus cinisque eius in mare deiectus. A Vaccaeis[4] exercitus Romanus caesus.

[1] Lavinii *Cluver*: Lanuvii MS.
[2] quoquo *Stephanus*: quoque MS.
[3] S. *add. Panvin*: *om.* MS.
[4] Vaccaeis *Oudendorp*: ab Achaeis MS.

Consulship of Marcus Aemilius and Gaius Hostilius Mancinus B.C. 137

24. When the auspices were taken at Lavinium, the chickens flew out of their coop into the Laurentine forest and could not be found. At Praeneste a blazing meteor appeared in the sky, and there was thunder from cloudless heavens. At Tarracina Praetor Marcus Claudius was burned up in his ship by a lightning bolt. The Fucine Lake overflowed the land for five miles in all directions. In the Graecostasis and assembly ground there was a flow of blood. On the Esquiline a colt was born with five feet. Several things were overthrown by lightning. As Consul Hostilius Mancinus was boarding ship in the harbour of Hercules on his way to Numantia, a cry was suddenly heard, "Stay, Mancinus!" When, after disembarking, he had later taken ship at Genoa, a snake that was found on the ship escaped from capture. The consul himself was defeated and not long after was handed over to the Numantines. (*Summary* LV; Valerius Maximus I. vi. 7.)

Consulship of Lucius Furius and Sextus Atilius Serranus B.C. 136

25. Regium was almost wholly consumed by fire without any trace of human malfeasance or carelessness. A maidservant bore a boy with four hands, feet, eyes, and ears, and double private parts. In the hot springs at Puteoli streams of blood issued. Several things were overthrown by lightning. The boy was burned by order of the soothsayers, and his ashes were thrown into the sea. A Roman army was cut to pieces by the Vaccaei. (*Summary* LVI.)

A.U.C. 619

Ser. Flacco Q. Calpurnio coss.

26. Mons Aetna maioribus solito arsit ignibus. Romae puer solidus posteriore naturae parte genitus. Bononiae fruges in arboribus natae. Bubonis vox primum in Capitolio dein circa urbem audita. Quae avis praemio posito ab aucupe capta combustaque; cinis eius in Tiberim dispersus. Bos locutus. In Numantinis res male gestae, exercitus Romanus oppressus.

A.U.C. 620

P. Africano C. Fulvio coss.

27. In Amiterno sol noctu visus, eiusque lux aliquamdiu fuit visa. Bos locutus et nutritus publice. Sanguine pluit. Anagniae servo tunica arsit et intermortuo igne nullum flammae apparuit vestigium. In Capitolio nocte avis gemitus similes hominis dedit. In aede Iunonis Reginae scutum Ligusticum fulmine tactum. Fugitivorum bellum in Sicilia exortum, coniuratione servorum in [1] Italia oppressa.

A.U.C. 621

P. Mucio L. Pisone coss.[2]

27a. Tiberius Gracchus . . .[3] legibus ferendis occisus. Proditum est memoria Tiberium Gracchum,

[1] in *add. Jahn*: *om.* MS.
[2] P. Mucio L. Pisone coss. *add. Ouaendorp*: *om.* MS.
[3] *lacunam ind. Jahn*: tr. pleb. *add. Rossbach*: in *add. Kornemann.*

Consulship of Servius Flaccus and Quintus Calpurnius B.C. 135

26. Mount Aetna flamed up with greater fires than usual. At Rome a boy was born without aperture in his fundament. At Bononia grain grew on trees. The cry of an owl was heard first on the Capitol and then about the city. After a reward had been offered this bird was caught by a fowler and burned; its ashes were scattered in the Tiber. An ox spoke. Before Numantia there was bad management and the Roman army was crushed. (*Summary* LVI; Orosius V. vi. 2–4; on the portent of grain, in general, cf. Pliny, *Natural History* XVIII. 166, and on owls, X. 34 f.)

Consulship of Publius Africanus and Gaius Fulvius B.C. 134

27. In Amiternum the sun was seen by night, and its light appeared for some length of time. An ox spoke, and was maintained at the public charge. There was a rain of blood. At Anagnia the tunic of a slave blazed up, and when the fire had died out no trace of flame was visible. On the Capitol at night a bird uttered groans which sounded human. In the temple of Queen Juno a Ligurian shield was struck by lightning. Runaway slaves began a war in Sicily, after a conspiracy of slaves in Italy had been crushed. (*Summary* LVI.)

Consulship of Publius Mucius and Lucius Piso B.C. 133

27a. Tiberius Gracchus was killed in connection with the passage of certain laws. It is preserved in the record that Tiberius Gracchus, on the day he

A.U.C. 621 quo die periit, tristia neglexisse omina, cum domi et in Capitolio sacrificanti dira portenderentur, domoque exiens sinistro ad limen offenso pede decusserit pollicem, et corvi fragmentum tegulae ante pedes eius proiecerint[1] ex stillicidio. In lacu Romano lacte rivi manarunt. Lunae terra quattuor iugerum spatio in profundum abiit et mox de caverna lacum reddidit. Ardeae terra pluit. Minturnis lupus vigilem laniavit et inter tumultum effugit. Romae bubo et alia avis ignota visa. In aede Iunonis Reginae clausis per biduum valvis infantis vox audita. Scuta novo sanguine maculata. Puella quadrupes nata. In agro Ferentino androgynus natus et in flumen deiectus. Virgines ter novenae canentes urbem lustraverunt.

A.U.C. 622

P. Popillio P. Rupilio coss.[2]

27b. In Italia multa milia servorum quae coniuraverant aegre comprehensa et supplicio consumpta. In Sicilia fugitivi Romanos exercitus necaverunt. Numantia diruta.

A.U.C. 624

Ap. Claudio M. Perperna coss.

28. Reate mulus cum quinque pedibus natus. Romae in Graecostasi[3] lacte pluit. Lupus et canis

[1] proiecerint *Stephanus*: proiecerunt MS.
[2] P. Popillio P. Rupilio coss. *ad. Oudendorp*: *om.* MS.
[3] Graecostasi *Munker*: agro Cortasi MS.

died, disregarded unfavourable omens, when evil was foreshadowed at his sacrifices both at home and on the Capitol. Furthermore, as he left his home he struck his left foot against the threshold and dislocated the great toe, and crows dropped a bit of tile from a rain-channel before his feet. In the Roman Pool streams of milk flowed. At Luna the earth over an area of two and a half acres disappeared into an abyss and presently produced a pool from the depths. At Ardea there was a rain of earth. At Minturnae a wolf slashed a watchman and escaped in the confusion. At Rome an owl was seen, as well as another and unknown bird. In the temple of Queen Juno the cry of a baby was heard for two days through the closed doors. Shields were stained with fresh blood. A girl was born with four feet. In Ferentine territory a hermaphrodite was born and cast into the river. Thrice nine maidens sang a chant and purified the city. (*Summary* LVIII; Plutarch, *Tiberius Gracchus* xvii; Valerius Maximus I. iv. 2 [3].) B.C. 133

Consulship of Publius Popillius and Publius Rupilius B.C. 132

27b. In Italy many thousand slaves who entered into a conspiracy were with difficulty arrested and destroyed by punishment. In Sicily the runaway slaves put Roman armies to death. Numantia was rased. (*Summary* LIX.)

Consulship of Appius Claudius and Marcus Perperna B.C. 130

28. At Reate a mule with five feet was born. At Rome there was a rain of milk in the Graecostasis.

A.U.C. 624 Hostiae pugnantes fulmine exanimati. Grex ovium in Apulia uno ictu fulmine exanimatus. Praetor populi Romani fulmine exanimatus. Terracinae sereno navis velum fulmine in aqua deiectum,[1] et impensas omnis quae ibi erant ignis absumpsit. Publius Crassus adversus Aristonicum dimicans occisus. Apollinis simulacrum lacrimavit per quadriduum. Vates portenderunt Graeciae fore exitium, unde deductum esset. Sacrificatum tum a Romanis donaque in templo posita. Phrygia recepta Asia Attali testamento legata Romanis. Antiocho regi Syriae ingenti exercitu dimicanti hirundines in tabernaculo nidum fecerunt. Quo prodigio neglecto proelium commisit et a Parthis occisus est.

A.U.C. 625

C. Sempronio M'. Aquilio coss.[2]

28a. . . . M. Fulvii Flacci triumviri . . . dissensione in legibus ferendis . . .[3] Angues duo nigri in cella Minervae allapsi civilem caedem portenderunt.

[1] Grex ovium in Apulia uno ictu fulmine exanimatus. Praetor populi Romani fulmine exanimatus. Terracinae sereno navis velum fulmine in aqua deiectum *Schlesinger*; Grex ovium in Apulia praetor populi Romani uno ictu fulmine exanimatus. Tarracinae sereno navis velum fulmine exanimatum in aquam deiectum MS : Grex ovium in Apulia fulmine exanimatus. Praetor populi Romani uno ictu fulmine exanimatus. Terracinae sereno navis velum in aqua deiectum *Rossbach*.

At Ostia a wolf and a dog were killed by lightning while fighting. A flock of sheep in Apulia was killed by a single stroke of lightning. A praetor of the Roman People was killed by lightning. At Terracina the sail of a ship was thrown into the water by lightning from a clear sky, and fire swept away all the stores which were there. Publius Crassus lost his life fighting against Aristonicus. The statue of Apollo wept for four days. Soothsayers prophesied that destruction would fall on Greece, whence the statue had been brought. A sacrifice was offered at that time by the Romans, and gifts were deposited in the temple. When Phrygia had been recovered, western Asia Minor was bequeathed to the Romans by the will of Attalus. When Antiochus, King of Syria, was on campaign with a huge army, swallows built a nest in his tent. He failed to heed this portent, joined battle, and was slain by the Parthians. (Attalus, *Summary* LIX; Apollo, Augustine, *City of God* III. 11; Dio XXIV. fr. 84. 2; Antiochus, Diodorus XXXIV–V. 15–17; Justinus XXXVIII. x. 9–10; Appian, *Syrian Wars* xi. 68.) B.C. 130

Consulship of Gaius Sempronius and Manius Aquilius B.C. 129

28a. . . . of Marcus Fulvius Flaccus of the Board of Three . . . discord over the passage of laws . . . Two black snakes slipped into the sanctuary of Minerva's temple, portending a slaughter of citizens. (*Summary* LIX.)

---

[2] C. Sempronio M'. Aquilio coss. *add. Jahn* : *om.* MS.
[3] *lacunas indicaverunt Jahn et H. J. Mueller.*

A.U.C. 628

M. Aemilio L. Aurelio coss.

29. Nocturna tempestate in Capitolio aliquot templa concussa sunt. Romae et circa fulmine pleraque deiecta sunt. Aetna mons terrae motu ignes super verticem late diffudit, et ad insulas[1] Liparas mare efferbuit et quibusdam adustis navibus vapore plerosque navalis exanimavit, piscium vim magnam exanimem dispersit, quos Liparenses avidius epulis appetentes contaminatione ventris consumpti, ita ut nova pestilentia vastarentur insulae. Quod prodigium aruspicum responso seditionem, quae post tempora ea fuit,[2] portendit.

A.U.C. 629

M.[3] Plautio M. Fulvio coss.

30. In arboribus fruges natae sunt. Oleo et lacte in Veiente pluit. Bubo in Capitolio visus. Arpis lapideus imber triduo . . .[4] apparuit locustarum ingenti agmine in Africa, quae a vento in mare deiectae fluctibusque eiectae odore intolerabili Cyrenis mortiferoque[5] vapore gravem pestilentiam fecerunt pecori; hominumque DCCC milia consumpta tabe proditum est. Fregellae, quae adversus Romanos coniuraverunt, dirutae. Ligures Sallyes trucidati.

[1] insulas *Jahn*: insulam MS.
[2] ea fuit *Rossbach*: patuit MS.: tempore patuit *Jahn.*
[3] M. *Oudendorp*: P. MS.
[4] *lacunam ind. Scheffer*: cecidit; vis *add. Haupt.*
[5] mortiferoque *Jahn*: mortifero MS.

Consulship of Marcus Aemilius and Lucius Aurelius

B.C. 126

29. During a storm at night many temples on the Capitol were shaken. At Rome and near by several things were overthrown by lightning. Mount Aetna, with an earthquake, scattered fire far and wide around its summit, and near the Liparae Islands the sea boiled up, burned certain ships, and stifled several mariners with fumes; it scattered about a large amount of dead fish. The Liparians took to them too greedily at their feasts, and were carried off by a poisoning of the stomach, so that the islands were devastated by an unheard-of plague. This portent, according to the answer of the soothsayers, prophesied the civil strife that occurred after these times. (Volcanism, Orosius V. x. 11; Strabo VI. ii. 11 [277]; Pliny, *Natural History* II. 203 [88].)

Consulship of Marcus Plautius and Marcus Fulvius

B.C. 125

30. Grain grew on trees. There was a rain of oil and milk in the neighbourhood of Veii. An owl was seen on the Capitol. At Arpi there was a rain of stones for three days . . . locusts appeared in a great swarm in Africa; when hurled into the sea by the wind and cast up by the waves, they produced by their unbearable stench and deadly effluvium a serious plague among livestock at Cyrene, and eight hundred thousand persons are reported to have been carried off by the putrefaction. Fregellae, which had conspired against the Romans, was rased. The Ligurian Sallyes were slaughtered. (*Summary* LX; locusts, Augustine, *City of God* III. 31; Orosius V. xi. 1–7; Fregellae, Velleius II. vi. 4.)

A.U.C. 630

C. Cassio Longino C. Sextio[1] coss.

31. In Graecostasi lacte pluit. Fulmine Crotone grex ovium cum cane et tribus pastoribus exanimatus. Saturae vitulus biceps natus. Tumultus in urbe fuit C.[2] Graccho leges ferente.

A.U.C. 632

Cn. Domitio C. Fannio coss.

32. In foro Vessano androgynus natus in mare delatus est. In Gallia tres soles et tres lunae visae. Vitulus biceps natus. Bubo in Capitolio visus. Aetnae[3] incendio Catina[4] consumpta. Sallyes et Allobroges devicti.

A.U.C. 633

L. Opimio Q. Fabio Maximo coss.

33. Grex luporum limites qui in agrorum divisione per C. Gracchum depositi erant dissipavit. Ipse Gracchus in Aventino occisus.

A.U.C. 635

L. Aurelio Cotta[5] L. Caecilio coss.

34. Androgynus in agro Romano annorum octo inventus et in mare deportatus. Virgines ter novenae in urbe cantarunt.

[1] Sextio *Hearn*: Sextilio MS.
[2] C. *add. Jahn*: *om.* MS.
[3] Aetnae *Oudendorp*: et ex MS.
[4] Catina *Oudendorp*: cathena MS.
[5] Cotta *Jahn*: et MS.

---

[1] This town-name does not appear elsewhere; "Saturnia" was suggested by Scaliger, "Astura" by Cluver.

Consulship of Gaius Cassius Longinus and Gaius Sextius

B.C. 124

31. In the Graecostasis there was a rain of milk. At Croton a flock of sheep with the dog and three shepherds perished by lightning. At Satura[1] a two-headed calf was born. There was rioting in Rome over the legislation of Gaius Gracchus. (*Summary* LX.)

Consulship of Gnaeus Domitius and Gaius Fannius

B.C. 122

32. In Forum Vessanum a hermaphrodite was born and was removed to the sea. In Gaul three suns and three moons were seen. A two-headed calf was born. An owl was seen on the Capitol. Catana was burned in an eruption of Aetna. The Sallyes and Allobroges were conquered. (*Summary* LXI; Orosius V. xiii. 3; Augustine, *City of God* III. 31; Pliny, *Natural History* II. 99.)

Consulship of Lucius Opimius and Quintus Fabius Maximus

B.C. 121

33. A pack of wolves scattered the boundary-stones which had been set up during the division of properties by Gaius Gracchus. Gracchus himself was slain on the Aventine. (*Summary* LXI.)

Consulship of Lucius Aurelius Cotta and Lucius Caecilius

B.C. 119

34. A hermaphrodite eight years old was found in Roman territory and was carried away to sea. Thrice nine maidens performed a chant in the city.

A.U.C. 636

M. CATONE Q. MARCIO[1] COSS.

35. Catone consule immolante exta tabuerunt, caput iocineris inventum non est. Lacte pluit. Terra cum mugitu tremuit. Examen apum in foro consedit. Sacrificium ex Sibyllinis.

A.U.C. 637

L. CAECILIO L. AURELIO COSS.

36. Fulmine Romae et circa pleraque tacta. Praeneste lacte pluit. Hastae Martis in regia motae. Priverni terra septem iugerum spatio in caverna desedit. Saturniae androgynus annorum decem inventus et mari demersus. Virgines viginti septem urbem carmine lustraverunt. Reliquum anni in pace fuit.

A.U.C. 640

M'.[2] ACILIO C. PORCIO COSS.

37. P. Elvius[3] eques Romanus a ludis Romanis cum in Apuliam[4] reverteretur, in agro Stellati filia eius virgo equo insidens fulmine icta exanimataque, vestimento deducto in inguinibus, exserta lingua, per inferiores locos ut ignis ad os emicuerit. Responsum

[1] Q. Marcio *Lycosthenes* : Quintio Marcio MS.
[2] M'. *Hearn* : M. MS.
[3] P. Elvius *Mommsen* : Pompeius Eluius MS.
[4] Apuliam *Scheffer* : Apulia MS.

---

[1] This name has perhaps strayed from the year 119, cf. above; the second consul was actually Quintus Mucius Scaevola.

Consulship of Marcus Cato and Quintus Marcius B.C. 118

35. When Consul Cato offered sacrifice, the entrails melted away, and no head was found on the liver. There was a rain of milk. The earth quaked with a bellowing sound. A swarm of bees settled in the forum. Sacrifice was offered in accordance with the Sibylline Books.

Consulship of Lucius Caecilius and Lucius Aurelius [1] B.C. 117

36. Several things were damaged by lightning in Rome and near by. At Praeneste there was a rain of milk. The spears of Mars in the Regia moved. At Privernum the earth sank into a hollow over an area of four and a half acres. At Saturnia a hermaphrodite ten years old was found and sunk in the sea. Twenty-seven maidens purified the city with a chant. The rest of the year was peaceful. (Privernum, Cicero, *On Divination* I. xliii. 97, a passage mentioning many other prodigies, including the three moons, above, 32.)

Consulship of Manius Acilius and Gaius Porcius B.C. 114

37. When Publius Elvius, a Roman knight, was returning to Apulia from the Roman Games, on the Stellate Plain his maiden daughter, while riding horseback, was struck lifeless by a thunderbolt, her dress was pulled awry to her groin, and her tongue protruded, as if the lightning had flashed over her lower limbs to her mouth. The soothsayers' answer

A.U.C. 640 infamiam virginibus et equestri ordini portendi, quia equi ornamenta dispersa erant. Tres uno tempore virgines Vestales nobilissimae cum aliquot equitibus Romanis incesti poenas subierunt. Aedes Veneri Verticordiae facta.

A.U.C. 641

C. Caecilio Cn. Papirio coss.

38. Albanus mons nocte ardere visus. Aedicula et signum de caelo tacta. Ara Salutis interrupta. Terra in Lucanis et Privernati late hiavit. In Gallia caelum ardere visum. Cimbri Teutonique Alpes transgressi foedam stragem Romanorum sociorumque fecerunt.

A.U.C. 643

P. Scipione L. Calpurnio coss.

39. Maxima pars urbis exusta cum aede Matris Magnae. Lacte per triduum pluit, hostiisque expiatum maioribus. Iugurthinum bellum exortum.

was that disgrace to virgins and to the order of knights was prophesied, since the trappings of the horse were scattered about. Three Vestal Virgins of most distinguished families, along with several Roman knights, at this one time suffered punishment for breach of chastity. A temple was built to Venus, Turner of Hearts. (*Summary* LXIII; Orosius V. xv. 20–22 [325 f.]; Plutarch, *Roman Questions* 83; Dio XXVI. fr. 87; Verticordia, cf. Ovid, *Fasti* IV. 157–60.) B.C. 114

Consulship of Gaius Caecilius and Gnaeus Papirius

B.C. 113

38. The Alban Mount seemed to be on fire by night. A small shrine and a statue were struck by lightning. The altar of Safety was broken. Wide cracks in the earth appeared in Lucania and the neighbourhood of Privernum. In Gaul the sky appeared to be on fire. The Cimbri and Teutoni crossed the Alps and inflicted a shameful slaughter on the Romans and their allies. (Pliny, *Natural History* II. 100 [33]; cf. *Summary* LXIII.—The Cimbri entered Illyricum.

Consulship of Publius Scipio and Lucius Calpurnius

B.C. 111

39. A very large part of the city was burned out, along with the temple of the Great Mother. There was a rain of milk for three days, and expiation was made with full-grown victims. The war with Jugurtha began. (*Summary* LXIV.)

A.U.C. 646

SERVIO[1] GALBA M. SCAURO COSS.

40. Avis incendiaria et bubo in urbe[2] visae. In laotomiis homo ab homine adesus. Ex Sibyllinis in insula Cimolia sacrificatum per triginta ingenuos patrimos et matrimos totidemque virgines. Multa milia hominum intumescente Pado et stagno Arretino obruta. Bis lacte pluit. Nursiae gemini ex muliere ingenua nati, puella integris omnibus membris, puer a parte priore alvo aperto ita ut nudum intestinum conspiceretur, idem posteriore natura solidus natus, qui voce missa expiravit. Contra Iugurtham prospere dimicatum.

A.U.C. 648

Q. SERVILIO CAEPIONE C.[3] ATILIO SERRANO COSS.

41. Amiterni cum ex ancilla puer nasceretur, ave dixit.[4] In agro Perusino et Romae locis aliquot lacte pluit. Inter multa fulmine icta Atellis digiti hominis quattuor tamquam ferro praecisi. Argentum signatum afflatu fulminis diffluxit. In agro Trebulano mulier nupta civi Romano fulmine icta nec exanimata. Fremitus caelestis auditus et pila caelo cadere visa. Sanguine pluit. Romae interdiu fax

[1] Servio *Broughton*: Sergio MS., *cf. Orosius IV. xxi. 3, 10.*
[2] urbe *Stephanus* : urbem MS.
[3] C. *add. Oudendorp* : *om.* MS.
[4] dixit *Scheffer* : dixit P. Sarrano G. Atilio Coss. MS.

Consulship of Servius Galba and Marcus Scaurus B.C. 108

40. A firebird and an owl were seen in the city. In the quarries one man was devoured by another. In accordance with the Sibylline Books, sacrifice was offered on Cimolos Island by thirty freeborn boys with living fathers and mothers, and as many maidens. Many thousand persons were overwhelmed in floods of the Po and the lake of Arretium. Twice there was a rain of milk. At Nursia twins were born to a free woman, a girl with all her members intact, and a boy with his belly open in front so that the bare intestine could be seen, whereas at the rear the child was without opening; he gave a cry and breathed his last. An encounter with Jugurtha was successful. (Firebird, Pliny, *Natural History* X. 36 [xvii].—Pliny cannot identify the bird; Jugurtha, *Summary* LXV.)

Consulship of Quintus Servilius Caepio and Gaius Atilius Serranus B.C. 106

41. At Amiternum, as a boy was being born to a serving-woman, he cried "Hail!" In the neighbourhood of Perusia and at several points in Rome there was a rain of milk. Among many things struck by lightning, at Atellae four of a man's fingers were cut off as if with a knife. Coined silver flowed away under a bolt of lightning. In the neighbourhood of Trebula a woman married to a Roman citizen was struck by lightning, but survived. An uproar in the sky was heard, and javelins seemed to fall from heaven. There was a rain of blood. At Rome a meteor was seen by day flying aloft. In the

A.U.C. 648 sublime volans conspecta. In aede Larum flamma a fastigio ad summum columen penetravit innoxia. Per Caepionem consulem senatorum et equitum iudicia communicata. Cetera in pace fuerunt.

A.U.C. 649

P. Rutilio Cn. Manlio coss.[1]

42. Trebulae Mutuscae ante quam ludi committerentur, canente tibicine angues nigri aram circumdederunt, desinente cantare dilapsi. Postero die exorti a populo lapidibus enecati. Foribus templi adapertis simulacrum Martis ligneum capite stans inventum. A Lusitanis exercitus Romanus caesus.

A.U.C. 650

C. Mario C. Flavio[2] coss.

43. Bubo extra urbem visus. Bos locuta. Trebulae Mutuscae simulacrum in templo, quod capite adaperto[3] fuit, opertum inventum. Nuceriae ulmus vento eversa sua sponte erecta in radicem convaluit. In Lucanis lacte, Lunae sanguine pluit. Arimini canis locutus. Arma caelestia tempore utroque[4] ab ortu et occasu visa pugnare et ab occasu vinci.

[1] Rutilio Cn. Manlio *Oudendorp* : Atilio et Cornelio Manilio MS.
[2] Flavio *Oudendorp* : Flacc. MS.
[3] adaperto *Heinsius* : adoperto MS.
[4] *sic* MS. : Tuderte Ameriaeque *Rossbach in scholio.*

---

[1] If this curious phrase is correct, it might mean either "night and morning," or "by day and by night," as Scheffer suggests; other editors emend the text, Rossbach taking the reading "at Tuder and Ameria" from the accounts of Pliny and Plutarch (see references below, and the critical note).

temple of the Lares a flame penetrated from the roof-top to the top of a column without doing damage. By the agency of Consul Caepio, juries were divided between the senate and the knights. Otherwise peaceful conditions prevailed. (Juries, Cicero, *Brutus* xliv. 161, 164; Cassiodorus, a.u.c. 648 = Livy, fr. (i) Hertz.) B.C. 106

Consulship of Publius Rutilius and Gnaeus Manlius B.C. 105

42. At Trebula Mutusca before the games were opened, as the flute-player was performing, black snakes surrounded the altar, but slipped away when he ceased to play. The next day they came out and were stoned to death by the people. When the doors of his temple were opened, a wooden statue of Mars was found standing on its head. A Roman army was slaughtered by the Lusitanians. (Snakes, Granius Licinianus xxxiii, p. 13 Flemisch.)

Consulship of Gaius Marius and Gaius Flavius B.C. 104

43. An owl was seen outside Rome. A cow spoke. At Trebula Mutusca an image in a temple, the head of which had been bare, was found veiled. At Nuceria an elm, overturned by the wind, straightened upon its root of its own accord and regained its strength. In Lucania there was a rain of milk, at Luna, of blood. At Ariminum a dog spoke. Weapons in the sky seemed to join battle at both times of day[1] from east and west; those from the west appeared to suffer defeat. According to an answer of the soothsayers, the people brought a

A.U.C. 650 Aruspicum responso populus stipem Cereri et Proserpinae tulit. Virgines viginti septem dona canentes tulerunt. Luna interdiu cum stella ab hora tertia usque ad horam septimam apparuit. A fugitivis et desertoribus in Thurinis regiones vastatae. Cimbri Alpes transgressi post[1] Hispaniam vastatam iunxerunt se Teutonis. Lupus urbem intravit. Fulminis ictu vultures super turrem exanimati. Hora diei tertia solis defectus lucem obscuravit. Examen apium ante aedem Salutis consedit. In comitio lacte pluit. In Piceno tres soles visi. In agro Vulsiniensi flamma e terra orta caelumque visa contingere. In Lucanis duo agni equinis pedibus nati, alter siminino capite. In Tarquiniensi lactis rivi terra scaturienti exorti.[2] Aruspicum responso signa oleaginea duo armata statuta supplicatumque. In Macedonia Thraces subacti.

A.U.C. 652

C. Mario Q. Lutatio coss.

44. Novemdiale sacrum fuit, quod in Tuscis lapidibus pluerat. Urbs aruspicum iussu lustrata. Hostiarum cinis per decemviros in mare dispersus, et per dies novem per magistratus circa omnia templa[3] et municipia pompa ducta supplicantum. Hastae Martis in regia sua sponte motae. Sanguine circa

[1] post *Burmann* : per MS.
[2] exorti *Stephanus* : exorta MS.
[3] per magistratus circa omnia templa *Rossbach* circa omnia templa per magistratus MS.: *fortasse* per *ante* municipia *addendum Rossbach.*

collection to Ceres and Proserpina. Twenty-seven maidens, chanting, brought gifts. The moon and a star appeared by day from the third to the seventh hour. Territory near Thurii was ravaged by runaway slaves and deserters. The Cimbri crossed the Alps after ravaging Spain, and united with the Teutoni. A wolf entered Rome. Vultures on a tower were struck dead by a lightning bolt. At the third hour of the day an eclipse of the sun brought on darkness. A swarm of bees settled in front of the temple of Safety. In the voting-ground there was a rain of milk. In Picenum three suns were seen. In the neighbourhood of Volsinii flame rising from the ground seemed to touch the sky. In Lucania two lambs were born with horses' feet; one of them had the head of a monkey. Near Tarquinii streams of milk sprang copiously from the earth. According to an answer from the soothsayers two armed olive-wood statues were set up and prayer was offered. In Macedonia the Thracians were subdued. (Cimbri, *Summary* LXVII; battle in sky, Plutarch, *Marius* xvii. 4; Pliny, *Natural History* II. lviii [148].) B.C. 104

Consulship of Gaius Marius and Quintus Lutatius B.C. 102

44. A nine-day ceremony was observed because it had rained stones in Etruria. The city was purified, by order of the soothsayers. The ashes of the victims were scattered in the sea by the Board of Ten, and for nine days a procession of suppliants was led by magistrates about all the temples and the outlying towns. The spears of Mars in the Regia moved of their own accord. There was a rain of blood

A.U.C. 652 amnem Anienem pluit. Examen apium in foro boario in sacello consedit. In Gallia in castris lux nocte fulsit. Puer ingenuus Ariciae flamma comprehensus nec ambustus. Aedes Iovis clusa fulmine icta. Cuius expiationem quia primus [1] monstraverat Aemilius Potensis aruspex, praemium tulit, ceteris celantibus quod ipsis liberisque exitium portenderetur. Piratae in Cilicia [2] a Romanis deleti. Teutoni a Mario trucidati.

A.U.C. 653

C. Mario M'. Aquilio coss.[3]

44a. Ancilia cum crepitu sua sponte mota. Servus Q.[4] Servilii Caepionis Matri [5] Idaeae se praecidit, et trans mare exportatus, ne umquam Romae reverteretur. Urbs lustrata. Capra cornibus ardentibus per urbem ducta, porta Naevia emissa relictaque. In Aventino luto pluit. Lusitanis devictis Hispania ulterior pacata. Cimbri deleti.

A.U.C. 654

C. Mario L. Valerio coss.

45. Fax ardens Tarquiniis late visa subito lapsu cadens. Sub occasu solis orbis clipei similis ab occi-

[1] primus *Scheffer*: prius MS.
[2] Cilicia *Sigonius*: Sicilia MS.
[3] C. Mario M'. Aquilio coss. *add. Oudendorp*: *om.* MS.
[4] Q. *Jahn*: que MS.
[5] Matri *Pighius*: matris MS.

around the Anio River. A swarm of bees settled in a shrine in the Cattle-Market. In a camp in Gaul a light shone at night. A freeborn boy at Aricia was enveloped in flame but not consumed. The temple of Jupiter, while closed, was struck by lightning. The expiation for this was first explained by the soothsayer Aemilius Potensis, and for this he received a reward; the other soothsayers had kept it secret because destruction of themselves and their children was portended. The pirates in Cilicia were wiped out by the Romans. The Teutoni were slaughtered by Marius. (*Summary* LXVIII; Plutarch, *Marius* xx f.) B.C. 102

Consulship of Gaius Marius and Manius Aquilius B.C. 101

44a. The sacred shields rattled and moved of their own accord. A slave of Quintus Servilius Caepio emasculated himself in devotion to the Great Mother, and was shipped across the sea, that he might never return to Rome. The city was purified. A she-goat with horns afire was led through the city, expelled by the Naevian Gate, and abandoned. On the Aventine it rained mud. The Lusitanians were subdued, and Farther Spain enjoyed peace. The Cimbri were wiped out. (*Summary* LXVIII; Plutarch, *Marius* xxv–xxvii.)

Consulship of Gaius Marius and Lucius Valerius B.C. 100

45. A blazing meteor was seen far and wide at Tarquinii, falling in a sudden plunge. At sunset a circular object like a shield was seen to sweep across

A.U.C. 654 dente ad orientem visus perferri.[1] In Piceno terrae motu domicilia ruinis prostrata, quaedam convulsa sede sua inclinata manserunt. Fremitus armorum ex inferno auditus. Quadrigae auratae in foro a pedibus sudaverunt. Fugitivi in Sicilia proeliis trucidati.

A.U.C. 655

M. Antonio A. Postumio coss.

46. Bubone in urbe visa urbs lustrata. Nimbis et procella plurima dissipata, fulmine pleraque tacta. Lanuvii in aede Iunonis Sospitae in cubiculo deae sanguinis guttae visae. Nursiae aedes sacra terrae motu disiecta. Lusitani rebellantes subacti. Sex. Titius[2] tribunus plebis de agris dividendis populo cum repugnantibus collegis pertinaciter legem ferret, corvi duo numero in alto volantes ita pugnaverunt supra contionem ut rostris unguibusque lacerarentur. Aruspices sacra Apollini[3] litanda et de lege, quae ferebatur, supersedendum pronuntiarunt. Fremitus ab inferno ad caelum ferri visus inopiam famemque portendit. Populus stipem, matronae thesaurum et virgines dona Cereri et Proserpinae tulerunt. Per virgines viginti septem

[1] perferri *Scheffer*: praeferri MS.
[2] Sex. Titius *Pighius*: Sextius MS.
[3] Apollini *Scheffer*: Apollinis MS.

from west to east. In Picenum houses were flattened B.C. 100
in pieces by an earthquake, while some, torn from their foundations, remained standing out of plumb. A clash of arms was heard from the depths of the earth. Gilded four-horse chariots in the Forum sweated at the feet. The runaway slaves in Sicily were butchered in battles. (Shield in sky, Pliny, *Natural History* II. 34 [100]; Sicily, *Summary* LXIX; Joannes Lydus, *On Signs* 4 [16].)

Consulship of Marcus Antonius and Aulus Postumius B.C. 99

46. When an owl was sighted in Rome, the city was purified. A great deal of damage was done by rain and wind, and several things were struck by lightning. At Lanuvium in the temple of Juno the Deliverer, drops of blood were seen in the chamber of the goddess. At Nursia a holy temple was broken apart by an earthquake. The Lusitanians took up arms again and were subdued. Sextus Titius, a tribune of the commons, persisted in offering legislation for the distribution of land against the opposition of his colleagues; thereupon crows, two in number, flying aloft fought so fiercely over the assembly as to tear each other with beak and claw. The soothsayers declared that a propitiatory offering should be made to Apollo, and that action on the law which was being proposed should be abandoned. A roar that seemed to rise from the depths of the earth to the sky foretold scarcity and famine. The people brought a collection, the matrons an offering of valuables, the maidens other gifts to Ceres and Proserpina. A chant was sung by twenty-seven maidens. Two

A.U.C. 655 cantitatum. Signa cupressea duo Iunoni Reginae posita. In Lusitania prospere a Romanis pugnatum.

A.U.C. 656

Q. Metello T.[1] Didio coss.

47. Bubone in Capitolio supra deorum simulacra viso cum piaretur, taurus victima exanimis concidit. Fulmine pleraque decussa. Hastae Martis in regia motae. Ludis in theatro creta candida pluit; fruges et tempestates portendit bonas. Sereno tonuit. Apud aedem Apollinis decemviris immolantibus caput iocineris non fuit, sacrificantibus anguis ad aram inventus. Item androgynus in mare deportatus. In circo inter pila militum ignis fusus. Hispani pluribus proeliis devicti.

A.U.C. 657

Cn. Cornelio Lentulo P. Licinio coss.

48. Supplicatum in urbe quod androgynus inventus et in mare deportatus erat. Pisauri terrae fremitus auditus. Muri pinnae sine terrae motu passim deiectae civiles portendere discordias. Nursiae simulacrum Iovis in partem sinistram conversum. Cupressea simulacra Iunonis Reginae posita per

[1] T. *Oudendorp*: Tullio MS.

images of cypress were dedicated to Juno the Queen. B.C. 99
In Lusitania the Romans conducted a successful campaign. (Titius, Valerius Maximus VIII. i. *damn.* 3, and cf. Cicero, *de Legibus* II. xii. 31 and vi. 14; *de Oratore* II. xi. 48; *Brutus* lxii. 225.)

Consulship of Quintus Metellus and Titus Didius B.C. 98

47. An owl was sighted on the Capitol above the images of the gods; while expiatory offerings were being made, the bull which was being offered dropped dead. Many things were overthrown by lightning. The spears of Mars in the Regia moved. During a festival it rained white chalk in the theatre; this foretold good crops and good weather. There was thunder from a clear sky. In the temple of Apollo, as the Board of Ten was offering sacrifice, no head appeared on the liver; as they made further sacrifice, a snake was found at the altar. Likewise a hermaphrodite was carried away to sea. In the circus fire flared on the pikes of the soldiers. The Spaniards were subdued in several battles. (Static electricity in circus, cf. Seneca, *Investigations into Nature* I. 1. 14.)

Consulship of Gnaeus Cornelius Lentulus and Publius Licinius B.C. 97

48. Prayers were offered in Rome because a hermaphrodite was discovered and carried out to sea. At Pisaurum a roaring in the earth was heard. The overthrow of the battlements of walls at many places, when there was no earthquake, foretold civil strife. At Nursia the image of Jupiter turned to the left. Images of cypress wood were set up to Juno

A.U.C. 657 virgines viginti septem, quae urbem lustraverunt. Celtiberi Maedi[1] Dardani subacti.

A.U.C. 658

CN. DOMITIO C. CASSIO COSS.

49. Lupus urbem ingressus in domo privata occisus. Bubo in Capitolio occisus. Fulmine pleraque decussa. Signa aurata Iovis cum capite columnaque disiecta. Faesulis sanguine terra manavit. Arretii mulieri e naso spicae farris natae, eadem farris grana vomuit. Urbe lustrata Ptolomaeus, rex Aegypti, Cyrenis mortuus S.P.Q. Romanum heredem reliquit.

A.U.C. 659

L.[2] CRASSO Q. SCAEVOLA COSS.

50. Caere lacte pluit. Lebadiae Eutychides in templum Iovis Trophonii degressus[3] tabulam aeneam extulit, in qua scripta erant quae ad res Romanas pertinerent. Fulminis afflatu pleraque animalia exanimata. Venafri hiatu terra alte subsedit. Vultures canem mortuum laniantes occisi ab aliis et comesi vulturibus. Agnus biceps, puer tribus manibus totidemque pedibus natus Ateste.[4] Hastae Martis in regia motae. Androgynus Urbino natus in mare deportatus. Pax domi forisque fuit.

[1] Maedi *Pighius*: Medi MS.
[2] L. *Jahn*: P. MS.
[3] degressus *Oudendorp*: digressus MS.
[4] Ateste *Rossbach*: At MS.: Atellae *Jahn*: *om. H. J. Mueller*.

---

[1] Scholars are not agreed whether *far* was true spelt (*triticum spelta*) or emmer (*triticum dicoccum*) or both. We may at least be sure that Obsequens was not scientifically precise. See N. Jasny, *The Wheats of Classical Antiquity*, Baltimore, Johns Hopkins Press, 1944, pp. 20, 120–3.

the Queen by twenty-seven maidens, who purified the city. The Celtiberians, Maedi, and Dardanians were overcome. (Celtiberians, *Summary* LXX.) B.C. 97

Consulship of Gnaeus Domitius and Gaius Cassius B.C. 96

49. A wolf entered Rome and was killed in a private house. An owl was killed on the Capitol. Several things were overthrown by lightning. Gilded statues of Jupiter were broken apart, along with their columns and capitals. At Faesulae blood trickled from the earth. At Arretium, ears of spelt [1] grew from a woman's nose, and she vomited kernels of spelt. After Rome had been purified, Ptolemy, King of Egypt, died at Cyrene and left the Roman senate and people as his heir. (*Summary* LXX.)

Consulship of Lucius Crassus and Quintus Scaevola B.C. 95

50. At Caere there was a rain of milk. At Lebadea, Eutychides went down into the shrine of Jupiter Trophonius and brought out a bronze tablet, on which were inscribed matters concerning the state of Rome. Many animals were killed by blasts of lightning. At Venafrum the ground opened and sank down to a great depth. Vultures tearing a dead dog were killed and eaten by other vultures. A two-headed lamb and a boy with three hands and three feet were born at Ateste. The spears of Mars in the Regia moved. A hermaphrodite born at Urbinum was carried away to sea. Peace reigned at home and abroad. (Oracle of Trophonius, cf. XLV. xxvii. 8 and the note.)

A.U.C. 660

C. Caelio[1] L. Domitio coss.

51. Novemdiale sacrum fuit quod in Volsca gente lapidibus pluerat. Vulsiniis luna nova defecit et non nisi postero die hora tertia comparuit. Puella biceps, quadripes, quadrimana, gemina feminea natura mortua nata. Avis incendiaria visa occisaque. In Vestinis in villa lapidibus pluit. Fax in caelo apparuit et totum caelum ardere visum. Terra sanguine manavit et concrevit. Canes saxa tegulas vulgo roserunt. Faesulis ingens multitudo inter sepulcra lugubri veste, pallida facie interdiu ambulare gregatim visa. Per Nasicam Hispaniae principes qui rebellabant supplicio consumpti, urbibus dirutis.

A.U.C. 661

C. Valerio M. Herennio coss.

52. Romae et circa fulmine pleraque decussa. Ancilla puerum unimanum peperit. Fregellis aedes Neptuni nocte patefacta. Maris vituli cum exta demerentur, gemini vitelli in alvo eius inventi. Arretii signum aeneum Mercurii sudavit. In Lucanis gregem vervecum, cum pasceretur et nocte in stabulo, flamma circumdata nihil adussit. Carseolis torrens sanguinis fluxit. Lupi urbem ingressi. Praeneste lana volitavit. In Apulia mula peperit.

[1] Caelio *Hearn*: Laelio MS.

---

[1] For this meaning of *vitellus*, see Plautus, *Asinaria* 667 (but this may be a comic invention); the alternative is "egg yolks."

Consulship of Gaius Caelius and Lucius Domitius B.C. 94

51. A nine-day ceremony was held because there had been a rain of stones among the Volscian people. At Volsinii a new moon was eclipsed and did not reappear till the third hour of the following day. A girl with two heads, four feet, four hands, and double female parts was born dead. A firebird was seen and killed. Among the Vestini it rained stones within a country house. A meteor appeared in the heavens, and the whole sky appeared to be on fire. The ground oozed blood and grew hard. Dogs gnawed stones and tiles at many points. At Faesulae a large crowd was seen among the graves, walking in a group by day with dark garments and pale faces. Under the leadership of Nasica the Spanish chieftains who revolted were disposed of by execution and their cities rased.

Consulship of Gaius Valerius and Marcus Herennius B.C. 93

52. At Rome and near by many things were overthrown by lightning. A maidservant bore a son with only one hand. At Fregellae the temple of Neptune was thrown open by night. When the entrails of a bull-calf were being removed, twin calflets [1] were found in its belly. At Arretium a bronze statue of Mercury sweated. In Lucania flame surrounded, without burning anything, a flock of wethers, both while they were feeding and in the fold at night. At Carseoli a torrent of blood flowed. Wolves entered Rome. At Praeneste wool flew through the air. In Apulia a mule foaled. A kite was caught in the

A.U.C. 661 Milvus in aede Apollinis Romae comprehensus Herennio consuli bis immolanti caput iocineris defuit. In sacro novemdiali cena deae posita a cane adesa antequam delibaretur. Vulsiniis prima luce flamma caelo emicare visa; cum in unum coisset, os flamma[1] ferrugineum ostendit, caelum visum discedere.[2] cuius hiatu vertices flammae apparuerunt. Lustrationibus prospere expiatum. Nam totus annus domi forisque tranquillus fuit.

A.U.C. 662

C. Claudio M. Perpenna coss.

53. Bubo in aede Fortunae Equestris comprehensus inter manus expiravit. Faesulis fremitus terrae auditus. Puer ex ancilla natus sine foramine naturae qua humor emittitur. Mulier duplici natura inventa. Fax in caelo visa. Bos locuta. Examen apium in culmine privatae domus consedit. Volaterris sanguinis rivus manavit. Romae lacte pluit. Arretii duo androgyni inventi. Pullus gallinaceus quadripes natus. Fulmine pleraque icta. Supplicatio fuit. Populus Cereri et Proserpinae stipem tulit. Virgines viginti septem carmen canentes urbem lustraverunt. Maedorum[3] in Macedonia gens provinciam cruente vastavit.

[1] flamma *Oudendorp*: flammae MS.
[2] discedere *Scheffer*: descendere MS.
[3] Maedorum *Scheffer*: Medorum MS.

temple of Apollo at Rome. Though Consul Herennius offered a second sacrifice, the head of the liver failed to appear. During a nine-day ceremony, the banquet spread for a goddess was devoured by a dog before it had been tasted. At Volsinii flame was seen to flash from the sky at dawn; after it had gathered together, the flame displayed a dark grey opening, and the sky seemed to divide; in the gap tongues of flame appeared. Expiation was successfully accomplished by ceremonies of purification. For the whole year was without disturbance at home and abroad. B.C. 93

Consulship of Gaius Claudius and Marcus Perpenna B.C. 92

53. An owl was caught in the temple of Knightly Fortune and breathed its last in the hands of its captors. At Faesulae a roaring in the ground was heard. A boy was born to a maidservant with no opening in his private parts where liquid is excreted. A woman was discovered with double private parts. A meteor was seen in the sky. A cow spoke. A swarm of bees settled on the gable of a private house. At Volaterrae a stream of blood flowed. At Rome it rained milk. At Arretium two hermaphrodites were discovered. A four-footed cock was born. Several things were struck by lightning. A day of prayer was held. The people brought a collection to Ceres and Proserpina. Twenty-seven maidens sang a chant and purified the city. The tribe of the Maedi in Macedonia caused bloody havoc in the province.

A.U.C. 663

L. Marcio Sex. Iulio coss.

54. Livio Druso tr. pl. leges ferente [1] cum bellum Italicum consurgeret, prodigia multa apparuerunt urbi. Sub ortu solis globus ignis a septemtrionali regione cum ingenti sono caeli emicuit. Arretii frangentibus panes cruor e mediis fluxit. In Vestinis per dies septem lapidibus testisque pluit. Aenariae terrae hiatu flamma exorta in caelum emicuit. Circa Regium terrae motu [2] pars urbis murique diruta. In Spoletino colore aureo globus ignis ad terram devolutus, maiorque factus e terra ad orientem ferri visus magnitudine solem [3] obtexit. Cumis [4] in arce simulacrum Apollinis sudavit. Aedis Pietatis in circo Flaminio clausa fulmine icta. Asculo [5] per ludos Romani trucidati. Cum ex agris in urbem pecora armentaque Latini agerent, strages hominum passim facta. Armenta in tantam rabiem concitata sunt ut vastando suos hostile imaginarentur bellum lacrimantesque canes [6] multis affectibus calamitatem praesagirent suis.

[1] Livio Druso tr. pl. leges ferente *Leopardus* : Libius Troso P. Tarquinius leges ferentes MS.
[2] terrae motu *ed. Basileensis prima* : terremota MS.
[3] magnitudine solem *Oudendorp* : magnitudinem Solis MS.
[4] Cumis *Scaliger* : Cuius MS.

Consulship of Lucius Marcius and Sextus Julius

B.C. 91

54. While the war of Italy was gathering during the legislative activity of Livius Drusus, tribune of the commons, many portents appeared in Rome. About sunrise a ball of fire flashed forth from the northern heavens with a great noise in the sky. At Arretium, as men were breaking loaves of bread, blood flowed from the middle of them. Among the Vestini there was a rain of stones and sherds for seven days. At Aenaria a flame rising from a crack in the ground flashed up to the sky. In an earthquake around Regium part of the city and of its wall was demolished. Near Spoletium a gold-coloured fireball rolled down to the ground; increased in size, it seemed to move off the ground towards the east, and was big enough to blot out the sun. In Cumae on the citadel an image of Apollo sweated. The temple of Duty in the Circus Flaminius was struck by lightning while closed. At Asculum during a festival the Romans were massacred. As the Latins were driving herds and flocks from the country to Rome, people perished on every side. The flocks were stirred to such madness that by ravaging their masters they foreshadowed a bitter war, and dogs weeping with many signs of emotion foretold disaster to their people. (*Summary* LXXI; Regium, Strabo VI. i. 6 [258]; omens, Orosius V. xviii; Augustine, *City of God* III. 23; Florus I. xxiv. 3; Cicero, *de Divinatione* I. xliv. 98 f.)

---

[5] Asculo *Scheffer*: A. Sylo MS.
[6] canes *add. in scholio Rossbach*: *om.* MS.

A.U.C. 664

L. Iulio Caesare P. Rutilio coss.

55. Metella Caecilia somnio Iunonem Sospitam profugientem, quod immunde sua templa foedarentur, cum suis precibus aegre revocatam diceret, aedem [1] matronarum sordidis obscenisque corporis coinquinatam ministeriis, in qua etiam sub simulacro deae cubile canis cum fetu erat,[2] commundatam supplicationibus habitis pristino splendore restituit. A Picentibus Romani barbaro more excruciati. Ubique in Latio clades accepta.[3] Rutilius [4] Lupus spretis religionibus, cum in extis caput non invenisset iocineris, amisso exercitu in proelio occisus.

A.U.C. 666

L. Sylla Q. Pompeio coss.

56. Pompedius Silo [5] in oppidum Bovianum, quod ceperat, triumphans invectus omen victoriae hostibus ostendit, quia triumphus in urbem victricem, non victam, induci solet. Proximo proelio amisso exercitu occisus. Mithridati adversus socios bellum paranti prodigia apparuerunt. Stratopedo, ubi senatus haberi solet, corvi vulturem tundendo rostris occiderunt. In eundem locum sidus ingens

[1] aedem . . . coinquinatam . . . in qua . . . commundatam *Oudendorp* : gregem . . . coinquinatum . . . in quo . . . commundatum MS.

[2] cum fetu erat *Scheffer* : confoetuerat MS.

[3] accepta *Scheffer* : accensa MS.

[4] Rutilius *Freinshem* : Lucilius MS.

[5] Pompedius Silo *Vossius* : Pompeius Sylo MS.

Consulship of Lucius Julius Caesar and Publius Rutilius

B.C. 90

55. Caecilia Metella related that she had dreamed that Juno the Deliverer was fleeing away because her precincts were being desecrated with filth, and that Metella had by her prayers with difficulty induced her to return. Metella cleaned out the temple, which was befouled by ladies' attention to dirty and vile physical needs, and in which under the very image of the goddess, a bitch had her lair and her litter; ceremonies of prayer were held, and the temple restored to its original lustre. Romans were barbarously tortured by the people of Picenum. Disaster befell everywhere in Latium. Rutilius Lupus scorned divine lore when he had failed to find the head of the liver among the entrails; he lost his army and fell in battle. (*Summary* LXXIII; Cicero, *de Divinatione* I. ii. 4; xliv. 99.)

Consulship of Lucius Sulla and Quintus Pompeius

B.C. 88

56. Pompedius Silo entered the city of Bovianum in triumphal procession after he had captured it; he thereby displayed an omen of victory for his enemies, because a triumphal procession is customarily led into the conquering city, not the conquered. In the next battle he lost his army and fell. As Mithridates was preparing for war against the allies of Rome, portents appeared to him. At Stratopedon,[1] where the senate usually meets, crows killed a vulture by striking it with their beaks. In the same place a

[1] This is not known as the name of a place; it means "the encampment," and may be an error; but it might be a portion of Rhodes, cf. the next note.

A.U.C. 666 caelo demissum. Isidis species visa sambucam[1] fulmine petere. Lucum Furiarum cum Mithridates succenderet, risus exauditus ingens sine auctore. Cum aruspicum iussu virginem Furiis immolaret, e iugulo puellae risus ortus turbavit sacrificium. Classis Mithridatis in Thessalia a Romanis[2] in proelio amissa.

A.U.C. 667

CN. OCTAVIO L. CINNA COSS.[3]

56a. Cinna et Mario per bella civilia crudeliter saevientibus Romae in castris Gnaei Pompei caelum ruere visum, arma signaque tacta, milites exanimati. Ipse Pompeius afflatus sidere interiit. Lectum eius populus diripuit, corpus unco traxit, quod discrimine civili perseverasset periclitanti patriae non succurrere, cum et imperium et maximos haberet exercitus.

[1] sambucam *add. Rossbach* : *om.* MS.
[2] *ita* MS. : a Romanis *om. H. J. Mueller* : a Rhodiis *Oudendorp* : incensa alia . . . demersa *Jahn.*
[3] Cn. Octavio L. Cinna coss. *Oudendorp* : *om.* MS.

---

[1] This was a special giant siege-engine used by Mithridates before Rhodes, cf. Appian, *Mithridatic Wars* iv. 26 f., from which passage Rossbach supplies the word here, see critical note.

huge star fell from the sky. A vision of Isis seemed to attack the "harp"[1] with a thunderbolt. When Mithridates set fire to a grove of the Furies, gigantic laughter was heard, with no one to utter it. When by order of the soothsayers, he was sacrificing a maiden to the Furies, laughter issuing from the throat of the girl disrupted the rite. The fleet of Mithridates was lost in battle with the Romans off Thessaly.[2] (Silo, cf. 61a.) B.C. 88

Consulship of Gnaeus Octavius and Lucius Cinna B.C. 87

56a. While Cinna and Marius were displaying a cruel rage in their conduct of the civil war, at Rome in the camp of Gnaeus Pompeius the sky seemed to fall, weapons and standards were hit, and soldiers struck dead. Pompeius himself perished by the blast of a heavenly body.[3] The people wrecked his bier, and dragged his corpse with a hook, because during the peril to his fellow-citizens, he continued to avoid coming to the rescue of his endangered fatherland, although he had both magistral authority and very large forces. (*Summary* LXXIX; Orosius V. xix. 18.)

[2] There is some confusion, grammatical as well as factual, in this statement; cf. the critical note and Appian, *Mithridatic Wars* iv. 25 and v. 29; and for the opening of Mithridates' campaign, *Summary* LXXVII.

[3] This curious phrase may be found in Pliny, *Natural History* II. 108, where the L.C.L. translation is "paralysed by a star"; and a similar phrase occurs in Petronius, *Satyricon* 2. One would suspect that it might cover many sorts of sudden seizure; but Orosius (see reference below) and Granius Licinianus (p. 22 F) interpreted it as meaning "struck by lightning."

A.U.C. 668

L. Cinna C. Mario coss.[1]

56b. Piraeum Sylla cum oppugnaret diuturno labore,[2] unus miles eius aggerem ferens exanimatus fulmine. Aruspex respondit quod caput iacentis in oppidum versum esset, introitum et victoriam Romanis significare. Post breve tempus Athenae et Piraeum a Sylla capta. Ilio a C. Fimbria incenso cum aedes quoque Minervae deflagrasset, inter ruinas simulacrum antiquissimum inviolatum stetit spemque restitutionis oppido portendit.

A.U.C. 671

L. Scipione C. Norbano coss.

57. Per Syllana tempora inter Capuam et Vulturnum ingens signorum sonus armorumque horrendo clamore auditus, ita ut viderentur duae acies concurrere per plures dies. Rei miraculo intentius[3] considerantibus vestigia equorum hominumque et recens[4] protritae herbae et virgulta visa molem ingentis belli portendere. In Etruria Clusii mater familiae vivum serpentem peperit, qui iussu aruspicum in profluentem deiectus adversa[5] aqua natavit. Lucius Sylla post quintum annum victor in Italiam reversus magno terrori fuit inimicis. Fraude[6] aeditui Capitolium una nocte conflagravit. Syllae crudelitate

[1] L. Cinna C. Mario coss. *add. Oudendorp* : *om.* MS.
[2] diuturno labore *hic posuit Rossbach* : *ante* quod caput *infra* MS. : *ibi* haud diuturno labore *Scheffer*.
[3] intentius *Scheffer* : ĩtus MS.
[4] recens *Scheffer* : recentes MS.
[5] adversa *Stephanus* : aversa MS.
[6] Fraude *add. Rossbach* *om.* MS. culpa *add. Scaliger*

Consulship of Lucius Cinna and Gaius Marius B.C. 86

56b. While Sulla was toiling day after day over the siege of Piraeus, one of his soldiers, who was bringing up earth for a mound, was struck dead by a thunderbolt. The soothsayer gave answer that because the head of the corpse pointed towards the city, the event indicated the entering in and victory of the Romans. After a short while Athens and Piraeus were taken by Sulla. When Ilium was burned by Gaius Fimbria, the temple of Minerva was also consumed, but amid the wreckage an image of great age remained standing unharmed, and foretold hope of restoration for the town. (*Summary* LXXXI; Ilium, fr. 17 and *Summary* LXXXIII.)

Consulship of Lucius Scipio and Gaius Norbanus B.C. 83

57. During the era of Sulla a great clash of standards and of arms, with dreadful shouting, was heard between Capua and Volturnum, so that two armies seemed to be locked in combat for several days. When men investigated this marvel more closely, the tracks of horses and of men and the freshly trampled grass and shrubs seemed to foretell the burden of a huge war. In Etruria at Clusium a matron bore a live snake, which by order of the soothsayers was cast into a stream and swam up against the current. Lucius Sulla returned victorious to Italy after five years and greatly terrified his enemies. By the malfeasance of a temple attendant the Capitol burned down in a single night. Through the cruelty of Sulla a horrible proscription of the

A.U.C. 671 foeda proscriptio principum fuit. Centena milia hominum consumpta Italico civilique bello relata sunt.

A.U.C. 677

MAM.[1] AEMILIO D. BRUTO COSS.

58. D.[2] Laelius legatus Pompei (cui prodigium Romae erat factum in lecto uxoris duo angues conspecti in diversumque lapsi, proxime Pompeio in castris sedenti accipiter super caput accesserat) in Hispania adversus Sertorium inter pabulatores occisus.

A.U.C. 678

CN. OCTAVIO C. SCRIBONIO COSS.

59. Reate terrae motu aedes sacrae in oppido agrisque commotae, saxa quibus forum strata erat discussa, pontes interrupti, ripae praelabentis[3] fluminis in aquam provolutae, fremitus inferni exauditi et post paucos dies, quae concussa erant corruerunt. Saxum vivum cum provolveretur, in praecipiti rupe immobile stetit. A Sertorio in Hispania exercitus Romani caesi. Adversum Maedos[4] varie dimicatum.

[1] Mam. *Oudendorp* : Marco MS.
[2] D. *Pighius* : Didius MS.
[3] praelabentis *Jahn* : labentis MS.
[4] Maedos *Scheffer* : Medos MS.

leading citizens took place. It is recorded that hundreds of thousands of persons were destroyed in the Italian and civil wars. (Battle, Augustine, *City of God* II. 25; snake, Appian, *Civil Wars* I. ix. 83, cf. Pliny, *Natural History* VII. 3 [34]; Sulla, *Summaries* LXXXV–LXXXVIII.) B.C. 83

Consulship of Mamercus Aemilius and Decimus Brutus B.C. 77

58. Decimus Laelius, a staff officer of Pompey, encountered a portent at Rome when two snakes were seen in his wife's bed, and then slipped away in different directions. As he sat at Pompey's side in camp a falcon approached above his head. Laelius lost his life among the foragers in Spain, in the campaign against Sertorius. (Frontinus, *Stratagems* II. v. 31, cf. fr. 19; Sallust, *Histories* II. 31 Maurenbrecher.)

Consulship of Gnaeus Octavius and Gaius Scribonius B.C. 76

59. In Reate an earthquake disturbed holy temples in the town and country, the paving stones in the market place were thrown apart, bridges were broken, the banks of the river which flows by the city were thrown into the water, noises were heard from the lower regions, and after a few days the structures which had been shaken collapsed. While a boulder was rolling along, it stopped motionless on a steep slope of rock. Roman armies were slaughtered by Sertorius in Spain. Battles against the Maedi had various outcomes. (Cf. *Summary* XCI, if the "Thracians" there are the Maedi above.)

A.U.C. 679

C.[1] Aurelio L. Octavio coss.

60. Sertorio in Hispania exercitum ducenti tale prodigium est factum: scuta equitum parte exteriore iaculaque et pectora equorum cruenta visa. Quod prosperum sibi interpretatus est Sertorius, quia exteriora hostili sanguine maculari solent. Continua ei proelia cum successu fuerunt.

A.U.C. 681

M. Varrone C. Cassio coss.[2]

60a. Cyzicum Mithridates cum oppugnaret, Aristagorae qui in summo magistratu erat Proserpina in quiete visa est dicere adversus tibicines se tubicinem[3] comparasse. Postero die turres hostium vento disiectae sunt. Ad immolandum bos sacra iniussa de montibus per hostium classem adnatavit seque ad aras percutiendam obtulit.

A.U.C. 691

M. Cicerone[4] C. Antonio coss.

61. Fulmine pleraque decussa. Sereno Vargunteius Pompeiis[5] de caelo exanimatus. Trabis ardens ab occasu ad caelum extenta. Terrae motu Spoletum totum concussum et quaedam corruerunt. Inter alia

[1] C. *Oudendorp*: Lucio MS.
[2] M. Varrone C. Cassio coss. *Oudendorp*: *om.* MS.
[3] tubicinem *H. Haupt*: tibicinem MS.
[4] Cicerone *Muretus*: Cesone MS.
Pompeiis *Scheffer*: Pompeius MS.

---

[1] This phenomenon (*dokos* in Greek) is mentioned by Pliny, *Natural History* II. 26 (96) and Joannes Lydus, *On Signs* 10b.

Consulship of Gaius Aurelius and Lucius Octavius B.C. 75

60. As Sertorius in Spain was leading his troops, the following portent took place: the shields of his cavalry appeared to be bloodstained on the outside, as well as their javelins and the chests of their horses. Sertorius interpreted this as favourable to himself, because the outside is usually stained with the blood of one's enemies. He had an uninterrupted series of successful battles. (Cf. *Summaries* XCI–XCIII.)

Consulship of Marcus Varro and Gaius Cassius B.C. 73

60a. When Mithridates was besieging Cyzicus, Proserpina appeared in a dream to Aristagoras, who held the highest magistracy, and said that she had provided a trumpeter to oppose the flute-players. On the following day, the towers of the besiegers were scattered by the wind. The heifer consecrated for sacrifice came down unbidden from the hills, swam through the hostile fleet, and presented herself at the altars for the stroke of the axe. (Plutarch, *Lucullus* x, with variations in details; cf. *Summary* XCV.)

Consulship of Marcus Cicero and Gaius Antonius B.C. 63

61. Several things were overthrown by lightning. Vargunteius was struck dead from a clear sky at Pompeii. A fiery timber[1] stretched up into the sky from the west. In an earthquake all Spoletum was shaken and some buildings collapsed. It was

A.U.C. 691 relatum,[1] biennio ante in Capitolio lupam Remi et Romuli fulmine ictam, signumque Iovis cum columna disiectum, aruspicum responso in foro repositum. Tabulae legum aeneae caelo tactae[2] litteris liquefactis. Ab his prodigiis Catilinae nefaria conspiratio coepta.

A.U.C. 692

D. Iunio L. Murena coss.

61a. C. Antonius procos.[3] cum in agro Pistorensi Catilinam devicisset, laureatos fasces in provinciam tulit. Ibi a Dardanis oppressus amisso exercitu profugit. Apparuit eum hostibus portendisse victoriam, cum ad eos laurum victricem tulerit, quam in Capitolio debuerat deponere.

A.U.C. 694

Quinto Metello L. Afranio coss.

62. Die toto ante sereno circa horam undecimam nox se intendit, deinde restitutus fulgor. Turbinis vi tecta deiecta. Ponte sublapso homines in Tiberim

[1] relatum *Lycosthenes*: relatu MS.
[2] caelo tactae *add. in scholio Rossbach*: *om.* MS.
[3] D. Iunio L. Murena coss. C. Antonius procos. *Jahn*: M. Cic. Gaio Antonio Coss. MS., *has lineas post res anni U.C.* 694 *ponens.*

reported among other things that two years before on the Capitol, the she-wolf of Remus and Romulus had been struck by lightning, and the statue of Jupiter with its column had been broken apart, but had been replaced in the Forum in accordance with an answer of the soothsayers. Bronze tablets containing laws were struck by lightning and the letters melted. With these portents the abominable conspiracy of Catiline began. (Cicero, *Catiline* III. viii. 18–20; Dio XXXVII. xxv. 1 f.; *Summary* CII; Pliny, *Natural History* II. 52 [137] gives the name of the man killed at Pompeii as Herennius, a name otherwise attested for the town.) B.C. 63

Consulship of Decimus Junius and Lucius Murena B.C. 62

61a. After Gaius Antonius as proconsul had inflicted final defeat on Catiline in the neighbourhood of Pistoria, he carried his laurel-wreathed *fasces* with him into his province. There he was crushed by the Dardani and fled after losing his army. This showed that he had given an omen of victory to his enemies when he brought to them the conqueror's laurel that he ought to have deposited on the Capitol. (*Summary* CIII; cf. 56.)

Consulship of Quintus Metellus and Lucius Afranius B.C. 60

62. Although the entire day had been clear up to that time, about the eleventh hour night spread over the sky, and then daylight was restored. Roofs were thrown down by the force of a tornado. When a bridge collapsed, people were thrown into the

A.U.C. 694 praecipitati. In agris pleraeque arbores eversae radicibus. Lusitani Gallaeci devicti.

A.U.C 701

Cn. Domitio M. Messala coss.[1]

63. Lupi in urbe visi. Nocturni ululatus flebiles canum auditi. Simulacrum Martis sudavit. Fulmen tota urbe pervagatum pleraque deorum simulacra decussit, homines exanimavit. Urbs lustrata. Propter dictaturam Pompeii ingens seditio in urbe fuit.

A.U.C. 700

L.[2] Domitio Appio Claudio coss.

64. M. Crassus ad Parthos profectus cum Eufratem transiret, multa prodigia neglexit. Cum etiam coorta tempestas signifero signum abreptum[3] mersisset gurgiti, et offundente se[4] nimborum caligine prohiberentur transire, pertinaciter perseverans cum filio et exercitu interiit.

A.U.C, 704

L. Paulo C. Marcello coss.

65. Mula pariens discordiam civium, bonorum interitum, mutationem legum, turpes matronarum

[1] Cn. Domitio M. Messala coss. *add. Oudendorp* : *om.* MS.
[2] L. *Oudendorp* : Gneo MS.
[3] abreptum *Oudendorp* : arreptum MS.
[4] se *add. Heinsius* : *om.* MS.

---

[1] Presumably a reference to Pompey's sole consulship in 52 B.C., and the riots over the trial of Milo.

[2] It is not clear why the order of years was not kept. An error in the transmission is possible, cf. critical note on 61a; or the whole account of Crassus' expedition may have been given in the year of the final disaster; Dio follows the same order as the MS. of Obsequens in reporting these prodigies.

[3] Or, "of goods," taking *bonorum* as neuter; but *interitus* suggests people rather than things, as would "decease" in English.

Tiber. In the country many trees were torn up by the roots. The Lusitanian Callaeci were subdued. (Defeat of Callaeci by Caesar, *Summary* CIII; Dio XXXVII. lviii.) B.C. 60

Consulship of Gnaeus Domitius and Marcus Messala B.C. 53

63. Wolves were seen in Rome. The mournful howling of dogs was heard by night. The image of Mars sweated. A thunderbolt strayed over the whole city, overthrowing many images of gods, and taking people's lives. The city was purified. Because of the dictatorship [1] of Pompey there was great civil disturbance in Rome. (Dio XL. xvii. 1.)

Consulship of Lucius Domitius and Appius Claudius B.C. 54[2]

64. When Marcus Crassus was crossing the Euphrates in his campaign against the Parthians, he disregarded many portents. Even when a storm came up, tore a standard from its bearer, and sank it in the stream, and the army was prevented from crossing by a black storm fog that came pouring down on them, Crassus obstinately pushed on and perished with his son and his army. (Dio XL. xviii; Florus I. xlvi. 4; Plutarch, *Crassus* xix. 3–5; *Summary* CVI.)

Consulship of Lucius Paulus and Gaius Marcellus B.C. 50

65. A foaling mule indicated civil strife, destruction of respectable citizens,[3] the overthrow of the constitution, and unseemly child-bearing among

A.U.C. 704 partus significavit. Incendium quo maxima pars urbis deleta est prodigii loco habitum. Inter Caesarem et Pompeium bella civilia exorta.

A.U.C. 706

C. Caesare P. Servilio coss.[1]

65a. Adversus Caesarem Pompeius in[2] Macedonia cum invitatis gentibus amicis instrueret aciem, a Dyrrhachio venientibus adversa fuerunt fulmina. Examen apium in signis perniciem portendit.[3] Nocturni terrores in exercitu fuere. Ipse Pompeius pridie pugnae diem[4] visus in theatro suo ingenti plausu excipi. Mox acie victus in Aegypto occisus. Eo ipso die plerisque locis signa sua sponte conversa constat,[5] clamorem crepitumque armorum Antiochiae, bis ut curreretur in muros, auditum Ptolemaideque,[6] sonum tympanorum Pergami. Palma viridis Trallibus in aede Victoriae sub Caesaris statua intra coagmenta lapidum magnitudine matura[7] enata. C. Cornelius augur Patavii eo die, cum aves admitterent, proclamavit rem geri et vincere Caesarem.

[1] C. Caesare P. Servilio coss. *add. Oudendorp* : *om.* MS.
[2] in *add. Scheffer* : *om.* MS.
[3] perniciem portendit *Rossbach in scholio*: portendit MS. consedit *Oudendorp*.
[4] diem *Scheffer* : die MS.
[5] constat *add. Rossbach* : *om.* MS.
[6] Ptolemaideque *Rossbach* : indeque MS.
[7] matura *Freinshem* : mature MS.

matrons. A fire by which a very large section of the city was destroyed was regarded as a portentous event. The civil wars between Caesar and Pompey had their beginning. (Fragments 31 and 32; *Summary* CIX.) B.C. 50

CONSULSHIP OF GAIUS CAESAR AND PUBLIUS SERVILIUS B.C. 48

65a. When Pompey was marshalling his line of battle against Caesar in Macedonia and had summoned some peoples friendly to himself, lightning flashes gave them an unfavourable omen as they were advancing from Dyrrhacium. A swarm of bees on the standards foretold ruin. There were panics at night in the army. Pompey himself on the day before the battle dreamed that he was being received in his own theatre with great applause. Immediately afterward he was defeated in battle, and was put to death in Egypt. On that very day, it is well known that in many places statues turned about of their own accord, battle-cries and the clash of arms were heard at Antioch, so that twice the walls were manned; the same sounds were heard at Ptolemaïs, and the noise of timbrels at Pergamum. A growing palm sprang up to full-grown size in Tralles in the temple of Victory, between the joints of the stones below the statue of Caesar. Gaius Cornelius, an augur, announced at Padua on that very day, since it was indicated by the birds, that the action was taking place, and that Caesar was conquering. (*Summaries* CXI and CXII; Valerius Maximus I. vi. 12; Florus II. xiii. 45; fragment 34.)

A.U.C. 708

C. Caesare M. Lepido coss.

66. Decem legionum [1] aquilae Gnaeo,[2] Cn. Pompeii filio, quae fulmina tenebant visae dimittere et in sublime avolare. Ipse adulescens Pompeius victus et fugiens occisus.

A.U.C. 710

C. Caesare M. Antonio coss.

67. Caesari dictatori exta sine corde inventa. Calpurnia uxor somniavit fastigium domus, quod S.C.[3] erat adiectum, ruisse. Nocte cum valvae cubiculi [4] clausae essent, sua sponte apertae sunt, ita ut lunae fulgore, qui intro venerat, Calpurnia excitaretur. Ipse Caesar viginti tribus vulneribus in curia Pompeiana a coniuratis confossus.

A.U.C. 710

M. Antonio P. Dolabella coss.

68. C. Octavius testamento Caesaris patris Brundisii se in Iuliam gentem adscivit. Cumque hora diei tertia ingenti circumfusa multitudine Romam intraret, sol puri ac sereni caeli orbe modico inclusus extremae lineae circulo, qualis tendi arcus in nubibus solet, eum [5] circumscripsit. Ludis Veneris Genetricis, quos pro collegio fecit, stella hora undecima crinita sub septentrionis sidere exorta convertit

[1] Decem legionum *Scheffer*: decimae legionis MS.
[2] Gnaeo *add. Jahn*: *om.* MS.
[3] S.C. *Freinshem*: sicut MS.
[4] cubiculi *Scheffer*: cubili MS.
[5] eum *Scheffer*: eam MS.

Consulship of Gaius Caesar and Marcus Lepidus

B.C. 46

66. The eagles of ten legions seemed to Gnaeus Pompeius, son of Gnaeus, to drop the thunderbolts they held and to fly away into the sky. Young Pompey himself was defeated and killed as he fled. (Cf. *Summary* CXV; Dio XLIII. xxxv. 3 f.)

Consulship of Gaius Caesar and Marcus Antonius

B.C. 44

67. Entrails without a heart were found at Dictator Caesar's sacrifice. His wife Calpurnia dreamed that the gable-top on his house, which had been added by decree of the senate, had fallen. By night when the doors of his bed-chamber were closed, they opened of their own accord, so that Calpurnia was awakened by the moonlight which streamed in brightly. Caesar himself was riddled with twenty-three wounds by the conspirators in Pompey's senate-house. (*Summary* CXVI; fr. 46.)

Consulship of Marcus Antonius and Publius Dolabella

68. In accordance with the will of his father Caesar, Gaius Octavius enrolled himself in the Julian clan at Brundisium. And when at the third hour of the day he entered Rome, surrounded by a huge crowd, the sun, enclosed within a small circle of clear and calm sky, surrounded Octavius with the end of an arc such as the rainbow usually displays in the clouds. At the festival of Mother Venus, which he conducted for the college, a comet appearing at the eleventh hour under the constellation of the Bear

A.U.C. 710 omnium oculos. Quod sidus quia ludis Veneris apparuit, divo Iulio insigne capitis consecrari placuit. Ipsi Caesari monstrosa malignitate Antonii consulis multa perpesso generosa fuit ad resistendum constantia. Terrae motus crebri fuerunt. Fulmine navalia et alia [1] pleraque tacta. Turbinis vi simulacrum, quod M. Cicero ante cellam Minervae pridie quam plebiscito [2] in exilium iret posuerat, dissipatum membris pronum iacuit, fractis humeris bracchiis capite; dirum ipsi Ciceroni portendit. Tabulae aeneae ex aede Fidei turbine evulsae. Aedis Opis valvae fractae. Arbores radicitus et pleraque tecta eversa. Fax caelo ad occidentem visa ferri. Stella per dies septem insignis arsit. Soles tres fulserunt, circaque solem imum corona spiceae [3] similis in orbem [3] emicuit, et postea in unum circulum sole redacto multis mensibus languida lux fuit. In aede Castoris nominum litterae quaedam Antonii et Dolabellae consulum excussae sunt, quibus utrisque alienatio a patria significata. Canum ululatus nocte ante pontificis maximi domum auditi,[4] ex his maximus a ceteris laniatus turpem infamiam Lepido portendit. Hostiae grex piscium in sicco reciproco maris fluxu relictus. Padus inundavit et intra ripam refluens ingentem viperarum vim

[1] et alia *add. Rossbach* : *om.* MS.
[2] plebiscito *hic posuit Scheffer* : *post* Cicero *supra* MS.
[3] spiceae . . . orbem *Scheffer* : spicae . . . urbem MS.
[4] domum auditi *Scheffer* : domum Lepidi auditi MS. : domum flebiles auditi *Jahn.*

drew the eyes of everyone. Since this star appeared at the festival of Venus, it was decided to dedicate it as a crown-jewel to the deified Julius. Though Caesar himself suffered much because of the unnatural malice of Consul Antony, he showed a gallant steadfastness in withstanding him. Earthquakes were frequent. The shipsheds and many other things were struck by lightning. By the violence of a tornado a statue, which Marcus Cicero had placed before the temple-chamber of Minerva on the day before he was exiled by decree of the commons, fell on its face with its limbs detached and its shoulders arms, and head broken; this foretold disaster to Cicero himself. Bronze tablets were torn by the tornado from the temple of Loyalty. The doors of the temple of Wealth were broken. Trees were torn up by the roots, and many roofs were overturned. A meteor in the sky was seen to travel towards the west. A conspicuous star blazed up for seven days. Three suns shone, and around the lowest sun a wreath like the wreath of heads of grain flashed into view surrounding it, and afterward when the sun had been reduced to a single orb, its light was sickly for many months. In the temple of Castor some letters were struck from the names of the consuls Antony and Dolabella, which meant that both would be estranged from the fatherland. The howling of dogs was heard by night before the residence of the Chief Pontiff, and the fact that the largest dog was torn by the others foretold unseemly disgrace to Lepidus. At Ostia a school of fish was stranded on dry land when a flooding sea in turn receded. The Po overflowed, and when it returned within its banks, left a great abundance of vipers. B.C. 44

A.U.C. 710 reliquit. Inter Caesarem et Antonium civilia bella exorta.

A.U.C. 711

C. Pansa A.[1] Hirtio coss.

69. Caesari cum honores decreti essent et imperium adversus Antonium, immolanti duplicia exta apparuerunt. Secutae sunt eum res prosperae. C. Pansae[2] cos. statua equestris Antonii[3] domi corruit. Equus phaleratus in ipsius conspectu festinans concidit. Quidam e populo sanguine victimarum prolapsus[4] respersam cruore palmam proficiscenti dedit. Funesta haec ipsi prodigia fuerunt, qui mox adversus Antonium dimicans in mortem vulneratus est. Armorum telorumque species a terra visa cum fragore ad caelum ferri. Signa legionis quae relicta a Pansa ad urbis praesidium erat[5] veluti longo situ inductis araneis vestiri[6] visa. Fulmine pleraque icta. In castris Caesaris luce prima in culmine praetorii super linteum consedit aquila, inde circumvolantibus minoribus avibus excita de conspectu abiit. Oraculo Apollinis vox

[1] A. *add. Oudendorp* : *om.* MS.
[2] Pansae *Oudendorp* : Pansa MS.
[3] *sic* MS.: aenea *Oudendorp* : anticae *Rossbach in scholio.*
[4] prolapsus *Scheffer* : prolapso MS.
[5] erat *Scheffer* : erant MS.
[6] vestiri *M. Haupt* : venire MS.

---

[1] The name of Antony which appears in the Latin is an intrusion for which no wholly satisfactory remedy has been proposed; see critical note. I translate without it, which secures agreement with Dio's account.

[2] Dio interprets the portents as applying to the state.

The civil wars between Caesar and Antony had their beginning. (Octavian, Pliny, *Natural History* II. 28 (98); Suetonius, *Augustus* 95; Orosius VI. xx. 5; comet, Dio XLV. vii. 1; cf. Vergil, *Georgics* I. 463–497; Ovid, *Metamorphoses* XV. 782–98, 847–51; Lucan, *Pharsalia* I. 522–83; Lydus, *On Signs* 10b; other omens, Dio XLV. xvii; three suns, Jerome on Eusebius II, *anno* 1973 [Mai, col. 429 f.]. Cf. *Summary* CXVII.) B.C. 44

Consulship of Gaius Pansa and Aulus Hirtius B.C. 43

69. When distinctions and military authority against Antony were conferred by vote on Caesar, double entrails appeared as he offered sacrifice. Success in his undertakings proceeded to attend him. A mounted statue of Consul Gaius Pansa collapsed at his home.[1] A horse with trappings, while dashing along before his very eyes, fell dead. One of the populace slipped in the blood of the victims and gave Pansa, as he was setting out, a palm spattered with gore. These portents were deadly to the consul himself, for presently as he was fighting against Antony, he was mortally wounded.[2] A vision of armour and weapons seemed to rise with a crash from earth to heaven. The standards of the legion which had been left by Pansa as a garrison for Rome were seen to be wrapped in spiderwebs spun over them, as though from long disuse. Several things were struck by lightning. In Caesar's camp at dawn an eagle lighted on the ridge of the headquarters above the awning, and then, being disturbed by smaller birds flying around it, disappeared from sight. At the oracle of Apollo a cry was heard,

A.U.C. 711 audita: lupis rabies hieme, aestate frumentum non demessum. Veteranis Caesari consulatum flagitantibus terribilis tumultus Romae fuit. Caesar cum in campum Martium exercitum deduceret, sex vultures apparuerunt. Conscendenti deinde rostra creato consuli iterum sex vultures conspecti veluti Romuli auspiciis novam urbem condituro signum dederunt. Reconciliatione inter Caesarem Antonium Lepidum facta foeda principum fuit proscriptio.

A.U.C. 712

M. Lepido Munatio Planco coss.

70. Mula Romae ad duodecim portas peperit. Canis aeditui mortua a cane tracta. Lux ita nocte [1] fulsit ut tamquam die orto ad opus surgeretur. In Mutinensi victoriae Marianae signum meridiem spectans sua sponte conversum in septentrionem hora quarta. Cum haec victimis expiarentur, soles tres circiter hora tertia diei visi, mox in unum orbem contracti. Latinis in Albano monte cum sacrificaretur, ex humero et [2] pollice Iovis cruor manavit. Per Cassium et Brutum in provinciis direptionibus sociorum bella gesta. Notatum est prodigii loco fuisse, quod P. Titius praetor propter dissensiones collegae magistratum abrogavit; et ante annum est

[1] nocte *add. Scheffer, Rossbach*: *om.* MS.
[2] humero et *Freinsheim*: humo a MS.

"Madness of wolves in the winter, in summer no reaping of grain." When the veterans demanded the consulship for Caesar, there was a dreadful disturbance at Rome. When Caesar was parading his forces on the Campus Martius, six vultures appeared. When thereafter he mounted the Rostra after his appointment as consul, again six vultures were seen and so, by the omen vouchsafed to a Romulus, gave the starting signal to the one who was about to found the city anew. After a reconciliation had been effected between Caesar, Antony, and Lepidus, there followed an atrocious proscription of the leading citizens. (Dio XLVI. xxxiii.; xlvi. 2; Suetonius, *Augustus* 95; *Summary* CXIX.) B.C. 43

Consulship of Marcus Lepidus and Munatius Plancus B.C. 42

70. A mule foaled in Rome by the Twelve Gates. The dead bitch of a sacristan was dragged off by a dog. Light shone so brightly at night that people got up to begin work as though day had dawned. In the neighbourhood of Mutina the memorial to the victory of Marius, which faced south, of its own accord turned towards the north at the fourth hour. While these omens were being averted by sacrifices, three suns were seen about the third hour of the day, which presently drew together into a single orb. At the Latin Festival on the Alban Mount, blood dripped from the shoulder and thumb of Jupiter while sacrifice was being offered. Campaigns were conducted under Cassius and Brutus in the provinces by plundering the allies. It was regarded as a portent that Publius Titius, as praetor, ejected a colleague from office because of disagreements; and

A.U.C. 712 mortuus. Constat neminem qui magistratum collegae abstulerat annum vixisse. Abrogaverunt autem hi: Lucius Iunius Brutus consul Tarquinio Collatino, Tib. Gracchus M. Octavio, Cn. Octavius L. Cinnae,[1] C. Cinna[2] tr. pl.[3] C. Marullo, Tullius . . .[4] Bruto et Cassio pugnam adversus Caesarem et Antonium molientibus in castris Cassii examen apium consedit. Locus aruspicum iussu interclusus interius ducto vallo. Vulturum et aliarum alitum quibus strages cadaverum pabulo est ingens vis exercitum advolavit. Puer in pompa Victoriae cultu cum ferretur, ferculo decidit. Lustratione lictor perversis fascibus lauream imposuit. Brutianis in proelium egredientibus Aethiops in porta occurrit et a militibus confossus. Cassius et Brutus interierunt.

C. Furnio C. Silano[5] coss.

A.U.C. 737 71. Sub Appennino in villa Liviae, uxoris Caesaris, ingenti motu terra intremuit. Fax caelestis a

[1] Cn. Octavius L. Cinnae *add. Rubino* : *om.* MS.
[2] C. Cinna *Scheffer* : Caecinnae MS.
[3] tr. pl. C. *Rupert* : P. Tarquinius P. MS.
[4] *lacunam ind. Jahn.*
[5] Silano *Oudendorp* : Syllano MS.

before a year had passed, Titius died. It is known that no one who had deprived a colleague of office has lived for a year afterward. The following acted in this manner: Lucius Junius Brutus, as consul, with Tarquinius Collatinus, Tiberius Gracchus with Marcus Octavius, Gnaeus Octavius with Lucius Cinna, Gaius Cinna, as tribune of the commons, with Gaius Marullus, Tullius . . . B.C. 42

As Brutus and Cassius were strenuously preparing for battle against Caesar and Antony, a swarm of bees settled in the camp of Cassius. The place was cut off by drawing the rampart farther in, on the order of the soothsayers. A huge throng of vultures and other birds which feed on the carnage of battle flew up to the army. A boy who was being carried in procession in the costume of Victory, fell from the barrow. At the purification, the lictor placed the laurel on the *fasces* when they were reversed. As Brutus' men marched out to battle an Ethiopian met them at the gate and was stabbed by the soldiers. Cassius and Brutus perished. (Omens in Italy, Dio XLVII. xl; Titius, Dio XLVI. xlix. 1 f. [43 B.C.]; Collatinus, II. ii; Octavius, *Summary* LVIII; Lucius Cinna, *Summary* LXXIX (this instance is included neither in Dio nor the Obsequens MS., see critical note); Marullus, Dio XLIV. ix. 3–x. 3; Tullius is not identifiable; omens at Philippi, Plutarch, *Brutus* xxxix. 1–3; xlviii; Appian, *Civil Wars* IV. xvii. 134; Florus II. xvii. 7. Cf. *Summary* CXXIV.)

Consulship of Gaius Furnius and Gaius Silanus B.C. 17

71. At the estate of Livia, the wife of Caesar, in the Apennines the earth trembled in a great quake.

A.U.C. 737 meridiano ad septentrionem extenta luci diurnae similem noctem[1] fecit. Turris hortorum Caesaris ad portam Collinam de caelo tacta. Insidiis Germanorum Romani[2] circumventi sub M. Lollio legato graviter vexati.

PAULO FABIO Q. AELIO COSS.

A.U.C. 743 72. In Germania in castris Drusi examen apium in tabernaculo Hostilii Rufi,[3] praefecti castrorum, consedit ita ut funem praetendentem praefixamque tentorio lanceam amplecteretur. Multitudo Romanorum per insidias subiecta est.

[1] noctem *Freinshem*: in nocte MS.
[2] Germanorum Romani *Scheffer*: Romanorum Germani MS.
[3] Rufi *Freinshem*: Rutilii MS.

A meteor reaching from south to north made night as bright as the light of day. A tower in the gardens of Caesar by the Colline Gate was struck by lightning. The Romans under the deputy Marcus Lollius were trapped into ambushes by the Germans and suffered severely. (Disaster to Lollius, 16 B.C., Dio LIV. xx. 4–6; Velleius II. 97; Suetonius, *Augustus* 23, cf. Tacitus, *Annals* I. 10. Dio LIV. xix. 7 mentions some portents omitted here.) B.C. 17

Consulship of Paulus Fabius and Quintus Aelius B.C. 11

72. In Germany in the camp of Drusus, a swarm of bees settled on the tent of Hostilius Rufus, the prefect of the camp, in such a way that it enveloped the forward guy rope and the spear planted before the tent. The whole force of Romans was crushed in an ambush. (*Summary* CXLII, end; Pliny, *Natural History* XI. 18 (55). Since Pliny points out that the immediate sequel to the bees was success by Drusus, either Obsequens has picked on some details of Drusus' campaign in order to support the conventional view that a swarm of bees is a bad omen, or else, as Rossbach suggests, the disaster was that of Varus, the lapse of time being disregarded.)

FOREWORD TO INDEX

This is primarily an index of names. An effort has been made to include every occurrence of every proper name in the extant books of Livy, in the summaries of the lost books, in the fragments, and in the Liber Prodigiorum of Obsequens. In many cases, however, particularly with place names, large blocks of pages have been included under a single inclusive reference. On the other hand, many passages are cited where a person or place is referred to but not named. For example, Livy may recount a year's campaign in Greece without the word 'Greece' appearing a single time; and more frequent are long passages where the minor characters are named, but the principal ones are referred to simply as 'the consul' and 'the other consul.' In addition, there are many articles dealing with political, social, religious, and military antiquities. These, however, do not pretend to be exhaustive.

Names of citizens are given in the fullest form known, whether or not Livy happens to use the cognomen or cognomina of the particular individual. The names in most cases have been taken from Broughton's *Magistrates of the Roman Republic.* This work has been of the greatest value, particularly in dividing the careers of persons of like names. The alphabetizing of personal names is based first on the nomina, then the cognomina, and finally the praenomina. When these are all alike, the order is chronological. In addition, all cognomina are listed in their alphabetical places with cross references to the nomina with which they are found. Where a Roman is mentioned in an article not his own, the triple name is used. By exception, the nomina are omitted with the Cornelii Scipiones, the Quinctii Flaminini, and the Claudii Marcelli; and the chief figures of the last days of the Republic are usually called by the names in common use today (e.g., Sulla, Caesar). Philip and Antiochus without qualifying number or expression are always Philip V and Antiochus III.

Items dealing with a country or city and those dealing with its people are usually combined in a single article in a single chronological order. Although this sometimes entails a clumsy shifting back and forth between singular and plural verbs, it should prove convenient since Livy uses the names of states and of their peoples interchangeably. In the few cases where a people play an important role quite apart from the state (as do, for example, the Numidians) they are given a separate article.

As far as practicable all items are dated. In any article items appearing before the first date are for some reason undateable. The dates should aid the user of the index in identifying the article in which he is interested, and still more in locating items within the longer articles. In the case of Romans who held office, the highest office with its date is given at the beginning of the article, unless this appears as the first item in the article.

Except in the earlier books Livy regularly makes separate mention of a man's election to an office and of his entry on the office. Unless there is special reason to note the election, the page reference to it is included with that of the entry on office, both being placed under the year of the office. Regular prorogation of office is not mentioned. It is to be assumed that a man's activities in the years immediately following a term as consul or praetor are as proconsul or propraetor unless otherwise indicated.

The index is based on the translation, the text having been consulted only when some problem was raised by the translation. Place names are given in the forms used by the translators where the latter agree. Where for a particular name different forms are used by different translators (or by the same translator on different pages), the Latin form is usually preferred, with cross references from the English or Greek forms where necessary. For headings of articles dealing with political and religious antiquities, English transliterations of Latin terms have been used when available; otherwise the Latin term has usually been kept.

RUSSEL M. GEER

I have taken advantage of the reprinting of this volume to add on pages 558–573 a table of parallel references, which will make it possible to use this Index with editions of Livy other than the present one.

1967 R. M. G.

ABBREVIATIONS

Praenomina

A.: Aulus
Ap.: Appius
C.: Gaius
Cn.: Gnaeus
D.: Decimus
K.: Caeso
L.: Lucius
Mam.: Mamercus
M': Manius
M.: Marcus
P.: Publius
Pro.: Proculus
Q.: Quintus
Ser.: Servius
Sex.: Sextus
Sp.: Spurius
T.: Titus
Ti.: Tiberius

Other Abbreviations

aed. cur.: *aedilis curulis*, curule aedile
aed. pl.: *aedilis plebeius*, plebeian aedile
c.: *circa*, about (with dates)
cens., censs.: *censor, censores*, censor, censors
cent.: *centurio*, centurion
civitas sine suf.: *civitas sine suffragio*, citizenship without vote
comit. cent.: *comitia centuriata*, assembly by centuries
comit. cur.: *comitia curiata*, assembly by *curiae*
comit. tr.: *comitia tributa*, assembly by tribes
cos., coss.: *consul, consules*, consul, consuls
cos. desig.: *consul designatus*, consul designate
cos. suf.: *consul suffectus*, consul elected to fill an unexpired term
curio max.: *curio maximus*, chief *curio*, a minor religious functionary
dict., *dictator rei gerendae causa*, dictator to govern the state
dict. clavi fig. c.: *dictator clavi figendi causa*, dictator to drive the nail
dict. comit. c.: *dictator comitiorum causa*, dictator to hold elections
is.: island
leg.: *legatus*, lieutenant, one holding delegated authority. (In the Index the abbreviation 'leg.' is used only when the term

legatus has its military meaning. For other meanings, the appropriate English word is used.)

mag. eq.: *magister equitum*, master of horse for a *dictator rei gerendae causa*

mag. eq. clavi fig. c.: master of horse for a *dict. clavi fig. c.*

mag. eq. comit. c.: master of horse for a *dict. comit. c.*

pont.: *pontifex*, pontiff

pont. max.: *pontifex maximus*, chief pontiff

pr., prr.: *praetor*, *praetores*, praetor, praetors

pr. pereg.: *praetor qui inter cives et peregrinos ius dicat*, praetor for judging cases involving non-citizens, ' foreign praetor '

pr. urb.: *praetor urbanus*, praetor for judging cases involving citizens, city praetor, urban praetor

pr. suf.: *praetor suffectus*, praetor elected to fill unexpired term

pref., or praef.: *praefectus*, prefect

pref. soc.: *praefectus sociorum*, prefect of allied troops

pref. urb.: *praefectus urbis*, prefect of the city (Rome)

prin. Sen.: *princeps Senatus*, senior member of the Senate

procos.: *proconsul*, proconsul

propr.: *propraetor*, propraetor

prov.: *provincia*, sphere of activity, province

qu.: *quaestor*, quaestor

rex sac.: *rex sacrorum* (or *sacrificulus*), king of sacrifices, a minor religious functionary

SC.: *Senatus consultum*, decree of the Senate

tr. (tribb.) mil.: *tribunus* (*tribuni*) *militum ad legiones*, military tribune (tribunes) serving with the legions

tr. (tribb.) mil. cos. p.: *tribunus* (*tribuni*) *militum consulari potestate*, military tribune (tribunes) with consular power

tr. (tribb.) pl.: *tribunus* (*tribuni*) *plebis*, tribune (tribunes) of the plebs

IIvir nav.: *duumvir navalis*, one of a board of two in charge of the fleet

IIvir sac.: *duumvir sacris faciundis*, member of a board of two for religious matters

IIIvir agr. assig. (dand., divid.): *triumvir* (*tresvir*) *agris assignandis* (*dandis*, *dividendis*), member of a board of three for assigning (distributing, dividing) lands

IIIvir col. deduc.: *triumvir* (*tresvir*) *coloniae deducendae*, member of a board of three for establishing a colony. (This is often given in the Index as ' IIIvir for ' with the name of the colony.)

ABBREVIATIONS

IIIvir mens.: *triumvir* (*tresvir*) *mensarius*, member of a board of three bank commissioners

Vvir agr. divid.: *quinquevir agris dividendis*, member of a board of five for dividing lands

Vvir mens.: *quinquevir mensarius*, member of a board of five bank commissioners

Xvir: *decemvir legibus scribendis*, member of a board of ten for codifying the laws

Xvir agr. divid.: *decemvir agris dividendis*, member of a board of ten for dividing lands

Xvir sac.: *decemvir sacrorum*, *decemvir sacris faciundis*, member of a board of ten for religious matters

As a matter of convenience in this Index the terms Vvir and Xvir are used for members of other boards of five or ten members performing certain designated functions.

INDEX

(References are by volume and page. Figures in parentheses are dates. Items between two page references belong with the reference which follows; those between two dates, with the date which precedes.)

Abbassius, Phrygian city: (189), **11**. 51

Abdera, in Thrace: (188) Cn. Manlius Volso at, **11**. 141; (170) stormed; restored, **13**. 17–19; (167) not in Macedonian republics, 347

Abelux, of Saguntum: (217) **5**. 273–7

Aborigines, of Latium: make treaty with Aeneas, **1**. 9–13

Abrupolis, Roman ally: (before 172) assailed by Perseus, **12**. 329, 409, 415–7

Aburius, C.: (171) envoy to Africa, **12**. 397

—, M., pr. 176: (187) tr. pl., opposes triumph of M. Fulvius Nobilior, **11**. 227–31; (176) pr. pereg., **12**. 227, 231

Abydus, in Troad: (200) destroyed by Philip, **9**. 43, 51–7, 91, 217; (198–197) his withdrawal demanded by Rhodes, 255, (196) and by Rome, 359; Antiochus moves from, 379, 381; (190) resists siege, **10**. 317, 325; Antiochus' fleet at, 331

Academy, at Athens: (200) **9**. 71–3

Acanthus, Macedonian port: (200) captured, **9**. 133; (167) in 2nd Macedonian republic, **13**. 351

Acarnania: location of, **9**. 321–3, **10**. 203; (211) restoration to Aetolian League promised, **7**. 93–5; prepares to resist Aetolia, 97–9, **12**. 403; (210) situation in, reported, **7**. 109; (208–207) fears Aetolians, **8**. 17; Punic fleet moves to, 31; (205) included in Roman peace with Philip, 253–5; (200) at war with Athens, **9**. 45; urged against Rome, 87; (198) T. Flamininus winters near, 205; (197) L. Flamininus at, 273; aids Philip, 313, 319–21, **12**. 403; submits, **9**. 321–3; (192) at Achaean council, **10**. 77; (191) part of, joins Antiochus, 191–3, **12**. 403; Antiochus leaves, **10**. 195; M. Porcius Cato near, 223; (189) Aetolians plunder, **11**. 15, 17; captures Aetolian envoys, 29; Oeniadae restored to, 37; (172) Roman envoys to, **12**. 403; (169) **13**. 63; Roman transports land in, 91; (167) partisans of Perseus in, investigated, 355–7, 365. *See* Alexander, Mnasilochus, Sopater.

accensi: (340) place of, in legion, **4**. 33, 39

Acerrae, in Campania: (332) granted *civitas sine suf.*, **4**. 71; (216) burned by Hannibal, **6**. 55–7, **7**. 213; prevents aid to Casilinum, **6**. 65; (210) rebuilding of, permitted, **7**. 213

Achaea: *see* Achaia.

Achaean League: friendship with Macedon, **12**. 269; (208) gains aid of Philip against Sparta, Aetolia, Attalus, **7**. 331–43; defeats Aetolians, 343; (207) Philip at council of, **8**. 17, 31–3; (205) on side of Philip in Roman treaty, 255; (200) declines his aid against Nabis; votes army, **9**. 73–7; (199) Philip demands oath, restores cities to, 163–5; (198) envoys of T. Flamininus, Rhodes, and Attalus at council of, 207–21, 281, **12**. 269; many withdraw from, **9**. 221–3; approves alliances with Attalus, Rome, and Rhodes; sends army, 223–5, 283; retires from Corinth and Argos, 225–33; (197) negotiates with Philip and Rome over Argos and Corinth, 251–

67; makes armistice with Nabis, 269–71; defeats Macedonians near Corinth, 313–9, 329; (196) obtains terms for Boeotia, 357–9; receives Corinth, 363, 369, 475; (195) aids in freeing Argos from Nabis, 477–505, 525; (194) promised Acrocorinth, 543; ransoms Romans, 547; (193) dominant in Peloponnese, **10**. 35–7, **11**. 103; sends aid to Gytheum, envoys to Rome, **10**. 37–9; (192) reports treaty violations by Nabis, 63; declares war on Nabis, 71; fleet defeated, 73–5; consults with allies, 77; Nabis twice defeated, 77–89, and shut up in Sparta, 103–5, **11**. 337; Sparta added to League, **10**. 111; Antiochus courts, 135–41, 173–5; war declared on him, 141–5; troops of, withdraw before him, 145–9; (191) Eleans join, 169, 245–7, 259; Messenians join on orders of Flamininus, 245–7, **12**. 65, 401–3; Zacynthus taken by, then by Rome, **10**. 249–53; council of, at Aegium, 257–9 (*cp*. **11**. 101); (190) plunders Aetolian coast, **10**, 303; (189) **11**. 21; (190) defeats Seleucus, **10**. 347–51; (189) assembly at Argos declares war on Sparta, **11**. 103–5; sends envoys to Rome, 107–9, 331; elects Philopoemen praetor, 109; imposes terms on Sparta, 109–15, 323; M. Fulvius Nobilior hears Spartans and, 115; (184) ignores Roman request for council, 323–5; Spartans complain of, 323, 331, 335; acts against Sparta defended before Roman envoys, 329–39; forced to yield by Rome, 339–41, (183) and to permit return of Spartan exiles; Sparta remains in, 371–3; Messenê secedes from, is defeated; Philopoemen killed, 373–9, **12**. 65; (182) envoys of, before Senate, 7; (181) 65; (174) vainly wooed by Perseus, 259–71, 307, 327, 401; (173) M. Marcellus calls council of, 307; (172) loyalty of, 401–3; furnishes troops, 425; P. Cornelius Lentulus returns from, 437; (171) Leonidas condemned by, 449; (169) Roman envoys compliment, **13**. 63; (167) partizans of Perseus in, called for trial, 355–7; (146) Rome defeats, **14**. 39, 41, 45. *See* Aratus, Aristaenus, Cycliadas, Lycon, Nicias, Nicostratus, Philopoemen; Corinth, Messenê, Patrae.

Achaeans: (197) in Rhodian army, **9**. 325–7; (190) in Roman army, **10**. 405, (189) **11**. 99, (171) **12**. 425, 463, 505, (149) **14**. 31

—, Harbour of the, on Hellespont: (190) **10**. 315–7

Achaia: colonizes Thurii, Tarentum, Metapontum, **6**. 397–9. *See* Achaean League.

—, Phthiotic: north of Thermopylae, **10**. 203; (196) freed, **9**. 365; granted to Thessaly, 369; (174) Perseus crosses, **12**. 257–9; (171) P. Licinius Crassus enters, 505. *See* Phthiotis.

Acharrae, in Thessaly: (198) **9**. 191

Acheron riv., in Epirus: (326) **4**. 93

Acheros riv., in Italy: (326) **4**. 97

Achillas: (48) kills Pompey, **14**. 141, 213

Achivi: spare Aeneas and Antenor, **1**. 9

Achradina, in Syracuse: (214) Syracusans gather in, **6**. 243–9, 257; magistrates flee to, 279; Romans attack city at, 283; (212) M. Marcellus takes, 435–7, 441, 447, 455–9

Acilius, C.: (c. 143) wrote history in Greek, **14**. 47; used by Q. Claudius Quadrigarius, **6**. 493, **10**. 41

—, L.: (181) leg. in Spain, **12**. 97–101

—, M': (218) IIIvir agr. adsig., **5**. 69–71

—, M': (210) envoy to Alexandria, **7**. 215; (208) in Senate, 311

— Balbus, M': (114) cos., **14**. 269

— Glabrio, M', cos. 191: a 'new man,' **10**. 471; (201) tr. pl., prevents taking Africa from P. Scipio (Afr.). **8**. 519; proposes plebiscitum for Punic peace, 529; (200) Xvir sac., **9**. 147; (197) aed. pl., 345; (196) pr. pereg., 341–3, 347; checks slave revolt, 373; (193) candidate for cos., **10**. 27; (191) cos. with Greece as prov., 69, 155, 157; vows games, 157–9; consults fetiales, 163; gathers forces at Brundisium, 165–7; aid offered by Philip, 167, **11**. 305, and Masinissa, **10**. 167; crosses to Greece, 195, 263; comes to

INDEX

Malian Gulf, 197–201, and Thermopylae, 205–9; harangues men, 209–13; vows temple to Pietas, **12**. 103–5; defeats Antiochus, **10**. 213–9, 249, 299, 435, **11**. 171, **12**. 391; moves through Greece, **10**. 219–57, 277; sacks Heraclea, 225–33; dictates terms to Aetolians, which they reject, 237–45; permits Philip to occupy Thessalian and Aetolian cities, 233, **11**. 287, 291–3, 299, including Demetrias, **10**. 251; grants truce to Aetolians, 257; at Achaean council, 257–9; refers Epirotes to Rome, 259; ends campaign, 259–61, **11**. 149; (190) sends Aetolian prisoners to Rome, **10**. 299; takes Lamia, 303–5, **11**. 305; attacks Amphissa, **10**. 305; succeeded by L. Scipio, 295, 297, 311, **11**. 147; triumphs, **10**. 427, **11**. 159; (189) sponsors SC. expelling Aetolian envoys, **10**. 435; seeks censorship; accused of retaining booty, 469–71

cilius Glabrio, M', cos. suf., 154: (181) dedicates temple vowed by father, **12**. 103–5

coridos Comê, in Asia Minor: (189) **11**. 49–51

crae, in Sicily: (214) **6**. 289

craephia, in Boeotia: (196) **9**. 357

craeus: *see* Zeus Acraeus.

criae, in Peloponnese: (192) **10**. 75

crillae, in Sicily: (214) **6**. 289

crocorinthus, citadel of Corinth: (196) Roman garrison on, **9**. 363, (194) removed from, 543, 547

cropolis, in Athens: treaty ratified on, **11**. 111; (167) L. Aemilius Paulus visits, **13**. 341

ctium, Acarnanian port: (169) transports land at, **13**. 91; (31) Octavius defeats Antony at, **14**. 163, **1**. 67

tors: (403) position of, in Etruria, **3**. 5, (364) in Rome, 363, (214) in Greece, **6**. 253

cuca, in Apulia: (214) **6**. 239

culeo: *see* Furius.

cutius, M.: (401) co-opted tr. pl., **3**. 37

cylla, African port: (195) **9**. 403

laeus, of Beroea: (169) envoy of Perseus to Gentius, **13**. 71–3

Adherbal, the sufete: (206) defeated, **8**. 125–7

—, of Numidia: (118) driven from kingdom by Jugurtha, restored by Rome, **14**. 75; (112) slain, 77

Adoreus, Mt., in Galatia: (189) **11**. 63

Adramytteum, in Mysia: (190) **10**. 347, 351

Adranodorus: (215) son-in-law of Hiero, guardian of Hieronymus, **6**. 187–91, 195; occupies Island, 243–5; accepts amnesty; elected to office, 245–9; killed, 253–61

Adriatic (Hadriatic) sea, *mare superum*: named from Hatria, **3**. 115; colony of Antenor on, **1**. 9; (321) road to Luceria skirts, **4**. 167; (302) losses of Cleonymus on, 363–7; (218) fleet sails, to Ariminum, **5**. 151; (216) allies enlisted from coast of, **6**. 81; (215) envoys of Philip brought from, 131; (181) visible from Mt. Haemus, **12**. 67; Philip surveys routes to, 69; (179) Scordisci on route to, 173; (178) fleet to protect, 185–7; (168) troops along, discharged, **13**. 255; transports on, scattered, 291–3. *Also* **7**. 363, **13**. 191.

Aebura, in Spain: (181) **12**. 93–101

Aebutia: (186) informs on Bacchanalian conspiracy, **11**. 249

Aebutius, M.: (178) tr. mil., **12**. 187

—, P.: (186) informs on Bacchanalian conspiracy, **11**. 243–57, 273–5

— Helva, L.: (463) cos., dies, **2**. 21–3

— —, M.: (442) IIIvir col. deduc., **2**. 295

— —, M.: (168) pr. for Sicily, **13**. 145, 147

— —, T.: (499) cos., mag. eq. at Lake Regillus, **1**. 279–81; triumphs, 285

— — Cornicen, Post.: (442) cos., seeks justice for Ardea, **2**. 295; (435) mag. eq., 327

— Parrus, T., pr. 178: (183) IIIvir col. deduc., **11**. 395; (178) pr. for Sardinia, **12**. 201; (176) 231; (173) Xvir agr. adsig., 303

Aecae, in Apulia: (214) **6**. 237

aediles, curule: (367, 366) established, **3**. 351, 357; insignia, 357–9; plebeian and patrician, 359; (304) elected by tribal assembly, **4**. 349, (213) **6**. 347; (299) in charge of grain, **4**. 399; (295) accuse usurers, 445; (292) give Roman games; pave road with fines of graziers, 541; (214) give four days of drama, **6**. 315; P. Scipio (Afr.) elected, below legal age, 345–7; (202) in charge of *aerarium*, **8**. 515; (189) condemn grain dealers, **11**. 115; (186) ordered to seek out Bacchic priests, 259; (184) barred from election of pr. suf., 343–7. *See* Roman games; finance.

aediles, plebeian: established, **2**. 269; (463) replace deceased coss., 23; (454) prosecute ex-cos., 105; (449) sacrosanct, 183–5; custodians of decrees, 185, 195; (428) empowered to curb foreign cults, 357; (389) direct rebuilding of Rome, **3**. 207; (367) refuse cost of longer games, 351; (216) former, named to Senate by dict., **6**. 79; (209) sons of living curule magistrates not eligible for, **7**. 301, **8**. 439; (204) with tr. pl. investigate Locrian affair, 287–9; (186) ordered to prevent Bacchic rites, **11**. 259. *See* Plebeian games; finance.

aediles, curule or plebeian: (345–343) accuse usurers, **3**. 455, (328) an adulterer, **4**. 85, (298) violators of land laws, 407; (308) adorn Forum, 323; (213) fail to suppress foreign cults, **6**. 343

Aefula, in Latium: (211) **7**. 35; (197) **9**. 243

Aegatian is.: (242) Punic fleet defeated off, **4**. 559, **5**. 29, 121, 379, **6**. 41, **8**. 487; (218) Punic fleet off, **5**. 145; (216) 383

Aegean sea: (191) **10**. 279; (190) 331; (187) **11**. 207; (168) **13**. 185

Aegimurus is., off Africa: (204) P. Scipio (Afr.) driven to, **8**. 315–7; (203) Hasdrubal captures transports at, 451–3

Aegina: (208) P. Sulpicius Galba and Attalus at, **7**. 335, 343; (207) **8**. 17, 29; (200) pursuit of Philip reaches, **9**. 45; Attalus at, 49, 73, 83, 97–9, (198–7) 269; (196) given Attalus, 361; (191) Eumenes at, **10**. 277; (172) **12**. 339, 343, 367

Aeginium, in Thessaly: (198) Flamininus fails to take, **9**. 195; (191) recovered from Athamanes, **10**. 197; (168) captured, **13**. 241; (16[?] sacked, 339

Aegium, Achaean town: (20[?] Achaean council meets at, **7**. 335 (207) **8**. 31; (192) **10**. 137; (19[?] 257–9; (173) **12**. 307; (169) **13**. 63 (189) council moved from, **11**. 101 (207) Philip sends Nicias to, **8**. 35 (192) ships launched at, **10**. 73; (18[?] slingers from, in Roman army, **1**[?] 99

Aelius, C.: (178) tr. mil., **12**. 187, 19[?]

—, P.: (409) first plebeian qu., **2**. 4[?]

—, Q.: (11) cos., **14**. 319

—, T.: (178) tr. mil., **12**. 187, 195

— Ligur (Ligus), P.: (172) cos., **1**[?] 317, **13**. 51, with Liguria as prov., **1**[?] 319–21; supports procos. M. Popiliu[s] Laenas, 319–21, 349; threatene[d] with fine, 351; inactive in Liguri[a] 353, 363–5; (167) Vvir for Illyria[n] peace, **13**. 299, 337–9

— Paetus, L.: (296) aed. pl., **4**. 447

— —, P.: (337) cos., **4**. 61; (32[?] mag. eq. com. c., 187; (300) one [of] first plebeian augurs, 389

— —, P., cos. 201: (208) augur, [?] 355, **12**. 253–5; (204) aed. pl., [?] 357–9; (203) pr. urb., 357, 36[?] 427–9, 445–7, 451; (202) mag. e[q.] com. c., conducts Cerialia, 51[5] (201) cos., 517, 533; does litt[le] against Boi, **9**. 7–9; appoints prop[r.] for Macedon, 9–11; Xvir agr. adsig[n.] holds elections, 13; (200) soldiers o[f] drafted, 25–7; (199) IIIvir t[o] investigate Narnia, 159; cens., 16[?] (193) envoy to Antiochus, 569 (174) dies, **12**. 253–5

— —, Q.: (217) consular candidat[e] **5**. 317; (216) pont., slain at Canna[e] **6**. 73

— —, Q., cos. 167: (177) tr. pl[.] defends A. Manlius Volso, **12**. 20[?] (174) augur, 255; (167) cos. wit[h] Gaul as prov., **13**. 295, 301, **14**. 24[?] raids Liguria, **13**. 403–5

— —, Sex., cos. 198: (200) aed. cur[.] **9**. 147; (199) IIIvir to investigat[e] Narnia, 159; (198) cos. with Ital[y] as prov., 173, 175; goes to Gau[l] 179; re-establishes Cremona an[d] Placentia, 233; holds elections, 237 (194) cens., 531–3, **10**. 23

— Tubero, P., pr. 201, 177: (202) ae[d.]

INDEX

pl., **8**. 515; (201) pr. for Sicily, 517, 521; (189) Xvir for settlement of Asia, **10**. 461–3, **11**. 123–35, 153, 161, 205, 301; (177) pr. ii urb., **12**. 207; IIIvir col. deduc., 225
Aelius Tubero, Q., (194) tr. pl., proposes Latin colonies, **9**. 551–3; IIIvir col. deduc., 553; (193) **10**. 25
— —, Q.: (168) given custody of Perseus, **13**. 267, 271
— —, Q., the annalist: (49–48) flees to Pompey, **14**. 209. Cited: (434) **2**. 331, (299) **4**. 391
Aemilia, wife of Africanus: (187) **11**. 201
—, a Vestal: (114) condemned, **14**. 75
Aemilian bridge: (179) piles for, **12**. 159
— column, with *rostra*, **12**. 347–9
— law: (434) limits terms of cens., **2**. 333; (310) violated **4**. 289–99
— portico: (193) built, **10**. 29; (174) repaired, **12**. 279
— tribe: (188) Formiae and Fundi in, **11**. 121
— way: (187) built, **14**. 5
Aemilianus: *see* Cornelius Scipio, Fabius Maximus.
Aemilius Barbula, Q.: (317) cos., takes Nerulum, **4**. 243–5; (311) cos. ii., ignores new Senate list, 277; defeats Etruscans, 281, 285–7
— Cerretanus, Q.: (323) cos., commands against Apulia, **4**. 143–5
— Lepidus, L., son of M., cos. 232: (216) gives funeral games for father, **6**. 103
— —, Mam., cos. 77: (88) leg., defeats Italians, **14**. 95
— —, M., cos. 232: (216) **6**. 103
— —, M.: pr. 218, 216, 213: (218) pr. for Sicily, **5**. 145–7, 151; (217) consular candidate, 317; (216) pr. suf., **6**. 69, 75; gives funeral games for father, 103; (213) pr. pereg. and for Luceria, 315, 347; suppresses foreign cults, 343–5, 383–5; accuses *publicani*, 349–51; (211) Xvir sac., **7**. 91
— —, M., cos. 187, 175: (201) envoy to Egypt, **9**. 7, 53; (200) delivers protest to Philip, 53–5; (199) pont., 173; (193) aed. cur., **10**. 29, **11**. 397; (191) pr. for Sicily, **10**. 69, 159–61, 297; (190) propr., 431; his son's victory at Magnesia, 415; consular candidate, 431; (189) **11**. 115, 147, 397, **12**. 147; (187) cos. with Liguria as prov., **11**. 143, 145–7, 161; protests continuance of procos. in East, 145–7; assails M. Fulvius Nobilior for Ambracian attack, 147–51; secures SC. for Ambracia, 151–3, 227; campaigns in Liguria, 153, 219, 223, 233–5, 277; vows temple, 223, **12**. 161; forces restoration of arms to Cenomani, **11**. 223–5; opposes triumph of Nobilior, 227–33; (183) IIIvir col. deduc., 395; (180) pont. max., **12**. 135, 143, **10**. 415; (179) cens. with Nobilior, ends feud, **12**. 143–7, 157–63; prin. Sen., 157; dedicates temples, 161–3; (178) punishes Vestals, **14**. 243; (177) IIIvir col. deduc., **12**. 225; (175) cos. ii, **14**. 245; victorious in Gaul and Liguria, **12**. 243–5; (174) prin. Sen. ii, 275; suppresses revolt in Venetia, 277; (173) Xvir agr. adsig., 303; (172) dictates vow, 373; (170) envoy to Gauls, **13**. 21; (169) prin. Sen. iii, 53; (164) iv, **14**. 11; (159) opposed by Cn. Tremellius; prin. Sen. vi, 13; (153–152) dies, 17
Aemilius Lepidus, M.: (190) tr. mil., **10**. 415–7
— —, M.: (126) cos., **14**. 265
— —, M.: (78) cos., driven from Italy by Sulla, **14**. 113–5
— —, M., the IIIvir: (46) cos., **14**. 309; (44) sons of, given as hostages to murderers of Caesar, 147; preempts office of pont. max., 147, 311; dogs howl before house of, 311; (43) in Gaul, member of 2nd IIIvirate, 151–3, 315; proscriptions, 153; (42) cos. ii, 315; (41) driven from Rome, 157; (36) attacks Octavius, 159
— —, M., son of the IIIvir: (31–30) plots against Octavius, killed, **14**. 163
— —, Q., son of M., cos. 232: (216) gives funeral games for father, **6**. 103
— — Livianus, Mam.: (77) cos., **14**. 299
— — Paulus, L.: (50) cos., **14**. 305
— — Porcina, M.: (137) cos., **14**. 57, 257; (136) Vaccaei defeat, 57
— Mamercus (or Mamercinus), C.: (394) tr. mil. c. p., **3**. 89; defeated

by Aequi, 99–101; (391) tr. mil. c. p. ii, defeats Volsinienses, 111–3

Aemilius Mamercus (or Mamercinus), L.: (484) cos., defeats Volsci, Aequi, **1**. 357; defeats land law, 357–9; (478) cos. ii, defeats Etruscans, 387; (473) cos. iii, 401; mobbed holding levy, 405–7

— —, L.: (389) mil. tr. c. p., **3**. 197, 201; (387) ii, 211; (383) iii, 269; (382) iv, 271

— —, L.: (377) tr. mil. c. p., defeats Latins, Volsci, **3**. 305–7; (368) mag. eq., 327; (366) cos., 357; (363) ii, 365; (355) interrex, 415; (352) mag. eq., 429

— —, Mam.: (438) tr. mil. c. p., **2**. 311–3; (437) dict., defeats Etruscans, 315–21, 361, 391; triumphs, 321; (434) dict. ii, against Etruscans, 331–3; limits censors' term, punished by cens., 333–5, 359, 363, **4**. 289–93; (428) IIIvir to investigate charges against Veii, **2**. 355; (426) dict. iii, defeats Etruscans, 359–71

— —, M. (or M'): (410) cos., **2**. 429; (405) tr. mil. c. p.; siege of Veii begins, 455; (403) tr. mil. c. p. ii, **3**. 3; (401) iii, 35; recovers camp, 43

— —, M.: (391) tr. mil. c. p., **3**. 111

— —, T. (or Ti.): (470) cos., **1**. 423, 425; (467) ii, supports land distribution, **2**. 3

— —, T. (or Ti.), cos. 339: (352) Vvir mens., **3**. 429; (341) pr., presents Samnite petition to Senate, **4**. 5; (339) cos., 49; at odds with Senate, 51–3

— — Privernas, L., cos. 341, 329: (342) mag. eq., **3**. 503; (341) cos., **4**. 3; plunders Samnium, 5; resigns, 11; (335) dict. comit. c., 67; (329) cos. ii, against Gauls, 79; (326) interrex, 93; (316) dict. for year, defeats Samnites, 245–7

— Numida, M': (211) Xvir sac., **7**. 91

— Papus, L., cos. 225: (220) cens., **6**. 73, 77–9, 211; (216) IIIvir mens., 73

— —, L.: (205) pr. for Sicily, **8**. 153, 155; (172) Xvir sac., **12**. 373

— —, M.: (320) dict. comit. c., **4**. 189

— —, M.: (210) curio max., **7**. 227, 235

— Paulus, L., cos. 219, 216: 219) cos., **5**. 335; colleague condemned, 317, 361; (218) envoy to Carthage, 49; incites Spaniards and Gauls, 55–9, 63; (216) cos. ii with C. Terentius Varro, 317–9; addresses people, 327; advised by Fabius Maximus, 327–33; campaign before Cannae, 333–49; opposes Varro's rashness, 337, 345–9; commands right at Cannae, 351; slain, 359–61, 365, 381, **6**. 35, 73, 155, **7**. 9, **8**. 119; buried by Hannibal, **5**. 373; pont., **6**. 73

Aemilius Paulus, L., cos. 182, 168: (194) IIIvir col. deduc., **9**. 535; (193) aed. cur., **10**. 29, **11**. 397; (191) pr. for Farther Spain, **10**. 69, 159–61, 165; (190) 297, 427–9; (189) defeats Lusitani, 469, 473; Xvir for Asian settlement, 461–3, **11**. 123–35, 153, 161, 205, 301; (187) opposes triumph of Manlius Volso, 153–61; (185) consular candidate, 319–21; (182) cos. with Liguria as prov., 397, **14**. 241, **12**. 3–5, 141; in Liguria, 53, 57; (181) defeats Ligurians, 77–89; triumphs, 105; (171) advocate of Spain, **13**. 7–9; (168) cos. ii with Macedon as prov., 145–51, 155–7, 385–7; directs reception of foreign envoys, 151; addresses *contio*, 159–63, 245; arrives in Macedon, 163, 187, 195; restores discipline, 197–203, 369, 377; defeats Perseus at Pydna, 205–35, 395, **10**. 469; sends news to Rome, **13**. 237; receives surrender of cities, 237–41, 395; moves to Pella, and Amphipolis, 241–3; victory known in Rome by rumour, then by envoys, 249–55; receives Perseus' envoys, 237, 257–9, then Perseus as captive, 267–71, 395; dismisses Numidians, 291–3; (167) procos., 297; Xviri appointed to advise, 299; orders sack of cities, 339; tours Greece, 339–45; meets Xviri at Amphipolis; receives Perseus, 345; announces terms, 347–59; holds festival, 359–63; permits plundering of Illyria and Epirus, 363–5; in Italy, 365; reserves spoil for treasury, 369; argument over triumph, 369–91; triumphs, 391–3, 397; gives games, **14**. 39, 41; bereft of sons by adop-

INDEX

tion and death, **13**. 235, 393, 397, **14**. 19, 39, 73; addresses *contio*, **13**. 393–7; (160) dies in poverty, **14**. 13

Aemilius Paulus, L.: (43) slain, **14**. 153

— —, M.: (302) cos., defeats Cleonymus, **4**. 363; mag. eq., defeated by Etruscans, 369–71

— —, M.: (255) cos., sets up *columna rostrata*, **12**. 347

— Potensis: (102) haruspex, **14**. 279

— Regillus, L.: (190) pr. for fleet, **10**. 285, 295, 297, 301–3, **13**. 319; naval operations against Antiochus in Aegean, **10**. 331–41; postpones negotiations, 345–7; at Adramyteum, 347; at Samos, 353; naval operations, 367–87; defeats Antiochus' fleet, 373–81; vows temple to Lares of Sea, **12**. 161; reports victory, **10**. 429–31; (189) granted naval triumph, 473

— —, M.: (217) pr. urb., carries out religious duties, **5**. 231, 311, **7**. 345; recalls cos. for elections, **5**. 313; (215) as flamen of Quirinus (?) unavailable for consulship, **6**. 197–9; (205) flamen of Mars, dies, **8**. 249, 359

— —, M.: (190) leg., **10**. 353

— Scaurus, L.: (190) leg., **10**. 381

Aenaria, Campanian is.: (328–7) **4**. 87; (91) **14**. 291

Aenea (Aenia): port town of Chalcidicê, **13**. 351; rites to Aeneas at, **12**. 11; (169) lands of, devastated, **13**. 123; (168) Perseus protects, 195–7; (167) sacked, 339. *See* Poris.

Aeneas, of Troy: established Trojans in Italy, **1**. 9–15; worshipped as Jupiter Indiges, 15; rites for, at Aenea, **12**. 11

– Silvius, king of Alba Longa, **1**. 17

Aenesidemus, of Dymae: (198) commands Achaeans in Argos, **9**. 231–3

Aenianes, in Thessaly: (197) Flamininus near, **9**. 283

Aenianes, Gulf of: *see* Malian Gulf.

Aenus, in Thrace: (200) Philip takes, **9**. 51, 91; (190) L. Scipio near, **10**. 387; (189) Antiochus' men ordered from, 479; (188) Cn. Manlius Volso near, **11**. 139; (185) Philip holds, 289–91; Eumenes claims, 301–9; (184) Philip ordered from, 323; (170) refuses Roman demands, **13**. 29; (167) Attalus claims, 309; not in Macedonian republics, 347

Aeolis: Gauls occupy, **11**. 55; (196) Antiochus claims, **9**. 379, 567; (193) **10**. 49; (190) Seleucus in, 313–5, 341; naval operations in, end, 325; continued protection needed, 363; withdrawal of Antiochus from, demanded, 393

Aepulo: (178–177) Histrian chief, **12**. 185, 219

Aequi: (534–10) Sex. Tarquin considers flight to, **1**. 185; Tarquin the Proud makes peace with, 191; (494) wars with, 313–21; (488) 351; (485) 357; (484) 357; (482) 361; (481) 361–3, 367, 373; (479) 381–5; (475) 399; (471) 415, 421; (470) 425; (469) 427; (468) 429–33; (467) granted peace, but invade Latium, **2**. 5; (466) wars with, 5; (465) 5–11; (464) 13–9; (463) 21–5, 33–5; (462) 31, 35; (461) 37; (460) feared while Ap. Herdonius holds Capitol, 53–5, 61, 69; (459) capture Tusculum; defeated at Mt. Algidus, 75, 79–81; granted peace, 83–5; (458) break treaty; defeated, 85–7, 95–7; (457) wars with, 101–3; (455) raid Tusculum; defeated, 103–5; (449) 125, 139, 193, 201–7; (447) levy against, suspended by civil strife, 221; (446) raid to Rome; defeated, 223–5, 231, 237–43; (445) murmur at fortification of Verrugo, 257; tribb. pl. accused of encouraging, 263; (444) war with, as a reason for tr. mil. c. p., 279; (432) discuss war, 337; (431) defeated at Mt. Algidus by dict. A. Postumius Tubertus, 339–53; (430) granted truce, 353; (425), 371; (421) inactive, 393–7; (418) war with, 403–11, 417; (415) 417; (414) 419; (410) 429; (409) 435–9; (408) 439; (397) **3**. 57; (396) peace granted to, 83; (394) war with, 99–101; (393) 103; (392) 109; (389) defeated by Camillus, 203, 219; (388) defeated, 209; (343) Campanians promise aid against, 459; (319) members of Roman Federation, **4**. 237; (304) aid Samnites; defeated, 345–9; (303) colony sent among, 361–3; (299)

defeated, 391. Typical enemies: **3.** 181, 185, 235, 471
Aequicoli: source of fetial law, **1.** 115; (298) colony planted among, **4.** 403
Aequimaelium: (438) site of house of Sp. Maelius, **2.** 309–11; (213) burned, **6.** 327–9; (189) building above, **11.** 95
aerarii: (214) Senators, equites, and/or citizens reduced to, by cens., **6.** 231; (209) **7.** 253; (204) **8.** 355–7; (173) **12.** 319; (168) **13.** 295
aerarium: (446) standards brought from, **2.** 237; (436–435) 327–9; (350) **3.** 433; (346) prisoners and spoil sold for, 451; (293) **4.** 537–9; (214) empty, **6.** 229–33; (210) Senators bring treasures to, **7.** 137–9; (209) gold from more sacred, used, 247–9; (207) booty carried in triumph and deposited in, **8.** 41; (190) **10.** 471; (189) **11.** 189–93; (167) **13.** 369, 377, 385; (202) thefts from, **8.** 515
Aëropus: (208) captures Lychnidus, **7.** 343
— : (205) Epirote magistrate, **8.** 253
Aesculapius: (292) summoned from Epidaurus, **4.** 543; (291) temple built, 547, **8.** 245–7; (180) gilded statue of, **12.** 115; (189) temple of, in Ambracia, **11.** 15, (170) in Antium, **13.** 17, (167) in Epidaurus, 343
—, a Punic god: (174) **12.** 257; (172) 357
Aesernia, Samnite town: (295) raided by Samnites, **4.** 477; (264) colony at, 553; (209) loyal, **7.** 245–7; (168) cavalry from, at Pydna, **13.** 225; (91–90) taken by Samnites, **14.** 89, 91, (81–80) by Sulla, 113
Aesis riv., in Umbria: (391) **3.** 121
Aeternius: *see* Aternius.
Aethalia is., near Ephesus: (190) **10.** 329
Aethopia, in Athamania: (189) **11.** 7–9
Aetna, Mt.: active, **7.** 113; (140) **14.** 255; (135) 259; (126) 265; (122) 267; (44) 215
Aetolians (Aetolian League): character of, **7.** 333, **9.** 121, 305, **10.** 141–3, **12.** 307; when putting question of war praetor of, does not state own opinion, **10.** 71; (212) Rome seeks friendship of, **6.** 431; (211) allied with Rome make war on Philip **7.** 91–101, 109, 141, **9.** 95, 215, **10** 97, **11.** 29; (209) Philip prepare attack on, **7.** 269, (208) and defeats 331–3; fail to make peace, 333–5 defend Elis, 339–41; death o Philip reported in; defeated by Achaeans, 343; (207) plunde neighbours; close Thermopylae, **8** 17–9; defeated by Philip, 27, 35 abandoned by Attalus, 29, (205) an by Rome; make peace with Philip 249–53, **9.** 5, 49, 85, 95, 311, **10.** 249 (200) reluctant to join allianc against Philip, **9.** 49, 83–99; declar war on Philip who repells then from Thessaly, 119–25; Rom refuses aid to, 133–5; (199) reliev Thaumaci, 161–3; (198) invad Thessaly, 189–93; lack harbour fo Roman winter quarters, 205; (198 197) invited to Opus by poor, ex cluded by rich, 249–51; at Roma conference with Philip, 251–61 (197) aid Flamininus at Cynos cephalae, 283, 287–95, 303, **10.** 33 37, 139–41, 177, 433–5, **11.** 27 plunder Philip's camp, **9.** 303 offended by Flamininus, hope t control Greece, 305–11, **10.** 253 hated by Acarnanians, **9.** 319–21 (196) territorial demands of, no met, 361–3, 369; send envoys t Rome, 371–3; (195) growin hostility of, 393–5, 407, 471, 475–7 525–9, 543–5; Nabis vainly await aid from, 517, 527; (193) try t rouse Nabis, Philip, and Antiochus **10.** 33–7, 53–5; (192) suspected 65–7, 89–93; ancient alliance c Athens with, 95; reject Roma terms and invite Antiochus, 93–9 143, 225, 233, 243, 425, **11.** 25 **13.** 317; plan revolutions in Gree cities; seize Demetrias, **10.** 99–103 127, 165, but fail to take Sparta 103–11, 365, or Chalcis, 111–5, 133- 5, 143; make Antiochus commander 129–33; win support of Athamania 135–7; at council of Achaeans, 137- 43; secure Chalcis, 145, 149; (191 Rome declares war on, 143–5, 163–5 273, **12.** 391; aid against, offered by Philip and Ptolemy, **10.** 167, and by Eumenes, 451; confer with Antio

chus, 173–81; campaign of, to Thermopylae, 181, 187–209; M' Acilius Glabrio defeats, at Thermopylae, 209–19, 225, 435, 441, 471, 475, and at Heraclea, 207, 217, 225–37, **11**. 305; defeat of, reported in Rome, **10**. 223; truce granted, 237–41; blamed by Philip for war, 243; assemble in Naupactus, 245, **11**. 287; supported by Elis, Megalopolis, **10**. 245, Samê, and Zacynthus, 275–7; fail to aid Demetrias, 251; make truce, send envoys to Rome, 253–7; (190) no settlement reached, 291–3; Glabrio continues in, 297; chief men of, brought to Rome, 299; seize Mt. Corax, 303–5; obtain truce by Athenian aid, 305–11; Glabrio triumphs over, 427; (189) falsely reported in revolt, 433; envoys dismissed, 433–5; assigned to cos. M. Fulvius Nobilior, 437–9; aid Amynander, **11**. 3–9; seek peace, 11; Nobilior moves against, 13–25; accept his terms, 25–33; peace made, 33–7, 95, 147, 149, **12**. 267; (188) Nobilior in, **11**. 117; (187) he triumphs over, 149–51, 225, 233, **12**. 143; (186) games vowed in, celebrated, **11**. 281, **12**. 141; (185) Philip claims cities from, **11**. 287–293; Thessalians seize town of, 297; (174) discord in, **12**. 271–3, 277, 297, 303–5; (173) council of, at Delphi, 307; (172) seek Perseus' aid, 327; send envoys to Rome, 363; receive Roman envoys, 401–3; elect Lyciscus general, 403; agents of Perseus in, 411, 417; (171) blamed for Roman defeat at Callinicus, 479; (169) discord in, **13**. 63; Stratus, a city of, withstands Perseus, 77–81; (167) Lyciscus and Tisippus kill leading men of, 345; conduct of, in war with Perseus investigated, 353–7. *See*: Alexander, Andronicus, Archidamus, Dinarchus, Dorimachus, Pantaleon, Phaeneas, Pyrrhias, Scopas, Thoas; Panaetolian council.

Aetolians: character of, **7**. 333, **9**. 121, 305, **12**. 307; often on both sides in Greek wars, **9**. 257; (196) agents in murder of Brachyllas, 351–3; (171) in army of Perseus, **12**. 449, of Rome, 463

Afranius, C.: (169) surrenders to Perseus, **13**. 67

—, L.: (60) cos., **14**. 303; (49) leg. of Pompey, surrenders, 137, 207; (47) refuses to command Pompeians; (46) slain at Thapsus, 143

— Stellio, C., pr. 185: (197) tr. pl., opposes triumph, **9**. 337–9; (185) pr., **11**. 285; (183) IIIvir col. deduc., 395–7

Africa (chiefly Carthage or its empire in Africa): (310) invaded by Agathocles, **8**. 183, (256–255) by M. Atilius Regulus, **4**. 555–7, **8**. 169, 181–3, 187, 317, **14**. 179; (249) P. Clodius Pulcher lost on voyage to, **14**. 181; (241) open to invasion, **5**. 121–3; (237–229) wars in, 5, 123; (219) invasion of, considered, 19; (218) assigned as prov. to Ti. Sempronius Longus, 47, 131; envoys sent to, 49; protected by Hannibal, 61–3; (217) Romans defeated in, 305; (216) fleet for, prepared, 323–5; P. Furius Philus returns from, **6**. 71; (215) T. Otacilius Crassus raids, 141, 201; (214) Bomilcar returns to, 291; (212) Bomilcar orders transports to, 447–9; (210) Hanno escapes to, **7**. 155; M. Valerius Messalla sent to, 217–21; Punic fleet returns to, 227; (209–208) M. Valerius Laevinus raids, 233, 303, 329–31; (207) **8**. 15; Hanno brings army from, to Spain, 3; (206) Masinissa returns to, 69–71, and promises aid in, 143; Mago prepares to cross to, 145; (205) P. Scipio (Afr.) after debate is permitted to cross to, 161–91, 245; preliminaries to invasion of, 207–11, 219–25, 229; (204) not assigned as prov., 257; invasion of, anticipated, 255–7, 277, 281, 285–9, 297–9; preparations made, 301–13; Scipio lands in, 313–9, 337–47, 369–71, 477, with L. Scipio as leg., **11**. 203, 205; (203) assigned to Scipio, **8**. 369; campaigns in, 373–431, 451–7; Cn. Servilius Caepio forbidden to cross to, 451; Hannibal and Mago recalled to, 427, 439–43, 465, 483–5, **9**. 23; Philip sends men to, **8**. 457; (202) assigned to Scipio, 461; fleet off, assigned to Ti. Claudius Nero,

INDEX

463, 511; Hannibal ready to surrender all outside, 481; Hannibal defeated in, 485–501, 515–7, **5**. 379, **11**. 179, 185, **13**. 381; Carthage to wage no war in or out of, **8**. 507; Romans in, rescued, **11**. 191; (201) assigned to Scipio, **8**. 517–21; fleet of Cn. Octavius off, 521; Scipio directed to make peace in, 529–33; grain sent from, **9**. 15; (200) 147; envoys sent to, 33, 37, 57–9; (195) Hannibal leaves, 403; (193) Hannibal will return to, if Antiochus attacks Rome, 571; Numidians claim land in, 577–9; stragglers from Scipio's army in, **10**. 7; Antiochus delays sending Hannibal to, 55, 123; (191) grain sought in, 161–3; (187) Scipio highly regarded in, **11**. 177; (182) affairs in, **12**. 55–7; (174) envoys return from, 255; (171) Masinissa hopes for all, 377; envoys from, in Rome, **13**. 13; (170) 25–7; (153–151) affairs in, **14**. 15–7, 19, 21; (149–147) 23–5, 29–31, 33, 37–9; (147) assigned as prov. to P. Scipio Aemilianus, 37. *See also*: **5**. 133, **6**. 17, 47, 87, 157, 325, **7**. 165, 169, 183, **8**. 71, 77–9, 119, 475, 525, **9**. 7, 11 3, 25, 35, 43, 143–5, 161, 177, **10**. 179, 415

Africa (chiefly non-Punic): (213) allies sought in, **6**. 329–33; (210) **7**. 215; (206) **8**. 73–9, 413; (202) Scipio's generous treatment of, **10**. 307, 389; (190) Masinissa chief king in, 365; (189) 451; (182) affairs in, **12**. 55–7; (174) 255–7; (168) Masinissa's departure from, not approved, **13**. 291; Numidian cavalry returned to, 291–3; (125) locusts and pestilence in, **14**. 69, 265; (118–105) affairs in, 75–81; (88) C. Marius and son go to, 97; (87) Marius recalled from, 99; (84) Q. Caecilius Metellus stirs war in; (83) C. Fabius Hadrianus burned alive in, 107; (80) campaigns of Pompey in, 113; (49) C. Scribonius Curio in, 139, 209; (48) M. Porcius Cato crosses deserts of; (47) Pompey's partizans in, 141; Caesar crosses to, 143, 145; (42) T. Sextius defeated in, 155; (40–38) campaigns in; (36) M. Aemilius Lepidus leaves, 159. *See* Numidia.

Africans (non-Punic): (219) in Punic armies in Spain, **5**. 33, (218) 61–3, (216) **6**. 87, 97–9, (210) **7**. 221, (209) 285, 289–91, (206), **8**. 59, 63, 85, 97, 123; (217) in Italy, **5**. 205, 213, (216) 351, 355–9, (207) **7**. 411, (204) **8**. 271; (212) in Sicily, **6**. 497; (205) in Africa, **8**. 185, 221–3, (202) 491, 495, 501

Africanus: *see* Cornelius Scipio, Cornelius Scipio Aemilianus; origin of name, **8**. 539

Agamemnon: at Aulis, **13**. 341

Agassae, in Macedon; (169) surrenders **13**. 113; (167) sacked for having supported Perseus, 339

Agathocles, of Syracuse: (310) invades Africa, **8**. 183

gathyrna, in Sicily: (210) **7**. 155–7, 255

agema: (190) unit in army of Antiochus, **10**. 407, (171) of Perseus, **12**. 447, 471

Agepolis: (168) Rhodian envoy, **13**. 255–7

Agesimbrotus, Rhodian admiral: (200) aids Romans, **9**. 135–9; (198–197) 197–201, 251

Agesipolis, exiled king of Sparta: (195) **9**. 483–5

agger: (403) used in siege, **3**. 25; (335) **4**. 65; (199) **9**. 161; (169) **13**. 71

Agraei: part of Aetolia, **9**. 257

agrarian law: *see* land law.

Agravonitae: (167) part of Illyricum, **13**. 337–9

Agrianes, Paeonian people: (207) in Macedonian army, **8**. 19, (197) **9**. 325–7, (171) **12**. 449, (169) **13**. 127

Agrigentum: (214) recovered by Himilco, **6**. 289, 301; (212) last point held by Carthage in Sicily, 429, 449, 495–501; (210) surrenders, **7**. 153–5, 161; (191) provincial boundary, **10**. 161

Agrippa Silvius: 10th king of Alba, **1**. 17

Ahala: *see* Servilius.

Aharna (Arna), in Umbria: (295) **4**. 453

Ahenobarbus: *see* Domitius.

Aius Locutius: (390) temple to, **3**. 169, 177

Alabanda, in Caria: (197) Rhodians

defeat Macedonians at, **9**. 325; (189) fort restored to, **11**. 41; (170) envoys from, **13**. 23–5; (167) Rhodes defeats, 333
Alander riv., in Phrygia: (189) **11**. 51, 61
Alba, valley of: (462) Hernici and Latins defeated near, **2**. 25
Alba Fucens, in land of Aequi: (303) colony at, **4**. 361; (302) Aequi attack, 363; (211) Hannibal near, **7**. 41; (209) refuses Roman demands, 243–7; (204) double levy imposed, **8**. 263–7; (203) internment at, of Syphax, 427, 539, (167) of Perseus, **13**. 397, (121) of king of Arverni, **14**. 73; (91) Italians attack, 89. Prodigy: (206) **8**. 47
Alba Longa: founded by Ascanius, **1**. 15, 79; kings of, 17; given to Numitor, 25; (753) Romulus sacrifices in manner of, 27; (715–672) Vestals derived from, 71; (672–640) war with, ends with alliance, 77–95; **4**. 19; treachery of, **1**. 95–105; destroyed; people transported to Rome, 105–9, 119, 181, **7**. 53, **12**. 147; chief men made Senators, **1**. 107, **2**. 271; ancestral rites continued, **1**. 111; (367) Gauls defeated near, **3**. 349; (360) plundered by Gauls, 389; (342) mutinous troops gather near, 501
Alba Silvius: 5th king of Alba Longa, **1**. 17
Alban citadel: (350–349) **3**. 439–41
– lake: (398–396) drained, **3**. 53–5, 59, 65, 173, 177. Prodigies: (398) 53–5; (209) **7**. 249
– mt.: site of Alba Longa, **1**. 15; (672–640) gods demand that rites on, be continued, 111, **3**. 177; (217) sacrifice to Jupiter Latiaris on, **5**. 191; (211) garrisoned, **7**. 35; triumph on, 81; (197) **9**. 339–41; (172) **12**. 351, **13**. 381; (176) cos. returns from, **12**. 233, **14**. 245; (168) temple of Moneta on, **13**. 295. Prodigies: (672–640) **1**. 111, **3**. 453; (212) **6**. 365; (209) **7**. 249; (113) **14**. 271. *See* Latin festival.
Albani, eastern tribe: (65) conquered, **14**. 125
Albingaunum, in Liguria: (205) **8**. 225
Albinius, L.: (390) saves Vestals, **3**. 139
Albinius, M.: (379) tr. mil. c. p., **3**. 299
Albinus Paterculus, L.: (493) one of first tribb. pl., **1**. 325
Albinus: *see* Junius Brutus, Postumius
Albius, C., of Cales: (206) leads mutiny at Sucro, **8**. 101, 111, 115–7, 121
Albula riv., old name of Tiber, **1**. 15
Alcê, in Spain: (179) **12**. 151–3
Alcibiades, of Athens: brings ruin, **8**. 169
—, of Sparta: (184) recalled from exile by Achaeans, then condemned to death, **11**. 329–333; pardoned, 341
Alco, of Saguntum: (219) seeks terms from Hannibal, **5**. 35–7
Alesia: (52) Gauls defeated at, **14**. 135
Aletrium, city of Hernici: (306) remains loyal, **4**. 333; retains laws, 339
Alexamenus, of Aetolia: (192) assassinates Nabis; slain, **10**. 101–11
Alexander, of Acarnania: (193) urges on Antiochus, **10**. 53–5; (191) at Stratus, 191; killed at Thermopylae, 219–21
—, of Aetolia: (197) rails against Philip, **9**. 255–7, (195) against Romans, 475
—, of Beroea: (181) agent of Philip in murder of Demetrius, **12**. 77
—, of Egypt: (33–31) son of Antony and Cleopatra, **14**. 163
—, of Epirus: (333–330) summoned by Tarentum, **4**. 11, 93; makes treaty with Rome, 69; campaigns in south Italy; slain, 69, 93–99, 231; contrasts Romans and Persians, 239
—, of Epirus: (198) brings Philip and Flamininus together, **9**. 181
—, of Macedon: uncle of Alexander of Epirus, **4**. 11, 99; his chances in Italy, 225–41; change in, after victories, 231; miraculous conception of, **7**. 73–5; praised by Hannibal, **10**. 43. *Also* **10**. 137, **12**. 451, 455, **13**. 267, 273
—, of Macedon, son of Perseus: (171) at review, **12**. 451; (167) prisoner in Rome, **13**. 367, 385, 389, in Alba Fucens, 397
—, of Megalopolis: (192) father-in-law of Amynander, **10**. 137

INDEX

Alexander Balas, of Syria: (c. 150) character of, **14**. 33; kills Demetrius I; killed by Demetrius II, 43; Syria claimed in name of son of, 45, (142) who is murdered, 55

Alexandria, in Egypt: (326) founded, **4**. 93; (216) Decius Magius taken to, **6**. 33; (214) Heraclia begs to be sent to, 259; (210) envoys to, **7**. 215; (201) **9**. 7, 53; (200) Aetolian mercenaries in, 125–7; (189) Macedonians in, become Egyptians, **11**. 59; (173) envoys to, **12**. 309, 367; (168) threatened by Antiochus, **13**. 151–3; envoys to and from Rome, 151–3, 277; Antiochus fails to take, 273, 277, 281; Ptolemy VI returns to, 279; (167) booty from, 363; (48–7) Caesar at, **14**. 141; library at, burned, 213; (31) M. Antony flees to; reduced by Octavius, 163

— Troas: (192) withstands Antiochus, **10**. 123; (190) 391

Alfaterna, *see* Nuceria Alfaterna.

Alfius, *see* Marius.

Algalsus: (168) cavalry commander, **13**. 189

Algidus, Mt., in Latium: (465) battle with Aequi near, **2**. 7–11; (459) 81; (458) 87, 93–7, 101; (457) 101–3; (455) 105; (449) 125, 139–41, 145, 201–9, 213; (447) 231; (431) 341–53; (418) 405; (392) **3**. 109; (218) *supplicatio* to Fortune on, **5**. 187; (211) Hannibal at, **7**. 35

Alienus, L.: (454) aed. pl., **2**. 105

Alimentus: *see* Cincius.

Aliphera, in Arcadia: (208–207) **8**. 33; (199) **9**. 165

Allia riv., in Latium: (390) Gallic victory at, **3**. 129–31, 135, 167, 181, **5**. 363–5, 393, **6**. 359, **11**. 57; troops defeated at, save Rome, **3**. 399, **6**. 361; (389) anniversary of, observed, **3**. 197; (380) Praenestini defeated on, 293–9

alliance (*foedus*): ritual for, **1**. 83–5; (753–717) with Laurentes, 51, (340) **4**. 47; (672–640) with Alba, **1**. 83–5; with Latins, 115; (534–510) 181; (495) 289; (493) 327, **3**. 395; (534–510) with Etruscans, **1**. 191; (508) 263; (486) with Hernici, 353; (459) with Aequi, **2**. 85–7; (444) with Ardea, 283; (354) with Samnites, **3**. 421, 459, 465–7; (341) **4**. 5; (320) Caudine peace not an, 195–9; (318) with Samnites, 241; (304) 345; (348) with Carthage, **3**. 449, **4**. 241; (326) with Apulia and Lucania, 99; (298) 401; (326) with Naples, 105; (304) with Marrucini, Marsi, Paeligni, Frentani, 349; (302) with Vestini, 367; (299) with Picenum, 395

alliance (*amicitia et societas*): (211) with Aetolians, **7**. 91–95

allies: (459) make up two thirds of army, **2**. 77; (217) loyalty of, **5**. 245; (216) 331; dismissed by Hannibal 389; (211) treatment of, **7**. 91; (177) **12**. 225; (173) 295–7; (91 demand citizenship, **14**. 89. *See* Latins, Social War.

Allifae, in Samnium: (326) in Samnite wars, **4**. 99; (310) 309–11; (307 331; (217) in Punic war, **5**. 245 259–61; (211) **7**. 33

Allobroges, Gauls: (218) aid Hannibal **5**. 89–91; (122–121) conquered, **14** 73, 267; (62) 127

Allobrogicus, *see* Fabius Maximus.

Allucius, a Celtiberian: (210) Scipio restores bride to, **7**. 191–5

Almana, in Macedon: (168) **13**. 175

Alopê, in Phthiotis: (171) **12**. 465

Alopeconnesus, in Thrace: (200) **9**. 51

Alorcus, a Spaniard: (219) envoy of Hannibal to Saguntum, **5**. 35–41

alphabet: invented by Evander, **1**. 2

Alps: width of, **14**. 233; crossed by Hercules, **3**. 119, (616–578) by Gauls 117–9, (391) 115–21, (218) by Hannibal, **5**. 65–9, 85–119, 125, 129 **6**. 95, 115, 153, **7**. 45, 367, without authority, **8**. 447; P. Scipio at foot of, **5**. 93, 121–3, **8**. 175–7; (215 Hasdrubal barred from, **7**. 161 (207) he crosses, 353, 355, 363–9 constant traffic over, 367; (205 Mago at foot of, **8**. 173, 197, 227–9 (203) 431–7; (186) crossed by envoys, **11**. 283, by Gauls, **14**. 241 (183) **11**. 391–3, (179) **12**. 163; (170 tribes of, complain, **13**. 19–21; (166 Gauls of, defeated, **14**. 11; (113 crossed by Teutons and Cimbri, 271 (105) by Cimbri, 79, 277, (101) 83 *Also*: **1**. 9, 13, **3**. 117, **5**. 139, 157 161, 173, **7**. 75, **8**. 467, **12**. 67, 235

INDEX

14. 15. *See* Gauls, Transalpine; Ligurians, Alpine; Salassi; Styni.

Alsium, maritime colony: (207) submits to levy, **7.** 363

Alyatti, in Galatia: (189) **11.** 61

Amadocus, of Thrace: (184) Philip captures, **11.** 327

Amarynthis, *see* Diana Amarynthis.

Ambarri, Gauls: (616–578) **3.** 119

ambassadors, *see* envoys.

Ambiani, Gauls: (57–6) subdued, **14.** 129

Ambigatus, Gallic chief: (616–578) **3.** 117

Ambiorix, Gallic chief: (54–3) **14.** 133

ambitus (bribery): (358) law against, **3.** 409; (181) **12.** 63; (159) **14.** 13

Ambracia, in Epirus: (198) supplies from, **9.** 195; (191) Amynander at, **10.** 199; **11.** 29; (189) joins Aetolians, 13; besieged by cos. M. Fulvius Nobilior, 13–33, who vows games, 231; siege equipment moved from, 97; (187) controversy over siege of, 147–53, 227–9; Nobilior triumphs over, 231–3; (171) Q. Minucius Scaevola sent to, **12.** 505; (169) C. Popilius at, **13.** 63, 79; Q. Marcius Philippus at, 91

Ambracian gulf: (198) fleet sent to, **9.** 193–5. *Also*: **11.** 13, **13.** 77

Ambrones, Germans: (102) defeated, **14.** 81

Ambrysus, in Phocis: (198) surrenders **9.** 205

Ambustus: *see* Fabius.

Ameriola, in Latium: (616–578), **1.** 137

Amiternum, Sabine town: (211) Hannibal at, **7.** 41; (205) promises men to Scipio, **8.** 195. Prodigies: (218) **5.** 185; (213) **6.** 317; (192) **10.** 61; (191) 263; (147) **14.** 253; (143) 255; (134) 259; (106) 273

—, in Samnium: (293) **4.** 509

Amphilochia: (197) in Aetolia, **9.** 257; (189) Aetolians recover, **11.** 11, 19; Perseus fails to regain, 19–21, 25, 33

Amphipolis, in Macedonia: (181) Perseus sent to, **12.** 77; (179) Philip dies at, 171–3; (172) Abrupolis raids to, 415; (170) refuses Roman demands, **13.** 29; (168) agents of Perseus and Eumenes at, 169; occupied by L. Aemilius Paulus after Pydna, 233–43; fleet winters at, 267, 271; (167) Paulus presents terms at, 345–7; capital of one of Macedonian republics, 349, 351; Paulus celebrates at, 359–63

Amphissa, in Locris: (190) M' Acilius Glabrio attacks, **10.** 305, 311; L. Scipio grants truce to, 307, 311

Ampius, C., pref. soc.: (201) **9.** 7–9

Amtorgis, in Spain: (212) **6.** 463–7

Amulius, son of Proca: drives Numitor from Alba Longa, **1.** 17; slain, 21–3

Amusicus, chief of Ausetani: (218) attacked by Cn. Scipio, **5.** 183

Amyclae, in Peloponnesus: (195) **9.** 489

Amynander, Athamanian king: (208) seeks peace with Philip for Aetolia, **7.** 333; (207 or 205) permits Philip to cross Athamania, **10.** 249; (205) at conference of Philip and Rome, **8.** 253; (200) offers aid, **9.** 81–3; saves Aetolians in Thessaly, 119–25; (198) plunders Thessaly, 191–3; summoned by Flamininus, 193; (197) at conference of Flamininus and Philip, 251; sent to Rome, 265; joins Flamininus, 285; at conference on Macedonian terms, 307; (196) retains forts, 371; (191) joins Antiochus, **10.** 135–7, 173, 177, 181, 187, 239, 249; attacked by Philip, 249, **11.** 287, 291; flees to Ambracia, **10.** 199, **11.** 3, 29, 287; surrender of, demanded, **10.** 239, 243; (189) recovers Athamania, **11.** 3–7; seeks peace with Rome, 9; urges Ambracian surrender, 29

Anabura, in Phrygia: (189) **11.** 51

Anagnia, in Latium: (307) Hernici declare war at, **4.** 333; (306) granted *civitas sine suffragio*, 339; (211) Hannibal near, **7.** 35. Prodigies: (211) **7.** 89; (210) 217; (204) **8.** 259; (203) 373; (169) **13.** 45–7; (167) 297, **14.** 245; (162) 249; (134) 259

Anapus riv., in Sicily: (214) **6.** 291

Anchises, father of Aeneas, **1.** 11

ancilia, shields of the Salii: **1.** 71; sacred to Mars Gradivus, **3.** 175–7; 'sent down from heaven,' 185; (368) cared for by patricians, 345; (190) are moved, **10.** 389; (101) move themselves, **14.** 83, 279

INDEX

Ancona, in Picenum : (178) **12.** 187
Ancus Marcius, 4th king: son of Sabine mother, **1.** 125; (640–616) elected king, 113; establishes rites, 113–5, and laws of war, 115–9; wars on Latins, 119–21, 181; builds public works, port, 121–3; dies, 127; instructor of Elder Tarquin, 129; (616) sons of, displaced by Tarquin, 127, **2.** 267, (578) return and assassinate him, **1.** 141–3, 147
Ancyra, in Galatia : (189) **11.** 83–5
—, in Illyricum : (169) **13.** 73
Andania, in Messenia : (191) **10.** 247
Andriscus : (153) pretended son of Perseus, **14.** 17, 27–9, or Philip, 31; sent to Rome, 17; (149) seizes Macedon, 27–9, 31; defeated, 31, (148) 35, 37, 41–3, 45, 253
Androcles, an Acarnanian: (197) agent of Philip, **9.** 319
—, officer of Perseus: (168) **13.** 195
Andronicus, an Aetolian: (167) beheaded, **13.** 357
—, a Macedonian: (190) officer of Antiochus at Ephesus, **10.** 331
— : (169) agent of Perseus, killed, **13.** 121
— : *see* Livius.
Andros, is. of Cyclades: (200) Macedon holds, **9.** 49; Rome gives, to Attalus, 129–31, 135; (198) ships of Attalus and Rhodes at, 197; (191) ships of Antiochus captured near, **10.** 221
Androsthenes, Macedonian general: (198) at Corinth, **9.** 225; (197) Achaeans defeat, 313–9
Anemurium, Cilician cape: (197) **9.** 333
Angeiae, in Thessaly : (198) **9.** 191
Anicius, Cn. : (168) leg. of L. Aemilius Paulus, besieges Aeginium, **13.** 241
—, M. : (216) holds Casilinum, **6.** 63–9
— Gallus, L., cos. 160 : (168) pr. pereg., **13.** 145, 147, with command in Illyricum, 157–9, 187–95, 255; (167) 297; legg. sent to advise, 299; in Epirus, 333–7; winters at Passaron, 339; queried about plunder, 363; returns to Rome, 365; triumphs, 369, 401–3, 385
Aniensis tribe : (299) formed, **4.** 393; (215) praerogative tribe, **6.** 197, 203
Anio aqueduct : 140) dedicated, **14.** 51
Anio riv., in Latium: (672–40) on route to Veii, **1.** 97; (616–578) Sabines defeated at, 131–3; (495) 301; (468) 429; (437) Veientes defeated at, **2.** 315; (435) 327; (390) Gauls camp on, **3.** 133; (361) T. Manlius Torquatus defeats Gaul at, 383–9, 349, **6.** 199; (211) Hannibal at, **7.** 37–9, 51, 159, **8.** 477. Prodigies : (102) **14.** 277–9. *Also*: **1.** 271, 323
Annalis : *see* Villius.
Annia, Paculla, a Campanian : (186) initiates men into Bacchic rites, **11.** 253
Annius, M. : (218) IIIvir agr. adsig., forced to flee by Boi, **5.** 69–71
— Luscus, T. : (172) envoy to Perseus, **12.** 359–63; (169) IIIvir col. deduc., **13.** 61
— —, T., cos. 153 : (133) opposes Ti. Gracchus, **14.** 63
— Milo, T., pr. 55 : (57) tr. pl., aids recall of Cicero, **14.** 129; (52) kills Clodius, exiled, 133; (48) slain, 139
— Setinus, L., pr. of Latium : (340) asserts Latin rights, **4.** 11–21
Antemnae, in Latium : (753–717) women of, seized, **1.** 35–7; attacks Rome; defeated; given citizenship, 39–43
Antenor, a Trojan : comes to Adriatic, **1.** 9
—, admiral of Perseus : (168) in Cyclades, **13.** 179–85; at Cassandria, 273; (167) near Lesbos, 357
antepilani: term defined, **4.** 31. *Also*: 39, 41
Anthedon, in Boeotia : (196) **9.** 355
Antias : *see* Valerius.
Anticyra, port of Locris : (211) taken, **7.** 99–101; (207) Philip crosses to, **8.** 33
—, port of Phocis : (198) Flamininus at, **9.** 205; (197) 269; 273; (196) 363
Antigonea, in Epirus : (199) Philip occupies, **9.** 165; (169) Macedonians plunder, **13.** 81–3. *See*: Creon, Menon, Patrocles.
—, in Macedon : (169) **13.** 123
Antigonus, general of Alexander, **12.** 67
—, son of Echecrates : (179) reveals to Philip Perseus' plot against

INDEX

Demetrius, **12**. 165–71; Perseus kills, 177

Antigonus, Macedonian noble: (179) agent of Philip, **12**. 173–5, (168) of Perseus, **13**. 175–7

—, son of Demetrius of Syria: (149) killed, **14**. 33

— Doson (Tutor), king of Macedon, 227–221: guardian of Philip; uncle of Antigonus son of Echecrates, **12**. 165, 169; aids Achaeans, **9**. 217, 223, 259, 487

Antimachus, officer of Perseus: (171) killed, **12**. 501

—, agent of Perseus: (169) negotiates with Eumenes, **13**. 131, 169

Antinoüs, of Passaron: (167) **13**. 335–7

Antiochia, on the Meander: (189) **11**. 41–3

—, on the Orontes: (197) Antiochus III at, **9**. 331; (196) 389; (193) **10**. 39; (195) Hannibal at, **9**. 407; (175) Antiochus IV builds temple at, **12**. 249. Prodigy: (48) **14**. 307

Antiochus III, the Great, king of Syria, 223–187: (203) makes treaty with Philip, **9**. 43; (198) invades Pergamum, withdraws, 175–7, 237, 333; (197) plans European invasion, 313, 329–31; checked in Cilicia by Rhodes, 331–5; vainly seeks aid of Eumenes, **10**. 449; (196) threatens liberty of Greeks, **9**. 351, 363, 383; ordered by Flamininus to withdraw, 367–9; Philip warned against, 371; moves to Thrace, 379–81; meets Roman Xviri at Lysimachia, 371, 383–7; returns to Seleucia, 387–9; (195) Flamininus procos. against, 393; Hannibal in service of, **8**. 509, **9**. 397–9, 403, 407, (193) 569–71, **10**. 41, 55–7, (190) 293, **11**. 381; (195) envoys of, referred to Senate, **9**. 479; war with, foreseen, 395, 507, 517; (194) 529; (193) 577; envoys of, in Rome, 561–9; envoys sent to, 569; agent sent to Carthage by, 573; Aetolians urge, against Rome, **10**. 33–7, 91; daughter of, marries Ptolemy, 39; Eumenes urges Rome against; Pisidae attacked by, 39–41; son of, dies, 45; Roman envoys meet, 45–51; decides on war, 51–57; (192) origins of war with, 63–119; war with, anticipated, 57–69, 89; Magnetes devoted to, 89–91; invited by Aetolians to free Greece, 93–9, 165, 177, 225, 233, **11**. 25, 27, 35, **13**. 317; reported entering Europe, **10**. 105; war with, made consular province, 121; crosses to Europe, 123–9; Aetolians make, general to free Greece, 129–33, 143; fails to win Chalcis, 133–5; wins support of Amynander, 135–7, 249, but not of Philip, **11**. 305; Achaeans declare war on, **10**. 137–45, **12**. 401; takes Chalcis and Euboea, **10**. 145–9, **13**. 317; (191) Rome declares war on, **10**. 155–9, 163–5, 263, **11**. 155, in order to free Greece, **10**. 211, 455–7; M' Acilius Glabrio commands against, 155–7, **11**. 149, **12**. 391; Philip, Eumenes, and Ptolemy promise aid against, **10**. 165–7, **11**. 305, **13**. 167; aids Elis, **10**. 169, **12**. 401–3; Epirotes equivocate, **10**. 169–71, 259; wins Boeotia, 145, 171–3, 219; Hannibal urges, to gain aid of Philip, 173–81; moves to Pherae; buries Macedonians slain at Cynocephalae, 181; attacks Thessalians, 181–9, **12**. 405; withdraws to Demetrias; winters at Chalcis, **10**. 189; marries a Chalcidian, 189, 201, 209–11; confers with Aetolians, 191; secures towns in Acarnania, 191–5, **12**. 403; garrisons of, in Athamania and Thessaly surrender, **10**. 199–201; defeated by Glabrio at Thermopylae, 201–19, 255, 275, 435, 471, **11**. 171, 285, **12**. 105, 391; withdraws to Ephesus, **10**. 221, 245, 249, 277, 299; promises aid to Aetolians, 235–7, 243; abandons Demetrias, 251–3; Glabrio ends campaign against, 259–61; moves to Chersonesus, 273–5; fleet of, defeated, 275–85, 313; (190) war with, assigned to L. Scipio, 285, 293, 305–7, **11**. 203; strengthens fleet, winters in Phrygia, **10**. 303, 313–5; hires Gallic auxiliaries, 313, 343, **11**. 39, 59, 61, 167–9; secures Phocaea, **10**. 315, 353; fleet of, defeats Rhodians, 315–25; naval operations, 325–41; raids Aegean, 331; retains Lycia, 335–9, **12**. 203; defeated before Pergamum, **10**. 343,

347–51, 443, 449; vainly seeks terms, 343–7; at Sardis, 351–3, 363; fails to win Prusias, 363–5; fails to take Colophon, 367–9, 373, 381; fleet of, defeated by Eudamus of Rhodes, 353–63, by L. Aemilius Regillus, 373–81, 473, **12**. 161; gains aid of Ariarathes, **10**. 381, 407, **11**. 121; fails to aid Phocaea, **10**. 385; vainly seeks peace, 389–95, 423; treats kindly son of Africanus, 389–91, 397–9, **11**. 177; defeated at Magnesia by L. Scipio, **10**. 399–419, **11**. 9, 39, 121, 149, 205, 291, 379, **12**. 25; flees to Apamea, **10**. 419; surrenders, 421–5; Glabrio triumphs over, 427, **11**. 159; (189) rumour in Rome of victory of, **10**. 433; still supported by Aetolians in Rome, 435; war with, assigned to Cn. Manlius Volso, 437; envoys of, before Senate, 441–3, 461; services against, reviewed by Eumenes, 443–53, and by Rhodians, 453–61; treaty with, ratified, 461–7, **11**. 167, 205–7; sends son to Rome as hostage, **12**. 287; driven from Asia west of Taurus, **10**. 443, 451, **11**. 25–7, 39, 147, 185, **12**. 419, 445; Glabrio accused of withholding booty of, **10**. 471; L. Scipio triumphs over, 475–7, **11**. 159, **13**. 383; sea peaceful after defeat of, **10**. 477; garrisons of, ordered from Aenos and Maronea, 479; Aetolians terrified at defeat of, **11**. 11; furnishes grain, 43, 123; (188) envoys of, come to Volso, 121–3; final terms of treaty with, 123–35; Rhodes rewarded for aid against, **9**. 329[1], **13**. 319, 327; Volso accused of breaking truce with, **11**. 153; expulsion of, increases Galatian danger, 163–7; (187) accounting for money taken from, required, 187–93; L. Scipio arbitrates between, and Eumenes, 283; generals of, in triumph of M. Fulvius Nobilior, 233; Seleucus succeeds, **12**. 287; (186) L. Scipio celebrates games vowed in war with, **11**. 283; (185) Philip and Eumenes claim cites taken from, 301–7; (185) votive gifts at tables of gods, **13**. 299; (167) Rhodes reviews aid against, 135, 315–27; Prusias asks lands taken from, 407. *Also*: **4**. 241, **10**. 453, **11**. 55, 145, 155, **12**. 85, 333, 385, 425, 427, **13**. 93, 167

Antiochus, son of Antiochus III: (193) dies in Syria, **10**. 39, 45

— IV Epiphanes, king of Syria, 175–163: (189) hostage in Rome, **12**. 287, 309, **13**. 151; (175) becomes king, **12**. 287; character of, 247–51, 287–9; (173) renews treaty, 309–11; (172) promises aid against Perseus, 367, 375; (171) plots against Egypt, 375; (168) ordered to end war with Egypt, **13**. 151–3; Perseus seeks aid of, 167; moves on Egypt, 273, 277–81; withdraws at demand of C. Popilius Laenas, 281–3, 323, 367; envoys of, submit at Rome, 285–7; (164) charged with conspiracy, **14**. 11; (163) dies, 11–3

— V Eupator: (162) killed, **14**. 13

— VI Epiphanes Dionysus: (138) killed, **14**. 55, 57

— VII Euergetes Sidetes, king of Syria, 138–129: (134) sends gifts to Aemilianus, **14**. 61; (130) at war with Parthia, 67; (129) killed, 263

Antipater: (278) vainly opposes Galatians, **11**. 53

—, nephew of Antiochus III: (190) at Magnesia, **10**. 409; envoy to L. Scipio, 421, (189) and to Rome, 461, 465–7

—, officer of Perseus: (171) **12**. 503

— : *see* Coelius.

Antipatrea, in Illyricum: (200) **9**. 81

Antiphilus, praetor of Boeotia: (197) delivers Thebes to Flamininus, **9**. 279–81

—, of Edessa: (171) infantry commander of Perseus, **12**. 449

Antipolis, Massilian town: (154) **14**. 15

Antissa, on Lesbos: (167) **13**. 357

Antistius, A.: (420) tr. pl., **2**. 399–401

—, L.: (379) tr. mil. c. p., **3**. 299

—, L.: (215) envoy, **6**. 135

—, M.: (319) tr. pl., **7**. 129

—, M.: (217) envoy to recall cos. C. Flaminius, **5**. 191

—, Sex.: (208) reports Hasdrubal crossing Alps, **7**. 355

—, Ti., tr. pl., 422: (423) commands dismounted cavalry, **2**. 391

INDEX

Antium, in Latium ; capital of Volsci, **3**. 223; (493) defeated, **1**. 327–9; (469) Volsci driven to, 427; (468) captured, 433; (467) colony proposed for, **2**. 3–5; (464) supports Aequi, 13; levy from, late, 15, 21; (461) leads Volsci and Aequi, 37–9; (459) Volsci defeated at, 75–9; revolt of, 81; (408) Aequi and Volsci defeated at, 439, 443; (406) army led to, 449; (390) Gauls flee to, **3**. 151; (386) revolts; Camillus defeats, 213–25, 291; (378) land near, raided, 303; (377) Latins flee to, 307; surrenders, 307–9; (349) plundered by Greeks, 441; (348) rebuilds Satricum, 449; (346) stirs Latin war, 449–51; (341) defeated, **4**. 3–5; (339) 49–51; (338) 53–5; receives colony and citizenship, 59, 237; ships of, decorate Rostra, 61; (317) receives code, 243; (207) maritime colony, exempt from levy, **7**. 363, (191) but subject to naval service, **10**. 163; (170) loot from Chalcis at, **13**. 15–7, 29; (87) Marius storms, **14**. 101. Prodigies: (217) **5**. 201; (206) **8**. 47; (203) 373; (163) **14**. 249

Antius, Sp.: (437) envoy to Fidenae, **2**. 313

Antonius, A.: (168) envoy to negotiate Perseus' surrender, **13**. 259

—, C., pr. 44: (49) leg. of Caesar, **14**. 137; (43) defeated by M. Brutus, 149, 153

—, L.: (41) cos., defeats Lepidus, defeated by Octavius, **14**. 157

—, M': (72) kills Sertorius, **14**. 119

—, M.: (334) mag. eq., **4**. 67–9

—, M.: (167) tr. pl., vetoes Rhodian war, **13**. 313–5; calls *contio*, 393

—, M., cos. 99: (102) pr., defeats pirates, **14**. 81; (99) cos., **14**. 281; (98) defends M' Aquilius, 87; (87) killed by Marius, 101

—, M., cos. 44, 34: (49) tr. pl., supports Caesar, driven from Rome, **14**. 137; (47) mag. eq., checks riots, 143; (44) cos., 309; crowns Caesar, 145; gives sons as hostages to conspirators, 147; begins war on Octavius, 147–9, 311–3; (43) defeated at Mutina, makes terms with Lepidus and Octavius, 149–51, 313–5; orders death of D. Brutus, joins IIIvirate, 151–3, 315; displays hands of Cicero, 217, 219; (42) defeats Brutus and Cassius, 155, 317; (41) wife and brother of, defeated by Octavius, 155–7; (40) reconciled with Octavius, marries Octavia, 157, 221–3; (39–38) leg. of, defeats Parthians, 157, 159, and Jews, 159; (36) revels with Cleopatra; repulsed by Parthians; (34) gives Armenia to son, 161; (32) divorces Octavia; (31) defeated at Actium, 163; (20) standards of, restored, 167

Antonius, Q.: (190) envoy to Phocaea, **10**. 385

— Balbus, Q.: (82) pr. in Sardinia, **14**. 109

— Creticus, M., pr. 74: (71) dies in Crete, **14**. 121

— Hibrida, C.: (63) cos., **14**. 201, 301; (62) defeats Catiline, 127, 303; (61) defeated by Dardani, 127–9, 303

— Merenda, Q.: (422) tr. mil. c. p., **2**. 391

— —, T.: (450) Xvir, **2**. 117; (449) 139

Antronae, in Thessaly: (174) Perseus at, **12**. 417; (171) surrenders, 505

Anxur, in Latium: (406) taken by Rome, **2**. 449–51, (402) by Volsci, **3**. 29, (401–400) by Rome, 35, 45, 47; (397) attacked by Volsci, 57; (342) troops at, mutiny, 501; (329) Roman colony, **4**. 85; (207) forced to submit to levy, **7**. 363. *See* Tarracina.

Aous riv., in Illyricum: (199) Philip defeated on, by P. Villius Tappulus, **9**. 165–9, (198) by Flamininus, 181–91, 215, 285, **10**. 209, **11**. 171

Apama, wife of Amynander, **10**. 137

—, wife of Seleucus I, **11**. 41

Apamea, in Phrygia: named for Apama, wife of Seleucus, **11**. 41; (193) Antiochus at, **10**. 45; (190) 343; 419; (189) Seleucus at, **11**. 51; (188) treaty with Antiochus signed at, 123; displaced persons called to, 127

Apelaurum, in Stymphalia: (197) **9**. 315

Apelles, agent of Philip: (181) sent to Rome, **12**. 65, 75; (179) suspected of Demetrius' murder, 165, 167, 305; (173) slain by Perseus, 305

INDEX

Apennines: (391) Gauls between Alps and, **3**. 115; twelve Etruscan cities each side of, 117; Boi and Lingones stay beyond, 121; (295) Samnites and Etruscans cross, **4**. 461; (218) Hannibal controls from Alps to, **5**. 157; (217) Hannibal fails to cross, 173–5, 199; C. Flaminius crosses, into Etruria, 193; (187) Ligurians driven across, **11**. 221–3; (17) earthquakes in, **14**. 317. *Also*: **5**. 161, **10**. 203, **12**. 243.
Aperantia, in Aetolia: (191) taken by Philip, **10**. 253–5, (189) by Aetolians, **11**. 11, (169) by Perseus, **13**. 81
Aphrodisias, in Cilicia: (197) taken by Antiochus, **9**. 333; (190) **10**. 353
Aphthir: (193) Numidian fugitive, **9**. 577
Apiolae, in Latium: (616–578) **1**. 129
Apion: *see* Ptolemy Apion of Cyrenê.
apocletes, inner council of Aetolian League: (192) **10**. 101; 133; (191) 241
Apodoti: (197) part of Aetolia, **9**. 257
Apollo: contest of Marsyas and, **11**. 41; (399) honoured at *lectisternium*, **3**. 49; (217) **5**. 235; (300) Xviri sac. oversee rites of, **4**. 385; (198) Argives invoke, **9**. 229; (180) offerings to, **12**. 115; (99) **14**. 281. Portents from: (205) **8**. 245; (199) **9**. 157; (182) **12**. 5, **14**. 241; (176) **12**. 233; (169) **13**. 47; (130) **14**. 263; (93) 287–9; (91) **14**. 291; (43) 313–5. Temples of, in Rome: (433) vowed, **2**. 213–5, 335; (431) dedicated, 353; (353) **3**. 427; (216) wreath deposited in, **6**. 33–5; (207) procession for Juno starts from, **7**. 361; (179) theatre near, **12**. 157; (194) Senate meets in, to receive envoys, **9**. 529, (189) to hear reports of generals, **10**. 473, (187) **11**. 225, (176) **12**. 235–7; (98) Xviri sacrifice in, **14**. 283; (93) prodigy in, 287–9. Temples and shrines of, outside Rome: at Caieta, **12**. 5, **14**. 241; at Cumae, **13**. 47, **14**. 291; at Delium, **10**. 147; at Delphi, *see* Apollo Pythius; at Gabii, **12**. 233; at Hiero Como, **11**. 41; at Sicyon, **9**. 273; at Velitrae, 157
—, Games of: (212) origin of, **6**. 385–7, **7**. 89; (209) conducted by pr. urb., 251; (208) 307; (184) **11**. 347; (208) date of, **7**. 307; (190) **10**. 301; (202) in Circus, **8**. 513; (190) eclipse during, **10**. 301
Apollo, Promontory of, in Africa: (203) **8**. 451
— Medicus: (179) temple of, **12**. 159
— Pythius: (534–10) gifts to, **1**. 195–7; (396) **3**. 73, 79–83, 87–9, (394) 97; (216) mission to, **5**. 385, **6**. 33–5; (205) omens from, **8**. 245; (191) sacrifice to, by Antiochus, **10**. 191, (172) by Eumenes, **12**. 335, (167) by L. Aemilius Paulus, **13**. 341, 395
— Zerynthius: (188) temple of, **11**. 139
Apollodorus, of Athens: (192) leads sedition favoring Antiochus, **10**. 145
Apollonia, in Aetolia: (207) **8**. 35
—, in Illyricum: (c. 270) envoys from, beaten, **4**. 553; (214) attacked by Philip, **6**. 303–7; (211) **7**. 95; (205) **8**. 251–3; (200) port for Illyricum or Macedon, **9**. 57, 65, 79, 117–9, (192) **10**. 69, (190) 305, (189) **11**. 11, (188) 143, (172) **12**. 343, 399, (171) 443, (169) **13**. 75, (168) 189, (167) 345; (197) auxiliaries from, **9**. 285; (171) **12**. 463; (168) **13**. 189; threatened by Gentius, 189–91; (167) given ships of Gentius, 403
—, in Thrace: (188) Cn. Manlius Volso at, **11**. 141; (179) Bastarnae return to, **12**. 177
Apollonides, of Syracuse: (214) urges alliance with Rome, **6**. 265
Apollonius: (190) naval commander under Hannibal, **10**. 357
—: (173) envoy of Antiochus IV, **12**. 309–11
appeal: (672–640) form of, **1**. 93; (509) secured by law, 243; (501) not valid against dictator, 277; (494) 313; (460) **2**. 73; (495) recognized by Ap. Claudius, **1**. 307; (460) not valid outside city, **2**. 71; (451) recognized by first Xvirate, 113, (450) but not by second, 119, (449) 139, 149, 161; restored, 175, 181–5; claimed by Ap. Claudius, 187–91; (440) hampers coss., 303; (310) cens. Ap. Claudius protected by, **4**. 299; (299) stricter sanctions for, 389–91; (210) denied by plebiscite, **7**. 129
Appian aqueduct: (312) built, **4**. 275

INDEX

Appian way: (342) mutinous troops on later, **3**. 503; (312) built, **4**. 275; (217) statue of Mars on, **5**. 203; pass on, secured by M. Minucius Rufus, 253–5; (216) scouting along, 379–81; (211) towns along, prepare supplies, **7**. 31; (52) Clodius slain on, **14**. 133

Appius: *see* Claudius.

April: (204) Megalesia on 12th, **8**. 261–3; (212) Latin Festival on 26th, **6**. 383, (168) on 12th, **13**. 151

Apronius, C.: (449) tr. pl., **2**. 181

Apsus riv., in Illyricum: (200) **9**. 79

Apuani, Ligurian tribe: (187) campaign against, **11**. 221–3; (186) 277–9; (185) 317–9; (182) threaten Pisa, **12**. 3; (180) defeated and transported, 113, 117–9, 127–9

Apuleius, L.: (391) tr. pl., convicts M. Furius Camillus, **3**. 113

—, Q.: (173) Xvir agr. adsig., **12**. 303

— Pansa, Q.: (300) cos., **4**. 377; attacks Nequinum, 391

— Saturninus, C.: (168) Vvir for dispute of Pisae and Luna, **13**. 287

— —, L., pr. 166: (173) Xvir agr. adsig., **12**. 303; (166) pr., **13**. 405; (145) envoy to Asia, **14**. 45

— —, L.: (100) tr. pl., **14**. 83–5

Apulia: (367) Gauls flee to, **3**. 349, 357; (349) 447; (326) Alexander of Epirus in, **4**. 95; Roman alliance with, 99, 105; (323) operations in, 143–5; (322) 155; (321) 165–7; (320) 207–9; (319) 217; (318–317) 243; (315) 249; (314) 267; (296) 413; (294) 489–99, 503–5; (217) **5**. 229, 261, 281–3, 309, 331; (216) 343, 379, 409; **6**. 3, 35, 77, 85–7; (215) 113, 115, 157–9, 163, 185; (214) 209, 237–41; (213) 317, 327; (212) 347, 421–3, **7**. 5, 7; (211) **6**. 501; **7**. 43; (210) 85, 111, 209–11; (209) 299; (208) 315; (207) 379–81, 393, 407, **8**. 41; (201) land in, distributed, **9**. 13; (190) a praetorian province, **10**. 295–7; (189) 439; (185) **11**. 309–11; (183) 363; (181) **12**. 59, 63; (185) slave war in, **11**. 309–11; (172) grain purchased in, **12**. 369. Compared with foes of Alexander, **4**. 231, 237. Prodigies: (214) **6**. 207; (173) **12**. 319; (130) **14**. 263; (114) 269; (93) 287. *See* Busa.

Apustius, L.: (215) leg. in Tarentum, **6**. 133

— Fullo, L., pr. 196: (201) aed. pl., **9**. 15; (200) leg. in Macedonia, 79–81; commands fleet, 127–39, 197; (196) pr. urb., 341–3, 347; (194–193) IIIvir col. deduc., 553; **10**. 25; (190) leg. to collect ships, 301; killed, 337

Aquae Calidae, in Africa: (203) **8**. 451–3

— Cumanae: (176) **12**. 233

— Sextiae, in Transalpine Gaul: (123) established, **14**. 73; (102) Teutones defeated at, 81

Aquileia, in Venetia: (186) Gauls settle near site of, **11**. 283, 365; (183–181) Latin colony at, 395, **12**. 81, 103; (178–177) base for Histrian invasion, 185–7, 197–9, 215–9, (171) for march on Illyricum, **13**. 5; (171–169) more settlers needed by 3–7, 61

Aquilii: (509) favor Tarquins, **1**. 229, 241

Aquilinus: *see* Herminius.

Aquilius, M', cos. 101: (100) ends slave war, **14**. 85; (98) acquitted of extortion, 87; (88) leg., routed by Mithridates, 97, 99

—, P.: (210) buys grain, **7**. 213

— Corvus, L.: (388) tr. mil. c. p., **3**. 209

— Gallus, L.: (176) pr. for Sicily, **12**. 227, 231

— Tuscus, C.: (487) cos., defeats Hernici, **1**. 351

Aquilonia: (293) Samnites defeated at, **4**. 505–29

Aquinum, in Latium: (211) **7**. 33

Ara Maxima: dedicated, **1**. 29; (312) ritual at, revealed, **4**. 275–7

Arabia: Alexander crosses, **13**. 273; (190) archers from, in Antiochus' army, **10**. 409; (168) Antiochus IV crosses, **13**. 281

Aradii: (192) in navy of Antiochus, **10**. 139

Arar riv., in Transalpine Gaul: (c. 12) **14**. 165

Aratthus riv., in Epirus: (169) **13**. 77

Aratus, of Sicyon, Achaean general: (213) death of, charged to Philip, **9**. 217

—, son of above: (209) murdered by Philip, **7**. 339, **9**. 217

INDEX

Arausio, in Transalpine Gaul: (105) **14**. 79

Arbocala, in Spain: (221) **5**. 13–5

Arcadia: (c. 370) Megalopolis formed by, **9**. 165; (184) Achaean council meets in, **11**. 329; (175) gifts of Antiochus IV to, **12**. 249. *See* Evander, Philopoemen.

arch: (216) leading to Campus, **5**. 321; (190) Africanus constructs, on Capitoline, **10**. 299

Archelaüs, of Acarnania: (197) pro-Roman, **9**. 319–21

—, of Egypt: (55) made king, exiled, **14**. 131

—, officer of Mithridates: (88) seizes Athens, **14**. 99, 103; (86) surrenders fleet, 103

archers, mounted: (192) in Antiochus' army, **10**. 137; (190) 407

Archidamus, of Aetolia: (199) saves Thaumaci, **9**. 161; (197) aids Flamininus at Cynocephalae, **10**. 141; (192) opposes Flamininus in Achaean council, 139–41

—, of Aetolia: (169) supports Perseus, **13**. 77–81; (168) 233

Archimedes: (214) at siege of Syracuse, **6**. 283–7; (212) 461

Archippus, of Argos: (195) expells Spartans, **9**. 523

Archo: (182) of Thessaly, slays children, **12**. 9–13

—: (174) pro-Macedonian Achaean, **12**. 265–71

Arcobarzanes, of Numidia: (153) enters Punic territory, **14**. 15–7

Ardaneae, in Apulia: *see* Herdonea.

Ardea, in Latium: mother city of Saguntum, **5**. 19; (534–510) army before, **1**. 197–201, roused by Brutus, 209; (446) land of, unjustly seized, **2**. 243–9, 293, (445) causing war, 257, (444) 279; treaty with, renewed, 281–3; (443) discord in, 287–95; (442) colony sent to, 295–7; (390) led by Camillus, defeats Gauls, **3**. 147–51; Camillus recalled from, 157, 163, 171; (339) Antiates raid, **4**. 49; (217) sacrifices at, **5**. 205; (209) fails to meet levy, **7**. 243–7; (204) forced to furnish extra quota, **8**. 263–7; (199) fails to get flesh from Latin Festival, **9**. 157; (186) Minius Cerrinius in custody at, **11**. 273. Prodigies: (198) **9**. 177; (133) **14**. 261

Ardiaei, Illyrians: (209) restoration of, demanded, **7**. 335

Ardyes, son of Antiochus: (197) **9**. 331

Arei, Africans: (197) in Rhodian army, **9**. 325

Aretho riv., in Epirus: (189) **11**. 13

Arethusa, Fountain of, in Syracuse: (212) Romans admitted near, **6**. 457

Areus, of Sparta: (184) repatriated, condemned, pardoned, **11**. 329, 333–5, 341

Arevaci, Spanish tribe: (76) **14**. 193, 195

Argei: (517–672) shrines, **1**. 75

Argenta, in Thessaly: (198) **9**. 193

Argentanum, in Bruttium: (203) **8**. 439

argentarii: (308) booths of, **4**. 323

Argestaean plain, in Macedon: (208) **7**. 343

Argiletum, in Rome: (715–672) **1**. 67

Argithea, in Athamania: (189) **11**. 3–9

Argos: mother city of Rhodes and Soli, **10**. 465, of Macedonian kings, **7**. 335, **9**. 223; (272) Pyrrhus dies in, **8**. 277, **9**. 23; (208) Philip at games in, **7**. 333, 337; (207) Spartans camp near, **8**. 17; (200) Philip controls, **9**. 23; Achaean council in, 73; (198) withdraws from council, 223; delivered to Philip, 229–33; (197) Achaeans demand freedom of, 255, 259–63; delivered to Nabis, 267–73; (195) 397; Achaeans demand freedom of, 471–7; Flamininus refrains from attacking, 479–83; freed from Nabis, 493–505, 511, 523–7; (193) new threat of Nabis, **10**. 55; (192) force against Nabis in, 75; (189) Achaean League meets in, **11**. 101; (172) **12**. 425; (167) L. Aemilius Paulus in, **13**. 343. *See*: Damocles, Philodemus.

—, Amphilochian: (189) **11**. 33

argyraspides: (190) in Antiochus' army, **10**. 407

Ariarathes V, of Cappadocia: (190) sends troops to Antiochus, **10**. 381, 407, **11**. 121; (189) supports Galatians, 91; (188) receives terms, 121–3; marries daughter to Eumenes, 131, **12**. 375; (181) sends envoys to Senate, 63–5; (172) son

INDEX

educated in Rome, 345–7; (171) opposes Perseus, 375; (163) dies, **14**. 11
Ariarathes VI, of Cappadocia: (163) king, **14**. 11; (158) expelled; restored, 13
Aricia, in Latium: (508) repells Arruns Porsinna, **1**. 265–7; (495) Aurunci defeated near, 301–3; (446) territory of, seized, **2**. 243–9; (338) defeated, **4**. 53; receives citizenship, 59; (87) stormed by Marius, **14**. 101. Prodigies: (216) **5**. 321; (213) **6**. 317; (202) **8**. 511; (193) **10**. 25; (152) **14**. 253; (102) 279. *See*: Turnus Herdonius.
Ariminum, in Umbria: (268) receives colony, **4**. 553; (218) Ti. Sempronius Longus at, **5**. 151–3; (217) C. Flaminius enters consulship at, 43, 187, 191; (213) in Second Punic War, **6**. 315; (210) **7**. 233; (209) 233, 245–7; (205) **8**. 155, 199, 227–9; (203) 369; (200) base against Gallic revolt, **9**. 31–3, 61, 141; (199) 155; (192) **10**. 63; (187) road built to, **11**. 223; (178) army at, suffers plague, **12**. 199; (49) Caesar at, **14**. 205. Prodigies: (194) **9**. 535; (104) **14**. 275
Arines: (210) commands New Carthage, **7**. 187
Ariobarzanes I, of Cappadocia: (92) restored to throne, **14**. 87; (89) 93; driven out by Mithridates, 95
Ariovistus, German chief: (58) invades Gaul, **14**. 129
Aristaenus, Achaean praetor: (198) favors Rome, **9**. 207–21; (197) at meeting with Philip, 251; urges Roman alliance on Boeotia, 281; (195) assails Aetolians, 477; attacks Spartans in Argos, 479–83; at conference with Rhodians, 495; urges Nabis to yield, 505
Aristagoras, of Cyzicus: (73) **14**. 301
Aristo: (214) reveals plot, **6**. 253–5
—, of Tyre: (193) agent of Hannibal in Carthage, **9**. 571–7
aristocracies: (171) in Greece favor Rome, **12**. 377–9
Aristodemus, tyrant of Cumae: (495) Tarquin the Proud dies at court of, **1**. 287; (492) retains Roman ships, 331
Aristomachus, of Croton: (215) pro-Punic, **6**. 181, 185
Aristonicus, son of Eumenes II: (131–130) seizes Pergamum, driven out, **14**. 65, 263
Aristoteles, prefect of Antiochus: (191) **10**. 221
Armenes, son of Nabis: (194) **9**. 551
Armenia: (69) L. Licinius Lucullus victorious in, **14**. 123; (36) M. Antonius retreats through, (34) and gives throne of, to son, 161. *See* Artavasdes, Tigranes.
Armilustrum, in Rome: (207) **7**. 359
arms and armour: (578) of legionaries, **1**. 151
army, distribution of: (218) **5**. 47–9; (217) 193, 237; (216) 319–21, **6**. 43–5; (215) 85–7, 105, 109, 113, 119–21; (214) 207–11; (213) 315–7; (212) 347–9; (211) **7**. 3–5; (210) 109–11; (209) 231–9; (208) 301–5; (207) 353, 357, 363–5; (206) **8**. 45; (205) 191; (204) 255–7; (203) 367–71; (202) 461–5; (201) 521–3; (200) **9**. 25–7; (199) 155; (198) 173–5; (197) 241; (196) 347; (195) 393; (194) 531; (193) 559–61; (192) **10**. 57–9; (191) 157–61; (190) 295–7; (189) 437–9; (188) **11**. 117–9; (187) 147, 153; (186) 275–7; (184) 341–3; (183) 363–5; (182) **12**. 3–5; (181) 59–61; (180) 109–15; (179) 139; (177) 211; (176) 229–33; (174) 251–3; (173) 293; (172) 321; (171) 381–3; (169) **13**. 43; (168) 157–9; (167) 297
Arna, *see* Ahrna.
Arniensis tribe: (387) formed, **3**. 213; (204) C. Claudius Nero a member of, **8**. 355
Arnus riv., in Etruria: (217) **5**. 205–7, 229
Arpi, in Apulia: (320) welcomes Romans, **4**. 209–11; (217) operations near, **5**. 229, 239; (216) **6**. 319, 325, **9**. 433; (215–214) **6**. 157, 185, 213; (213) 319–27, 397, **7**. 161; (194) Roman colony near, **9**. 533–5. Prodigies: (217) **5**. 201; (125) **14**. 265
Arpinum, city of Volsci: (305) retaken from Samnites, **4**. 345; (303) given citizenship, 361, (188) **11**. 119–21. Prodigy: (203) **8**. 373

INDEX

Arrenius, C.: (210) tr. pl., delays elections, **7**. 223–5
—, L.: (210) tr. pl., delays elections, **7**. 223–5; (208) praef. soc., 319, 321
Arretium, in Etruria: (311) not allied with Samnites, **4**. 285; (310) 30 yr. truce, 309; (302) civil strife in, 367–9, 377; (294) 40 yr. truce, 501; (217) C. Flaminius at, **5**. 205–11; (209) revolt checked at, **7**. 299; (208) assigned as prov. to C. Hostilius Tubulus, 303, 305; revolt in, checked, 307–11; (205) promises Scipio equipment, **8**. 193; urban legions at, 199; (200) forces assemble at, **9**. 61; (193) 559, **10**. 9; (187) road built to, **11**. 223. Prodigies: (198) **9**. 177; (192) **10**. 61; (108) **14**. 273; (96) 285; (93) 287; (92) 289; (91) 291
Arrius, Q., pr. 73: (72) propr., defeated by Spartacus, **14**. 119
Arruns, of Clusium: (391) brings Gauls into Etruria, **3**. 115
—, *see* Tarquinius, Porsinna.
Arsaces, of Parthia: (92) seeks Roman friendship, **14**. 87
Arsanias riv.: (68) **14**. 199
Arsian forest: (509) **1**. 239
Arsinoê III Cleopatra: (210) **7**. 215
—, sister of Ptolemy XII: (46) **14**. 213
Artatus riv., in Illyricum: (169) **13**. 71
Artavasdes, of Armenia: (34) imprisoned, **14**. 161
Artemis: (191) temple of, in Heraclea, **10**. 227
Artemon: (171) officer of Perseus, **12**. 471
Artena: early Etruscan city, **2**. 457
—, Volscian town: (404) taken, **2**. 457
Arthetaurus, an Illyrian: (172) Perseus kills, **12**. 329, 409–13
Arverni, Gallic tribe: (616–578) enter Italy, **3**. 119; (207) aid Hasdrubal, **7**. 367; (121) defeated, **14**. 73. *See* Bituitus, Vercingetorix; Gergovia.
Arvina: *see* Cornelius, Cornelius Cossus.
Arx: *see* Citadel.
Ascanius: founds Alba Longa, **1**. 11, 15–7
Asclepiodotus: (171) general of Perseus, **12**. 449, (169) **13**. 97, 107, 113
Ascordus riv., in Macedon: (169) **13**. 113
Ascua, in Spain: (216) **6**. 91
Asculum, in Picenum: (91) Romans killed in, **14**. 89, 291; (89) captured, 95, 107
Ascuris, Lake, in Thessaly: (169) **13**. 95–9
Asellio: *see* Sempronius.
Asellius, M., tr. pl., 422: (423) cavalry leader; (422) tr. pl., **2**. 391
Asellus: *see* Claudius.
Asia: Macedonian conquests in, **4**. 225, **9**. 5, **12**. 451, 455, **13**. 271–3; unwarlike character of people of, **4**. 239, **13**. 323; danger from luxury of, **9**. 421, **11**. 61, 219, 235–7
Asia (*i.e.*, Asia Minor): (230) Attalus defeats Galatians in, **9**. 335; (205) stone of Great Mother brought from, **8**. 245–7, **10**. 261; (201) discontent in, **9**. 7; (197) Rhodes demands Philip free ports of, 255; (196) Philip and Antiochus warned from Greek cities of, 359–69, 379–87; (195) Hannibal in, 407; (193) Rome demands freedom for Greek cities of, 561–7; counterclaims of Antiochus in, 565, **10**. 47–9, 137–9; (191) Antiochus raises forces from, 181, 203, 209–13, 221; Aetolian envoys to, 235–7; Hannibal warns that Romans will cross to, 273–5; (190) assigned to L. Scipio, 293–5, 307, **11**. 203; naval operations off, **10**. 313–41, 351–87; Romans first cross to, 301, 387–9, 431; operations in, 389–421; Antiochus required to withdraw from, west of Taurus, 391–5, 423, 443, **11**. 27, 165–7; envoys from, in Rome, **10**. 421, 427; aid of Pegamum in, 445–51; (189) assigned to Cn. Manlius Volso, 437–41, 477; affairs of, settled by Senate, 461–7; Scipio granted triumph over, 473–7; Scipios tarry in, **11**. 9; Galatians a threat to, 51–7; campaign of Volso in, 37–95; (188) 117, 121–3, 135–43, 161–75; settlement of, 123–35; (187) Volso ordered to leave, 145–7; he triumphs over, 175, 235; (182) wars in, settled, **14**. 7; (172) power of Perseus in, **12**. 325, 329, 333–5, 361; envoys sent to, 347, 427–9; most of,

loyal, 365–7, (171) 373; (170) envoys from, **13**. 21–5; (168) called next object of Rome, 167; (167) envoys from, 311; support for Perseus in, investigated, 357; Roman envoys in, 367; (145) **14**. 45; (92) P. Rutilius protects, from *publicani*, 87; (88) seized by Mithridates, 99; (87–86) 103; (85) recovered by C. Flavius Fimbria, (84) and by Sulla, 105; (82) war in, renewed, 109; (43) C. Trebonius killed in, 151. *Also*: **8**. 29, **9**. 139, 197, 325, 329, 335, 373, 387, **10**. 95, 97, 131, 177, 209, 441, 457–9, 465, **11**. 3, 11, 33, 177–9, 187, 189, 207–9, 283, **12**. 7, 257, 263, 339, 385, 419, **13**. 133, 273, 279, 319, 333, 359, 361, **14**. 65, 161, 263. *See* Pergamum, Attalus.
Asiaticus: (189) title requested by L. Scipio, **10**. 473
Asina: *see* Cornelius Scipio.
Asinius Pollio, C., cos. 40: (43) joins M. Antonius, **14**. 151
Asnaus mts., in Illyricum: (199) **9**. 165
Asopus riv., in Malis: (191) **10**. 225
Aspendus, in Pamphilia: (190) aids Rhodes, **10**. 355; (189) granted peace, **11**. 49
Asper: *see* Trebonius.
assembly, no right of, in early Rome, **11**. 261. *See comitia, concilium.*
assessments, of luxuries: (184) **11**. 359
Astapa, in Spain: (206) **8**. 91–5
Astii, Thracians: (188) attack Romans, **11**. 137; (172) gain alliance, **12**. 347
Astraeum, in Paeonia: (181) **12**. 77
Astragon, in Caria: (197) **9**. 325
Astura riv., in Latium: (338) **4**. 53–5
Astymedes, of Rhodes: (167) envoy to Rome, **13**. 331
asylum: on Capitoline, **1**. 33, 219; in Greece, **10**. 147
Atalantê is., near Chalcis: (192) **10**. 113–5
Atanagrus, in Spain: (218) **5**. 183
Atella, in Campania: (216) deserts Rome, **5**. 409; (211) surrenders, **7**. 61; (210) punished, 129–33, 213. Prodigies: (207) 357–9; (106) **14**. 273. *See* Magius, Oppia.
Atellan farce: (364) **3**. 363
Atellus, *see* Mamilius.
Aternius Varus Fontinalis, A.: (454) cos., **2**. 105; (448) co-opted tr. pl., 219
Atesis, Alpine riv.: (102) **17**. 83
Atestê, in Venetia: (95) **14**. 285
Athacus, in Macedonia: (200) **9**. 103
Athamania, in Epirus: (207) Philip crosses, **10**. 249; (200) opposes Philip, **9**. 119–25; (198) plunders Thessaly, 191–3; (197) supports Flamininus, 285, **10**. 177; (191) joins Antiochus, 177, 187–9; towns recovered from, 197–9, and given to Philip, **11**. 287–91, 305; subject to Philip, **10**. 199–201, 249, 255, **11**. 3, 289; (189) recovered by Amynander, **10**. 435, **11**. 3–11, 33, (185); Philip ordered to give up, 289–91, 297–9, 305; (171) P. Licinius Crassus crosses, **12**. 461. *Also* **11**. 13. *See* Amynander.
Athena: (200) Philip violates shrines of, in Athens, **9**. 89; (192) prayer to, at Ilium by Antiochus, **10**. 127, (190) by propr. C. Livius Salinator, 317, by cos. L. Scipio, 397, (167) in Athens by procos. L. Aemilius Paulus, **13**. 343; (85) image of, survives sack of Troy, **14**. 187, 297; (192) temple of, at Sparta, **10**. 111
Athena Alcedemos: (171) Perseus sacrifices to, **12**. 447
Athena Itonia: (191) temple of, **10**. 219
Athenaeum, in Athamania: (189) **11**. 7; (185) 297
Athenaeus, brother of Eumenes: (189) joins cos. Cn. Manlius Volso, **11**. 39–41; (188) brings fleet to Hellespont, 135; (183) in Rome, 367; (171) with Eumenes, **12**. 463–5; (168) congratulates Rome, **13**. 287; (167) escorts L. Aemilius Paulus in Greece, 339
Athenagoras, pref. of Philip: (200) attacks L. Apustius, **9**. 81; at Athacus, 103–5; defeats Dardani, 119, 125; (199) on Mt. Asnaus, 165–7; (197) at Cynocephalae, 293–5
—, general of Perseus, (168) **13**. 195
Athens: (454–451) laws of, studied, **2**. 107–9; (449) treaty with Persia, **9**. 331; 413) defeated at Syracuse, **6**.

437, 453, **8**. 169, 183; (335) inveighs against Alexander, **4**. 233; (209) urges Aetolian peace on Philip, **7**. 333; (205) included in treaty with Philip, **8**. 255; (201) Philip infringes on, **9**. 7, 17, 21, **13**. 317; (200) seeks aid of Egypt, **9**. 27, of Rome, 17, 43; political, military, and naval operations, 43–9, 65–91, 127–9; (198) guarded by fleet, 197; at Achaean council, 207–9, 217; (196) witnesses acts of Flamininus in Boeotia, 357–9; gains islands, 361; (195) praises Rome's aid, 473–5; (192) receives Roman envoys, **10**. 89; represents Rome at Aetolian council, 95–7; checks sedition favoring Antiochus, 145; (191) grain distributed in, 221; (190) pleads for Aetolians, 307–9; (189) **11**. 11, 29, 33; treaty ratified in, 111; (182) victims of Philip seek, **12**. 11; Antiochus Epiphanes works on temple of Jupiter in, 249; (174) excludes Macedonians, 259; (170) envoys from, **13**. 21–3; (167) L. Aemilius Paulus visits, 341–3; (88) occupied for Mithridates, **14**. 99; (87) freed by Sulla, 103, 297; (49) has only two warships, 205; (46) M. Marcellus murdered in, 145. *Also*: **9**. 421–3, **10**. 111, 115, 331, **11**. 131, **13**. 323, 381

Athens, long walls of: (200) **9**. 79

athletes: (186) first shown in votive games, **11**. 281

Athos, Mt.: on Pallenê, **13**. 125; (168) harbours of, 181; (167) 351

Atilius, C.: (216) IIvir for temple of Concord, **6**. 73

—, L.: (311) tr. pl., proposes election of tribb. mil. by soldiers, **4**. 279

—, L.: (216) qu., slain at Cannae, **5**. 363

—, L.: (215) pref., escapes from Locri, **6**. 177

—, L., pr. 197: (210) tr. pl., **7**. 129; (197) pr. for Sardinia, **9**. 239

—, L.: (168) in Samothrace, **13**. 261

—, M.: (216) IIvir for temples of Concord, **6**. 73

— Calatinus, A.: (258) cos., escapes Punic fleet, **4**. 555; (249) first dict. outside Italy, 557

Atilius Luscus, L.: (444) in first college of tribb. mil. c. p., **2**. 279–81

— Priscus, L.: (399) tr. mil. c. p., **3**. 47; (396) ii, 63

— Regulus, M.: (335) cos., **4**. 65–7

— —, M.: (294) cos., against Samnites, **4**. 481–5, 489–99, 503–5, 509; (293) pr., 533

— —, M.: cos. 267, 256: (256) cos., defeats Punic fleet, invades Africa, **4**. 555; (255) defeated and captured; his mission to Rome and his death, **4**. 557, **8**. 169, 181–3, 317, 479–81, **14**. 179

— —, M., cos. 227, 217: (217) cos. suf., **5**. 289, 341; takes army of Fabius, 305–7, 333; names dict. comit. c., 313, 317; (216) procos., 313, 335; IIIvir mens., **6**. 73; (214) cens., 211, 229–33; accused by tr. pl.; abdicates on death of colleague, 313

— —, M.: (213) pr. urb. and pereg., **6**. 315; moves against foreign cults, 343–5, 385; (211) leg., at siege of Capua, **7**. 21–3, 127–9; (210) envoy to Ptolemy IV, 215

— Serranus, A., cos. 170: (194) aed. cur., **9**. 555; (192) pr. for Spain, for Macedon and fleet, **10**. 29, 59; naval operations, 63–5, 111, (191) 161, 191, 195, 221, 277; (173) pr. ii urb., **12**. 283, 293, 303, 309, 313–7; (172) envoy in Epirus, 369, 399–405; confers with Perseus, 405–21, 429; ends Boeotian league, 421–5; at Achaean assembly, 425; reports to Senate, sent to Larisa, 433–7; (170) cos. in Liguria and Gaul, **13**. 13⁷, 33; proclaims elections, 39

— —, C.: (218) pr., relieves pr. L. Manlius Volso, **5**. 73; gives army to cos. P. Scipio, 113; makes vow, 187; (217) gives army to cos. C. Flaminius, 193; candidate for cos.; pont., 317

— —, C.: (185) pr., **11**. 285

— —, C.: (106) cos., **14**. 273

— —, M., pr. 174: (190) IIIvir col. deduc., **10**. 429; (189) 469; (174) pr. for Sardinia, **12**. 251, (173) 293

— —, Sex.: (136) cos., **14**. 257

Atina, Volscian city: (313) captured, **4**. 273; (293) plundered, 509

Atinian Law: (149) **14**. 35

INDEX

Atinius, C., pr. 188 : (194) tr. mil., **9**. 539; (188) pr. for Farther Spain, **11**. 115–7, (187) 239, (186) killed, 279
—, C. : (186) Bacchanalian leader, **11**. 269
—, M. : (212) pref. soc. at Thurii, **6**. 399–401; (194) slain by Boi, **9**. 539
—, M. : (186) Bacchanalian leader, **11**. 269
— Labeo, C., pr. 195 : (197) tr. pl., secures colonies, **9**. 243; opposes triumphs of coss., 337–9; forces vote on Macedonian peace, 345–7; (195) pr. pereg., 391–3
— —, C. : (190) pr. for Sicily, **10**. 285, 295–7
— — Macerio, C. : (131) tr. pl., attacks cens., **14**. 67
Atintania, in Epirus : (208) return of, demanded, **7**. 335; (205) annexed to Macedon, **8**. 253; (167) **13**. 353
Atius, L. : (178) tr. mil., **12**. 193–5
Atratinus : *see* Papirius, Sempronius.
Atrax, in Thessaly : (198) resists Flamininus, **9**. 195, 201–5, 285; (191) resists Antiochus, **10**. 185; M. Baebius Tamphilus at, 195
Atrebates, Belgic tribe : (57–56) **14**. 129
Atreus, L., of Fregellae : (169) **13**. 47
atria (markets) : (184) built, **11**. 361
Atrinum, in Italy : (213) **6**. 327
Atrium Libertatis : (212) hostages held in, **6**. 367; (194) rebuilt, **9**. 533; (169) censors transact business in, **13**. 59; (168) 293–5
— Publicum, on Capitol : (214) **6**. 207
— Regium : (210) burned, **7**. 103–5; (209) rebuilt, 253
Atrius, C., of Umbria : (206) leads mutineers at Sucro, **8**. 101, 111, 115–7, 121
Attalis, Athenian tribe : (200) **9**. 47
Attalus I Soter, king of Pergamum, 241–197 : defeats Galatians, **9**. 335, **11**. 55, 59; (211) allied with Rome and Aetolia, **7**. 93, 141, **10**. 447; (209) praetor of Aetolians, **7**. 331; (208) brings fleet to Aegina, 333–5, 343, **8**. 17; (207) takes various cities, 17–23, 27; at Aetolian council, 19; surprised by Philip, 27, 33; called home by threat of Prusias, 29–31, 35; (205) helps Rome get stone of Great Mother, 247–9; included in treaty with Philip, 255; (201) reports discontent in Asia, **9**. 7; (200) naval operations against Philip, 43–55; aids Athens, 71–3; winters at Aegina, 83, 97; (199) naval operations, 127–39; (198) threatened by Antiochus, 175–7, 237; naval operations, 197–201, 223–7, 283; envoy of, at Achaean council, 207–11; sends crown to Rome, 237; (197) represented at council at Nicaea, 251–61; winters at Aegina, 269; confers with Nabis, rejoins fleet, 269–73; falls ill at Thebes, 279–83, **10**. 447; dies at Pergamum, **9**. 335; character and achievements, 335, **11**. 301, **13**. 167; succeeded by son Eumenes, **9**. 361, 369, **10**. 463, **11**. 133
Attalus II Philadelphus, son of Attalus I, king of Pergamum, 160–139 : (192) in Rome, **10**. 67; (190) defends Pergamum, 343, 347–9; at Magnesia, 417; (189) with Cn. Manlius Volso against Galatians, **11**. 39–43, 67–71, 81, 157; agent of Volso in negotiations, 85–7; (182) lives in harmony with King Eumenes, **12**. 23–5; (172) in Rome, lays charges against Perseus, 321; on false news of Eumenes' death acts the king, 339; (171) serves against Perseus, 463, 467, 473, 499, 505, (169) **13**. 103, 133, 155, (168) 181–3, 213, 273; congratulates Rome, 287; (167) ambitions checked, 303–11; negotiates with Galatians, 367; (149) helps Nicomedes, **14**. 31; (148) envoys sent to, 35
— III Philometor Euergetes, king of Pergamum, 139–133; (133) leaves kingdom to Rome, **14**. 63, 65, 263
—, of Syracuse : (212) prevents betrayal to Rome, **6**. 431
Attenes, prince of Turdetani : (206) deserts Hasdrubal, **8**. 67
Attica : south of Thermopylae, **10**. 203–5; (208–207) Philip off, **8**. 35; (200) Acarnanians plunder, **9**. 45; Philip plunders, 77–9, 89, 217; Roman fleet off, 131; (198) 201; (167) L. Aemilius Paulus in, **13**. 341; (194) Attic coins, **9**. 551; (190) **10**. 427; (189) 473; 475; (187) **11**. 233; 237; (188) Attic talents, 129

INDEX

Attius Tullius, Volscian chief: (491) joins Coriolanus, **1**. 335–45, 351
— Varus, P., pr. c. 53: (49) leg. of Pompey, defeated, **14**. 139
Attus Navius: (616–578) augur, **1**. 131–3
Atys Silvius: 6th king of Alba, **1**. 17
auctoritas patrum: (716) for election of king, **1**. 63; (672) 75; (640) 113; (578) 147; (534) 173; (415) necessary for laws and elections, **2**. 417; (368) **3**. 345–7; (367) granted to first plebeian cos., 349–51; (356) dict. triumphs without, 415; (339) to be given in advance for measures of *comitia cent.*, **4**. 53; (188) not needed for grant of citizenship by people, **11**. 119; an empty form in late republic, **1**. 63. *See* Senate.
Audax: (139) murders Viriathus, **14**. 53
Audena riv., in Liguria: (175) **12**. 243
Aufidena, in Samnium: (298) **4**. 403
Aufidius, Cn.: (170) tr. pl., **13**. 31–3
Aufidus riv., in Apulia: (216) **5**. 347
Aufugum, in Bruttium: (203) **8**. 439
Auginus mt., in Liguria: (187) **11**. 221
Augurinus: *see* Genucius, Minucius.
augurs: consulted by Romulus, **1**. 65; (715–672) created by Numa, 65–7, **2**. 269; (616-578) influence of, increases, **1**. 131–3; (460) inaugurate *templum* outside Rome, **2**. 71; (453) co-opted, 107; (180) **12**. 135; (167) **13**. 405; (437) gives signal for battle, **2**. 317; (426) permit tr. mil. c. p. to name dict., 359; (368) always patrician, **3**. 345; (300) opened to plebeians, number increased, **4**. 379–89; (204) mere youth elected, **8**. 359; (196) forced to pay taxes, **9**. 389; (81–80) number increased, **14**. 111. Deaths and/or appointments of: (463) **2**. 25–7; (453-2) 107; (300) **4**. 389; (216) **6**. 103; (213) 345; (211) **7**. 91; (210) 227; (208) 355; (204) **8**. 359; (203) 459–61; (196) **9**. 391; (195) 395; (183) **11**. 365; (180) **12**. 135; (174) 253; (170) **13**. 41; (167) 405
August (Sextilis): (463) coss. take office on 1st, **2**. 21; (462) on 11th, 27; (176) cos. suf. elected on 5th; Latin festival repeated on 11th, **12**. 233
Augustus Caesar: *see* Julius Caesar Octavius.
Aulerci, Gauls: (616–578) enter Italy, **3**. 119
Aulis, in Boeotia: Agamemnon at, **13**. 341; (192) in war against Antiochus, **10**. 113, 143, 147, 149; (167) L. Aemilius Paulus at, **13**. 341
Aulius, M': (208) pref. soc., slain, **7**. 319–21
— Cerretanus, Q.: (323) cos., **4**. 143; (319) ii, defeats Ferentani, 219–21; (315) mag. eq., defeats Samnites, slain, 247–51
Aurelius, C.: (216) leg. of M. Marcellus, **6**. 55
—, L.: (196) qu., taxes priests, **9**. 389
— Cotta, C., cos. 200: (202) pr. urb., **8**. 461–3; (200) cos. with Italy as prov., **9**. 13–9, 33–9, 145–7, **12**. 391; commands in Gaul, **9**. 65, 139, 155, 171; protests triumph of L. Furius Purpurio, 145
— —, C.: (75) cos., **14**. 301; removes restrictions from tribb. pl., 197
— —, L.: (181) tr. mil., **12**. 85–7
— —, L.: (144) cos., **14**. 45; (138) accused by Scipio Aemilianus, 57
— —, L.: (119) cos., **14**. 267, 269
— —, L.: (70) pr., restores juries to *equites*, **14**. 121
— —, M.: (216) aed. pl., **6**. 103; (212) leg. at Puteoli, 425; (204–200) Xvir sac., **8**. 359, **9**. 147; (203) envoy to Philip, **8**. 459, (201) 523–5, **9**. 11, 17
— —, M.: (189) leg. of L. Scipio, **10**. 441–3
— —, M.: (74) cos., defeated by Mithridates, **14**. 117
— Orestes, L.: (126) cos., **14**. 265; defeats Sardi, 69
— Scaurus, C.: (186) pr. for Sardinia, **11**. 235, 241
— —, M.: (108) cos. suf., **14**. 273; (105) leg., killed by Cimbri, 79
Aurinx, in Spain: (214) **6**. 311
Aurunca: *see* Suessa Aurunca.
Aurunci (Ausones): (503–502) defeated, **1**. 271–5; (495) 301–3, 311; (345) **3**. 451–3, 471; (340) yield, **4**. 61; (337) expelled by Sidicini, 61, 273; (336) defeated, 63–7; (314) 259–61
Aurunculeius, C.: (209) pr. for Sardinia, **7**. 225–7, 231–3; (208)

303; (207) tr. mil. at Grumentum, 375
Aurunculeius, L.: (190) pr. urb., **10.** 285, 295, 303, 429; (189) Xvir for settlement of Asia, 461–3, **11.** 123–35, 153, 161, 205, 301
— Cotta, L.: (54) leg. of Caesar, **14.** 133
Auruncus: *see* Cominius.
Ausetani, Spanish tribe: (218) defeated by Hannibal, **5.** 67, by Cn. Scipio, 183; (211) Hasdrubal among, **7.** 65; (205) revolt of, suppressed, **8.** 213–9; (195) surrender, **9.** 467; (183) Celtiberians in land of, defeated, **11.** 397
Ausona, city of Aurunci: (314) **4.** 259
Ausones: *see* Aurunci.
auspices: (716) at Numa's inauguration, **1.** 67; (534–10) forbid displacement of Terminus by Jupiter, 191; (445) not possessed by plebeians, **2.** 259–61, 275; (368) **3.** 345; (392) new, obtained by interregnum, 111; (388) 211; (390) neglected before Allia, 129; taken within pomerium, 179; (325) **4.** 115; (293) false report of, valid for one receiving it, 515–7; (247) scorned, 559; (223) C. Flaminius made cos. without, **5.** 189; (217) Flaminius, cos. ii, leaves city without, 189, 201; cannot be taken by private citizen, 201, (207) or by leg., **7.** 385; of two coss. serving together, one only has the, **8.** 39
Austicula, in Campania: (215) **6.** 135
Autlesbis, Thracian chief: (171) attacks Cotys, **12.** 503
Autricones, Spanish tribe: (76) Sertorius attacks, **14.** 193–5
Autronius Paetus, P.: (66) cos. desig., condemned for *ambitus*, **14.** 125[7]
Auximum, in Picenum: (174) walled by cens., **12.** 279–81. Prodigies: 255; (172) 349
Avaricum, in Aquitania: (52) **14.** 135
avaritiae nomine: (153) praetors condemned, **14.** 15
Avectius, tribune of Nervii: (11–10) under Drusus, **14.** 167
Aventine Hill, in Rome: named, **1.** 17; (753) Remus seeks augury on, 25; (715–672) altar on, 73; (640–616) settled by Latins, 119–21; (494) plebeians meet on, 307, (494–493) secede to, 323; (456) opened to settlement, **2.** 103, 109; (449) plebeians secede to, 167–71, 205, 229, **3.** 507, **4.** 291, **9.** 439; tribb. pl. elected on, **2.** 179–81; (396) temple to Juno Regina on, **3.** 79–81, 177, (218) **5.** 187, (217) 203, (207) **7.** 359; (214) temple of Libertas on, **6.** 227; (211) Numidian deserters quartered on, **7.** 37; (186) homes of Aebutia and Hispala Faecenia on, **11.** 249; (184) new sewers on, 361; (182) temple of Luna on, **12.** 5; (121) C. Gracchus slain on, **14.** 73, 267. Prodigies: (216) **5.** 321; (207) **7.** 359–61; (193) **10.** 25; (188) **11.** 119, **14.** 239; (182) **12.** 5; (101 **14.** 279
Aventinensis: *see* Genucius.
Aventinus, 12th king of Alba, **1.** 17
Avernus, Lake: (214) Hannibal moves to, **6.** 213, 239
Axilla: *see* Servilius.
Axius riv., in Macedon: (183) city founded on tributary of, **11.** 391; (168) Perseus at, **13.** 175, 233; (167) divides two Macedonian republics, 349
Axylon, in Asia Minor: (189) **11.** 63
Azorus, in Thessaly: (171) surrenders to Perseus, **12.** 457; (169) Q. Marcius Philippus near, **13.** 95

Babylonia: Macedonians in, corrupted, **11.** 59
Bacchanalian conspiracy: (186) discovered and suppressed, **11.** 241–75; (184) 353, (181) **12.** 63
Bacchium, is. off Aeolis: (190) **10.** 353
Bacchus: (186) rites of, described, **11.** 241–7, 253; rites permitted, 271–3
Badius, a Campanian: (212) defeated in single combat, **6.** 411–5
Baebian law: for election of praetors, **12.** 139
Baebius, A.: (167) pref., aids slaughter of Aetolians, **13.** 345; condemned, 353
—, L.: (169–168) envoy to Macedon, **13.** 149, 153–5
—, Q.: (200) tr. pl., opposes war, **9.** 19
— Dives, L., pr. 189: (203) envoy to

INDEX

Carthage, **8**. 453–5; (189) pr. for Nearer Spain, **10**. 431, 437–9; slain, 467
Baebius Herennius, Q.: (217) tr. pl., supports C. Terentius Varro, **5**. 315–7
— Sulca, Q., pr. 175: (173) envoy to Macedon and Egypt, **12**. 309
— Tamphilus, Cn., cos. 182: (204) tr. pl., accuses censs., **8**. 357; (200) aed. pl., **9**. 147; (199) pr. for Gaul, 147, 155, 171; (186) IIIvir col. deduc., **11**. 285; (185) consular candidate, 319–21; (182) cos., 397, **12**. 141, **14**. 241; in Liguria, **12**. 3–5; gains ovation, 53; holds elections, 57; (181) procos. at Pisae, 63, 79–81
— —, Cn.: (168) pr. urb., **13**. 145–7; (167) envoy on Illyrian peace, 299–301, 337–9
— —, M., cos. 181: (194) IIIvir col. deduc., **9**. 533–5; (192) pr. for Hither Spain, **10**. 29, 59; for Macedon and fleet, 59–61, 65–9, 157; (191) warned by Philip of Antiochus, 181; meets Philip, aids Larisa, 187, 195; occupies Thessalian towns, 195–7; in attack on Heraclea, 225–7; (185) envoy to reconcile Philip and Greeks, **11**. 291–309; (184) reports to Senate, 321; (181) cos. with Liguria as prov., **12**. 57–9, 81, 89, 105, 107, 117; holds elections, 107; (180) defeats Ligurians, triumphs, 113, 117–21
— —, Q.: (219) envoy to Hannibal and to Carthage, **5**. 19, 25–31, 45; (218) envoy to declare war, 49; vainly tries to raise Gauls and Spaniards, 55–9, 63
Baecula, in Spain: (209) Hasdrubal defeated near, **7**. 283–9, 293; (206) P. Scipio (Afr.) at, **8**. 55
Baeculonius, A.: (178) signifier, **12**. 195
Baesadines, Spanish commander: (195) defeated, **9**. 395
Baesidiae, in Bruttium: (203) **8**. 439
Baetica, in Spain: (207) **8**. 9
Baetis riv., in Spain: (206) Hasdrubal checked at, **8**. 67–9; Hanno defeated at, 89, 123
Baeturia, in Spain: (197) revolt of, expected, **9**. 337; (185) Romans in, **11**. 311
Baga, king of Mauri: (204) aids Masinissa, **8**. 323
Bagradas riv., in Africa: (255) Regulus checked at, **14**. 179; (203) Roman envoys escorted to, **8**. 455
Balanos, Gallic chief: (169) offers aid against Macedon, **13**. 133
Balari, Sardinians: (178–177) defeated, **12**. 201, 221–3
Balbus: *see* Acilius, Antonius, Fonteius, Naevius.
Baldo, in Spain: (197) **9**. 337
Balearic (Baliaric) is.: origin of name, **14**. 71; (217) seek peace, **5**. 269; (215) Punic fleet driven on, **6**. 121, 139–41; (206) Mago winters on, **8**. 149, 173, 197; (122–121) Q. Caecilius Metellus attacks, **14**. 71; (218) mercenaries from, in Punic army, **5**. 63, 163–5, (217) 213, (216) 323, 351, (210) **7**. 209, (209) 285, 295, (206) **8**. 63, (202) 491; (206) skill of, as slingers, 149–51, (189) **11**. 99
Balearicus: *see* Caecilius Metellus.
Balius, companion of Hercules, **14**. 71
Ballista, Mt., in Liguria: (187) Ligurians defeated on, **11**. 223; (180) **12**. 127; (176) 239, 241; (179) crossed by Q. Fulvius Flaccus, 163
ballistae and catapults: (219) **5**. 33; (211) **7**. 23; (200) **9**. 135; (198) 183
bank commissioners: *see* triumviri mensarii, quinqueviri mensarii.
bankruptcy: (352) Vviri for, **3**. 429
Bantia, in Apulia: (208) **7**. 315
Bantius, L., of Nola: (216) pro-Punic leader; pr. M. Marcellus wins, **6**. 49–51
Baphyrus riv., in Macedon: (169) **13**. 111
Barbanna riv., in Illyricum: (168) **13**. 191–3
Barbatus: *see* Cornelius Scipio, Horatius.
Barbula: *see* Aemilius.
Barcine faction, in Carthage: (229) secures Spanish command for Hasdrubal, **5**. 5–7; (221) sends Hannibal to Spain, 9; (219) opposes Roman peace, 27; (216) supports Hannibal, **6**. 37, 43; (203) urges continued war, **8**. 387; (201) 527; (193) agent of Hannibal approaches, **9**. 573

INDEX

Barcine family, in Carthage: (215) generals from, **6**. 139; (206) **8**. 53
Bargullum, in Epirus: (205) **8**. 253
Bargusii, Spanish tribe: (218) favour Rome, **5**. 55; subdued by Hannibal, 67
Bargyliae, in Caria: (197) Macedonian withdrawal from, demanded, **9**. 255, refused, 261; Macedonians flee to, 327; (196) Philip to withdraw from, 359, 501; P. Cornelius Lentulus at, 371, 383
—, Gulf of: (190) **10**. 339
Barium, Apulian port: (181) **12**. 61
Barnosthenes, Mt., near Sparta: (192) **10**. 77, 87–9
basilica Fulvia (or Aemilia): (179) contracted for, **12**. 159
— Portia: (184) erected, **11**. 361
Bassania, in Illyricum: (168) **13**. 189
Bassus: *see* Caecilius.
Bastarnae, Sarmatians: (182) allied with Philip, **12**. 15, 171, 323; (179) cross Danube, 171–3; defeated by Thracians, enter Dardania, 175–7; (175) Perseus stirs, against Dardanians, 245–7, 263, **13**. 259; (29) Crassus attacks, **14**. 165.
Bastetani, Spanish tribe: (207) L. Scipio among, **8**. 11; (190) L. Aemilius Paulus among, **10**. 427–9
Bastia: (81–0) husband of, proscribed, **14**. 113
Bato, a Dardanian: (200) aids P. Sulpicius Galba, **9**. 81
battering ram: (219) **5**. 21–3; (200) **9**. 135; (195) 491; (191) **10**. 227; (190) 305; 383; (189) **11**. 15–21; 97; (171) **12**. 489
bears: (169) in games, **13**. 149
Begorritis, Lake, in Macedon: (171) **12**. 457
Belbinates ager, in Arcadia: (189) **11**. 113
Belgae: (57–6) subdued, **14**. 129
Belligenes, a Spaniard: (212) agent in delivery of Syracuse, **6**. 455, **7**. 83
Bellona: (340) addressed in *devotio*, **4**. 37; (296) vows and prayers to, 429–31. Temple of, outside *pomerium*: (211) Senate in, to consider triumph or ovation, **7**. 79; (207) **8**. 37–9; (206) 151; (200) **9**. 139; (197) 337; (191) **10**. 267; (187) **11**. 153; (185) 309; (178) **12**. 201; (173) 315; (172) 351; 371; (203) foreign envoys received in, **8**. 445; (202) 515; (197) **9**. 343; (171) **12**. 397
Bellovaci, Gauls: (51) defeated by Caesar, **14**. 135, (46) by D. Brutus, 143
Bellovesus: (616–578) leads Gauls, **3**. 117–21
Bellus: (168) Illyrian envoy, **13**. 193
Bellus, Mt., in Africa: (204) **8**. 329
Belus: father of Dido, **14**. 177
Bendis, temple of: (188) **11**. 139
Beneventum, in Samnium: once called Maleventum, **4**. 271; (268) colony at, 553; (217) Hannibal raids, **5**. 243; (214) Ti. Sempronius Gracchus defeats Hanno at, **6**. 213–27, 233, 235, 237, **7**. 9; (212) Q. Fulvius Flaccus takes Hanno's camp at, **6**. 389–95; Ap. Claudius Pulcher and Flaccus near, 397, 401–3; Gracchus dies at, 409–11; Hannibal leaves, 415; (209) loyal, **7**. 245–7
Bergae, in Bruttium: (203) **8**. 439
Bergistani, in Spain: (195) revolt of, subdued, **9**. 459–61, 469
Beroea, in Macedon: (168) surrenders, **13**. 237; (167) in 3d Macedonian republic, 349, 353. *See* Adaeus, Alexander, Hippias, Midon.
Berones, Spanish tribe: (76) **14**. 193, 195
Bessi, Thracians: (183) **11**. 389
Bestia: *see* Calpurnius.
Beudos Vetus, in Phrygia: (189) **11**. 51
Bevus riv., in Illyricum: (200) **9**. 99
Bianor, of Acarnania: (197) supports Rome, **9**. 319–21
Bibaculus: *see* Furius.
Bibulus: *see* Calpurnius, Publicius.
Bigerra, in Spain: (214) **6**. 309
Bilistages: (195) chief of Ilergetes, seeks aid, **9**. 447–9
Bisaltae, Thracians: (168) refuse aid to Perseus, **13**. 237; (167) in first Macedonian republic, 347–51
Bithynia: (c. 275) Galatians cross, **11**. 53; (190) Roman threat to, **10**. 363; (189) rivers of, **11**. 63; (183) Hannibal dies in, **14**. 241; (88) Mithridates holds, 97; (84) 105; (75–74) 117; (73) Mithridates driven from, 119. *See* Nicomedes, Prusias.

INDEX

Bithynicus: *see* Pompeius.
Bithys, of Thrace: (167) hostage, **13.** 399, 401
Bitias: (c. 260) Punic admiral, **14.** 177
Bitocus, a Galatian: (63) **14.** 127
Bituitus, king of Arverni: (121) defeated, **14.** 73
Bituriges, Celts: (616–578) in Italy; **3.** 117–9; (52) Caesar takes city of, **14.** 135
Black Rocks, in Spain: (211) **7.** 65
Blaesus: *see* Sempronius.
Blanda, in Lucania: (214) **6.** 237
Blasio: *see* Cornelius.
Blattius: (210) betrays Salapia, **7.** 143–5
Blossii, of Capua: (210) plot of, **7.** 211
Blossius, *see* Marius.
Bocchus, king of Moors: (106–105) aids, then betrays Jugurtha, **14.** 79
Boebê, marsh in Thessaly: (200) **9.** 119
Boeotia: south of Thermopylae, **10.** 203; (208) Philip crosses, **7.** 333, 343; (207) **8.** 19, 31; seeks aid of Philip, 17–9; Philips sends army across, 35; (205) joins in Roman treaty, 255; (200) Philip crosses, **9.** 69, 79; Andrians transported to, 131; (198) Macedonian prisoners transported to, 201; Flamininus winters near, 205; Macedonians cross, 227; (197) joins Roman alliance, 279–83, **10.** 447, 451; men of, in Macedonian forces, **9.** 313; (196) recovers pro-Macedonian citizens, 351; roused against Rome, 355–9; (192) sought by Aetolians and Antiochus, **10.** 135, 145–7; (191) 171–5; Antiochus' troops winter in, 191; cos. M' Acilius Glabrio reproves, 219, 233; (172) allied with Perseus, **12.** 325–9, 403–5, 411, 417; Roman envoys end League of, 401–5, 421–5, 433; Perseus seeks new alliance with, 431–3; P. Lentulus sent to, 437; (171) men of, serve Perseus, 449; military operations in, 463–5, 489–91, 505, (169) **13.** 91; (167) pro-Roman informers in, 355; (146) aids Achaeans at Thermopylae, **14.** 41. *See* Neon.
Bogud, king of Moors: (47–46) **14.** 211, 213
Boi, Gauls: settle north of Apennines, **3.** 121; expel Etruscans, **10.** 469; (218) revolt, capture land commissioners, **5.** 69–71, 155, **7.** 301, **8.** 439; send envoys to Hannibal, **5.** 85; (217) watched, 311; (216) defeat pr. L. Postumius Albinus, **6.** 83; (201) repulse pref. C. Ampius, **9.** 7–9; (200) sack Placentia, Cremona, 31; (197) aid Gauls; surrender to cos. Q. Minucius Rufus, 245–9, 337, 341; (196) defeat cos. M. Marcellus, 373–5, 379; he and cos. L. Furius Purpurio defeat, 375–7, 393; (195) defeated by cos. L. Valerius Flaccus, 471, 527, (194) 535, by Ti. Sempronius Longus, 535–41, (193) by cos. L. Cornelius Merula, 559, **10.** 9–17, 33, (192) by coss. C. Domitius Ahenobarbus and L. Flamininus, 63, 119; Flamininus kills a captured, **11.** 357; (191) defeated by cos. P. Scipio Nasica, **10.** 157, 261, 265–73, 295; (190) dispossessed, 295; colonies decreed for lands of, 429, (189) and established at Bononia, 469, (183) at Parma and Mutina, **11.** 395
Boiorix, leader of Boi: (194) **9.** 537
—, a Cimbrian: (105) kills leg. M. Aurelius Scaurus, **14.** 79
Bolae, in Latium: (415–414) captured, **2.** 417–9; (413) lands of, not distributed, 419, 425; (389) recovered, **3.** 203
Bomilcar, Punic admiral: (215) at Locri, **6.** 143; (214) at Syracuse, 291; (212) 441; driven to Tarentum, 445–9
Bononia (Bologna) in Cisalpine Gaul: (189) Latin colony, **10.** 469; (187) Ligurians raid; road from, to Arretium, **11.** 223. Prodigy: (135) **14.** 259
Booths, New, in Forum: (449) **2.** 159
booty: (616–578) offered to Vulcan, **1.** 135, (341) to Lua Mater, **4.** 5, (295) to Jupiter Victor, 473, (167) to Mars, Minerva, and Lua Mater, **13.** 361; (414) withheld from soldiers, causing mutiny, **2.** 419–23; (389) distributed to soldiers, **3.** 201; (385) 239, *et saepe*; (388) reserved for state, seized by soldiers, 209;

INDEX

(293) placed in *aerarium*, **4**. 537; (203) is property of Roman people, **8**. 417–9. *See aerarium.*
Bora, Mt., in Macedon: (167) **13**. 349
Bosporus: (66–65) Mithridates in, **14**. 125. *See* Machares.
Bostar: (217) Punic governor of Saguntum, **5**. 275–7
—: (215) Punic envoy to Philip, captured, **6**. 117–9; punished, 131–3
—: (211) Punic commander in Capua, **7**. 19, 45
Bottiaea, in Macedon: (211) **7**. 97
Bovianum, in Samnium: (313, 311) taken, **4**. 271, 281; (305) 341–3; (298) 403; (293) Samnites flee to, 521, 529; (212) Roman camp near, **6**. 391; (88) Pompedius Silo enters, **14**. 293. *See* Numerius Decimus.
Bovillae, in Latium: (292) road to, paved, **4**. 541; (52) Clodius slain at, **14**. 133
Bowls, golden: (389) dedicated on Capitol, **3**. 207; (217) offered by Naples, **5**. 309, (216) by Paestum, 321
Brachyllus, of Boeotia: (196) anti-Roman Boeotarch, murdered, **9**. 351–5, **10**. 135, 171
Braneus, chief of Allobroges: (218) aids Hannibal, **5**. 91
Brennus, Gallic chief: (390) at Allia, **3**. 129; leaves Rome, 163–5
—, —: (278) enters Dardania, **11**. 51
Bribery: *see ambitus.*
Bridges, over Tiber: (640–616) pile, built, **1**. 121; (508) held by Horatius, 249–51; (390) *sacra* carried over, **3**. 139; (192) two, swept away, **10**. 61
Bridge, pontoon: (218) over Po, **5**. 139, 141
Britain: (55–4) twice invaded by Caesar, **14**. 131, 203, 205; (13) Augustus returns from, 223
Brixia (Brescia), in Cisalpine Gaul: (391) Cenomani settle at, **3**. 119–21; (218) aids Rome, **5**. 73; (197) envoys sent to, **9**. 245
'Bronze Shields': (168) in Perseus' army, **13**. 227
Bruanium, in Macedon: (200) **9**. 115
Brundisium: (302) Cleonymus rounds, **4**. 363; (246) colony at, 559; (215) M. Valerius Laevinus commands fleet at, **6**. 113, 115, 163, (214) 207 209, 215, 239, 303; (212) not taken by Hannibal, 427; (209) loyal, **7**. 245–7; (200) port for crossings to Greece or Macedon, **9**. 43; (198) 179; (194) 549; (192) **10**. 65–9; (191) 165; (190) 301; (180) **12**. 131; (172) 343; 367–9; 399; (171) 443; (170) **13**. 33; (169) 91; (168) 149; 395; 255; 293; (167) 409; (191) allotted to A. Cornelius Mammula, **10**. 159; (181) complains of pirates, **12**. 59; (171) fleet inspected at, 383, 395; (44) Octavius enrolled in Julian clan at, **14**. 309; (40) Octavius and Antony make peace at, 223. *See* Dasius, Rammius.
Bruttii: (333) defeated by Alexander of Epirus, **4**. 93–5; (282–1) by Rome, 549; (280) support Pyrrhus, **9**. 23; (280–272) defeated by Rome, **4**. 551, **6**. 205; (216) desert Rome, **5**. 409, **6**. 35; attack Petelini, 69–71, 101; take Croton, 101, (215) 179–85; operations of Hanno among, 131, 143, 147, 157, 175, (214) 217, 237; aid Hannibal, 341, 219, 221; (213) some of, return to Rome, 341; (212) Hanno and Mago in, 389, 395, 399, 405; (211) Hannibal in, **7**. 17, 43–5, 161, 203; (210) threatened by Rhegium, 157; (209) assigned to Q. Fulvius Flaccus, 231; ravaged, 255; promised fair treatment, 267; Hannibal withdraws to, 267–9; Tarentum betrayed by, 269–75; (208) T. Quinctius Crispinus leaves, 313–5; Hannibal in, 329; (207) assigned to Flaccus and C. Claudius Nero, 353, 357; Hannibal in, 363, 373, 413, **8**. 51; Hanno sent to, **7**. 379; (206) assigned to L. Veturius Philo and Q. Caecilius Metellus, **8**. 43, 49, (205) to Metellus and P. Licinius Crassus, 153–5, 191, 195, 249; operations in, 175, 185, 199, 229; (204) assigned to P. Sempronius Tuditanus, 255–7, 349; some cities of, submit, 357; (203) allotted to Cn. Servilius Caepio, 367–9; many towns of, surrender, 439; Hannibal abandons, 441; (202) troops from, with Hannibal at Zama, 491; allotted to C. Livius Salinator, 463, (201) to M. Valerius

INDEX

Falto, 517, 521, (200) to Q. Minucius Rufus, **9**. 19, 25, who investigates conspiracies, 37, (199) 155–7; (194) Roman and Latin colonies in, 535, 553; (192) assigned to M. Baebius Tamphilus, **10**. 59, 65–7; colony in, 119; (191) allotted to A. Cornelius Mammula, 121–3, 159, 297, 301, (190) to M. Tuccius, 295–7, (189) 439, (188) **11**. 117; (173) temple of Juno Lacinia in, **12**. 299. Prodigy: (199) **9**. 157

Brutulus: *see* Papius.

Brutus: *see* Junius.

Bubulcus: *see* Junius.

Bucar, a Numidian: (204) deserts Masinissa, **8**. 329–33

Budares, Spanish commander: (195) defeated, **9**. 395

Bullis, on Illyrian coast: (191) vantage point against Italy, **10**. 179; (168) men from, in Roman army, **13**. 189

Bulotus riv., near Locri: (205) **8**. 235

Bursa, citadel of Carthage: **9**. 577

Bursaones: (76) Sertorius plunders, **14**. 195

Busa, Apulian woman: (216) aids Romans after Cannae, **5**. 373, 377

Buteo: *see* Fabius.

Buxentum, in Lucania: (197–194) Roman colony established at, **9**. 243, 529, 533; (186) re-established, **11**. 285

Bylazora, in Paeonia: (168) **13**. 175

Byzacium, in Africa: (195) **9**. 403

Byzantium: (278) Gauls cross from, **11**. 51–3; (197) return of Perinthus to, demanded, **9**. 255; (184) Philip feigns aid to, **11**. 327; (172) Perseus aids, **12**. 329, 411, 417, 429. *See* Heraclides.

Cacus: steals Hercules' cattle, **1**. 27–8

caduceus: (168) envoy's staff, **13**. 237

Cadusii, from Media: (192) **10**. 137, 143

Caecilia Metella: (88) Sulla's wife, **14**. 185; (90) dream of, 293

Caecilius, A.: (189) aed. pl., **11**. 117

— (or Caelius), C.: (90) pr., subdues Salluvii, **14**. 91

—, M.: (200) leg., **9**. 61

—, M.: (173) Xvir agr. adsig., **12**. 303; (172) envoy to secure grain, 369

Caecilius, Q.: (439) tr. pl., **2**. 311

— Bassus: (47) supports Pompey, **14** 143

— Denter, L.: (182) pr. for Sicily, **11** 397, **12**. 3

— —, M.: (173) envoy to Macedo and Egypt, **12**. 309

— Metellus, L., cos. 251, 247: (250 defeats Carthaginians, **4**. 557; (242 pont. max., holds flamen Mart. i city, 559, **10**. 439; saves *sacra*, **4** 559

— —, L., cos. 68: (70) pr., defeat pirates, **14**. 121

— —, M. (or L.), tr. pl., 213: (216 would abandon Italy, **5**. 373–5 (214) qu., degraded, **6**. 229–31, **7** 253; (213) tr. pl., attacks censs., **6** 313

— —, M., pr. 206: (208) aed. pl., **7** 357; (206) pr. urb., pereg., **8**. 43–5 (205) envoy for stone of Grea Mother, 247–9

— —, Q., cos. 206: (216) pont., **6**. 73 (209) aed. pl., **7**. 301; (208) aed cur., 355; (207) leg., brings news o Metaurus, 409; mag. eq. com. c. **8**. 43; (206) cos. in Bruttium, 41–3 49–51; restores farmers, 47–9 (205) 191, 195, 243–5; dict. com. c. 243, 249; (204) leg. for Locriar affair, 285–9; (203) support Africanus, 449; (202) 461; (201 Xvir agr. adsig., **9**. 13; (193 criticises cos., **10**. 21–3; (185–184 commissioner to Macedon and Greece, **11**. 291–309, 321–3, 331 369; (179) reconciles M. Aemilius Lepidus and M. Fulvius Nobilior **12**. 143–7

— — Balearicus, Q.: (123) cos. **14** 71

— — Calvus, L.: (142) cos., **14**. 255

— — Caprarius, C.: (113) cos., **14** 271

— — Celer, Q., cos. 60: (62) wife of, debauched by Clodius, **14**. 127; (60) cos., 303; pont., 127

— — Creticus, Q., cos. 69: (68–67) procos. in Crete, **14**. 123, 201; (67) resents Pompey, 123; (66) organizes Crete, 125

— — Delmaticus, L.: (119) cos., **14**. 267; (119–117) subdues Dalmatians, 75

INDEX

Caecilius Metellus Denter, L., cos. 284 : (283) pr., defeated by Gauls, **4**. 549
— — Diadematus, L. : (117) cos., **14**. 269; (115–114) cens., removes 32 senators, 75
— — Macedonicus, Q., cos. 143 : (168) reports Pydna, **13**. 237, 249–53; (148) propr., defeats Andriscus, **14**. 35, 37; (146) defeats Achaeans, triumphs, 41–3; (143–142) cos., procos., in Spain, 45–7, 255; (131–130) cens., proposes law requiring all to marry; attacked by C. Atinius Labeo, 65–7
— — Nepos, Q.: (98) cos., **14**. 283
— — Numidicus, Q. : (109) cos., defeats Jugurtha, **14**. 77; (100) driven from Rome by Marius; restored, 85
— — Pius, Q., cos. 80 : (89) leg., defeats Marsi, **14**. 95; (88) pont. max.; marries daughter to Sulla, 185; (84) supports optimates; defeated in Africa, 107; (76–74) opposes Sertorius, 115–9, 193–5
— — — Scipio Nasica, Q. (also called P. Scipio) : (52) cos., **14**. 133; (47) Pompeian commander in Africa, 141; (46) defeated, 143
Caecus : *see* Claudius.
Caedicius, C.: (293) leg., **4**. 515, 519
—, L. : (475) tr. pl., accuses Sp. Servilius Structus, **1**. 397
—, M. : (391) hears prophecy of Gallic sack, **3**. 113, 177
—, Q. : (390) cent., **3**. 153–5
Caelian hill : (672–640) added by Hostilius, **1**. 107, 119; (508) army leaves by, 255
Caelimontana porta : (508) **1**. 255[1]; (193) **10**. 23–5
Caelimontanus, *see* Verginius, — Tricostus.
Caelius, C. : *see* Caecilius, C.
— Caldus, C. : (94) cos., **14**. 287
— Rufus, M. : (48) pr., joins Milo, **14**. 139
Caeni, Thracians : (188) **11**. 137
Caenina, in Latium : (753–717) people of, at Consualia, **1**. 35; defeated, 39–41
Caeno, Volscian town : (469) **1**. 427
Caepio : *see* Servilius.
Caerê, in Etruria : home of Etruscan king, **1**. 13; (510) exiled Tarquins at, 209; (397) Romans cross territory of, **3**. 57; (390) *sacra* taken to, 139, 169, 423–5; treaty with, 169; (353) attacks Rome, granted peace, 421–5; (310) K. Fabius Ambustus educated at, **4**. 301; (302) Etruscan interpreters from, 371; (205) promises Africanus supplies, **8**. 193. Prodigies : (218) **5**. 185–7; (217) 201; (216) 321; (208) **7**. 307; (206) **8**. 47; (174) **12**. 255; (163) **14**. 249; (147) 253; (95) 285. *See* Artena.
Caesar, Garden of : (17) **14**. 319
Caesar : *see* Julius.
Caesetius Flavus, L. : (44) tr. pl., opposes Caesar, is exiled, **14**. 145
caetrati, targeteers : (200) in Macedonian army, **9**. 105; (192) in Achaean army, **10**. 75, 83, 87; (190) in Antiochus' army, 409
Caiatia, in Campania : (295) Samnites defeated near, **4**. 477–9; (217) Hannibal at, **5**. 245; (216) M. Marcellus at, **6**. 47
Caïcus riv., in Mysia : (190) Antiochus camps at, **10**. 343; L. Scipio at, 397
Caieta, in Latium : (43) Cicero unable to sail from, **14**. 217. Prodigies : (213) **6**. 316[3]; (182) **12**. 5, **14**. 241
Calabria : (215–214) coast of, defended, **6**. 117, 211, 303; (172) grain from, **12**. 369; (171) fleet for Macedon off, 439
Calagurris, in Spain : (186) Celtiberians defeated near, **11**. 279–81; (76, 74) allied to Sertorius, **14**. 195, 117
Calatia, in Campania : (321) Romans near, **4**. 165; (313) captured, 273; (306) Samnites take, 333; (216) deserts Rome, **5**. 409; (211) surrenders, **7**. 61; (210) punished, 129–33; Atellans settled at, 213; (174) walls of, rebuilt, **12**. 279–81. Prodigies : (172) **12**. 349; (167) **13**. 297, **14**. 245
Calatinus : *see* Atilius.
Calavii, of Capua : (314) accused of conspiracy, **4**. 263
—, of Capua : (210) punished for arson, **7**. 105
Calavius, A., of Capua : (321) **4**. 185
—, Pacuvius, of Capua : (216) holds

INDEX

Capua, **6**. 5–11; saves Hannibal, 23–9
Caldus: *see* Caelius.
calendar: (715–672) designed by Numa, **1**. 69; (304) posted by Cn. Fulvius, **4**. 349–51; (190) dislocation of, **10**. 301[4]; (168) **13**. 215[1]; 87–8. *See* the various months.
Cales, in Campania: (336–334) captured, colony sent to, **4**. 65–7; (296) Samnites plunder, 433; (217) Hannibal at, **5**. 245, 287; Romans flee to, 253; (215) city legions mobilize at, **6**. 105; Fabius Maximus at, 127; (214) M. Marcellus at, 217; (213) political prisoners placed at, 321; (211) **7**. 57–61; Hannibal at, 33; Hannibal plunders, 51; (209) fails to meet requisitions, 241–7; (204) forced to furnish extra quota, **8**. 263–7. Prodigy: (214) **6**. 207. *See* C. Albius.
Caletranus ager: (183) **11**. 395–7
Callaeci: *see* Gallaeci.
Callaicus: *see* Junius Brutus.
Callicrates, of Achaia: (174) pro-Roman, **12**. 261–5, 269; (167) in danger, **13**. 357
Callicritus, of Thebes: (172) assassinated, **12**. 329, 411–3
Callicula, Mt., in Campania: (217) Hannibal outwits Q. Fabius Maximus at, **5**. 251–9
Callidromum, Mt., above Thermopylae: (191) Aetolians driven from, **10**. 205–9, 215
Callifae, in Samnium: (326) **4**. 99
Calligenes: (179) conceals Philip's death, **12**. 171
Callimedes, pref. of Ptolemy: (200) betrays Aenus to Philip, **9**. 51
Callinicus, in Thessaly: (171) victory of Perseus at, **12**. 471–7
Callipeucê, pass into Macedon: (169) **13**. 107
Callipolis, Aetolian town: (191) **10**. 245
—, Thracian town: (200) **9**. 51
Callippus: (168) Perseus' admiral, **13**. 179
Callithera, in Thessaly: (198) **9**. 191
Callo: (215) reveals conspiracy against Hieronymus, **6**. 189–91
Calor riv., near Beneventum: (214) Hanno near, **6**. 217; 212 Ti. Sempronius Gracchus slain in, 409–11
Calpurnia, wife of Caesar: (44) **14**. 215, 309
Calpurnius, C.: (216) envoy from troops surrendering at Cannae, **5**. 407
—, L.: (198) envoy to Achaeans, **9**. 207–9
— Bestia, L.: (111) cos., **14**. 271; makes treaty with Jugurtha, 77
— Bibulus, M.: (59) cos., opposes Caesar, **14**. 127; (51) procos. in Syria, 135
— Flamma, M.: (258) tr. mil. rescues army, **4**. 555, **5**. 399
— Piso, C.: (211) pr. urb., **6**. 501, **7**. 13, 37, 59, 79, 89; (210) in Etruria, 109; in Capua, 223; (209) in Etruria, 231, 299, 303–5
— —, C., cos. 180: (186) pr. for Farther Spain, **11**. 235, 241, 279; (185) defeats Spaniards, 311–7; (184) triumphs, 341–3, 353–5; (181) IIIvir col. deduc., **12**. 89; (180) cos. for Liguria, 107–9; dies of plague or poison, 115–7
— —, Cn.: (139) cos., **14**. 53
— —, Q.: (135) cos., **14**. 259
— — Caesoninus, L.: (148) cos., **14**. 37, 253
— — Frugi, L., cos. 133, the annalist. Cited: (534–510) **1**. 193; (494) 323; (471) 415; (305) **4**. 341; (299) 391, (212) **6**. 493
— — —, L., cos. 15: (13–11) subdues Thracians, **14**. 167
Calussa: *see* Cornelius.
Calvinus: *see* Domitius, Sextius, Veturius.
Calvius Cicero, C.: (454) tr. pl., convicts T. Romilius, **2**. 105
Calvus: *see* Caecilius Metellus, Cornelius Scipio, Licinius, Rutilius.
Calycadnus, cape in Cilicia: (188) **11**. 127
Calydon, in Aetolia: (191) **10**. 191
Camars: old name of Clusium, **4**. 455
Cambunian mts., in Macedon: (171) crossed by Perseus, **12**. 457, (170) by cos. A. Hostilius Mancinus, **13**. 95; (169) held for Perseus, 95–7
camels: (190) in Antiochus' army, **10**. 409

INDEX

Camenae: (715–672) grove dedicated to, **1**. 75
Cameria, in Latium: (616–578) **1**. 137
Camerinum, in Umbria: (310) offers aid against Etruscans, **4**. 303; (205) sends cohort to P. Scipio (Afr.), **8**. 195
Camerinus: *see* Sulpicius.
Camillus: *see* Furius.
camp, fortified: (168) importance of, **13**. 221–3; (197) **9**. 287–9
Campania: fertile soil of, **3**. 497; wealth of, 459; character of, 457, 469, **4**. 183, **6**. 13; boundary of, **5**. 251; (476) grain from, **1**. 395; (423) Capua taken by Samnites or, **2**. 377, **3**. 497, **8**. 117; (420–419) Cumae taken by, **2**. 403; (361–360) Gauls in, **3**. 389; (343) aid Sidicini; defeated by Samnites, 455–7, 469, 481; seek Roman aid, 457–63, 469; give selves to Rome, 463–5, **4**. 5, 9; aided against Samnites, **3**. 467–9, **9**. 93; (342) Roman garrisons in, plot, **3**. 495–501; (341) pillage Samnium, **4**. 7–9; (340) join Latins against Rome, 9, 15, 17, 41–3; surrender; knights become citizens, 47–9; (338) *civitas sine suffragio* given, 61, **6**. 15, **7**. 125, **9**. 93; (328) threaten revolt, **4**. 87; (327) Samnites challenge Rome in, 89; (321) receive Romans after Caudine Forks, 183; (319) in Roman Federation, 237; (314) revolt, 259, 267; (313) Romans move on, 271; (310) 311; (308) gladiators in, 323; (305) Samnites raid, 341; (296) Samnites defeated in, 431–7; (295) cavalry from, used against Gauls, 461, 473; (294) Samnites raid, 481; (280) legion of, seizes Rhegium, 549, 553; (217) Hannibal devastates, **5**. 243–7, 287; (216) deserts Rome after Cannae, 409, **6**. 3–33, 107, 411; military operations in, 45–69; (215) M. Marcellus sent to, 107; Philip's envoys captured in, 115–9; military operations in, 121–31, 135–7, 143–59, 163, 175, (214) 211–3, 215–7, 227–9, 233–7, (213) 327–9, (212) 387–403, 411–9, 425–9, (211) **7**. 15–31, 41–3; punishment of, after fall of Capua, 61–5, 125–33, **11**. 149; (209) lands in, leased, **7**. 251; (208) cos. dies in, 345; (205) lands of, sold, **8**. 195–7; (201) assigned as province to M. Valerius Falto, **9**. 27; (194) Roman colonies in, 533; (189) censors list certain, in Rome, **11**. 95, 119; (188) receive *ius connubii*, 119; (173) public and private lands in, divided, **12**. 293–5, 313, 317, 345; (172) victims offered in, 349. Prodigies: (208) **7**. 305; (177) **12**. 223; (174) 255; (166) **14**. 245. *See* Capua, Casilinum, Cumae, Nola; Badius, Minius Cerrinius, Paculla Annia.
Campi Macri, in Cis-Alpine Gaul: (176) **12**. 239–41; (168) **13**. 283
Campus Martius: (716) Romulus vanishes from, **1**. 57; (578–534) army purified in, 155; (509) land of Tarquins becomes the, 231; (462) booty displayed in, **2**. 35; (449) Senate meets in, 213; (458) army assembles in, 93; (446) 237; (435) census taken in new building in, 329; (384) *comitia centuriata* meets in, **3**. 265; (200) **9**. 19–25; (366) elections in, **3**. 357; (355) 419; (304) **4**. 353; (215) **6**. 197, 203; (211) **7**. 71; (218) Hannibal aims at, **5**. 89; (217) slaves conspire in, 309–11; (214) temple of Vulcan in, **6**. 207; (193) altar of Mars in, **10**. 29; (179) **12**. 143; (189) flooded, **11**. 95; (179) censors sit in, **12**. 143; temple to Lares of Sea in, 161; (167) captured ships beached beside, **13**. 401; (44) Caesar's body carried toward, **14**. 147; (43) Octavius parades troops in, 315. Burials in: (78) Sulla, 113; (54) Julia, 133; (43) Hirtius and Pansa, 151. Prodigies: (216) **5**. 321; (214) **6**. 207; (189) **11**. 95; (152) **14**. 251; (43) 315
Canae, in Aeolis: (191) fleet winters at, **10**. 285; (190) 315, 325
Canastraeum: on Pallenê, **13**. 125; (200) fleet makes for, **9**. 133
candidata toga: (432) forbidden, **2**. 339
Caninius Rebilus, C.: (171) pr. for Sicily, **12**. 371, 383
— —, M.: (170) envoy to Macedon, **13**. 39, 41; (167) to Thrace, 401

INDEX

Canna riv., in Apulia: (216, 212) **6**. 385

Cannae, in Apulia: prophecy of disaster at, **6**. 385; (216) Hannibal's victory at, **5**. 345–73; news of, reaches Rome, 377–83, and Carthage, **6**. 35–7; Senate refuses to ransom those surrendering at, **5**. 389–409; Hannibal frees captured allies, 389, **6**. 49, 213, 377; allies desert Rome after, **5**. 409, **6**. 3, 13, 35–7, 103, 319, **7**. 203, **8**. 183–5; after, Hannibal moves to Samnium, **6**. 3, not to Rome, **5**. 369, 383, **6**. 63, **7**. 27, 29, **8**. 443; punishment of survivors of, *see* Cannae, legions of; (215) war less active after, **6**. 121; Roman recovery, **4**. 239; leadership of M. Marcellus, **6**. 105, **7**. 207; Philip joins Hannibal after, **6**. 115; punishment of those wishing to desert Italy after, **5**. 373–5, **6**. 229–31, 313, **7**. 253. *Also* **6**. 15, 41, 51, 57–9, 61, 73, 85, 145, 147, 149, 155, 165, 193, 203, 229, 315, 359, 361, 405, 425, 485, 499, **7**. 11, 45, 159–61, 257, 369, 405, **8**. 443, 477, **9**. 433

Cannae, legions of: (216) survivors of Cannae sent to Sicily, **6**. 85, to serve without pay, 105; (214) joined by others, 231; (212) plea for discharge refused, 357–65; (211) hold Sicily, **7**. 5, 11, (210) 111, (209) 233, 241, 253, (208) 303, (206) **8**. 45, (204) 257; join forces of P. Scipio (Afr.), 303–5

cannibalism: (216) Carthaginians charged with, **6**. 17; (108) in quarries, **14**. 273

Cantabri, Spaniards: (151) **14**. 19

Cantilius, L.: (216) executed, **5**. 385

Canuleius, C.: (445) tr. pl., secures law permitting intermarriage, **2**. 257–77

—, M.: (420) tr. pl., attacks the Sempronii, **2**. 401

— Dives, L., pr. 171: (174) envoy to Aetolians, **12**. 273; (171) pr. for Spain, 371, 383; investigates charges against governors, **13**. 7, 11; founds colony in Spain, 11–3

Canusium, in Apulia: (318) submits, **4**. 243; (216) fugitives from Cannae at, **5**. 365–7, 371–7, 381–3, 393, 397–9, 403, **6**. 13; M. Marcellus takes command at, **5**. 385–7; (209) Hannibal and Marcellus at **7**. 255 (207) Hannibal moves to, 381

Capena, in Etruria: (402) aids Vei against Rome, **3**. 29–31; (401) 35 43; (399) 49; (398) 53; (397) 57 61; (396) 65–7; (395) grantec peace, 83, 95, (389) and citizenship 207; (211) grove of, plundered by Hannibal, **7**. 41. Prodigies: (217 **5**. 201; (210) **7**. 217; (196) **9**. 349

Capena porta, of Rome: (672–640 Horatius meets sister at, **1**. 91 (459) army musters outside, **2**. 77 (350) **3**. 433; (295) walk from paved, **4**. 447; (189) **11**. 95; (216 Senate to meet at, **6**. 109–11; (211 Q. Fulvius Flaccus enters by, **7**. 35 (205) temples dedicated near, **6**. 495 **8**. 249; (187) funeral of Africanu near, **11**. 191, 197. Prodigy: (196 **9**. 349

Capenus, a Sequanian: (43) murder D. Junius Brutus, **14**. 153

Capetus, Silvius: 8th king of Alba, **1** 17

Capito: *see* Fonteius.

Capitol (Capitoline Hill), in Rome (753–17) Sabines on, **1**. 45, 119, **9** 429; (460) occupied by Ap Herdonius, **2**. 53–71, 75; (419 slaves conspire to seize, 403; (390 held against the Gauls, **3**. 135–65 171–85, 231, 241, 249, 265–7, 341, **4** 175, **11**. 57; men of, institute Capitoline games, **3**. 169; (384 patricians forbidden to live on, 267 (340) T. Manlius Imperiosus threatens Latins on, **4**. 19, **6**. 75; (323 crowded with armed men, **4**. 145 (c. 230) Senators flee to, **14**. 181 (213) foreign cults on, **6**. 343; (211 garrison on, **7**. 35–7; Aetoliar treaty set up on, 95; (210) levy on **7**. 123–5; (207) matrons summoned to, 359; (193) quotas for allies assigned on, **9**. 559; (189) treaty with Antiochus struck on, **10**. 461; Spartans accused of breaking treaty ratified on, **11**. 111; (187) Africanus goes to, 179–81; (179) censors escorted to, **12**. 147; (133) Ti. Sempronius Gracchus slain on, **14**. 63; (83) buildings on, burned, 297, **3**. 207, **6**. 493; (44) Caesar's murderers seize, **14**. 147. General references

INDEX

to, as centre of city: (509) **1**. 243, 249, (479) 387, (446) **2**. 231, (445) 263, (393) **3**. 107, (384) 265, 267, (340) **4**. 17, (325) 133, (216) **5**. 367. Buildings on: (189) Aequimelium, **11**. 95; (140) aqueduct, **14**. 51; (190) arch, **10**. 299; (214) Atrium publicum, **6**. 207; (172) columna rostrata, **12**. 347; (174) portico, 279; (388) substructure, **3**. 209–11; (215) temples of Mens and Venus, **6**. 107, 113; (616–578) of Jupiter, *see* Jupiter Optimus Maximus, temple of; (186) of Ops, **11**. 281. Offerings and dedications on, by citizens: (389) **3**. 207; (380) 299; (368) 343; (358) 407; (305) **4**. 345; (212) **6**. 493; (206) **8**. 153; (204) 359; (202) 515; (196) **9**. 375; (192) **10**. 123; (189) **11**. 115; (187) 199; (172) **12**. 349; (167) **13**. 343; by non-citizens: (495) **1**. 289; (449) **2**. 193; (342) **3**. 495; (216) **5**. 325; (205) **8**. 159; (198) **9**. 237; (191) **10**. 259; (170) **13**. 23; (169) 135; (168) 289–91; (167) 315; 407. Senate meets on: (460) **2**. 73; (340) **4**. 17, **6**. 75; (215) 105; (214) 205; (211) **7**. 3; (205) **8**. 155; (202) 461; (198) **9**. 173; (187) **11**. 201; (172) **12**. 433; (166) **14**. 247. Tribal assembly meets on: (212) **6**. 351; (196) **9**. 345; (195) 413; (194) 553; (169) **13**. 57; (167) 371–3. Triumphator mounts the: (753–17) **1**. 41; (300) **4**. 385; (207) **8**. 41; (187) **11**. 169; (171) **12**. 441; (167) **13**. 387; 397; (62) **14**. 303. Vows taken by coss. on, (217) **5**. 191, 201; (200) **9**. 43; (187) **11**. 169–71; (177) **12**. 217; (174) 277; (172) 371; (171) 441; (167) **13**. 387. Prodigies (458) **2**. 101; (390) **3**. 185; (214) **6**. 207; (212) 365; (203) **8**. 373; (197) **9**. 243; (194) 535; (192) **10**. 61; (186) **11**. 281; (182) **12**. 5, **14**. 241; (179) **12**. 141, **14**. 243; (172) **12**. 347; (166) **14**. 247; (135, 134) 259; (133) 261; (126, 125) 265; (122) 267; (98) 283; (96) 285; (63) 303

Capitoline Games: (390) established, **3**. 169, 177

Capitolinus: *see* Maelius, Manlius, — Volso, Quinctius, — Cincinnatus, — Poenus, Sestius, Tarpeius Montanus.

Cappadocia: (190) men from, in army of Antiochus, **10**. 407, (189) of Gauls **11**. 91; (88) seized by Mithridates, **14**. 97; (84) freedom of, demanded, 105. *See* Ariarathes, Ariobarzanes.

Capra, swamp in Campus Martius: (716) **1**. 57

Caprarius: *see* Caecilius Metellus.

Capua, in Campania: reputation of, **3**. 495–7, **6**. 25, 63, 153; called Volturnum by Etruscans, **2**. 377; (423) taken by Samnites, 377, **4**. 507, or Campanians, **3**. 497, **8**. 117; (411) Samnites of, refuse grain to Rome, **2**. 427; (343) Samnites defeat Campanians near, **3**. 457; surrenders to Rome, 457–65, **7**. 49; protected, **3**. 467–77, 491–5; (342) Roman troops plot to take, 495–9; (340) defeated, **4**. 21, 45–7; (338) receives *civitas sine suffragio*, 61; (321) receives Romans after Caudine disaster, 183–5; (318) receives laws, 243; (314) pro-Samnite faction in, 259–67; (217) promised to Hannibal, **5**. 243; supply base for Rome, 255; (216) internal condition, **6**. 5–13; offers aid, 13–7; admits Hannibal, 5, 17–33, 37, 45, 59, 149–51, **9**. 433; opposition to Hannibal in, **6**. 23–33, 57; refuses to receive refugees from Nuceria, 49; (216–215) Hannibal winters in, 61–3, 153–5, **7**. 211; (215) Hannibal camps near, **6**. 115, 127; Romans camp near, 135–7, 159, 197–9; (214) Hannibal reinforces, 211–3; cos. Q. Fabius Maximus escorts Campanians to, 235–7; (213) nobles of, surrender, 327; (212) siege of, by coss. Q. Fulvius Flaccus and Ap. Claudius, 389–91, 397, 401, 411–29, 501, **7**. 49, (211) 3, 13–31, 35; surrenders, 43–57, 61, 69, 79, 91, 119, 139–41, 161, **12**. 345; treatment of, **7**. 55–65; (210) nobles of, punished for arson in Rome, 105; assigned to Flaccus, 105–9, 119, 127, 211–3, 223, **8**. 169; punishment of, **7**. 125–33, 311, **9**. 87, 91–5; (209) allotted to pr. T. Quinctius Crispinus, **7**. 231–3, 303; contrasted with Romans, 243; cos. Flaccus in, 253; (208) assigned to Flaccus, 301–3; Crispinus in, 329; (207) assigned to C. Hostilius

INDEX

Tubulus, 353, 357, 373; troops from, called to Rome, 383; (206–204) assigned to Tubulus, **8**. 45, 257; (199) censors sell tax-contracts for, and land in, **9**. 169; (167) Prusias at, **13**. 405–7; (73) slaves at, escape under Spartacus, **14**. 117–9. Prodigies: (217) **5**. 203; (209) **7**. 249; (208) 305; (207) 359; (203) **8**. 373; (198) **9**. 177; (193) **10**. 25; (179) **12**. 141–3; (177) 213; (163) **14**. 249; (83) 297. *See* Campania.

Capussa, king of Numidia: **8**. 321, 325

Capys, Samnite leader: (423) captures Capua, **2**. 377

— Silvius, 7th king of Alba, **1**. 17

Carales, Sardinian port: (215) Roman forces at, **6**. 137–41; (210) Carthaginians raid near, **7**. 227; (202) Roman fleet refits at, **8**. 513

Caralitis marsh, in Lycia: (189) **11**. 47

Caranus, 1st king of Macedon, **13**. 271

Caravandis, Illyrian city: (168) **13**. 189

Caravantius, Illyrian leader: (168) raids Cavii, **13**. 187–9, 193; captured, 195, 337; (167) led in triumph, 403

Carbo: *see* Papirius.

carcer (prison): (640–616) built, **1**. 121–3; (449) **2**. 193; (194) *carcer inferior*, **9**. 533. *Also*: **2**. 193, 197. *See* Latumiae, Tullianum.

carceres (starting stalls in Circus): (329) first, **4**. 79; (174) additional, **12**. 279

Caria: (197) Antiochus plans to seize cities of, **9**. 331; (196) Philip surrenders, to Rhodes, 361; (190) Rhodian fleet guards, **10**. 355; (189) part of, given Rhodes, 463–5, **11**. 133, **13**. 315; fears Galatians, **11**. 57; (169) freed by Rome, **13**. 137; (167) 331, 333; (197) men of, in army of Philip, **9**. 325, (190) of Antiochus, **10**. 409. *Also*: **10**. 337, **11**. 43

Caria Hydrela: (189) given Eumenes, **10**. 465

Carinae, in Rome: (211) **7**. 35; (191) **10**. 263

Carmenta (Carmentis) mother of Evander, **1**. 29; 390) shrine of, **3**, 157

Carmentalis porta: (479) on road to Veii, **1**. 387; (213) fire near, **6**. 327, 365; (207) procession for Juno Regina enters, **7**. 361

Carmo, in Spain: (197) **9**. 337

Carni, Alpine tribe: (170) outraged by cos., compensated, **13**. 5, 19–21

Carnuns, in Illyria: (171 **13**. 3

Carnutes, Gauls: (616–578) **3**. 119

carpentum, 2-wheeled car: (395) used by matrons, **3**. 89; (195) **9**. 421

Carpetani, Spanish tribe: (221) conquered by Hannibal, **5**. 15–7; (219) 35; (218) desert Hannibal in Alps, 67; (185) Roman forces among, **11**. 311; (181) **12**. 95, 101

Carseoli, town of the Aequi: (302, 298) colony founded at, **4**. 369, 403; (209) unable to meet Roman demands, **7**. 243–7; (204) extra quotas required, **8**. 263–7; (167) Bithys of Thrace held in, **13**. 399, 401. Prodigy: (93) **14**. 287

Cartala, in Spain: (221) **5**. 13

Carteia, Spanish port: (206) Roman fleet at, **8**. 123–7; (171) Latin colony at, **13**. 13

Carthage, Carthaginians, Phoenicians, Punici: origin and early history, **4**. 553, **9**. 407, **14**. 177; 'Carthage' means 'New Town', 177; *sufetes* highest officials in, **8**. 149; (431) first invades Sicily, **2**. 353; (342) congratulates Rome on Samnite victory, **3**. 495; (348) treaty made with Rome, 449, **4**. 241, **5**. 31, (306) renewed, **4**. 341; (280) 551; (226) **5**. 7; (289) war with Agathocles, **8**. 183; (273) aids Tarentum, **4**. 551; (264) Rome aids Mamertines against, 553, **13**. 317; (264–242) First Punic War, **4**. 553–9, **5**. 3, 121, 279, 341, 379, **13**. 381, **14**. 179; atrocities, **8**. 51; (242) peace terms, **5**. 7, 121–3; (237–21) growth of, in Spain, 5–7, 17, 45–7, 55–7, **8**. 213; Ebro riv. as limit, **5**. 7, **9**. 451; (219) envoys to, from Rome, **5**. 19, and Hannibal, 25–7; refuses terms, 27–31; takes Saguntum, 19–25, 31–43; (218) war declared on, 45–55, 59, **11**. 155; Hannibal sends troops to, **5**. 63; cross the Ebro, 57–9, 65, the Pyrenees, 65–9, the Rhone, 75–85, the Alps, 87–113; operations in Po

INDEX

valley, 113–45, 153–73, in Spain, 179–85; naval operations, 145–53; (217) operations in Italy, 173–9, 205–23, 229, 239–61, 277–85, 295–303, 307–11, in Spain, 269–77, **11**. 203; naval operations, **5**. 261–9, 305; (216) operations in Italy, 335–73, **6**. 3–33, 45–71, 85, 101–3, in Sicily and Sardinia, 71–3, 103, in Spain, 87–101; naval operations, **5**. 383; cruel treatment of prisoners by, 395; victory of Cannae reported in, **6**. 35–7; debate in, on reinforcements, 37–43; sends troops to Sardinia and Spain, 43, 93, 111–3; (215) Philip makes treaty with, 115–9, 131–5, **7**. 95, **9**. 7, 35, 473; operations in Italy, **6**. 121–31, 135–7, 143–63, 175–85, in Sardinia, 137–41, in Sicily, 185–97, in Spain, 163–9; sends reinforcements to Italy, 147, 201; (214) operations in Italy, 211–29, 233–41, in Sicily, 241–301, 359, in Spain, 307–13, (213) in Italy, 319–29, 341, in Spain and Numidia, 329–35, (212) in Italy, 365-83, 387–429, **7**. 9, in Sicily, **6**. 363, 429–63, 495–501, **7**. 119–23, **9**. 85, in Spain, **6**. 463–95, (211) in Italy, **7**. 15–57, in Sicily, 83–5, in Spain, 65-77; naval operations, 79; Marcellus triumphs over, on Alban Mt., 81; (210) general situation of, 139–41; operations in Africa, 215, 219–23, in Italy, 141–5, 151, 203–15, 299, in Sardinia, 227, in Sicily, 151–7, 217–9, 239, in Spain, 157–97, (209) in Italy, 253–79, in Spain, 279–97, in Greece, 269; Latins consider peace with, 241; (208) naval preparations by, 303; operations in Africa, 329–31, in Italy, 313-29, naval operations, 331, 335–7; (207) operations in Italy, 363–413, in Spain, **8**. 3–15; naval operations, 15, 31, 33; (206), operations in Italy, 49–53, in Spain, 53–151, 171, 181, **9**. 463; (205) debate in Senate on attacking, **8**. 161–91; operations in Africa, 209–11, 219–25, 229, **10**. 451, in Italy, **8**. 197–9, 225–9, in Sicily, 207–9, 229–43, 267-81, in Spain, 211–9; naval operations, 197, 199, 225–7; (204) operations in Africa, 257, 297–347, in Italy, 349–51, in Sicily, 293–7; secures alliance with Syphax, 297–301; Scipio accused of forgetting, 285; (203) operations in Africa, 373–423, **13**. 385; vainly seeks terms, **8**. 423–7, 445-9; operations in Italy, 431–43; recalls Hannibal 439–43; seeks mercenaries in Spain, 443; naval operations, 395–401, 451–3, 455; operations in Africa, 453–9, (202) 465–505, 511, **11**. 179, 185; terms dictated to, **8**. 505–9; armistice granted to, 509–11; (201) envoys of, in Rome, 515–9, 527; peace granted to, 523–33, **9**. 5–7, 15, 21, 93, 95, 307, **10**. 167–9, 459, **12**. 355, 359, 445, **13**. 315; saved from destruction, **8**. 533; pays first tribute, 535–7; P. Scipio Africanus triumphs over, 537–9, **11**. 159, 181, **13**. 383; (200) Philip's aid to, causes Macedonian war, **9**. 5–7, 35, 473; instigates Gallic revolt, 31–3, 247, 341; envoys in, 33, 57; (199) pays tribute, 157–9; some hostages returned to, 159; (198) hostages of, stir up slaves, 233–7; (196) revolt in Spain not instigated by, 347; (195) rejects alliance with Antiochus; Hannibal leaves, 397–407, **11**. 175, 191; many ships of, at Cercina, **9**. 403–5; dispute with Numidia, 403; envoys in, 403–7; (193) Hannibal plots rising in, 569-75; rivalry of nobles and senators in, 575; Masinissa claims tributaries of, 575–9, **10**. 451; (192) Hannibal not sent to, by Antiochus, 123–7; (191) grain from, for war with Antiochus, 161–3, 167–9; ships of, in Roman fleet, 167, 275, 281–3; (188) envoys in Rome beaten, **11**. 145; senate of, said to crucify generals, 169 (*cp*. **5**. 409); (182) dispute with Masinissa, **12**. 55–7, 107; (181) hostages returned to, 107; (174) envoys of Rome and of Perseus in, 255–7; (172) complains of Masinissa, 355–9; (171) protected by Rome, 377; Rome asks, for cavalry and elephants, 395–7; ships of, in Roman fleet, 465; Masinissa warns against, **13**. 13; (170) grain from, 25–27; (168) hostages not asked from, 291; (157) dispute with Masinissa,

INDEX

14. 15; (153–150) preliminaries of Third Punic War, 15–21; (150) attacks Masinissa, 21; (149) forced into war, 23–5, 29–31; siege of, begins, 25; (148) Phameas Himilco deserts; Hasdrubal charged with treason, 33; cities near, stormed, 35; (147–146) blockaded and destroyed, 37–41, 65, 253, **13**. 235; P. Scipio Aemilianus triumphs over, **14**. 43; (123–2) colony planted at, 71

Carthalo: (217) cavalry commander of Hannibal, **5**. 253; (216) 361; envoy, 389–91; (212) **6**. 411; (209) commands in Tarentum, **7**. 275

Carventum, in Latium: (410) seized by Aequi and Volsci, **2**. 429; recovered, 431; (409) seized by Aequi, 437–9

Carvilius, C., of Spoletium: (169) parleys with Perseus, **13**. 67–9

—, L.: (212) tr. pl., indicts publican, **6**. 351–5

—, Sp.: (212) tr. pl., indicts publican, **6**. 351–5

—, Sp.: (171) answers Perseus' envoys, **12**. 397–9

— Maximus, Sp.: (299) aed. cur., **4**. 391–3

— —, Sp.: (293) cos., **4**. 509, **6**. 205; takes Samnite towns, **4**. 509–11, 525–33; receives Etruria as province, 535; triumphs, 539

— —, Sp., cos. 234, 228: (216) proposes admitting Latins to Senate, **6**. 75; (211) augur, dies, **7**. 91

Caryae, in Peloponnese: (195) Flamininus at, **9**. 483; (192) Philopoemen at, **10**. 77

Carystus, in Euboea: (200) plundered by fleet, **9**. 131; (198) surrenders, 197–201, 213; (196) freed, 369; (192) aids Chalcis, **10**. 113–5

—, in Liguria: (173) **12**. 311

Casander: (184) Philip's agent in destruction of Maronea, **11**. 325–7

Casca: *see* Servilius.

Cascantini, Spanish tribe: (76) **14**. 195

Casilinum, in Campania: (217) Hannibal reaches, by error, **5**. 243–5; garrisoned by Q. Fabius Maximus, 251, 255, 287; (216) Marcellus leaves, **6**. 45–7; Hannibal takes, 57–69, 75, **8**. 443; (214) Fabius takes, **6**. 217, 233–7; (212) base fo siege of Capua, 419, 425

Casinum, in Latium: (217) Hanniba fails to reach, **5**. 243–5; (211) h camps before, **7**. 33. Prodigies (208) 305; (166) **14**. 247.

Cassander, general of Alexander (316) founds Cassandrea, **13**. 125

Cassandrea, on Pallenê: (316) founde by Cassander, **13**. 123–5; (208–207 Philip builds ships at, **8**. 35; (200 Roman fleet repulsed by, **9**. 133 (169) Perseus garrisons, **13**. 83 C. Marcius Figulus fails to take, 123 9; (168) Perseus launches fleet a 181; Antenor sails to, 273; (167 a flourishing city, 351

Cassignatus: (171) commands Gala tians under Eumenes, **12**. 467–9

Cassinum: *see* Casinum.

Cassius Longinus, C., cos. 171: (178 tr. mil., **12**. 199; (174) pr., 251 (173) Xvir agr. adsig., 303; (171 cos. with Italy as prov., 371, 37 379–85; moves from Gaul o Macedon without authority, **13**. 3–5 recalled, 5–7; plunders on rout 19–21; (170) tr. mil. in Macedo 19; (168) in charge of Gentius, 19

— —, C.: (124) cos., **14**. 267

— —, C.: (96) cos., **14**. 285

— —, C., cos., 73: (72) defeated b Spartacus, **14**. 119

— —, C., pr. 44: (52) qu., defeat Parthians, **14**. 135; (44) pr conspires against Caesar, 147; (43 condemned, 151; controls Syria confers with M. Brutus, 153 hostility of Octavian, 217; (42 plunders allies, 315; kills self a Philippi, 317, 155

— —, L.: (107) cos., defeated b Gauls, **14**. 77–9

— —, Q., cos. 164: (167) pr. urb., **13** 297–9, 369; conducts Perseus t Alba, 397; gives ships to Greeks 403; grants Senate to Prusias, 405 7

— —, Q.: (49) tr. pl., support Caesar, driven from Rome, **14**. 137 (48) cruelty of, in Spain, 139; (47 plans revolt, 211

— Vecillinus, Sp.: (502) cos., take Pometia, triumphs, **1**. 273–5; (501 first mag. eq., 275–7; (493) cos. i

INDEX

makes Latin treaty, 327–9; (486) cos. iii, favours plebeians, 353–5; (485) executed for seeking throne, 355–9, **2**. 307–9, **3**. 253, 259

Castor, temple of: (499) vowed, **1**. 285; (484) dedicated, 357; (340) memorial to Campanian knights in, **4**. 47–9; (306) honorary statue before, 339; (44) letters struck from names of Antony and Dolobella on, **14**. 311

Castra (or Castrum Portorium): (199) **9**. 169

— Aelia, in Spain: (77) **14**. 189

— Claudiana: *see* Claudian Camp.

— Pyrrhi: *see* Pyrrhus, Camp of.

castramentation: (c. 270) first taught by Pyrrhus, **10**. 43

Castrum, in Picenum: (290) **4**. 547

— Album, in Spain: (229) Hamilcar dies at; (214) Romans at, **6**. 307

— Novum, in Etruria: (191) **10**. 163

— Salerni, in Campania: (197) **9**. 243

Castulo, in Spain: (217) Cn. Scipio advances to pass of, **5**. 269; (214) goes over to Rome, **6**. 309; (211) revolts on death of the Scipios, **8**. 79; (206) P. Scipio (Afr.) at, 55; reduced, 79, 87

—, Forest of: (211) Mago retires beyond, **7**. 77; (209) P. Scipio (Afr.) crosses, 293–5

Castus, officer of Spartacus: (71) killed, **14**. 119, 199

Casus riv., in Asia Minor: (189) **11**. 45

Catana (Catina), in Sicily: (209) grain brought to, **7**. 239; (122) burned by Mt. Aetna, **14**. 267

cataphracti: (192) armoured cavalry of Antiochus, **10**. 137, (190) 407, 413, 415

catapults: *see* ballistae.

Catilina: *see* Sergius.

Catius, Q.: (210) aed. pl., **7**. 229; (207) leg. of C. Claudius Nero, 383; (205) envoy to Delphi, **8**. 193

Catmelus: (178) commands Gauls under A. Manlius Volso, **12**. 187

Cato: *see* Hostilius, Porcius.

Cattle market: *see* Forum Boarium.

Catulus: *see* Lutatius.

Caudex: *see* Claudius.

Caudine pass: (321) Samnite victory at, **4**. 167–85, 189–207, 215, 219, 221, 239, 301, 311, **5**. 249, **6**. 145, 361, **10**. 31; (214) Q. Fabius Maximus raids region of, **6**. 237

Caudine peace: (321) **4**. 163, 185, 205, 315; a *sponsio*, not a *foedus*, 177–9, 195–9; (320) discussed in Senate, 189–99, 205; hostages for, held, 207; released, 215–9

Caudinus: *see* Cornelius Lentulus.

Caudium, in Samnium: (321) Samnites camp near, **4**. 165; (320) *fetiales* at, 199; (319) Samnites defeated at, 219; (314) 267–71; (215) Marcellus raids near, **6**. 143

Caulares riv., in Lycia: (189) **11**. 47

Caulonia, in Bruttium: (209) vainly besieged, **7**. 255, 269, 277

Caunus, in Caria: (197) protected by Rhodes, **9**. 335; (167) revolts from Rhodes, reduced, **13**. 333

Caura: (143) **14**. 255

cavalry: (753–17) three centuries of, organized by Romulus, **1**. 153; (616–578) strength doubled by Tarquin, 133; (578–534) twelve new centuries of Servius, 153; (403) serve on own horses, **3**. 27; (401) paid, 45–7; (264) first used overseas, **4**. 553; (171) drawn from leading young men, **12**. 481. Examples of use of: (674–640) **1**. 109; (616–578) 135; (426) **2**. 239; (322) **4**. 151–3; (216) **5**. 353–61; (211) **7**. 15–7; (205) **8**. 213–9; (203) 403–5; (499) dismounted, **1**. 283–5; (449) **2**. 211; (423) 381–5; (381) **3**. 281; (362) 379–81; (315) **4**. 249; (310) 317; (426) with horses unbridled, **2**. 367–9; (325) **4**. 115; (180) **12**. 125. *See equites, cataphracti*, Numidians.

Cavii, Illyrians: (168) **13**. 187–9

Celaenae, in Phrygia: **11**. 41–3

Celathara, in Thessaly: (198) **9**. 191

Celeiates, Ligurians: (197) **9**. 245

Celer: *see* Caecilius Metellus.

celeres: bodyguards of kings, **1**. 57, 207

Celetrum, in Macedon: (200) **9**. 117

Celines, Gallic tribe: (200) **9**. 31

celoces, light war-ships: (219) **5**. 47

Celtiberians: (218) in Punic army, **5**. 127, 169; (217) give hostages; attack Punic Spain, 271, 273; (213) in Roman army, **6**. 335; (212) 463, 465; desert the Scipios, 465–7, **7**. 163, **8**. 171; (207) aid Carthaginians, 3; defeated and scattered,

3–9; (206) raid Suessetani, 99; treated kindly by P. Scipio (Afr.), 391–3; (203) in army of Syphax and Hasdrubal, 387–93; (195) defeated, **9**. 445; hired by Turduli against Rome, 461–5; (193) defeated, **10**. 21; (187) take up arms, **11**. 239; (186) defeated, 279–81; (184) two triumphs over, 355; (183) defeated, 397, **14**. 241; (182) **12**. 3, 55; (181) 93–103, 107–11, 115; (180) 121–7, 139–41, 299, 319; (179) 149–57; (178) 287, 203, 273; (174) revolt; are subdued, 273–5, 283, **14**. 245; (152–151) defeated, 19; (142) 47; (103) drive Cimbri from Spain, 81; (97) defeated, 87, 285; (77–6) attacked by Sertorius, 193. *See* Allucius.

Celts: (391) division of Gauls, **3**. 117

Cenaeum, Euboean promontory: (191) **10**. 219–21

Cenchreae, port of Corinth: (208–207) Philip sails from, **8**. 35; (198) occupied by Flamininus, **9**. 201, 207, 213, 225, **12**. 269; (197) Attalus joins fleet at, **9**. 273

Cenomani, Gauls: (391) cross Alps and settle, **3**. 119–21; (218) aid Romans at Trebia, **5**. 163–5; (200) sack Placentia and Cremona, **9**. 31; (197) take up arms, 243–7; defeated, 337, 341; (187) disarmed while at peace, **11**. 223–5

censor, census: (578–534) census instituted, **1**. 149, **2**. 85, 269; (443) first censors, **2**. 285; (435) first census in Campus Martius, 329. Term: (434) limited to 18 months by Aemilian law, 333–5, (310) which Ap. Claudius defies, **4**. 289–99; (169) census conducted on Dec. 18th, **13**. 143; (168) request for 'usual extension of term' vetoed by tr. pl., 295. Eligibility: (351) first plebeian elected, **3**. 431–3; **4**. 387; (339) one must be plebeian, 53; (210–209) men not *consulares* elected, **7**. 227, 251; (131) two plebeians, **14**. 65. Election: (310) both must receive majority, **4**. 297–9; (392) cens. suf. elected, **3**. 109–11, **4**. 297; (380) cens. must resign if colleague dies, **3**. 289–91, **4**. 295; (214) **6**. 313; (210) **7**. 227–9; (214) cos. designated by lot to hold election of censs., **6**. 205. Duties and powers: (443) **2**. 285–7; (310) **4**. 291–9; (214) **6**. 229–33; (209) **7**. 251–3; (204) **8**. 351–7; (184) **11**. 355–61; (179) **12**. 143–7; (169–168) **13**. 49–61, 143. Conflicts with tribb. pl.: (310) **4**. 289–99; (213) **6**. 313; (204) **8**. 357; (169) **13**. 55–61. Population figures and/or completion of *lustrum*: (578–534) **1**. 155; (465) **2**. 11; (459) 85; (319) **4**. 237; (299) 393; (292) 541; (289) 547; (280, 275) 551; (264) 553; (252) 557; (247) 559; (224, 220) 561; (208) **7**. 355; (204) **8**. 353; (193) **10**. 23; (188) **11**. 121; (178) **12**. 289; (173) 319; (167) **13**. 413; (164) **14**. 11; (159) 13; (154) 15; (141) 49; (136) 59; (129) 65; (124) 69; (114) 75; (70) 121; (46) 145

Censorinus: *see* Marcius.

census, provincial: (13) **14**. 165

Centenius, C.: (217) propr., captured by Hannibal, **5**. 227

— Paenula, M.: (212) centurion, defeated by Hannibal, **6**. 417–9, 423

Cento: *see* Claudius.

Centobriga, Celtiberian city: (143) **14**. 47

Centumalus: *see* Fulvius.

centuries: *see comitia centuriata.*

centurion: (473) former, refuses to serve in lower rank, **1**. 405; (446) elected by cohorts, **2**. 237; (342) former tribb. mil. barred from service as; *centurio primus*, later called *primi pili*, **3**. 511; (180) role of, in paying troops, **12**. 129; (171) vainly claim old rank on recall to service, 383–95 (cp. **14**. 207); career of a, **12**. 389–95

Cephallania, Ionian is.: (191) fleet off, **10**. 191; A. Postumius commands on, 195; (190) piracy near, 331; (189) excluded from Aetolian peace, **11**. 31, 37; M. Fulvius Nobilior moves to, **10**. 437, **11**. 33, 95–101, 105, 149; (187) Nobilior reports victories on, 225; he triumphs, 233; (172) envoys pass through, **12**. 401; (171) fleet at, 439, 463. Prodigies: (163) **14**. 249; (140) 255

Cephalus, of Epirus: (169) supports Perseus, **13**. 65; (167) slain, 337

INDEX

Cepnati, Thracians: (172) **12**. 347
Cerceii, in Latium: (198) **9**. 233
Cercetius, Mt., in Epirus: (198) **9**. 193
Cercina, is. in Lesser Syrtis: (217) spared, **5**. 305; (195) Hannibal flees to, **9**. 403–5
Cercinium, in Thessaly: (200) **9**. 119
Cerco: *see* Lutatius.
Cerdiciates, Ligurians: (197) **9**. 245
Cerdubelus, Spanish commander: (206) surrenders Castulo, **8**. 87
Ceremia, in Illyricum: (171) **13**. 3
Ceres: (485) property of Sp. Cassius consecrated to, **1**. 355; (217) in *lectisternium* with Mercury, **5**. 235; (216) rite of, omitted, 383, **9**. 435; (214) worshipped at Henna, **6**. 297; (202) dict. conducts festival of, **8**. 515; (200) mysteries of, at Eleusis, **9**. 45, 139; (191) Books demand fast for, **10**. 263; (104) collection (*stips*) for, **14**. 275–7; (99) 281; (92) 289. Temple of Ceres, Liber, and Libera in Rome: (449) aedd. pl. sell confiscated property at, **2**. 183, receive decrees of Senate at, 185, (296) make dedications from fines at, **4**. 447, (210) **7**. 229, (208) 357, (197) **9**. 345; (174) prayer at, **12**. 281. Prodigies: (206) **8**. 47; (182) **12**. 5
Cerindones, Spaniards: (76) **14**. 195
Cermalus, in Rome: (196) **9**. 349
Cerretanus: *see* Aemilius, Aulius.
Cerrinii, Herennius and Minius, Campanians: (186) leaders in Bacchic conspiracy, **11**. 253, 269, 273
Certima, Celtiberian town: (179) **12**. 149–51
Certis riv.: name for Baetis riv., **8**. 89
Cesennia: (305) **4**. 345
Cethegus: *see* Cornelius.
Chaereas: (179) agent of Philip, **12**. 167
Chaeronea, in Boeotia: (192) Aetolians at, **10**. 133; (191) Antiochus at, 191; (172) envoys from, **12**. 421
Chalbus, chief of Tartesii: (216) **6**. 89
Chalcedon, in Bithynia: (171) triremes of, in Roman fleet, **12**. 465; (74) M. Aurelius Cotta defeated near, **14**. 117
Chalcioecus, temple of Athena in Sparta: (192) Aetolians slain at, **10**. 111
Chalcis: in Euboea, **8**. 21; mother city of Cumae, **4**. 85–7; (208) Philip moves to, **7**. 333; (207) Philip strengthens, **8**. 19; P. Sulpicius Galba fails to take, 23–5, 33, 35; (200) held by Philip, **9**. 65; C. Claudius Cento raids, 65–9; Philip asks Achaean garrison for, 75; (198) Carystus garrisoned from, 197; Philocles in, 199; (197) one of the 'fetters of Greece', 265, 475; (196–195) Rome holds, 361–3, 475; (194) Flamininus evacuates, 543, 547–9, **10**. 49; (192) Roman envoys in, 89; Aetolians fail to take, 101, 111–7, 133–5, 143, 165, 183; garrisoned by Eumenes, 115–7; anecdote of, 141; in spite of reinforcements, 145–7, surrenders to Antiochus, 149, 171–3, 179, **13**. 317; (191) Antiochus in, **10**. 169–71, 173, 189, 195, 201, 217, leaving at approach of M'. Acilius Glabrio, 221; Flamininus at, 247; (190) P. Scipio (Afr. f.) sails from, 389; (172) envoy C. Valerius Laevinus near, **12**. 343; conference of Romans and Boeotians at, 421–5; (171) Roman and allied forces at, 425, 463–5; (170) envoys from, accuse governors, **13**. 27–33; (169) fleet at, 91, 95; (168) envoys to Egypt sail from, 185; (167) L. Aemilius Paulus at, 341; (146) aids Achaeans; is destroyed, **14**. 41. *See* Eubulidas.
Chaldaeans (astrologers): (139) ordered from Italy, **14**. 53
Chamates: (44) supposititious son of C. Marius, **14**. 147
Chaonia, in Epirus: (199) Philip occupies, **9**. 165; (169) supplies men for Roman army, **13**. 75, 83
Characa, in Tempê: (169) **13**. 109
Chariclitus, Rhodian admiral: (190) defeats Hannibal, **10**. 357–61
Charidemus: (149) **14**. 31
Charilaus, of Palaepolis: (326) surrenders Palaepolis, **4**. 101–3
chariots: (295) used by Gauls, **4**. 467; scythed, used by early Romans, **14**. 175, (190) by Antiochus, **10**. 409–17
Chariteles: murdered by Philip, **9**. 217
Charopus, of Epirus: (199) gives information, **9**. 167; (198) 183, 193

INDEX

Chauci, Germans: (12) subdued, **14.** 167

Chaunus mts., in Celtiberia: (179) **12.** 155

Chelidoniae, Cilician cape: (197) **9.** 331; (196) 387

Chersonesus, Thracian: (c. 275) occupied by Galatians, **11.** 53; (200) Philip moves towards, **9.** 51; (196) occupied by Antiochus, 381, as part of inheritance, 385, 565; (191) Antiochus sets out for, **10.** 275; (190) L. Scipio crosses, 387; occupied, 395, 455; (188) given to Eumenes, **11.** 133, 301, 307; Cn. Manlius Volso gathers ships at, 135

Cherusci, Germans: (12) **14.** 167

chickens, sacred: (368) signs from, **3.** 345; (325) **4.** 115; (320) 213; (293) 513–7; (216) **5.** 341; (209) **7.** 277; (176) **12.** 243; (249) ordered drowned, **4.** 557–9, **14.** 181; (137) flee coop, 55, 257. *See pullarius.*

Chimarus: (168) agent of Perseus, **13.** 169

Chios: (208) sends Philip envoys, **7.** 333–5; (197) Attalus demands replacement of ships lost off, **9.** 253; (191) Roman fleet at, **10.** 279, 285; (190) 331, 381–3; (179) **12.** 161; (190) granary of Romans, **10.** 369; pirates plunder, 369–71; (188) loyalty of, **11.** 133; (168) Perseus drives transports of Eumenes on, **13.** 181–3

chronological difficulties of early history, **1.** 285

Chumstinctus: (11–10) tribune of Nervii, **14.** 167

Cia: (200) Rhodians at, **9.** 49

Ciani: *see* Cios.

Cibyra, in Asia Minor: (189) forced to give supplies, **11** 45–7; (167) aids Caunians against Rhodes, **13.** 333

Cicereius, C.: (173) pr. for Sardinia and Corsica, **12.** 283, 293, 311; (172) triumphs on Alban Mt., 351; envoy to Illyricum, 365; (167) dedicates temple to Moneta, 311, **13.** 295; (167) adviser on Illyrian peace, 299, 337–9

Cicero: *see* Calvius, Tullius.

Cicurinus: *see* Veturius, — Crassus, — Geminus.

Cierium, in Thessaly: (198) surrenders to Flamininus, **9.** 195; (191) captured by Antiochus, **10.** 185; surrenders to M' Acilius Glabrio, 199

Cilicia: (197) Antiochus seizes cities of, **9.** 331–3; (193) Antiochus in, **10.** 39; (190) he gets ships and men in, 335, 409; (102) pirates of, defeated, **14.** 81, 279; (78–75) 115, 117; (67) 123; (66) Pompey takes, from Tigranes, 125. *Also*: **10.** 355, **11.** 65. *See* Soli.

Cilnii, of Arretium: (302) cause dissension, **4.** 367–9; reconciled to plebs, 377

Cimbii, port in Spain: (206) **8.** 149

Cimbri: (113) defeat Cn. Papirius Carbo, **14.** 75, 271, (109) M. Junius Silanus, 77; (106) capture M. Aurelius; (105) defeat Cn. Manlius and Q. Servilius Caepio at Arausio, 79; (104–103) feared in Rome; plunder Gaul and Spain, 81, 277; (103) return to Gaul, 81; (101) defeated by Q. Lutatius Catulus and C. Marius, 81–3, 279

Cimetra, Samnite city: (296) **4.** 413

Ciminian forest, in Etruria: (310) Q. Fabius Maximus crosses, **4.** 301–5, 309–11, 315, 447

Ciminius, Mt., in Etruria: (310) **4.** 305

Cimolos, is. in Aegean: (108) **14.** 273

Cincian law: **9.** 423, **8.** 289[2]

Cincibilus, Gallic king: (170) complains of Roman plundering, **13.** 19–21

Cincinnatus: *see* Manlius, Quinctius.

Cincius, P.: (217) commands fleet, **5.** 305

— Alimentus, L., the historian: (210) pr. for Sicily and fleet, **7.** 89, 109, 111, 217, (209) 233, 239; (208) besieges Locri, 315, 327; envoy to cos., 329; captured by Hannibal, **5.** 111. Cited: (363) **3.** 367; (218) **5.** 111

— —, M.: (204) tr. pl., aids investigation at Locri, **8.** 287–9; (193) at Pisae, reports Ligurians in arms, **9.** 557–9

Cineas: (280) envoy of Pyrrhus, **4.** 549, **9.** 423

Cingilia, town of Vestini: (325) **4.** 113

Cinna: *see* Cornelius, Helvius.

Circê: (534–510) claimed as ancestress by Octavius Mamilius, **1.** 173

INDEX

Circeii, in Latium: called Circeium, **14**. 227; (534–510) colonists sent to, **1**. 195, (488) expelled from, 345; (385) aids Volsci, **3**. 235, 239, 255, (383) 269; (340) home of Latin praetor, L. Numisius, **4**. 11; (209) fails to meet Roman demands, **7**. 243–7; (204) required to furnish increased quota, **8**. 263–7
Circeium, Cape: site of Circeii, **14**. 227
circus: games of, antedate drama, **3**. 361
Circus Flaminius: *see* Flaminian Circus.
— Maximus: (616–578) marked out, **1**. 129; (534–510) seats constructed, 193; (330) *carceres* built, **4**. 79; (295) temple of Venus near, 479; (212) games of Apollo in, **6**. 387 (cp. **8**. 513); (202) votive games in, **8**. 465; flooded, 513; (196) arch built in, **9**. 349; (191) temple to Juventas in, **10**. 263; (174) new equipment in, **12**. 279. Prodigy: (182) 5, **14**. 241
Cirrha, port of Delphi: (172) **12**. 335
Cirta, in Numidia: (204) Masinissa near, **8**. 335; (203) he takes, 407; (201) presented to him, 537; (112) Adherbal besieged in, **14**. 77
Cissis, in Spain: (218) **5**. 181
Cissus, Ionian port: (191) **10**. 279–81
citadel (Arx) in Rome: standard displayed on, to summon *comitia centuriata*, **11**. 261; (753–717) held by Sabines, **1**. 43–7, 119; (460) seized by Ap. Herdonius, **2**. 53–67; (419) slave plot to take, checked, 403; (390) held against Gauls, **3**. 131–65, 169, 171, 175, 183, 231, 241, 249, 341; men of, on college for Capitoline games, 169; (384) secret meeting of plebs on, 261; patricians barred from living on, 267; (345) temple of Juno Moneta on, 453; (323) crowded with armed men, **4**. 145; (217) temple of Concord on, **5**. 311; (211) garrisoned, **7**. 35–7; (201) foliage from, used by fetiales, **8**. 531. References to, as center of Rome: **1**. 243, **2**. 231, 263, **4**. 133, 385
Cithaeron, Mt., in Greece: (200) **9**. 77
Citium, in Macedon: (171) **12**. 447–51
Citium, Mt., in Epirus: (169) **13**. 77
citizenship (*civitas*): (640–616) granted to many Latins, **1**. 121, (509) individuals, **1**. 235, (458) **2**. 99, (210) **7**. 219, (509) freed slaves, **1**. 235, (445) cities or tribes, **2**. 265, (389) **3**. 207, (381) 289, (338) **4**. 57–61, (329) 81–5, (303) 361, (before 216) **6**. 15, (188) **11**. 119, (89) **14**. 101, 105–7, (340) Campanian knights, **4**. 47, (215) **6**. 107; (306) Hernici prefer own laws to, **4**. 339, 347; (304) enforced as punishment, 347; (216) not accepted, **6**. 69; (195) refused to Latins in Roman colony, **9**. 529; (188) SC. not needed for grant of, by people, **11**. 119; (177) conditions for grant to Latins, Samnites, and Paelignians, **12**. 207–15; illegally gained, 207–11; (91) extension to all Italy proposed, **14**. 89; granted, 101, 105–7
citizenship without vote (*civitas sine suffragio*): (338) **4**. 61; (332) 71; (306) 339; (188) replaced by full rights, **11**. 119
Cius, in Bithynia: (200) mistreated by Philip, **9**. 91, 217, 257–9; (196) Prusias ordered to free, 359. *See* Herodorus.
Civil War: (51–44) **14**. 135–47, 305–11
Clampetia, in Bruttium: (204) recovered from Carthage, **8**. 357, 439
Clastidium, cis-Alpine town: (222) M. Marcellus defeats Gauls at, **4**. 561, **7**. 313, **8**. 249; (218) magazine at, surrendered to Hannibal, **5**. 143; (197) yields to cos. Q. Minucius Rufus, **9**. 243–5, 249
Claudia: (247) fined, **4**. 559
— Quinta: (204) receives Idaean Mother, **8**. 261
Claudian camp, above Suessula: (215) urban legions sent to, **6**. 105; Q. Fabius Maximus at, 137, 163; (212) C. Claudius Nero called from, 425
— tribe, Old: (505) **1**. 271
— violence: (185) **11**. 321
Claudii: (505–503) of Sabine origin, admitted to patriciate, **1**. 271, **2**. 267, **4**. 387; (449) traditionally hostile to plebs, **2**. 195–9; (439) 309; (416) 415; (368) **3**. 337; (310) **4**. 291–3; (296) 413–5
Claudius, C.: (310) leg., **4**. 301
—, C.: (211) flamen of Jupiter, abdicates, **7**. 91

INDEX

Claudius, L.: 174) pr. for Sicily, **12**. 253
—, M.: (449) client of Xvir Ap. Claudius, claims Verginia, **2**. 145–57; exiled, 199
—, M.: (137) pr., killed by lightning, **14**. 257
—, P.: (207) pref. soc. at Grumentum, **7**. 375
—, P.: 196) tr. mil., slain by Boi, **9**. 373
—, Q.: (218) tr. pl., limits size of senators' ships, **5**. 189
— Asellus: (215) fights duel with Campanian, **6**. 159–61, 197–9
— —, Ti.: (207) tr. mil. at Grumentum, **7**. 375; (205) aed. pl., **8**. 249
— —, Ti.: (206) pr. for Sardinia, **8**. 43–5
— —, Ti.: (140) tr. pl., tries to hold cos. from province, **14**. 51
— Caecus, Ap., cos. 307, 296; (312) cens., builds roads and aqueduct, revises senate list, **4**. 275–7, appointing sons of freedmen and distributing *humiles* in all tribes, 353; (310) continues as sole cens., 289–99; (307) cos., 331, 341; (300) opposes lex Ogulnia, 381–9; (298) interrex, 399; (296) cos. ii, 413–5; bickers with colleague through Etruscan campaign, 423–31; reports danger, 439; more competent in Rome than in field, 443; (295) pr., 443, in Etruria, 451–3; at Rome, exaggerates Etruscan danger, 455; opposes Q. Fabius Maximus, 459; defeats Samnites, 477–9; (280) opposes terms with Pyrrhus, 549–51; blindness of, 277, 549
— Caudex, Ap.: (264) cos., **9**. 3
— Cento (Centho), Ap., pr. 175: (179) aed. cur., **12**. 179; (174) procos., defeats Celtiberians, 275; receives ovation, 281–3; (172) envoy to Perseus, 359–63; (170) leg., campaigns without success in Illyricum, **13**. 35–7, 41, 75, (169) and Epirus, 75–7, 81–3; (168) 155; replaced, 157, 189
— —, C., cos. 240: (217) interrex, **5**. 313; (213) dict. com. c., **6**. 345
— —, C.: (200) leg., protects Athens, **9**. 43; raids Chalcis, 65–9
Claudius Crassus, Ap.: (424) tr. mil. c. p., **2**. 373; praef. urb., 377
— —, Ap., tr. mil. c. p., 403: (416) hostile to plebs, **2**. 413; (403) **3**. 9; tr. mil. c. p., 3; in Rome, addresses people during siege of Veii, 9–25; (396) urges sale of spoil of Veii, 69–71; (368) opposes re-election of tribb. pl. C. Licinius Stolo and L. Sextius, 337–47
— — Inregillensis, Ap., cos. 349: (362) dict., defeats Hernici, **3**. 377–81; (349) cos., 439; dies, 443
— — — Sabinus, Ap., Xvir, 451–449: (471) cos., hostile to plebs, **1**. 409–15; defeated by Volsci because of mutiny, 415–21; (470) opposes land law; accused by plebs; dies (?), 423–5; (451) cos. ii, **2**. 109; Xvir leg. scrib., 109–11, 413; presides at own re-election, 115–7; tyrannical plans of, 117–21, **4**. 291; (449) presides over stormy Senate, **2**. 129–37; remains in city, 139; lust of, for Verginia, 143–61, 171, 205; accused by L. Verginius in camp, 163–7; resigns, 179; accused by Verginius, 187–91, **3**. 263; appeal of, denied, **2**. 191–3; kills self; property confiscated, 197
— Flamen, Q.: (208) pr. for Tarentum, **7**. 299, 301, 329; (207) 357, 363, 373; sends envoys of Hasdrubal to C. Claudius Nero, 381; (206) in Tarentum, **8**. 45, 49
— Glaber, C.: (73) pr., defeated by Spartacus, **14**. 119
— Glicia, M.: (249) dict., **4**. 557
— Hortator, C.: (337) mag. eq., **4**. 63
— Inregillensis, C.: (337) dict. **4**. 63
— — Sabinus, C.: (460) cos., **2**. 51; opposes Ap. Herdonius, 53–65, 67; prevents consideration of Terentilian law, 65; opposes re-election of coss., 75; (451) candidate for Xviri, 117; opposes Xvir Ap. Claudius, 131–3; (449) seeks grace for Claudius, 195–7, **3**. 263; opposes grant of triumph by people, **2**. 215; (445) urges arming the coss., 277
— Lepidus, M.: (189) envoy of propr. in Aetolia to Senate, **10**. 433
— Marcellinus, M.: (185) pr., **11**. 285
— Marcellus, C.: (50) cos., **14**. 305

INDEX

Claudius Marcellus, M.: (331) cos., **4.** 71; (327) dict. com. c., 91

— —, M., cos. 222, 215, 214, 210, 208: (222) cos., defeats Gauls, **4.** 561; vowing temple to Honor and Valor, **7.** 313, **8.** 249; (216) pr. for Sicily, **5.** 319, and the fleet, 385; goes to Canusium, 387; withstands Hannibal at Nola, **6.** 45–55, 153, 499, **7.** 115, 207; moves to Suessula, **6.** 55–7; unable to aid Casilinum, 65; reports to Senate, 79, 85; (215) cos. suf., resigns because of *vitium*, 107–9, **7.** 301; procos., **6.** 105; goes to Nola, 109, 137; raids land of Hirpini and Samnites, 143–5; drives Hannibal back from before Nola, 149–57; 163; (214) cos. iii, 203–5, 313; saves Nola, 215–7, 227–9; slave volunteers, 219; takes Casilinum, 235–7; ill at Nola, 237–9; receives Sicily as prov., 241, 295; sends envoys to Syracuse, 263, 267; takes Leontini, 269–71, **7.** 115; letter from, forged, **6.** 275; lays siege to Syracuse, 283–5, 289–91; recovers some cities, 287–9; winters, 301; (213) procos. for Sicily, 315–7; (212) 349; forwards petition of legions of Cannae, 357–65; resumes siege of Syracuse, 429–43; pestilence in army of, 443–5; Bomilcar withdraws before, 447–9; takes Syracuse, 449–63, **7.** 121; grief at death of Archimedes, **6.** 461; settles affairs of Sicily, 495; transports spoils to Rome, 495, **7.** 81, 121–3, 275; defeats Hanno, **6.** 497–501; (211) procos. for Sicily, **7.** 5; triumphs on Alban Mt., granted ovation, 79–83; (210) cos. iv, 87, 101; accused of cruelty by Sicilians, 101–3, 111–23, 127, **11.** 149; veterans of, discharged, **7.** 111; becomes patron of Syracuse, 125; receives fleet and Italy as prov., 111–5; conducts levy, 123, takes Salapia, 143–5, 203; sends ships to fleet, 147; receives refugees from Herdonea, 207; follows Hannibal into Apulia, 207–13; names dict. com. c., 223; suggests loans to state by citizens, **8.** 267, **9.** 41; restores M. Livius Salinator to city, **7.** 347; (209) procos., 231–3; receives funds from sacred treasury, 249; defeated by Hannibal, 253–9; defeats Hannibal, 259–67, 315; prevents Etruscan revolt, 299; (208) cos. v, 297–9, **8.** 465, with Italy as prov., **7.** 301; joins army at Venusia, 313; slain, 317–23, 327, 345, 115, **8.** 119; augur, **7.** 355; ring of, used by Hannibal, 323–7, (205) veterans of, enlisted by P. Scipio (Afr.), **8.** 209

Claudius Marcellus, M.: (216) aed. pl., **6.** 103

— —, M., cos. 196: (208) tr. mil., escapes when father is slain, **7.** 319–21; delivers eulogy for father, 323; leads his army to Venusia, 329; (205) dedicates temple, **6.** 495, **8.** 249; (204) tr. pl., assigned to Locrian investigation, 287–9; (200) aed. cur., **9.** 147; (198) pr. for Sicily, 173, 175, 237; (196) cos. with Italy as prov., 341, 345–7; campaigns against Gauls, 373–7; triumphs, 377–9; pontiff, 389, **12.** 225; presides at elections, **9.** 391; (195) envoy to Carthage, 403; (193) leg. against Boi, **10.** 11; accuses coss., 17, 21–3; (189) cens., 469–73, **11.** 95, 121, **12.** 213; (177) dies, **12.** 225

— —, M., cos. 183: (188) pr. urb., **11.** 115, 117, enforces fetial law, 145; (183) cos. **14.** 241, with Liguria as prov., **11.** 363–5, 391–5; persuades Gauls to return home, **14.** 5, **11.** 391–3, 283; holds elections, 397; (182) procos. for Gaul, **12.** 5, 53, 79–81; (173) envoy to Aetolians and Achaeans, 307; (169) leg. in Macedon, **13.** 97–9; Xvir sac., dies, 149

— —, M., cos. 166, 155, 152: (177) pontiff, **12.** 225; (171) tr. pl., 387; (169) pr. for Spain, **13.** 39, 49, 53; (168) takes Marcolica, 257; (166) cos., 403, **14.** 245; defeats Gauls, 11; (152) cos. iii, 251; reduces Celtiberians, 19; (148) envoy to Masinissa; drowns, 33, 37

— —, M.: (90) captured by Samnites, **14.** 91

— —, M.: (51) cos., proposes law for Caesar's return, **14.** 135; 46) murdered, 145

INDEX

Claudius Marcellus, M., son of Octavia: (23) dies, **14**. 167

— Nero, Ap., pr. 195: (197) tr. mil., at conference with Philip, **9**. 261; returns to Rome, 265; (195) pr. for Farther Spain, 391–3, 445, 461; (189) Xvir for settlement of Asia, **10**. 461–3, **11**. 123–35, 153, 161, 205, 301

— —, C., cos. 207: (214) commands cavalry before Nola, **6**. 227–9; (212) pr. for Campania, 345, 347; joins in siege of Capua, 425; (211) commands cavalry in Campania, **7**. 19; takes troops to Spain, 65, 75; tricked by Hasdrubal, 65–9, 387; replaced, 77; (209) leg. at Canusium, 263; (208) elected cos., reconciled with colleague elect, 347–53; (207) cos., 357, **9**. 39; moves to Venusia, **7**. 371–3; defeats Hannibal at Grumentum, 373–7; follows Hannibal to Metapontum and Canusium, 377–81; captures Hasdrubal's messengers, 381; marches to join cos. M. Livius Salinator, 381–3, 387–93, causing panic in Rome, 383–7, 407; with Salinator defeats Hasdrubal, 393–405, **8**. 175; returns to Apulia, **7**. 407; thanksgiving decreed in Rome; sends head of Hasdrubal to Hannibal, 411; celebrates joint triumph with Salinator, **8**. 37–41; names dict. com. c., 43; resigns army to successor, 45, 49; (204) cens., quarrels with colleague, 351–7, **11**. 225; contracts for temple of Idaean Mother, **10**. 261; (201) leg. to Ptolemy Epiphanes, **9**. 7

— —, Ti., cos. 202: (204) pr. for Sardinia, **8**. 249, 255, 257; sends grain to Africa, 347; (202) cos. with African fleet as prov., 457, 461–3, 519, 533; celebrates votive games, 465; ordered to Africa with fleet, 511; (201) brings fleet home, 513

— —, Ti.: (181) pr. for Sicily, **12**. 59; (172) (?) envoy to east, 347, 365–7, 427–9

— —, Ti.: (178) pr. pereg., **12**. 179; defends Liguria, 197; (177) procos. for Liguria, 221–3 (176) 227–9; (172) (?) envoy to east, 347, 365–7, 427–9

— —, Ti.: (167) pr. for Sicily, **13**. 297

Claudius Pulcher: *see* Claudius Glaber, pr. 73

— —, Ap., cos. 212: (216) tr. mil., leads survivors of Cannae, **5**. 373, 377; father-in-law of Pacuvius Calavius of Capua, **6**. 7; (215) pr. for Sicily, 81, 105, 109, 133, 345; fails to take Bomilcar, 143; raises siege of Regium, 177–9; sends envoy to Hieronymus, 193; concentrates forces, 197; (214) leg., sends Syracusan envoys to Marcellus, 263; protects allies, 267; called to Leontini, 271; sends envoys to Syracuse, 281; at Pachynum, 291; seeks consulship, 301; (212) cos., 345–7, **7**. 307; in Samnium, **6**. 389–91, 395–7, and Campania, 401–3, 411, 415–9, 425; holds elections, 501; (211) continues siege of Capua, 501, **7**. 3, 19; wounded, 23, 31; takes Capua; dies, 51, 57, 61, 127

— — Ap., cos. 185: (196) leg. of Flamininus, **9**. 357, (195) 489, (194) 547, (191) of M. Baebius Tamphilus, **10**. 187–9, 195, of M' Acilius Glabrio, 227, 245; (187) pr. for Tarentum, **11**. 143–5; (185) cos., 283, 385, **13**. 299, with Liguria as prov., **11**. 311, 317–9, 341; supports brother for consulship, 319–21; (184) heads embassy to Philip, 323–7, and Achaeans, 329–41; (174) envoy to Aetolians, **12**. 273; (173) settles discord in Thessaly, and Perrhaebia, 307

— —, Ap.: (143) cos., **14**. 47, 255; subdues Salassi, 47; (140) prevents extra levy, 51; (133) IIIvir agr. assig., 63

— —, Ap.: (130) cos. suf., **14**. 261

— —, Ap., cos. 79: (87) propr., loses army to Cinna, **14**. 99; (77–76) procos., defeats Thracians, 115

— —, Ap.: (54) cos., **14**. 305

— —, C., cos. 177: (195) augur, **9**. 395, **13**. 405; (180) pr. suf. pereg., investigates poisonings, **12**. 117, and piracy, 133; (177) cos. with Histria as prov., 207, 211; limits acquisition of citizenship, 211–5, 319; leaves for province without proper forms, 215–7; returns to Rome; takes over province, 217–9; defeats Histrians and Ligurians, 221–3, 237;

INDEX

triumphs, 225; holds elections, 227; (176) defeats Ligurians, 227, 235–9; (171) leg. of P. Licinius Crassus against Perseus, 443; **13**. 3[1]; (169) censor, 49–55, 143; accused by tr. pl., tried, acquitted, 55–61; disagrees with colleague about freedmen in city tribes, 293–5; (168) request for usual extension of term vetoed, 295; (167) envoy to advise on Macedonian terms, 299, 345–7, 355; summons Achaean partizans for trial, 355–7; dies, 405
Claudius Pulcher, C.: (92) cos., **14**. 289
— —, P.: (249) cos., drowns sacred chickens; defeated by Punic fleet, **4**. 557, 559, **5**. 341, **14**. 181
— —, P., cos. 184: (189) aed. cur., condemns grain dealers, **11**. 115; (188) pr. pereg., 115–7; (185) candidate for cos., aided by brother, 319–21; (184) cos., 321, 385, **14**. 7, with Liguria as prov., **11**. 341, 363; introduces envoys of Philip, Eumenes, and Thrace, 321–3; inactive, 363; (181) IIIvir col. deduc., **12**. 89
— Quadrigarius, Q., the historian: translates Annals of Acilius, **6**. 493, **10**. 41. Cited: (367) **3**. 349; (330) **4**. 77; (321) 179; (294) 503; (212) **6**. 493; (197) **9**. 303; (196) 361; 375; (193) **10**. 41; (189) **11**. 81; (188) 141–3; (169) **13**. 137–9
— Sabinus Inregillensis, Ap., cos. 495: (504) a Sabine, comes to Rome; becomes Senator, **1**. 271, **4**. 387; (495) cos., raids Volsci, **1**. 287; enforces law of debt, 293–5, 303–7, 309; quarrels with colleague, 305–7; (494) urges appointing dictator against plebs, 313; (480) suggests checking tribunes by tribunes, 363–5, **2**. 413
Clausal riv., in Illyricum: (168) **13**. 191
Clausus, Attius, original name of Ap. Claudius Sabinus Inregillensis
clavus (nail): (363) driven into temple of Jupiter Optimus Maximus, **3**. 365–7; (331) **4**. 73; (363) into temple of Nortia, **3**. 367. *See* dictator clavi figendi causa.
Clazomenae, in Ionia: (188) **11**. 133
Cleomedon: (198) envoy of Philip to Achaeans, **9**. 213, 215, 219
Cleomenes III, tyrant of Sparta: (222) defeated by Antigonus Doson, **9**. 483, 487, **12**. 165
Cleon, leader of slave revolt, (136) **14**. 59
Cleonae, in Argolis: (197) plundered by Macedonians, **9**. 313; Achaeans move to, 315–7; (195) Flamininus at, 479
Cleonymus, the Spartan: (302) raid of, on Thuriae fails, **4**. 363; defeated by Veneti, 365–7
Cleopatra, wife of Alexander of Epirus: (326) receives his ashes, **4**. 97–9
—, *see* Arsinoê III Cleopatra
— I, of Egypt: (190) congratulates Rome on defeat of Antiochus, **10**. 299–301
— II, of Egypt: (168) protests actions of Antiochus IV, **13**. 151–3; thanks Rome for aid, 285–7; (131) drives Ptolemy VIII from Egypt, **14**. 67
—, daughter of Ptolemy VI: (148–147) marries Demetrius Nicator, **14**. 43; (126–125) murders him, 71
— III, of Egypt: (131) violated by Ptolemy VIII, **14**. 67
— VII, of Egypt: (48) driven out by Ptolemy XIII, **14**. 139; restored by Caesar, 141; (36) revels with M. Antonius; (34) son of Antonius and, made king of Armenia, 161; (33–31) Antonius' passion for, 163; (30) prisoner of Octavius, 223; commits suicide; Octavius triumphs over, 163
Cleoptolemus, of Chalcis: (191) marries daughter to Antiochus, **10**. 189
Cleuas, general of Perseus: (169) **13**. 77, 81–3
clients: (504) Ap. Claudius Sabinus brings many, **1**. 271; (491) used by patricians against plebs, 335; (461) **2**. 49; (472) lose power in tribal assembly, **1**. 409; (440) Sp. Maelius buys grain in Etruria through, **2**. 301; (391) unable to protect M. Furius Camillus, **3**. 113
Clitae, in Cassandrea: (169) **13**. 125
Clitoris, in Arcadia: (184) **11**. 329
Clivius Urbius, *see* Urbius, Clivius

INDEX

Clivus Capitolinus: (460) leads to Capitoline, **2**. 63; (174) paved, **12**. 279
— Publicius: (211) leads to Aventine, **7**. 37; (207) 361; (203) burned, **8**. 459
Cloacina, shrine of: (449) **2**. 159
Clodianus: *see* Cornelius Lentulus.
Clodius Licinus, C., the historian. Cited: (204) **8**. 295
— Pulcher, P., tr. pl. 58: (63) acquitted; (59) becomes plebeian, **14**. 127; (58) tr. pl., exiles Cicero, 129; (52) slain, 133
Cloelia: (508) courage of, **1**. 261–3, **4**. 203
Cloelii: (672–640) from Alba, **1**. 107
Cloelius, P.: (c. 220) first to marry within 7th degree, **14**. 181
— Gracchus: (458) leader of Aequi, **2**. 87; captured, led in triumph, 97–9
— Siculus, P.: (378) tr. mil. c. p., **3**. 303
— —, P.: (180) rex. sac., **12**. 135
— —, Q.: (498) cos., **1**. 285
— —, Q.: (378) cens., **3**. 303
— —, T.: (444) tr. mil. c. p., abdicates because of *vitium*, **2**. 279–81; (442) IIIvir col. deduc., **2**. 295–7
— Tullus: (438) envoy to Fidenae, **2**. 313
Clondicus: (179) chief of Bastarnae, **12**. 177; (168) demands pay from Perseus before serving, **13**. 175–7
clothing: (190) as tribute, **10**. 315; (169) as military supply, **13**. 141
Cluilian trench: (672–640) Albans camp at, **1**. 79; (488) Volsci at, 345
Cluilius, an Aequian: (443) leads Volsci, defeated, **2**. 289–93
—, C.: (672–640) Alban king, **1**. 77–81
Clunia, in Spain: (75) **14**. 115
Clupea, African port: (208) Punic fleet defeated off, **7**. 329–31
— in Africa: (204) Masinissa defeated near, **8**. 331
Clusium, in Etruria: (508) Lars Porsinna of, threatens Rome, **1**. 245–7; (c. 396) refuses to aid Veii, **3**. 121; (391) seeks Roman aid against Gauls, **3**. 115, 121–3; envoys to, fight Gauls, 123–7; (295) Gauls defeat L. Scipio near, **4**. 455, 459–61; deserters from, come to Q. Fabius Maximus, 461; defeated by Cn. Fulvius Maximus, 463, 475; (205) promises P. Scipio (Afr.) supplies, **8**. 193; (82) Sulla defeats Carbo near, **14**. 109. Prodigy: (83) **14**. 297
Cluvia, Pacula, of Capua: (210) aids Roman captives, **7**. 127–9
Cluviae, in Samnium: (311) **4**. 281
Cluvius, Sp.: (172) pr. for Sardinia, **12**. 317, 321
— Saxula, C.: (173) pr. ii, pereg., **12**. 283, 293; (168) leg. at Pydna, **13**. 225
Clytus, praetor of Acarnania: (191) supports Antiochus, **10**. 191–3
Cnidus, in Macedon: (200) **9**. 81
—, in Caria: **9**. 81; (190) obeys propr. C. Livius Salinator, **10**. 335; ship of, with Rhodians, 353–5; (c. 150) Demetrius I of Syria sends son to, **14**. 43
Cnossos, in Crete: (68–67) **14**. 123. See Syllus.
Cobulatus riv., in Lycia: (189) **11**. 47
Cocceius Nerva, L.: (40) reconciles M. Antonius and Octavian, **14**. 221–3
Cocles: *see* Horatius
Codrio, in Macedon: (200) **9**. 81
Coela, name for Euboean gulf, **9**. 137
Coelê Syria: *see* Syria, Coelê
Coelius, L.: (169) leg. in Illyricum, **13**. 75
— Antipater, L., the historian. Cited: (218) **5**. 111; 137; 139; (217) 307; (216) **6**. 19; (211) **7**. 41; (208) 323; (205) **8**. 199; (204) 305; 315–7; 343
— Caldus, C.: *see* Caelius Caldus, C.
Coenus, of Perrhaebia: (168) aids L. Aemilius Paulus, **13**. 207
cohort: (446) elects centurions, **2**. 237; (362) 400 men in, **3**. 379; (293) **4**. 515
cohortes alariae: (293) **4**. 515
— *extraordinariae*: (194) **9**. 539; (181) **12**. 83
— *repentinae*: (178) **12**. 187
— *subsidiariae*: (314) **4**. 269
coinage: (406) no silver, **2**. 455; (269) silver first used for, **4**. 553; (216) shortage of, **6**. 73
Colchis: (66) **14**. 125
Collatia, in Latium: (616–578) taken

1. 135–7; (510) Lucretia ravished at, 199–207
Collatinus: *see* Tarquinius
Collina tribus: (220) freedmen assigned to, **4.** 561
Colline gate: (508) force posted at, **1.** 255; (477) battle with Etruscans near, 393; (468) Sabines almost reach, 429; (449) plebeians enter through, **2.** 171; (435) forces of Veii and Fidenae near; Romans muster outside, 327; (426) Romans from Veii camp before, 361; (390) Gauls enter, **3.** 141; (380) Praenestini advance on, 293; (360) battle with Gauls near, 389–91; (337) Vestal buried alive near, **4.** 63; (216) **5.** 385; (211) armies camp near, **7.** 35–7; Hannibal rides toward, 37; (202) preparations for games of Apollo outside, **8.** 513; (181) temple of Venus Erycina near, **12.** 103; (82) Sulla defeats Samnites at, **14.** 109, 173. Prodigies: (177) **12.** 213; (17) **14.** 319
Colobatus riv., *see* Cobulatus riv.
colonies: (753–717) sent out by Romulus, **1.** 43
—, Latin: (300) relieve pressure at Rome, **4.** 379; (209) 12, refuse to meet quotas, **7.** 243–5, (204) are required to furnish doubled quotas, **8.** 263–7, and conduct own census, 353; (197) supporters of Hannibal barred from, **9.** 343. Establishment of: (753) Crustumium, Antemnae, **1.** 43; (534–510) Signia, Circeii, 195; (494) Velitrae, 319; (492) Norba, 331; (442) Ardea, **2.** 295; (418) Labici, 411; (395) on Volscian frontier, **3.** 83; (385) Satricum, 251; (383) Nepete, 269; (379) Setia, 301; (334) Cales, **4.** 67; (328) Fregellae, 85, 89; (313) Suessa, Pontiae; (312) Interamna Sucasina, 273; (303) Sora, Alba (in Aequis), 361; (302, 298) Carseoli, 369, 403; (299) Narnia, 393; (290) Castrum, Hadria, 547; (273) Cosa, Posidonia, 551; (268) Ariminum, Beneventum, (264) Aesernia, 553; (240) Spoletium, 559; (220) Cremona, Placentia, 561, **10.** 429; (194) in Bruttium; near Thurii, **9.** 553; (193) Castrum Frentinum, **10.** 25; (189) Bononia, 429, 469; (181) Aquileia, **11.** 395, **12.** 103; Gravisca, 89; (180) Pisa, 135–7; (171) Carteia, **13.** 13; (121) Carthage (Junonia), **14.** 71
colonies, Roman: (207) effort to levy soldiers from, **7.** 363; (195) citizenship denied Latins in, **9.** 529. Establishment of: Fidenae, **1.** 97, **2.** 313; (640–616) Ostia, **1.** 123; (467) Antium, **2.** 5; (338) **4.** 59; (329) Anxur (Tarracina), 85; (296) Minturnae, Sinuessa, 439; (290) Sena, 547; (248) Brundisium, Fregenae, 559; (194) Buxentum, Croton, Liternum, Puteoli, Salernum, Sipontum, Tempsa, Volturnum, **9.** 533–5; (192) Vibo, **10.** 119; (184) Pisaurum, Potentia, **11.** 361–3; (183) Mutina, Parma, Saturnia, 395–7; (177) Luna, **12.** 225
Colophon: *see* Notium.
Columen, in Latium: (459) **2.** 81
columna rostrata Aemilia: (172) destroyed by lightning, **12.** 347–9
Combolomarus: (189) Galatian chief, **11.** 67
Combulteria, in Campania: (215) **6.** 135
Comê Macra, in Thessaly: (198) **9.** 191
Comenses, Gallic tribe: (196) support Insubres, defeated, **9.** 375, 379
comet: (147) **14.** 253; (44) 309–11
Cominium, in Samnium: (293) besieged and taken, **4.** 509–11, 515, 519, 525–9
— Ocritum, in Samnium: (212) **6.** 395
Cominius, L.: (325) tr. mil., **4.** 115
— Auruncus, Post.: (501) cos., **1.** 275; (493) ii, fights Volsci, 327–9
Cominus, *see* Pontius.
comitia centuriata: original formation of, **1.** 149–55; assemble when standard is displayed on citadel, **11.** 261; meet under auspices, **1.** 133, **2.** 71, **3.** 179; preceded by *contio*, **9.** 19–21, **13.** 313; (578–534) first meeting of, **1.** 155; meet in Campus Martius, **1.** 155; (384) **3.** 265; (355) 419; (304) **4.** 353; (215) **6.** 197; (200) **9.** 19–21; (460) meeting of, at Lake Regillus feared, **2.** 71; (510) called by pref. urb., **1.** 209, (509) by cos., **1.** 225, *and often*,

(210) by dict., **7**. 223; (510) elect coss., **1**. 209; (390) **3**. 179; (355) 419; (297) **4**. 403–5; (296) 439; (215) **6**. 197, 203; (210) **7**. 223; (190) **10**. 431; (509) elect cos. suf., **1**. 225; (299) **4**. 397; (399) elect tribb. mil. c. p., **3**. 47; (396) 63; (390) 179; (366) elect praetors, 357; (384) try cases of treason (*perduellio*), **3**. 265–7; (169) **13**. 59–61; (451) adopt Laws of Ten Tables, **2**. 113 (*cp*. 121); (449) decree that plebiscites shall bind the people, 183, 229; (427) act on war and peace, **2**. 357; (200) **9**. 17–25; (171) **12**. 379–81, 397; (339) *auctoritas patrum* to be given in advance, **4**. 53 (*cp*. **3**. 347); (304) corrupted by cens. Ap. Claudius, **4**. 353; (204) tribes as units in, **8**. 355; (179) change in organization of, **12**. 159

comitia curiata : (716) receive right to name king, **1**. 63; (640) elect Ancus, 113, (534) but not Tarquinius Superbus, 173; (390) recall Camillus, **3**. 157; deal with war, 179; (368) tribb. pl. would free, from *auctoritas patrum*, 347; (310) confer *imperium* on dict., **4**. 315

comitia tributa : (393) meet in Forum, **3**. 107, (304) **4**. 353, (357) before Sutrium, **3**. 411; (357) meetings outside city prohibited, **3**. 411; (461) meet on *dies comitiales*, **2**. 39; (472) called by trib. pl., **1**. 407, (449) **2**. 217, (170) **13**. 33, (449) by pont. max., **2**. 179, (357) by cos., **3**. 411; (471) patricians removed from, **1**. 421; (311) urban plebs distributed in all tribes of, (304) then restricted to four urban tribes, **4**. 353; (179) composition of, changed, **12**. 159; (472–471) plebeian magistrates elected in, **1**. 407–15; (449) **2**. 217; (491) act as court, **1**. 331–5; (461) **2**. 49; (323) **4**. 145; (189) **10**. 439–41; (180) **12**. 135; (170) **13**. 31, 33; (383) vote declaration of war, **3**. 269; (205) ratify peace, **8**. 255; (201) 529; (449) grant triumph, **2**. 215; (356) **3**. 415, **4**. 503; (300) increase number of priests, 389; (204) make provincial assignments, **8**. 257; (202) 461; (201) 519. *See : populus* (usually the same as *comitia tributa*), *concilium plebis* (often not distinguished by Livy from the *tributa*), tribe.

Comitium : (385) dict. summons M. Manlius to, **3**. 245; (217) crowd turns to, **5**. 223; (216) crowded, 397; scourging in, 385; (214) **6**. 237; (212) 367; (208) covered, **7**. 355; (204) coss. receive envoys in, **8**. 269; (187) statues in, **11**. 199; (181) ' Books of Numa ' burned in, **12**. 93. Prodigies : (194) **9**. 535; (104) **14**. 277

commercium : (338) many Latins lose, **4**. 61; (167) of Macedonian republics limited, **13**. 349

Compasium : (184) Achaeans kill Spartans at, **11**. 331

Compsa, in Samnium : (216) delivered to Hannibal, **6**. 3; (214) taken by cos. Q. Fabius Maximus, 237. Prodigies : (213) 317; (154) **14**. 251

Comum, in cis-Alpine Gaul : (196) **9**. 375

concilium plebis : (449) meets in Flaminian Meadows, **2**. 181; (212) meets on Capitol, **6**. 351; (169) **13**. 57; (460) convened by tr. pl., **2**. 57; (449) 181; (210) **7**. 221; (194) **9**. 553; (167) **13**. 369; (449) acts of, made binding on state, **2**. 183, 229; (311) urban plebs distributed to all tribes in, (305) then confined to four urban tribes, **4**. 353; (212) Latins in, vote in tribe picked by lot, **6**. 351; (472–471) plebeian magistrates elected in, **1**. 407–15; (449) **2**. 217; (304) **4**. 353; (213) **6**. 347; (471) quieted by T. Quinctius, and dismissed, **1**. 413; formed from *comitia tributa* by removal of patricians, 421, 411; (460) lex Terentilia proposed in, **2**. 57; (454) ex-consuls accused before, 105; (449) passes laws after expulsion of Xviri, 181; (371) considers laws of tribb. pl. Licinius and Sextius, **3**. 317; (368) 327–9, 333; threatened by dictator, 329–31; (362) ex-dictator accused before, 367, 371; (357) limits usury, 409; (217) elects co-dictator, **5**. 289–91; (212) ratifies exile, **6**. 351–5; (210) selects dict. com. c., **7**. 221–3; (209) acts on

Campanian lands, 251; (201) provincial command referred to, **8**. 521; (200) considers exemption for priest, **9**. 149; (196) ratifies peace, 345; (194) establishes Latin colonies, 553; (187) P. Scipio Africanus accused before, **11**. 181–5; (169) considers public contracts, **13**. 57; (167) grants *imperium* to *triumphator*, 369–73, 391. *See*: *comitia tributa*, plebiscite
concilium populi: *see populus*
Concord: (304) temples of, in precinct of Vulcan, **4**. 351, (217–216) and on Citadel, **5**. 311, **6**. 73; (214) altar of, in Syracuse, 245, 247. Prodigies: (211) **7**. 89; (183) **11**. 397, **14**. 241; (181) **12**. 61, **14**. 241
Condylus, above Tempê: (169) **13**. 109
Congonnetiacus, prince of Arverni: (121) arrest of, decreed, **14**. 73
Conpulteria, in Samnium: (214) **6**. 237
'Conquerors': *see* Nicatores
Conribilo, Spanish chief: (192) captured, **10**. 65
conscripti, *patres*: (509) term explained, **1**. 221
Consentia, in Bruttium: (326) taken by Alexander of Epirus, **4**. 95–7, (216) by Himilco, **6**. 101; (214) revolts to Hannibal; (213) returns to Rome, 341; (206) ravaged, **8**. 49; (204) submits, 357; (203) 439
Considius, Q.: (476) tr. pl., proposes land law; accuses T. Menenius Agrippa, **1**. 395
Consualia: (753–717) held by Romulus, **1**. 35
consuls: (510) first, elected, **1**. 209, **2**. 269; (509) original power of, **1**. 221; (469) plebs refuse to vote for, 429; (462) restriction on power of, proposed, **2**. 31 (*see* Terentilian law); (460) successive terms banned, 73–5; (458) dict. forces, to abdicate, 99; (455–454) tried and condemned after term, 105; (446) one, yields supreme command to other, 237; (445) patricians thwart demand for plebeian, 257–77, but permit substitution of tribb. mil. c. p., 277–9; (434) tribb. pl. prevent election of, 335; (409) 437; (375–371) **3**. 319; (392) Senate forces both, to abdicate, 111; (375–367) after long conflict, 317–47, (367) opened to plebeians, 349; (366) L. Sextius first plebeian, 349, 357, **4**. 387; (362) L. Genucius first plebeian, to conduct war, **3**. 375; (355) patricians only elected, 415; (354) 419; (353) 421; (351) 431; (349) 439; (343) 455; (349) dict. com. c. M. Furius Camillus declares self elected, 439, and on death of colleague rules as sole, 443; (348) M. Valerius Corvus becomes, at age 23, 447, 505; (342) election of two patrician, and re-election within ten years forbidden, 513, **4**. 405, **7**. 349; (340) Senate forces both, to abdicate, **4**. 11; Latins demand that one, be Latin, 13, 17, **6**. 19; (327) first prorogation of consular *imperium*, **4**. 91; (320) enter office on day of election, 189; (296) effort to elect two patrician, 413–5; (291) interrex returns self as, **7**. 225; (217) C. Flaminius enters office away from Rome, without formalities, **5**. 187–91, 201; division of army between, called usual, 293; one, elected, controls election of colleague, 317; re-election of, permitted, **7**. 225; (216) hold command on alternate days, **5**. 337, 349, *cp*. 293; Campanians demand share in, **6**. 19; (215) preserve *imperium* by not entering city, 197, 203; role of *centuria praerogativa* in election, 197, 203; (210) **7**. 223; (214) elected *in absentia*, **6**. 205; (213) 313; (212) elected without previous curule office, 501; (199) **9**. 171–3; (210) election of, described, **7**. 221–7; dict. com. c. returns self as, 223–5; (209) pr. elected, 299; (190) one, elected, presides over election of colleague, **10**. 431; (178) prorogued *imperium* prevents prosecution of, **12**. 199–201; (177) conflict between, and procos., 215–21; (176) cos. suf. cannot hold elections of, 243; (c. 151) second term forbidden, **14**. 59; (147) Scipio Aemilianus elected, before legal age, 25–7, 35, (134) and permitted a second term, 59; (85–84) Cn. Papirius Carbo and L. Cornelius Cinna appoint selves, for two years; (84) Carbo sole, 105;

(82) C. Marius becomes, at age 20, 107; (70) Pompey elected, without previous office, 121; (52) Pompey sole, 133; Caesar permitted to seek election *in absentia*, 135; (43) Octavian becomes, at 19, 151. Date of election: (188) Feb. 18th, **11**. 143; (187) before Mar. 5th, 235; (179) Mar. 13th, **12**. 179; (172) Feb. 18th, 371; (170) Jan. 26th, **13**. 39; (176) of cos. suf., Aug. 3rd, **12**. 233. Date of entry on office: (463) Aug. 1st, **2**. 21; (462) Aug. 11th, 27; (450) May 15th, called regular date, 117–9; (423) Dec. 13th, 377; (329) July 1st, **4**. 79: (217) Mar. 15th, **5**. 199, *et saepe*; (153) changed to Jan. 1st, **14**. 15. Formalities for entry on office: (217) **5**. 187–201; (177) **12**. 215–7

Contenebra, in Etruria: (388) **3**. 209

Contestania, Spanish tribe: (76) **14**. 193–5

contio: (186) begun with prayer, **11**. 259; (300) before tribal assembly, **4**. 381–9; (167) **13**. 371–91; (200) before *comitia centuriata*, **9**. 19–25; (186) to hear cos. *in re* Bacchic conspiracy, **11**. 259

Contrebia, in Spain: (181) surrenders, **12**. 101–3; (77) taken by Sertorius, **14**. 187–9, 193

— Leucada, in Spain: (76) **14**. 195

contributions: (210) by citizens to state, **7**. 135–9; (204) repaid, **8**. 267; (200) **9**. 41–3; (196) 389

conubii, ius: *see* marriage, right of.

co-optation: (493) of tribunes, **1**. 325; (449) **2**. 219; (439) 311; (401) **3**. 37; (448) of tribunes forbidden, **2**. 221; (180) into sacred colleges, **12**. 133–5

Copaic swamp, in Boeotia: (196) **9**. 357

copper: (167) mining of, permitted in Macedon, **13**. 349

Cora, in Latium: (503) Latin colony, revolts, **1**. 271; (495) gives hostages, 287; (330) Privernates plunder, **4**. 75; (211) prepares supplies, **7**. 31

Coracesium, in Asia Minor: (197) **9**. 333

Corax, Mt., in Greece: (191) M' Acilius Glabrio crosses, **10**. 245; (190) Aetolians seize, 303–5

Corbio, in Latium: (488) Volsci take, **1**. 345; (458) Aequi ordered to leave, **2**. 97; (457) Aequi slay Roman garrison in, 101; destroyed, 103; (446) Volsci and Aequi withdraw to, 225; Romans camp by, 237

Corbio, in Spain: (184) **11**. 353

Corbis, a Spaniard: (206) kills cousin in duel, **8**. 89

Corculum: *see* Cornelius Scipio Nasica.

Corcyra, Illyrian town: (180) **12**. 133

—, is. in Ionian sea: (211) limits Aetolian and Roman spheres, **7**. 93; M. Valerius Laevinus winters at, 95, 99; (209) Punic fleet at, 269; (200) naval base during war with Philip, **9**. 57, 65, 127, 139, (199) 167, (198) 197, 227, (197) 269, 319, 321; (198) on route between Italy and Greece, 179, 193, (191) **10**. 223, 275, (172) **12**. 399, 401, 409, (171) 439, (169) **13**. 91, (167) 395; (191) Hannibal urges Antiochus to base fleet on, **10**. 179; (189) Aetolians to deliver fugitives to, **11**. 35; (168) troops at, discharged, **13**. 255; (167) captured ships presented to, 403

Cordova, in Spain: (48) **14**. 139

Coreli, Thracians: (188) **11**. 137

Corfinium, Paelignian city: (49) **14**. 137

Corinth: ancient home of Tarquins, **1**. 123, 165, **2**. 267; (c. 272) Nicaea transported to, **10**. 73; (208) region of, plundered, **7**. 337; (208–207) Philip at, **8**. 31, 35; (200) **9**. 21, 65, 73, 77; offered to Achaeans by Philip 75, (198) and by Rome, 207; vainly attacked by Flamininus and Attalus, 201, 207, 225–33; (197) Achaeans vainly demand that Philip free, 255, 259–67; one of fetters of Greece, 265, 475; Flamininus at gate of, 271–3; Achaeans defeat Macedonians near, 313–9; (196) status of, uncertain, 361–3; Flamininus proclaims freedom of Greece at, 365; returned to Achaeans, 363, 369, 475, **10**. 49; (195) ornaments from, in Rome, **9**. 421; Flamininus confers with allies at, 471–7; (194) 543–7; garrison withdrawn from, 547–9; (192) envoys in, **10**. 99; Flamininus in, 115–7; (191) 247; (173) Aetolian hostages in, **12**. 307;

INDEX

(172) Eumenes brought to, 339; (167) L. Aemilius Paulus at, **13**. 343; (147) envoys molested in, **14**. 39, 41; (146) destroyed by L. Mummius, 41, 45; (142) art works from, in Italy, 47
Corinth, Gulf of: (208–207) Punic fleet in, **8**. 31–3; (191) M. Porcius Cato sails through, **10**. 223; (189) Illyrians raid, **11**. 21; (171) Roman fleet in, **12**. 463; (169) **13**. 91. *Also*: **7**. 101, **9**. 205
—, Isthmus of: (198) Attalus leads army across, **9**. 225; (172) ships drawn over, **12**. 339. *Also*: **9**. 217, **13**. 343, **14**. 41
Coriolanus: *see* Marcius
Corioli, Volscian town: (493) captured, **1**. 327–9, **2**. 245; (488) recovered by Volsci and Coriolanus, **1**. 345
Cormasa, in Asia Minor: (189) **11**. 49
corn: *see* grain.
Cornelia: (331) charged with brewing poison, **4**. 73
—: (187) wife of P. Cornelius Scipio Nasica, **11**. 199
—: (187) wife of Ti. Sempronius Gracchus, **11**. 199–201
—, wife of Pompey: her opinion of Crassus, **14**. 211; (48) flees to Cyprus, 141
Cornelia gens: (193) fails to win consulship for P. Scipio Nasica, **10**. 29; (187) praised by Nasica, **11**. 203
— tribus: (188) Arpinates in, **11**. 121
Cornelii: (319) worthy foes for Alexander the Great, **4**. 229
— Scipiones: (187) tombs of, **11**. 197
Cornelius, A.: (459) qu., **2**. 81–3
—, C.: (387) tr. mil. c. p., **3**. 211
—, C., of Padua: (48) foresees Pharsalus, **14**. 207–9, 307
—, Cn.: (174) flamen Dialis, **12**. 283
—, P.: (389) tr. mil. c. p., **3**. 197; (385) ii, 231
— Arvina, P., cos. 306: (310) IIvir nav., **4**. 311; (306) cos., defeats Samnites, 333–41; (292) cens., 541
— Blasio, Cn., pr. 194: (199) in Spain as procos., **9**. 149; (196) granted ovation, 349; (194) pr. for Sicily, 527, 531
— —, P.: (170) envoy to Carnians, Histrians, and Iapydes, **13**. 19–21, (168) to Pisae and Luna, 287
Cornelius Calussa, P.: (c. 332) pont. max., **6**. 355
— Cethegus, C., cos. 197: (200) procos. in Spain, **9**. 145–9; (199) aed. cur., 147–9, 173; (197) cos. with Italy as prov., 237–41; defeats Insubres, 243–7; vows temple to Juno Sospita, 247; triumphs, 337–41; (194) cens., 531–3, **10**. 23; dedicates temple to Juno Matuta, **9**. 553; (193) envoy to Africa, 579
— —, C.: (154–151) condemned for debauching a free bondwoman, **14**. 21–3
— —, C.: (63) joins Catiline, **14**. 127
— —, L.: (149) attacked by Ser. Sulpicius Galba, **14**. 27
— —, M., cos. 204: (213–196) pont., **6**. 345, **9**. 389–91; (213) aed. cur., **6**. 345–7; (212) conducts election of pont. max., 355; (211) pr. for Apulia, 501; in Sicily, subdues mutiny, **7**. 83–5; (210) in Sicily, 101–3, 111; (209) cens., 251–3, 355; (204) cos., **8**. 249, **10**. 261, 263, with Etruria as prov., **8**. 255–7, 349–51, 357; holds elections, 357; (203) defeats Mago in Gaul, 369, 431–5; (196) dies, **9**. 389–91
— —, M., cos. 160: (171) leg. to restrain cos. C. Cassius Longinus, **13**. 7; (169) IIIvir for re-establishing Aquileia, 61; (160) cos., drains Pomptine marshes, **14**. 13
— —, P., cos. 181: (187) aed. cur., **11**. 239; (185) pr., 285; (181) cos. with Liguria as prov., **12**. 59; musters reserves at Pisa, 81, 89; Ligurian peace referred to, 105; inactive, 107, 117; (180) receives surrender of Ligurian Apuani, 113, 117–9; triumphs, 119–21; (173) Xvir agr. assig., 303. (As cos. and procos. mis-called 'Lentulus.')
— —, P.: (184) pr. urb. and pereg., **11**. 321, 341, 347; acts against Bacchanalian conspiracy, 353.
— Cinna, L., cos. 87: (89) leg., defeats Marsi, **14**. 95; (87) cos., driven from Rome, 99, 317; returns with Marius, 99–101, 295; (86) cos. ii, 101–5; (85) appoints self cos. for two years; exiles citizens; (84) killed by own soldiers, 105

INDEX

Cornelius Cossus, A., cos. 428 : (437) tr. mil., kills Etruscan king, **2**. 319–21; dedicates *spolia opima*, 321–5, 361–3, 365; (431) pont. max., dictates vows to dict., 345; (428) cos., 323–5, 355; (426) tr. mil. c. p., 357–9; names dict.; made mag. eq., 359–71

— —, A. : (413) cos., **2**. 423

— —, A. : (385) dict., defeats Volsci, **3**. 233–41; triumphs, 251; opposes M. Manlius Capitolinus, 243–51

— —, A. : (369) tr. mil. c. p., **3**. 321; (367) ii, 347

— —, Cn. : (414) tr. mil. c. p., **2**. 417; (409) cos., 433

— —, Cn. : (406) tr. mil. c. p., **2**. 447–9; (404) ii, 455; (401) iii, **3**. 35; plunders near Capena, 43; grants cavalry triple pay, 45–7

— —, P. : (415) tr. mil. c. p., **2**. 417

— —, P. : (408) tr. mil. c. p., **2**. 439–41

— —, P. : (395) tr. mil. c. p., **3**. 83

— — Arvina, A., cos. 343, 332 : (353) mag. eq. against Caerê, **3**. 423; (349) mag. eq. com. c., 447; (343) cos., 455, **4**. 479; trapped by Samnites, saved by P. Decius Mus, **3**. 469, 477–81; with Decius, defeats Samnites, 487–91; triumphs, 495; (332) cos. ii, **4**. 69; (322) dict., defeats Samnites, 147–53; triumphs, 155; another version, 155–7; (320) fetial, surrenders sponsors of Caudine peace, 201–3

— Dolabella, Cn. : (208–180) rex sac., **7**. 355, **12**. 133

— —, L. : (180) IIvir nav., unwilling to become rex sac., **12**. 133–5; (178) commands in south Adriatic, 187

— —, P., cos. suf. 44 : (47) tr. pl., incites riots, **14**. 143; (44) cos. suf., 309; letters struck from name of, 311; (43) kills C. Trebonius, 151; defeated by C. Cassius, kills self, 153

— Lentulus, Cn., cos. 201 : (216) tr. mil. at Cannae, **5**. 359–61; (212) qu., buries Ti. Sempronius Gracchus, **6**. 411, and brings his army to Capua, 415; (205) aed. cur., **8**. 249; (201) cos., 517, 533; desires Africa as prov., receives fleet, 517–9, 533; vetoes SC. for Punic peace, 529; commands fleet, 537; (200) **9**. 43; (199) IIIvir to supplement colony at Narnia, 159; (196) Xvir for Macedonian peace, 343, 359–61, 367–71, 381–3, 395, 479, 561; (184) dies, an augur, **11**. 365

Cornelius Lentulus, Cn. : (199) procos. in Spain, **9**. 149. *See* Cn. Cornelius Blasio, pr. 194.

— —, Cn. : (146) cos., **14**. 41

— —, Cn. : (97) cos., **14**. 283

— —, L. : (327) cos., commands against Samnites, **4**. 87–93; (321) leg., favors Caudine surrender, 175–7; (320) dict., defeats Samnites, 219

— —, L., pr. 211 : (213–173) Xvir sac., **6**. 345, **12**. 319 *; (211) pr. for Sardinia, **6**. 501, **7**. 5, 111; (209) leg. of Marcellus at Canusium, 263

— —, L., cos. 199 : (205) aed. cur., **8**. 249; (206–200) procos. in Spain, 151, 213–9, 249, 257, 371, 521; granted ovation, **9**. 59–61; (199) cos., with Italy as prov., 145–7, 155; appoints IIIviri to investigate Narnia, 159; conducts election of cens., 169; supersedes pr. Cn. Baebius Tamphilus in Gaul; holds elections, 171; (198) in Gaul, 175, 179, 233; (196) envoy to Antiochus and Ptolemy, 381–3, 387

— —, L. : (198) pr. urb., **9**. 235. *See* L. Cornelius Merula, cos. 193.

— —, L. : (168) brings news of Pydna, **13**. 237, 249–53

— —, P. : (214) pr. for Sicily, **6**. 203, 207, 213; (213) 317; (212) 349, **7**. 5; commands legions of Cannae and other disciplinary units, **6**. 357, **7**. 5

— —, P. : (181) cos., **12**. 59. *See* P. Cornelius Cethegus, cos. 181

— —, P., cos. suf. 162 : (172) envoy to Greece and Macedon, **12**. 399–403; sent to Thebes with troops, 437; (171) tr. mil., 443; besieges Haliartus, 463–5; (169) aed. cur., **13**. 149; (168) envoy to Perseus, 259

— —, Ser. : (303) cos., **4**. 361

— —, Ser. : (207) aed. cur., **8**. 43; (205) tr. mil. in Spain, 215–7

— —, Ser., pr., 169 : (172) envoy to Greece and Macedon, **12**. 399–403,

* This first item may belong to the next L. Cornelius Lentulus.

425; (169) pr. for Sicily, **13**. 39–41, 53
Cornelius Lentulus Caudinus, L., cos. 237: (217) pont. max., advises vote on Sacred Spring, **5**. 231–3; (213) dies, **6**. 345
— — —, L.: (209) aed. cur., **7**. 301
— — —, P., pr. 203: (210) arbitrates award of mural crown, **7**. 185; (203) pr. for Sardinia, **8**. 357, 369, 371, 451, 521; (202) crosses to Utica with ships, 501; (196) Xvir for Macedonian peace, **9**. 343, 359–61, 367–71, 381–3, 395, 479, 561; (189) Xvir for settlement of Asia, **10**. 461–3, **11**. 123–35, 153, 161, 205, 301
— — Clodianus, Cn.: (72) cos., defeated by Spartacus, **14**. 119; (70–69) cens., 121
— — Lupus, L.: (156) cos., **14**. 251
— — Spinther, P., cos. 57: (49) captured by Caesar, freed, **14**. 137
— — Sura, P., cos. 71: (63) pr. ii, joins Catiline, **14**. 127
— Maluginensis, M.: (450) Xvir, **2**. 117; (449) 139
— —, M.: (436) cos., **2**. 325
— —, M.: (392) cens. suf. with dire results, **3**. 109–11, **4**. 297
— —, M.: (369) tr. mil. c. p., **3**. 321; (367) ii, 347
— —, P.: (404) tr. mil. c. p., **2**. 455
— —, P.: (397) tr. mil. c. p., **3**. 57–9; (394) ii, 89; (390) iii, 127
— —, Ser.: (485) cos., **1**. 355; (453) flamen of Quirinus, dies, **2**. 107
— —, Ser.: (386) tr. mil. c. p., **3**. 213, 217; (384) ii, 255; (382) iii, 271; (380) iv, 289; (370) vi, 319; (368) vii, 327; (361) mag. eq., 383
— — Uritinus, L.: (459) cos., left to defend city, **2**. 75–79; captures Antium, triumphs, 81–3; (449) supports Xviri, 133–7
— Mammula, A.: (217) pr., vows Sacred spring, **9**. 395; (216–215) propr. for Sardinia, **6**. 71–3, 111, 119
— —, A.: (191) pr. for Bruttium, **10**. 69, 159, 297, 301; (190) propr. for Aetolia, 297; (189) 433
— —, M.: (173) envoy to Macedon and Egypt, **12**. 309
— —, P.: (180) pr. for Sicily, **12**. 107, 109
Cornelius Merenda, Cn.: (194) pr. for Sardinia, **9**. 527, 531
— —, P.: (217) candidate for cos., **5**. 317
— Merula, Cn.: (189) Xvir for settlement of Asia, **10**. 461–3, **11**. 123–35, 153, 161, 205, 301
— —, L., cos. 193: (198) pr. urb., **9**. 173, 175; suppresses slave rising in Setia, 235; (194) IIIvir for colony at Tempsa, 535; (193) cos. with Gaul as prov., 555–7, 561, **10**. 57; defeats Boi, 9–15; recalled for elections, 17, 21, 29; refused a triumph, 17, 21–3
— Rufinus, P.: (333) dict., resigns because of *vitium*, **4**. 67–9
— —, P., cos. 290: (275) removed from Senate, **4**. 551
— Rutilus Cossus, P.: (408) dict., defeats Aequi and Volsci, **2**. 443; (406) tr. mil. c. p., 447–9
— Scapula, P.: (328) cos., **4**. 85. (*See* P. Cornelius Scipio Barbatus.)
— Scipio, Cn.: (177) pr. for Gaul, **12**. 207
— —, L., cos. 350: (352) interrex, **3**. 427; (350) cos., 433
— —, L.: (259) cos., defeats Sardinians, **4**. 555
— —, L.: (174) pr. pereg., expelled from Senate, **12**. 277
— —, L.: (167) qu., escorts Prusias, **13**. 405–9
— —, P.: (396) mag. eq., **3**. 67; (395) tr. mil. c. p., 83; (392) interrex, 111; (389) 197
— —, P.: (366) first aed. cur., **3**. 357; (350) mag. eq. com. c., 439
— —, P.: (218) cos. with Spain as prov., **5**. 17, 43, 47–9, 73–5, **8**. 533, **9**. 343; cavalry of, defeated on Rhone, **5**. 75, 83–5; sends army to Spain, returns to Italy, 93, 113–5, **8**. 175–7; checks Gauls in Po valley, **5**. 113–5; addresses army, 115–23; defeated by Hannibal at Ticinus riv., wounded, 133–7, 169, **6**. 35, **8**. 475; moves to Trebia, **5**. 139–43; joined by cos. Ti. Sempronius Longus, 153; vainly opposes immediate battle, 155–7; defeated, 159–67; moves to Cremona, 169; (217) joins Cn. Scipio in Spain, 271–3, **8**. 131, 155; at Saguntum, **5**. 273–7; (216)

commands fleet, **6**. 87; checks Hasdrubal, 95–101, **7**. 161; (215) reports victory, **6**. 163; raises siege of Iliturgi and Intibili, 167–9; (214) surrounded, rescued by Cn., 307–9; (213) looks to Africa, 329, **7**. 215; (212) recovers nearly all Spain, **6**. 349, 463–5, **8**. 171; defeated and slain, **6**. 467–71, 477, 481, 485, **7**. 9, 71, 157–9, 371, **8**. 79, 119, 157, 169–71, 181–3, 211, 477, **11**. 203; grief in Rome and Spain, **6**. 477; armies of, and Cn. united after their deaths, 477–9; Spain revolts, **8**. 79

Cornelius Scipio, P. (Africani f.): (190) captured by Antiochus, **10**. 389–91; returned, 393–9, 433; (180) co-opted augur, **12**. 135; (before 167) adopts son of L. Aemilius Paulus, **13**. 235, 379, **14**. 19

— — Aemilianus, P., cos. 147, 134; (before 167) adopted by P. Scipio (Africani f.), **13**. 235, 397, **14**. 19; (168) with natural father, L. Aemilius Paulus, at Pydna, **13**. 235, (167) on tour of Greece, 339, and in triumph, 391; (151) tr. mil. at siege of Intercatia, **14**. 19; (149–148) displays valour, 25, 31; (148) wins Himilco over to Rome, 33; distributes Numidia to sons of Masinissa, 33, 37; stands for aed., elected cos., 35, 37; (147) cos., besieges Carthage, 37–9, 253; (146) sacks Carthage, celebrates games, 39, 41; triumphs, 43; receives name 'Africanus,' **13**. 235; (142) cens., **12**. 159; (138) accuses L. Aemilius Cotta, **14**. 57; (134) cos. ii for Numantine war, 59, 61, 259; rejects gifts of Antiochus VII, 61; (133) captures Numantia, triumphs, 65; (129) opposes re-election of tribb. pl., 67; dies, 67–9

— — Africanus, P., cos. 205, 194: stories of birth, **7**. 73–5; (218) saves father at Ticinus, **5**. 137; (216) tr. mil., leads survivors at Cannae, 373–7; (213) aed. cur., **6**. 345–7; (211) elected procos. for Spain, **7**. 71–5, **8**. 157, 285; (210) gathers forces in Spain, **7**. 75–9, 157–65; captures New Carthage, 165–87, 231; recovers Spanish hostages, 187–91; treatment of captives, 191–5; at Tarraco, receives envoys from tribes, 195–7; *supplicatio* voted by Senate, 229–31; (209) procos., 235; wins support of many Spaniards, 279, 281–3, **10**. 307, 365; defeats Hasdrubal, brother of Hannibal, at Baecula, **7**. 279–89, **8**. 173–5; frees Spanish prisoners and Massiva, **7**. 289–93; **8**. 157; occupies Pyrenees, **7**. 293; much of Spain submits to, 293–5; fame in Rome, 297; (208) sends ships to Sardinia, 303; (207) sends troops to cos. M. Livius Salinator, 365; holds most of eastern Spain, **8**. 3; armies of, defeat Hanno, 3–9, and take Orongis, 9–15; (206) defeats Hasdrubal, son of Gisgo, at Ilipa, 55–69, 319, at Tarraco, 69–71; hopes for conquest of Africa, 71–3; visits Syphax and makes treaty, meets Hasdrubal, 73–9, 221, 297–9, 413; captures Iliturgi and Castulo, 79–87; holds games at New Carthage, 87–9; illness of, leads to revolt of allies, 97, and mutiny, 99–103, 281–3, which is suppressed, 103–23; defeats rebels, 129–41; meets Masinissa, 141–5; returns to Tarraco, 145, and Rome, 151–3; (205) cos., 153, **10**. 261; presents Saguntine envoys, **8**. 155–7; presses for invasion of Africa, 153, 161, 189, 245, 441, 443; opposed by Q. Fabius Maximus, 161–77; replies, 177–89; receives as prov. Sicily with permission to cross to Africa, 153–5, 189–91; celebrates votive games, 155, 193; accepts volunteers, moves to Sicily, 193–7, 207; prepares for crossing, 207–11; fear of, in Africa, 197, 221, 223; Spanish tribes revolt on withdrawal of, 211; Masinissa urges, to make speed, 223–5, 229; postpones crossing to recover Locri, 229–37, 277; finds Q. Pleminius innocent, 241–3, 269, 281; (204) procos., 255; attacked in Senate for Locrian affair, 281–5; senatorial investigation, 285–93, **11**. 177, 183; directed to cross to Africa, **8**. 293, 297; loses support of Syphax, 299–303; size of army, 303–11; crosses, 311–7; defeats Punic cavalry, 319; joined by

INDEX

Masinissa, 319–21, 337; defeats Hanno, 339–43; occupies Salaeca, 343; fails to take Utica, 345–7; winters, 347; (203) procos., 369; continues siege of Utica, 375, 379, 387, 389; unsuccessful negotiations with Syphax, 375–9; twice defeats Syphax and Hasdrubal son of Gisgo, 379–85, 389–93, 465; moves on Carthage, returns to defend fleet, 393–401; Syphax, a prisoner before, 413–5; requires Masinissa to give up Syphax' wife, 411, 415–9; proclaims Masinissa king, 421–3, 429–31; receives Punic envoys, grants armistice, 423–7; sends Punic envoys to Rome, 445–9; granted authority on terms, 449, 511; protests violation of armistice, 453; dismisses envoys, 457; (202) naval command shared with cos., 461–3, 505; faces Hannibal, 465–9; displays forces to Punic scouts, 471; confers with Hannibal, 471–85; defeats Hannibal at 'Zama,' 487–501; sends fleet to Carthage, returns to Utica, 501–3; dictates terms, 503–9; **9**. 577; sends Punic envoys to Rome, 509–11; (201) naval command shared with cos., 519–23; holds Macedonians in chains, 523–5; makes peace, 529–33, **12**. 357; restores Masinissa to kingdom, **8**. 537, **10**. 365; returns to Rome, triumphs, **8**. 537–9, **10**. 475, **11**. 159, 181, **13**. 381–3; source of name 'Africanus,' **5**. 137, **8**. 539; land secured for veterans, **9**. 11–3, 143–5; sends grain from Africa, 15; (200) cos. P. Sulpicius Galba enlists men from army of, 25; celebrates votive games, 143; (199) cens., 169; made princeps senatus, 531, **11**. 383; (195) defends Hannibal, **9**. 401–3; (194) cos. ii, with Italy as prov., 527–31, 561; conducts votive games, **8**. 295; princeps senatus, **9**. 531, **11**. 383; assists colleague against Boi, **9**. 537, 541, 555; suggests reserved seats for Senators at games, 555; (193) envoy in dispute between Carthage and Numidia, 577–9; stragglers from army of, still in Africa, **10**. 7; fails to win election for Nasica, 27; envoy to Ephesus, meets Hannibal, 41–5; (190) leg. of brother, L. Scipio, 285, 293, **11**. 167, 177, **12**. 25; constructs arch on Capitoline, **10**. 299; enlists veterans, 301; sent to Greece by L., 307; makes Aetolian truce, 307–11; ascertains loyalty of Philip, 311–3; in Thessaly, 339; prevents Prusias joining Antiochus, 363–5; Antiochus fears, 365; a Salian priest, 389; resists Antiochus' envoy, 389, 393–5; son of, captured by Antiochus, returned, 389–99, 433, **11**. 177, 187; sick on day of Magnesia, **10**. 397, **11**. 187, 205; at Sardis, answers envoys of Antiochus, **10**. 421–5; (189) falsely reported captured, 433; Amynander sends envoys to, **11**. 9; princeps senatus, 95, 383; (187) with L., prosecuted by Petillii, 175–81, 219; leaves city on plea of illness, seconded by Ti. Sempronius Gracchus, 181–5; conclusion of trial, 201–11; spends rest of life at Liternum, 185–7; (187, 183) various accounts of last days and death, 189–91, 195–201, 379, 383–7, **13**. 381; daughters of, married to P. Scipio Nasica and Gracchus, **11**. 199–201; (169) basilica on site of house of, **13**. 143; (168) grandfather by adoption of son of L. Aemilius Paulus, 235, **14**. 19; personal appearance and character, **7**. 73, **8**. 77, 143, 281–5, 417, **10**. 313, **11**. 187; statue on family tomb, 197

Cornelius Scipio Asiaticus, L., cos. 190: (207–206) leg. of P. Scipio (Afr.) in Spain, **8**. 9–15, 71, 119, **11**. 203, (205) in Sicily, **8**. 233, (204) in Africa, 307, **11**. 203; (202) escorts Punic envoys to Rome, **8**. 511, 515; (193) pr. for Sicily, **9**. 555, 557; (192) candidate for cos., **10**. 69; (191) reports victory at Thermopylae, 223; (190) cos., 285, 291, **14**. 239, with Greece as prov., **10**. 293, 295, 299, and P. as leg., 293, **11**. 167, 185, **12**. 25; moves to Greece, **10**. 301, 305–7; succeeds M' Acilius Glabrio, 311, **11**. 147, 235; grants Aetolian truce, **10**. 307–11; crosses Macedon and Thrace, 311–3, 339, 343, 387, **11**. 141, 305–7; not yet in Asia when

INDEX

Antiochus seeks terms, **10**. 345; wins Prusias' support, 363–5; at Lysimachia, 387; crosses Hellespont, 383, 387–9, 429–31, 449; defeats Antiochus at Magnesia, 395–419, **11**. 149, 203–5; cities surrender to, **10**. 419–21; dictates terms to Antiochus, 421–5, **11**. 43, 123, 153, 167, 205–7, **12**. 201–3; receives envoys of Amynander, **11**. 9; winters, **10**. 425; (189) falsely reported captured, 433; succeeded by Cn. Manlius Volso, 437, **11**. 37–9, 147, 235; sends envoy to Senate, **10**. 441–3; treaty of, with Antiochus ratified, 461; requests name Asiaticus, 473; triumphs, 473–7, **11**. 159, 205; (187) excuses brother's absence, 181–3; accused of embezzlement, convicted, 187–203, 235; defended by P. Scipio Nasica, 203–7; goods sold to pay fine, person protected by Ti. Sempronius Gracchus, 199, 201, 209–11; (186) envoy to Antiochus; celebrates votive games, 283; (184) candidate for cens., 347–9; deprived of horse by cens. M. Porcius Cato, 359; (183) envoy to Prusias, 399; statue on tomb of family, 197

Cornelius Scipio Asiaticus, L.: (83) cos., **14**. 297; loses army to Sulla, 107

— — Asina, Cn.: (260) cos., defeated and captured by Carthage, **4**. 555

— — —, P., cos. 221: (218) IIIvir agr. assig., **5**. 69–71; (217) interrex, 313; (211) would defend city only, **7**. 29

— — Barbatus, L.: (298) cos., defeats Etruscans, **4**. 399–403; (297) leg., defeats Samnites, 411; (295) propr., defeated by Gauls, 455, 459–61; leg. at Sentinum, 471, (293) at Aquilonia, 515, 521–3

— — —, P.: (328) cos. **4**. 85; (306) dict. com. c., 341; (304) pont. max., 351. (*See* P. Cornelius Scapula.)

— — Calvus, Cn., cos. 222: (218) leg. of P. Scipio in Spain, **5**. 93, 117, **8**. 131, 155, **12**. 25; defeats Hanno, **5**. 179–81, and Spanish tribes, 181–5; (217) defeats Punic fleet, 263–7; secures islands and north Spain, 267–71; joined by P., 271–3; (216) **6**. 87; checks Hasdrubal, 95–101; (215) asks for supplies, 163; defeats Punic forces, 167–9; (214) rescues P., 307–13; (213) seeks alliance in Africa, 329, **7**. 215; (212) undertakes aggressive war, **6**. 349, 463–7; defeated and slain, 471–7, 481, 485, 489, **7**. 9, 157–9, 371, **8**. 79, 119, 157, 169–71, 181–3, 211, 259, 477, **11**. 203; L. Marcius holds forces of, **6**. 477–9; (211) successor named, **7**. 7; (206) veterans of, under P. Scipio (Afr.), **8**. 131, 171; father of P. Scipio Nasica, **8**. 259, **11**. 203

Cornelius Scipio Hispallus, Cn., cos. 176: (199–176) pont., **9**. 173, **12**. 233; (179) pr. pereg., 139; (176) cos. with Pisae as prov., 227–9; dies, 233, **14**. 245

— — Maluginensis, M.: (176) pr. for Spain; excused from prov., **12**. 227, 231; (174) removed from Senate, 275–7

— — Nasica, P., cos. 191: (204) as best Roman, receives Idaean Mother, **8**. 259–61, **10**. 29, 261, 271; (200) IIIvir col. deduc., **9**. 145; (197) aed. cur., 345; (194) pr. for Farther Spain, 527, 531, (193) **10**. 3–5, 27; vows games, 5, 261; candidate for cos., 25–9, 69; (191) cos., 69, 155, 163, with Italy, 157, and Gaul as prov., 261; celebrates votive games, 261; expiates portents, 263–5; defeats Boi, 265–7; triumphs, 267–73; (190) transports Boi, 295; (189) candidate for cens., 469; sets up chariot on Capitol, **11**. 115; (187) son-in-law of Africanus, 199; defends L. Scipio Asiaticus, 203–7; (184) candidate for cens., 347–9; (183) envoy to Prusias, 399; IIIvir col. deduc., 395, (181) **12**. 103; (171) advocate for Spain, **13**. 7–9

— — —, P.: (94) pr. for Spain, **14**. 287

— — — Corculum, P., cos. 162, 155: (169) aed. cur., **13**. 149; (168) tr. mil. under L. Aemilius Paulus, 207–9, 211[1]; 213, 219; occupies Amphipolis, 241; (167) raids Illyricum, 363–5; (162) cos., **14**. 249; (155) cos. ii, defeats Dalmatians, 15; (153–149) opposes Punic war, 17, 19, 21, 23; (151) instigates destruction of theatre, 21

INDEX

Cornelius Scipio Nasica Serapio, P.: (138) cos., imprisoned by tr. pl., **14**. 53, 55; (133) leads mob against Ti. Gracchus, 63
— — — —, P.: (111) cos., **14**. 271
— Sisenna, P.: (183) pr. urb., **11**. 363
— Sulla, Faustus: (46) supports Pompey, killed, **14**. 143
— —, P.: (212) pr. urb. and pereg., **6**. 345–7, 385, 397, 417, 425, 427, 501; first to celebrate Games of Apollo, **7**. 307
— —, P.: (186) pr. for Sicily, **11**. 235, 241
— —, Ser: (174) propr. in Sardinia, **12**. 251; (167) Xvir on peace in Macedon, **13**. 299, 339, 345–7, 355
— — Felix, L., cos. 88, 80: the name 'Felix', **8**. 539; (105) qu., captures Jugurtha, **14**. 79; (92) propr., restores Ariobarzanes; receives Parthian envoys, 87; (89) leg., defeats Samnites, 93; (88) cos., 185, 293; marries Caecilia Metella, 185; drives Marius and Sulpicius from Rome; restores order, 97, 187; (86) defeats Mithridates in Greece; takes Piraeus and Athens, 103, 297; (85) defeats Thracians; (84) receives envoys of Senate; makes peace with Mithridates, 105; preparations in Rome against, 105, 107; portents, 297; (83) returns to Italy, 107–9, 297; (82) defeats Marius; occupies Rome, 109; defeats Samnites, 109–11, 173; (81–80) dict., reforms constitution, proscribes enemies, 111–3, 297; (78) dies, 113
Cornicen: *see* Aebutius, Helva, Oppius.
Corniculum, in Latium: home of Servius Tullius, **1**. 141, **2**. 267; (616–578) captured by Elder Tarquin, **1**. 137, 141
Cornificius, Q.: (42) procos., defeats T. Sextius, **14**. 155
Cornus, in Sardinia: (215) **6**. 137, 141
Cornutus: *see* Sulpicius Camerinus.
Corolamus, leader of Boi: (196) defeats M. Claudius Marcellus, **9**. 373
coronae: (292) given for valour, worn at Roman games, **4**. 541; (384) *civicae* and *murales*, possessed by M. Manlius Capitolinus, **3**. 265; (210) *murales*, awarded at capture of New Carthage, **7**. 183–5; (36) *navalis*, given M. Vipsanius Agrippa, **14**. 161; (343) *obsidialis*, given to P. Decius Mus, **3**. 491. *See also*: crowns, wreaths.
Coronê, in Messenia: (183) **11**. 373
Coronea, in Boeotia: (196) violence in, punished, **9**. 357, **10**. 171; (191) plundered, 219; (172) favors Perseus, **12**. 425, 431–3; (171) aids Haliartus, 489; harasses Thebans, 505; Senate recompenses, **13**. 17, 85
Corragus, of Macedon: (189) supporter of Eumenes, **11**. 41; (171) **12**. 503
Corrhagum, in Illyricum: (200) **9** 79–81
Corsica: (259) campaign in, **4**. 555; (c. 236) 559, **5**. 45; (217) 305; (202) **8**. 513; (181) **12**. 63, 105–7; (174) 251; (173) 311, 351; (167–160) **14**. 11
Cortona, in Etruria: (310) truce with, **4**. 309; (217) Hannibal near, **5**. 213
Cortuosa, in Etruria: (388) **3**. 209
Coruncanius, Ti., cos. 280: (c. 255) first plebeian pont. max., **4**. 557
Corvinus: *see* Valerius Maximus, — Messala.
Corvus: *see* Aquilius, Valerius Maximus.
Corycus, cape in Cilicia: (197) **9**. 333
—, cape and port in Ionia: (191) Antiochus defeated off, **10**. 281, 313; (190) 377; Roman fleet off, 327–9
Corylenus, in Asia Minor: (190) **10**. 353
Cos, is. in Aegean: (190) C. Livius Salinator at, **10**. 335; ships of, in Rhodian fleet, 323, 353–5
Cosa, Etruscan port: (202) **8**. 513; (273) colony at, **4**. 551; (217) Punic fleet off, **5**. 237–9; (209) loyal, **7**. 245–7; (199, 197) new citizens for, **9**. 159, 343
Cosconius, C.: (89) defeats Samnites, **14**. 93
—, M.: (203) tr. mil., slain, **8**. 435
—, M.: (135) pr., defeats Scordisci, **14**. 59
Cossus: *see* Cornelius, — Rutilus.
Cossyra, is. off Sicily: (82) **14**. 111
Cotta: *see* Aurelius, Aurunculeius.
Cotto, agent of Philip: (179) **12**. 173–5
Cotto, in Asia Minor: (190) **10**. 353
Cotys, Thracian king: (171) supports Perseus, **12**. 377, 449; at Callinicus,

467, 471; defends Thrace, 503; (169) allied with Perseus, **13**. 65; (168) after Pydna with Perseus, 231, who plans flight to, 263–5; (167) son returned to, 399–401

Cranii, people of Cephallania: (189) **11**. 97

Crannon, in Thessaly: (191) captured by Antiochus, **10**. 185; M' Acilius Glabrio at, 201; (171) Romans at, **12**. 493–5

Crassipes: *see* Furius.

Crassus: *see* Claudius, Licinius, Otacilius, Papirius, Rutilius, Veturius.

Crastinus, C.: (48) soldier of Caesar, **14**. 207

Crater: *see* Nicaea, wife of Crater.

credit: (215) corporations furnish supplies on, **6**. 165–7, **9**. 433

Cremastê: *see* Larisa Cremastê.

Cremera riv.: (478) Etruscans checked at, **1**. 387–9; (477) Fabians defeated near, 389–91, 395, **2**. 3, **4**. 315, on July 18th, **3**. 197

Cremo, ridge in Alps: (218) **5**. 111–3

Cremona, in Cis-Alpine Gaul: (220) colony at, **4**. 561, **5**. 69; (218) P. Scipio winters at, 169; (209) loyal, **7**. 245–7; escapes in Punic War, **9**. 31; (206) plundered by Gauls, **8**. 49; (200) **9**. 31, 61; L. Furius Purpurio defeats Gauls at, 61–5; (198) people of, forced to return, 233; (197) expresses gratitude to C. Cornelius Cethegus, 339–41; (195) rebuilt, 471; (190) **10**. 429; (168) cohort from, at Pydna, **13**. 225

Creon of Antigonea: (168) general of Perseus, **13**. 195–7

Cretan arms: (171) Achaeans use, **12**. 463

— mercenaries, in armies of: (192) Achaeans, **10**. 73, 81–5, (183) **11**. 373; (190) Antiochus, **10**. 407; (207) Attalus, **8**. 27; (171) Eumenes, **12**. 467; (200) Philip, **9**. 103–9, 115–7, (197) 313, 325; (171) Perseus **12**. 449, 467, 471, 495, (170) **13**. 27, 35, (168) 233, 239; (217) Rome, **6**. 273, (197) **9**. 271–3, 285, (190) **10**. 405, 411–3, (189) **11**. 71, (171) **12**. 395, **13**. 27; (195) Sparta, **9**. 485, (192) **10**. 83; (214) Syracuse, **6**. 273–5

Crete: (195) Nabis to retain no part of, **9**. 513; (189) Q. Fabius Labeo in, **10**. 477–9; (174) civil war on, **12**. 273; (172) envoys sent to, 347; (171) 397; (170) Cretan envoys in Rome, **13**. 27; (168) hostages of Perseus and Eumenes to be sent to, 171; (149) Andriscus claims Cretan rearing, **14**. 27–9; (72–71) M. Antonius Creticus unsuccessful in, 121; (68–67) cities in, stormed by Q. Caecilius Metellus, claimed by Pompey, 123, 125, 199–201. *See also*: Cydas, Euphanes, Evander, Leusus, Oroandes; Cretan arms, Cretan mercenaries.

Creusa, wife of Aeneas, **1**. 15

Creusa, on Gulf of Corinth: (191) **10**. 223; (171) **12**. 465; (169) **13**. 91

Crispinus: *see* Quinctius.

Crispus: *see* Sallustius.

Crito, of Boeotia: (215) envoy of Philip to Hannibal, **6**. 135

Critolaus, of Achaia: (147) molests envoys; (146) kills self, **14**. 41

Crixus: (73–72) leads gladiators' revolt, **14**. 117–9

Croto: *see* Maecilius.

Croton, in Bruttium: (c. 530) home of Pythagoras, **1**. 65; (c. 500) defeated by Locri, **8**. 279; (c. 389) captured by Dionysius, **6**. 183; (c. 275) depopulated after war with Pyrrhus, 181; (216) deserts Rome, **5**. 409; (216–215) captured by Brutii, **6**. 101, 179–85; (210) supplies oarsmen, **7**. 147; (204) Hannibal at, **8**. 349; (203) 439; (194) Roman colony at, **9**. 535. Prodigy: (124) **14**. 267

crowns, golden: (495) presented to Jupiter Capitolinus by Latins, **1**. 289; (449) **2**. 193; (343) by Carthage, **3**. 495; (198) by Attalus, **9**. 237; (191) by Philip, **10**. 259; (170) by Alabanda; by Lampsacus; **13**. 23; (169) by Pamphylia, 133–5; (167) by Rhodes, 331; (437) presented to Jupiter by dict. at public cost, **2**. 323; (205) sent to Delphi, **8**. 193; (393) carried in triumph, **4**. 535; (194) **9**. 551; (189) **10**. 473; 475; (187) **11**. 233 (cp. 31); 237; (184) 355; (181) **12**. 105; (180) 137; (185) carried in ovation, **11**.

309; (182) **12.** 55; (361) given soldiers for valour, **3.** 389; (349) 447; (343) 489; (293) **4.** 529; (210) given by P. Scipio (Afr.) to C. Laelius, **7.** 187; (203) **8.** 423; by Scipio to Masinissa, 421. *See* wreath, *corona.*

crucifixion: (258) of Punic general by troops, **4.** 555; (217) of guide by Hannibal, **5.** 245; of slaves, 309–11; (196) **9.** 373; (206) of sufetes of Gades, **8.** 149; (201) of deserters, 533

Crustumeria, in Latium: (753–717) people of, at Consualia, **1.** 35; defeated, 39; receives colony, 43; (616–578) captured, 137; (499) 279; (449) Romans entrench near, **2.** 141. Prodigies: (177) **12.** 211, 223.

Crustumina tribus: (171) **12.** 389

Crustuminian mts.: (390) **3.** 129

— plains: (468) **1.** 429

Crustumium: *see* Crustumeria.

Cuballum, in Galatia: (189) **11.** 63

Culcha, Spanish chief: (206) sends troops to procos. P. Scipio (Afr.), **8.** 55; (197) revolts, **9.** 335–7

Culleo: *see* Terentius.

Cumae, in Campania: settled from Chalcis; mother city of Palaepolis (Naples), **4.** 85–7; (508) defeats Arruns Porsinna, **1.** 265–7; (495) Tarquin the Proud dies in, 287; (508) grain purchased from, 247; (492) 331; (433) **2.** 337; (420) taken by Campanians, 403, (411) who prevent sale of grain, 427; (338) granted citizenship without vote, **4.** 61, 237; (216) receives Nucerian refugees, **6.** 49; (215) loyal Campanian knights become *municipes* of, 107; Ti. Sempronius Gracchus thwarts plot in, 121–7; Hannibal abandons siege of, 127–31, 153, **7.** 9, **8.** 443; Gracchus at, **6.** 131, 163; (214) Hannibal devastates lands of, 215; (212) Q. Fulvius Flaccus moves to, 417; (180) permitted to use Latin, **12.** 135; (176) Cn. Cornelius Scipio Hispallus dies at, 233, **14.** 245. Prodigies: (212) **6.** 365; (208) **7.** 305; (202) **8.** 511; (169) **13.** 46; (91) **14.** 291

Cunctator: *see* Fabius Maximus Verrucosus.

Curatius, P.: (401) tr. pl., **3.** 39

Cures, Sabine town, whence the term 'Quirites,' **1.** 49; (716) home of Numa, 63, 125

curia, the Senate house: **1.** 169, 339, **4.** 551, **5.** 397, *et saepe*; (672–640) built, **1.** 107; (534) Tarquin the Proud throws Servius from, 167–9; (187) statues in, **11.** 199; (174) portico added to, **12.** 279. *See* Hostilia curia.

curiae, named for Sabine women, **1.** 51. *See comitia curiata.*

Curiatii, of Alba: (672–640) combat with Horatii, **1.** 83–95; made Senators, 107

Curiatius, C.: (138) tr. pl., names Scipio Nasica, 'Serapio,' **14.** 53; imprisons coss., 55

— Fistus Trigeminus, P.: (453) cos., **2.** 107; (451) Xvir, 109

Curio: *see* Scribonius.

curio maximus: (463) **2.** 27; (209) first held by plebeian, **7.** 235. *Also*: **7.** 227; **12.** 253–5

Curius, M': (199) tr. pl., withdraws veto on election of Flamininus, **9.** 171–3

— Dentatus, M': (290) cos., triumphs over Samnites and Sabines, **4.** 547; (275) cos. ii, defeats Pyrrhus, triumphs, 551, **13.** 383; worthy to meet Alexander, **4.** 229

Cursor: *see* Papirius.

cursus honorum: (180) ages for office-holding first set, **12.** 137–9; (70) Pompey freed from, **14.** 121. For earlier irregularities, *see, e.g.*: (212) **6.** 501; (205) **8.** 153 (cp. **6.** 345–7, **7.** 71); (199) **9.** 171–3; (184) **11.** 343–5

Curtian lake: (753–717) named, **1.** 49, (362) **3.** 373–5

Curtius, M.: (362) throws self into Curtian lake, **3.** 373–5

—, Mettius, Sabine leader: (753–717) holds Citadel, **1.** 45–7; escapes by Curtian lake, 49, **3.** 373–5

— Philo, C.: (445) cos., **2.** 257; opposes intermarriage of orders, 259–63, 275; holds faulty election, 281

curule chair: of Etruscan origin, **1.** 31; (473) used by cos., 401, (366) pr., and aed. cur., **3.** 357–9, (390) and by those who had held such

offices, 139; (300) **4**. 383; (212) **6**. 355; (210) granted as honour to Syphax, Ptolemy, **7**. 215, (203) Masinissa, **8**. 421, (200) **9**. 35, (172) and Eumenes, **12**. 335
curule magistrates, former: (216) placed in Senate by dictator, **6**. 79; (203) sons of, barred from plebeian office during life of father, **8**. 439
Curvus: *see* Fulvius, Titinius.
Cusibis, in Spain: (192) **10**. 65
Cutiliae, Sabine town: (211) **7**. 41
Cutina, in Central Italy: (325) **4**. 113
Cyclades: naval operations in: (195) **9**. 483; (191) **10**. 277; (168) **13**. 181, 185
Cycliadas, Achaean leader: (208) meets Philip, **7**. 339; (200) general, answers Philip, **9**. 75–7; (198) expelled, 207; (197) with Philip confers with Flamininus, 251
Cydas, of Crete: (197) commands archers, **9**. 285; (169–168) Eumenes' agent in negotiations with Perseus, **13**. 131, 169
Cydonia, in Crete: (189) in local war, **10**. 477; (68–67) taken, **14**. 123
Cylarabis, near Argos: (195) **9**. 481
Cyllenê, port of Elis: (209) **7**. 339
Cymê, in Aeolis: (190) revolts to Seleucus, **10**. 325; (188) tax-free, **11**. 133
Cymenes, in Thessaly: (198) **9**. 191
Cyneatis, citadel of Samê: (189) **11**. 101
Cynosarges, suburb of Athens: (200) **9**. 73
Cynoscephalae, Thessalian range: (197) Flamininus defeats Philip at, **9**. 291–303, 319, 323, 333, **10**. 181
Cynus, Locrian port: (207) **8**. 25
Cyparissia, in Messenia: (198) **9**. 217
Cyphaera, in Thessaly: (198) **9**. 191
Cyprius vicus, in Rome: (578–534) **1**. 169
Cyprus: (196) Antiochus fails to reach, **9**. 387–9; (168) Antiochus IV claims, **13**. 279–81; Roman envoys at, 283; (131) Ptolemy VIII flees to, **14**. 67; (57) annexed, 131; (48) kin of Pompey flee to, 141
Cypsela, Thracian port: (200) occupied by Philip, **9**. 51, (188) by Cn. Manlius Volso, **11**. 135
Cyrenê: 216) ship of Decius Magius driven to, **6**. 31; (193) Aphthir in, **9**. 577; (163–145) Ptolemy VIII rules, **14**. 13, 43; (125) locusts cause pestilence in, 265; (96) Ptolemy Apion dies in, making Rome his heir, 87, 285
Cyretiae, in Thessaly: (200) taken by Aetolians, **9**. 119, (191) **10**. 187, by propr. M. Baebius Tamphilus, 195, (171) by Perseus, **12**. 457
Cyrtii, people of Asia Minor: (190) in army of Antiochus, **10**. 407–9, (171) of P. Licinius Crassus, **12**. 473
Cyrus the Great: early life happier, **4**. 227
Cythnos, is. of Cyclades: (200) held by Macedonians, **9**. 49; withstands Romans, 131
Cyzicus, on Propontis: (200) ships of, at Abydus, **9**. 53; (175) gifts of Antiochus IV to, **12**. 249; (73) Mithridates defeated before, **14**. 119, 301

Daedala, in Peraea: (190) **10**. 355
Dahae, mercenaries of Antiochus: (192) **10**. 137, 143, (190) 399, 407
Dalmatia: (155, 156) subdued, **14**. 15; (118) 75; (35–33) 161, 163; (11–10) 167
Damarata, daughter of Hiero: (214) **6**. 247, 257
Damasippus: *see* Junius Brutus.
Damippus, of Sparta: (212) **6**. 431
damiurgi: (198) Achaean officials, **9**. 221; (189) **11**. 101
Damius, admiral of Eumenes: (168) **13**. 181
Damocles, of Argos: (195) plots against Nabis, **9**. 479–81
Damocritus, Aetolian leader: (200) supports Philip, **9**. 97, then Rome, 119–27; (193) incites Nabis, **10**. 35; (192) insults Flamininus, 99, 233, **11**. 33; seeks Nabis' death, **10**. 105; (191) captured, 233; (190) imprisoned, 299; kills self, 427
Damoteles, Aetolian envoy: (189) negotiates peace, **11**. 25–33
Danube (Hister) riv.: (184) Philip rouses tribes along, **11**. 327; (181) visible from Mt. Haemus, **12**. 67; (179) Bastarnae cross, 171–3; (168) Gallic mercenaries return to, **13**. 177

INDEX

Daorsi, Illyrians: (167) **13**. 337
Daphnê, in Syria: (195) **9**. 407
Dardania, west of Mt. Scordus, **13**. 191; (c. 275) Galatians in, **11**. 51; (211) at war with Philip, **7**. 97; (208) 343; (207) **8**. 37; (200) aid Rome against Philip, **9**. 81–3, 99, 103; invade Macedon, 113, 119; defeated by Philip, 125; (197) 329; (189) mercenaries from, **10**. 433; (179–174) Philip stirs Bastarnae against, **12**. 173–7, 245–7, 263; (169) conquered by Perseus, **13**. 85, 65, 73, 259; sought by Gentius, 187; (167) vainly ask return of Paeonia, 349–51; (97) defeated, **14**. 285; (75) 115; (73) 117; (62) crush C. Antonius, 303
Dardanus, on Hellespont: (190) yields, **10**. 317, 395–7; (188) given freedom, **11**. 133
Darius III of Persia: (331) Alexander defeats, **4**. 231
Darsa, in Asia Minor: (189) **11**. 49
Dasius, of Brundisium: (218) betrays supplies to Hannibal, **5**. 143
—, of Salapia: (210) pro-Punic leader, **7**. 143–5
— Altinius: (216) delivers Arpi to Hannibal, (213) then to Rome, **6**. 319–23
Dassarenses, in Illyricum: (167) **13**. 337
Dassaretii, in Illyricum: (208) Aeropus attacks, **7**. 343; (200) Rome defeats Macedonians among, **9**. 99–101, 117; (198) avoided by Romans, 179; (191) Philip and M. Baebius Tamphilus meet among, **10**. 187, 195; (172) Roman troops among, **12**. 399; (170) **13**. 35; (167) granted tax exemption, 337
Daulis, in Phocis: (198) **9**. 205
debt: (385) agitation against laws of, **3**. 233, 241; (380) 289–93; (378) 303; (377) 305, 311–3; (375) Licinian-Sextian laws on, proposed, 317, 323, (367) and passed, 349; (354) agitation continues, 421; (352) Vviri for liquidating debts, 427–9; (347) interest rate reduced, 449; (326) imprisonment for, forbidden, **4**. 107–11; (173) causes disorder in Aetolia and Thessaly, **12**. 305–7; (172) abolition of, promised by Perseus, 331. *See* usury.
debtor slavery: (495) causes riots, **1**. 289–97, 303–7
December: (423) coss. take office on 13th, **2**. 377; (169) census conducted on 13th, **13**. 143
decemviri agris dividendis: (201) for lands in Samnium and Apulia, **9**. 13, (200) 143–5, (173) in Liguria and Gaul, **12**. 303
decemviri legibus scribundis: (452) elected, **2**. 109; (451) rule justly; prepare ten tables of law, 109–113; (450) evil rule of second, 113–23, 269, (449) who retain power, 123–67; forced by foreign danger to call Senate, 123–9, which defies them, 129–37, but permits levy, 139; defeated, 139; crimes against Siccius, 141–3, and Lucretia, 143–63; forced to resign, 163–79, 227, **6**. 353; punishment of, **2**. 195–99, 227, 309
decemviri sacrorum (or *sacris faciundis*): (369) replace IIviri; partly plebeian, **3**. 327, (367) 347; (300) duties of, **4**. 385; (213) vacancies on board filled, **6**. 345; (211) **7**. 91; (210) 227; (209) 235; (204) **8**. 359; (200) **9**. 147; (180) **12**. 135; (174) 253–5; (173) 319; (172) 373; (169) **13**. 149; (217) supervise *lectisternium*, **5**. 235; (212) direct special rites, **6**. 387; (207) **7**. 361; (188) **11**. 119; (187) 153; (183) 367; (142) **14**. 255; (102) 277; (98) 283. *See* Sibylline Books.
decemviri stiltibus iudicandis: (449) made inviolate, **2**. 183–5
Decianus: *see* Plautius.
Decidius Saxa, L.: (40) leg. of M. Antonius, **14**. 157
Decimius, C., pr. 169: (171) envoy to Crete, **12**. 397; (169) pr. pereg., **13**. 39, 53, 143; (168) envoy to Antiochus IV and Ptolemy, 153, 185 275–7, 285
—, L.: (172) envoy to Gentius, **12**. 399–401, 429
—, M.: (172) envoy to east, **12**. 347, 365–7
—, Numerius, Samnite leader: (217) aids against Hannibal, **5**. 283–5
— Flavus, C.: (209) tr. mil., **7**. 265

INDEX

Decimius Flavus, C.: (184) pr. urb., **11.** 321, 341–5
Decius, L.: (415) tr. pl., **2.** 417
—, M.: (311) tr. pl., **4.** 277–9
—, Q. (or P.): (120) tr. pl., accuses L. Opimius, **14.** 73
— Mus, P., cos. 340: (352) Vvir mens., **3.** 429; (343) tr. mil., saves army, 477–87, **5.** 399; honoured, **3.** 489–91, 495; (340) cos., **4.** 11; devotes self in battle with Latins, 21–3, 35–43, 45, 199, 381–3, 467–9, 477; worthy to face Alexander, 229
— —, P., cos. 312, 308, 297, 295: (312) cos., **4.** 273–5; (310) leg. in victory over Samnites, 321–25; (308) cos. ii, against Etruscans, 325–7; (306) mag. eq. com. c., 341; (304) cens., 353; (300) supports law opening priesthoods to plebs, 381–9; first plebeian pont., 389; (297) cos. iii, against Samnites, 407–13; (296) 415–25, 431–3; (295) cos. iv, 441–3, 481, **6.** 205; protests assignment of prov. without lot, **4.** 447–51, 457–9; joins Fabius in Etruria, 455–7; devotes self at Sentinum, 461–77; Ap. Claudius Caecus receives army of, 477; worthy to face Alexander, 229
— Subulo, P.: (169) IIIvir for Aquileia, **13.** 61; (168) reports Gallus' victory, 255
— Vibellius: *see* Vibellius, D.
decorations, military: (343) **3.** 489–91; (293) **4.** 529–31. *See coronae.*
decuries: (716) Senate divided into, **1.** 61
dedication of temple: (304) permission of Senate or tribb. pl. required for, **4.** 351
Deiotarus, tetrarch of Galatia: (74) opposes Mithridates, **14.** 117
Delium, in Boeotia: (200) Andrians transported to, **9.** 131; (192) Romans attacked at, **10.** 147, 171; (172) Boeotian treaty with Perseus displayed at, **12.** 325–7
Delos: (196) given to Athens, **9.** 361; (191) Roman fleet at, **10.** 277–9; (175) gifts of Antiochus IV to, **12.** 249; (168) Macedonians, Romans, and Pergameans at, **13.** 185; C. Popilius Laenas at, 273
Delphi: (534–510) officially consulted, **1.** 195–7; (398–394) **3.** 53–9, 79, 89, 97; (216) **5.** 385, **6.** 33; (205) **8.** 247; (394) gifts to, **3.** 89, 97–9; (205) **8.** 193, 245; (279) Gauls plunder, **11.** 165, **12.** 175–7; (191) Antiochus at, **10.** 191; (174) Perseus at, **12.** 257, 263–5, 417; (174, 173) Roman envoys and Aetolians at, 273, 307; (172) Boeotian treaty of Perseus recorded at, 325–7; Perseus plots death of Eumenes at, 335–41, 373, 411, 477, **13.** 261–3; (167) Aemilius Paulus at, 339–41, 395; statues of Paulus to be set up at, 341
Demaratus, father of Tarquin the Elder: **1.** 123, **2.** 267
Demeter, temple of, at Eleusis: (200) attacked by Philip, **9.** 89
Demetrias, in Thessaly: one of the 'fetters of Greece,' **9.** 265; (208) Philip at, **7.** 343; (207) **8.** 17, 21, 27, 35; (200) **9.** 69, 97–9, 135; (198–197) 251; he refuses to yield, 265; (196) held by Rome, 361–3, (195) 475; (194) evacuated by Flamininus, 543, 549, **10.** 49, 91; (192) Roman envoys at, 89; seized by Aetolia, 101–3, 111, 117, 125–7, 165; occupied by Antiochus, **13.** 317, **10.** 127–9, 133, 143, (191) 173, 189; Glabrio sends captives to, 201; possible refuge for Antiochus, 221; surrenders to Philip, 251–3, **11.** 287; (185) Philip diverts trade to, 295; (181) Philip at, **12.** 77; (179) 163–5; 171; (171) threatened by Rome, 505; (169) **13.** 129–31; (168) agents of Perseus and Eumenes at, 169; (167) Aemilius Paulus at, 345
Demetrias, Gulf of: (207) **8.** 21
Demetrium, in Phthiotis: (207) **8.** 23
—, port of Samothrace: (168) **13.** 265
Demetrius of Pharus: (217) surrender of, demanded, **5.** 311
— II, of Macedon: (c. 230) attacked by Dardanians, **9.** 81
—, younger son of Philip, **11.** 387, **12.** 17; (197–196) hostage in Rome, **9.** 311, 361, **11.** 327, **12.** 49; (194) in Flamininus' triumph, **9.** 551; (191) returned, **10.** 259; (183) agent of Philip in Rome, **11.** 327, 367–71, **12.** 33, 49; under influence of Flamininus, 33; gains concessions, **11.** 387–9; (182) quarrels with

Perseus, **12**. 13–53, 65; suspected by Philip, 15–7; supported by pro-Romans, 35; (181) dismissed from campaign, 67–9; trapped and accused by Perseus; murdered by order of Philip, 73–7, 263, 267, 323, 449, **13**. 309; (179) Philip discovers innocence of, **12**. 165–9
)emetrius I Soter, of Syria: (163) hostage in Rome; escapes; slays Antiochus V; becomes king; (158) expels Ariarathes, **14**. 13; (150) sends Andriscus to Rome, 27–9; killed by Alexander Balas, 21, 43; (148) son of, killed, 33
– II Nicator, of Syria: (144) kills Alexander Balas, **14**. 43; Diodotus defeats, 43–5; (125) wife kills, 71
)emocrates, of Tarentum: (210) commands fleet, **7**. 147; (209) slain, 271–3
)emosthenes, the orator: **4**. 233; **14**. 231
)entatus: *see* Curius.
)enter: *see* Caecilius, — Metellus, Livius.
)entheleti, Thracian people: (183) Philip attacks, **11**. 389; (181) **12**. 71–3
)erdas: (205) Epirote magistrate, **8**. 253
)eserters: (208) Roman, in Punic army, **7**. 325; **9**. 227; (201) punishment of, **8**. 533; (200) **9**. 33; (198) Italian, in Philip's army, 227
)esudaba, in Macedon: (168) **13**. 175
)euriopus, in Paeonia: (183) **11**. 391
)evotio: (390) of Senators, **3**. 141–3; (362) of M. Curtius, 373; (340) of P. Decius Mus in Latin war, **4**. 21–3, 35–9; formula for, 37, 43; (295) of P. Decius Mus at Sentinum, 467–9; (191) Ligurian formula of, **10**. 265
)exagoridas, of Gytheum: (195) **9**. 491–3
)iadem: (44) offered to Caesar, **14**. 145
)iaeus: (146) Achaean leader, **14**. 41, 45
)iana: (578–534) heifer offered to, **1**. 159; (399) honoured in *lectisternium*, **3**. 49; (217) **5**. 235; (295) hind of, gives omen, **4**. 463; (212) Syracuse attacked during feast of, **6**. 431. Temples and shrines of, in Rome: (578–534) site of, on Vicus Cyprius, **1**. 169; (187) vowed by M. Aemilusi Lepidus, **11**. 223, (179) and dedicated, **12**. 161. Temples and shrines outside Rome: (200) at Abydus, **9**. 53; (210) at Anagnia, **7**. 217; (167) at Aulis, **13**. 341; (578–534) at Ephesus, **1**. 157
Diana Amarynthis: (192) at Eretria, **10**. 113
— Tauropolos: (168) in Amphipolis, **13**. 235
Dicaearchus, an Aetolian: (193) sent to rouse Antiochus against Rome, **10**. 35–7; (191) surrender of, demanded, 239; (189) accused of rousing Aetolia, **11**. 33
—, of Plataea: (197) proposes Boeotian alliance with Rome, **9**. 281
dictator: (501) origin of office, **1**. 275–7, **2**. 269; not subject to appeal, **1**. 277; (494) 313; (435) named at night, **2**. 327; (408) 443; (327) **4**. 91; (216) **6**. 77; (435) named on advice of Senate by cos., **2**. 327, (310) **4**. 313–5, *and often*; (426) named by tr. mil. c. p., **2**. 359; (356) first, from plebs, **3**. 413, **4**. 387; (458) term normally limited to 6 mo., **2**. 99; (310) **4**. 295; (325) seeks punishment of mag. eq. who fought against orders, **4**. 115–37, 369; (316–315) term of 12 mo., 245, 247, 255; (310) *imperium* confirmed by *comit. cur.*, 315; (249) first army led outside Italy by, 557; (217) office almost forgotten, **5**. 227, 237; elected by *populus*, 227, 307; (210) **7**. 221–3; (217) two dictators, **5**. 287–303; (216) can mount horse only by special law, **6**. 43; without mag. eq. to revise senate, 77; (210) must be named on Roman soil, **7**. 221; (208) 329; (81–80) Sulla as, reconstitutes state, **14**. 111; (44) Caesar made, for life, 145; office abolished, 147. *Dictator clavi figendi causa*: (363) **3**. 365; (331) **4**. 73; (313) 273. *Dictator comitiorum causa*: (361) **3**. 383 (?); (351) 429–31; (350) 439; (349) 447; (335) **4**. 67; (327) 91; (321) 187–9; (306) 341; (217) **5**. 313; (213) **6**. 345; (210) **7**. 221; (208) 345; (207) **8**. 43; (205) 243, 249; (203) 461; (202) 515. *Dictator ludorum causa*: (344)

3. 455; (322) **4**. 155; (208) **7**. 345. *Dictator qui senatus legeret*: (216) **6**. 77–9. *Dictator rei gerendae causa*: (501) **1**. 275; (499) 279; (494) 315; (458) **2**. 89–91; (439) 303–5; (437) 315; (435) 327; (434) 331; (431) 341–3; (426) 359; (418) 409; (408) 443; (396) **3**. 67; (390) 157; (389) 199; (385) 233; (380) 295; (368) 327; 331; (367) 347; (362) 377; (361) 383; (360) 389; (358) 395; (356) 413; (353) 423; (352) 429; (345) 451–3; (342) 503; (340) **4**. 49; (339) 51; (337) 63; (334–333) 67; (332) 69; (325–324) 113; (322) 147, 155; (320) 219; (316) 245; (315) 247; (314) 261; (313) 271; (312) 275; (310–309) 315; (302–301) 363; 369; (287) 547; (249) 557; (217) **5**. 227; 287–301; (216) 387; (203) **8**. 451

dictator: (460) officer in Tusculum, **2**. 61

Dictynneum, in Sparta: (195) **9**. 519

Didas, of Paeonia: (181) Philip's agent in murder of son, **12**. 69, 73, 77, 449; (171) commands under Perseus, 449, 471; governs Paeonia, 471

Didius, T.: (98) cos., **14**. 283; (97) defeats Celtiberians, 87

Dido: queen of Carthage, **14**. 177

Dierus, in Macedon: (169) **13**. 99

dies fasti et nefasti: (715–672) designated by Numa, **1**. 69

Diespiter: (672–640) prayer to, **1**. 85

Digitius, Sex.: (210) receives mural crown, **7**. 183–5

—, Sex.: (194) pr. for Nearer Spain, **9**. 527, 531; (193) **10**. 3, 7; (190) leg. to collect ships, 301; (174) envoy to Macedon, **12**. 257; (172) envoy to purchase grain, 369

—, Sex.: (170) tr. mil., **13**. 39

Diiovis: (200) temple to, vowed, **9**. 63

Dimallum, on Illyrian coast: (205) **8**. 251–3

Dinarchus, of Aetolia: (169) **13**. 79

Dinocrates: (197) prefect of Philip, **9**. 325–9

—: (183) general of Messenê, **11**. 377

Dinomenes, of Syracuse: (215) conspires against Hieronymus, **6**. 195; (214) becomes magistrate, 249, 271

Dinon: (168–167) pro-Macedonian Rhodian, **13**. 165, 185–7, 317

Diocles, of Aetolia: (192) **10**. 101–3

Diodorus, of Amphipolis: (168) **13**. 235

Diodotus Tryphon: (146) makes Antiochus VI king, **14**. 45; (138) murders him, 55, 57

Diomed, plain of: (212) **6**. 385

Dionysius the Great, of Syracuse: **6**. 189, 247; (c. 389) takes Croton, 183

Dionysodorus: (198–197) envoy of Attalus to Philip, **9**. 251–5

Diophanes, Achaean general: pupil of Philopoemen, **10**. 347; (191) summoned by Flamininus, 247; yields Zacynthus, 249–51; (190) defeats Seleucus, 347–51; (189) envoy to Rome, **11**. 107

Dioscorides: (48) envoy of Ptolemy, **14**. 211

Dioxippus: (200) mercenary leader, **9**. 69–71

Dipo, in Spain: (185) **11**. 311

Dipylon gate, of Athens: (200) **9**. 71

Dis, Father: (252, 149) games for, **14**. 23, 31

Ditalco: (139) murders Viriathus, **14**. 53

Dium, in Macedon: (211) Philip turns back at, **7**. 99; (197) he drills troops at, **9**. 283; (172) Perseus and Romans confer near, **12**. 405–21; (169) campaign against Perseus near, **13**. 97–121; (168) he meets Gentius' envoys at, 165

Dives: *see* Baebius, Canuleius, Licinius Crassus.

Dodona: *see* Zeus of.

Dolabella: *see* Cornelius.

Dolichê, in Macedon: (171) Perseus takes, **12**. 457; (169) Romans near, **13**. 95

Dolopia: (198) Aetolians threaten, **9**. 191; (196) Flamininus frees, 369; (191) Philip and Aetolians fight for, **10**. 253–5, (189) 435, **11**. 11, 19, 25, 33, 297; (174) reduced by Perseus, **12**. 257, 263, 267, 329, 411, 417. *See* Artemon.

Domitius Ahenobarbus, Cn., cos. 192: (196) aed. pl., **9**. 391, 553; (194) pr. urb., 527, 529; conducts elections, dedicates temple, 553; (192) cos. **10**. 27–9, **11**. 37, with Italy, then

INDEX

Gaul as prov., **10**. 57–63, 119; (191) 265; (190) leg. at Magnesia, 403
Domitius Ahenobarbus, Cn., cos. suf., 162: (172) pont., **12**. 373; (169) envoy to Macedon, **13**. 149, 153–5; (167) Xvir to advise Aemilius, 299, 339, 345–7, 355–7
— —, Cn.: (122) cos., **14**. 267; (121) defeats Allobroges, 73; (115) cens., 75
— —, Cn., cos. 96: (103) pont. max., **14**. 81; (96) cos., 285
— —, Cn.: (80) proscribed, **14**. 113
— —, L.: (94) cos., **14**. 287
— —, L.: (54) cos., **14**. 305; (49) captured by Caesar, freed, 137
— Calvinus, Cn.: (332) cos., **4**. 69
— —, Cn., cos. 53: (48) campaigns against Parthia, **14**. 141
— —, M., pr. 80: (79–78) leg., defeated in Spain, **14**. 115
— — Maximus, Cn., cos. 283: (299) aed. cur., **4**. 391; (280) first plebeian cens. to close *lustrum*, 551
Donuca, Mt.: (179) Thracians flee to, **12**. 175
Dorimachus, of Aetolia: (211) confirms Roman promises, **7**. 93
Doris: (208–207) Philip takes towns in, **8**. 29; (172) Perseus crosses, **12**. 329–31
Doriscus, in Thrace: (200) **9**. 51
Dorsuo: *see* Fabius.
Dorulatus, leader of Boi: (194) **9**. 535
Doson: *see* Antigonus.
dowry: (160) repaid from estate of deceased husband, **14**. 13
drama: (364) early, in Italy, **3**. 361–5; (214) at Roman games, **6**. 315; (201) **9**. 13; (194) at Megalesia, 555; (191) **10**. 263; (173) at dedication of temple, **12**. 319
Draudacum, in Illyricum: (169) **13**. 69
Drepana, in Sicily: (242) **8**. 167
Dromos, plain near Sparta: (195) **9**. 485
drought and crop failure: (181) **12**. 89, **14**. 243
Druentia, riv. of Gaul: (218) **5**. 91, 93
Drumiae, in Doris: (207) **8**. 29
Drusus: *see* Livius.
Drusus, Nero Claudius: (15–11) conducts war in Germany; takes census, **14**. 165–7; (11) defeated, 319; (9) defeats Germans, dies, 167
Drymussa, is. off Clazomenae: (188) **11**. 133
Ducarius: (217) slays C. Flaminius, **5**. 219
Duillius, C.: (352) Vvir mens., **3**. 429
—, C.: (260) cos., first to celebrate naval triumph, **4**. 555
—, K.: (450–449) Xvir, **2**. 115–7, 139
—, K.: (336) cos., **4**. 63; (334) IIIvir for Cales, 67
—, M.: (470) tr. pl., **1**. 415; accuses Ap. Claudius, 423–5; (449) favours re-election of Xvir Ap. Claudius, **2**. 115; leads against Xviri, 171–3; tr. pl. ii, 181; restores appeal, 185; limits power of tribb. pl., 199, 217–9
—, M.: (357) tr. pl., limits interest rate, **3**. 409
— Longus, Cn.: (399) tr. mil. c. p., **3**. 47
duplicarii: (471) military rank, **1**. 421
duplication of office: (342) forbidden, **3**. 513
Duria, Alpine pass: Gauls cross, **3**. 119
Durnium, in Illyricum: (168) **13**. 189
Duronia, a matron: (186) wishes to initiate son in Bacchic rites, **11**. 243–9
Duronia, Samnite town: (293) **4**. 509
Duronius, L.: (181) pr. for Apulia, **12**. 59; suppresses Bacchic rites, 63; (180) returns from Illyricum, 131–3
duumviri aedi locandae: (345) **3**. 453; (217) **5**. 311
duumviri aedi dedicandae: (216) **6**. 73; (215) 103, 107; (194) **9**. 553; (192) **10**. 123; 191) 261–3; (181) **12**. 103–5
duumviri navales: (311) to construct and command fleet, **4**. 277; (282) 549; (181) **12**. 59–61, 83; (180) 133; (178) 185–7; (176) 237
duumviri perduellionis: (672–640) instituted for treason trial, **1**. 93; (384) condemn M. Manlius, **3**. 267
duumviri sacris faciundis: (436) direct ritual, **2**. 327; (433) consult Sibylline books, 335; (390) **3**. 167–9; (399) institute first *lectisternium*, 47–9; (387) dedicate temple, 213; (369) replaced by Xviri sacrorum, 327, 347
Dymae, in Achaea: (208) Philip at, **7**. 339, 343; (198) recently plundered

by Rome, aided by Philip, **9**. 223, 219; (189) slingers from, in Roman army, **11**. 99. *See* Aenesidemus.
Dyniae, in Phrygia: (189) **11**. 51
Dyrrachium (Epidamnus), port of Illyricum: (205) Romans at, **8**. 251; (200) **9**. 79; (171) **12**. 439; (169) hostages of Parthini sent to, **13**. 75; (168) envoys blown back to, 149; auxiliaries from, 189; threatened by Gentius, 189–91; (167) ships of Gentius given to, 403; (48) Caesar besieges Pompey at, **14**. 139, 307

eagle, as standard of legion: (46) **14**. 309
earth, and water: mark of submission, **10**. 53
Earth, Mother: *see* Tellus.
earthquake: (461) **2**. 35; (436) 327; (203) **8**. 373; (193) **9**. 557; (192) **10**. 61; 119; (179) **12**. 179, **14**. 243; (174) **12**. 281; (118, 117) **14**. 269; (100, 99) 281; (97) 283; (91) 291; (76) 299; (63) 301; (44) 311; (17) 317
Ebro (Hiberus) riv., in Spain: (226) boundary between Rome and Carthage, **5**. 7, 13, **9**. 451; *cp*. **5**. 17, 19, 53, 55, 131, 157, 287, **6**. 93, **7**. 197, **8**. 159; (218) Hannibal crosses, **5**. 45–7, 59, 65–9, 87, 331, without authority, **8**. 447; operations of Cn. Scipio north of, **5**. 179–85; (217) 263–75; (216) of P. and Cn. Scipio near, **6**. 87–9, 95; (214) 307; (212) L. Marcius faces Hasdrubal son of Gisgo north of, 479; (211) C. Claudius Nero at, **7**. 65; Hasdrubal son of Hamilcar winters near, 77; (210) P. Scipio (Afr.) begins campaign at, 157–65; **8**. 171; (206) tribes south of, protected, 99; Scipio crosses, 133; (195) operations near, **9**. 451, 459–61, 467; (193) **10**. 3; (183) **11**. 397; (77–76) Sertorius on, **14**. 189, 195
Eburones, Gauls: (54, 53) **14**. 133
Ebusus, Spanish is., (217) **5**. 267–9
Ecetra, city of Volsci: (495) makes terms, **1**. 299–301; (464) aids Aequi, **2**. 13; (461) Antiates meet at, 37; (406) operations near, 449; (404) 457; (378) **3**. 303
Echecrates: (179) brother of Antigonus III Doson, **12**. 165
Echedemus, of Acarnania: (197) agent of Philip, **9**. 319
—, of Athens: (190) envoy, **10**. 309
Echinus, in Thessaly: (197) Philip holds, **9**. 257, but yields to Aetolians, 309; (195) withheld from Aetolians, 475
eclipse, lunar: clashing of bronze at, **7**. 19; (168) announced before Pydna, **13**. 215–7; (94) of new moon **14**. 287
—, solar: (202) **8**. 511; (190) **10**. 301 (188) **11**. 119; (104) **14**. 277
Edesco, a Spaniard: (209) joins P. Scipio (Afr.), **7**. 279
Edessa, in Macedon: (167) **13**. 349, 353
Egeria: (715–672) Numa consults, **1**. 69, 75
Egerius: *see* Tarquinius.
Egnatius, Gellius, a Samnite: (296) defeated in Etruria, **4**. 421–31, 437; (295) slain at Sentinum, 473, 479
—: *see* Marius.
Egypt: (326) Alexandria founded in, **4**. 93; effect of, on Macedonians, **11**. 59; (200) treaty of Antiochus and Philip to partition, **9**. 43; Aetolian mercenaries in, 127; (198–197) Flamininus demands restoration of lands of, 253; (196) Antiochus threatens, 387, 395–7; (168) Antiochus IV occupies, **12**. 375, **13**. 277–81, but yields to C. Popilius Laenas, 273, 281–3, 167; (131) disturbed condition of, **14**. 67; (96) Ptolemy Apion bequeaths, to Rome, 87, 285: (48) Pompey killed on reaching, 141, 307; Cleopatra restored to throne of, 141; (46) Caesar triumphs over, 145, 213. *See* Ptolemy, Cleopatra.
Elaea, port of Pergamum: (193) Roman envoys at, **10**. 39; (191–190) military and naval operations about, 279, 325, 341–7, 353, 397; Africanus ill, taken to, 397, 421, **11**. 205; (188) Eumenes' fleet sails from, 135; (169) **13**. 123; (168) Perseus destroys ships leaving, 181–3
Elaeus, in Thrace: (200) submits to Philip, **9**. 51, (190) to C. Livius Salinator, **10**. 317
Elatia, in Phocis: (208–207) Philip

INDEX

moves to, **8**. 27–9; (198) Flamininus takes, **9**. 205–7, 215, 227–9, 249, **12**. 269; (197) Flamininus at, **9**. 269, 279–85, (196) 351, 357, 363, (195) 477–9, 527, (194) 541, 547; (191) Antiochus flees to, **10**. 217; (190) M' Acilius Glabrio at, 303
‹latia, in Thessaly: (171) **12**. 459
‹lba, is.: (202) **8**. 513
‹ection: (716) of king, in *comit. cent.*, presided over by interrex, **1**. 63; (510) of coss. in *comit. cent.*, presided over by praef. urb., 209, (509) by cos., 225, *et saepe*, (463) by interrex, **2**. 27 (*see* interrex), (361) by dictator, **3**. 383 (*see* dictator comit. c.); (438) rank in office fixed by plurality in, **2**. 311–3; (460) presiding officer may refuse to accept votes, 73–5; (433) tribb. pl. prevent election of coss., 335; (421) 397; (414) 423; (375–371) **3**. 319; (199) **9**. 171–3; (56) **14**. 131; (396) procedure in, **3**. 63; (215) **6**. 197, 203; (211) **7**. 85–7; (210) 221–7; (207) **8**. 41–3; (296) candidates elected in absentia, **4**. 443; (205) **8**. 249; (53) **14**. 133; (52) 135; (189) influence of presiding officer on, **11**. 115; (187) 147; (185) 319–21; (188) date of, **11**. 143; (179) **12**. 179; (172) 371; (170) **13**. 39; (166) corruption in, **14**. 247; (202) prevented by storm, **8**. 515; (179) **12**. 179; (139) use of ballot required in, **14**. 53. *See comitia centuriata*, *— curiata*, *— tributa*, *concilium plebis*; and the several magistrates.
‹*ephantomachae*: (168) in Perseus' army, **13**. 227–9
‹ephants: (280) in Pyrrhus' army, **4**. 549; (250) in triumph of L. Caecilius Metellus, 557; (221) in Hannibal's army, **5**. 15, (218) cross Rhone, 81–3, and Alps, 101–3, 109; at Trebia, 163–7; (217) Hannibal carried on one surviving, 175, 207; (216) new, sent to Hannibal, **6**. 43; in Punic armies, 61, 287, 501, etc.; (211) in ovation of M. Marcellus, **7**. 81; (201) Carthage required to surrender, **8**. 505–7, 533; (200) first used by Rome against Philip, **9**. 107; (198) 237; (197) 295, 299; (198) supplied by Masinissa 237; (191) **10**. 167; (171) **12**. 375, etc.; (196 Philip forbidden to have, **9**. 359–61; (192) in Antiochus' army, **10**. 127, 187, etc.; (191) in army of M' Acilius Glabrio, 197, (190) of L. Scipio, 405, (189) of Cn. Manlius Volso, **11**. 71; (188) Antiochus surrenders, 127, 131; (171) used against Perseus, **12**. 395, etc.; (218) device for transporting, across river, **6**. 81–3, (207) for killing, **7**. 403, (169) for moving down hill, **13**. 103–5; displayed in games, 149
elephants, African: (190) **10**. 405
—, Indian: (192) **10**. 93–5; (190) 405
Eleusis, in Attica: (200) mysteries at, violated, **9**. 45; Philip's attack on, fails, 73, 77–9, 89–91
— in Egypt: (168) **13**. 281
Elicius: *see* Jupiter Elicius.
Elimea, Macedonian city: (169) **13**. 77
Elimea (Elimiotis), Macedonian district: (200) P. Sulpicius Galba moves on, **9**. 117; (171) Perseus in, **12**. 457; (167) in 4th republic, **13**. 353
Elis, in Greece: (211) joins Romano-Aetolian alliance, **7**. 93; (209–208) Aetolians and Romans hold, against Philip and Achaeans, 339–43; (208–207) Philip protects, from Sparta, **8**. 29; (205) with Rome in treaty with Philip, 255; loses Triphylia, **9**. 165; (191) aided by Antiochus against Achaeans, **10**. 169; supports Antiochus, **12**. 401–3; outside Achaean league, **10**. 245–7, 257–9; added to league, **12**. 403; (189) council meets at, **11**. 107; (172) charged by Achaeans with having supported Philip, **12**. 401–3
Elpeüs riv., in Thessaly: (169) Perseus camps on, **13**. 115–7; (168) 153, 165, 173, 177, 197; L. Aemilius Paulus tries to cross, 205–11, 223
Elvius, P.: (114) **14**. 269
Elymaeans: (192) in Antiochus' army **10**. 137, 143, (190) 407, 409
emancipation of son: (357) **3**. 411
Emathia, in Macedon: (182) Philip moves population from coast to, **12**. 7–9; (170) rejects Roman demands, **13**. 29; (168) raided, 235–7
Emporia, in Africa: (204) P. Scipio (Afr.) sails for, **8**. 309, 337; (193) Masinissa endangers, **9**. 575

INDEX

Emporiae, Spanish port: colony of Phocaea, **7**. 75; divided between Greeks and Spaniards, **9**. 441–5; (218) Cn. Scipio at, **5**. 179–83; (211) P. Scipio (Afr.) lands at, **7**. 75, **8**. 171; (195) M. Porcius Cato lands at, **9**. 441, 447, defeats Spaniards near, 451–9
Empulum, in Latium: (355) **3**. 417
Eneti: follow Antenor to Venetia, **1**. 9
Ennius, Q.: lines of, on Fabius Maximus, **8**. 459; (187) statue of, **11**. 197
envoys: (509) rights of, **1**. 231; (172) **12**. 363; (205) treatment of foreign, in Rome, **8**. 159–61; (172) **12**. 365. *See ius gentium.*
Eordaea, in Macedon: (200) cos. P. Sulpicius Galba moves to, **9**. 115–7, 295; (171) Perseus at, **12**. 457; (167) in 4th Macedonian republic, **13**. 353
Epanterii: (205) **8**. 197–9
Ephesus: (196) Antiochus in, **9**. 379–81, 387; (195) Hannibal joins him in, 407; (193) 571; **10**. 39; they confer with envoys P. Villius Tappulus and Africanus in, 41–51; (191) goods of, as spoil of Thermopylae, 213; Antiochus returns to, 221, 273, 277; naval operations off, 285, (190) 319–21, 327–35, 339–41, 353, 365–7, 379–81, **12**. 161; surrenders to L. Scipio, **10**. 421, who winters at, 425, **11**. 9; (189) fleet based at, **10**. 477–9; (188) **11**. 131; (189) Cn. Manlius Volso at, before Galatian campaign, 37–9, and after, 93; (188) Eumenes and Roman envoys reach, 123; given to Eumenes 133–5
Epicadus: (168) killed by Gentius, **13**. 187
—: (168) commands Parthini in Roman army in Illyricum, **13**. 189
Epicrates, of Rhodes: (190) admiral under L. Aemilius Regillus, **10**. 331, 335
Epicydes, of Carthage and Syracuse: (215) sent by Hannibal to Syracuse, **6**. 191–5; (214) foments revolt, 251–3; elected magistrate, 261–3; joins brother in Leontini, 267–9; flees to Herbesus, 271; seizes Syracuse and declares war on Rome, 273–83, 451–3, **7**. 115–7; leads defence of Syracuse, **6**. 289, (212) 429–49, **7**. 115; sails to Agrigentum, **6**. 447–51, and continues war, 495–501; (210) flees to Africa, **7**. 155; (209) troops trained by, in Roman army, 239
Epicydes Sindon: (212) prefect of Epicydes of Syracuse, **6**. 449
Epidamnus: Greek name for Dyrrachium, **13**. 75
Epidaurus, in Argos: (292) Aesculapius brought from, **4**. 543; (167) L. Aemilius Paulus visits, **13**. 343
Epidius Marullus, C.: (44) tr. pl. opposes Caesar, expelled from office, **14**. 145–7, 317
Epiphanes: *see* Antiochus IV, Ptolemy V.
Epipolae, quarter of Syracuse: (212) **6**. 435
Epirus: in NW Greece, **9**. 321, **10**. 203; (326) ashes of Alexander of sent to, **4**. 97; (275) M' Curius Dentatus triumphs over, **13**. 383; (211) Acarnanians appeal to, **7**. 97–9; (205) agent of Philip in making peace, **8**. 253–5, **9**. 253; (200) an appendage of Macedon, 23; entered by P. Sulpicius Galba, 57, (199) by Macedonians, 165, (198) by Flamininus, 179; proposes peace terms, 181; assists Flamininus, 193–5; Philip driven from passes of, 189, 195–7, 215–7, 285, 295; (194) Romans cross, 547–9; (192) M. Baebius Tamphilus sent to, **10**. 69; leaders of, at Achaean council, 77; (191) seeks Antiochus' friendship, 169–71; pardoned for this, 259; (190) L. Scipio crosses, 305; (189) supports M. Fulvius Nobilior at Ambracia, **11**. 11–5; (188) Cn. Manlius Volso crosses, 143; (184) prisoner conducted through, 327; (174) relations of, with Perseus, **12**. 267; (172) troops and envoys sent to, 343, 399–403; (171) P. Licinius Crassus crosses, 461; (169) Phanote in, resists Ap. Claudius Cento, **13**. 75–7; invites Perseus to move on Aetolia, 77; men of, in both armies, 81, 83; furnishes grain, 141; (167) part of, supports Perseus, 363, but surrenders to L. Anicius Gallus, 335–7, who winters in, 339; partisans

INDEX

of Perseus from, to be tried in Rome, 355, 365–7; L. Aemilius Paulus despoils, 363–5; fourth Macedonian republic borders on, 349; (44) C. Octavius in, **14**. 147; (43) M. Junius Brutus defeats C. Antonius in, 149; (43–42) Sex. Pompeius gathers slaves and exiles in, 155; (31) Octavius crosses to, 163. *See* Alexander, Cephalus, Charopus, Menestas, Pyrrhus.

Eposognatus, a Galatian: (c. 191) refuses to aid Antiochus, **11**. 61; (189) tries to restrain Tectosagi, 61–5

Equites, equestrian order: (753–717) Romulus forms three centuries of, **1**. 51; (672–640) number of, increased by Tullus Hostilius, 107, (616–578) and by Elder Tarquin, 131–3, who assigns seats in theatre to, 129; (578–534) increased to 18 centuries by Servius; vote first in *comitia centuriata*, 153; (509) L. Junius Brutus selects Senators from, 221; (411) serve as envoys, **2**. 427–9; (403) serve at Veii on own horses, **3**. 25, 27; (304) parade of, before censs. instituted, **4**. 353; (214) list of, revised by censs., **6**. 231; (209) **7**. 253; (194) **9**. 533; (189) **11**. 95; (210) make voluntary loans for navy, **7**. 139; (207) prerogative of, in consular elections, **8**. 41; (204) each cens. orders other to sell his horse, 353–5; (184) L. Scipio Asiaticus deprived of horse, **11**. 359; (174) many removed, **12**. 281; (171) a training school for Senators, 481; (169) many removed, **13**. 55; 12 centuries of, in *comitia centuriata*, 59; (123–122) 600, made Senators by C. Gracchus, **14**. 71; (106) courts divided between Senators and, 275; (92) use control of courts unjustly, 87; (91) share courts with Senate, 89; (81–80) Sulla recruits Senate from, 111; (70) courts transferred to; Pompey made cos. while still, 121; (67) front rows in theatre reserved for, 123. For *equites* in military sense *see* cavalry.

Eretria, in Euboea: (198) captured, **9**. 197–9, 213; (196) status of, uncertain, 361, freed, 369; 194 garrison withdrawn from, 549; (192) thwarts Aetolian attempt on Chalcis, **10**. 113–5

Eretria, in Thessaly: (198) destroyed by Philip, **9**. 189; (197) Flamininus camps near, 291

Eretum, Sabine town: (458) Sabines defeated near, **2**. 89, 99, (449) camp at, 125, and defeat Romans, 139; (211) Hannibal passes through, **7**. 41. Prodigy: (211) 89.

Ergavica, in Spain: (179) **12**. 155

Ergetium, in Sicily: (211) **7**. 83–5

Ericinium, in Thessaly: (191) recovered, **10**. 197; (185) Perrhaebia claims, **11**. 297

Erigonus riv., in Paeonia: (200) Philip camps on, **9**. 115, (185) founds Perseis on, **11**. 391

Eritium, in Thessaly: (191) **10**. 195–7

Eriza, in Asia Minor: (189) **11**. 45

Erythrae, in Locris: (208–207) **8**. 33–5

—, in Ionia: **10**. 369; (191) fleet of Antiochus moves to, 279; Roman fleet passes, 285; (190) Romans from, try to rouse Aeolis, 315; ships of, in Roman fleet, 325; Romans and Eumenes sail to, 327; (188) rewarded for loyalty, **11**. 133; (168) Perseus destroys Eumenes' transports near, **13**. 181–3

Eryx, Mt., in Sicily: (241) Hamilcar confined on, **5**. 29, 121–3, **8**. 167. *See* Venus.

Esquiline gate, in Rome: (508) Etruscans ambushed at, **1**. 253–5; (446) Volsci and Aequi raid toward, **2**. 225, 229; (381) troops assemble outside, **3**. 275; (211) **7**. 35–7. Prodigies: (196) **9**. 349; (177 **12**. 213

— hill: (578–534) Servius establishes home on, **1**. 155, 171; (494) plebs meet on, 307; (446) Aequi almost take, **2**. 229; (211) Q. Fulvius Flaccus leads army to, **7**. 35; Numidian deserters cross to, 37. Prodigies: (165) **14**. 247; (137) 257

— tribe: (220) freedmen assigned to, **4**. 561; (168) **13**. 293–5

Esquilinus: *see* Minucius, Sergius, Verginius, — Tricostus.

Ethiopian: (42) as portent, **14**. 317

Etitovius: Gallic chief: (c. 575) enters Italy, **3**. 119–21

INDEX

Etleva, Illyrian queen : (168) **13**. 195
Etna, Mt. : *see* Aetna, Mt.
Etruria : early power of, **1**. 13, 109, **3**. 115–7, 185; defeated by Aeneas, **1**. 13, 15; separated from Latins by Tiber, 15–7; lictors, curule chairs, purple-bordered togas from, 31–3; (672–640) danger from, 81, 109; (640–616) Lucumo leaves, 123–5; skill of, in augury, 125, (578–534) 155–7; (616–578) defeated by Gauls, **3**. 115, 119, 121; horses and boxers from, **1**. 131; (578–534) truce with, expires, defeated by Servius, 149; (534–510) treaty renewed, 191; soothsayers and artisans called from, 191–5; Tarquin the Proud in exile in, 209, (509) fail to restore Tarquin, 235–9; occupy the Janiculum, checked by Horatius Cocles, 247–51, **3**. 341; invest city, various traditions, **1**. 251–67; settlement of, in Vicus Tuscus, 267; (492) corn from, 331; (480) Veientes and, defeated, 365–79; (479) danger from, 383; (477–476) defeat the Fabii, occupy the Janiculum, 387–93, 397; (461) K. Quinctius an exile among, **2**. 49; (460) danger from, 55; (441–440) grain from, 299; (437) defeated, 315–21; (435) 329; (434) refuse aid to Veii, 331–3; (433) grain sought from, 337; (432) discuss war, 337; (426) defeated, 359–71; (423) admit Samnites into Capua (Volturnum), 377, **3**. 497, **4**. 507, **8**. 117; (411) sell grain, **2**. 427; (406) danger from, 447; (405) fail to aid Veii, 455; (403) **3**. 3–5, 15–19, 23; (402) some, aid Veii, 29; (397) 61, 65; no soothsayers from, at Rome, 53; (396) Veii, wealthiest city of, captured, 79; (391) attacked by Gauls, 115, 121; Roman envoys at Clusium aid, 123–5, 153; (390) plunder Roman lands, defeated, 151–3; (389) attack Rome; defeated by Camillus, 199–207, 219; (388) towns of, taken, 209; (386) danger from, 213, 217; driven from Nepetê and Sutrium by Camillus, 225–9; (382) feared, 271; (364) scenic entertainment from, 361; (358) plunder Roman lands, 393; (356) defeated at salt works, 413–5; (353) raid salt works, 421–3; (352) feared without cause, 429; (319) in part in Roman Federation, **4**. 237; (312) feared, 273–5; (311) defeated before Sutrium, 281, 285–9; (310) 289, 299–309; literature of, studied in Rome, 301–3; chief cities granted truce, 309; Samnites consider march into, 311–3; defeated, 315–9, 323–5; (308) 325–31; (302) after a victory are defeated, 367–77, and granted truce, 377–9; (299) fail to get Gallic aid, 393–5, 403; defeated, 395–7; (298) 401–3; (297) some cities of, seek peace, 407; (296) Samnites and, defeated, 415–7, 421–31; new danger from, 437–41; (295) Q. Fabius Maximus and P. Decius Mus contend for command against, 447–59; defeated by Fabius and Decius, 459–79, and by Cn. Fulvius, 461, 475; (294) Samnites plan campaign in, 481; three cities of, gain truce, 501; various accounts of operations in, 501–5; (293) defeated, 531–5, 539; (284–281) 549; (280–278) 551; (218) P. Scipio coasts along, **5**. 75; (217) Hannibal unable to enter, 173–5; C. Flaminius in, 193; Hannibal plunders, 209–11; Romans flee to, after Trasumennus, 223–5; (212) allotted to M. Junius Silanus, **6**. 347–9; (211) **7**. 3–5; (212) grain from, for armies, **6**. 397, 419, 425, (210) **7**. 213; assigned to C. Calpurnius Piso, 109, 223, (209) 231, with urban legions, 237; revolt in, checked by Marcellus, 299; (208) assigned to C. Hostilius Tubulus, 303, 309–11, and C. Terrentius Varro, 309–11; men of, in Marcellus' army, 319–21; (207) Varro continued in, 351–3, 357; haruspices summoned from, 359; advance of Hasdrubal to, feared, 363, **8**. 43; (206) assigned to M. Livius Salinator, 45, (205) 199, 227; promises aid to P. Scipio (Afr.), 193; booty from, taken to Carthage, 199; (204) assigned to M. Cornelius Cethegus, 255, 349–51, 357; (203) allotted to C. Servilius Geminus, 367–9, 437–9; conspiracy in, suppressed, 461; (202) allotted to M. Servilius Geminus,

463, (201) 521; (200) troops transferred from, **9**. 33, 61, 141–3; L. Furius Purpurio sent to, 139; (196) slave rising in, suppressed, 373; (193) allotted to P. Porcius Laeca, 393; troops for Ligurian war assembled in, 561; (192) spoil taken by Ligurians in, **10**. 63; (191) Hannibal urges Antiochus to attack, 179; (190) allotted to P. Junius Brutus, 295–7; (189) 439, 467; colonies established on land once held by, 469; (183) **11**. 395; (181) **12**. 89; (177) 225; (187) Africanus serves in, **11**. 197; (186) Bacchic rites in, 241–3; (89) revolt in, suppressed, **14**. 93; (88) soothsayers from, 185; (63) Catiline raises army in, 127. As typical enemy: **3**. 185, 471, **4**. 237, **6**. 15. Prodigies: (102) **14**. 277; (83) 297. *See* Fidenae, Nortia, Twelve Cities, Veii, Voltumna; Porsinna.

Ettritus: (168) killed by Gentius, **13**. 187

Etuta: (168) wife of Gentius, **13**. 187

Euboea: S. of Thermopylae, **10**. 203, facing harbours of Macedon, **13**. 351–3; (209) Philip in, **7**. 333, 343; (207) complains to Philip of Aetolians, **8**. 17; Philip plans signal fires on, 21, 25; Attalus and P. Sulpicius Galba move to, 21–5; Philip leaves, 35; (200) Philocles leaves, **9**. 77; fleet and Attalus at, 131–3; (199) Philip tempts Achaeans to, 213; (198) fleets of Attalus, Rhodes, and Rome at, 197; cities of, taken, 201, 213; (196) proclaimed free by Flamininus, 365; (194) council of, called, 549; (192) Chalcis, key to, **10**. 113; Antiochus' conquest of, 147–9, (191) belittled by Hannibal, 175, 179; yields to M' Acilius Glabrio, 221; (182) fugitives from Philip seek, **12**. 11; (172) Roman envoys to, 401; (167) visited by L. Aemilius Paulus, **13**. 341. *See* Chalcis, Cenaeum, Oreus.

Euboean gulf (Coela): (200) **9**. 137

– straits: (200) **9**. 67

– talents: (190) **10**. 423; (189) **11**. 31

Eubulidas, of Chalcis: (190) Antiochus required to surrender, **10**. 425, (188) **11**. 131

Euctus: (168) with Perseus, **13**. 233

Eudamus: (190) Rhodian admiral, **10**. 327; in Roman council at Samos, 335; defeats Hannibal off Sida, 355–61; advises Romans at Samos, 367–9; defeats Antiochus off Myonnesus, 373–81; (168) at Tenedos, **13**. 181

Euergetes: *see* Antiochus VII, Attalus III, Ptolemy III.

Euganei: Antenor drives, from Venetia, **1**. 9

Eugenium, in Illyricum: (205) **8**. 253

Euhydrium, in Thessaly: (198) **9**. 189

Eulaeus: (168) with Perseus, **13**. 233

Eulyestae: (171) **12**. 447

Eumenes II, of Pergamum: (196) favoured in Roman treaty with Philip, **9**. 361, 369, **10**. 363; (195) assists Flamininus against Sparta, **9**. 483, 491, 495, 511, 525; (193) urges war with Antiochus, **10**. 39–41, 51, **13**. 167; (192) reports Antiochus' advance, **10**. 67; meets Flamininus in Euripus, goes to Athens, 115–7; sends men to Chalcis, 145, who soon retire, 149; (191) shares naval victory over Antiochus, 277–85; (190) tries to rouse Aeolis against Antiochus, 313–5; joins C. Livius Salinator, 315, 325–7; shares naval operations, 327–31, 333–5, 341; recalled to Pergamum, 341–3; joins L. Aemilius Regillus in council, 345–7, and in naval operations, 353; aids Scipio's crossing of Hellespont, 353, 367–9, 387, 449; brings supplies, 397; forces of, at Magnesia, 405, 411–3, 417–9; favours peace, 421; promised reparation, 423–5; (189) addresses Senate, asking for pro-Syrian cities, 425–7, 443–53; opposed by Rhodes, 453–61; receives certain lands, 463–5, **11**. 307; in Rome during Galatian war, 39, 123; Eposognatos loyal to, 61; (188) Galatians to receive terms from, 123, 135, 163; favoured in settlement with Antiochus, 127–35, 167, 209, 305; marries daughter of Ariarathes, 131, **12**. 375; disputes of, with Antiochus referred to Senate, **11**. 135, or to L. Scipio, 283; assists return of Cn. Manlius Volso, 135; (185) claims Thracian cities held by Philip, 289, 301–9, (184) 321–3, (183) 367; Prusias aided against, 367, 379; (182) envoys of, before Senate, **12**. 7; harmony of, and Attalus, 23–5; (181) envoys of, before Senate, 63; (174) receives messages from Greek cities, 257; (173) some Greeks prefer Perseus to, 305; makes charges against Perseus, 309, 321–31, 343, 361, 419, 429; envoys of Perseus and Rhodes attack, before Senate, 331–5; agents of Perseus wound, near Delphi, 335–9, 373, 411–3, 437, 477, **13**. 93, 261–3, charges of, against Perseus proved, **12**. 339–41; at Pergamum, prepares for war, 343; rejects Perseus' overtures, 367; (171) ally of Rome against Perseus, 373, 453; brings fleet to Chalcis, 463; with P. Licinius Crassus in Thessaly, 463, 467–77, 499, 505; general of, attacks Cotys, 503; (169) gives little naval aid to C. Marcius Figulus, **13**. 123–33, 155; negotiations with Perseus reported, 131, 305, **14**. 11; returns to Pergamum, **13**. 131; (168) Perseus seeks aid of, 167–9, 179; wishes a negotiated peace, 169–73; ships of, in minor actions, 181–5; congratulates Rome on defeat of Perseus, 287; (167) sends Attalus to Rome, 303–11; still childless, 307; seriously ill, 367; at war with Galatians, 367, 411; excluded from Rome, **14**. 11; (164) charged by Prusias with plundering, 11; Andriscus avoids, 29; unfavourable account of, by Valerius Antias, **13**. 133. *See* Aristonicus, Athenaeus, Attalus; Pergamum.

Eumenes: (168) garrison commander of Perseus, **13**. 195

Eunomus: (192) Thessalian praetor, **10**. 117

Eunus: (134) leads Sicilian slave revolt, **14**. 59

Eupalium, in Locris: (207) **8**. 35

Eupator: *see* Antiochus V.

Euphanes: (191) officer of Antiochus, **10**. 169

Euphranor: (174) Macedonian governor, killed by Dolopians, **12**. 417

—: (169) officer of Perseus, **13**. 131

Euphrates riv.: (54) **14**. 133, 305

Eupolemus, an Aetolian: (189) commands against Rome, **11**. 15, 19; (174) kills returning exiles, **12**. 271–3

Euripus: (208) P. Sulpicius Galba avoids currents of, **8**. 21–5; (200) Chalcidian pirates held at, **9**. 65; importance of, to Philip, 67–9; (192) on Aetolian route to Chalcis, **10**. 113–5; Flamininus meets Eumenes at, 115; Antiochus and Aetolian envoys cross, 133, 143, 183; Achaeans cross, with aid to Chalcis, 145; Roman post on, surrenders, 149; (191) Hannibal belittles capture of, 179; (167) visited by L. Aemilius Paulus, **13**. 341

Euromus, in Asia Minor: (197) Philip's withdrawal from, demanded, **9**. 255, 359; (167) Rhodes retains, **13**. 333

Europe: **4**. 225, **7**. 331, **9**. 5, 313, 359, 363, 369, 383–5, 395, 507, 529, 565, 571, **10**. 33, 53, 97, 105, 133–9, 165, 177, 209, 391–3, 423, 443, 449, 455, **11**. 125, 133, 135, 145, 207, **12**. 373, 455, **13**. 271–3, 361

Eurotas riv., in Sparta: (195) Flamininus at, **9**. 487, 491; (192) Philopoemen defeats Nabis near, **10**. 85–7; Nabis murdered near, 10[…]

Euryalus, in Syracuse, (212) **6**. 437–4[…]

Eurydicê: (168) Gentius' mother, **13**. 187

Eurylochus, chief of Magnetes: (192) in council at Demetrias, **10**. 91–3; seizes Demetrias for Aetolians, 101–3, 111; warns Romans from Demetrias, 117; meets Antiochus, 127; (191) kills self, 253

Eurymedon riv.: (196) Antiochus near mouth of, **9**. 387; (190) Rhodian fleet at, **10**. 355

Eurymenae, in Thessaly: (185) **11**. 291–3

Euthymidas, of Chalcis: (192) exiled, fails to seize Chalcis, **10**. 111–5

Eutychides: (95) enters shrine of Jupiter at Lebadea, **14**. 285

Evander, an Arcadian: establishes Lupercalia, **1**. 21, **14**. 227, and Greek cult of Hercules, **1**. 27–31; invents letters, 29

—, of Crete: (172) assaults Eumenes for Perseus, **12**. 335–9, 475–7, **13**[…]

261–3; (171) warns Perseus after Callinicus, **12**. 475–7; (168) flees with him, **13**. 233, 239; murdered by him, 261–3
Eversa, of Thebes: (172) opposes Perseus, killed, **12**. 329, 411
execution: (509) described, **1**. 233
exile, to avoid penalty: (461) **2**. 49; (212) **6**. 355; (211) **7**. 13–5; (187) **11**. 181–3; (171) **13**. 9–11
extraordinarii milites: (193) **10**. 11, 13

Fabiae: (377) wives of Ser. Sulpicius Rufus and C. Licinius Stolo, **3**. 313–5
Fabii: (484) hated by plebs, **1**. 357; (480) gain fame against Etruscans, 373, 379–81; (479) undertake war with Veii, 383–7; almost wiped out at Cremera, 389–91, 93, **3**. 197; (390) sacrifice annually on Quirinal, 155, 175; (319) worthy opponents for Alexander, **4**. 229
Fabius, L.: (203) envoy to Carthage, **8**. 453–5
—, M.: (335) escapes from Cales, **4**. 65–7
—, M. (or Caeso): (310) enters Ciminian forest, **4**. 301
— Ambustus, Caeso (or C.), tr. mil. c. p., 404, 401, 395, 390: (409) qu., **2**. 433; (404) tr. mil. c. p., 455; (401) ii, **3**. 35; recovers camp at Veii, 43; (395) tr. mil. c. p. iii, 83; (391) envoy to Clusium, 121–7; (390) tr. mil. c. p. iv, neglects auspices, defeated by Gauls, 127–31
— —, C.: (358) cos., **3**. 393; defeated by Etruscans, 407; (355) interrex, 415
— —, C.: (315) mag. eq., **4**. 251–3
— —, M.: (391) father of Caeso, N., and Q., envoys to Clusium, **3**. 121–7
— —, M.: (381) tr. mil. c. p., **3**. 273; (377) aids son-in-law, C. Licinius Stolo, 313–7; (369) 321; tr. mil. c. p. ii, 321
— —, M.: (360) cos., defeats Hernici, **3**. 389–91; (356) cos. ii, defeats Etruscans, 413; (355) interrex, 415; (354) cos. iii, 419; (351) interrex, 431; dict. comit. c., 433; (325) appeals for son, **4**. 129–33, 137
— —, M.: (322) mag. eq., **4**. 147, 151–3
Fabius Ambustus, N.: (406) tr. mil. c. p., **2**. 447; captures Anxur, 449–51; (391) envoy to Clusium, **3**. 121–7; (390) tr. mil. c. p., neglects auspices, defeated by Gauls, 127–31
— —, Q.: (412) cos., **2**. 427
— —, Q., tr. mil. c. p., 390: (391) envoy to Clusium, slays Gallic chief, **3**. 121–7; (390) tr. mil. c. p., neglects auspices, defeated by Gauls, 127–31; (389) accused of violating *ius gentium*, dies, 197
— —, Q.: (344) mag. eq., **3**. 455; (321) dict. comit. c., **4**. 187
— Buteo, M., cos. 245: (216) dict. to revise Senate, **6**. 77–9
— —, M., pr. 201: (203) aed. cur., distributes grain, **8**. 459; (201) pr. for Sardinia, 517, 521–3
— —, N.: (173) pr. for Hither Spain, **12**. 283, 293; dies at Massilia, 301–3
— —, Q., pr. 196: (197) sent to Rome, **9**. 265; (196) pr. for Farther Spain, 341, 347, 393
— —, Q., pr. 181: (185) qu. in Spain, **11**. 309; (181) pr. for Gaul, **12**. 59, 81; (180) 115; IIIvir col. deduc., 135–7; (168) Vvir between Pisae and Luna, **13**. 287
— Dorsuo, C.: (390) sacrifices on Quirinal, **3**. 153–5, 175
— —, M.: (345) cos., captures Sora, **3**. 451–3; (340) interrex, **4**. 11; (334) IIIvir col. deduc., 67
— Hadrianus, C.: (84) pr. in Africa; (83) burned alive, **14**. 107
— Labeo, Q., cos. 183: (196) qu., forces priests to pay taxes, **9**. 389; (189) pr. for fleet, **10**. 431, 437, 477–9, **11**. 303; (188) destroys Antiochus' ships, 131; triumphs, **10**. 479, **11**. 163; (185) candidate for cos., 319–21; (184) IIIvir col. deduc., 363, 397; (183) cos. with Liguria as prov., 363, 397, **14**. 241; (192) **12**. 3–5; (180) pont., 133; (167) Xvir on Macedonian terms, **13**. 299, 339, 345–7, 355; sent to destroy Antissa, 357
— Maximus, Q., cos. 213: (217) son of Cunctator, **5**. 279–81; (216) tr. mil., survives Cannae, 373; (215) aed. cur., **6**. 203; (214) pr. for Apulia, 203, 209; at Luceria and Ardaneae, 213, 239; (213) cos.,

313–5, 347, **9**. 433, with Apulia as prov., **6**. 317, 327; makes father dismount, 317–9; punishes Dasius Altinius, 319–21; takes Arpi, 323–7; (209) leg., gathers forces for Sicily, **7**. 237–9; (208) sent to Venusia, 329; (207) envoy of M. Livius Salinator to Senate, **8**. 37

Fabius Maximus, Q.: (203–196) augur, **8**. 461, **9** .391, 395

— —, Q.: (181) pr. pereg., **12**. 59; levies Latins for Liguria, 81–3, 89; answers Ligurians, 105

— — Aemilianus, Q., cos. 145: son of L. Aemilius Paulus, **13**. 397; (168) leg. of Paulus, 207–9, 237, 249–53; (167) 339, 363, 365; follows Paulus in triumph, 391; (145) cos., against Viriathus, **14**. 45

— — Allobrogicus, Q.: (121) cos., **14**. 267; defeats Allobroges and Arverni, 73

— — Gurges, Q., cos. 292, 276, 265: (297) tr. mil., **4**. 409–11; (295) aed. cur., builds temple to Venus, 479; (292) cos., 541; defeats Samnites, triumphs, 547; father of Cunctator, **8**. 459

— — Rullianus, Q., cos. 322, 310, 308, 297, 295: (331) aed. cur., accuses women poisoners, **4**. 71; (325) mag. eq. of L. Papirius Cursor, 113; defeats Samnites against orders, 115–7, 369; barely escapes punishment, 119–39; (322) cos., 147; defeats Samnites, 155; (320) interrex, 189; (319) worthy opponent of Alexander, 227; (315) dict. for year, 245–7, 253–5; takes Saticula, 247–9; defeats Samnites, 251–3; (310) cos. ii, 289; defeats Etruscans, 299–301; crosses Ciminian forest, 303–5, 311; defeats Etruscans, 305–9: names Papirius dict., 313–5; defeats Etruscans, triumphs, 323–5; (308) cos. iii, 325, 341; defeats Samnites and Umbrians, 325–31; (307) 331–3; (304) cens., puts *humiliores* in urban tribes, institutes parade of equites, 353; (302) mag. eq., 369 (?); (299) aed. cur. ii, 391; imports grain, 399; (297) cos. iv, 403–7; defeats Samnites, 407–13; refuses to present own name at election, 413–5; (296) in Samnium, Lucania, 415, 421–3, 431; (295) cos. v, 441–3, **6**. 205; with P. Decius Mus, **4**. 447–59, defeats Etruscans and Samnites at Sentinum, 461–73; celebrates Decius' funeral, 473–5; triumphs, 475–7; ends term, 481; (292) leg. of son, 547; grandfather of Cunctator, **8**. 459

Fabius Maximus Servilianus, Q.: (142) cos., **14**. 255; (141–140) in Spain, defeats Viriathus, 47, 49, 51

— — Verrucosus (Cunctator), Q., cos. 233, 228, 215, 214, 209: (218) envoy to Carthage, and Spain, **5**. 49–59, 63; (217) dict. ii, by election, 227, 307; takes up religious matters, 229–31; vows temple to Venus Erycina, 235; takes command, 235–9; avoids battle, 239–45, 251; assailed by mag. eq., M. Minucius Rufus, 241–51, 335, **13**. 379; camps near Hannibal, **5**. 251–5, who escapes through Callicula, 255–61, 339; follows Hannibal, 261; criticism of, at Rome, 277–81, 327, 347; Hannibal spares farm of, 279; Minucius wins victory in absence of, 281–3, 315; Hannibal imitates, 283; Numerius Decimus mistaken for, 283–5; holds election for cos. suf., 287–9; Minucius given equal power, 285–7, 289–95, 313, **8**. 163–5; saves Minucius, who resumes rank, **5**. 297–303, 315; ends term, 305–7; (216) advises cos. L. Aemilius Paulus, 327–35, 361; advises Senate after Cannae, 379–81; elected pont., **6**. 73; opposes Latins as Senators, 75–7; IIvir for temple of Venus Erycina, 103, 107; (215) cos. suf., 109, **9**. 413; at Teanum, **6**. 109; orders grain brought to towns, 113; in Campania, 127–9, 135–7, 157–63; fortifies Puteoli, 197, 419; holds election; elected cos., 197–203, **7**. 225; (214) cos. iv, **6**. 205, 313; holds election of censs., 211; takes Casilinum, 213, 217, 233–7; plunders Samnium, 237–9, holds elections, 313–5; (213) leg. of son, 317–23; (211) opposes moving troops to Rome, **7**. 29–31; proposed as cos., 87; (209) cos. v, 223–5, **8**. 263; near Tarentum, **7**. 231, 233;

sends forces to Sicily, 237–9; rebukes Latins, 241–5; encourages Senate, 245–7; receives sacred funds, 249; prin. sen., 251–3; takes Tarentum, 253–5, 267–79, 297, 311–3; in Senate, favors Tarentines, 299, 311; (208) reconciles coss. elect, 349–53; (207) advises cos. M. Livius Salinator, 371; (205) opposes P. Scipio's African expedition, **8**. 161–77, 465; Scipio answers, 177–89; (204) examines Locrians, 281; proposes SC. against Q. Pleminius and Scipio, 283–5; prin. sen., 351; dies, 459–61; his character and career, 163–5, 177–9, 459; **13**. 161, 379

Fabius Paulus: (11) cos., **14**. 319

— Pictor, Q., the annalist: (216) envoy to Delphi, **5**. 385, **6**. 33. Cited: (578–534) **1**. 155; (534–510) 193; (488) 351; (294) **4**. 503–5; (217) **5**. 223

— —, Q., pr. 189: (189–167) flam. Quir., **10**. 431, **13**. 405; (189) pr. for Sardinia, **10**. 431, 437, then pereg., 439–41

— Vibulanus, Caeso, cos. 484, 481, 479; (485) qu., **1**. 355–7; (484) cos., opposes land law, 357–9; (481) cos. ii, defeats Aequi in spite of mutiny, 361–3, 417; (480) in Etruscan battle, 375; (479) cos. iii, proposes SC. distributing land, fights Aequi and Veientes, 381–3; leads Fabii against Veientes, 385

— —, M.: (483) cos., **1**. 359; (480) ii, 363; defeats Etruscans, 367–79

— —, M.: (442) cos., **2**. 295; (437) leg. against Etruscans, 315, 321; (433) tr. mil. c. p., 335; (431) leg. against Aequi and Volsci, 347–51

— —, N.: (421) cos., defeats Aequi, **2**. 395; (415) tr. mil. c. p., 417; (407) ii, 445

— —, Q.: (485) cos., sells booty for treasury, **1**. 355–7; (482) cos. ii, 361; (480) killed in Etruscan battle, 375, 379

— —, Q.: (479) sole survivor of Cremera; (467) cos., **2**. 3–5; (465) ii, defeats Aequi, 5–11; (462) pref. urb., defends city, 29, 31; (459) cos. iii, defeats Volsci, 75–9, and Aequi, 79–81; triumphs, 83; opposes re-election of tribb. pl., 83; (458) envoy to Aequi, 87; pref. urb., convenes Senate, 99; takes over army of L. Minucius, 101; (450–449) Xvir leg. scrib., 117, 139

Fabius Vibulanus, Q.: (423) cos., **2**. 377, 385; (414) tr. mil. c. p. ii, 417; (413) interrex, 423

Fabrateria, Volscian city: (330) **4**. 73–5

Fabricius Luscinus, C., cos. 282, 278: (280) envoy to Pyrrhus, **4**. 549; (278) cos. ii; (275) cens., 551

— —, C.: (195) pr. urb., **9**. 391, 393; (190) leg., collects ships, **10**. 301

Faecenia: *see* Hispala.

Faesulae: (217) fertility of, **5**. 209. Prodigies: (96) **14**. 285; (94) 287; (92) 289

Faesus: *see* Minucius.

Fair God, Cape of the, in Africa: (204) **8**. 315

Falerii, Etruscan city: *see* Faliscans.

Falerna tribus: (318) added, **4**. 243

Falernian district: (349) Gauls occupy, **3**. 447; (340) distributed to plebs, **4**. 47, 51; (296) Samnites plunder, 431; protected by colonies, 439; (217) Hannibal plunders, **5**. 245–7, 251, 287

Faliscans: (437) support Veii and Fidenae, **2**. 315, **3**. 29; defeated, **2**. 317–21, 361; (436) invaded, 325; (435) quiet, 327; (434) call Etruscan Council, 331; (402) attack Romans at Veii, **3**. 29–31, 41, 95; (401) plundered, 35, 43; (399) defeated at Veii, 49–51; (398) continue war, 53; (397) 57, 61; (396) 63–7; (395) 83; (394) defeated by Camillus, 89–93, 147; surrender; Camillus spurns treachery of tutor, 93–7, **6**. 319, **12**. 435; (389) some, become citizens, **3**. 207; (358) aid Tarquinienses, 409; (356) defeated, 413–5; (353) 425–7; (351) receive 40 yr. truce, 431; (343) ask for treaty, 495; (328) Romans in, mistreated, **4**. 87; (298) territory of, invaded, 401–3; (297) sue for peace, 407; (295) army posted near, 461–3; (293) join Etruscans, 533; receive year's truce, 539; (241) revolt of, subdued, 559. *See* L. Opicernicus.

Falto: *see* Valerius.

famine, in Rome: (492) **1**. 329–31; (456) **2**. 103; (453) 107; (440) 299; (433) 337; (428) 355; (411) 427; (392) **3**. 109; (390) 161; (383) 269; (298) **4**. 399; (165) **14**. 247; (142) 255
Fannius, C.: (187) tr. pl., refuses aid to L. Scipio, **11**. 209
—, C.: (122) cos., **14**. 267
Fas: (340) prayer to Jus and, **4**. 19
fasces: (509) one cos. only has, **1**. 221; cos. P. Valerius lowers, 241; (501) axes in, of dictator, 277; (473) of cos., broken by mob, 407; (451) one Xvir has 12, others have none, **2**. 111; (450) each Xvir has 12 with axes, 119; (449) of Appius, broken by mob, 161; (339) cos. with, names dict., **4**. 51; (320) cos. having the, presides over Senate, 189; (215) with axes, carried by cos. in Campus Martius, **6**. 203; (212) of Ti. Sempronius Gracchus sent to Hannibal, 409; (82) 24, carried before Sulla, **14**. 111; (62) laurel crowned, should be deposited on Capitol, 303; (42) laurel on, in lustration of camp, 317
Fathers: *see* Senate, Senators.
Faucia, a curia: (310) **4**. 315
Faunus: (196, 194) temple to, **9**. 391, 553
Faustulus: rescues Romulus and Remus, **1**. 19–23
Faventia, in cis-Alpine Gaul: (82) **14**. 109
Faveria, Histrian town: (177) **12**. 221
Februarius: honoured in time of pestilence, **14**. 227
February: (188) coss. elected on 18th, **11**. 143; (172) **12**. 371
Felix: *see* Cornelius Sulla.
Felsina, city of Boi: (196) **9**. 377
Fenectane plains: (339) **4**. 49
Feralia, a festival: (193) **10**. 19
Ferentani: *see* Forentum.
Ferentina, Grove of: (534–510) Latins meet at, **1**. 175, 183; (349) **3**. 441
Ferentine water: (534–510) Turnus Herdonius drowned in, **1**. 181; (491) Volsci gather at source of, 341
Ferentinum: (413) captured; given to Hernici, **2**. 425–7, 439; (404) Volsci defeated near, 457; (361) captured, **3**. 381–3; (306) refrains from war, **4**. 333; own laws restored to, 339; (296) captured, 421; (211) Hannibal passes near, **7**. 35; (199) Punic hostages at, **9**. 159; (195) request of, *re* citizenship denied, 529. Prodigy: (133) **14**. 261
Feretrius: *see* Jupiter.
feriae in triduum: (464) to avert omens, **2**. 21
Feritrum, Samnite town: 294) **4**. 487–9
Feronia: (217) gift to, by freedwomen, **5**. 203–5; (672–640) sanctuary of, near Capena, **1**. 109; (211) **7**. 41. Prodigies: (210) **7**. 217; (196) **9**. 349
fescennine verses: (364) **3**. 361
fetiales: (672–640) ritual for treaty; treaty made with Alba, **1**. 83–5; (640–616) ritual for demanding restitution, 115–9; restitution demanded from Latins, 119, (427) Veii, **2**. 357, (407) 445, (362) Hernici, **3**. 395, (361) Tibur, 383, (357) Faliscans, 409, (343) Samnites, 467, (327) Palaepolis, **4**. 87, (304) Aequi, 347, (293) Etruscans, 533; (326) declare war on Samnites, 99; (321) none present at Caudine pass, 177–9; (320) deliver up sponsors of Caudine peace, 199–203; (298) order Samnites from Lucania, 401; (201) sent to Africa to make peace; formula of, **8**. 531; (200) consulted on form for declaring war, **9**. 25; (191) **10**. 163–5; (188) deliver citizens to Punic envoys, **11**. 145; (187) forms of, neglected, 155, 159–61
'fetters of Greece,' (197) **9**. 265
Ficana, in Latium: (640–616) **1**. 119
Ficulea Vetus, in Latium: (616–578) **1**. 137
Ficulensis via: (449) old name for Via Nomentana, **2**. 173
Fidenae, Etruscan town: (753–717) defeated, **1**. 51–5; becomes Roman colony, 97, **2**. 313; (672–640) revolts, is defeated, **1**. 97–9, 103; (499) besieged, 279; (449) Romans entrench near, **2**. 141; (437) goes over to Veii, 313–5, **3**. 29; defeated, **2**. 317–21, 361; (435) taken, 327–31, 337, 357, 405; (428) new colonists sent to, 355, (426) are killed, and new war begins, 359–61, **3**. 15;

INDEX

sacked, **2**. 363–71, 391; (390) possible site for new Rome, **3**. 183. *Also* 127.
Fidenas: *see* Sergius, Servilius, — Priscus.
Fidentia, in cis-Alpine Gaul: (82) **14**. 109
Fides: (715–672) cult of, **1**. 75; (44) temple of, **14**. 311
Figulus: *see* Marcius.
Fimbria: *see* Flavius.
finance, public: (296) aedd. build public works from fines, **4**. 447; (295) 479; 485; (292) 541; (202) **8**. 515; (196) **9**. 391; (194) 553; (193) **10**. 29; (192) 123; (189) **11**. 115–7; (179) revenue assigned censs. for public works, **12**. 147, 157–61; (169) **13**. 143; (215) financial difficulties, **6**. 163–7; (214) 211; 231–3. *See* aediles, censors, *publicani*, *quinqueviri mensarii*; *aerarium*; *portoria*, tithe, *tributum*.
fire, as instrument of war: (426) **2**. 365–7; (389) **3**. 201; (190) **10**. 323–5, 377
fires: (390) in Rome, **3**. 143–5, 195; (213) **6**. 327–9; (210) **7**. 103–5; (203) **8**. 459; (192) **10**. 121; (178) **14**. 243; (148) 37, 253; (111) 271; (84) **6**. 493; (50) **14**. 205, 307; (136) in Regium, 257
Firmum, in Picenum: (209) loyal, **7**. 245–7; (168) cohort from, at Pydna, **13**. 225
Fish market (*Forum Piscatorium*): (210) fire spreads to, **7**. 103
Flaccinator: *see* Folius.
Flaccus: *see* Fulvius, Tarquitius, Tremellius, Valerius.
Flamen: *see* Claudius.
amines: (715–672) placed over sacrifices, **1**. 75; (640–616) 119; (409) a patrician priesthood, **2**. 435; (390) carry *sacra* to Caerê, **3**. 135–9, 423–5. *Flamen Dialis*: (715–672) Numa performs duties of, then appoints a, **1**. 71; (368) a patrician priesthood, **3**. 345; (390) not permitted to leave city, **3**. 179; (183) **11**. 363; (209) appointed by pont. max., **7**. 235; (200) cannot take oath, **9**. 147–9; (209) sits in Senate, **7**. 237. Vacancies and appointments: (211, 209) 91, 235; 174) **12**. 283. *Flamen Martialis*: (715–672) Numa appoints first, **1**. 71; (242) not permitted to leave city. **4**, 559, **10**. 439. Vacancies and appointments: (204) **8**. 359; (169, 168) **13**. 149, 295. *Flamen Quirinalis*: (715–672) Numa appoints first, **1**. 71; (390) carries *sacra* to Caerê, **3**. 137–9; (215) not permitted to leave city, **6**. 199; (189) **10**. 439–41. Vacancies and appointments: (453) **2**. 107; (190) **10**. 431; (167 **13**. 405
Flaminian Circus: (220) built by cens. C. Flaminius, **4**. 561, in Flaminian meadows, **2**. 181; (209) charges against Marcellus heard in, **7**. 297; (206) altar of Neptune in, **8**. 47; (187) military decorations presented in, **11**. 233; (179) temples of Juno and Diana in, **12**. 161, **14**. 251; (167) preparations for triumph made in, **13**. 389; (156) temple of Fortune in, **14**. 251; (91) temple of Pietas in, 291. Prodigies: (206) **8**. 47; (156) **14**. 251
— meadows: (449) plebeians meet in, **2**. 181; Senate meets in, 213–5
— way: (220) built by cens. C. Flaminius, **4**. 561; (217) dict. Q. Fabius Maximus meets army on, **5**. 237; (187) joined by Aemilian way, **11**. 223
Flamininus: *see* Quinctius.
Flaminius, C., cos. 223, 217: character of, **5**. 209–11; (232) tr. pl., quarrels with Senate, 187–9; (223) cos., quarrels with Senate, 187–9; defeats Gauls, triumphs, 189–91, 219, **6**. 45; (220) cens., **4**. 561, **6**. 73, 77–9, 211; builds circus and way, **4**. 561; (217) cos. ii, **5**. 43, 169, **7**. 345, **9**. 395; with Placentia as prov., **5**. 187; takes office in Ariminum, neglecting ritual, 187–93, 43, 199–201, 231; reaches Arretium, 205; defeated at Trasumennus by Hannibal, killed, 209–19, 223, 225, 241, 261, 285, 321, 329, 341, 347, **6**. 35, 155, **7**. 9, 225, **8**. 119; cos. suf. for, **5**. 287
—, C., cos. 187: (210) qu. of P. Scipio (Afr.), in Spain, **7**. 181, 189; (196) aed. cur., distributes grain, **9**. 391; (193) pr. for Hither Spain, 555–9,

10. 5–7, 19–21; (192) 59, 63–5; (191) 161; (190) 297; (187) cos. with Liguria as prov., **11.** 143, 145, 153; defends M. Fulvius Nobilior, 149–51; defeats Ligurians, 219–23, 277; builds road, 223; holds elections, 233–5; (183–181) IIIvir for Aquileia, 395, **12.** 103

Flamma: *see* Calpurnius.

Flavius, Cn.: (304) aed. cur. although freedman's son, **4.** 349–51; publishes *ius civile* and calendar, dedicates temple to Concord, 351

—, M., tr. pl. 327, 323: (328) gives dole; (327) tr. pl., **4.** 85; (323) ii, proposes trial of Tusculans, 145

— Fimbria, C.: (104) cos., **14.** 275

— —, C.: (87) supporter of Marius, **14.** 101; (86) leg. of C. Valerius Flaccus, whom he kills, 103; (85) wins victories in Asia, kills self, 105, 297

Flavoleius, M.: (480) a centurion, **1.** 371–3

Flavus: *see* Decimius, Lucretius.

—, a Lucanian: (212) betrays Ti. Sempronius Gracchus, **6.** 403–9

fleet: *see* naval antiquities, *duumviri navales*.

flint: (672–640) used as sacrificial knife, **1.** 85; (218) **5.** 135; (202) **8.** 531; (189) used for paving, **11.** 95; (174) **12.** 277–81

floods, of Tiber: (363) **3.** 365; (203) **8.** 459; (202) 513; (193) **10.** 23; (192) 61; (189) **11.** 95

Floronia (Florentia), a Vestal: (216) punished for unchastity, **5.** 385, 413

Flumentane gate: (384) *concilium populi* meets outside, **3.** 267; (193) buildings near, swept away by Tiber, **10.** 23; (192) 61

flute players: (311) at sacrifice, **4.** 279–81

oedus: *see* alliance.

Folius Flaccina (or Flaccinator), M.: (433) tr. mil. c. p., **2.** 335; (390) pont. max., dictates *devotio*, **3.** 141

— —, M.: (318) cos., **4.** 241; (314) mag. eq., 263; tried, acquitted, 265–7; (313) mag. eq., 271

Fonteius, M.: (166) pr., **13.** 405

—, Ti.: (212) leg. of P. Scipio in Spain, **6.** 469; commands on his death, 477–9; (211) **7.** 65

Fonteius Balbus, P.: (168) pr. for Spain, **13.** 145–7

— Capito, C., cos. suf. 33; (37) agent of M. Antonius, **14.** 221

— —, P.: (169) pr. for Sardinia, **13.** 39, 53

— —, T.: (178) pr., **12.** 179; (177–176) in Spain, 231

Fontinalis gate: (193) **10.** 29

Forentum, in Apulia: (319) defeated, **4.** 221[1]; (317) 243

Formiae, in Latium: (338) granted citizenship without vote, **4.** 61; (327) Samnites seek aid of, 89; (295) Samnites raid, 477; (217) Hannibal may winter near, **5.** 255; (216) slave from, warns Romans, 341–3; (188) granted vote, **11.** 119–21; (184) road construction at, 361; (43) Cicero comes to, **14.** 217. Prodigies: (199) **9.** 157; (197) 243; (192) **10.** 61; (182) **12.** 5; (163) **14.** 249

Fors Fortuna: (578–534, 293) temples to, built, **4.** 539. Prodigy: (209) **7.** 249

Fortuna: (218) *supplicatio* to, **5.** 187; (672–640) powerful over human affairs, **1.** 81; (508) 257–9; (491) 333; (423) **2.** 379; (401) **3.** 43; (394) 93; (390) 127; 143–5; 147–9; (386) 225; (343) 485; (326) **4.** 99; (325) 111; (320) 207–9; (319) 227; (315) 247; (314) 257; (310) 311; (298) 405; (297) 409; (295) 465, 471; (257–253) 555; (223) **5.** 209; (218) 125–7; 133; (217) 293; (216) 337; (212) **6.** 485; (210) **7.** 157; (202) **8.** 475; 483; (197) **9.** 335; (187) **11.** 159; (168) **13.** 225. Temples of: (196) in Forum Boarium, **9.** 349, (213) burned, **6.** 329, (212) rebuilt, 365, (169) prodigy at, **13.** 47; (209) in Capua, **7.** 249, (208) 305; (216) in Praenestê, **6.** 69, (173) **12.** 295, (167) **13.** 407

— Equestris: (180) temple to, vowed, **12.** 125, (179) contracted for, 141, (173) constructed, 299, dedicated, 319. Prodigies: (156) **14.** 251; (92) 289

— Muliebris: (488) temple to, **1.** 351

— Primigenia: (204) temple to, vowed, **8.** 349, (194) dedicated, **9.** 553. Prodigy: 169) **13.** 47

INDEX

Foruli, Sabine town: (211) **7.** 41–3
Forum Aesi: (163) **14.** 249
—Boarium (Bovarium): (296) temples of Hercules and of Pudicitia Patricia in, **4.** 443; (216) human sacrifices in, **5.** 385–7; (207) procession of Juno crosses, **7.** 361; (204) street from, paved, **8.** 351; (196) arches built before temples of Fortune and Mater Matuta in, **9.** 349; (192) fire in, **10.** 121. Prodigies: (214) **6.** 207; (102) **14.** 279
— Olitorium: temples in, dedicated (218) to Spes, **5.** 185; (194) to Juno Matuta, **9.** 553; (181) to Pietas, **12.** 103
— Romanum: (753–717) Romans and Sabines fight in, **1.** 47, **9.** 429, **12.** 145; (670–616) prison built above, **1.** 123; (616–578) building sites about, distributed, 131; drained, 137; (578–534) Tullia rides through, 169; (495) riot in, 291–5; (494) plebs avoid, 307; (473) trial of coss. in, 403; (390) Gauls enter, **3.** 141, 145; (362) Curtian lake opens in, 373; (338) statues set up in, **4.** 55; (306) 339; (338) beaks of ships ornament Rostra in, 61; (314) traitors beheaded in, 257; (310) money-changers in; *tensae* conducted through, 323; (304) *comit. trib.* meets in, 353; (280) mutinous troops beheaded in, **8.** 115; (217) crowded, **5.** 223; (216) gladiators at funeral games in, **6.** 103; (213) effort to expell new cults from, 343, **11.** 265; (211) Senate in continuous session in, **7.** 35; (210) fire in, 103, 107; Capuans examined in, 105–7; (209) buildings in, restored, 253; (207) procession of Juno Regina crosses, 361; (195) crowded with women, **9.** 413, 417; (187) Africanus returns to, to save brother, **11.** 197; (183) banquet in, 365–7; prophecy that tents will be set up in, 367; (178) fire in area about, **14.** 243; (174) assembly in, undertakes vow, **12.** 255; (167) judgment seat of pr. urb., **13.** 405; (82) Q. Lucretius Ofella killed in, **14.** 113. Prodigies: (214) **6.** 209; (196) **9.** 349; (194) 535; (174) **12.** 255; (118) **14.** 269; (100) 281; (63) 303
Forum Vessanum: (122) **14.** 267
Fossa Graeca, in Campania: (205) **8.** 195
— Quiritium: (640–616) **1.** 121
Founder, Hut of (*casa Romuli*): **3.** 183
freedmen: (304) Cn. Flavius, son of a, becomes aed., **4.** 349; sons of, admitted to Senate by Ap. Claudius, 353; (296) serve in army, 437; (220) assigned to four tribes, 561; **13.** 293; (217) serve in fleet and in city garrison, **5.** 239; (191) enrolled as *socii navales*, **10.** 161; (181) **12.** 61; (172) 367; (171) 383; (169) **13.** 45; (186) status of, **11.** 245; (171) colony of, for children of soldiers and Spanish women, **13.** 11–3; (168) placed in single tribe, 293–5; (89) begin to serve in army, **14.** 93; (84) distributed in all tribes, 107
Fregellae, in Latium: captured from Volsci by Samnites, **4.** 89; (328) colony sent to, 85, 89; (320) seized by Samnites, 207; (313) recovered, 271, 283; (211) delays Hannibal, **7.** 33–5; (209) remains loyal, 245–7; (208) 319–21; (190) troops from, in Asia, **10.** 391; (177) Samnites move to, **12.** 209; (169) not technically Roman territory, **13.** 47; (125) revolts, is reduced, **14.** 69, 265. Prodigies: (211) **7.** 89; (206) **8.** 47; (197) **9.** 243; (169) **13.** 47; (93) **14.** 287. *See* M. Trebellius.
Fregenae, in Etruria: (248) maritime colony, **4.** 559; (191) **10.** 163
Frentani, in Central Italy: (304) obtain alliance, **4.** 349; (207) prepare for C. Claudius Nero, **7.** 383. *Cp.* **4.** 220[2].
Frentinum castrum: (193) **10.** 25
Fresilia, town of Marsi: (302) **4.** 369
Friniates, Ligurians: **12.** 243; (187) defeated, **11.** 221, 223
Frugi: *see* Calpurnius Piso.
Frusino, in Latium: (303) tampers with Hernici, punished, **4.** 361; (211) Hannibal at, **7.** 35. Prodigies: (207) 359; (203) **8.** 373; (202) 511; (200) **9.** 39; (197) 243; (162) **14.** 249; (147) 253
Fucinus, Lake: (408) fort at, taken, **2.** 443; (137) overflows, **14.** 257
Fufetius: *see* Mettius Fufetius.
Fugifulae, in Lucania: (214) **6.** 237

Fulcinius, C.: (438) envoy to Fidenae, killed, statue on Rostra, **2**. 313
Fullo: *see* Apustius.
Fulvia, wife of M. Antonius; (41) stirs up Perusine war, **14**. 155–7
Fulvius, C.: (218) qu., captured by Ligurians, given to Hannibal, **5**. 177–9
—, Cn.: (190) pr. pereg., **10**. 285, 295
—, Cn.: (167) pr. for Hither Spain, **13**. 297
—, Q.: (197) tr. pl., prevents assignment of Macedon to coss., **9**. 239–41
—, Q.: (180) co-opted IIIvir epulo while *praetextatus*, **12**. 133
— Centumalus, M.: (192) pr. urb., **10**. 29, 59, 69; prepares fleet for Sicily, 61, 67, 69
— — Maximus, Cn., cos. 211: (214) aed. cur., gives first festival with drama, **6**. 315; (213) pr. at Suessula, 315, 347; Campanian nobles surrender to, 327; (211) cos., 501, **7**. 3; faces Hannibal outside city, 37–9; holds elections, 69, 85; (210) in Apulia, 111; defeated and slain near Herdonea, 203–7, **8**. 119; (209) surviving troops of, sent to Sicily, **7**. 233, 237–9
— Curvus, C.: (296) aed. pl., **4**. 447
— —, L.: (322) cos., **4**. 147; (316) mag. eq., 245
— —, M.: (305) cos. suf., captures Bovianum, **4**. 343
— Flaccus, C.: (211) leg. of brother, Q., at Capua, **7**. 19, 55, 127; (209) and in Etruria, 237
— —, C.: (134) cos., **14**. 259; assigned to slave revolt, 59
— —, Cn.: (212) pr. for Apulia, **6**. 345–7; defeated by Hannibal near Herdonea, 421–3, **7**. 5, 205; convicted of treason, goes into exile, 7–15; surviving troops sent to Sicily, 5, 11, 233, 239
— —, L.: (174) removed from Senate by brother, Q., **12**. 277
— —, M., tr. pl. 199: (201) Xvir agr. divid., **9**. 13; (199) tr. pl., vetoes, then permits election of Flamininus, 171–3
— —, M.: (184) IIIvir col. deduc., **11**. 363; (181) leg. of brother, Q. (cos. 179), **12**. 95; (171) envoy of Senate to C. Cassius Longinus, **13**. 7, (170) to Macedon, 39, 41
Fulvius Flaccus, M., cos. 125: (130–129) IIIvir agr. divid., **14**. 67–9, 263; (125–124) cos. and procos. against Salluvii, 69, 265; (121) killed with C. Gracchus, 73
— —, Q., cos. 237, 224, 212, 209: (217) leg. of Cn. Servilius Geminus, **5**. 239; (216) pont., **6**. 73; (215) pr. urb., 81, 105; commands home fleet, 113; raises army for Sardinia, 119–21; accepts Sardinian captives, 141; arranges supplies for Spain, 165; (214) pr. urb. *extra sortem*, 203; (213) mag. eq. comit. c., 345; (212) cos. iii, 345, **7**. 307, bids tribb. pl. dismiss assembly, **6**. 351; not elected pont. max., 355; takes Hanno's camp, 389–97; enters Campania, 401–3, 411–7; besieges Capua, 419, 425–7, 501; (211) 501, **7**. 3, 13, 19–25; writes letter defending brother, Cn., 13; moves to defend Rome, 29–35, **8**. 169; given *imperium* within city, **7**. 35; drives Hannibal from walls, 35–9; takes Capua, 43–57; in spite of colleague puts leading Capuans to death, 57–61, 105–7, 127; other Campanian cities surrender to, 61, 129, 133; (210) command continued, 109, 111, 233; Capuans accuse, before Senate, 119, 127, **11**. 149; his camp at Capua fired, **7**. 211–3; dict. comit. c., 223–7; (209) cos. iv with Lucania and Bruttium as prov., 225, 231, 237, 249; rebukes rebellious Latins, praises loyal colonies, 241–7, **8**. 263; holds elections for censs., **7**. 251; at Capua, 253; Hirpini and Lucani surrender to, 267; holds elections, 297–9; (208) procos. for Capua, 301–3, 313; (207) in Bruttium, 353, 357; receives army at Capua, 373; called to Lucania by C. Claudius Nero, 381; (205) opposes Africa as prov. for P. Scipio (Afr.), **8**. 189
— —, Q., cos. 180: (197) accompanies Philip's envoys to Rome, **9**. 265; (189) aed. pl., **11**. 115–7; (187) pr. for Sardinia, 143–5; (181) leg. of L. Aemilius Paulus, **12**. 85; candi-

date for cos.; (180) cos. suf., 117; defeats Ligurians, 127–9
Fulvius Flaccus, Q., cos. 179: (184) aed. cur. elect, seeks praetorship, **11**. 343–7; (182) pr. for Hither Spain, 397, **12**. 3, 7, 53–5; (181) 59; defeats Celtiberians, 93–103; (180) 121–7; vows temple to Fortune and games to Jupiter, 125, 299; returns with part of army, 107–15, 127; triumphs, 137, 179, 393; co-opted pont., 135, 373; (179) cos., 137, 353, **13**. 271, **14**. 243, with Liguria as prov., **12**. 139; celebrates votive games, 139–41; defeats Ligurians and Gauls, 163; triumphs; holds elections, 177–9; (174) cens., 275–81, 317; expells brother, L., from Senate, 277; prevented by Senate from using roof tiles of temple of Juno Lucina for temple of Fortune, 299–301, 373; dedicates temple, 319; (172) hangs self, 373; (169) censors bar from bidding those who had contracts with, **13**. 55
— —, Ser.: (135) cos., **14**. 259; defeats Vardaei, 59
— Gillo, Q., pr. 200: (203) leg., conducts Punic envoys, **8**. 445, 449, 455–7; (202) aed. cur., 515; (200) pr. for Sicily, **9**. 13, 19, 25–7
— Maximus Centumalus, Cn., cos. 298: (302) leg., engages Etruscans, **4**. 371–7; (298) cos., defeats Samnites, triumphs, 399–403; (295) propr., against Etruscans, 461–3, 475
— Nobilior, M., cos. 189: (196) aed. cur., distributes grain, **9**. 391; (193) pr. for Farther Spain, 555–9, **10**. 21, (192) 59, 63–5; (191) 159–61; receives ovation, 223–5, 267; (190) elected cos., 431; presides over election of colleague, preventing election of M. Aemilius Lepidus, 431, **11**. 147, **12**. 147; (189) cos., with Aetolia as prov., **10**. 433, 437, **11**. 11, 147; takes Ambracia, 11–31; sends Aetolian envoys to Rome, 33, 37; moves to Cephallania, 33, 95–7; at meeting of Achaean league, 101; bids Achaeans and Spartans send envoys to Rome, 105–7; prevents election of Lepidus, 115, 147; (188) procos. for Aetolia, 115, (187) 145; recalled, 147; attacked for siege of Ambracia, 147–51; triumphs in spite of cos. Lepidus, 225–33, **12**. 143; (186) celebrates votive games, **11**. 231, **12**. 141, presenting first athletic contests, **11**. 281; (184) candidate for cens., 347–9; (179) cens. with Lepidus; reconciled with him, **12**. 143–7, 157–9, 163
Fulvius Nobilior, M.: (180) tr. mil., banished for dismissing legion at Pisa, **12**. 129–31
— —, M.: (171) tr. pl., **12**. 387
— —, Q., cos. 153; (184) IIIvir col. deduc., **11**. 363; (149) defends Ser. Sulpicius Galba, **14**. 27
— Paetinus Nobilior, Ser.: (255) cos., **12**. 347
— Paetus, M.: (299) cos., **4**. 391
Fundanius, M.: (195) tr. pl., proposes abrogation of Oppian law, **9**. 413–5
— Fundulus, M.: (213) aed. pl., **6**. 347
Fundii: (338) granted citizenship without vote, **4**. 61, 77; (330) allied with Rome's enemies, 75–7; (327) Samnites seek aid of, 89; (188) granted vote, **11**. 119–21; (174) temple of Jupiter at, **12**. 281
funeral laudations: history confused by, **4**. 157
Furies: (88) Mithridates offers human sacrifice to, **14**. 295
Furius, C.: (178) IIvir nav. in Adriatic, **12**. 185–7; (170) leg. at Issa, **13**. 33–5
—, L.: (318) pr., gives laws to Capua, **4**. 243
—, L.: (308) tr. pl., opposes Ap. Claudius Caecus, **4**. 331
—, Q.: (449) pont. max., holds election of tribb. pl., **2**. 179–81
—, Sex.: (488) cos., proposes envoy to Coriolanus, **1**. 345–7
—, Sp.: (378) tr. mil. c. p., plunders Volscian lands, **3**. 301–3
— Aculeo, C., qu. 190: (187) convicted with L. Scipio, **11**. 193, 201–3
— Bibaculus, L.: (216) qu., **5**. 363
— Camillus, L., cos. 349: (350) dict. com. c., elected cos., **3**. 439; (349) cos., defeats Gauls and Greeks, 443–9; (345) dict., defeats Aurunci, 453
— —, L.: (338) cos., reduces Latins, **4**. 53–7; (325) cos. ii, ill, names dict., 111–3

INDEX

Furius Camillus, M., dict. 396, 390, 389, 368, 367 : (403) tr. mil. c. p. (?) **3**. 3; (401) tr. mil. c. p., 35, 43; (398) ii, 51–3; (397) interrex, 61; (396) dict., takes Veii, 67–77; vows tithe to Apollo, temple to Juno, games, 67, 73, 81–3, 87–9, 109; sells captives for *aerarium*, 77; triumphs; dedicates temple to Mater Matuta, 79–81; (394) tr. mil. c. p. iii, defeats Faliscans, 89–97; (393) supports mutual veto of tribb. pl., 105; opposes re-establishment of Veii, 105–7; dedicates temple to Juno, 109, 73, 79–81; (392) interrex, 111; (391) exiled on account of spoils of Veii, 113, 149, **6**. 353, **13**. 381; (390) leads Ardeates against Gauls, **3**. 147–51; recalled, made dict., 153–7, **4**. 177, **5**. 211, **7**. 349, **3**. 195; defeats Gauls, 163–7, 231, **4**. 203, **5**. 247–9; triumphs, **3**. 167, 407, **4**. 219; rebuilds shrines, **3**. 167–9; opposes transfer to Veii, 169–85; (389) interrex, 197; dict., defeats Volsci, Aequi, Etruscans; triumphs, 199–207, 211, 235; (386) tr. mil. c. p. iv, 213; with supreme power; defeats Antiates, 215–23; recovers Sutrium and Nepetê, 225–9; (385) M. Manlius Capitolinus rouses plebs against, 231; (384) tr. mil. c. p. v, 255; (381) vi, 273, 289; averts disaster due to L. Furius Medullinus, defeats Volsci, 275–83; asks for Medulinus as aid against Tusculum, 283–7, **4**. 131; (368) dict. to check tribb. pl. Licinius and Sextius, **3**. 327–31; possible candidate for cos., 341; (367) dict., defeats Gauls, triumphs, 347–9; proposes praetorship, 351; (366) his son, Sp., the first pr., 357; (365) dies; his character and fame, 359, **4**. 229, **9**. 143; (358) games vowed by, celebrated, **3**. 407–9

— —, Sp. : (366) first pr., **3**. 357

— Crassipes, M., pr. 187, 173 : (201) sent to Senate by M. Aurelius Cotta, **8**. 525; (200) leg. of L. Furius Purpurio, **9**. 61; (194, 192) IIIvir for Vibo, 553, **10**. 119; (187) pr. for Gaul, **11**. 143–5, 223–5; (173) pr. ii, **12**. 283, for Sicily, 293

— Fusus, Agr. : 446) cos., **2**. 223; defeats Aequi and Volsci, 235–43; unable to protect Aricia and Ardea from plebs, 243–53

Furius Fusus, Agr.: (391) tr. mil. c. p., defeats Sappinates, **3**. 111

— —, Sp. : (481) cos., **1**. 361

— Luscus, M. : (187) aed. pl., **11**. 239

— Medullinus, L. : (474) cos., opposes land law, **1**. 401; (473) accused, 401–3

— —, L. : (432) tr. mil. c. p., **2**. 337; (425) ii, 371; (420) iii, 399

— —, L. : (413) cos., investigates murder of P. Postumius Albinus, **2**. 423; occupies Ferentinum, 425–7; (409) cos. ii, 433; (407) tr. mil. c. p., 445; (405) ii, 455; (398) iii, **3**. 53; (397) iv, 57; (395) v, 83; (394) vi, 89; (391) vii, 111

— —, L. : (400) tr. mil c. p., **3**. 45

— —, L. : (381) tr. mil. c. p., saved from defeat by Camillus, **3**. 273–83; Camillus asks for, as aid, 283–5, **4**. 131; (370) tr. mil. c. p. ii, **3**. 319

— — Fusus, P. : (472) cos., **1**. 407; (467) IIIvir agr. dand., **2**. 5; (464) leg. of brother, Sp.; killed, **2**. 17

— — —, Sp. : (464) cos., defeated by Aequi, **2**. 11–7; (461) testifies for K. Quinctius, 43

— Paculus (Pacilus), C. : (412) cos., **2**. 427

— — Fusus, C. : (441) cos., **2**. 297; (435) cens., 329; takes vengeance on dict. Aemilius Mamercinus, 335, 359, 363, **4**. 291–3; (426) tr. mil. c. p., leads unsuccessful war against Veii, **2**. 357–9

— Philus, L. : (171) pr. for Sardinia, **12**. 371, 383; pont.; (170) dies, **13**. 41–3

— —, L. : (136) cos., **14**. 257

— —, P., cos. 223 : (216) pr. urb., **5**. 319; calls Senate after Cannae, 379; takes over fleet, 387; wounded in African raid, **6**. 71; (214) cens., 211; severe on military shirkers, 229–33, 313; dies, 313; an augur, 345

— —, P. : (216) loses hope after Cannae, **5**. 373

— —, P. : (174) pr. in Hither Spain, **12**. 251; (173) 303; (171) accused; goes into exile, **13**. 9

— Purpurio, L., cos. 196 : (210) tr. mil., **7**. 209; 200) pr. for Gaul, **9**.

13, 19, 25, 31–3; defeats Gauls, 61–5; vows temple to Jupiter, 63, 553, **10**. 123; envoy to Aetolian council, **9**. 83, 91–5; triumphs over Gauls, 139–43; (196) cos., 341, with Italy as prov., 345–7; defeats Boii, 375–7; lets contract for temple of Jupiter, 553, **10**. 123; (189) Xvir for Asian settlement, 461–3, **11**. 123–35, 153, 161, 205, 301; (187) opposes triumph of Cn. Manlius Volso, **11**. 153–61; proposes financial investigation of eastern wars, 189; (184) candidate for cens., 347–9; (183) envoy to warn Gauls, 393–5

Furnius, C.: (17) cos., **14**. 317

Fusius, Sp.: (672–640) pater patratus in making Alban peace, **1**. 85

Fusius: variant of Furius, **2**. 13

Fusus: *see* Furius, — Medullinus, — Paculus.

Gabii, in Latium: (534–510) Sex. Tarquin takes, **1**. 183–9, (510) flees to, 209; (462) Volsci waste fields of, **2**. 29; (390) Gauls defeated near, **3**. 167, 297, **5**. 249; possible site for new Rome, **3**. 183; (383) Praenestini attack, 271; (380) 293; (211) Hannibal at, **7**. 35. Prodigies: (214) **6**. 207; (176) **12**. 233; (163) **14**. 249

Gabinian cincture: (390) worn at family sacrifice, **3**. 155, (340) in *devotio*, **4**. 37, 381

— way: (508) Etruscans ambushed on, **1**. 255; (463) Volsci and Aequi on, **2**. 23; (390) Gauls defeated on, **3**. 167

Gabinius: (167) pref. of Scodra, **13**. 333–5

—, A.: (139) tr. pl., secures electoral reform, **14**. 53

—, A.: (89) leg., defeats Lucanians, killed, **14**. 95

—, A., cos. 58: (55) restores Ptolemy, **14**. 131

Gades: Spanish port, **6**. 333, **7**. 169, 295, **10**. 213; (218) Hannibal pays vows at, **5**. 61, 65; (211) Hasdrubal son of Gisgo retires to, **7**. 77; (207) Hasdrubal and Mago retire to, **8**. 3, 7–9, 15; (206) 53, 69–71, 97; Romans fail to take, 97, 123–7; Masinissa at, 141, 145; surrenders on terms, 145, 149–51, **9**. 159; (49) granted citizenship, **14**. 137

Gaetulians: (216) in Punic army, **6**. 59

Gala, king of Maesuli, father of Masinissa: at war with Syphax, **6**. 333, **7**. 293, **8**. 327, **12**. 55; dies, **8**. 321; soldiers of, support Masinissa, 325. *See* Masinissa.

Galaesus riv., in Calabria: (212) **6**. 379

Galatia, in Campania: (211) **7**. 19

Galatians, Gauls, Gallograeci: character of, **10**. 313, **11**. 55–61, 71–5, 157, 163–9; (279) sack Delphi, **11**. 165, **12**. 175–7; (278) migrate into Asia Minor, **11**. 51–5, 59–61, **12**. 263; (230) defeated by Attalus I, **9**. 335, **11**. 55, 59; (189) campaign of Cn. Manlius Volso against, **10**. 441, 477, **11**. 37–51, 55–95, 121, 147, 149; (188) terms given to, 121–3, 135; (187) authority for war against, questioned, 153–61, justified by Manlius, 161–73, who triumphs, 175, 235–9; (167) Eumenes asks aid against, **13**. 305–9; ignore peace effort, 367; Prusias asks lands of, 407; at war with Eumenes, 411. Serve in armies of: (197) Rhodes, **9**. 325; (190) Antiochus, **10**. 313, 343, 399, 407–9, **11**. 39, 59, 167; (171) Eumenes, **12**. 467–9, 473, (169) **13**. 133, 181–3; Perseus, 129, (168) 173–9, 185. *See* Bitocus, Deiotarus, Bastarnae, Tectosages, Tolostobogii, Trocmi.

Galba: *see* Sulpicius.

Galeagra, tower in Syracuse, (212). **6**. 431

Galepsus, in Thrace: (168) **13**. 239

Galeria tribus: (210) **7**. 223

Gallaeci (Callaeci), in Spain: (136 defeated by D. Junius Brutus, **14**. 57, (60) by Caesar, 305, *cp*. 127

Galli, priests of Great Mother: (190) in Sestus, **10**. 317; (189) in Pessinus, **11**. 63–5

Gallic gulf, Gulf of Genoa: (211) P. Scipio (Afr.) sails past, **7**. 75; (203) Punic envoys enter, **8**. 437; (195) M. Porcius Cato passes, **9**. 441

— pyres: (390) **3**. 161–3, **5**. 249

Gallus: *see* Anicius, Aquilius, Lucretius, Ogulnius, Sulpicius, Volumnius Amintinus.

INDEX

games, funeral, with gladiators: (264) **4**. 553; (216) **6**. 103; (206) **8**. 87; (200) **9**. 147; (183) **11**. 365; (174) **12**. 283–5

—, votive: (449, 441) of Xviri, **2**. 297, (431, 424) of A. Postumius Tubertus, 343–5, 371–3; (396, 392) of M. Furius Camillus, **3**. 67, 109; (360) of Q. Servilius Ahala, 389; (217) vowed by pr. on order of Sibylline Books, **5**. 231, 235, (208) celebrated, **7**. 345, (203–202) **8**. 373, 465, (194) **9**. 531; (206, 205) of P. Scipio (Afr.), **8**. 155, 193; (205, 200) **9**. 143; (200, 194) of P. Sulpicius Galba, first, without fixed value, **9**. 29, 533; (193, 191) of P. Scipio Nasica, **10**. 5, 261; (191) of M' Acilius Glabrio, 159; (190, 186) of L. Scipio, **11**. 283; (189, 186) of M. Fulvius Nobilior, 231, 281, **12**. 141; (180, 179) of Q. Fulvius Flaccus, 125, 141–3; (172) of C. Popilius Laenas, 371

Games: *see* Apollo, Games of; Capitoline games; Consualia; Megalesia; Isthmian, Nemean, Olympic, Roman, Saecular, Taurian games.

Gannicus: (71) follower of Spartacus, **14**. 119, 199

Ganymedê: (48) led in Caesar's triumph, **14**. 213

Garamantes, African tribe: (204) **8**. 337

Garuli, Spanish tribe: (175) **12**. 243

Gaulotus: (189) Galatian chief, **11**. 67

Gauls: (295) character of, **4**. 465; (217) **5**. 207; (194) **9**. 541; (193) **10**. 13; (167) **13**. 353; (218) in Roman army, **5**. 75, 85, 137, 141, 159, 165, (216) **6**. 43, (207) **7**. 365, (178) **12**. 187, 193, 197–9, (168) **13**. 157; (218) in Punic armies, **5**. 95, 111, 141, 153, 159, 167, (217) 173, 205–7, (216) 351–7, **6**. 95, (214) 311, (212) 375, (207) **7**. 381, 399, 403–5, (206) **8**. 145, (205) 197–9, 225–7, (203) 433–5, (202) 489–91, (200) **9**. 33; (171) in army of Perseus, **12**. 449, 453; (71) in army of Spartacus, **14**. 119; (218) prisoners of Hannibal fight duel, **5**. 123–5; (216) man and woman buried alive after Cannae, 385–7; (88) Marius' murder attempted by a, **14**. 97

Gauls, Gaul (cis-Alpine), Ariminum: enter Po valley, **3**. 115–21, **5**. 87–9; (397) hold much of Etruria, **3**. 61; (391) coming of, foretold, 113, 169, 173, 177; Clusium seeks aid against, 115, 121; Roman envoys fight, 121–7, 173; (390) march on Rome, 127–9; defeat Romans at Allia, 129–33, 295, **4**. 177, **5**. 393, **11**. 57; occupy Rome, slaughter Senators, burn city, **3**. 135–45, 77, 85, 111, 173, 181, 201, 349, 423, **4**. 315, 327, **5**. 89, **14**. 229, destroying records, **3**. 195; vainly attack Citadel and Capitol, 145–9, 171, 341; M. Furius Camillus cuts off party of, 147–51; C. Fabius Dorsuo passes through, 153–5; driven from Capitol by M. Manlius Capitolinus, 157–61, 231, 241, **11**. 57; suffer from pestilence, **3**. 161–3; accept ransom, withdraw, are defeated by Camillus, 163–7, 219, 231, 295–7, 417, 443, **4**. 175–7, 185, 203, **5**. 247–9, 391–3, **7**. 159, **13**. 381; matrons contribute ransom gold, **3**. 169, **9**. 429; (387) temple to Mars, vowed in war with, dedicated, **3**. 213; (385) patricians accused of holding gold recovered from, 243, 249, *cp*. 169; (367) Camillus defeats, 347–9; (366) reported gathering, 357; (361) defeated by T. Quinctius Poenus, 383–9, T. Manlius Torquatus defeating champion, 385–9, **6**. 199, **11**. 57; raid into Campania, **3**. 389; (360) defeated by Q. Servilius Ahala, 389–91, **4**. 59–61, (358) by C. Sulpicius Peticus, **3**. 395–407, (350) by M. Popilius Laenas, 433–9, (349) by L. Furius Camillus, 441–7, M. Valerius Corvus defeating champion, 443–5, **6**. 199, **11**. 57; (before 345) driven to the shore and their ships, **3**. 471; (332) rising of, dreaded, **4**. 69; (329) 79; (312) 273; (302) 365; (299) Etruscans seek aid of, 393–5, 403; (296) aid Etruscans and Samnites, 417, 421, 437–41; (295) attack Romans near Clusium, 459–61; defeated by Q. Fabius Maximus and P. Decius Mus at Sentinum, 461–77, **6**. 205; (284) put envoys to death; defeat L. Caecilius Metellus, **4**. 549; (223) defeated by C. Flaminius, 561, **5**. 45,

171, 189, 219, **6**. 45, (222) by M. Marcellus, **4**. 561, **7**. 313, **8**. 249; (220) colonies planted in, at Placentia and Cremona, **4**. 561, (218) are resented, **5**. 69–71; defeat L. Manlius Volso, 47–9, 71–3, 129; invite Hannibal into Italy, 85, 153; Hannibal encounters, 111–3, and seeks aid of, 115, 133, 141, 153; P. Scipio prevents, from joining Hannibal, 115; seek aid of Scipio and Ti. Sempronius Longus, 153–5; Cenomani alone loyal to Rome, 163; (217) turn against Hannibal, 199; Cn. Servilius Geminus opposes, 229, 233, 307; Hannibal considers return to, 307–9; (216) 343; desert Rome after Cannae, 409; defeat L. Postumius Albinus, 319, **6**. 81–5; (214) trophies of, in Syracuse serve as arms, 243; assigned to M. Pomponius Matho, 207–9, 315; (213) to P. Sempronius Tuditanus, 315, (212) 349, (211) **7**. 5, (210) to M. Valerius Laevinus, 109–11, (209) to L. Veturius Philo, 231, 249, (208) 303, (207) to M. Livius Salinator and L. Porcius Licinus, 353, 357, 365, **8**. 37; aid Hasdrubal, **7**. 353–5, 363–9, 385–7; C. Claudius Nero moves toward, 385; Hasdrubal defeated in, 393–405, **8**. 41; (206) assigned to Q. Mamilius Turrinus, 45; plunder Placentia and Cremona, 49; (205) Mago in, 221–9; allotted to Sp. Lucretius, 155, 227, (204) to L. Scribonius Libo with Lucretius and M. Livius Salinator, 255–7, (203) to M. Cornelius Cethegus, 369, who defeats Mago in, 431–7; Mago recalled from, 425, 437; C. Servilius Geminus enters, 437–9; (202) allotted to M. Sextius Sabinus, 463, (201) to P. Aelius Paetus; Boi defeat and kill C. Ampius, **9**. 7–9; (200) allotted to L. Furius Purpurio, 19, 25, who defeats, 31–3, 61–5, vowing temple to Jupiter, 63, 553, and triumphing, 139–45; Hamilcar leads army of, 57; C. Aurelius Cotta goes to, 65; (199) defeat Cn. Baebius Tamphilus, 155, 171; (198) C. Helvius and Sex. Aelius Paetus in, 175, 179, 233, 237; (197) C. Cornelius Cethegus and Q. Minucius Rufus defeat, 241–9, 339–41, Cethegus vowing temple to Juno, 247, 553; Macedon protects Greece from, 307–9; (196) defeated by M. Claudius Marcellus, 373–5, (195) by L. Valerius Flaccus, 393, 471, 501, (194) 535; fight close battle with Ti. Sempronius Longus, 537–41; Africanus leaves, 555; (193) defeated by L. Cornelius Merula, 557, **10**. 9–15; (192) allotted to L. Quinctius Flamininus, 59; his profligate acts in, **11**. 355–7; (191) Hannibal urges Antiochus to arouse, **10**. 179; defeated by P. Scipio Nasica, 261, 265–73; (190) C. Laelius to enroll colonists for, 429; (189) assigned to Laelius 439, **11**. 117; (188) allotted to C. Livius Salinator, 117, (187) to M. Furius Crassipes, 145, who is forced to restore lands wrongfully taken, 223–5; contrast between, and Galatians, 157; Africanus dreaded in, 177; C. Flaminius builds road in, 223; (186) trans-Alpine Gauls cross into, 283; (183) 363–5; (184) colony established at Pisaurum, 361–3; (183) allotted to L. Julius Caesar, 363–5; (182) assigned to M. Claudius Marcellus, **12**. 5, 53, 79, 81; (181) Latin colony established at Aquileia, 103; allotted to Q. Fabius Buteo, 59, 81, (180) 115, (178) to A. Manlius Volso, 184[4], 205, (177) to Cn. Scipio and C. Valerius Laevinus, 207, or to C. Claudius Pulcher, 221–7; (176) 227; (175) M. Aemilius Lepidus and P. Mucius Scaevola win victories in, 243–5; (173) lands in, distributed to individuals, 303; (171) allotted to C. Cassius Longinus, **13**. 3; (170) A. Atilius Serranus visits, 33; (168) allotted to C. Licinius Crassus, 145, 283–5, 299, (167) to Q. Aelius Paetus, 297, 301; (154) win victories, **14**. 251; (150) Lusitanians sold in, 27; (78–77) held by M. Junius Brutus, 115; (44) M. Antonius moves to, 149; (29, 12) census of, taken, 165. Prodigies: (218) **5**. 185; (173) **12**. 297; (122) **14**. 267; (113) 271; (102) 279. *Also* **12**. 85. *See* Boi, Brixiani, Celines, Cenomani, Insubres, Libui, Scordisci.

INDEX

Gauls, Gaul (trans-Alpine) : (c. 227) invade Italy, defeated, **4**. 559; (219, 218) Hannibal and Rome try to rouse, **5**. 45–7, 57–9, 65; (218) Hannibal crosses, 61, 67–9, 75–97, 127–9, **8**. 467; campaign of P. Scipio in, **5**. 75, 83–5, 115–21; (211) P. Scipio (Afr.) coasts along, **7**. 75, **8**. 171; (208) Hasdrubal in, **7**. 295, 353–5; (186) invade Venetia, **11**. 283, **14**. 241; (183) **11**. 365; repulsed by M. Marcellus, 365, 391–5, **14**. 241; (182) reported arming, **12**. 57; (179) enter Italy, ordered out, 163; (170) complain of C. Cassius Longinus, **13**. 19–21; (169) offer aid against Perseus, 133; (166) defeated by M. Marcellus, **14**. 11; (152) successful campaigns in, 253; (143) Sibylline Books require sacrifice in hostile territory before campaign in, 255; (121) Allobroges and Arverni defeated, **14**. 73; (107) defeat L. Cassius Longinus, 77–9; (105) Cimbri return to, 81; (90) revolt in, crushed, 91; (74) Pompey withdraws to, 117; (58–51) operations of Caesar in, 129–35; (46) he triumphs over, 145; (43) Antony flees into, 151; (29, 12) census taken in, 165. *See* Allobroges, Arverni, Bellovaci, Ebruones, Helvetii, Nitobroges, Tigurni, Treveri.

Gaurium, port of Andros : (200) **9**. 129

Gaurus, Mt., in Campania : (343) **3**. 469

Gavillius Novellus, Cn. and L., of Aquileia : (178) report Roman disaster, **12**. 197

geese of Juno : (390) save Capitol, **3**. 159

Geganii, of Alba : (672–640) enrolled in Senate by Hostilius, **1**. 107

Geganius Macerinus, L. : (378) tr. mil. c. p., moves against Volsci, **3**. 303

— —, M. : (447) cos., **2**. 221; (443) ii, 285; defeats Volsci, triumphs, 289–93; (437) cos. iii, 315; (435–434) cens., 329; punishes dict. Mam. Aemilius Mamercinus for limiting term, 335, 363, **4**. 291–3; (431) leg., **2**. 347

— —, M. : (367) tr. mil. c. p., **3**. 347

— —, Pro. : (440) cos., **2**. 297

— —, T. : (492) cos., **1**. 329

Gellius : *see* Statius, Egnatius.

— Publicola, L. : (72) cos., defeated by Spartacus, **14**. 119; (70–69) cens., 121

Gelo, of Syracuse : son of Hiero, **6**. 189; (216) pro-Punic leader, 103. *See* Harmonia, Heraclia.

Geminus : *see* Servilius, Veturius.

Genius : (218) sacrifice to, **5**. 187

Genoa (Genua) : (218) P. Scipio lands at, **5**. 93; (205) Mago captures and sacks, **8**. 197, 225, 369; (203) Sp. Lucretius rebuilds, 369; (197) Q. Minucius Rufus at, **9**. 243; (137) C. Hostilius Mancinus takes ship at **14**. 257

Gentius, king of Illyricum : (180) charged with piracy, **12**. 131–3, (172) and with aiding Perseus, 365, (171) 377; sought as ally, 401; ships of, seized, 439; (170) suspected, **13**. 33; (169) Perseus unwilling to pay, for wanted services, 69–73, 83, (168), 163–7, 173, 179, 185, 189, 195, 241; imprisons Roman envoys, 179, 189; murders brother, 187; plunders Apollonia and Dyrrachium, 189–91; war with, an appendage of that with Perseus, 267; (167) surrenders to L. Anicius Gallus, 187–95, 203–5, 255, 333, 337, **14**. 245; sent to Rome, **13**. 195; held at Rome, 367; Anicius triumphs over, 299, 385, 401–3; sent to Spoletium, then to Iguvium for safe-keeping; ships of, given to Greek cities, 403

Genua : *see* Genoa.

Genucius, C. : (300) first plebeian augur, **4**. 389

—, Cn. : (473) tr. pl., accuses coss., murdered, **1**. 401–5

—, L. : (342) tr. pl., proposes law banning interest, **3**. 511–3

—, L. : (210) envoy to Syphax, **7**. 215

—, M. : (193) tr. mil.; Boi slay, **10**. 15

—, T. : (476) tr. pl., introduces land law, **1**. 395–7

— Augurinus, Cn. : (399) tr. mil. c. p., **3**. 47; (396) ii; Faliscans defeat, 63–5

— —, M. : (445) cos., opposes *lex Canuleia*, **2**. 257–63

— —, T. : (451) cos. elect.; Xvir, **2**. 109

— Aventinensis, Cn. : (363) cos., **3**. 365

INDEX

Genucius Aventinensis, L.: (365) cos., **3**. 359; (362) ii, 367; first plebeian cos. to conduct war; Hernici ambush and slay, 375
— —, L.: (303) cos., wipes out brigands in Umbria, **4**. 361
Genusus riv., in Illyricum: 168) **13**. 189
Geraesticus, port of Teos: (190) **10**. 371–3
Geraestus, port of Euboea: (200) **9**. 131
Gereonium, in Apulia: (217) abandoned; Hannibal destroys, **5**. 261, 281; mag. eq. M. Minucius Rufus defeats Hannibal near, 281–5; (216) Hannibal delays at, 309, 331–3, 347
Gergithus: (188) given to Ilium, **11**. 133
Gergovia, in Gaul: (52) **14**. 135
Germany: woods of, dreaded, **4**. 301; (71) slaves from, with Spartacus, **14**. 119; (58) driven from Gaul by Caesar, 129; (55) he invades, 131; (53) 133; (17) M. Lollius defeated in, 319; (12–9) campaigns of Drusus in, 165–7, 319; (9 A.D.) P. Quinctilius Varus defeated in, 169
Gerronius, in Macedon: (200) **9**. 81
Geryon: slain by Hercules, **1**. 27, **14**. 71
Gibraltar, Straits of: (206) C. Laelius defeats Adherbal in, **8**. 125–7, **14**. 225. *See* Hercules, Pillars of.
Gillo: *see* Fulvius.
Gisgo: (215) envoy of Hannibal to Philip, **6**. 117; captured, 119, 131–3
—: (202) opposes peace, **8**. 507
—: (153) stirs Carthage against Rome, **14**. 17
Gitana, in Epirus: (172) **12**. 403
Glabrio: *see* Acilius.
gladiators: (c. 264) first shown in Rome, **4**. 553; (206) free men as, in Spain, **8**. 87–9; (175) in Greece, **12**. 251; (73) Spartacus leads revolt of, **14**. 117–9. *See* games, funeral.
Glaucia: *see* Servilius.
Glaucias: (169) envoy of Perseus to Gentius, **13**. 73
Gnosii, in Crete: (189) enslave Romans, **10**. 477–9
gold: (189) relation to silver, **11**. 37; (167) mining of, in Macedon forbidden, **13**. 349
Gomphi, in Thessaly: (198) Amynander takes, **9**. 121, 191–3; Flamininus near, 195; (191) M. Baebius Tamphilus and Philip recover, **10**. 197; (189) Philip at, **11**. 7–9; (171) P. Licinius Crassus rests at, **12**. 461
Gonni (Gonnus), in entrance to Tempê: **12**. 483, 503; (197) Philip flees to, **9**. 301; (191) Ap. Claudius occupies, **10**. 187–9; (171) surrenders to Perseus, **12**. 459; P. Licinius Crassus fails to take, 503–5; (169) **13**. 109
Gonnocondylum, in Perrhaebia: (185) **11**. 295–7
Gordium, in Bithynia: (189) **11**. 65
Gordiutichi, in Caria: (189) **11**. 43
Gorgopas: (195) surrenders Gytheum, **9**. 491–3
Gortynii, Cretans: (197) in army of Flamininus, **9**. 285; (189) release Roman slaves, **10**. 477–9
Gracchuris (Graccuris), in Spain: (174) established, **12**. 287; (76) Sertorius plunders, **14**. 195
Gracchus: *see* Cloelius, Sempronius, Veturius.
Gradivus: *see* Mars.
Graecostasis, in Rome. Prodigies: (137) **14**. 257; (130) 261; (124) 267
grain, corn: imported from (508) Volsci and Cumae, **1**. 247; (492, 491) Etruria, Cumae, Sicily, 329–33; (486) Sicily, 355; (476) Campania, 395; (474) Veii, 401; (440) Etruria, **2**. 299–301; (433) Etruria, Campania, Sicily, 337; (412) Sicily, Etruria, 427; (216) Sicily, **5**. 323; (212) Etruria, **6**. 397; Africa, 463; (210) Syracuse, **7**. 123; (204) Sicily, Sardinia, **8**. 347; (202) 511; (201) Africa, **9**. 15; (200) 147; (495) centurion in charge of, **1**. 303–5; (491) Senate fixes price of, 333; (477) scarce after Etruscans cross Tiber, 393; (441) L. Minucius made pref. annonae; hoarding of, prohibited, **2**. 299; (440) Sp. Maelius gives, free, 301, 309; (216) Hiero sends, as gift, **5**. 323; scarce in Hannibal's army, 335–7, 343; (215) gathered from farms into fortified cities, **6**. 113; state obtains, on credit, 165, **9**. 433; (205) sent to army in Sicily, **8**. 209–11; (203) sold by aedd. cur., 459; (201) **9**. 15;

(200) 147; (189) hoarders of, fined, **11**. 115; (170) demanded from Athens, **13**. 21–3; (123) distributed under law of C. Gracchus, **14**. 71, (91) of M. Livius Drusus, 89; (57) controlled by Pompey, 129. *See* famine.

grain law: (123) of C. Gracchus, **14**. 71; (91) of M. Livius Drusus, 89

grappling-irons: (210) **7**. 149; (203) **8**. 401; (191) **10**. 283

Gratidianus: *see* Marius.

Gravisca, in Etruria: (181) colony at, **12**. 89. Prodigy: (176) 233

grazers: (296) condemned, **4**. 447; (293) 541; (196) **9**. 391; (193) **10**. 29

Great Harbour, of Syracuse: (214) Bomilcar enters, **6**. 291; (212) fortified, 441

— Mother: *see* Idaean Mother.

— Plain, in Africa: (203) **8**. 391

Greece, the Greeks: besiege Troy, **3**. 15; (534–510) Tarquin the Proud sends envoys to, **1**. 195; (454) laws of, studied, **2**. 107; (349) raiders from, on Latin coast, **3**. 441–3, 447–9; exhausted by civil wars, 449; (336) included in Macedon, **13**. 273; (302) fleet from, seizes Thuriae, **4**. 363–7; (293) Aesculapius summoned from, **4**. 543, 547, **8**. 245–7; (279) Gauls plunder, **11**. 165; (215) Hannibal will aid Philip in, **6**. 117; (213) assigned to M. Valerius Laevinus, 317; (212) 349, **8**. 247; (211) **7**. 5, 109; affairs in, 91–101; allotted to P. Sulpicius Galba, 85 101; (209) 233; (209–208) Philip enters, 331, **9**. 35; affairs in, **7**. 331–43; (208–207) Galba continued in, 305; affairs in, **8**. 17–37; (205) assigned to P. Sempronius Tuditanus, 249; peace made, 249–55; (203) Philip attempts to enslave, 457, **13**. 317; (200) Ptolemy V will send no army to, **9**. 27; Rhodes and Attalus leave, to Rome, 49; P. Sulpicius Galba in, 17, 43–57, 65–139; Philip calls Macedonians Greek, 87; danger from him to, 89; often at war with Macedon, 101; (199) campaign of P. Villius Tappulus[1] in, 167–9; (198) Aetolians bring Romans to, 373, **10**. 37, 243; Flamininus' campaign in, **9**. 179–233, 237, **10**. 27, **11**. 31; (198–197) Philip's withdrawal from, demanded **9**. 249–65; power of Nabis in, 265–73; (187) Flamininus' campaign in (Cynocephylae), 279–305; Aetolians claim credit, 305, 371–3, **10**. 33; peace conference for, **9**. 305–13; affairs in, 313–35; Flamininus continued in, 345–7; (196) affairs in, 351–73; freedom of, proclaimed at Isthmian games, 363–7, 473, 501–3, **10**. 47, 49, 91, 97, 211, 253–5, 393, **12**. 455, **13**. 31; Antiochus warned from, **9**. 369, 379–87; (195) danger to, from Antiochus, Nabis, and Aetolians, 395–7; danger to Roman character from, 421; Flamininus' campaign against Nabis, 393, 471–527; (194) Flamininus reviews achievements in, 541–7, leaves, 547–9, **10**. 33, and triumphs, **9**. 549–51; Roman slaves in, freed, 547; (193) envoys from Antiochus and, 561–9; Antiochus urged by Hannibal to attack, 571; affairs in, leading to war with Antiochus, **10**. 33–57; Antiochus offers, to Philip, **11**. 305; (192) A. Atilius Serranus sent to, with fleet, **10**. 63, 65; Flamininus and other envoys sent to, 65; affairs in, leading to war, 65–119, **13**. 279; Antiochus sails to, **10**. 123–49; 175; condition of, under Rome, 135; (191) allotted to M' Acilius Glabrio, **10**. 155–7; preparations for campaign in, 161–9; Antiochus in, 169–97; Glabrio's campaign in (Thermopylae, Heraclea), 197–237, 259–61, 299; affairs of the Aetolians, 237–45, 253–7, of the Achaeans, 245–51, 257–61, of Philip, 251–3; Hannibal warns Antiochus Romans may cross from, 273–5; C. Livius Salinator brings fleet to, 275–85, 339; (190) assigned to L. Scipio with Africanus as leg., 285, 291–5, **11**. 177–9; his campaign against Antiochus (Magnesia), **10**. 299–427; (189) fate of, discussed before Senate by agents of Antiochus, Eumenes, and Rhodes, 441–67; Galatians a threat to, **11**. 57, 61; Aetolian campaign of M. Fulvius Nobilior, **10**. 437, **11**. 9–37, 95–101;

INDEX

affairs of the Achaeans, 101–15; (188) Q. Fabius Labio returns to, 131; colonies of, in Thrace aid Cn. Manlius Volso, 141; (187) Nobilior recalled from, 147; coss. vainly desire, as prov., 145, 161; (185) increasing friction between Philip and, 285–309; (184) envoys in, 321–41; (183) Achaeans and Lacedaemonians, 371–9; (182) Q. Marcius Philippus reports on, **12**. 7; cruelty of Philip in, 7–13; (181) envoys from, in Rome, 63–5; (174) Perseus seeks support of, 257–73, (173) 297, 303–5, (172) 321–43, 377, 417, 449; (173) M. Marcellus and other envoys in, 307–11; (172) envoys from, heard, 363, 397; troops sent to, 399–401, 425, 437, 451–3; envoys to Perseus and, 399–433, report, 433–7; (171) campaign of P. Licinius Crassus and C. Lucretius Gallus in, 381–5, 439–505, **13**. 15–7, 27–33; (170) assigned to A. Hostilius Mancinus and L. Hortensius, 17, 19, 91, 95; envoys from, 21–5; (169) allotted to Q. Marcius Philippus, 43, 53; SC. limiting requisitions in, 61; Roman envoys in, 61–3; campaign of Ap. Claudius Centho in, 75–83; Philippus' campaign in, 91–133, 139–43; (168) allotted to L. Aemilius Paulus, 145–9, 155–63; his campaign in (Pydna), 163–271, 385; all, injured by war with Perseus, 255–7; (167) envoys from, 311; Aemilius tours, 339–45, 359–61, dictates peace terms, 347–53, administers justice, 353–9; rival parties in cities of, 353–7; leading men of, in custody in Rome, 367–9; (148–144) affairs of, **14**. 41–3; (130) destruction of, foretold, 263; (88) agent of Mithridates in, 99; (49) Caesar moves into, 139; (43) M. Junius Brutus in, 149, 153; (42) Octavius and Antony cross to, 155

Greece, Greeks, Western: (420) Campanians take Cumae from, **2**. 403; (327) Publilius Philo's campaigns against Samnites and, **4**. 87–91; (326) 99–107; (319) members of Roman Federation, 237; (280–275)support Pyrrhus, **9**. 23; (216) man and woman sacrificed after Cannae, **5**. 385–7; desert Rome, 409; Hanno and Bruttii attack, **6**. 101; (215) 175, 179; (212) Tarentum and Thurii, chief cities of, 367; Syracuse, most beautiful city of, 453; (200) may support Philip, **9**. 23; (195) in Emporiae, 441–3; (194) colonies on land once held by, 535; (193) under Roman domination, **10**. 47–9. *See* Croton, Emporiae, Sinopê, Syracuse, Tarentum, Tempsa, Thurii, Vibo.

Greek art and culture: influence of, **11**. 241; (211) works of, in Syracusan triumph of M. Marcellus, **6**. 495, **7**. 81; (204) Africanus' love for, **8**. 285; (194) works of, in Flamininus' triumph, **9**. 551; (186) Greek actors in votive games, **11**. 281, (175) in shows given by Antiochus IV, **12**. 249–51; (170) works of, in Macedonian booty, **13**. 17; skill in giving games, 361; (148) Masinissa trains son in, **14**. 33; (Augustan age) training in, given Romans, **4**. 303

— historians cited: (319) **4**. 233; (204) **8**. 315; (199) **9**. 169; (183) **11**. 379

— language: (216) response from Delphi in, **6**. 33; (209) used for making compounds, **7**. 251; (205) Hannibal sets up inscription in, **8**. 199; (181) writings in, in 'chests of Numa,' **12**. 89–91; (169) Dyrrachium called Epidamnus in, **13**. 75; used by L. Aemilius Paulus, 271; (167) Cn. Octavius translates peace terms into, 347; (141) C. Acilius writes Roman history in, **14**. 47, translated by Q. Claudius Quadrigarus, **6**. 493, **10**. 41

— religious customs: (753) sacrifice to Hercules, **1**. 27; (292) palms presented to victors in Roman games, **4**. 541; cult of Aesculapius, 543, **8**. 245–7; (212) offerings to Apollo, **6**. 387; (208) Olympic games, **7**. 351; (204) wearing of fillets and olive branches, **8**. 269; (186) Bacchic rites, **11**. 241

Grumentum, in Lucania: (215) Punic defeat at, **6**. 131; (207) **7**. 373–7

Gulussa, son of Masinissa: (172) envoy, **12**. 355–9; (171 **13**. 13;

INDEX

(151) reports Punic war preparations, **14**. 19; (149) 21; Punic rejection of, a pretext for war, 23; (148) receives part of father's realm, 33, 37; aids Rome against Carthage, 33–5
Gurges: *see* Fabius Maximus.
Gymnesii: (123) Greek name for Baleares, **14**. 71
Gyrto: (191) not occupied by Antiochus, **10**. 185; (171) occupied by T. Minucius Rufus, **12**. 459
Gytheum, port of Sparta: (195) taken by Flamininus, **9**. 491–3, 507, 517, (192) by Nabis, **10**. 35–9, 69–77, **11**. 333; A. Atilius Serranus approaches, **10**. 111

Hadria (Hatria), in Picenum: gives name to Adriatic sea, **3**. 115; (290) colony at, **4**. 547; (217) Hannibal plunders, **5**. 229; (209) loyal, **7**. 245–7. Prodigies: (214) **6**. 209; (194) **9**. 535
Hadrianus: *see* Fabius.
Hadriatic sea: *see* Adriatic sea.
Hadrumetum, in Africa: Punic port, **9**. 405; (202) Hannibal at, **8**. 469, 499, 501
Haedui (Aedui), Gauls: (616–578) enter Italy, **3**. 119; (121) Salluvii raid, **14**. 73; (58) seek Caesar's aid, 129
Haemus, Mt., in Thrace: (181) **12**. 67–71
Haliacmon riv., in Macedon: (171) **12**. 457
Haliartus, in Boeotia: (172) favors alliance with Perseus, **12**. 425, 431; (171) C. Lucretius Gallus takes, 463–5, 489–91
Halicarnassus: (197) Rhodes preserves liberty of, **9**. 335; (190) Rhodians send to, for stores, **10**. 319; C. Livius Salinator visits, 335
Halys riv., in Galatia: (189) Galatians forced to withdraw beyond, **11**. 55, 87, 93; (188) set as limit for Antiochus, 125
Hamae, in Campania: (215) **6**. 121–7
Hamilcar Barca: (247–241) Punic leader in First Punic war, **5**. 29, 31, 129, **8**. 165–7, 467; (241) makes treaties with Rome, **5**. 121–3; (237) crosses to Spain, 5, 9, postponing attack on Rome, 13; a constant cause of war, 27, 5; binds Hannibal to hate Rome, 5, **10**. 55–7; (229–228) dies, **5**. 5, **6**. 307; appears reborn in Hannibal, **5**. 9. *See* Hasdrubal, Hannibal, Mago, sons of; Hasdrubal, son-in-law of.
Hamilcar, son of Gisgo: (218) surrenders Melita, **5**. 151
—: (215) Locri surrenders to, **6**. 175–7; (205) holds citadel of Locri, **8**. 233, 237, 271
—, pref. of fleet: (210) ravages Sardinia, **7**. 227
—: (200) survivor of Hasdrubal's army, raises Gauls, **9**. 31–3; outlawed, 57; defeated and killed by L. Furius Purpurio, 63; (197) or defeated and led in triumph by C. Cornelius Cethegus, 247, 341
Hammonius: (149) virtual ruler of Syria, **14**. 33
Hampsicora, of Sardinia: (215) sends secretly to Carthage, **6**. 111; T. Manlius Torquatus defeats, 137–41
Hannibal: (258) defeated, **4**. 555
—, son of Hamilcar: importance of war with, **5**. 3; not of African origin, **6**. 15; boyhood in father's camp, **5**. 129; swears enmity to Rome, 5, **10**. 55–7; (228–221) serves in Spain under Hasdrubal; his character, **5**. 7–13; marries, **6**. 309; (221–219) defeats Spanish tribes, **5**. 13–7, 59; (219) attacks Saguntum, 17–25, 29; rebuffs Roman envoys, 17–9, 25–7; supported by Punic senate, 27–31, 49, *cp*. **8**. 447; takes Saguntum, **5**. 31–43, **8**. 157, **9**. 21, 57; chronological problem, **5**. 43–5; (218) Rome renews charges against, and declares war, 49–53, 131, **11**. 155; secures some Gallic support, **5**. 57–9; winters, 43, 59; leaves Spanish hostages in Saguntum, 273; provides for defence of Africa, 61–3, and Spain, 63–5; crosses Ebro, 65–9, leaving Hanno in Spain, 67, 179–81; crosses Pyrenees, 67–9, 75, 87, 181; wins Gallic support, 69, 75, **6**. 95; crosses Rhone, **5**. 75–83; defeats Roman cavalry, 83–5; encourages men for Alpine crossing, 85–9; settles contentions of Allo-

INDEX

broges, 91; crosses Druentia, 91–3; crosses Alps, 93–111, 115, 117–9, **6**. 115, **7**. 387; his forces, **5**. 111; possible routes, 111–3; takes city of Taurini, 113–5; P. Scipio meets, 93, 115–23, **8**. 177; encourages men, **5**. 123–33; defeats Scipio at Ticinus riv., 133–9, 43; crosses Po, 139–41; camps near Trebia riv., secures Clastidium, 141–5; plunders Gallic lands, 153–5; defeats Ti. Sempronius Longus on Trebia, 151, 157–69; Scipio goes to Spain, 179, **8**. 155; wounded near Placentia, **5**. 169–71, **7**. 369; captures Victumulae, **5**. 171–3; (217) fails to cross Apennines, 173–5, 199; returns toward Placentia, 175; fights drawn battle with Sempronius, 175–7; withdraws to Liguria, 177–9; loses Gallic support, 199, **7**. 385–7; disguises self, **5**. 199; loses eye crossing marshes of Arno, 205–7; defeats C. Flaminius at Lake Trasumennus, 209–23; dismisses captured allies, 223, 243, **6**. 213, 273, 377; captures cavalry of C. Centenius, **5**. 227; plunders Umbria and Apulia, 229; vainly offers battle to Q. Fabius Maximus, 237–41, **8**. 165; plunders in Samnium, **5**. 243; misled by guide on way to Campania, 243–5; camps by Volturnus, seeks winter quarters, 245–51; outwits Fabius and crosses above Callicula, 251–9; takes Gereonium, 261, 281; worried by Fabian tactics, 277–9, **8**. 459; exchanges prisoners, **5**. 279; spares farm of Fabius, 279, 287; M. Minucius defeats, 281–5, 291; adopts policy of Fabius, 283; defeats Minucius, who is saved by Fabius, 295–9, 303; considers retirement to cis-Alpine Gaul, 307–9, 343; a tr. pl. charges that patricians brought on war with, 315; (216) possible invasion of Africa to weaken, 323; less dangerous to Rome than cos. C. Terentius Varro, 329, 333; difficulties of supply at Gereonium, 331, 335, 343–5; fails to draw Romans into ambush, 337–43; moves to Cannae, 343–5; there defeats L. Aemilius Paulus and Varro, 347–73 (*see* Cannae); takes prisoners, 371, 401; master of nearly all Italy, 379, 409, **8**. 183–5; fails to follow up victory, **5**. 367–9, 381–3, 389, **7**. 27, 39, **8**. 443; dismisses captured allies, **5**. 389, **6**. 213, 377; sends Romans under parole to arrange ransom, **5**. 389–97, some of whom fail to return, 407–9, **6**. 231; ransom refused, **5**. 397–405, **9**. 419; in need of money, **5**. 405; sells prisoners, **9**. 547; Arpi betrayed to, **6**. 319; moves into Samnium, leaving booty at Compsa, 3; fails to take Neapolis, 3–5; admitted into Capua, 5–33, 37, 59, **7**. 131, **9**. 93; Mago reports victories of, in Carthage, **6**. 35–7; Hanno questions their value, 37–43; reinforcements voted, 43; fails to win Neapolis and Nola; takes Nuceria, freeing non-Romans, 45–9; M. Marcellus checks, before Nola, 49–55, 499, **7**. 115, 207; plunders Acerrae, **6**. 55–7; fails to take Casilinum, 57–61; winters in Capua, 61; (215) effect of Capua on his men, 63, 155, **7**. 211; takes Casilinum on terms, **6**. 63–9; resisted by Petelia, 71; Roman disasters in Gaul of little consequence compared with war with, 85; Scipios fear Spanish troops for, 95; makes treaty with Philip, 117, 135, **9**. 21, 407, **13**. 317; envoys captured and brought to Rome, **6**. 117–9, 131–3; moves against Ti. Sempronius Gracchus, 127–9; returns to Tifata, 129–31; Fabius recovers Campanian cities from, 135–7; Samnites appeal to, 143–7; fails to win Nola, 135, 147–51; Marcellus defeats, before Nola, 151–7, 499; winters in Apulia, 157–9, 185; sends Hanno to Bruttium, 157, 179; makes terms with Locri, 177–9, **8**. 229, 269, and with Hieronymus of Syracuse, **6**. 191–7, 251–3, **7**. 115–7; transports population from Croton to Locri, **6**. 179, 185; T. Otacilius Crassus with fleet fails to intercept supplies, 201; (214) to relieve Capua vainly attacks Puteoli, 211, 215; is promised aid in Tarentum, 213–5; fails to take Nola, 215–7, 227–9,

235; kept from Beneventum and Cumae by Gracchus, **7**. 9; soldiers of, captured at Casilinum, **6**. 233, 237; moves to Tarentum, which fails to rise, 239–41; winters at Salapia, 241; agents of, in Syracuse, 251, 253; urges active war in Sicily, 287; (213) war with, assigned to Q. Fabius Maximus (son of Cunctator) and Gracchus, 315; punishes family of Dasius of Arpi, 321–3; recovers troops from Arpi, 325–7; spends summer in Sallentine region, 341; victorious in Italy, **9**. 433; (212) war with, assigned to Q. Fulvius Flaccus and Ap. Claudius Pulcher, **6**. 347; Tarentum, except citadel, delivered to, 365–83, **7**. 149, 273, 351; orders Hanno to provide grain for Campanians, **6**. 387–9; promises them aid, 395–7, 401–3; joined by Metapontum, 397, and part of Lucania, 403–5; buries Gracchus with honour, 409–11; fights drawn battle with coss. near Capua, 403, 415–7; defeats M. Centenius Paenula in Lucania, 417–9, and Cn. Fulvius Flaccus near Herdonea, 421–3, **7**. 9; moves to Tarentum, then to Brundisium, **6**. 427–9, 501; sends Muttines to Sicily, 495–7; (211) postpones attack on Tarentum, moves to defend Capua, **7**. 15–7; fails to relieve Capua by battle before city, 17–27, 51, or by march on Rome, 27–43, 51, 159–61, **8**. 445, 475–9, **9**. 93; abandons Capua, withdraws to Bruttium, **7**. 43–53, 141; some Capuans desert to, 107; powerless to aid Italian allies, 65, 85, but still dangerous, 87; Philip disregards treaty with, 95; (210) plunders wherever he passes, 103; war with, assigned to M. Valerius Laevinus, 109, 111, then to M. Marcellus, 113–5; misfortunes of Syracuse due to, 121; fails to prevent delivery of Salapia to Rome, 141–5, 203; loses superiority in cavalry, 145; withdraws into Bruttium, 161, 203; garrisons of, at Marmoreae and Meles lost, 203; defeats Cn. Fulvius Centumalus near Herdonea, 203–7; engages Marcellus in Lucania, 207–9, and Apulia, 209, 213; Hasdrubal plans to join, 221; Italy withstands, with difficulty, 229; (209) Latin revolt aids, 241–5; Fabius, first citizen of Rome, *Hannibale iudice*, 251; Marcellus defeats, near Canusium, 253–67, 297; withdraws toward Bruttium, 267–9; moves too late to save Tarentum, 269, 277; fails to trap Fabius, 277; *nobiles* charged with prolonging war with, 299; (208) moves from Lacinium to Apulia, 315; sets ambushes, slays Marcellus, 315–23; fails in plot against Salapia, 323–7; raises siege of Locri, 327–9; C. Claudius Nero too violent for war with, 347; (207) war with, allotted to Claudius, 353, 357, 371; to be kept busy in Bruttium, 363; moves slowly from winter quarters, 365–73; C. Claudius Nero defeats, 373–7; withdraws to Canusium, 377–81; Hasdrubal's envoys to, captured, 381; left unguarded by Claudius, 383–5, 393, **8**. 41; Hasdrubal fears for, **7**. 395–7; Hasdrubal's head thrown into camp of, 411; withdraws to Bruttium, 413, **8**. 37; (206) war with, assigned to L. Veturius Philo and Q. Caecilius Metellus, 43, who do nothing, 51; army of, described, 51–3, **4**. 239; Mago ordered from Spain to aid, **8**. 145; in Italy, 79, 159; (205) Fabius urges that, be defeated in Italy, 161–77, P. Scipio (Afr.) that, be forced to defend Carthage, 79, 177–89; war with, assigned to P. Licinius Crassus and Metellus, 191; supply ships of, captured, 199; spends summer near temple of Juno Licinia, erects inscription, 199; **12**. 301; fame in Spain, **8**. 211; Mago fails to meet, 221–3; loses Locri, 233–7, 269, 277, 281; (204) Scipio charged with avoiding, 285; Scipio hopes to draw, from Italy, 285, 311, 477; uncle of wife of Maesulian king, 323; defeated, returns to Croton, 349; (203) war with, allotted to Cn. Servilius Caepio, 367–9; Punic senate recalls, 387, 393–5, 427, 437; blamed for war, 423, 447; engages Caepio near Croton, 439; leaves Italy, 439–45, 449–51, **9**. 23, **12**. 445;

reaches Africa, **8.** 457, 465; receives aid from Macedon, 457, 491, 523–5, **9.** 7, **13.** 317; (202) fear of, in Rome, **8.** 465–9; vain conference with Scipio, 469–87; Scipio defeats, at 'Zama,' 485–501, 515–7, **5.** 137, 379, **10.** 27, **11.** 157–9, 179, 185, **12.** 85; urges acceptance of terms, **8.** 503, 507–9, **9.** 307, **10.** 423; takes refuge with Antiochus (?), **8.** 509; comments on terms, 535–7; defeat of, reported to Ptolemy, **9.** 7; Scipio triumphs over, **8.** 537–9, **11.** 159, **13.** 383; (200) Philip not to be compared with, **9.** 21; Venusia weakened by war with, 145; (199) veterans of war with, mutiny, 161; (198) Italians from army of, join Philip, 227; (195) quarrels with judges, leaves Carthage, 397–405, **11.** 175, 191; joins Antiochus, **9.** 403–7, 397–9, **10.** 37, 293, 441; (194) urges Antiochus against Rome, **9.** 529, **11.** 381, (193) and to invade Italy, **9.** 569–71; plots Punic revolt, 571–5; confers with envoy, **10.** 41, 55; reputed conversation with Scipio, 41–5; recovers confidence of Antiochus, 55–7; (192) Antiochus abandons plan to send, to Carthage, 123–7, 55; compared with Antiochus, 139; (191) urges Antiochus to attack Italy, 173–81; praised by Antiochus as prophet, 203; warns that Rome will invade Asia, 273–5; with Antiochus' fleet; defeated, 313, 355–61, **13.** 319; (190) with Antiochus at Magnesia, **11.** 205; surrender of, demanded, **10.** 425; (189) compared with Antiochus, 475; Antiochus surrenders, by treaty, **11.** 131; takes refuge with Prusias, 379; (183) commits suicide, 379–83, 399, **14.** 241; death of, compared with those of Scipio and Philopoemen, **11.** 379, 385–7

Hannibal: (215) envoy of Hannibal son of Hamilcar to Syracuse, **6.** 191–3

—, son of Bomilcar: (215) defeated, **6.** 167

Hanno*: (259) cos. L. Scipio defeats, **4.** 555

Hanno: anti-Barcine leader, (221) opposes Hannibal's going to Spain, **5.** 9; (219) urges Punic senate to check Hannibal, 27–31; (216) shows emptiness of Hannibal's gains, **6.** 37–43; advocates peace, **8.** 527; (203) rejoices at Hannibal's recall, 441

—: (218) Hannibal leaves, in Spain, **5.** 67, 179; Cn. Scipio defeats, 179–81

—, son of Bomilcar: (218) with Hannibal at Rhone, **5.** 77–81

—: (215) defeated, withdraws to Bruttium, **6.** 131, 143; goes to Nola, 147–51; returns to Bruttium, 157; attacks Greek cities, 175; Croton surrenders to, 179–85; (214) T. Sempronius Gracchus defeats, at Beneventum, 217–23; defeats allies, withdraws to Bruttium, 237; (213) defeats T. Pomponius Veientanus, 341, 349; (212) near Beneventum; gathers grain for Capua, 389–91; Q. Fulvius Flaccus takes camp of, 391–5; aids revolt of Thurii, 395, 399

—: (215) captured in Sardinia, **6.** 139

—: (212) survives capture of Syracuse, **6.** 495; commands in Agrigentum, 495–7; (210) **7.** 153–5; flees to Africa, 155

—: (211) commands in Capua, **7.** 19, 45

—: (207) commands in Metapontum; sent to Bruttium, **7.** 379

—: (207) brings troops to Spain, **8.** 3; M. Junius Silanus defeats, 3–9, 15

—: (206) gathers forces for Mago, **8.** 97, 123

—: (204) slain, **8.** 319, 337, 343

—, son of Hamilcar: (204) cavalry commander, defeated and slain by P. Scipio (Afr.), **8.** 337–43

—, son of Hamilcar: (168) requested by Masinissa as hostage, **13.** 291

Harmonia: (214) Gelo's daughter, wife of Themistus; killed, **6.** 253, 257

Harpalus: (172) envoy of Perseus, **12.** 331–5

Harpasus riv., in Asia Minor: (189) **11.** 41

* Identification and separation of the Punic leaders of this name is often conjectural.

INDEX

Harsa: *see* Terentilius.

haruspices: (398) from Etruria, **3**. 53; captured at Veii, 53–5, 59; (340) consulted, **4**. 23; (212) **6**. 403; (209) **7**. 277; (208) 319; (207) 359; (200) **9**. 17; (199) 157; (192) **10**. 61; (191) 155; 263; (182) **12**. 5; (177) 225; (172) 347–9; (171) 379; (152) **14**. 251–3; (126) 265; (104) 275–7; (102) 277; 279; (99) 281; (86) 297; (63) 303; (42) 317

haruspicy: (208) liver without head, **7**. 319; (203) **8**. 373; (176) **12**. 227–9; (154) **14**. 251; (118) 269; (98) 283; (93) 289; (90) 293; (176) liver melted, **12**. 229, **14**. 245; (44) victim without heart, 309

Hasdrubal *, son-in-law of Hamilcar Barca: (237–229) under Hamilcar in Spain, **5**. 5, 9; (229–221) succeeds Hamilcar, 5–7; Hannibal trained under, 7–13; makes treaty with Rome, 7, 51–5; delays attack on Rome, 13; (221) killed; succeeded by Hannibal, 7–9

—, son of Hamilcar: (218) Hannibal leaves, in Spain, **5**. 63, 93, 119, 179; retires south of Ebro, 181–5; (217) Cn. Scipio defeats, 263–7; retires into Lusitania, 269; Celtiberians defeat, 271; (216) builds fleet, **6**. 87–9; defeats Tartessi, 89–93; ordered to Italy, 93–5; Cn. and P. Scipio defeat, 95–101, **7**. 161; (215) **6**. 167; (214) defeats pro-Roman Spaniards, 307; fights series of battles with P. and Cn. Scipio, 307–13; (212 or 211) defeats Cn. Scipio, 463–7, 471–7; perhaps defeated by L. Marcius, 493; silver shield with likeness of, on Capitoline, 493; (211) escapes C. Claudius Nero by trick, **7**. 65–9; winters near Saguntum, 77; (210) troops for, hired in Africa, 221; Senate fears march of, to Italy, 229; (209) P. Scipio (Afr.) defeats near Baecula, 279, 283–9; marches toward Pyrenees, 289; Scipio fails to hinder, 293, **8**. 173–5; confers with other leaders, **7**. 293–7; invents way of killing elephants, 403; (208) reported nearing Italy, 353–5, (207) 363–5, 369–71; crosses Alps, **7**. 367–9, **8**. 3; abandons siege of Placentia, **7**. 369, 381; messengers of, to Hannibal captured, 381–3; faced by M. Livius Salinator and C. Claudius Nero; moves to Metaurus riv., 391–9; defeated and slain, 399–405, **8**. 41, 51, 199, **10**. 263; head of, thrown into Hannibal's camp, **7**. 411–3; fame of, as general, 385; allies of, in Italy punished, **8**. 43, 45; gifts from spoils of, sent to Delphi, 193; (200) Hamilcar, survivor of army of, raises Gauls, **9**. 31–3

Hasdrubal: (217) officer of Hannibal at Callicula, **5**. 257, (216) at Cannae, 353, 357

—, son of Gisgo: (214) with Hasdrubal and Mago, sons of Hamilcar, defeated by P. and Cn. Scipio, 307–313; (212 or 211) with them defeats the Scipios, 463–77; follows L. Marcius across Ebro, 479–83; (211) withdraws to Gades before P. Scipio (Afr.), **7**. 77; (209) too late for battle at Baecula, 293–5; plans to retire and avoid battle, 295; (207) withdraws to Gades, **8**. 3, 7–9; makes raids, 11; scatters army, 9, 15; (206) Scipio defeats, near Silpia (or Baecula), 53–67, 319; escapes to Gades, 67–71; meets Scipio at court of Syphax, 75–9, 297–9, 413; (204) marries daughter to Syphax, 297–301, 407–9, 413, 465, **12**. 55; ablest general in Africa, **8**. 317–9, 423, 465; urges Syphax to war with Masinissa, 327; with Syphax relieves Utica, 337–9, 345–7; (203) Scipio defeats, 375–85; escapes to Carthage, 385–7; Scipio defeats, 389–93

—: (203) Punic admiral, tows transports to Carthage, **8**. 453–5

—: (149) ambushes Romans, **14**. 25; (147) mistreats prisoners, 253; (146) defeated, surrenders Carthage, 37–9; wife of, kills self, 39, 41; P. Scipio Aemilianus triumphs over, 43

—, son of Gulussa: (148) Carthaginians kill, for treason, **14**. 33, 37

* Identification and separation of the Punic leaders of this name is often conjectural.

INDEX

Hasdrubal Calvus: (215) sent to Sardinia, **6**. 113; driven to Balearic is., 121; T. Manlius Torquatus defeats, on Sardinia, 139; T. Otacilius Crassus scatters fleet of, 141

— Haedus: (201) opponent of Hannibal in Carthage; envoy to Rome, **8**. 527–9; upbraids Hannibal, 535

Hasta, in Spain: (186) **11**. 279

hastae Martiae: *see* Mars, spears of.

hastati: (350) **3**. 435; (340) **4**. 31–9, etc.

Hatria: *see* Hadria.

Hebrus riv., in Thrace: (188) **11**. 139

Hegeas, of Neapolis: (216) **6**. 5

Hegesianax: (193) envoy of Antiochus, **9**. 563–9

Hegesilochus, of Rhodes: (172) pro-Roman magistrate, **12**. 427

Helen of Troy: **1**. 9

Hellespont: (278) Galatians cross, **11**. 53–5; (200) Philip moves to, **9**. 49; (198–197) Rhodes demands Philip withdraw from, 255; (196) Antiochus takes cities of, 379–81; (192) Antiochus crosses, **10**. 67, 137; (191) Antiochus leaves, for Ephesus, 277; (190) L. Scipio at, 313, 317; Rhodian and Roman fleets join at, 325; ships of Antiochus raid from, 331; Scipio crosses, 345, 353, 367, 369, 381, 387–9, 395, 397, 423, 449, **11**. 305; (188) Cn. Manlius Volso crosses, 135. *Also*: **11**. 65; **13**. 353

Helo, in Spain: (192) **10**. 65

Helorus, in Sicily: (214) **6**. 287

Helva: *see* Aebutius.

Helvetii: (107) Tigurini withdraw from, **14**. 79: (63) Caesar conquers, 129

Helvius, C.: (203) tr. mil., **8**. 435

—, C., pr. 198: (199) aed. pl., **9**. 173; (198) pr. for Gaul, 173, 175, 179, 233; (189) envoy of Cn. Manlius Volso to Moagetes, **11**. 45; in Galatian war, 69, 75, 79

—, M.: (209) tr. mil., **7**. 259

—, M., pr. 197: (198) aed. pl., **9**. 239; (197) pr. for Farther Spain, 239, 241; reports war, 335–7; (195) defeats Celtiberians; receives ovation, 445–7; (194) IIIvir col. deduc., 533–5

— Cinna, C.: (44) tr. pl., removes colleague from office, dies, **14**. 317

Heniochi, beyond the Euxine: (66) **14**. 125

Henna, in Sicily: (214) surrender to Himilco prevented, **6**. 293–301

Hephaestia, on Lemnos: (196) **9**. 371

Heptagoniae, in Sparta: (195) **9**. 519

hepteres: (190) in Antiochus' fleet, **10**. 357–61, 377

Hera: (208) games for, at Argos, **7**. 333–5

Heraclea, in Athamania: (189) **11**. 5

—, in Bithynia: (171) **12**. 465

—, in Lucania: (c. 530) Pythagoras gathers youths in, **1**. 65; (c. 330) Alexander of Epirus takes, **4**. 95; (280) Pyrrhus defeats Romans at, **5**. 393, **6**. 359; (214) Hannibal gets grain from, 241

—, in Macedon: (181) **12**. 77

— Minoa, in Sicily: (214) Himilco at, **6**. 287–9; (212) Punic transports sent to Africa from, 449; Numidians mutiny at, 497–9

— Sinticê, in Paeonia: (167) **13**. 347–9. *See* Asclepiodotus.

— Trachinia, above Thermopylae: (208–207) Aetolian council at, **8**. 19–21, 29; Philip drives Aetolians to, 27; (200) Aetolians, Attalus, and L. Apustius confer at, **9**. 133–5; (197) Aetolians and Flamininus at, 283; (191) Aetolians occupy, **10**. 205–7, 211, 217; M' Acilius Glabrio takes, 207, 225–37, 245, **11**. 287; (190) he moves from, **10**. 305

Heracleum, in Thessaly: (169) Perseus raids, **13**. 97; Q. Marcius Philippus camps near, 107; M. Popilius Laenas takes, 117–21; fleet sails from, 121; (168) L. Aemilius Paulus sends forces to, 207

Heraclia: (214) daughter of Hiero, slain, **6**. 257–61

Heraclides: (200) admiral of Philip, **9**. 49, 99, 135; Philip imprisons, 165

—, of Byzantium: (190) envoy of Antiochus, **10**. 389–95

Heraclitus Scotinus: (215) envoy of Philip to Hannibal, **6**. 135

Heraea, in Arcadia: (208–207) Philip restores, to Achaeans, **8**. 31–3, (199) **9**. 163–5, (196) 369

Heraeum, port of Leucas: (197) **9**. 321

Herbesus, in Sicily: (214) Hippocrates and Epicydes flee to, **6**. 271;

Syracuse attacks, 273; surrenders to Marcellus, 287
Herculaneum, Samnite town: (293) **4**. 533–5
Hercules: crosses Alps, **3**. 119, **5**. 121; slays Cacus, dedicates Great Altar, **1**. 27–31; leaves Balius on Balearic is., **14**. 71; buried on Mt. Oeta, **10**. 245; (753) worshipped by Romulus with Greek rites, **1**. 27; Potitii carry on rites of, 29–31, **4**. 275–7; (399) honoured at *lectisternium*, **3**. 49; (312) public slaves perform rites of, **4**. 275–7, 295–7; (305) statue of, on Capitol, 345; (296) prayer to, 425; (198) **9**. 229; (191) M' Acilius Glabrio sacrifices to, on Mt. Oeta, **10**. 245; (189) statue of, in temple, **11**. 115. Temples of: (198) at Ardea, **9**. 177; (200) at Cynosarges, 73; (296) in Rome, **4**. 443; (218) **5**. 187; (199) **9**. 157; (189) **11**. 115; (179) **12**. 159; 211) outside Colline gate, **7**. 37.
—, Harbour of: (137) **14**. 257
—, Pillars of: (218) **5**. 127; (216) **6**. 15
—, Spring of: (217) **5**. 201
— (i.e., Melkarth): (218) Hannibal pays vow to, **5**. 61
Hercynian highlands, in Germany: (616–578) **3**. 117
Hercynna, shrine of, in Lebadia: (167) **13**. 341
Herdonea (Ardaneae) in Apulia: (216) joins Hannibal, **7**. 203; (214) Fabius camps at, **6**. 239; (212) near, Hannibal defeats Cn. Fulvius Flaccus, **6**. 421–3, 427, (210) and Cn. Fulvius Centumalus, **7**. 203–5; people of, turn against Hannibal; are transported, 205–7
Herdonius, Ap., a Sabine: (460) occupies Capitol, is slain, **2**. 53–67
—, Turnus, of Aricia: (534–510) opposes Tarquin the Proud; slain, **1**. 175–81
Herennius, C.: (218) IIIvir col. deduc., **5**. 69–71
—, M.: (93) cos., **14**. 287–9
— Bassus, of Nola: (215) rejects Hanno's offer, **6**. 149–51
—: *see* Baebius, Cerrinius, Pontius.
Herennuleius (Herennius ?): (76) officer of Sertorius, **14**. 191
Hergates, Spanish tribe: (175) **12**. 243
Herius Asinius: *see* Hierius Asinius.
— Pettius, of Nola: (215) rejects Hanno's offer, **6**. 149–51
Hermaeum, in Boeotia: (192) **10**. 147
Hermandica, in Spain: (221) **5**. 13–5
Herminius, Sp.: (448) cos., **2**. 219
— Aquilinus, T., cos. 506: (508) holds bridge with Horatius, **1**. 251; ambushes Etruscans, 255; (506) cos., 267; (499) leg., killed at Lake Regillus, 283
Hermionê, port in Argolis: (200) **9**. 127, 129
Hernici: (534–510) possible refuge for Sex. Tarquin, **1**. 185; (495) allied with Volsci, 287–9; (487) C. Aquilius defeats, 351; (486) receive treaty, 353; (475) aid against Veii; defeat Volsci and Aequi, 399; (468) aid against Volsci and Aequi, 431; (464) relieve Romans besieged by Aequi, **2**. 13–21; (463) Aequi and Volsci raid, 21–3; aid against Volsci and Aequi, 25–7; (462) 27–31; (461) charged with false reports of danger, 37; (459) aid against Volsci, 75–7; (449) congratulate Romans on harmony, 193; Aequi and Volsci raid, 201; (446) a match for Aequi and Volsci, 225; (431) aid against Aequi and Volsci, 339, 343, 351; (424) Volscian threat to, reported, 375; (423) 377; (413) Volsci plunder, 425; receive Ferentinum, 425–7, 439; (410) Aequi and Volsci raid, 429; (409) 435; (396) serve at Veii, **3**. 67; (389) revolt, 199; (387) war with, considered, 213; (386) aid Antiates, whom Camillus defeats, 217–23; reparation demanded from, 229–31; (385) join Volsci, 231–5, 239; release of, captured in Volscian defeat refused, 255; plebs call war with, a Senatorial trick, 247; (380) 291; (366) defection of, rumoured, 357; (363) war with, prevented, 367; (362) ambush L. Genucius, 375–7; defeated by C. Sulpicius, 377, and by Ap. Claudius Crassus, 377–81; (361) lose Ferentinum, 381–3; (360) war with, assigned to M. Fabius Ambustus, 389; (358 C. Plautius

Proculus defeats, 393, 407, 471; (307) some, aid Samnites, **4**. 333; (306) Q. Marcius Tremulus defeats, 333–5, 339, 345; retain own laws with right of marriage, 339, 347; (303) Frusinates fined for tampering with, 361
Herodicus, of Thessaly: (182) Philip kills children of, **12**. 9–13
Herodorus, of Cius: (192) **10**. 111–5
—: (181) friend of Demetrius; tortured to death by Philip, **12**. 75
Herophon: (168) agent of Perseus to Eumenes, **13**. 169, 179
Hersilia, wife of Romulus: **1**. 43
Hexapylon, gate of Syracuse: (214) **6**. 243; 277–9; 283; 301; (212) 433–5
hexeres: (205) in fleet of P. Scipio (Afr.), **8**. 241, (190) of Antiochus, **10**. 357, 377
Hibera, in Spain, (216) **6**. 95–7
Hiberi, an eastern people: (66) **14**. 125
Hiberus riv.: *see* Ebro riv.
Hibrida: *see* Antonius.
Hicesias: *see* Leon.
Hiempsal: (118) Jugurtha kills, **14**. 75
Hiera Comê, in Asia Minor: (189) **11**. 41
Hierius Asinius: (90) general of Marrucini, slain, **14**. 91
Hiero II, of Syracuse: (264–263) allied with Carthage; defeated, **4**. 553; becomes ally, **6**. 265, 459; presented with Gallic and Illyrian arms, 243; (218) warns of Punic ships, **5**. 145; receives Ti. Sempronius Longus, 149–51; (216) sends supplies and men; urges invasion of Africa, 321–5; appeals for aid, 383; furnishes supplies, **6**. 73, 133–5; suspected in death of son, Gelo, 103; (215) dies; Hieronymus succeeds, 185–93, 255; loyalty of, to Rome, 265, 437, 451, 453–5, 459, **7**. 115, 119, 123; his wise rule over Syracuse, **6**. 245, 287, 441; (213) kingdom of, as prov., 315–7; (212) 349; (209) **7**. 239. *See* Damarata, Heraclia, Gelo.
Hierocles, of Agrigentum: (191) transfers Zacynthus to Achaeans, **10**. 249
Hieronymus, of Syracuse: (215) succeeds Hiero, **6**. 185–9; conspiracy against, 189–91; allied with Hannibal, 191–5, 251, 265, 273, 451–3, **7**. 115–7; sends envoy to Ptolemy, **6**. 257; assassinated, 195, 241, 245, 255, 259
Hierta, king of Numidia: (81) **14**. 113
Hilernus: (193) Spanish king, captured, **10**. 21
Himera riv., in Sicily: (215) boundary between Hannibal and Hieronymus, **6**. 193; (212) Marcellus defeats Epicydes and Hanno on, 497–501
Himilco: (217) Punic admiral, defeated near mouth of Ebro riv., **5**. 263–7
—: (216) Punic senator, supports Hannibal, **6**. 37–43
—: (216) replaces Hasdrubal in Spain, **6**. 93–5
—: (216) pref. of Hannibal, **6**. 101
—: (214) recovers Agrigentum, **6**. 287–9, and Murgantia, 291–3; fails at Henna, 293, 299; returns to Agrigentum, 301; (212) dies of pestilence before Syracuse, 439–45
—: (206) commands in Castulo, **8**. 87
—: *see* Maharbal, Phaneas.
Hippacra: *see* Hippo Diarrhytus.
Hippias, of Beroea: (172) Perseus gives, as hostage, **12**. 409; (171) commands phalanx, 447, 475; (169) fails to hold pass above Lake Ascuris, **13**. 97–107, 113; (168) surrenders to L. Aemilius Paulus, 237
—: (171) Thessalian general, **12**. 459
—: (169) envoy of Perseus to Gentius, **13**. 163
Hippo Diarrhytus (Hippacra), in Africa: (205) C. Laelius plunders, **8**. 219[1]. *See* Muttines.
— Regius, in Africa: (205) C. Laelius plunders, **8**. 219–25 (*but cp.* 219[1]); (204) Masinissa established between, and Cirta, 335
Hippocrates: (215) Hannibal sends, and Epicydes to Syracuse, **6**. 191–3; attacks cities held by Rome, 195; (214) foments Syracusan revolt, 251–3, 261–3; involves Leontini in war, 267–9; flees to Herbesus, 271; seizes control of Syracuse, leading to Roman siege, 273–83, 287, 451, 453, **7**. 115–7; defeated by Marcellus; joins Himilco, **6**. 289–91; returns to

Murgantia, 301; (212) at Agrigentum, 429; plot against, fails, **7.** 115; attacks Romans before Syracuse; dies of pestilence, **6.** 439–45, 451; Muttines replaces, 495–7
Hippolochus, of Larisa: (191) surrenders to Antiochus, **10.** 183–5
Hirpini: (217) Hannibal leaves, **5.** 243; (216) desert Rome, 409; Hannibal invited to land of, **6.** 3; (215) M. Valerius Laevinus recovers towns of, 131; secure aid of Hannibal, 143–7; (209) surrender to Q. Fulvius Flaccus, **7.** 267; (89) Sulla defeats, **14.** 93
Hirtius, A.: (43) cos., **14.** 313; defeats Antony at Mutina; slain, 151
Hirtuleius, L., qu., 79: (78) follower of Sertorius, defeats L. Manlius, **14.** 115; (75) Q. Caecilius Metellus Pius defeats, 191–3, 115
Hispala Faecenia: (186) freedwoman, aids discovery of Bacchanalian conspiracy, **11.** 243–57, 273–5
Hispallus: *see* Cornelius Scipio.
Hister riv.: *see* Danube riv.
Histiaeus: (168) garrison commander of Perseus, **13.** 197
Histrians: (302) savage people beyond Adriatic, **4.** 363; (221) subjugated, 561, **5.** 45; (183) M. Marcellus in, **11.** 395, 397; (181) assigned to L. Duronius, **12.** 59; Q. Fabius Buteo campaigns against, 81; (178) A. Manlius Volso attacks, without authority, 185–7, 205; capture camp at Timavis, 187–91, but are driven out, 191–97; panic at Rome, 197–9; M. Junius Brutus moves against, 199, then is questioned about, 205; (177) L. Minucius Thermus reports on, 207; allotted to C. Claudius Pulcher, 211–3, who dismisses Brutus and Volso, 215–9; he defeats, 219–23, **14.** 243, and triumphs over, 225; Latins sent to, 227; (171) Aquileia asks protection from, **13.** 5; outraged by C. Cassius Longinus; (170) compensated, 5, 19–21
Homer: cited, **10.** 347; **14.** 197
Homolium, in Thessaly: (172) **12.** 405
Honour (*Honor*), temple of, outside Porta Capena: (222) vowed by M. Marcellus, **7.** 313; (205) dedicated by his son, **6.** 495, **8.** 249
Hope (*Spes*), temple of, outside Porta Carmentalis: (477) Etruscans raid to, **1.** 393; (218) lightning strikes, **5.** 185; (213) burned, **6.** 327–9; (212) rebuilt, 365; (179) portico near, **12.** 159
Horatia: (672–640) weeps for dead Curiatius; killed by brother, **1.** 91, 95
Horatian spears: commemorate victory of Horatii, **1.** 93
Horatii: (672–640) overcome Curiatii, **1.** 83–93
— : (510) leaders against kings, **2.** 129
Horatius, M.: (378) tr. mil. c. p., **3.** 303
—, P.: (672–640) pleads for son, P., **1.** 93–5
—, P.: (672–640) survives combat with Curiatii, **1.** 89; kills sister; convicted; freed on appeal, 91–5
— Barbatus, L.: (425) tr. mil. c. p., **2.** 371
— —, M., cos. 449: (449) assails Xviri, **2.** 129–31, 135, 137; forces Xvir Ap. Claudius to withdraw, 161; secures resignation of Xviri, 167, 171–81; cos., restores democracy, 181–7; defeats Sabines, 193, 207–13; granted triumph by people, 213–5, 243, **4.** 503; opposes reelection, 217; (445) abstains from debate on plebeian coss., **2.** 277
— Cocles: (508) holds bridge against Porsinna, **1.** 249–53, 263
— Pulvillus, C. (or M.): (477) cos., **1.** 391–3; (457) ii., defeats Aequi, **2.** 101–3; (453) augur; dies of pestilence, 107
— —, L.: (386) tr. mil. c. p., **3.** 213; campaigns against Volsci, 217, 225
— —, M.: (509) cos. suf., **1.** 243–5; dedicates temple of Capitoline Jupiter, 245, **3.** 367
Horreum, in Epirus: (167) **13.** 335–7
horses: (214) herds of, in southern Italy, **6.** 241; (170) Gallic envoys each permitted to take ten, from Italy, **13.** 21
horses, public: (578–534) *equites* given money for, **1.** 153. *See equites.*
horse-trappings, silver: (210) ex-magistrates retain, **7.** 137

INDEX

Hortensius, L. : (422) tr. pl., **2**. 391–3
—, L. : (170) pr. for Greece and fleet, **13**. 17; wanton acts of, in Abdera and Chalcis rebuked, 17–9, 29–33
—, Q. : (287) dict., brings back seceding plebeians, **4**. 547
—, Q., pr. 45 : (42) killed at Philippi, **14**. 155
Hostilia, Curia : (672–640) Tullus Hostilius builds, **1**. 107; (390) Senate meets in, **3**. 187; (216) **5**. 379. *See curia.*
Hostilia, Quarta : (180) poisons husband, cos. C. Calpurnius Pisa, **12**. 117
Hostilius, C. : (168) envoy to Antiochus IV, **13**. 153, 185, 285
—, Hostius : (753–717) killed by Sabines, **1**. 45, 75; grandfather of Tullus Hostilius, 75
—, Tullus, 3rd king of Rome : (672–640) becomes king, **1**. 75; lacks interest in ritual, 111; campaigns against Alba, 77–91; demands Alban aid at Veii, 91; establishes trial for treason with appeal, 93–5, **4**. 129; defeats Veii and Fidenae, **1**. 95–9; establishes Salian priests and shrines to Pallor and Panic, 99; punishes Mettius Fufetius, 101–5; incorporates Alba, 105–7, 115, 181, **4**. 19; builds Curia Hostilia, **1**. 107; defeats Sabines, 107–11; tries to avert pestilence by secret rites; killed by lightning, 111–3
— Cato, A. : (207) pr. for Sardinia, **7**. 351, 357, **8**. 45; (201) Xvir agr. divid., **9**. 13; (190) leg. of L. Scipio, **11**. 193; (187) convicted with Scipio, 193, 201–3
— —, C. : (207) pr. urb. and pereg., **7**. 351, 357, 411
— —, L. : (201) Xvir agr. divid., **9**. 13; (190) leg. of L. Scipio; (187) accused with Scipio; acquitted, **11**. 193
— Mancinus, A., cos. 170 : (180) pr. urb., **12**. 107–9; (170) cos., receives complaints from Abdera, **13**. 17; goes to Macedon through Camburnian mts., 19, 95; supplies sent to, 25–7; sends Ap. Claudius Cento into Illyricum, 35; ineffective in Macedon, 41; (169) envoys sent by, return, 63; maintains order in Thessaly, 91–3; remains with Q. Marcius Philippus, 93
Hostilius Mancinus, A. : (149) envoy to Prusias and Attalus, **14**. 35, 31–3
— —, C. : (137) cos., **14**. 57; Numantines defeat; Senate rejects his peace terms, 55, 257; (136) delivered to Numantines, 57, 257
— —, L. : (217) cavalry officer of Q. Fabius Maximus, slain, **5**. 251–3
— —, L. : cos. 145 : (148) leg. at Carthage, **14**. 37; (145) cos., 45
— Rufus : (11) pref. of camp., **14**. 319
— Tubulus, C. : (209) pr. urb., **7**. 225–7, 231, 233[1], 251; (208) propr. for Etruria, 303, 305; takes hostages, 307–11; transferred to Tarentum, 351, 353, (207) then to Capua, 353, 357; attacks Hannibal's column, 371–3; (206) in Capua, **8**. 45; (204) 257
Hostus, of Sardinia : (215) defeated and slain by T. Manlius Torquatus, **6**. 137–41
humiles : (312) distributed in all tribes; (304) placed in four urban tribes, **4**. 353. *See* freedmen.
Hyampolis, in Phocis : (198) **9**. 205
Hybla, in Sicily : (211) **7**. 83–5
Hyblaea : *see* Megara Hyblaea.
Hybristas, of Sparta : (190) pirate, **10**. 331
Hydramitis, in Crete : **14**. 29
Hydrela, in Caria : (189) **10**. 465
Hydruntum, in Calabria : (191) **10**. 223
Hypata, in Greece : (191) M' Acilius Glabrio wastes, **10**. 201, 207; Aetolians occupy, 205, 211; Aetolian council in, 235; 237; 241–5; (190) 307–9; (174) exiles returning to, slain, **12**. 271–3
Hypsaeus : *see* Plautius.
Hyrcanian plain, in Asia Minor : (190) **10**. 399

Iamphorynna, in Maedica : (211) **7**. 97–9
Iapydae, Illyrian tribe : (170) compensated for acts of C. Cassius Longinus, **13**. 19–21; (129) defeated by C. Sempronius Tuditanus and D. Junius Brutus, **14**. 69, (35) by Octavius, 161
Iasus, in Caria : (197) Philip required

to withdraw from, **9**. 255, 261, (196) 359, 501; (190) Antiochus holds, **10**. 339–41

Ibes, in Spain: (206) **8**. 89

Icilian law: (456) opens Aventine to plebs, **2**. 103; (453) not to be abrogated, 109

Icilii: (409–408) plebeian leaders, **2**. 433–9

Icilius: (449) summons L. Verginius, **2**. 153

—, L.: (456) tr. pl., secures law opening Aventine, **2**. 103, 109, 427; (455) tr. pl. ii, 103; (451) supports re-election of Xvir Ap. Claudius Crassus, 115; (449) defends Verginia, his betrothed, against Claudius, 145–61; rouses people, 159–61, and army, 169–71; presents plebeian demands, 175–7; tr. pl. iii, 181, 223, 261, wins triumphs for L. Valerius Potitus and M. Horatius Barbatus by popular vote, 215

—, L.: (412) tr. pl., agitates for land law, **2**. 427

—, Sp.: (470) tr. pl., **1**. 415

Icos, is. off Thessaly: (200) **9**. 131

Idaean Mother (Magna Mater): (205) Sibylline books direct introduction of, **8**. 245; P. Scipio Nasica as 'best citizen' welcomes, 247–9, 259–61, **10**. 29, 261, 271; matrons carry, to Palatine, **8**. 261–3, **9**. 421, 429; (204) temple of, contracted for, **8**. 351, (191) and dedicated, **10**. 261–3; (190) Galli, servants of, 317; (189) **11**. 63; (111) temple of, burned, **14**. 271; (101) slave emasculates self for, 279

Iguvium, in Umbria: (167) **13**. 403

Ilercaones, Spanish tribe: (76) **14**. 191–5

Ilerda, in Spain: (49) **14**. 137

Ilergavonenses, Spanish tribe: (217) **5**. 271

Ilergetes, Spanish tribe: (218) in army of Hasdrubal Barca, **5**. 63, 183; Hannibal subdues, 67; Cn. Scipio exacts hostages from, 183; (217) roused against Rome, 269; (210) P. Scipio (Afr.) recovers hostages of, **7**. 189; (206) subdued by Scipio, **8**. 111, 121, 129–41, (205) by L. Cornelius Lentulus and L. Manlius Acidinus, 211–9; 195) ask aid of M. Porcius Cato, **9**. 447–9. *See* Indibilis.

Iliberri, north of Pyrenees: (218) **5**. 67–9

Ilienses, Sardinian tribe: (181) revolt, **12**. 63; defeated by M. Pinarius Rusca, 107, (178–177) by Ti. Sempronius Gracchus, 201, 221–3; (Augustan period) not pacified, 107

Ilipa, in Spain: (193) **10**. 5

Iliturgi(s), in Spain: (215) P. and Cn. Scipio raise Punic siege of, **6**. 167; (214) 309; (211) Hasdrubal Barca camps near, **7**. 65; revolts on death of the Scipios, **8**. 79, 103; (206) P. Scipio (Afr.) destroys, 79–87; (195) M. Helvius captures, **9**. 445

Ilium: Roman descent from, **1**. 15, **10**. 397, **11**. 133; (205) in Macedonian treaty, **8**. 255; (192) sacrifice at, by Antiochus, **10**. 127, (190) by C. Livius Salinator, 317, 397; (188) Rhoeteum and Gergithus added to, **11**. 133; (85) C. Flavius Fimbria burns, **14**. 105, 297. *See* Troy.

Illyricum: (359–336) part of, subject to Philip II, **13**. 273; (302) Cleonymus shuns, **4**. 363; (c. 300) Gauls in, **11**. 59; (c. 233) defeated, **4**. 559; (219) 561, **5**. 45; spoils of, given to Hiero, **6**. 243; (217) tribute demanded from, **5**. 311; (211–200) often at war with Philip, **7**. 95–7, **9**. 101, **10**. 209; (200) invade Macedon, **9**. 119; (197) in Philip's army, 313, **10**. 209 Philip willing to cede, to Rome, **9**. 253, 261; kept out of Greece by Macedon, 307–9; (196) given to Pleuratus, 371; (191) compared with eastern soldiers, **10**. 209; (183) source of Erigonus riv., **11**. 391; (180) accused of piracy, **12**. 131–3; (178) IIviri navales to oppose, 185–7; (172) Issaeans accuse, 365; Roman army in, 373, 399; sought as ally against Perseus, 401, 429; (171) C. Cassius Longinus tries to reach Macedon through, **13**. 3–5; (170) unsuccessful campaign against, 33–7, 75; (169) Perseus conquers, 65–75, 259; Ap. Claudius Cento winters in, 83, 155; (168) L. Anicius Gallus sent to, 157; allied with

INDEX

Perseus, 163–7, 179, 185; Gauls scattered throughout, 173; Gallus defeats, 187–95, 203–5, 255, 299, 405; (167) 297; **14**. 245; left free; divided into three parts, **13**. 299–303, 315, 333–9; borders on 4th Macedonian republic, 349; industrious farmers in 3rd republic, 353; L. Aemilius Paulus ravages those of, who aided Perseus, 363; Gallus triumphs, 401–3, 385; ships of, given to Greek cities, 403; (156) Dalmatians plunder, **14**. 15; (135) Ser. Fulvius Flaccus defeats Vardaei in, 59; (113) Cimbri raid, 75; (49) Pompeians defeat C. Antonius in, 137; (34–33) Dalmatians defeated in, by Octavius; (29) he triumphs, 163. *See* Arthetaurus, Gentius, Pineus, Pleuratus, Scerdilaedus; Parthini, Penestae, Tralles; Mt. Scordus.

Ilotae (Helots ?): (195) **9**. 487

Ilvates, Ligurian tribe: (200) attack Placentia and Cremona, **9**. 31; (197) surrender to Q. Minucius Rufus, 245, 249

imagines: (439) false titles under, confuse records, **2**. 311; (322) **4**. 157; (217) **5**. 307

Imbrinium, in Samnium: (325) **4**. 115

Imbros: (196) Philip surrenders, to Athens, **9**. 361; (192) Antiochus at, **10**. 127

imperator: (304) only, or cos. may dedicate temple, **4**. 351; (211) army may not choose, **7**. 7; (209) P. Scipio (Afr.) hailed as, by army, 291

Imperiosus: *see* Manlius, — Capitolinus.

imperium: (431) holder of, may impose death penalty, **2**. 351–3; (340) **4**. 25–9; (418) held by coss. on alternate days, **2**. 407; (216) **5**. 337; (310) conferred by *comitia curiata*, **4**. 315; (211) when Hannibal threatens Rome, granted within city to procos., **7**. 35, and to former dictt., coss., censs., 39; granted within city for day of ovation, 81, (167) or triumph, **13**. 369, 375, 389; (173) granted to pr. elect to combat locusts, **12**. 319; (203) dict. named to recall cos. by his *maius imperium*, **8**. 451; (103) of defeated procos. is abrogated, **14**. 79–81; (43) granted Octavius by Senate, 149

Inachus riv., in Acarnania: (169) **13**. 77, 79

Inarimê, in Lydia: (c. 74) **14**. 197

India: (323) unwarlike people of, **4**. 231, 237, 239; once possessed by Macedon, **12**. 455, **13**. 273; (192) elephants from, **10**. 93–5; (190) 405; (189) **11**. 45

Indian ocean: *see* Red sea.

Indibilis, chief of Ilergetes: (217) Cn. Scipio defeats, **5**. 269–71; (212) commands the Suessetani, **6**. 469; (210) daughters of, among hostages freed by P. Scipio (Afr.), **7**. 189; (209) supports Scipio, 279–81, 291; (206) revolts on news of Scipio's illness, **8**. 97–9, 111–3, 117, 129, 145, 173; defeated by Scipio, 105–7, 129–41; (205) revolts, 211–3; slain, 217

Indiges: *see* Jupiter Indiges.

Indigites di: (340) addressed in *devotio*, **4**. 37

Indus riv., in Asia Minor: (189) **11**. 45

Infernal marshes (Stagna Inferna), in Epirus: (326) **4**. 93

Ingauni, Ligurian tribe: (205) Mago son of Hamilcar aids, **8**. 197; (203) Mago fears treachery from, 437; (201) P. Aelius Paetus makes treaty with, **9**. 9; (185) defeated by Ap. Claudius Pulcher, **11**. 317–9, (181) by L. Aemilius Paulus, **12**. 77–81, 87, 105; (180) A. Postumius Albinus explores coast of, 129. *See* Ligurians.

Inlucia, in Spain: (193) **10**. 19

Inregillensis: *see* Claudius, — Crassus.

Inregillus: (504) home of the Claudii, **1**. 271

Insani montes, in Sardinia: (202) **8**. 513

Insteius, C.: (76) pref. of Q. Sertorius, recruits cavalry, **14**. 195

—, L.: (77) leg. of Q. Sertorius, **14**. 189

Insteius vicus, in Rome: (214) **6**. 207

Insubres, pre-Gallic: (391) **3**. 119

—, Gallic tribe: (391) cross Alps, **3**. 119; (223) C. Flaminius defeats, **5**. 219; (218) Boi rouse, **5**. 69; at war with Taurini, 113; Romans enter land of, 133; (217) envoys sent to, 311; (200) attack Cremona and

Placentia, **9.** 31; (199) defeat Cn. Baebius Tamphilus, 171; (197) C. Cornelius Cethegus defeats, 243–9, 337, 341; (196) M. Marcellus defeats, 375, 393; L. Furius Purpurio withdraws before, 377; (194) L. Valerius Flaccus defeats, 535. *See* Ducarius.
Insula, part of Syracuse: *see* Nasos.
Intemelii, Ligurian tribe: (180) **12.** 129
Interamna Sucasina, in Latium: (313–312) colony at, **4.** 273; (294) resists Samnites, 499; (293) Sp. Carvilius Maximus takes over army at, 509; (211) Hannibal passes, **7.** 33; (209) unable to meet Roman demands, 243–7; (204) forced to furnish extra quotas, **8.** 263–7
intercalary month: (715–672) introduced by Numa, **1.** 69; (189) precedes Kal. of March, **10.** 475; (170) begins on 3rd day after Terminalia, **13.** 41, (167) on day after Terminalia, 405
Intercatia, in Spain: (151) **14.** 19–21
interregnum: (716) first, after Romulus, **1.** 61–3; term of interrex limited to 5 days, 61; (310) **4.** 295; (672) after Numa, **1.** 75; (640) after Tullus Hostilius, 113; (578) none after Elder Tarquin, 167; (462) because of pestilence, **2.** 27; (449) for election after Xvirate, 181; (444) when tribb. mil. c. p. resign because of *vitium*, 281–3; (397) **3.** 61; (421) caused by struggle between orders, **2.** 397; (414) 423; (370) **3.** 319; (356) 415; (352) 427; (351) 429–31; (344) 455; (392) to obtain fresh auspices, 111; (387) 211; (332) **4.** 69; (389) lest magistrates of 390 preside, **3.** 195–7; (340) when coss. resign to permit early elections, **4.** 11; (332) when appointment of dict. com. c. is voided by *vitium*, 69; (327) 93; (320) 189; (217) **5.** 313; (298) for no known reason, **4.** 399; (193) proposed but avoided, **10.** 17
Intibili, in Spain: (215) **6.** 167–9
Inuus: Roman name for Lycean Pan, **1.** 21
Iolcus, in Thessaly: (169) **13.** 129, 131
Ion, of Thessalonica: (171) officer of Perseus, **12.** 471; (168) delivers children of Perseus to Cn. Octavius, **13.** 265–7
Ionia: crossed by Meander riv., **11.** 41–3; (278) Tolostobogii occupy, 53–5; (196) Antiochus fears cities of, will claim independence, **9.** 379; (193) not slaves of a king, 567; Antiochus claims, **10.** 47–9; (190) needs protection, 363; withdrawal of Antiochus from, demanded, 393; (189) except free cities, restored to Eumenes, 463
Ionian sea: (215) between Macedon and Italy, **6.** 115; (171) fleet crosses, **12.** 439
Iphigenia: sacrificed at Aulis, **13.** 341
Iresiae, in Thessaly: (198) **9.** 189
iron: (205) from Populonium, **8.** 193; (167) mining of, permitted in Macedon, **13.** 349
Isalca: (216) pref. of Hannibal, **6.** 59
Isara riv., in Gaul: (218) **5.** 89
Isaurians, in Cilicia: (75–74) **14.** 117
Isidorus: (191) admiral of Antiochus, moves to Demetrias, **10.** 219–21, 253
Isiondenses, in Pamphylia: (189) **11.** 47–9
Isis: (88) vision of, **14.** 295
Island, of Rhone and Isara: (218 89
—, part of Syracuse: *see* Nasos.
—, in Tiber: (509) formed, **1.** 231–3; (292) temples to Aesculapius, **4.** 547, (196) to Faunus, **9.** 391, (194) and to Jupiter on, 553
Ismenias: (172) pro-Macedonian Boeotian leader, **12.** 405, 421–3
Issa, Illyrian is.; (200) ships of, join Romans, plunder Euboean coast, **9.** 131, 219; (190) men from, in army of C. Livius Salinator, **10.** 337; (172) envoys of, accuse Illyrians, **12.** 365; (171) *lembi* of, in Roman fleet, 439; (170) forces for Illyrian war sent to, **13.** 33–5; (167) granted tax exemption, 337
Isthmian games: character of, **9.** 363–5; (196) Flamininus proclaims liberty of Greece at, 359, 365–7
Istra: *see* Terentius.
Italy: fame of Etruria fills, **1.** 13; (302) harbourless on east coast, **4.** 363; (237–229) Hamilcar plans to invade, **5.** 5; (218) Hannibal moves toward 63–105; he displays, to

men from top of Alps, 105, and promises land in, 133; (216) Hasdrubal's invasion of, **6**. 93–7, is checked by the Scipios, 97–101; (212) 463; (215) assigned to Carthage by treaty of Philip and Hannibal, 117; (214) very few natives of, in Hanno's army, 221; (208) Hasdrubal invades, **7**. 353–5, (207) 363–9; (206–205) Mago invades, **8**. 145, 197–9, 223; (205) Philip urged to invade, 223; (203) Hannibal and Mago recalled from, 437–43; (91–87) citizenship extended to all, **14**. 89, 101; *et passim*.

Itonia: *see* Athena Itonia.

Iulus: son of Aeneas; ancestor of Julii, **1**. 15

— : *see* Julius.

Janiculum: view from, **5**. 249; (640–616) annexed, **1**. 121; Lucumo comes to, 125; (508) Porsinna occupies, 249, 253, **3**. 341; he retires from, **1**. 261, 265; treaty with him made on, 269; (477) Etruscans defeated on, 393–5, 397; (390) flight through, before Gauls, **3**. 137–9; (287) plebs secede to, **4**. 547; (214) legions reported on, vanish, **6**. 209; (181) 'books of Numa' found on, **12**. 89; (87) Marius attacks, **14**. 101

January: (170) elections on 26th and 28th, **13**. 39; (153) coss. take office on 1st of, **14**. 15

Janus: (340) addressed in *devotio*, **4**. 37; (174) three statues of, **12**. 281; (715–672) temple of, built by Numa; (235) closed by T. Manlius Torquatus, (29) by Augustus, **1**. 67

— Quirinus: (640–616) invoked by fetial, **1**. 117

Jerusalem: (63) Pompey takes, **14**. 127, 201; no image in temple at, 203

Jews: (63) defeated by Pompey, **14**. 127, (38) by M. Antonius, 159

Juba, of Mauretania: (49) defeats C. Scribonius Curio, **14**. 139; (47) urges destruction of Utica, 141; (46) Caesar defeats, 143

judges, order of, in Carthage: (195) Hannibal attacks excessive power of, **9**. 399–401

Jugarius vicus, in Rome: (213) fire in, **6**. 327–9; procession for Juno Regina enters Forum by, **7**. 361. Prodigy: (192) **10**. 61

iugum: *see* yoke.

Jugurtha: (118) adopted son of Micipsa of Numidia, drives out foster brothers, **14**. 75; (112) war declared on, 77, 271; (110) in Rome, murders Massiva; defeats A. Postumius Albinus, 77; (109–108) defeated by Q. Caecilius Metellus, 77, 273, (106–105) by Marius; betrayed by Bocchus, 79; (104) in Marius' triumph, 81

Julia: (54) daughter of Caesar, wife of Pompey, dies, **14**. 133

Julian gens: claims Iulus as ancestor, **1**. 15; (672–640) from Alba, 107

Julius, C.: (447) cos., **2**. 221; (435) ii, 327; (434) iii, 331

—, C.: (352) dict., **3**. 429

—, L.: (183) pr. for Gaul, **11**. 363

—, L.: (166) pr. **13**. 405

— Caesar, C., dict. 48–44: (61) subdues Lusitanians; forms IIIvirate; (59) cos., secures agrarian laws, **14**. 127; (58–50) procos., in Gaul, Germany, and Britain, 129–35, 165; (50–49) drives Pompey from Italy, 135–7, 205, 307; (49) campaigns in Spain, 137, 207, in Greece, 139; (48) cos. ii, defeats Pompey at Pharsalus, 139, 207–9; portents, 207–9, 307; pardons all who yield, 139, 207, 209; escapes plots in Alexandria; dictator, 141; (47) war against, renewed in Africa and Spain, 141–3; (46) cos. iii, 309; defeats Scipio and Juba at Thapsus, 143; excoriates Cato, 215; (46–45) conducts four triumphs; defeats sons of Pompey, 145, 213; establishes colony at Emporiae, **9**. 441; (45) gable ornament on house of, **14**. 215; (44) cos. v, 309; omens before and after death of, 215, 309–11; assassinated, 145–7, 217, 309; his will, 147, 309; judgment on, 217; had planned Macedonian war, 147; star dedicated to, 311; statue of, at Tralles, 307; (12) altar to, at confluence of Arar and Rhone, 165; (9) Drusus buried in tomb of, 169

INDEX

Julius Caesar, L.: (90) cos., **14**. 293; Samnites defeat; defeats Samnites, 91; (87) Marians kill, 101
— —, L.: (43) proscribed, **14**. 153
— —, Sex.: (208) pr. for Sicily, **7**. 299–303; sent to Capua, 329
— —, Sex., cos. 157: (181) tr. mil. of L. Aemilius Paulus, **12**. 85; (170) envoy to Abdera, **13**. 17
— —, Sex.: (47) leg. of Caesar, **14**. 143
— — Octavius (Augustus), C.: (44) adopted son and heir of Caesar, **14**. 147, 217, 309–11; (43) receives *imperium* from Senate, 149, 313; defeats M. Antonius before Mutina, 149–51, 309–13; cos. suf., 151, 315; forms IIIvirate with Antony and M. Aemilius Lepidus; their proscriptions, 151–3, 217, 315; (42) defeats M. Junius Brutus and C. Cassius Longinus at Philippi, 155, 317; (41) checks mutiny in Italy, 155–7; (40) defeats L. Antonius; makes terms with Antony, 157, 221–3; plot of Q. Salvidenus against, 157; (40, 38, 36) defeats Sex. Pompeius, 159–61; (35–32) defeats Iapydae, Dalmatians, Pannonians, 161–3; restores temple of Jupiter Feretrius; words of, heard by Livy, **2**. 323; (33–31) defeats Antony at Actium; takes Alexandria; triumphs, **14**. 163, 223; (31–30) Lepidus conspires against, 163; (29) closes temple of Janus, **1**. 67–9; (27) organizes state; takes name 'Augustus,' **14**. 163–5; (27–26, 19) reduces Spain, **8**. 53, **14**. 165; (18–17 ?) reads to Senate speech of Q. Caecilius Metellus on marriage, 65; (17) celebrates Saecular games, 223–5; (13) returns from Britain, 223; (9) pronounces eulogy of Drusus, 169; (c. 1) rebuilds city, 205; (A.D. 14) dies; Book CXXI of Livy published, 153. Prodigies accompanying career of, 309–19. *See* Octavia, Livia, Tiberius Nero, Drusus, Vipsanius Agrippa.
— — Strabo, C., aed. cur., 90: (87) killed by Marians, **14**. 101
— Iulus, C.: (489) cos., **1**. 347[1]
— —, C.: (482) cos., **1**. 361; (451) Xvir, **2**. 109–11; (449) envoy to plebeians on Aventine, 167
Julius Iulus, C.: (408) tr. mil. c. p., **2**. 439–41; (405) ii, 455; (392) cens. dies in office, **3**. 109, **4**. 297
— —, L.: (438) tr. mil. c. p., **2**. 313; (431) mag. eq., 343; (430) cos., 353–5
— —, L.: (403) tr. mil. c. p., **3**. 3
— —, L.: (401) tr. mil. c. p., **3**. 35; (397) ii, 57–9
— —, L.: (388) tr. mil. c. p., **3**. 209; (379) ii, 299
— —, Sex.: (424) tr. mil. c. p., **2**. 373
— —, Vop.: (473) cos., **1**. 401; calls Senate when riot follows levy, 405–7
— Mento, Cn.: (431) cos., **2**. 339; forced to name dict.; remains in city, 341–3; dedicates temple of Apollo, 353
— Proculus: (716) reports message fromRomulus, **1**. 59–61
— Vercondaridubnus, C.: (12) Haeduan priest of divus Julius, **14**. 165
July (Quinctilis): (391) magistrates take office on first of, **3**. 111; (329) **4**. 79; (389) business banned on 18th, anniversaries of Allia and of Cremera, **3**. 197–9; (304) parade of *equites* on 15th, **4**. 353; (208) Games of Apollo on 5th or 13th, **7**. 307, (190) on 11th, **10**. 301
June: (215) grain to be brought to towns before 1st, **6**. 113; (171) Latin festival on 1st, **12**. 395
Junii: (510) leaders against Tarquins, **4**. 229
Junius, C.: (423) tr. pl., **2**. 385–7
—, D.: (212) leg., commands at mouth of Volturnus, **6**. 425
—, L.: (167) Xvir on Macedonian terms, **13**. 299, 339, 345–7, 355
—, Q.: (439) tr. pl., **2**. 311
— Brutus, D.: (194) IIIvir for Sipontum, **9**. 533–5
— —, D.: (77) cos., **14**. 299
— —, L., cos. 509: (534–510) sent to Delphi, **1**. 195–7; (510) drops feigned stupidity; leads against Tarquins, 203–9, 219; (509) cos., 209; dictates oath to people; enrolls senators, 221; urges cos. Tarquinius Collatinus to resign, 223–5, **14**. 317; exiles all Tarquins, **1**. 225; punishes those plotting for Tarquins, including own sons, 229–35, **2**. 307, **4**. 133; killed fighting the

INDEX

Tarquins, **1**. 237–9, **14**. 317; funeral, **1**. 239–41, 271; successor to, 241–5

Junius Brutus, M., cos. 178 : (195) tr. pl., supports Oppian law, **9**. 413; yields, 439; (191) pr. urb. and pereg., **10**. 69, 159 ; prepares fleet, 161, 297; calls Senate for report on Thermopylae, 223; dedicates temple to Idaean Mother, 261–3; (189) Xvir for Asian terms, 461–3, **11**. 123–35, 153, 161, 205, 301; (178) cos., **12**. 179, **13**. 9, 271, **14**. 243, with Liguria as prov., **12**. 199; raises forces for Histria, 197–9; winters at Aquileia, 199; in Rome, questioned on Histria, 205; (177) defeats Histrians, 211–5; sent home by C. Claudius Pulcher, 217–9; (172) envoy to Asia, 427–9; (169) candidate for cens., **13**. 49

— —, M., pr. 88 : 82) kills self, **14**. 111

— —, M., tr. pl. 83 : (78–77) leg., slain by Pompey in cis-Alpine Gaul, **14**. 115

— —, M. : (44) pr., leader in plot against Caesar, **14**. 147; (43) condemned, 151; in Greece, 149–153; plunders allies, 315; Octavius' hostility for, 217; kills self at Philippi, 155, 317

— —, P., pr. 190 : (195) tr. pl., supports Oppian law, **9**. 413; yields, 439; (192) aed. cur., **10**. 123; (190) pr. for Etruria, 285, 295–7, (189) 439; sent to Farther Spain, 467

— —, Ti. and T. : (509) put to death by father for plotting return of Tarquins, **1**. 229–35, **2**. 307

— — Albinus, D., pr. 45 : (49) leg. of Caesar, **14**. 137; (46) 143; (44) leader of plot against Caesar, 147; occupies Mutina; (43) besieged, 149; siege raised; triumph granted, 151; (43) condemned; put to death, 151–3

— — Callaicus, D. : (138) cos. with Spain as prov.; tribb. pl. imprison, for refusing exemptions, **14**. 53, 55; gives land to soldiers of Viriathus, 53; (137–136) defeats Lusitanians, 55, 57, 69; (129) leg., defeats Iapydae, 69

— — Damasippus, L. : (82) pr. urb., **14**. 109

Junius Brutus Scaeva, D., cos. 325 : (339) mag. eq., **4**. 51; (325) cos., defeats Vestini, 111–5

— — —, D., cos. 292 : (293) leg., **4**. 525; (292) cos., 541; (264) gladiators at funeral games of, 553

— — —, D. : (264) shows first gladiators at funeral of father, **4**. 553

— Bubulcus Brutus, C. : (317) cos., **4**. 243; (313) ii, 271; captures Nola, Atina, and Calatia, 273; (312) mag. eq., 275; (311) cos. iii, ignores new Senate list, 277; defeats Samnites, 281–5; vows temple to Safety (*Salus*), 339–41, 363; (310) mag. eq. against Samnites, 315, 321; (307–306) cens., contracts for temple, 339–41; (302) dict., defeats Aequi and Sallentini; dedicates temple, 363

— — —, C. : (291) cos., **7**. 225

— Pennus, M., pr. 201 : (205) aed. pl., **8**. 249; (201) pr. urb., 517; appoints Xviri agr. divid., **9**. 13

— —, M., cos. 167 : (172) pr. for Nearer Spain, **12**. 317, 321, 343–5; (167) cos. with Pisae as prov., **13**. 295, 301, **14**. 245; excludes Rhodian envoys, **13**. 311; raids Ligurians, 403

— Pera, M., cos. 230 : (216) dict., levies army of youths, slaves, and convicts, **5**. 387–9, **6**. 43–5; admits envoys from survivors of Cannae, **5**. 391; leaves Rome, **6**. 43–5, 57; returns for auspices, 65; with army, 75, 85, 109; holds elections, 79–81

— Pullus, C. : (249) cos., **14**. 181

— Silanus, C. : (17) cos., **14**. 317

— —, M., pr. 212 : (216) pref., holds Naples, **6**. 47; (212) pr. for Etruria, 345, 347–9, 419; (211) **7**. 3–5; (210) goes to Spain with P. Scipio (Afr.), 75–7, 165, 187, **8**. 119; (209) **7**. 235; (208) 303; (207) defeats Hanno and Mago, **8**. 3–9; (206) brings auxiliaries to Castulo, 55; at Baecula, 61; attacks Punic camp, 69; gains Masinissa, 69–71; remains at New Carthage, 73; feigns attack on Lacetani, 107; sent to Tarraco, 141

— —, M. : (196) pref. soc., slain by Boi, **9**. 373

— —, M. : (109) cos.; Cimbri defeat, **14**. 77

INDEX

Junius Silanus Manlianus, D.: (141) pr., accused of robbing Macedonians, **14**. 49, 51
Juno: (302) beaks of Cleonymus' ships in temple of, at Patavium, **4**. 367
— Acraea: (198) cape near Sicyon sacred to, **9**. 227. *See* 477[1].
— Lacinia, temple of, near Croton: **6**. 183; (280) not violated by Pyrrhus, (205) or Hannibal, **12**. 301; (215) envoys of Philip and Hannibal at, **6**. 115–7; (205) Hannibal sets up inscription at, **8**. 199, (203) slays Italic troops at, 441; (173) roof tiles of, stolen by Q. Fulvius Flaccus; returned by order of Senate, **12**. 299–301, 373
— Lucina (Rome), temple of: (190) struck by lightning, **10**. 299, **14**. 239
— Matuta (Rome), temple of: (197) vowed by C. Cornelius Cethegus; (194) dedicated, **9**. 553
— Moneta (Rome), temple of: on Citadel, **3**. 267; (345) vowed by Camillus; (344) dedicated, 453; (444) linen rolls in, cited, **2**. 283; (437) 323; (434) 331; (196) prodigy in, **9**. 349. Temple to, on Alban mt.: (173) vowed by C. Cicereius, **12**. 311; (168) dedicated, **13**. 295
— Regina (Rome, the Capitoline): (460) associated with Jupiter Capitolinus and Minerva, **2**. 57; (385) **3**. 249; (217) **5**. 203; (197) **11**. 179; (390) geese of, save Capitol, **3**. 159; (389) Camillus dedicates bowls to, 207; (217) shares couch with Jupiter at *lectisternium*, **5**. 235; (195) invoked by Achaean praetor, **9**. 477. Temple of, in Flaminian circus: (187) vowed, **11**. 223; (179) dedicated, **12**. 161; (156) lightning near, **14**. 251
— — (Veii; Rome on the Aventine): (396) Camillus vows temple in Rome to, **3**. 73; Veii entered through temple of, 75; brought to Rome, 77–9; temple for, built on Aventine, 81; (392) dedicated, 109, 177; (218–217) statue dedicated to, **5**. 187; (217) special ceremonies for, 203; (207) **7**. 361; (200) **9**. 39; (207) cypress images dedicated to, **7**. 361; (99, 97) **14**. 281–5. Prodigies in temple of: (207) **7**. 359; (134) **14**. 259; (133) 261
Juno Sospita (Lanuvium): (338) temple and grove of, to be common to Lanuvium and Romans, **4**. 59; (218) offerings to, **5**. 187; (217) 203. Prodigies in temple of: (218–217) **5**. 185; (215) **6**. 109; (214) 207; (204) **8**. 259; (200) **9**. 39; (181) **12**. 61, **14**. 241; (99) 281
— — (Rome): (197) temple to, vowed by C. Cornelius Cethegus, **9**. 247; (194) dedicated (?) 553[1]; (90) cleansed by Caecilia Metella, **14**. 293
Jupiter: *for Jupiter as special divinity of Rome, see* Jupiter Optimus Maximus. *For Jupiter as translation of Zeus, see* Zeus.
Jupiter, flamen of: *see* flamen Dialis.
—, temples of: (174) at Fundi and at Pisaurum, contracted for, **12**. 281. Prodigies in temples of, in (213) Aricia, **6**. 317; (208) Caerê, **7**. 307; Cumae, 305; (199) Formiae, **9**. 157; (198) Lanuvium, 177; (207) Minturnae, **7**. 357; (191) **10**. 263; (97) Nursia, **14**. 283; (199) Ostia, **9**. 157; (206) Satricum, **8**. 47; Tarracina, **8**. 47; (179) **12**. 141; (210) Tusculum, **7**. 217
— Capitolinus: *see* Jupiter Optimus Maximus.
— Elicius (Rome): (715–672) Numa dedicates altar to, **1**. 73; (640) provoked by faulty ritual, strikes Tullus Hostilius with lightning, 113
— Feretrius (Rome): (672–640) *fetiales* pray to, **1**. 85; (640–616) 115–7; (340) witness to treaties, **4**. 25; (218) **5**. 135; (211) **7**. 31. Temple of: (753–717) *spolia opima* dedicated in, by Romulus, **1**. 41, (437) by A. Cornelius Cossus, **2**. 321–5, 363–5; (640–616) Ancus Marcius enlarges, **1**. 123; (32) Augustus rebuilds, **2**. 323
— Imperator (Praenestê): (380) statue of, brought to Capitol, **3**. 299
— Indiges: name of Aeneas after death, **1**. 15
— Latiaris, temple of, on Alban mt.: (217) C. Flaminius avoids usual sacrifice at, **5**. 191. Prodigies: 209) **7**. 249; (42) **14**. 315

INDEX

Jupiter Optimus Maximus (Rome)*: father of Hercules, **1**. 29; (753–747) answers Romulus' prayer, 45–7; (716) prayer to, 67; (495) golden crowns sent to, 289; (491) requires repetition of games, 337–9; (480) soldiers swear by, 373, 375; (449) honoured by name 'king,' **2**. 129; protects plebeian officers, 183–5; Latins and Hernici bring crown to, 193; protector of Rome, 205; (445) 261; (437) golden crown offered to, 321–3; (419) reveals slave conspiracy, 403; (390) rescued by M. Manlius, **3**. 253; Capitoline games in honour of, 169; shrine erected to, because of warning voice, 191 (*but cp.* 169); (385) M. Manlius made equal to, in name, 253; invoked by Manlius, 249, (384) 265, (340) by Latins, **4**. 15, against Latins, 19–21, in *devotio*, 37, (311) in battle, 283; (300) robes of, worn by triumphator, 385; (295) invoked, 451; (217) votive games and special ceremonies for, after Trasumenes, **5**. 203, 231–5; in *lectisternium*, 235; (216) oath by, 375; (213) banquet for, on account of Plebeian games, **6**. 347; (208) **7**. 357; (204) **8**. 359; (202) 515; (201) **9**. 15; (199) 173; (212) cited in verses of Marcius Vates, **6**. 385; (206) P. Scipio (Afr.) prays to, **8**. 117; (205) Saguntine envoys give gold crown to, 159; (200) games vowed to, **9**. 29; (193) **10**. 5; (191) 159; (189) **11**. 231, 281; (180) **12**. 125, 141, 143; (172) 349; 371–3; (199) P. Villius Tappulus vows temple to, **9**. 169; (195) invoked by Achaean praetor, 477; (192) two temples to, vowed by L. Furius Purpurio, are dedicated, 553, **10**. 123; (187) Africanus prays to, in memory of Zama, **11**. 179; (179) in *lectisternium*, **12**. 179, **14**. 243; (176) Q. Petilius Spurinus makes imperfect sacrifice to, at beginning of term, **12**. 227–9; (175) Antiochus Epiphanes builds temple to, in Antioch, 249; (174) inscription to, in temple of Mater Matuta, 283; (170) envoys of Alabanda bring gifts to, **13**. 23; (168) Masinissa refused permission to sacrifice to, 289–91. Temple of, on Capitoline: (616–578) Elder Tarquin vows, **1**. 139, 191; (534–510) Tarquin the Proud builds, 183–5, 191–3; (509) M. Horatius dedicates, 245, **3**. 367; (460) Ap. Herdonius occupies, **2**. 57–9, 67–9; (390) Romans seek protection in, **3**. 173; gold recovered from Gauls deposited in, 169; couch spread for Jupiter in, 175; (389) Camillus dedicates golden bowls at Juno's feet in, 207; (380) image of Jupiter Imperator of Praenestê brought to, 299; chapel of Minerva in, 299; (363) 365; tablet directing driving the nail affixed to, 365; (358) triumphator and troops approach, 401; (342) golden crown from Carthage deposited in, 495; (311) flute players forbidden to feast in, **4**. 279; (296) statue of Jupiter in chariot on roof of; silver vessels for, 445; (217) C. Flaminius avoids, **5**. 191; (216) statue of Victory set up in, 325; (211) P. Scipio (Afr.) frequently visits, **7**. 73; (200) he forbids statue of self in, **11**. 199; (196) M. Claudius Marcellus deposits gold necklace in, **9**. 375; (193) gilded shields on roof of, **10**. 29; (192) 123; (191) Philip permitted to make offerings in, 259; (179) M. Aemilius Lepidus cleans and restores, **12**. 157; defeat of Antiochus commemorated in, 163; (169) Pamphylian envoys offer gifts for, **13**. 133–5; (83) burned, **3**. 207; (70) restored, **14**. 121–3. Prodigies: (c. 277) **4**. 551; (186) **14**. 241; (166) 247; (156, 152) 251; (102) 279; (96) 285; (63) 303. *See also* Capitol.

Jupiter Stator (Rome), temple of: (753–717) vowed by Romulus, **1**. 45–7, **4**. 505; home of Elder Tarquin near, **1**. 145; (294) vowed by M. Atilius Regulus, **4**. 497, 505; (207) maidens learn hymn in, **7**. 359

*** Including general references to Jupiter as guardian of Rome and to Jupiter Capitolinus.**

INDEX

Jupiter Vicilinus (Compsa), temple of: (213) prodigy in, **6**. 317
— Victor (Rome): (295) Q. Fabius Maximus vows temple to, **4**. 473; (293) L. Papirius Cursor vows thimbleful of mead to, 523–5
—, a Punic god: (218) sends dream to Hannibal, **5**. 65
Jupiter gate, in Capua: (211) **7**. 55
juries: (106) divided between Senators and *equites*, **14**. 275; (92) controlled by *equites*, 87; (91) divided, 89; (70) transferred to *equites*, 121
Jus: (340) prayer to Fas and, **4**. 19
ius gentium: (509) protects envoys, **1**. 231; (438) **2**. 313; (340) **4**. 21; (203) **8**. 457; (189) **11**. 87; (389) Q. Fabius indicted for violating, **3**. 197
iustitium: (465) decreed, **2**. 11; (464) 17–9; (458) 93; (431) 343; (426) 361; (389) **3**. 199; (386) 217; (361) 383; (345) 453; (302) **4**. 369–71; (296) 437; (320) by common consent before decree, 187
Juventa(s): (534–510) shrine of, not to be moved, **1**. 211, **3**. 185; (218) *lectisternium* to, **5**. 187; (207) temple to, vowed, (191) and dedicated, **10**. 263
Juventius, T.: (197) tr. mil., lost in Liguria, **9**. 339
— Thalna (Talna), L.: (185) leg. in Spain, **11**. 315; (184) reports to Rome, 341
— —, M', cos. 163: (170) tr. pl., convicts C. Lucretius Gallus for conduct in Macedon, **13**. 31, 33; (167) pr. pereg., 297, 299; without consulting Senate, brings to assembly bill for war with Rhodes, 313–5; (163) cos., **14**. 249
— —, P., pr. 149; (148) propr., defeated in Thessaly by Andriscus, **14**. 35, 37
— —, T.: (194) pr. pereg., **9**. 527, 531; (172) leg. to buy grain, **12**. 369

Kalendae: day after, avoided for rites, **3**. 199
king, kingship: (716) people demand a, on death of Romulus, **1**. 63; (717) elected by assembly under interrex; approved by Senate, 63; (672) 75; (640) 113; (616) Elder Tarquin first to canvas for, 127–9; (578) Servius gains, without vote, 147; (534) Tarquin the Proud becomes, by force, 171–3; (510) expelled, 209, 219, 225, 267–9, **2**. 129, 269; (509) rights and insignia of, pass to coss., **1**. 221; (509) P. Valerius charged with seeking, 241–3; (403) Etruscans object to king at Veii, **3**. 3–5; (384) M. Manlius Capitolinus condemned for seeking, 263–7
king of sacrifices: *see* rex sacrorum.
kings, Atrium of the: (210) burned **7**. 103–5; rebuilt, 253
kite, as portent: (166) **14**. 247; (93 287–9
Knossos *see* Cnossos.

Labeatê, Lake, in Illyricum: (168) **13**. 191–3
Labeatis (Labeatae) Illyrian tribe: (169) under Gentius, **13**. 69; (168) envoy of Perseus meets Gentius among, 165; Scodra, strongest town of, 191; kin of Gentius arrested among, 195; (167) separated from rest of Illyricum, 337
Labeo: *see* Atinius, Fabius.
Labican way: (423) **2**. 389
Labici, in Latium: (488) Volsci under Coriolanus take, **1**. 345; (463) Aequi and Volsci cross, **2**. 25; (458) Aequi raid, 87; (419) join Aequi, 403–5; Q. Servilius Priscus defeats; (418) colony sent to, 409–11; (415) attacked by Bolani, 417, (397) by Aequi, **3**. 57, (383) by Praenestini, 271, (360) by Gauls, 389; (211) Hannibal passes, **7**. 35
Labienus, T.: (39) leads Parthians into Syria; slain, **14**. 157–9
Lacedaemon, Laconia, Sparta: ruled by two kings, **12**. 23; (490) Persians demand submission of, **10**. 53; (480) at Thermopylae, 205, 207, 211; (302) spoils of, in temple of Juno at Patavium, **4**. 367; (after 235) ruled by tyrants, **9**. 483–5, 499–501; they build first walls for, 517; (226) defeats Megalopolis, 223, **11**. 113; (222) Macedon defeats, at

Sellasia, **9**. 487; (212) allied with Aetolians, **6**. 431; (211) Aetolian treaty with Rome open to, **7**. 93; (208) Machanidas of, attacks Achaeans, 331; (207) **8**. 17, but withdraws, 31; (205–192) *see* Nabis, tyrant of Lacedaemon; (192) after assassination of Nabis, brought into Achaean league, **10**. 111, **11**. 337–9; war with, alienates Philopoemen and Flamininus, **10**. 135–7; (191) Achaeans debate return of exiles to, 257–9; (189) effort to recover coast cities from exiles, **11**. 101–3, 333–5, leads to intervention of Achaia and Rome, 103–11; submits to Achaean terms, 111–5; (184) complains of Achaean treatment, 323; relations with Achaia discussed before Roman commissioners, 329–41; (183) Senate directs, to remain in Achaean league, 371–3; (182) Senate receives envoys from, **12**. 7, (181) and from exiles, 65; (167) L. Aemilius Paulus visits, **13**. 343. Character of, **9**. 499, **10**. 205, **11**. 59, **13**. 323. *See also* Agesipolis, Armenes, Cleonymus, Damippus, Hybristas, Leonides, Machanidas, Nabis, Xanthippus.

Lacerius, C.: (401) co-opted tr. pl., **3**. 37

Lacetani, Spanish tribe: (218) Hannibal subdues, **5**. 67; Cn. Scipio defeats, 183; (206) revolt, **8**. 97–9, 107, 111, 139; (195) surrender to M. Porcius Cato, **9**. 467–9

Lacinium, Cape, in Bruttium: (208) Hannibal moves to, **7**. 315; (191) fleet purified at, **10**. 275

Laconia: *see* Lacedaemon.

Laconicus: (192) briefly king of Sparta after Nabis, **10**. 109–11

Lacumazes: (204) titular king of Maesulii, **8**. 321–3; Masinissa defeats, then makes terms with, 323–7

Lacus Romanus: (133) **14**. 261

Laeca: *see* Porcius.

Laeetani, Spanish tribe: (218) Cn. Scipio subdues, **5**. 179; (206) revolt, **8**. 97[2]

Laelius, C., cos. 190: (210) leg. of P. Scipio (Afr.) in Spain, **8**. 119; at capture of New Carthage, **7**. 165, 181–7; reports to Rome, 195, 229–31; (209) at Baecula, 281, 287–9; (206) confers with Syphax, **8**. 73–5; captures Iliturgi, 81–5; defeats Adherbal in Straits, 97, 123–7; commands cavalry in defeat of Ilergetes, 133–7; (205) raids Africa; meets Masinissa, 211, 219–25, 301; in Sicily, 225, 229; (204) commands fleet for Africa, 307, 337; (203) destroys Syphax' camp, 381–3; captures Syphax, 393, 401–7, 411, 415; brings him to Rome, 423, 427; in Senate for discussion of Punic peace, 427, 445–9; returns to Scipio, 455–7; (202) qu. of Scipio at Zama, 489, 493, 497; reports to Rome, 501; may command fleet, 523; (197) aed. pl., **9**. 345; (196) pr. for Sicily, 341–3, 347; (193) candidate for cos., **10**. 27–9; (190) cos., 285, 291, **14**. 239, with Italy as prov., **10**. 293, 295; enrolls colonists for Gaul, 429; (189) in Gaul, 439, **11**. 117; (174) envoy to Macedon, **12**. 257, (170) to trans-Alpine Gaul, **13**. 21

Laelius, D.: (77) leg. of Pompey in Spain, killed, **14**. 299

— Sapiens, C.: (140) cos., **14**. 51, 255

Laenas: *see* Popilius.

Laetorius, C.: (471) tr. pl., **1**. 409–11

—, C., pr. 210: (216) aed. cur., **6**. 103; (212) sent by Senate to coss., 425; (210) pr. for Gaul, **7**. 89, 233; (209) Xvir sac., 235; (205) leg. of P. Sempronius Tuditanus in Aetolia, **8**. 251, (200) of pr. L. Furius Purpurio in defeat of Gauls, **9**. 61; (194) IIIvir col. deduc., 535

— L.: (202) aed. pl., **8**. 515

—, M.: (495) a centurion, dedicates temple to Mercury, **1**. 305

Laevi, Ligurian tribe: **3**. 121; (196) raided by Boi, **9**. 377

Laevinus: *see* Valerius.

Lagum, in Asia Minor: (189) **11**. 47

Lamia, in Malis: **9**. 163; (209) Philip defeats Aetolians at, **7**. 331–3; (192) Antiochus at, **10**. 129, 143, musters troops at, 145, (191) 203; Philip attacks, 233–5, 303, **11**. 287, 305; Nicander brings money to, **10**. 243; (190) M' Acilius Glabrio takes, 303–5, **11**. 287

Lampsacus, on Hellespont: (196) resists Antiochus, **9**. 379–81; (193)

INDEX

he claims inherited rights in, **10**. 47–51, 391; (192) resists Antiochus, 123; (170) ally of Rome, **13**. 23–5

Lampsus, in Thessaly: (198) **9**. 193

Lampter, in Phocaea: (190) **10**. 383

Lanatus: *see* Menenius.

land laws and distributions: (486) proposed by cos., **1**. 353–5, (484) by tribb. pl., 357–9; (483) 359; (481) 361; (480) 363; (479) supported by K. Fabius, blocked by Senate, 381; (476) tribb. pl. propose, 395; (474) 401; (470) 423; (469) foreign danger checks agitation for, 427; (467) land distribution at Antium proposed by Q. Fabius Vibulanus and adopted, **2**. 3–5; (441) proposed, 297; (421) 397; (416) 411–7; (413) 425; (412) 427; (410) 429; (406) 447–9; (401) **3**. 43; (393) Veientine land distributed, 107–9; (388) distribution of Pomptine land proposed, 211; (386) 213; (385) typical means of stirring plebs, 233; (375) L. Sextius and C. Licinius Stolo propose limitations on public lands, 317; (369) 321–3; (367) their laws passed, 349, 353; (340) land distributed after victory over Latins, **4**. 47, 51; (298) aedd. prosecute holders of too much land, 407; (296) graziers condemned, 447; (293) 541; (196) **9**. 391; (193) **10**. 29; (201) public lands distributed, **9**. 11–3; (200) 143–5; (199) 155; (173) bounds between public and private lands disputed, **12**. 293–5, 313, 317; land distributed to citizens and Latins, 303; (172) leases required on public lands, 345; (133) land law of Ti. Sempronius Gracchus, **14**. 61–3; (123–122) of C. Sempronius Gracchus, 71; (100) of L. Apuleius Saturninus, 85; (99) of Sex. Titius, 281; (91) of M. Livius Drusus, 89; (59) of Caesar, 127

Lanuvium, in Latium: (458) exile at, **2**. 99; (431) Romans camp near, 345; (389) Volsci defeated near, **3**. 201; (383) revolts, 269; (339) aids Pedani against Rome, **4**. 51; (338) C. Maenius defeats, 53; granted citizenship, 59; (176) magistrate of, causes *vitium* in Latin festival, **12**. 233; (87) Marius storms, **14**. 101. Prodigies: (198) **9**. 177; (193) **10**. 25; (174) **12**. 255; (173) 297; (167) **13**. 297, **14**. 245; (166) 247; (147) 253. *See* Juno Sospita.

Laodicê, daughter of Seleucus IV: (172) wife of Perseus, **12**. 325[2]

—, sister of Demetrius: (149) Hammonius kills, **14**. 33

Laodicea, in Syria: (43) **14**. 153

Lapathus, in Thessaly: (169) **13**. 97, 109

Lapicini, Spanish tribe: (175) **12**. 243

Larcius, Sp., cos. 507: (508) holds bridge with Horatius, **1**. 251; fights Etruscans, 255; (507) cos., 267

—, T., cos. 501: *see* Largius, T.

—, T.: (498) cos., **1**. 285

— Flavus, Serg.: (490) cos. **1**. 347[1]

Larentia: foster mother of Romulus, **1**. 19

lares: (672–640) of Alba, abandoned, **1**. 105; (340) addressed in *devotio*, **4**. 37; (106) flame in temple of, **14**. 275

Lares of the Sea: (179) temple of, **12**. 161–3

Largius, T.: (501) cos., **1**. 275; dict., frightens Sabines, 275–7; (494) advises relief for debtors, 311–3

Larinum, in Apulia: (217) M. Minucius Rufus camps at, **5**. 281; (207) prepares for C. Claudius Nero, **7**. 383; (168) troops at, discharged, **13**. 255

Larisa, above Argos: (198) **9**. 231

—, in Thessaly: **9**. 137, **12**. 483; (207) Philip's army at, **8**. 17, 19; (200) complains of Philip, **9**. 91; (198) Flamininus near, 195; Philip occupies 257, (197) but is willing to surrender, to Aetolians, 261; Philip near, 289; he has records at, burned; Flamininus moves toward, 303; (191) negotiations between Antiochus and Thessalian council at, **10**. 181–3; Antiochus releases men of, taken at Scotusa, 185; Antiochus attacks, 185–9; Ap. Claudius Pulcher relieves, 187–9, 195; M' Acilius Glabrio meets council in, 197–201; (174) Perseus visits, **12**. 417; (172) Thessalian council, envoys of Rome, and of Perseus at, 405–7, 423; A. Atilius sent to hold, 437; (171) hostages received by,

INDEX

457; P. Licinius Crassus leads army, to, 461–3, 505; (169) A. Hostilius Mancinus at, **13**. 63; Sp. Lucretius sent from, 111

Larisa Cremastê, in Thessaly: (200) taken by L. Apustius, **9**. 137; (197) Philip gives, to Aetolians, 309; (171) Q. Marcius Philippus attacks, **12**. 465

Larisus riv., in Achaia: (209) **7**. 339

Lars Porsinna: *see* Porsinna.

Las, on Laconian coast: (189) **11**. 103–5

Latin colonies: *see* colonies, Latin.

— federation: *see* Latins.

— festival (Latin games): (397) held on Alban mt., **3**. 59–61; (217) **5**. 201; (212) **6**. 383; (199) **9**. 157; (179) **12**. 141; (176) 233; (174) 279; (168) **13**. 163; (42) **14**. 315; (223, 217) proclaimed by new coss. who remain in city until celebration of, **5**. 189–91, 201; (212) **6**. 383; (187) **11**. 153; (176) **12**. 235; (169) **13**. 53; (168) 145, 151, 157, 163; (199) meat from, distributed to Latin cities, **9**. 157; (190) **10**. 299; (397) proclaimed by improperly elected magistrates, **3**. 59; (340) treaty with Laurentes to be renewed annually after, **4**. 47; (217) cos. C. Flaminius avoids, **5**. 189–91, 201; (176) vitiated by failure of Latin magistrate, **12**. 233. Celebrated: (397) **3**. 59–61; (396) 65; (212) on Apr. 26th, **6**. 383; (199) **9**. 157; (190) **10**. 299; (187) **11**. 153; (179) **12**. 141; (176) on May 5th and Aug. 11th, 233–5; (172) 321; (171) on June 1st, 395; (169) **13**. 53; (168) as soon as possible, 145, 157, on March 31st, 163, or Apr. 12th, 151. Prodigy at: (42) **14**. 315

— language: works in, cited by Livy, (204) **8**. 315; (199) **9**. 169; (183) **11**. 379; (672–640) taught the Fidenates by colonists, **1**. 99; (211) men speaking, used by Hannibal, **7**. 25; (208) 325; (181) 'chests of Numa' contain writings in Greek and, **12**. 89–91; (180) Cumae permitted to use, officially, 135; (167) L. Aemilius Paulus gives peace terms in, **13**. 347; (c. 75) Q. Claudius Quadrigarius translates Acilius' annals into, **6**. 493

Latin name, *socii Latini nominis*: *see* Latins.

— way: (488) Coriolanus and Volsci follow, **1**. 345; (294) Samnites attack colonies on, **4**. 499; (217) Q. Fabius Maximus on, **5**. 239; (216) scouts sent along, 379–81; (211) Hannibal follows, **7**. 31–3

Latinius, T.: (491) dreams of defective games, **1**. 337

Latins (Latin Federation, Latin name, Latin allies, Latium): name given to Aborigines and Trojans, **1**. 13; under Aeneas, defeat Etruscans, 13–7; under woman's regency, 15; (753) large population of, 25; (672–640) Tullus Hostilius makes treaty with, 115, **4**. 19; (640–616) Ancus Marcius defeats, **1**. 115–21; many, become citizens, 121, **12**. 147; (616–578) Tarquin the Elder defeats, **1**. 129; (578–534) join Romans in building temple to Diana, 157–9; (534–510) Tarquin the Proud checks Turnus, and makes new treaty with, 173–83, **4**. 19; Sex. Tarquin ready to wander among, **1**. 185; (508) Aricia seeks aid of, 265; (501) 30 cities of, conspire, 275; (499) Praeneste leaves, 279; defeated at Lake Regillus, 279–87, **3**. 295; (495) closely united with Rome, 289; report Volscian advance, 295; (494) refused permission to arm, 315, **2**. 67; protected, **1**. 315; Sp. Cassius makes treaty with, 327–9, **3**. 395; (486) included in Cassius' proposed land distribution, **1**. 353; (475) auxiliaries before Veii, defeat Aequi and Volsci, 399; (467, 466) Aequi raid, **2**. 5; (464) relieve Roman camp, 15–21; (463) Volsci and Aequi defeat, 23–5; (460) aid against Ap. Herdonius, 61–5, 67; (459) serve against Volsci, 75–7; (449) congratulate Rome on harmony; warn of Volsci and Aequi, 193; Aequi and Volsci raid, 201; (446) 225; (431) serve against Aequi and Volsci, 339, 343, 351; (423) report Volscian preparations, 377; (410) Aequi and Volsci raid, 429; (409) 435; (396) serve against Veii, **3**. 67; (390) gather at Veii against

INDEX

Gauls, 155; (389) revolt, 199; (387) 213; (386) some of, aid Volscian attack, 213, 229; Q. Servilius Fidenas faces, 215–7; Camillus defeats Volsci and, at Satricum, 219–23, 471; fail to furnish soldiers, 229–31; (385) join Volsci, 231–5; some, captured with Volsci, 239; Rome postpones war with, 239–41; M. Manlius Capitolinus blames Senate for war with, 247; (385) Rome refuses to release prisoners, 255; (383) loyalty of, still questioned, 269; (380) danger from, belittled, 291, 295; (379) revolt with Praenestini, 301; (377) join Volsci; are defeated near Satricum, 305–7; quarrel with Antiates, 307–9; burn Satricum, 309, 449; besiege Tusculum; defeated, 309–11; (358) peace made on old terms, 395; (353) report Volscian attack, 421; (350) Gauls defeated in, 433–9; called enemies who may become friends, 437; (349) refuse aid to Rome, 441; (346–345) Rome fears attack by, 449–53; (343) attack Paeligni, 495, **4**. 15; (342) disregard treaty, **3**. 513; (341) with Campanians and Sidicini plunder Samnium, **4**. 7–9, 15; no longer under control, 9, 15; (340) leaders of, called to Rome, 11; L. Annius Setinus, praetor of, asserts rights of, 13–17; demand share in Senate and in offices, 15, 17, **6**. 19, 75; Senate votes war on, **4**. 19–21, 237; P. Decius Mus and T. Manlius Imperiosus defeat, 21–45, 469; similarities with Romans, 23, 29–35; Manlius defeats, near Trifanum, 45–7; territory of, distributed, 47, 51; (339) Q. Publilius Philo defeats, in Fenectane plains, 49–51; (338) L. Furius Camillus and C. Maenius reduce towns of, 53–5; Senate discusses fate of, 55–7; different cities given different terms, 57–61; (319) a part of the Federation, 237; (307) prisoners parcelled out to, 333; (217) Hannibal releases captured, **5**. 223, (216) 365; remain loyal, **6**. 41; admission of, to citizenship and to Senate considered, 75; (212) vote in tribe picked by lot, 351; (211) possible complicity in Capuan revolt, **7**. 57; prisoners from Capua distributed among, 63; (210) no Campanian to be reckoned as a, 131; (209) begin to complain, 241; (206) war removed from, **8**. 47–9; (200) named with Romans in prayer, **9**. 15, 25; (198) guard Punic prisoners and hostages, 237; (195) not subject to Oppian law, 437; enrolled in Roman colonies without citizenship, 529; (193) method of levying troops from, 559–61; law of usury extended to, **10**. 19; (187) share certain exemptions with Romans, **11**. 151; migrants from, to Rome forced to return, 225; (180) suffer from Illyrian pirates, **12**. 133; share in bonus, 137; (179) burdened by games of Ti. Sempronius Gracchus, 141; (177) those illegally claiming citizenship, sent to own cities, 207–15, 319; receive smaller donatives, 225, (173) and land allotments, 303; (177) sent back to Histria after triumph, 227; (171) Latin rights given to colony in Spain, **13**. 13; (167) and citizens share equally in donatives, 403; (91) flocks and herds of, turn on masters, **14**. 291; (90) disaster everywhere in, 293; (295) serve in Roman armies, **4**. 461, (294) 487, (225) 561, (218) **5**. 163, (217) 223, (216) 323, 325, 387, **6**. 57, (211) **7**. 65, (209) 241, (206) **8**. 63, 131, (205) 221, (204) 283, (201) 521, (200) **9**. 25–7, 31, 61, (198) 173–5, (197) 241, (196) 347, 375, (195) 393, 459, (193) 559–61, (192) **10**. 57–9, 121, 123, (191) 161, 165, (190) 295–7, 403, (189) 439, (188) **11**. 117, (186) 275–7, (184) 343, (182) **12**. 3–5, (181) 59, 63, 83, 89, 101, (180) 113, 127, 137, (179) 139, (178) 197, (177) 211, (176) 229–33, (174) 251, (173) 293, (172) 367–9, (171) 395, (170) **13**. 33, (169) 43, (168) 157, 229, 285, (91) **14**. 89

Latins Ancient (*Prisci Latini*): colonies planted by Latinus Silvius, **1**. 17; (640–616) Ancus Marcius defeats, and gives citizenship to, 115–21, **12**. 147; (616–578) Elder Tarquin subdues, **1**. 137

INDEX

Latinus, king of Aborigines: makes peace with Aeneas, **1**. 9–11; killed, 13
— Silvius, 4th king of Alba, **1**. 17
Latona: (399) honoured at *lectisternium*, **3**. 49, (212) at festival of Apollo, **6**. 387
Laudiceni: (197) in Rhodian army, **9**. 325
laurel: (394) letter wreathed with, announces victory, **3**. 101; (168) **13**. 251; (167) men in triumph crowned with, 385
Laurentum, in Latium: Aeneas comes to, **1**. 9–11; (753–717) envoys of, maltreated by T. Tatius; peace preserved, 51; (349) Greek pirates raid, **3**. 441; (340) treaty with, to be renewed annually, **4**. 47; (190) meat due, at Latin festival not given, **10**. 299. Prodigy: (137) **14**. 257
Lautulae, pass in Latium: (342) mutineers near, **3**. 501, 511; (315) Samnites defeated at, **4**. 251–3, 259; (217) M. Minucius Rufus secures, **5**. 253[1]
Lautumiae (Quarries), prison in Rome: (210) fire near, **7**. 103; (198) special guards for, **9**. 237; (190) 43 Aetolian chiefs thrown into, **10**. 299; (184) markets near, **11**. 361
Lavinia, daughter of Latinus: betrothed to Turnus, married to Aeneas, **1**. 11; regent for Ascanius, 15
Lavinium, in Latium: Aeneas founds, **1**. 11, 79; named for Lavinia, 11; flourishes, 15, 25; Alba planted from, 79; (753–717) T. Tatius killed at; Romulus renews treaty with, 51; (509) L. Tarquinius Collatinus retires to, 225; (488) Coriolanus and Volsci recover, 345; (390) Romans still perform rites in, **3**. 177; (340) too late in aiding Latins, **4**. 45; (211) prepares supplies for Q. Fulvius Flaccus, **7**. 31. Prodigy: (137) **14**. 257.
law: (753) given by Romulus, **1**. 31; (318–317) codes drawn up for Capua and Antium, **4**. 243; (304) *formulae* of civil, published, 349–51. *See* Twelve Tables of the Law.
Lebadea, in Boeotia: 167) temple of Zeus Trophonius at, **13**. 341, (95) **14**. 285
Lechaeum, port of Corinth: (198) **9**. 225–7
lectisternium: (399) celebrated at Rome, **3**. 47–9; (364) 361; (348) 449; (326) **4**. 99; (218) **5**. 187; at Caerê, 187; (217) at Rome, 203–5; 231, 235; (179) **12**. 179; (191) customarily celebrated for greater part of year, **10**. 155. Prodigy at, (179) **12**. 179.
Lecton, cape in Asia Minor: (190) **10**. 397
legion: (340) formation of, **4**. 31–5; (203) **8**. 391; (202) 489; (197) **9**. 279; (190) **10**. 403–5; (381) size of, and/or total number of, **3**. 273; (349) 441; (340) **4**. 33; (319) 237; (270) **8**. 115; (218) **5**. 47–9; (216) 319–21; (214) **6**. 209; (211) **7**. 3–5; (210) 109–11; (208) 305; (207) 357; (204) **8**. 305; (203) 371; (202) 463; (201) 523; (200) **9**. 27; (194) 531; (193) **10**. 7; (190) 403; (184) **11**. 343; (182) **12**. 3; (181) 59; 113–5; (180) 113–5; (177) 211; (174) 251–3; (171) 381; 453; (169) **13**. 43–5; (168) 157–9; (167) 297
Legion, First: (296) **4**. 423, (295) 463, (217) **5**. 293, (216) 373, (214) **6**. 291, (212) 423, (210) **7**. 209, (207) 377, (191) **10**. 165, (181) **12**. 83, (180) 127, (178) 199, (171) 385, 395. Second: (296) **4**. 423, (295) 453–5, 465, (217) **5**. 293, (216) 373, (196) **9**. 373, (195) 455–7, (194) 539, (193) **10**. 13–5, (186) **11**. 277, (180) **12**. 127, 129, (178) 187–93, (172) 369, (171) 385, (168) **13**. 215, 227, 229, (167) 369–71. Third: (296) **4**. 423, (295) 463, (217) **5**. 293, (216) 373, 387, (212) **6**. 393–5, (210) **7**. 209, (207) 375, (191) **10**. 165, (181) **12**. 83, (180) 127, (178) 187–95, (176) 237, (171) 385. Fourth: (296) **4**. 423, (295) 465, (217) **5**. 293, (197) **9**. 339, (194) 539, (180) **12**. 127, (178) 197, (171) 385, (44) **14**. 149. Fifth: (295) **4**. 463, (210) **7**. 205, (204) **8**. 305, (185) **11**. 313, 317, (181) **12**. 99. Sixth: (295) **4**. 463, (211) **7**. 19, (210) 205, (204) **8**. 305. Seventh: (181) **12**. 99. Eighth: (185) **11**. 313. Eleventh: (203) **8**.

435. Twelfth and Thirteenth: (205) **8**. 215, (203) 433–5. Eighteenth: (209) **7**. 257, 263. Nineteenth and Twentieth: (207) **7**. 365. Martian: (44) **14**. 149. Naval: (216) **5**. 387. Urban: (216) **6**. 43, 87, (215) 105, (213) 317, 347–9, (212) 349, 355, (210) **7**. 109–11, (209) 237, (208) 309, 353, (207) 383, (205) **8**. 199, (203) 371, (200) **9**. 27, (196) 373, (194) 531, (193) 559, **10**. 7, (191) 157, (190) 295, (171) **12**. 395

Legion of Cannae: *see* Cannae, legions of.

legislation, process of: *see comitia centuriata*, *comitia tributa*, *concilium plebis*, *populus*; *auctoritas patrum*, *plebiscitum*, *senatus consultum*.

Lemnus: (207) **8**. 17–9

Lentulus: *see* Cornelius.

—: (73) gladiatorial school of, **14**. 117

Leon, of Athens: (192) pro-Roman, **10**. 145; (189) envoy to Rome, **11**. 33

Leon, in Sicily: (214) **6**. 301

Leonides: (171) officer of Perseus, **12**. 449

Leonnatus: (171) officer of Perseus, **12**. 447; 475

Leontini, in Sicily: (215) Hieronymus killed at, **6**. 195, 241; (214) his treasure taken from, 249; soldiers may be called from, 247; Hippocrates involves, in war with Rome, 267–9; Marcellus takes, 271, 275–83, **7**. 115, and garrisons, **6**. 301

leopards: (169) in games, **13**. 149

Lepidus: *see* Aemilius, Claudius.

Leptis, in Africa: (203) Hannibal lands at, **8**. 457; (193) Masinissa endangers, **9**. 575

Lesbos: (167) **13**. 357

Letum, Mt., in Liguria: (180) Ligurians defeated on, **12**. 127; (176) 239–41

Leucadia (Leucata): a peninsula of Acarnania, now an island, **9**. 321–3, **10**. 205; (211) rounded by M. Valerius Laevinus, **7**. 99, (169) by C. Marcius Figulus, **13**. 91

Leucas, on Leucadia: (197) Acarnanian council at, **9**. 319–21; L. Quinctius Flamininus takes, 321–3; (196) Aetolians demand restoration of, 369; (195) 407; Flamininus leaves, 483; (191) loyal to Rome, **10**. 191; Roman fleet strengthens, 195; (167) removed from Acarnanian league, **13**. 357

Leuci, in Peloponnese: (192) **10**. 75

Leusus, of Crete: (189) joins Cn. Manlius Volso, **11**. 41

levy: (481) hindered by tribb. pl. **1**. 361; (480) 363; (445) **2**. 257–9, 273, 277; (410) 429; (409) 435–7; (380) **3**. 293; (378) 303; (418) from ten tribes chosen by lot, **2**. 405; (345) without exemptions, **3**. 453; (329) **4**. 79; (151) **14**. 19; (296) of every sort of men, **4**. 437; (275) goods of men refusing, are sold, 551; (217) urban, **5**. 239; (212) by two commissions, **6**. 355–7; age for, reduced, 357; (186) exemption from, as reward, **11**. 273–5; (178) *extra ordinem*, as usual in crisis, **12**. 197; (169) by prr. when coss. fail, **13**. 49. *See lex sacrata.*

lex sacrata: (431) levy under, by Aequi and Volsci, **2**. 339, (310) by Etruscans, **4**. 317, by Samnites, 321, (293) 505, (191) by Ligurians, **10**. 265

Liber, Libera: *see under* Ceres.

Liberty, Hall of: *see* Atrium Libertatis.

—, temple of: (238) Ti. Sempronius Gracchus builds; (214) painting placed in, **6**. 227

Libethrum, in Macedon: (169) **13**. 107

Libitina: (181) overwhelmed by plague, **12**. 61, **14**. 241; (175) 245; (174) **12**. 253. Prodigy in grove of: (166) **14**. 247

Libo: *see* Poetelius, Scribonius.

Libui, Gallic tribe: enter Italy, **3**. 121; (196) Boi raid, **9**. 377

Liburnia, on Adriatic: (302) **4**. 363

Libyphoenicia: (218) **5**. 63. *See* Muttines.

Licabrum, in Spain: (192) **10**. 63–5

Licinia: (151) murders husband, **14**. 17–9

—: (114) Vestal, condemned for unchastity, **14**. 75

Licinian laws: (375) on debt, land and consulship, proposed by tribb. pl. C. Licinius Stolo and L. Sextius Lateranus, **3**. 317; (376–367) controversy over, 317–49; (367) passed,

INDEX

349–51. *Also*: 411, 427, 433, 439, 455, **4**. 381, **9**. 423.

Licinius, C.: (493) one of first tribb. pl., **1**. 325

—, M.: (209) tr. mil. of Marcellus, killed, **7**. 259

—, M.: (149) envoy to Attalus, **14**. 35, 31–3

—, Sex.: (138) tr. pl., imprisons coss., **14**. 55

—, Sex.: (87) tr. pl., cast from Tarpeian rock by Marius, **14**. 101–3

—, Sp.: (481) tr. pl., supports land law, **1**. 361–3

— Calvus, C., cos. 361: (368) first plebeian mag. eq., **3**. 333 (*but cp.* **4**. 387); (361) cos., takes Ferentinum, **3**. 381–3; names dict. com. c., 383

— —, P.: (400) first plebeian tr. mil. c. p., **3**. 45–7, 325; (396) declines 2nd term in favour of son, 63; in Senate, urges free sharing of booty of Veii, 69, 71, 77

— —, P.: (396) tr. mil. c. p., **3**. 63, 69, 77

— Crassus, C., cos. 168: (172) pr. urb., **12**. 317, 321; investigates M. Popilius Laenas, 351–5; restores Ligurian freedom, 353; directs naval levy, 367; calls troops from Liguria, 369; (171) leg. of brother, P., 471; (168) cos. with Italy as prov., **13**. 145–9, 159, 283; provides men and supplies for Macedon, 151, 157–9, 255; receives news of Pydna; discharges troops, 251–5; (167) in Gaul, 283, 299–301; Xvir on Macedonian peace, 299, 339, 345–7, 355

— —, L.: (95) cos., **14**. 285

— —, M.: (179) blocks aqueduct, **12**. 159

— —, M., cos. 30: (29–28) campaigns in Thrace, **14**. 165

— —, P., cos. 171: (176) pr. for Spain, **12**. 227, 231, but excused for religious reasons, 231, 385; (171) cos., 371, 373, 379–81, with Macedon as prov., 385, 395; conducts levy, hears disputes about rank, 385–95; orders Perseus' envoys to withdraw, 397–9; in Macedon, 439–43, 453, 461–3; Perseus defeats, at Callinicus, 467–79, 483; rejects Perseus' terms, 485–7; various operations, 491–505; cruelty and greed of, **13**. 15, 21–3, 85; demands Cretan archers, 27; (167) envoy to Galatians, 367

Licinius Crassus, P.: (97) cos., **14**. 283; (87) kills self; Fimbria kills son of, 101

— — Dives, M., cos. 70, 55: (72–71) propr., defeats Spartacus, **14**. 119, 199; (70) cos., restores power of tribb. pl., 121; (60) joins IIIvirate, 127; (55) cos., with Syria as prov., 131; (54–53) defeated and killed by Parthians, 133, 135, 305; (20) standards of, returned, 167; 'ill-starred house of,' 211

— — —, P., cos. 205: (212–183) pont. max., **6**. 355, **11**. 365, **14**. 7; (210) mag. eq. com. c., **7**. 223; cens., 227; restores M. Livius Salinator to Senate, 347; resigns on colleague's death, 227–9; (209) as pont. max. forces C. Valerius Flaccus to become flamen Dialis, 235; (208) pr. pereg., 299–301; (206) as pont. max. punishes Vestal, **8**. 47; (205) cos., 153, **10**. 261, with Bruttium as prov., **8**. 153–5, 169, 191, 195, 243, 249; as pont. max. cannot leave Italy, 155, 187; names dict. com. c., 243–5, 249; (204) in Bruttium, 255; defeats Hannibal near Croton, 349; reputation of, 367–9; (200) as pont. max. disallows vow for indefinite sum, **9**. 29, (194) requires repetition of 'sacred spring,' 531, (191) dictates vow for games, **10**. 159, (189) prevents Q. Fabius Pictor, pr. and flamen, from leaving Italy, 439–41; (183) dies; funeral with gladiators, **11**. 365

— — — Mucianus, P.: (131) cos. and pont. max., leaves Italy; defeated and killed by Aristonicus, **14**. 65, 263

— Lucullus, C.: (196) tr. pl., IIIvir epulonis, **9**. 389; (191) IIvir for temple of Juventas, **10**. 263

— —, L.: (202) aed. cur., **8**. 515

— —, L.: (151) cos.; tribb. pl. imprison, for strict levy; defeats Spanish tribes, **14**. 19

— —, L.: (74) cos., defeats Mithridates, **14**. 117; (73) 119; (72) 121;

(69) 123, 199; (70) makes Machares of Bithynia a 'friend,' 121; (68) troops of, mutiny, 123

Licinius Lucullus, M.: (186), pr. pereg., **11**. 235, 241, 269

— Macer, C., the historian: (444) cited, **2**. 283; (437) 323; (434) 331; (361) **3**. 383; (310) **4**. 315; (304) 351; (299) 391

— Murena, L.: (82) propr., renews war with Mithridates, **14**. 109

— Nerva, A., pr. 166: (178) tr. pl., attacks A. Manlius Volso, **12**. 199–201, 205; (171) envoy to Crete, 397; (169–168) IIIvir on Macedon, **13**. 149, 153–5; (166) pr., 405

— —, C.: (168) reports victory of L. Anicius Gallus, **13**. 255; (167) leg. of Gallus in Illyricum, 335; returns hostages to Thrace, 401

— —, C.: (167) pr. for Farther Spain, **13**. 297

— Pollio, L.: (208) sent by Senate to T. Quinctius Crispinus, **7**. 329

— Stolo, C., cos. 365: (376) tr. pl., **3**. 313–7; proposes popular laws; prevents elections, 317–9; (375–370) tr. pl. ii-vii, 319; (369) viii, 321–3; (368) ix, 327; defies other tribb. pl. and dict., 327–31; candidate for re-election, 333–5; attacked by Ap. Claudius Crassus, 337–47; first plebeian mag. eq., **4**. 387 (*but cp*. **3**. 333); (367) tr. pl. x; his laws passed, **3**. 347, 349, 353, 417; (364) cos., 359; (357) condemned for violating own land law, 411. *See* Licinian law.

— Strabo, M.: (178) tr. mil., killed by Histrians, **12**. 189–91

— Tegula, P.: (200) composes hymn to Juno Regina, **9**. 39

— Varus, C., cos. 236: (219-218) envoy to declare war on Carthage, **5**. 49; returns via Spain and Gaul, 55–9, 63

— —, P., pr. 208: (210) aed. cur., **7**. 229; (208) pr. urb., 299, 301; commands home fleet, 305; proposes annual games to Apollo, 307; escorts flamen C. Valerius from Senate, 237; brings news of Metaurus, 409

Licinus: *see* Clodius, Porcius.

lictors: (753) of Etruscan origin; 12 used by Romulus, **1**. 31–3; (672–640) inflict punishment, 93; (509) 233; (473) of plebeian birth, 405; 12 for each cos., 405; (213) **6**. 317; (450, 449) each Xvir has 12, **2**. 119, 173; (377) accompany tr. mil. c. p., **3**. 313; (340) inflict military punishment, **4**. 29; (321) disgraced cos. deprived of, 181; (295) accompany cos. in field, 453, 469; (213) **6**. 317; (208) **7**. 321; (217) cos. appears before dict. without, **5**. 237; (200) attend provincial governors, **9**. 85; wear military cloaks in field, 43; (177) **12**. 217, 219; (167) **13**. 387. *See* fasces.

Ligur (Ligus): *see* Aelius.

Liguria (Ligustini): (238) first campaign against, **4**. 559; (218) slave from, saves P. Scipio, **5**. 137; in Punic army, 63, 111, (217) 173, (207) **7**. 365, 399–405, (206) **8**. 145, (202) 489–91, (200) **9**. 33; (217) Hannibal retires to, **5**. 177–9; envoys to, protest aid to Hannibal, 311; (205) Mago, son of Hamilcar, allies self with, **8**. 197–9, and is promised troops, 225–7; (203) allotted to C. Servilius Geminus, 367–9; (200) sack Placentia, **9**. 31; (197) Q. Minucius Rufus defeats, 243–5, 339, and triumphs on Alban mt., 341; (196) M. Marcellus triumphs over, 377–9; (195) allotted to P. Porcius Laeca, 393; (194) Africanus in (?), 541; (193) rises; allotted to Q. Minucius Thermus, 557–9, **10**. 7–9, 15; L. Cornelius Merula crosses, 9; Thermus almost cut off in, 29–33; (192) defeated by Thermus, 57–9, 61–3, by L. Quinctius Flamininus, 61, 63, 119; (191) Hannibal urges Antiochus to rouse, 179; Thermus repells, 265–9, (190) 295, but is denied triumph, 427; (189) kill L. Baebius Dives en route to Spain, 467; (188) allotted to M. Valerius Messala, **11**. 117, 143; (187) defeated by M. Aemilius Lepidus and C. Flaminius, 145–7, 161, 219–23, **12**. 161; (186) defeat Q. Marcius Philippus, **11**. 275–9; (185) Ap. Claudius Pulcher and M. Sempronius Tuditanus defeat, 317–9, **14**. 7; (184) assigned to P.

INDEX

Claudius Pulcher and L. Porcius Licinus, **11**. 341, **12**. 103, (183) to M. Marcellus and Q. Fabius Labeo, **11**. 363, 397, (182) to L. Aemilius Paulus and Cn. Baebius Tamphilus, **12**. 3–5, 53, 57, and Labeo, 5; some seek to surrender to Marcellus, 53; (181) assigned to P. Cornelius Lentulus and M. Baebius Tamphilus, 59, 107; Paulus defeats, 77–89, **14**. 243, and triumphs, **12**. 105; pirates on coast of, defeated, 59, 87; seek peace, 105; (180) assigned to A. Postumius Albinus and C. Calpurnius Piso, 109, 115; surrender to Lentulus and Tamphilus, 113–21, who triumph, 121; Albinus and Piso defeat, 127–9; (179) assigned to L. Manlius Acidinus and Q. Fulvius Flaccus, 139; Flaccus defeats, 163, and triumphs, 177–9; (178) M. Junius Brutus leaves, 199; (177) C. Claudius Pulcher defeats, 221–3, 237, and triumphs, 225; Luna founded in, 225; revolt, seize Mutina, 225–7, 235; (176) allotted to Q. Petilius Spurinus, 227–9; defeated by Pulcher, 235–9, by Spurinus and C. Valerius Laevinus, 239–43, **14**. 245, (175) by M. Aemilius Lepidus and P. Mucius Scaevola, **12**. 243–5; (173) assigned to L. Postumius Albinus and M. Popilius Laenas, 293; Laenas attacks, and sells those who have surrendered, defying the Senate, 311–7, 371; land in, distributed, 303; (172) disputes *re*, continue in Senate, 319–21; assigned to C. Popilius Laenas and P. Aelius Ligur, 321, 363–5; some, restored to freedom, 353; Laenas reports on, 371; (171) in Roman army, 395; (170) A. Atilius Serranus inactive in, **13**. 33; (167) Q. Aelius Paetus and M. Junius Pennus ravage, 403; (166) C. Sulpicius Gallus defeats, **14**. 11, 247; (166–160) varying success in, 11; (154) plunder Massilia; Q. Opimius defeats, 15; (125–123) M. Fulvius Flaccus defeats trans-Alpine, 69. *See also*: Apuani, Friniates, Ilvates, Ingauni, Laevi, Sallyes, Statellates.

Ligurian mts.: (218) sailed past by cos. P. Scipio, **5**. 75; (195) by cos. M. Porcius Cato, **9**. 441

Ligurian shield: (168) used by Roman *velites*, **13**. 209; (134) in temple of Juno Regina, **14**. 259

Ligurians, Alpine: (205) **8**. 173, 197

Ligurius, Cn.: (197) tr. mil., slain, **9**. 339

Ligus (Ligur): *see* Aelius.

Ligustini: *see* Ligurians.

Ligustinus, Sp.: (171) veteran centurion, his career, **12**. 389–95

Ligynae, in Thessaly: (198) **9**. 193

Lilybaeum, in Sicily: (218) saved from Punic danger, **5**. 145–51; (217) Roman fleet at, 305; (216) Punic fleet threatens, 383; P. Furius Philus comes to, **6**. 71; (215) Roman fleet at, 141; (212) 463; (210) **7**. 219; (208) 331; (207) **8**. 15; (204) P. Scipio (Afr.) gathers forces in, 303–13, (201) returns to, 537; (200) subject to Rome, **9**. 85; (82) Pompey cuts off M. Junius Brutus from, **14**. 111

Limnaeum, in Thessaly: (191) **10**. 197–9

Limnê (*ad Limnen*), city in Pisidia: (189) **11**. 47

linen: (205) from Tarquinii for sails, **8**. 193

— books, of temple of Moneta: (444) cited from Licinius Macer, **2**. 283; (437) 323; (434) 331

Linen Legion, of Samnites: (293) **4**. 509, 521

Lingones, Gallic tribe: enter Italy, **3**. 121

lions: (186) in votive games, **11**. 281

Liparae is.: (394) envoys to Delphi taken to, by pirates, **3**. 97; (218) ships from Carthage fail to reach, **5**. 145; (126) volcanic action near, **14**. 265

Liris riv.: (296) Minturnae planted at mouth of, **4**. 439; (211) broken bridge over, delays Hannibal, **7**. 33; (210) Campanians settled west of, 131

Lissus, in Illyricum: (169) Gentius at, **13**. 73; (168) 187–9

Litana, forest in Gaul: (216) L. Postumius Albinus ambushed in, **6**. 81–3; (195) L. Valerius Flaccus defeats Boi in, **9**. 471, 527

Liternum, in Campania: (217) Hanni-

bal near, **5**. 255; (215) Ti. Sempronius Gracchus drills army near, **6**. 123; (194) Roman colony at, **9**. 533; (187) Africanus retires to, **11**. 181, (183) dies and is buried at, 185–7, 195–7, **13**. 381
Liternus riv.: (197) **9**. 243
Litubium, in Liguria: (197) **9**. 245
lituus: augur's rod, **1**. 67
Livia, wife of Augustus: (17) **14**. 317
Livianus: *see* Aemilius Lepidus.
Livius, L.: (321) sponsor of Caudine peace; (320) tr. pl., opposes surrender of sponsors, **4**. 193; resigns, is led to Caudium, 199
—, T., the historian: prefaces of, **1**. 3–9; **3**. 195; **5**. 3; **9**. 3–5; his purpose, **1**. 5–7
— Andronicus, L.: (240) composes plays, **3**. 363; (207) and hymn to Juno Regina, **7**. 359, 361, **9**. 39
— Denter, M.: (302) cos., **4**. 363; (299) one of first plebeian pontiffs, 389; (295) dictates ritual of *devotio*, 467–9; propr., 469
— Drusus, C.: (147) cos., **14**. 39, 253
— —, M.: (112) cos., defeats Scordisci, **14**. 75–7
— —, M.: (91) tr. pl., stirs plebs and Italians; death of, **14**. 87–9, 291
— Macatus, M.: (214) pref. of Tarentum, **6**. 239; (210) **7**. 145, 151, (209) 311; (208) Senate considers reward or punishment of, 311–3, 347
— Salinator, C., cos. 188: (211–170) pont., **7**. 91, **13**. 41–3; (204) aed. cur., **8**. 359; (202) pr. for Bruttium, 461, 463, 521; (198) leg., gives up command of fleet, **9**. 197; (193) leg. against Boi, **10**. 13; candidate for consul, 27; (191) pr. for fleet, 69, 159–63, 273–7, **13**. 317–9; defeats fleet of Antiochus, **10**. 281–3, 385; winters at Canae, 285, 315; (190) with fleet in Aegean, 315–7, 325–33; wins battle near Phoenicus, 335–9; goes to Italy, 339; envoy to Bithynia, 365; (188) cos., **11**. 115, **14**. 239, with Gaul as prov., **11**. 117, 147; (170) dies, **13**. 41
— —, M. cos. 219, 207: (218) envoy to Carthage to declare war, **5**. 49; returns via Spain and Gaul, 55–9, 63; convicted for acts as cos., 317, **7**. 347, **8**. 355; marries daughter of Pacuvius Calavius of Capua, **6**. 7; (210) restored to city and Senate, **7**. 347; (208) defends M. Livius Macatus, 347; elected cos.; reconciled with colleague, C. Claudius Nero, 349–53; (207) cos., 357, **9**. 39, with Gaul as prov., **7**. 353; conducts strict levy, 361–5; goes to prov., 369, 371; with Nero; defeats Hasdrubal, 389–405, 411, **8**. 175; triumphs, 37–41; vows temple to Juventas, **10**. 263; dict. com. c., **8**. 43; investigates Etruscans and Umbrians, 43; (206–204) in Etruria, 45, 199, 227, 255–7; (204) cens. with Nero; their quarrels, 351–7, **11**. 225; fixes price of salt, **8**. 351–3; contracts for temples of Idaean Mother and of Juventas, **10**. 261–3; (203) in Senate, **8**. 447–9
loan, to state: (210) **7**. 135–9; (200) partly repaid in land, **9**. 41; (196) payment completed, 389
Locri, in Bruttium: ancient war with Croton, **8**. 279; (275) Pyrrhus plunders, 275; (216) deserts Rome, **5**. 409, **6**. 101, 143; (215) makes peace with Hannibal, 175–9; Crotonians moved to, 185; (214) possible refuge for Hippocrates and Epicydes, 251, 269; (208) siege of, given up by T. Quinctius Crispinus, **7**. 313–5, by L. Cincius Alimentus, 315–7, 327; (205) Rome recovers, **8**. 229–37, 269; Q. Pleminius, leg. of P. Scipio (Afr.), maltreats, 237–43, 267–97, **11**. 177; SC. for investigation, **8**. 287; Pleminius found guilty, 289–95, **9**. 533; restoration promised, **8**. 289–91; (200) thefts from shrine of Persephonê at, **9**. 37, 41, (199) punished, 155–7; (191) furnishes ships, **10**. 275; (171) **12**. 439
Locris: south of Thermopylae, **10**. 203; (211) M. Valerius Laevinus take Anticyra in, **7**. 99–101, 109; (207) P. Sulpicius Galba in, **8**. 25; (198) joins Philip, **9**. 501; Flamininus in, 205, 213, 215, 249; (197) Philip must withdraw from, 265; (196) proclaimed free by Flamininus, 365, 501; annexed to Aetolians, 369
locusts, plagues of: (203) about Capua, **8**. 373; (173) in Pomptine region,

12. 297; in Apulia, 319; (125) in Africa, **14**. 69, 265
Lollius, M.: (16) leg.; Germans trap, **14**. 319
Longarus, a Dardanian: (c. 230) wars against Demetrius II of Macedon, **9**. 81
Longinus: *see* Cassius.
Longula, Volscian town: (493) captured by Post. Cominius, **1**. 327, (488) by Cn. Marcius Coriolanus and Volsci, 345; (310) L. Papirius Cursor faces Samnites near, **4**. 315
Longuntica, Spanish port: (217) **5**. 267
Longus: *see* Duillius, Manlius Volso, Sempronius, Sulpicius, Tullius.
Longus vicus, in Rome: (296) **4**. 445
Lonorius: (c. 278) leads Galatians into Asia, **11**. 51–3
Loracina riv., in Latium: (170) **13**. 15–7
Loretanus portus: (202) **8**. 513
Loryma, opposite Rhodes: (190) L. Aemilius Regillus and fleet at, **10**. 341; (168) envoys pass, **13**. 273–5
lot: provinces assigned by, *passim*; (295) argument on use of, for consular provinces, **4**. 447–51; (190) senatorial action in place of, **10**. 293; (176) *vitium* in casting, **12**. 239–41
Lower sea: *see* Tuscan sea.
Lua mater: (341) spoils dedicated to, **4**. 5; (167) **13**. 361
Luca, in Etruria: (217) **5**. 177
—, a Volscian town: (331) **4**. 73
Lucania: (332–326) Alexander of Epirus often defeats, **4**. 69, 93–5; (326) exile from, murders him, 93–7, 231; makes alliance with Rome, 99, 105–7; abandons alliance, 107, 111, 399; (317) Roman campaign in, 237, 243; (298) gains alliance against Samnites, 399–403; (296) Q. Fabius Maximus suppresses insurrection in, 423; (294) cohort from, 483; (c. 287) Thurii assisted against, 547; (c. 282) defeated, 549; (c. 278) 551; (c. 275) supports Pyrrhus, **8**. 115, **9**. 23; (c. 272) defeated, **4**. 551, **6**. 205; (216) deserts Rome, **5**. 409, **6**. 35; (215) Ti. Sempronius Longus defeats Hanno in, 131; (214) in Punic army, 219–21; in Roman army, 237; Q. Fabius Maximus takes town in, 237; (213) Ti. Sempronius Gracchus in, 317, 327, 341; T. Pomponius Veientanus plunders, 349; (212) Gracchus in, 349; he is slain in, 403–11, 419–21; Hannibal follows Ap. Claudius Pulcher into, 417, and defeats M. Centenius Paenula in, 417–9; (211) he withdraws through, **7**. 43; (210) M. Marcellus in, 207; (209) surrenders to Q. Fulvius Flaccus, 231, 267; (208) T. Quinctius Crispinus in, 313; (207) C. Claudius Nero defeats Hannibal in, 353, 373–7; Flaccus in, 381; Nero feigns march into, 383–5; Hannibal takes followers from, to Bruttium, 413; (206) returns to Roman allegiance, **8**. 49–51; (91) rebels, **14**. 89; (89) kills A. Gabinius, 95. Prodigies: (200) **9**. 39; (113) **14**. 271; (104) 275; 277; (93) 287. *See* Flavus, Statilius.
Lucanus: (89) leg., defeats Samnites, **14**. 93
Luceres: (753–717) equestrian century, **1**. 51, 131; one of original tribes, **4**. 379
Luceria, in Apulia: (321) false news of attack on, **4**. 165–7; (320) Samnites defeated at, 207–19, 223, **5**. 249; (314) joins Samnites; recovered, **4**. 261; (294) M. Atilius Regulus in doubtful battle with Samnites near, 489–91, 499, 503–5; (217) Hannibal plunders near, **5**. 229; (215) M. Valerius Laevinus camps near, **6**. 115, 131; Ti. Sempronius Gracchus at, 163, 185; (214) 207, 209, 213, 217; Q. Fabius Maximus at, 213, 239; (213) allotted to M. Aemilius Lepidus, 315, 347; (209) remains loyal, **7**. 245–7
Lucilius, Sex., tr. pl., 87: (86) **14**. 101[6]
Lucina: *see* Juno Lucina.
Lucretia, wife of Tarquinius Collatinus: (510) Sex. Tarquinius violates, **1**. 199–203; kills self, 203, **2**. 143; corpse of, rouses citizens, 205–7
Lucretius, L.: (218) qu., ambushed by Ligurians, delivered to Hannibal, **5**. 177–9
—, M.: (210) tr. pl., **7**. 221

INDEX

Lucretius, M.: (207) leg., brings forces from Spain against Hasdrubal, **7.** 365

—, M.: (172) tr. pl., requires leases on public lands, **12.** 345; (171) leg., gathers ships, 439; besieges Haliartus, 463–5

—, P.: (506) cos., **1.** 267

—, Sp., pr. 205: (206) aed. pl., **8.** 153; (205) pr. for Gaul, 153, 155; with M. Livius Salinator confronts Mago, 199, 227; (204) in Gaul, 255–7; (203) rebuilds Genua, 369; (200) envoy to Africa, **9.** 37, 57

—, Sp.: (172) pr. for Farther Spain, **12.** 317, 321, 343–5; (169) leg., occupies forts above Tempê, **13.** 111, 115

— Flavus Tricipitinus, L.: (393) cos., opposes colonization of Veii; defeats Aequi, **3.** 103; (391) tr. mil. c. p., 111–3; (388) ii, 209; (383) iii, 269; (381) iv, 273

— Gallus, C., pr. 171: (181) IIvir nav., **12.** 83; (171) pr. for fleet, 371, 383–5, 395; reaches Corinthian gulf, 439, 463; takes Haliartus and Thebes; returns to fleet, 489–91; demands grain from Athens, **13.** 21–3; (170) charged with greed and cruelty, 15–7, 29; decorates temple of Aesculapius with booty, 17; assembly condemns, 29–33

— Ofella, Q.: (82) of Sulla's party, **14.** 111; stands for cos., killed by Sulla, 113

— Tricipitinus, Hostius: (429) cos., **2.** 355

— —, L.: (462) cos., **2.** 27; defeats Aequi and Volsci, 27–31, 45; triumphs, 35; (459) pref. urb., 81

— —, P.: (419) tr. mil. c. p., **2.** 403; (417) ii, 411

— —, Sp., cos. suf., 509: (510) father of Lucretia, **1.** 203–7; pref. urb., holds first election, 209; (509) urges cos. Tarquinius Collatinus to retire, 225; cos. suf.; dies, 243–5

— —, T.: (508) cos., **1.** 245; attacks Etruscans, 255; (504) cos. ii, triumphs over Sabines, 271

Lucullus: *see* Licinius, Terentius Varro.

Lucumo: *see* Tarquin the Elder.

—: (391) seduces wife of Arruns, **3.** 115

Ludi Magni: *see* Roman games; games, votive.

Luna, in Etruria: (193) Ligurians plunder near, **9.** 557; (195) port on way to Spain, 441, (186) **11.** 279, (185) 319; (177) a Roman colony, **12.** 225; (175) Ligurians plunder, 243; (170) Latin allies winter at, **13.** 33; (168) quarrels with Pisae, 287. Prodigies: (142) **14.** 255; (133) 261; (104) 275

Luna, temple of, on Aventine: (182) **12.** 5

Lupercalia: Evander establishes, **1.** 21, to prevent sterility in women, **14.** 227; (44) M. Antonius runs in, 145

Lupus: *see* Cornelius Lentulus, Rutilius.

Luscinus: *see* Fabricius.

Luscus: *see* Annius, Atilius, Furius, Postumius Albinus.

Lusitania, in Spain: (218) Punic troops in, **5.** 127; in Hannibal's army, 169; (217) Hasdrubal, son of Hamilcar, retires to, 269; (209) Hasdrubal, son of Gisgo, retires to, **7.** 295; (193) P. Scipio Nasica defeats, **10.** 3–5; (190) defeat L. Aemilius Paulus, 427–9; (189) Paulus defeats, 469; (187) in arms, **11.** 239; (186) C. Atinius defeats, 279; (184) C. Calpurnius Piso and L. Quinctius Crispinus triumph over, 353–5; (183) quiet, 397; (181) defeated by P. Manlius, **12.** 103, (179) by L. Postumius Albinus, 149, (178) who triumphs, 203–5; (167–160) campaigns against, **14.** 11; (154) 21, 251; (151–149) surrender to Ser. Sulpicius Galba; enslaved; Galba tried for treatment of, 21, 27, 31, 45; (147) defeated, 41; (147–146) Viriathus seizes, 43, 45; (143) harass Q. Caecilius Metellus, 47; (141) Q. Fabius Maximus Servilianus recovers, 47, 49; (140) ambush leg. Q. Occius, 51; (138) ravaged, 57; (137) D. Junius Brutus subdues, 55, 69; (105) slaughter Roman army, 275; (101) subdued, 279; (99) 281; 283; (76) Q. Caecilius Metellus in, 195; (61) Caesar subdues, 127. *See* Gallaeci.

INDEX

lustratio, purification: (578–534) of city by Servius, **1**. 155; (460), omitted because of death of cos., **2**. 75; (459) of army, **2**. 77; (189) **11**. 37–9; (176) **12**. 239; (42) **14**. 317; (458) of Capitol because of portent, **2**. 101; (218) of Rome because of portent, **5**. 187; (193) **10**. 25; (186) **11**. 281; (172) **12**. 347; (166, 165) **14**. 247; (102) 277; (101) 279; (99) 281; (96) 285; (93) 289; (53) 305; (133) of city, by 27 maidens, 261; (117) 269; (97) 285; (92) 289; (191) of fleet, **10**. 275; (182) of Macedonian army, **12**. 17–9; (169) **13**. 77. For regular *lustra*, *see* censors. *See also* Maidens.

Lutarius: (278) leads Gauls into Asia, **11**. 51–3

Lutatius Catulus, C.: (242) cos., defeats Punic fleet, **4**. 559, **5**. 249, **6**. 41, **8**. 153, 165, **10**. 439, **13**. 381; makes abortive treaty with Carthage, **5**. 51–3, **8**. 447

— —, C., cos. 220: (218) IIIvir agr. adsig., captured by Boi, **5**. 69–71, **8**. 439; (203) rescued, 439

— —, Q.: (102) cos., **14**. 277; driven from Alps by Cimbri, 83; (101) procos.; with C. Marius, defeats Cimbri, 83

— —, Q.: (78) cos., drives colleague from Italy, **14**. 113–5; (70) dedicates temple of Jupiter on Capitol, 121–3

— Cerco, C.: (173) envoy to Macedon and Egypt, **12**. 309

— —, Q.: (241) cos., **8**. 533

Luxinius, Spanish chief: (197) rises, **9**. 337

luxury, Asiatic: (187) introduced, **11**. 235–7

Lycaonia: (189) Cn. Manlius Volso plunders, **11**. 157; (188) restored to Eumenes, **10**. 455, 463, **11**. 125, 133

Lyceum, outside Athens: (200) **9**. 73

Lychnidus, in Illyricum: (208) Aeropus captures, **7**. 343; (196) Philip gives, to Pleuratus, **9**. 369–71; (170) base of Ap. Claudius Cento, **13**. 35–7; (169) L. Coelius returns to, 75; (168) Claudius in danger near, 155; assigned to L. Anicius Gallus, 157

Lycia: (197) Antiochus plans to occupy coast of, **9**. 331, **12**. 203; (196) he comes to, **9**. 387; (190) naval operations off, **10**. 335–41, 355; Hannibal fears to pass, 361; men of, serve Antiochus, 409; fleet of Antiochus brought to, 421; (189) given to Rhodes, 463, 465, **11**. 133, **12**. 201–3, **13**. 315; (188) Q. Fabius Labeo leaves, **11**. 131; (178) Rhodians ordered not to ill-treat, **12**. 203; (174) harassed by Rhodians, 273; (172) 333; (169) granted freedom by Rome, **13**. 137–9, 331–3. *See* Zeuxis.

Lyciscus: (172) Aetolian praetor, **12**. 403; (167) kills leading Aetolians, **13**. 345

Lyco, in Spain: (190) **10**. 427–9

Lycon: (171) officer of Perseus, **12**. 449

Lycortas, of Megalopolis: (192) officer of Philopoemen, **10**. 83; (189) envoy to Rome, **11**. 107; (184) Achaean praetor, addresses Romans, 329–39; (183) praetor, 379

Lyctus, in Crete: (68–67) **14**. 123

Lycurgus, the law-giver: **9**. 501; (189) Achaeans abolish laws of, **11**. 113–5, 323, 331, 335

—, tyrant of Sparta: (221) **9**. 483

Lydia: (190) cavalry from, serves Antiochus, **10**. 409; Antiochus places Timo over, 419; (189) restored to Eumenes, 463, **11**. 133; (171) auxiliaries from, in Roman army, **12**. 453

Lymphaeum, in Bruttium: (203) **8**. 439

Lyncestae, in Macedon: (167) **13**. 353

Lyncus mts.: (211) Philip crosses, **7**. 97; (200) P. Sulpicius Galba makes base on, **9**. 99; (198) Flamininus avoids, 179; Philip in, 189

Lysias, guardian of Antiochus V Eupator: (162) instigates murder of Cn. Octavius, **14**. 249; slain by Demetrius, 13

Lysimachia, in Aetolia: (191) Antiochus holds conference near, **10**. 191

—, on Propontis: (c. 278) Galatians occupy, **11**. 53; (198) Philip fails to hold, **9**. 257–9; (196) Thracians sack; Antiochus restores, 381, 385, 387, 565; he meets Roman envoys at, 383, 561, 569; (193) he gives, to

Seleucus, **10**. 45; (191) Seleucus at, 177; soldiers of Antiochus conducted to, 253; (190) he withdraws garrison from, 381, 387, 391, 395; L. Scipio in, 387; (188) given to Eumenes, **11**. 133, 301, 307; Cn. Manlius Volso establishes base in, 135

Lysimachus, general of Alexander: (281) Seleucus defeats, **9**. 565; (196) Antiochus claims former realm of, 385–7

—: (182) adviser of Philip, **12**. 21

Lysinoë, in Asia Minor: (189) **11**. 49

Lysis riv., in Asia Minor: (189) **11**. 47

Macatus: *see* Livius.

mace, ivory, of Senators: (390) **3**. 143

Macedon (*for further references for the years* 217–179 *see* Philip V; *for* 179–167 *see* Perseus.) Aeneas in, **1**. 9; (348) Greece trembles before, **3**. 449; fame of kings of, **10**. 35, **13**. 271–3; **14**. 33; (319) could not have conquered Italy, **4**. 225–41; (215) makes treaty with Hannibal, **6**. 117–9; envoys of, captured, 131–3; preparations against, 133–5, 163–5; (214) Tarentum, port for, 215; war with, 301–7; (213) assigned to M. Valerius Laevinus, 317; (211) his campaigns against, **7**. 91–101, 109; allotted to P. Sulpicius Galba, 85; (210) 101; (209) 233; (208) 305; (209–7) his campaigns against, 331–43, **8**. 17–37; Dardanians invade, **7**. 343, **8**. 37; Maedi threaten, 17–9; (205) terms of peace with, 251–5; (203) Greek and Roman envoys to, 457–9; (201) account of second war with Philip begins, **9**. 5; war with, referred to coss., 7; fleet ordered to, 11; (200) allotted to P. Sulpicius Galba, 17, 29; war with, declared, 17–25, 31; operations against, 41–57, 65–139, 157, 167; Dardanians invade, 113; (199) allotted to P. Villius Tappulus, 155; operations against, 159–69, **10**. 209; (198) allotted to Flamininus, **9**. 167, 173–5; operations against, 179–205, 225–33; Achaeans won from, 207–225; (197) assigned to Flamininus, 239–43; vain peace talks, 251–65, 283; only Acarnanes loyal to, 319; operations against, 283–305, 335, 501; defeated at Cynoscephalae, 291–303, **10**. 181; peace conference; **9**. 305–13; defeated by Achaeans, 313–9, and by Rhodians, 323–9; defeat Dardani, 329; peace with, ratified, 343–5; (196) assigned to Flamininus, 345–7; peace terms, 359–73, 543–5, **11**. 207, 295, 303–5; (195) troops for, **9**. 393; coast of, safe, 505; (194) Roman army in, to be demobilized, 529–31; Flamininus triumphs over, 549–51; (193) possible aid of, for Antiochus, **10**. 55; (192) assigned to A. Atilius Serranus, 59; M. Baebius Tamphilus moves troops to, 65–9, 157; formerly masters of Demetrias, 91, and of Euboea, 113–5; throne of, promised Philip of Athamania, 137; (191) support of, needed by Antiochus, 175–9; Ap. Claudius Pulcher crosses, 187; captures Aetolians returning from Antiochus, 243; Antiochus' troops conducted through, 253; cities outside, restored to Philip, 365; (190) L. Scipio crosses, 311–3, 343, **11**. 305–7; (189) driven from Athamania, 5–9; Aetolians establish buffer states against, 11; plunders Amphilochia and Dolopia; withdraws, 21, 25; (188) Cn. Manlius Volso returns through, 141–3; (185) causes of war with Perseus, 285–309; (184) Ap. Claudius sent to, 323–9; (183) charges against, 367–71; Q. Marcius Philippus sent to, 371, 373; Demetrius favoured by, 387–91; (182) Philippus reports on, **12**. 7; Perseus plots against Demetrius, 7–53; (181) 65–77; (179) he seizes throne, 163–77; (175) affairs of, 245–7; (174) 257–71; (173) reported preparing war, 297, 303–9; (172) Eumenes urges war against, 321–31, 419; envoys of, in Rome, 331, 335; war with, delayed, 343; preparations for war with, 347, 359–69; Philippus envoy to, 399–421, 429–37; (171) war with Perseus determined on, 373–87, 397, 437–9; allotted to P. Licinius Crassus, 381, 385, 397; he sets out, 439–43;

INDEX

Perseus' preparations, 443–57; operations in, 457–505; C. Cassius Longinus moves on, without authority, **13**. 3–7; (170) 19; A. Hostilius Mancinus in, 25, 27; Numidian, Punic, and Cretan aid against, 13, 27, 289; lack of success in, 33–41; (169) allotted to Q. Marcius Philippus, 43, 53; military preparations, 43–5, 49–55; operations in, 61–83, 91–143, 153–55; (168) allotted to L. Aemilius Paulus, 143–9; he makes preparations, 155–63, and defeats Perseus, 163–277, 287, 395–7, **14**. 39; (167) assigned to Paulus, **13**. 295–7; envoys to assist in settlement of, 299; settlement discussed in Senate, 301–3; freed; divided into four parts, 303, 315, 333, 347–53, 363; constitution of, 353, 357–9; Paulus returns from, with army, 359–69; he triumphs after opposition, 369–93, 401; Prusias congratulates Rome on defeat of, 405–7; Eumenes' doubtful role in, **14**. 11; those who have served in, oppose Rhodian claims, 329; (154–150) Andriscus claims throne of, **14**. 17, 27–31; (148) Q. Caecilius Metellus recovers, 35, 253; (143) L. Tremellius Scrofa defeats pretender in, 47; (142) Romans defeated in, 255; (140) complains of D. Junius Silanus, 49, 51; (104) Thracians subdued in, 277; (92) Maedi plunder, 289; (90) Thracians raid, 93; (89) 95; (87, 86) Mithridates occupies; Thracians raid, 103; (48) Pompey gathers forces in, 307; (44) Caesar plans war in, 147. *See* Alexander, Andronicus, Andriscus, Antigonus, Caranus, Perseus, Philip; and the several Roman generals named above.

Macedon, Gulf of: (169) **13**. 125

Macedonians, in alien service: (202) in army of Hannibal, **8**. 491, 523–5; (195) of Flamininus, **9**. 483; (191) of Antiochus, **10**. 191, 213–5; (190) of Antiochus and Scipio at Magnesia, 405; (189) of Aetolians, 433; of Antipater, **11**. 53; become Egyptians in Egypt, 59;

Macella, in Sicily: (211) **7**. 83–5

Macer: *see* Licinius.

Macerinus: *see* Geganius.

Machanidas, of Sparta: (208) harasses Achaeans, **7**. 331; (207) **8**. 17; withdraws, 29–33

Machares, of Bosporus: (70) becomes *amicus*, **14**. 121

Macra riv.: (185) Liguria opened to, **11**. 319; (180) people near, defeated, **12**. 127

Macra Comê, in Thessaly (?): (198 **9**. 191

Macris, is. near Samos: (190) Antiochus' fleet at, **10**. 327, 373–5

Madamprus, in Lycia: (189) **11**. 47

Maduateni, Thracian tribe: (188) **11**. 137

Madytus, in Thrace: (200) surrenders to Philip, **9**. 51, (196) to Antiochus, 381

Maecenas, C.: (40) agent of Octavius, **14**. 221

Maecia tribe: (332) added, **4**. 69; (204) not condemned by M. Livius Salinator, **8**. 355

Maecilius, L.: (470) tr. pl., **1**. 415

—, Sp.: (416) tr. pl. iv, proposes land law, **2**. 411–7

— Croto, Ti.: (215) leg., conducts legions of Cannae, **6**. 105

Maecius, Geminus: (340) Tusculan commander, slain by T. Manlius, **4**. 23–9

—, Octavius: (293) leg., commands auxiliaries at Aquilonia, **4**. 519

Maedica, in Thrace: (211) Philip attacks, **7**. 97; (208–207) threatens Macedon, **8**. 17; (181) Philip attacks, **12**. 67–9, 73; (172) allied against Perseus, 347; (168) Gauls in, **13**. 175; (97) defeated, **14**. 285; (92) plunders Macedon, 289; (76) war with, 299

Maelius, Q., tr. pl., 320: (321) sponsor of Caudine peace; (320) tr. pl., opposes surrender of sponsors, **4**. 193; resigns, is led to Caudium, 199

—, Sp.: (440) seeks kingship; slain, **2**. 299–313, **3**. 253, 257–9

—, Sp.: (436) tr. pl., attacks L. Minucius and C. Servilius Ahala, **2**. 325

— Capitolinus, P.: (400) tr. mil. c. p., **3**. 45

INDEX

Maenium, a market: (184) built, **11**. 361

Maenius, C.: (338) cos., defeats Latins, **4**. 53–5; (314) dict. to investigate conspiracies; resigns, 261–7, 295

—, C.: (180) pr. for Sardinia, **12**. 107, 109, 137; investigates poisonings, 117, 137

—, P.: (396) tr. mil. c. p., **3**. 63

—, Q.: (170) pr., makes proclamation about Abdera, **13**. 17; enrolls Lampsacenes as allies, 25; promises protection to Chalcis, 31–3

—, T.: (186) pr. urb., **11**. 235, 241, 269, 277, 285; (180) tr. mil., reports victories in Spain, **12**. 107

Maeonia, in Lydia: **14**. 197

Maesesses, Spanish tribe: (207) **8**. 11

Maesian forest: (640–616) **1**. 123

Maesulii, Numidian tribe: (213–204) account of, **8**. 321–37; (213) defeat Syphax, **6**. 333; (203) welcome Masinissa, **8**. 401–3. *See* Capussa, Gala, Lacumazes, Masinissa, Mazaetullus, Syphax.

Maevius, M.: (203) tr. mil., **8**. 435

Magaba, Mt., in Galatia: (189) **11**. 65

Magalus, chief of Boi: (218) meets Hannibal, **5**. 85

magister equitum: (368) first plebeian, **3**. 333–5, **4**. 387; (325) Q. Fabius Maximus, fights against orders of dict., **4**. 115–39; (217) elected, **5**. 227

magister vicorum: (195) **9**. 435

magistrates: (202) Rome without curule, **8**. 515; (183) Livy cites books of the, **11**. 385; (180) minimum ages for, **12**. 137–9

Magius, Cn., of Atella: (214) medix tuticus of Campanians, **6**. 233

—, Decius, of Campania: (216) defies Hannibal, **6**. 21–3; surrendered to him, 29–31; escapes to Ptolemy, 31–3

— Cilo, Cn. (or P.): (46) murders M. Marcellus, **14**. 145

Magna Mater: *see* Idaean Mother.

Magnesia, in Thessaly: **10**. 203, **13**. 125; (196) freed, **9**. 365, 369; (192) envoys at council of, **10**. 89–93; refuses to return to alliance, 117; welcomes Antiochus, 127; (185) controversy over cities of, **11**. 287–93; (171) Perseus near, **12**. 461; he negotiates with, 503; not fitted for wintering, 505; (169) freight ships at, **13**. 113–5

Magnesia ad Maeandrum, in Ionia: (190) Antiochus gathers rowers at, **10**. 321; surrenders to L. Scipio, 421; he winters at, 425; (189) Cn. Manlius Volso at, **11**. 39

— ad Sipylum, in Lydia: (191) Antiochus gathers forces at, **10**. 279; (190) L. Scipio defeats Antiochus near, **10**. 399–419, **11**. 205; surrenders to Scipio, **10**. 419; assigned to Eumenes, 463–5; (87) resists Mithridates, **14**. 103

Magnus: *see* Pompeius.

Mago, brother of Hannibal: (218) crosses Po, **5**. 139–141; at Trebia, 159–61, 165; (217) at Arno riv., 205; (216) at Cannae, 353; in Samnium, **6**. 3; in Bruttium, 35; reports to Carthage, 35–43; (215) takes troops to Spain, 43, 111–3; P. and Cn. Scipio defeat, 167; (214) defeats Spaniards, 307; recruits troops, 311; (212) defeats P. Scipio, 463–71, and Cn. Scipio, 471–7; L. Marcius defeats, 493; (211) withdraws before P. Scipio (Afr.), **7**. 77; (209) goes to Balearic is., 293–5; (207) M. Junius Silanus defeats, **8**. 3–9; (206) conducts levies, 53; Scipio defeats, 55–7, 173; gathers forces at Gades, 71, 97, 123–7, 131; permits Masinissa to enter Spain, 141; ordered to Italy, 145; winters on Balearic is., 149–51, 197; (205) crosses to Liguria, 173, 197–9; inactive, 221–9; (204) 255–7; Etruscans favour, 351; (203) destroys Genua, 369; defeated; dies, 431–7; recalled to Carthage, 437–43, 449; (200) survivor of army of, **9**. 33

—: (215) envoy of Hannibal to Philip, **6**. 117–9, 131–3

—: (215) captured in Spain, **6**. 139

—: (212) commands in Bruttium; aids revolt of Thurii, **6**. 399; plots against Ti. Sempronius Gracchus, 405, 409; commands in Campania, 411, 423; (208) in Locri, **7**. 327

—: (210) surrenders New Carthage, **7**. 179, 187; sent to Rome, 195

Maharbal, general of Hannibal: (219)

before Saguntum, **5**. 35; (218) at Ticinus, 133; (217) at Trasumenus, 221; in Falernia, 245; (216) at Cannae, 353; urges march on Rome, 367–9; fails to take Casilinum, **6**. 59, 61
maidens: (190) ten youths and ten, perform sacrifice, **10**. 299; (207) twenty-seven, sing chant and purify city, **7**. 359–61; (200) **9**. 39; (133) **14**. 261; (119) 267; (117) 269; (104) 277; (99) 281; (97) 283–5; (92) 289
Malacini, in Spain: (197) **9**. 337
Malea, Cape: (200) rounded by Romans, **9**. 127, 139, (198) 197, (191) **10**. 273, 277, (171) **12**. 463; (195) controlled by Nabis, **9**. 505, 513
Maleventum: (314) Samnites flee to, **4**. 271; (296) Apulians defeated near, 413. *See* Beneventum.
Malian gulf (Gulf of Aenianes): south of Thessaly, **10**. 203–5; (207) Philip raids shores of, **8**. 21; (200) Attalus enters, **9**. 133; (197) Philip and Flamininus confer by, 251; (192) Thoas gathers forces at, **10**. 113; operations of Antiochus and Romans near, 129; (191) 191, 201, 219, 225–7, 243; (190) 307. *See* Nicaea, Phalara, Thaumaci.
Malis, in Greece: (172) **12**. 411
Malitiosa Silva: (672–640) **1**. 109
Malleolus: *see* Publicius.
Mallius Maximus, Cn.: *see* Cn. Manlius Maximus, cos. 105.
Malloea (Maloea) in Thessaly: (200) occupied by Aetolians, **9**. 119–21, (191) by Antiochus, **10**. 187, by Philip, 195–7, (185) **11**. 297, (171) by P. Licinius Crassus, **12**. 505
Maluginensis: *see* Cornelius, — Scipio.
Mamercinus: *see* Aemilius, Pinarius.
Mamercus: *see* Aemilius, Pinarius.
Mamertines, in Messana: (264) aided by Rome, **4**. 553, **8**. 117, 483, **9**. 21
Mamilius, L., of Tusculum: (460) aids against Ap. Herdonius, **2**. 61, 67; (458) granted citizenship, 99
—, Octavius, of Tusculum: descended from Ulysses and Circê; (534–510) son-in-law of Tarquin the Proud, **1**. 173; (506) gives Tarquin refuge, 269; (501) leads Latin revolt, 275; (499) killed at Lake Regillus, 279–83
Mamilius Atellus, C., pr. 207: (209) first plebeian curio max., **7**. 235; (208) aed. pl., 357; (207) pr. for Sicily, 351, 357, 365, **8**. 45; (203) envoy to Philip, 459; (174) dies, **12**. 253
— Turrinus, Q., pr. 206: (207) aed. pl., **8**. 43; (206) pr. pereg., 43–5; then for Gaul, 45, 49
Mammula: *see* Cornelius.
Mancinus: *see* Hostilius.
Mandonius, Spanish chief: (217) Cn. Scipio defeats, **5**. 269–71; (210) wife of, before P. Scipio (Afr.), **7**. 189–91; (209) supports Rome, 279–83; (206) rebells, **8**. 97, 105, 111, 113, 117, 129, 173; Scipio suppresses, 107, 129–41; delivered to Romans, 219
Manduria, in Calabria: (209) **7**. 267
Manes, Di: (340) addressed in *devotio*, **4**. 21, 37; (295) 467, 469
Manilius, C.: (66) tr. pl., **14**. 125
—, M' (or M.): (149) cos., **14**. 183, 31; begins siege of Carthage; defeated, 25, 29–31; (148) takes cities, 35, 37
—, P.: (167) Xvir on Illyrian terms, **13**. 299–301, 337–9
—, Sex.: (449) tr. mil., commands on Aventine, **2**. 171
maniple: (340) term explained, **4**. 31–3
Manlian gens: (384) name 'Marcus' banned in, **3**. 267
— orders: **2**. 353, **4**. 29
— pass, in Spain: (180) **12**. 121
Manlius, A.: (208) tr. mil., slain, **7**. 319–21
—, C.: (474) cos., makes truce with Veii, **1**. 401; opposes tribb. pl., 401–3
—, C.: (379) tr. mil. c. p.; Volsci defeat, **3**. 299-301; (342) mutineers seize, 513
—, Cn.: (72) pr.; Spartacus defeats, **14**. 119
—, L.: (216) envoy of survivors of Cannae, **5**. 407
—, L.: (188) strikes Punic envoy, **11**. 145
—, L.: (168) qu., escorts envoys of Masinissa, **13**. 287–91
—, L.: (79–78) procos. in Spain; defeated by Hirtuleius, **14**. 115

Manlius, P., pr. 195, 182: (196–180) IIIvir epulonis, **9.** 389, **12.** 133; (195) pr. for Nearer Spain, **9.** 391, 393; defeats Turdetani, 461–7; (182) pr. ii, **11.** 397, for Farther Spain, **12.** 3, 7, 53–5; (181) defeats Lusitani, 59, 103; (180) dies on return, 131–3

— Acidinus (L.f.): (171) tr. mil., **12.** 443

— — (M.f.): (171) tr. mil., **12.** 443

— —, L.: (210) pr. urb., **7.** 89, 213–5; (208) envoy to Greece, 351; (207) commands in Umbria, 407–9; (206) propr. or procos. in Spain, **8.** 151; (205) 213–9; (204) 257; (203) 371; (201) 521; (200) **9.** 149; (199) ovation prevented, 169–71

— —, M.: (171) son of, a tr. mil., **12.** 443

— — Fulvianus, L., cos. 179: (188) pr. for Nearer Spain, **11.** 115–7; (187) reports insurrections, 239; (186) defeats Celtiberians, 279–81; (185) granted ovation, 309; (183) envoy to warn Gauls, 393–5; (181) IIIvir for Aquileia, 395, **12.** 103; (179) cos., 137, 353, **13.** 271, **14.** 243, with Liguria as prov., **12.** 139, 163; (171) son of, a tr. mil., 443

— Capitolinus, A.: (389) tr. mil. c. p., **3.** 197, 201; (385) ii, 231; (384) deserts brother, M., 263; (383) tr. mil. c. p., iii, 269; (370) iv, 319

— —, L.: (422) tr. mil. c. p., **2.** 391

— —, M.: (434) **2.** 331

— —, M.: (392) cos., celebrates games, defeats Aequi, abdicates, **3.** 109–11; (390) roused by geese, saves Capitol, 159–61, 231, 241, 249, 253, 385, **11.** 57; (387) interrex, **3.** 211; (385) advocates debt reforms, 231–3, 241–5; defies dict., imprisoned, released, 245–55; (384) addresses plebs, 255–61; condemned, executed, 261–7; pestilence follows his death, 267–9; (345) temple to Juno Moneta on site of house of, 453, 267.

— —, P.: (379) tr. mil. c. p.; Volsci defeat, **3.** 299–301; (368) dict., 331–3; (367) tr. mil. c. p. ii, 347

— —, T.: (384) deserts brother, M., **3.** 263

— — Imperiosus, Cn.: (359) cos., repulses Tiburtes, **3.** 393; (357) cos. ii, against Faliscans, 409–11; (356) interrex, 415; (351) cens., 432[1]; (345) mag. eq., 453

Manlius Capitolinus Imperiosus, L.: (363) dict. clavi fig. c., conducts levy, **3.** 365–7; (362) attacked by tr. pl.; saved by son, L., 367–73, 385

— Cincinnatus, Cn.: (480) cos., **1.** 363; defeats Etruscans, slain, 367–79

— Imperiosus Torquatus, T., cos. 347, 344, 340: (362) saves father from tr. pl., **3.** 369–73, 385; tr. mil., 373; (361) defeats Gallic champion, 349, 385–9, 445, 447, **6.** 199, **11.** 57; (353) dict. against Caerê, **3.** 423; refuses to hold elections under Licinian-Sextian laws, 427; (349) dict. com. c., 447; (347) cos., 449; (344) ii, 453; (340) iii, **4.** 11; pleads with Latins, 17; urges Latin war, 19–21, **6.** 75; with P. Decius Mus plans *devotio*, **4.** 21–3, 383; condemns son for leaving ranks, 27–9, 49, 119, 133, **2.** 353; defeats Latins, **4.** 35–41; buries Decius, 43; defeats Latins and Volsci, 47; Aurunci surrender, 61; names dict., 49; worthy to oppose Alexander, 227–9

— Maximus, Cn.: (105) cos.; Cimbri defeat, **14.** 79, 275

— Naevius: (351) cens., **3.** 433, 432[1]

— Torquatus, A., cos. 164: (167) pr. for Sardinia, remains in Rome, **13.** 297

— —, L.: (295) leg.; Gauls defeat, **4.** 459

— —, T.: (340) defeats Latin champion; condemned by father, T., for leaving ranks, **4.** 23–9, 45, 139

— —, T.: (299) cos., **4.** 391, 395–7

— —, T.: (235) cos., conquers Sardinia, **6.** 121; closes temple of Janus, **1.** 67; (216) opposes ransom of survivors of Cannae, **5.** 397–405; opposes admission of Latins to Senate, **6.** 75; (215) propr., conquers Sardinia, 121, 137–41; (212) pont., **8.** 515; candidate for pont. max., **6.** 355; (211) refuses consulship, **7.** 85–9, 349; (210) in Senate, attacks Marcellus, 123; (209) senior ex-censor, but not princeps

senatus, 251; (208) dict. for elections and games, 345–51, **8**. 371–3, 465; (202) dies, 515
Manlius Torquatus, T., cos. 165: (170) pont., **13**. 43; (165) cos., **14**. 247; (140) condemns son, 49, 51
— — Atticus, A.: (241) cos., **8**. 533
— Volso, A., Xvir, 451: (454) envoy to Athens, **2**. 107; (451) Xvir, 109
— —, A., cos. 178: (194) IIIvir col. deduc., **9**. 553; (193) **10**. 25; (178) cos., **12**. 179, **13**. 9, 271, **14**. 243, against Histrians, **12**. 185–99, 207, 217; tribb. pl. attack, 199–201; (177) 205; defeats Histrians, 199–201, 215–9; C. Claudius Pulcher attacks, 217–9
— —, Cn., cos. 189: (197) aed. cur. **9**. 345; (195) pr. for Sicily, 391–3; (193) candidate for cos., **10**. 27; (192) 69; (189) cos., 431–3, with Asia as prov., 437, 441, 477, **11**. 147; defeats Galatians, 37–51, 55–95, 149, 153–73, 219, (188) 115–7; receives envoys, 121–3; treaty with Antiochus, 131, 153; dictates terms to Galatians, 135; crosses Thrace, 135–43, 159, 171–3; (187) recalled by Senate, 145–7; granted triumph after debate, 153–75, 205; investigation of, demanded, 189; triumphs, 235–9; (184) candidate for cens., 347–53
— —, L.: (218) pr. for Gaul, **5**. 47–9; Boi defeat, 71–3, 129; vows temple to Concord, 311, **6**. 73; gives army to P. Scipio, **5**. 113; (217) candidate for cos., 317
— —, L.: (197) pr. for Sicily, **9**. 239; (189) leg. of brother, Cn., against Galatians, **11**. 69, 75, 79, (188) 123, 131
— —, L.: (149) envoy to Syria, **14**. 33, 35
— —, M.: (420) tr. mil. c. p., **2**. 399
— —, P.: (400) tr. mil. c. p., **3**. 45
— —, P.: (210) pr. for Sardinia, **7**. 89, 111, 227, 233
— — Capitolinus, A.: (405) tr. mil. c. p., **2**. 455; (402) ii, **3**. 27; (397) iii, 57; (394) envoy to Delphi, 97
— — Longus, L.: (256) cos., **8**. 317
mantlets: *see vineae*.
Mantua, in cis-Alpine Gaul: (214) **6**. 207
manumission: (177) restrictions on, **12**. 213–5; (171) **13**. 11–3; (357) tax on, **3**. 411; (209) **7**. 247–9; (210) by state, as reward, **7**. 105. *See* freedmen.
Manus, slave of the Capuan Calavii: (210) accuses his masters, **7**. 105
Marcellus, Marcellinus: *see* Claudius.
March: (189) preceded by intercalary month, **10**. 475; (194) animals born in, and April offered in Sacred Spring, **9**. 531; (217) consular term begins on 15th, **5**. 187, 199, *et saepe*; (187) elections before the 5th, **11**. 235, (179) on the 11th and 12th, **12**. 179; (168) Latin Festival on 31st, **13**. 163
Marcia, Vestal: (114) condemned, **14**. 75
Marcian aqueduct: (140) **14**. 51
— shield: in Capitol, (212) **6**. 493
Marcius, valley in Liguria: (186) **11**. 277–9
Marcius: *see* Ancus, Numa.
—, Cn.: (389) tr. pl., accuses Q. Fabius Ambustus, **3**. 197
—, M.: (210) rex. sac., dies, **7**. 227, 355
—, M.: (193) tr. mil., slain, **10**. 15
—, Q.: (193) tr. mil., slain, **10**. 15
— Censorinus, L.: (149) cos., **14**. 25, 31, 183; begins siege of Carthage, returns for elections, 25
— Coriolanus, Cn.: (493) takes Corioli, **1**. 327–9; (491) accused by tribb. pl., welcomed by Volsci, 331–5, 397; plots against Rome, 335–9; (488) leads Volsci against Rome; yields to mother, 345–51, 353, 403, **3**. 507, **9**. 429
— Figulus, C., cos., 162, 156: (169) pr. for fleet, **13**. 39, 53; in Aegean, 91, 95, 121–33; (162) cos., **14**. 249; (156) ii, 251; defeats Dalmatians, 15
— —, T.: (169) palm in house of, **13**. 47
— Philippus, L.: friend of Philip, **12**. 405
— —, L.: (91) cos., **14**. 291; (82) leg. of Sulla, 109
— —, Q., cos. 186, 169: (188) pr. for Sicily, **11**. 115, 117; (186) cos., 235, **12**. 113; investigates Bacchanalian conspiracy, **11**. 241, 257–73; Ligurians defeat, 275–9; absent at end of

term, 283; (183) envoy to Macedon and Greece, 373; (182) **12**. 7; (180) Xvir sac., 135, (174) 255; (172) envoy to Epirus and Thessaly, 399–405; confers with Perseus, 405–21, 429; envoy to Boeotia, 421–5, and Argos, 425; reports to Senate, 433–7; sent to Greece with fleet, 437; (171) 465; (169) cos. ii, **13**. 39, with Macedon as prov., 43, 53; charged with lax levy, 49; in Thessaly, 91–5; in Macedon, 95–121, 129–31, 153, 339; asks for supplies, 139–41; (167) adviser on Macedonian terms, 299, 339, 345–7, 355

Marcius Philippus, Q.: (169) leg. of father, Q., **13**. 97–9

— Ralla, M.: (204) pr. urb., **8**. 249, 255; (203) commands fleet, 371; (202) escorts Punic envoys, 511, 515

— —, Q.: (196) tr. pl., prevents recall of Flamininus, **9**. 345–7; (194) IIvir for temple of Fortuna Primigenia, 553, (192) of Jupiter, **10**. 123

— Rex, P.: (171) envoy to restrain cos. C. Cassius Longinus, **13**. 7

— —, Q.: (118) cos., **14**. 269; routs Styni, 75

— Rutulus, C., cos. 357, 352, 344, 342: (357) cos., defeats Privernates, **3**. 409–11; (356) first plebeian dict., 413–5, 431–3, **4**. 387; triumphs by order of people, **3**. 415, **4**. 503; (352) cos. ii, **3**. 427; (351) first plebeian cens., 431–3, **4**. 387; (344) cos. iii, **3**. 453; (342) iv, suppresses mutiny, 497–501; worthy to oppose Alexander, **4**. 227

— —, C., cos. 310: (311) tr. pl., **4**. 277–9; (310) cos., 289; meets Samnites, wounded, 309–15; (300) one of first plebeian pontiffs and augurs, 389; (295) leg. at Sentinum, 471; (293) cens., 541

— Scilla, Q.: (172) tr. pl., forces trial of M. Popilius Laenas, **12**. 351–3

— Septimus, L.: (212) rallies army after deaths of P. and Cn. Scipio; defeats Hasdrubal, **6**. 477–93, **7**. 5–7, 141, **8**. 119, 171; (211) is refused title of propr., **7**. 7; turns army over to C. Claudius Nero, 65; honoured by P. Scipio (Afr.), 77; (206) serves under him, **8**. 61, 73, 79, 87–97, 123, 127, 141, **9**. 159

Marcius Sermo, M.: (172) tr. pl., forces trial of M. Popilius Laenas, **12**. 351–3

— Tremulus, Q.: (306) cos., defeats Hernici and Samnites, **4**. 333–9; Piso omits, 341

— vates: (212) books of, with prophecies on Cannae, found, **6**. 383–7

Marcolica, in Spain: (168) **13**. 257

Mare nostrum: (207) **8**. 3

Marenê, in Thrace: (171) **12**. 503

Marica, Grove of: (207) **7**. 357

marine risks: (212) shared by state, **6**. 349

Maritime circus, in Anagnia: (307) **4**. 333

Marius, C., cos. 107, 104–100, 86: (106) procos., defeats Jugurtha, **14**. 79; (104) cos. ii, 275; triumphs, 81; (102) cos. iv, defeats Teutoni, 81, 277–9; (101) cos. v, 173; defeats Cimbri, triumphs, 83, 279; (100) cos. vi, 279; supports Senate against Saturninus and Glaucia, 83–5; (90) leg., defeats Marsi, 91, (89) 91–3; (88) given Mithridatic command; driven from Rome by Sulla, 95–7, 187; (87) occupies Rome, 99–101, 295; (86) cos. vii, institutes reign of terror, dies, 101–3; (84) followers of, support Carbo, 107; (44) Chamates claims to be son of, 147; (42) memorial of, near Mutina, 315

—, C., cos. 82: (88) exiled, **14**. 97; (82) made cos. by violence, 107, 173; causes death of Senators; defeated by Sulla, 109; kills self, 111

—, M.: (76) qu. of Sertorius, **14**. 195

— Alfius, *medix tuticus* of Campanians: (215) plots treachery, slain, **6**. 125

— Blossius, of Capua: (216) welcomes Hannibal, **6**. 21–3

— Egnatius, Samnite leader: (89) killed, **14**. 93

— Gratidianus, M., pr. 85: (82) Sulla kills, **14**. 111

Marmoreae, in Italy: (210) **7**. 203

Maronea, on Thracian coast: (200) Philip takes, **9**. 49–51, 91; (190) L. Scipio crosses near, **10**. 387; (189) garrison of Antiochus ordered from, 479; (188) furnishes grain, **11**. 141; (185) Philip occupies, 289–

91; he disputes possession with Eumenes, 301–9; (184) his garrison ordered from, 323; he destroys, 325–7; (170) bars out Romans, **13**. 29; (167) Attalus claims, 309; not in 1st Macedonian republic, 347

marriage: (753–717) origin of cry 'Thalassio,' **1**. 37; (443) widow claims to control daughter's, **2**. 287–9; (220) within 7th degree, **14**. 181; (171) of first cousins, **12**. 389

marriage, right of (*ius conubii*): (753–717) Romulus seeks, with neighbours, **1**. 33–5; (450) between orders, denied by Twelve Tables, **2**. 269–71, **4**. 293, (445) permitted, **2**. 257–77; (338) with Roman citizens, denied to Latins, **4**. 61, (216) long possessed by Campanians, **6**. 13, **9**. 93, (188) granted Campanians, **11**. 119, (171) not possessed by provincials, **13**. 11; (306) between Hernic cities, limited, **4**. 339; (167) between Macedonian republics, denied, **13**. 349

Marrucini: (325) potential enemies, **4**. 111; (304) seek alliance, 349; (217) Hannibal among, **5**. 229; (211) **7**. 41–3; (207) warned to aid C. Claudius Nero, 383; (205) in fleet of P. Scipio (Afr.), **8**. 195; (168) at Pydna, **13**. 225; (91) rebel, **14**. 89; (90) defeated, 91; (89) 95. Prodigy: (214) **6**. 209

Mars: father of Romulus and of Roman people, **1**. 5, 17, **2**. 205, **4**. 463; (509) land of Tarquins consecrated to, **1**. 231; (343) P. Decius Mus sacrifices to, **3**. 491; (340) addressed in *devotio*, **4**. 37, 43; (311) called on in battle, 283; (217) vow to, renewed, **5**. 231; with Venus in *lectisternium*, 235; (167) Macedonian arms offered to, **13**. 361. Altar of, in Campus: (193) **10**. 29; (179) censs. sit near, **12**. 143. Flamen of: *see flamen Martialis*. Grove of, near Crustumerium: (177) **12**. 211. Sacred shields of: *see ancilia*. Spears of, in Regia: (181) are shaken, **12**. 61, **14**. 241; (117) 269; (102) 277; (98) 283; (95) 285. Spears of, in Praeneste: (214) **6**. 209. Statue of, on Appian way: (217) **5**. 203. Temple of, on Via Appia, outside Porta Capena: (387) **3**. 213; (350) 433; (296) **4**. 447; (293) 541; (189) **11**. 95. Temple of, at Capua: (208) **7**. 305, (193) **10**. 25. Personification of war: **4**. 45, 89, 119, 341, **5**. 3, **8**. 89, **10**. 423, **12**. 333, 441; or of warlike character, **5**. 29, 239, **11**. 61. Portents from, or from his attributes: (295) **4**. 463; (217) **5**. 203; (214) **6**. 209; (208) **7**. 305; (193) **10**. 25; (177) **12**. 211; (105) **14**. 275; (53) 305; *see also* Spears of Mars, *above*.

Mars Gradivus: (715–672) Numa establishes Salii as priests of, **1**. 71; (480) military oath by, 373–5; (390) sacred shields of, **3**. 175–7

Marsi, Italian tribe: (340) Romans cross territory of, **4**. 21; (325) potential enemies, 111; (319) members of Federation, 237; (310) Samnites threaten, 313; (308) join Samnites; defeated, 325; (304) made allies, 349; (302) crushed; treaty renewed, 369; (217) Hannibal among, **5**. 229; (211) **7**. 41–3; (205) in fleet of P. Scipio (Afr.), **8**. 195; (196) in army of M. Marcellus, **9**. 375; (91) rebel, **14**. 89; (90–89) defeated, 91–3; (89) seek peace, 95

Marsyas, the satyr: **11**. 41

Marsyas riv., in Asia minor: (189) **11**. 41

Martius, Campus: *see* Campus Martius.

Masaesulians, African tribe: (206) subject to Syphax, **8**. 73; (204) Masinissa defeats, 325, 333; (203) 405

Masgaba, son of Masinissa: (168) envoy to Rome, **13**. 287–91, 409

Masinissa, son of Gala, king of Numidia: (213) defeats Syphax of Numidia, **6**. 333; (212) harasses P. Scipio, 467–71; (210) takes Numidians to Carthage, **7**. 219; (209) P. Scipio (Afr.) captures and returns nephew of, 291–3, **8**. 143; plunders Spain, **7**. 295–7; (206) Scipio repulses raid of, **8**. 55–7; shifts sides, 69–71, **10**. 451; meets Scipio, promises aid in Africa, **8**. 141–5, 185; (206–205) fails to recover kingdom from Syphax, 321–37, 413; (205) a doubtful ally, 173; becomes bitter enemy of Carthage, 221;

meets Laelius in Africa, 225, 337; urges that Scipio cross to Africa, 229, 301; (204) joins him in Africa, 319–21, 337; aids in defeating Hanno, 339–43, (203) and Syphax and Hasdrubal, 381–83, 389–93; recovers kingdom, 401–7, **10**. 365, **13**. 289, 291; marries Sophoniba, wife of Syphax, **8**. 407–11; rebuked by Scipio he sends her poison, 415–21; hailed as king, 421–3; envoys of, sent to Rome, 423, 429–31, 445; (202) at Zama, 471, 489, 493, 497; tyrannical rule of, 491; restored to kingdom by terms of peace, 507, 537; (200) aid of, for Macedonian war asked, **9**. 33–5, and given, 57–9, (198) 237; (195) quarrels with Carthage, 403; (193) 575; envoys of Carthage and, in Rome, 579; (191) offers aid for war with Antiochus, **10**. 167; (182) Rome fails to end dispute of, with Carthage, **12**. 55–7; (181) holds disputed territory, 107; (174) envoys return from, 255–7; (172) Punic charges against, answered by son, Gulussa, 355–9; (171) sends aid for war with Perseus, 375–7, 395–7, 453, **13**. 13, (170) 25–7; (168) Masgaba, son of, in Rome, 287–91, 409; Senate refuses request of, for Punic hostage, 291; Misagenes, son of, ill at Brundisium, 291–3; (157) envoys sent to settle dispute of, with Carthage, **14**. 15; (153) 15, 17; (151) envoys return with Gulussa; defeats Carthaginians, 21; (149) Punic attacks on, lead to Third Punic War, 23; (148) vigour in old age, 21, 33; dies; M. Marcellus, envoy to, drowned, 33, 37

Maso: *see* Papirius.

Massicus, Mt., in Campania: (217) **5**. 245

Massilia: c. 600) ounded rom Phocaea, **3**. 119, **9**. 441; old allies of Rome, 443; (218) inform Rome of Hannibal's acts, **5**. 57, 69; furnish guides for P. Scipio, 75, (217) and scout ships for Cn. Scipio, 263; (211) ships of, escort P. Scipio (Afr.), **7**. 75–7; (208) report Hasdrubal in Gaul, 353–5; (189) report slaying of L. Baebius Dives, **10**. 467; remain thoroughly Greek, 459; acquire Gallic disposition, **11**. 59; (181) complain of Ligurian pirates, **12**. 59; boundary of naval command, 61; (173) N. Fabius Buteo dies at, 301–3; (154) attacked by Ligurians, **14**. 15, (125) by Salluvii, 69; (49) surrenders to Caesar, 137

Massiliota: *see* Terentius.

Massiva, nephew of Masinissa: (209) P. Scipio (Afr.) captures and returns, **7**. 291–3, **8**. 143

—, Numidian prince: (111) Jugurtha kills, **14**. 77

Mastanabal, son of Masinissa: (149) receives part of Numidia, **14**. 33, 37

Mater deorum: *see* Idaean Mother.

Mater Matuta, temple of, in Rome: (396) vowed and dedicated, **3**. 67, 81; (213) burned, **6**. 329; (212) rebuilt, 365; (196) arch dedicated before, **9**. 349; (174) inscription for Ti. Sempronius Gracchus in, **12**. 283. Temple of, at Satricum: (377) spared in sack, **3**. 309; (346) 451. Prodigies: (377) **3**. 309; (206) **8**. 47

Materina, Umbrian canton (308) **4**. 329

Matho: *see* Naevius, Pomponius.

Matienius, C.: (138) punished for desertion, **14**. 53

Matienus, C. (or M.), pr. 173: (181) IIvir navalis, **12**. 83; captures Ligurian ships, 87; (173) pr. for Farther Spain, 283, 293; (171) accused; goes into exile, **13**. 9–10

—, P.: (205) tr. mil., attacks Locri, **8**. 231; Q. Pleminius kills, 239–43, 277–9

matrons, Roman: (395) bring gold to treasury, **3**. 87–9; (390) 169; (389) repaid, 207; (331) convicted of poisoning, **4**. 71–3; (207) make contributions from dowries, **7**. 359–61; (195) Oppian law on dress of, repealed after discussion, **9**. 413–41

Mauri, Moors: (218) in Punic army, **5**. 63, (217) 247, (216) 323, **6**. 17, 91, 99, (214) 221, 241, (202) **8**. 491, 493; (206) Masaesulians border on, **8**. 73; escort Masinissa, 323. *See* Baga, Bocchus, Juba.

Maurusii, Numidians: 213) Syphax flees to, **6**. 333

INDEX

Mavors: (217) named on lot, **5**. 203
Maximus: *see* Carvilius, Fabius, Fulvius Centumalus, Manlius, Sulpicius Galba, Valerius.
May: (495) temple of Mercury consecrated on 15th of, **1**. 287; (450) official terms begin on 15th of, **2**. 117–9; (449) 123, 135; (191) troops gather at Brundisium on 15th of, **10**. 165; prr. set out for prov. in, 165; (176) Latin Festival on 5th of, **12**. 233
Mazaetullus: (before 204) rules Maesulii, **8**. 321–23; Masinissa defeats, 325–7
Meander riv., in Asia Minor: course of, **11**. 41–3; (189) boundary in territorial settlement, **10**. 463–5; (188) **11**. 133; (189) Cn. Manlius Volso crosses, 39–41. *See* Antiochia, Magnesia.
meat, dole of: *see visceratio.*
Mecium, ad, near Lanuvium: (389) **3**. 201
Medes: (192) in army of Antiochus, **10**. 137, 143, (190) 407; (36) M. Antonius invades, **14**. 161
Meduacus riv., in Venetia: (302) **4**. 365
Medullinus: *see* Furius.
Medio, in Acarnania: (191) **10**. 191–5
Mediolanium (Milan): Gauls found, **3**. 119; (194) Gauls defeated near, **9**. 535
medix tuticus: (215) Campanian magistrate, **6**. 125, (214) 233 (211) **7**. 25–7
Medullia, in Latium (640–616) captured, **1**. 121; (616–578) 137
Megalesia: (204) festival for Idaean Mother, **8**. 261–3; (194) drama at, **9**. 555; (191) **10**. 263
Megalopolis, in Arcadia: (370) Arcadians found, **9**. 165; (226) Sparta defeats; Antigonus Doson restores, **9**. 223; (208–207) Aliphera restored to, **8**. 33, (199) **9**. 165; (198) withdraws from Achaean council, 223; (192) Philopoemen plunders near, **10**. 77; Aetolians enslaved at, 111; (191) Flamininus at, 247; (189) portico at, rebuilt; land restored to, **11**. 113; (175) Antiochus Epiphanes aids, **12**. 249; (174) Achaean council at, 271; (167) L. Aemilius Paulus at, **13**. 343. *See* Alexander, Diophanes, Lycortas, Philip.
Megara, in Greece: (208–207) Philip passes, **8**. 31; (200) **9**. 73; Romans prevent raids by way of, 65
— Hyblaea, in Sicily: (214) Syracusan mutiny at, **6**. 271–5; Marcellus destroys, 275, 287
Megellus: *see* Postumius.
Megistê, harbour in Lycia: (190) Rhodian fleet at, **10**. 355, 361, 421
Melambium, in Thessaly: (197) **9**. 291
Melas riv., in Malis: (191) **10**. 227
— riv., in Thrace: (188) **11**. 135
Meleon, in Epirus: (169) **13**. 81
Meles: (210) Marcellus takes, **7**. 203
Meliboea, in Thessaly: (191) recovered from Athamanes, **10**. 197; (169) M. Popilius Laenas attacks, **13**. 129–31; (168) Cn. Octavius captures, 241
Melita (Malta): (218) **5**. 151
Melkarth: (218) Hannibal pays vow to, **5**. 61[1]
Memmius, C., pr. 172: (174) envoy to Aetolians, **12**. 273; (172) pr. for Sicily, 317, 321, 367
—, C., pr. 104: (100) L. Apuleius Saturninus kills, **14**. 85
—, T.: (170) envoy to tribes injured by C. Cassius Longinus, **13**. 21
Memnon, an Achaean: (198) **9**. 221–3
Memphis, in Egypt: (168) **13**. 277, 281
Mendaeus, port of Cassandrea: (200) **9**. 133
Menecrates: (168) Perseus' agent, **13**. 169
Menelais, in Dolopia: (185) **11**. 297
Menelaus, Mt., near Sparta: (195) **9**. 489
Menenius, L.: (357) tr. pl., carries law on usury, **3**. 409
—, M.: (410) tr. pl., obstructs levy, **2**. 429–31
—, M.: (384) tr. pl., attacks M. Manlius Capitolinus, **3**. 261–3
— Lanatus, Agr.: (503) cos., triumphs over Aurunci, **1**. 271–3; (494) tells story of belly to plebs, 323–5; (493) dies, 329; his popularity, 397
— —, Agr., cos. 439: (442) IIIvir col. deduc., **2**. 295–7; (439) cos., 301; (419) tr. mil. c. p., 403; (417) ii, 411

Menenius Lanatus, C. (or T.): (452) cos., **2**. 107; opposes law for Xvirate, 109
— —, L.: (440) cos., **2**. 297
— —, L. (or Licinus): (387) tr. mil. c. p., **3**. 211–3, 212[1]; (380) ii, 289, 288[2]; (378) iii, 303
— —, T.: (477) cos.; Etruscans defeat, **1**. 391–3; (476) tr. pl. accuse; dies of shame, 395–7, 401, 403
Menestas, of Epirus: (191) surrender of, demanded, **10**. 239; (189) accused of rousing Aetolians, **11**. 33
Menippus, general of Philip: (208) left in Greece, **7**. 343; (207) sent to Chalcis, **8**. 19
—, general of Antiochus: (193) envoy to Flamininus, **9**. 563–9, (192) to Aetolians, **10**. 93–5; sent to occupy Euboea, 145–9; (191) in Perrhaebia, 187, Aetolia, 191
Menix, is. of Lesser Syrtis: (217) **5**. 305
Menon, of Antigonea: (171) general of Perseus, **12**. 471
Menophilus, of Perrhaebia: (168) informant of L. Aemilius Paulus, **13**. 207
Mens, temple to: (217) vowed, **5**. 231, 235; (215) dedicated, **6**. 107, 113
Mentissa, in Spain: (211) **7**. 65
Mento: *see* Julius.
mercenary soldiers: (213) first used by Rome, **6**. 335; (212) 465–7
merchants, guild of: (495) **1**. 305
Mercury: envoys called bearers of wand of, **14**. 227; (495) temple of, consecrated, **1**. 287, 303–5; (399) honoured in *lectisternium*, **3**. 49; (217) **5**. 235; (93) statue of, sweats, **14**. 287
—, Hill of, in Spain: (210) **7**. 171
—, Promontory of, in Africa (Cape Bon): (204) **8**. 313
Merenda: *see* Antonius, Cornelius.
Meropus range: (199) **9**. 165
Merula: *see* Cornelius.
Mesembria, on Euxine: (179) **12**. 177
Messala (Messalla): *see* Valerius, — Maximus.
Messana (Messina), in Sicily: (288) Mamertines seize, **8**. 117; (264) Romans cross straits to aid, **9**. 85, **13**. 317; (218) Hiero brings Punic ships to, **5**. 145; Ti. Sempronius Longus comes to, 149; (215) Ap. Claudius Pulcher at, **6**. 143, 177–9; (205) P. Scipio (Afr.) at, **8**. 233–7, 241–3, (204) 289–91; (200) subject to Rome, **9**. 85; (43–42) Sex. Pompeius occupies, **14**. 155
Messana, straits of: **8**. 467; (218) currents in, **5**. 145; (205) **8**. 233; (191) Roman fleet moves through, **10**. 275; (171) **12**. 439
Messapia: (c. 331) **4**. 95
Messenê, in Peloponnese: (208) Aetolians demand return of Pylos to, **7**. 335; Achaeans defeat Aetolians near, 343; (205) on side of Rome in treaty with Philip, **8**. 255; (201) captured by Nabis, **9**. 503; (before 200) Philip's cruelty in, 91, 217; (195) Nabis required to make restitution to, 511; (191) forced by Flamininus to join Achaean League, **10**. 245–7; (183) secedes; forced back into League, **11**. 373–9, **12**. 65, 403; (172) charged by Achaeans with having supported Philip and Antiochus, **12**. 401–3
Messius, Vettius, Volscian leader: (431) defeated, **2**. 349–51
Metapontum, port of Lucania: (c. 530) Pythagorians at, **1**. 65; (326) bones of Alexander of Epirus brought to, **4**. 97; (216) deserts Rome, **5**. 409; (214) Hannibal brings grain from district of, **6**. 241; (212) left by Roman garrison, goes over to Hannibal, 381, 397–9; (210) seizes Roman ships, **7**. 151; Herdoneans transported to, 207; (209) Hannibal's trick at, fails, 277–9; (207) Hannibal withdraws to, 379–81, and transports people to Bruttium, 413
Metaurus riv., in Picenum: (207) **7**. 397; Hasdrubal defeated on the, 395–407
Metellus: *see* Caecilius.
Meteon, in Illyricum: (168) envoy of Perseus at, **13**. 165; kin of Gentius arrested in, 195
Methres, father of Dido: **14**. 177
Methymna, in Lesbos: (167) **13**. 357
Metrodorus, of Rhodes, (168) agent of Perseus, **13**. 165–7
Metropolis, in Thessaly: (198) repulses

INDEX

Aetolians, **9**. 191; surrenders to Flamininus, 195; (191) Antiochus takes, **10**. 185; surrenders to M' Acilius Glabrio, 199
Metropolis, in Phrygia: (189) **11**. 51
Metilius, M.: (416) tr. pl., proposes land law, **2**. 411–7
—, M.: (401) tr. pl., **3**. 39
—, M.: (217) tr. pl., proposes co-dictatorship of M. Minucius, **5**. 285–7; (212) envoy to coss., **6**. 425
Metius: *see* Statius.
Mettius Curtius, Sabine: (753–717) holds Citadel; escapes by Curtian lake, **1**. 45–9, **3**. 373–5
— Fufetius, of Alba: (672–640) dict. of Alba, consults with Tullus Hostilius, **1**. 79–85; yields, 91; aids Veii and Fidenae, 95–9; punished, 101–5
Mevania, in Umbria: (308) **4**. 327
Mezentius, Etruscan king: Aeneas defeats, **1**. 13–5
Micipsa, son of Masinissa: (148) shares in kingdom, **14**. 33, 37; (118) dies, 75
Micythio(n), of Chalcis: (192) leader against Aetolians and Antiochus, **10**. 113–5, 135, 147–9; (170) reports outrages, **13**. 27–9, 33
Midon, of Beroea: (171) general of Perseus, **12**. 471, (168) **13**. 197, 237
Milan: *see* Mediolanium.
Miletus, in Ionia: **11**. 43; (190) obeys C. Livius Salinator, **10**. 335; L. Aemilius Regillus sails past, 339; (188) sacred land restored to, **11**. 133; (170) promises aid against Macedon, **13**. 23
Milionia, city of Marsi: (302) captured, **4**. 369; (294) 485–7
Milionius, of Lavinium: (340) warns his people, **4**. 45
Milo: *see* Annius.
Miltiades, a rhetorician: **14**. 231
Milyas, in Lycia: (189) restored to Eumenes, **10**. 463, (188) **11**. 133
Minatius, Staius, a Samnite: (296) **4**. 435
Mincius riv., in cis-Alpine Gaul: (197) Gauls and Romans camp on, **9**. 245. Prodigy: (214) **6**. 207
Minerva: (460) member of Capitoline triad, **2**. 57, (385) **3**. 249, (217) **5**. 203, (187) **11**. 179; (217) with Neptune in *lectisternium*, **5**. 235; (167) spoil dedicated to, **13**. 361. Shrine of, on Capitoline: (380) **3**. 299, (363) 365–7, (129) **14**. 263, (44) 311. Temple of, at Terracina: (166) **14**. 247. *See* Athena.
Minerva, Promontory of: (181) bounds naval commands, **12**. 61; (172) rites at, 347–9
Minervium, in Italy: (167) **13**. 297
mines (*cunicula*): (435) used in attack on Fidenae, **2**. 329, (396) on Veii, **3**. 69, 73–5, (200) on Abydus, **9**. 51, on Oreus, 135, (191) on Lamia, **10**. 233–5; (216) and counter-mines used at Casilinum, **6**. 61, (189) at Ambracia, **11**. 21–5
Minius: *see* Cerrinus.
Minnio, friend of Antiochus: (193) meets envoys, **10**. 47–9; (190) at Magnesia, 409
Minturnae, in Latium: (340) Latins flee to, **4**. 41, 47; (314) delivered to Rome, 259–61; (296) colony at, 439; (207) forced to submit to levy, **7**. 363; (191) **10**. 163; (88) C. Marius captured near, **14**. 97. Prodigies: (207) **7**. 357–9; (191) **10**. 263; (169) **13**. 47; (133) **14**. 261
Minucia, Vestal: (337) buried alive, **4**. 63
Minucius, M.: (401) tr. pl., **3**. 39
—, M.: (216) tr. pl., proposes bill for bank commissioners, **6**. 73
—, P.: (193) tr. mil., against Boi, **10**. 13
—, Q.: (193) tr. mil., against Boi, **10**. 13; (174) leg., with ships, **12**. 273
— Augurinus, M.: (497) cos., **1**. 285; (491) ii, 331; expells Volsci from Rome, 339–41
— —, P.: (492) cos., **1**. 329–31
— —, Ti.: (305) cos., defeats Samnites, triumphs, **4**. 341–3
— Esquilinus, Q.: (457) cos., **2**. 101–3
— — Augurinus, L.: (458) cos., **2**. 85; blockaded by Aequi, 89; leg. of Cincinnatus, 95–101, **4**. 131; (450) Xvir, **2**. 117; (449) commands against Aequi, 139; (440) pref. annonae, 299; (439) 301, 305; honoured; co-opted tr. pl., 311; accused of death of Sp. Maelius, 311, 325
— Faesus, M.: (300) plebeian augur, **4**. 389

INDEX

Minucius Molliculus, Ti.: (180) pr. pereg., **12**. 107, 109; dies, 115, 117
— Myrtilus, L.: (188) strikes Punic envoys; surrendered, **11**. 145
— Rufus, M., cos. 221: (217) elected mag. eq. for Q. Fabius Maximus, **5**. 227; differs with him, 241, 247–51, 335, **13**. 379; camps near Hannibal, **5**. 253–5; left in command, 261; defeats Hannibal, 281–5, 315; made equal to dict., 285–7, 291; divides army, 293–5; saved by Fabius, 295–9; resumes old rank, 299–303, 307, **8**. 163–5; (216) slain at Cannae, **5**. 363
— —, M.: (197) pr. pereg., **9**. 239; (194–192) IIIvir col. deduc., 553, **10**. 119; (193) envoy to Africa, **9**. 579
— —, M., cos. 110: (109–108) defeats Thracians, **14**. 77
— —, Q., cos. 197: (210) leg. of Ap. Claudius Pulcher, **7**. 127; (201) aed. pl., **9**. 15; (200) pr. for Bruttium, 13, 19, 25; investigates sacrilege at Locri, 37, 41, (199) 155–7; (197) cos. with Italy as prov., 237–41; defeats Gauls, 243–9, 337–9; tribb. pl. prevent triumph, 337–9; triumphs on Alban mt., 339–41; (189) Xvir for Asian settlement, **10**. 461–3, **11**. 123–35, 153, 161, 205, 301; (183) envoy to warn Gauls, 393–5
— —, T.: (171) occupies Gyrton, **12**. 459
— Thermus, L.: (180) leg., reports on Spain, **12**. 107–13, (177) on Histria, 207
— —, Q., cos. 193: (201) tr. pl., prevents recall of P. Scipio (Afr.), **8**. 519; introduces bill for Punic peace, 529; (198) aed. cur., **9**. 239; (197, 194) IIIvir for colonies, 243, 533; (196) pr. for Nearer Spain, 341–3, 347, 393, 445, 461; (195) triumphs, 395, 447; (193) cos., with Liguria as prov., 555–61, **10**. 7–9, 15–7, 29–33; (192) defeats Ligurians, 57–63; (191) 265–9; (190) 295; refused a triumph, 427; (189) Xvir for Asian settlement, 461–3, **11**. 123–35, 153, 161, 205, 301, 307; (188) envoy to Antiochus, 131; Thracians kill, 139, 159, 173
Minurus: (139) murders Viriathus, **14**. 53
Misagenes, son of Masinissa: (171) aids against Perseus, **12**. 375, 483, 499, 505, (169) **13**. 103; (168) ill at Brundisium, 291–3
Misenum, Cape: (214) Hannibal wastes region of, **6**. 215
Mithridates, son of Antiochus: (197) **9**. 331
Mithridates VI of Pontus: (88) victories of, in Cappadocia and Bithynia, **14**. 95, 97; C. Marius, commander against, 95–7; seizes Asia, slaughters citizens, 99, 103; portents appear to, 293–5; defeated on sea, 295; (87) attacks Magnesia, 103; (86) defeated by Sulla, 103; (85) by C. Flavius Fimbria, 105; (84) makes peace, 105, 113; (82) war with, renewed, 109; (75–74) makes treaty with Sertorius; defeats M. Aurelius Cotta, 117; (73) besieges Cyzicus, 301; L. Licinius Lucullus defeats, 117, 119, (72) 121, (69) 123; (68) saved by mutiny, 123; (66–65) Cn. Pompeius drives, to Bosporus, 125; (63) kills self, 125–7, 201; (58) Pompey triumphs over sons of, 129. *See* Machares, Pharnaces.
Mitylenê: (190) triremes of, join Romans, **10**. 325; Roman fleet at, 353; (80) destroyed, **14**. 113. *See* Peraea.
Mitys riv., in Macedon: (169) **13**. 113
Mnasilochus, of Acarnania: (191) supports Antiochus, **10**. 191–5; (190) surrender of, demanded, 425; (188) **11**. 131
Moagetes, of Cibyra: (189) forced to pay tribute, **11**. 45–7
Moeniacoeptus, Gallic chief: (214) in Punic army, **6**. 311–3
Moericus, a Spaniard: (212) admits Romans to Syracuse, **6**. 455–61, **7**. 81–3, 115, 119
Moesia: (29) **14**. 165
Molliculus: *see* Minucius.
Molossis (Molottis), in Epirus: **4**. 93; (198) Philip in, **9**. 189; (167) cities of, surrender, **13**. 335
Moneta: *see* Juno Moneta.
Montani: *see* Epanterii, Salassi.
Monunius, chief of Dardani: (168) **13**. 187
moon: *see* eclipse, lunar.

INDEX

Moors : *see* Mauri.
Mopselus : (171) Perseus camps at, **12**. 483, 495, 503
Mopsii, of Compsa : (216) pro-Roman, **6**. 3
Morcus : (168) Gentius' envoy to Rhodes, **13**. 165
Morzius, of Paphlagonia : (189) with Galatians, **11**. 91
mourning : (216) after Cannae, limited, **5**. 383
Mucian meadows : (508) **1**. 261
Mucianus : *see* Licinius Crassus Dives.
Mucius, C. : (97) procos. in Asia, **14**. 87
– Scaevola, C. : (508) in Etruscan camp, burns hand to show courage, **1**. 255–63
– —, P., cos. 175 : (179) pr. urb. to investigate poisonings, **12**. 139; (175) cos., **14**. 245[1]; defeats Gauls and Ligurians, **12**. 243–5; (169) candidate for cens., **13**. 49
– —, Q. : (215) pr. for Sardinia, **6**. 81, 105, 109–11; ill, 119–21, 137; (214) propr. in Sardinia, 207; (213) 317; (212) 349, **7**. 5; (209) Xvir sac.; dies, 235; (179) two sons of, are prr., **12**. 139
– —, Q., cos. 174 : (179) pr. for Sicily, **12**. 139; (174) cos., 251[3], **13**. 9, **14**. 245[1]; holds levy, **12**. 253; departs for prov., 277; (171) leg. of P. Licinius Crassus, **12**. 443, 473, 505
– —, Q., cos. 95 : (97) procos. in Asia, **14**. 87[6]; (95) cos., 285; (82) pont. max.; C. Marius kills, 109
Mugillanus : *see* Papirius.
muleteers : (358) as cavalry, **3**. 407
Mulvian bridge : (207) **7**. 409
Mummius, L., pr. 177 : (187) tr. pl., vetoes, then permits, investigation of the Scipios, **11**. 189, 191; (177) pr. for Sardinia, **12**. 207; investigates fraudulent citizens, 213–5
–, L. : (146) cos., defeats Achaeans, sacks Corinth, **14**. 41, 45; (145) triumphs, 45; (142) cens., builds Tiber bridge, **12**. 159; distributes Greek art, **14**. 47
–, Q. : (187) tr. pl., vetoes, then permits, investigation of the Scipios, **11**. 189, 191
Munatius, C. : (173) Xvir agr. adsig., **12**. 303
Munatius Plancus, L. : (42) cos., **14**. 315; (43) joins M. Antonius, 151
Munda, in Spain : (214) Punic defeat at, **6**. 309–11; (179) Ti. Sempronius Gracchus storms, **12**. 149; (45) Caesar defeats sons of Pompey at, **14**. 145
Murcia, altar of, in Rome : (640–616) **1**. 121
Murena : *see* Licinius.
Murgantia, in Samnium : (296) P. Decius Mus captures, **4**. 419, 421
Murgantia, Sicilian port : (214) fleet off, **6**. 263
Murgantia (Murgentia), in Sicily : (214) betrayed to Himilco, **6**. 293, 297; Hippocrates returns to, 301; (211) revolts, **7**. 83; reduced, 85
Mus : *see* Decius.
Musca : *see* Sempronius.
Mutila, in Histria : (177) **12**. 221
Mutilum, in cis-Alpine Gaul : (201) C. Ampius near, **9**. 9; (196) L. Furius Purpurio retires from, 377
Mutilus : *see* Papius.
Mutina, in cis-Alpine Gaul : (218) IIIvir agr. adsig. flee to, **5**. 69–71; **7**. 301; Boi and Insubres attack, **5**. 69–71; (193) Boi defeated near, **10**. 11–5; (183) Roman colony at, **11**. 395; (177) Ligurians capture, **12**. 227, 239; (176) recovered, 235; (44) D. Junius Brutus occupies; (43) M. Antonius besieges, **14**. 149; siege raised, 151. Prodigy : (42) 315
mutinies in Roman forces : (342) in Campania, **3**. 495–513; (206) in Spain, **8**. 99–123; (205) at Locri, 241–3, 277; (199) in Macedon, **9**. 161; (180) in Spain, **12**. 109; (74) in army of Lucullus, **14**. 117; (68) 123
Muttines, a Libyphoenician : (212) commands Numidians in Sicily, **6**. 495–9; (211) **7**. 83; (210) betrays Agrigentum, 153, 219; (209) cavalry of, in Sicily, 239; (190) with cos. L. Scipio in Thrace, **11**. 143
Mycenica, in Argos : (197) **9**. 269
Mylae, in Thessaly : (171) **12**. 457–9
Mylas riv., in Sicily : (214) Syracusans turned back from, **6**. 271, 277
Mylassa, in Caria : (188) granted tax exemption, **11**. 133; (167) Rhodes defeats, **13**. 333
Myndus, in Caria : (197) Rhodes pre-

INDEX

serves liberty of, **9**. 335; (190) C. Livius Salinator visits, **10**. 335

Myonnesus, cape near Ephesus: (190) fleet of Antiochus defeated near, **10**. 327, 369–81, 387, 429

Myrina, in Mysia: (196) **9**. 359

Myrtilus: *see* Minucius.

Mysia: (189) restored to Eumenes, **10**. 463–5, **11**. 133; (190) in army of Antiochus, **10**. 407, (171) of Perseus, **12**. 467

Mytilenê: *see* Mitylenê.

Nabis, of Sparta: (205) on Rome's side in treaty with Philip, **8**. 255, **9**. 499; (201) captures Messenê, 503; (200) Philip promises Achaeans aid against, 73–7, 213; (198) endangers Achaeans, 207, 213, 219; (197) receives Argos from Philip, 267–71, 473, 501; allied with Rome, 269–73; returns to Sparta, 273; (195) Flamininus, procos. against, 393, 397, decides to free Argos from, 471–7, and defeats, 477–93; defends self before Flamininus, 495–9, who answers, 499–505; agrees to leave Argos, 505; Greeks give Flamininus power to treat with, 505–11; refuses terms, 511–7; renews war, 517–23; accepts terms, retaining Sparta, 523–7, 543, **10**. 51–5, 103, 363–5, **11**. 207; another account of war with, **9**. 527; peace with, ratified, 529; (194) Flamininus defends policy toward, 543; son of, in triumph, 551; (193) Aetolians seek aid of, **10**. 33–7; Achaeans warn; besieges Gytheum, 37–9; aid from, for Antiochus expected, 53–5; (192) violates terms, 59, 63; besieges Gytheum, raids Achaean fields, 69–71; prepares fleet, 73; Philopoemen defeats, 75–85; shut in Sparta, 85–9, 103; Aetolians assassinate, 101–11, 365

Naevian gate: (508) Etruscans attacked at, **1**. 255. Prodigy: (101) **14**. 279

Naevius, M., tr. pl. 184: (187) accuses Africanus, **11**. 195–7, 383–5

— Balbus, L.: (168) Vvir for dispute of Pisae and Luna, **13**. 287

Naevius Crista, Q.: (214) pref. soc., defeats Macedonians at Apollonia, **6**. 303–7

— Matho, Q., pr. 184: (194) IIIvir for Vibo, **9**. 553, (192) **10**. 119; (184) pr. for Sardinia; investigates poisoning, **11**. 321, 341, 353

nail: *see clavis*.

Naples: *see* Neapolis.

Nar riv., in Central Italy: (299) **4**. 393. Prodigy: (194) **9**. 535

Naraggara, in Africa: (202) **8**. 473. *See* Zama.

Narbo, in Gaul: (27) **14**. 165

Narnia, in Umbria: (299) colony at **4**. 391–3; (209) claims inability to meet levy, **7**. 241–3, 247; (207 opposing Hasdrubal at, considered 383; horsemen of, report victory on Metaurus, 407; (204) required to furnish extra levy, **8**. 263–7 (199) extra colonists for, **9**. 159

Narrows (Stena) in Epirus: (199) **9** 165

Nasica: *see* Caecilius Metellus Piu Scipio, Cornelius Scipio.

Nasos (Insula), in Syracuse: (214 Andranodorus occupies, **6**. 243–9 255; wall of, overthrown, 249 (212) Epicydes on, 435; leader elected for, 455; Romans occupy 457–61, **7**. 81–3

—, in Acarnania: (211) **7**. 95, 97

Natta: *see* Pinarius.

Naupactus, Aetolian port: **7**. 331, **10** 73; (211) M. Valerius Laevinus at **7**. 99–101; (209) Roman fleet at 335–9, (200) Aetolian council at **9**. 85, 119; (194) **10**. 33; (191 Antiochus moves to, 191; compelled to revolt, 239; cos. M' Acilius Glabrio besieges, 245, 251, 277, **11** 287; truce at, **10**. 253–7; (190 siege not renewed, 303–5

Naustathmus, harbour of Phocaea (190) **10**. 383

Nautius, Sp.: (293) leg., feign attack, **4**. 515, 519; honoured, 529

— Rutulus (Rutilus), C.: (475) cos campaigns against Volsci, **1**. 397–9 (458) cos. ii, **2**. 85; defeats Sabines 89, 99–101

— —, C. (or Sp.): (411) cos. **2**. 427

— —, Sp.: (488) cos. **1**. 345–7

— —, Sp.: 424) tr. mil. c. p., **2**. 37

INDEX

Nautius Rutulus, Sp.: (419) tr. mil. c. p., **2**. 403; (416) ii, 411; (404) iii, 455–7
— —, Sp.: (316) cos., remains in Rome, **4**. 245–7
naval antiquities: (311) IIviri nav. elected to equip fleet, **4**. 277 (*see* duumviri navales); (219) strength of navy, **5**. 47–9; (205) **8**. 195; (192) **10**. 69; (172) **12**. 367, 439; (214) siege engines mounted on ships, **6**. 285; (209) **7**. 269; (203) **8**. 397; (198) **9**. 197–9; (214) crews secured at private cost, **6**. 211; (210) **7**. 133–9, **9**. 433; (210) rigging removed before battle, **7**. 147; (191) **10**. 281; (210) training of crews, **7**. 195–7; (192) **10**. 73; (206) trireme and quinquereme compared, **8**. 75, 125, 127; (205) fleet for P. Scipio (Afr.) built in 45 days, 195, 211; (204) its equipment, 307–9; (191) freedmen enrolled for fleet, exemptions denied, **10**. 161–3; ships demanded from naval allies, 275; ships beached and walled in for winter, 285, 321; (190) damaged ships towed from battle, 361; fire carried on prows, 377–9; (178) market established on shore, **12**. 187, 191; (172) old ships reconditioned, freedmen enrolled, 367; (170) sailors quartered in private homes, **13**. 29; (168) ships placed in ship sheds, **12**. 367; **13**. 253–5. Types of ships: *moneres*, **11**. 127; *biremes*, **6**. 303; *triremes*, **7**. 145–7, **8**. 75, etc.; *quadriremes*, **8**. 195, 455, etc.; *quinqueremes*, **5**. 47, 49, etc.; *hexeres*, **8**. 241, **10**. 357, 377; *hepteres*, 357–61, 377; with 16 banks of oars, **9**. 359, **13**. 369; *actuariae*, **5**. 83, **11**. 127; *apertae*, **9**. 65, 219, etc.; *celoces*, **5**. 47, **10**. 369; *cercuri*, **9**. 331; *constratae*, **10**. 133, 277; *hippagogus*, **13**. 181–3; *lembi*, **6**. 303, **9**. 219, etc.; *longae*, **3**. 97, **5**. 47, etc.; *onerariae*, **8**. 197, 307, etc.; *praetoriae*, **8**. 307, **10**. 75, 359–61; *pristes*, **10**. 73, **13**. 181; *rostratae*, **8**. 191, 197, **10**. 277, etc., *speculatoriae*, **8**. 397, **10**. 75, 275, 277; *tectae*, **9**. 197, 219, etc.
navalia: (Augustan age) on the Tiber, **2**. 91
Navius: *see* Attus.
—, Q.: (211) centurion, devises new tactics, **7**. 15–7, 21
Neapolis (Naples): settled from Cumae, **4**. 85; (327) Roman forces near, 91; makes treaty, 105; (319) in Federation, 237; (217) offers 20 golden bowls to Rome, **5**. 309, 321; (216) withstands Hannibal, **6**. 3–5, 45–7, 127; receives refugees from Nuceria, 49; (215) supplies grain, 159; (214) Hannibal plunders lands of, 215, 227; (204) Q. Pleminius goes toward, for exile, **8**. 289; (193) subject to Rome, **10**. 47–9; (191) Roman and allied ships at, 275; (180) Ligurians transported by way of, **12**. 127; (171) fleet sails from, 439
—, quarter of Syracuse: (212) **6**. 439
—, in Thrace: (188) **11**. 141
Nemea, riv. in Greece: (197) **9**. 315
Nemean games: (209) Philip presides at, **7**. 333, 337, 339; (195) renewed after freeing of Argos, **9**. 525
Neocretans: (190) **10**. 409
Neon, of Thebes: (168) flees with Perseus, **13**. 233; (167) beheaded, 357
Nepetê, in Etruria: (396) Etruscans defeated near, **3**. 67; (386) betrayed to Etruscans, recovered, 225–9; (383) colony sent to, 269; (297) envoys from, report on Etruscans, **4**. 407; (210) Campanians sent to, **7**. 131–3; (209) claims inability to meet levy, 241–7; (204) forced to meet extra quota, **8**. 263–7
Nepheris, in Africa: (147) **14**. 37–9
Nepos: *see* Caecilius Metellus.
Neptune: (753–717) Consualia in honour of, **1**. 35; (399) at *lectisternium*, **3**. 49; (217) **5**. 235; (210) P. Scipio (Afr.) bids men follow, **7**. 175; (206) altar of, in Circus, **8**. 47; (93) temple of, at Fregellae, **14**. 287
Neptuniae aquae: (184) **11**. 361
Nequinium (Narnia), in Umbria: (300–299) taken by treachery; Narnia founded on site of, **4**. 391–3
Nero: *see* Claudius.
Nerulum, in Lucania: (317) **4**. 243
Nerva: *see* Cocceius, Licinius.
—, Emperor: **14**. 221
Nervii: (57–56) **14**. 129–31. *See* Avectius, Chumstinctus.

INDEX

Neryllus, L.: (181) books of Numa found on land of, **14**. 9
Nesattium, in Histria: (177) **12**. 219–21
Nessus riv., in Macedon: (167) bounds first Macedonian republic, **13**. 347; Bisaltae live beyond, 351.
New Carthage, in Spain: (221–220) Hannibal winters in, **5**. 13; (219–218) 43, 59, 65, 111; (217) Hasdrubal leaves, 263; region of, plundered, 267; (210) description of, **7**. 165–7; P. Scipio (Afr.) captures, 165–87, 281, 285, 303, **8**. 15, 117, 145, 171; various accounts of capture, **7**. 187–9, 231; Scipio drills men at, 195–7; capture of, belittled by Carthaginians, 197, reported to Senate, 229; (206) Scipio and C. Laelius sail from, **8**. 73–5; Scipio at, 79, 87–9, 97; mutineers from Sucro sent to Scipio in, 105–11; Laelius and L. Marcius Septimus return to, 127; Scipio addresses army at, 129–33; Mago's attack on, fails, 145–7; (180) M. Fulvius Nobilior banished beyond, **12**. 131
nexus: *see* debtor slavery.
Nicaea, wife of Crater: (272) **10**. 73
Nicaea, in Locris: (208–207) Attalus and procos. P. Sulpicius Galba move to, **8**. 21; (197) Philip and procos. Flamininus confer at, **9**. 251, 261
—, town of Massilians: (154) **14**. 15
Nicander, of Aetolia: (193) tries to rouse Philip against Rome, **10**. 35–7; (191) comes from Antiochus; well treated by Philip, 243; (189) praetor of Aetolians, **11**. 3; plunders Acarnania, 15; fails to relieve Ambracia, 17–9
—, a pirate: (190) serves Antiochus, **10**. 321–3
Nicanor, a Macedonian: (197) at Cynoscephalae, **9**. 297
Nicator: *see* Demetrius, Seleucus.
Nicatores: (169) troops of Perseus, **13**. 71
Nicephorium, at Pergamum: (197) Attalus demands that Philip restore, **9**. 253, 259
Nicias, praetor of Achaeans: (208–207) sent by Philip to Aegium **8**. 35
—, minister of Perseus: (169) destroys treasure; killed by Perseus, **13**. 121
Nico Perco, of Tarentum: (212) betrays Tarentum to Hannibal, **6**. 367–77, **7**. 149; (210) commands ship, 149; (209) slain in capture of Tarentum, 273.
Nicodamus, an Aetolian: (189) leads Aetolians into Ambracia, **11**. 17–21
Nicomedes I, of Bithynia: (c. 270) **11**. 53
— II, of Bithynia: (167) brought to Senate by father, Prusias, **13**. 405–11; (149) kills father, becomes king, **14**. 31, 35
— IV, of Bithynia: (89) Rome places, on throne, **14**. 93; (88) Mithridates overthrows, 95; (75–74) makes Rome heir, 117
Nicostratus, Achaean praetor: (197) with Flamininus confers with Nabis; makes truce, **9**. 269–71; at Sicyon, drives out marauding Macedonians, 313–9
Nile riv.: (168) Antiochus crosses, **13**. 151; he demands lands at mouth of, 281; (48–47) boat of Ptolemy XIII sinks in, **14**. 141
Ninnii Celeres, of Capua: (216) entertain Hannibal, **6**. 23
Nisuetae, African tribe: (197) **9**. 325
Nitiobroges, Gallic tribe: (107) **14**. 77–9
nobiles: (217) accused of prolonging Punic war; although plebeian, despise plebs, **5**. 315; oppose *novus homo* as cens., **11**. 351
Nobilior: *see* Fulvius.
Nola, in Campania: (327) garrisons Palaepolis, **4**. 87, causing latter to give self to Rome, 99–105; (313) captured, 271–3; (216) Hannibal fails to take, **6**. 45–9; M. Marcellus defeats Hannibal before, and occupies, 49–57, 153, 499; men of, prevent Marcellus aiding Casilinum, 65; (215) he holds, 109, 135–7, 143–7; with aid from, he defeats Hannibal, 147–57; grain from, sent to army, 159; Marcellus keeps garrison in, 163; (214) commons of, fail in plot to betray city, 215–7; Marcellus defeats Hannibal before, 227–9; Marcellus leaves and returns to, 235–9; 203) Hannibal regrets

INDEX

'growing old before,' **8**. 443; (90) Samnites capture, **14**. 91
Noliba, in Spain: (192) **10**. 65
Nomentana via: (449) **2**. 173
Nomentum, Latin town: (616–578) captured, **1**. 137; (437) Etruscans defeated near, **2**. 361, *cp*. 317; (435) 329, 357; (338) receives citizenship, **4**. 59
Nones: day after, avoided for rites, **3**. 199
Norba, in Latium: (492) colony at, **1**. 331; (342) Privernates raid, **3**. 513; (341) reports revolt of Privernum, **4**. 3; (330) Privernates raid, 75; (209) loyal, **7**. 245–7; (199) Punic hostages removed from, **9**. 159; (198) slave rising at, fails, 233
Norbanus, C.: (83) cos., **14**. 297; Sulla defeats, 107; (81–80) proscribed, kills self, 113
Nortia, Etruscan goddess: annual nails driven in temple of, **3**. 367
nota: (204) of censors, **8**. 351; (184) **11**. 355
Notium, port of Colophon: (190) Antiochus' siege of, fails, **10**. 367–9, 373, 381; (188) tax exempt, **11**. 133
Nova Carthago: *see* New Carthage.
— Classis, in Spain: (217) **5**. 271
— via, in Rome: (616–578) Tanaquil addresses crowd in, **1**. 145; (391) voice in, foretells Gallic sack, **3**. 113; (390) temple to Aius Locutius on, 169, 177
Novellus: *see* Gavillius.
novemdiale sacrum: (672–640) for purification after a shower of stones, **1**. 111; (218) **5**. 187; (215) **6**. 109; (212) 365; (211) **7**. 91; (207) 357–9; (204) **8**. 259; (202) 511; (194) **9**. 535; (193) **10**. 25; (191) 263; (188) **11**. 119, **14**. 239; (186) **11**. 281, **14**. 239; (169) **13**. 149; (102) **14**. 277; (94) 287; (93) 289
Novensiles divi: (340) addressed in *devotio*, **4**. 37
novus homo: (314) *nobiles* lay charges against, **4**. 263; (217) contrasted with *plebeius nobilis*, **5**. 315; (189) *nobiles* oppose a, for censor, **10**. 471; (184) **11**. 351; (101) Marius a, **14**. 83
Nuceria Alfaterna in Campania: (310) fields of, plundered, **4**. 311; (308) captured, 325; (216) Hannibal plunders, **6**. 47–51, 149–51, **7**. 213; (210) men of, settled at Atella, 213. Prodigy: (104) **14**. 275
Numa Marcius: (715–672) pont., **1**. 71
— Pompilius, king of Rome: son of Pompo, **12**. 89; a Sabine, **1**. 63, 125, 127, **2**. 267, 269; character and training of; not a pupil of Pythagoras, **1**. 63–5, **12**. 91; (716) elected king, **1**. 65–7; (715–672) closes temple of Janus, 67–9; establishes laws, rituals, calendar, priesthoods, 67–73, 149, **2**. 269, **14**. 183; dedicates altars and groves, **1**. 73–5; death of, 75; (640) commentaries of, consulted by Tullus Hostilius, 113; (640–616) honoured by Ancus Marcius, his grandson, 113–5, 125; (181) 'books of,' found, **12**. 89–93
Numantia, in Spain: (141) treaty of Q. Pompeius with, repudiated, **14**. 49, 51; (138) defeats M. Popillius Laenas, 53, 57, (137) and C. Hostilius Mancinus, 55, 257, who is surrendered when his treaty is rejected, 57–9, 257; (135) Romans crushed before, 259; P. Scipio Aemilianus elected cos. to end war with, 59; (134–133) he captures, 61, 65, 183, 261
Numicius Priscus, T.: (469) cos., defeats Volsci and Sabines, **1**. 427
Numicus riv., in Latium: **1**. 15
Numida: *see* Aemilius.
Numidia: (213) Syphax of, allied with Rome, **6**. 329–31; (209) Massiva, prince of, captured and freed, **7**. 291–3, **8**. 143; (206) Masinissa, prince of, meets Hannibal, 141–3; (205) a doubtful ally, 171–3; (204) sensuality of, 299, 409–11; Syphax of, allied with Carthage, 297–301; Masinissa fails to secure throne of, 321–37; (203) P. Scipio (Afr.) destroys winter quarters of, 377–85; defeated by Scipio, 389–93, by Laelius and Masinissa, 401–11, 427; Masinissa king of, 421–3; captives from, freed, 427–31; (202) under Vermina, defeated by Scipio, 503; (200) aids Rome against Philip, **9**. 33–5, 57–9, 198) 237; 195) dis-

putes of Carthage and, 403; (193) claims of, to Punic lands, 577–9; (191) grain bought in, **10**. 161–3; (172) Carthage complains of, **12**. 355–7; (171) sends aid against Perseus, 375, 395–7, 483, **13**. 13, 289; (153) raids Punic territory, **14**. 15–7; (118) divided on death of King Micipsa, 75; (112–109) claimed by Massiva, whom Jugurtha kills, 77; (109–108) Q. Caecilius Metellus devastates, 77; (106–105) Jugurtha driven from, 79. *See* Gala, Gulussa, Hierta, Jugurtha, Masinissa, Misagenes, Syphax; Maesulii, Masaesulii, Maurusii.
Numidian cavalry: (204) foremost type in Africa, **8**. 339; (216) two horses used by some, **6**. 97; (193) described, **10**. 31–3; (218) in Punic armies, **5**. 63, 83–5, 133, 137, 141–3, 153, 161–5, 169, (217) 205, 245, 247, 253, 283, (216) 341, 347–51, 357, 367–71, **6**. 5, 17, 43, 89–91, 97–9, (215) 147, (214) 213, 221, 241, (213) 331, (212) 371–3, 409, 467–75, 497–501, (211) **7**. 15, 25, 27–9, 35, 45–7, 83, (210) 145, 153, 205, 219, (209) 285, (208) 317–9, 327, (207) 379, 381, (206) **8**. 49, 57, 143–5, (205) 185, 229, 235, (204) 271, 339, (203) 389, 391, 433, (202) 491–3; (215) in Roman armies, **6**. 157, (211) **7**. 37–9, (209) 239, (207) 365, (203) **8**. 381–3, 391–3, (202) 489, 493, 497, (200) **9**. 35, 57, (193) **10**. 31–3, (190) **11**. 143, (171) **12**. 395–7, 453, 483, 499, 505, (169) **13**. 141, (168) 289
Numisius, C.: (177) pr. for Sicily, **12**. 207
— Circeiensis, L.: (340) praetor of Latium, called to Rome, **4**. 11; encourages Latins, 45
— Tarquiniensis, T.: (167) Xvir for Macedonian settlement, **13**. 299, 339, 345–7, 355
Numistro, in Lucania: (210) **7**. 207–9
Numitor Silvius, king of Alba: father of Rhea; Aumulius expels, **1**. 17; Romulus restores, 21–5
Numitorius, L.: (470) tr. pl., **1**. 415
—, P., tr. pl. 449: (449) great-uncle of Verginia, **2**. 149, 181; son of, summons L. Verginius, 153; displays body of Verginia, 159; leads secession, 169; tr. pl., 181; prosecutes Sp. Oppius, 197
Nunnius, A.: (100) rival of L. Apuleius Saturninus, slain, **14**. 83–5
Nursia, in Sabinum: (205) promises men to P. Scipio (Afr.), **8**. 195. Prodigies: (190) **10**. 299, **14**. 239; (108) 273; (99) 281; (97) 283
Nymphaeum, in Illyricum: (172) Cn. Sicinius near, **12**. 399; (171) P. Licinius Crassus near, 443, 455
Nymphius, of Palaepolis: (326) gives up city to Rome, **4**. 101–5

Oaeneum, city of Penestae: (169) **13**. 69–71
oath: (381) tr. mil. c. p. excused by 'oath on score of health,' **3**. 273; (216) first formal military oath administered by the tribb. mil., **5**. 325. Senatorial action under oath: *see* Senate.
Obba, in Africa: (203) **8**. 389
Oblivion riv., in Spain: (137) **14**. 55, 57
obsecratio: 436) in time of pestilence, **2**. 327
Occius, Q.: (143) leg. of Q. Caecilius Metellus in Spain, **14**. 47[6], 51
Ocean (i.e., the Atlantic): Numidians and Moors live near, **5**. 63, **6**. 15; (218) Hannibal marches from, to Italy, **5**. 127, **6**. 15; (211) Hasdrubal son of Gisgo withdraws to, **7**. 77; (209) Spain toward, loyal to Carthage, 295; (207) Carthaginians retire to, **8**. 3, 9; (206) 53, 69, 159, 181; Mago assembles ships on, 97; C. Laelius sails into, 123; Gades on island in, 131; P. Scipio (Afr.) and L. Marcius Septimus approach, 141; Mago returns toward, 147; he withdraws from, 151; (138) Spain subdued as far as, **14**. 55; (56–54) C. Caesar conquers Veneti beside, and twice crosses, to Britain, 131
Ocriculum, in Umbria: (308) received into friendship, **4**. 331; (217) Q. Fabius Maximus and Cn. Servilius Geminus at, **5**. 237; (203) renews allegiance, **8**. 439
Octavia, sister of Augustus: (40) marries M. Antonius, **14**. 157; (32) divorced, 163; (11) dies, 167

INDEX

Octavius: *see* Julius Caesar, Mamilius.
—, Cn., pr. 205: (206) aed. pl., **8**. 153; (205) pr. for Sardinia, 153–5; captures transports, 199; (204) propr. for fleet, 257, 347; (203) off Sardinia, 371; reaches Promontory of Apollo, 451; (202) P. Scipio (Afr.) orders, to Utica, 501–3; (201) gives over ships, 521–3, 537, **9**. 11; (200) envoy to Africa, 37, 57; (194) IIIvir col. deduc., 535; (192) envoy to Greece, **10**. 65, 89–93, 97–9, 111; (191) sent to support Acarnania, 195
—, Cn., cos. 165: (169) envoy to Greece, **13**. 61–3; (168) Xvir. sac., 149; pr. for fleet, 145–7, 151, 157, 163; brings fleet to Oreüs, 187, 195; on Macedonian coast, 205–7, 241, 259; receives Perseus' surrender, 265–7; (167) translates terms into Greek, 345–7; transports booty to Rome, 363; receives naval triumph, 369, 385, 397; (165) cos., **14**. 247; (162) envoy to Syria, killed, 249
—, Cn.: (87) cos., drives cos. L. Cornelius Cinna from city, **14**. 99; defeats Cinna and Marius; killed by Cinna, 101, 317
—, Cn.: (76) cos., **14**. 299
—, L.: (75) cos., **14**. 301
—, M.: (133) tr. pl., vetoes land law of Ti. Sempronius Gracchus; removed from office, **14**. 63, 317
October: (402) tribb. mil. c. p., take office on 1st of, **3**. 31–3, 41
Odomanticê, in Paeonia: (168) **13**. 257
Odrysae, Thracians: (183) Philip attacks, **11**. 389; expel Macedonians, 391. *See* Cotys.
Oeniadae, in Acarnania: (211) captured by M. Valerius Laevinus; given to Aetolia, **7**. 95, 97; (189) returned to Acarnania, **11**. 37
Oenus riv., in Laconia: (195) **9**. 487
Oeta, Mt., in Thessaly: **10**. 205, 225, 233; (191) M' Acilius Glabrio sacrifices to Hercules on, 245; (190) he leads army over, 305; (174) Perseus crosses, **12**. 257, 263
Oezalces, uncle of Masinissa: (c. 210) brief reign of, over Maesuli, **8**. 321, 325, 327; Mazaetullus marries widow of, 323
Ofella: *see* Lucretius.
Ogulnius, Cn.: (300) tr. pl.; law of, opens priesthoods to plebeians, **4**. 379, 389; (296) aed. cur., dedicates monuments from fines, 445–7
—, M.: (210) buys Etruscan grain, **7**. 213; (196) tr. mil.; Boi kill, **9**. 373
— Gallus, M.: (182) pr. urb., **11**. 397, **12**. 3, 53
— —, Q., cos. 269: (300) tr. pl.; law of, opens priesthoods to plebeians, **4**. 379, 389; (296) aed. cur., dedicates monuments from fines, 445–7
Olbia, in Sardinia: (210) **7**. 227
Olcades, Spanish tribe: (221) **5**. 13–7
Olcinium, in Illyricum: (167) under C. Licinius, **13**. 335; freed and made tax exempt, 337–9
Old plains: *see* Veteres campi.
Old shops: *see* Veteres.
Olonicus: (169) leads Spanish revolt, killed, **13**. 85, 15[2]
Olympia, in Elis: (209) treaty of Rome and Aetolians set up at, **7**. 95; (195 ?) a treaty ratified at, **11**. 111; (167) L. Aemilius Paulus visits, **13**. 343
Olympias: sister of Alexander of Epirus, mother of Alexander the Great, **4**. 11; (326) ashes of Alexander of Epirus sent to, 97–9
Olympias (Gonnocondylum), in Perrhaebia: (185) **11**. 295–7
Olympic festival: (207) at Elis, **8**. 29; (208) L. Manlius Acidinus envoy to, **7**. 351
Olympio: (168) envoy of Gentius, **13**. 165
Olympium, temple of Zeus outside Syracuse: (214) **6**. 281
Olympus, Mt., between Macedon and Thessaly: (169) **13**. 111, 115
— mts., in Galatia: (189) Cn. Manlius Volso drives Galatians from, **11**. 65–81, 85, 91
Onchestus riv., in Thessaly: (197) **9**. 291
Onesimus, a Macedonian: (169) rewarded for aid to Rome, **13**. 141–3
Onomastus, agent of Philip: (184) destroys Maronea, **11**. 325; Rome demands surrender of, 325–7; (182) Philip consults, *re* his sons, **12**. 21
Onusa, in Spain: (218) Hannibal

passes, **5**. 65; (217) Cn. Scipio sacks, 267
Opicernius, L., of Falerii: (186) in Bacchanalian conspiracy, **11**. 269
Opillia: *see* Oppia.
Opimia, a Vestal: (216) punished, **5**. 385
Opimius, L., cos. 121: (125) pr., reduces Fregellae, **14**. 69; (121) cos., 267; slays C. Sempronius Gracchus; (120) acquitted, 73
—, Q.: (154) cos., **14**. 251; subdues Ligurians, 15
— Pansa, L.: (294) qu.; Samnites kill, **4**. 483
Opiter: *see* Verginius.
Opitergini, Gauls: (49) **14**. 137–9
Oppia, or Opillia, a Vestal: (483) punished, **1**. 359, 437
—, Vestia, of Atella: (210) in Capua, prayed for Romans during siege, **7**. 127–9
Oppian law: (195) repealed, **9**. 413–41
Oppius, C.: (449) tr. pl., **2**. 181
—, C.: (215) tr. pl., carries Oppian law on women's dress, **9**. 413
—, M.: (449) tr. mil., commands plebeians on Aventine, **2**. 171
—, Q.: (88) procos. in Syria; Mithridates imprisons, **14**. 99
— Cornicen, Sp.: (450) Xvir, **2**. 117; remains in Rome, 139; aids Ap. Claudius, convenes Senate, 161–3, 167; arrested, kills self, 197–9
— Salinator, L., pr. 191: (197) tr. pl., prevents assignment of Macedon as consular prov., **9**. 239–41; (193) aed. pl., **10**. 67; (192) commands fleet off Sicily, 67, 69; (191) pr. for Sardinia, 69, 159, 161; (190) 297
Ops, temple of. Prodigies: (186) **11**. 281; (148) **14**. 37; (44) 311
Opus, in Locris: (208–207) Attalus sacks; Philip recovers, **8**. 25–9, 33, 35; (197) asks Roman aid, **9**. 249–51
Orange: *see* Arausio.
Orbitanium, in Lucania: (214) **6**. 237
Orchomenus, in Arcadia: (199) **9**. 163–5
Orestes: *see* Aurelius.
Orestis, between Epirus and Macedon: (209) Dardanians hold, **7**. 343; (200) P. Sulpicius Galba attacks, **9**. 117; (196) freed from Macedon, 369; (172) given a garrison. **12**, 403
Oretani, Spanish tribe: (219) Hannibal suppresses revolt of, **5**. 35; (193) attacked by C. Flaminius, **10**. 19–21, (192) by M. Fulvius Nobilior, 65
Oreus, in Euboea: (208–207) Attalus and P. Sulpicius Galba sack, **8**. 21–31; Philip organizes, 35; (200) he asks Achaean garrison for, **9**. 75; Attalus and Roman fleet take, 119, 135–7; (196) freed, 361, 369; (194) garrison withdrawn from, 547–9; (190) P. Scipio (Afr. f.) captured near, **10**. 389–91; (169) supply port for Thessaly and Macedon, **13**. 131–3; (168) 187
Orgessum, in Illyricum: (200) **9**. 79–81
Orgiago (Origiaco, Ortiago): (189) Galatian chief, **11**. 67; wife of, kills centurion, 83–5
Oricum, port of Illyricum: (214) Philip captures; M. Valerius Laevinus recovers, **6**. 303–7; (211) Philip raids toward, **7**. 95; (194) army of Flamininus sails from, **9**. 547–9; (167) L. Aemilius Paulus gathers forces at, **13**. 363–5
Origines by M. Porcius Cato, cited: (195) **9**. 429; (167) **13**. 331
Oriundes riv., in Illyricum: (168) **13**. 191
Oroanda, in Pisidia: (189) envoys of, buy peace from Cn. Manlius Volso, **11**. 61, 157, and report Galatian movements, 65–7; (188) L. Manlius Volso sent to collect from, 123, 131
Oroandes, of Crete: (168) deserts Perseus at Samothrace, **13**. 263–5
Orongis, in Spain: (207) **8**. 9–15
Oropus, in Attica: (167) **13**. 341
Orsua, a Spaniard: (206) slain in duel with cousin, **8**. 89
Orthobula: (174) poisons husband, **12**. 273
Orthosia, in Caria: (167) **13**. 333
Ortiago: *see* Orgiago.
Ortona, in Latium: (481) Aequi attack, **1**. 361; (457) M. Horatius Pulvillus recovers, from Aequi, **2**. 103
Osca in Spain: (195) coins from, **9**. 445–7; (194) 535; (180) **12**. 137
Osci, Samnites: Atellan farce borrowed from, **3**. 363; 296) men

speaking dialect of, used as spies, **4**. 433
Osphagus riv., in Macedon: (200) **9**. 115
Ossa, Mt., in Thessaly: (171) Perseus in foothills of, **12**. 461; (169) M. Popilius Laenas near, **13**. 129
Ostia: (640–616) Ancus Marcius founds, **1**. 123; (492) grain from coast north of, 331; (428) Fidenates banished to, **2**. 355; (340) Antiates raid, **4**. 49; (319) Greek cities south of, in Federation, 237; (217) supplies for Spain sent from, **5**. 237; Cn. Servilius Geminus at, to guard coast, 239; (216) Hiero sends supplies to, 321; Roman fleet at, 385, 387; (215) ships from, sail for Tarentum, **6**. 133; (212) grain shipped from, 419; (208) old ships at, repaired, **7**. 305; (207) exempt from levy, 363; (204) P. Scipio Nasica meets Idaean Mother at, **8**. 261; (191) denied exemption from naval service, **10**. 163; (87) C. Marius sacks, **14**. 101. Prodigies: (209) **7**. 249; (208) 305–7; (199) **9**. 157; (130) **14**. 263; (44) 311
Otacilius Crassus, T., pr. 217, 214: (217) pr. for Sicily and fleet, **5**. 285, 305; vows temple to Mens, 235; (216) command continued, 325; reports Punic danger, 383, **6**. 71; aided by Hiero, 71–3; (215) IIvir for temple of Mens, 107, 113; command continued, 113; raids near Carthage, 141; named for cos. by praerogative century, 197; Q. Fabius Maximus opposes his election, 199–203; (214) pr. ii, for fleet, 203, 207, 211, 213; (213) 317; (212) 349, 463; (211) **7**. 5; named as cos. by praerogative century, 85, 89; dies in Sicily, 89; pontiff and augur, 91, 227; (210) fleet of, given to M. Marcellus, 109
Otho: *see* Roscius.
Ottolobus (Ottolobum) in Thessaly: (200) P. Sulpicius Galba defeats Philip near, **9**. 107–13, 119; (169) Q. Marcius Philippus plans to enter Macedon by, **13**. 97
Oufentina tribus: *see* Ufentina tribus.
ovatio: (211) described, **7**. 81; (410) license permitted during, **2**. 431; (200) granted for victory won under another's *imperium*, **9**. 59–61; (195) 445; (211) granted to general returning without army, **7**. 81; (185) **11**. 309; (461) granted for minor victory, **2**. 35; (421) 395; *et saepe*.
Ovile, voting enclosure: (211) **7**. 87
Oxeae, is. opposite Cephallania: (208–207) **8**. 31

Paccius: (209) Bruttian envoy, **7**. 267
—, Ovius: (293) celebrates Samnite ritual, **4**. 507
Pachynum, Sicilian cape: (214) Punic fleet off, **6**. 263, 287; Ap. Claudius Pulcher meets troops at, 291; (212) Bomilcar held at, 447–9; (191) boundary of naval commands, **10**. 161
Pacula (Paculla): *see* Annia, Cluvia.
Paculus (Pacilus): *see* Furius.
Pacuvius: *see* Calavius.
Padua: *see* Patavium.
Paeligni, in Central Italy: (343) Latins attack, **3**. 495, **4**. 15; (340) Romans cross, 21; (325) hostile if Vestini are molested, 111; (319) members of Federation, 237; (308) defeated, 325; (304) obtain alliance, 349; (295) attack Samnites after Sentinum, 475, 479; (217) Hannibal plunders, **5**. 229, 261; (212) in attack on Hanno's camp, **6**. 393–5; (211) Hannibal crosses, **7**. 41–3; (205) in fleet of P. Scipio (Afr.), **8**. 195; (177) many move to Fregellae, **12**. 209; (168) at Pydna, **13**. 225, 229, 231; (91) rebel, **14**. 89; (90) defeated, 91; (89) surrender, 95
Paeonia, in Macedon: (c. 300) Gauls cross, **11**. 59; (197) Philip defeats Dardani in, **9**. 329, (183) founds, Perseis in, **11**. 391, (182) moves people into, **12**. 7–9, (181) and calls army to, 65–7; Didas governs, 69, 73; Demetrius plans flight through, 73, 75, is sent to, 77; (171) in army of Perseus, 449; (168) Perseus orders Gauls into, **13**. 175; (167) in 2nd and 3rd Macedonian republics, 349–51. *See* Didas.
Paestum (Posidonia): (332) Alexander of Epirus leaves, **4**. 69; (273)

colony at, 551; (216) offers Rome gold, **5**. 321; (210) supplies ships, **7**. 147; (209) loyal, 245–7
Paetinus: *see* Fulvius.
Paetus: *see* Aelius, Autronius, Fulvius.
pages, royal, of Perseus: (168) **13**. 233; surrender, 265
painting: (214) mural, in temple of Liberty, **6**. 227
Palaepharsalus, in Thessaly: (198) Philip destroys, **9**. 189; (169) A. Hostilius Mancinus camps at, **13**. 91
Palaepolis, near Naples: from Cumae, **4**. 85–7; (328–327) offends Romans; Nolani and Samnites occupy, 87; Romans near, 91; (326) surrenders to escape own allies, 99–105; government of, transferred to Neapolis (Naples), 105
Palatina tribus: (220) freedmen in, **4**. 561
Palatine hill: origin of name, **1**. 21; Romulus seeks augury on, 25, 45, fortifies, 27; Sabines drive Romans to, 45–7; original Romans occupy, 119; (640–616) settlement between Aventine and, 121; (508) center of city, 249; (330–329) Meadows of Vaccus on, **4**. 75, 81; (204) Idaean Mother taken to temple of Victory on, **8**. 261–3, **10**. 261; contract let for temple of Mother on, **8**. 351. Prodigies: (202) 511; (163) **14**. 249
Palenses, of Cephallania: (189) **11**. 97
Palinurus, on Samos: (190) **10**. 321
Palisade, in Tempê: (169) **13**. 109
Palladium: in temple of Vesta, **3**. 175[2]
Pallanteum, in Arcadia: **1**. 21
Pallantium: old name of Palatine, **1**. 21
Pallenê, cape of Chalcidicê: (316) Cassander founds Cassandrea on, **13**. 125; (200) Attalus sails for, **9**. 133; (169) C. Marcius Figulus meets Eumenes on, **13**. 123; (167) a fertile land, 351
Pallor: (672–640) temple to, vowed, **1**. 99
palms: (293) first given at Roman games, **4**. 541
Palpud: *see* Pulpud.
Palumbinum, in Samnium: (293) **4**. 533
Pamphilidas, Rhodian admiral: 190) in defeat of Hannibal off Sida, **10**. 355–63
Pamphylia, in Asia Minor: Taurus mts. divide, **11**. 135; (196) Antiochus delayed in, **9**. 387; (192) men of, in Antiochus' forces, **10**. 139, (190) 409; Rhodians defeat Hannibal off, 355–61, **13**. 319; (189) Cn. Manlius Volso enters, grants peace for a price, **11**. 43, 49; (188) Antiochus sends supplies to Volso in, 123; Eumenes and Antiochus dispute over, 135; (169) grant of friendship renewed, **13**. 133–5
Pan, Lycaean: Lupercalia in honour of, **1**. 21
Panaetolian council: (200) hears envoys of Macedon, Athens, and Rome, **9**. 83–97; has power of war and peace, 97; (192) hears advocates of Antiochus and Rome, **10**. 95–7
Pandosia, in Bruttium: (326) Alexander of Epirus killed at, **4**. 93–9; (204) submits to Rome, **8**. 357
—, in Epirus: (before 330) **4**. 93
Panic: (672–640) temple vowed to, **1**. 99
Pannonia: (35) subdued by Octavius, **14**. 161, (11–10) by Tiberius, 167
Panormus (Panhormus), on Samos: (190) Polyxenidas defeats Pausistratus off, **10**. 319–25, 373, 377
—, in Sicily: (214) legion brought to, **6**. 291; (205) fleet of P. Scipio (Afr.) at, **8**. 211
Pansa: *see* Apuleius, Titinius, Vibius.
Pantaleon, of Aetolia: (172) defends Eumenes, **12**. 337
Pantauchus, of Macedon: (172) hostage, **12**. 409; (168) Perseus' envoy to Gentius, **13**. 163–5, 179, 189–91; brings news of Gentius' defeat, 203; surrenders to L. Aemilius Paulus, 237
panthers: (186) in votive games, **11**. 281
Paphlagonia: Eneti expelled from, **1**. 9
Papinus, Mt., in Gaul: (168) **13**. 283
Papiria tribus: (323) hostile to Pollian tribe, **4**. 145
Papirius, L.: (326) money lender, **4**. 109
—, M.: (390) senator, killed by Gauls, **3**. 143

INDEX

Papirius, M.: (352) Vvir on debt, **3.** 429
—, P.: (380) tr. mil. c. p., **3.** 289
—, Sp.: (293) discloses trickery of the *pullarii*, **4.** 515; rewarded for bravery, 529
— Atratinus, M.: (411) cos., **2.** 427
— Carbo, C.: (168) pr. for Sardinia, **13.** 145–7, and pr. pereg., 285, 287
— —, C., cos. 120: (131) tr. pl., fails to secure law for re-election of tribb. pl., **14.** 67; (130) IIIvir agr. divid., 67–9
— —, Cn.: (113) cos., **14.** 271; Cimbri rout, 75
— —, Cn., cos. 85, 84, 82: (87) officer of Marius, **14.** 101; (84) cos. ii; sole cons., prevents peace, 105; secures SC. disbanding all armies, 107; (82) cos. iii, 173; Sulla drives, from Italy, 109; Pompey puts, to death, 111
— Crassus, C.: (384) tr. mil. c. p., **3.** 255
— —, L.: (436) cos., attacks Veientes and Falisci, **2.** 325; (430) cos. ii, proposes limiting fines, 353–5
— —, L.: (368) tr. mil. c. p., **3.** 327
— —, L., cos. 336, 330: (340) pr.; dictator, **4.** 49; (336) cos., 63; (330) ii, 73; defeats Privernum, 75; holds elections, 77–9; (325) pref. urb. under dict., 139
— —, L., cens. 318: (332) pr., proposes partial franchise for Acerra, **4.** 71
— —, M.: (441) cos., **2.** 297
— —, M.: (332) dict., **4.** 69
— —, Sp.: (382) tr. mil. c. p., defeats Velitrae, **3.** 271–3
— Cursor, L.: (393) cens., has *suffectus* elected when colleague dies, **4.** 297, **3.** 109–11; (387) tr. mil. c. p., **3.** 211; (385) ii, 231
— —, L., cos. 326, 320, 319, 315, 313: (340) mag. eq., **4.** 49; (326) cos., 93; (325) dict. against Samnites, 113; punishes mag. eq. for victory won against orders, 115–37, 369; defeats Samnites, grants peace, triumphs, 139–43; (320) cos. ii, 189; defeats Samnites, takes Luceria, 207–19; possibly mag. eq. in this campaign, 219; (319) cos. iii, 219–21; takes Satricum, triumphs, 221–3; (315) cos. iv, 247[1]; (313) v, 271; (310) dict., defeats Samnites, triumphs, 313–23; vows temple to Quirinus, 537; character and fame, 223–5, 227–9, 505, 511, **5.** 249; father of L., cos. 293, **4.** 505, 537
Papirius Cursor, L., cos. 293, 272: (299) aed. cur., **4.** 391; (293) cos., 505; defeats Samnites, 509–25; presents decorations, 529; takes Saepinum, 531, 535; triumphs; gives spoil to treasury, 535–7; dedicates temple to Quirinus vowed by father, 537; holds elections, 541; (292) pr., 541; (272) cos. ii, **6.** 204
— Maso, C.: (218) IIIvir agr. adsig., driven to Mutina by Boi, **5.** 69–71; (213) Xvir sac.; dies, **6.** 345
— —, C.: (213) pont.; dies, **6.** 345
— —, L.: (176) pr. urb., **12.** 227, 229–31
— Mugillanus, L.: (444) cos. suf., **2.** 283; (443) one of first cens., 287; (427) cos. ii, 357; (422) tr. mil. c. p., 391; (421) interrex, 397–9
— —, L.: (382) tr. mil. c. p., **3.** 271
— — (or Cursor), L.: (326) cos., **4.** 93; battles Samnites, 99; (319) cos. ii, 219–21
— —, M.: (418) tr. mil. c. p., **2.** 405; quarrels with colleagues; Aequi defeat, 405–7; (416) tr. mil. c. p. ii, 411
— Turdus, C.: (178) tr. pl., attacks A. Manlius Volso, **12.** 199–201, 205
Papius Brutulus, Samnite: (322) breaks truce, kills self, **4.** 155
— Mutilus, Samnite: (81) proscribed, kills self, **14.** 113
Papus: *see* Aemilius.
Parachelois, in Athamania: (185) **11.** 297
Parilia: (182) **12.** 5
Parma: (183) Roman colony, **11.** 395; (176) C. Claudius Pulcher at, **12.** 237
Parmenio: (168) Gentius' envoy to Rhodes, **13.** 165
Parnassus, Mt., in Phocis: (172) **12.** 337–9
Paroreia, in Thrace: (189) road to, fixed as Macedonian boundary, **11.** 303; (171) Paeonians from, in Perseus' army, **12.** 449
Paros, one of Cyclades: (200) Philip

holds, **9**. 49, 91; (196) given to Athens, 361
Parrus: *see* Aebutius.
Parthenius, Mt., in Arcadia: (195) **9**. 483
Parthia: Macedonians in, degenerate, **11**. 59; (130–129) slay Antiochus VII of Syria, **14**. 67, 263; (92) seek friendship, 87; (66) 125; at war with Armenia, 125; (55) assigned to M. Licinius Crassus, 131; (53) he fights against portents, is slain, 133, 305; (51) C. Cassius Longinus defeats, 135; (40–38) invade Syria; are driven out, 157–9; (36) repulse M. Antonius, 161; (20) restore standards of Crassus and Antony, 167; typical enemies, **4**. 233. *See* Arsaces, Phraates.
Parthini, in Illyricum: (205) roused against Philip, **8**. 251; fall to Rome in treaty, 253; (196) taken from Philip, given to Pleuratus, **9**. 371; (169) give hostages, **13**. 75; Roman army winters among, 83; (168) in Roman forces, 189
Passaron, in Epirus: (167) surrenders to L. Anicius Gallus, **13**. 335–7; he winters there, 339; L. Aemilius Paulus comes to, 363
Patara, in Lycia: (196) Antiochus at, **9**. 387; (190) Romans advised to win, **10**. 335; withstands C. Livius Salinator, 335–9, and L. Aemilius Regillus, 339–41; Rhodian fleet at, 361–7; Polyxenidas brings Antiochus' fleet to, 421; (188) Antiochus' ships destroyed at, by terms of treaty, **11**. 131
Patavium, in Venetia: (302) drives out Cleonymus, **4**. 365–7; (175) M. Aemilius Lepidus checks revolt of, **12**. 277; (48) victory of Caesar announced at, on day of battle, **14**. 207–9, 307
pater patratus: (672–640) role in making peace, **1**. 83–5, (640–616) and war, 117–9
Paterculus: *see* Albinus,
Patrae, in Achaia: (208) Aetolians cross to, **7**. 331; (192) Philopoemen escapes to, **10**. 75; (191) tr. mil. M. Porcius Cato at, 223; (189) Achaean ships at, **11**. 21; slingers from, 99. *See* Tiso.
patres: *see* patricians, Senate.
patres conscripti: (509) origin of term **1**. 221; (494) term of address to Senate, 309–11; *et saepe*.
patria potestas: 140) father tries son, **14**. 49, 51
patricians: (753) origin of name, **1**. 33; (672–640) Albans and (505–503) Sabines become, by royal appointment or by co-option, 107, 271, **2**. 271, **4**. 387; (509) claim sole control of offices and auspices, **2**. 259–61, 269, (368) **3**. 345, (362) 375, (300) **4**. 387; (493) ineligible for tribb. pl., **1**. 325, **2**. 339; (488) Coriolanus spares lands of, **1**. 345; (471) removed from *comitia tributa*, 421; (467) oppose distribution of land, **2**. 3; (448) two, co-opted as tribb. pl., 219; use violence against tribb. pl., 221–3; (450) marriage with plebeians forbidden, 269–71, **4**. 293; (445) marriage with plebeians permitted, **2**. 257–77; proposal that coss. need not be, 257; tribb. mil. c. p. to be either plebeian or, 277; (445–399) all tribb. mil. c. p. are, **3**. 45; (444) elect interrex, **2**. 281; (421) 397; (395) oppose colonization of Veii, **3**. 85–7; (385) M. Manlius Capitolinus first, to be demagogue, 233; charged with concealing Gallic gold, 243; (384) forbidden to live on Citadel or Capitol, 267; (377) seem to regain control of tribb. mil. c. p., 313; (377–367) oppose Licinian-Sextian laws, 313–49; (370) only five Xviri sac. to be, 327; (367) only one cos. to be, 325, 349, 357; praetor and aed. cur. to be, 351, 357; (355) two coss. from, 415; (354) 419; (353) 421; (351) 431; (349) 439; (343) 455; (300) vainly oppose admission of plebeians to priesthoods, **4**. 379–89; (296) try to elect both coss., 413–5; (296) shrine of Patricia Pudicitia open only to matrons of, 443–5; (209) legality of transfer from, to plebeians, **7**. 301[1]; (203) **8**. 439
Patrocles, of Antigonea: (171) commander of Perseus, **12**. 471
patrons, of colony: (317) make laws for colony, **4**. 243
patrum auctoritas: see *auctoritas patrum*.

INDEX

Paullulus: *see* Postumius Albinus.
Paulus: *see* Aemilius, — Lepidus, Fabius.
Pausanias, of Epirus: (198) brings together Philip and Flamininus, **9**. 181
—, of Pherae: (191) sent to Antiochus, **10**. 183
Pausistratus, Rhodian praetor: (197) defeats Macedonians, **9**. 323–7; (191) commands Rhodian ships, **10**. 285, (190) 315; deceived and defeated by Polyxenidas, 317–27
Pavor: (647–640) shrine to, **1**. 99
payment for military service: (424) proposed, **2**. 375; (406) granted; special tax levied, 451–5, **3**. 5, 9, 13; change in formation and equipment caused by, **4**. 31; (403) relation of, to year round service, **3**. 11–3; (401) difficulty in finding funds for, 35; (400) triple pay for cavalry, 45–7; (394) money for, exacted by terms of surrender, 97; (391) 113; (293) booty not used for, but deposited in treasury, **4**. 537
peace, methods of making: (672–640) **1**. 83–5; (205) **8**. 253–5; (201) 529–33; (197–196) **9**. 305–13, 343–5, 359–61, 367–71; (194) 529; (190–189) **10**. 345–7, 421–7, 461; (141) **14**. 49
Pedanius, T.: (212) heroism of, **6**. 393–5
Pedasa, in Caria: (196) **9**. 359
Pedum, in Latium: (488) Coriolanus takes, **1**. 345; (358) Gauls near, **3**. 395; (339–338) taken, **4**. 51–5; receives franchise, 59
Pelagonia, in Macedon: **11**. 391; (211) Philip crosses, **7**. 97; (200) Perseus holds passes of, **9**. 83, 99–103; P. Sulpicius Galba brings grain from, 113–5; (167) in 4th Macedonian republic, **13**. 349, 353
Pelium, in land of Dassaretii: (200) **9**. 117
Pella, in Macedon: described, **13**. 241; (211) Philip winters in, **7**. 95, 99; (190) Ti. Sempronius Gracchus visits, **10**. 311; (172) chief city of Perseus, **12**. 415; (171) 447, 503; (169) royal treasury at, **13**. 107, 121, (168) 165, 173, 179, 241; Perseus flees to, 231–3; surrenders to L. Aemilius Paulus, 237, 241–3; (167) capital of 3d Macedonian republic, 349, 353; booty from; Paulus camps near, 363
Pellaeum, near Pella: (167) **13**. 363
Pellenê, in Achaia: (197) **9**. 313–7. *See* Pisias, Timocrates.
Pellinaeum, in Thessaly: (191) occupied by Athamanes, **10**. 187; recovered, 197–9
Peloponnesus: (753) Evander an exile from, **1**. 29; (200) Philip controls, **9**. 23; he seeks hostages from, 75; (196) cities of, restored to Achaeans, 369; (195) Nabis a threat to, 397; cities of, except Argos, freed, 473; Aetolian threat to, 477; (193) Achaeans lord it in, **10**. 35; natural area for Achaean league, 251; (184) **11**. 337; (189) M. Fulvius Nobilior comes to, 101–7; (184) commissioners sent to, 323, 329; (183) all, to remain in Achaean league; Q. Marcius Philipus sent to, 373; (174) Perseus seeks admission to, **12**. 265; (172) envoys try to rally, against Perseus, 401–3, 425; (169) decree of Senate read in cities of, **13**. 61; many in, charged with Macedonian sympathy, 355. *Also*: **9**. 205, 217–9, **10**. 169, 205, 245, 275, 303, 451, **11**. 333, 387, **12**. 307. *See* Achaeans, Argos, Lacedaemon, Nabis.
Pelops, king of Sparta: alliance with, **9**. 499
peltasts (*caetrati*): (200) in Philip's army, **9**. 105; (197) 285, 297
Pelusium, in Egypt: (168) Antiochus IV wins victory at, **13**. 151; he claims, 279–81
Penates, of Alba: (672–640) abandoned, **1**. 105
—, of Capua: (212) Romans attack, **6**. 413
—, of Rome: (167) portents in temple of, on Velia, **13**. 297; (165) **14**. 247
Penestae, Illyrian tribe: (169) Perseus occupies cities of, **13**. 65–9, 73–5; Romans take hostages from, 75; in Macedonian army, 83, 127
Peneüs riv., in Thessaly: (198) Flamininus marches to, **9**. 195; (172) conference with Perseus at, **12**. 405–21; (171) P. Licinius Crassus camps near, 463; Romans retreat

across, 477–83; (169) increases difficulty of Tempê, **13**. 109; (167) bounds 3d Macedonian republic, 349
Pennus: *see* Junius.
Pentri, Samnite tribe: (311) capital of, taken, **4**. 281; (216) loyal, **5**. 409
Peparethus is., off Thessaly: (207) Philip sends men to, **8**. 19, 21; Attalus and procos. P. Sulpicius Galba move from, 21; (200) Philip destroys, **9**. 83
Pera: *see* Junius.
Peraea, opposite Rhodes: (197) return of, demanded by Rhodes, **9**. 255, and promised by Philip, 259–61; Rhodes recovers, 323–9, (190) and defends, **10**. 355
—, colony of Mitylenê: (190) Antiochus attacks, **10**. 353
Perco: *see* Nico Perco.
perduellio (treason): (672–640) trial for, **1**. 93; 103–5; (486–485) 355; (384) **3**. 263–7; (211) **7**. 7–15; (169) **13**. 59–61
Perga, in Pamphylia: (188) **11**. 123
Pergamum: (263) kingdom established, **12**. 305, **13**. 307; (205) envoys come to, for Great Mother, **8**. 247; (200) Philip raids, **9**. 135; (197) Attalus I dies in, 335; (193) envoys to Antiochus visit Eumenes II at, **10**. 39–41, 45–7; (190) Antiochus attacks, 343–7, 449; Achaeans raise siege of, 347–51; (172) Eumenes returns to, **12**. 343; called a danger to Greece by Perseus, 419; (171) Philetaerus left at, 463; (169) Eumenes returns to, **13**. 131; (167) Eumenes ill at, 367; (133) Attalus III leaves, to Rome, **14**. 63, 263; (131) Aristonicus seizes, 65; (85) C. Flavius Fimbria captures, 105; (48) timbrels in, tell of Pompey's death, 307. *See* Attalus, Eumenes.
Perinthus, in Thrace: (197) Rhodians ask return of, to Byzantium, **9**. 255; (196) Philip agrees to withdraw from, 359
Perpenna (Perperna), M.: (168) envoy to Gentius, imprisoned, **13**. 179, 189; freed, 195
—, M.: (130) cos., **14**. 261; defeats Aristonicus, 65
—, M.: (92) cos., **14**. 289
— Vento, M., pr. 82: (76) officer of Sertorius, sent against Cn. Pompey, **14**. 191–3; (75) Q. Caecilius Metellus defeats, 115; (72) murders Sertorius; Pompey executes, 119
Perranthes, hill above Ambracia: (189) **11**. 13
Perrhaebia: pass into Thessaly, **10**. 203, **13**. 177, 207; people of Atrax came from, **9**. 195; (200) Aetolians and Athamanes raid, 119–21; (196) Flamininus frees, 365, 369; (191) Aetolians enter, **10**. 187; Philip recovers some cities of, 195–7, 253, 255; (185) controversy over these cities, **11**. 289–99, 303–5, (184) 323; (173) civil discord in, **12**. 305–7; (172) Perseus promises to abolish debt in, 331; (171) Perseus takes, 397, 457; P. Licinius Crassus recovers, 505; (169) Q. Marcius Philippus enters, **13**. 95; (168) L. Aemilius Paulus plans to occupy passes into, 207
Perseis, in Paeonia: (183) Philip founds, **11**. 391
Persephonê: *see* Proserpina.
Perses, of Macedon: *see* Perseus.
Perseus: (211) holds Thermopylae for Philip, **7**. 97
—, son of Philip: (213–212) born of uncertain parentage, **11**. 387, **12**. 17, 27; (200) occupies passes into Pelagonia, **9**. 83, 99–103; (189) fails to recover Amphilochia from Aetolians, **11**. 19–21, 33; (185) basic causes of war with, 285–309; (183) hostility of, toward brother, Demetrius, 387–9; city Perseis named for, 391; (182) quarrels with Demetrius; nourishes Philip's hatred for Demetrius and for Rome, **12**. 13–53, 65, 69, 261–3; (181) climbs Mt. Haemus with Philip, 67; attacks Petra, 73; secures Demetrius' death, 75–7, 305, **13**. 93, 309; receives Thracian hostages, **12**. 77; (179) Philip discovers guilt of, and plans to disinherit, 165–71; plots Philip's death, **13**. 93; seizes power on Philip's death, **12**. 171; executes Antigonus, son of Echecrates, 177; (178) accepted by Rome, 267, **13**. 271; (175) denies rousing Bastarnae, **12**. 245, 263; (174) sends envoys to Carthage, 255–7; accumulates trea-

sure for war, 327, **13**. 391; enters Greece with armed force, **12**. 257–9, 263, 329–31, 397, 411, 417, **13**. 317; makes treaty with Boeotians, **12**. 325, 403–5, 411, 417–9, 421–3; vainly seeks friendship with Achaia, 259–71, 327; Aetolians seek aid of, 327, 411, 417; aids Byzantines, 329, 411, 417; (173) warlike acts of, reported in Rome, 297; Greeks prefer, to Eumenes, 303–5; reputed murderer of wife, 305; envoys sent to, 309; (172) war with, expected, 321; charges of Eumenes against, 307–9, 321–31, 343, 419; married to daughter of Seleucus, 325; envoys of Rhodes and of, provoke Senate, 331–5; plots murder of Eumenes, 335–9, 343, 373, 411, 413, 437; plots of, revealed by Rammius of Brundisium, 339–43, 413; declared an enemy but war postponed, 343–7, 359–63; basic causes of war with, **11**. 285–309; Gentius supports, **12**. 365; tries to win Roman allies in East, 365–7; preparations for war with, 367–9; attitude of eastern kings toward, 373–7; commons in Greek states favour, 377–9; envoys try to rouse Greeks against, 399–405; confers with envoys, 405–19; sends envoys to Rome, 421, 429; Boeotian league rejects alliance with, 421–5, 431–3; envoys to Asia win support against, 427–9; sends envoys to Byzantium, 429; Rhodes refuses aid to, 429–31; occupation of Larisa by, anticipated, 437; (171) war against, declared, 379–81, and troops provided, 381–95; envoys of, are ordered from Italy, 397–9, 437–9; P. Licinius Crassus sets out against, 441–3; makes active preparations for war, 443–57; advances, 457–61, 465; defeats Crassus at Callinicus, 467–81; offers terms which are rejected, 483–7; supporters of, defeated in Boeotia, 489–91; fails in attacks on Romans from Sycurium, 487, 493–5, and Mopselus, 495–503; retreats to Pella and Thessalonica, 503; sends Cotys to Thrace, 503; (170) Lampsacus abandons, **13**. 23–5; Cretan archers in army of, 27; services of Chalcis against, 27–9; war with, fought for freedom of Greece, 31; holds Uscana, 35; successes of, reported to Senate, 39–41; (169) takes points on Illyrian borders, 63–71; sends envoys to Gentius, 71–3; returns to Macedon, 75; fails to take Stratus, 77–81; refuses money to Gentius, 73, 83, 173, 179, and Gauls, 173–9; sends garrison to Cassandrea, 83, 125; gains successes in Thrace, Dardania, and Illyricum, 85; Q. Marcius Philippus sets out against, 91–5; occupies passes from Thessaly, 95–7; camps at Dium, 97; fails to check Philippus, 97–107, 139–41; withdraws to Pydna, 107–13; reoccupies Dium, camps on Elpeus, 115; puts ministers to death, 121; sends aid to Meliboea and Demetrias; negotiations with Eumenes rumoured, 131; Agassae returns to, 339; Prusias pleads cause of, 135; Rhodians urge peace with, 135–7, 323, 327, but are rebuked, 139; (168) holds Pieria, avoids battle, 153–5; secures alliance with Gentius, 163–5, 173, 179, 185, 189; wins support from Rhodes, 165–7, 185–7; seeks aid of Eumenes and Antiochus, 167–9; refuses Eumenes' offer to negotiate for a price, 169–73; miserly character of, 73, 173–9; fleet of, in the Cyclades, 179–85; skirmishes with L. Aemilius Paulus, 187, 195–7, 203–11; delays battle, 217, 225; Paulus defeats, at Pydna, **4**. 241, **10**. 469, **13**. 225–33, 395, **14**. 41, 245; flees to Pella, then Amphipolis, **13**. 231, 233; sends envoys to Paulus; seeks aid of Bisaltae, 237; goes to Samothrace, 239, 243, losing treasure, 391; defeat of, known in Rome, 249–53; Rhodian peace efforts called aid to, 255–7; sends envoys to Paulus, 257–9; kills Evander the Cretan, 261–3; surrenders to Cn. Octavius, 263–7, 395; sent to Paulus, 267–71, 287; Rhodians decree death for any who have aided, 277; aid of Masinissa against, 289–93; offerings *ad omnia pulvinaria* for victory over, 299; Eumenes not faithful to, 305;

Rhodians seek pardon for aid to, 311, 317–31; supporters of, in Greek states, 335–43, 355–7, 363; meets Paulus in Apollonia; children of, in Amphipolis, 345; kingdom of, divided; subjects of, freed, 347–51; Illyrians attacked for aid to, 363; brought to Rome with children, 367, for triumph, 379, 383, 385, 389; after opposition, Paulus triumphs over, 369–93, 397, 401, and celebrates games, **14**. 41; Octavius granted naval triumph over, **13**. 369, 397; sent to Alba, 397–9; Cotys pardoned for aid to, 399; Prusias congratulates Rome on victory over, 405; (160) Paulus, conqueror of, dies, **14**. 13; (153) Andriscus claims to be son of, 17, 27–9, 31

Persians: (480) demand surrender of Sparta, **10**. 53; fight Spartans at Thermopylae, 205–7; (449) Athenian treaty with, **9**. 331; (336–324) Alexander defeats, **13**. 273; his men adopt customs of, **4**. 231; unwarlike nature of, 237–9

Persius, C.: (210) leads raids from Tarentum, **7**. 151

Perusia, in Etruria: (310) Q. Fabius Maximus defeats Etruscans near; granted truce, **4**. 309; breaks truce; Fabius defeats, 323; (295) defeated by Cn. Fulvius Maximus, 475, by Fabius, 477; (294) makes 40 yr. truce, 501; (216) cohort from, at Casilinum, **6**. 59, 69; (205) promises supplies to P. Scipio (Afr.), **8**. 193; (40) Octavius defeats L. Antonius at, **14**. 157. Prodigy: (106) 273

Pessinus, in Phrygia: (205) Great Mother brought from, **8**. 245–9, **9**. 421; (189) Galli from, **11**. 63–5

pestilence: frequent, in Rome, **14**. 227; (672–640) in Rome, **1**. 111; (466) **2**. 5; (463–462) 21–7; (453) 107; (436–435) 325–7; (433) 335; (428) 355; (412) 427; (399) **3**. 47, 51; (392) 109; (390) among Gauls in Rome, 161; (384–383) in Rome, 267–9; (365–364) 359; (348) 449; (332–331) **4**. 69–73; (328) 87; (295) 479; (293–291) 541–3, 547; (212) in army, **6**. 443–5; (208) in Rome, **7**. 307; (205) in army, **8**. 199, 243–5; (190) in fleet off Asia, **10**. 355; (187) in Rome, **11**. 153; (181–180) **12**. 61–3, 115–7, 133, **14**. 241; (178) **12**. 199; (175–174) 253–5, **14**. 245; (165) 247; (142) 255; at Luna, 255; (125) in Africa, 69, 265

Petelia, in Bruttium: (216) resists Carthaginians, **6**. 69–71; Himilco takes, 101; (208) Romans ambushed near, **7**. 317

Peteline grove, outside Rome: (384) trial of M. Manlius Capitolinus in, **3**. 267; (342) *populus* meets in, 511

Peticus: *see* Sulpicius.

Petilius, L.: (181) 'books of Numa' found on land of, **12**. 89–93; **14**. 9[1]

—, L.: (168) envoy to Gentius, imprisoned, **13**. 179, 189; released, 195

—, Q.: (187) tr. pl., with Q. Petilius Spurinus accuses the Scipios, **11**. 175–85, 195–7; secures law for financial accounting, 187–91, 209, 235

— Spurinus, Q., cos. 176: (187) tr. pl., with Q. Petilius accuses the Scipios, **11**. 175–85, 195–7; secures law for financial accounting, 187–91, 209, 235; (181) pr. urb., **12**. 59; enrolls and discharges *legiones tumultuariae*, 81–3, 89; directs burning of 'books of Numa,' 91–3; (176) cos., for Liguria; makes unpropitious sacrifices; repeats Latin games, 227–9, 233; elects cos. suf., 233, 237; killed in Liguria, 237–41, **14**. 245

Petitarus riv., in Aetolia: (169) **13**. 81

Petra, pass in Macedon: (185) Thessalians and Perrhaebians occupy, **11**. 297; (168) Perseus garrisons, **13**. 197; L. Aemilius Paulus slips through, 395

—, in Thrace: (181) **12**. 73, 75

Petreius, M.: (49) leg. of Pompey, surrenders at Ilerda, **14**. 137; (47) refuses to command in Spain; (46) kills self, 143

Petronius, M.: (145) envoy to Asia, **14**. 45

Pettius: *see* Herius.

Phacium, in Thessaly: (198) Philip destroys, **9**. 189; (191) M. Baebius Tamphilus takes, **10**. 195

Phacus, citadel of Pella: **13**. 241; (169) Perseus destroys treasure in, 107, 121

INDEX

Phaeca, in Thessaly: (198) **9**. 191
Phaeneas, an Aetolian: (197) with Flamininus in conference with Philip, **9**. 251–7; commands Aetolians, 283; demands harsh terms for Philip, 309–11; (192) introduces Antiochus in Aetolian council, **10**. 129; opposes Thoas, 131; (191) envoy to M' Acilius Glabrio, 239–41; appeals to Flamininus, 257; (189) envoy to M. Fulvius Nobilior, accepting terms, **11**. 25–33
Phaestum, in Thessaly: (191) **10**. 195
Phalanna, in Boeotia: (171) Perseus at, **12**. 459; Romans at, 495
phalanx, Macedonian: characteristics of, **9**. 115, 285, 297–301, **10**. 215, 405–7, 413–5, **13**. 229
Phalara, on Maliac gulf: (209) Philip and Greek envoys at, **7**. 333–5; (192) Antiochus at, **10**. 129; (191) Nicander at, 243
Phalasarnae: *see* Susus of.
Phaloria, in Thessaly: (198) Flamininus burns, **9**. 193–5; (191) M. Baebius Tamphilus recovers from Athamanes, **10**. 197; (185) Philip and Thessalians both claim, **11**. 291–3
Phameas Himilco: (148) deserts to Rome, **14**. 33
Phanae, on Chios: (191) Roman fleet near, **10**. 279; (168) Eumenes' horse transports make for, **13**. 181; Perseus' fleet anchors off, 185, leaves, 273
Phanotê, in Epirus: (169) resists Ap. Claudius Cento, **13**. 75–7, 81; (167) surrenders to L. Anicius Gallus, 335
Phanotea, in Locris: (198) **9**. 205
Pharae: (192) gate of Sparta, **10**. 87–9
Pharcado, in Thessaly: (200) **9**. 121
Pharnaces I, of Pontus: (182) sends envoys, **12**. 7; (181) 63
— II, of Pontus: (64–63) makes war on father, **14**. 125; (48) repulses Cn. Domitius Calvinus, 141; (47) Caesar defeats, 143
Pharos: *see* Demetrius of.
Pharsalia, in Thessaly: (197) Romans in, **9**. 291; (48) Caesar defeats Pompey in, **14**. 139, 209
Pharsalus, in Thessaly: (198–197) Philip promises, to Aetolians, **9**. 257, 261, 309; (196) Aetolians demand, 369, (195) 407, 475; (191) surrenders to Antiochus, **10**. 187, then to M' Acilius Glabrio, 201
Pharsalus, Old: *see* Palaepharsalus.
Phaselis, port of Lycia: (190) **10**. 355, 361
Pheneus, in Arcadia: (207) **8**. 31
Pherae, in Thessaly: (198) excludes Philip, **9**. 189; (197) Flamininus at, 289; (191) Antiochus musters troops at, **10**. 181; yields to Antiochus, 183–7, to M' Acilius Glabrio, 201; (171) Perseus raids, **12**. 465–7
Pherinium, in Thessaly: (198) **9**. 193
Phila, between Macedon and Thessaly: (171) Perseus garrisons, **12**. 503; (169) he raids to, **13**. 97; Roman camp near, 99, 115–7; (168) 203
Philadelphus: *see* Attalus II, Ptolemy II.
Philadelphus: (33–31) son of Antony and Cleopatra, **14**. 163
Phileas of Tarentum: (212) aids escape of Tarentine hostages, **6**. 365–7
Philemenus, of Tarentum: (212) betrays city to Hannibal, **6**. 367–77; (209) his death, **7**. 273–5
Philetaerus, of Pergamum: (171) brother of Eumenes, left in Pergamum, **12**. 463
Philip II, king of Macedon, 359–336: **11**. 113; growth of Macedon under, **12**. 455, **13**. 267, 271–3
Philip V, king of Macedon, 221–179: (217) envoys to, demand release of Demetrius of Pharos, **5**. 311; (215) makes treaty with Hannibal, **6**. 115–7, **7**. 141, **9**. 21, 407; treaty known in Rome, **6**. 117–9, 131–3; Roman counter-measures, 133–5; new envoys of, to Hannibal, 135; M. Valerius Laevinus sent against, 133, 163; (214) 207, **9**. 21; Tarentum important port for, **6**. 215; war with, begins, 301–3; operations of, about Apollonia against Laevinus, 303–7, **7**. 87, 109; (212) envoy from Syracuse to, captured, **6**. 431; (211) kept busy by Aetolians and Thracians, **7**. 91–9, **9**. 215; (210) oarsmen needed against, **7**. 135; (209) Punic fleet sent to aid, 269, 335; defeats Aetolians; prevents landing of Attalus; makes truce, 331–3; goes

to Argos for Nemean games, 333–5, 337–9; peace negotiations with Aetolians, 335–7; repulses Roman fleet, 337; fails to take Elis; takes Pyrgus, 339–41; recalled to meet invasions of Dassaretii and Dardani, 343; (207) gathers army at Demetrias, **8**. 17–9; operations against Aetolia, 19–31, 35, **10**. 249; meets envoys of Ptolemy and Rhodes, **8**. 29; gives Zacynthus to Amynander, **10**. 249; addresses Achaean council, **8**. 31–3; turns to Dardanian war, 35–7; (205) urged by Carthage to invade Italy, 223; makes treaty with Aetolians, 249–51, **9**. 5, 49, 85, 87, 311, and with Rome, **8**. 253–5; (203) sends Carthage aid, 457, 523–5, **9**. 7, 35, **13**. 317; envoys sent to, on Greek complaint, **8**. 457–9; (202–201) stern reply to envoys of, 517, 523–7; (201) Egypt asked not to aid, **9**. 7; (200) war with, voted, 9–11, 15–25; and allotted to P. Sulpicius Galba, 17; causes of war with, **8**. 457, **9**. 5–7, 19–25, 35, 471–3, **13**. 317; fetials consulted, **9**. 25, **10**. 163–5; **11**. 155[5]; Athens asks aid of Egypt against, **9**. 27; Masinissa asked for cavalry against, 35; meets Rhodians and Attalus at sea, 43, 45; makes treaty with Antiochus, 43, **10**. 55; causes of Athenian war with, **9**. 45–7; begins war with empty treasury, **13**. 391; operations on Hellespont and in Asia, **9**. 49–57, 135, 385; rejects Roman protests, 53–5; returns home, 57; operations in central Greece, 65–79; at Achaean council, 73–5; withdraws to Macedon, 77–9, 83; loots Sciathus and Peparethus, 83, 131–3; envoys of, address Aetolian council, 83–7; answered by Athenians, 89–91, and Romans, 91–5; council takes no action, 97; assembles army and navy, 97–9; Galba defeats, in minor battles, 99–113, 215; retires to mountains, 113–7; Aetolians declare war on; are defeated, 119–25; pref. of, defeats Dardanians, 119, 125–7; Athenian hatred for, 127–9, 209; Attalus bound to aid against, 133; end of season's campaign, 139; (199) abandons siege of Thaumaci; winters in Macedon, 161–3; throws Heraclides into prison; sends envoys to Achaeans, 163–5; drills army; occupies passes, 165–7; campaign of P. Villius Tappulus against, 167–9; (198) war with, allotted to T. Quinctius Flamininus, 175, 167, 169, 179; aid of Attalus against, endangers Pergamum, 175–7; makes vain peace proposals, 181–3; Flamininus defeats, at Aous riv., 183–7, 195–7, **10**. 207, **11**. 171; withdraws to Macedon, **9**. 187–9, 215–7; establishes base at Tempê, 195; Achaean council, after debate, 207–23, votes alliance with Rhodes, Pergamum, and Rome against, 223–5, 475, **12**. 401; naval support against, furnished by Rhodes, **10**. 453, **12**. 427, **13**. 317, 319, 327, by Pergamum, **10**. 451, **13**. 167; supported by Thessaly, Phocis, Locris, **9**. 501, **12**. 405, Elis and Messenê, 401–3, Acarnania, 403, and Lampsacus, **13**. 23, but not openly by Boeotia, **9**. 351, **12**. 325; Italians in army of, **9**. 227; Argos delivered to, 229–33, 501; holds Corinth, 233; (198–197) abortive negotiations with Flamininus, 251–65; terms rejected in Rome, 265, 283; (197) gives Argos to Nabis, 265–7, 497, 505; alliance with Rome against, made by Nabis, 269–73, 495–501, and by Boeotia, 281–3; renews alliance with Acarnanians, 319–21; musters army at Dium, 283–7; moves to Pherae, 289–91; Flamininus defeats, at Cynoscephalae, 291–303, **10**. 181; flees to Macedon; sends agents to Flamininus, **9**. 303; Romans and allies discuss terms for, 305–9; Aetolians not satisfied, 305–11; yields to demands; sends envoys and son, Demetrius, to Rome, 309–11; intends to hold Corinth, 313, 475; Rhodians recover Peraea from, 323–9; defeats Dardani, 329; Antiochus plans to aid, 329–33, **10**. 95, Flamininus reports victory; Xviri named to make terms with, **9**. 343, 395; (196) assembly ratifies peace, 345; Boeotia thanks, for recovery of bodies,

INDEX

351; terms of peace with, 359–63, 475, 563, **10**. 49, 365, **11**. 207, **12**. 361, 363, 381, 451, 483, 485; Greek cities once held by, freed, **9**. 363–7, 501, 567–9, **10**. 211, 455–9, **12**. 455, **13**. 31; Antiochus warned to leave cities once held by, **9**. 369; Pleuratus and Amynander receive forts of; seeks alliance with Rome, 371; Aetolians magnify their aid against, 373, **10**. 139–41, 177, 435, **11**. 27; end of war with, **9**. 373, 335; Antiochus seizes former possessions of, 383–5; (195) sends aid to Flamininus against Sparta, 483; forced to withdraw from Iasus and Bargyliae, 501; (195–194) Flamininus reorganizes cities freed from, 541–3; he triumphs over, 549–51, **11**. 159, **13**. 383; (193) Aetolians incite, against Rome, **10**. 33–7; Antiochus claims former cities of, 49, 211; Alexander of Acarnania promises Antiochus aid of, 53–5; (192) son of, in Rome; importance of, to Rome, 91; Aetolians plan to replace, with Antiochus, 91, 95; (191) offers aid against Antiochus, 165–7, 181, **11**. 305, **13**. 167; Antiochus needs aid of, **10**. 175–9, **11**. 305; makes agreement with M. Baebius Tamphilus, **10**. 187–9, 195; takes Thessalian towns, 195–9, and Athamania, 199–201, 249, **11**. 287, 291; garrisons of Antiochus volunteer to serve under, **10**. 201; besieges Lamia, but Romans receive surrender, 233–5, 303, **11**. 287, 305; urges Aetolians to submit, **10**. 243; recovers Demetrias, Dolopia, Aperantia, Perrhaebia, 251–7, **11**. 287; makes offerings on Capitol; Demetrius returned, **10**. 259; tribute cancelled, 365; (190) Ti. Sempronius Gracchus tests loyalty of, 311; reads Roman treaty twice daily, **13**. 141; aids Romans crossing Macedon, **10**. 313; (189) prefects of, misgovern Athamania, **11**. 3; loses Athamania, 3–9, and Dolopia, 11; tries to set Rome against Aetolians, 33; (188) suspected in attack on Cn. Manlius Volso, 137; 185) responsible for war with Pyrrhus, 285–309, **12**. 53; denied right to punish rebels, **11**. 285, 303–5; strengthens Macedon, 287–91; accused of occupying certain cities, defends self, 291–307; cities in Thessaly, Perrhaebia, and Athamania taken from, 299, 305; indecisive answer to claims of, 307–9; (184) envoys of, before Senate, 321–3; directed to give up coast, 323, 389; withdraws from Maronea; destroys city, 325–7; sends Demetrius to Rome; defeats Thracians; incites Histrians, 327; (183) nearby tribes complain of, in Rome, 367; Demetrius wins favour for, in Rome, 367–71; Perseus, elder son of, by concubine, 387; displeased by favour shown Demetrius, 387–9; forced to withdraw from Thrace, 389; leads army beyond Thrace; founds Perseis, 389–91; (182) envoys of, received by Senate; Q. Marcius Philippus reports on, **12**. 7; prepares for war, 7, 261–3, 451; cruelty of, rouses anger in Macedon, 9–13; suspicion of Rome and of Demetrius fanned by Perseus, 13–7; makes alliance with Bastarnae, 15, 171–5, 323; Perseus and Demetrius quarrel before, 21–51; postpones decision, 51–3; (181) envoys of, before Senate, 63–5; summons army to Paeonia, 65–7; sends Demetrius to Macedon, 67–9; climbs Mt. Haemus, 69–71; returns to Macedon, 71–3; orders murder of Demetrius, 73–7, 261–7, 323; (179) discovers his innocence, 163–9, 305; makes Antigonus son of Echecrates his heir, 169–71; dies at Amphipolis, 163, 171, 175, 323; plot of Perseus against, **13**. 93. Friendship of, and father of Q. Marcius Philippus, **12**. 405. *Also*: **4**. 241, **8**. 247, **9**. 397, 525, **10**. 39, 105, 139, 363, **11**. 145, 149, 157, **12**. 85, 391, 425, **13**. 315, **14**. 39. *See* Demetrius, Perseus; Macedon.

—, praetor of Epirus: (205) at peace conference, **8**. 253

— of Megalopolis: (205) governor of Zacynthus, **10**. 249; (192) Aetolians and Antiochus promise Macedonian

throne to, 137; (191) Antiochus sends, to collect bones at Cynoscephalae, 181; commands at Pellinaeum, 197; surrenders to M' Acilius Glabrio, 199
Philip: (192) favourite of L. Quinctius Flamininus, **11**. 355–7
—: (190) officer of Antiochus, **10**. 409
—, brother and adopted son of Perseus: (171) at review, **12**. 451; (168) with Perseus after Pydna, **13**. 239; surrendered, 267; (167) in Rome for triumph, 345, 367, 385, 389
—: (169) officer of Perseus, **13**. 127
—: (149) *see* Andriscus, pretended son of Perseus.
—: (142) second false Philip, **14**. 47
Philippei: (194) coins, carried in triumph, **9**. 551; (189) **10**. 475–7; (187) **11**. 233; 237
Philippi, in Macedon: (42) **14**. 155, 317
Philippopolis, in Thessaly: (185) Philip claims, **11**. 291–3; (183) he takes, 389
Philippus: *see* Marcius.
Philistion: (212) slain in Syracuse, **6**. 449
Philo: *see* Curtius, Publilius, Veturius.
—, of Chalcis: (190, 188) Antiochus surrenders, **10**. 425, **11**. 131
Philocles, of Macedon: (200) pref. of Chalcis, plunders Attica, **9**. 49, 77–9; (198) fails to relieve Eretria, 199; reinforces Corinth, 227–9; receives surrender of Argos, 229–33; (197) delivers Argos to Nabis, 267, 271, 505; confers with Flamininus, 273; (181) envoy to Rome *re* Demetrius, **12**. 65; returns with false charges, 75; (179) arrested for death of Demetrius, 165–7
Philocrates: (167) Rhodian envoy, **13**. 331
Philodemus, of Argos: (212) surrenders Euryalus to Marcellus, **6**. 437–41
Philometor: *see* Ptolemy VI.
— Euergetes: *see* Attalus III.
Philopator: *see* Ptolemy IV, Seleucus IV.
Philopoemen, of Megalopolis, praetor of Achaean League: mercenary leader in Crete, **10**. 73; (200) Cycliadas follows, as praetor, **9**. 75; (192) praetor, addresses Achaeans, **10**. 71; Nabis defeats fleet under, 71–5; plunders Spartan territory, 75–7; defeats Nabis, 77–89; wins Lacedaemonians to alliance, 111; ill will between Flamininus and, 89, 135–7; (190) pupil of, brings Achaeans to Pergamum, 347; (189) praetor, calls assembly of League at Argos, **11**. 101; demands punishment of Spartan attackers of Las, 103–5; sends Lycortas to Rome, 107; re-elected praetor, 109; enters Lacedaemon; fails to protect surrendered Spartans, 109–11, 331–3; forces Sparta to destroy walls and give up laws, 333–5; (184) Lycortas, agent of, before Roman commission, 331; (183) praetor, captured by Messenê, 373–5; put to death, 375–9, 385–7; character and reputation, **10**. 79–81, 89, 347, **11**. 379
Philostratus: (169) Epirote general, **13**. 81–3
Philotas: (190) pref. of Abydus, **10**. 325
Philus: *see* Furius.
Phlius, in N.E. Peloponnese: (207) Philip moves to, **8**. 31; (197) Macedonians plunder, **9**. 313–7
Phocaea, in Ionia: described, **10**. 383; mother city of Massilia, **3**. 119, and Emporiae, **7**. 75, **9**. 441; (191) fleets of Rome and Eumenes at, **10**. 279, 285; (190) 313–5; anti-Roman uprising in, 315, 385; betrayed to Seleucus; C. Livius Salinator fails to take, 325, 353; surrenders, 383–7; fleet winters at, 387; (188) receives old territory and own laws, **11**. 133
Phocis, in central Greece: **10**. 203; (207) Philip in, **8**. 21, 27; (198) allied to Philip, **9**. 501; Flamininus winters in, seizing various points, 205, 213, 215, 227–9, 249; Philip to withdraw troops from, 265; (197) Flamininus crosses, 279; (196) freed, 365, 501; annexed to Aetolians, 369; (192) Antiochus crosses, **10**. 133; (191) 191, 195; M' Acilius Glabrio crosses, 219; 257
Phoebeum, in Sparta: (195) **9**. 519

INDEX

Phoenicê, in Epirus: (205) **8**. 253
Phoenicia: (193) Antiochus and Ptolemy in, **10**. 39; (190) Antiochus sends Hannibal to, for ships, 313; (66) Pompey takes, from Tigranes, **14**. 125
Phoenicians: *see* Carthage.
Phoenicus, in Ionia: (191) **10**. 285
—, in Lycia: (190) **10**. 337
Phraates II, of Parthia: (131) at war with Antiochus VII, **14**. 67
Phraates III, of Parthia: (66) Pompey renews friendship with; at war with Tigranes of Armenia, **14**. 125
Phrygia: (205) stone of Great Mother from, **8**. 247–9, **9**. 421; (190) Antiochus winters in, **10**. 313; cavalry from, in army of Antiochus, 409; (189) after defeat of Antiochus Rome gives, to Eumenes, 455, 463, **11**. 133; cos. Cn. Manlius Volso campaigns in, 51, 57, 59, 157; (171) in Roman army, **12**. 453; (130) Rome recovers, **14**. 263; (88) Mithridates invades, 97; (74) his officers crushed in, 117. Also **10**. 465, **11**. 41, 63.
Phrygius riv., in Lydia: (190) **10**. 399–401
Phthiotis, in Thessaly: (197) Flamininus in, **9**. 285, 291. *See* Alopê, Demetrium, Eretria, Thebes, Zelasium.
Phylacê, in Epirus: (167) **13**. 335–7
Picenum: (299) alliance with, **4**. 395, 237; reports new Samnite war, 397; (268) defeated; receives colony at Ariminium, 553; (217) Hannibal plunders, **5**. 229; (216) troops raised in, **6**. 43; (215) assigned to C. Terentius Varro, 113; (214) 207, 209; (213) 317, 347; (207) C. Claudius Nero sets out for, **7**. 383–5; (184) colony at Potentia in, **11**. 361–3; (91) first to rebel, **14**. 89; (90) tortures Romans, 293; (89) Cn. Pompeius Strabo defeats, 91. Prodigies: (218) **5**. 185–7; (194) **9**. 535; (192) **10**. 61; (186) **11**. 281, **14**. 239; (104) 277; (100) 281
Pictor: *see* Fabius.
Pieria, coastal region north of Thessaly: (185) Thessalians seize Petra in, **11**. 297; (169) Q. Marcius Philippus in, **13**. 113–5; 121; (168) Perseus holds, 153; he flees through, 233
Pietas: (181) temple of, in Forum Olitorium, **12**. 103–5; (91) in Flaminian circus, **14**. 291
Pile bridge: *see* bridge, over Tiber.
pilus: military unit, **4**. 31
Pinarii: (753) ministers of cult of Hercules, **1**. 29–31
Pinarius, L.: (214) prevents surrender of Henna, **6**. 293–301
— Mamercinus Rufus, L.: (472) cos., **1**. 407
— Mamercus, L.: (432) tr. mil. c. p., **2**. 337
— Mamertinus Rufus, P.: (489) cos., **1**. 347[1]
— Natta, L., pr. 349: (363) mag. eq. clav. fig. c., **3**. 365; (349) pr., opposes Greek raids, **3**. 443
— Rusca, M.: (181) pr. for Sardinia, **12**. 59, 63, 79; defeats Corsicans and Ilienses, 105–7
Pineus, king of Illyricum: (217) tribute or hostages demanded from, **5**. 311
piracy, pirates: (302) on east coast of Adriatic, **4**. 363–5; (190) **10**. 331; plunder Chios, 369–71; (181) from Histria and Liguria, **12**. 59; (180) from Illyricum, 131–3; (102) M. Antonius drives, to Cilicia, **14**. 81, 279; (75) P. Servilius Vatia storms cities of, in Cilicia, 117; (70) L. Caecilius Metellus suppresses, in Sicily, 121; (67) Pompey drives, from sea and grants lands to, 123
Piraeus, in Attica: (200) Attalus and Roman fleet at, **9**. 45, 65, 67, 129, 137; Romans from, defend Athens, 73; resists Philip, 77–9, 89–91; (198) L. Flamininus moves from, 197; Attalus returns to, 227; (192) Achaeans send troops to, **10**. 145; (191) captured ships of Antiochus sent to, 221; Roman fleet at, 275–7; (190) L. Aemilius Regillus at, 331; (188) Q. Fabius Labeo returns by way of, **11**. 131; (167) walls of, seen by L. Aemilius Paulus, **13**. 341; (86) Sulla captures, **14**. 297
Pirustae, Illyrian tribe: (167) **13**. 337
Pisae, (Pisa) in Etruria: (218) P. Scipio at, **5**. 113; (195) allotted to P.

Porcius Laeca, **9.** 393; (193) Ligurians enter lands of, 557–9; Q. Minucius Thermus occupies, **10.** 7–9, 15; (192) he defeats Ligurians near, 61–3; (188) allotted to M. Valerius Messala, **11.** 117; (187) Ligurians raid lands of, 221–3; (185) M. Sempronius Tuditanus sets out from, 317–9; (182) Ligurians endanger, **12.** 3; L. Aemilius Paulus and Cn. Baebius Tamphilus winter at, 57, 63, (181) 79–81; (180) Ligurians attacked from, 127–9; irregularities in military pay at, 129–31; land for Latin colony at, 135; (178) assigned to Ti. Claudius Nero, 197–9, (177–176) 221, 227; (176) allotted to Cn. Scipio Hispallus, 227–9; forces for Liguria gather at, 237; (175) plundered, 243; (173) army for Liguria winters at, 315; (170) **13.** 33; (168) quarrels with Luna, 287; (167) allotted to M. Junius Pennus, 297, 301

Pisaurum, in Umbria: (184) colony established, **11.** 361–3; (174) censors contract for temple and streets at, **12.** 281. Prodigies: (163) **14.** 249; (97) 283

Piscatorium Forum: (210) **7.** 103

Piscina publica: (215) **6.** 111

Pisias, of Pellenê: (198) pro-Roman Achaean, **9.** 221–3

Pisidia: (193) Antiochus attacks, **10.** 39, 41; (190) men of, with Antiochus at Magnesia, 409; (189) Rome controls, 455; Caria facing, given to Rhodes, 465; surrenders to Cn. Manlius Volso, **11.** 43, 49; he plunders, 157

Pisistratidae: (200) decrees against, applied to Philip, **9.** 129

Pisistratus, of Boeotia: (196) pro-Roman, executed, **9.** 351–5

Piso: *see* Calpurnius.

Pista, in Illyricum: (167) **13.** 337

Pistoria, in Etruria: (62) **14.** 303

Pisuetae, from Caria: (197) **9.** 325

Pithecusae, is. off Naples: **4.** 87

Pityusa, is. off Spain: (206) **8.** 149

Pius: *see* Caecilius Metellus.

Placentia, in Cispadine Gaul: (219) colony at, **4.** 561, **5.** 69–71; (218) P. Scipio comes to, 113; he returns to, after Ticinus, 139; Hannibal near, 141; after Trebia, Romans escape to, 167, (218–217) and winter, 169, 187; withstands Hannibal, 171, **7.** 369; (217) Hannibal moves toward, **5.** 175; (209) remains loyal, **7.** 245–7; (207) withstands Hasdrubal, 369, 381; (206) Gauls raid, **8.** 49; (200) **9.** 31, 63; (206) men of, forced to return to, **8.** 49; (198) **9.** 233; (197) thanks C. Cornelius Cethegus, 339, 341; (195) L. Valerius Flaccus rebuilds, 471; (194) Ti. Sempronius Longus withdraws to, 541; (193) Ligurians plunder, 559; (192) L. Quinctius Flamininus slays convict at, **11.** 357–9; (190) new colonists for, **10.** 429; (187) road from, **11.** 223; (180) A. Postumius Albinus at, **12.** 131; (178) emergency cohort raised at, 187, 189; (168) cavalry from, at Pydna, **13.** 225

Plaetorius, C.: (172) envoy to Gentius, **12.** 365

Plancus: *see* Munatius.

Plataea: *see* Dicaearchus of.

Plator: (208–207) general of Philip, betrays Oreüs, **8.** 21–5

—: (168) Gentius' brother, **13.** 187

Plautius: (87) leg.; Samnites defeat, **14.** 101

—, C.: (146) pr.; Lusitanians defeat, **14.** 43

— Decianus, C.: (329) cos., defeats Privernum, triumphs, **4.** 79–81; opposes its destruction, 81–5

— Hypsaeus, L.: (189) pr. for Nearer Spain, **10.** 431, 437–9

— —, M.: (125) cos., **14.** 265

— —, P.: (52) candidate for cos., **14.** 133

— Proculus, C.: (358) cos., defeats Hernici, **3.** 393, 407; names dict., 395; (356) mag. eq. for C. Marcius Rutulus, 413

— —, P.: (328) cos., **4.** 85

— Venox (or Venno), C.: (347) cos., **3.** 449; (341) ii, defeats Privernum, Antium, **4.** 3–5; resigns to make way for new coss., 11

— —, C.: (312–311) cens., **4.** 275–7, 289, 293

— —, L.: (330) cos., **4.** 73; attacks Fundi and Privernum, 77; (322) pr., 155

INDEX

Plautius Venox, L.: (318) cos. **4**. 241–3
Plautus: *see* Sergius.
Plebeian games: repeated one or more times: (216) **6**. 103; (213) 347; (209) **7**. 299; (208) 357; (207) **8**. 43; (205) 249; (204) 359; (203) 461; (202) 515; (201) **9**. 15; (200) 147; (199) 173; (197) 345; (196) 391; (189) **11**. 117; (187) 239
plebeians, of Ardea: (443) invite Volscian intervention, **2**. 287–91
—, of Rome: (534–510) oppressed by king, **1**. 193; (508) favoured by Senate during life of Tarquin the Proud, 247–9, (495) then oppressed, 287; refuse military service because of debt, 289–95; calmed by promises, 295–7; riot because of laws of debt, 303–7; (494) meet on Aventine, defy coss., 307–13; calmed by M' Valerius Maximus, 313–15; Senate repudiates his pledge to, 321; (494–493) secession of, to Sacred Mount leads to creation of tribb. pl., 323–7; (491) force Cn. Marcius Coriolanus into exile, 331–7; (486) seek land law, 353–5; (484) 357; (483) 359; (481) refuse military service, 361–3; (480) roused to fight by Etruscan jeers, 365–73; the Fabii win favour of, 379–81; (474) demand land law, 401; (473) protect Volero Publilius from lictors, 403–7; (472–471) officers of, elected in tribal assembly, 407–15; (471) disobey coss. in field, 415–21; (469) demand land law, 427; abstain from consular election, 429; (462) seek to limit consular power, **2**. 31–7 (*see* Terentilian law); condemn ex-coss., 105; (451) excluded from first Xvirate, 107–9; (450–449) oppressed by second Xvirate, 119–23; (449) secede to Aventine, 167; then to Sacred Mount, 171–3; recalled by L. Valerius Potitus and M. Horatius, 173–9; elect tribb. on Aventine, 181; (446) quelled by T. Quinctius Capitolinus, 223–33; (445) marriage between, and patricians legalized; share in consulship demanded, 257–77; new office of tribb. mil. c. p. open to, 277–9; (439) a *transitio ad plebem*, 311; (395) demand distribution of Veientine land or emigration to Veii, **3**. 83–5; (393) Veientine land distributed to, 107–9; (386–385) find leader in M. Manlius Capitolinus, 231–69; (383) on promise of land, vote for war, 269; (377) oppressed by debt, 311–3; (377–367) after long struggle, win admission to consulship, 313–351; (326) receive new liberty with end of imprisonment for debt, **4**. 107–9; (296) women of, excluded from shrine of Patricia Pudicitia, 443; (287) secede to Janiculum, 547. First elected to offices: (409) qu., **2**. 433; (400) tr. mil. c. p., **3**. 45, 325; (368) mag. eq., 333; (367) Xvir sac., 347; (366) cos., 357; (365) aed. cur., 359; (356) dict., 413–5; (351) cens., 431–3; (337) pr., **4**. 63; (300) pont. and aug., 379–89; (129) both cens., **14**. 65. (362) First pl. cos. commands under own auspices, **3**. 375; (280) first pl. cens. closes lustrum, **4**. 551; (400) first mention of pl. Senator, **3**. 45
plebeian tribunes: *see* tribuni plebis.
plebiscites: (449) made binding on whole people, **2**. 183, 229; (339) **4**. 51–3; (415) authorized by *senatus auctoritas*, **2**. 417. Individual *plebiscita*: (449) for punishment of any leaving people without tribb., **2**. 185; (445) permitting intermarriage, 259, 275–7; (368) fining dict. M. Furius Camillus, **3**. 331; (357) *re* usury, 409; (342) *re* usury, re-election, plebeian coss., 511–3; (311) for election of tr. mil. *ad legiones*, and IIviri nav., **4**. 277–9; (296) to prorogue *imperium*, 443; (217) for election of co-dictator, **5**. 289–91, 303; (212) confirming exile, **6**. 355; (211) **7**. 15; (210) *re* treatment of Campanians, 129; for appointment of dict. com. c., 221–3; (200) for election of 'procoss.' for Spain, **9**. 149; (194) establishing Latin colonies, 553; (193) extending Roman laws of usury to Latins, **10**. 19; (172) *re* treatment of Ligurians, **12**. 351; (188) without *senatus auctoritas*, for grant of citizenship, **11**. 119

Pleiades: (218) setting of, **5**. 103
Pleiae, in Laconia: (192) **10**. 75–7
Pleminius, Q.: (205) leg., aids capture of Locri, **8**. 231–3; atrocities in Locri, 237–43; acts investigated and punished, 267–95, **9**. 37, 533; partiality of P. Scipio (Afr.) for, **8**. 269, 281, **11**. 177; Q. Fabius Maximus proposes decree against, **8**. 281–3; in custody, 289; death of, 295–7, **9**. 533
Plestina, city of Marsi: (302) **4**. 369
Pleuratus, Illyrian king: (200) son of Scerdilaedus, offers aid to P. Sulpicius Galba, **9**. 81–3; invades Macedon, 101–3, 113, 119; (196) Flamininus gives Lychnidus and Parthini to, 369–71; (189) raids Aetolia, **11**. 21; father of Gentius, **13**. 187
—, son of Gentius: (168) sent to Rome with father, **13**. 195
—, an Illyrian: (169) envoy of Perseus to Gentius, **13**. 71–3; sends Illyrians to Perseus, 127
—, Thracian king: (211) treaty of friendship open to, **7**. 93; (209) Aetolians demand return of Ardiaei to, 335; (208–207) takes field, **8**. 17; (205) on side of Rome in treaty with Philip, 255
Plistica, Samnite town: (316–315) **4**. 245–9
Plitê, in Pisidia: (189) **11**. 61
Plotius, A.: (90) leg., defeats Umbrians, **14**. 93
Pluinna, in Macedon: (200) **9**. 115
Po riv.: Etruscans once beyond, **3**. 117; (c. 391) Boi and Lingones cross, 121; (224) Romans cross for first time, **4**. 561; (220) Placentia and Cremona established on, **5**. 69; (218) Gauls drive L. Manlius to, 73; P. Scipio returns to, 93, 113–5; Hannibal points out plains of, 105; blocks retreat for Hannibal before Ticinus, 125; after Ticinus crossed by Scipio, 139, and Hannibal, 139–41; Gauls hold land between Trebia and, 153; (218–217) Scipio crosses; supplies brought up, 169; (200) Gauls cross, **9**. 31; (197) most tribes S. of, submit, 245; Boi cross, 245, 337; (196) M. Marcellus crosses, 375; Boi cross, 377; 195) L. Valerius Flaccus near, 471; (194) Boi cross, 535; (193) Ligures plunder along, 559; (172) land beyond, given to Ligures, **12**. 353; (108) overflows, **14**. 273; (49) Opitergini from beyond, allied to Caesar, 137; (44) overflows, 311
Poeni: *see* Carthaginians.
Poenine pass, in Alps: named from local god, **5**. 113; (c. 391) Boi and Lingones cross, **3**. 121; (218) a possible route of Hannibal, **5**. 111–3
Poeninus: god of Poenine pass, **5**. 113
Poenus: *see* Quinctius, — Cincinnatus.
Poetelius: (441) tr. pl. ii, agitates for land law, **2**. 297
—, P.: (210) envoy to Syphax, **7**. 215
—, Q.: (450) Xvir, **2**. 117; shares command against Sabines, 139
— Balbus, C.: (360) cos., triumphs over Gauls and Tiburtes, **3**. 389–91
— Libo, M.: (314) cos., takes Sora, **4**. 253–7; subdues Ausones, 259–61; conducts trials, 265–7; defeats Samnites at Caudium, 267–71; winters, 271
— — Visolus, C., cos. 346, 326: (358) tr. pl., secures first law on bribery, **3**. 409; (346) cos., 449; (326) ii, **4**. 93; against Samnites, 99
— — —, C.: (313) dict., takes Fregellae and Nola, 271–3
Poetneum: (185) Athamanes claim, **11**. 297
poison: (203) kept by kings, **8**. 419
poisoning: (331) convictions for, **4**. 71–3; (184) **11**. 341, 353; (180) **12**. 117, 137; (179) 139; (151) **14**. 17–9
Politorium, in Latium: 640–616) **1**. 119–21
Pollentia: (187) statue of, **11**. 239
Pollia tribus: (323) hated by Papirian tribe, **4**. 145; (204) M. Livius Salinator a member of, **8**. 353–5
Pollio: *see* Asinius, Licinius.
Polluted field: *see* Sceleratus campus.
Polusca, Volscian town: (493) captured, **1**. 327; Coriolanus and Volsci recover, 345
Polyaenus, of Syracuse: (214) urges moderation, **6**. 245, 247
Polyaratus, of Rhodes: (168–167) favours Perseus, **13**. 165–7, 185–7, 317
Polybius, the historian, cited: (201)

INDEX

8. 539; (197) **9**. 303; (194) 547; (191) **10**. 219; (183) **11**. 383; (167) **13**. 409–11
Polyclitus: (212) left in Syracuse by Epicydes; slain, **6**. 449
Polycratia: (208) wife of Aratus, **7**. 339
Polyphantas, general of Philip: (209) in Greece, **7**. 343; (207) **8**. 19
Polyxenidas, admiral of Antiochus: a Rhodian exile, **10**. 317; (192) sent against Chalcis, 145; (191) refits fleet, 181, 275; defeated near Cissus, 277–85; (190) equips new fleet, 313; deceives and defeats Rhodians, 317–25, 373; Romans avoid, 325–9; at Ephesus, 329, 335, 353; defeated off Myonnesus, 367–81; goes to Syria, 421
pomerium: defined, **1**. 155–7; (578–534) Servius Tullius extends, 155; (390) sacred rites within, **3**. 179
Pometia: *see* Suessa Pometia.
Pompedius Silo, Q.: (88) Italic leader in Social War; killed, **14**. 95, 293
Pompeii, in Campania: (310) fleet at, **4**. 311. Prodigy: (63) **14**. 301
Pompeius, L.: (171) tr. mil., **12**. 495–7
—, Q.: (141) cos., subdues Termestini, **14**. 49; Numantines defeat, 51; (136) leg., 183; (131–130) cens., 65
— Bithynicus, A., pr. 45: (42) Sex. Pompeius murders, **14**. 155
— Magnus, Cn., cos. 70, 55, 52: (83) joins Sulla, **14**. 107; (82) sent to Sicily by Senate, 111; in Africa; celebrates triumph while *eques*, 113; (78) kills M. Junius Brutus in Gaul; (77) sent to Spain with *imperium*, 115; (77–74) unsuccessful against Sertorius, withdraws to Gaul, 115, 117, 119, 191–3, 197, 299; (73) successful against Sertorius, 117; (72) defeats M. Perperna Vento; ends Spanish war, 119; (70) cos., restores power of tribb. pl., 121; (67) defeats pirates; offends Q. Caecilius Metellus, 123; (66) defeats Mithridates; receives Tigranes' surrender; (65–64) organizes Pontus, 125; (63) captures Jerusalem, 127, 201; (60) forms triumvirate with Caesar and Crassus, 127; (58) triumphs; hailed as Magnus, 129, **8**. 539; (57) aids recall of Cicero; receives supervision of grain, **14**. 129; (55) cos. ii, with Spain as prov. for five years, 131; (54) Julia, wife of, dies, 133; (52) cos. without colleague, 133, 305; (51) has army in Italy, 135–7; (50) begins war with Caesar, 307; (49) tribb. pl. flee to, 209; driven from Italy, 137; legg. of, in Spain, Africa, and Illyricum defeated, 137, 139; T. Labienus supports, 157; (48) besieged at Dyrrachium, 139, 307; defeated at Pharsalus, 139; words of wife to, 211; deserted by Fortune, **4**. 227; Cicero in camp of, **14**. 139; flees to Egypt, murdered, 141; portents, 307; (47) P. Scipio takes over forces of, 141; follower of, stirs war in Syria, 143; Caesar slain in Senate house of, 147, 309
Pompeius Magnus, Cn.: (47) renews war with Caesar in Spain, **14**. 141–3; (45) defeated and slain, 145, 309, **9**. 441
— — Pius, Sex.: (48) flees to Cyprus, **14**. 141; (45) survives defeat at Munda, 145, **9**. 441; (43–38) a pirate, **14**. 155, 159; (39) makes terms with Octavius and Antony; breaks peace; (36) Agrippa defeats, 159; (36–35) killed, 161
— Rufus, Q.: (88) cos., **14**. 185, 293; opposes Marius; murdered by Cn. Pompeius Strabo, 97
— —, Q.: (88) killed fighting Marius, **14**. 97
— Strabo, Cn.: (89) cos., defeats Italians, **14**. 91, 93, (88) 95; takes Asculum, 95, 107; murders Q. Pompeius Rufus, 97; (87) supports Cn. Octavius against Marius, 99; killed from heaven, 295
Pompilius: *see* Numa Pompilius.
—, Sex.: (420) tr. pl., angered at election of patricians, **2**. 399–401
Pompo: supposed father of Numa, **12**. 89
Pomponius, M.: (449) tr. pl., **2**. 181
—, M.: (362) tr. pl., accuses L. Manlius Imperiosus, **3**. 367, 371
—, M., pr. 161: (167) tr. pl., vetoes Rhodian war, **13**. 313–5
—, Q.: (395) tr. pl., vetoes colonization of Veii, **3**. 85; (393) fined, 103
—, Sex.: (218) leg. for fleet, **5**. 151

* Pomponius Matho, M., cos. 231: (217) mag. eq. com. c., disqualified by *vitium*, **5**. 313; (211) pontiff; dies, **7**. 91

* — —, M.: (217) pr., announces Trasumenus, **5**. 223; (204) augur and Xvir sac.; dies, **8**. 359

* — —, M.: (216) pr. pereg., **5**. 319, 379, **6**. 79; (214) in Cisalpine Gaul, 207, 315; M. Marcellus calls, to Nola, 227

— —, M., pr. 204: (207) aed. pl., **8**. 43; (205) leg. to Delphi, 193; (204) pr. for Sicily, 249, 255–7, 311; investigates Locrian affair, 287–93, **9**. 37; interviews P. Scipio (Afr.), **8**. 293–5; aids his departure, 303, 307; (203) commands fleet, 371; (202) 463

— Rufus, M.: (399) tr. mil. c. p., **3**. 47

— Veientanus, T.: (213) praef. soc., plunders Bruttium and Lucania; Hanno slays, **6**. 341, 349

Pomptina tribus: (358) formed, **3**. 407

Pomptine (Pontine) district: (492) grain sought from; colony in, **1**. 331; (433) grain sought from, **2**. 337; (388) tribb. pl. propose distribution of, **3**. 211; (386) 213; report Antiates in arms, 213; (385) Volsci invade, 233; (383) Vviri to distribute land in, 269; (349) L. Furius Camillus in, against Gauls, 443; (173) locusts in, **12**. 297

Pomptine marshes: (160) drained, **14**. 13

Pomptinus, C., pr. 63: (61) subdues Allobroges, **14**. 127

Pontiae, is. off Campania: (313) colony on, **4**. 273; (209) loyal, **7**. 245–7

pontifex maximus: (449) holds tribunal elections, **2**. 179–81; (431) dictates vow, 345, (200) **9**. 29, (172) **12**. 373, (390) formula for *devotio*, **3**. 141, (340) **4**. 37, (295) 467–9, (304) for dedication, 351; (420) punishes Vestal, **2**. 401–3; (206) **8**. 47; (c. 253) first plebeian, **4**. 557; (242) prevents cos. from sailing, 559, **10**. 439; (217) requires popular vote on Sacred Spring, **5**. 231; (216) punishes paramour of Vestal, 385; (212) regularly an ex-magistrate; elected by popular vote, **6**. 355; (103) **14**. 81; (209) names flamen Dialis, **7**. 235; (206) may not leave Italy though cos., **8**. 153–5, 187; (200) college of pontiffs reverses decision of, **9**. 29; (189) prevents flamen leaving Italy, **10**. 439–41; (183) elected by other pontiffs, **11**. 365; (180) **12**. 135; portents referred to, 115; appoints rex sac., 133–5; (131) takes prov. outside Italy; killed, **14**. 65

pontifices: (715–672) created by Numa, **1**. 71–3, **2**. 269; (640) publish commentaries of Numa, **1**. 113; (368) exclusively patrician, **3**. 345; (449) **2**. 267; (300) opened to plebeians, number increased, **4**. 379–89; (207) direct special rites, **7**. 359; (196) wear *toga praetexta*; forced to pay back taxes, **9**. 389; (183) chosen by co-option; elect pont. max., **11**. 365; (180) **12**. 135; (181) announce shaking of spears, 61; (176) prescribe expiation, 233. Deaths and/or appointments of: (390) **3**. 141; (300) **4**. 389; (216) **6**. 73; (213) 345; (211) **7**. 91; (210) 227; (203) **8**. 459–61; (202) 515; (199) **9**. 173; (196) 389–91; (183) **11**. 365; (180) **12**. 135; (177) 225; (176) 233; (174) 253; (172) 373; (170) **13**. 41–3

pontiffs, college of: (204) rules on expiation, **8**. 287, (203) 373, (187) on disposal of sacred spoil, **11**. 151, (176) on *vitium*, **12**. 233; (200) appeal to, from decision of pont. max., **9**. 29; (81) size of, increased by Sulla, **14**. 111

pontifical law: (181) in 'Books of Numa,' **12**. 91

Pontificus, Ti.: (480) tr. pl., proposes land laws, **1**. 363–5

Pontine district: *see* Pomptine district.

Pontinus: *see* Pomptinus.

Pontius, C., Samnite leader: (321) rouses people, **4**. 163–5; defeats Romans at Caudine Forks; sends them under yoke, 165–83, 217; (320) refuses to accept surrender of sponsors of peace, 201–5; loses

* In dividing the careers of these three (or two) men, certainty is impossible.

reputation, 205; possibly captured at Luceria, 219
Pontius, C., Samnite leader: (292) led in triumph, **4**. 547
—, Herennius, a Samnite: (321) father of C. Pontius, **4**. 163; his advice at Caudine surrender, 171–3, 205
— Cominus: (390) messenger from Veii, **3**. 157
Pontus: (73) L. Licinius Lucullus defeats Mithridates in, **14**. 119; (72) 121; (65–64) organized as province, 125; (46) Caesar triumphs over, 145. *See* Mithridates, Pharnaces, Phraates.
Pontus Euxinus, Black Sea: (181) reputedly visible from Haemus, **12**. 67; (171) two triremes from, join Romans, 465
Popilius (Popillius): (43) murders Cicero, **14**. 153
—, T.: (211) leg. at Capua, **7**. 23
— Laenas, C., cos. 172, 158: (172) cos. **12**. 317, **13**. 51, with Liguria as prov., **12**. 321; defends brother, M., in Senate, 319–21; delays departure for prov., 349–51; inactive in Liguria, 351–3, 363–5; sends troops to Macedon, 369; in Rome, 369–73; (169) envoy to Greece, **13**. 61–3; prevents surrender of Stratus, 63, 79; (168) envoy to Antiochus IV and Ptolemy VIII, 153; at Delos, 185, 273; at Rhodes, 273–7; in Egypt demands immediate answer from Antiochus, 281–3, 323; reports, 285
— —, M., cos. 359, 356, 354 (?), 350, 348: (359) cos., repulses Tiburtes, **3**. 393; (357) secures conviction of C. Licinius Stolo under own law, 411; (356) cos. ii, defeats Tiburtes, 413; (354) cos. (?), 419; (350) cos. iii, defeats Gauls, 433–9; (349) triumphs, 439; (348) cos. iv, 447
— —, M.: (316) cos., **4**. 245
— —, M., cos. 173: (180) IIIvir for Pisae, **12**. 135–7; (176) pr. 227; excused from prov., Sardinia, 231; (174) envoy to Aetolians, 273; (173) cos., 283, **13**. 9, with Liguria as prov., **12**. 293; defeats Ligurians, 311–3; ignores SC. freeing captives sold as slaves, 313–7; vainly demands *ovatio*, 317; (172) brother, C., defends, 319–21; procos., fights surrendered Ligurians, 349–51; twice tried, escapes conviction, 351–5; (171) counsel for veteran centurions, 387; (169) tr. mil. in Macedon, **13**. 91, 103–7, 111; captures Heracleum, 117–21; driven from Meliboea, 129–31
Popilius Laenas, M.: (139) cos.; (138) Numantines defeat, **14**. 53
— —, P.: (210) envoy to Syphax, **7** 215
— —, P.: (180) IIIvir for Pisa, **12**. 135–7
— Sabellus, C.: (178) bravery of, **12**. 195
Poppaedius Silo: *see* Pompedius Silo.
Populonium, in Etruria: (205) promises P. Scipio (Afr.) iron, **8**. 193; (202) storm drives Ti. Claudius Nero to, 513
populus: (358) with senatorial approval, passes law, **3**. 409; (208) **7**. 307; (181) **12**. 63; (406) with senatorial approval, declares war, **2**. 447; (327) **4**. 87; (293) 533; (219) **5**. 47; (191) **10**. 155; cp. (187) **11**. 155; (201) makes peace, **8**. 529; (198) **9**. 223–5; (390) creates dictator, **3**. 157; (217) **5**. 227; (327–326) approves prorogation of *imperium*, **4**. 91; (215) **6**. 105; (208) **7**. 303; (449) grants triumph without senatorial approval, **2**. 215; (356) **3**. 415; (211) with senatorial approval, grants *imperium* for day of ovation, **7**. 81; (470) tries criminal cases, **1**. 423; (384) **3**. 267; (295) **4**. 479; (189) hears appeal from decision of pont. max., **10**. 439–41; (180) **12**. 133–5; (189) may grant citizenship without senatorial approval, **11**. 119
Porcia, basilica: (184) erected, **11**. 361
Porcina: *see* Aemilius Lepidus.
Porcius Cato, C.: (114) cos., **14**. 269; Scordisci defeat, 75
— —, C.: (56) tr. pl., blocks elections, **14**. 131
— —, L., cos. 89: (90) propr., defeats Etruscans; (89) cos., killed fighting Marsi, **14**. 93
— —, M., cos. 195, cens. 184–3: (204) qu. with fleet, **8**. 307; (199) aed. pl.,

9. 173; (198) pr. for Sardinia, 173–5; expells usurers from prov., 237; secures lex Porcia protecting citizens, 4. 389; (195) cos., with Spain as prov., 9. 391–3, 531; opposes abrogation of lex Oppia, 415–29; Spanish campaign of, 441–71, 531, 10. 3, 12. 391; thanksgiving decreed for, 9. 471, 527; (194) triumphs, 535; (193) dedicates shrine to Victoria, 10. 25; (191) leg. of M' Acilius Glabrio at Thermopylae, 207–9, 215; reports victory, 223; (189) candidate for cens., 469–71; (187) supports Petilli against Scipios, 11. 187–91; (184) cens., 347–61, 383–5; removes 7 senators including L. Flamininus, 355–9; takes horse from L. Scipio Asiaticus, 359; places high assessments on luxuries, 359–61; (178) advocates Voconian law, 12. 289; (171) named advocate by Spains, 13. 7–9; (167) supports Rhodian plea, 329; (153) son's funeral shows poverty of, 14. 17; (153–151) urges Punic war, 17, 19, 21, 23–5; (149) praises Aemilianus, 25; supports effort to free Lusitanians; assails Q. Fulvius Nobilior, 27; *Origines* of, 13. 331, 14. 27; witticism of, 33, 35; character of, 11. 349–51

Porcius Cato, M.: (118) cos., 14. 269

— — (Uticensis), M., pr. 54: (57) annexes Cyprus; (56) candidate for pr.; opposes grant of provinces for ten years, 14. 131; (52) opposes Caesar's candidacy *in absentia*; candidate for cos., 135; (49) driven from prov., 205; (48) in Africa; (47) commands at Utica, 141; kills self, 143; praised by Cicero, blamed by Caesar, 215

— —, M.: (46) pardoned, 14. 143

— Laeca, P., pr. 195: (199) tr. pl., vetoes ovation, 9. 169–71; (196) one of first elected IIIviri epulones, 389; (195) pr. for Pisae, 391, 393

— Licinus, L., pr. 207: (211) leg., commands before Capua, 7. 23; (210) aed. pl., 229; (207) pr. for Gaul, 351, 357; reports Hasdrubal in Alps, 365; commands centre at Metaurus, 393–9; army of, protects Gaul, 8. 37, 45

Porcius Licinus, L., cos. 184: (193) pr. for Sardinia, 9. 555–7; (184) cos., 11. 319–23, 385; with Liguria as prov., 341; vows temple, 12. 103; prevents candidacy of aed. for pr., 11. 343–7; inactive, 363; (183) in Liguria, 363, 391

— —, L.: (181) dedicates temple vowed by father, L., 12. 103; (172) brings fleet to Brundisium, 369

Poris: (182) wife of, slays children, 12. 9–13

Porsinna (Porsenna), Arruns: (508) attacks Aricia; defeated, 1. 265–7

—, Lars, of Clusium: (508) camps on Janiculum, 1. 245–55, 3. 341; escapes attack of C. Mucius Scaevola, 1. 255–61; makes terms, demanding hostages, 261; Cloelia escapes from, 263, 4. 203; sends son against Aricia, 1. 265; gives up cause of Tarquins, 267–9; explanation of 'selling goods of Porsinna,' 263–5. *Also*: 4. 417, 7. 159

Porta Capena, etc.: *see* Capena, Caelimontana, Carmentalis, Collina, Esquilina, Flumentana, Fontinalis, Jovis, Naevia, Romana, Trigemina Porta.

portents and prodigies: Livy's reason for recording, 13. 45; (672–640) reported and expiated, 1. 111; (616–578) 139; (578–534) 159; (534–510) 191; 195; (483) 359; (470) 425; (464) 2. 19–21; (461) 35–7; (458) 101; (399) 3. 51; (398) 53–5, 177; (391) 113, 177; (390) 187; (349) 445; (344) 453; (340) 4. 19; (295) 463; 479; (293) 517; (219) 5. 65; (218) 135; 185–7; (217) 201–5; 211–3; (216) 321; 385–7; (215) 6. 109; 129; 135; (214) 207–9; (213) 317; (212) 365; 403; (211) 7. 89–91; (210) 217; (209) 249–51; (208) 305–7; (207) 357–61; (206) 8. 45–7; (205) 245; (204) 257–9; (203) 373; (202) 511–3; (200) 9. 37–9; (199) 157; (198) 177–9; (197) 243; (196) 347–9; (194) 535; (193) 557; 10. 23–5; (192) 61; 119–21; (191) 263–5; (190) 297–9; (188) 11. 119; (187) 239; (186) 281–3; (183) 365–7; 397; (182) 12. 5–7; (181) 61–3; (180) 115; (179) 141–3; 179; (177) 211–3; 223–5; 176) 233; (174)

253–5; (173) 297–9; 319; (172) 347–9; (169) **13**. 45–9; 149; (167) 297; (190–11) **14**. 239–319
porticoes: (616–578) about Forum, **1**. 131; (193) near Porta Trigemina, **10**. 29; (192) 123; (179) **12**. 159; (174) 279; (189) in Megalopolis, **11**. 113
portoria, port dues: (508) plebs freed from, **1**. 247; (199) contract for, let, **9**. 169; (187) Romans exempt from, imposed by Ambraciots, **11**. 151; (179) instituted by cens., **12**. 159
Posideum: (169) cape of Pallenê, **13**. 125
Posidonia: *see* Paestum.
Postumia, a Vestal: (420) acquitted, **2**. 401–3
Postumius, soothsayer: (88) foretells good fortune of Sulla, **14**. 187
—, C.: (168) tr. mil., receives surrendering Macedonians, **13**. 265
—, L.: (90) pr.; Samnites kill, **14**. 91
—, M.: (403) tr. mil. c. p., **3**. 3
—, M., of Pyrgi: (212) dishonest publican; punished, **6**. 349–55
— Albinus, A.: (242) cos., **6**. 41, and flamen of Mars; pont. max. holds, in city, **4**. 559, **10**. 439
— —, A.: (151) cos.; tribb. pl. imprison, for strict levy, **14**. 19
— —, A., cos. 99: (110) leg.; Jugurtha defeats, **14**. 77; (99) cos., 281; (89) leg., killed by own men, 93
— —, L., cos. 234, 229: (216) pr. for Gaul, **5**. 319; elected cos. iii; ambushed and slain, **6**. 81–3, 87, 107–9, **7**. 9, **8**. 119
— —, L., cos. 173: (180) pr. for Farther Spain, **12**. 107–9, 121; (179) 139; defeats Vaccaei, 149, 157; (178) triumphs, 201, 203; (173) cos., 283, **13**. 9, with Liguria as prov., **12**. 293; surveys public lands in Campania, 293–7, 313, 317, 345; requires Latins to be counted in own cities, 319; holds elections, 317; (171) envoy to Masinissa and to Carthage, 397; (169) candidate for cens., **13**. 49; (168) tr. mil. at Pydna, 227; (167) leg. sent to sack Aenia, 339
— —, L., cos. 154: (168) flamen of Mars, **13**. 295; (154) cos., defies auspices, dies, **14**. 251
Postumius Albinus, Sp., cos. 186: (189) pr. urb. and pereg., **10**. 431, 437, 467; (186) cos., **11**. 235, **12**. 113; suppresses Bacchanalian conspiracy, **11**. 241, 243, 249–79; holds elections, 283–5; (184) augur, 365, **12**. 135; (180) dies, 135
— — Caudinus, Sp., cos. 334, 321: (334) cos., wastes lands of Sidicini; names dict., **4**. 67; (332) cens., adds tribes, 69–71; (327) mag. eq. com. c., 91; (321) cos. ii, 163; Samnites defeat, at Caudine Pass, 165–81; passes under yoke, 181; names dict. com. c., 187; (320) urges surrender of sponsors of peace, 189–99; calling self Samnite, strikes fetial, giving cause for war, 201–5
— — Luscus, A., cos. 180: (191) leg. at Cephallania, **10**. 195; (187) aed. cur., **11**. 239; (185) pr., 285; (180) cos., **12**. 107, 117, with Liguria as prov., 109, 113; presents envoys from Spain to Senate, 107; directed to vow gifts and statues, 115; defeats Ligurians, 127–9; disciplines men, 129–31; (174–173) cens., 275–81, 317–9; (169) all receiving contracts from, barred by next cens., **13**. 55; (173) Xvir sac., **12**. 319; (171) envoy to Crete, 397; (168) envoy to arrange surrender of Perseus, **13**. 259; (167) Xvir on Macedonian terms, 299, 339, 345–7, 355; placed over Perseus, 345
— — Magnus, Sp.: (148) cos., **14**. 37, 253
— — Paullulus, Sp., cos. 174: (183) pr. for Sicily, **11**. 363; (174) cos., **12**. 251³, **13**. 9; holds levy; leaves for prov., **12**. 253, 277; (172) envoy to Asia, 427–9
— — Regillensis, A.: (397) tr. mil. c. p., **3**. 57–9; (381) ii, 273
— — —, L.: (389) tr. mil. c. p., **3**. 197; (381) ii, 273
— — —, M.: (426) tr. mil. c. p., **2**. 357; defeated at Veii, 359, 385; (423) fined, 391; (403) tr. mil. c. p., ii, **3**. 3
— — —, M.: (414) tr. mil. c. p., **2**. 417–9; defeats Aequi; withholds booty from troops, who kill him, 419–25
— — —, Sp.: 394) tr. mil. c. p., **3**.

89; defeats Aequi, 99–101; (380) cens.; dies, 291
Postumius Albus Regillensis, A., cos. 496: (499) dict., defeats Latins at Lake Regillus, **1**. 279–85, 287; vows temple to Castor, 285, 357; triumphs; (496) cos., 285; (495) leads cavalry, 301
— — —, A., cos. 464: (484) IIvir for temple vowed by father, **1**. 357; (464) cos., **2**. 11–5; defeats Aequi, 15–9; (458) envoy to Aequi, 87
— — —, Sp., (466) cos., **2**. 5; (454) sent to Athens to study laws, 107; (451) Xvir, 109; (446) leg. against Aequi and Volsci, 237–9
— — —, Sp., (432) tr. mil. c. p., **2**. 337; (431) leg. of dict. A. Postumius Tubertus, 345–9
— Megellus, L., cos. 305, 294, 291: (305) cos., triumphs over Samnites, **4**. 341–3; (295) propr., commands near Rome, 461; plunders Etruria, 463; (294) cos. ii, 481; dedicates temple to Victory, 485; in Samnium 485–9, and Etruria, 499–501; triumphs despite Senate and tribb. pl., 501–3; defeated in Apulia (?), 503; (293) leg. of cos. Sp. Carvilius; indicted by tr. pl. but escapes, 539; (291) cos. iii, elected while interrex, **7**. 225; (290) convicted for using soldiers as labourers, **4**. 547
— Tempsanus, L.: (185) pr. for Tarentum, **11**. 285, 309; checks rising of shepherds, 309–11; (184) 353
— Tubertus, A., dict. 431: (434) mag. eq., **2**. 331; (431) dict., defeats Aequi and Volsci; triumphs, 343–53, 391; condemns son to death (?), 351
— —, P.: (505) cos., triumphs over Sabines, **1**. 269; (503) cos. ii, triumphs over Aurunci and Pometia, 271–3
— Tympanus, L.: (194) qu.; Boi slay, **9**. 539
Potensis: *see* Aemilius.
Potentia, in Picenum: (184) colony at, **11**. 361–3; (174) water supply for, **12**. 281
Pothinus: (48) instigates Ptolemy XIII to kill Pompey, **14**. 141
Potidaea: *see* Cassandria.
Potidania, in Aetolia: (207) **8**. 35
Potitii: (753) priests of Hercules, **1**. 29–31; (312) teach ritual to public slaves, die, **1**. 31, **4**. 275–7, 295–7
Potitus: *see* Valerius.
praefectus annonae: (440) L. Minucius Esquilinus Augurinus named, **2**. 299, (439) 301–13
— *iure dicundo*: (211) sent from Rome to Capua, **7**. 63
— *urbis*: (534–510) appointed by king; (509) holds first consular election, **1**. 209; (465) governs city in absence of coss., **2**. 11; (462) 29, 31; (459) 81; (458) 99–101; (424) 377. *Cp.*: (404) **2**. 15; (418) 405; (325) **4**. 139; (215) **6**. 203
Praenestê, in Latium: (499) supports Rome against Latins, **1**. 279; (462) Volsci plunder fields of, **2**. 29; (383) disloyal, **3**. 271; (382–379) defeated by T. Quinctius Cincinnatus, 271–3, 291–301; (358) Gauls near, 395, **4**. 59–61; (339–338) aid Pedani against Rome, 51–3; (338) deprived of lands, 59–61; (319) L. Papirius Cursor and praetor of, 225; (217) Q. Fabius Maximus traverses, **5**. 239; (216) levy from, holds Casilinum, **6**. 57–9, 67–9; (207) C. Claudius Nero and M. Livius Salinator meet at, **8**. 37; (198) slave rising at, **9**. 235; (173) L. Postumius Albinus demands service from, **12**. 295–7; (171) P. Furius Philus in exile at, **13**. 9; (167) Prusias makes offerings at, 407–9; (82) Marius kills self at, **14**. 109–11; Sulla orders death of all at, 111. Prodigies: (217) **5**. 201; (214) **6**. 209; (166) **14**. 245; (140) 255; (137) 257; (117) 269; (93) 287
praerogativa centuria: (396) in election, **3**. 63; (296) **4**. 441; (215) **6**. 197, 203; (211) **7**. 85–7
praetexta toga: (366) worn by prr. and aedd. cur. as well as by coss., **3**. 357–9
praetextati: (216) called to service, **5**. 387
Praetextatus: *see* Sulpicius.
praetor: cos. once called, **2**. 185; *praetor maximus* required for driving nail, **3**. 365; (367) a patrician office with judicial powers

of coss., 351, 357–9; elected under same auspices as coss., **2**. 185, **4**. 121–3; (350) exercises military command, one cos. being ill, **3**. 433; (337) open to plebeians, **4**. 63, 387; (332) proposes *lex* granting *civitas*, 71; (318) draws up code for Capua, 243; (242) number of, increased to two, (228) to four, 559; (217) calls Senate in absence of coss. or dict., **5**. 225; (216) **6**. 75; (187) **11**. 153; *et saepe*; (213) duties of pr. urb. and pereg. combined, **6**. 315; (212) 347; (207) **7**. 357; (206) **8**. 43–5; (192) **10**. 121; (191) 159; (189) 437; (184) **11**. 347; (212) conducts special election, **6**. 365; (194) **9**. 553; (173) **12**. 303; (211) calls *comit. cent.* for treason trial, **7**. 13; (204) SC. directs, to investigate acts of procos., **8**. 287; (198) number of, increased to six, **9**. 239; (181) directed by SC. to forbid levy by coss., **12**. 89; (180) only four elected, 139; (176) excused from foreign service for religious reasons, 231, 385; (171) directed by SC. to name agents against cos., **13**. 5–7. *See* provinces, assignment of.

praetor: (322) Samnite official, **4**. 155

Praetutii, in Picenum: (217) Hannibal plunders, **5**. 229; (207) prepare for C. Claudius Nero, **7**. 383

Prasiae, Attic port: (200) **9**. 131

Praxo, of Delphi: (172) aids Perseus against Eumenes, **12**. 335, 341

prayer: formula of, before *contio*, **11**. 259

Priatic plain, in Thrace: (188) **11**. 141

Priene, in Caria: (189) **11**. 43

priests, deaths and/or appointments of: (463) **2**. 25–7; (453) 107; (390) **3**. 141; (300) **4**. 389; (216) **6**. 73; 103; (213) 345; (211) **7**. 91; (210) 227; (209) 235; (208) 355; (204) **8**. 357–9; (203) 459–61; (202) 515; (200) **9**. 147; (199) 173; (196) 389–91, 395; (190) **10**. 431; (184–183) **11**. 365; (180) **12**. 133–5; (177) 225; (174) 253–5; (173) 319; (172) 373; (170) **13**. 41–3; (169) 149; (167) 405

primi pili: first centurion, **3**. 511; (495) elected to dedicate temple, **1**. 305; (340) in Roman and Latin armies, **4**. 35; (212) given independent command; defeated, **6**. 417–9

princeps senatus: (209) traditionally the senior ex-censor, **7**. 251; appointment of, 251–3; (204) **8**. 351; (199, 194) **9**. 531; (189) **11**. 95; (184) 383; (179) **12**. 157; (174) 275; (169) **13**. 53; (164) **14**. 11; (159) 13

principes: term explained, **4**. 31–3

Prinnê, in Asia Minor: (190) **10**. 353

prisci Latini: *see* Latins, Ancient.

Priscus: *see* Atilius, Numicius, Servilius, Tarquinius.

prison: *see carcer*.

prisoners: (216) enlisted, **6**. 45

prisoners of war: (346) treatment of, **3**. 451; (307) **4**. 333; (212) **6**. 361; exchanges of, in First and Second Punic Wars, **5**. 279; (216) attitude towards ransoming, 389–409; (431) sold as slaves, **2**. 351; (396) **3**. 77; (389) 207; (346) 451; (307) **4**. 333; (198) **9**. 233; (173) sold by general, freed by Senate, **12**. 315; (171) **13**. 85; (169) sold by Perseus, 69; (147) maltreated by Hasdrubal, **14**. 253

Privernas: *see* Aemilius Mamercinus.

Privernates: (358) raid Roman territory, **3**. 407; (357) plundered, 409; (342) attack Norba and Setia, 513; (341) revolt, are reduced, **4**. 3; (340) territory taken from, distributed, 47; (330–329) defeated, 75–81, 145; made citizens, 81–5; (327) Samnites seek aid of, 89.

Prodigies: (209) **7**. 249; (200) **9**. 39; (173) **12**. 297; (163) **14**. 249; (117) 269; (113) 271

Proca Silvius: king of Alba, **1**. 17

procedure, judicial: (672–640) in treason trial, **1**. 93; (459) question of fact referred to private judge, **2**. 83; (212) in trial of dishonest *publicani*, **6**. 349–55; (187) in trial of L. Scipio, **11**. 191–9, 201–3, 209; (186) in trials after Bacchanalian conspiracy, 267–71

proconsul: (464) *imperium proconsule* granted to former cos., **2**. 15; (326) consular *imperium* first prorogued, **4**. 91, 105; (211) retain *imperium* in city only by special SC., **7**. 35;

INDEX

privatus sent to Spain as, 69–73; (206) **8.** 151; triumph refused to such *privatus* procos., 151; (200) **9.** 59–61; (204) not expected to leave prov., **8.** 283; (200) **9.** 141; (187) relation of cos. and, **11.** 145–7
Proculus : *see* Julius, Plautius.
Proerna, in Thessaly : (191) **10.** 201
Propontis : Galatians occupy, **11.** 51; Sangarius riv. enters, 63
propraetor : (211) L. Marcius assumes title of, **7.** 7; (201) *privatus* named, for fleet, **9.** 11
proscriptions : (82) by Sulla, **14.** 109–13; (43) by Second IIIvirate, 153, 315
Proserpina : (214) worshipped at Henna, **6.** 297, 301; (104) collection for, **14.** 275–7; (99) 281; (92) 289; (73) foretells destruction of Mithridates' siege works, 301. Temple of, in Locri : (c. 510) protected from Crotonians, **8.** 279; (c. 276) robbed by Pyrrhus, 239, 275–7, (205) by Q. Pleminius, 239, 277–9, 283, 287, **9.** 37; (200) money stolen from, 37, 157
province : (204) governor not expected to leave, without permission, **8.** 283; (200) **9.** 141; (178) **12.** 205; (171) one cos. not to enter, of other, **13.** 3–7; investigation of extortion in, 7–11; (55) assigned for five years, **14.** 131
provinces (i.e. spheres of action), assignment of : (464) **2.** 13–5; (459) 77; (458) 87; (449) 193; (421) 395; (395) **3.** 83; (393) 103; (391) 111; (382) 271; (381) 273; (379) 299; (362) 375; (360) 389; (358) 393; (357) 409; (356) 413; (353) 421; (351) 431; (350) 433; (342) 497; (341) **4.** 3; (339) 49–51; (335) 65; (329) 79; (327) 87; (325) 111–3; (323) 143; (320) 207; (311) 281; (308) 325; (307) 331; (306) 333; (305) 341; (299) 395–7; (298) 401; (297) 407; (295) 447–51, 457–9; (294) 481; (293) 509, 533–5; (218) **5.** 47; (217) 187; (216) 319; (215) **6.** 85–7, 105, 113; (214) 203–7; (213) 315–7; (212) 347–9; (211) 501, **7.** 3–5; (210) 109–11; (209) 231–5; (208) 301–5; (207) 353, 357; (206) **8.** 43–5; 205) 153–5, 191; (204) 255–7; (203) 367–71; (202) 461–3; (201) 517–21; (200) **9.** 17–9; (199) 155; (198) 173–5; (197) 239–41; (196) 345–7; (195) 391–3; (194) 529–31; (193) 557; (192) **10.** 57–9; (191) 121, 155–61; (190) 293–7, **11.** 203; (189) **10.** 437–9; (188) **11.** 117; (187) 143–7; (186) 241; (185) 285 [1]; (184) 341; (183) 363–5; (182) **12.** 3–5; (181) 59; (180) 109–15; (179) 139; (178) 185[1,3,5]; (177) 207, 211–3; (176) 227–33; (175) 243[3]; (174) 251; (173) 293; (172) 321; (171) 371, 381–5; (170) **13.** 13[4]; (169) 39–41, 53; (168) 145–7, 285; (167) 295–7; (166) 405
Proxenus, of Hypatia : (174) poisoned, **12.** 271–3
Prusias I, king of Bithynia, c. 236–186 : (208) allied with Philip, **7.** 335, **9.** 257–9; (207) enters Pergamum, **8.** 29; (205) on Philip's side in Roman treaty, 255; (196) required to free Ciani, **9.** 359; (190) rebuffs Antiochus, **10.** 363–5; (189) lands occupied by, returned to Eumenes, 463, **11.** 133
— II, king of Bythinia, 186–148 : (183) Eumenes complains of aid to, **11.** 367; Hannibal flees to, kills self, 379–83, 399; (172) married to sister of Perseus, **12.** 325, (171) but remains neutral, 373–5; (169) aids Rome, **13.** 123, 167; envoys of, in Rome, 135; (167) at Rome, seeks alliance and land, 405–9; (164) envoys of, accuse Eumenes, **14.** 11; (149) son kills, 31, 35; servile nature of, **13.** 409–11, **14.** 33
prytanis : (172) Rhodian magistrate, **12.** 427
Pseudophilippus : *see* Andriscus.
Pteleum, in Thessaly : (200) Attalus takes, **9.** 137; (192) Antiochus' fleet at, **10.** 127; (174) Perseus visits, **12.** 417; (171) P. Licinius Crassus razes, 505
Ptolemaïs : (48) **14.** 307
Ptolemy II Philadelphus, king of Egypt, 285–246 : (c. 273) alliance with, **4.** 551
— III Euergetes, king of Egypt, 246–221 : (246–241) seizes Syrian lands, **9.** 385, **10.** 49

INDEX

Ptolemy IV Philopator, king of Egypt, 221–205 : (216) frees Decius Magius, **6**. 33; envoys sent to, by Syracuse, 257, (210) by Rome, **7**. 215; (208) urges Aetolian peace on Philip, 333, **8**. 29; (204) Antiochus and Philip covet wealth of, **9**. 43, 253

— V Epiphanes, king of Egypt, 210–180 : (201) envoys to, **9**. 7; (200) Athens asks aid of, 27; prefect of, betrays Aenus to Philip, 51; hires Aetolian mercenaries, 127; (198–197) Flamininus orders Philip to return cities to, 253; (197) Antiochus III occupies cities of, in Asia, 331–5; (196) he is warned to withdraw from cities of, 369, 381–3; makes treaty with Antiochus, 385; reported dead, 387; (193) marries Antiochus' daughter, **10**. 39; (191) offer of supplies against Antiochus refused, 165–7; (190) urges Rome into Asia, 299–301

— VI Philometor, king of Egypt, 180–145 : (173) envoy to, **12**. 309; (172) loyal, 367; (171) Antiochus IV plots to recover Coelê Syria from; guardians of, promise Rome aid against Perseus, 375; (168) Antiochus feigns to restore, **13**. 151, 277, 281; makes terms with brother, Ptolemy VIII Euergetes, and returns to Alexandria, 277–9; Antiochus prepares war on, 279–81; Rome imposes peace on Antiochus and, 283, 323, 367, 409; envoys of, thank Senate, 285–7; (164–163) expelled by Euergetes, then restored, **14**. 11; (159) rules Egypt while Euergetes rules Cyrenê, 13; (148) killed aiding Demetrius II, 43

— VIII Euergetes, king of Egypt, 170–163, 145–132, 127–116 : (169) envoys of, protest acts of Antiochus IV, **13**. 151–3; comes to terms with brother, Philometor, 277–9; Antiochus prepares war on, 279–81; (164–163) expels, then re-admits Philometor, **14**. 11; (163) king of Cyrenê, 13; (145) king of Egypt on Philometor's death, 43; (131) flees to Cyprus, kills son, 67

— XII Theos, king of Egypt, 80–51 : (56) flees to Rome; restored by A. Gabinius, **14**. 131

Ptolemy XIII, king of Egypt, 51–47 : (48) drives sister, Cleopatra, from Egypt, **14**. 139; orders murder of Pompey; (48–47) Caesar defeats, 141; brother of Arsinoê, 213

— Apion, king of Cyrenê : (96) makes Rome his heir, **14**. 87, 285

—, of Telmessus : (189) land of, not given to Rhodes or Eumenes, **10**. 465

public lands : *see* land laws.

publicani : (215) furnish supplies on credit, **6**. 165–7; (213) a, becomes pref. soc., 341, 349; dishonesty of, in marine risks, 349–55; (184) protest contracts of M. Porcius Cato and L. Valerius Flaccus, **11**. 361; (167) necessity for, and danger of, in provinces, **13**. 303

Publicius Bibulus, C. : (209) tr. pl., accuses Marcellus of prolonging war, **7**. 297–9

— —, L. : (216) tr. mil., survives Cannae, **5**. 373

— Malleolus : (101) a matricide, **14**. 83

Publicola : **3**. 473; *see* Gellius, Valerius, — Potitus.

Publilia : (151) poisons husband, **14**. 17–9

Publilia tribus : (358) formed, **3**. 407

Publilius, C. : (326) imprisoned for debt, **4**. 107–11

—, Q. : (384) tr. pl., assails M. Manlius Capitolinus, **3**. 261–3

—, T. : (299) plebeian augur, **4**. 389

—, Volero, tr. pl., 472, 471 : (473) former centurion, refuses to serve in ranks, **1**. 405–7; (472) tr. pl., introduces bill electing plebeian officials in *tributa*, 407–9; (471) tr. pl. ii; bill of, is passed, 409–15

— Philo, Q., cos. 339, 327, 320, 315 : (352) Vvir mensarius, **3**. 429; (339) cos., triumphs over Latins, **4**. 49–51; dict., makes constitutional changes, 51–3; (336) first plebeian pr., 63, 387; (335) mag. eq. com. c., 67; (332) cens., 69; (327) cos. ii, 87; first to have *imperium* extended *pro consule*, 91, 105; (326) triumphs after fall of Palaepolis, 101, 105; (320) cos. iii, calls Senate *re* Caudine peace, 189; defeats Samnites, 207–17 and Apulians, 217; contra-

dictory traditions, 219; (315) cos. iv, 247[1]; (314) accused, acquitted, 267; worthy to meet Alexander, 227
Publilius Philo, Volero: (399) tr. mil. c. p., **3**. 47
— Volscus, L.: (400) tr. mil. c. p., **3**. 45
Pudicitia Patricia: (296) plebeian matrons barred from shrine of, **4**. 443–5
— Plebeia: (296) shrine of, established, **4**. 445
Pudpud: *see* Pulpud.
Pulchri promuntorium, in Africa: (204) **8**. 315
Pulex: *see* Servilius.
pullarius: (325) warns dict. L. Papirius Cursor, **4**. 115; (320) reports favourable signs, 213; (293) reports falsely; slain in battle, 515–7
pulli: *see* chickens, sacred.
Pullus: *see* Junius.
Pulpud (Pudpud, Palpud): town, **14**. 213
Pulvillus: *see* Horatius.
pulvinaria: (217) six, displayed for the 12 gods, **5**. 235; (218) prayers and/or gifts at all, 187; (217) 203; (210) **7**. 217; (209) 251; (203) **8**. 445; (200) **9**. 29; (199) 157; (193) 557; (185) **10**. 159, **13**. 299; (181) **12**. 61; (167) **13**. 299
Punic: *see* Carthaginian.
Punic fraud: (221) **5**. 11; (217) 221; (212) **6**. 489; (211) **7**. 65–9; (208) 345; (203) **8**. 447; 453–7; 481; (202) 483; 487; (195) **9**. 495; (193) 573; (172) **12**. 435
— War, First: follows war with Pyrrhus, **3**. 455; unspeakable acts of Punic commanders in, **8**. 51; Roman navy in, **5**. 247, **12**. 347; Africa often invaded in, **8**. 187; exchanges of prisoners in, **5**. 279; final victory in, after defeats, 117, **6**. 41, **7**. 159; (264) begins under Ap. Claudius Caudex, cos., **9**. 3; (264–242) course of, **4**. 553–9; (264) cause of, **8**. 483, **13**. 317; (252) games for Father Dis during, **14**. 23; (249) P. Claudius Pulcher defeated in, **5**. 341; (242) ended by C. Lutatius Catulus, **8**. 153, 165, **13**. 381; (241) peace made, gates of Janus opened, **1**. 67, **8**. 533
Punic War, Second: background of, **5**. 3–17; (219) course of, 17–49; (218) 49–173, 179–87; (217) 173–9, 187–321; (216) 321–409, **6**. 3–103; (215) 105–205; (214) 205–315; (213) 315–47; (212) 347–501; (211) **7**. 3–101; (210) 101–231; (209) 231–301; (208) 301–55; (207) 357–413, **8**. 3–43; (206) 43–153; (205) 153–255; (204) 255–359; (203) 367–461; (202) 461–517; (201) 517–533; (203) peace negotiations to end, 425–7; 445–9; (202) 473–85, 503–11; (201) 515–7, 522–31; peace formally made, 531–3; (200) Rome weakened by, for Macedonian war, **9**. 23, 27, 41, 95; elephants taken in, used in Macedon, 107; (198) slave war caused by captives of, 233–7; (193) Rome fears new Punic war, 569. *Also*: **9**. 3–5, 31, 215, 329, 347, 413, 499–501, 527, 547, 553, **11**. 187, 205, **13**. 267, 291, 379, 381
— —, Third: (154–150) preliminaries of, **14**. 15–21; (149) course of, 23–27, 29–31; (149–148) 33–5, 37; (147–146) 37–41, 253; (146) end of, 39, 41
punishments, cruel and unusual: (672–640) Mettius Fufetius torn between chariots, **1**. 103–5; (534–510) Turnus Herdonius drowned, 181; (509) traitors flogged and beheaded, 233; (217) spy's hands cut off, **5**. 309; (211) **7**. 45–7; (101) matricide sewn in sack and drowned, **14**. 83. *See* crucifixion.
punishments, military: (471) cowards scourged and beheaded, **1**. 419–21; (390) guard thrown from Rock, **3**. 161; (302) cohorts left outside camp without tents, **4**. 371; (270) legion that seized Rhegium beheaded, 553, **8**. 115; (214) required to take meals standing, **6**. 225; (209) barley issued as food, **7**. 261; (206) mutineers beheaded, **8**. 107–23; (201) deserters beheaded or crucified, 533; (180) legion put on half pay, **12**. 131; (138) deserters beaten *sub furca* and sold, **14**. 53, 57
Pupinia, near Rome: (308) P. Decius Mus at, **4**. 327; (211) Hannibal near, **7**. 35
Pupius, C.: (217) IIvir for building temple of Concord, **5**. 311

INDEX

Pupius, L., pr. 183 : (185) aed.; (184) candidate for pr. suf., **11**. 343; (183) pr. for Apulia, 363; begins Bacchanalian investigation, **12**. 63

—, P.: (409) plebeian qu., **2**. 433

purification : *see lustratio.*

purple : (195) limits on use of, **9**. 435–7

Purpurio : *see* Furius.

Puteoli, in Campania : hot springs at, **14**. 257; (215) importance of; fortified, **6**. 197, 419; (214) Hannibal attacks, 213–5; (212) grain depot at, 419, 425; (211) army for Spain embarks at, **7**. 65, 75; (203) Punic envoys land at, **8**. 445; (199) contract for tax at, **9**. 169; (197, 194) Roman colony at, 243, 529, 533; (168) Masgaba passes through, **13**. 287; 291. Prodigies: (190) **10**. 299; (177) **12**. 213; (136) 257

Pydna : in Thessaly, **13**. 123; (169) people of Dium moved to, 107; Perseus flees to, 111; (168) L. Aemilius Paulus defeats Perseus at, 211–37, 395; city surrenders, 237; Paulus leaves, 241; news of victory at, reaches Rome, 249–53

Pygela, port near Ephesus : (190) **10**. 321

Pylae : *see* Thermopylae.

Pylaemenes : slain at Troy, **1**. 9

Pylaic council of Aetolians : (200) competent on war and peace, **9**. 97; (196) meets at Thermopylae, 371

Pylus, in Messenia : (208) **7**. 335

Pyra, tomb of Hercules : (191) **10**. 245

Pyrenaeus, port in Spain : (195) **9**. 441

Pyrenees mts. : in Spain, **7**. 169; (218) Hannibal subdues tribes south of, **5**. 67; he crosses, 67, 75, 87, 181, **6**. 153; Cn. Scipio sails by, **5**. 179; (209) Hasdrubal marches toward, **7**. 289; P. Scipio (Afr.) occupies, 293; (103–102) Cimbri cross, **14**. 81

Pyrenees, promontory of : (211) **7**. 75

Pyrgi, in Etruria : (191) not exempt from naval service, **10**. 163. *See* Postumius, M.

Pyrgus, in Elis : (209) **7**. 341–3

Pyrrheum, in Ambracia : (189) Romans attack, **11**. 15; Aetolians counter-attack from, 17–9

Pyrrhias, praetor of Aetolians : (209) Philip defeats, **7**. 331–3; (200) at council at Heraclea, **9**. 133

Pyrrhus, king of Epirus, 297–272 : maternal grandfather of Hieronymus of Syracuse, **6**. 193; war with, follows Samnite wars, **3**. 455; (280) enters Italy to aid Tarentum, **4**. 549, **6**. 21, **9**. 11; Greeks and some Italians support, **6**. 143, 145, **9**. 23, **10**. 43, 459; defeats P. Valerius Laevinus, **4**. 549, **5**. 393, **6**. 359; sends Cineas to Rome, **4**. 549, **9**. 423; releases captives without ransom, **4**. 549, **5**. 395; not received in city to discuss peace, **4**. 549–51; second indecisive battle with, 551; Rome warns, of poisoner, 551, **6**. 319, **11**. 383, **12**. 435; legion sent to protect Rhegium from, **8**. 115, **9**. 91; temple of Juno in Bruttium respected by, **12**. 301; destroys Croton, **6**. 181; (279–275) in Sicily; (275) returns to Italy, **4**. 551; plunders temple of Proserpina at Locri, **8**. 239, 275–7; M' Curius Dentatus drives, from Italy, **4**. 551, **8**. 277, **13**. 383; killed in Argos, **4**. 551, **8**. 277, **9**. 23; less dangerous than Philip, **9**. 21–3; a great general, **10**. 43, 177, **14**. 175; palace of, in Ambracia, **11**. 15[1], 31

—, Camp of, in Elis : (198) **9**. 189

—, Camp of, in Laconia : (192) **10**. 77–9

Pythagoras, the philosopher : not a teacher of Numa, **1**. 63–5, **12**. 91; (c. 530) taught in Italy, **1**. 65; (181) teachings of, in ‘Books of Numa’, **12**. 91

—, son-in-law of Nabis : (195) commands in Argos, **9**. 479; slaughters Argives, 503, 525; joins Nabis in Sparta, 493, 521; envoy to Flamininus, 495, 523; (192) under Nabis, **10**. 85

Pytho, a Macedonian : (169) commands at Cassandrea, **13**. 127

Pythoüs, in Thessaly : (171) surrenders to Perseus, **12**. 457; (169) Q. Marcius Philippus considers pass by, **13**. 95; (168) Perseus garrisons, 197; L. Aemilius Paulus plans attack on, 209, 211[1]

INDEX

Quadrigarius: *see* Claudius.
quadrireme: *see* naval antiquities.
quaestor: office created after beginning of Republic, **2**. 269; (485) prosecute for treason, **1**. 355, (459) and for perjury, **2**. 81–3, (458) 85; (446) bring standards from *aerarium*, 237; (350) **3**. 433; (439) sell goods of condemned, **2**. 309; (187) **11**. 201–3, 209; (421) increased to four; opened to plebeians on equal terms, **2**. 395–9, 433; (409) first plebeian, 433, **3**. 325; (410) receive booty for *aerarium*, **2**. 431; (394) **3**. 91; (210) **7**. 181; (c. 266) increased to eight, **4**. 553; (216) former, made Senators, **6**. 79; (205) sell part of Campanian land, **8**. 195; (202) normally assigned to prov. by lot, exceptionally by SC., 489; (196) collect back taxes, **9**. 389; (180) receive unexpended military funds, **12**. 129; (173) receive tribute from Antiochus Epiphanes, 309; (167) escort foreign kings, **13**. 405–7
—, an officer in Carthage: (195) **9**. 399
quaestoria porta: gate of camp, **9**. 539, **12**. 85
Quarries: *see* Lautumiae.
Quies: (423) shrine of, **2**. 389
Quinctilis: *see* July.
Quinctilius, Cn.: (331) dict. clavi fig. c., **4**. 73
—, Sex.: (453) cos. **2**. 107
— Varus, M.: (403) tr. mil. c. p., **3**. 3
— —, M.: (203) son of P., **8**. 433
— —, P.: (203) pr. for Ariminium, **8**. 357, 369, 463; defeats Mago, 431–5; (169) flamen Martialis; dies, **13**. 149
— —, P.: (166) pr., **13**. 405
— —, P.: (9 A.D.) leg., defeated by Germans, **14**. 169
— —, T.: (185) leg. in Spain, **11**. 315; (184) reports victories, 341
Quinctian meadows: (458) once farm of L. Quinctius Cincinnatus, **2**. 91
Quinctii: (672–640) Albans, made Senators by Hostilius, **1**. 107; (319) worthy to oppose Alexander, **4**. 229
Quinctius, D.: (210) commands fleet at Rhegium; defeated and slain, **7**. 145–51
—, L.: (326) tr. mil., commands troops in Palaepolis, **4**. 101–3
Quinctius Capitolinus, Cn.: (366) first aed. cur,. **3**. 357
— —, L.: (385) tr. mil. c. p., **3**. 231
— — Barbatus, T., cos. 471, 468, 465, 446, 443, 439; (471) cos., **1**. 409; calms plebeians, 411–3; defeats Aequi, 415, 421; (468) cos. ii, defeats Volsci and Aequi, 429–33, **2**. 5; (467) IIIvir agr. div., 5; (465) cos. iii, defeats Aequi, 5–11; completes lustrum, 11; (464) defeats Aequi, 15–9; (461) defends Caeso Quinctius, 43, 47; (458) qu., urges trial of M. Volscius Fictor, 85; (451) candidate for Xvir, 117; (446) cos. iv, rebukes plebeians, 223–35; levies army with no exemptions, 235–7, 259; defeats Aequi and Volsci, 237–43; unable to protect Aricia and Ardea from plebs, 243–9; (445) opposes violence, 277; (444) interrex, 283; (443) cos. v, 285; esteemed by all, 293–5; (439) cos. vi, 301; names dict. against Sp. Maelius, 303; (437) leg. of Mam. Aemilius Mamercinus at Fidenae, 315, 317; (423) appeals for T. Quinctius Cincinnatus Poenus, 391
— — —, T.: (421) cos., **2**. 395; (405) tr. mil. c. p., 455
— Cincinnatus, Caeso: (464) military service of, **2**. 43; (462) 45; (461) opposes passage of Terentilian law; tr. pl. A. Verginius accuses, 41–9; released on bond; goes into exile, 47–9, 67; father, L., sells lands to pay forfeit, 49; (460) return of, rumoured, 51; father of, cos. suf., 65; (459) M. Volscius Fictor convicted of perjury against, 83, 85, 99
— —, C.: (377) tr. mil. c. p., **3**. 305
— —, L., cos. suf. 460, dict. 458, 439: (461) pleads for son, Caeso, **2**. 45; sells lands, lives in hovel, 49; (460) cos. suf., represses plebeians, blames Senate, 65–73; refuses re-election, 73–5; (458) dict., notified on his farm, 89–91; decrees *iustitium*, 93; defeats Aequi, 93–7; suspends cos. L. Minucius, 97–9, **4**. 131; triumphs; prevents tribunal interference with trial of M. Volscius; resigns, **2**. 99; (451) candidate for Xvir, 117; (445) opposes violence, 277; (439) dict. against Sp. Maelius, 303–9, 313, **3**.

INDEX

257; (423) memory of, venerated, **2.** 391

Quinctius Cincinnatus, L., tr. mil. c. p. 438, 425, 420: (438) tr. mil. c. p., **2.** 313; (437) mag. eq. of Mam. Aemilius Mamercinus, 315–7; (425) tr. mil. c. p. ii, 371; (420) iii, 399

— —, L., tr. mil. c. p., 386, 377: (386) tr. mil. c. p., **3.** 213; commands in city, 217, then against Volsci, 225; (377) tr. mil. c. p. ii, 305; relieves Tusculum, 309–11

— —, Q.: (415) tr. mil. c. p., **2.** 417; (405) ii, 455

— —, Q.: (369) tr. mil. c. p., **3.** 321

— — Capitolinus, T., tr. mil. c. p., 388, 385, 384: (388) tr. mil. c. p., **3.** 209; (387) IIvir sac., dedicates temple of Mars, 213; (385) tr. mil. c. p. ii, 231; mag. eq. for A. Cornelius Cossus, 233, 237; (384) tr. mil. c. p. iii, 255; (380) dict. in internal crisis, 295; defeats Praenestini, triumphs, 397–9

— — —, T.: (368) tr. mil. c. p., **3.** 327

— — Poenus, T., cos. 431, 428: (431) cos., **2.** 323, 339; Aequi and Volsci defeat; names A. Postumius Tubertus dict., 341–3; loses arm in victory, 345–53, 391; resents colleague's dedication of temple, 353; (428) cos. ii, 355; (427) cos. (?) 357; (426) tr. mil. c. p.; disagreement with others leads to disaster at Veii, 357–9; leg. of Mam. Aemilius Mamercinus, 363–71, 391; (423) tried for Veientine defeat, acquitted, 385, 391

— Crispinus, L.: (186) pr. for Nearer Spain, **11.** 235, 241; (185) defeated, then victorious, 311–7; not permitted to bring army home, 341–3; triumphs, 353–5; (183) IIIvir col. deduc., 395

— —, T., cos. 208: (214–213) commands fleet and old camp before Syracuse, **6.** 301; (212) 441–3; (209) pr. for Capua, **7.** 225, 231–3, 303; (208) cos., 299, **8.** 465, with Italy as prov., **7.** 301; attempts siege of Locri; joins M. Marcellus in Apulia, 313–5; wounded ,317–21; retires, 323–5; at Capua, names dict. com. c., 329, 345, and dies, 345, 351, **8.** 119

Quinctius Crispinus, T.: (212) defeats Campanian in single combat, **6.** 411–5

— Flamininus, Caeso: (217) IIvir for temple of Concord, **5.** 311

— —, C.: (177) pr. pereg., **12.** 207

— —, L., cos. 192: (213) augur, **6.** 345, *cp.* **13.** 41; (201) aed. cur., **9.** 13–5; (199) pr. urb., 147, 155; (198) leg. of brother, T., 321, 547, commanding fleet, 197, **10.** 27; joins allied fleets; takes Eretria, **9.** 197–9; sends envoy to Achaeans, 207; Achaean envoys sent to, 225; fails to take Corinth, 207, 225–7; winters at Corcyra, 227, 269; (197) continued in command of fleet, 241; with T. confers with Nabis, 269–71; tries to win Acarnanians, 273, 319; takes Leucus, Acarnania, 321–3, (195) takes Gytheum, 483, 491–3; at interview with Nabis, 495; commands fleet, 525; (194) assembles transports, 547; (192) cos. by aid of T., **10.** 25–9, **12.** 25, with Italy, then Gaul as prov., **10.** 57–9; plunders Boi, 61–3; profligacy of, **11.** 355–9; holds elections, **10.** 69; plunders Liguria, 119; conducts levy for 191, 121–3, 157, 159, 165; (191) leg. of M' Acilius Glabrio, 157; (184) removed from Senate, **11.** 355–9; (170) dies, **13.** 41

—, T., cos. 198, cens. 189: (205–204) propr. at Tarentum, **8.** 257; (201) Xvir agr. divid., **9.** 13; (200) IIIvir for Venusia, 145; (199) qu. 171; (198) cos., 171–3, 167, **11.** 37, with Macedon as prov., **9.** 175, **12.** 391; crosses to Greece, **9.** 167, 177–9, **11.** 31; defeats Philip by Aous riv., **9.** 181–7, 195–7, **11.** 171; occupies Thessaly, **9.** 193–7, 201–5, 215–7; takes Elatia, 205–7, 227–9, **12.** 269; seeks support of Achaeans, **9.** 207; winters, 249; (197) procos., 241; confers with Philip near Nicaea, 249–65; Senate gives full discretion to, 265; makes alliance with Nabis, 269–71; confers with Philocles, 271–3; summons Attalus, 279; gains Theban alliance, 281; at Aetolian council, 283; in Phthiotis, 283–7; defeats Philip at Cynoscephalae, 289–305, 343, **10.**

141, **11**. 149; dictates terms, the Aetolians objecting, **9**. 305–13, **10**. 253, 365, **11**. 207, 285, **12**. 483; Senate appoints Xviri to assist, in making terms, **9**. 343; (196) procos., 347; permits Boeotians to recover citizens, 351; punishes Boeotian brigandage, 357–9, **10**. 171; confers with Xviri, **9**. 359–63, 367–71; at Isthmian games proclaims freedom of Greece, 363–7, **10**. 97, **11**. 337; Antiochus sends envoy to, **9**. 387; winters, 471; (195) procos., 393; Senate refers to, the problems of Aetolia, 407, **10**. 131, and Nabis, **9**. 397, 471; decides on war with Nabis, 471–7; fails to take Argos, 477–81; sends Antiochus' envoys to Senate, 479; moves on Sparta, 481–91; aids brother, L., in capture of Gytheum, 493; confers with Nabis, 495–505; urges allies to make peace with Nabis, 505–11; gives terms to Nabis, 511–3, **10**. 365; attacks Sparta, **9**. 517–23; Nabis accepts terms, 523; places Laconian coast under Achaeans, **10**. 37, **11**. 103; the oppressed in Peloponnese flee to, 333; ill-will between Philopoemen and, **10**. 135–7; at Argos, **9**. 525; another version of war with Nabis; at Elatia; Senate decrees thanksgiving, 527, (194) ratifies peace, and orders, to return with army, 529–31; reorganizes Greece; removes garrisons, 541–9; triumphs 549–51, **11**. 159; obtains Senate for envoys of Greece and Asia, **9**. 561, 567–9; confers with Antiochus' envoys, 561–7, **10**. 45; wins consulship for L., 27; ambassador to Greece, 65; advises Achaeans to await Roman aid, 71; at council of Magnetes, 89–93; tries to prevent Aetolian invitation to Antiochus, 95–101, 233; at Chalcis, 111; at Corinth and Demetrias, 115–7; at Achaean council, 137–45; sends troops to Athens, and Chalcis, 145–7, who are attacked by Antiochus, 147; (191) sends Cn. Octavius to Thyrreum, 195; veterans of, serve against Antiochus, 209; orders Messenia to join Achaean league, 247; awards Zacynthus to Rome, 249–53; secures truce between Aetolians and M' Acilius Glabrio, 253–7; at Achaean council, 257; at Rome, supports Aetolian envoys, 291; (189) cens., 469, 473, **11**. 95, 121, **12**. 213; (185) Philip charged with attack on envoys to, **11**. 295, 297; (184) L., brother of, removed from Senate, 355; harmony between L. and, **12**. 25; influences Philip's son, Demetrius, 33, 41, 65; (183) envoy to Prusias, **11**. 379–83, 399; (181) forged letter of, used against Demetrius, **12**. 75–7, 165–7; (174) games in memory of, 285

Quinctius Flamininus, T., cos. 150: (174) gives games in honour of father, T., **12**. 285; (167) envoy to Thrace, **13**. 401; augur, 405

— Poenus Capitolinus Crispinus, T., cos. 354, 351; (367) mag. eq. to Camillus, **3**. 347; (361) dict. com. c. or for Gallic war, 383–9; (360) mag. eq. to Q. Servilius Ahala, 389; (354) cos., 419; (351) ii, 431; (342) forced to lead mutineers, 501–3, 513; secures compromise, 503–9; (334) IIIvir col. deduc., **4**. 67

Quinquatrus, festival of Minerva: (210) **7**. 103; (168) **13**. 153

quinqueremes: *see* naval antiquities.

quinqueviri agris dividendis: (383) **3**. 269

— *finibus cognoscendis*: (168) **13**. 287

— *mensarii*: (352) **3**. 429

— *muris reficiendis*: (212) **6**. 365

— *uls cis Tiberim*: (186) maintain order, **11**. 259

Quirina tribus: (c. 242) formed, **4**. 559

Quirinal hill: (578–534) Servius adds, to city, **1**. 155; (390) Fabian rites on, **3**. 155, 175; (194) temple of Fortuna Primigenia on, **9**. 553. Prodigies: (166, 165) **14**. 247

Quirinus: (390) sacred shields of Mars and, **3**. 175–7; (340) addressed in *devotio*, **4**. 37; (167) triumph celebrated on festival of, **13**. 401. Temple of: (435) Senate meets in, **2**. 327; (329) opposite shrine of Semo Sangus, **4**. 81; (293) dedicated, 537; (206) struck by lightning, **8**. 47. *See* Janus; flamen Quirinalis.

Quirites: origin of name, **1**. 49; used as term of address in *contio*, e.g., **1**.

INDEX

59; as synonym for citizen, e.g., **2.** 59, **7.** 9; in formal expression, e.g., **1.** 83–5, **4.** 23, 37, **5.** 233, **12.** 233
Quirites' ditch: *see* Fossa Quiritium.

Rabuleius, M': (450) Xvir, **2.** 117; (449) shares Sabine command, 139
Racilia: (458) Cincinnatus' wife, **2.** 91
Raecius, M.: (208) envoy to Massilia, **7.** 355
—, M.: (170) pr., raises troops, **13.** 35; ordered to summon Senators, 39
Raeti, Alpine tribe: akin to Etruscans, **3.** 117; (15) Tiberius and Drusus overcome, **14.** 165
Ralla: *see* Marcius.
Rammius, L., of Brundisium: (172) accuses Perseus, **12.** 341–3, 411, 413
Ramnes: one of early tribes, **4.** 379
— (Ramnenses), equestrian century: (753–717) Romulus forms, **1.** 51, 131; (618–578) Elder Tarquin doubles, 133
Raphia, in Phoenicia: (193) **10.** 39
raven: (349) aids M. Valerius Corvus against Gaul, **3.** 445.
Raving mts: *see* Insani montes.
Rea Silvia: *see* Rhea Silvia.
Reatê, Sabine town: (211) Hannibal in, **7.** 41–3; (205) provides men for P. Scipio (Afr.) **8.** 195. Prodigies: (212) **6.** 365; (211) **7.** 89; (203) **8.** 373; (190) **10.** 299, **14.** 239; (182) **12.** 5, **14.** 241; (179) **12.** 143; (169) **13.** 47; (162) **14.** 249; (130) 261; (76) 299
recuperatores: (210) to decide award of mural crown, **7.** 183; (171) for claims for extortion in Spain, **13.** 7–11
Red sea (i.e., Indian Ocean): (327–325) Macedonian conquests extend to, **12.** 455, **13.** 273; (191) Roman rule may reach, **10.** 213
re-election: (342) within ten years forbidden, **3.** 513
Regia: (148) burned, **14.** 253; (117) spears of Mars in, 269, (102) 277, (98) 283, (95) 285
Regillensis: *see* Postumius Albanus.
Regillus: *see* Aemilius.
Regillus, Sabine town: **2.** 195
—, Lake: (499 or 496) A. Postumius Albus defeats Latins at, **1.** 279–85, 289, 319, **3.** 199, 295, **4.** 19, 25; (460) L. Quinctius Cincinnatus calls armed assembly at, **2.** 71
Regium: *see* Rhegium.
Regulus: *see* Atilius.
religatio: (180) M. Fulvius Nobilior banished beyond New Carthage, **12.** 131
religion: (715–672) Numa organizes, **1.** 71–3
religions, foreign: (428) forbidden, **2.** 357; (213) **6.** 343–5; (186) **11.** 265
Remens, near Veii: (173) **12.** 297
Remus: son of Rhea Silvia and Mars, **1.** 17; childhood and youth of, 17–23; founds Rome; slain by Romulus, 25; (61) lightning strikes she-wolf of Romulus and, **14.** 303
Rethogenes: (143) a Celtiberian, joins Romans, **14.** 47
Rex: *see* Marcius.
rex sacrorum (*rex sacrificulus*, king of sacrifices): (509) in charge of certain rites, **1.** 221–3; (449) retains regal title, **2.** 129; (310) **4.** 295; (368) not open to plebeians, **3.** 345; (210) vacancy not filled, **7.** 227; (208) filled, 355; (180) incompatible with military duties; method of filling office, **12.** 133–5
Rhea Silvia, daughter of Numitor: a Vestal; mother of Romulus and Remus by Mars, **1.** 17–9
Rhegium (Regium) in Bruttium: (c. 280) seized by Campanian legion sent as guard, **4.** 549, **8.** 115–7, **9.** 91–3; (c. 270) freed, **4.** 553, **9.** 93; in Federation, **9.** 87, **10.** 47–9; (216) loyal, **6.** 101; (215) resists Hanno, 175–9; (211) Hannibal moves on, **7.** 43–5; (210) fleet at, 145–7; troops placed in, ravage Bruttium, 157; (209) 255; (205) Locrians in, plot recovery of Locri, **8.** 229–31, 239; (204) Q. Pleminius brought from Naples to, 289–91; (191) supplies ships for C. Livius Salinator, **10.** 275, (171) for war with Perseus, **12.** 439; (136) almost destroyed by fire, **14.** 257, (91) by earthquake, 291, (44) by Aetna, 215
Rhine riv.: (55) Caesar crosses, **14.** 131; (12–9) Drusus subdues Germans across, 165, 167

INDEX

Rhinocolura, between Egypt and Syria: (168) **13**. 281
Rhion (Rhium), strait of Gulf of Corinth: (209) Aetolians cross, **7**. 331; (208–207) Punic fleet shuns, **8**. 31
Rhizon, in Illyricum: (167) supports Rome, **13**. 335–9
Rhoda, in Spain: (195) **9**. 441
Rhodes: of Argive origin, **10**. 465; (209) envoys from, urge Aetolian peace on Philip, **7**. 333–5; (207) **8**. 29; (201) envoys from, congratulate Rome on Punic defeat, **13**. 315, report discontent in Asia, **9**. 7; (200) with Attalus, defeats Philip at sea, 43–9, 283, then relaxes efforts, 49–55; honoured in Athens, 47–9; sends ships to Athens, 65; with Romans, raids Chalcis, 67; P. Sulpicius Galba sends envoys to, 83; fleet of, joins Romans, 135, 139; (198) operations about Euboea, 197–201, and Corinth, 201, 207, 283, **10**. 453; envoys of, at Achaean council, **9**. 207–11, which approves alliance with, 223; (198–197) demands of, presented to Philip, 251, 255, who answers, 259–61; (197) defeats Macedonians; recovers Peraea but not Stratonicea, 323–9; checks Antiochus, 331–5; congratulates Rome on Philip's defeat, **13**. 315; (196) Carian cities given to, **9**. 361; (195) aids attack on Nabis, 483, 491, 495, 525; included in proposed peace, 511; (191) fleet of, joins Roman after defeat of Polyxenidas; dismissed, **10**. 277, 285, (190) 313, 315; L. Scipio wins friendship of, **11**. 209; Polyxenidas defeats fleet of, **10**. 315–27, 331, 367, 373, **13**. 319; sends new fleet to Samos, **10**. 327–33, **13**. 319; guards strait of Cephallania, **10**. 331; at Roman council on Samos; C. Livius Salinator visits, 335; he dismisses, 339; fleet of, with L. Aemilius Regillus, 339–45, 353; favours peace, 345; defeats Hannibal off Sida, 353–61, **13**. 319; with Roman fleet, **10**. 361–3, defeats Polyxenidas off Myonnesus, 373–81; returns home, 381–3; ships of, at Megistê, 421; (189) envoys of, in Rome, 443, **13**. 315; Eumenes attacks, before Senate, **10**. 445–7; envoys of, answer Eumenes, 453–61; receives Lycia and part of Caria, 463–5, **11**. 133, **13**. 315; fails to get Soli, **10**. 465–7; aids Aetolians seeking peace, **11**. 11, 29, 33; (188) rights of, within kingdom of Antiochus to be respected, 127–9; (182) complains of slaughter in Sinopê, **12**. 7; (178) ordered to cease ill-treating Lycians, 203; (175) gifts of Antiochus IV to, 249; (174) harasses Lycia, 273; (172) envoy of, in Rome answers Eumenes, 333–5; friendship with, renewed, 347; drawn unwillingly into war with Perseus, **13**. 135; suspected of aiding him, **12**. 367, **13**. 139; prepares naval aid for Rome, **12**. 427–9; refuses to aid Perseus, 429–33; (171) Rome sends home ships of, 465, **13**. 321; (169) envoys of, urge peace with Perseus, 135–7, 323–5; accused of treachery; Lycia and Caria freed from, 137–9; (168) Perseus and Gentius send envoys to, 165–7, 185; Perseus dismisses captured ships of, 181; agrees to try to end war, 185–7; sends envoys to L. Aemilius Paulus, 205; Senate rebukes envoys of, 255–7; C. Popilius and C. Decimus in, 273–5; agrees to punish those responsible, 275–7; (167) envoys of, rebuffed after defeat of Perseus, 311–3; declaration of war on, vetoed, 313–5; defends conduct, 315–29; required to give up Caria and Lycia, 331–3; seeks alliance in place of 'friendship,' 331–3; suppresses Caunian revolt, 333; (164) enters alliance, **14**. 11; (100) Metellus Numidicus in exile at; a philosophical centre, 85; (88) resists Mithridates, 99; (82) procos. C. Norbanus, one of proscribed, in, 113. *See* Epicrates, Eudamus.
Rhoduntia, above Thermopylae: (191) Aetolians occupy and hold, **10**. 207–9, 215
Rhoeteum, on Hellespont: (190) surrenders to C. Livius Salinator, **10**. 317; L. Scipio moves to, 395–7; (188) given to Ilium, **11**. 133
Rhone riv.: (218)P. Scipio at mouth

of, sends cavalry upstream, **5**. 75, 83–5, 117–9; Hannibal crosses, 75–83, 87, 111, 125, **7**. 367; he moves up, to 'Island,' **5**. 89; Scipio at Hannibal's camp on, 93, 115–7, 119–21; Cn. Scipio sails to Spain from, 179; (103) Cimbri plunder between Pyrenees and, **14**. 81; (12) altar of divine Caesar on, 165
Rhotrine springs: (189) **11**. 49
Rimini: *see* Ariminum.
ring (*anulus*): worn by Senator, his wife, and children, **7**. 137
Roman colonies: *see* colonies.
— games (*ludi Romani*, *ludi magni*), annual: (616–578) Elder Tarquin institutes, **1**. 131; (322) dictator to give signal at, **4**. 155; (293) military crowns first worn at; palms first awarded at, 541; (201) drama at, **9**. 13; (194) Senators given separate seats at, 533, 555; (168) begin on Sept. 15; news of Pydna reaches Rome during, **13**. 249–51. Celebrated with one or more repetitions: (491) **1**. 337; (367) **3**. 351; (216) **6**. 103; (213) 347; (210) **7**. 229; (209) 299; (208) 355; (207) **8**. 43; (205) 249; (204) 359; (203) 461; (202) 515; (201) **9**. 13–5; (200) 147; (199) 173; (198) 239; (197) 345; (196) 391; (194) 555; (189) **11**. 117; (187) 239; (179) **12**. 179; (168) **13**. 249–51. Prodigy at: (187) **11**. 239; (114) **14**. 269
— games, votive: (194) celebrated, **9**. 533
Romana porta, at Capua: (179) **12**. 141–3
Rome, Romans: *passim*.
Rome, city of, as divinity: (170) temple to, at Alabanda, **13**. 23
Romilius Rocus Vaticanus, T.: (455) cos., **2**. 103; defeats Aequi; (454) condemned for withholding booty, 105; (451) Xvir, 109
Romularis: *see* Ruminalis.
Romulea, Samnite city: (296) **4**. 419–21
Romuli casa (hut of Romulus): (390) **3**. 183
Romulus: son of Mars and Rhea Silvia, **1**. 5, 17; cast into Tiber; nursed by wolf or by Larentia, 19; early life of, 19–21; makes Numitor king, 21–3; founds Rome, 25, **2**. 129, 309, **3**. 85, 359, **14**. 315; slays Remus, **1**. 25; establishes laws, 31; opens sanctuary; appoints Senators, 33; seizes Sabine women, 33–9, **9**. 429; kills king of Caenina; dedicates *spolia opima*, **1**. 39–41, **2**. 321, 325, 365; defeats Antemnates and Crustumii; makes them citizens, **1**. 41–3; vows temple to Jupiter Stator, 45–7, **4**. 505; defeats Sabines, **1**. 45–9; shares throne with T. Tatius, 49, 191, **2**. 267, **3**. 347, **12**. 145; divides people into *curiae*, **1**. 51; gives equal suffrage to all, 153; forms three centuries of *equites*, 51, 131, 153; renews covenant with Lavinium, 51; defeats Fidenae and Veii, 51–7; disappears; is deified, 57–9, 171; appears to Proculus Julius, 59–61; (460) prayer to, **2**. 59; (63) lightning strikes she-wolf of Remus and, **14**. 303. *Also*: **1**. 71, 75, 115, **2**. 269, **3**. 167, **4**. 463, **14**. 227
Romulus Silvius, 11th king of Alba, **1**. 17
rorarii: (340) young soldiers, **4**. 31, 39
Roscius, L.: (438) envoy to Fidenae; slain, **2**. 313
— Otho, L., pr. 63: (67) tr. pl., reserves theatre seats for *equites*, **14**. 123
rostra, in Patavium: (302) **4**. 367
—, in Rome: (438) envoys slain at Fidenae honoured with statues on, **2**. 313; (338) named from beaks of ships of Antium, **4**. 61; (325) dict. removes mag. eq. from, 129; (216) M. Fabius Buteo names Senators from, **6**. 77–9; (187) P. Scipio Africanus accused from, **11**. 179–81; no eulogy on him from, 191; he forbade his statue on, 199; (186) coss. mount, for *contio*, 259; (87) heads of Marius' victims on, **14**. 101; (44) Caesar's body burned before, 147; (43) Cicero's head and hand displayed on, 153, 219; vultures appear as Octavius mounts, 315
Rubicon riv., N. of Ariminum: (49) **14**. 205
Rufinus: *see* Cornelius.
Rufrium, Samnite town: (326) **4**. 99

INDEX

rufuli: *tribb. mil. ad leg.* appointed by the general, **3**. 373
Rufus: *see* Hostilius, Minucius, Pinarius, Pompeius, Pomponius, Rutilius, Salvidienus, Sulpicius.
Rullianus: *see* Fabius Maximus.
Ruminalis: fig tree of Romulus and Remus, **1**. 19; (296) statue of Romulus, Remus, and wolf at, **4**. 445–7
Rupilius, P.: (132) cos., ends slave war in Sicily, **14**. 65
Rusca: *see* Pinarius.
Ruscino, N. of Pyrenees: (218) **5**. 67–9
Rusellae, in Etruria: (302) Etruscans defeated near, **4**. 371–77; (294) captured, 501; (205) promises supplies to P. Scipio (Afr.), **8**. 193
Rusucmon, Punic port: (203) **8**. 399
Rutilius, M.: (c. 220) loses bride, **14**. 181
—, P.: (169) tr. pl., attacks censors, **13**. 55–61; disenfranchised, 143
— Calvus, P.: (166) pr., **13**. 405
— Crassus, Sp.: (417) tr. mil. c. p., **2**. 411
— Lupus, P.: (90) cos., scorns sign, **14**. 293; Marsi defeat and slay, 91, 293
— Rufus, P., cos. 105, historian: cited and rejected, **11**. 383; (105) cos. **14**. 275; (97) leg. of C. Mucius, unjustly condemned for extortion, 87
Rutilus (Rutulus): *see* Cornelius, Marcius, Nautius, Sempronius, Verginius Tricostus.
Rutulians: defeated by Aeneas, **1**. 11–3; first settlers at Saguntum, **5**. 19; (534–510) war prepared against, **1**. 197; (442) land at Ardea granted to, **2**. 295

Sabatina tribus: (387) added, **3**. 213
Sabatini, Campanians: (210) **7**. 129–33
Sabellians: *see* Samnium.
Sabellus: *see* Popilius; Samnites.
Sabines: (753–717) Romans seize women of, **1**. 35–9; attack Rome, occupying citadel, 43–7, 75, **2**. 59–61, **9**. 429; women of, make peace, **1**. 47–9; become one people with Romans, 49, 125, **2**. 267, 271, **12**. 147; settle on Capitoline and Citadel, **1**. 119; (716) fear loss of power on Romulus' death, 61; Numa from, becomes king, 61–7, **2**. 267; (672–640) Tullus Hostilius defeats, 107–11; Ancus Marcius son of a, 125; (616–578) Elder Tarquin defeats, 131–9; (578–534) sacrifice to Diana by, forestalled, 159; (505–504) defeated, 269–71; Ap. Claudius from, 271, **2**. 267, **4**. 387; (501) violence of, in Rome, **1**. 275, 341; tacit truce with, 277; (495–494) veterans of wars with, 291–3, 311; raid Roman fields, 301, 305; (494) defeated, 313, 317–9; (479) always hostile, 383; (475) defeated, 397–9; (470) fields of, raided, 425; (469) raid to walls, 427; (468) defeated, 429; (460) attack by, feared, **2**. 55; (458) raid to walls, 87; defeated, 89, 99–101; (457) indecisive campaign, 101–3; (449) raid and withdraw, 123–5, 131; defeat Xvir Q. Fabius Vibulanus, 139–41; Roman army in land of, joins plebeians on Aventine, 169–71; defeated by M. Horatius Barbatus, 193, 207–13, 243; (343) subjugated, **3**. 471; (319) in Federation, **4**. 237; (310) Samnites consider march through, 313; (290) rebel; are defeated, 547; (217) Q. Fabius Maximus crosses, **5**. 239; (205) promise P. Scipio (Afr.) soldiers, **8**. 195. Prodigies: (578–534) **1**. 159; (216) **5**. 321; (214) **6**. 207; (200) **9**. 39; (196) 349; (174) **12**. 281. *Also*: **3**. 437, **12**. 389. *See* T. Tatius.
Sabinus: *see* Claudius, Sextius, Titurius.
sacred laws: *see lex sacrata.*
Sacred Mount: (494–493) plebeians secede to, **1**. 323–7, 333, 413, **2**. 53, 171–3, 205, 229, **3**. 507, **4**. 291, **9**. 439; first tribb. pl. elected on, **1**. 325–7, **2**. 181; (449) plebeians move from Aventine to, **2**. 171–3, 205, 229
sacred spring: (217) vowed; formula for, **5**. 231–5; (195) celebrated, **9**. 395; (194) repeated, 531–3
Sacred way: (508) statue of Cloelia on, **1**. 263; (169) censors order wall on, destroyed, **13**. 55

INDEX

Sacriportus, in Latium: (82) **14.** 109
sacrosanctity: (452) of tribb. pl. not to be touched by Xviri, **2.** 109; (449) nature of, 183–5; (44) granted to Caesar, **14.** 145
Saecular games (Festival of the Age): (249) celebrated for 3d time, **14.** 23, 181; (149) for 4th time, 23, 31, 183, (17) by Augustus, 223–5
Saepinum, in Samnium: (293) L. Papirius Cursor takes, **4.** 531, 535
Safety: *see* Salus.
Sagalassenes, Pisidians: (189) **11.** 49
Saguntia, in Spain: (195) **9.** 465
Saguntum, in Spain: location and origin, **5.** 19–21; (226) Rome and Carthage guarantee independence of, 7; (221) Hannibal decides to attack, 13, the Turdetani giving a pretext, 17, **6.** 313, **8.** 157; appeals to Senate, which sends envoys, 17–9; withstands Punic siege, 19–25, 27–31; Romans vainly protest in Carthage, 25–31, 131, 247; (219) Hannibal takes, 31–43, 59, 87, 89, 115, 121, **6.** 61, **9.** 53, 447–9; date of siege, **5.** 43–5; fall of, told in Rome, 45, causes Punic war, 45–7, **6.** 313, **8.** 155, 483, **9.** 57; legal position of, **5.** 49–55; failure to save, costs Rome allies, 55–7, **9.** 21; (217) P. and Cn. Scipio move on, **5.** 273–7; (214) recovered, **6.** 313; (211) Hasdrubal winters near, **7.** 77; (205) envoys of, in Rome, **8.** 155–61; (203) envoys bring Punic prisoners to Rome, 443; Punic envoys call Hannibal's attack on, unauthorized, 447
Salaeca, in Africa: (204) Hanno occupies, **8.** 339; P. Scipio (Afr.) takes, 343
Salapia, Apulian port: (214–213) Hannibal winters at, **6.** 241, 327; (210) delivered to cos. M. Marcellus, **7.** 143–5, 203, 325; (208) repels Hannibal, 325–7
Salaria via: (361) **3.** 383
Salassi: Alpine tribe, **5.** 113; (143) inflict disaster, **14.** 255; subdued, 47; (25) 165
Salê, in Thrace: (188) **11.** 141
Salernum: (195) Roman colony at, **9.** 529, (194) 533
Salganea, on Euripus: 192) Euthymidas driven from, **10.** 113–5; Antiochus takes, 133, 147–9
Salii: (715–672) Numa establishes 12 for Mars, **1.** 71, (672–640) and Tullus 12 for Quirinus, 99; (409) patrician, **2.** 435; (190) Africanus, one of, leaves army on day shields are moved, **10.** 389
Salinae, salt works: (640–616) Ancus Marcius establishes, near Ostia, **1.** 123; (390) Etruscans defeated at, **3.** 153; (356) 413–5; (353) Etruscans raid, 423
—, in Rome: (213) **6.** 327
Salinator: origin of name, **8.** 351–3. *See* Livius, Oppius.
Sallentini, in S.E. Italy: (307) defeated, **4.** 331; (302) 363; (269) submit, 553; (244) colony sent into land of, 559; (215) M. Valerius Laevinus to protect, **6.** 163; (214) Numidians plunder, 241; (213) small towns of, join Hannibal, 341; (209) Q. Fabius Maximus in, **7.** 267; (208) assigned to Q. Claudius, 301; (207) 357, 373; C. Hostilius Tubulus attacks Hannibal among, 371–3
Sallustius Crispus, C., pr. 46, the historian: criticism of **14.** 229
Salluvii, Gauls: enter Italy, **3.** 121; (125) defeated, **14.** 69; (123) 73; (90) 91. *See* Ligurians; Toutomotulus.
Sallyes, Ligurians: (125) defeated, **14.** 265; (122) 267
Salonius, C.: (194) IIIvir col. deduc., **9.** 535; (173) Xvir agr. divid., **12.** 303
—, P.: (342) tr. mil. or centurion, opposes mutiny, **3.** 511
— Sarra, Q.: (192) pr. for Sardinia, **10.** 29, 59
salt: (508) monopoly in, becomes public, **1.** 247; (204) price of, raised by censors, **8.** 351–3; (167) Macedonian republics but not Dardanians forbidden to import, **13.** 349–51. *See* Salinae.
salt-cellar (*salinum*) (210) ex-curule magistrates retain, **7.** 137
Salui, Gauls: oppose Massilienses, **3.** 119; (218) P. Scipio coasts by, **5.** 75
Salus (Safety): (311 temple to,

vowed, (306) contracted for, **4**. 341, (302) and dedicated by C. Junius Bubulcus, 363; (180) statue vowed to, to avert pestilence, **12**. 115; (176) no good omen in sacrifice to, 229. Portents in temple of: (206) **8**. 47; (166) **14**. 247; (113) 271; (104) 277

Salvidienus Rufus Salvius, Q., cos. desig., 39: (42) leg. of Octavius; Sex. Pompeius defeats, **14**. 155; (39) condemned for treason, kills self, 157

sambuca: (88) siege engine, **14**. 295

Samê, on Cephallania: (198) fleet at, **9**. 197; (191) C. Livius Salinator plunders, **10**. 275–7; (189) M. Fulvius Nobilior takes, **11**. 97–101

Samnite: a type of gladiator, **4**. 323

Samnium, Samnites, Sabellians: (423) take Capua, **2**. 377, **3**. 497, **4**. 507; (411) prevent grain purchases, **2**. 427; (354) make alliance, **3**. 421, 455, 459, 465; (343) causes of First Samnite War, 455–69; attack Campanians, 455–63, who give selves to Rome, 465–7, **4**. 5, **7**. 49; ordered to cease attacks on allies, **3**. 467, **6**. 15, **9**. 93; war on, declared, **3**. 467–9, **4**. 479; defeated by M. Valerius Corvus, **3**. 469–77, 491–5, 505, by A. Cornelius Cossus and P. Decius Mus, 469, 477–91, **5**. 399; Campanians protected from, **3**. 495, 497; (342) quiet, 499; war with, costs Rome allies, 513; (341) L. Aemilius Mamercus plunders, **4**. 5; obtain peace, 5–7; attacked by Roman allies, 7–9; (340) allied with Rome against Latins and Campanians, 9–17, 21, 41–5; (332) Alexander of Epirus defeats, 67–9; (330) warned not to molest Fabrataria and Luca, 73–5; (329) relations with Rome precarious, 81; (328) 87; (327) L. Cornelius Lentulus commands against, 87, 91; raise army, defy envoys, 87–9; (326) war declared on, 99; Palaepolis drives out, 99–105; allied with Lucanians, 105–7, and Vestini, 111; (325) L. Papirius Cursor dict. against, 113; defeated by Q. Fabius Maximus, 115–9, by Cursor, 139–43; granted year's truce, 143; wasted, 143–5; (322 defeated by A. Cornelius Cossus or Fabius, 147–55; (321) shut Romans in Caudine Pass, 163–71; reject advice of Herennius Pontius, 171–3; send Romans under yoke, 173–85, **5**. 249; (320) refuse to accept sponsors of Caudine surrender, **4**. 189–205; seize Fregellae, 207; defeated by Q. Publilius Philo; flee to Luceria, 207–11; defeated by Cursor or Lentulus, 211–9, **5**. 249, **6**. 361; (319) garrison of, in Satricum betrayed, **4**. 221–3; (318) truce for two years with, 241–3; (316) defeated by L. Aemilius Mamercus, 245, (315) by Fabius, 245–53; (314) Ausones and Luceria recovered from, 259–61; M. Poetelius Libo and C. Sulpicius Longus defeat, at Caudium, 267–71; (313) capture Fregellae; flee, 271; (312) war with, ended; renewed on rumours of Etruscan war, 273–5; (311) take Cluviae, 281; C. Junius Bubulcus defeats, 281–5, 339–41; (310) C. Marcius Rutulus takes Allifae from, 309–11; rejoice in reported Roman loss in Ciminian forest, 311–3; fight drawn battle with Rutulus, 313; defeated by Cursor, P. Decius Mus, and M. Valerius Corvus, 319–25, 505; (309) arms of, displayed in triumph, 319, 323; (308) defeated by Fabius, 325–9, (307) 331–3, (306) by P. Cornelius Arvina and Q. Marcius Tremulus, 333–9, (305) by L. Postumius Megellus and Ti. Minucius Augurinus, 341–5; (304) ancient treaty with, renewed, 345–7; (303) colony in land of, 361; (300) quiet, 379; (299) seek allies, 397; (298) invade Lucania, 399; war on, declared, 401; Cn. Fulvius defeats, 401, 403; Etruscans join, 403; (297) Fabius and Decius defeat, near Tifernum, 407–13; (296) Decius drives, into Etruria, 415–7; he takes cities of, 417–21; L. Volumnius Flamma Volens and Ap. Claudius Caecus defeat Etruscans and, 421–37; colonies established for protection against, 439, **5**. 247; (295) command against, discussed, **4**. 455–9; defeated by Fabius and Decius at Sentinum 461–77 by

INDEX

Volumnius at Mt. Tifernus, 465, 475, and near Caiatia, 477–9; Fabius triumphs over, 475–7; continue war, 479–81; (294) M. Atilius Regulus and L. Postumius Megellus defeat, 481–99; Postumius triumphs over without permission, 501–3; various accounts of year, 503–5; (293) levy of, under special vow, 505–9, 513; defeated by Sp. Carvilius Maximus at Amiternum, 509, by L. Papirius Cursor at Aquilonia, 511–25, 529, **6**. 205; Carvilius takes cities of, **4**. 525–35; Papirius defeats, at Saepinum and triumphs, 531, 535–9; (292) defeated by Q. Fabius Gurges, (290) by M' Curius Dentatus; treaty with, renewed, 547; (282) revolt; are defeated, 549; (278) support Pyrrhus, **6**. 143, **9**. 23; (272) successful campaigns against, **4**. 551; (268) colony sent to Beneventum in, 553; (217) Hannibal crosses, **5**. 243; support Roman winter quarters, 255; Hannibal feigns march through, 261; aid M. Minucius Rufus at Larinum, 283–5; Hannibal master of, 287, (216) 379, 409, **6**. 35; he moves to, after Cannae, 3; (215) seek Punic aid against M. Marcellus, 143–7; in Punic army, 145; (214) Q. Fabius Maximus plunders, 237; (212) Roman armies in, 389; (211) Hannibal crosses, **7**. 41, 43; (210) Marcellus in, 203, 207; (207) in Roman army, 381; (201) Xvir agr. assig. in, **9**. 13; (200) expected to support Philip, 23; (180) Ligurians settled in, **12**. 119, 127–9; (177) come to Fregellae, 209; (168) cavalry from, at Pydna, **13**. 225; (91) rebel, **14**. 89; (90) defeat L. Julius Caesar; defeated by him, 91, (89) by L. Cornelius Sulla, and by C. Cosconius and Lucanus, 93; (87) join Marius and Cinna; defeat Plautius, 101; (82) Sulla defeats, at Colline gate, 109, 173; (81–80) Sulla i n, 113. Climate of, **4**. 535. *Also*: **3**. 509, **4**. 237, 307, **6**. 15, **7**. 159, **8**. 115

Samos: (200) complains of Philip's cruelty, **9**. 91; (197) Rhodes protects, 335; (190) naval operations near, **10**. 317–43, 353–5, 361, 367–73, **12**. 161, **13**. 319; (171) four triremes from, join Romans, **12**. 465

Samothrace: a sacred island, **13**. 261–3; (172) Perseus' conference at, **12**. 361; (171) possible refuge for him, 445; (168) he offers to place funds in, **13**. 171; he flees to, after Pydna, 239, 243, 253, 259–65, 391, and surrenders, 265–7, 309, 395; (167) his children moved from, 345

Sanctuary: *see* Asylum.

sanctuary, right of: (192) at Delium, **10**. 147; (168) at Samothrace, **13**. 261

Sangarius riv., in Bithynia: (189) **11**. 63

Sangus Semo (Dius Fidius): (329) shrine of, in Rome, **4**. 81; (199) in Veliternum, **9**. 157

Sapinia tribe, Umbrian district: (201) on way to Boi, **9**. 9; (196) 377

Sappinates, in Etruria: (392) raid Roman lands, **3**. 109; (391) plundered, 111

Sapriportis, near Tarentum: (210) **7**. 147

Sardinia, Sardi: (259) L. Scipio conquers, **4**. 555; (235) T. Manlius Torquatus subdues revolt in, 559, **5**. 45, **6**. 121; occupation of, a cause of Second Punic War, **5**. 5, 117, 123, 127, 131, 157, 379, **8**. 475, 481; (217) pr. sent to, **5**. 285; Cn. Servilius Geminus takes hostages from, 305; (216) A. Cornelius Mammula reports lack of money and grain in, **6**. 71–3; (215) allotted to Q. Mucius Scaevola, 105, 109, 119; Carthage sends Hasdrubal Calvus to, 111–3, 121; rebellion brewing in, 111, 119, **7**. 159; T. Manlius Torquatus sent to, **6**. 119–21; he defeats Carthaginians, 137–41; T. Otacilius Crassus defeats Punic fleet off, 141; paid taxes in kind before war, now pays nothing, 165; (214) Scaevola continued in, 207, 209; (213) 317; (212) 349, **7**. 5; grain from, **6**. 419, 425; (211) allotted to L. Cornelius Lentulus, 501, **7**. 5; (210) to P. Manlius Volso, 111; Punic fleet crosses to, 227; (209) allotted to C. Aurunculeius, 231,

233; (208) 303; (207) to A. Hostilius Cato, 357, **8**. 45; (206) to Ti. Claudius Asellus, 45; (205) to Cn. Octavius, 155, 199, 257; (204) to Ti. Claudius Nero, 255, 257, who sends grain to army, 347; (203) to P. Cornelius Lentulus Caudinus, 369; fleet organized for, 371; sends supplies to P. Scipio (Afr.), 375, 451; Punic fleet defeated off, 437; (202) Hannibal gives up, 481; grain from, 511; Ti. Claudius Nero storm bound on, 513; (201) allotted to M. Fabius Buteo, 517, 521, 523; (200) to M. Valerius Fallo, **9**. 27; (199) to L. Villius Tappulus; veterans of wars in, receive lands, 155; (198) allotted to M. Porcius Cato, 175, who sends supplies to Greece, expels usurers, 237; (197) to L. Atilius, 239; (196) to Ti. Sempronius Longus, 347; (195) 393; (194) to Cn. CorneliusMerenda, 531; (193) to L. Porcius Licinus, 557; (192) to Q. Salonius Sarra, **10**. 59; (191) to L. Oppius Salinator, 121, 159, 161; Antiochus urged to attack Italy opposite, 179; second tithe imposed, 161; (190) Salinator continued in; second tithe imposed, 297; (189) allotted to Q. Fabius Pictor, who remains in Rome; second tithe imposed, 437–41; (188) allotted to C. Stertinius, **11**. 117; (187) to Q. Fulvius Flaccus, 145; (186) to C. Aurelius Scaurus, 241; (184) to Q. Naevius Matho, 341, 353; (183) to Cn. Sicinius, 363; (182) to C. Terentius Istra, **12**. 3; (181) to M. Pinarius Rusca, 59, 79, who defeats rebels, 63, 107; (180) to C. Maenius, 109, 117, 137; (179) to C. Valerius Laevinus, 139; (178) to T. Aebutius; disorders in, 201; (177) to L. Mummius, then to Ti. Sempronius Gracchus, 207, 211–3; envoys from, 207; successes of Gracchus in, 221–3, (176–175) 231, 235–7, 283; (176) allotted to M. Popilius, who declines, 231; (174) to M. Atilius Serranus, but left to Ser. Cornelius Sulla, 251; (173) to C. Cicereius, 293, who wins victory, 311; (172) to Sp. Cluvius, 321; (171) to L. Furius Philus, 371, 383; second tithe imposed, 383; (169) allotted to P. Fonteius Capito, **13**. 39–41, 53; (168) to C. Papirius Carbo, 145–7, who stays in Rome, 285; (167) to A. Manlius Torquatus, who stays in Rome, 297; made praetorian province for 166, 405; (126–123) L. Aurelius Orestes subdues, **14**. 69; (82) L. Marcius Philippus, leg. of Sulla, seizes, 109; (78) M. Aemilius Lepidus tries to stir civil war in, 113–5. Prodigy: (217) **5**. 201

Sardinians, skin-clad (Sardi Pelliti): (215) **6**. 137

Sardis: (197) Antiochus sends forces to, **9**. 331; (190) Antiochus' base, **10**. 343, 353, 363, 365, 381, 419; L. Scipio receives envoys at, 421; (167) Eumenes' army at, **13**. 367

sarisae: (191) long spears of *phalangitae*, **10**. 213; (190) 415

Sarpedon, Cilician cape: (188) **11**. 127

Sarra: *see* Salonius.

Sarus riv., in Cilicia: (196) **9**. 387–9

Sassula, in Latium: (354) **3**. 419

Saticula, in Samnium: (343) A. Cornelius Cossus camps near, **3**. 469, 477; (316) L. Aemilius Mamercus attacks, **4**. 245; (315) Q. Fabius Maximus Rullianus takes, 247–9, **6**. 15; (216) M. Claudius Marcellus traverses, 47; (209) loyal, **7**. 245–7

Satricum, in Latium: (488) Coriolanus and Volsci take, **1**. 345; (386) Latins and allies defeated at, **3**. 217–23; (385) colony at, 251; (381) Volsci and Praenestini plunder, 273; Romans nearly defeated before, 275–85, 291; (377) Latins and Volsci withdraw to, 305–7; Latins burn, 309; (348) Antiates rebuild, 449; (346) M. Valerius Corvus destroys, 451; (341) Volsci defeated near, **4**. 3; (320) joins Samnites, 207; (319) L. Papirius Cursor recovers, 221–3, **7**. 129. Prodigy: (206) **8**. 47

Satura, unknown town: (124) **14**. 267

saturae: early dramatic form, abandoned by Livius Andronicus, **3**. 361–3

Saturn, temple of: (497) dedicated, **1**. 285; (217) sacrifice at, **5**. 205; (174) portico from, **12**. 279. Prodigy: (174) 255

INDEX

Saturnalia: (497) established, **1**. 285; (217) feast at, **5**. 205; (202) Vermina, Syphax' son, defeated on first day of, **8**. 503
Saturnia, in Etruria: (183) Roman colony, **11**. 395–7. Prodigies: (172) **12**. 349; (117) **14**. 269
Saturninus: *see* Apuleius.
Saverrio: *see* Sulpicius.
Savo, in Liguria: (205) **8**. 197
Saxa: *see* Voconius.
Saxa Rubra, on Flaminian way: (478) **1**. 387
Saxula: *see* Cluvius.
Scaea, in Thessaly: *see* Tripolis.
Scaeva: *see* Junius Brutus.
Scaevola: *see* Mucius.
Scantinius, P.: (216) pontiff, dies, **6**. 73
Scantius, M.: (293) tr. pl., indicts L. Postumius, **4**. 539
—, M.: (149) **14**. 37
Scaptia tribus: (332) formed, **4**. 69
Scaptius, P.: (446) a plebeian, urges seizure of lands of Aricia and Ardea, **2**. 243–9
Scapula: *see* Cornelius.
Scarphea, in Locris: (197) Flamininus in, **9**. 283; (191) Antiochus' army pursued to, **10**. 217
Scaurus: *see* Aemilius, Aurelius.
Sceleratus campus: (337) **4**. 63
Sceleratus vicus: (534) **1**. 171
Scerdilaedus, Illyrian king: (211) alliance open to, **7**. 93; (209) Aetolia demands Ardiaei be restored to, 335; recognizes Philip's helmet, 343; (207) in arms, **8**. 17. *See* Pleuratus.
—, son of Gentius: (168) sent to Rome with father, **13**. 195
Sciathus, Aegean is.: (200) Philip sacks, **9**. 83; Roman fleet at, 131–3; (192) Antiochus' fleet at, **10**. 127; (169) C. Marcius Figulus winters at, **13**. 131
Scilla: *see* Marcius.
Scipio: *see* Caecilius Metellus Pius, Cornelius.
school, elementary: (449) for girls, in Forum, **2**. 145
Scodra, in Illyricum: (169) Perseus' envoys at, **13**. 73; (168) L. Anicius Gallus takes, 191–5; (167) 333–5; he and commissioners confer at; tax imposed on, 337
Scopas, Aetolian leader: (211) confirms promises of M. Valerius Laevinus, **7**. 93; plans to invade Acarnania, 97–9; with Laevinus takes Anticyra, 99–101; (200) hires troops for Ptolemy V, **9**. 127
Scordisci, Celts in Thrace and Illyricum: (179) permit passage of Bastarnae to Italy, **12**. 173–5; (175) aid them against Dardanians, 245–7; (156) defeated, **14**. 251; (c. 141) defeat Romans, 51; (135) M. Cosconius defeats, 59; (114) defeat C. Porcius Cato, 75; (112) M. Livius Drusus defeats, 75–7
Scordus, Mt.: highest in Illyricum, **13**. 191; (169) Gentius' envoys cross, 73
scorpiones: (214) in defence of Syracuse, **6**. 285; (211) of Capua, **7**. 23
Scotussa, in Thessaly: (207) Philip at, **8**. 19–21, 27; (197) he and Flamininus both approach, **9**. 291; (191) soldiers of Larisa retire to, **10**. 183; surrenders to Antiochus, 185, to M' Acilius Glabrio, 201
Scribonius, C.: (181) pref. soc. in defeat of Celtiberians, **12**. 97
—, L.: (216) envoy of Cannae captives to Senate, **5**. 407
— Curio, C.: (196) aed. pl., convicts grazers, **9**. 391; builds temple to Faunus from fines, 391, 553; (193) pr. urb., 555, 557, 561, **10**. 17; (174) curio maximus, **12**. 255
— —, C.: (76) cos., **14**. 299; (75) defeats Dardanians, 115; (73) 117
— —, C.: (50) tr. pl., opposes, then supports Caesar, **14**. 137; (49) leg. in Africa, 139, 209
— Libo, L., pr. 204: (216) tr. pl., **5**. 407, **6**. 73; IIIvir mensarius, 73; (204) pr. pereg. and for Gaul, **8**. 249, 255, 369
— —, L., pr. 192: (194) aed. cur., introduces drama at Megalesia; provides seats for Senators at Roman games, **9**. 555; (192) pr. pereg., **10**. 29, 59; directed to prepare fleet, 61; (186) IIIvir for reestablishing Sipontum and Buxentum, **11**. 285
— —, L.: (149) tr. pl., proposes law to free Lusitanians, **14**. 27
Scrofa: *see* Tremellius.

INDEX

Scultenna riv., in Liguria: (177) C. Claudius Pulcher defeats Ligurians on, **12**. 223, 237
Scyllaeum, cape of Argolis: (200) Roman fleet at, **9**. 127; (191) **10**. 277
Scyros, Aegean is.: (200) Roman fleet passes, **9**. 131; (196) given to Athens in Macedonian treaty, 361
secession of plebs: *see* plebeians.
Sedetani, Spanish tribe: (206) Mandonius and Indibilis enter land of, **8**. 97–9, 129; (205) Ilergetes and Ausetani in land of, 213; (200) victory of C. Cornelius Cethegus in land of, **9**. 145; (195) surrender to M. Porcius Cato, 467
Seduni Veragri, Alpine tribe: (218) **5**. 113
Segestica, in Spain: (195) **9**. 463
Segovesus: (616–578) Gallic leader, moves to Hercynian mts., **3**. 117
Segovia, in Spain: (76) **14**. 195
Selepitani, in Illyricum: (167) **13**. 337
Seleucia, in Cilicia: (196) Antiochus returns to, **9**. 389; (144) Demetrius II flees to, **14**. 45
—, on Tigris: **11**. 59
Seleucus I Nicator, king of Syria, 312–280: (281) gains Thrace, **9**. 385, 565. *See* Apama.
— IV Philopater, king of Syria, 187–175: (196) Antiochus gives Lysimachia to, **9**. 385–7, **10**. 45; (191) Hannibal urges that, watch Macedon, 177–9; (190) opposes Romans in Aeolis, 313–5, 325, 341; fails to take Pergamum, 343, 347–53, 449; at Magnesia, 409; flees to Apamea, 419; (189) brings grain to Cn. Manlius Volso, **11**. 43; furnishes guides, 51; (187) king of Syria, **12**. 287; gives daughter to Perseus, 325; (175) dies, 287. *See* Demetrius I Soter.
—, son of Demetrius II Nicator: (125) murdered by mother, **14**. 71
Selinus, in Cilicia: (197) **9**. 333
Sellasia, in Laconia: (195) **9**. 487
Selymbria, on Propontis: (196) **9**. 381–3
Semigermani: (218) block Poenine pass, **5**. 113
Sempronia: (129) suspected in death of husband, Scipio Aemilianus, **14**. 69
Sempronian basilica: (169) Ti. Sempronius Gracchus builds, **13**. 143
— law: *see* Ti. Sempronius Gracchus, tr. pl., 133
Sempronianus: *see* Veturius Gracchus.
Sempronius, P.: (194) pref. soc., slain by Boi, **9**. 539
—, Ti.: (167) tr. pl., **13**. 371
— Asellio, A.: (89) pr. urb., slain by mob of usurers, **14**. 93
— Atratinus, A.: (497) cos., **1**. 285; (491) ii, 331; expels Volsci, 339–41
— —, A.: (444) one of first tribb. mil. c. p.; resigns because of *vitium*, **2**. 279–81
— —, A.: (425) tr. mil. c. p., **2**. 371; (420) ii, 399; (416) iii, 411
— —, A.: (380) mag. eq., **3**. 295, 297
— —, C.: (423) cos., **2**. 377; Volsci defeat, 377–85, 395; tribb. pl. attack, 385–9; returns to city, 391; (422) prosecuted by one tr. pl., saved by others, 391–3; (420) condemned, 401
— —, L.: (444) cos. suf., **2**. 283; (443) one of first censors, 287
— Blaesus, C.: (211) tr. pl., convicts Cn. Fulvius Flaccus for treason, **7**. 7–15; (210) leg. in Etruria, 223
— —, C., pr. 184: (187) aed. pl., **11**. 239; (184) pr. for Sicily, 321, 341; (170) leg. to free Abdera, **13**. 17
— —, P.: (191) tr. pl., opposes, then permits triumph of P. Cornelius Scipio Nasica, **10**. 267–71
— —, Ti.: (217) qu., lost on African coast, **5**. 305
— Gracchus, C., tr. pl., 123–122: (133) IIIvir agr. adsig., **14**. 63; (132–130) 67–9; (131) supports law for re-election of tr. pl., 67; (123) tr. pl., secures various reforms, 71, 267; (122) tr. pl. ii, founds colonies, 71; (121) seizes Aventine; L. Opimius kills, 73, 267; wolves scatter stones set up by, 267
— —, P.: (189) tr. pl., prosecutes M' Acilius Glabrio, **10**. 471–3
— —, Ti., cos. 238: (246) aed. pl., builds temple to Libertas, **6**. 227
— —, Ti., cos. 215, 213: (216) aed. cur., **6**. 81, 103; mag. eq. to M. Junius Pera, **5**. 387, **6**. 103; floats supplies to Casilinum, 65–7; elected cos., 79–81; calls Senate, 85; directed

to name IIviri for temple of Eryx, 103; (215) cos., 105, **9**. 413, 433; postpones election of cos. suf., **6**. 107; receives legions of *volones* (slave volunteers), 109, 113, 123; defeats Campanians at Hamae, 123–5; escapes Hannibal at Cumae, 127–31; sends to Rome captured envoys of Philip and Hannibal, 131–3; near Capua, 135; winters in Apulia, 163, 185; (214) in Luceria with *volones*, 207, 209; defeats Carthaginians at Beneventum; frees *volones*, 213, 217–27, 233, 363, **7**. 9; in Lucania, **6**. 235, 237; (213) cos. ii, 313, in Lucania, 317, 327, 341; names dict. com. c., 345; (212) in Lucania, 349; slain in ambush, 403–11, 415, **8**. 119; *volones* desert after death of, **6**. 419–21

Sempronius Gracchus, Ti.: (204–174) augur, **8**. 359; **12**. 253–5

— —, Ti., cos. 177, 163, cens. 169: (190) sent by L. Scipio to test Philip, **10**. 311; (187) tr. pl., prevents prosecution of Africanus, **11**. 183–5, 197–9; marries his daughter, 199–201; forbids imprisonment of L. Scipio, 201, 209; supports triumph of M. Fulvius Nobilior, 229–31; (185) envoy to reconcile Philip and Greeks, 291–309, (184) 321; (183) IIIvir for Saturnia, 397; (182) aed. cur., spends lavishly on games, **12**. 141; (180) pr. for Nearer Spain, 107–13, 121, 127, 393; (179) 139; defeats Celtiberians, 149–57, (178) who surrender, 273, 287; founds Gracchuris, 287; triumphs, 201–5; (177) cos. with Sardinia as prov., 207, 213; defeats Ilienses, 221–3; (176) in Sardinia, 231, 235–7; triumph commemorated by inscription, 283; (169) cens., **13**. 49; assists levy, 49–51, 53–5; choses Senate, 53; bars contractors under last censors from bidding, 55; prosecuted for resisting tribb. pl., acquitted, 55–61; (168) conducts strict census, 55, 143, 295; purchases home of Africanus for Basilica Sempronia, 143; enrolls all freedmen in Esquiline tribe, 293–5; tribb. pl. veto extension of term of, 295; (163) cos. ii, **14**. 249

Sempronius Gracchus, Ti.: (133) tr. pl., removes opposing tr., **14**. 63, 317; carries land law; appoints self to land commission; divides bequest of Attalus among colonists; seeks re-election, 61–3; disregards omens; is slain, 63, 259–61, 317; judgment of Aemilianus on, 67; brother of C., 71

— —, T.: (196) pref. soc., **9**. 373

— Longus, C.: (174) Xvir sac., **12**. 255

— —, P.: (184) pr. for Farther Spain, **11**. 321, 341; (183) 363; ill, 397; (182) **12**. 3; dies, 7, 55

— —, Ti.: (218) cos., **5**. 17, 43–5, **8**. 533, **9**. 343, 527, with Sicily and Africa as prov., **5**. 47; arrives in prov., 145, 149; operations at Melita, 149–51; Hannibal defeats, and P. Scipio at Trebia, 143, 151–69, 43; presides over elections, 169, 43–5; winters at Placentia, 169, 171; (217) meets Hannibal near Placentia; retires to Luca, 175–7; gives army to C. Flaminius, 193; (215) defeats Hanno near Grumentum, **6**. 131; (210) Xvir sac., dies, **7**. 227; impetuosity of, **5**. 153, 157–9, 241, 261, 347

— —, Ti., cos. 194: (210–174) augur, Xvir sac., **7**. 227, **12**. 253; (200) tr. pl., opposes *ovatio* for L. Cornelius Lentulus, **9**. 59–61; (198) aed. cūr., 239; (197–194) IIIvir col. deduc., 243, 533; (196) pr. for Sardinia, 341, 347; (195) 393; (194) cos. with Italy as prov., 527–31; celebrates 'sacred spring,' 531; fights Boi; retires to Placentia, 537–41; (193) reports Gallic rising, 559; Latins in army of, to serve again, 561; leg. or procos. against Boi, **10**. 11, 13, 23; (191) leg. of M' Acilius Glabrio at Heraclea, 225, 229; (184) candidate for cens., **11**. 347–9; (174) dies, **12**. 253

— Musca, T.: (168) Vvir to settle disputes of Pisa and Luca, **13**. 287

— Rutilus, C.: (189) tr. pl., prosecutes M' Acilius Glabrio, **10**. 471–3

— —, T.: (186) involved in Bacchic cult, **11**. 243–9

— Sophos, P., cos. 304, cens. 299: 310 tr. pl., vainly opposes Ap.

Claudius, **4**. 289–99; (304) cos., 345; defeats Aequi, triumphs, 345–9; (300) one of first plebeian pont., 389; (299) cens., adds two tribes, 393; (296) pr. in command of city, 437; appoints IIIviri col. deduc., 439

Sempronius Sophos, P.: (252) cens., **4**. 557

— —, P.: (204) cos.. vows temple to Fortuna; (199) cens., **9**. 553

— Tuditanus, C., pr. 197: (198) aed. pl. **9**. 239; (197) pr. for Nearer Spain, 239–41, 349; (196) defeated and slain, 345–7, 389; pont., 389

— —, C.: (129) cos., defeated by Iapydae, **14**. 69

— —, M.: (210) tr. mil. (?), **7**. 183–5

— —, M., cos. 185: (193) tr. pl., extends usury law to Latins, **10**. 19; (189) pr. for Sicily, 431, 437–9; (188) brings fleet home, **11**. 117; (185) cos., 283, 321, 385, **13**. 299, with Liguria as prov., **11**. 311, 317–9, 341, **14**. 7; defeats Apuani; conducts elections, **11**. 319–21; (184) candidate for cens., 349; (183–174) pont., 365, **12**. 253

— —, P., cens. 209, cos. 204: (216) tr. mil., leader of Cannae survivors, **5**. 365–7, 399–401, **6**. 315; (214) aed. cur., first gives drama at festival; (213) pr. for Gaul, 315; takes Atrinum, 327; (212) propr., 349; (211) **7**. 5; (209–208) cens., 251–3, 355; (205) procos. in Greece, **8**. 251–3; makes treaty with Philip, 253–5; (204) cos., 249, 255, **10**. 261–3, with Bruttium as prov., **8**. 255–7; defeats Hannibal; vows temple to Fortuna Primigenia, 349, **9**. 553[2]; takes Bruttian cities, **8**. 357; (203) in Bruttium, 367, 463; (201) envoy to Ptolemy V, **9**. 7

Sena, in Umbria: (c. 289) maritime colony at, **4**. 547, **7**. 363; (207) levy from, 363; C. Claudius Nero and M. Livius Salinator meet at, 391

Senate: (753) formed by Romulus, **1**. 33; (716) rules after his death, 61; (534–510) Tarquin the Proud ignores, 173; (509) debates restoration of Tarquins, 227; (508) liberal to poor, 247–9; (495) begins oppression of poor, 287 (*see* patricians, plebeians); (449) resists Xviri, **2**. 121, 127–31, 173; etc.

Membership: (753) Romulus appoints, **1**. 33; (672–640) Tullus adds Albans, 107; (616–578) Elder Tarquin adds *patres minorum gentium*, 129; (534–510) decreased by Tarquin the Proud, 173; (509) L. Junius Brutus adds new members, *patres conscripti*, 221; (504) Ap. Claudius, a Sabine, enrolled, 271; (400) first mention of plebeian in, **3**. 45; (340) Latins demand share in, **4**. 15–9; (312) Ap. Claudius tries to add sons of freedmen, 353; (216) right to, gained by office holding, **5**. 363; **6**. 79; proposal to add Latins rejected, 75–7; vacancies after Cannae filled by special dict., 75–9; (209) flamen claims ancient right to, **7**. 237; list of, revised by censors, 251–3; (199) **9**. 169; (194) 531–3; (189) **11**. 95; (184) 355–9; (179) **12**. 157; (174) 275–7; (169) **13**. 53; (191) *ius sententiam dicendi* of prospective members, **10**. 163; (123) recruited from *equites* by tr. pl. C. Sempronius Gracchus, **14**. 71, (81) by Sulla, 111

Procedure: (320) convened by cos. with fasces, **4**. 189, (462) by praef. urb., **2**. 31, (458) 99, (449) by Xviri, 125–7, (424) by tr. mil. c. p., 375; (216) by tr. pl., **5**. 407, (210) **7**. 221, (216) by pr. urb., **6**. 79, (178) **12**. 201, etc., (216) by mag. eq., **6**. 85; (640–616) individual Senators called on in fixed order for *sententiae*, **1**. 117–9, (449) **2**. 129, (329) **4**. 85, (204) **8**. 281–7, (203) 447–9; (204) giving of *sententiae* not completed in one day, 283–5; (449) Senator demands right to speak on state of nation, **2**. 129, 137; (396) tr. mil. c. p. calls on father to speak first, **3**. 69; (216) non-Senators removed before *sententiae*, **5**. 397; (210) Senate acts under oath, **7**. 129; (201) **8**. 519; (172) **12**. 351; (205) Senators must give *sententia*, **8**. 189–91; (191) Senators kept in Rome, **10**. 163; (170) **13**. 39; (186) certain actions require quorum of 100, **11**. 271, (172) of 150, **12**. 373. *See* princeps senatus. *For place of*

INDEX

meeting, *see* Curia, Capitol, temple of Apollo, temple of Bellona.

Activity of: *Administrative and Legislative Matters*: (205) deals with the state, the enrolment of armies, the assignment of posts, **8**. 161; *see* provinces, assignment of; armies, distribution of; triumphs; etc. *Foreign affairs*: (444) receives envoys, **2**. 281; (205), **8**. 155–61; 237; (203) 443–9; (202) 515–7, (206) 523–9; (182) **12**. 7; (181) 105; (172) 321–35; 345–7; *see* peace, treaties of; war, declaration of; etc. *Judicial matters*: (413) refers investigation of murder to tribb. pl., **2**. 423, (303) of conspiracy to coss., **4**. 361; (210) directed by plebiscite to judge Campanians, **7**. 129; (205) punishment of tribb. mil. referred to, **8**. 241–3; (204) orders investigation of Locrian affair, 287; (92–91) shares juries with *equites*, **14**. 87–9. *Religious matters*: (399) orders consultation of Sibylline Books, **3**. 47 (*see* Sibylline books); (390) competent in religion, 169; (212) votes festivals and sacrifices after discovery of books of Marcius, **6**. 387; (181) orders 'Books of Numa' burned, **12**. 93; (172) orders votive games, 371; etc. *Senatus auctoritas* (*patrum auctoritas*): (716) for election of kings, **1**. 63; (672) 75; (640) 113; (578) 147; (534) 173; (415) required for laws and elections, **2**. 417; (368) **3**. 345–7; (368) Licinius and Sextius would free assemblies from, 347; (339) must be granted in advance, **4**. 53; (188) not needed for grant of citizenship, **11**. 119; becomes empty form, **1**. 63; examples of: (358) **3**. 409; (210) **7**. 129; (193) **10**. 19; (181) **12**. 63

senate: (460) in Tusculum, **2**. 61

Senators: (753) called *patres*, **1**. 33; (616–578) are assigned places in circus, 129; (534–510) Tarquin the Proud slaughters, 221; (503) poverty of some, 271; (493) 329; (495) coss. protect, from mob, 293; (390) await Gauls in Forum, **3**. 135–43; (210) contribute private wealth to state, **7**. 135–9, **9**. 433; (194) seats reserved for, at Roman games, 533, 555

senatus consultum: (211) to cos., contains words 'if he sees fit,' **7**. 61

senatus consultum ultimum: (464) during war with Aequi, **2**. 15; (384) during sedition of M. Manlius Capitolinus, **3**. 261; (121) against C. Sempronius Gracchus, **14**. 73; (49) against Caesar, 137

Senones, Gauls: (616–578) enter Italy, **3**. 119; (390) attack Clusium, then Rome, 121; (283) slay envoys; defeat L. Caecilius, **4**. 549

Sentinum, in Umbria: (295) Etruscans and Samnites defeated at, **4**. 461–77, 479

Sentius, C., pr. 94: (92) Thracians defeat, **14**. 87

Seppius Loesius: (211) last *medix tuticus* of Capua, **7**. 25–7, 43–7

September: (363) nail driven on 13th of, **3**. 365; (168) Roman games begin on 15th, **13**. 249–51

Septimus: *see* Marcius.

Sequani, Gauls: (58) **14**. 129. *See* Capenus.

Serapio: *see* Cornelius Scipio Nasica.

Serapion: (48) envoy, **14**. 211

Sergia: (331) a poisoner, **4**. 73

Sergius, L.: (203) envoy to Carthage, **8**. 453–5

—, M.: (205) tr. mil.; P. Scipio (Afr.) sends to Locri, **8**. 231; Q. Pleminius kills, for aiding Locrians, 239–43, 277–9

— Catilina, L., pr. 68: (63) omens before conspiracy of, **14**. 301–3; conspires; Cicero drives, from Rome, 127; (62) C. Antonius defeats, 303.

— Esquilinus, M.: (450) Xvir, **2**. 117; (449) commands against Aequi, 139

— Fidenas, L.: (437) cos., defeats Veientes, **2**. 315; (433) tr. mil. c. p., 335; (429) cos. ii; (428) investigates raids by Fidenates, 355; (424) tr. mil. c. p. ii, 373; (418) iii; Aequi defeat, 405–9

— —, L.: (397) tr. mil. c. p., **3**. 57; (394) envoy to Delphi, 97

— —, M': (404) tr. mil. c. p., **2**. 455; (402) ii, **3**. 27; defeated at Veii, 29–31, 39–41; term shortened by SC., 33, 41; (401) fined, 39–43, 45, 49

Sergius Fidenas Coxo, C.: (387) tr. mil. c. p., **3**. 211; (385) ii, 231; (380) iii, 289
— Plautus, C.: (200) pr. urb., **9**. 13, 19; (199) distributes lands to soldiers, 155
— Silus, M.: (197) pr. urb., **9**. 239, 249, or pereg., 337; reads to Senate dispatches from Gaul, 249, Spain, 337, and Greece, 343
— —, M.: (168) leg. at Pydna, **13**. 225
serpent (*serpens*): 256) in Bagradas riv. opposes M. Atilius Regulus, **4**. 555, **14**. 179. *See* snake (*anguis*).
Serranus: *see* Atilius.
Serrheum, in Thrace: (200) **9**. 51
Sertorius, Q., pr. 83: (87) attacks Rome with Marius, **14**. 99–101; (78–77) proscribed; raises civil war in Spain, 115; (77) reduces Contrebia; strengthens forces, 187–93; reduces various tribes, 115, 193–5; Cn. Pompeius sent against, 299, without success, 115; (76) 299; (75) 115, 197, 301; Q. Caecilius Metellus Pius defeats, 115; his cruelty, 115–7; (74) allied with Mithridates; defeats Pompey and Metellus; (73) Pompey defeats, 117; (72) M. Perperna murders, 119
Servilianus: *see* Fabius Maximus.
Servilii: (672–640) from Alba, enrolled as patricians by Hostilius, **1**. 107
Servilius, M.: (181) tr. mil. in Liguria, **12**. 83; (170) pont., **13**. 43
—, P.: (201) Xvir agr. adsig., **9**. 13
—, Q.: (91) pr. *pro consule*, killed, **14**. 89
— Ahala, C.: (439) mag. eq., **2**. 305; slays Sp. Maelius, 305–7, **3**. 261; tribb. pl. accuse, **2**. 311; (436) 325
— —, C., cos. 427: *see* Servilius Axilla.
— —, C.: (408) tr. mil. c. p., **2**. 439; names dict. for war with Aequi; becomes mag. eq., 441–3; (407) tr. mil. c. p. ii, 445; (406) leg. at capture of Anxur, 451; (402) tr. mil. c. p. iii, **3**. 27; shortens term, 33, 41
— —, C.: (389) mag. eq., **3**. 199; M. Manlius Capitolinus saves, 265
— —, Q., cos. 365, 362, 342: (365) cos., **3**. 359; (362) ii, 367; names Ap. Claudius dict., 377; (360) dict., vows great games; defeats Gauls at Colline gate, 389–91; (355) interrex, 415; (351) mag. eq. comit. c., 433; (342) cos. iii, 497, 499
Servilius Axilla (Ahala, Priscus, or Structus), C.: (427) cos., **2**. 357; (418) tr. mil. c. p.; disputes command with others, 405; names father, Q., dict., becomes mag. eq., 407–9; (417) tr. mil. c. p., ii, 411
— Caepio, Cn., cos. 203: (213–174) pont., **6**. 345, **12**. 253; (207) aed. cur., **8**. 43; (205) pr. urb., 153–5, 197, 199; (203) cos., 357, with Bruttium as prov., 367–9; conducts votive games, 371–3; opposes Hannibal, 439; prevented from crossing to Africa, 451; (195) envoy to Carthage, **9**. 403; (192) envoy to Greece, **10**. 65, 89–99, 111; (174) dies, **12**. 253
— —, Cn., cos. 169: (179) aed. cur., **12**. 179; (174) pr. for Farther Spain, 251, 303; (172) envoy to Perseus, 359–63; (169) cos., **13**. 39, with Italy as prov., 43, 53; charged with lax levy, 49; holds elections, 143–5; sends envoys to Macedon, 149; (168) in Gaul, enrolls cavalry for Macedon, 157
— —, Cn.: (141) cos., **14**. 49; (125) cens. 69[8]
— —, Q.: (140) cos., **14**. 51, 255; (139) in Spain, kills Viriathus, 49, 53
— —, Q.: (106) cos., **14**. 273; divides juries between Senators and equites, 275; (105) Cimbri defeat, at Arausio, 79; (101) slave of, emasculates self, 279
— —, Q., pr. 91: (90) eg. of P. Rutilius; ambushed and slain, **14**. 91
— Casca, C.: (212) tr. pl., **6**. 351
— Fidenas, Q.: (402) tr. mil. c. p., **3**. 27; (398) ii, 53; (397) interrex, 61; (395) tr. mil. c. p. iii, 83; (390) iv, 127; defeated at Allia by Gauls, 129–31; (388) tr. mil. c. p. v, 209; (386) vi, 213; commands near city, 215–7
— —, Q.: (382) tr. mil. c. p., **3**. 271; (378) ii, 301–3; (369) iii, 321
— Geminus, C.: (before 218) pr., **8**. 439; (218) IIIvir agr. adsig., en-

slaved by Boi, **5**. 69–71, **7**. 301, **8**. 439; (203) freed by son, C., 439
Servilius Geminus, C., cos. 203: (212) leg., brings supplies to Tarentum, **6**. 397; (211 ?) tr. pl., **7**. 301, **8**. 439; (210) pont., **7**. 227; (209) aed. pl., 301; (208) mag. eq. com. c., 345; aed. cur., 345, 355; (206) pr. for Sicily and fleet, **8**. 43, 45, 191; (203) cos., 357, with Etruria and Liguria as prov., 367–9; conducts votive games, 371–3; in Gaul, rescues father, from slavery, 437–9; plebeian offices of, regularized, 439; not recalled for peace discussion, 447–9, but possibly for elections, 461; (202) in Etruria, 463; dict. com. c.; conducts Cerialia, 515; (201) Xvir agr. adsig., **9**. 13; (194) IIvir for temple to Jupiter on Island, 553; (183) pont. max., **11**. 365; (180) seeks to avert gods' wrath, **12**. 115; tries to force IIvir nav. to resign and become rex. sac., 133–5; Xvir sac. and pont. max., dies of pestilence, 135
— — Cn.: (217) cos., **5**. 43, 169, 199, 341, **7**. 225, 345, **9**. 395; absent from city, unable to name dict. after Trasumenus, **5**. 227–9, 307; gives legions to Q. Fabius Maximus; commands at Ostia, 237–9; sails to Corsica, Sardinia, Africa, 285, 305; returns at end of Fabius' term, 305; with cos. suf. M. Atilius Regulus follows Fabian tactics, 307, 333; names dict. com. c., 313, 317; (216) procos., 313; at Cannae, 335, 345, 351; slain, 363
— Glaucia, C.: (100) pr., supports tr. pl. L. Apuleius Saturninus, killed, **14**. 85
— Priscus, C., tr. mil. c. p. 418: *see* Servilius Axilla, C.
— —, P.: (463) cos., **2**. 21–5
— —, Sp.: (378) cens. to investigate debt, **3**. 303
— — Fidenas, Q., dict. 435, 418: (435) dict., defeats Etruscans, takes Fidenae, **2**. 327–9, 405, **3**. 365[1]; (431) urges naming of dict., **2**. 341; (428) IIIvir to investigate charges against Fidenae, **2**. 355; (418) bids son, C. Servilius Axilla, yield command and raise army in city, 405–7; named dict. by son; defeats Aequi, 409–11; (416) praises Ap. Claudius, 413–5
Servilius Priscus Structus, P.: (495) cos., **1**. 287; calms debtors, 293–7; defeats Volsci and Sabines, 287, 297–301; fails to satisfy debtors, 303–7, 311, 315
— — —, Q.: (468) cos., **1**. 429; (466) ii, **2**. 5; (465) pref. urb., 11; (459) qu., accuses M. Volscius, 81–3
— Pulex Geminus, M., cos. 202: (211) aug., **7**. 91; (204) aed. cur., **8**. 359; (203) mag. eq., elected cos., 451, 457; (202) cos. with Etruria as prov., 461–3; celebrates votive games, 465; directed to remain near Rome, 511; names dict. com. c.; goes to Etruria, 513–5; (201) in Etruria, 521; Xvir agr. adsig., **9**. 13; (197–194) IIIvir for colonies, 243, 533; (167) supports triumph for L. Aemilius Paulus, **13**. 373–91
— Structus, C., tr. mil. c. p. 418: *see* Servilius Axilla, C.
— —, Sp.: (476) cos.; cos. A. Verginius saves, from Veientes, **1**. 393–5; (475) prosecuted; acquitted, 397, 401
— —, Sp.: (368) tr. mil. c. p., **3**. 327
— — Ahala, C.: (478) cos., **1**. 387
— Vatia Isauricus, P., cos. 79: (78–77) defeats Cilicians, **14**. 115, (75–74) 117
Servius Romanus: (404) a slave, betrays Artena to Rome, **2**. 457
— Tullius, of Corniculum: father of king Servius Tullius, **1**. 141
— —, 6th king of Rome, 578–534: a contemporary of Pythagoras, **1**. 63–5; son of slave, or of chief of Corniculum, 139–43, 167, 169, **2**. 267, 269; (616–578) flame on head of, **1**. 139; honoured, 139–41; (578) on Tarquin's death seizes power, 143–7, 165, 223; recognized by Senate, not by people, 147; (578–534) wins favour in Etruscan war; institutes census; divides people into classes and centuries, 149–53, **2**. 269; forms four urban tribes, **1**. 153–5; closes *lustrum*, 155; extends *pomerium*; builds wall, 155–7; persuades Latins to accept Rome as capital, 157–9; divides conquered lands;

recognized by people, 159–61; consecrates temple to Mater Matuta, **3**. 67, to Fors Fortuna, **4**. 539; (534) overthrown by Tullia and Tarquin the Proud, **1**. 161–71, 207; Senatorial supporters of, put to death, 171; (509) first coss., elected by 'commentaries of,' 209
Sestius, P.: (451) tried for murder, **2**. 111
—, P.: (414) qu., wounded by mob, **2**. 421–3
— Capitolinus Vaticanus, P.: (452) cos., **2**. 107; introduces law for Xvirate, 109; (451) Xvir, 109
Sestus, on Hellespont: (198–197) garrisoned by Philip, **9**. 255; (196) yields to Antiochus, 381, (190) to Rome, **10**. 317
Setia, in Latium: Latin colony, **8**. 263 (cp. **4**. 11, **7**. 243); (379) additional colonists for, **3**. 301; (342) Privernates waste, 513; (341) reports revolt of Privernum, **4**. 3; (330) Privernates waste, 75; (211) prepares supplies for Roman army, **7**. 31; (209) unable to furnish men or money, 241–7; (204) forced to furnish extra quota, **8**. 263–7; (198) slave revolt at, suppressed; Punic hostages at, **9**. 233–7. Prodigy: (204) **8**. 259. *See* L. Annius.
Setinus: *see* Annius.
Sewer, Great: (616–578) constructed by Elder Tarquin, **1**. 137; (534–510) by Tarquin the Proud, 193
sewers: (184) repaired and built by censs., **11**. 361
Sexetani, Spanish tribe: (197) **9**. 337
Sextilia, a Vestal: (273) punished, **4**. 551
Sextilis: *see* August.
Sextilius, C.: (379) tr. mil. c. p., **3**. 299
—, M., of Fregellae: (209) spokesman for loyal colonies, **7**. 245
Sextius, M.: (414) tr. pl., proposes land law, **2**. 419–21
—, T., pr. 45(?): (42) Q. Cornificius defeats, in Africa, **14**. 155
— Calvinus, C.: (124) cos., **14**. 267; (123) defeats Salluvii, founds Aquae Sextiae, **14**. 73
— Sabinus, M., pr. 202: (203) aed. pl., **8**. 461; (202) pr. for Gaul, 461–3, 521
— Sextinus Lateranus, L., cos. 366; (376) tr. pl., **3**. 315–7; (375–371) ii–vi, advocates anti-patrician reforms; vetoes patrician elections, 317–9; (370) tr. pl. vii, permits elections, 319–21; (369) tr. pl. viii, advocates reforms, 321–7; (368) tr. pl. ix, ignores vetoes of colleagues and authority of dictator, 327–31; candidate for 10th term, 333–47; (367) tr. pl. x, secures law opening consulate and Xvirate sacris faciundis to plebeians, 347–9, 417; (366) first plebeian cos., 349, 357, **4**. 387
shepherds: (185) rising of, in Apulia suppressed, **11**. 309–11; (184) 353
shields: (308) as offensive weapons, **4**. 329; (168) guards forbidden to carry, **13**. 199; Ligurian, used by *velites*, 209
shields of Mars: *see ancilia.*
ships: (217) Senators may not own sea-going, **5**. 189; (167) Macedonians may not cut timber for, **13**. 351. *See* naval antiquities.
shops: (216) closed in mourning, **6**. 85
Shops, Old: *see* Veteres.
Sibyl of Cumae: comes to Italy, **1**. 29; (187) verses of, **11**. 155; (149) **14**. 31; (140) 51
Sibylline Books: (461) consulted, **2**. 37; (436) 327[1]; (433) 335; (399) order first *lectisternium*, **3**. 47–9, 51; (390) consulted, 167–9; (348) 449; (344) 453; (295) **4**. 479; (292) order introduction of Aesculapius, 543; (218) consulted, **5**. 185–7; (217) 203–5; 231; 235; (216) 321; after Cannae, order human sacrifice, 385–7; (212) consulted, **6**. 387; (205) order introduction of Idaean Mother, **8**. 245; (200) consulted, **9**. 39; (193) 557; **10**. 25; (191) 263–5; (190) 299; (187) **11**. 155; (181) **12**. 61–3, **14**. 243; (180) **12**. 115; (179) 143; (174) 255; (173) 297–9; (172) 347; (169) **13**. 47–9; (167) 297; (165) **14**. 247; (149) direct Saecular Games, 23, 31; (143) consulted, 255; (140) 51; (118) 269; (108) 273. *See* duumviri *and* decemviri sacris faciundis.
Siccius, Cn.: (470) tr. pl., **1**. 415; prosecutes. Ap. Claudius 423–5,
— Dentatus, L., tr. pl., 454: (449) Xviri murder, **2**. 141–3, 169, 171

INDEX

Sichaeus, husband of Dido: called Sicharbal, **14**. 177
Sicilian sea: (197) **9**. 321
— strait: mythical monsters in, **8**. 273; Etruscan power extended to, **1**. 13; (394) pirates near, **3**. 97. *See* Messana.
Sicilinum, town of Herpini: (215) **6**. 131
Sicily: Aeneas in, **1**. 9; (492, 491) corn from, 331–3; (486) 355; (433) **2**. 337; (411) 427; (431) first Punic army in, 353; (415–413) Athenian disaster in, **8**. 169, 183; (406–357) Dionysius tyrant of, **6**. 183; (348) raiders from, **3**. 449; (311–308) Punic forces in, **8**. 183; (278–275) Pyrrhus in, **4**. 551, **8**. 275; (264) Romans enter, to aid Mamertines, **4**. 553, **8**. 117, **9**. 85, **13**. 317; (242) A. Postumius Albinus prevented from going to, **10**. 439; (264–242) the stake of the First Punic War, **8**. 187, 483; (241) taken by Rome, **5**. 117, 121, 127, 379, **8**. 475; pays taxes in kind, **6**. 165; divided between Rome and Carthage, **7**. 239; (219) Roman seizure of, a cause of Second Punic War, **5**. 5, 123, 131, 157; (218) allotted to T. Sempronius Longus, 47, 149–51; Hannibal fears invasion via, 61; military and naval operations in, 145–53; Sempronius summoned from, 143, 153, 169; (217) pr. in, but not needed, 285; Cn. Servilius Geminus returns to, after African defeat, 305; (216) assigned to M. Marcellus, 319, T. Otacilius Crassus commands fleet, 325; Crassus reports from, 383, **6**. 71; Campanian *equites* sent to, 13, 19–21; they become citizens, 107; survivors of Cannae guard, 85–7; trend away from Rome in, 103, **7**. 159; (215) allotted to Ap. Claudius Pulcher with Cannae legions, **6**. 105, 109, 113, 193, 197, 345; Crassus commands fleet, 113; money intended for, diverted, 133–5; pays no taxes, 165; confusion in, after Hiero's death, 185–97; (214) assigned to P. Cornelius Lentulus, 207, 209, 213, **7**. 5; Crassus commands fleet in, **6**. 211, 213; men added to Cannae legions as punishment, 231; operations in, 241–301; Marcellus sent to, 241, 263; siege of Syracuse begins, 283; Carthage begins active war in, 287–93, 363; many cities alienated from Rome, 301; (213) Lentulus and Marcellus continued in, 315–7; (212) 349; Cannae legions seek active duty in, 357–65; Tarentum requests Punic ships from, 381; operations in, to capture of Syracuse, 429–63, to Marcellus' last battle in, 495–501, **7**. 87, 91, 139; (211) allotted to C. Sulpicius Piso, **6**. 501, **7**. 5; Marcellus' command in, extended, 5; Cannae legions still in, 5, 11; fleet for, assigned to T. Otacilius Crassus, 5, 89; Punic fleet leaves; Marcellus leaves, 79, 83, M. Cornelius Cethegus succeeding, 83–5, 103; land in, given to Moericus; new Punic forces in, 83; (210) men from, attack Marcellus in Rome, 101–3, 107, 111–9, 127, 133; allotted to Marcellus with Cannae legions, 109, 111, then to M. Valerius Laevinus, 113, 125; Marcellus answers charges, 119–23; his acts in, ratified, 123; he becomes patron of Syracuse, 125; Laevinus in, 151, 231; all, a province, 161, 217–9, **9**. 85, 93, **10**. 47; oarsmen needed for, **7**. 135; operations in, 151–7, 255; shipment of grain from, resumed, 145–7, 155, 219; Laevinus recalled, 213, 217–9; Punic preparations against; Laevinus returns to, 219–23; (209) assigned to Laevinus and L. Cincius Alimentus with reinforcements and Cannae legions, 233, 237–41, 253, 329; (208) assigned to Sex. Julius Caesar, 301–3; Laevinus commands fleet, 303, 329–31; siege engines from, sent to Locri, 313–5, 327; refugees from, recalled, 351; (207) allotted to C. Mamilius, 357, 365; victories in, 369–71; Laevinus defeats Punic fleet off, **8**. 15; (206) allotted to C. Servilius Geminus with Cannae legions; Laevinus leaves, 45; Senate complains of too much attention to cultivation of, 47–9; (205) allotted to L. Aemilius Papus; assigned to P. Scipio (Afr.) with permission to go to Africa, 153–5,

191; he prepares for Africa in, 207–11, 221–5; Carthage urges Philip against, 223; (204) allotted to M. Pomponius Matho with Cannae legions, 255–7, 287; Scipio prepares for Africa in, 297–313, 369–71; spoils of Africa sent to, 319, 343; sends supplies to Africa, 343, 345, 347; (203) 375; 451; allotted to P. Villius Tappulus, 369–71; Cn. Servilius Caepio forbidden to leave, for Africa, 451; (202) allotted to Cn. Tremelius Flaccus; Tappulus commands fleet, 463; Hannibal ready to give up, 481; grain from, lowers Roman prices; Ti. Claudius Nero ordered to, on way to Africa, 511; (201) allotted to P. Aelius Tubero, 517, 521; Tappulus commands fleet, 523; cos. to sail to, 519; Scipio and fleet return via, 537; Cn. Octavius brings fleet from, **9**. 11; (200) allotted to Q. Fulvius Gillo, 19, 25–7, (199) to L. Valerius Flaccus, 155; veterans of, 155, 161; (198) allotted to M. Claudius Marcellus, 175; he sends supplies for army in Greece, 237; (197) allotted to L. Manlius Volso, 239, (196) to C. Laelius, 347; sends grain to Rome, 391; (195) allotted to Cn. Manlius Volso, 393, (194) to Cn. Cornelius Blasio, 531, (193) to L. Scipio, 557; C. Flaminius raises troops in, **10**. 7; (192) allotted to L. Valerius Tappo, 59; rumours that Antiochus will attack; reinforced, 65–9; (191) allotted to M. Aemilius Lepidus, 121, 159–61, 431; tithe doubled, 161; fleet moves toward, 275; (190) allotted to C. Atinius Labeo; tithe doubled, 295–7; (189) allotted to M. Sempronius Tuditanus; tithe doubled, 437–9; (188) allotted to Q. Marcius Philippus, **11**. 117, (187) to L. Terentius Massiliota, 145; Africanus highly regarded in, 177; (186) allotted to P. Cornelius Sulla, 241, (184) to C. Sempronius Blaesus, 341, (183) to Sp. Postumius Albinus, 363; new island formed near, 397–9, **14**. 241; (182) allotted to L. Caecilius Denter, **12**. 3, (181) to Ti. Claudius Nero, 59, (180) to P. Cornelius Mammula, 109, (179) to Q. Mucius Scaevola, 139, (177) to C. Numisius, 207, (176) to L. Aquilius Gallus, 231, (174) to L. Claudius, 253, (173) to M. Furius Crassipes, 293, (172) to C. Memmius, 321; ships fitted out in, 367–9; (171) allotted to C. Caninius Rebilus; tithe doubled, 371, 383; (169) freedmen enrolled in, for navy, **13**. 45; allotted to Ser. Cornelius Lentulus, 39–41, 53, (168) to M. Aebutius Helva, 145–7; men from, desert fleet, 155; (167) allotted to Ti. Claudius Nero, 297, (166) to a pr., 405; (146) spoils of Carthage given to, **14**. 39; (134) slave wars in, 59, 259; (133) 63; (132) 65, 261; (100) 85, 281; (82) Pompey sent to, by SC., 111; (70) L. Caecilius Metellus defeats pirates and slaves in, 121; (48) Cicero in, 209; (43–39) Sex. Pompeius occupies, 155, 159; (39) assigned to him; (37, 36) he is driven to, 159. Prodigies: (217) **5**. 201; (214) **6**. 209; (183) **11**. 397, **14**. 241. *See* Syracuse.

Sicimina, Mt., in Gaul: (168) **13**. 283

Sicinius, C.: (449) tr. pl., **2**. 181

—, C.: (170) envoy to Carni, Histri, and Iapydes, **13**. 21

—, Cn., pr. 183, 172: (185) aed. pl.; (184) candidate for pr. suf., **11**. 343; (183) pr. for Sardinia, 363; (177) IIIvir col. deduc., **12**. 225; (173) pr. elect, given *imperium* against locusts, 319; (172) pr. pereg., 317, 321, 347; levies and transports troops to Macedon, 343, 367–9, 399, 437; frees Ligurians, 353; (171) in Macedon, 369, 383, 397

—, L.: (387) tr. pl., proposes land law, **3**. 213

—, T.: (487) cos., against Volsci, 351

—, T.: (395) tr. pl., proposes migration to Veii, **3**. 85

— Bellutus, L., tr. pl., 493; (494) leads plebs to Sacred mt., **1**. 323; (493) tr. pl., 325–7, 333, **2**. 181

Siculus: *see* Cloelius.

Sicyon, on Corinthian gulf: (209) Philip's death near, reported, **7**. 337, 343; (198) conference with Achaeans at, **9**. 207–25; Achaeans camp near, 225; Philip's troops

near, 227; Attalus and Flamininus at, 269; honours Attalus, 273; (197) Achaeans at, 313; Macedonians raid; are repelled, 313–9; (192) Achaean council at, **10**. 71; (167) procos. L. Aemilius Paulus at, **13**. 343. *See* Aratus.
Sida, Pamphylian port: (193) Antiochus attacks Pisidae about, **10**. 39; (192) men of, in his fleet, 139; (190) Rhodians defeat Syrians off, 355–61
Sidicini, of Central Italy: (343) Samnites attack; Campanians defend, **3**. 455–7, 461, 469, 481 (*but cp.* **6**. 15); (341) Samnites attack with Roman approval, **4**. 5–7; try to surrender to Rome, 7; Latins aid, 7–9, 13–7; (337) defeat Aurunci, 61; (336–332) war with Rome, 63–9; (297) P. Decius Mus marches into Samnium through, 407; (216) slave from, warns of Hannibal's trick, **5**. 341–3; (211) Hannibal plunders, **7**. 33; ordered to surrender Capuans, 59
Sidon: (192) men of, in Antiochus' fleet, **10**. 139; (190) 379
siege engines: (502) used against Pometia, **1**. 273, (403) Veii, **3**. 17, (219) Saguntum, **5**. 33, (214) Casilinum, **6**. 235, Syracuse, 283–7, (208) Locri, **7**. 327, (200) Oreus, **9**. 135, (199) Thaumaci, 161, (197) Leucas, 321–3, (195) Segestica, 463, Gytheum, 491, (189) Ambracia, **11**. 15–25, Samê, 97–9, (184) Corbio, 353, (171) Haliartus, **12**. 489–91; (386) needed against Antium, **3**. 223; (211) carried in ovation, **7**. 81; used on shipboard, 101; (209) 269; (210) captured in New Carthage, 181, 187; (198) used in battle, **9**. 183
Sigeum, on Hellespont: (168) **13**. 181
signa: *see* standards; statues.
Signia, in Latium: (534–510) colony founded by Tarquin the Proud, **1**. 195; (495) re-established, 287; (362) scatters Hernici, **3**. 381; (340) joins Latins against Rome, **4**. 11; (328) Fregellae on land of, 85; (209) loyal, **7**. 245–7; (199) Punic hostages at, **9**. 159
Silana, in Thessaly: (191) **10**. 197
Silanus: *see* Junius.
Silenus, the historian: (210 cited, **7**. 187
Silius, Q.: (409) plebeian qu., **2**. 433
Silpia (Ilipa), in Spain: (206) P. Scipio (Afr.) defeats Punic forces at, **8**. 53–67
Silus: *see* Sergius.
Silvanus: (509) voice of, proclaims victory, **1**. 239
silver: (275) senator removed for owning 10 lbs. of, **4**. 551; (189) relation of, to gold, **11**. 37; (167) mining of, forbidden in Macedon, **13**. 349
Silvius, son of Ascanius: 2d king of Alba Longa, **1**. 17
—: cognomen of Alban kings, **1**. 17
Sinda, in Pisidia: (189) **11**. 47
Sinopê: on the Euxine, **11**. 65; (182) slaughter in, **12**. 7
—: old name of Sinuessa, **4**. 439
Sintia, in Dardania: (211) **7**. 97
Sintica, in Macedon: (168) **13**. 241. *See* Heraclea Sintica.
Sinuessa, in Latium: (296) maritime colony, **7**. 363, **5**. 247; replaces Sinopê, **4**. 439; (217) Hannibal at, **5**. 247, 255; (215) Ti. Sempronius Gracchus mobilizes at, **6**. 113, 123; (207) forced to submit to levy, **7**. 363; (191) **10**. 163; (174) cens. contracts for construction at, **12**. 281. Prodigies: (215) **6**. 109; (209) **7**. 249–51, 359; (200) **9**. 39; (198) 177–9; (174) **12**. 255
—, Baths of: (217) **5**. 245
Sipontum, in Apulia: (c. 330) Alexander of Epirus takes, **4**. 95; (194) Roman colony at, **9**. 533–5; (186) new colonists for, **11**. 285
Sipylus, in Lydia: *see* Magnesia ad Sipylum.
Sirae, in Paeonia: (168) **13**. 257, 259[1]
Sisenna: *see* Cornelius.
Sister's Beam, in Rome: (672–640) **1**. 95
sixteen bank ship: *see* naval antiquities.
skins, inflated: (218) for crossing rivers, **5**. 79; 139
slave insurrections: (460) occupy Capitol under Ap. Herdonius, **2**. 53–65; (419) discovered and quelled, 403; (217) participants in, crucified, **5**. 309–11; (198) at Setia, **9**. 233–5; (196) in Etruria, 373; (185) in Apulia, **11**. 309–11; (134–132) in

Italy and Sicily, **14**. 59, 63, 65, 259, 261; (104) in Thurii, 277; (100) in Sicily, 85, 281; (73) led by Crixus and Spartacus, 117–21, 199
slave volunteers (*volones*); (216) purchased by state and enrolled as soldiers, **5**. 389, 393, **6**. 43, (214) as oarsmen, **9**. 433; (215–212) serve with distinction under Ti. Sempronius Gracchus, **6**. 109, 123, 209, 363, **7**. 9; (214) earn freedom by valour, **6**. 217–27; (212) desert on his death, 419–21, 425; (207) recalled, **7**. 363–5; (206–205) **8**. 45, 199
slaves: (346) captives sold as, **3**. 451: (337) evidence of, admitted, **4**. 63; (220–203) Gauls hold Roman captives as, **8**. 439; (194) Romans held as, in Greece, **9**. 547, (189) in Crete, **10**. 477
slingers (218) Balearic, in Hannibal's army, **5**. 63; (216) 323; (210) **7**. 209; (206) Balearic, attack Mago's fleet; their skill, **8**. 149–51; (216) offered to Rome by Hiero, **5**. 323; (214) on Roman fleet besieging Syracuse, **6**. 283; (207) in Roman army, **7**. 365; (191) in Antiochus' army, **10**. 213; (190) 407; (189) Achaean, in Roman army; their peculiar slings, **11**. 99; (171) in Perseus' army, using dart-slings, **12**. 497
Smyrna: *see* Zmyrna.
snake (*anguis*): (356) carried by Etruscan priest, **3**. 413; (292) of Aesculapius brought to Rome, **4**. 547; (236) father of P. Scipio (Afr.), **7**. 73–5. *See* serpent (*serpens*).
Social war: (90) portents before, **14**. 291; (91) begins, 89; (90) continues, 91; (89) 91–5
socii navales: (198) desert to Philip, **9**. 227
Soli, Cilician port: of Argive origin, **10**. 465; (197) Antiochus recovers, **9**. 333; (189) not granted to Rhodes, **10**. 465–7
Solo, in Gallia Narbonensis: (61) **14**. 127
Solon, of Athens: (454) envoys study laws of, **2**. 107
—, officer of Perseus: (168) **13**. 237
Solonium, in Latium: (340) **4**. 49
Solovettius, a Galatian: (167) commands at Synnada, **13**. 367
Sopater, of Acarnania: (200) Macedonian commander in Chalcis, **9**. 67
—, a Macedonian: (203) sent to Carthage by Philip, **8**. 457; (201) captured, 523–5
—, officer of Perseus: (171) **12**. 503
—, of Syracuse: (214) made magistrate on Hieronymus' murder, **6**. 249; attacks Themistus and Adranodorus, 255–7
Sophoniba, daughter of Hasdrubal: (204) marries Syphax, **8**. 297–301, **12**. 55; (203) influences his policy, **8**. 387, 403; he blames, for desertion of Rome, 413–5; after Syphax' capture, marries Masinissa, 407–11; when forced to leave him, poisons self, 415–21
Sophos: *see* Sempronius.
Sora, in Latium: (345) taken, **3**. 453; (315) joins Samnites, **4**. 249; (314) recovered, 253–9, 283; (306) Samnites take, 333; (305) recovered, 345; (303) colony sent to, 361; (297) army moves through, 407; (294) L. Postumius Megellus gathers army at, 485; (209) unable to furnish men and money, **7**. 241–7; (204) forced to furnish extra quota, **8**. 263–7
sortitio: *see* provinces, assignment of.
Sosilas, of Rhodes: (195) at conference with Nabis, **9**. 495
Sosis, of Syracuse: (214) assassinates Hieronymus; rouses people, **6**. 241–5, 249, 437–9; tries to take Herbesus, 271–3; (212) agent of M. Claudius Marcellus, 437–9; **7**. 81–3, 115, 119; (211) shares ovation of Marcellus, 81–3
Sositheus, of Magnesia: (215) envoy of Philip to Hannibal, **6**. 135
Sospita: *see* Juno Sospita.
Soter: *see* Attalus I; Demetrius I.
Sotimus: (326) officer of Alexander of Epirus, **4**. 97
sources for early Roman history: **1**. 5; falsified by family records, **2**. 311; **4**. 157; **5**. 307; (390) destroyed by fire, **3**. 195
Spain: spread of Punic power in, **5**. 5–17, 45–7; (219) capture of Saguntum, 9–25, 31–45; Roman envoys sent to, 17–9; Hannibal claims all, 59, 67, 87, 127–9, **8**. 467;

INDEX

Hanno in charge of passes from, **5.** 67; Roman defence of, a cause of war, **8.** 483; prompt aid to Saguntum would have limited war to, **9.** 21; (218) assigned to P. Scipio, **5.** 47, 93, 119, 131, **8.** 175–7; envoys in, **5.** 25, 55–9; Hannibal leaves, 59–67; Cn. Scipio sent to, 93, 117; Hannibal promises land in, to men, 133; Rome claims, north of Hibrus riv., 157; Cn. Scipio lands in, 179; operations in, 179–85; (217) supplies for army in, captured, 237–9; operations under Cn. Scipio in, 261–71; envoys come to Scipio from all, 269; P. Scipio arrives in, 271, **8.** 155; operations in, **5.** 271–7; hostages of, held by Carthage, freed, 273–7; (216) Punic reinforcements for, voted, **6.** 43; operations in, 87–103; Himilco replaces Hasdrubal, 93–5; Hasdrubal, defeated by Scipios, abandons march from, to Italy, 95–101, **7.** 369; (215) Mago diverted from Italy to, **6.** 111–3; supplies for, furnished on credit, 163–7; nearly all revolts to Rome, 169, **9.** 463; (214) operations in, **6.** 307–13; (213) 329–35, 341; Numidians join Rome, 331–3, **7.** 215; (212) assigned to Scipios, **6.** 349; all, held by Rome, 455; (212 or 211) operations in, 463–95; defeat and death of the Scipios, 469–77, **7.** 71, 139, 141, 159, 369, **8.** 119, 179, 183, 259, **11.** 203; victory of L. Marcius, **6.** 477–95, **8.** 119; (211) people to name commander for, **7.** 7; troops for, **7.** 41, 141; C. Claudius Nero goes to, 65; Hasdrubal Barca feigns to leave, 65–9; no tribes of, return to Rome, 69; P. Scipio (Afr.) elected procos. for, 69–75, **8.** 179–81, 285; he sets out for, with M. Junius Silanus, **7.** 75–9; (210) affairs in, 157–203; Scipio assumes command, 157–63, **8.** 171, takes New Carthage, **7.** 165–79, 231, frees hostages held there, 165, 169, 181, 187–91; Punic troops to be sent to, for invasion of Italy, 221; C. Laelius reports to Senate on, 229–31; (209) Scipio and Silanus continued in, 235; funds from sacred treasury used for, 249; operations in, 279–97; victory at Baecula, 283–89, Hasdrubal quits, for Italy, 289, 295, all, submits to Scipio, 279, 289–95, 397, Masinissa comes to, to aid Carthage, 293, **8.** 321–3, 327, conference of Punic leaders, 295; (208) Scipio and Silanus continued in, 303; (207) 357; troops sent to Italy, 365; Hasdrubal's long experience in, 385–7; war in, after Hasdrubal's departure, **8.** 3–15; L. Scipio leg. in, 9–15, **11.** 203; (206) operations in, **8.** 53–153; Punic levies, 53, Scipio's victory at Silpia, 55–71, 317–9, 487, Carthaginians driven from, 71, 75, 77, 111, 117, Silanus and Septimius defend, while Scipio visits Syphax, 73, 297, 413, Scipio attacks certain cities, 79–87, 133–7, revolt and mutiny on news of his illness, 97–123, 155, 281, 285, Masinissa joins him, 141–3, 417, last Punic army driven from, 145–7, 153, 159, 469, 477, **11.** 185; Scipio's treatment of, **8.** 157, 417, **10.** 307, 365, 389; assigned to L. Cornelius Lentulus and L. Manlius Acidinus, **8.** 151; Scipio reports to Senate on, 151; (205) Q. Fabius Maximus belittles his achievements, 171–5; he answers, 179–81, 185; tribal uprising in, suppressed by Lentulus and Acidinus, 211–9; (204) they are continued in, 249, 257; (203) 371; supplies sent to Scipio from, 375; Punic abandonment of, a condition of peace, 425; grain sent to Italy from, 459; (202) Hannibal ready to give up, 481; (201) replacement of Lentulus and Acidinus in, urged, 521; (200) Lentulus granted ovation on return from, **9.** 59–61; land distributed to veterans of, 143–5, 155; C. Cornelius Cethegus victor in, 145, 147; assigned by plebiscite to Cn. Cornelius Lentulus (or Blasio) and L. Stertinius, 149; (199) Acidinus denied ovation on return from, 169–71; (198) veterans of, sought for Macedonian war, 177; (197) divided into two provinces, 239–41 (*see* Spain, Farther, and Spain, Nearer); (187) Scipio Africanus regarded in, as sole source of Roman power, **11.** 177; (172) made single province, **12**. 371; (171) allotted to C. Canuleius Dives, 383; charges of corruption in, investigated, **13**. 7–11; limits placed on governors' powers, 11; (170) uprising in, ended, 15, 85; (169) allotted to M. Marcellus, 39–41, 45, 53, 257, (168) to P. Fonteius Balbus, 145–7; (167) divided into two provinces, 295–7; (55) assigned for five years to procos. Pompey, **14**. 131; (49) Caesar's wars in, 137; (48) troops in, desert to Caesar, 139; (47) Pompeian forces in, 141–3; (45) Caesar defeats sons of Pompey and triumphs, 145; (27–25) Augustus' campaigns in, 165. *Also*: **12**. 85, **13**. 383. *See* Farther Spain, Nearer Spain, Bergistani, Carpetani, Celtiberi, Ilergetes, Lacetani, Lusitani, Oretani, Sedetani, Suessetani, Turdetani, Vaccaei, Vettones; Castulo, Contrebia, Emporiae, Gades, Iliturgi, New Carthage, Numantia, Saguntum; Ebro riv., Tagus riv.; Indibilis, Mandonius.

Spain, Farther: (197) allotted to M. Helvius, **9**. 239–41; war begins, 331, 335–7, 347; (196) allotted to Q. Fabius Buteo, 347; L. Stertinius returns from, 349; (195) allotted to Ap. Claudius Nero, 393, 445; Helvius gains ovation on return, 445; Nero's men sent to Nearer Spain, 461; (194) allotted to P. Scipio Nasica, 531; (193) his victories, **10**. 3–5, 27, 261; allotted to M. Fulvius Nobilior, **9**. 557; his victories, **10**. 21, 33; (192) allotted to A. Atilius Serranus, then to Nobilior, 59; his victories, 63–5; (191) he receives ovation, 223–5, 267; allotted to L. Aemilius Paulus, 121, 159–61; (190) 297; Lusitani defeat him, 427–9; (189) allotted to L. Baebius Dives, 437–9; on his death, to P. Junius Brutus, 467–9; Paulus defeats Lusitani, 469, receives *supplicatio*, 473, and brings wealth, **14**. 13; (188) allotted to pr. C. Atinius, **11**. 117–9; his victories, **14**. 239; (187) he reports rising, **11**. 239, (186) wins victories, is slain, 279; allotted to C. Calpurnius Piso, 241, 279; (185) his victories ,311–7, 341, 353; (184) allotted to P. Sempronius Longus, 341–3, 353; (183) 363, 397; (182) he dies in, **12**. 7, 55; allotted to P. Manlius, 3–7, 53–5; (181) 59, 103; (180) 131, 133; M. Fulvius Nobilior banished to, 131; allotted to L. Postumius Albinus, 109, 121; (179) 139; he defeats Vaccaei, 157, **14**. 243; (178) he triumphs, 201–5; (177–176) T. Fonteius Capito in, 231; (176) allotted to M. Scipio Maluginensis, who is excused, 231 (*but cp.* 275–7); (174) to Cn. Servilius Caepio, 251, (173) to M. (or C.) Matienus, 293, (172) to Sp. Lucretius, 321, 345; (171) Matienus accused by; goes into exile, **13**. 7–11; limits placed on governor's power, 11; (171–168) joined with Nearer Spain, **12**. 371 (*see* Spain); (167) separated again, **13**. 295–7; allotted to C. Licinius Nerva, 297; (166) to a praetor, 405; (160–153) unsuccessful wars in, cause change in calendar, **14**. 15; (147–146) Viriathus defeats M. Vetilius, 43; (141) Q. Fabius Maximus Servilianus defeats Viriathus, 49, (140–139) then recognizes his independence; his murder instigated by Q. Servilius Caepio, 49–51, 55; (138) deserter from army in, condemned; lands in, given to men of Viriathus, 53; (137) D. Junius Brutus subdues Lusitanians, 55, 57, (136) and Gallaeci, 57; (101) pacified, 279; (94) P. Scipio Nasica checks revolt, 287; (78–77) Q. Sertorius raises great war in, 115; (77) Pompey sent to; (77–74) victories of Sertorius, 115–7, 187–97, 299–301; (73–72) Pompey ends war in, 117, 119

Spain, Nearer (Hither): (207) P. Scipio (Afr.) withdraws to, **8**. 15; (197) allotted to C. Sempronius Tuditanus, **9**. 239–41; (196) he is defeated, 345–7; allotted to Q. Minucius Thermus, 347; Cn. Cornelius Blasio gains ovation for victories in, 349; (195) allotted to M. Porcius Cato and P. Manlius, 391–3; Thermus' victory in, 395; Cato's campaign in, 441–71, 529, 531, **12**. 391; he recovers all, this

INDEX

side of Hiberus, **9**. 459; *supplicatio* for victories in, 471, 527; (194) allotted to Sex. Digitius, 531; Cato leaves, **10**. 3, and triumphs, **9**. 535; Digitius defeated, **10**. 3; (193) allotted to pr. C. Flaminius, **9**. 557, **10**. 5–7, 19–21, 33, (192) to M. Baebius Tamphilus, then to Flaminius, 59, 63–5, (191) 161, (190) 297, (189) to L. Plautius Hypsaeus, 437–9, (188) to L. Manlius Acidinus, **11**. 117–9, (187) 239; (186) he defeats Celtiberians, 279–81; allotted to L. Quinctius Crispinus, 241, 277; (185) he wins victory in Central Spain, 311–7, 341; Acidinus gains ovation on return, 309; (184) allotted to A. Terentius Varro, 341–3; he takes Corbio, 353, (183) defeats Celtiberians, 363, 397; (182) allotted to pr. Q. Fulvius Flaccus, **12**. 3–7, 53–5; (181) 59; his victories, 93–103, 107–9; (180) 121–7; allotted to Ti. Sempronius Gracchus, 109–13; Fulvius triumphs on return, 113, 137, 141, 393; Gracchus' victories in, 287, 393; (179) 139; he makes peace, 147–57, 273; (178) he triumphs, 201–5; (177) assigned to M. Titinius Curvus, 211, 273; (176) allotted to P. Licinius Crassus, who is excused, 231, (174) to P. Furius Philus, 251; Ap. Claudius Centho suppresses revolt in, 273–5, 281–3; (173) allotted to Num. Fabius Buteo, 293; he dies and Philus continues in, 301–3; (172) allotted to M. Junius Pennus, 321, 343–5; (171) envoys from, complain of ill treatment; SC. limits governors' powers, **13**. 7–11; M. Titinius accused of extortion in, 9; joined with Farther Spain, **12**. 371 (*see* Spain); (167) separated from Farther Spain, **13**. 295–7; allotted to Cn. Fulvius, 297; (166) to a pr., 405; (160–153) unsuccessful wars in, cause change in calendar, **14**. 15; (152) continued failures in, cause confusion in Rome, 19; victories in, claimed by M. Marcellus, (151) by L. Licinius Lucullus, 19, 253; (144) Q. Caecilius Metellus Macedonicus seeks, as prov., 45; (141) Q. Pompeius defeated by Numantines, defeats Termestini, 49, 51; (137) Numantines defeat C. Hostilius Mancinus, 55; (134) Numantine war, 61; (104) Cimbri ravage, 81, 277, (103) are driven out by Celtiberians, 81; (98–97) T. Didius defeats Celtiberians, 87, 283

Spaniards: (218) in Punic army, **5**. 59–61, 77–9, 139–41, (217) 205, 213, 259–61, (216) 337, 343, 351–7, **6**. 43, (215) 157, (214) 213, 253–5, (213) 327, 335, (212) 465, (211) **7**. 19–25, (210) 209, (209) 263, (207) 399–401, (206) **8**. 59–67, 123, (203) 387–9, 443; (215) in Roman army, **6**. 157, (213) 327, 335, (212) 465, (207) **7**. 365, (206) **8**. 59–67; (212) take part in funeral of Ti. Sempronius Gracchus, **6**. 409; two, aid in delivery of Syracuse, 455–9, **7**. 83–5; (195) status of, in Emporiae, **9**. 441–5; (171) colony of children of Roman soldiers and women of, **13**. 11–3

Spanish sword: (361) worn by T. Manlius Torquatus in duel with Gaul, **3**. 385; (216) used for thrusting, **5**. 351; (200) used by Roman cavalry, **9**. 101; (189) used by *velites*, **11**. 75

Sparta: *see* Lacedaemon.

Spartacus: (73) with Crixus heads rebelling gladiators; defeats C. Claudius Pulcher and P. Varenus, **14**. 117–9; (72) defeats Cn. Cornelius Lentulus; L. Gellius Publicola and Q. Arrius; C. Cassius Longinus and Cn. Manlius, 119; (71) M. Licinius Crassus defeats, 119–21, 199

spear: (397) booty sold *sub hasta*, **3**. 59; (389) captives sold *sub hasta*, 207. *See* Mars, spears of.

Spercheus riv., in Thessaly: (191) M' Acilius Glabrio at, **10**. 201; (190) 303

Sperchiae, in Thessaly: (198) **9**. **191**

Spes: *see* Hope.

Spinther: *see* Cornelius Lentulus.

Spoletium, in Umbria: (c. 240) colony at, **4**. 559; (217) repulses Hannibal, **5**. 229; (209) loyal, **7**. 245–7; (167) refuses to accept custody of Gentius, **13**. 403. Prodigies: (214) **6**. 209; (91) **14**. 291; (63) 301. *See* C. Carvilius.

spolia opima: (753–717) first, dedicated by Romulus, **1**. 41; (715–672) law of Numa on, **14**. 183; (437) dedicated by cos. or tr. mil. A. Cornelius Cossus, **2**. 321–5, 363, 365; (222) by M. Marcellus, **4**. 561

sponsio: (321) terms at Caudine pass a, **4**. 177–9, 189–91, and not binding on state, 193–9

—, a judicial challenge: (184) of M. Porcius Cato to L. Quinctius Flamininus, **11**. 359; (before 179) of M. Aemilius Lepidus to M. Fulvius Nobilior, **12**. 147

Spurillius, Ti.: (422) tr. pl., **2**. 391

Spurinus: *see* Petilius.

square, hollow: (200) Romans advance in a, **9**. 109

standards (*signa*, *vexilla*): (446) brought from treasury at time of levy, **2**. 237; (435) 327–9; (350) **3**. 433; (446) hurled into midst of enemy, **2**. 241; (431) 351; (386) **3**. 221; (212) **6**. 393; (211) **7**. 21; (194) **9**. 539; (178) **12**. 195; (209) barley issued to cohorts losing, **7**. 261

Statellates, in Liguria: (173) M. Popilius Laenus makes unauthorized war on, **12**. 311–7; (172) 349; he evades order to free captured, 351–5

Statilius, Marius, a Lucanian: (216) spies on Hannibal's empty camp, **5**. 339–41, 345

Statius, T.: (475) tr. pl., fails to convict Sp. Servilius, **1**. 397

— Gellius: (305) Samnite leader, **4**. 343

— Metius: (214) commands Campanians and Carthaginians in Casilinum, **6**. 233–7

— Trebius, of Compsa: (216) betrays Compsa to Hannibal, **6**. 3

Stator: *see* Jupiter Stator.

Statorius, Q., centurion: (213) envoy of the Scipios to Syphax; drills his army, **6**. 329–31, **8**. 403; (202) commands army, 465

statues: (439) gilded, in honour of L. Minucius, **2**. 311; (438) murdered envoys honoured by, 313; (380) of Jupiter Imperator, brought to Capitol, **3**. 299; (338) equestrian, of Camillus and C. Maenius, **4**. 55, (306) of Q. Marcius Tremulus, 339; (305) of Hercules, on Capitol, 345; (296) of Jupiter in chariot on Capitol roof, 445; of wolf and twins at fig tree, 445–7; (218) bronze, for Juno on Aventine, **5**. 187; (217) of Mars, of wolves, 203; (212) Greek, from Syracuse, **6**. 495, **7**. 117, **9**. 421, (209) from Tarentum, **7**. 275; (210) set up by aedd. from fines, 229; (202) **8**. 515; (200) **9**. 147; (197) 345; (208) three, given Ceres by aedd. pl., **7**. 357; (207) cypress, carried to temple of Juno Regina, 361; (99) **14**. 283; (97) 283–5; (198) ancient, found at Eretria, **9**. 199; (196) gilded, on arches in Forum Boarium, 349; (189) of Hercules, **11**. 115; Africanus forbids public, of self, 199; (182) on Capitol and in Circus, **12**. 5; (181) first gilded, in Italy, 105 (*but cp.* **2**. 311, **9**. 349); (179) on Capitol, overthrown by storm, **12**. 141; (169) of Apollo at Cumae, **13**. 47; (104) of olive wood, **14**. 277; (58) placed by Cicero before shrine of Minerva, 311

Stellate district, in Campania: (305) Samnites raid, **4**. 341; (295) they are defeated near, 477–9; (217) Hannibal comes to, by error, **5**. 245. Prodigies: (163) **14**. 249; (114) 269

Stellatina tribus: (387) added, **3**. 213

Stellio: *see* Afranius.

Stena, pass in Epirus: (199) **9**. 165

Stertinius, C.: (188) pr. for Sardinia, **11**. 115, 117

—, L.: (199–197) procos. in Farther Spain, **9**. 149, 349; (196) Xvir for Macedonian peace, 343, 359–61, 367–71, 381–3, 395, 479, 567

—, L.: (168) qu., meets son of Masinissa at Brundisium, **13**. 293

Stimula, grove of: (186) **11**. 251

stipendium (tax): (196) unpaid, collected from priests, **9**. 389; (187) arrears of, paid from money carried in triumph, **11**. 239. *See* tributum.

Stobi, in Paeonia: (197) Philip defeats Dardani near, **9**. 329; (183) he founds Perseis near, **11**. 391; (181) he summons army to, **12**. 65–7; (167) salt trade to, **13**. 351

stockade (*vallum*): (197) Roman and Macedonian, **9**. 287–9

Stolo: *see* Licinius.

Strabo: *see* Julius Caesar, Licinius, Pompeius.

INDEX

Straits (of Gibraltar): (206) **8**. 123–7
Stratius: (167) sent to Rome with Attalus, **13**. 305–9
Strato: (42) aids M. Brutus' suicide, **14**. 155
Stratonicê, wife of Eumenes: (172) Attalus courts, **12**. 339
Stratonicea: (197) Rhodians defeat Macedonians near, **9**. 325–9; (196) Philip surrenders, to Rhodes, 361
Stratonidas: (196) involved in murder of anti-Roman Boeotarch, **9**. 353
Stratopedon, in Rhodes: (88) **14**. 293–5
Stratus, in Aetolia: (191) army assembled at, by Antiochus, **10**. 191, (189) by Aetolians, **11**. 15–7; (169) strongest city of Aetolia, **13**. 77; Perseus fails to take, 77–81
Structus: *see* Servilius, — Priscus.
Strymon, in Thessaly: (198) **9**. 193
Strymon riv., in Macedon: (171) Paeonians from valley of, **12**. 449; (168) Thracians cross, **13**. 237; *lembi* of Perseus in, 239; (167) boundary between Macedonian republics, 347; Bisaltae live on, 351; L. Aemilius Paulus crosses, 363
Stuberra, on Macedonian frontier: (200) P. Sulpicius Galba brings grain to, **9**. 113–5; (169) base of Perseus, **13**. 65, 69–73. *See* Thrysis of.
Stymphalia, Arcadian district: (197) **9**. 315
Styni, Alpine tribe: (118) **14**. 75
Subertanum, Forum: (211) **7**. 89
subitarii milites: (464) **2**. 15; (201) **9**. 7; (181) **12**. 81, 89
Subota, is. near Chios: (168) **13**. 181
Subulo: *see* Decius.
Subura, street in Rome: (461) **2**. 47
Suburana tribus: (220) freedmen assigned to, **4**. 561
Sucasina: *see* Interamna.
Sucro, in Spain: (206) mutiny at, **8**. 99–123, 285
Suessa Aurunca, in Latium: (337) Aurunci occupy, **4**. 61; (313) colony at, 273; (294) cohort from, 483; (211) Hannibal near, **7**. 33; (209) unable to furnish men and supplies, 243–7; (204) forced to supply extra quota, **8**. 263–7. Prodigies: (199) **9**. 157; (198) 177
— Pometia, in Latium: (616–578) sons of Ancus in exile at, **1**. 147; (534–510) Tarquin the Proud takes, 183, and builds temple of Jupiter Capitolinus from spoils, 193; (503) a Latin colony, revolts to Aurunci, 271–3; (502) recovered and razed, 273–5; (495) Volsci give children of, as hostages, 287; P. Servilius Priscus sacks, 299–301
Suessetani, in Spain: (212) defeat P. Scipio, **6**. 469–71; (206) Celtiberians plunder, **8**. 99; (195) serve under M. Porcius Cato, **9**. 467–9; (184) A. Terentius Varro takes Corbio of the, **11**. 353
Suessiones, in Gaul: (57–56) **14**. 129
Suessula, in Campania: (343) Samnites defeated at, **3**. 491–5; (338) citizenship without vote given, **4**. 61; (327) Samnites challenge Romans to fight near, 89; (216) camp above, used by M. Marcellus, **6**. 47, 57, (215) 105, 109, by Q. Fabius Maximus, 137, 159, 163, (214) by Marcellus, 217, by M. Pomponius Matho, 227, (213) by Cn. Fulvius Centumalus, 315, 327, by Q. Fabius Maximus, 317, 323, (212) by C. Claudius Nero, 347, 425, (211) **7**. 19. Prodigy: (212) **6**. 365
sufetes, Punic magistrates: (206) in Gades, **8**. 149; (203) in Carthage, 387; (193) **9**. 573–5
Suismontium, Mt., in Liguria; (187) **11**. 223
Sulca: *see* Baebius.
Sulla: *see* Cornelius.
Sulmo, Paelignian town: (211) **7**. 41
Sulpicia: (186) aids in revealing Bacchanalian conspiracy, **11**. 249–55
Sulpicius, C.: (211) pr. for Sicily, **6**. 501, **7**. 5
—, L.: (181) tr. mil. under L. Aemilius Paulus, **12**. 83
— Camerinus, C.: (382) tr. mil. c. p., **3**. 271; (380) cens., 291
— —, P., Xvir 451: (454) envoy to Athens, **2**. 107; (451) Xvir, 109; (449) Senate sends, to plebs, 167; (446) leg. against Aequi, 239
— —, Ser.: (393) cos., opposes migration to Veii, **3**. 103; (391) tr. mil. c. p., 111; (387) interrex, 211
— — Cornutus, Q.: (490) cos., **1**. 347[1]

INDEX

Sulpicius Camerinus Cornutus, Q.: (402) tr. mil. c. p., **3**. 27; (398) ii, 53
— — —, Ser.: (500) cos., **1**. 279; (463) curio max., dies, **2**. 27
— — —, Ser.: (461) cos., **2**. 35, 39–41
— — Praetextatus, Q.: (434) cos., **2**. 331; (431) leg., 347
— — Rufus, Ser.: (345) cos., **3**. 451; takes Sora, 453
— Galba, C.: (202–199) pont., **8**. 515, **9**. 173
— —, C., pr. 171: (174) pont., **12**. 253; (171) pr. urb., 371, 383, 395, **13**. 5–7
— —, Ser.: (209) aed. cur., **7**. 301; (205) envoy for stone of Idaean Mother, **8**. 247–9; (203–199) pont., 461, **9**. 173
— —, Ser.: (194) **9**. 533
— —, Ser., pr. 187: (189) aed. cur., fines grain dealers, **11**. 115; (187) pr. urb., 143, 145; presides over Senate, 153, 189, 191, 231; (185) candidate for cos., 319–21
— —, Ser., cos. 144: (167) tr. mil. of L. Aemilius Paulus, **13**. 369; opposes triumph of Paulus, 369–91; (151) pr.; Lusitanians defeat, **14**. 21; (149) decree freeing Lusitanians enslaved by, fails, 27, 31; M. Porcius Cato attacks, **11**. 351; (144) cos., **14**. 45
— —, Ser.: (108) cos., **14**. 273
— —, Ser.: (91) pr., escapes Lucanians, **14**. 89; (90) defeats Paeligni, 91; (89) leg., crushes Marrucini, 95
— — Maximus, P., cos. 211, 200: (211) cos., with Apulia as prov., **6**. 501, **7**. 3, 85; faces Hannibal's march on Rome, 37–39; elects procos. for Spain, 69; prov. changed to Macedon and fleet, 85, 109, 111; (210) 101; (209) 233, 249; sends troops to Aetolians, 331; plunders Sicyon and Corinth, 337; defends Elis, 339–41; (208–207) command continued, 303–5; winters at Aegina, 343, **8**. 17; operates on coast, 17–29, 33; (205) P. Sempronius Tuditanus succeeds, 251; (203) dict. to keep Cn. Servilius Caepio from Africa, 451; holds elections, 461; (200) cos. ii, with Macedon as prov., **9**. 13–7, **12**. 391; favours war with Philip, **9**. 17–25; consults fetiales; enlists volunteers, 25; vows games and gift to Jupiter, 29, 533[2]; reaches Macedon, 43, 167; winters around Apollonia, 57, 65, 79; (199) sends L. Apustius to plunder, 79; seeks allies, receives envoys, 81–3; crosses land of Dassaretii, 99, 239–41; meets Philip in minor battles, 99–119, 215, 295; ends campaign, 139, 155; reports portent, 157; (197) leg. of Flamininus, 243; Xvir for making peace, 343, 359–61, 367–71, 381–3, 395, 479, 561–7; (193) envoy to Antiochus, 569, **10**. 39; ill, remains at Pergamum, 41; meets Antiochus' agent, 47–51; returns to Rome, 51, 63
Sulpicius Gallus, C., cos. 166: (181) reports Ligurian victory, **12**. 87–9; (171) advocate for Spain, **13**. 7–9; (169) pr. urb., 39, 53, 141, 145; conducts levy, 49, 53; (168) tr. mil., warns of lunar eclipse before Pydna, 215–7; (167) commands winter camp, 339; rebuked for laxity, 345; (166) cos., 403, **14**. 245; defeats Ligurians, 11; (149) Ser. Sulpicius Galba is guardian of son of, 27
— Longus, C., cos. 337, 323, 314: (337) cos., fails to aid Aurunci, **4**. 61; opposes election of first plebeian pr., 63; (323) cos. ii, 143–5; (314) iii, 253; takes Ausonian towns, 255–61; conducts treason trials, 267; defeats Samnites at Caudium, 267–71; besieges Bovianum, 271; (312) dict. against Etruscans, 275; worthy to meet Alexander, 227
— —, Q.: (390) tr. mil. c. p., **3**. 127; makes unacceptable sacrifice, 129, 199; Gauls defeat, at Allia, 129–31; proposes to punish negligent guards, 161; arranges Gallic withdrawal, 163–5
— Peticus, C., cos. 364, 361, 355, 353, 351: (364) cos., **3**. 359; (362) leg. of dead cos., defeats Hernici, 377–81; (361) cos. ii, takes Ferentinum, 381–3; (358) dict., defeats Gauls, triumphs, 395–407; (356) interrex, 415; (355) cos. iii, 415; plunders Tarquinii, 417; (353) cos. iv, 421;

reports Etruscan raids, 421–3; (352) interrex, 429; (351) cos. v, 431
Sulpicius Praetextatus, Ser.: (370) tr. mil. c. p., **3**. 319; (368) ii, 327
— Rufus, P.: (88) tr. pl., supports Marius, killed, **14**. 95–7
— —, Ser.: (388) tr. mil. c. p., **3**. 209; (384) ii, 255; (383) iii, 269; (377) iv, 305; relieves Tusculum, 309–11; marries daughter of M. Fabius Ambustus, 313–5
— —, Ser.: (51) cos., **14**. 135
— Saverrio, P.: (304) cos., **4**. 345; defeats Aequi, triumphs, 345–9; (299) cens., 393; interrex, 399
Summanus, temple of: (197) **9**. 243
sumptuary law: *see* Oppian law.
Sun: (181) altar to, **12**. 71
Sunium, cape in Attica: (208–207) Philip rounds, **8**. 35; (200) Romans keep pirates beyond, **9**. 65; Roman fleet at, 67; (198) 201
suovetaurilia: (578–534) offered by Servius after first census, **1**. 155; (340) to be offered if spear of *devotio* is captured, **4**. 43
Superbus: *see* Tarquinius.
superstition: (428) growth of, **2**. 355–7; (213) **6**. 343–5
superum mare: *see* Adriatic sea
supplicatio: (463) atonement in time of pestilence, **2**. 27; (292) **4**. 543; (208) **7**. 307; *et saepe*; (344) atonement because of prodigies, **3**. 455; (296) **4**. 443; (218) **5**. 187; *et saepe*; (206) because fire of Vesta had gone out, **8**. 47; (178) **14**. 243; (90) at cleansing of temple, 293; (219) prayer for success in war, **5**. 47; (217) 235; (203) **8**. 369; (200) **9**. 25, 29; (191) **10**. 159; (190) 431; (181) prayer for rain, **14**. 243; (449) thanksgiving, **2**. 213; (396) **3**. 79–81; (296) **4**. 437; (293) 531; (212) **7**. 79–81; *et saepe*
Sura: *see* Cornelius Lentulus.
Surenas, of Parthia: (53) defeats M. Licinius Crassus, **14**. 133
sureties: (461) first required, **2**. 47–9
surgery: (147) trepanning skull, **14**. 43; (142) for removal of stone, 55; for tumours, 203
surrender: (616–578) formula for, **1**. 137; (191) Greek and Roman terms of, contrasted, **10**. 237–41
Susus, of Phalasarnae: (171) commands Cretans for Perseus, **12**. 449
Sutrium, on Etruscan border: (389) Etruscans take; M. Furius Camillus recovers, **3**. 203–7; (386) 225–7; (357) assembly by tribes in camp before, 411; (311) Etruscans defeated at, **4**. 285–9; (310) 299–301; 305–9; (297) envoys of, report Etruscan wish for peace, 407; (210) Campanians settled in, **7**. 131–3; (209) unable to furnish men and money, 243–7; (204) forced to meet extra quota, **8**. 263–7
Sybaris: (210) **7**. 147. *See* Thurii.
Sycurium, near Tempê: (171) base of Perseus, **12**. 459–61, 465, 469, 487, 493–5
Sylleum, in Pamphylia: (189) **11**. 47
Syllus, of Cnossos: (171) commands Cretans for Perseus, **12**. 449
synhedri: (167) senators of new Macedonian republics, **13**. 359
Synnada, in Phrygia: (189) Cn. Manlius Volso comes to, **11**. 51; (167) Galatians muster at; they confer with Romans at, **13**. 367
Syphax, king of Masaesulii (Numidians): (213) an enemy of Carthage and friend of Rome, **6**. 329–31; a centurion trains army of, 331, **8**. 403; defeats Carthaginians, **6**. 331; Masinissa defeats, 333; (210) exchanges envoys with Rome, **7**. 215; assists Mazaetullus against Masinissa, **8**. 323–7; drives Masinissa from kingdom, 327–9, 413, **10**. 365, **12**. 55, 57; (206) P. Scipio (Afr.) seeks friendship of, **8**. 73; Scipio and Hasdrubal son of Gisgo at court of, 75–7, 297, 413; makes alliance with Scipio, 79, 185, 299; (205) of doubtful loyalty, 171–3, 221–5; (204) marries Sophoniba, daughter of Hasdrubal, 297–9, 415, **12**. 55; defeats Masinissa, **8**. 329–37; allied with Carthage, 297–9, **9**. 35; sends envoys to Scipio, **8**. 299–303; (204) Carthage asks aid of, 337–9; raises siege of Utica, 345–7; (203) treats unsuccessfully with Scipio, 375–81; defeated by Scipio and Masinissa; escapes, 381–7;

influence of Sophoniba upon, 387, 403; continues war, 387–9; Scipio defeats, at Great Plains, 389–93, 465, **11**. 185; Laelius and Masinissa capture, **8**. 401–7, 411, 417–9, 469, 477, **13**. 267; wife of, marries Masinissa, **8**. 407–11, 417–9; brought before Scipio, blames wife, 411–5; Masinissa to succeed, 423; Laelius takes, to Rome, 423, 427, **13**. 385; interned in Alba Fucens, **8**. 427; victory over, reported in Senate, 427–9; (201) Masinissa granted lands of, 537, **9**. 33–5, **10**. 365, 451; Scipio triumphs over, **8**. 537–9, **11**. 159, 181; dies before triumph, **8**. 539. *See* Vermina, Arcobarzanes.

Syracuse: (415–413) defeats Athens, **6**. 437; (c. 310) Agathocles of, invades Africa, **8**. 183; (264) Rome assists Mamertines against, **4**. 553; (218) fleet of, aids Rome, **5**. 145; (216) Punic fleet plunders lands of, 383; (215) Hieronymus succeeds Hiero, **6**. 185–9; he makes terms with Hannibal, 191–5, **7**. 117; he is killed, **6**. 195; Ap. Claudius Pulcher camps on frontier of, 197; (214) disturbances in, 241–79; M. Marcellus sends envoys to, 263; alliance with Rome voted, 265–7; army late for capture of Leontini, 269–71; Hippocrates and Epicydes gain control, deserting Rome, 273–9, 287, **7**. 115; Marcellus begins siege of, **6**. 279–93, 301; defended by Archimedes' engines, 283–7; Punic force withdraws from, 291–3; (212) Marcellus continues in command, 349, 363; final operations against, 429–59; vain negotiations for surrender, 429–31, 437; sends envoy to Philip, 431; pestilence in armies outside, 443–5; Bomilcar fails to aid, 441, 447–9; negotiations for surrender, 449–55; Moericus betrays, 455–9, **7**. 81–3; surrenders to Marcellus, **6**. 459, 495, **7**. 91, 111–21, 161, **8**. 209; he addresses people, **6**. 459–61; he permits plundering, 461–3, **7**. 117, 123; supplies brought to, **6**. 463; he returns to, 501; (211) spoils of, carried in ovation, **7**. 81–3, used to adorn Rome, 121, 123, 275, **11**. 229, create craze for art, **6**. 495, **9**. 421; (210) Marcellus accused by, before Senate, **7**. 111–9, **11**. 149; his defence, **7**. 119–23; his acts in, ratified, 123–5; he becomes patron of, 125; M. Valerius Laevinus settles affairs of, 151; (205) P. Scipio (Afr.) in, **8**. 211, 231, 243, 285, (204) 293–5, 301, **11**. 177; (200) cited as example of Roman 'protection,' **9**. 85, **10**. 47–9; Roman answer to this, **9**. 91–3. Prodigy: (177) **12**. 223–5. *See* Achradina, Epipolae, Euryalus, Hexapylon, Island (Nasos), Neapolis, Tycha; Adranodorus, Dinomenes, Epicydes, Gelo, Hiero, Hieronymus, Hippocrates, Sopater, Sosis, Themistus, Theodotus.

Syria: unwarlike people of, **10**. 143, 209, **11**. 59; kings of, pay tribute to Galatians, 55; (203–187) relations with Rome, *see* Antiochus III; (193) Antiochus sends son to, **10**. 39; (190) in confusion, 301; fleet comes from, 313, 355; cavalry of, at Magnesia, 409; Polyxenidas returns to, 421; (168) open to attack, **13**. 167; Antiochus IV returns to, 277, 285; (162) Cn. Octavius, envoy to, assassinated, **14**. 249; (149) Philip (Andriscus) in, 29; civil war in, 11; (154–150) 21; (149) 33; (144) 43, 45; (142) 55, 57; (130) war with Parthia, 67; (125) civil war in, 71; (118–115) 75; (101) 83; (99–91) 87; (66) Pompey takes, from Tigranes, 125; (54) assigned for five years to M. Licinius Crassus, 131; (52) Parthians enter, but are defeated by C. (or Q.) Cassius Longinus; (51) M. Calpurnius Bibulus in, 135; (47) war against Caesar stirred in, 143; (43) Longinus gains control of, 153; (40) Parthians overrun, 157; (38) P. Ventidius Bassus defeats Parthians in, 157–9. *See* Antiochus, Seleucus, Demetrius; Eunus, Polyxenidas.

Syria, Coelê (Hollow Syria): (198) Antiochus III seizes cities in, **9**. 331; (171) Antiochus IV hopes to recover, **12**. 375; (168) he enters, **13**. 279–81

Syrtis, Lesser: (204) Masinissa flees to, **8**. 337; (193) he plunders shores of, **9**. 575

INDEX

Tabae, in Pisidia : (189) **11**. 43

tabernaculum : (444) faulty, voids election, **2**. 281

Tabernae Novae : (210) **7**. 103

tactics, military (battles described): (753–717) against Fidenates, **1**. 53; (499) at Lake Regillus, 279–85; (446) against Volsci and Aequi, **2**. 237–43; (385) **3**. 237–9; (358) against Gauls, 403–7; (350) 435–9; (340) against Latins, **4**. 31–41; (322) against Samnites, 147–53; (314) 269–71; (310) against Etruscans, 299–301; (302) 373–7; (297) against Samnites, 407–13; (295) at Sentinum, 463–75; (293) cavalry, 519–21; (218) at Trebia, **5**. 159–69; (217) at Trasumennus, 213–25; (216) at Cannae, 351–67; of P. and Cn. Scipio in Spain, **6**. 97–101; (209) of P. Scipio (Afr.) in Spain, **7**. 283–9; (206) **8**. 59–67; 133–7; (205) 215–9; (207) at the Metaurus riv., **7**. 399–405; (202) at 'Zama,' **8**. 489–501; (197) at Cynoscephalae, **9**. 293–303; (195) in Spain, 453–9; (190) at Magnesia, **10**. 403–19; (189) against Galatians, **11**. 67–81, 89–93; (181) in Spain, **12**. 95–101; (171) at Callinicus, 471–7; (168) at Pydna, **13**. 213–31

tactics, naval : (191) **10**. 281–5; (190) 357–61; 375–81

Tagus riv., in Spain : (221) Hannibal defeats tribes near, **5**. 15–7; (209) Hasdrubal retires along, **7**. 289; (192) M. Fulvius Nobilior advances to, **10**. 65; (185) C. Calpurnius Piso and L. Quinctius Crispinus win victories on, **11**. 311–7

Tamiani : (197) in Rhodian army, **9**. 325

Tamphilus : *see* Baebius.

Tanagra, in Boeotia : (196) murderers of Brachyllas flee to, **9**. 353; (192) Romans attacked near, **10**. 147

Tanaquil, wife of Tarquinius Priscus : character and influence, **1**. 123–7; (616–578) foretells future of Servius, 139; (578) secures throne for him, 145–7, 165

Tannetum, in cis-Alpine Gaul : (218) L. Manlius Volso retires to, **5**. 73; Boi capture IIIviri agr. adsig. near, **8**. 439

Tappo : *see* Valerius.

Tappulus : *see* Villius.

Tarentini, a kind of cavalry : (192) in armies of Philopoemen and of Nabis, **10**. 81, 83, (190) of Antiochus, 409

Tarentum : of non-Roman origin, **7**. 243; (332) seeks aid of Alexander of Epirus, **4**. 93–5; (326) Palaepolis expects aid from, 101, 105; Romans at gates of, 105; causes Lucanian revolt, 105–7, 111; (320) envoys of, seek peace for Samnites, 211–5; (282) Rome declares war on, 549; (280) aided by Pyrrhus, 549, **6**. 21, **9**. 23, **10**. 459, (273) and by Carthage, **4**. 551, **5**. 29; Rome ransoms prisoners from, **5**. 393; (272) war with, ends, **4**. 553, **6**. 205; (216) deserts Rome, **5**. 409; (215) assigned to M. Valerius Laevinus, **6**. 113; port of, guarded, 115; base for operations against Philip, 133–5; (214) betrayal of, promised to Hannibal, 213–5, 239; he approaches, 229, but withdraws, 239–41; (213) he hopes for betrayal of, 341; (212) hostages of, escape from Rome; are captured, 365–7; conspirators deliver, to Hannibal, 367–77, 397–9, **7**. 141, 147, 149, 311–3, **9**. 433, except for citadel, **6**. 377–83, **7**. 139, 147, under M. Livius Macatus, 145, 151, 311; Hannibal at, **6**. 387–9; citadel holds out, 397, 427, **7**. 17, 79; (211) Hannibal moves from, 17, 45; withdrawal of Punic fleet requested by, 79; (210) citadel holds out, 145–51, 213; (209) assigned to Q. Fabius Maximus, 231–3, 239–41, 303; he takes, 249, 253–5, 267–77, 297, 313; auspices save him from plot, 277; sues for peace, 299; (208) assigned to Q. Claudius, 301; Senate confines people of, to city, 311; Roman garrisons from, ambushed, 315–7; danger to, after Marcellus' death, 329; T. Quinctius Crispinus dies in, 345; people of, invited home, 351; (207) assigned to C. Hostilius Tubulus, 351, 353, then to Q. Claudius, 357, 363; Hannibal moves from, 373; Hasdrubal's messengers captured near, 381; (206) Claudius continues in, **8**. 45; (205, 204) assigned to Flamininus, 257; (200) subject to Rome, **9**. 87; (193) **10**. 47–9; (192) M. Baebius Tamphilus ordered to, 65–7; (191) allotted to A. Cornelius Mammula, 159; (189) Spartan discipline lacking in, **11**. 59; (187) allotted to Ap. Claudius Pulcher, 145; (185) to L. Postumius Tempsanus, 309; (184) he checks conspiracies, 353; (181) complains of piracy, **12**. 59; (178) in command of L. Cornelius Dolabella, 187; (169) land near given to Onesimus, **13**. 143

Tarentum, in Rome: (149) games for Father Dis at the, **14**. 23, 31

targeteers: *see caetrati*.

Tarpeia: (753—717) betrays Capitol to Sabines, who kill her, **1**. 43–5

Tarpeian mt.: the Capitoline, **1**. 191

— rock: (390) M. Manlius Capitolinus repels Gauls from, **3**. 253, 385 (*cp*. 157–159); death by being hurled from, inflicted on negligent guard, 161, (384) on Capitolinus, 267; (214) on prisoners, **6**. 237–9; (212) on recovered hostages, 367; (88) on slave, **14**. 97; (87) on Sex. Licinius, 101–3; (131) tribb. pl. save Q. Caecilius Metellus from, 67

Tarpeius, Sp., commander of Capitoline: (753–717) father of Tarpeia, **1**. 43

— Montanus Capitolinus, Sp.: (454) cos., **2**. 105; (449) sent by Senate to plebeians, 167; (448) co-opted tr. pl., 219

Tarquinia, sister of Tarquinius Superbus: (534–510) mother of L. Junius Brutus, **1**. 195

Tarquinii, in Etruria: (640–616) home of Tarquinius Priscus, **1**. 123–5, 165, **2**. 267; (509) aids Tarquinius Superbus, **1**. 235–9; (397) defeated, **3**. 57–9; (388) land of, invaded, 209; (358) defeats Rome, sacrifices prisoners, 393, 407–9, 419–21; (356) defeated at Salinae, 413–5; (355) lands of, plundered, 417; (354) defeated, 419–21; (353) gains Caeretes as allies, 421–5; (351) granted 40 year truce, 431; (308) frightened by P. Decius Mus, seeks truce, **4**. 325; (211) Cn. Fulvius Flaccus in exile at, **7**. 15; (205) promises P. Scipio (Afr.) sails, **8**. 193; (181) Gravisca founded on territory of, **12**. 89. Prodigies: (210) **7**. 217; (104) **14**. 277; (100) 279

Tarquinii (the family): (509) too fond of sovereignty, **1**. 223; exiled, 225, **2**. 143; plot of, suppressed; property of, confiscated, **1**. 227–31; (508) Porsinna fails to restore, 245–69; (501) coss. suspected of supporting, 275; (499) defeated at Lake Regillus, 279–85; (492) Aristodemus of Cumae, heir of, 331; cited as typical enemies of plebeians, **2**. 43, 129, **3**. 339, **4**. 293

Tarquinius, Arruns, brother of Priscus, father of Egerius, **1**. 123

—, Arruns, son (or grandson) of Priscus: (578–534) marries daughter of Servius, **1**. 147; killed by wife and brother, 161–3

—, Arruns, son of Superbus: (534–510) envoy to Delphi, **1**. 195–7; (509) joins father in exile, 209; L. Junius Brutus and, slay each other, 237–9

—, Sextus, son of Superbus: (534–510) delivers Gabii to Rome, **1**. 185–9; left at Rome, 197; (510) violates Lucretia, 199–203, 207; killed at Gabii, 209

—, T., son of Superbus: (534–510) envoy to Delphi, **1**. 195–7; (509) joins father in exile, 209; (499) commands exiles at Lake Regillus, 281

— Collatinus, L., son of Egerius: (510) wagers with Tarquins on virtue of wives, **1**. 199–201; swears vengeance on Sextus, 203, 205; (509) cos., 209; resigns because of name, 223–5, **2**. 307, **14**. 317

— Egerius: nephew of Priscus, **1**. 123; (616–578) commands in Collatia, 137; (534–510) father of Collatinus, 199

— Priscus, L.: originally called Lucumo, **1**. 123; (640–616) comes from Tarquinii to Rome, 123–7, 165, **2**. 267–9; (616–578) secures throne, **1**. 127–9, 223; increases Senate, 129; adds equestrian centuries, 131–3; subdues Latins and Sabines, 129–37; builds walls, sewers, foundations for temple of Capitoline Jupiter, 131, 137–9, 191; accepts Servius Tullius as son-in-law, 139–41; father or grandfather of Tarquinius Superbus, 161, 165; murdered by sons of Ancus, 141–7, 167; Gauls enter Italy during reign of, **3**. 117

Tarquinius Superbus, L., son or grandson of Priscus, **1**. 161, 165; marries Tullia, 147, 161; (534) plots against Arruns Tarquinius and Servius Tullius, 161–71; seizes throne, 171–3; (534–510) seeks favour of Latins, 173–5; secures death of Turnus Herdonius, 175–81; makes new Latin treaty, 181–3, **4**. 19; begins Volscian war; takes Suessa Pometia, **1**. 183; takes Gabii by trickery, 183–91; makes peace with Aequi and Etruscans, 191; constructs temple of Jupiter Capitolinus and public works, 191–3; people murmur, 193–5; founds colonies, 195, 287; disturbed by prodigy, sends to Delphi, 195; L. Junius Brutus swears oath of vengeance on, 205; (510) removed from throne; exiled at Caere, 207–9, 219, 223, 333; (509) plot to restore, fails, 227–35; leads Etruscans against Rome, 235–9; (508–506) Lars Porsinna fails to restore, 245–69; (499) wounded at Lake Regillus, 279; (495) dies at Cumae, 287. Reign of, as date, **14**. 81

Tarquitius Flaccus, L.: (458) mag. eq., **2**. 91–3

Tarracina, in Latium: (217) pass above, secured against Hannibal, **5**. 253–5; (212) escaped hostages captured at, **6**. 367; (204) Great Mother reaches, **8**. 259; (191) naval exemptions denied to, **10**. 163; (179) mole constructed at, **12**. 157; (40) agents of Octavian and M. Antony confer at, **14**. 221. Prodigies: (213) **6**. 317; (210) **7**. 217; (206) **8**. 47; (204) 259; (191) **10**. 263; (179) **12**. 141; (166) **14**. 247; (163) 249; (137) 257; (130) 263. *See* Anxur.

Tarraco, Spanish port: (218) Hasdrubal defeats Cn. Scipio near, **5**. 181; base for Scipio, 181, 185, (217) 263, 271, (211) for C. Claudius Nero, **7**. 65, for P. Scipio (Afr.), 75–7, **8**. 171, (210) **7**. 157, 175, 197, 229, (209) 281, 293, (207) **8**. 15, (206) 55, 69–73, 79, 141, 145, (195) for M. Porcius Cato, **9**. 459, (180) for Ti. Sempronius Gracchus, **12**. 121, 127

Tartesii: *see* Turdetani.

Tatius, T., Sabine king: (753–717) bribes Tarpeia, seizes Capitol, **1**. 39, 43–5; vows shrines, 191; rules jointly with Romulus, 49–51, 125, 127, **2**. 267, **3**. 347, 375, **12**. 145; settles Sabines in Rome, **1**. 109; gives name to century of equites; mistreats Laurentian envoys, 51; killed at Lavinium, 51, 61

Taulantia, in Illyria: (167) **13**. 337

Taurasini, Samnites: (180) **12**. 119

Taurea: *see* Vibellius.

Taurian games: (186) celebrated, **11**. 281

Taurianum, in Bruttium: (213) **6**. 341

Taurine passes: (616–578) **3**. 119

Taurini Galli: (218) **5**. 111–5

Tauropolos: (168) Diana called, in Amphipolis, **13**. 235

Taurus mts., in Asia Minor: (193) Antiochus crosses, **10**. 39; (190) he is required to withdraw beyond, 393, 423, 443, 451, 459, 463, 467, **11**. 25–7, 39, (188) 125, 135, 163–5, 185, 207, **12**. 419, 445; (189) Galatians control tribes this side of, **11**. 53–5, 93; Cn. Manlius Volso anxious to leave, 93; (188) he receives envoys from tribes this side of, 121, is with difficulty restrained from crossing, 155, (187) claims to have pacified all this side of, 163; Sibylline prophecy against crossing, 155; form boundary of Roman power, 165

Taurus riv.: (189)**11**. 49

taxes: *see portoria*, *tributum*, *stipendium*, tithe; censors.

Taygetus, Mt., in Laconia: (195) **9**. 491

Teanum Apulum, in Apulia: (318) **4**. 243

Teanum Sidicinum, in Campania: (216) M. Marcellus sends naval legion to, **5**. 387; (216–215) M. Junius Pera winters at, **6**. 81, 109; (211) Capuan senators executed at, **7**. 57–9. Prodigy: (166) **14**. 247

Teates: *see* Teanum Apulum.
Tecmon, in Epirus: (167) **13**. 335–7
Tectosagi, Galatians: in interior of Asia Minor, **11**. 53–5; (189) reported in arms, 63–7; make treacherous attack on Cn. Manlius Volso; are defeated, 83–93
Tegea, in Arcadia: (195) Flamininus passes, **9**. 483; (192) Achaean council in, **10**. 77; (189) **11**. 113; (192) Aetolians flee from Sparta to, **10**. 111; (175) Antiochus Epiphanes builds theatre in, **12**. 249
Tegula: *see* Licinius.
Telemnastus, of Crete: (192) commands auxiliaries for Philopoemen, **10**. 83
Telesia, in Samnium: (217) Hannibal takes, **5**. 243; (214) Q. Fabius Maximus recovers, **6**. 237
Telesinus: (82) dies with younger Marius, **14**. 111
Tellenae, in Latium: (640–616) **1**. 119
Tellus (Earth): (340) addressed in *devotio*, **4**. 21, 37; (295) 467, 469. Temple of, **1**. 355
Telmessus, in Lydia: (189) assigned to Eumenes, **10**. 465; (188) occupied by Q. Fabius Labeo, **11**. 131; given to Eumenes, 133–5. *See* Ptolemy of.
—, Gulf of: (190) **10**. 337
Temenites gate, of Tarentum: (212) **6**. 373
Tempanius, Sex., tr. pl. 422: (423) pref., defeats Volsci by dismounting cavalry, **2**. 381–5, 391; (422) praises C. Sempronius Atratinus, 387–91; tr. pl., 391
Tempê, in Thessaly: (198) Philip establishes base in, **9**. 195; (197) he flees to, 301; peace councils at, 309–13; (196) 371; (191) Ap. Claudius Pulcher occupies, **10**. 187–9: (185) dispute between Philip and Thessalians heard at, **11**. 291–9; (171) Perseus occupies approaches to, **12**. 459, 483, 503; (169) **13**. 109–11; points about, taken by Sp. Lucretius, 111, 115, and M. Popilius Laenas, 117
templum: (716) marked by augur, **1**. 67
Tempsa, in Bruttium: (194) **9**. 535
Tempsanus: *see* Postumius.
Tempyra, in Thrace: (188) **11**. 139–41
Ten Tables of Laws: (451) adopted by *comit. cur*., **2**. 111–3
Tencteri, German tribe: (12) **14**. 167
Tendeba, in Stratonicea: (197) **9**. 325
Tenedos, is. in Aegean: (200) Rhodian fleet at, **9**. 51; (168) Perseus' fleet at, **13**. 179–81
Tenos, is. of Cyclades: (191) **10**. 221
tensae: (390) ceremonial cars, **3**. 139; (310) **4**. 323
Teos, in Ionia: (190) prepares supplies for Antiochus, **10**. 369; yields to L. Aemilius Regillus, 371–3
Terentilian law: (462) limiting consular power, proposed by C. Terentilius Harsa, **2**. 31–5; (461) advocated by tribb. pl., 35–9, 49–51; (460) 57, 73; (459) 81; (458) 85, 101; (457) 101; (455) 103; (454) abandoned, 105
Terentilius Harsa, C.: (462) tr. pl., proposes law limiting consular power, **2**. 31–5
Terentina tribus: (299) added, **4**. 393
Terentius, Q.: (217) envoy to forbid C. Flaminius assuming office at Ariminum, **5**. 191
— Culleo, Q., pr. 187: (201) war prisoner, freed, **8**. 533, 539, **11**. 191; (195) envoy to Carthage, **9**. 403; (187) pr. pereg., **11**. 143–5; conducts trial of L. Scipio, 191–5, 201, 209; forces Latins from Rome, 225; Cn. Manlius Volso avoids trial before, 235; (185) candidate for cos., 319; (171) envoy to Carthage and Masinissa, **12**. 397
— Istra, C.: (182) pr. for Sardinia, **11**. 397, **12**. 3; (181) IIIvir for Gravisca, 89
— Massiliota, L., pr. 187: (200) aed. pl., **9**. 147; (196) Xvir for Macedonian settlement, 343, 359–61, 367–71, 381–3, 395, 479, 561; (187) pr. for Sicily, **11**. 143–5; (180) tr. mil., reports Spanish victories, **12**. 107
— Tuscivicanus, P.: (167) Vvir for Illyrian settlement, **13**. 299–301, 337–9
— Varro, A., pr. 184: (189) envoy of Aetolian propr.; conducts Aetolian envoys home, **10**. 433–5; (184) pr. for Nearer Spain, **11**. 321, 341, 353;

(183) 363; defeats Celtiberians, 397; (182) command continued, **12**. 7, 55; gains ovation, 55; (172) envoy to Illyricum, 365; (167) Xvir for Macedonian settlement, **13**. 299, 339, 345–7, 355
Terentius Varro, C., cos. 216 : (218) pr., **5**. 289; (217) supports law making mag. eq. equal to dict., 289–91, 313; (216) cos., 313–9; delivers truculent harangues, 327; Q. Fabius Maximus warns L. Aemilius Paulus against, 327–33; Paulus and, command army on alternate days, 335–7; saved from trap by omen, 341–3; with Paulus, follows Hannibal to Cannae, 345–7; orders battle, 349; commands left, 351; defeated, 351–61; escapes to Venusia, 361–3, 399, **6**. 35, 359–61, **7**. 11; asks troops from Capua, **6**. 13–7; moves to Canusium with survivors, **5**. 377; reports to Senate, 381–3; called to Rome; names M. Junius Pera dict., 385–7; thanked for not despairing of state, 409, **6**. 359; active, 43; names dictator to fill Senate, 77–9; in Apulia, 85; (215) 87; army of, sent to Tarentum, 113, 133; in Picenum, 113; (214) 207, 209; (213) 317, 347; (208) propr. in Etruria, **7**. 309–11, 351; (207) 357, **8**. 45; (203) envoy to Philip, 459, (200) to Africa, **9**. 37, 57; IIIvir col. deduc., 145
— —, M. : (49) leg. of Pompey, surrenders to Caesar, **14**. 137, 139
— — Lucullus, M., cos. 73 : (72) subdues Thracians, **14**. 121
Terina, in Bruttium : (326) **4**. 95
Termessus, in Pisidia : (189) buys peace from Cn. Manlius Volso, **11**. 47–9
Termestini, in Spain : (141) **14**. 49
Terminalia : (170) followed by intercalary month, **13**. 41; (167) 405
Terminus (Termo) : (534–510) shrine of, not moved, **1**. 191, 211, **3**. 185
Terra Mater : *see* Tellus.
Terracina : *see* Tarracina.
testudo : (403) shed used in siege, **3**. 17; (200) **9**. 135; (195) 491; (295) military formation with interlocked shields, **4**. 471, 473; (293) 521, 525, (200) **9**. 117; (195) 521; (169) **13**. 117–21. Cp. **9**. 203
Tetraphylia, in Acharnania : (189) **11**. 5
Teuma, in Thessaly : (198) **9**. 191
Teuticus : (168) envoy of Gentius, **13**. 193
Teutoni : (113) and Cimbri cross Alps, defeat Romans, **14**. 271; (104) Cimbri join, 277; (103) 81; (102) C. Marius defeats, at Aquae Sextiae, 81, 279
Thabusium, in Asia Minor : (189) **11**. 45
Thalassius : (753–717) wedding cry from name of, **1**. 37
Thalna : *see* Juventius.
Thapsus, in Africa : (204) battle between Numidians at, **8**. 323
—, on African coast : (195) Hannibal avoids, in flight, **9**. 403–5; (46) Caesar defeats Pompeians at, **14**. 143
Thasos, is. in Aegean : (200) complains of Philip, **9**. 91; (196) Philip to withdraw from, 359; Xviri for Macedonian settlement at, 371, 383
Thaumaci, in Phthiotis : (199) Philip abandons siege of, **9**. 161–3; (198) Aetolians occupy, 191; (191) M' Acilius Glabrio takes, **10**. 201; (190) L. Scipio at, 311
theatre : (179) at temple of Apollo contracted for, **12**. 157; (174) stage built by cens., 277–9; (151) under construction, thrown down by P. Scipio Nasica, **14**. 21; (67) seats in, reserved for *equites*, 123
Thebê, plain of, in Mysia : (190) **10**. 347
Thebes, in Boeotia : (335) razed by Alexander the Great, **4**. 233; (197) joins Roman alliance, **9**. 279–83; Attalus ill in, 281, 335; (196) roused against Rome by murder of Brachyllas, 353–5; (192) Euthymidas of Chalcis in, **10**. 111–5; (191) Antiochus welcomed in, 171; (before 172) Perseus murders envoys of, to Rome who had opposed him in Boeotian council, **12**. 329, 411, 413; makes alliance with Perseus, **13**. 357, **12**. 325–7; (172) factions in; alliance with Perseus repudiated, 421–5, 431; P. Cornelius Lentulus sent to, 437; (171) surrenders to C. Lucretius Gallus, 491; calls P.

Licinius Crassus to Boeotia, 505; (169) SC. read in, **13**. 61; (146) destroyed for aiding Achaeans, **14**. 41
Thebes, in Phthiotis: (208–207) Philip takes, **8**. 29; (198–197) he holds, against Aetolians, **9**. 257, 261; (197) Flamininus fails to take, 287–9, 311; yielded by Philip, claimed by Aetolia and Rome, 309–11; (196) not granted to Thessalians, 369; (185) Philip destroys trade of, **11**. 293–5
Theium, in Athamania: (189) **11**. 5
Themistus, Gelo's son-in-law: (214) joins plot against Hieronymus; is killed, **6**. 253–61
Theodotus, of Egypt: (48) tutor of Ptolemy XIII, instigates Pompey's murder, **14**. 141
—, of Passaron: (167) opposes surrender to Rome, slain, **13**. 335–7
—, of Passaron: (167) urges surrender to Rome, **13**. 335–7
—, of Rhodes: (167) sent to seek Roman alliance, **13**. 331
—, of Syracuse: (215) conspires against Hieronymus, **6**. 191, 249; (214) tries to rouse Syracusans, 241–5
Theogenes: (168) garrison commander of Perseus, **13**. 197
Theondas: (168) chief magistrate of Samothrace, **13**. 261–3
Theos: *see* Ptolemy XII.
Theoxena, a Thessalian: (182) victim of Philip, **12**. 9–13
Theoxenus: (197) Achaean commander, **9**. 325
Thera, is. of Sporades: (197) **9**. 325
Thermopylae (Pylae): described, **10**. 203–5, **9**. 163; (208–207) Philip drives Aetolians from, **8**. 19, 27; (200) Philip's gateway to Greece, **9**. 69; (197) Flamininus moves through, 283; (196) Pylaic council meets at, 371; (191) Antiochus fortifies, **10**. 205, 275, **13**. 317; M' Acilius Glabrio defeats him at, **10**. 207–19, 249, 471, 475, **11**. 171, 285, **12**. 105; Glabrio at, **10**. 221, 225, 233; (146) Q. Caecilius Metellus defeats Achaeans at, **14**. 41
Thermus: *see* Minucius.
Thespiae, in Boeotia: (191) news of Thermopylae sent from, **10**. 223; (172) Boeotian exiles at, **12**. 423
Thesprotian Gulf, in Epirus: (326) **4**. 93
Thesprotians: (169) in Roman army, **13**. 75, 83
Thessalonica, in Macedon: (197) Philip in, **9**. 329; (181) **12**. 77; (179) 171; (185) Roman commissioners meet in, **11**. 301; (182) cruelty of Philip in, **12**. 9–13; (171) Perseus at, 503; (169) his orders to burn dockyards of, not obeyed, **13**. 107, 121; C. Marcius Figulus attacks, 121–3; ships from, reinforce Cassandrea, 129; (168) Macedonian and Illyrian envoys for Rhodes leave, 165; horses taken from Eumenes brought to, 183; Perseus strengthens, 195; plundering coast of, proposed, 205; surrenders to L. Aemilius Paulus, 237; (167) capital of 2d Macedonian republic, 349; a flourishing city, 351. *See* Ion.
Thessaly: north of Thermopylae, **10**. 203; (211) Philip seeks allies in, **7**. 97; (209) he passes through, 333; 343; (205) on side of Macedon in Roman treaty, **8**. 255; (200) Aetolians and Athamanes plunder, **9**. 121; (198) 191–3; Philip retains, 181–3; he withdraws into, plundering, 187–9, 255–7; operations of Flamininus in, 191–5, 201–5, 213–7, 311, **12**. 405; (197) **9**. 283–305, 329, 343; (196) declared free, 365, 369, 501, **10**. 49, **12**. 405; (194) Flamininus in, **9**. 547–9; (192) Romans seek aid of, against Aetolians and Antiochus, **10**. 89; (191) his council debates on, 173–81; he enters, 181–9; M. Baebius Tamphilus and Philip take towns in, 195–7, **11**. 287, 291–3, 305; (190) L. Scipio crosses, **10**. 305, 311, 339; (188) Cn. Manlius Volso enters, **11**. 143; (185) Philip's rights in, disputed before Senate, 287–91, and before Roman commissioners, 291–7; he replies, 297–9, 303; (184) envoys of, before Senate, 321–3; new commission sent to, 323; (182) sufferings of, at hands of Philip, **12**. 9–13; (174) Perseus enters, 257–9, 263, 267, 329–31, 397, 411, 417; (173) envoys from, report

on Macedon, 303; Rome settles civil discord in, 305–7; (172) envoys from, in Rome, 363; envoys sent to council of, 401–5; A. Atilius Serranus sent to, against Perseus, 437; (171) operations against Perseus in, 459–63, 503–5, **13**. 3, 257; (170) A. Hostilius Mancinus winters in, 63, 91–3; routes from, to Macedon closed in winter, 63–5; (169) operations of Q. Marcius Philippus in, 91–5, 109–21, 133; (168) danger from Gauls in, 177–9; envoys from, congratulate L. Aemilius Paulus, 243; (167) he crosses, 339; harbours of Macedon face, 351; (149) Andriscus turned back from, **14**. 31, 35; (148) he defeats P. Iuventius Thalna in, 35, 37; (88) Mithridates loses fleet off, 295; (86) he enters, 103; (48) Pompey retreats into, 139. Thessalian cavalry in Macedonian army: (334) **4**. 237; (197) **9**. 295, 313, 325; in Roman army: (195) 483, (192) **10**. 117, (171) **12**. 463, 473–9. *See* Eunomus, Theoxena; Demetrias.

Thessaly, Hollow: (199) **9**. 163

Thetideum, in Thessaly: (197) **9**. 291–3

Theudoria, in Athamania: (189) **11**. 5

Thoas, an Aetolian: (193) complains of injuries, **10**. 33; (192) brings Antiochus' envoy to Aetolia, 93–5; secures Aetolian invitation to Antiochus, 99, 425, **11**. 33; fails to take Chalcis, **10**. 101, 111–5; warns Antiochus against Hannibal, 123–7; in Aetolian council, 131; (191) in Antiochus' council, 177; censured by Antiochus, 201–3; sent to him as envoy; remains, 235–7; (190) surrender of, demanded, 425; (188) **11**. 131

Thrace: (336) part of, subject to Philip II, **13**. 273; (c. 275) Galatians cross, **11**. 51, 59; (211) wars of Philip V against, **7**. 97; (208–207) **8**. 17–9; (200) **9**. 49, 259, **10**. 209; (before 196) destroy Lysimachia, **9**. 381, 387; (197) a danger to Greece, 307–9; (196) L. Stertinius, Xvir for Macedonian peace, goes to, 371; Antiochus claims right to territory recovered in, 381–7, 565; (191) Hannibal urges him to invade, **10**. 177; his defeated troops cross, 253; (190) Philip escorts army of L. Scipio through, 311–3, **11**. 305–7, gaining cities for himself, 287; attack on Scipio's army in, foiled, 141–3; invalid soldiers left in, **10**. 387; (189) garrisons of Antiochus ordered from, 479; (188) Cn. Manlius Volso attacked while crossing, **11**. 135–43, 159, 171–3, 219; (185) Philip settles men of, in Macedon, 289, **12**. 7–9; possession of cities of, disputed by Philip and Eumenes, **11**. 301–9; (184) 325–7; (183) 367; Philip forced to leave, 389, **12**. 31, but crosses, against Odrysae, **11**. 389–91; (181) Perseus sent to receive hostages from, **12**. 77; (179) Perseus in, at Philip's death, 171; Bastarnae enter, 173–7; (175) aid Bastarnae against Dardanians, 245–7; (172) various tribes of, allied with Rome, 347, (171) or with Perseus, 377, 503, **13**. 399; Macedonians trained in wars with, **12**. 451; successes of Perseus in, **13**. 85; (168) Gauls plunder, 177; Perseus plans escape to, 263; (167) hostages returned to, 401; (149) Andriscus driven into, **14**. 35; (135) Roman wars in, 59; (114) 75; (112) 75–7; (109–108) 77; (104) 277; (92) 87; (90) Macedon raided from, 93; (89) 95; (87, 86) 103; (85–84) Roman wars in, 105; (77–76, 75) 115; (73) 117; (72) 121; (61–60) 127–9; (43) 153; (28) 165; (13–11) 167. *See* Autlesbis, Cotys.

Thracians as auxiliaries: (197) in Achaean army, **9**. 315–7, (183) **11**. 373; (189) in Aetolian army, **10**. 433; (200) in Macedonian army, **9**. 77, 115, (198) 231–3, 285, **10**. 209, (197) **9**. 295, 313, 325, (184) **11**. 325, (172) **12**. 327, (171) 449, 453, 467, 473, 477, 495, (168) **13**. 225–7, 235–9; (190) in Roman army, **10**. 405, (189) **11**. 71

Thrasippus: (171) commander under Perseus, **12**. 447

Thraso, guardian of Hieronymus: (215) pro-Roman; executed, **6**. 189–91

Thrausi, Thracians (188) **11**. 141

Thronium, in Locris : (208–207) Philip takes, **8**. 29; (198–197) he and cos. Flamininus confer at, **9**. 263; (197) Flamininus at, 283; (192) base for Aetolian attack on Chalcis, **10**. 113–5; (191) ships of Antiochus at, 219

Thucydides, the historian : cited, **14**. 229

thunder storm : (470) foils attack on Aequi, **1**. 425; (279) destroys Gauls at Delphi; (179) aids Thracians against Bastarnae, **12**. 175–7

Thuriae, in Calabria : (302) **4**. 363

Thurii (Sybaris) in Bruttium : (319) in Federation, **4**. 237; (287) assisted against Lucanians, 547; (212) hostages of, escape; are captured and executed, **6**. 365–7, 397–9; joins Hannibal, 397–401; (210) oarsmen from, **7**. 147; destroys Roman ships, 151; Hannibal transports people of Herdonea to, 207; (208) gives information to Hannibal, 317; (194) Latin colony near, **9**. 553; (104) fugitive slaves raid, **14**. 277

Thurrus, a Celtiberian : (179) supports Rome, **12**. 153–5

Thyatira, in Lydia : (190) C. Livius Salinator plunders, **10**. 315; Antiochus at, 353, 397–9; surrenders, 419

Thymbres riv., in Phrygia : (189) **11**. 63

Thyrreum, in Acarnania : (191) saved from Antiochus, **10**. 191–5; (189) Aetolian envoys brought to, **11**. 29; (169) Roman envoys at, **13**. 63

Thyrsis, of Stuberra : (181) agent of Philip in murder of Demetrius, **12**. 77

Tiber riv. : Hercules drives cattle across, **1**. 27; once called Albula; separates Romans and Etruscans; Silvius Tiberinus drowned in, 15–7; Romulus and Remus cast into, 19; (753–717) checks Fidenates, 53; crossed in attack on Veii, 55; (672–640) Veientes cross, 97; (640–616) first bridge over, 121; Ostia at mouth of, 123; (616–578) Sabines driven into, 135; drains built to, 137; (578–534) bath in, as purification, 159; (509) grain from Tarquins' field thrown into, forms island, 231–3; (508) a defence for city, 249; Horatius Cocles swims, 251–3; Lars Porsinna camps on, 253; Cloelia swims, 261–3; (492) grain brought down, 331; (411) **2**. 427; (477) crossed in Etruscan wars, **1**. 393; (476) 393–5; (437) **2**. 321; (426) 361, 363, 369; (440) many cast selves into, in famine, 299; (400) closed by severe winter, **3**. 47; (390) after Allia Romans cross, 129–31; messenger to Capitol floats down, 157; (356) C. Marcius Rutulus crosses, on rafts, 415; (349) Greeks raid mouth of, 441; (338) rebellious Latins exiled beyond, **4**. 59; (329) 81; (296) Etruscans hope to recover all north of, 417; (249) sacred chickens thrown into, **14**. 181; (217) Q. Fabius Maximus and Cn. Servilius Geminus meet on, **5**. 237; (211) P. Scipio (Afr.) sails from mouth of, **7**. 75; (210) Campanians sent beyond, 131; (204) P. Scipio Nasica receives Idaean Mother at mouth of, **8**. 261; (193) wharf built on, **10**. 29; (192) two bridges over, swept away, 61; fire on shore of, 121; (191) ashes of portentous cattle thrown into, 263; (190) Damocritus, escaped from prison, pursued along, 427; (186) matrons in Bacchic rites run to, **11**. 255; *Vviri uls cis Tiberim* maintain order, 259; (179) bridge over, and temple and portico near, contracted for, **12**. 157–9; (174) stairs from, built, 279; (168) ships moored in, beached on news of Pydna, **13**. 253–5; (167) L. Aemilius Paulus sails up, 369; (156) pontiff's house blown into, **14**. 251; (60) bridge over, fails, 303–5. Floods in : **1**. 19; (415) **2**. 417; (363) **3**. 365; (215) **6**. 205; (202) **8**. 513; (193) **10**. 23; (192) 61; (189) **11**. 95. *Also* ; **1**. 261, **2**. 91, **3**. 183, **5**. 89, **10**. 99, **14**. 259.

Tiber, Island in : *see* Island, in Tiber.

Tiberinus Silvius : 9th king of Alba Longa, drowned in Albula (Tiber), **1**. 17

Tiberius Nero : (15) overcomes Raeti, **14**. 165, (11–10) Dalmatians, and Pannonians; (9) brings home Drusus' body, 167

Tibur, in Latium : (449) M. Claudius goes into exile at, **2**. 199; (361) closes gates to Romans, **3**. 383;

INDEX

accepts Gallic alliance, 389; (360) defeated, 389–91; (359) 393; (356) 413; (355) 417; (354) surrenders; is treated with clemency, 419; (339) aids Pedani against Rome, **4**. 51; (338) defeated and deprived of land, 53–5, 59–61; (311) returns flute players, 279; (217) Q. Fabius Maximus holds levy at, **5**. 237–9; (201) Syphax dies at, **8**. 539; (171) M. (or C.) Matienus in exile at, **13**. 9–11

Tichius, above Thermopylae: (191) Aetolians hold, **10**. 207–9, 215

Ticinus riv., in Cis-alpine Gaul: (616–578) Gauls defeat Etruscans near, **3**. 119; Gauls settle on, 121; (218) Hannibal defeats P. Scipio on, **5**. 115–41, 43, 169

Tifata, Mt., above Capua: (343) Samnites attack Campanians from, **3**. 457; (215) Hannibal camps on, **6**. 127, 131, 137, 147, (214) 213, (211) **7**. 17–9; 199) land at foot of, sold, **9**. 169

Tifernum, in Samnium: (305) Samnites defeated near, **4**. 341; (297) 407–13

Tifernus, Mt., in Samnium: (295) Samnites defeated on, **4**. 475, 479

Tigranes I, of Armenia: (72) Mithridates VI flees to, **14**. 121; (69–68) L. Licinius Lucullus defeats, 123, 199; (66) wars of, with Parthia, and with his own son; surrenders to Pompey, 125

—, son of Tigranes I: (66) rebels against father, **14**. 125; (58) Pompey triumphs over, 129

Tigranocerta: (69) **14**. 199

Tigurini Galli: (107) **14**. 79

Timarum, in Thessaly: (198) **9**. 193

Timasicrates, of Rhodes: (190) meets L. Aemilius Regillus, **10**. 331

Timasitheus, Liparaean magistrate: (394) sends captured envoys to Delphi, **3**. 97–9

Timavus, Lake, in Venetia: (178) **12**. 185–7

Timocrates, of Pellenê: (195) rules Argos for Nabis, **9**. 493, 523–5

Timon, of Phthiotic Thebes: (197) fails to betray city, **9**. 287

— : (190) rules Lydia for Antiochus, **10**. 419

Timotheus: (171) agent of Perseus, **12**. 503

Tisaeus, Mt., in Thessaly: (208–207) **8**. 21

Tisippus: (167) accused of slaughter of Aetolians, **13**. 345

Tiso, of Patrae: (192) Achaean admiral, defeated by Nabis, **10**. 73–5

tithes, doubled: (191) from Sicily and Sardinia, **10**. 161; (190) 297; (189) 437–9; (171) **12**. 383; (176) from Sardinia, 235

Tithronion, in Doris: (208–207) **8**. 29

Titienses, equestrian century: (753–717) created; named for T. Tatius, **1**. 51; (618–578) doubled, 131–3

—, one of ancient tribes, **4**. 379

Titinius, C.: (193) tr. pl., opposes triumph of L. Cornelius Merula, **10**. 23

—, M.: (449) tr. pl., **2**. 181

—, M.: (302) mag. eq., **4**. 363

—, M.: (178) pr. urb., **12**. 199, 201

—, P.: (200) leg. in defeat of Gauls, **9**. 61

—, Sex.: (439) tr. pl., attacks execution of Sp. Maelius, **2**. 311

— Curvus, M., pr. 178: (193) tr. pl., opposes triumph of L. Cornelius Merula, **10**. 23; (178) pr. for Nearer Spain, **12**. 179, **13**. 9; (177) **12**. 211; (176) 231, 273–5; (171) tried for extortion, **13**. 9

— Pansa Saccus, L.: (400) tr. mil. c. p., **3**. 45; (396) ii, 63–5

Titium atrium: (184) built, **11**. 361

Titius, P.: (42) pr., expels colleague, dies, **14**. 315–7

—, Sex.: (99) tr. pl., offers land laws, **14**. 281

Titurius Sabinus, Q.: (54) leg. of Caesar, **14**. 133

toga candida: (432) use of, forbidden, **2**. 339; (184) not worn by office-holding candidate, **11**. 343

— *picta*: (300) worn by triumphators, **4**. 383–5; (203) **8**. 421–3; given to Masinissa, 421–3

— *praetexta*: (753) of Etruscan origin, **1**. 31; (473) worn by magistrates, 401, (300) **4**. 383, (209) by flamens, **7**. 237, (196) by IIIviri epulones and pontiffs, **9**. 389, (195) by officials, priests, and boys, 435

Toletum in Farther Spain: (193) M.

Fulvius Nobilior defeats tribes near, **10**. 21; (192) he captures, 65; (185) C. Calpurnius Piso and L. Quinctius Crispinus defeated near, **11**. 311
Tolostobogii, Galatians: (c. 275) occupy Aeolis and Ionia, **11**. 53–5; (189) occupy Olympus range, 65–7; Cn. Manlius Volso defeats, 51, 67–81, 91
Tolumnius, Lars, king of Veii: (438) aids revolt at Fidenae, **2**. 313; kills envoys, 313, 447; defeated; slain by A. Cornelius Cossus, 317–25, 363, 365
tormenta: (214) devised by Archimedes for defence of Syracuse, **6**. 285; (168) used by Perseus from river bank, **13** 209
Torona, Cape, in Chalcidicê: (200) **9**. 133
Toronê, in Chalcidicê: (169) C. Marcius Figulus attacks, **13**. 129; (167) in 2d Macedonian republic, 351
—, Gulf of: (169) **13**. 125
Torquatus: *see* Manlius, — Imperiosus.
Toutomotulus, king of Salluvii: (121) flees to Allobroges, **14**. 73
trade: *see commercium.*
Tralles, in Caria: (190) surrenders to L. Scipio, **10**. 421; he winters at, 425; (188) given to Eumenes, **11**. 133–5. Prodigy: (48) **14**. 307
Tralles (Tralli), Illyrian tribe: (209) in Philip's army, **7**. 341, (200) **9**. 103, (197) 285; (190) in Roman army, **10**. 405, (189) **11**. 71; (190) in Antiochus' army, **10**. 407–9
Trasumennus, Lake: (217) Hannibal defeats cos. C. Flaminius at, **5**. 213–27, 331, 379, **6**. 5, 61, 147, 155, 165, 203, **7**. 45, 159, 225, 257, 369, **8**. 443, 477; Hannibal frees allies captured at, **5**. 243, 389, **6**. 213, 273, 377; he arms men with spoils of, **5**. 351
treason: *see perduellio.*
treasury: *see aerarium.*
treaty: (672–640) ancient ritual for making, **1**. 83–5; (318) ratification by *populus* required, **4**. 241–3; (198) **9**. 223–5; (203) procedure for discussion of, in Senate, **8**. 445–9. *See* alliance, *sponsio.*
Trebellius, M.: (169) agent of L. Coelius, **13**. 75
—, Q.: (210) centurion, awarded mural crown, **7**. 183–5
Trebia, in Campania: (216) **6**. 47
Trebia riv., in Cis-alpine Gaul: (218) Hannibal and P. Scipio camp near, **5**. 141–5, 153; Gauls occupy land between Po and, 153; victory of Hannibal at, 155–69, 43–5, 175, **6**. 61, 147, 155, **7**. 159, 369; Hannibal frees allies captured at, **5**. 389; he arms men with spoils of, 351
Trebium, in Latium: (488) **1**. 345
Trebius: *see* Statius.
Trebonian law: (401) violated, **3**. 37–9, 43. *See* L. Trebonius Asper.
Trebonius, C., cos. 45: (55) tr. pl., secures law assigning provinces to Pompey and Crassus, **14**. 131; (49) leg. of Caesar, besieges Massilia, 137; (46) propr. for Spain, 211; (44) conspires against Caesar, 147; (43) killed in Asia, 151
—, Cn.: (401) tr. pl., defends Trebonian law, **3**. 37–9
—, M.: (383) tr. mil. c. p., **3**. 269
—, T.: (293) leg. of L. Papirius Cursor against Samnites, **4**. 515, 519
— Asper, L.: (448) secures law that tribb. pl. be elected, not co-opted, **2**. 221. *See* Trebonian law.
Trebula, in Campania: (303) receives citizenship, **4**. 361; (215) Q. Fabius Maximus recovers, from Hannibal, **6**. 135. Prodigy: (106) **14**. 273
— Mutusca, in Samnium. Prodigies: (105, 104) **14**. 275
Tremellius (Tremelius), C.: (173) Xvir agr. adsig., **12**. 303
—, Cn., pr. 159: (168) tr. pl., not made senator, vetoes extended term for censs., **13**. 295; (159) pr., opposes pont. max., fined, **14**. 13
— Flaccus, Cn., pr. 202: (205) envoy to bring Idaean Mother, **8**. 247–9; (203) aed. pl., 461; (202) pr. for Sicily, 461, 463, 521.
— Scrofa, L.: (142) qu., routs Macedonian pretender, **14**. 47
Tremulus: *see* Marcius.
Treveri (Gauls): (54) attack camp of leg. Q. Tullius Cicero; procos. Caesar defeats, **14**. 133
triarii, veteran soldiers forming re-

INDEX

serve: (437) **2.** 321; (350) **3.** 435; (340) **4.** 31–3
Triarius: *see* Valerius.
tribe (*tribus*, a political division): three ancient, **4.** 379; (578–534) four urban, formed, **1.** 153–5, called Esquilina, Palatina, Suburana, Collina, **4.** 561; (495) increased to twenty-one, **1.** 287; (418) levy from ten, **2.** 405; (311) *humiles*, distributed in all, (304) then returned to urban, **4.** 353; (220) freedmen assigned to urban, 561, (168) to one tribe, **13.** 293; (204) *comit. cent.* based on tribes, **8.** 355; (179) composition of, changed, **12.** 159, **1.** 153. Formation of new tribes: (387) Stellatina, Tromentina, Sabatina, Arniensis, **3.** 213; (358) Pomptina, Publilia, 407; (332) Maecia, Scaptia, **4.** 69; (318) Ufentina, Falerna, 243; (299) Aniensis, Terentina, 393; (241) Velina, Quirina, 559. *See* the tribes named and also: Aemilia, Claudia, Cornelia, Crustumina, Galeria, Papiria, Pollia, Pupinia, Voturia.
tribuni militum (*ad legiones*): (449) irregularly elected by plebeians, **2.** 169–71; (362) elected for first time, **3.** 373; (342) no, may become centurion in same legion, 511; (311) sixteen, to be elected for four legions, **4.** 277; (207) **7.** 357; (171) appointed by coss. and pr. from Senate, **12.** 383, 395; appoint first centurion, 395; (169) of four added legions, elected, **13.** 43; (168) of eight legions, half elected, half appointed, from ex-magistrates, 155–7
tribuni militum consulari potestate: (445) three, patrician or plebeian, may replace coss., **2.** 277–9; (438) increased to six, 311–3, (403) to eight, **3.** 3; only patricians elected, 7; (418) have military command on successive days, **2.** 407; (402) take office Oct. 1st instead of Dec. 13th, **3.** 31–3, 41; (400) first plebeian elected, 45, 325; (391) take office July 1st, 111; (381) may be excused from serving on score of health, 273; (375) abolition of, proposed by tribb. pl. L. Sextius and C. Licinius Stolo, 317; (367) abolished, 351. Elected for years as follows: (444) **2.** 279; (438) 311–3; (434 ?) 331; (433) 335; (432) 337; (426) 357; (425) 371; (424) 373; (422) 391; (420) 399; (419) 403; (418) 405; (417, 416) 411; (415) 417; (414) 417–9; (408) 439; (407) 445; (406) 447; (405) 455; (404) 455–6; (403) **3.** 3; (402) 27–9; (401) 35; (400) 45; (399) 47; (398) 51–3; (397) 57; (396) 63; (395) 83; (394) 89; (391) 111; (390) 127; (389) 197; (388) 209; (387) 211–3; (386) 213; (385) 231; (384) 255; (383) 269; (382) 271; (381) 273; (380) 289; (379) 299; (378) 301–3; (377) 305; (370) 319; (369) 321; (368) 327; (367) 347
tribuni plebis: (493) two elected and made inviolate, **1.** 325–7, **2.** 269, **4.** 291; (491) secure conviction of Cn. Marcius Coriolanus, **1.** 333–5; (484) propose land law, 357, *et saepe*; (481) obstruct levy, 361, *et saepe*; one may be used by Senate to check others, 361–5, **2.** 413–5, *et saepe*; (476) accuse former magistrates, **1.** 395–7, *et saepe*; (473) sacrosanctity fails to protect, 403; (472–471) to be elected in *comitia tributa*; number increased to five, 407–15; (461–457) re-elected, **2.** 51, 83–5, 101; (460) powerless outside city, 71; SC. forbids re-election of, 73; (457), increased to ten, and re-election forbidden, 101–3; (455) re-elected, 103; (449) power of, suspended under Xviri, 123, 149, 161; Senate submits to Xviri through hatred of, 137; restoration of, demanded, 173–5; pont. max. holds election of, on Aventine, 179–81; sacrosanctity of, restored, 183–5; one, prevents re-election of nine, 215–9; five elected, co-opt others, including patricians, 219; (448) co-option of, forbidden, 221, 311; (447) fail to protect plebeians, 221–3; (445) first use veto against Senate, 277; (431) command coss. to obey Senate, 341–3; (421) veto SC. for election of coss, 397; (414) 423; prevent Senatorial investigation of mutiny, 423; (410) nine, aid coss. against

tenth, 429–31; (408) refuse to aid Senate against tr. mil. c. p., 441, (402) give such aid, **3**. 33; (401) fill number by co-option, 35–9; (393) former, condemned for having supported Senate, 103–5; (376–367) C. Licinius Stolo and L. Sextius re-elected, 319, 321, 327, 347; (375–371) some, oppose Licinian–Sextian laws, 317; (358) with authority of Senate present law to *populus*, 409, *et saepe*; (310) carry orders of Senate to cos., **4**. 305; (249) vainly forbid departure of cos., **14**. 181; (216) one, presides over Senate, **5**. 407; (210) **7**. 221; (216) former, made Senators, **6**. 79; (212) impose fine on *publicani*, 351; lay capital charge against those disturbing their action, 353–5; (205) may protect Senator refusing to give *sententia*, **8**. 189–91; (204) two, with pr. investigate Locrian affair, 287–9; (203) son of former curule magistrate ineligible for, during father's life, 439; (187) Africanus uses violence against, **11**. 197–9; proper relations of coss. and, 229–31; (183) term of, begins Dec. 10th, 385; (181) refer 'books of Numa' to Senate, **12**. 93; (172) with authority of Senate secure plebiscite for investigation of consular campaign, 351; (170) conduct trial before *tributa*, **13**. 31–3, (169) before *centuriata*, 57–9; (167) normally permit discussion before veto, 313–5; (151) imprison coss. for strict levy, **14**. 19; (138) 53, 55; (149) Atinian law concerning, 35; (133) one, secures recall of another, 63; (131–130) law permitting re-election of, rejected, 67; (81–80) power of, weakened by Sulla, 111, (71) restored, 121; (75) made eligible for higher office, 197

tribus: *see* tribe.

tribute: (167) Macedonian, equal half of regal tax, **13**. 347, 349. *See* tithe.

tributum (war tax): (578–534) based on census, **1**. 155; (508) burden of, assumed by rich, 247; (495) plebeians oppressed by, 291; (401) **3**. 35–7; (396) 71; (406) required for new payment to soldiers; tribb. pl. promise to protect any refusing to pay, **2**. 453; (401) **3**. 43; (400) they permit, 47; (394) not required, 97; (378) 303; (347) 449; (390) required to pay Gallic ransom, 243–5, (377) to build wall of hewn stone, 305; (293) to pay soldiers, booty having been placed in *aerarium*, **4**. 537; (215) doubled, **6**. 105; income from, diminished by military disasters, 165; (210) people exhausted by, **7**. 135, **8**. 267. *See stipendium*.

Tricastini, in Transalpine Gaul: (616–578) territory of, invaded by Gauls, **3**. 119, (218) crossed by Hannibal, **5**. 91

Tricca, in Thessaly: (198) Philip moves to, **9**. 189; (191) recovered from Athamanes, **10**. 197; (185) held by Philip, claimed by Thessaly, **11**. 291–3

Tricipitinus: *see* Lucretius, — Flavus.

Tricorii, Transalpine Gauls: (218) **5**. 91

Tricostus: *see* Verginius.

trientabulum: (200) land allotted in discharge of public debt, **9**. 43

Trifanum, in Latium: (340) **4**. 47

Trigemina porta, in Rome: (439) statue outside, **2**. 311; (193) portico built outside, **10**. 29; (192) 123; (179) **12**. 159; (174) warehouse outside and portico inside, paved, 279

Triphylia, in Elis: (208–207) Philip gives, to Achaeans, **8**. 33; (199) **9**. 163–5; (198) he comes to 'camp of Pyrrhus' in, 189; (196) restored to Achaeans, 369

Tripolis, in Laconia: (192) **10**. 77

—, in Perrhaebia: (191) Aetolians waste, **10**. 187; (171) surrenders to Perseus, **12**. 457; recovered, 505

— Scaea, in Thessaly: (171) **12**. 463

trireme: *see* naval antiquities.

triumph: (753–717) celebrated by Romulus, **1**. 41; (480) refused by M. Fabius Vibulanus because of brother's death, **1**. 379; (449) denied by Senate, granted by people, **2**. 213–5; (356) **3**. 415; (294) **4**. 503; (223) **5**. 189; (437) rude songs sung at, **2**. 321; (410) 431; (343) **3**. 495; (421) ovation in lieu of, **2**. 395; (211) **7**. 81; (200) **9**. 59; (195) 445; (185) **11**. 309; (356)

INDEX

people grant, to plebeian dict., **3**. 415; (339) cos. leaves army in field to seek a, **4**. 51; (326) first granted to a procos., 105; (295) gifts to soldiers after, 477; (294) conditions for granting, 501–3; (211) **7**. 79–81; (206) **8**. 151; (200) **9**. 59–61; 139–45; (195) 445; (187) **11**. 153, 159–63, 173–5; (185) 309; (294) cos. triumphs against will of Senate and seven tribb. pl., **4**. 503; (293) vast treasure carried in, and deposited in *aerarium*, 537; treasure distributed, 539; (211) Senate meets in temple of Bellona to consider, **7**. 79 (*see* Bellona); (197) of two coss. must be considered separately, **9**. 337–9; gifts to soldiers after, 341, *et saepe*; (190) triumph without a returned army, **10**. 427; (187) form of decree for, **11**. 169; (180) granted when no war had been waged, **12**. 121; (167) *imperium* in city given for day of, **13**. 369; (80) Pompey triumphs while *eques*, **14**. 113. Descriptions of: (458) **2**. 99; (396) **3**. 81; (300) **4**. 385; (191) **10**. 271–3; (189) 475–7; (187) **11**. 233; 237–9; (167) **13**. 385–93; 401–3. Dress of triumphator: (203) **8**. 421–3

triumph, naval: (260) granted, **4**. 555; (189) **10**. 473; (167) **13**. 369, 397

triumphs on Alban mt.: (211) **7**. 81; (197) **9**. 339, 341; (172) **12**. 351; (167) **13**. 381

Triumvirate, First: (62 formed, **14**. 127

— Second: (43) formed, **14**. 151, 153, 315; Cicero leaves Rome before arrival of, 217; proscriptions of, 315; (36) M. Lepidus loses place on, 159–61, 163; (32) end of, 163

triumviri (*tresviri*): (212) to aid in levy, **6**. 357; to recover *sacra*; to rebuild temples, 365

— *agris dividendis*: (467) **2**. 5; (133) **14**. 63; (129) 67

— *capitales*: (c. 290) first created, **4**. 547; (213) fail to control superstition, **6**. 343; (186) directed to maintain order, **11**. 259, 269

— *coloniae deducendae*: (442) **2**. 295–7; (383) **3**. 269; (334) **4**. 67; (313) 273; (218) **5**. 69–71; (200)**9**. 145; (199) 159; (197) 243; (194) 533–5; 553; (193) **10**. 25; (192) 119; (190) 429; (189) 469; (186) **11**. 285; (183) 395; (181) **12**. 103; (180) 135–7; (177) 225; (169) **13**. 61; (122) **14**. 71

triumviri epulones: (196) first elected, **9**. 389; (180) a *praetextatus* co-opted to, **12**. 133

— *mensarii*: (216) to meet financial emergency, **6**. 73; (214) offer pay for slaves freed as soldiers, 233; (210) receive voluntary offerings, **7**. 137

Trocmi, Galatians: (c. 275) receive coast of Hellespont, **11**. 53–5; (189) join other Galatians, 65–7; Cn. Manlius Volso defeats, 89–93

Trogili, harbour of Syracuse: (212) **6**. 431

Troilum, in Etruria: (293) **4**. 539

Tromentina tribus: (387) formed, **3**. 213

Troy: sacrifice of Iphigenia before voyage to, **13**. 341; Greeks capture, **1**. 9, **3**. 15; survivors of, led to Adriatic by Antenor, **1**. 9, to Laurentium by Aeneas, 9–13, 79, **6**. 385; (85) statue of Athena unhurt in sack of, **14**. 187. *See* Ilium.

—: name given to colonies of Antenor, and of Aeneas, **1**. 9

Tubero: *see* Aelius.

Tubertus: *see* Postumius.

Tubulus: *see* Hostilius.

Tuccia, a Vestal: (c. 235) convicted, **4**. 559

Tuccius, M., pr. 190: (192) aed. cur., prosecutes usurers; makes dedications, **10**. 123; (190) pr. for Apulia and Bruttium, 285, 295–7; (189) 439; (188) **11**. 117; (186) IIIvir col. deduc., 285

Tuditanus: *see* Sempronius.

Tullia, daughter of Servius Tullius: (578) wife of Tarquin the Proud, **1**. 147; (534) murdered by sister, 161–3

—, daughter of Servius Tullius: (578) marries Arruns Tarquinius, **1**. 147; (534) murders sister and Arruns, marries Tarquin the Proud, 161–3; plots overthrow of Servius, 163–5, 169–71, 207; (510) flees, 209

Tullianum: (204) **8**. 295–7

Tullius: *see* Attius, Servius.
Tullius, Sex: (358) first centurion, demands battle with Gauls, **3**. 397–405; (357) in defeat of Privernates, 411
— Cicero, M.: (63) cos., **14**. 201, 301; extirpates Catilinarian conspiracy, 127; (58) sets up statue at temple of Minerva, 311; exiled, 129; (57) recalled, 129; (48) in Pompey's camp or in Sicily on day of Pharsalia, 139, 209; receives letter from Caesar, 209; (46) wrote eulogy of M. Porcius Cato, 215; (44) statue set up by, blown over, 311; (43) opposes M. Antony, 219; death of, 153, 217–21; character of, 219–21, 231. Cited: (99) 87
— Cicero, Q.: (54) leg. of Caesar, defends camp, **14**. 133
— Longus, M': (500) cos., **1**. 279
Tullus: *see* Cloelius, Hostilius.
tumultuariae legiones: (181) of citizens, **12**. 81
tumultuarii milites: (193) raised in Spain, **10**. 7, (192) in Sicily, 67
tumultus: (193) Senate declares state of, **9**. 561
tunica palmata: (300) worn by *triumphatores*, **4**. 383; (203) given to Masinissa, **8**. 421–3
Turda, in Spain: (195) **9**. 395
Turdetani (Turduli), in Nearer Spain: (219) quarrel of, with Saguntum a cause of Punic War, **5**. 17, 37, **6**. 313, **8**. 157; (214) Rome subdues, **6**. 313; (209) P. Scipio (Afr.) defeats, **8**. 157
— (Tartesii, Turduli), in Farther Spain: (216) Hasdrubal defeats, **6**. 89–93; (206) desert Hasdrubal, **8**. 67; (195) M. Porcius Cato and P. Manlius subdue, **9**. 459–67
Turdus: *see* Papirius.
Turnus, king of Rutulians: **1**. 11–3
— Herdonius: *see* Herdonius, Turnus.
turres: (403) used in siege of Veii, **3**. 17, (335) Cales, **4**. 65, (219) Saguntum, **5**. 33, (215) Cumae, **6**. 129, (198) Atrax, **9**. 203, (191) Heraclea, **10**. 227
Turrinus: *see* Mamilius.
Tuscan (Tyrrhenian, Lower) sea: name indicates extent of Etruscan power, **3**. 115; 411) grain from shore of, **2**. 427; (349) Gauls move to, **3**. 447; (319) allies hold coast of, **4**. 237; (216) Hannibal moves to, **6**. 3; (215) Macedonian envoys brought to, 131; (211) P. Scipio (Afr.) crosses, **7**. 75; (180) Ligurians transported along, **12**. 127
Tuscans: *see* Etruria.
Tuscivicanus: *see* Terentius.
Tusculan estate, of Cicero: (43) **14**. 217
Tusculum, in Latium: (506) Tarquin the Proud retires to; (505) danger from, **1**. 269; (499) Latins defeated near, 279; (463) Aequi and Volsci move on, **2**. 25, 29; (460) forces of, aid against Ap. Herdonius, 61–7, 79, 103; (459) citadel of, captured by Aequi, recovered by Roman aid, 79–81; (458) Aequi raid, 87; (455) 103; (449) 125, 135; Romans flee to, 141; (443) defeat Volsci, 293; (431) A. Postumius Tubertus camps near, 345; (419) directed to watch Aequi and Labicani, 403, (418) who plunder them, 405; Romans flee to, 407–9; (394) **3**. 101; (383) Praenestini invade, 271; (381) accused of aiding Volsci; attacked by Rome, 283–5, 291; submit; become citizens, 285–9, 309; (377) saved from Latins by Rome, 309–11; (370) 319–21; (360) Gauls plunder, 389; (353) M. Valerius Publicola camps near, 423; (342) T. Quinctius Poenus lives near, 501; (340) cavalry of, in Latin army, **4**. 23; (338) most of, retain citizenship, 59; (323) acquitted for aid to Latins, 145; (211) Hannibal not admitted, **7**. 35. Prodigies: (210) **7**. 217; (190) **10**. 299, **14**. 239; (176) **12**. 233. *See* L. Mamilius, Octavius Mamilius.
Tuscus: *see* Aquilius.
Tuscus vicus: (508) Etruscans settle on, **1**. 267; (207) procession for Juno Regina leaves Forum by, **7**. 361. Prodigy: (196) **9**. 349
Tutia riv., near Rome: (211) **7**. 41
Twelve Cities of Etruria: elect king, **1**. 33; (434) hold council, **2**. 331; (403) elect priest, **3**. 5; (391) two leagues, 117; (352) appoint dict., 429
Twelve Tables of the Law: (449) en-

graved on bronze, **2**. 195; (445) forbid intermarriage of orders, 269–71, 275; (389) published, **3**. 197; (356) cited, 415; (195) **9**. 431–3
Tycha, in Syracuse: (214) Theodotus and Sosis cross, **6**. 243; (212) M. Marcellus plunders, 439
Tymphaeis, in Macedon: (167) **13**. 353
Tyndareus, in Sicily: (191) **10**. 161
Tynes (Tunis) in Africa: (203) P. Scipio (Afr.) occupies, **8**. 395, 423; (202) he meets Punic envoys at, 503
Tyre, in Phoenicia: (195) Hannibal flees to, **9**. 405–7; (193) Carthaginians frequent, 573; (192) men of, in Antiochus' navy, **10**. 139. *See* Aristo.
Tyresius, a Spaniard: (143) Q. Occius conquers, **14**. 47
Tyrrhenian sea: *see* Tuscan sea.
Tyscon, in Phrygia: (189) **11**. 61

Ufentina tribus: (318) added, **4**. 243
Ulysses: (534–510) reputed ancestor of Mamilius of Tusculum, **1**. 173
ultimate decree: *see Senatus consultum ultimum.*
Umbria: (before 390) Gauls enter, **3**. 121; (319) in Federation, **4**. 237; (310) promise aid against Etruscans, 303; resent Ciminian expedition, 305, 309; (308) join Etruscans; Q. Fabius Maximus defeats, 327–31; (303) L. Genucius Aventinensis and Ser. Cornelius Lentulus attack brigands in, 361; (299) M. Fulvius Paetus takes Nequinium in, 391–3; Narnia colonized against, 393; (296) joins Samnites and Etruscans, 421, 437–41; (295) defeated by L. Scipio near Clusium, 459–61, by P. Decius Mus and Q. Fabius Maximus at Sentinum, 461–75, 479; (269) submits, 553; (217) Hannibal victor in, **5**. 227–9; (207) Hasdrubal plans to meet him in, **7**. 383; news of Metaurus reaches Rome from, 407; possible aid for Hasdrubal in, **8**. 43; (205) promises aid to P. Scipio (Afr.), 195; (201) force against Boi crosses, **9**. 9; (90) A. Plotius defeats, **14**. 93. Prodigy: (186) **11**. 283, **14**. 241. *See* C. Atrius.
Unlucky way, in Rome: (479) **1**. 387

Upper sea: *see* Adriatic sea.
Urbicna, in Spain: (182) **12**. 55
Urbinum, in Umbria: (95) **14**. 285
Urbius clivus, in Rome: (534) **1**. 171
Uria, in Calabria: (171) **12**. 439
Uscana, in Illyricum: (170) resists Rome, **13**. 35–7; (169) surrenders to Perseus, 65–9, 75; L. Coelius attacks, 75
usury: (357) rate of, fixed, **3**. 409, 421; (347) rate reduced, 449; (342) abolition of, proposed, 511–3; (344) usurers prosecuted by aedd., 455; (296) **4**. 445; (192) **10**. 123; (198) usurers expelled from Sardinia, **9**. 237; (193) laws against, extended to Latins, **10**. 19; (89) usurers kill pr. urb., **14**. 93
Utens riv., in Cisapline Gaul: (391) **3**. 121
Utica: (212) T. Otacilius Crassus takes Punic supplies at, **6**. 463; (210) lands of, plundered by M. Valerius Messala, **7**. 219, (207) by M. Valerius Laevinus, **8**. 15; (204) P. Scipio (Afr.) attacks, 319, 339, 345–7; (203) 375, 379, 387; he is diverted from, 389; Punic fleet gains advantage before, 393–401, 455; (202) P. Cornelius Lentulus brings fleet to, 501; Scipio at, after Zama, 501–3; (149) surrenders, **14**. 23; offers quarters for troops, 29; (47) M. Porcius Cato protects, 141; (46) he kills self at, 143
Uzentini, in Calabria: (216) **5**. 409

Vaccaei, Spaniards: (220) Hannibal conquers, **5**. 13–7; (193) defeated by M. Fulvius Nobilior, **10**. 21, (179) by L. Postumius Albinus, **12**. 149, 157, (178) 287, (151) by L. Licinius Lucullus, **14**. 19; (136) defeat M. Aemilius Lepidus, 57, 257; (134) P. Scipio Aemilianus raids, 61; (76) Sertorius seeks recruits from, 195
Vaccus, Meadows of, on Palatine: (330) **4**. 75
Vacuna, temple of, in Sabine country: (214) **6**. 207
vades: *see* surety.
Valentia, in Spain: (138) **14**. 53
Valerii: (510) leaders in expelling kings, **2**. 129, **4**. 229; (509, 449, 300)

introduce laws strengthening appeal, **4**. 389
Valerio–Horatian laws: (449) secure plebeian rights, **2**. 181–7
Valerius, M': (501) possibly first dict., **1**. 277; (?) **2**. 24[4]
—, M.: (672–640) fetial, **1**. 85
—, M.: (463) augur, **2**. 25
—, M.: (340) pont., dictates *devotio* to P. Decius Mus, **4**. 37
— M.: (167) reports portent, **13**. 297
—, Vol.: father of P. and M. Valerius Publicola, **1**. 203, 276, and of M' Valerius Maximus, 315
— Antias, the historian, cited: (464) **2**. 19; (434) 331; (212) **6**. 493; (210) **7**. 187; (205) **8**. 199; (204) 343; (203) 375; 439; (202) 471–3; (199) **9**. 167; (197) 303; (196) 361; 375; (195) 445; 457; (193) **10**. 7; (191) 219; 263; 265–7; (189) 433; 479; **11**. 81; (187) 175; 193; (186) 283; (184) 353; 357–9; (183) 383–5; 399; (181) **12**. 91; (174) 277; (172) 321; (169) **13**. 133; (167) 403; (105) **14**. 79. His untrustworthiness, **8**. 439, **9**. 303, **10**. 219, 267, **11**. 81, 353, **13**. 133, 403
— —, L.: (215) transports captured envoys to Rome, **6**. 119
— Corvus: *see* Valerius Maximus Corvus.
— Falto, M., pr. 201: (205) envoy to secure Idaean Mother, **8**. 247–9, 259; (203) aed. cur., 459; (201) pr. for Bruttium, 517, 521, and Campania; (200) propr. for Sardinia, **9**. 27
— Flaccus, C.: (331) cos., **4**. 71
— —, C., pr. 183: (209) compelled to be flamen Dialis **7**. 235–7; gains admission to Senate, 237; (199) aed. cur., brother taking oath for him, **9**. 147–9; 173; (184) seeks vacant praetorship, **11**. 343–7; (183) pr. pereg. while flamen, 363, 391
— —, C.: (93) cos., **14**. 287
— —, L.: (331) mag. eq. clavi fig. c., **4**. 73; (321) mag. eq. com. c., 189
— —, L., cos. 195, cens. 184: (212) tr. mil., rebukes men, **6**. 393; (209) ill-disposed to brother C., **7**. 235; (201) aed. cur., **9**. 13–5; (200) leg. in defeat of Gauls, 61–3; takes oath for brother, flamen Dialis and aed. cur., 147–9; (199) pr. for Sicily, 147, 155; (196–180) pont., 389–91, **12**. 133; (195) cos. with Italy as prov., **9**. 391–3; defeats Boi; rebuilds cities, 471, 527; holds elections, 527; *ver sacrum* improperly performed, 395, 531; (194) defeats Gauls, 535; (191) leg. at Thermopylae, **10**. 207–9, 215, and at Heraclea, 225; envoy to Aetolians, 237, 241; (190) IIIvir col. deduc., 429, 469; (189) candidate for cens., 469–71; (184) cens., **11**. 347–61, 383–5; builds buildings, 361; princeps senatus, 383; (180) dies, **12**. 133
Valerius Flaccus, L.: (152) cos., **14**. 251
— —, L.: (100) cos., **14**. 279; (86) princeps senatus; sends envoys to procos. Sulla, 105
— — L.: (86) cos. suf., sent to replace Sulla; killed, **14**. 103; (68) soldiers of, desert L. Licinius Lucullus, 123
— — P., cos. 227; (219) envoy to Hannibal and Carthage, **5**. 19, 25, 31, 45; (216) leg. at Nola, **6**. 55; (215) pref. classis, captures Philip's envoys, 117–9; at Tarentum, 133; (214) leg., commands at Brundisium, 303; (211) urges defence of Rome, **7**. 31
— Laevinus, C., cos. suf., 176: (189) agent in Aetolian peace, **11**. 29, 33; (179) pr. for Sardinia, **12**. 139; (177) pr. ii, for Gaul, 207; (176) cos. suf., defeats Ligurians, 237–43; (174) envoy to Aetolians, 273, (173) to Macedon and Egypt, 309; (172) brings home charges against Perseus, 339–43; (169) candidate for cens. **13**. 49
— —, M., cos. 220, 210: (215) pr. peregr., **6**. 81, 105; sent to Apulia, 109, 113; tricked by Philip's envoys, 115, 119; recovers towns of Hirpini, 131; commands fleet against Macedon, 133, 163; (214) 207, 209, 239, 303; recovers Oricum from Philip, 303–7; (213) propr. for Greece and Macedon, 317, **9**. 21; (212) **6**. 349; (211) **7**. 5, 85, 99–101; elected cos. ii; his reputation, 87;

INDEX

negotiates Aetolian treaty, 91–5, **11**. 29; (210) cos. ii; accompanied to Rome by Capuans, **7**. 105–7; reports on Macedon, 109; receives Italy as prov., then Sicily, 109–15; veterans of, discharged, 111; restores M. Livius Salinator to city, 347; lays before Senate Syracusan complaints against Marcellus, 117, 123–5; urges contributions for fleet, 135–9, **8**. 267, **9**. 41; settles Syracusan affairs; takes Agrigentum and other towns, **7**. 151–7; recalled for elections, 213–5; reports to Senate, 217–21; fails to provide for elections, 221–3; (209) procos. for Sicily and fleet, 231–3, 239–41, 255, 269; (208) 303; raids African coast, 329–31; as patrician ineligible as colleague of C. Claudius Nero, 349; (207) procos. for Sicily and fleet, **8**. 15, 45; (205) leads legions to Arretium, 199; envoy to secure stone of Idaean Mother, 247–9; (204) suggests return of private contributions, 267; (203) urges rejection of Punic envoys, 449; (201) propr., takes fleet to Macedon, **9**. 11; (200) sends dispatches to Rome, 17; funeral games for, with gladiators, 147

Valerius Laevinus, M., pr. 182 : (200) gives funeral games for father, M., **9**. 147; (182) pr. pereg., **11**. 397, **12**. 3; (181) leg. in Liguria, 83 ; (171) leg. at Callinicus, 473

— —, P. : (280) cos.; Pyrrhus defeats, **4**. 549

— —, P. : (200) gives funeral games for father, M., **9**. 147

— Maximus, M' : (501) dict. **1**. 277 (?); (494) dict. in struggle over debts, **1**. 315; triumphs over Sabines, 317–9; resigns when Senate refuses aid to debtors, 321

— — Corvinus, M., cos. 312, 289 : (312) cos., appoints IIIviri col. deduc., **4**. 273; ends Samnite war, 275; (307) cens., 341; (297) tr. mil. against Samnites, 409–11

— — Corvus M., cos. 348, 346, 343, 335, 300, 299 : (349) tr. mil., by aid of raven defeats Gaul, **3**. 443–7 **6**. 199, **11**. 57; (348) cos. at age 23, **3**. 447; (346) ii, defeats Volsci, 449–51; (343) cos. iii, 455; defeats Samnites in Campania, triumphs, 469–77, **4**. 479, **3**. 491–5; (342) dict., ends mutiny, 503–13; (340) interrex, **4**. 11; (335) cos. iv, defeats Sidicini, 65–7; (332) interrex, 69; (325) leg. of L. Papirius Cursor, 139; (321) interrex, 139; (310) leg. of Cursor, 321, 325; (308) pr. iv, 325; (302) dict., defeats Marsi and Etruscans, triumphs, 369–77; (300) cos. v, 377; proposes stronger law of appeal, 389–91; defeats Aequi, 391; (299) cos. vi suf., against Etruscans, 397; character of, **3**. 473; worthy to meet Alexander **4**. 227–9

Valerius Maximus Lactuca, M., cos. 456 : (458) qu., **2**. 85; (456) cos., 103

— — Lactucinus, M. : (398) tr. mil. c. p., **3**. 51; (395) ii, 83

— — Messala, M' : (252) cens., **4**. 557

— Messala (Messalla), M., cos. 226 : (210) praef. classis, plunders African coast, **7**. 217–9, 229; proposed as dict. com. c., 221; (209) praef. classis, 233–5

— —, M., cos. 188 : (193) pr. pereg., **9**. 555–7; (190) candidate for cos., **10**. 431; (188) cos., **11**. 115, **14**. 239, with Pisa and Liguria as prov., **11**. 117, 143, 147; holds elections, 143; (174) envoy to Macedon, **12**. 257; (172) Xvir sac., 373

— — Corvinus, M., cos. suf., 31 : (43) secures brother's pardon, **14**. 153

— Poplicola : *see* — Publicola.

— Potitus, C. : (370) tr. mil. c. p., **3**. 319

— —, C. : (331) cos., **4**. 71

— —, L., cos. 483, 470 : (485) qu., prosecutes Sp. Cassius, **1**. 355; (483) cos., 359; (470) ii, opposes land law; wars against Aequi, 423–5; (464) praef. urb., **2**. 15

— —, L., cos. 449 : (449) opposes Xviri, **2**. 129, 135–7; after death of Verginia forces Ap. Claudius to withdraw, 161; envoy to plebeians; demands resignation of Xviri, 167, 171–3; negotiates settlement, 175–9; cos., secures plebeian rights, 181–7, 201, 217; defeats Aequi on Mt. Algidus, 193, 201–7, 243; triumph refused by Senate, granted by

people, 213–5, 243, **4**. 503; opposes own re-election, **2**. 217; (445) refrains from debate on plebeian coss., 277
Valerius Potitus, L., cos. 393, 392: (414) tr. mil. c. p., **2**. 417; (406) ii, 447–9; with colleagues defeats Volsci, 449–51; (403) iii, **3**. 3; (401) iv, 35, 45; (398) v, plunders Falerii, 51–3; (397) interrex, 61; (394) envoy to Delphi, 97; (392) cos., defeats Aequi, triumphs, 109; abdicates because of plague; interrex, 111; (390) mag. eq., 163; (387) interrex, 211
— — Publicola, P., tr. mil. c. p. 386, 384, 380, 377, 370, 367: (386) tr. mil. c. p., **3**. 213; second to M. Furius Camillus, 215–29; (384) tr. mil. c. p. ii, 255; (380) iii, 289; (377) iv, defeats Latins and Volsci, 305–7; (370) tr. mil. c. p., v, 319; (367) vi, 347
— — Volusus, C., cos. 410: (415) tr. mil. c. p., **2**. 417; (410) cos., conducts levy in spite of tr. pl., 429–31; sells spoil; granted ovation; insulted by soldiers, 431; (407) tr. mil. c. p. ii, 445; (404) iii, 455
— Publicola, L.: (394) tr. mil. c. p., **3**. 89; (390) mag. eq., 163; (389) tr. mil. c. p. ii, 197; (387) iii, 213; (383) iv, 269; (380) v, 289
— —, M., cos. 355, 353: (358) mag. eq. of C. Sulpicius Peticus, **3**. 395, 407; (355) cos., 415–7; (353) ii, 421; recalled from Volscian wars, names dictator against Etruscans, 423
— —, M.: (43) pardoned by Brutus and Cassius, **14**. 153
— —, P., cos. 509, 508, 506, 504: (510) joins Sp. Lucretius and L. Junius against Tarquins, **1**. 203–5; (509) cos. suf., 225; arrests supporters of Tarquins, 231; defeats Etruscans, triumphs, 237–9, **2**. 59, 205; celebrates funeral of L. Junius Brutus, **1**. 239–41; accused of plots; called 'Publicola,' 241–3; secures laws of appeal, 243, 315; defeats Etruscans; (508) cos. ii, 245; defends Rome, 253–5; (506) cos. iii, 267; (504) iv, defeats Sabines; (503) dies, 271
— —, P., cos. 475, 460: (475) cos., defeats Veientes and Sabines **1**. 397–9; (462) interrex, **2**. 27; (460) cos. ii, 51; slain attacking Ap. Herdonius on Capitol, 53–71, 75
Valerius Publicola, P.: (352) cos., **3**. 427; (350) pr., 433; (332) mag. eq., **4**. 69
— Tappo, C.: (188) tr. pl., proposes citizenship for Formiae, Fundi, Arpinum, **11**. 119–21
— —, L., pr. 192: (195) tr. pl., would abrogate Oppian law, **9**. 413, 415, 427–39; (192) pr. for Sicily and fleet, **10**. 29, 59, 67; (191) 161; (190) IIIvir for Placentia, Cremona, Bononia, 429, 469
— Triarius, C.: (68–67) leg., defeated by Mithridates, **14**. 123
— Volusus, M.: (505) cos., triumphs over Sabines, **1**. 269, 277; (499) slain at Lake Regillus, 281
vallum (wall): (458) stakes for, carried by soldiers, **2**. 93; (197) **9**. 287–9
Vardaei, in Illyricum: (135) **14**. 59
Vareia, in Spain: (76) **14**. 195
Varenus, P.: (73) pr., defeated by Spartacus, **14**. 119
Vargunteius: (63) lightning kills, **14**. 301
Varro: *see* Terentius.
Varus: *see* Aternius, Attius, Licinius, Quinctilius.
Vascones, Spanish tribe: (76) **14**. 195
Vatia: *see* Servilius.
Vatican hill, near Rome: (295) **4**. 461–3
Vatinius, P., cos. 47: (55) pr., **14**. 131; (43) procos.; M. Junius Brutus takes army of, 149
Vecilius, Mt.: (449) **2**. 163
Vecillinus: *see* Cassius.
Veientanus: *see* Pomponius.
Veii: (753–717) defeated by Romulus, makes 100 year truce, **1**. 55–7, 109; (672–640) war with, foreseen, 91; attack by, repulsed, 97–9; aids Sabines unofficially, 109; (640–616) Ancus Marcius takes Maesian forest from, 123; (578–534) Servius Tullius defeats, 149; (509) defeated with Tarquin the Proud, 235–9; P. Valerius Publicola leads against, 245; (508, 506) Lars Porsinna returns lands taken for, 261, 269; (483) war with, 359; (482, 481) 361; (480) joined by other Etrus-

INDEX

cans; defeated by M. Fabius Vibulanus and Cn. Manlius Cincinnatus, 365–81; (479) make raids, 381–3; Fabii undertake war with, 383–7; (478) defeated, 387; (477) slay all Fabii but one, 389–91; (476) occupy Janiculum, 393–5; (475) P. Valerius Publicola defeats Sabines and, 397–9; (474) 40 year truce with, 401; (460) feared, **2.** 55, 61; (445) plunder Roman frontier, 257; tribb. pl. accused of encouraging, 263; (444) war with, as reason for tribb. mil. c. p., 279; (437) defeated by L. Sergius Fidenas, 313–5, by Mam. Aemilius Mamercinus, 315–21, 361; (436) raided, 325; (435) Q. Servilius Priscus defeats, 327–9; truce with, 357; (434) seek Etruscan aid, 331–3; (432) 337; (428–427) raids of, unpunished, 355–7; (426) victorious because of Roman dissension, 359, 385–7, 391, 407; Mamercinus defeats, 359–71; naval battle with (?), 371; (425) 20 year truce, 371, 397; (415) flooded Tiber checks, 417; (407) truce with, ends, 445; (406) war declared on, 447, 455; its causes, **3.** 15; (405) besieged, **2.** 455; (404) 457; (403) **3.** 3–27; elect king, 3, 19; seek Etruscan aid, 3–5, 17, 19, 23; Roman disunion aids, 23; Roman volunteer army rebuilds siege works before, 25–7; (402) with Capenates and Faliscans, take Roman camp, 29–31, 39–41, 95, (401) which tribb. mil. c. p. M' Aemilius Mamercus and K. Fabius Ambustus recover, 35, 43; (399) reinforcements for, defeated, 49–51; (398) no action at, 53; prophecy that, will fall when Alban lake is drained, 53–5, 173, 177, (397) confirmed by Delphi, 59; besieged, 57, 59; Etruscans refuse aid to, 61, 121; (396) panic in Roman camp before, 65; M. Furius Camillus takes command against, 65–7, makes vows, 67, 73, 81, 87–9, consults Senate *re* booty, 69–71; he captures, and gives city over to plundering, 71–9, 93, 95, 147, 173, 219; use of mine in capture, 69, 73–5, 223; gods of, removed to Rome, 73, 77–9, 177; Camillus triumphs over, 81–3; (395) plebeians propose migration to, 83–5, opposed by patricians, 85; land of, subject to Camillus' vow to Apollo, 87–9; (393) Senate opposes re-establishment of, 103–7, but grants land at, to plebeians, 107–9; (392) vows of Camillus paid, 109; (391) he is convicted *re* spoils of, 89, 113; (390) Romans flee to, after Allia, 131–3, 147, 399, **6.** 361; they defeat Etruscan raiders, **3.** 151–3; Camillus becomes dict. at, 155–7, **4.** 177, **5.** 211, 249; messengers pass between Rome and, **3.** 157, 161; mag. eq. L. Valerius ordered to bring army from, 163; plebeian effort to move to, fails, 167–87; (389) tr. mil. L. Aemilius Mamercinus opposes Etruscans near, 201; granted citizenship; Romans in, forced to return, 207; (385) farm of M. Manlius Capitolinus near, 243; (329) muster at, on rumour of Gallic war, **4.** 79; (210) Campanians forced to settle at, **7.** 131–3. *Also*: **3.** 127, 241. Prodigies: (207) **7.** 357; (198) **9.** 177; (174) **12.** 255; (173) 297; (169) **13.** 149; (166) **14.** 245–7; (125) 265. *See* Lars Tolumnius.

Velabrum, in Rome: (207) **7.** 361

Velia, hill in Rome: (509) **1.** 241–3; (167) temple of Penates on, **13.** 297

—, Samnite city: (293) cos. Sp. Carvilius Maximus takes, **4.** 531–3; (210) required to furnish ships, **7.** 147

Velina tribus: (241) added, **4.** 559

velites: (189) equipment of, **11.** 75; (211) serve in combination with cavalry, **7.** 15–7, (200) **9.** 103–5, (202) with heavy armed, **8.** 489

Velitrae, in Latium: (494) Volsci pursued into, **1.** 317; colony sent to, 319, (492) reinforced, 331; (385) colonists from, aid Volsci, **3.** 235, 239, 255; (383) unpunished, 269; (382) defeated, 271–3; (380) legions at, 291, 299; (370) besieged, 319–21; (369) 321, 327; (368) 333; (367) 347; (358) raid Roman lands, 407; (340) join Latin revolt, **4.** 11; (339) support Pedani, 51; (338) C. Maenius routs, 53; punished, 59, 81; colony sent to, 59; 323) Tusculans accused

of aiding, 145. Prodigies: (202) **8**. 511; (199) **9**. 157; (198) 177
Vellocasses, Celts: (103) **14**. 81
Venafrum, in Campania: (95) **14**. 285
Veneti, in Transalpine Gaul: (56) **14**. 131
Venetia, at head of Adriatic: founded by Antenor, **1**. 9; (391) not occupied by Etruscans, **3**. 117; (302) repulses Cleonymus, **4**. 363–7; description of, 365; (186) Transalpine Gauls found city in, **11**. 283; (174) cos. M. Aemilius Lepidus suppresses revolt in, **12**. 277
Venno, Venox: *see* Plautius.
Ventidius Bassus, P., cos. suf. 43: (39) leg., defeats Parthians, **14**. 157–9; (38) 159
Vento: *see* Perpenna.
Venus: mother of Aeneas, **1**. 11; (217) with Mars in *lectisternium*, **5**. 235; (197) Attalus demands restoration of temple of, **9**. 253, 259; (178) temple of, in Rome, burned, **14**. 243
— Erycina: (217) temple to, ordered by Sibylline books, **5**. 231, vowed by Q. Fabius Maximus, 235, (215) dedicated, **6**. 103, 107; (181) temple to, near Colline gate, dedicated, **12**. 103, **8**. 513
— Genetrix: (44) Caesar honoured before temple of, **14**. 145; comet at festival of, 309–11
— Obsequens: (295) temple to, near Circus, **4**. 479; (204) public works near temple of, **8**. 351; (174) **12**. 279
— Verticordia: (114) temple to, **14**. 271
Venusia, in Apulia: (216) cos. C. Terentius Varro flees to, after Cannae, **5**. 361–3, 375–7, 393, 397, **6**. 361; Capuan envoys reach Varro at, 13; (210) M. Marcellus overtakes Hannibal near, **7**. 209; (209) loyal, 245–7; Marcellus leaves army at, 297, 301; (208) he takes command at, 313–5; after his death, army led back to, 329; (207) C. Claudius Nero moves from, 373; Nero and Hannibal fight near, 379–81; (200) new colonists for, **9**. 145
ver sacrum: *see* sacred spring.
Vercellium town of Herpini: (215) **6**. 131
Vercingetorix, an Arvernian: (52) **14**. 135
Vercondaridubnus: *see* Julius.
Verginia: (449) claimed as slave by M. Claudius, **2**. 143–7; awarded to him by Xvir Ap. Claudius, 147–57; slain by her father, 159, 165, 191, 199, 205
—: (296) excluded from patrician shrine, builds shrine of Pudicitia Plebeia, **4**. 443–5
Verginius A., tr. pl. 461–458: (461) tr. pl., supports Terentilian law by attacking K. Fabius, **2**. 41–3, 47, 49; (460) tr. pl. ii, 51; hinders levy, 67, 57; (459) tr. pl. iii, 73; (458) iv, 83, 85; (457) v, 101
—, A.: (395) tr. pl., vetoes law to colonize Veii, **3**. 85; (394) tr. pl., 89; (393) fined, 103–5
—, L., tr. pl. 449: (449) father of Verginia, **2**. 143–53; Ap. Claudius decides against, 153–7; slays daughter, returns to camp, 159, 163–7; refuses election as trib. mil., 169; tr. pl., 181; accuses Ap. Claudius, 187–93, 197; urges lighter penalty for M. Claudius, 199
—, L.: (207) tr. mil., conducts Hasdrubal's envoys, **7**. 381
—, P.: (494) a Senator, supports moderate debt reform, **1**. 311–3
— Caelimontanus, A.: (469) cos., campaigns against Aequi and Sabines, **1**. 427; (467) IIIvir agr. div., **2**. 5
— Esquilinus, Opiter: (473) cos., **1**. 401; holds levy, causing riot, 405–7
— Tricostus, L.: (435) cos., names dict. against Veii, **2**. 327; (434) cos. ii, 331
— —, L.: (389) tr. mil. c. p., **3**. 197
— —, Optiter: (502) cos., triumphs over Pometia, **1**. 273–5
— — Caelimontanus, A.: (494) cos., **1**. 307–11; defeats Volsci, 315–7
— — —, Sp.: (456) cos., **2**. 103
— — — T.: (496) cos., **1**. 285
— — —, T.: (448) cos., **2**. 219
— — Esquilinus, L.: (402) tr. mil. c. p., **3**. 27; refusal to aid colleague causes defeat at Veii, 31–3, 39–41; forced to shorten term, 33, 41; (401) condemned, 35, 39–45, 49
— — Rutilus, A.: (476) cos., defeats

INDEX

Veientes on Janiculum, **1**. 393–5; (475) testifies for colleague, 397
Verginius Tricostus Rutilus, Pro.: (486) cos., opposes land law favouring Latins, **1**. 353–5
— — —, T.: (479) cos.; Veientes defeat **1**. 381–3; (463) augur; dies, **2**. 25–7
Vermina, son of Syphax: (204) defeats Masinissa, **8**. 335–7; (202) defeated by procos. P. Scipio (Afr.), 503, 517; (200) seeks recognition as king, **9**. 35–7; accepts terms, 59
Verona, in Cisalpine Gaul: **3**. 121
Verrucosus: *see* Fabius Maximus.
Verrugo, in land of Volsci: (445) fortified by Rome, **2**. 257; (409) recaptured from Volsci, 437, 439; (407) Roman garrison of, slain, 445; (394) Roman garrison of, flees **3**. 99–101
Vertomarus: (222) Gallic chief, slain by M. Marcellus, **4**. 561
Verulae, in Latium: (306) does not join Hernici, **4**. 333; declines citizenship, 339
Vescelia, in Farther Spain: (192) **10**. 65
Vescellium, town of Herpini: (215) **6**. 131
Vescia, in Latium: (340) Latins flee to, **4**. 45; (314) nobles deliver, to Rome, 259–61; (296) Samnites plunder, 431; colonies planted to protect, 439; (295) Samnites raid, 477; (293) L. Papirius Cursor winters in, 537
Veseris riv., in Campania: (340) **4**. 35, 469
Vesta: (217) with Vulcan in *lectisternium*, **5**. 235. Temple of, in Rome: (393) especially sacred, **3**. 107; (390) eternal fire in, 175, 185; (353) Caerites invoke Vestals in, 423; (242) burned, **4**. 559; (210) saved from fire, **7**. 105, 107; (206) fire in, goes out, **8**. 47; (178) **12**. 287, **14**. 243; (82) Q. Mucius Scaevola killed fleeing to, 109. Prodigy: (391) **3**. 113
Vestal virgins: Rhea Silvia becomes a, **1**. 17; (715–612) created by Numa, 71; (390) carry *sacra* to Caere, **3**. 135–9, 423–5; moved from Rome only by Gauls, 179; 483) punished or unchastity, **1**. 359; (337) **4**. 63; (273) 551; (c. 233) 559; (216) **5**. 385; (114) **14**. 75, 271; (420) tried and acquitted, **2**. 401–3; (206) scourged for letting fire out, **8**. 47; (178) **14**. 243
Vestia: *see* Oppia.
Vestini, in Central Italy: (325) join Samnites, **4**. 111; D. Junius Brutus defeats, 111–5; (319) part of Federation, 237; (302) treaty with, 367; (168) in guard before battle of Pydna, **13**. 225; (91) revolt, **14**. 89; (89) surrender to Cn. Pompeius Strabo, 93, 95. Prodigies: (94) 287; (91) 291
Vesuvius, Mt., in Campania: (340) **4**. 35
Vetelia, in Latium: (488) **1**. 345
Veteres (Old Shops), in Rome: (169) **13**. 143
Veteres campi (Old Plains), in Lucania: (212) **6**. 409
Vetilius, M.: (147) pr., killed by Viriathus, **14**. 43
veto, consular: (201) used against SC., **8**. 529
veto, tribunician: (445) first recorded use of, against Senate, **2**. 277; (167) not used before discussion of measure, **13**. 313–5. *See tribuni plebei.*
Vettii, in Macedon: (167) **13**. 353
Vettones, Spanish tribe: (193) M. Fulvius Nobilior defeats, **10**. 21; (192) 65
Veturia: (488) induces her son, Cn Marcius Coriolanus, to withdraw **1**. 347–51
Veturius (Vetusius) Calvinus, T., cos. 334, 321: (334) cos., proposes colony at Cales; names dict., **4**. 67; (321) cos. ii, 163; trapped by Samnites at Caudine pass, 165–77; goes under yoke, 177–83; at Rome, names dict. com. c., 185–9; (320) surrender of, to Samnites proposed, 189–99, but refused by Samnites, 199–205
— Cicurinus, C.: (455) cos., **2**. 103; defeats Aequi; (454) condemned for selling booty, 105, 107; (453) coopted augur, 107
— Crassus Cicurinus, C.: (377) tr. mil. c. p., **3**. 305; (369) ii, 321

Veturius Crassus Cicurinus, L. : (451) Xvir, **2**. 109
— — —, L. : (368) tr. mil. c. p., **3** 327; (367) ii, 347
— — —, M. : (399) tr. mil. c. p., **3**. 47
— Geminus Cicurinus, C. : (499) cos., **1**. 279
— — —, T. : (494) cos., **1**. 307; checks riot, 309–11; defeats Aequi, 315, 319–21; unable to control plebs, 323
— — —, T. : (462) cos., defeats Aequi and Volsci, **2**. 27, 31; gains ovation, 35
— Gracchus Sempronianus, T. : (174) augur, **12**. 255
— Philo, L., cos. 220 : (217) dict. com. c., **5**. 313; disqualified by *vitium*, 313, 317; (210) cens., **7**. 227; restores M. Livius Salinator to Senate, 347; dies in office, 227
— —, L., cos. 206 : (211) leg. at sack of Capua, **7**. 127; (210) aed. cur., 229; (209) pr. pereg. and for Gaul, 225, 231, 249; (208) in Gaul, 303; (207) brings news of Metaurus, 409–11; (206) cos. with Bruttium as prov., **8**. 41–3; restores farmers, 47–9; recovers Lucania, 49–51; conducts elections, 153; (205) command not prorogued, 191, 195; mag. eq. com. c., 249; (202) escorts Punic envoys to Rome, 511, 515–7
— —, Ti. : (204) flamen Martialis, **8**. 357–9
Vetusius : *see* Veturius.
vexillum : (340) term defined, **4**. 31–3
Via Aemilia, Flaminia, Gabina, Latina, Lavicana, Nova, Nomentana, Sacra, Salaria : *see* Aemilian way, etc.
via quintana : (178) in camp, **12**. 191
Vibellius, D. : (282) tr. mil., leads mutiny in Regium, **4**. 549, **8**. 115
— Taurea, Cerrinus, of Capua : (216) supports Hannibal, **6**. 25; (215) bloodless duel with Claudius Asellus, 159–61, 197–9; defies Q. Fulvius Flaccus; kills self, **7**. 59–61
Vibius, a Bruttian : (209) seeks terms of surrender, **7**. 267
— Accaus : (212) praef. soc. in capture of Hannibal's camp; rewarded, **6**. 393–5
— Pansa Caetronianus, C., cos. 43 : (48) flees to Pompey, **14**. 209; (43) cos., defeated by Antony; dies, 151; portents before the battle, 313
Vibius Virrius, of Capua : (216) proposes to deliver Italy to Hannibal, **6**. 17, **7**. 47; (211) in Capua, opposes surrender, 47–53; kills self, 53–5
Vibo, in Bruttium : (218) Punic fleet plunders near, **5**. 151; (201) fleet crosses to Macedon from, **9**. 11; (192) colony at, **10**. 119
Vibulanus : *see* Fabius.
Vica Pota : temple of, **1**. 243
Vicilinus : *see* Jupiter Vicilinus.
victimarii : (181) supply fire for burning 'Books of Numa,' **12**. 93
Victoria : (294) cos. L. Postumius Megellus dedicates temple to, **4**. 485; (216) Hiero sends statue of, **5**. 323–5; (211) statues of, on temple of Concord, **7**. 89; (204) Idaean Mother taken to temple of, on Palatine, **8**. 261; (193) shrine to Victoria virgo near temple of, **10**. 25; (42) boy dressed as, in army of Brutus and Cassius, **14**. 317. Prodigies in temples of : (163) 249; (48) 307
— virgo : (193) shrine to, dedicated, **10**. 25
Victoriae mons, in Spain : (214) **6**. 307
Victumulae, in Cisalpine Gaul : (219) Romans use, as magazine, **5**. 171; (218) Hannibal occupies, 133, 171–3
Vicus Cyprius, Insteius, Jugarius, Longus, Tuscus : *see* Cyprius vicus, etc.
villa publica, outside Rome : (203) envoys entertained in, **8**. 445; (197) **9**. 343; (194) rebuilt, 533; (82) Sulla slays citizens in, **14**. 111
Villius, Ap. : (449) tr. pl., **2**. 181
—, P. : (196) struck by lightning, **9**. 349
— Annalis, L., pr. 171 : (180) tr. pl. proposes law fixing ages for office, **12**. 137–9; (171) pr. pereg., 371, 383
— Tappulus, L., pr. 199 : (213) aed. cur., accuses matrons, **6**. 347; (199) pr. for Sardinia, **9**. 147, 155
— —, P., cos. 199 : (204) aed. pl., **8**. 357 . 359; (203) pr. for Sicily and fleet, 357, 369–71; (202) 463; (201) 523; Xvir agr. divid., **9**. 13; (199) cos. with Macedon as prov., 145–7,

155; quells mutiny, 159–61; winters in Corcyra; camps near Aous riv., 167–9, 241; (198) Flamininus sends, home, 179; (197) leg. of Flamininus, 243; Xvir for Macedonian peace, 343, 359–61, 367–71, 381–3, 395, 479, 561; (196) visits Antiochus, 371, 383; (195) reports danger from him, 507; (193) envoy to him, 569, **10**. 39–41, 45–51, 55; returns to Rome, 61, 63; (192) envoy to Greece, 65, 89–93, 97–9, 111, 117
Viminal hill, in Rome: (578–534) **1**. 155
Vindalium, in Gallia Narbonensis: (121) **14**. 73
Vindicius, a slave: (509) informs of plot of the Vitelli, **1**. 231, 235
vindicta: (509) slaves freed by, **1**. 235
vineae (penthouse, sheds): (502) used in attacks on walls, **1**. 273; (403) **3**. 25; (335) **4**. 65; (294) 485; (219) **5**. 21–3; (218) 183; (216) **6**. 61; (214) 235; (200) **9**. 135; (199) 161; (195) 463; (192) **10**. 65; (189) **11**. 23; (184) 353; (177) **12**. 219
vinegar: (218) rock crumbled by, **5**. 109
Vipsanius Agrippa, M., cos. 37, 28, 27: (40) Octavius' agent, negotiates with Antony, **14**. 221; (36) defeats Sex. Pompeius, 159; receives first mural crown, 161; (12) dies, 165
Viriathus, Spanish chief: (147–146) seizes Lusitania, **14**. 43; (142) 255; (140) Q. Fabius Maximus Servilianus defeats, then makes peace with, 45, 49, 51, 255; (139) murdered; men of, receive land, 49, 53; (138) murderers of, not rewarded, 55
Viromandui, Gauls: (57–56) **14**. 129
Virrius: *see* Vibius.
Virtus: (222) temple vowed to, by M. Marcellus, (208) constructed, **7**. 313, (205) dedicated, **8**. 249
visceratio: (328) dole of meat at funeral, **4**. 85; (183) **11**. 365
Vismarus: (214) pro-Punic Gaul, **6**. 311–3
Vitellia: (509) wife of L. Junius Brutus, **1**. 229
Vitellia, in Latium: (393) **3**. 103
Vitellii: (509) plot return of Tarquins, **1**. 229–31, 241
vitium: (444) in election of tribb. mil. c. p., **2**. 281; (397) **3**. 59; (380) in election of cens., 291; (368) in appointment of dict., **3**. 331; (337) **4**. 63; (333) 69; (327) 91; (321) 187; (217) **5**. 313, 317; (292) in election of tribb. pl., **4**. 541, (215) of cos., **6**. 109, (202) of aed. pl., **8**. 515; (180) prevents inauguration of rex sac., **12**. 133–5; (176) in allotment of provinces, 239–41; in auspices, 241–3; (168) in setting day for muster, **13**. 283
Vitruvius Vaccus, of Fundi: (329) leads Privernates against Rome; captured, **4**. 75–9; house of, on Palatine destroyed; put to death, 81
Voconius Saxa, Q.: (169) tr. pl., secures law forbidding inheritance by women, **12**. 289.
Vocontii, in Transalpine Gaul: (218) **5**. 91
Volaterrae, in Etruria: (298) Etruscans defeated near, **4**. 401; (205) promises supplies to P. Scipio (Afr.), **8**. 193; (81–80) Sulla takes, **14**. 113. Prodigy: (92) 289
Volcae, on Rhone: (218) **5**. 75
Volcanus: *see* Vulcan.
Volceii, in Lucania: (209) **7**. 267
Volciani, Spanish tribe: (218) **5**. 55
Volero: *see* Publilius.
volones: *see* slave volunteers.
Volsci, in Central Italy: (534–510) 200 years war with, begins, **1**. 183–5; (508) corn from, 247; (495) war with, 287–9, 295–301; (494) relief for veterans of wars with, 311; defeated, 313–9; (493) 327–9; (492) refuse to sell grain, 331; (491) welcome Cn. Marcius Coriolanus, 335–7; driven from Rome, 339–41; roused against Rome, 341–5; Coriolanus leads, on Rome, 345–7, **3**. 507, **9**. 429; quarrel with Aequi, **1**. 351; (487) war with, 351; (485, 484) 357; (483) 359; (479) 383–5; (477) 393; (475) Latins and Hernici defeat, 399–401; (471) war with, 415–21; (469) raid toward Rome; defeated, 427; (468) Antium taken from, 429–33, **2**. 5; (467) in colony at Antium, 5; (464) war with, 13; (463) 21–5; (462) 27–35; (461) danger from, called patrician invention, 37; (460)

feared while Ap. Herdonius holds Capitol, 53–5, 61, 69; (459) Q. Fabius Vibulanus defeats, at Mt. Algidus, 75–81; (449) war with, 193, 201–7, 243; (447) 221; (446) T. Quinctius Capitolinus drives back, 223–43; (445) murmur, 257; tribb. pl. accused of encouraging, 263; (444) war with, a possible cause for tribb. mil. c. p., 279; (443) plebeians of Ardea seek aid of; defeated before Ardea, 287–93; (442) colony to defend Ardea against, 295; (432) Aequi and, discuss war, 337; (431) A. Postumius Tubertus defeats, on Mt. Algidus, 339–53, 391; (430) internal strife among, 353; (424) war with, 375; (423) defeat C. Sempronius Atratinus, 377–89, 393–5; (413) abandon Ferentinum, 425–7; (410) volunteers of, with Aequi, 429; (409) wars with, 435–9; (408) 439, 443; (407) recover Verrugo, 445–7; (406) wars with, 447–51; (405) 455; (404) 457; (402) recover Anxur, **3**. 29; (401) Anxur attacked by Rome, 35, 43–5, (400) and taken, 47; (397) besiege Anxur, 57; (396) peace granted to; (395) plebeians spurn colony in lands of, 83; (389) M. Furius Camillus defeats, 199–203, 211, 219, and triumphs, 207, 219; (386) he again defeats, 219–25, 229, 289; (385) A. Cornelius Cossus defeats, 231–9, and triumphs, 251; war with, a pretence for naming dict., 247; Latins rebuked for aiding, 255; (383) war with, 269; (381) Camillus defeats, 273–83; (379) fail to pursue victory, 299–301; (378) raids by, 303; (377) defeated at Satricum, 305–9; (353) attack Latium, 421–3; (349) Gauls scatter among, 447; (348) rebuild Satricum, 449; (346) defeated at Satricum, 451; (345) war with, 453; (343) Campanians promise aid against, 459; (341) defeated near Satricum, **4**. 3–5; (340) aid Latins against Rome, 11, 17, 45–7; (338) Antium in land of, taken, 53–5; (330) gain protection against Samnites, 73–5; (328) colonies established on former lands of, at Fregellae, 85, 89, (313) at Pontiae, 273, (303) at Sora, 361; (319) part of Federation, 237. Prodigy: (94) **14**. 287. *Also*: **3**. 181, 185, 471, 505, 509. *See* Messius; Antium.

Volscius Fictor, M., tr. pl. before 461: (461) charges Caeso Quinctius Cincinnatus with brother's murder, **2**. 45–7; (459–458) convicted of perjury, 81–3, 85, 99

Volscus: *see* Publilius.

Volsinii, Etruscan city: (392) attacks Roman territory, **3**. 109; (391) defeated, granted truce, 111–3; (363) yearly nails driven in temple at, 367; (308) P. Decius Mus takes strongholds of, **4**. 325; (294) L. Postumius Megellus defeats; truce granted, 501; (c. 290) wars with, 547; (c. 265) 553. Prodigies: (208) **7**. 307; (104) **14**. 277; (94) 287; (93) 289

Volso: *see* Manlius.

Voltumna, shrine of, in Etruria: (434) Etruscan council at, **2**. 331; (432) 337; (405) 455; (397) **3**. 61; (389) 199

Volturnum, old name of Capua: **2**. 377

—, port near Capua: (211) fighting near, **7**. 23; (197, 194) Roman colony at, **9**. 243, 533. Prodigies: (191) **10**. 263; (83) **14**. 297

Volturnus riv., in Campania: runs through Casilinum, **5**. 251, **6**. 59; (340) Falernian land to, distributed to plebeians, **4**. 47; (296) Samnites camp at, 433; (295) they raid near, 477; (217) Hannibal camps by, **5**. 245; (216) M. Marcellus crosses, **6**. 47; flood in, checks him, 65; supplies floated to Casilinum on, 65–7; (215) crossed by Ti. Sempronius Gracchus, 123, by Q. Fabius Maximus, 127, 135; (214) Marcellus delayed by, 217; (212) grain depot at mouth of, 419, 425; (211) allied cavalry moves toward, **7**. 19; crossed by Hannibal, 29–33, 51, by Q. Fulvius Flaccus, 31–3; (210) some Campanians transported to, 131; (197, 194) colony at mouth of, **9**. 243, 533

Volturnus wind: (216) aids Hannibal at Cannae, **5**. 345, 353

Volumnia: (488) urges husband, Q.

INDEX

Marcius Coriolanus, to withdraw, **1.** 347–51
Volumnius Amintinus Gallus, P.: (461) cos., **2.** 35; tribb. pl. hinder levy by, 39–41; (460) attacks Ap. Herdonius on Capitol, 63; (458) envoy to Aequi, 87
— Flamma Violens, L.: (307) cos., commands against Sallentini, **4.** 331, 341; (296) cos. ii, 415; in Samnium, 421–3; moves to Etruria; aids defeat of Samnites and Etruscans in spite of colleague, 423–31; defeats Samnites near Volturnus riv., 431–7; urges election of P. Decius Mus and Q. Fabius Maximus, 439–41; wife of, excluded from shrine of Pudicitia Patricia, 443–5; (295) in Samnium at time of Sentinum, 443, 455–7, 465, 475; defeats Samnites near Caiatia, 477–9; (293) leg. in defeat of Samnites at Aquilonia, 515, 521; worthy to oppose Alexander, 229
Volustana mt., in Macedon; (169) **13.** 97
Volusus: *see* Valerius, — Potitus.
Vortumnus, statue of: (169) **13.** 143
voting: (179) method of, changed, **12.** 159
votive games: *see* games, votive.
votive offerings: temples as votive offerings: (433, 431) to Apollo, **2.** 335, 353; (296) to Bellona, **4.** 429–31; (499 or 496) to Castor, **1.** 357; (217, 216) to Concord, **5.** 311, **6.** 73; (187, 179) to Diana, **11.** 223, **12.** 161; (180, 179, 173) to Fortuna Equestris, **12.** 125, 141, 299, 319; (204, 194) to Fortuna Primigenia, **8.** 349, **9.** 553; (222) to Honor, **7.** 313; (197, 194) to Juno Matuta, **9.** 553; (345, 344) to Juno Moneta, **3.** 453; (173, 168) **12.** 311, **13.** 295; (396, 392) to Juno Regina, **3.** 73, 81, 109; (187, 179) **11.** 223, **12.** 161; (197, 194) to Juno Sospita, **9.** 247, 553[1]; (199) to Jupiter, 169; (200, 196, 194, 192) 63, 553, **10.** 123; (616–578, 534–510) to Jupiter Optimus Maximus, **1.** 139, 191–3; (753–717) to Jupiter Stator, 45–7, **4.** 505; (294) 497, 505; (295) to Jupiter Victor, 473; (190, 179) to Lares of the Sea, **12.** 161; (217 215 to Mens, **5.** 231, 235, **6.** 107, 113; (672–640) to Pallor and Pavor, **1.** 99; (191, 181) to Pietas, **12.** 103–5; (311, 306, 302) to Salus, **4.** 341, 363; (217, 215) to Venus Erycina, **5.** 231, 235, **6.** 103, 107; (184, 181) **12.** 103; (222, 205) to Virtus, **7.** 313, **8.** 249. Other offerings: (396–394) tithe of spoil of Veii to Apollo, **3.** 81–3, 87–9, 97–9; (293) thimbleful of mead to Jupiter, **4.** 523–5; (218, 217) to Mars, by direction of the Books, **5.** 187, 231; (180) statues to Apollo, Aesculapius, and Salus, **12.** 115
Voturia tribe: (211) junior century of, consults seniors, **7.** 85–9
vows: (200) taken by coss. at beginning of term, **9.** 43; (187) **11.** 169–71; (177) **12.** 215–9; (174) 277; (171) 441; (167) **13.** 387; (217) avoided by cos. C. Flaminius, **5.** 191, 201
Vulcan (Volcanus): (616–578) captured arms dedicated to, **1.** 135; (215) **6.** 157; (203) **8.** 385; (177) **12.** 223; (340) arms dedicated to, in *devotio*, **4.** 43; (217) with Vesta in *lectisternium*, **5.** 235; (304) temple of Concord in precinct of, **4.** 351. Prodigies in precinct of: (183) **11.** 367, **14.** 241; (181) **12.** 61, **14.** 241; in temple of: (214) **6.** 207; (197) **9.** 243; (195) 535
—, isle of, between Italy and Sicily: (218) Punic fleet at, **5.** 145, departs from, 151
Vulsinienses: *see* Volsinii.
Vulturnus riv.: *see* Volturnus riv.

walls, of Rome: (753) built by Romulus, **1.** 25, 33; (640–616) by Ancus Marcius, 121; (616–578) by Tarquin the Elder, 131, 137; (578–534) by Servius Tullius, 155–7; (377) special tax for, **3.** 305; (353) repaired, 427; (212) Vviri to restore, **6.** 365
war, declaration of: (640–616) formula for, instituted by Ancus Marcius, **1.** 115–9; (427) by *comitia centuriata* on authority of Senate, **2.** 357; (406) 447; (362) **3.** 375; (219) **5.** 47; (200) **9.** 17–25; (171) **12.** 379–81, 397; (383) by *comitia tributa*,

on authority of Senate, **3**. 269; (189) war begun without authority by cos. Cn. Manlius Vulso, **11**. 155; (178) by cos. A. Manlius Vulso, **12**. 185[4], 205; (167) question of, referred to people by pr. without Senatorial authority, **13**. 313. *See* fetiales.
water supply: (312) Ap. Claudius Caecus builds aqueduct, **4**. 275; (184) censs. cut off public water from private property, **11**. 361; (179) landowner blocks construction of aqueduct, **12**. 159; (174) censs. build aqueduct at Potentia, 281; (170) private, **13**. 15; (140) Anio dedicated, and Marcia extended to Capitol, **14**. 51
wax: (181) exacted from Corsica, **12**. 105–7; (173) 311
wealth: (195) Nabis redistributes, in Sparta, **9**. 497–9, 501–3
whetstone: (616–578) augur cuts, **1**. 131–3
White Shield phalanx: (168) in army of Perseus, **13**. 227
White Temple, at Capua: (198) lightning strikes, **9**. 177; (179) **12**. 141–3
widows: (214) funds of wards and, placed in *aerarium*, **6**. 233, **9**. 429, 433
winter: (403) siege of Veii continues through, **3**. 5; (401) 37; (399) of unusual severity, 47; (179) **12**. 141
wolf: nurses Romulus, **1**. 19
wolves: (217) images of, on Appian way, **5**. 203; (63) on Capitol, **14**. 303
women, position of: (195) discussed, **9**. 413–39
wood-dealers' quarter, in Rome: (192) **10**. 123
wreaths: (193) worn by populace in ceremonies, **9**. 557; (191) **10**. 263–5; (180) **12**. 115; (169) **13**. 49; (207) worn by Xviri, **7**. 361; (216) laurel, brought from Delphi, **6**. 33–5. *See* crowns, *coronae*.

Xanthippus, of Sparta: (255) Punic general, defeats M. Atilius Regulus, **4**. 557, **8**. 183
Xenarchus, Achaean praetor: (174) seeks Perseus' favour, **12**. 259–61; brother of Archo, 265
Xeno: (190) governs Sardis for Antiochus, **10**. 419
—: (189) general of Philip, **11**. 5–9
Xenoclides: (192) prevents Aetolian seizure of Chalcis, **10**. 113–5; leads Achaeans to Chalcis, 145; vainly opposes surrender to Antiochus, 149
Xenophanes: (215) Philip's envoy to Hannibal, deceives M. Valerius Laevinus, **6**. 115–7; brought to Rome by P. Valerius Flaccus, 117–9, 131–3
Xenophon, an Achaean: (197) with Flamininus at conference with Philip, **9**. 251
Xychus: (179) gives evidence on death of Demetrius, Philip's son, **12**. 167
Xylines Comê, in Pamphylia: (189) **11**. 49
Xyniae, in Thessaly: (198) abandoned in fear of Aetolians, **9**. 191; (197) Aetolians join Flamininus at, 283; (185) Thessalian seizure of, charged by Philip, **11**. 297

year: *see* calendar.
Year, Great: (88) completion of, **14**. 185.
yoke: (458) description of; defeated Aequi sent beneath, **2**. 97; (443) Volsci sent beneath, 291–3; (321) Roman army sent beneath, after Caudine treaty, **4**. 181–3, 191; (320) Samnites sent beneath, 219; (307) 333; (294) 499
youths, ten: (190) and ten maidens in ritual, **10**. 299

Zacynthus, is. off Elis: Saguntum a colony of, **5**. 19; (211) M. Valerius Laevinus takes, **7**. 95; (191) C. Livius Salinator plunders, **10**. 275–7; Rome and Achaeans both claim, 249–51; ceded to Rome, 251, 253
Zama, in Africa: (202) Hannibal moves to, **8**. 469–71; P. Scipio (Afr.) defeats Hannibal at 'Zama', 485–501 (*cp*. 543–54), **5**. 379; news of, reaches Rome, **8**. 515–7; (187) Africanus breaks off trial on anniversary of, **11**. 179–83

INDEX

Zelasium, cape of Phthiotis: (200) **9**. 135
Zeno, of Demetrias: (192) pro-Roman, at council of Magnetes, **10**. 93
Zephyrium, in Cilicia: (197) **9**. 333
Zerynthius: (188) Thracian name for Apollo, **11**. 139
Zeus: (200) temple of, at Piraeus attacked by Philip, **9**. 89; (198) name of, pronounced at opening of Argive assembly, 229; (181) Philip dedicates altar to, on Mt. Haemus, **12**. 71; (169) temple of, at foot of Mt. Olympus, **13**. 111; (167) statue of, at Olympia, 343
Zeus Acraeus: (189) temple of, in Athamania, **11**. 7
— of Dodona: (326) foretells death of Alexander of Epirus, **4**. 93
— Nikaios: (169) Perseus camps at temple of, **13**. 77
— Olympius: (175) Antiochus IV builds temples of, in Athens and in Antioch, **12**. 249; (214) temples of, in Syracuse, **6**. 243, 281
— Trophonius, temple of, at Lebadia: 167 procos. L. Aemilius Paulus visits, **13**. 341; (95) bronze tablet in, **14**. 285
Zeuxippus, of Boeotia: (196) pro-Roman, slays rival, exiled, **9**. 351–5
Zeuxis: (197) pro-Roman praetor of Acarnanians, **9**. 319–21
—: (190) general of Antiochus at Magnesia, **10**. 409
—: (190) envoy of Antiochus, **10**. 421–5
Ziboetas, of Bithynia: (189) driven out by brother and Galatians, **11**. 53
Zmyrna (Smyrna), in Asia Minor: (196) refuses to submit to Antiochus, **9**. 379, **10**. 453; (193) he claims inherited rights in, 47–51; (192) he fails to take, 123; (190) ships and soldiers of, serve Rome, 335, 337; Antiochus offers to withdraw from, 391; (189) Senate praises envoys of, 453; (188) rewarded for loyalty, **11**. 133; (43) M. Junius Brutus and C. Cassius Longinus confer at, **14**. 153
Zoippus . of Syracuse: (215 pro-Punic guardian of Hieronymus, **6**. 187, 189; (214) in voluntary exile in Egypt, 257–9

TABLE OF PARALLELS

The following table will make possible the use of this index with editions of Livy other than the present one. The Roman numerals in the left of each pair of columns are the volumes of the Loeb edition, and the figures that follow are the pages of the translation. The lower-case Roman numerals in the other column are the books of Livy, and the figures that follow give the chapter and section with which the corresponding Loeb page begins. In most cases the section will have begun on the preceding page.

I	i	I	i	I	i	I	ii
3	Pr. 1	79	23.1	155	43.13	231	4.5
5	Pr. 4	81	23.6	157	44.4	233	5.3
7	Pr. 9	83	24.1	159	45.3	235	5.9
9	Pr. 13	85	24.5	161	46.1	237	6.3
11	1.6	87	25.1	163	46.6	239	6.9
13	2.1	89	25.7	165	47.2	241	7.4
15	2.6	91	25.13	167	47.7	243	7.9
17	3.5	93	26.5	169	48.1	245	8.5
19	4.2	95	26.10	171	48.6	247	9.1
21	4.9	97	27.1	173	49.3	249	9.7
23	5.5	99	27.7	175	50.1	251	10.5
25	6.3	101	28.1	177	50.7	253	10.11
27	7.3	103	28.6	179	51.3	255	11.5
29	7.7	105	28.10	181	51.8	257	12.2
31	7.12	107	29.5	183	52.5	259	12.8
33	8.3	109	30.4	185	53.4	261	12.15
35	9.2	111	31.1	187	53.11	263	13.6
37	9.9	113	31.6	189	54.4	265	14.1
39	9.15	115	32.2	191	55.1	267	14.7
41	10.4	117	32.6	193	55.6	269	15.2
43	11.1	119	32.12	195	56.3	271	16.2
45	11.8	121	33.3	197	56.9	273	16.8
47	12.6	123	33.8	199	57.3	275	17.5
49	13.1	125	34.4	201	57.10	277	18.5
51	13.6	127	34.9	203	58.5	279	19.1
53	14.4	129	35.3	205	59.1	281	19.7
55	14.9	131	35.9	207	59.6	283	20.5
57	15.4	133	36.4	209	59.12	285	20.11
59	16.2	135	37.2			287	21.5
61	16.8	137	38.1			289	22.4
63	17.7	139	38.6			291	23.2
65	18.2	141	39.5			293	23.7
67	18.7	143	40.3	219	1.1	295	23.13
69	19.4	145	41.1	221	1.6	297	24.3
71	20.1	147	41.5	223	2.1	299	25.1
73	20.6	149	42.2	225	2.6	301	25.6
75	21.3	151	43.1	227	3.1	303	26.6
77	22.3	153	43.8	229	3.6	305	27.5

TABLE OF PARALLELS

I	ii
307	27.12
309	28.3
311	29.1
313	29.8
315	30.3
317	30.10
319	31.2
321	31.7
323	32.1
325	32.9
327	33.2
329	33.8
331	34.3
333	34.9
335	35.2
337	35.7
339	36.4
341	37.3
343	38.1
345	38.6
347	39.9
349	40.3
351	40.9
353	41.1
355	41.7
357	42.1
359	42.6
361	43.1
363	43.7
365	44.2
367	44.8
369	45.2
371	45.8
373	45.13
375	46.4
377	47.2
379	47.7
381	47.12
383	48.5
385	48.10
387	49.6
389	49.12
391	50.6
393	51.1
395	51.7
397	52.4
399	53.1
401	53.5
403	54.5
405	55.1
407	55.6
409	56.3
411	56.9

I	ii
413	56.15
415	57.4
417	58.7
419	59.4
421	59.10
423	61.1
425	61.7
427	63.1
429	64.1
431	64.8
433	65.3

II	iii
3	1.1
5	1.4
7	2.3
9	2.10
11	3.4
13	4.1
15	4.7
17	5.3
19	5.9
21	5.14
23	6.5
25	7.1
27	7.6
29	8.6
31	8.11
33	9.6
35	9.12
37	10.6
39	10.12
41	11.4
43	11.11
45	12.4
47	13.2
49	13.8
51	14.4
53	15.3
55	15.9
57	16.5
59	17.4
61	17.10
63	18.4
65	18.10
67	19.4
69	19.9
71	20.2
73	20.8
75	21.5
77	22.2

II	iii
79	22.8
81	23.4
83	24.3
85	24.10
87	25.5
89	26.1
91	26.8
93	27.1
95	28.1
97	28.7
99	29.2
101	29.7
103	30.5
105	31.3
107	31.8
109	32.7
111	33.7
113	34.2
115	35.2
117	35.8
119	36.2
121	36.7
123	37.5
125	38.3
127	38.9
129	38.13
131	39.6
133	40.3
135	40.10
137	41.1
139	41.7
141	42.3
143	43.3
145	44.2
147	44.9
149	45.2
151	45.9
153	46.5
155	47.1
157	47.5
159	48.3
161	48.8
163	49.6
165	50.5
167	50.11
169	51.1
171	51.9
173	52.2
175	52.9
177	53.4
179	54.2
181	54.9
183	55.2

II	iii
185	55.8
187	55.15
189	56.6
191	56.11
193	57.4
195	57.9
197	58.4
199	58.9
201	59.4
203	60.6
205	60.11
207	61.7
209	61.13
211	62.6
213	63.2
215	63.7
217	64.3
219	64.8
221	65.3
223	65.9
225	66.4
227	67.3
229	67.9
231	68.4
233	68.8
235	69.2
237	69.6
239	70.2
241	70.8
243	70.14
245	71.5
247	72.2
249	72.7

	iv
257	1.1
259	1.5
261	2.5
263	2.11
265	3.2
267	3.9
269	3.14
271	4.5
273	4.10
275	5.5
277	6.3
279	6.9
281	7.2
283	7.7
285	8.1
287	8.6

TABLE OF PARALLELS

II	iv
289	9.6
291	9.13
293	10.4
295	10.9
297	11.6
299	12.7
301	13.2
303	13.8
305	13.13
307	14.5
309	15.4
311	16.1
313	16.7
315	17.7
317	17.12
319	18.7
321	19.5
323	20.3
325	20.9
327	21.5
329	22.2
331	23.1
333	24.1
335	24.6
337	25.3
339	25.11
341	26.3
343	26.9
345	27.1
347	27.8
349	28.2
351	28.8
353	29.6
355	30.3
357	30.9
359	31.2
361	31.7
363	32.4
365	32.10
367	33.4
369	33.10
371	34.3
373	35.4
375	35.9
377	36.4
379	37.5
381	38.1
383	39.2
385	39.8
387	40.5
389	41.2
391	41.8
393	42.3
395	42.10
397	43.6
399	43.12
401	44.6
403	44.11
405	45.5
407	46.3
409	46.8
411	47.4
413	48.2
415	48.10
417	48.16
419	49.7
421	49.12
423	50.3
425	51.2
427	51.8
429	52.7
431	53.7
433	53.13
435	54.7
437	55.4
439	55.8
441	56.8
443	57.3
445	57.10
447	58.3
449	58.12
451	59.5
453	60.1
455	60.5
457	61.4

III	v
3	1.1
5	1.4
7	2.4
9	2.11
11	3.5
13	4.2
15	4.10
17	5.4
19	5.10
21	6.4
23	6.10
25	7.1
27	7.7
29	8.2
31	8.8
33	9.1
35	10.1
37	10.7
39	11.2
41	11.8
43	11.14
45	12.6
47	12.12
49	13.5
51	13.13
53	14.5
55	15.6
57	16.1
59	16.6
61	17.3
63	18.1
65	18.7
67	19.2
69	19.9
71	20.5
73	21.1
75	21.8
77	21.15
79	22.5
81	23.3
83	23.11
85	24.6
87	25.2
89	25.9
91	26.3
93	26.9
95	27.6
97	27.12
99	28.4
101	28.8
103	29.1
105	29.7
107	30.2
109	30.8
111	31.6
113	32.5
115	33.1
117	33.9
119	34.4
121	35.1
123	35.6
125	36.5
127	36.10
129	37.6
131	38.4
133	39.1
135	39.6
137	39.13
139	40.7
141	41.2
143	41.9
145	42.4
147	43.2
149	43.8
151	44.6
153	45.4
155	46.1
157	46.7
159	47.2
161	47.7
163	48.3
165	48.8
167	49.5
169	50.2
171	50.8
173	51.4
175	52.1
177	52.7
179	52.13
181	53.2
183	53.7
185	54.4
187	55.1

	vi
195	1.1
197	1.5
199	1.11
201	2.6
203	2.12
205	3.4
207	3.10
209	4.6
211	4.12
213	5.7
215	6.6
217	6.13
219	7.1
221	7.5
223	8.7
225	9.2
227	9.9
229	10.3
231	10.9
233	11.6
235	12.2
237	12.8
239	13.3
241	14.1
243	14.7
245	14.12

TABLE OF PARALLELS

III	vi
247	15.5
249	15.10
251	16.3
253	17.1
255	17.6
257	18.2
259	18.8
261	18.14
263	19.6
265	20.5
267	20.10
269	20.16
271	21.6
273	22.3
275	22.8
277	23.5
279	23.11
281	24.6
283	24.10
285	25.5
287	25.11
289	26.6
291	27.4
293	27.8
295	28.3
297	28.9
299	29.6
301	30.4
303	31.1
305	31.7
307	32.6
309	33.2
311	33.8
313	34.2
315	34.7
317	35.4
319	35.8
321	36.5
323	36.11
325	37.5
327	37.10
329	38.4
331	38.8
333	39.1
335	39.7
337	40.1
339	40.7
341	40.13
343	40.19
345	41.4
347	41.9
349	42.5
351	42.10

III	vii
357	1.1
359	1.5
361	2.2
363	2.8
365	2.13
367	3.6
369	4.3
371	5.2
373	5.8
375	6.5
377	6.11
379	7.4
381	8.1
383	9.1
385	9.7
387	10.7
389	10.13
391	11.6
393	11.11
395	12.7
397	12.12
399	13.4
401	13.9
403	14.4
405	14.10
407	15.5
409	15.12
411	16.4
413	17.1
415	17.7
417	18.1
419	18.9
421	19.3
423	19.8
425	20.4
427	20.8
429	21.5
431	22.2
433	22.9
435	23.4
437	23.10
439	24.7
441	25.3
443	25.9
445	26.2
447	26.8
449	26.14
451	27.5
453	28.2
455	28.7
457	29.4
459	30.3
461	30.10
463	30.17
465	31.1
467	31.6
469	32.1
471	32.8
473	32.15
475	33.6
477	33.14
479	34.3
481	34.10
483	35.2
485	35.8
487	36.3
489	36.10
491	37.2
493	37.8
495	37.15
497	38.5
499	38.9
501	39.6
503	39.13
505	40.3
507	40.8
509	40.15
511	41.1
513	42.1

IV	viii
3	1.1
5	1.5
7	2.2
9	2.10
11	3.3
13	3.10
15	4.5
17	4.12
19	5.7
21	6.4
23	6.11
25	7.2
27	7.9
29	7.17
31	8.2
33	8.8
35	8.14
37	9.3
39	9.9
41	10.3
43	10.9
45	11.2
47	11.9
49	11.16
51	12.6
53	12.15
55	13.6
57	13.13
59	14.1
61	14.9
63	15.4
65	16.2
67	16.10
69	17.3
71	17.12
73	18.7
75	19.1
77	19.9
79	20.1
81	20.7
83	21.1
85	21.8
87	22.6
89	23.2
91	23.9
93	23.15
95	24.4
97	24.11
99	24.17
101	25.6
103	25.13
105	26.5
107	27.5
109	28.1
111	28.8
113	29.6
115	29.14
117	30.7
119	30.13
121	31.6
123	32.3
125	32.11
127	32.18
129	33.7
131	33.13
133	33.20
135	34.4
137	35.1
139	35.7
141	36.2
143	36.9
145	37.5
147	38.1
149	38.7
151	38.12
153	39.4

TABLE OF PARALLELS

IV	viii
155	39.11
157	40.3
	ix
163	1.1
165	1.7
167	2.3
169	2.10
171	3.2
173	3.9
175	4.3
177	4.9
179	5.2
181	5.8
183	6.2
185	6.10
187	7.6
189	7.14
191	8.4
193	8.13
195	9.5
197	9.11
199	9.19
201	10.7
203	11.5
205	11.11
207	12.5
209	12.11
211	13.6
213	14.1
215	14.7
217	14.15
219	15.6
221	15.11
223	16.7
225	16.13
227	17.1
229	17.8
231	17.15
233	18.5
235	18.10
237	18.18
239	19.6
241	19.12
243	20.4
245	21.1
247	22.1
249	22.7
251	23.2
253	23.11
255	24.1
257	24.8

IV	ix
259	24.15
261	25.8
263	26.7
265	26.14
267	26.20
269	27.6
271	27.11
273	28.4
275	29.2
277	29.9
279	30.4
281	30.10
283	31.7
285	31.14
287	32.3
289	32.11
291	33.7
293	34.5
295	34.11
297	34.18
299	34.25
301	35.5
303	36.3
305	36.9
307	37.2
309	37.8
311	38.1
313	38.6
315	38.13
317	39.3
319	39.10
321	40.6
323	40.14
325	40.20
327	41.6
329	41.14
331	41.20
333	42.6
335	43.3
337	43.11
339	43.18
341	43.25
343	44.8
345	44.16
347	45.6
349	45.14
351	46.2
353	46.10
	x
361	1.1
363	1.7

IV	x
365	2.4
367	2.10
369	3.2
371	4.2
373	4.9
375	5.3
377	5.9
379	6.2
381	6.8
383	7.4
385	7.9
387	8.3
389	8.11
391	9.5
393	9.12
395	10.6
397	11.1
399	11.9
401	12.1
403	12.7
405	13.6
407	13.13
409	14.6
411	14.13
413	14.21
415	15.8
417	16.3
419	17.1
421	17.7
423	18.3
425	18.9
427	19.2
429	19.10
431	19.17
433	20.2
435	20.8
437	20.15
439	21.7
441	21.14
443	22.6
445	23.4
447	23.12
449	24.6
451	24.14
453	25.4
455	25.11
457	25.18
459	26.6
461	26.12
463	27.4
465	27.11
467	28.7
469	28.14

IV	x
471	29.5
473	29.11
475	29.19
477	30.8
479	31.6
481	31.14
483	32.6
485	33.5
487	34.2
489	34.9
491	35.2
493	35.9
495	35.18
497	36.6
499	36.12
501	37.1
503	37.8
505	37.14
507	38.6
509	38.12
511	39.6
513	39.14
515	40.5
517	40.11
519	41.3
521	41.9
523	41.14
525	42.7
527	43.6
529	43.13
531	44.5
533	45.3
535	45.11
537	46.4
539	46.10
541	47.1
543	47.6
Summaries	
547	xi
549	xii
549	xiii
551	xiv
553	xv
553	xvi
555	xvii
555	xviii
557	xix
559	xx

TABLE OF PARALLELS

V	xxi
3	1.1
5	1.4
7	2.4
9	3.2
11	4.2
13	4.10
15	5.6
17	5.14
19	6.3
21	7.3
23	8.1
25	8.9
27	9.4
29	10.6
31	10.11
33	11.3
35	11.10
37	12.4
39	13.1
41	13.8
43	14.4
45	15.6
47	16.6
49	17.7
51	18.4
53	18.11
55	19.4
57	19.11
59	20.8
61	21.5
63	21.12
65	22.4
67	23.1
69	24.3
71	25.3
73	25.10
75	26.3
77	26.7
79	27.5
81	28.2
83	28.7
85	29.3
87	30.2
89	30.8
91	31.5
93	31.10
95	32.6
97	32.12
99	33.6
101	34.1
103	34.8
105	35.6
107	36.3

V	xxi
109	37.1
111	37.6
113	38.7
115	39.4
117	40.1
119	40.9
121	41.4
123	41.11
125	42.1
127	43.5
129	43.13
131	44.3
133	44.8
135	45.6
137	46.4
139	47.1
141	47.6
143	48.5
145	48.9
147	49.7
149	50.2
151	50.11
153	51.7
155	52.6
157	53.2
159	53.8
161	54.3
163	54.9
165	55.6
167	56.1
169	56.8
171	57.6
173	57.13
175	58.7
177	59.4
179	59.10
181	60.7
183	61.5
185	61.11
187	62.6
189	63.2
191	63.7
193	63.14
	xxii
199	1.1
201	1.5
203	1.11
205	1.18
207	2.4
209	3.1
211	3.7

V	xxii
213	3.13
215	4.4
217	5.2
219	5.8
221	6.6
223	7.1
225	7.9
227	8.1
229	8.7
231	9.7
233	10.1
235	10.6
237	11.1
239	11.6
241	12.5
243	12.12
245	13.5
247	14.2
249	14.9
251	14.14
253	15.4
255	15.11
257	16.6
259	17.4
261	18.4
263	19.2
265	19.8
267	19.12
269	20.7
271	21.4
273	22.3
275	22.9
277	22.16
279	23.2
281	23.8
283	24.6
285	24.12
287	25.6
289	25.14
291	26.2
293	27.3
295	27.11
297	28.9
299	29.1
301	29.8
303	30.3
305	31.1
307	31.8
309	32.3
311	33.2
313	33.9
315	34.2
317	34.9

V	xxii
319	35.4
321	36.4
323	37.4
325	37.11
327	38.6
329	39.2
331	39.8
333	39.16
335	40.1
337	40.8
339	41.7
341	42.5
343	42.11
345	43.5
347	43.11
349	44.6
351	45.6
353	46.5
355	47.4
357	47.9
359	48.5
361	49.6
363	49.14
365	50.3
367	50.9
369	51.2
371	51.9
373	52.5
375	53.5
377	54.1
379	54.8
381	55.4
383	56.2
385	57.1
387	57.6
389	57.11
391	58.7
393	59.7
395	59.12
397	59.19
399	60.7
401	60.12
403	60.19
405	60.25
407	61.3
409	61.9
VI	xxiii
3	1.1
5	1.6
7	2.3

TABLE OF PARALLELS

VI	xxiii
9	3.1
11	3.10
13	4.5
15	5.5
17	5.11
19	6.3
21	7.2
23	7.8
25	8.4
27	9.2
29	9.9
31	10.4
33	10.11
35	11.5
37	11.11
39	12.7
41	12.15
43	13.5
45	14.2
47	14.10
49	15.4
51	15.11
53	16.4
55	16.11
57	17.1
59	17.9
61	18.4
63	18.10
65	19.2
67	19.11
69	19.17
71	20.6
73	21.4
75	22.3
77	22.9
79	23.5
81	24.3
83	24.9
85	25.1
87	25.9
89	26.4
91	26.11
93	27.7
95	28.3
97	28.11
99	29.7
101	29.16
103	30.9
105	30.17
107	31.7
109	31.13
111	32.3
113	32.11

VI	xxiii
115	33.1
117	33.9
119	34.5
121	34.13
123	35.5
125	35.12
127	36.1
129	36.10
131	37.8
133	38.4
135	38.12
137	39.7
139	40.6
141	41.2
143	41.10
145	42.5
147	42.12
149	43.6
151	43.13
153	44.5
155	45.3
157	45.10
159	46.9
161	47.2
163	48.1
165	48.6
167	49.3
169	49.12
	xxiv
175	1.1
177	1.5
179	1.12
181	2.7
183	3.3
185	3.11
187	4.2
189	4.9
191	5.9
193	6.2
195	6.9
197	7.8
199	8.3
201	8.12
203	8.18
205	9.6
207	10.3
209	10.10
211	11.5
213	12.2
215	13.2
217	13.9

VI	xxiv
219	14.4
221	15.3
223	16.1
225	16.9
227	16.17
229	17.5
231	18.4
233	18.11
235	19.2
237	19.10
239	20.7
241	20.15
243	21.4
245	21.12
247	22.7
249	22.14
251	23.4
253	23.11
255	24.7
257	25.4
259	26.3
261	26.12
263	27.4
265	28.1
267	28.9
269	29.6
271	30.1
273	30.10
275	31.2
277	31.11
279	32.4
281	33.2
283	33.8
285	34.6
287	34.13
289	35.5
291	36.2
293	36.8
295	37.6
297	38.2
299	38.9
301	39.6
303	40.2
305	40.8
307	40.15
309	41.5
311	42.2
313	42.8
315	43.6
317	44.4
319	44.10
321	45.6
323	45.14

VI	xxiv
325	46.5
327	47.7
329	47.15
331	48.6
333	48.13
335	49.7
	xxv
341	1.1
343	1.6
345	1.12
347	2.6
349	3.4
351	3.12
353	4.1
355	4.9
357	5.6
359	6.2
361	6.10
363	6.17
365	7.3
367	7.10
369	8.5
371	8.12
373	9.7
375	9.15
377	10.6
379	11.3
381	11.9
383	11.16
385	12.3
387	12.10
389	13.1
391	13.8
393	14.2
395	14.8
397	15.1
399	15.7
401	15.13
403	15.20
405	16.7
407	16.14
409	16.22
411	17.5
413	18.5
415	18.12
417	19.5
419	19.14
421	20.4
423	21.3
425	22.1
427	22.8

TABLE OF PARALLELS

VI	xxv
429	22.16
431	23.6
433	23.14
435	24.4
437	24.11
439	25.3
441	25.9
443	26.4
445	26.12
447	27.4
449	27.12
451	28.6
453	29.1
455	29.7
457	30.3
459	30.10
461	31.5
463	31.11
465	32.6
467	33.4
469	34.3
471	34.11
473	35.3
475	36.2
477	36.11
479	37.2
481	37.10
483	37.15
485	38.4
487	38.11
489	38.19
491	39.3
493	39.11
495	39.18
497	40.5
499	40.12
501	41.7

VII	xxvi
3	1.1
5	1.5
7	2.1
9	2.7
11	2.14
13	3.4
15	3.12
17	4.6
19	5.4
21	5.11
23	6.1
25	6.7
27	6.14
29	7.6
31	8.4
33	9.1
35	9.8
37	10.2
39	10.7
41	11.5
43	11.11
45	12.8
47	12.15
49	13.2
51	13.9
53	13.15
55	14.2
57	14.8
59	15.7
61	15.14
63	16.5
65	16.12
67	17.6
69	17.13
71	18.4
73	18.11
75	19.7
77	19.13
79	20.7
81	21.3
83	21.10
85	21.17
87	22.8
89	22.14
91	23.6
93	24.5
95	24.12
97	25.3
99	25.11
101	26.2
103	26.7
105	27.3
107	27.10
109	28.1
111	28.8
113	29.3
115	29.9
117	30.6
119	30.12
121	31.5
123	31.11
125	32.6
127	33.3
129	33.10
131	34.2
133	34.10
135	35.5
137	36.2
139	36.9
141	37.5
143	38.3
145	38.10
147	39.4
149	39.12
151	39.18
153	40.1
155	40.10
157	40.17
159	41.6
161	41.12
163	41.18
165	42.1
167	42.7
169	43.2
171	44.1
173	44.6
175	45.4
177	46.1
179	46.7
181	47.4
183	48.2
185	48.8
187	48.14
189	49.6
191	49.14
193	50.6
195	50.13
197	51.7

VII	xxvii
203	1.1
205	1.6
207	1.13
209	2.6
211	2.12
213	3.5
215	4.4
217	4.11
219	5.3
221	5.11
223	5.17
225	6.5
227	6.12
229	6.18
231	7.4
233	7.10
235	7.17
237	8.6
239	8.13
241	8.19
243	9.7
245	9.13
247	10.4
249	10.11
251	11.4
253	11.12
255	12.3
257	12.9
259	12.15
261	13.5
263	13.11
265	14.6
267	14.13
269	15.4
271	15.10
273	15.16
275	16.4
277	16.9
279	16.16
281	17.5
283	17.12
285	18.2
287	18.10
289	18.16
291	19.2
293	19.9
295	20.3
297	20.8
299	21.2
301	21.9
303	22.4
305	22.10
307	23.3
309	24.1
311	24.7
313	25.5
315	25.11
317	26.4
319	26.11
321	27.4
323	27.12
325	28.4
327	28.10
329	29.1
331	29.7
333	30.2
335	30.9
337	30.16
339	31.6
341	32.2

TABLE OF PARALLELS

VII	xxvii
343	32.9
345	33.6
347	34.1
349	34.8
351	35.1
353	35.8
355	36.2
357	36.9
359	37.3
361	37.9
363	38.2
365	38.9
367	39.4
369	39.9
371	40.4
373	40.10
375	41.4
377	42.1
379	42.8
381	42.16
383	43.7
385	44.1
387	44.7
389	45.5
391	45.12
393	46.5
395	46.12
397	47.6
399	47.10
401	48.8
403	48.15
405	49.4
407	50.1
409	50.9
411	51.5
413	51.12

VIII	xxviii
3	1.1
5	1.6
7	2.3
9	2.12
11	3.2
13	3.9
15	3.16
17	5.1
19	5.7
21	5.15
23	6.2
25	6.10
27	7.3

VIII	xxviii
29	7.9
31	7.15
33	8.2
35	8.8
37	8.14
39	9.6
41	9.12
43	10.1
45	10.9
47	11.1
49	11.8
51	11.15
53	12.7
55	12.14
57	13.6
59	14.1
61	14.8
63	14.16
65	15.2
67	15.10
69	16.3
71	16.11
73	17.3
75	17.12
77	18.3
79	18.11
81	19.5
83	19.11
85	19.18
87	20.7
89	21.3
91	22.1
93	22.8
95	22.14
97	23.5
99	24.4
101	24.10
103	25.1
105	25.7
107	25.15
109	26.7
111	26.15
113	27.8
115	27.14
117	28.5
119	28.11
121	29.1
123	29.10
125	30.3
127	30.9
129	31.3
131	32.3
133	32.9

VIII	xxviii
135	33.5
137	33.13
139	34.3
141	34.10
143	35.4
145	35.12
147	36.5
149	37.1
151	37.7
153	38.5
155	38.12
157	39.5
159	39.12
161	39.19
163	40.4
165	40.11
167	41.4
169	41.12
171	42.2
173	42.8
175	42.15
177	42.20
179	43.4
181	43.11
183	43.18
185	44.4
187	44.10
189	44.17
191	45.6
193	45.12
195	45.18
197	46.5
199	46.11

	xxix
207	1.1
209	1.7
211	1.14
213	1.21
215	2.2
217	2.10
219	2.17
221	3.7
223	3.15
225	4.7
227	5.4
229	5.9
231	6.6
233	6.12
235	7.3
237	7.9

VIII	xxix
239	8.7
241	9.3
243	9.8
245	10.3
247	11.1
249	11.7
251	12.1
253	12.7
255	12.14
257	13.4
259	14.2
261	14.9
263	14.14
265	15.6
267	15.13
269	16.4
271	17.4
273	17.11
275	17.19
277	18.6
279	18.12
281	18.18
283	19.4
285	19.10
287	20.3
289	20.11
291	21.5
293	21.11
295	22.5
297	22.10
299	23.4
301	23.10
303	24.6
305	24.12
307	25.5
309	25.11
311	26.4
313	27.2
315	27.9
317	27.14
319	28.8
321	29.4
323	29.12
325	30.6
327	30.13
329	31.7
331	32.1
333	32.8
335	32.14
337	33.6
339	34.2
341	34.9
343	34.16

TABLE OF PARALLELS

VIII	xxix
345	35.6
347	35.12
349	36.4
351	36.10
353	37.3
355	37.8
357	37.15
359	38.6
	xxx
367	1.1
369	1.5
371	2.1
373	2.8
375	3.1
377	3.7
379	4.4
381	4.11
383	5.7
385	6.5
387	7.2
389	7.10
391	8.3
393	8.8
395	9.7
397	10.2
399	10.8
401	10.16
403	11.1
405	11.8
407	12.5
409	12.11
411	12.18
413	13.3
415	13.11
417	14.2
419	14.9
421	15.5
423	15.12
425	16.6
427	16.13
429	17.6
431	17.13
433	18.3
435	18.9
437	19.1
439	19.7
441	19.12
443	20.7
445	21.6
447	22.1
449	23.2

VIII	xxx
451	24.1
453	24.9
455	25.3
457	25.10
459	26.4
461	26.10
463	27.4
465	27.10
467	28.3
469	28.8
471	29.2
473	29.7
475	30.4
477	30.10
479	30.17
481	30.23
483	31.1
485	31.8
487	32.4
489	32.10
491	33.5
493	33.12
495	34.2
497	34.9
499	35.2
501	35.8
503	36.4
505	36.9
507	37.3
509	37.10
511	38.3
513	38.9
515	39.4
517	40.2
519	40.8
521	40.16
523	41.6
525	42.4
527	42.11
529	42.18
531	43.4
533	43.10
535	44.4
537	44.11
539	45.3
IX	xxxi
3	1.1
5	1.5
7	1.9
9	2.6

IX	xxxi
11	3.2
13	4.1
15	4.5
17	5.5
19	6.1
21	7.1
23	7.8
25	7.15
27	8.8
29	9.5
31	10.1
33	11.1
35	11.8
37	11.16
39	12.5
41	13.1
43	13.8
45	14.6
47	14.12
49	15.6
51	16.3
53	17.3
55	18.1
57	18.7
59	19.4
61	20.6
63	21.10
65	22.2
67	23.2
69	23.11
71	24.7
73	24.15
75	25.3
77	25.10
79	26.7
81	27.2
83	28.2
85	29.3
87	29.10
89	30.1
91	30.10
93	31.7
95	31.13
97	32.1
99	33.2
101	33.8
103	34.6
105	35.3
107	36.4
109	36.11
111	37.9
113	38.5
115	39.4

IX	xxxi
117	39.13
119	40.6
121	41.5
123	41.13
125	42.7
127	43.4
129	44.5
131	45.4
133	45.12
135	46.4
137	46.11
139	47.1
141	48.2
143	48.9
145	49.5
147	49.12
149	50.8
	xxxii
155	1.1
157	1.8
159	2.2
161	3.2
163	4.3
165	5.4
167	5.13
169	6.6
171	7.4
173	7.10
175	8.3
177	8.11
179	9.3
181	10.1
183	10.8
185	11.6
187	12.3
189	13.2
191	13.10
193	14.2
195	15.1
197	16.1
199	16.10
201	17.2
203	17.10
205	18.1
207	19.1
209	19.11
211	20.6
213	21.6
215	21.13
217	21.20
219	21.26

TABLE OF PARALLELS

IX	xxxii	IX	xxxiii	IX	xxxiv	IX	xxxiv
221	21.34	325	18.2	429	5.6	535	45.3
223	22.5	327	18.12	431	5.11	537	46.2
225	23.2	329	18.21	433	6.8	539	46.10
227	23.9	331	19.7	435	6.14	541	47.5
229	24.3	333	20.3	437	7.3	543	48.2
231	25.4	335	20.12	439	7.10	545	49.6
233	25.10	337	21.7	441	8.4	547	50.2
235	26.8	339	22.5	443	9.4	549	51.1
237	26.17	341	23.4	445	9.12	551	52.4
239	27.6	343	24.2	447	10.6	553	53.1
241	28.5	345	25.1	449	11.8	555	54.1
243	28.12	347	25.9	451	13.1	557	54.8
245	29.6	349	26.6	453	13.9	559	56.2
247	30.7	351	27.5	455	14.7	561	56.11
249	31.1	353	28.3	457	15.4	563	57.5
251	32.3	355	28.11	459	16.2	565	58.1
253	32.13	357	29.3	461	17.1	567	58.8
255	33.5	359	29.10	463	17.9	569	59.4
257	33.14	361	30.7	465	19.1	571	60.4
259	34.6	363	31.5	467	19.10	573	61.7
261	35.1	365	32.2	469	20.8	575	61.15
263	35.11	367	32.9	471	21.8	577	62.6
265	36.8	369	34.2	473	22.7	579	62.13
267	38.1	371	34.11	475	23.3		
269	38.9	373	35.11	477	24.1		
271	39.8	375	36.7	479	25.1		
273	40.5	377	37.1	481	25.9	X	xxxv
		379	37.9	483	26.7	3	1.1
		381	38.6	485	26.14	5	1.5
	xxxiii	383	39.1	487	27.8	7	2.2
279	1.1	385	40.1	489	28.4	9	3.1
281	1.6	387	40.6	491	28.12	11	4.2
283	2.9	389	41.8	493	29.9	13	5.2
285	3.10	391	42.5	495	30.3	15	5.11
287	4.5	393	43.2	497	31.5	17	6.4
289	5.9	395	44.1	499	31.14	19	7.1
291	6.6	397	44.7	501	32.2	21	7.7
293	7.4	399	45.7	503	32.9	23	8.6
295	7.11	401	46.7	505	32.16	25	9.3
297	8.6	403	47.5	507	33.6	27	10.2
299	9.1	405	48.3	509	34.1	29	10.8
301	9.10	407	49.1	511	34.9	31	11.3
303	10.6			513	35.8	33	11.10
305	11.3			515	36.4	35	12.4
307	12.1		xxxiv	517	37.4	37	12.13
309	12.10	413	1.1	519	38.4	39	13.2
311	13.8	415	1.6	521	39.4	41	13.8
313	13.15	417	2.6	523	39.12	43	14.5
315	14.9	419	2.14	525	40.7	45	14.12
317	15.7	421	3.7	527	41.6	47	15.7
319	15.16	423	4.4	529	42.5	49	16.5
321	16.9	425	4.12	531	43.7	51	16.13
323	17.7	427	4.19	533	44.4	53	17.7

TABLE OF PARALLELS

X	xxxv
55	18.5
57	19.4
59	20.6
61	20.14
63	21.7
65	22.5
67	23.5
69	24.1
71	25.2
73	25.11
75	26.7
77	27.6
79	27.14
81	28.4
83	28.11
85	29.7
87	30.4
89	30.9
91	31.4
93	31.13
95	32.4
97	32.12
99	33.6
101	34.2
103	34.8
105	35.4
107	35.10
109	35.19
111	36.8
113	37.6
115	38.6
117	39.2
119	40.1
121	40.7
123	41.7
125	42.4
127	42.13
129	43.7
131	44.7
133	45.8
135	46.8
137	47.4
139	48.6
141	48.13
143	49.7
145	50.2
147	50.9
149	51.5
	xxxvi
155	1.1
157	1.6

X	xxxvi
159	2.2
161	2.8
163	3.1
165	3.9
167	4.1
169	4.9
171	5.5
173	6.3
175	7.1
177	7.7
179	7.15
181	8.1
183	9.2
185	9.11
187	10.4
189	10.11
191	11.3
193	11.11
195	12.7
197	13.4
199	14.2
201	14.9
203	15.2
205	15.8
207	16.4
209	17.1
211	17.7
213	17.14
215	18.4
217	19.3
219	19.11
221	20.5
223	21.3
225	21.11
227	22.8
229	23.5
231	24.4
233	24.11
235	25.4
237	26.5
239	27.8
241	28.4
243	29.1
245	30.1
247	31.3
249	31.10
251	32.4
253	33.3
255	34.3
257	34.10
259	35.7
261	35.14
263	36.4

X	xxxvi
265	37.5
267	38.6
269	39.7
271	40.4
273	40.11
275	41.4
277	42.4
279	43.5
281	43.13
283	44.8
285	45.4
	xxxvii
291	1.1
293	1.6
295	2.1
297	2.6
299	3.2
301	3.9
303	4.5
305	5.2
307	6.2
309	6.7
311	7.6
313	7.14
315	8.5
317	9.7
319	10.3
321	10.11
323	11.6
325	11.13
327	12.5
329	13.1
331	13.9
333	14.3
335	15.4
337	16.4
339	16.13
341	17.6
343	18.3
345	18.10
347	19.5
349	20.4
351	20.12
353	21.4
355	22.2
357	23.4
359	23.10
361	24.5
363	25.1
365	25.9
367	26.3

X	xxxvii
369	26.12
371	27.5
373	28.2
375	28.11
377	29.7
379	30.4
381	30.10
383	31.7
385	32.5
387	32.12
389	33.5
391	34.5
393	35.5
395	36.3
397	37.1
399	37.7
401	38.4
403	39.3
405	39.9
407	40.3
409	40.11
411	41.3
413	41.9
415	42.4
417	43.3
419	43.9
421	44.7
423	45.8
425	45.15
427	45.21
429	46.7
431	47.3
433	48.1
435	49.2
437	50.1
439	50.9
441	51.5
443	52.1
445	52.8
447	53.4
449	53.11
451	53.18
453	53.27
455	54.6
457	54.13
459	54.20
461	54.28
463	55.4
465	56.2
467	56.8
469	57.4
471	57.10
473	58.1

TABLE OF PARALLELS

X	xxxvii
475	58.7
477	59.4
479	60.5

XI	xxxviii
3	1.1
5	1.5
7	1.11
9	2.9
11	3.3
13	3.9
15	4.6
17	5.3
19	5.9
21	6.7
23	7.6
25	7.11
27	8.4
29	9.1
31	9.8
33	9.13
35	10.6
37	11.6
39	12.2
41	12.9
43	13.7
45	13.13
47	14.9
49	15.4
51	15.12
53	16.4
55	16.11
57	17.3
59	17.9
61	17.16
63	18.3
65	18.9
67	19.2
69	20.3
71	20.10
73	21.5
75	21.11
77	22.3
79	22.9
81	23.5
83	24.1
85	24.8
87	25.5
89	25.12
91	26.3
93	27.1

XI	xxxviii
95	28.1
97	28.6
99	29.2
101	29.9
103	30.6
105	31.2
107	32.2
109	32.10
111	33.8
113	34.3
115	34.9
117	35.6
119	36.3
121	36.9
123	37.6
125	38.1
127	38.5
129	38.11
131	38.17
133	39.7
135	39.16
137	40.6
139	40.12
141	41.5
143	41.12
145	42.5
147	42.11
149	43.3
151	43.10
153	44.6
155	45.2
157	45.9
159	46.4
161	46.11
163	47.5
165	47.11
167	48.5
169	48.11
171	48.16
173	49.7
175	50.1
177	50.9
179	51.4
181	51.12
183	52.6
185	52.11
187	53.8
189	54.3
191	54.9
193	55.4
195	55.10
197	56.4
199	56.9

XI	xxxviii
201	57.2
203	58.1
205	58.9
207	59.3
209	60.1
211	60.9

	xxxix
219	1.1
221	1.6
223	2.5
225	3.1
227	4.2
229	4.9
231	5.4
233	5.12
235	6.1
237	6.8
239	7.3
241	8.1
243	8.8
245	9.4
247	10.4
249	11.2
251	12.2
253	13.2
255	13.10
257	14.2
259	14.8
261	15.4
263	15.11
265	16.4
267	16.10
269	17.4
271	18.3
273	18.9
275	19.4
277	20.2
279	20.10
281	21.9
283	22.5
285	23.2
287	23.8
289	24.2
291	24.9
293	25.3
295	25.9
297	25.16
299	26.6
301	27.1
303	27.7
305	28.2
XI	**xxxix**
307	28.8
309	29.2
311	29.9
313	30.7
315	31.3
317	31.11
319	32.2
321	32.9
323	33.2
325	33.8
327	34.7
329	35.5
331	36.3
333	36.9
335	36.15
337	37.6
339	37.14
341	37.20
343	38.8
345	39.3
347	39.9
349	40.2
351	40.9
353	41.3
355	42.2
357	42.9
359	43.3
361	44.3
363	44.10
365	45.5
367	46.3
369	47.1
371	47.8
373	48.3
375	49.3
377	49.11
379	50.7
381	51.2
383	51.9
385	52.3
387	52.8
389	53.6
391	53.14
393	54.7
395	55.1
397	55.9
399	56.6

XII	xl
3	1.1
5	1.5

TABLE OF PARALLELS

XII	xl	XII	xl	XII	xli	XII	xlii
7	2.4	113	36.4	217	10.5	323	11.1
9	3.3	115	36.10	219	10.11	325	11.7
11	4.6	117	37.3	221	11.6	327	12.6
13	4.14	119	38.1	223	12.6	329	13.1
15	5.5	121	38.8	225	13.3	331	13.8
17	5.12	123	39.6	227	14.1	333	14.3
19	6.6	125	40.4	229	14.9	335	14.9
21	7.7	127	40.11	231	15.5	337	15.5
23	8.6	129	41.4	233	15.11	339	16.4
25	8.14	131	41.9	235	16.7	341	17.1
27	9.1	133	42.3	237	17.4	343	17.8
29	9.9	135	42.9	239	18.1	345	18.6
31	10.1	137	43.1	241	18.8	347	19.6
33	10.8	139	44.1	243	18.14	349	20.3
35	11.3	141	44.8	245	19.2	351	21.3
37	12.2	143	45.3	247	19.7	353	22.1
39	12.9	145	46.3	249	20.3	355	22.7
41	12.16	147	46.11	251	20.10	357	23.6
43	13.3	149	47.1	253	21.3	359	24.3
45	14.2	151	47.7	255	21.9	361	25.1
47	14.9	153	48.5	257	22.1	363	25.8
49	15.5	155	49.6	259	22.6	365	26.1
51	15.11	157	50.6	261	23.4	367	26.7
53	16.2	159	51.4	263	23.9	369	27.4
55	16.7	161	52.1	265	23.16	371	28.1
57	17.3	163	52.6	267	24.4	373	28.9
59	18.1	165	54.2	269	24.10	375	29.3
61	18.7	167	54.9	271	24.16	377	29.9
63	19.5	169	55.8	273	25.4	379	30.5
65	20.1	171	56.7	275	26.1	381	30.10
67	21.1	173	57.2	277	27.2	383	31.3
69	21.7	175	57.7	279	27.5	385	31.9
71	22.3	177	58.3	281	27.10	387	32.6
73	22.11	179	59.2	283	28.2	389	33.3
75	23.4			285	28.11	391	34.3
77	24.1					393	34.9
79	25.2		xli			395	34.15
81	25.9	185	1.1		xlii	397	35.7
83	26.7	187	1.3	293	1.1	399	36.6
85	27.6	189	2.3	295	1.6	401	37.1
87	27.15	191	2.9	297	1.12	403	37.8
89	28.8	193	3.3	299	2.7	405	38.5
91	29.5	195	3.10	301	3.5	407	39.1
93	29.11	197	4.7	303	4.1	409	39.7
95	30.3	199	5.6	305	5.2	411	40.5
97	31.1	201	6.2	307	5.8	413	40.10
99	31.9	203	6.8	309	6.3	415	41.6
101	32.7	205	7.2	311	6.11	417	41.12
103	33.7	207	8.1	313	7.7	419	42.4
105	34.4	209	8.7	315	8.5	421	43.1
107	34.12	211	8.10	317	9.3	423	43.7
109	35.4	213	9.5	319	10.1	425	44.3
111	35.11	215	9.11	321	10.10	427	45.1

TABLE OF PARALLELS

XII	xlii
429	45.6
431	46.4
433	46.10
435	47.5
437	47.8
439	48.3
441	48.10
443	49.7
445	50.5
447	50.11
449	51.5
451	51.11
453	52.8
455	52.14
457	53.4
459	54.3
461	54.9
463	55.6
465	56.3
467	57.1
469	57.9
471	58.4
473	58.12
475	59.3
477	59.8
479	60.4
481	61.2
483	61.10
485	62.7
487	62.14
489	63.3
491	63.7
493	64.1
495	64.8
497	65.6
499	65.11
501	66.4
503	66.9
505	67.6

XIII	xliii
3	1.1
5	1.5
7	1.11
9	2.5
11	2.11
13	3.3
15	4.1
17	4.6
19	4.13
21	5.6
23	6.3
25	6.9
27	6.13
29	7.7
31	8.1
33	8.7
35	9.5
37	10.3
39	11.1
41	11.8
43	11.13
45	12.7
47	13.3
49	13.8
51	14.5
53	15.1
55	15.7
57	16.5
59	16.10
61	16.14
63	17.3
65	18.1
67	18.7
69	19.1
71	19.7
73	19.14
75	20.4
77	21.5
79	21.9
81	22.8
83	23.4

XIII	xliv
91	1.1
93	1.5
95	2.1
97	2.9
99	3.3
101	4.1
103	4.9
105	5.4
107	5.10
109	6.4
111	6.12
113	7.2
115	7.10
117	8.6
119	9.5
121	9.9
123	10.6
125	11.2
127	11.7
129	12.4
131	13.4
133	13.11
135	14.3
137	14.10
139	15.1
141	16.2
143	16.7
145	17.2
147	17.9
149	18.4
151	19.4
153	19.11
155	20.3
157	21.2
159	21.10
161	22.7
163	22.13
165	23.2
167	23.10
169	24.7
171	25.3
173	25.11
175	26.6
177	26.12
179	27.6
181	28.1
183	28.8
185	28.15
187	29.7
189	30.7
191	30.14
193	31.7
195	31.15
197	32.8
199	33.4
201	33.10
203	34.7
205	35.3
207	35.9
209	35.15
211	35.23
213	36.8
215	37.1
217	37.7
219	38.1
221	38.9
223	39.5
225	40.2
227	40.8
229	41.4
231	42.1
233	42.9
235	44.1
237	44.8
239	45.8
241	46.1
243	46.9

XIII	xlv
249	1.1
251	1.7
253	2.3
255	2.9
257	3.5
259	4.2
261	5.2
263	5.9
265	6.2
267	6.9
269	7.4
271	8.5
273	9.4
275	10.5
277	10.12
279	11.2
281	11.9
283	12.5
285	12.11
287	13.6
289	13.12
291	14.1
293	14.8
295	15.5
297	16.1
299	16.6
301	17.4
303	18.2
305	19.2
307	19.9
309	19.14
311	20.2
313	20.9
315	21.6
317	22.4
319	22.11
321	23.4
323	23.10
325	23.17
327	24.4
329	24.11
331	25.3
333	25.9
335	26.2

TABLE OF PARALLELS

XIII	xlv	XIII	xlv	XIII	xlv	XIII	xlv
337	26.8	357	31.9	377	37.6	397	41.8
339	26.15	359	32.2	379	37.11	399	42.4
341	27.6	361	32.8	381	38.4	401	42.11
343	27.11	363	33.5	383	38.11	403	43.5
345	28.6	365	34.2	385	39.2	405	44.2
347	29.1	367	34.10	387	39.8	407	44.7
349	29.7	369	35.2	389	39.13	409	44.13
351	29.12	371	35.8	391	39.19	411	44.20
353	30.4	373	36.4	393	40.5		
355	31.4	375	37.1	395	41.2		

THE LOEB CLASSICAL LIBRARY

VOLUMES ALREADY PUBLISHED

Latin Authors

AMMIANUS MARCELLINUS. Translated by J. C. Rolfe. 3 Vols.

APULEIUS: THE GOLDEN ASS (METAMORPHOSES). W. Adlington (1566). Revised by S. Gaselee.

ST. AUGUSTINE: CITY OF GOD. 7 Vols. Vol. I. G. E. McCracken. Vols. II and VII. W. M. Green. Vol. III. D. Wiesen. Vol. IV. P. Levine. Vol. V. E. M. Sanford and W. M. Green. Vol. VI. W. C. Greene.

ST. AUGUSTINE, CONFESSIONS OF. W. Watts (1631). 2 Vols.

ST. AUGUSTINE, SELECT LETTERS. J. H. Baxter.

AUSONIUS. H. G. Evelyn White. 2 Vols.

BEDE. J. E. King. 2 Vols.

BOETHIUS: TRACTS and DE CONSOLATIONE PHILOSOPHIAE. Rev. H. F. Stewart and E. K. Rand. Revised by S. J. Tester.

CAESAR: ALEXANDRIAN, AFRICAN and SPANISH WARS. A. G. Way.

CAESAR: CIVIL WARS. A. G. Peskett.

CAESAR: GALLIC WAR. H. J. Edwards.

CATO: DE RE RUSTICA. VARRO: DE RE RUSTICA. H. B. Ash and W. D. Hooper.

CATULLUS. F. W. Cornish. TIBULLUS. J. B. Postgate. PERVIGILIUM VENERIS. J. W. Mackail.

CELSUS: DE MEDICINA. W. G. Spencer. 3 Vols.

CICERO: BRUTUS and ORATOR. G. L. Hendrickson and H. M. Hubbell.

[CICERO]: AD HERENNIUM. H. Caplan.

CICERO: DE ORATORE, etc. 2 Vols. Vol. I. DE ORATORE, Books I and II. E. W. Sutton and H. Rackham. Vol. II. DE ORATORE, Book III. DE FATO; PARADOXA STOICORUM; DE PARTITIONE ORATORIA. H. Rackham.

CICERO: DE FINIBUS. H. Rackham.

CICERO: DE INVENTIONE, etc. H. M. Hubbell.

CICERO: DE NATURA DEORUM and ACADEMICA. H. Rackham.

CICERO: DE OFFICIIS. Walter Miller.

CICERO: DE REPUBLICA and DE LEGIBUS. Clinton W. Keyes.

CICERO: DE SENECTUTE, DE AMICITIA, DE DIVINATIONE. W. A. Falconer.

CICERO: IN CATILINAM, PRO FLACCO, PRO MURENA, PRO SULLA. New version by C. Macdonald.

CICERO: LETTERS TO ATTICUS. E. O. Winstedt. 3 Vols.

CICERO: LETTERS TO HIS FRIENDS. W. Glynn Williams, M. Cary, M. Henderson. 4 Vols.

CICERO: PHILIPPICS. W. C. A. Ker.

CICERO: PRO ARCHIA, POST REDITUM, DE DOMO, DE HARUSPICUM RESPONSIS, PRO PLANCIO. N. H. Watts.

CICERO: PRO CAECINA, PRO LEGE MANILIA, PRO CLUENTIO, PRO RABIRIO. H. Grose Hodge.

CICERO: PRO CAELIO, DE PROVINCIIS CONSULARIBUS, PRO BALBO. R. Gardner.

CICERO: PRO MILONE, IN PISONEM, PRO SCAURO, PRO FONTEIO, PRO RABIRIO POSTUMO, PRO MARCELLO, PRO LIGARIO, PRO REGE DEIOTARO. N. H. Watts.

CICERO: PRO QUINCTIO, PRO ROSCIO AMERINO, PRO ROSCIO COMOEDO, CONTRA RULLUM. J. H. Freese.

CICERO: PRO SESTIO, IN VATINIUM. R. Gardner.

CICERO: TUSCULAN DISPUTATIONS. J. E. King.

CICERO: VERRINE ORATIONS. L. H. G. Greenwood. 2 Vols.

CLAUDIAN. M. Platnauer. 2 Vols.

COLUMELLA: DE RE RUSTICA. DE ARBORIBUS. H. B. Ash, E. S. Forster and E. Heffner. 3 Vols.

CURTIUS, Q.: HISTORY OF ALEXANDER. J. C. Rolfe. 2 Vols.

FLORUS. E. S. Forster.

FRONTINUS: STRATAGEMS and AQUEDUCTS. C. E. Bennett and M. B. McElwain.

FRONTO: CORRESPONDENCE. C. R. Haines. 2 Vols.

GELLIUS. J. C. Rolfe. 3 Vols.

HORACE: ODES and EPODES. C. E. Bennett.

HORACE: SATIRES, EPISTLES, ARS POETICA. H. R. Fairclough.

JEROME: SELECTED LETTERS. F. A. Wright.

JUVENAL and PERSIUS. G. G. Ramsay.

LIVY. B. O. Foster, F. G. Moore, Evan T. Sage, and A. C. Schlesinger and R. M. Geer (General Index). 14 Vols.

LUCAN. J. D. Duff.

LUCRETIUS. W. H. D. Rouse. Revised by M. F. Smith.

MANILIUS. G. P. Goold.

MARTIAL. W. C. A. Ker. 2 Vols. Revised by E. H. Warmington.

MINOR LATIN POETS: from PUBLILIUS SYRUS to RUTILIUS NAMATIANUS, including GRATTIUS, CALPURNIUS SICULUS, NEMESIANUS, AVIANUS and others, with "Aetna" and the "Phoenix." J. Wight Duff and Arnold M. Duff. 2 Vols.

Minucius Felix. Cf. Tertullian.

Nepos Cornelius. J. C. Rolfe.

Ovid: The Art of Love and Other Poems. J. H. Mosley. Revised by G. P. Goold.

Ovid: Fasti. Sir James G. Frazer

Ovid: Heroides and Amores. Grant Showerman. Revised by G. P. Goold

Ovid: Metamorphoses. F. J. Miller. 2 Vols. Revised by G. P. Goold.

Ovid: Tristia and Ex Ponto. A. L. Wheeler.

Persius. Cf. Juvenal.

Pervigilium Veneris. Cf. Catullus.

Petronius. M. Heseltine. Seneca: Apocolocyntosis. W. H. D. Rouse. Revised by E. H. Warmington.

Phaedrus and Babrius (Greek). B. E. Perry.

Plautus. Paul Nixon. 5 Vols.

Pliny: Letters, Panegyricus. Betty Radice. 2 Vols.

Pliny: Natural History. 10 Vols. Vols. I–V and IX. H. Rackham. VI.–VIII. W. H. S. Jones. X. D. E. Eichholz.

Propertius. H. E. Butler.

Prudentius. H. J. Thomson. 2 Vols.

Quintilian. H. E. Butler. 4 Vols.

Remains of Old Latin. E. H. Warmington. 4 Vols. Vol. I. (Ennius and Caecilius) Vol. II. (Livius, Naevius Pacuvius, Accius) Vol. III. (Lucilius and Laws of XII Tables) Vol. IV. (Archaic Inscriptions)

Res Gestae Divi Augusti. Cf. Velleius Paterculus.

Sallust. J. C. Rolfe.

Scriptores Historiae Augustae. D. Magie. 3 Vols.

Seneca, The Elder: Controversiae, Suasoriae. M. Winterbottom. 2 Vols.

Seneca: Apocolocyntosis. Cf. Petronius.

Seneca: Epistulae Morales. R. M. Gummere. 3 Vols.

Seneca: Moral Essays. J. W. Basore. 3 Vols.

Seneca: Tragedies. F. J. Miller. 2 Vols.

Seneca: Naturales Quaestiones. T. H. Corcoran. 2 Vols.

Sidonius: Poems and Letters. W. B. Anderson. 2 Vols.

Silius Italicus. J. D. Duff. 2 Vols.

Statius. J. H. Mozley. 2 Vols.

Suetonius. J. C. Rolfe. 2 Vols.

Tacitus: Dialogus. Sir Wm. Peterson. Agricola and Germania. Maurice Hutton. Revised by M. Winterbottom, R. M. Ogilvie, E. H. Warmington.

Tacitus: Histories and Annals. C. H. Moore and J. Jackson. 4 Vols.

TERENCE. John Sargeaunt. 2 Vols.

TERTULLIAN: APOLOGIA and DE SPECTACULIS. T. R. Glover. MINUCIUS FELIX. G. H. Rendall.

TIBULLUS. Cf. CATULLUS.

VALERIUS FLACCUS. J. H. Mozley.

VARRO: DE LINGUA LATINA. R. G. Kent. 2 Vols.

VELLEIUS PATERCULUS and RES GESTAE DIVI AUGUSTI. F. W. Shipley.

VIRGIL. H. R. Fairclough. 2 Vols.

VITRUVIUS: DE ARCHITECTURA. F. Granger. 2 Vols.

Greek Authors

ACHILLES TATIUS. S. Gaselee.

AELIAN: ON THE NATURE OF ANIMALS. A. F. Scholfield. 3 Vols.

AENEAS TACTICUS. ASCLEPIODOTUS and ONASANDER. The Illinois Greek Club.

AESCHINES. C. D. Adams.

AESCHYLUS. H. Weir Smyth. 2 Vols.

ALCIPHRON, AELIAN, PHILOSTRATUS: LETTERS. A. R. Benner and F. H. Fobes.

ANDOCIDES, ANTIPHON. Cf. MINOR ATTIC ORATORS.

APOLLODORUS. Sir James G. Frazer. 2 Vols.

APOLLONIUS RHODIUS. R. C. Seaton.

APOSTOLIC FATHERS. Kirsopp Lake. 2 Vols.

APPIAN: ROMAN HISTORY. Horace White. 4 Vols.

ARATUS. Cf. CALLIMACHUS.

ARISTIDES: ORATIONS. C. A. Behr. Vol. I.

ARISTOPHANES. Benjamin Bickley Rogers. 3 Vols. Verse trans.

ARISTOTLE: ART OF RHETORIC. J. H. Freese.

ARISTOTLE: ATHENIAN CONSTITUTION, EUDEMIAN ETHICS, VICES AND VIRTUES. H. Rackham.

ARISTOTLE: GENERATION OF ANIMALS. A. L. Peck.

ARISTOTLE: HISTORIA ANIMALIUM. A. L. Peck. Vols. I.–II.

ARISTOTLE: METAPHYSICS. H. Tredennick. 2 Vols.

ARISTOTLE: METEOROLOGICA. H. D. P. Lee.

ARISTOTLE: MINOR WORKS. W. S. Hett. On Colours, On Things Heard, On Physiognomies, On Plants, On Marvellous Things Heard, Mechanical Problems, On Indivisible Lines, On Situations and Names of Winds, On Melissus, Xenophanes, and Gorgias.

ARISTOTLE: NICOMACHEAN ETHICS. H. Rackham.

ARISTOTLE: OECONOMICA and MAGNA MORALIA. G. C. Armstrong (with METAPHYSICS, Vol. II).

ARISTOTLE: ON THE HEAVENS. W. K. C. Guthrie.

ARISTOTLE: ON THE SOUL, PARVA NATURALIA, ON BREATH. W. S. Hett.

ARISTOTLE: CATEGORIES, ON INTERPRETATION, PRIOR ANALYTICS. H. P. Cooke and H. Tredennick.

ARISTOTLE: POSTERIOR ANALYTICS, TOPICS. H. Tredennick and E. S. Forster.

ARISTOTLE: ON SOPHISTICAL REFUTATIONS.
On Coming to be and Passing Away, On the Cosmos. E. S. Forster and D. J. Furley.

ARISTOTLE: PARTS OF ANIMALS. A. L. Peck; MOTION AND PROGRESSION OF ANIMALS. E. S. Forster.

ARISTOTLE: PHYSICS. Rev. P. Wicksteed and F. M. Cornford. 2 Vols.

ARISTOTLE: POETICS and LONGINUS. W. Hamilton Fyfe; DEMETRIUS ON STYLE. W. Rhys Roberts.

ARISTOTLE: POLITICS. H. Rackham.

ARISTOTLE: PROBLEMS. W. S. Hett. 2 Vols.

ARISTOTLE: RHETORICA AD ALEXANDRUM (with PROBLEMS. Vol. II). H. Rackham.

ARRIAN: HISTORY OF ALEXANDER and INDICA. Rev. E. Iliffe Robson. 2 Vols. New version P. Brunt.

ATHENAEUS: DEIPNOSOPHISTAE. C. B. Gulick. 7 Vols.

BABRIUS AND PHAEDRUS (Latin). B. E. Perry.

ST. BASIL: LETTERS. R. J. Deferrari. 4 Vols.

CALLIMACHUS: FRAGMENTS. C. A. Trypanis. MUSAEUS: HERO AND LEANDER. T. Gelzer and C. Whitman.

CALLIMACHUS, Hymns and Epigrams, and LYCOPHRON. A. W. Mair; ARATUS. G. R. Mair.

CLEMENT OF ALEXANDRIA. Rev. G. W. Butterworth.

COLLUTHUS. Cf. OPPIAN.

DAPHNIS AND CHLOE. Thornley's Translation revised by J. M. Edmonds: and PARTHENIUS. S. Gaselee.

DEMOSTHENES I.: OLYNTHIACS, PHILIPPICS and MINOR ORATIONS I.–XVII. AND XX. J. H. Vince.

DEMOSTHENES II.: DE CORONA and DE FALSA LEGATIONE. C. A. Vince and J. H. Vince.

DEMOSTHENES III.: MEIDIAS, ANDROTION, ARISTOCRATES, TIMOCRATES and ARISTOGEITON I. and II. J. H. Vince.

DEMOSTHENES IV.–VI: PRIVATE ORATIONS and IN NEAERAM. A. T. Murray.

DEMOSTHENES VII: FUNERAL SPEECH, EROTIC ESSAY, EXORDIA and LETTERS. N. W. and N. J. DeWitt.

DIO CASSIUS: ROMAN HISTORY. E. Cary. 9 Vols.

Dio Chrysostom. J. W. Cohoon and H. Lamar Crosby. 5 Vols.

Diodorus Siculus. 12 Vols. Vols. I.–VI. C. H. Oldfather. Vol. VII. C. L. Sherman. Vol. VIII. C. B. Welles. Vols. IX. and X. R. M. Geer. Vol. XI. F. Walton. Vol. XII. F. Walton. General Index. R. M. Geer.

Diogenes Laertius. R. D. Hicks. 2 Vols. New Introduction by H. S. Long.

Dionysius of Halicarnassus: Roman Antiquities. Spelman's translation revised by E. Cary. 7 Vols.

Dionysius of Halicarnassus: Critical Essays. S. Usher. 2 Vols. Vol. I.

Epictetus. W. A. Oldfather. 2 Vols.

Euripides. A. S. Way. 4 Vols. Verse trans.

Eusebius: Ecclesiastical History. Kirsopp Lake and J. E. L. Oulton. 2 Vols.

Galen: On the Natural Faculties. A. J. Brock.

Greek Anthology. W. R. Paton. 5 Vols.

Greek Bucolic Poets (Theocritus, Bion, Moschus). J. M. Edmonds.

Greek Elegy and Iambus with the Anacreontea. J. M. Edmonds. 2 Vols.

Greek Lyric. D. A. Campbell. 4 Vols. Vol. I.

Greek Mathematical Works. Ivor Thomas. 2 Vols.

Herodes. Cf. Theophrastus: Characters.

Herodian. C. R. Whittaker. 2 Vols.

Herodotus. A. D. Godley. 4 Vols.

Hesiod and The Homeric Hymns. H. G. Evelyn White.

Hippocrates and the Fragments of Heracleitus. W. H. S. Jones and E. T. Withington. 4 Vols.

Homer: Iliad. A. T. Murray. 2 Vols.

Homer: Odyssey. A. T. Murray. 2 Vols.

Isaeus. E. W. Forster.

Isocrates. George Norlin and LaRue Van Hook. 3 Vols.

[St. John Damascene]: Barlaam and Ioasaph. Rev. G. R. Woodward, Harold Mattingly and D. M. Lang.

Josephus. 10 Vols. Vols. I.–IV. H. Thackeray. Vol. V. H. Thackeray and R. Marcus. Vols. VI.–VII. R. Marcus. Vol. VIII. R. Marcus and Allen Wikgren. Vols. IX.–X. L. H. Feldman.

Julian. Wilmer Cave Wright. 3 Vols.

Libanius. A. F. Norman. 3 Vols. Vols. I.–II.

Lucian. 8 Vols. Vols. I.–V. A. M. Harmon. Vol. VI. K. Kilburn. Vols. VII.–VIII. M. D. Macleod.

Lycophron. Cf. Callimachus.

Lyra Graeca, J. M. Edmonds. 2 Vols.

Lysias. W. R. M. Lamb.

Manetho. W. G. Waddell.

Marcus Aurelius. C. R. Haines.

Menander. W. G. Arnott. 3 Vols. Vol. I.

Minor Attic Orators (Antiphon, Andocides, Lycurgus, Demades, Dinarchus, Hyperides). K. J. Maidment and J. O. Burtt. 2 Vols.

Musaeus: Hero and Leander. Cf. Callimachus.

Nonnos: Dionysiaca. W. H. D. Rouse. 3 Vols.

Oppian, Colluthus, Tryphiodorus. A. W. Mair.

Papyri. Non-Literary Selections. A. S. Hunt and C. C. Edgar. 2 Vols. Literary Selections (Poetry). D. L. Page.

Parthenius. Cf. Daphnis and Chloe.

Pausanias: Description of Greece. W. H. S. Jones. 4 Vols. and Companion Vol. arranged by R. E. Wycherley.

Philo. 10 Vols. Vols. I.–V. F. H. Colson and Rev. G. H. Whitaker. Vols. VI.–IX. F. H. Colson. Vol. X. F. H. Colson and the Rev. J. W. Earp.

Philo: two supplementary Vols. (*Translation only.*) Ralph Marcus.

Philostratus: The Life of Apollonius of Tyana. F. C. Conybeare. 2 Vols.

Philostratus: Imagines; Callistratus: Descriptions. A. Fairbanks.

Philostratus and Eunapius: Lives of the Sophists. Wilmer Cave Wright.

Pindar. Sir J. E. Sandys.

Plato: Charmides, Alcibiades, Hipparchus, The Lovers, Theages, Minos and Epinomis. W. R. M. Lamb.

Plato: Cratylus, Parmenides, Greater Hippias, Lesser Hippias. H. N. Fowler.

Plato: Euthyphro, Apology, Crito, Phaedo, Phaedrus, H. N. Fowler.

Plato: Laches, Protagoras, Meno, Euthydemus. W. R. M. Lamb.

Plato: Laws. Rev. R. G. Bury. 2 Vols.

Plato: Lysis, Symposium, Gorgias. W. R. M. Lamb.

Plato: Republic. Paul Shorey. 2 Vols.

Plato: Statesman, Philebus. H. N. Fowler; Ion. W. R. M. Lamb.

Plato: Theaetetus and Sophist. H. N. Fowler.

Plato: Timaeus, Critias, Clitopho, Menexenus, Epistulae. Rev. R. G. Bury.

Plotinus: A. H. Armstrong. 7 Vols. Vols. I.–V.

Plutarch: Moralia. 16 Vols. Vols I.–V. F. C. Babbitt. Vol. VI. W. C. Helmbold. Vols. VII. and XIV. P. H. De Lacy and B. Einarson. Vol. VIII. P. A. Clement and H. B. Hoffleit. Vol. IX. E. L. Minar, Jr., F. H. Sandbach, W. C. Helmbold. Vol. X. H. N. Fowler. Vol. XI. L. Pearson and F. H. Sandbach. Vol. XII. H. Cherniss and W. C. Helmbold. Vol. XIII 1–2. H. Cherniss. Vol. XV. F. H. Sandbach.

Plutarch: The Parallel Lives. B. Perrin. 11 Vols.

Polybius. W. R. Paton. 6 Vols.

Procopius. H. B. Dewing. 7 Vols.

Ptolemy: Tetrabiblos. F. E. Robbins.

Quintus Smyrnaeus. A. S. Way. Verse trans.

Sextus Empiricus. Rev. R. G. Bury. 4 Vols.

Sophocles. F. Storr. 2 Vols. Verse trans.

Strabo: Geography. Horace L. Jones. 8 Vols.

Theocritus. Cf. Greek Bucolic Poets.

Theophrastus: Characters. J. M. Edmonds. Herodes, etc. A. D. Knox.

Theophrastus: Enquiry into Plants. Sir Arthur Hort, Bart. 2 Vols.

Theophrastus: De Causis Plantarum. G. K. K. Link and B. Einarson. 3 Vols. Vol. I.

Thucydides. C. F. Smith. 4 Vols.

Tryphiodorus. Cf. Oppian.

Xenophon: Cyropaedia. Walter Miller. 2 Vols.

Xenophon: Hellencia. C. L. Brownson. 2 Vols.

Xenophon: Anabasis. C. L. Brownson.

Xenophon: Memorabilia and Oeconomicus. E. C. Marchant. Symposium and Apology. O. J. Todd.

Xenophon: Scripta Minora. E. C. Marchant. Constitution of the athenians. G. W. Bowersock.